CHAMBERS

C000094140

THESAURUS

CHAMBERS

CHAMBERS
An imprint of Chambers Harrap Publishers Ltd
7 Hopetoun Crescent
Edinburgh, EH7 4AY

www.chambers.co.uk

Previously published in a different format as *Chambers Paperback Thesaurus*
First published by Chambers Harrap Publishers Ltd 2003

A CIP catalogue record for this book is available from the British Library.

ISBN 0550 10151 9

Designed and typeset by Chambers Harrap Publishers Ltd, Edinburgh
Printed and bound in Great Britain by Mackays of Chatham Ltd

Contents

Contributors

Project Editor
Mary O'Neill

Editor
Martin H. Manser

Publishing Manager
Patrick White

Prepress
Marina Karapanovic

Supplement adapted from material by
Hazel Norris

Preface

A thesaurus is a book that contains lists of synonyms – that is, words that have a similar meaning to another word. A thesaurus allows you to look up a common word and find a range of words that have the same or nearly the same meaning. *Chambers Paperback Thesaurus* is one of a series of thesauruses drawn from the extensive *Chambers Dictionary* database. It lists over 180,000 synonyms for common English words, allowing you to find a suitable word for every occasion. This new edition has been revised and updated to include the most recent and useful words and terms.

Looking up a word in this thesaurus may help you to find a more exact term for an essay or report, a livelier phrase for a speech, or a simpler expression for a letter. This will enable you to say what you have to say using the full range of words available to you. Moreover, browsing through a thesaurus also offers you a fascinating insight into the richness and variety of the English language.

But this book offers much more than lists of alternative words. It also contains lists of antonyms – words that have an opposite meaning. This allows you the further option of describing things in terms of their opposites. For example, you can describe something that is dull not only as 'boring', but also as 'not interesting'.

Another feature of this thesaurus is the inclusion of over 250 panels containing related words. For example, look up the word 'dance' and you will find not only a number of alternative words (*ball, hop, knees-up...*) but also a list of various types of dance (*waltz, quickstep, foxtrot...*). An added supplement gives words grouped by ending, eg *-logy* or *-ship*. These features complement the lists of synonyms to help create a thesaurus that is even more useful as a resource for solving puzzles and word games.

Another special supplement gives guidance on using the words in the thesaurus well and avoiding potential pitfalls, making *Chambers Paperback Thesaurus* a complete as well as convenient guide to today's vocabulary.

How to use the Thesaurus

Chambers Paperback Thesaurus has been designed to allow you to find the information you want quickly and easily. The entries are arranged in alphabetical order, so you can go straight to the word you are looking for without having to search in an index.

The lists of synonyms are arranged according to shades of meaning or in order from the most common to the least frequently used or the most specialized term.

Some synonyms are followed by a label which indicates that the word is restricted in use to certain occasions. Thus some words are only appropriate in informal contexts and should not be used in business correspondence or formal writing. Similarly, formal words might not be appropriate for more general use. Another label indicates that a word is restricted to American English.

If the word you want can be used in a number of different senses, you will find these senses are clearly distinguished. Each sense is numbered and introduced either by a phrase in italics giving an example of the word in use, or by a 'key' synonym in capital letters. These features mean that it is easy for you to work out which sense of the word you are interested in.

Antonyms or opposite words are introduced by the symbol ◨ . Where there is more than one part of speech in an entry, the antonyms are listed after the part of speech to which they apply. Where there are several senses of a word, the antonyms are numbered to indicate to which senses they apply.

Some entries include additional information, such as synonyms for related idioms and phrasal verbs (introduced by the symbol ◇) or panels of related words. The diagram on the facing page shows how these features appear in the text.

Headwords are shown in bold letters at the beginning of each entry.

Different meanings are shown in numbered sections, introduced either by a phrase in italics showing the word in use or by a key synonym in capitals.

Parts of speech, eg noun, verb, are shown by abbreviations.

Idioms and phrasal verbs are grouped alphabetically at the end of some entries. These are indicated by the symbol ◇.

Synonyms or alternative words are listed with the most commonly used ones before less frequent and more specialized terms, or arranged by shades of meaning.

Antonyms, words that mean the opposite of the headword, are introduced by the symbol ☒.

Lists of related words are shown in panels after some entries.

Labels in italics indicate when words are restricted to certain areas of language.

frontier *n* border, boundary, borderline, limit, edge, perimeter, confines, marches, bounds, verge.

frosty *adj* **1** ICY, frozen, freezing, frigid, wintry, cold, chilly. **2** UNFRIENDLY, unwelcoming, cool, aloof, standoffish, stiff, discouraging.
☒ warm.

froth *n* bubbles, effervescence, foam, lather, suds, head, scum.
➤ *v* foam, lather, ferment, fizz, effervesce, bubble.

frown *v* scowl, glower, lour, glare, grimace.
➤ *n* scowl, glower, dirty look (*infml*), glare, grimace.
◇ **frown on** disapprove of, object to, dislike, discourage.
☒ approve of.

frozen *adj* iced, chilled, icy, icebound, ice-covered, arctic, ice-cold, frigid, freezing, numb, solidified, stiff, rigid, fixed.
☒ warm.

frugal *adj* thrifty, penny-wise, parsimonious, careful, provident, saving, economical, sparing, meagre.
☒ wasteful, generous.

fruit

Varieties of fruit include: apple, Bramley, Cox's Orange Pippin, Golden Delicious, Granny Smith, crab apple; pear, William, Conference, Asian pear; orange, Jaffa, mandarin, mineola, clementine, satsuma, tangerine, kumquat, Seville; apricot, peach, plum, persimmon, sharon fruit, nectarine, cherry, sloe, damson, greengage, grape, gooseberry, goosegog (*infml*), physalis, rhubarb, tomato; banana, pineapple, olive, lemon, lime, ugli fruit, star fruit, lychee, date, fig, grapefruit, kiwi fruit, mango, papaya, pawpaw, guava, passion fruit, avocado; melon, honeydew, cantaloupe, casaba, Galia, watermelon; strawberry, raspberry, blackberry, bilberry, loganberry, elderberry, blueberry, boysenberry, cranberry; redcurrant, blackcurrant.

Abbreviations used in the Thesaurus

adj	adjective
adv	adverb
conj	conjunction
fml	formal
infml	informal
interj	interjection
n	noun
prep	preposition
®	trademark
sl	slang
US	American English
v	verb

Aa

abandon *v* **1** DESERT, leave, forsake, jilt, ditch (*infml*), leave in the lurch (*infml*), maroon, strand, leave behind, scrap. **2** *abandon ship*: vacate, evacuate, withdraw from, quit. **3** RENOUNCE, resign, give up, forgo, relinquish, surrender, yield, waive, drop.
₤ 1 support, maintain, keep. **3** continue.

abandoned *adj* **1** DESERTED, unoccupied, derelict, neglected, forsaken, forlorn, desolate. **2** DISSOLUTE, wild, uninhibited, wanton, wicked.
₤ 1 kept, occupied. **2** restrained.

abandonment *n* **1** DESERTION, leaving, forsaking, jilting, neglect, scrapping. **2** RENUNCIATION, resignation, giving up, relinquishment, surrender, sacrifice, waiver, dropping, discontinuation.

abashed *adj* **1** ASHAMED, shamefaced, embarrassed, mortified, humiliated, humbled. **2** CONFUSED, bewildered, nonplussed, confounded, perturbed, discomposed, disconcerted, taken aback, thrown (*infml*), dumbfounded, floored (*infml*), dismayed.
₤ 2 composed, at ease.

abate *v* **1** DECREASE, reduce, lessen, diminish, decline, sink, dwindle, taper off, fall off. **2** MODERATE, ease, relieve, alleviate, mitigate, remit, pacify, quell, subside, let up (*infml*), weaken, wane, slacken, slow, fade.
₤ 1 increase. **2** strengthen.

abbey *n* monastery, priory, friary, seminary, convent, nunnery, cloister.

abbreviate *v* shorten, cut, trim, clip, truncate, curtail, abridge, summarize, précis, abstract, digest, condense, compress, reduce, lessen, shrink, contract.
₤ extend, lengthen, expand, amplify.

abbreviation *n* shortening, clipping, curtailment, abridgement, summarization, summary, synopsis, résumé, précis, abstract, digest, compression, reduction, contraction.
₤ extension, expansion, amplification.

abdicate *v* renounce, give up, relinquish, surrender, cede, yield, forgo, abandon, quit (*infml*), vacate, retire, resign, step down (*infml*).

abdomen *n* belly, guts, stomach, tummy (*infml*), paunch, midriff.

abdominal *adj* ventral, intestinal, visceral, gastric.

abduct *v* carry off, run away with, run off with (*infml*), make off with, spirit away, seduce, kidnap, snatch, seize, appropriate.

aberration *n* deviation, straying, wandering, divergence, irregularity, nonconformity, anomaly, oddity, peculiarity, eccentricity, quirk, freak, lapse, defect.
₤ conformity.

abhor *v* hate, detest, loathe, abominate, execrate, shudder at, recoil from, shrink from, spurn, despise.
₤ love, adore.

abhorrence *n* hate, hatred, aversion, loathing, abomination, horror, repugnance, revulsion, disgust, distaste.
₤ love, adoration.

abhorrent *adj* detestable, loathsome, abominable, execrable, heinous, obnoxious, odious, hated, hateful, horrible, horrid, offensive,

repugnant, repellent, repulsive, revolting, nauseating, disgusting, distasteful.
🔁 delightful, attractive.

abide *v* 1 BEAR, stand, endure, tolerate, put up with, stomach, accept. 2 REMAIN, last, endure, continue, persist.
◇ **abide by** 1 *abide by the rules*: obey, observe, follow, comply with, adhere to, conform to, submit to, go along with, agree to. 2 FULFIL, discharge, carry out, stand by, hold to, keep to.

ability *n* 1 CAPABILITY, capacity, faculty, facility, potentiality, power. 2 SKILL, dexterity, deftness, adeptness, competence, proficiency, qualification, aptitude, talent, gift, endowment, knack, flair, touch, expertise, know-how (*infml*), genius, forte, strength.
🔁 1 inability. 2 incompetence, weakness.

abject *adj* 1 CONTEMPTIBLE, worthless, low, mean, ignoble, dishonourable, deplorable, despicable, vile, sordid, debased, degenerate, submissive, servile, grovelling, slavish. 2 MISERABLE, wretched, forlorn, hopeless, pitiable, pathetic, outcast, degraded.
🔁 1 proud, exalted.

ablaze *adj* 1 BLAZING, flaming, burning, on fire, ignited, lighted, alight, illuminated, luminous, glowing, aglow, radiant, flashing, gleaming, sparkling, brilliant. 2 IMPASSIONED, passionate, fervent, ardent, fiery, enthusiastic, excited, exhilarated, stimulated, aroused, angry, furious, raging, incensed, frenzied.

able *adj* capable, fit, fitted, dexterous, adroit, deft, adept, competent, proficient, qualified, practised, experienced, skilled, accomplished, clever, expert, masterly, skilful, ingenious, talented, gifted, strong, powerful, effective, efficient, adequate.
🔁 unable, incapable, incompetent, ineffective.

able-bodied *adj* fit, healthy, sound, strong, robust, hardy, tough, vigorous, powerful, hale, hearty, lusty, sturdy,

strapping, stout, stalwart, staunch.
🔁 infirm, delicate.

abnormal *adj* odd, strange, singular, peculiar, curious, queer, weird, eccentric, paranormal, unnatural, uncanny, extraordinary, exceptional, unusual, uncommon, unexpected, irregular, anomalous, aberrant, erratic, wayward, deviant, divergent, different.
🔁 normal, regular, typical.

abnormality *n* oddity, peculiarity, singularity, eccentricity, strangeness, bizarreness, unnaturalness, unusualness, irregularity, exception, anomaly, deformity, flaw, aberration, deviation, divergence, difference.
🔁 normality, regularity.

abolish *v* do away with, annul, nullify, invalidate, quash, repeal, rescind, revoke, cancel, obliterate, blot out, suppress, destroy, eliminate, eradicate, get rid of (*infml*), stamp out, end, put an end to, terminate, subvert, overthrow, overturn.
🔁 create, retain, authorize, continue.

abolition *n* annulment, nullification, invalidation, quashing, repeal, abrogation, cancellation, obliteration, suppression, eradication, extinction, end, ending, termination, subversion, overturning, dissolution.
🔁 creation, retention, continuance.

abominable *adj* loathsome, detestable, hateful, horrid, horrible, abhorrent, execrable, odious, repugnant, repulsive, repellent, disgusting, revolting, obnoxious, nauseating, foul, vile, heinous, atrocious, appalling, terrible, reprehensible, contemptible, despicable, wretched.
🔁 delightful, pleasant, desirable.

abominate *v* hate, loathe, detest, abhor, execrate, despise, condemn.
🔁 love, adore.

abomination *n* hate, hatred, aversion, loathing, abhorrence, repugnance, revulsion, disgust, distaste, hostility, offence, outrage,

disgrace, anathema, horror, evil, curse, plague, torment, bête noire.
🔒 adoration, delight.

abort v miscarry, terminate, end, stop, arrest, halt, check, frustrate, thwart, nullify, call off, fail.
🔒 continue.

abortion n miscarriage, termination, frustration, failure, misadventure.
🔒 continuation, success.

abortive adj failed, unsuccessful, fruitless, unproductive, barren, sterile, vain, idle, futile, useless, ineffective, unavailing.
🔒 successful, fruitful.

abound v be plentiful, proliferate, flourish, thrive, swell, increase, superabound, swarm, teem, run riot, overflow.

about prep 1 REGARDING, concerning, relating to, referring to, connected with, concerned with, as regards, with regard to, with respect to, with reference to. 2 CLOSE TO, near, nearby, beside, adjacent to. 3 ROUND, around, surrounding, encircling, encompassing, throughout, all over.
➤ adv 1 about twenty: around, approximately, roughly, in the region of, more or less, almost, nearly, approaching, nearing. 2 run about: to and fro, here and there, from place to place.
◇ **about to** on the point of, on the verge of, all but, ready to, intending to, preparing to.

above prep over, higher than, on top of, superior to, in excess of, exceeding, surpassing, beyond, before, prior to.
🔒 below, under.
➤ adv overhead, aloft, on high, earlier.
🔒 below, underneath.
➤ adj above-mentioned, above-stated, foregoing, preceding, previous, earlier, prior.

above-board adj honest, legitimate, straight, on the level, fair, fair and square, square, true, open, frank, candid, guileless, straightforward,

forthright, truthful, veracious, trustworthy, honourable, reputable, upright.
🔒 dishonest, shady (*infml*), underhand.

abrasion n graze, scratch, scratching, scraping, scrape, scouring, grating, grinding, abrading, chafing, chafe, friction, rubbing, erosion, wearing away, wearing down.

abrasive adj scratching, scraping, grating, rough, harsh, chafing, frictional, galling, irritating, annoying, sharp, biting, caustic, hurtful, nasty, unpleasant.
🔒 smooth, pleasant.

abreast adj acquainted, informed, knowledgeable, in the picture, up to speed (*infml*), au courant, up to date, in touch, au fait, conversant, familiar.
🔒 unaware, out of touch.

abridge v shorten, cut (down), prune, curtail, abbreviate, contract, reduce, decrease, lessen, summarize, précis, abstract, digest, condense, compress, concentrate.
🔒 expand, amplify, pad out.

abridgement n 1 SHORTENING, cutting, reduction, decrease, diminishing, concentration, contraction, restriction, limitation. 2 SUMMARY, synopsis, résumé, outline, précis, abstract, digest, epitome.
🔒 1 expansion, padding.

abroad adv 1 OVERSEAS, in foreign parts, out of the country, far and wide, widely, extensively. 2 AT LARGE, around, about, circulating, current.
🔒 1 at home.

abrupt adj 1 abrupt departure: sudden, unexpected, unforeseen, surprising, quick, rapid, swift, hasty, hurried, precipitate. 2 SHEER, steep, precipitous, sharp. 3 BRUSQUE, curt, terse, short, brisk, snappy, gruff, rude, uncivil, impolite, blunt, direct.
🔒 1 gradual, slow, leisurely.
3 expansive, ceremonious, polite.

abscond v run away, run off, make off, decamp, flee, fly, escape, bolt, quit, clear out (*infml*), disappear, take French leave.

absence *n* **1** NON-ATTENDANCE, non-appearance, truancy, absenteeism, non-existence. **2** LACK, need, want, deficiency, dearth, scarcity, unavailability, default, omission, vacancy.
₣ 1 presence, attendance, appearance. **2** existence.

absent *adj* **1** MISSING, not present, away, out, unavailable, gone, lacking, truant. **2** INATTENTIVE, daydreaming, dreamy, faraway, elsewhere, absent-minded, vacant, vague, distracted, preoccupied, unaware, oblivious, unheeding.
₣ 1 present. **2** alert, aware.

absent-minded *adj* forgetful, scatterbrained, absent, abstracted, withdrawn, faraway, distracted, preoccupied, absorbed, engrossed, pensive, musing, dreaming, dreamy, inattentive, unaware, oblivious, unconscious, heedless, unheeding, unthinking, impractical.
₣ attentive, practical, matter-of-fact.

absolute *adj* **1** UTTER, total, complete, entire, full, thorough, exhaustive, supreme, consummate, definitive, conclusive, final, categorical, definite, unequivocal, unquestionable, decided, decisive, positive, sure, certain, genuine, pure, perfect, sheer, unmixed, unqualified, downright, out-and-out, outright, thorough. **2** OMNIPOTENT, totalitarian, autocratic, tyrannical, despotic, dictatorial, sovereign, unlimited, unrestricted.

absolutely *adv* utterly, totally, dead, completely, entirely, fully, wholly, thoroughly, exhaustively, perfectly, supremely, unconditionally, conclusively, finally, categorically, definitely, positively, unequivocally, unambiguously, unquestionably, decidedly, decisively, surely, certainly, infallibly, genuinely, truly, purely, exactly, precisely.

absorb *v* **1** TAKE IN, ingest, drink in, imbibe, suck up, soak up, consume, devour, engulf, digest, assimilate,

understand, receive, hold, retain. **2** ENGROSS, involve, fascinate, enthral, monopolize, preoccupy, occupy, fill (up).
₣ 1 exude.

absorbing *adj* interesting, amusing, entertaining, diverting, engrossing, preoccupying, intriguing, fascinating, captivating, enthralling, spellbinding, gripping, riveting, compulsive, unputdownable (*infml*).
₣ boring, off-putting.

abstain *v* refrain, decline, refuse, reject, resist, forbear, shun, avoid, keep from, stop, cease, desist, give up, renounce, forgo, go without, deny oneself.
₣ indulge.

abstemious *adj* abstinent, self-denying, self-disciplined, disciplined, sober, temperate, moderate, sparing, frugal, austere, ascetic, restrained.
₣ intemperate, gluttonous, luxurious.

abstinence *n* abstaining, abstention, abstemiousness, self-denial, non-indulgence, avoidance, forbearance, refraining, refusal, restraint, self-restraint, self-control, self-discipline, sobriety, teetotalism, temperance, moderation, frugality, asceticism.
₣ indulgence, self-indulgence.

abstract *adj* non-concrete, conceptual, intellectual, hypothetical, theoretical, unpractical, unrealistic, general, generalized, indefinite, metaphysical, philosophical, academic, complex, abstruse, deep, profound, subtle.
₣ concrete, real, actual.
➤ *n* synopsis, outline, summary, recapitulation, résumé, précis, epitome, digest, abridgement, compression.
➤ *v* **1** SUMMARIZE, outline, précis, digest, condense, compress, abridge, abbreviate, shorten. **2** EXTRACT, remove, withdraw, isolate, detach, dissociate, separate.
₣ 1 expand. **2** insert.

abstraction *n* **1** IDEA, notion, concept, thought, conception, theory, hypothesis, theorem, formula, generalization, generality.

2 INATTENTION, dream, dreaminess, absent-mindedness, distraction, pensiveness, preoccupation, absorption. **3** EXTRACTION, withdrawal, isolation, separation.

absurd *adj* ridiculous, ludicrous, preposterous, fantastic, incongruous, illogical, paradoxical, implausible, untenable, unreasonable, irrational, nonsensical, meaningless, senseless, foolish, silly, stupid, idiotic, crazy, daft (*infml*), farcical, comical, funny, humorous, laughable, risible, derisory.
E3 logical, rational, sensible.

abundant *adj* plentiful, in plenty, full, filled, well-supplied, ample, generous, bountiful, rich, copious, profuse, lavish, exuberant, teeming, overflowing.
E3 scarce, sparse.

abuse *v* **1** MISUSE, misapply, exploit, take advantage of, oppress, wrong, ill-treat, maltreat, hurt, injure, molest, damage, spoil, harm. **2** INSULT, swear at, defame, libel, slander, smear, disparage, malign, revile, scold, upbraid.
E3 1 cherish, care for. **2** compliment, praise.
➤ *n* **1** MISUSE, misapplication, exploitation, imposition, oppression, wrong, ill-treatment, maltreatment, hurt, injury, molestation, damage, spoiling, harm. **2** INSULTS, swearing, cursing, offence, defamation, libel, slander, disparagement, reproach, scolding, upbraiding, tirade.
E3 1 care, attention. **2** compliments, praise.

abusive *adj* insulting, offensive, rude, scathing, hurtful, injurious, cruel, destructive, defamatory, libellous, slanderous, derogatory, disparaging, pejorative, vilifying, maligning, reviling, censorious, reproachful, scolding, upbraiding.
E3 complimentary, polite.

abyss *n* gulf, chasm, crevasse, fissure, gorge, canyon, crater, pit, depth, void.

academic *adj* **1** SCHOLARLY, erudite, learned, well-read, studious, bookish, scholastic, pedagogical, educational, instructional, literary, highbrow. **2** THEORETICAL, hypothetical, conjectural, speculative, notional, abstract, impractical.
➤ *n* professor, don, master, fellow, lecturer, tutor, student, scholar, man of letters, woman of letters, pedant.

accelerate *v* quicken, speed, speed up, pick up speed, step up, expedite, hurry, hasten, precipitate, stimulate, facilitate, advance, further, promote, forward.
E3 decelerate, slow down, delay.

accent *n* pronunciation, enunciation, articulation, brogue, twang (*infml*), tone, pitch, intonation, inflection, stress, emphasis, accentuation, intensity, force, cadence, rhythm, beat, pulse, pulsation.

accentuate *v* accent, stress, emphasize, underline, highlight, intensify, strengthen, deepen.
E3 play down, weaken.

accept *v* **1** *accept a gift*: take, receive, obtain, acquire, gain, secure. **2** ACKNOWLEDGE, recognize, admit, allow, approve, agree to, consent to, take on, adopt. **3** TOLERATE, put up with, stand, bear, abide, face up to, yield to.
E3 1 refuse, turn down. **2** reject.

acceptable *adj* satisfactory, tolerable, moderate, passable, adequate, all right, OK (*infml*), so-so (*infml*), unexceptionable, admissible, suitable, conventional, correct, desirable, pleasant, gratifying, welcome.
E3 unacceptable, unsatisfactory, unwelcome.

acceptance *n* **1** TAKING, accepting, receipt, obtaining, getting, acquiring, gaining, securing. **2** ACKNOWLEDGEMENT, recognition, admission, concession, affirmation, concurrence, agreement, assent, consent, permission, ratification, approval, stamp of approval, OK (*infml*), adoption, undertaking, belief, credence.
E3 1 refusal. **2** rejection, dissent.

accepted *adj* authorized, approved, ratified, sanctioned, agreed, acknowledged, recognized, admitted,

confirmed, acceptable, correct, conventional, unorthodox, traditional, customary, time-honoured, established, received, universal, regular, standard, normal, usual, common.
Ea unconventional, unorthodox, controversial.

access *n* admission, admittance, entry, entering, entrance, gateway, door, key, approach, passage, road, path, course.
Ea exit, outlet.

accessible *adj* 1 REACHABLE, get-at-able (*infml*), attainable, achievable, possible, obtainable, available, on hand, ready, handy, convenient, near, nearby. 2 FRIENDLY, affable, approachable, sociable, informal.
Ea 1 inaccessible, remote. 2 unapproachable.

accessory *n* 1 EXTRA, supplement, addition, appendage, attachment, extension, component, fitting, accompaniment, decoration, adornment, frill, trimming.
2 ACCOMPLICE, partner, associate, colleague, confederate, assistant, helper, help, aid.

accident *n* 1 CHANCE, hazard, fortuity, luck, fortune, fate, serendipity, contingency, fluke. 2 MISFORTUNE, mischance, misadventure, mishap, casualty, blow, calamity, disaster.
3 *road accident*: collision, crash, shunt (*sl*), prang (*sl*), pile-up.

accidental *adj* unintentional, unintended, inadvertent, unplanned, uncalculated, unexpected, unforeseen, unlooked-for, chance, fortuitous, flukey, uncertain, haphazard, random, casual, incidental.
Ea intentional, deliberate, calculated, premeditated.

acclaim *v* praise, commend, extol, exalt, honour, hail, salute, welcome, applaud, clap, cheer, celebrate.
➤ *n* acclamation, praise, commendation, homage, tribute, eulogy, exaltation, honour, welcome, approbation (*fml*), approval, applause, ovation, clapping, cheers, cheering,

shouting, celebration.
Ea criticism, disapproval.

accommodate *v* 1 LODGE, board, put up, house, shelter. 2 OBLIGE, help, assist, aid, serve, provide, supply, comply, conform. 3 ADAPT, accustom, acclimatize, adjust, modify, fit, harmonize, reconcile, settle, compose.

accommodating *adj* obliging, indulgent, helpful, co-operative, willing, kind, considerate, unselfish, sympathetic, friendly, hospitable.
Ea disobliging, selfish.

accommodation *n* housing, shelter, board, lodging, digs (*infml*).

> *Types of accommodation include*: flat, apartment, bedsit, bedsitter, dormitory (*US*), hostel, halls of residence, rooms, shelter, pad (*infml*), squat (*infml*); bed and breakfast, board, guest house, hotel, youth hostel, villa, timeshare, self-catering, motel, inn, pension, boarding-house; barracks, billet, married quarters. *see also* **house**; **room**.

accompany *v* 1 ESCORT, attend, convoy, chaperon, usher, conduct, follow. 2 COEXIST, coincide, belong to, go with, complement, supplement.

accomplice *n* assistant, helper, abettor, mate, henchman, conspirator, collaborator, ally, confederate, partner, associate, colleague, participator, accessory.

accomplish *v* achieve, attain, do, perform, carry out, execute, fulfil, discharge, finish, complete, conclude, consummate, realize, effect, bring about, engineer, produce, obtain.

accomplished *adj* skilled, professional, practised, proficient, gifted, talented, skilful, adroit, adept, expert, masterly, consummate, polished, cultivated.
Ea unskilled, inexpert, incapable.

accomplishment *n* 1 *the accomplishment of a task*: achievement, attainment, doing, performance, carrying out, execution, fulfilment, discharge, finishing, completion, conclusion, consummation, perfection, realization, fruition, production. **2** SKILL, art, aptitude, faculty, ability, capability, proficiency, gift, talent, forte. **3** EXPLOIT, feat, deed, stroke, triumph.

accord v **1** AGREE, concur, harmonize, match, conform, correspond, suit. **2** GIVE, tender, grant, allow, bestow, endow, confer.

▪ **1** disagree. **2** deny.

➤ n accordance, agreement, assent, unanimity, concert, unity, correspondence, conformity, harmony, sympathy.

▪ conflict, discord, disharmony.

according to in accordance with, in keeping with, obedient to, in conformity with, in line with, consistent with, commensurate with, in proportion to, in relation to, after, in the light of, in the manner of, after the manner of.

accordingly adv in accordance, in accord with, correspondingly, so, as a result, consequently, in consequence, therefore, thus, hence, appropriately, properly, suitably.

accost v approach, confront, buttonhole, waylay, stop, halt, detain, importune, solicit.

account n **1** an account of what happened: narrative, story, tale, chronicle, history, memoir, record, statement, report, communiqué, write-up, version, portrayal, sketch, description, presentation, explanation. **2** LEDGER, book, books, register, inventory, statement, invoice, bill, tab, charge, reckoning, computation, tally, score, balance.

Terms used in accounting and finance include: above the line, accounting period, accounts rendered, accounts payable, accounts receivable, accrual basis, allowable expense, annual accounts, annual report, appreciation, APR (= Annual Percentage Rate), asset-stripping, audit, authorized capital, bad debt, balance sheet, below the line, benefit in kind, bookkeeping, break-even point, budgetary control, capital expenditure, capital gain, capitalization, cash flow, circulating capital, collateral, compound interest, consolidated accounts, cost accounting, cost-benefit analysis, creative accounting, credit control, creditor, current assets, current liabilities, debit, debt/equity ratio, debtor, deferred credit, deferred expenditure, deferred liability, deficit, depreciating asset, depreciation, direct costs, disinvestment, dividend, double-entry bookkeeping, earnings per share, equity, fiduciary loan, fictitious assets, financial year, first cost, fiscal year, fixed assets, fixed capital, fixed costs, fixtures and fittings, floating capital, frozen assets, funds flow statement, gearing, going concern, gross margin, gross profit, gross receipts, grossing up, historic cost, income, intangible assets, interim accounts, ledger, liability, liquid assets, liquidation, liquidity, loan capital, loss, net assets, net profit, nominal capital, overheads, outgoings, payroll, petty cash, poison pill, profit and loss account, rate of return, realization of assets, refinance, replacement cost, reserves, return on capital, revenue expenditure, ring fencing (funds), running costs, secured loan, simple interest, statutory income, statutory returns, takeover, hostile takeover, tangible assets, tax loss, taxable profits, total costs, trading account, trial balance, turnover, unit costs, variable costs, wasting asset, watering, white knight, windfall profit, write off.

◇ **account for** explain, elucidate, illuminate, clear up, rationalize, justify, vindicate, answer for, put paid to, destroy, kill.

accountable adj answerable, responsible, liable, amenable, obliged, bound.

accumulate v gather, assemble, collect, amass, aggregate, cumulate, accrue, grow, increase, multiply, build up, pile up, hoard, stockpile, stash (*infml*), store.
☒ disseminate.

accumulation n gathering, assembly, collection, growth, increase, build-up, conglomeration, mass, heap, pile, stack, stock, store, reserve, hoard, stockpile.

accuracy n correctness, precision, exactness, authenticity, truth, veracity, closeness, faithfulness, fidelity, carefulness.
☒ inaccuracy.

accurate adj correct, right, unerring, precise, exact, well-directed, spot-on (*infml*), faultless, perfect, word-perfect, sound, authentic, factual, nice, true, truthful, veracious, just, proper, close, faithful, well-judged, careful, rigorous, scrupulous, meticulous, strict, minute.
☒ inaccurate, wrong, imprecise, inexact.

accusation n charge, allegation, imputation, indictment, denunciation, impeachment, recrimination, complaint, incrimination.

accuse v charge, indict, impugn, denounce, arraign, impeach, cite, allege, attribute, impute, blame, censure, recriminate, incriminate, criminate, inform against.

accustomed adj used, in the habit of, given to, confirmed, seasoned, hardened, inured, disciplined, trained, adapted, acclimatized, acquainted, familiar, wonted, habitual, routine, regular, normal, usual, ordinary, everyday, conventional, customary, traditional, established, fixed, prevailing, general.
☒ unaccustomed, unusual.

ache v 1 HURT, be sore, pain, suffer, agonize, throb, pound, twinge, smart, sting. 2 YEARN, long, pine, hanker, desire, crave, hunger, thirst, itch.
➤ n 1 PAIN, hurt, soreness, suffering, anguish, agony, throb, throbbing, pounding, pang, twinge, smarting, stinging. 2 YEARNING, longing, craving, desire, itch.

achieve v accomplish, attain, reach, get, obtain, acquire, procure, gain, earn, win, succeed, manage, do, perform, carry out, execute, fulfil, finish, complete, consummate, effect, bring about, realize, produce.
☒ underachieve, miss, fail.

achievement n 1 *the achievement of our aims*: accomplishment, attainment, acquirement, performance, execution, fulfilment, completion, success, realization, fruition. 2 ACT, deed, exploit, feat, effort.

acid adj 1 SOUR, bitter, tart, vinegary, sharp, pungent. 2 ACERBIC, caustic, corrosive, stinging, biting, mordant, cutting, incisive, trenchant, harsh, hurtful.

Types of acid include: acetic (or ethanoic), acrylic, amino, aqua fortis, aqua regia, arachidonic, ascorbic, benzoic, boric, carbolic, chloric, citric, DNA (deoxyribonucleic acid), fatty, folic, formic (or methanoic), hydrochloric, hydrocyanic, lactic, malic, nalidixic, nitric, nitrohydrochloric, nitrous, palmitic, pectic, phenol, phosphoric, prussic, RNA (ribonucleic acid), salicylic, spirits of salt, stearic, sulphuric, tannic, tartaric, uric.

Amino acids include: alanine, arginine, asparagine, aspartic acid, cysteine, glutamic acid, glutamine, glycine, histidine, isoleucine, leucine, lysine, methionine, phenylalanine, proline, serine, threonine, trytophan, tyrosine, valine.

acknowledge v 1 *acknowledge an error*: admit, confess, own up to, declare, recognize, accept, grant, allow, concede. 2 GREET, address, notice, recognize. 3 *acknowledge a letter*: answer, reply to, respond to, confirm.
☒ 1 deny. 2 ignore.

acknowledged adj recognized, accepted, approved, accredited, declared, professed, attested, avowed, confirmed.

acknowledgement n 1 ADMISSION, confession, declaration, profession, recognition, acceptance. 2 GREETING, salutation, notice, recognition. 3 ANSWER, reply, response, reaction, affirmation. 4 GRATITUDE, thanks, appreciation, tribute.

acquaint v accustom, familiarize, tell, notify, advise, inform, brief, enlighten, divulge, disclose, reveal, announce.

acquaintance n 1 AWARENESS, knowledge, understanding, experience, familiarity, intimacy, relationship, association, fellowship, companionship. 2 FRIEND, companion, colleague, associate, contact.

acquire v buy, purchase, procure, appropriate, obtain, get, cop (sl), receive, collect, pick up, gather, net, gain, secure, earn, win, achieve, attain, realize. relinquish, forfeit.

acquisition n purchase, buy (infml), procurement, appropriation, gain, securing, achievement, attainment, accession, takeover, property, possession.

acquit v absolve, clear, reprieve, let off, exonerate, exculpate, excuse, vindicate, free, liberate, deliver, relieve, release, dismiss, discharge, settle, satisfy, repay. convict.

acquittal n absolution, clearance, reprieve, exoneration, exculpation, excusing, vindication, freeing, liberation, deliverance, relief, release, dismissal, discharge. conviction.

acrid adj pungent, sharp, stinging, acid, burning, caustic, acerbic, biting, cutting, incisive, trenchant, sarcastic, sardonic, bitter, acrimonious, virulent, harsh, vitriolic, nasty, malicious, venomous.

acrimonious adj bitter, biting, cutting, trenchant, sharp, virulent, severe, spiteful, censorious, abusive, ill-tempered. peaceable, kindly.

acrimony n bitterness, rancour, resentment, ill-will, petulance, gall, ill temper, irascibility, trenchancy, sarcasm, astringency, acerbity, harshness, virulence.

act n 1 DEED, action, undertaking, enterprise, operation, manoeuvre, move, step, doing, execution, accomplishment, achievement, exploit, feat, stroke. 2 put on an act: pretence, make-believe, sham, fake, feigning, dissimulation, affectation, show, front. 3 LAW, statute, ordinance, edict, decree, resolution, measure, bill. 4 TURN, item, routine, sketch, performance, gig (sl).
➤ v 1 BEHAVE, conduct, exert, make, work, function, operate, do, execute, carry out. 2 PRETEND, feign, put on, assume, simulate, mimic, imitate, impersonate, portray, represent, mime, play, perform, enact.
◇ **act on** 1 act on orders: carry out, fulfil, comply with, conform to, obey, follow, heed, take. 2 AFFECT, influence, alter, modify, change, transform.

acting adj temporary, provisional, interim, stopgap, supply, stand-by, substitute, reserve.
➤ n theatre, stagecraft, artistry, performing, performance, play-acting, melodrama, dramatics, theatricals, portrayal, characterization, impersonation, imitating.

action n 1 ACT, move, deed, exploit, feat, accomplishment, achievement, performance, effort, endeavour, enterprise, undertaking, proceeding, process, activity, liveliness, spirit, energy, vigour, power, force, exercise, exertion, work, functioning, operation, mechanism, movement, motion. 2 killed in action: warfare, battle, conflict, combat, fight, fray, engagement, skirmish, clash. 3 LITIGATION, lawsuit, suit, case, prosecution.

activate v start, initiate, trigger, set off, fire, kick-start (infml), switch on, set in motion, mobilize, propel, move, stir, rouse, arouse, stimulate, motivate, prompt, animate, energize, impel, excite, galvanize. deactivate, stop, arrest.

active *adj* **1** BUSY, occupied, on the go (*infml*), industrious, diligent, hard-working, forceful, spirited, vital, forward, enterprising, enthusiastic, devoted, engaged, involved, committed, militant, activist. **2** AGILE, nimble, sprightly, light-footed, quick, alert, animated, lively, energetic, vigorous. **3** IN OPERATION, functioning, working, running.
▣ **1** passive. **2** inert, dormant. **3** inactive.

activity *n* **1** LIVELINESS, life, activeness, action, motion, movement, commotion, bustle, hustle, industry, labour, exertion, exercise. **2** OCCUPATION, job, work, act, deed, project, scheme, task, venture, enterprise, endeavour, undertaking, pursuit, hobby, pastime, interest.

actor *n* actress, play-actor, film actor, movie actor (*US*), comedian, tragedian, ham (*infml*), player, performer, artist, luvvie (*infml*), impersonator, mime.

actual *adj* **1** REAL, existent, substantial, tangible, material, physical, concrete, positive, definite, absolute, certain, unquestionable, indisputable, confirmed, verified, factual, truthful, true, genuine, legitimate, bona fide, authentic, realistic. **2** CURRENT, present, present-day, prevailing, live, living.
▣ **1** theoretical, apparent, imaginary.

actually *adv* in fact, as a matter of fact, as it happens, in truth, in reality, really, truly, indeed, absolutely.

acumen *n* astuteness, shrewdness, sharpness, keenness, quickness, penetration, insight, intuition, discrimination, discernment, judgement, perception, sense, wit, wisdom, intelligence, cleverness, ingenuity.

acute *adj* **1** SEVERE, intense, extreme, violent, dangerous, serious, grave, urgent, crucial, vital, decisive, sharp, cutting, poignant, distressing.
2 *an acute mind*: sharp, keen, incisive, penetrating, astute, shrewd, judicious, discerning, observant, perceptive.
▣ **1** mild, slight.

adamant *adj* hard, resolute, determined, set, firm, insistent, rigid, stiff, inflexible, unbending, unrelenting, intransigent, unyielding, stubborn, uncompromising, tough, fixed, immovable, unshakable.
▣ hesitant, flexible, yielding.

adapt *v* alter, change, qualify, modify, adjust, convert, remodel, customize, fit, tweak, tailor, fashion, shape, harmonize, match, suit, conform, comply, prepare, familiarize, acclimatize.

adaptable *adj* alterable, changeable, variable, modifiable, adjustable, convertible, conformable, versatile, plastic, malleable, flexible, compliant, amenable, easy-going.
▣ inflexible, refractory.

adaptation *n* alteration, change, shift, transformation, modification, adjustment, accommodation, conversion, remodelling, reworking, reshaping, refitting, revision, variation, version.

add *v* append, annex, affix, attach, tack on, join, combine, supplement, augment.
▣ take away, remove.
◇ **add up 1** ADD, sum up, tot up, total, tally, count (up), reckon, compute. **2** AMOUNT, come to, constitute, include. **3** *it doesn't add up*: be consistent, hang together, fit, be plausible, make sense, be reasonable, mean, signify, indicate.
▣ **1** subtract.

addict *n* **1** ENTHUSIAST, fan, buff (*infml*), fiend, freak, devotee, follower, adherent. **2** DRUG-ADDICT, user (*infml*), dope-fiend (*infml*), junkie (*infml*), druggie (*infml*), tripper (*sl*), mainliner (*sl*).

addicted *adj* dependent, hooked, obsessed, absorbed, devoted, dedicated, fond, inclined, disposed, accustomed.

addiction *n* dependence, craving, habit, monkey (*sl*), obsession.

addition *n* **1** ADDING, annexation, accession, extension, enlargement, increasing, increase, gain. **2** ADJUNCT,

supplement, additive, addendum, appendix, appendage, accessory, attachment, extra, increment.
3 SUMMING-UP, totting-up, totalling, counting, reckoning, inclusion.
🔁 **1** removal. **3** subtraction.
◇ **in addition** additionally, too, also, as well, besides, moreover, further, furthermore, over and above.

additional *adj* added, extra, supplementary, spare, more, further, increased, other, new, fresh.

address *n* **1** RESIDENCE, dwelling, abode, house, home, lodging, direction, inscription, whereabouts, location, situation, place. **2** SPEECH, talk, lecture, sermon, discourse, dissertation.
➤ *v* lecture, speak to, talk to, greet, salute, hail, invoke, accost, approach, buttonhole.

adept *adj* skilled, accomplished, expert, masterly, experienced, versed, practised, polished, proficient, able, adroit, deft, nimble.

adequate *adj* enough, sufficient, commensurate, requisite, suitable, fit, able, competent, capable, serviceable, acceptable, satisfactory, passable, tolerable, fair, respectable, presentable.
🔁 inadequate, insufficient.

adhere *v* **1** STICK, glue, paste, cement, fix, fasten, attach, join, link, combine, coalesce, cohere, hold, cling, cleave to.
2 *adhere to the agreement*: observe, follow, abide by, comply with, fulfil, obey, keep, heed, respect, stand by.

adherent *n* supporter, upholder, advocate, partisan, follower, disciple, satellite, henchman, hanger-on, votary, devotee, admirer, fan, enthusiast, freak, nut.

adhesion *n* adherence, adhesiveness, bond, attachment, grip, cohesion.

adhesive *adj* sticky, tacky, self-adhesive, gummed, gummy, gluey, adherent, adhering, sticking, clinging, holding, attaching, cohesive.
➤ *n* glue, gum, paste, cement.

adjacent *adj* adjoining, abutting,

touching, contiguous, bordering, alongside, beside, juxtaposed, next-door, neighbouring, next, closest, nearest, close, near.
🔁 remote, distant.

adjoin *v* abut, touch, meet, border, verge, neighbour, interconnect, link, connect, join, combine, unite, couple, attach, annex, add.

adjourn *v* interrupt, suspend, discontinue, break off, delay, stay, defer, postpone, put off, recess, retire.
🔁 assemble, convene.

adjournment *n* interruption, suspension, discontinuation, break, pause, recess, delay, stay, deferment, deferral, postponement, putting off, dissolution.

adjudicate *v* judge, arbitrate, umpire, referee, settle, determine, decide, pronounce.

adjust *v* **1** MODIFY, change, adapt, alter, convert, dispose, shape, remodel, fit, accommodate, suit, measure, rectify, regulate, balance, temper, tune, fine-tune, tweak, fix, set, arrange, compose, settle, square. **2** ACCUSTOM, habituate, acclimatize, reconcile, harmonize, conform.
🔁 **1** disarrange, upset.

adjustment *n* **1** MODIFICATION, change, adaptation, alteration, conversion, remodelling, shaping, fitting, accommodation, rectification, regulation, tuning, fixing, setting, arranging, arrangement, ordering, settlement. **2** HABITUATION, orientation, acclimatization, naturalization, reconciliation, harmonization, conforming.

ad-lib *v* improvise, extemporize, make up, invent.
➤ *adj* impromptu, improvised, extempore, extemporaneous, off-the-cuff, unprepared, unpremeditated, unrehearsed, spontaneous, made up.
🔁 prepared.
➤ *adv* impromptu, extempore, extemporaneously, off-the-cuff, off the

top of one's head, spontaneously, impulsively.

administer v 1 *administer an organization*: govern, rule, lead, head, preside over, officiate, manage, run, organize, direct, conduct, control, regulate, superintend, supervise, oversee. 2 GIVE, provide, supply, distribute, dole out, dispense, measure out, mete out, execute, impose, apply.

administration n 1 ADMINISTERING, governing, ruling, leadership, management, execution, running, organization, direction, control, superintendence, supervision, overseeing. 2 GOVERNING BODY, regime, government, ministry, leadership, directorship, management, executive, term of office.

administrative adj governmental, legislative, authoritative, directorial, managerial, management, executive, organizational, regulatory, supervisory.

admirable adj praiseworthy, commendable, laudable, creditable, deserving, worthy, respected, fine, excellent, superior, wonderful, exquisite, choice, rare, valuable.
🖪 contemptible, despicable, deplorable.

admiration n esteem, regard, respect, reverence, veneration, worship, idolism, adoration, affection, approval, praise, appreciation, pleasure, delight, wonder, astonishment, amazement, surprise.
🖪 contempt.

admire v esteem, respect, revere, venerate, worship, idolize, adore, approve, praise, laud, applaud, appreciate, value.
🖪 despise, censure.

admirer n 1 FOLLOWER, disciple, adherent, supporter, fan, enthusiast, devotee, worshipper, idolizer. 2 SUITOR, boyfriend, girlfriend, sweetheart, lover.
🖪 1 critic, opponent.

admissible adj acceptable, tolerable, tolerated, passable, allowable,

permissible, allowed, permitted, lawful, legitimate, justifiable.
🖪 inadmissible, illegitimate.

admission n confession, granting, acknowledgement, recognition, acceptance, allowance, concession, affirmation, declaration, profession, disclosure, divulgence, revelation, exposé.
🖪 denial.

admit v 1 CONFESS, own (up), grant, acknowledge, recognize, accept, allow, concede, agree, affirm, declare, profess, disclose, divulge, reveal. 2 LET IN, allow to enter, give access, accept, receive, take in, introduce, initiate.
🖪 1 deny. 2 shut out, exclude.

admittance n admitting, admission, letting in, access, entrance, entry, acceptance, reception, introduction, initiation.
🖪 exclusion.

adolescence n teens, puberty, youth, minority, boyhood, girlhood, development, immaturity, youthfulness, boyishness, girlishness.

adolescent adj teenage, young, youthful, juvenile, puerile, boyish, girlish, immature, growing, developing.
➤ n teenager, youth, juvenile, minor.

adopt v take on, accept, assume, take up, appropriate, embrace, follow, choose, select, take in, foster, support, maintain, back, endorse, ratify, approve.
🖪 repudiate, disown.

adorable adj lovable, dear, darling, precious, appealing, sweet, winsome, charming, enchanting, captivating, winning, delightful, pleasing, attractive, fetching.
🖪 hateful, abominable.

adore v love, cherish, dote on, admire, esteem, honour, revere, venerate, worship, idolize, exalt, glorify.
🖪 hate, abhor.

adorn v decorate, deck, bedeck, ornament, crown, trim, garnish, gild, enhance, embellish, doll up, enrich, grace.

adult *adj* grown-up, of age, full-grown, fully grown, developed, mature, ripe, ripened.
Ea immature.

adulterate *v* contaminate, pollute, taint, corrupt, defile, debase, dilute, water down, weaken, devalue, deteriorate.
Ea purify.

advance *v* **1** PROCEED, go forward, move on, go ahead, progress, prosper, flourish, thrive, improve, push the envelope (*infml*). **2** ACCELERATE, speed up, hasten, send forward. **3** FURTHER, promote, upgrade, foster, support, assist, benefit, facilitate, increase, grow. **4** *advance an idea*: present, submit, suggest, allege, cite, bring forward, offer, provide, supply, furnish. **5** *advance a sum of money*: lend, loan, pay beforehand, pay, give.
Ea **1** retreat. **2** retard. **3** impede.
➤ *n* **1** PROGRESS, forward movement, onward movement, headway, step, advancement, furtherance, breakthrough, development, growth, increase, improvement, amelioration. **2** DEPOSIT, down payment, prepayment, credit, loan.
Ea **1** retreat, recession.
◊ **in advance** beforehand, previously, early, earlier, sooner, ahead, in front, in the lead, in the forefront.
Ea later, behind.

advanced *adj* leading, foremost, cutting-edge, state-of-the-art, ahead, forward, precocious, progressive, forward-looking, avant-garde, ultra-modern, sophisticated, complex, higher.
Ea backward, retarded, elementary.

advancement *n* furtherance, promotion, preferment, betterment, improvement, development, growth, rise, gain, advance, progress, headway.
Ea demotion, retardation.

advantage *n* **1** ASSET, blessing, benefit, good, welfare, interest, service, help, aid, assistance, use, avail, convenience, usefulness, utility, profit, gain, start.

2 LEAD, edge, upper hand, superiority, precedence, pre-eminence, sway.
Ea **1** disadvantage, drawback, hindrance.

advantageous *adj* beneficial, favourable, opportune, convenient, helpful, useful, worthwhile, valuable, profitable, gainful, remunerative, rewarding.
Ea disadvantageous, adverse, damaging.

adventure *n* exploit, venture, undertaking, enterprise, risk, hazard, chance, speculation, experience, incident, occurrence.

adventurous *adj* daring, intrepid, bold, audacious, headstrong, impetuous, reckless, rash, risky, venturesome, enterprising.
Ea cautious, chary, prudent.

adverse *adj* hostile, antagonistic, opposing, opposite, counter, contrary, conflicting, counter-productive, negative, disadvantageous, unfavourable, inauspicious, unfortunate, unlucky, inopportune, detrimental, harmful, noxious, injurious, hurtful, unfriendly, uncongenial.
Ea advantageous, favourable.

adversity *n* misfortune, ill fortune, bad luck, ill luck, reverse, hardship, hard times, misery, wretchedness, affliction, suffering, distress, sorrow, woe, trouble, trial, tribulation, calamity, disaster, catastrophe.
Ea prosperity.

advertise *v* publicize, promote, push, plug (*infml*), praise, hype (*sl*), trumpet, blazon, herald, announce, declare, proclaim, broadcast, publish, display, make known, inform, notify.

advertisement *n* advert (*infml*), ad (*infml*), commercial, publicity, promotion, promo (*infml*), plug (*infml*), hype (*sl*), display, blurb, announcement, notice, poster, bill, placard, leaflet, handbill, circular, handout, flyer, propaganda.

advice *n* **1** WARNING, caution, do's and don'ts, injunction, instruction, counsel, help, guidance, direction, suggestion, recommendation, opinion, view. **2** NOTIFICATION, notice, memorandum, communication, information, intelligence.

advisable *adj* suggested, recommended, sensible, wise, prudent, judicious, sound, profitable, beneficial, desirable, suitable, appropriate, apt, fitting, fit, proper, correct.
🖬 inadvisable, foolish.

advise *v* **1** COUNSEL, guide, warn, forewarn, caution, instruct, teach, tutor, suggest, recommend, commend, urge. **2** NOTIFY, inform, tell, acquaint, make known, report.

adviser *n* counsellor, consultant, authority, guide, teacher, tutor, instructor, coach, helper, aide, right-hand man, mentor, confidant(e), counsel, lawyer.

advocate *v* defend, champion, campaign for, press for, argue for, plead for, justify, urge, encourage, advise, recommend, propose, promote, endorse, support, uphold, patronize, adopt, subscribe to, favour, countenance.
🖬 impugn, disparage, deprecate.
➤ *n* defender, supporter, upholder, champion, campaigner, pleader, vindicator, proponent, promoter, speaker, spokesperson.
🖬 opponent, critic.

affable *adj* friendly, amiable, approachable, open, expansive, genial, good-humoured, good-natured, mild, benevolent, kindly, gracious, obliging, courteous, amicable, congenial, cordial, warm, sociable, pleasant, agreeable.
🖬 unfriendly, reserved, reticent, cool.

affair *n* **1** BUSINESS, transaction, operation, proceeding, undertaking, activity, project, responsibility, interest, concern, matter, question, issue, subject, topic, circumstance, happening, occurrence, incident, episode, event. **2** *have an affair*: relationship, liaison, intrigue, love affair, romance, amour.

affect *v* **1** CONCERN, regard, involve, relate to, apply to, bear upon, impinge upon, act on, change, transform, alter, modify, influence, sway, prevail over, attack, strike, impress, interest, stir, move, touch, upset, disturb, perturb, trouble, overcome. **2** ADOPT, assume, put on, feign, simulate, imitate, fake, counterfeit, sham, pretend, profess, aspire to.

affectation *n* airs, pretentiousness, mannerism, pose, act, show, appearance, façade, pretence, sham, simulation, imitation, artificiality, insincerity.
🖬 artlessness, ingenuousness.

affected *adj* assumed, put-on, feigned, simulated, artificial, fake, counterfeit, sham, phoney (*infml*), contrived, studied, precious, mannered, pretentious, pompous, stiff, unnatural, insincere.
🖬 genuine, natural.

affection *n* fondness, attachment, devotion, love, tenderness, care, warmth, feeling, kindness, friendliness, goodwill, favour, liking, partiality, inclination, penchant, passion, desire.
🖬 dislike, antipathy.

affectionate *adj* fond, attached, devoted, doting, loving, tender, caring, warm, warm-hearted, kind, friendly, amiable, cordial.
🖬 cold, undemonstrative.

affirm *v* confirm, corroborate, endorse, ratify, certify, witness, testify, swear, maintain, state, assert, declare, pronounce.
🖬 refute, deny.

affirmative *adj* agreeing, concurring, approving, assenting, positive, confirming, corroborative, emphatic.
🖬 negative, dissenting.

afflict *v* strike, visit, trouble, burden, oppress, distress, grieve, pain, hurt, wound, harm, try, harass, beset, plague, torment, torture.
🖬 comfort, solace.

affliction *n* distress, grief, sorrow,

misery, depression, suffering, pain, torment, disease, illness, sickness, plague, curse, cross, ordeal, trial, tribulation, trouble, hardship, adversity, misfortune, calamity, disaster.
🖭 comfort, consolation, solace, blessing.

affluence *n* wealthiness, wealth, riches, fortune, substance, property, prosperity, opulence, abundance, profusion, plenty.
🖭 poverty.

affluent *adj* wealthy, rich, moneyed, loaded (*sl*), flush (*infml*), well-off, prosperous, well-to-do, opulent, comfortable.
🖭 poor, impoverished.

afford *v* 1 HAVE ENOUGH FOR, spare, allow, manage, sustain, bear. 2 PROVIDE, supply, furnish, give, grant, offer, impart, produce, yield, generate.

affront *v* offend, insult, abuse, snub, slight, provoke, displease, irritate, annoy, anger, vex, incense, outrage.
🖭 compliment, appease.
➤ *n* offence, insult, slur, rudeness, discourtesy, disrespect, indignity, snub, slight, wrong, injury, abuse, provocation, vexation, outrage.
🖭 compliment.

afraid *adj* frightened, scared, alarmed, terrified, fearful, timorous, daunted, intimidated, faint-hearted, cowardly, reluctant, apprehensive, anxious, nervous, timid, distrustful, suspicious.
🖭 unafraid, brave, bold, confident.

after *prep* following, subsequent to, in consequence of, as a result of, behind, below.
🖭 before.

again *adv* once more, once again, another time, over again, afresh, anew, yet again, encore.

against *prep* 1 *against the wall*: abutting, adjacent to, close up to, touching, in contact with, on. 2 OPPOSITE TO, facing, fronting, in the face of, confronting, opposing, versus, opposed to, in opposition to, anti, hostile to,

resisting, in defiance of, in contrast to.
🖭 2 for, pro.

age *n* 1 ERA, epoch, day, days, generation, date, time, period, duration, span, years, aeon. 2 OLD AGE, maturity, elderliness, seniority, dotage, senility, decline.
🖭 2 youth.
➤ *v* grow old, mature, ripen, mellow, season, decline, deteriorate, degenerate.

agency *n* 1 *recruitment agency*: bureau, office, department, organization, business, work. 2 MEANS, medium, instrumentality, power, force, influence, effect, intervention, action, activity, operation, mechanism, workings.

agent *n* 1 SUBSTITUTE, deputy, delegate, envoy, emissary, representative, rep (*infml*), broker, middleman, go-between, intermediary, negotiator, mover, doer, performer, operator, operative, functionary, worker. 2 INSTRUMENT, vehicle, channel, means, agency, cause, force.

aggravate *v* 1 *aggravate a problem*: exacerbate, worsen, inflame, increase, intensify, heighten, magnify, exaggerate. 2 (*infml*) ANNOY, irritate, vex, irk, exasperate, incense, provoke, tease, pester, harass, bug (*infml*).
🖭 1 improve, alleviate. 2 appease, mollify.

aggregate *n* total, sum, amount, whole, totality, entirety, generality, combination, collection, accumulation.
➤ *adj* cumulative, accumulated, collected, combined, united, added, total, complete, composite, mixed, collective.
🖭 individual, particular.

aggression *n* 1 ANTAGONISM, provocation, offence, injury, attack, offensive, assault, onslaught, raid, incursion, invasion, intrusion. 2 AGGRESSIVENESS, militancy, belligerence, combativeness, hostility.
🖭 1 peace, resistance. 2 passivity, gentleness.

aggressive *adj* argumentative, quarrelsome, contentious, belligerent, hostile, offensive, provocative, intrusive, invasive, bold, assertive, in-your-face (*infml*), pushy, go-ahead, forceful, vigorous, zealous, ruthless, destructive. **E3** peaceable, friendly, submissive, timid.

aggrieved *adj* wronged, offended, hurt, injured, insulted, maltreated, ill-used, resentful, pained, distressed, saddened, unhappy, upset, annoyed. **E3** pleased.

aghast *adj* shocked, appalled, horrified, horror-struck, thunderstruck, stunned, stupefied, amazed, astonished, astounded, startled, confounded, dismayed.

agile *adj* active, lively, nimble, spry, sprightly, mobile, flexible, limber, lithe, fleet, quick, swift, brisk, prompt, sharp, acute, alert, quick-witted, clever, adroit, deft. **E3** clumsy, stiff.

agitate *v* **1** ROUSE, arouse, stir up, excite, stimulate, incite, inflame, ferment, work up, worry, trouble, upset, alarm, disturb, unsettle, disquiet, discompose, fluster, ruffle, flurry, unnerve, confuse, distract, disconcert. **2** SHAKE, rattle, rock, stir, beat, churn, toss, convulse. **E3** **1** calm, tranquillize.

agitator *n* troublemaker, rabble-rouser, revolutionary, stirrer (*sl*), inciter, instigator.

agony *n* anguish, torment, torture, pain, spasm, throes, suffering, affliction, tribulation, distress, woe, misery, wretchedness.

agree *v* **1** CONCUR, see eye to eye, get on, settle, accord, match, suit, fit, tally, correspond, conform. **2** CONSENT, allow, permit, assent, accede, grant, admit, concede, yield, comply. **E3** **1** disagree, differ, conflict. **2** refuse.

agreeable *adj* pleasant, congenial, likable, attractive, delightful, enjoyable, gratifying, satisfying, palatable,

acceptable, proper, appropriate, suitable, fitting, in accord, consistent. **E3** disagreeable, nasty, distasteful.

agreement *n* **1** SETTLEMENT, compact, covenant, treaty, pact, contract, deal, bargain, arrangement, understanding. **2** *be in agreement*: concurrence, accord, concord, unanimity, union, harmony, sympathy, affinity, compatibility, similarity, correspondence, consistency, conformity, compliance, adherence, acceptance. **E3** **2** disagreement.

agricultural *adj* agronomic, agrarian, farming, farmed, cultivated, rural, pastoral, bucolic.

> *Types of agricultural implement and machinery include*: axe, chainsaw, clover broadcaster, fertilizer distributor, field sprinkler, fork, hayfork, pitchfork, hoe, mattock, potato planter, rake, hayrake, reaping hook, saw, scythe, shovel, sickle, spade, wheelbarrow, whetstone; all-terrain vehicle (ATV), baler, bale wrapper, cultivator, drill, corn drill, seed drill, fertilizer spreader, fork-lift truck, front end loader, harrow, combination seed-harrow, disc harrow, harvester, combine harvester, hedgecutter, irrigator, milking machine, mower, flail mower, muckspreader, potato planter, plough, reversible plough, wheel plough, power lift, rotary hoe, Rotovator®, scarifier, slurry tanker, sprayer, tedder, tractor, trailer.

agriculture *n* agronomics, farming, husbandry, cultivation, culture, tillage.

ahead *adv* forward, onward, leading, at the head, in front, in the lead, winning, at an advantage, advanced, superior, to the fore, in the forefront, in advance, before, earlier on.

aid *v* help, assist, succour, rally round, relieve, support, subsidize, sustain, second, serve, oblige, accommodate, favour, promote, boost, encourage, expedite, facilitate, ease.

☒ hinder, impede, obstruct.

➤ n help, assistance, prop, support, relief, benefit, subsidy, donation, contribution, funding, grant, sponsorship, patronage, favour, encouragement, service.

☒ hindrance, impediment, obstruction.

ailing adj unwell, ill, sick, poorly, indisposed, out of sorts (*infml*), under the weather (*infml*), off-colour, suffering, languishing, sickly, diseased, invalid, infirm, unsound, frail, weak, feeble, failing.

☒ healthy, thriving, flourishing.

ailment n illness, sickness, complaint, malady, disease, infection, disorder, affliction, infirmity, disability, weakness.

aim v 1 POINT, direct, take aim, level, train, sight, zero in on (*infml*), target. 2 *aim to achieve*: aspire, want, wish, seek, resolve, purpose, intend, propose, mean, plan, design, strive, try, attempt, endeavour.

➤ n aspiration, ambition, hope, dream, desire, wish, plan, design, scheme, purpose, motive, end, intention, object, objective, target, mark, goal, direction, course.

aimless adj pointless, purposeless, unmotivated, irresolute, directionless, rambling, undirected, unguided, stray, chance, random, haphazard, erratic, unpredictable, wayward.

☒ purposeful, positive, determined.

air n 1 ATMOSPHERE, oxygen, sky, heavens, breath, puff, waft, draught, breeze, wind, blast. 2 APPEARANCE, look, aspect, aura, bearing, demeanour, manner, character, effect, impression, feeling.

➤ v 1 *air a room*: ventilate, aerate, freshen. 2 *air an opinion*: utter, voice, express, give vent to, make known, communicate, tell, declare, reveal, disclose, divulge, expose, make public, broadcast, publish, circulate, disseminate, exhibit, display, parade, publicize.

aircraft

Types of aircraft include: aeroplane, plane, jet, jumbo, Concorde, airbus, helicopter, monoplane, two-seater, air-ambulance, freighter, aquaplane, seaplane, glider, hang-glider, microlight, hot-air balloon; fighter, spitfire, bomber, kite (*infml*), jump jet, dive-bomber, chopper (*sl*), spy plane, delta-wing, swing-wing, troop carrier, airship, turbojet, VTOL (vertical take-off and landing), warplane, zeppelin.

airless adj unventilated, stuffy, musty, stale, suffocating, stifling, sultry, muggy, close, heavy, oppressive.

☒ airy, fresh.

airy adj 1 ROOMY, spacious, open, well-ventilated, draughty, breezy, blowy, windy, gusty. 2 CHEERFUL, happy, light-hearted, high-spirited, perky, lively. 3 NONCHALANT, offhand.

☒ 1 airless, stuffy, close, heavy, oppressive.

aisle n gangway, corridor, passage, passageway, alleyway, walkway, path, lane.

alarm v frighten, scare, startle, put the wind up (*infml*), terrify, panic, unnerve, daunt, dismay, distress, agitate.

☒ reassure, calm, soothe.

➤ n 1 FRIGHT, scare, fear, terror, panic, horror, shock, consternation, dismay, distress, anxiety, nervousness, apprehension, trepidation, uneasiness. 2 DANGER SIGNAL, alert, warning, distress signal, siren, bell, alarm-bell.

☒ 1 calmness, composure.

alarming adj frightening, scary, startling, terrifying, unnerving, daunting, ominous, threatening, dismaying, disturbing, distressing, shocking, dreadful.

☒ reassuring.

alcohol n drink, booze (*sl*), liquor, spirits, hard stuff (*sl*), intoxicant.

alcoholic adj intoxicating, brewed, fermented, distilled, strong, hard.

➤ n drunk, drunkard, inebriate, hard drinker, dipsomaniac, wino (*sl*), alkie (*sl*).

alcove *n* niche, nook, recess, bay, corner, cubby-hole, compartment, cubicle, booth, carrel.

alert *adj* attentive, wide-awake, watchful, vigilant, on the lookout, sharp-eyed, observant, perceptive, sharp-witted, on the ball (*infml*), active, lively, spirited, quick, brisk, agile, nimble, ready, prepared, careful, heedful, circumspect, wary.
🔁 slow, listless, unprepared.
➤ *v* warn, forewarn, notify, inform, tip off, signal, alarm.

algae

Types of algae and lichen include: anabaena, badderlocks, bladderwrack, bull kelp, carrageen, Ceylon moss, chlorella, conferva, desmid, diatom, dinaflagellate, dulse, euglena, fucoid, fucus, gulfweed, Irish moss, kelp, laminaria, laver, lecanora, nostoc, nullipore, oak moss, oarweed, peacock's tail, redware, reindeer moss, rock tripe, rockweed, sargassum, sea lace, sea lettuce, sea tangle, sea wrack, Spanish moss, spirogyra, stonewort, wrack.

alias *n* pseudonym, false name, assumed name, nom de guerre, nom de plume, pen name, stage name, nickname, moniker (*sl*), sobriquet.
➤ *prep* also known as, also called, otherwise, formerly.

alibi *n* defence, justification, story, explanation, excuse, pretext, reason.

alien *adj* strange, unfamiliar, outlandish, incongruous, foreign, exotic, extraterrestial, extraneous, remote, estranged, separated, opposed, contrary, conflicting, antagonistic, incompatible.
🔁 akin.
➤ *n* foreigner, immigrant, newcomer, stranger, outsider.
🔁 native.

alight[1] *v* descend, get down, dismount, get off, disembark, land, touch down, come down, come to rest, settle, light, perch.
🔁 ascend, board.

alight[2] *adj* lighted, lit, ignited, on fire, burning, blazing, ablaze, flaming, fiery, lit up, illuminated, bright, radiant, shining, brilliant.
🔁 dark.

align *v* **1** STRAIGHTEN, range, line up, make parallel, even (up), adjust, regulate, regularize, order, co-ordinate. **2** ALLY, side, sympathize, associate, affiliate, join, co-operate, agree.

alike *adj* similar, resembling, comparable, akin, analogous, corresponding, equivalent, equal, the same, identical, duplicate, parallel, even, uniform.
🔁 dissimilar, unlike, different.
➤ *adv* similarly, analogously, correspondingly, equally, in common.

alive *adj* **1** LIVING, having life, live, animate, breathing, existent, in existence, real. **2** LIVELY, animated, spirited, awake, alert, active, brisk, energetic, vigorous, zestful, vivacious, vibrant, vital.
🔁 **1** dead, extinct. **2** lifeless, apathetic.

all *adj* **1** EACH, every, each and every, every single, every one of, the whole of, every bit of. **2** COMPLETE, entire, full, total, utter, outright, perfect, greatest.
🔁 **1** no, none.
➤ *n* everything, sum, total, aggregate, total amount, whole amount, whole, entirety, utmost, comprehensiveness, universality.
🔁 nothing, none.
➤ *adv* completely, entirely, wholly, fully, totally, utterly, altogether, wholesale.
◇ **all right** *adj* **1** SATISFACTORY, passable, unobjectionable, acceptable, allowable, adequate, fair, average, OK (*infml*). **2** *are you all right?*: well, healthy, unhurt, uninjured, unharmed, unimpaired, whole, sound, safe, secure.
🔁 **1** unacceptable, inadequate.
➤ *adv* satisfactorily, well enough, passably, unobjectionably, acceptably, suitably, appropriately, adequately,

reasonably, OK (*infml*).

🔁 unsatisfactorily, unacceptably.

allay *v* alleviate, relieve, soothe, ease, smooth, calm, tranquillize, quiet, quell, pacify, mollify, soften, blunt, lessen, reduce, diminish, check, moderate.

🔁 exacerbate, intensify.

allegation *n* accusation, charge, claim, profession, assertion, affirmation, declaration, statement, testimony, plea.

allege *v* assert, affirm, declare, state, attest (*fml*), maintain, insist, hold, contend, claim, profess, plead.

alleged *adj* supposed, reputed, putative, inferred, so-called, professed, declared, stated, claimed, described, designated, doubtful, dubious, suspect, suspicious.

allegiance *n* loyalty, fidelity, faithfulness, constancy, duty, obligation, obedience, devotion, support, adherence, friendship.

🔁 disloyalty, enmity.

allergic *adj* sensitive, hypersensitive, susceptible, affected, incompatible, averse, disinclined, opposed, hostile, antagonistic.

🔁 tolerant.

alleviate *v* relieve, soothe, ease, palliate, mitigate, soften, cushion, dull, deaden, allay, abate, lessen, reduce, diminish, check, moderate, temper, subdue.

🔁 aggravate.

alliance *n* confederation, federation, association, affiliation, coalition, league, bloc, cartel, conglomerate, consortium, syndicate, guild, union, partnership, marriage, agreement, compact, bond, pact, treaty, combination, connection.

🔁 separation, divorce, estrangement, enmity, hostility.

allocate *v* assign, designate, budget, allow, earmark, set aside, allot, apportion, share out, distribute, dispense, mete.

allocation *n* allotment, lot, apportionment, measure, share, portion, stint, ration, quota, budget, allowance, grant.

allot *v* divide, ration, apportion, share out, distribute, dispense, mete, dole out, allocate, assign, designate, budget, allow, grant, earmark, set aside.

allotment *n* division, partition, allocation, apportionment, measure, percentage, lot, portion, share, stint, ration, quota, allowance, grant.

all-out *adj* complete, full, total, undivided, comprehensive, exhaustive, thorough, intensive, thoroughgoing, wholesale, vigorous, powerful, full-scale, no-holds-barred, maximum, utmost, unlimited, unrestrained, resolute, determined.

🔁 perfunctory, half-hearted.

allow *v* **1** PERMIT, let, enable, authorize, sanction, approve, tolerate, put up with, endure, suffer. **2** ADMIT, confess, own, acknowledge, concede, grant. **3** *allow two hours for the journey*: allot, allocate, assign, apportion, afford, give, provide.

🔁 **1** forbid, prevent. **2** deny.

◇ **allow for** take into account, make provision for, make allowances for, provide for, foresee, plan for, arrange for, bear in mind, keep in mind, consider, include.

🔁 discount.

allowance *n* **1** ALLOTMENT, lot, amount, allocation, portion, share, ration, quota. **2** REBATE, reduction, deduction, discount, concession, subsidy, weighting. **3** PAYMENT, remittance, pocket money, grant, maintenance, stipend, pension, annuity.

alloy *n* blend, compound, composite, amalgam, combination, mixture, fusion, coalescence.

allure *v* lure, entice, seduce, lead on, tempt, coax, cajole, persuade, win over, disarm, charm, enchant, attract, interest, fascinate, captivate, entrance, beguile.

🔁 repel.

➤ *n* lure, enticement, seduction,

temptation, appeal, attraction, magnetism, fascination, glamour, captivation, charm, enchantment.

allusion *n* mention, reference, citation, quotation, remark, observation, suggestion, hint, intimation, implication, insinuation.

ally *n* confederate, associate, leaguer, consort, partner, sidekick, colleague, co-worker, collaborator, helper, helpmate, accomplice, accessory, friend.

▣ antagonist, enemy.

➤ *v* confederate, affiliate, league, associate, collaborate, join forces, band together, team up, fraternize, side, join, connect, link, marry, unite, unify, amalgamate, combine.

▣ estrange, separate.

almighty *adj* **1** OMNIPOTENT, all-powerful, supreme, absolute, great, invincible. **2** ENORMOUS, severe, intense, overwhelming, overpowering, terrible, awful, desperate.

▣ **1** impotent, weak.

almost *adv* nearly, well-nigh, practically, virtually, just about, as good as, all but, close to, not far from, approaching, nearing, not quite, about, approximately.

alone *adj* only, sole, single, unique, solitary, separate, detached, unconnected, isolated, apart, by oneself, by itself, on one's own, lonely, lonesome, deserted, abandoned, forsaken, forlorn, desolate, unaccompanied, unescorted, unattended, solo, single-handed, unaided, unassisted, mere.

▣ together, accompanied, escorted.

aloof *adj* distant, remote, offish, standoffish, haughty, supercilious, unapproachable, inaccessible, detached, forbidding, cool, chilly, cold, sympathetic, unresponsive, indifferent, uninterested, reserved, unforthcoming, unfriendly, unsociable, formal.

▣ sociable, friendly, concerned.

aloud *adv* out loud, audibly, intelligibly,

clearly, plainly, distinctly, loudly, resoundingly, sonorously, noisily, vociferously.

▣ silently.

alphabet

Alphabets and writing systems include: American Sign Language (ASL), Braille, British Sign Language (BSL), Byzantine, Chalcidian alphabet, cuneiform, Cyrillic, devanagari, estrangelo, finger-alphabet, futhark, Glagol, Glossic, Greek, Gurmukhi, hieroglyphs, hiragana, ideograph, initial teaching alphabet (i.t.a.), International Phonetic Alphabet (IPA), kana, kanji, katakana, Kufic, linear A, linear B, logograph, nagari, naskhi, ogam, pictograph, romaji, Roman, runic, syllabary.

Communications code words for the letters of the alphabet are: Alpha, Bravo, Charlie, Delta, Echo, Foxtrot, Golf, Hotel, India, Juliet, Kilo, Lima, Mike, November, Oscar, Papa, Quebec, Romeo, Sierra, Tango, Uniform, Victor, Whisky, X-ray, Yankee, Zulu.

also *adv* too, as well, and, plus, along with, including, as well as, additionally, in addition, besides, further, furthermore, moreover.

alter *v* change, vary, diversify, modify, tweak, qualify, shift, transpose, adjust, adapt, convert, turn, transmute, transform, reform, reshape, remodel, recast, revise, amend, emend.

▣ fix.

alteration *n* change, variation, variance, difference, diversification, shift, transposition, modification, adjustment, adaptation, conversion, transformation, transfiguration, metamorphosis, reformation, reshaping, remodelling, revision, amendment.

▣ fixity.

alternate *v* interchange, reciprocate,

rotate, take turns, follow one another, replace each other, substitute, change, alter, vary, oscillate, fluctuate, intersperse.

➤ *adj* alternating, every other, every second, interchanging, reciprocal, rotating, alternative.

alternative *n* option, choice, selection, preference, other, recourse, substitute, back-up.

➤ *adj* substitute, second, another, other, different, unorthodox, unconventional, fringe, alternate.

altitude *n* height, elevation, loftiness, tallness, stature.

🖪 depth.

altogether *adv* totally, completely, entirely, wholly, fully, utterly, absolutely, quite, perfectly, thoroughly, in all, all told, in toto, all in all, as a whole, on the whole, generally, in general.

altruistic *adj* unselfish, self-sacrificing, disinterested, public-spirited, philanthropic, charitable, humanitarian, benevolent, generous, considerate, humane.

🖪 selfish.

always *adv* every time, consistently, invariably, without exception, unfailingly, regularly, repeatedly, continually, constantly, perpetually, unceasingly, eternally, endlessly, evermore, forever, ever.

🖪 never.

amalgamate *v* merge, blend, mingle, commingle, intermix, homogenize, incorporate, alloy, integrate, compound, fuse, coalesce, synthesize, combine, unite, unify, ally.

🖪 separate.

amateur *n* non-professional, layman, ham (*infml*), dilettante, dabbler, enthusiast, fancier, buff (*infml*).

🖪 professional.

➤ *adj* non-professional, lay, unpaid, unqualified, untrained, amateurish, inexpert, unprofessional.

🖪 professional.

amaze *v* surprise, startle, astonish,

astound, stun, stupefy, daze, stagger, floor (*infml*), dumbfound, flabbergast (*infml*), shock, dismay, disconcert, confound, bewilder.

amazement *n* surprise, astonishment, shock, dismay, confusion, perplexity, bewilderment, admiration, wonderment, wonder, marvel.

ambassador *n* emissary, envoy, legate, diplomat, plenipotentiary, consul, deputy, representative, agent, minister, apostle.

ambiguity *n* double meaning, double entendre, equivocality, equivocation, enigma, puzzle, confusion, obscurity, unclearness, vagueness, woolliness, dubiousness, doubt, doubtfulness, uncertainty.

🖪 clarity.

ambiguous *adj* double-meaning, equivocal, multivocal, double-edged, back-handed, cryptic, enigmatic, puzzling, confusing, obscure, unclear, vague, indefinite, woolly, confused, dubious, doubtful, uncertain, inconclusive, indeterminate.

🖪 clear, definite.

ambition *n* 1 ASPIRATION, aim, goal, target, objective, intent, purpose, design, object, ideal, dream, hope, wish, desire, yearning, longing, hankering, craving, hunger. 2 *a woman of ambition*: enterprise, drive, push, thrust, striving, eagerness, commitment, zeal.

🖪 2 apathy, diffidence.

ambitious *adj* 1 ASPIRING, hopeful, desirous, intent, purposeful, pushy, bold, assertive, go-ahead, enterprising, driving, energetic, enthusiastic, eager, keen, striving, industrious, zealous. 2 FORMIDABLE, hard, difficult, arduous, strenuous, demanding, challenging, exacting, impressive, grandiose, elaborate.

🖪 1 lazy, unassuming. 2 modest, uninspiring.

ambivalent *adj* contradictory,

conflicting, clashing, warring, opposed, inconsistent, mixed, confused, fluctuating, vacillating, wavering, hesitant, irresolute, undecided, unresolved, unsettled, uncertain, unsure, doubtful, debatable, inconclusive.

amble v walk, saunter, toddle (*infml*), stroll, promenade, wander, drift, meander, ramble.
Ea stride, march.

ambush n waylaying, surprise attack, trap, snare, cover, hiding-place.
➤ v lie in wait, waylay, surprise, trap, ensnare.

amenable *adj* accommodating, flexible, open, agreeable, persuadable, compliant, tractable, submissive, responsive, susceptible, liable, responsible.
Ea intractable.

amend v revise, correct, rectify, emend, fix, repair, mend, remedy, redress, reform, change, alter, adjust, modify, qualify, enhance, improve, ameliorate, better.
Ea impair, worsen.

amendment n revision, correction, corrigendum, rectification, emendation, repair, remedy, reform, change, alteration, adjustment, modification, qualification, clarification, addendum, addition, adjunct, improvement.
Ea impairment, deterioration.

amends n atonement, expiation, requital, satisfaction, recompense, compensation, indemnification, indemnity, reparation, redress, restoration, restitution.

amiable *adj* affable, friendly, approachable, genial, cheerful, good-tempered, good-natured, kind, obliging, charming, engaging, likable, pleasant, agreeable, congenial, companionable, sociable.
Ea unfriendly, curt, hostile.

amid *prep* amidst, midst, in the midst of, in the thick of, among, amongst, in the middle of, surrounded by.

amnesty n pardon, forgiveness, absolution, mercy, lenience, indulgence, reprieve, remission, dispensation, immunity, oblivion.

among *prep* amongst, between, in the middle of, surrounded by, amid, amidst, midst, in the midst of, in the thick of, with, together with.

amount n quantity, number, sum, total, sum total, whole, entirety, aggregate, lot, quota, supply, volume, mass, bulk, measure, magnitude, extent, expanse.
◇ **amount to** add up to, total, aggregate, come to, make, equal, mean, be tantamount to, be equivalent to, approximate to, become, grow.

amphibian

Amphibians include: frog, bullfrog, tree frog, toad, horned toad, midwife toad, natterjack, newt, eft, salamander, congo eel, axolotl.

ample *adj* large, big, extensive, expansive, broad, wide, full, voluminous, roomy, spacious, commodious, great, considerable, substantial, handsome, generous, bountiful, munificent, liberal, lavish, copious, abundant, plentiful, plenty, unrestricted, profuse, rich.
Ea insufficient, inadequate, meagre.

amplify v enlarge, magnify, expand, dilate, fill out, bulk out, add to, supplement, augment, increase, extend, lengthen, widen, broaden, develop, elaborate, enhance, boost, intensify, strengthen, deepen, heighten, raise.
Ea reduce, decrease, abridge.

amputate v cut off, remove, sever, dissever, separate, dock, lop, curtail, truncate.

amuse v entertain, divert, regale, make laugh, tickle (*infml*), crease (*infml*), slay (*infml*), cheer (up), gladden, enliven, please, charm, delight, enthral, engross, absorb, interest, occupy, recreate, relax.
Ea bore, displease.

amusement n entertainment, diversion, distraction, fun, enjoyment,

pleasure, delight, merriment, mirth, hilarity, laughter, joke, prank, game, sport, recreation, hobby, pastime, interest.
E3 boredom, monotony.

amusing *adj* funny, humorous, hilarious, comical, laughable, ludicrous, droll, witty, facetious, jocular, jolly, enjoyable, pleasant, charming, delightful, entertaining, interesting.
E3 dull, boring.

anaemic *adj* bloodless, ashen, chalky, livid, pasty, pallid, sallow, whey-faced, pale, wan, colourless, insipid, weak, feeble, ineffectual, enervated, frail, infirm, sickly.
E3 ruddy, sanguine, full-blooded.

anaesthetize *v* desensitize, numb, deaden, dull, drug, dope, stupefy.

analogy *n* comparison, simile, metaphor, likeness, resemblance, similarity, parallel, correspondence, equivalence, relation, correlation, agreement.

analyse *v* break down, separate, divide, take apart, dissect, anatomize, reduce, resolve, sift, investigate, study, examine, scrutinize, review, interpret, test, judge, evaluate, estimate, consider.

analysis *n* breakdown, separation, division, dissection, reduction, resolution, sifting, investigation, enquiry, study, examination, scrutiny, review, exposition, explication, explanation, interpretation, test, judgement, opinion, evaluation, estimation, reasoning.
E3 synthesis.

analytic *adj* analytical, dissecting, detailed, in-depth, searching, critical, questioning, enquiring, inquisitive, investigative, diagnostic, systematic, methodical, logical, rational, interpretative, explanatory, expository, studious.

anarchic *adj* lawless, ungoverned, anarchistic, libertarian, nihilist, revolutionary, rebellious, mutinous,

riotous, chaotic, disordered, confused, disorganized.
E3 submissive, orderly.

anarchist *n* revolutionary, rebel, insurgent, libertarian, nihilist, terrorist.

anarchy *n* lawlessness, unrule, misrule, anarchism, revolution, rebellion, insurrection, mutiny, riot, chaos, pandemonium, disorder, confusion.
E3 rule, control, order.

anathema *n* aversion, abhorrence, abomination, object of loathing, bête noire, bugbear, bane, curse, taboo, proscription.

anatomy

> *Anatomical terms include*: aural, biceps, bone, cardiac, cartilage, cerebral, cranial, crural, dental, diaphragm, dorsal, duodenal, elbow, epidermis, epiglottis, Fallopian tubes, foreskin, gastric, genitalia, gingival, gristle, groin, gullet, hamstring, helix, hepatic, hock, intercostal, jugular, lachrymal, ligament, lumbar, mammary, membral, muscle, nasal, neural, ocular, oesophagus, optical, pectoral, pedal, pulmonary, renal, spine, tendon, triceps, umbilicus, uterus, uvula, voice-box, vulva, windpipe, wisdom tooth, womb. *see also* **bone**.

ancestor *n* forebear, forefather, progenitor, predecessor, forerunner, precursor, antecedent.
E3 descendant.

ancestral *adj* familial, parental, genealogical, lineal, hereditary, genetic.

ancestry *n* ancestors, forebears, forefathers, progenitors, parentage, family, lineage, line, descent, blood, race, stock, roots, pedigree, genealogy, extraction, derivation, origin, heritage, heredity.

anchor *v* moor, berth, tie up, make fast, fasten, attach, affix, fix.

> *Types of anchor include*: car, double fluked, grapnel, kedge, killick,

mushroom, navy, sea, stocked, stockless, yachtsman.

ancient *adj* **1** OLD, aged, time-worn, age-old, antique, antediluvian, prehistoric, fossilized, primeval, immemorial. **2** OLD-FASHIONED, out of date, antiquated, archaic, obsolete, bygone, early, original.
≊ 1 recent, contemporary. **2** modern, up to date.

anecdote *n* story, tale, yarn, sketch, reminiscence.

angel *n* **1** *angel of God*: archangel, cherub, seraph, divine messenger, principality. **2** DARLING, treasure, saint, paragon, ideal.
≊ 1 devil, fiend.

The nine orders of angels are: seraph, cherub, throne, domination/dominion, virtue, power, principality, archangel, angel.

angelic *adj* cherubic, seraphic, celestial, heavenly, divine, holy, pious, saintly, pure, innocent, unworldly, virtuous, lovely, beautiful, adorable.
≊ devilish, fiendish.

anger *n* annoyance, irritation, antagonism, displeasure, irritability, temper, pique, vexation, ire, rage, fury, wrath, exasperation, outrage, indignation, gall, bitterness, rancour, resentment.
≊ forgiveness, forbearance.
➤ *v* annoy, irritate, aggravate (*infml*), wind up (*infml*), vex, irk, rile, miff (*infml*), needle, nettle, bother, ruffle, provoke, antagonize, offend, affront, gall, madden, enrage, incense, infuriate, exasperate, outrage.
≊ please, appease, calm.

angle *n* **1** CORNER, nook, bend, flexure, hook, crook, elbow, knee, crotch, edge, point. **2** ASPECT, outlook, facet, side, approach, direction, position, standpoint, viewpoint, point of view, slant, perspective.

angry *adj* annoyed, cross, irritated,

aggravated (*infml*), displeased, uptight, irate, mad (*infml*), enraged, incensed, infuriated, furious, raging, passionate, heated, hot, exasperated, outraged, indignant, bitter, resentful.
≊ content, happy, calm.

animal *n* creature, mammal, beast, brute, barbarian, savage, monster, cur, pig, swine.

Animals include: cat, dog, hamster, gerbil, mouse, rat, rabbit, hare, fox, badger, beaver, mole, otter, weasel, ferret, ermine, mink, polecat, hedgehog, squirrel, horse, pig, cow, bull, goat, sheep; monkey, lemur, gibbon, ape, chimpanzee, orang-utan, baboon, gorilla; seal, sea lion, dolphin, walrus, whale; lion, tiger, cheetah, puma, panther, cougar, jaguar, ocelot, leopard; aardvark, armadillo, wolf, wolverine, hyena, mongoose, skunk, racoon, wombat, platypus, koala; deer, antelope, gazelle, eland, impala, reindeer, elk, caribou, moose; wallaby, kangaroo, bison, buffalo, gnu, camel, zebra, llama, panda, giant panda, bear, grizzly bear, polar bear, giraffe, hippopotamus, rhinoceros, elephant. *see also* **amphibian**; **bird**; **butterfly**; **cat**; **cattle**; **dog**; **fish**; **horse**; **insect**; **invertebrate**; **mammal**; **marsupial**; **mollusc**; **monkey**; **reptile**; **rodent**.

adj bestial, brutish, inhuman, savage, wild, instinctive, bodily, physical, carnal, fleshly, sensual.

animate *adj* alive, living, live, breathing, conscious.
≊ inanimate.

animated *adj* lively, spirited, buoyant, vibrant, ebullient, vivacious, alive, vital, quick, brisk, vigorous, energetic, active, passionate, impassioned, vehement, ardent, fervent, glowing, radiant, excited, enthusiastic, eager.
≊ lethargic, sluggish, inert.

animosity *n* ill feeling, ill-will, acrimony, bitterness, rancour, resentment, spite, malice, malignity, malevolence, hate, hatred, loathing, antagonism, hostility, enmity, feud. 🔁 goodwill.

annex v **1** ADD, append, affix, attach, fasten, adjoin, join, connect, unite, incorporate. **2** ACQUIRE, appropriate, seize, usurp, occupy, conquer, take over.

annexe n wing, extension, attachment, addition, supplement, expansion.

annihilate v eliminate, eradicate, obliterate, erase, wipe out, liquidate (*infml*), murder, assassinate, exterminate, extinguish, raze, destroy, abolish.

anniversary

> *Names of wedding anniversary include*: 1st cotton, 2nd paper, 3rd leather, 4th flowers/fruit, 5th wood, 6th iron/sugar, 7th copper/wool, 8th bronze/pottery, 9th pottery/willow, 10th tin, 11th steel, 12th silk/linen, 13th lace, 14th ivory, 15th crystal, 20th china, 25th silver, 30th pearl, 35th coral, 40th ruby, 45th sapphire, 50th gold, 55th emerald, 60th diamond, 70th platinum.

annotation n note, footnote, gloss, comment, commentary, exegesis, explanation, elucidation.

announce v declare, proclaim, report, state, reveal, disclose, divulge, make known, notify, intimate, promulgate (*fml*), propound, publish, broadcast, advertise, publicize, blazon. 🔁 suppress.

announcement n declaration, proclamation, report, statement, communiqué, dispatch, bulletin, notification, intimation, revelation, disclosure, divulgence, publication, broadcast, advertisement.

announcer n broadcaster, newscaster, newsreader, commentator, compère, master of ceremonies, MC, town crier, herald, messenger.

annoy v irritate, rile, aggravate (*infml*), wind up (*infml*), piss off (*sl*), displease, anger, vex, irk, madden, exasperate,

tease, provoke, ruffle, trouble, disturb, bother, pester, plague, harass, bug (*infml*), molest. 🔁 please, gratify, comfort.

annoyance n **1** NUISANCE, pest, disturbance, bother, trouble, bore (*infml*), bind, pain (*infml*), headache (*infml*), tease, provocation. **2** *express one's annoyance*: irritation, aggravation (*infml*), displeasure, anger, vexation, exasperation, harassment. 🔁 **2** pleasure.

annoyed adj irritated, cross, displeased, angry, vexed, piqued, exasperated, provoked, harassed. 🔁 pleased.

annoying adj irritating, aggravating (*infml*), vexatious, irksome, troublesome, bothersome, tiresome, trying, maddening, exasperating, galling, offensive, teasing, provoking, harassing. 🔁 pleasing, welcome.

annul v nullify, invalidate, void, rescind, abrogate, suspend, cancel, abolish, quash, repeal, revoke, countermand, negate, retract, recall, reverse. 🔁 enact, restore.

anoint v **1** OIL, grease, lubricate, embrocate, rub, smear, daub. **2** BLESS, consecrate, sanctify, dedicate.

anomalous adj abnormal, atypical, exceptional, irregular, inconsistent, incongruous, deviant, freakish, eccentric, peculiar, odd, unusual, singular, rare. 🔁 normal, regular, ordinary.

anomaly n abnormality, exception, irregularity, inconsistency, incongruity, aberration, deviation, divergence, departure, freak, misfit, eccentricity, peculiarity, oddity, rarity.

anonymous adj unnamed, nameless, unsigned, unacknowledged, unspecified, unidentified, unknown, incognito, faceless, impersonal, nondescript, unexceptional. 🔁 named, signed, identifiable, distinctive.

answer *n* 1 REPLY, acknowledgement, response, reaction, rejoinder, retort, riposte, comeback, retaliation, rebuttal, vindication, defence, plea. 2 SOLUTION, explanation.
➤ *v* 1 REPLY, acknowledge, respond, react, retort, retaliate, refute, solve. 2 *answer one's needs*: fulfil, fill, meet, satisfy, match up to, correspond, correlate, conform, agree, fit, suit, serve, pass.
◇ **answer back** talk back, retort, riposte, retaliate, contradict, disagree, argue, dispute, rebut.

answerable *adj* liable, responsible, accountable, chargeable, blameworthy, to blame.

antagonism *n* hostility, opposition, rivalry, antipathy, ill feeling, ill-will, animosity, friction, discord, dissension, contention, conflict.
🔁 rapport, sympathy, agreement.

antagonist *n* opponent, adversary, enemy, foe, rival, competitor, contestant, contender.
🔁 ally, supporter.

antagonistic *adj* conflicting, opposed, adverse, at variance, incompatible, hostile, belligerent, contentious, unfriendly, ill-disposed, averse.
🔁 sympathetic, friendly.

antagonize *v* alienate, estrange, disaffect, repel, embitter, offend, insult, provoke, annoy, irritate, anger, incense.
🔁 disarm.

anthem *n* hymn, song, chorale, psalm, canticle, chant.

anthology *n* selection, collection, compilation, compendium, digest, treasury, miscellany.

anticipate *v* 1 FORESTALL, pre-empt, intercept, prevent, obviate, preclude. 2 EXPECT, foresee, predict, forecast, look for, await, look forward to, hope for, bank on, count upon.

anticlimax *n* bathos, comedown, let-down, disappointment, fiasco.

antics *n* foolery, tomfoolery, silliness, buffoonery, clowning, frolics, capers, skylarking, playfulness, mischief, tricks, monkey-tricks, pranks, stunts, doings.

antidote *n* remedy, cure, counter-agent, antitoxin, neutralizer, countermeasure, corrective.

antipathy *n* aversion, dislike, hate, hatred, loathing, abhorrence, distaste, disgust, repulsion, antagonism, animosity, ill-will, bad blood, enmity, hostility, opposition, incompatibility.
🔁 sympathy, affection, rapport.

antique *adj* antiquarian, ancient, old, veteran, vintage, quaint, antiquated, old-fashioned, outdated, archaic, obsolete.
➤ *n* antiquity, relic, bygone, period piece, heirloom, curio, museum piece, curiosity, rarity.

antiquity *n* ancient times, time immemorial, distant past, olden days, age, old age, oldness, agedness.
🔁 modernity, novelty.

antiseptic *adj* disinfectant, medicated, aseptic, germ-free, clean, pure, unpolluted, uncontaminated, sterile, sterilized, sanitized, sanitary, hygienic.
➤ *n* disinfectant, germicide, bactericide, purifier, cleanser.

antisocial *adj* asocial, unacceptable, disruptive, disorderly, rebellious, belligerent, antagonistic, hostile, unfriendly, unsociable, reserved, retiring, uncommunicative, withdrawn, alienated, unapproachable.
🔁 sociable, gregarious.

anxiety *n* worry, concern, care, distress, nervousness, apprehension, dread, foreboding, misgiving, uneasiness, restlessness, fretfulness, impatience, suspense, tension, stress.
🔁 calm, composure, serenity.

anxious *adj* worried, concerned, nervous, apprehensive, afraid, fearful, uneasy, restless, fretful, impatient, in suspense, on tenterhooks, tense, taut,

distressed, disturbed, troubled, tormented, tortured.
Fª calm, composed.

apart *adv* **1** SEPARATELY, independently, individually, singly, alone, on one's own, by oneself, privately, aside, to one side, away, afar, distant, aloof, excluded, isolated, cut off, separated, divorced, separate, distinct. **2** *tear apart*: to pieces, to bits, into parts, in pieces, in bits, piecemeal.
Fª 1 connected. **2** together.

apathetic *adj* uninterested, uninvolved, indifferent, unemotional, emotionless, cool, impassive, unmoved, unconcerned, cold, unfeeling, numb, unresponsive, passive, listless, unambitious.
Fª enthusiastic, involved, concerned, feeling, responsive.

apathy *n* uninterestedness, indifference, coolness, impassivity, unconcern, coldness, insensibility, passivity, listlessness, lethargy, sluggishness, torpor, inertia.
Fª enthusiasm, interest, concern.

ape *v* copy, imitate, echo, mirror, parrot, mimic, take off (*infml*), caricature, parody, mock, counterfeit, affect.
➤ *n* monkey, chimpanzee, gibbon, gorilla, baboon, orang-utan.

aplomb *n* composure, calmness, equanimity, poise, balance, coolness, confidence, assurance, self-assurance, audacity.
Fª discomposure.

apocryphal *adj* unauthenticated, unverified, unsubstantiated, unsupported, questionable, spurious, equivocal, doubtful, dubious, fabricated, concocted, fictitious, imaginary, legendary, mythical.
Fª authentic, true.

apologetic *adj* sorry, repentant, penitent, contrite, remorseful, conscience-stricken, regretful, rueful.
Fª unrepentant, impenitent, defiant.

apology *n* acknowledgement, confession, excuse, explanation, justification, vindication, defence, plea.
Fª defiance.

appal *v* horrify, shock, outrage, disgust, dismay, disconcert, daunt, intimidate, unnerve, alarm, scare, frighten, terrify.
Fª reassure, encourage.

appalling *adj* horrifying, horrific, harrowing, shocking, outrageous, atrocious, disgusting, awful, dreadful, frightful, terrible, dire, grim, hideous, ghastly, horrible, horrid, loathsome, daunting, intimidating, unnerving, alarming, frightening, terrifying.
Fª reassuring, encouraging.

apparatus *n* machine, appliance, gadget, device, contraption, equipment, gear, tackle, outfit, tools, implements, utensils, materials, machinery, system, mechanism, means.

apparent *adj* seeming, outward, visible, evident, noticeable, perceptible, plain, clear, distinct, marked, unmistakable, obvious, manifest, patent, open, declared.
Fª hidden, obscure.

apparently *adv* seemingly, ostensibly, outwardly, superficially, plainly, clearly, obviously, manifestly, patently.

apparition *n* ghost, spectre, phantom, spirit, chimera, vision, manifestation, materialization, presence.

appeal *n* **1** REQUEST, application, petition, suit, solicitation, plea, entreaty, supplication, prayer, invocation.
2 ATTRACTION, allure, interest, fascination, enchantment, charm, attractiveness, winsomeness, beauty, charisma, magnetism.
➤ *v* **1** *appeal for help*: ask, request, call, apply, address, petition, sue, solicit, plead, beg, beseech, implore, entreat, supplicate, pray, invoke, call upon.
2 ATTRACT, draw, allure, lure, tempt, entice, invite, interest, engage, fascinate, charm, please.

appear *v* **1** ARRIVE, enter, turn up, attend, materialize, develop, show (up),

come into sight, come into view, loom, rise, surface, arise, occur, crop up, come to light, come out, emerge, issue, be published. **2** SEEM, look, turn out. **3** *appear in a show*: act, perform, play, take part.
F3 1 disappear, vanish.

appearance *n* **1** APPEARING, arrival, advent, coming, rise, emergence, début, introduction. **2** LOOK, expression, face, aspect, air, bearing, demeanour, manner, looks, figure, form, semblance, show, front, guise, illusion, impression, image.
F3 1 disappearance.

appendix *n* addition, appendage, adjunct, addendum, supplement, epilogue, codicil, postscript, rider.

appetite *n* hunger, stomach, relish, zest, taste, propensity, inclination, liking, desire, longing, yearning, craving, eagerness, passion, zeal.
F3 distaste.

appetizing *adj* mouthwatering, tempting, inviting, appealing, palatable, tasty, delicious, yummy (*infml*), scrumptious (*infml*), succulent, piquant, savoury.
F3 disgusting, distasteful.

applaud *v* clap, cheer, acclaim, compliment, congratulate, approve, commend, praise, laud, eulogize, extol.
F3 criticize, censure.

applause *n* ovation, clapping, cheering, cheers, acclaim, acclamation, accolade, congratulation, approval, commendation, praise.
F3 criticism, censure.

appliance *n* machine, device, contrivance, contraption, gadget, tool, implement, instrument, apparatus, mechanism.

Types of domestic appliance include: washing machine, washer, washer-drier, tumble dryer, clothes airer, iron, steam iron, steam press, trouser press; dishwasher, vacuum cleaner, upright cleaner, cylinder cleaner, wet-and-dry cleaner, Hoover®, floor polisher, carpet sweeper, carpet shampooer; oven,

Aga®, barbecue, cooker, Dutch oven, electric cooker, fan oven, gas stove, kitchen range, microwave oven, stove, hob, hotplate, grill, electric grill, griddle, rotisserie, spit, waffle iron, deep fryer, slow cooker, sandwich maker, toaster; food processor, mixer, blender, liquidizer, ice-cream maker, juicer, juice extractor, food slicer, electric knife, knife sharpener, kettle, tea/coffee maker, percolator, coffee mill, electric tin opener, timer, water filter; refrigerator, fridge (*infml*), icebox, fridge-freezer, freezer, deep freeze; hostess trolley, humidifier, ionizer, fire extinguisher.

applicable *adj* relevant, pertinent, apposite, apt, appropriate, fitting, suited, useful, suitable, fit, proper, valid, legitimate.
F3 inapplicable, inappropriate.

applicant *n* candidate, interviewee, contestant, competitor, aspirant, suitor, petitioner, inquirer.

application *n* **1** REQUEST, appeal, petition, suit, claim, inquiry. **2** RELEVANCE, pertinence, function, purpose, use, value. **3** DILIGENCE, industry, assiduity, effort, commitment, dedication, perseverance, keenness, attentiveness.

apply *v* **1** REQUEST, ask for, requisition, put in for, appeal, petition, solicit, sue, claim, inquire. **2** *apply oneself to a task*: address, buckle down, settle down, commit, devote, dedicate, give, direct, concentrate, study, persevere. **3** USE, exercise, utilize, employ, bring into play, engage, harness, ply, wield, administer, execute, implement, assign, direct, bring to bear, practise, resort to.
4 REFER, relate, be relevant, pertain, fit, suit. **5** *apply ointment*: put on, spread on, lay on, cover with, paint, anoint, smear, rub.

appoint *v* **1** NAME, nominate, elect, install, choose, select, engage, employ, take on, commission, delegate, assign, allot, designate, command, direct, charge, detail. **2** DECIDE, determine,

arrange, settle, fix, set, establish, ordain, decree, destine.
▪ **1** reject, dismiss, discharge.

appointment n **1** ARRANGEMENT, engagement, date, meeting, rendezvous, interview, consultation. **2** JOB, position, situation, post, office, place. **3** NAMING, nomination, election, choosing, choice, selection, commissioning, delegation.

appraisal n valuation, rating, survey, inspection, review, examination, once-over (*infml*), evaluation, assessment, estimate, estimation, judgement, reckoning, opinion, appreciation.

appreciate v **1** ENJOY, relish, savour, prize, treasure, value, cherish, admire, respect, regard, esteem, like, welcome, take kindly to. **2** *appreciate in value*: grow, increase, rise, mount, inflate, gain, strengthen, improve, enhance. **3** UNDERSTAND, comprehend, perceive, realize, recognize, acknowledge, sympathize with, know.
▪ **1** despise. **2** depreciate. **3** overlook.

appreciation n **1** ENJOYMENT, relish, admiration, respect, regard, esteem, gratitude, gratefulness, thankfulness, indebtedness, obligation, liking, sensitivity, responsiveness, valuation, assessment, estimation, judgement. **2** GROWTH, increase, rise, inflation, gain, improvement, enhancement. **3** UNDERSTANDING, comprehension, perception, awareness, realization, recognition, acknowledgement, sympathy, knowledge.
▪ **1** ingratitude. **2** depreciation.

appreciative adj **1** GRATEFUL, thankful, obliged, indebted, pleased. **2** ADMIRING, encouraging, enthusiastic, respectful, sensitive, responsive, perceptive, knowledgeable, conscious, mindful.
▪ **1** ungrateful.

apprehension n dread, foreboding, misgiving, qualm, uneasiness, anxiety, worry, concern, disquiet, alarm, fear, doubt, suspicion, mistrust.

apprehensive adj nervous, anxious, worried, concerned, uneasy, doubtful, suspicious, mistrustful, distrustful, alarmed, afraid.
▪ assured, confident.

apprentice n trainee, probationer, student, pupil, learner, novice, beginner, starter, recruit, newcomer.
▪ expert.

approach v **1** ADVANCE, move towards, draw near, near, gain on, catch up, reach, meet. **2** APPLY TO, appeal to, sound out. **3** BEGIN, commence, set about, undertake, introduce, mention. **4** RESEMBLE, be like, compare with, approximate, come close.
➤ n **1** *the approach of winter*: advance, coming, advent, arrival. **2** ACCESS, road, avenue, way, passage, entrance, doorway, threshold. **3** APPLICATION, appeal, overture, proposition, proposal. **4** ATTITUDE, manner, style, technique, procedure, method, means.

appropriate adj applicable, relevant, pertinent, to the point, well-chosen, apt, fitting, meet (*fml*), suitable, fit, befitting, becoming, proper, right, correct, spot-on (*infml*), well-timed, timely, seasonable, opportune.
▪ inappropriate, irrelevant, unsuitable.
➤ v **1** SEIZE, take, expropriate, commandeer, requisition, confiscate, impound, assume, usurp. **2** STEAL, pocket, filch, pilfer, purloin, embezzle, misappropriate.

approval n **1** ADMIRATION, esteem, regard, respect, good opinion, liking, appreciation, approbation (*fml*), favour, recommendation, praise, acclaim, acclamation, commendation, honour, applause. **2** AGREEMENT, concurrence, assent, consent, permission, leave, sanction, authorization, licence, mandate, go-ahead, green light (*infml*), blessing, OK (*infml*), certification, ratification, validation, confirmation, support.
▪ **1** disapproval, condemnation.

approve v **1** ADMIRE, esteem, regard, like, appreciate, favour, recommend,

praise, commend, acclaim, applaud.
2 *approve a proposal*: agree to, assent to, consent to, accede to, allow, permit, pass, sanction, authorize, mandate, bless, countenance, OK (*infml*), ratify, rubber-stamp (*infml*), validate, endorse, support, uphold, second, back, accept, adopt, confirm.
  🔄 **1** disapprove, condemn.

approximate *adj* estimated, guessed, rough, inexact, loose, close, near, like, similar, relative.
  🔄 exact.
  ➤ *v* approach, border on, verge on, be tantamount to, resemble.

approximately *n* roughly, around, about, circa, more or less, loosely, approaching, close to, nearly, just about.

apt *adj* **1** RELEVANT, applicable, apposite, appropriate, fitting, suitable, fit, seemly, proper, correct, accurate, spot-on (*infml*), timely, seasonable. **2** CLEVER, gifted, talented, skilful, expert, intelligent, quick, sharp. **3** LIABLE, prone, given, disposed, likely, ready.
  🔄 **1** inapt. **2** stupid.

aptitude *n* ability, capability, capacity, faculty, gift, talent, flair, facility, proficiency, cleverness, intelligence, quickness, bent, inclination, leaning, disposition, tendency.
  🔄 inaptitude.

arbitrary *adj* **1** RANDOM, chance, capricious, inconsistent, discretionary, subjective, instinctive, unreasoned, illogical, irrational, unreasonable. **2** DESPOTIC, tyrannical, dictatorial, autocratic, absolute, imperious, magisterial, domineering, overbearing, high-handed, dogmatic.
  🔄 **1** reasoned, rational, circumspect.

arbitrate *v* judge, adjudicate, referee, umpire, mediate, settle, decide, determine.

arbitration *n* judgement, adjudication, intervention, mediation, negotiation, settlement, decision, determination.

arbitrator *n* judge, adjudicator, arbiter, referee, umpire, moderator,

mediator, negotiator, intermediary, go-between.

arch *n* archway, bridge, span, dome, vault, concave, bend, curve, curvature, bow, arc, semicircle.

> *Types of arch include*: basket handle, convex, corbel, equilateral, four-centre, Gothic, horseshoe, keel, lancet, Norman, ogee, parabolic, round, segmental, shouldered, skew, stilted, tented, trefoil, Tudor.

  ➤ *v* bend, curve, bow, arc, vault, camber.

archaeology

> *Archaeological terms include*: agger, amphitheatre, amphora, artefact, barrow, beaker, blade, bogman, bowl, bracteate, burin, cairn, cartouche, cave art/rock art, cist, cromlech, cup, dolmen, earthwork, eolith, flake, flask, flint, handaxe, henge, hieroglyph, hill fort, hoard, hypocaust, incised decoration, jar, jug, kitchen-midden, kurgan, ley lines, loom weight, lynchet, megalith, microlith, mosaic, mound, mummy, neolith, obelisk, palmette, palstave, papyrus, potassium-argon dating, radiocarbon dating, rock shelter, sondage, spindle, stele, stone circle, tell, tumulus, urn, vallum, whorl.

archaic *adj* antiquated, old-fashioned, outmoded, old hat (*infml*), passé, outdated, out of date, obsolete, old, ancient, antique, quaint, primitive.
  🔄 modern, recent.

archetype *n* pattern, model, standard, form, type, prototype, original, precursor, classic, paradigm, ideal.

architect *n* designer, planner, master builder, prime mover, originator, founder, instigator, creator, author, inventor, engineer, maker, constructor, shaper.

architecture

> *Architectural and building terms include*: alcove, annexe, architrave,

baluster, barge-board, baroque, bas-relief, capstone, casement window, classical, coping stone, Corinthian, cornerstone, cornice, coving, dado, decorated, dogtooth, dome, Doric, dormer, double glazing, drawbridge, dry-stone, duplex, Early English, eaves, Edwardian, elevation, Elizabethan, façade, fanlight, fascia, festoon, fillet, finial, flamboyant, Flemish bond, fletton, fluting, French window, frieze, frontispiece, gable, gargoyle, gatehouse, Georgian, Gothic, groin, groundplan, half-timbered, Ionic, jamb, lintel, mullion, Norman, pagoda, pantile, parapet, pinnacle, plinth, Queen Anne, rafters, Regency, reveal, ridge, rococo, Romanesque, roof, rotunda, roughcast, sacristy, scroll, soffit, stucco, terrazzo, Tudor, Tuscan, wainscot, weathering. *see also* **arch**; **roof**; **tower**; **wall**; **window**.

archives *n* records, annals, chronicles, memorials, papers, documents, deeds, ledgers, registers, roll.

ardent *adj* fervent, fiery, warm, passionate, impassioned, fierce, vehement, intense, spirited, enthusiastic, eager, keen, dedicated, devoted, zealous.
◨ apathetic, unenthusiastic.

arduous *adj* hard, difficult, tough, rigorous, severe, harsh, formidable, strenuous, tiring, taxing, fatiguing, exhausting, backbreaking, punishing, gruelling, uphill, laborious, onerous.
◨ easy.

area *n* locality, neighbourhood, environment, environs, patch, terrain, district, region, zone, sector, department, province, domain, realm, territory, sphere, field, range, scope, compass, size, extent, expanse, width, breadth, stretch, tract, part, portion, section.

argue *v* 1 QUARREL, squabble, bicker, row, wrangle, haggle, remonstrate, join issue, fight, feud, fall out, disagree,

dispute, question, debate, discuss. **2** REASON, assert, contend, hold, maintain, claim, plead, exhibit, display, show, manifest, demonstrate, indicate, denote, prove, evidence, suggest, imply.

argument *n* 1 QUARREL, squabble, row, wrangle, controversy, debate, discussion, dispute, disagreement, clash, conflict, fight, feud. **2** REASONING, reason, logic, assertion, contention, claim, demonstration, defence, case, synopsis, summary, theme.

argumentative *adj* quarrelsome, contentious, polemical, opinionated, belligerent, perverse, contrary.
◨ complaisant.

arid *adj* 1 *arid landscape*: dry, parched, waterless, desiccated, torrid, barren, infertile, unproductive, desert, waste. **2** DULL, uninteresting, boring, monotonous, tedious, dry, sterile, dreary, colourless, lifeless, spiritless, uninspired.
◨ 1 fertile. 2 lively.

arise *v* 1 ORIGINATE, begin, start, commence, derive, stem, spring, proceed, flow, emerge, issue, appear, come to light, crop up, occur, happen, result, ensue, follow. **2** RISE, get up, stand up, go up, ascend, climb, mount, lift, soar, tower.

aristocracy *n* upper class, gentry, nobility, peerage, ruling class, gentility, élite.
◨ common people.

aristocrat *n* noble, patrician, nobleman, noblewoman, peer, peeress, lord, lady.
◨ commoner.

aristocratic *adj* upper-class, highborn, well-born, noble, patrician, blue-blooded, titled, lordly, courtly, gentle, thoroughbred, élite.
◨ plebeian, vulgar.

arm[1] *n* limb, upper limb, appendage, bough, branch, projection, extension, offshoot, section, division, detachment, department.

arm[2] *v* provide, supply, furnish, issue,

equip, rig, outfit, ammunition, prime, prepare, forearm, gird, steel, brace, reinforce, strengthen, fortify, protect.

armoured *adj* armour-plated, steel-plated, iron-clad, reinforced, protected, bullet-proof, bomb-proof.

armoury *n* arsenal, ordnance depot, ammunition dump, magazine, depot, repository, stock, stockpile.

arms *n* **1** WEAPONS, weaponry, firearms, guns, artillery, instruments of war, armaments, ordnance, munitions, ammunition. **2** COAT-OF-ARMS, armorial bearings, insignia, heraldic device, escutcheon, shield, crest, heraldry, blazonry.

army *n* **1** ARMED FORCE, military, militia, land forces, soldiers, troops, legions, cohorts. **2** MULTITUDE, throng, host, horde.

Units in the armed services include:
task-force, militia, garrison;
air force: wing, squadron, flight;
army: patrol, troop, corps, platoon, squad, battery, company, brigade, battalion, regiment;
marines: Royal Marines, commandos;
navy: fleet, flotilla, squadron, convoy.
see also **rank**[1].

---

aroma *n* smell, odour, scent, perfume, fragrance, bouquet, savour.

aromatic *adj* perfumed, fragrant, sweet-smelling, balmy, redolent, savoury, spicy, pungent.

around *prep* **1** SURROUNDING, round, encircling, encompassing, enclosing, on all sides of, on every side of. **2** *around a dozen*: approximately, roughly, about, circa, more or less.

➤ *adv* **1** EVERYWHERE, all over, in all directions, on all sides, about, here and there, to and fro. **2** CLOSE, close by, near, nearby, at hand.

arouse *v* rouse, startle, wake up, waken, awaken, instigate, summon up, call forth, spark, kindle, inflame, whet, sharpen, quicken, animate, excite, prompt, provoke, stimulate, turn on (*sl*),

galvanize, goad, spur, incite, agitate, stir up, whip up.
🔁 calm, lull, quieten.

arrange *v* **1** ORDER, tidy, range, array, marshal, dispose, distribute, position, set out, lay out, align, group, class, classify, categorize, sort (out), sift, file, systematize, methodize, regulate, adjust. **2** ORGANIZE, co-ordinate, prepare, fix, plan, project, design, devise, contrive, determine, settle. **3** *arrange music*: adapt, set, score, orchestrate, instrument, harmonize.
🔁 **1** untidy, disorganize, muddle.

arrangement *n* **1** ORDER, array, display, disposition, layout, line-up, grouping, classification, structure, system, method, set-up, organization, preparation, planning, plan, scheme, design, schedule. **2** AGREEMENT, settlement, contract, terms, compromise. **3** ADAPTATION, version, interpretation, setting, score, orchestration, instrumentation, harmonization.

array *n* ARRANGEMENT, display, show, exhibition, exposition, assortment, collection, assemblage, muster, order, formation, line-up, parade.
➤ *v* **1** ARRANGE, order, range, dispose, group, line up, align, draw up, marshal, assemble, muster, parade, display, show, exhibit. **2** CLOTHE, dress, robe, deck, adorn, decorate.

arrest *v* **1** *arrest a criminal*: capture, catch, seize, nick (*sl*), run in, apprehend, detain. **2** STOP, stem, check, restrain, inhibit, halt, interrupt, stall, delay, slow, retard, block, obstruct, impede, hinder.

arrival *n* appearance, entrance, advent, coming, approach, occurrence.
🔁 departure.

arrive *v* reach, get to, appear, materialize, turn up, show up (*infml*), roll up (*infml*), enter, come, occur, happen.
🔁 depart, leave.

arrogant *adj* haughty, supercilious, disdainful, scornful, contemptuous, superior, condescending, patronizing, high and mighty, lordly, overbearing, high-handed, imperious, self-important, presumptuous, assuming, insolent, proud, conceited, boastful.

F3 humble, unassuming, bashful.

art *n* **1** FINE ART, painting, sculpture, drawing, artwork, craft, artistry, draughtsmanship, craftsmanship. **2** SKILL, knack, technique, method, aptitude, facility, dexterity, finesse, ingenuity, mastery, expertise, profession, trade. **3** ARTFULNESS, cunning, craftiness, slyness, guile, deceit, trickery, astuteness, shrewdness.

Schools of art include: abstract, action painting, Aestheticism, Art Deco, Art Nouveau, Barbizon, Baroque, Bohemian, Byzantine, classical revival, classicism, Conceptual Art, concrete art, Constructivism, Cubism, Dadaism, Etruscan art, Expressionism, Fauvism, Florentine, folk art, Futurism, Gothic, Hellenistic, Impressionism, junk art, Mannerism, medieval art, Minimal Art, Modernism, the Nabis, Naturalism, Neoclassicism, Neoexpressionism, Neoimpressionism, Neo-Plasticism, Op Art, plastic art, Pop Art, Postimpressionism, Post-Modernism, Purism, quattrocento, Realism, renaissance, Rococo, Romanesque, Romanticism, Suprematism, Surrealism, Symbolism, Venetian, Vorticism. *see also* **painting**; **picture**; **sculpture**.

Arts and crafts include: painting, oil painting, watercolour, fresco, portraiture; architecture, drawing, sketching, caricature, illustration; graphics, film, video, animation, animatronics, digital design; sculpture, modelling, woodcarving, woodcraft, marquetry, metalwork, enamelling, cloisonné, engraving, etching, pottery, ceramics, mosaic, jewellery, stained glass, photography, lithography, calligraphy, collage,

origami, spinning, weaving, batik, silk-screen printing, needlework, tapestry, embroidery, patchwork, crochet, knitting. *see also* **embroidery**.

artful *adj* cunning, crafty, sly, foxy, wily, tricky, scheming, designing, deceitful, devious, subtle, sharp, shrewd, smart, clever, masterly, ingenious, resourceful, skilful, dexterous.

F3 artless, naïve, ingenuous.

article *n* **1** *article in a magazine*: feature, report, story, account, piece, review, commentary, composition, essay, paper. **2** ITEM, thing, object, commodity, unit, part, constituent, piece, portion, division.

articulate *adj* distinct, well-spoken, clear, lucid, intelligible, comprehensible, understandable, coherent, fluent, vocal, expressive, meaningful.

F3 inarticulate, incoherent.

➤ *v* say, utter, speak, talk, express, voice, vocalize, verbalize, state, pronounce, enunciate, breathe.

articulation *n* saying, utterance, speaking, talking, expression, voicing, vocalization, verbalization, pronunciation, enunciation, diction, delivery.

artificial *adj* false, fake, bogus, counterfeit, spurious, phoney (*infml*), pseudo, specious, sham, insincere, assumed, affected, mannered, forced, contrived, made-up, feigned, pretended, simulated, imitation, mock, faux, synthetic, plastic, man-made, manufactured, non-natural, unnatural.

F3 genuine, true, real, natural.

artisan *n* craftsman, craftswoman, artificer, journeyman, expert, skilled worker, mechanic, technician.

artist

Types of artist include: architect, graphic designer, designer, draughtsman, draughtswoman, graphic artist, illustrator, cartoonist, animator, photographer, printer, engraver, goldsmith, silversmith, blacksmith, carpenter, potter, weaver, sculptor, painter; craftsman, craftswoman, master.

artiste *n* performer, entertainer, variety artist, vaudevillian, comic, comedian, comedienne, player, trouper, actor, actress, thespian.

artistic *adj* aesthetic, ornamental, decorative, beautiful, exquisite, elegant, stylish, graceful, harmonious, sensitive, tasteful, refined, cultured, cultivated, skilled, talented, creative, imaginative.
Ea inelegant, tasteless.

artistry *n* craftsmanship, workmanship, skill, craft, talent, flair, brilliance, genius, finesse, style, mastery, expertise, proficiency, accomplishment, deftness, touch, sensitivity, creativity.
Ea ineptitude.

as *conj, prep* **1** WHILE, when. **2** SUCH AS, for example, for instance, like, in the manner of. **3** BECAUSE, since, seeing that, considering that, inasmuch as, being.
◊ **as for** with reference to, as regards, with regard to, on the subject of, in connection with, in relation to, with relation to, with respect to.

ascend *v* rise, take off, lift off, go up, move up, slope upwards, climb, scale, mount, tower, float up, fly up, soar.
Ea descend, go down.

ascent *n* **1** ASCENDING, ascension, climb, climbing, scaling, escalation, rise, rising, mounting. **2** SLOPE, gradient, incline, ramp, hill, elevation.
Ea **1** descent.

ascertain *v* find out, learn, discover, determine, fix, establish, settle, locate, detect, identify, verify, confirm, make certain.

ascribe *v* attribute, credit, accredit, put down, assign, impute, charge, chalk up to.

ashamed *adj* sorry, apologetic, remorseful, contrite, guilty, conscience-stricken, sheepish, embarrassed, blushing, red-faced, mortified, humiliated, abashed, humbled.
Ea shameless, proud, defiant.

aside *adv* apart, on one side, in reserve, away, out of the way, separately, in isolation, alone, privately, secretly.
➤ *n* digression, parenthesis, departure, soliloquy, stage whisper, whisper.

ask *v* **1** REQUEST, appeal, petition, sue, plead, beg, entreat, implore, clamour, beseech, pray, supplicate, crave, demand, order, bid, require, seek, solicit, invite, summon. **2** INQUIRE, query, question, interrogate, quiz, press.

asleep *adj* sleeping, napping, snoozing, fast asleep, sound asleep, dormant, resting, inactive, inert, unconscious, numb, dozing.

aspect *n* angle, direction, elevation, side, facet, feature, face, expression, countenance, appearance, look, air, manner, bearing, attitude, condition, situation, position, standpoint, point of view, view, outlook, prospect, scene.

aspiration *n* aim, intent, purpose, endeavour, object, objective, goal, ambition, hope, dream, ideal, wish, desire, yearning, longing, craving, hankering.

aspire *v* aim, intend, purpose, seek, pursue, hope, dream, wish, desire, yearn, long, crave, hanker.

aspiring *adj* would-be, aspirant, striving, endeavouring, ambitious, enterprising, keen, eager, hopeful, optimistic, wishful, longing.

assassin *n* murderer, killer, slayer, cut-throat, executioner, hatchet man (*infml*), gunman, hit-man (*sl*), liquidator (*sl*).

assassinate *v* murder, kill, slay, dispatch, hit (*sl*), eliminate (*sl*), liquidate (*sl*).

assault *n* **1** ATTACK, offensive, onslaught, blitz, strike, raid, invasion, incursion, storm, storming, charge. **2** *charged with assault*: battery, grievous bodily harm, GBH (*infml*), mugging (*sl*), rape, abuse.

➤ *v* attack, charge, invade, strike, hit, set upon, fall on, beat up (*infml*), mug (*sl*), rape, molest, abuse.

assemble *v* **1** GATHER, congregate, muster, rally, convene, meet, join up, flock, group, collect, accumulate, amass, bring together, round up, marshal, mobilize. **2** CONSTRUCT, build, put together, piece together, compose, make, fabricate, manufacture.
ⓔ **1** scatter, disperse. **2** dismantle.

assembly *n* **1** GATHERING, rally, meeting, convention, conference, convocation, congress, council, group, body, company, congregation, flock, crowd, multitude, throng, collection, assemblage. **2** CONSTRUCTION, building, fabrication, manufacture.

assert *v* affirm, attest, swear, testify to, allege, claim, contend, maintain, insist, stress, protest, defend, vindicate, uphold, promote, declare, profess, state, pronounce, lay down, advance.
ⓔ deny, refute.

assertion *n* affirmation, attestation, word, allegation, claim, contention, insistence, vindication, declaration, profession, statement, pronouncement.
ⓔ denial.

assertive *adj* bold, confident, self-assured, forward, pushy, insistent, emphatic, forceful, firm, decided, strong-willed, dogmatic, opinionated, presumptuous, assuming, overbearing, domineering, aggressive.
ⓔ timid, diffident.

assess *v* gauge, estimate, evaluate, appriase, review, judge, consider, weigh, size up, compute, determine, fix, value, rate, tax, levy, impose, demand.

assessment *n* gauging, estimation, estimate, evaluation, appraisal, review, judgement, opinion, consideration, calculation, determination, valuation, rating, taxation.

asset *n* strength, resource, virtue, plus (*infml*), benefit, advantage, blessing, boon, help, aid.
ⓔ liability.

assets *n* estate, property, possessions, goods, holdings, securities, money, wealth, capital, funds, reserves, resources, means.

assign *v* **1** ALLOCATE, apportion, grant, give, dispense, distribute, allot, consign, delegate, name, nominate, designate, appoint, choose, select, determine, set, fix, specify, stipulate. **2** ATTRIBUTE, accredit, ascribe, put down.

assignment *n* commission, errand, task, project, job, position, post, duty, responsibility, charge, appointment, delegation, designation, nomination, selection, allocation, consignment, grant, distribution.

assist *v* help, aid, abet, rally round, co-operate, collaborate, back, second, support, reinforce, sustain, relieve, benefit, serve, enable, facilitate, expedite, boost, further, advance.
ⓔ hinder, thwart.

assistance *n* help, aid, succour, co-operation, collaboration, backing, support, reinforcement, relief, benefit, service, boost, furtherance.
ⓔ hindrance, resistance.

assistant *n* helper, helpmate, aide, right-hand man, auxiliary, ancillary, subordinate, backer, second, supporter, accomplice, accessory, abettor, collaborator, colleague, partner, ally, confederate, associate.

associate *v* **1** AFFILIATE, confederate, ally, league, join, amalgamate, combine, unite, link, connect, correlate, relate, couple, pair, yoke. **2** *associate with bad company*: socialize, mingle, mix, fraternize, consort, hang around (*infml*).
➤ *n* partner, ally, confederate, affiliate, collaborator, co-worker, mate, colleague, peer, compeer, fellow, comrade, companion, friend, sidekick (*infml*), assistant, follower.

association *n* **1** ORGANIZATION, corporation, company, partnership, league, alliance, coalition, confederation, confederacy, federation, affiliation, consortium, cartel, syndicate, union, society, club, fraternity, fellowship, clique, group, band. **2** BOND, tie, connection, correlation, relation, relationship, involvement, intimacy, friendship, companionship, familiarity.

assorted *adj* miscellaneous, mixed, varied, different, differing, heterogeneous, diverse, sundry, various, several, manifold.

assortment *n* miscellany, medley, potpourri, jumble, mixture, variety, diversity, collection, selection, choice, arrangement, grouping.

assume *v* **1** PRESUME, surmise, accept, take for granted, expect, understand, deduce, infer, guess, postulate, suppose, think, believe, imagine, fancy. **2** AFFECT, take on, feign, counterfeit, simulate, put on, pretend. **3** *assume command*: undertake, adopt, embrace, seize, arrogate, commandeer, appropriate, usurp, take over.

assumed *adj* false, bogus, counterfeit, fake, phoney (*infml*), sham, affected, feigned, simulated, pretended, made-up, fictitious, hypothetical.
☒ true, real, actual.

assumption *n* presumption, surmise, inference, supposition, guess, conjecture, theory, hypothesis, premise, postulate, idea, notion, belief, fancy.

assurance *n* **1** ASSERTION, declaration, affirmation, guarantee, pledge, promise, vow, word, oath. **2** CONFIDENCE, self-confidence, aplomb, boldness, audacity, courage, nerve, conviction, sureness, certainty.
☒ 2 shyness, doubt, uncertainty.

assure *v* affirm, guarantee, warrant, pledge, promise, vow, swear, tell, convince, persuade, encourage, hearten, reassure, soothe, comfort, boost, strengthen, secure, ensure, confirm.

assured *adj* **1** SURE, certain, indisputable, irrefutable, confirmed, positive, definite, settled, fixed, guaranteed, secure. **2** SELF-ASSURED,

confident, self-confident, bold, self-possessed, audacious, assertive.
☒ 1 uncertain. **2** shy.

astonish *v* surprise, startle, amaze, astound, stun, stupefy, daze, stagger, floor (*infml*), dumbfound, flabbergast (*infml*), shock, confound, bewilder.

astonishment *n* surprise, amazement, shock, dismay, consternation, confusion, bewilderment, wonder.

astounding *adj* surprising, startling, amazing, astonishing, stunning, breathtaking, jawdropping (*infml*), stupefying, overwhelming, staggering, shocking, bewildering.

astray *adv* adrift, off course, lost, amiss, wrong, off the rails (*infml*), awry, off the mark.

astute *adj* shrewd, prudent, sagacious, wise, canny, knowing, intelligent, sharp, penetrating, keen, perceptive, discerning, subtle, clever, crafty, cunning, sly, wily.
☒ stupid, slow.

asylum *n* haven, sanctuary, refuge, shelter, retreat, safety.

asymmetric *adj* unsymmetrical, unbalanced, uneven, crooked, awry, unequal, disproportionate, irregular.
☒ symmetrical.

atheism *n* unbelief, non-belief, disbelief, scepticism, irreligion, ungodliness, godlessness, impiety, infidelity, paganism, heathenism, free-thinking, rationalism.

atheist *n* unbeliever, non-believer, disbeliever, sceptic, infidel, pagan, heathen, free-thinker.

athlete *n* sportsman, sportswoman, runner, gymnast, competitor, contestant, contender.

athletic *adj* fit, energetic, vigorous, active, sporty, muscular, sinewy, brawny, strapping, robust, sturdy, strong, powerful, well-knit, well-proportioned, wiry.
☒ puny, wimpy (*infml*).

athletics *n* sports, games, races, track events, field events, exercises, gymnastics.

atmosphere *n* **1** AIR, sky, aerospace, heavens, ether. **2** AMBIENCE, environment, surroundings, aura, feel, feeling, mood, spirit, tone, tenor, character, quality, flavour.

> *The different layers of the atmosphere are*: troposphere, stratosphere, mesosphere, thermosphere, ionosphere, exosphere.

atom *n* molecule, particle, bit, morsel, crumb, grain, spot, speck, mite, shred, scrap, hint, trace, scintilla, jot, iota, whit.

> *Subatomic particles include*: photon, electron, positron, neutrino, anti-neutrino, muon, pion, kaon, proton, anti-proton, neutron, anti-neutron, lambda particle, sigma particle, omega particle, psi particle.

atrocious *adj* shocking, appalling, abominable, dreadful, terrible, horrible, hideous, ghastly, heinous, grievous, savage, vicious, monstrous, fiendish, ruthless.
F3 admirable, fine.

atrocity *n* outrage, abomination, enormity, horror, monstrosity, savagery, barbarity, brutality, cruelty, viciousness, evil, villainy, wickedness, vileness, heinousness, hideousness, atrociousness.

attach *v* **1** *attach a label*: affix, stick, adhere, fasten, fix, secure, tie, bind, weld, join, unite, connect, link, couple, add, annex. **2** ASCRIBE, attribute, impute, assign, put, place, associate, relate to, belong.
F3 **1** detach, unfasten.

attachment *n* **1** ACCESSORY, fitting, fixture, extension, appendage, extra, supplement, addition, adjunct, codicil. **2** FONDNESS, affection, tenderness, love, liking, partiality, loyalty, devotion, friendship, affinity, attraction, bond, tie, link.

attack *n* **1** OFFENSIVE, blitz, bombardment, invasion, incursion, foray, raid, strike, charge, rush, onslaught, assault, battery, aggression, criticism, censure, abuse. **2** SEIZURE, fit, convulsion, paroxysm, spasm, stroke.
➤ *v* **1** INVADE, raid, strike, storm, charge, assail, assault, set about, set upon, fall on, lay into, do over (*sl*). **2** CRITICIZE, censure, blame, denounce, revile, malign, abuse.
F3 **1** defend, protect.

attacker *n* assailant, mugger (*sl*), aggressor, invader, raider, critic, detractor, reviler, abuser, persecutor.
F3 defender, supporter.

attain *v* accomplish, achieve, fulfil, complete, effect, realize, earn, reach, touch, arrive at, grasp, get, acquire, obtain, procure, secure, gain, win, net.

attainment *n* accomplishment, achievement, feat, fulfilment, completion, consummation, realization, success, ability, capability, competence, proficiency, skill, art, talent, gift, aptitude, facility, mastery.

attempt *n* try, endeavour, shot (*infml*), go (*infml*), stab (*infml*), bash (*infml*), push, effort, struggle, bid, undertaking, venture, trial, experiment.
➤ *v* try, endeavour, have a go (*infml*), aspire, seek, strive, undertake, tackle, venture, experiment.

attend *v* **1** *attend a meeting*: be present, go to, frequent, visit. **2** ESCORT, chaperon, accompany, usher, follow, guard, look after, take care of, care for, nurse, tend, minister to, help, serve, wait on. **3** PAY ATTENTION, listen, hear, heed, mind, mark, note, notice, observe.
◇ **attend to** deal with, see to, take care of, look after, manage, direct, control, oversee, supervise.

attendance *n* **1** PRESENCE, appearance. **2** TURNOUT, audience, house, crowd, gate.

attendant *n* aide, helper, assistant, auxiliary, steward, waiter, servant, page, retainer, guide, marshal, usher, escort,

companion, follower, guard, custodian.
➤ *adj* accompanying, attached, associated, related, incidental, resultant, consequent, subsequent.

attention *n* alertness, vigilance, concentration, heed, notice, observation, regard, mindfulness, awareness, recognition, thought, contemplation, consideration, concern, care, treatment, service.
Ea inattention, disregard, carelessness.

attentive *adj* **1** ALERT, awake, vigilant, watchful, observant, concentrating, heedful, mindful, careful, conscientious.
2 CONSIDERATE, thoughtful, kind, obliging, accommodating, polite, courteous, devoted.
Ea 1 inattentive, heedless.
2 inconsiderate.

attitude *n* feeling, disposition, mood, aspect, manner, bearing, pose, posture, stance, position, point of view, opinion, view, outlook, perspective, approach.

attract *v* pull, draw, lure, allure, entice, seduce, tempt, invite, induce, incline, appeal to, interest, engage, fascinate, enchant, charm, bewitch, captivate, excite.
Ea repel, disgust.

attraction *n* pull, draw, magnetism, lure, allure, bait, enticement, inducement, seduction, temptation, invitation, appeal, interest, fascination, enchantment, charm, captivation.
Ea repulsion.

attractive *adj* pretty, fair, fetching, good-looking, handsome, beautiful, gorgeous, stunning, glamorous, lovely, pleasant, pleasing, agreeable, appealing, winsome, winning, enticing, seductive, tempting, inviting, sexy (*infml*), interesting, engaging, fascinating, charming, captivating, magnetic.
Ea unattractive, repellent.

attribute *v* ascribe, accredit, credit, impute, assign, put down, blame, charge, refer, apply.
➤ *n* property, quality, virtue, point,

aspect, facet, feature, trait, characteristic, idiosyncrasy, peculiarity, quirk, note, mark, sign, symbol.

auburn *adj* red, chestnut, tawny, russet, copper, Titian.

audible *adj* clear, distinct, recognizable, perceptible, discernible, detectable, appreciable.
Ea inaudible, silent, unclear.

audience *n* spectators, onlookers, house, auditorium, listeners, viewers, crowd, turnout, gathering, assembly, congregation, fans, devotees, regulars, following, public.

audit *n* examination, inspection, check, verification, investigation, scrutiny, analysis, review, statement, balancing.

augur *v* bode, forebode, herald, presage, portend, prophesy, predict, promise, signify.

auspices *n* aegis, authority, patronage, sponsorship, backing, support, protection, charge, care, supervision, control, influence, guidance.

auspicious *adj* favourable, propitious, encouraging, cheerful, bright, rosy, promising, hopeful, optimistic, fortunate, lucky, opportune, happy, prosperous.
Ea inauspicious, ominous.

austere *adj* **1** STARK, bleak, plain, simple, unadorned, grim, forbidding.
2 SEVERE, stern, strict, cold, formal, rigid, rigorous, exacting, hard, harsh, spartan, grave, serious, solemn, sober, abstemious, self-denying, restrained, economical, frugal, ascetic, self-disciplined, puritanical, chaste.
Ea 1 ornate, elaborate. **2** genial.

austerity *n* plainness, simplicity, severity, coldness, formality, hardness, harshness, solemnity, abstemiousness, abstinence, economy, asceticism, puritanism.
Ea elaborateness, materialism.

authentic *adj* genuine, true, real, actual, certain, bona fide, legitimate, honest, valid, original, pure, factual,

accurate, true-to-life, faithful, reliable, trustworthy.
🔁 false, fake, counterfeit, spurious.

authenticate *v* guarantee, warrant, vouch for, attest, authorize, accredit, validate, certify, endorse, confirm, verify, corroborate.

authenticity *n* genuineness, certainty, authoritativeness, validity, truth, veracity, truthfulness, honesty, accuracy, correctness, faithfulness, fidelity, reliability, dependability, trustworthiness.
🔁 spuriousness, invalidity.

author *n* **1** WRITER, novelist, dramatist, playwright, composer, pen, penman, penwoman. **2** CREATOR, founder, originator, initiator, parent, prime mover, mover, inventor, designer, architect, planner, maker, producer.

authoritarian *adj* strict, firm, disciplinarian, severe, harsh, rigid, inflexible, unyielding, dogmatic, doctrinaire, absolute, autocratic, dictatorial, despotic, tyrannical, oppressive, domineering, imperious.
🔁 liberal.

authoritative *adj* scholarly, learned, official, authorized, legitimate, valid, approved, sanctioned, accepted, definitive, decisive, authentic, factual, true, truthful, accurate, faithful, convincing, sound, reliable, dependable, trustworthy.
🔁 unofficial, unreliable.

authority *n* **1** SOVEREIGNTY, supremacy, rule, sway, control, dominion, influence, power, force, government, administration, officialdom. **2** AUTHORIZATION, permission, sanction, permit, warrant, licence, credentials, right, prerogative. **3** *an authority on antiques*: expert, guru (*infml*), pundit, connoisseur, specialist, professional, master, scholar.

authorize *v* legalize, validate, ratify, confirm, license, entitle, accredit, empower, enable, commission, warrant,

permit, allow, consent to, sanction, approve, give the go-ahead.

autocracy *n* absolutism, totalitarianism, dictatorship, despotism, tyranny, authoritarianism, fascism.
🔁 democracy.

autocrat *n* absolutist, totalitarian, dictator, despot, tyrant, authoritarian, (little) Hitler (*infml*), fascist.

autocratic *adj* absolute, all-powerful, totalitarian, despotic, tyrannical, authoritarian, dictatorial, domineering, overbearing, imperious.
🔁 democratic, liberal.

automatic *adj* **1** AUTOMATED, self-activating, mechanical, mechanized, programmed, self-regulating, computerized, push-button, robotic, self-propelling, unmanned. **2** SPONTANEOUS, reflex, knee-jerk (*infml*), involuntary, unwilled, unconscious, unthinking, natural, instinctive, routine, necessary, certain, inevitable, unavoidable, inescapable.

autonomy *n* self-government, self-rule, home rule, sovereignty, independence, self-determination, freedom, free will.
🔁 subjection, compulsion.

auxiliary *adj* ancillary, assistant, subsidiary, accessory, secondary, supporting, supportive, helping, assisting, aiding, extra, supplementary, spare, reserve, back-up, emergency, substitute.

available *adj* free, vacant, to hand, within reach, at hand, accessible, handy, convenient, on hand, ready, on tap, off-the-shelf (*infml*), obtainable.
🔁 unavailable.

avalanche *n* landslide, landslip, cascade, torrent, deluge, flood, inundation, barrage.

avant-garde *adj* innovative, innovatory, pioneering, experimental, unconventional, left-field (*infml*), far-out (*sl*), way-out (*sl*), progressive, advanced, forward-looking, enterprising, inventive.
🔁 conservative.

avarice n covetousness, rapacity, acquisitiveness, greed, greediness, meanness.
🔁 generosity, liberality.

avaricious adj covetous, grasping, rapacious, acquisitive, greedy, mercenary, mean, miserly.
🔁 generous.

avenge v take revenge for, take vengeance for, punish, requite, repay, retaliate.

average n mean, mid-point, norm, standard, rule, par, medium, run.
🔁 extreme, exception.
➤ adj mean, medial, median, middle, intermediate, medium, moderate, satisfactory, fair, mediocre, middling, indifferent, so-so (*infml*), passable, tolerable, undistinguished, run-of-the-mill, ordinary, everyday, common, usual, normal, regular, standard, vanilla (*infml*), typical, unexceptional.
🔁 extreme, exceptional, remarkable.

averse adj reluctant, unwilling, loth, disinclined, ill-disposed, hostile, opposed, antagonistic, unfavourable.
🔁 willing, keen, sympathetic.

aversion n dislike, hate, hatred, loathing, detestation, abhorrence, abomination, horror, phobia, reluctance, unwillingness, disinclination, distaste, disgust, revulsion, repugnance, repulsion, hostility, opposition, antagonism.
🔁 liking, sympathy, desire.

avert v turn away, deflect, turn aside, parry, fend off, ward off, stave off, forestall, frustrate, prevent, obviate, avoid, evade.

aviation n aeronautics, flying, flight, aircraft industry.

Aviation terms include: aeronautics, aeroplane, aerospace, aileron, aircraft, airfield, airline, air miss, airplane (*US*), airport, airship, airspace, air station, air steward, airstrip, air traffic control, airway, altitude, automatic pilot, biplane, black box, captain, chocks away (*infml*), cockpit, console, control tower, crash dive, crash-landing, dive, drag, fixed-wing, flap, flight, flight crew, flight deck, flight recorder, fly-by, fly-by-wire, fly-past, fuselage, George (*sl*), glider, ground control, ground speed, hangar, helicopter, hop, hot-air balloon, jet, jet engine, jet propulsion, jetstream, joystick, jumbo jet, landing, landing gear, landing strip, lift-off, loop-the-loop, Mach number, maiden flight, mid-air collision, monoplane, night-flying, nose dive, overshoot, parachute, pilot, plane, pressurised cabin, prang (*sl*), propeller, rotor blade, rudder, runway, solo flight, sonic boom, sound barrier, spoiler, supersonic, swing-wing, take-off, taxi, test flight, test pilot, thrust, touchdown, undercarriage, undershoot, vapour trail, vertical take-off and landing (VTOL), windsock, wingspan. *see also* **aircraft**.

avid adj eager, earnest, keen, enthusiastic, fanatical, devoted, dedicated, zealous, ardent, fervent, intense, passionate, insatiable, ravenous, hungry, thirsty, greedy, grasping, covetous.
🔁 indifferent.

avoid v evade, elude, sidestep, dodge, shirk, duck (*infml*), escape, get out of, bypass, circumvent, balk, prevent, avert, shun, abstain from, refrain from, steer clear of.

avoidable adj escapable, preventable.
🔁 inevitable.

avowed adj sworn, declared, professed, self-proclaimed, self-confessed, confessed, admitted, acknowledged, open, overt.

awake v awaken, waken, wake, wake up, rouse, arouse.
➤ adj wakeful, wide-awake, aroused, alert, vigilant, watchful, observant, attentive, conscious, aware, sensitive, alive.

awakening n awaking, wakening,

waking, rousing, arousal, stimulation, animating, enlivening, activation, revival, birth.

award *v* give, present, distribute, dispense, bestow, confer, accord, endow, gift, grant, allot, apportion, assign, allow, determine.

➤ *n* prize, trophy, decoration, medal, presentation, dispensation, bestowal, conferral, endowment, gift, grant, allotment, allowance, adjudication, judgement, decision, order.

aware *adj* conscious, alive to, sensitive, appreciative, sentient, familiar, conversant, acquainted, informed, up to speed (*infml*), enlightened, au courant, knowing, knowledgeable, cognizant, mindful, heedful, attentive, observant, sharp, alert, on the ball (*infml*), clued-up (*infml*), shrewd, sensible.
🄴 unaware, oblivious, insensitive.

awe *n* wonder, veneration, reverence, respect, admiration, amazement, astonishment, fear, terror, dread, apprehension.
🄴 contempt.

awe-inspiring *adj* wonderful, sublime, magnificent, stupendous, overwhelming, breathtaking, stupefying, stunning, astonishing, amazing, impressive, imposing, majestic, solemn, moving, awesome, formidable, daunting, intimidating, fearsome.

🄴 contemptible, tame.

awful *adj* terrible, dreadful, fearful, frightful, ghastly, unpleasant, nasty, horrible, hideous, ugly, gruesome, dire, abysmal, atrocious, horrific, shocking, appalling, alarming, spine-chilling.
🄴 wonderful, excellent.

awkward *adj* **1** CLUMSY, gauche, inept, inexpert, unskilful, bungling, ham-fisted, unco-ordinated, ungainly, graceless, ungraceful, inelegant. **2** CUMBERSOME, clunky (*infml*), unwieldy, inconvenient, difficult, fiddly, delicate, troublesome, perplexing. **3** *feeling awkward in their presence*: shy, uncomfortable, ill at ease, embarrassed. **4** OBSTINATE, stubborn, unco-operative, irritable, touchy, prickly, rude, unpleasant.
🄴 **1** graceful, elegant. **2** convenient, handy. **3** comfortable, relaxed. **4** amenable, pleasant.

axe *n* hatchet, chopper, cleaver, tomahawk, battle-axe.
➤ *v* **1** CUT (DOWN), fell, hew, chop, cleave, split. **2** CANCEL, terminate, discontinue, remove, withdraw, eliminate, get rid of, throw out, dismiss, discharge, sack (*infml*), fire (*infml*).

axiom *n* principle, fundamental, truth, truism, precept, dictum, byword, maxim, adage, aphorism.

axis *n* centre-line, vertical, horizontal, pivot, hinge.

axle *n* shaft, spindle, rod, pin, pivot.

Bb

babble v **1** CHATTER, gabble, jabber, cackle, prate, mutter, mumble, murmur. **2** *the stream babbled*: burble, gurgle.
➤ n chatter, gabble, clamour, hubbub, gibberish, burble, murmur.

baby n babe, infant, suckling, child, tiny, toddler, rugrat (*sl*), ankle-biter (*sl*), sprog (*sl*).
➤ adj miniature, small-scale, mini (*infml*), midget, small, little, tiny, minute, diminutive.

babyish adj childish, juvenile, puerile, infantile, silly, foolish, soft (*infml*), sissy (*infml*), baby, young, immature, naïve.
✿ mature, precocious.

back n rear, stern, end, tail, tail end, hind part, hindquarters, posterior, backside, reverse.
✿ front, face.
➤ v **1** GO BACKWARDS, reverse, recede, regress, backtrack, retreat, retire, withdraw, back away, recoil. **2** SUPPORT, sustain, assist, side with, champion, advocate, encourage, promote, boost, favour, sanction, countenance, endorse, second, countersign, sponsor, finance, subsidize, underwrite.
✿ **1** advance, approach. **2** discourage, weaken.
➤ adj rear, end, tail, posterior, hind, hindmost, reverse.
✿ **1** front.
◇ **back down** concede, yield, give in, surrender, submit, retreat, withdraw, back-pedal, do a U-turn.
◇ **back out** abandon, give up, chicken out (*infml*), withdraw, pull out (*infml*), resign, recant, go back on, cancel.
◇ **back up** confirm, corroborate, substantiate, endorse, second, champion, support, reinforce, bolster, assist, aid.
✿ let down.

backbone n **1** SPINE, spinal column, vertebrae, vertebral column, mainstay, support, core, foundation, basis. **2** COURAGE, mettle, pluck, nerve, grit, character, determination, resolve, tenacity, steadfastness, toughness, stamina, strength, power.
✿ **2** spinelessness, weakness.

backfire v recoil, rebound, ricochet, boomerang, miscarry, fail, flop.

background n **1** SETTING, surroundings, environment, context, circumstances. **2** HISTORY, record, credentials, experience, grounding, preparation, education, upbringing, breeding, culture, tradition.

backing n support, accompaniment, aid, assistance, helpers, championing, advocacy, encouragement, moral support, favour, sanction, promotion, endorsement, seconding, patronage, sponsorship, finance, funds, grant, subsidy.

backlash n reaction, response, repercussion, reprisal, retaliation, recoil, kickback, backfire, boomerang.

backlog n accumulation, stock, supply, resources, reserve, reserves, excess.

backsliding n lapse, relapse, apostasy, defection, desertion, defaulting.

backward adj **1** *a backward step*: retrograde, retrogressive, regressive. **2** SHY, bashful, reluctant, unwilling, hesitant, hesitating, wavering, slow, behind, behindhand, late, immature, underdeveloped, retarded, subnormal, stupid.
✿ **1** forward. **2** precocious.

bacteria *n* germs, bugs (*infml*), viruses, microbes, micro-organisms, bacilli.

bad *adj* **1** UNPLEASANT, disagreeable, nasty, undesirable, unfortunate, distressing, adverse, detrimental, harmful, damaging, injurious, serious, grave, severe, harsh. **2** EVIL, wicked, sinful, criminal, corrupt, immoral, vile. **3** *bad workmanship*: poor, inferior, substandard, shoddy, imperfect, faulty, defective, deficient, unsatisfactory, useless. **4** ROTTEN, mouldy, decayed, spoilt, putrid, rancid, sour, off, tainted, contaminated. **5** *a bad child*: naughty, mischievous, ill-behaved, disobedient.
Ea 1 good, pleasant, mild, slight. **2** virtuous. **3** skilled. **4** fresh. **5** well-behaved.

badge *n* identification, emblem, device, insignia, sign, mark, token, stamp, brand, trademark, logo.

badly *adv* **1** GREATLY, extremely, exceedingly, intensely, deeply, acutely, bitterly, painfully, seriously, desperately, severely, critically, crucially. **2** WICKEDLY, criminally, immorally, shamefully, unfairly. **3** WRONG, wrongly, incorrectly, improperly, defectively, faultily, imperfectly, inadequately, unsatisfactorily, poorly, incompetently, negligently, carelessly. **4** UNFAVOURABLY, adversely, unfortunately, unsuccessfully.
Ea 3 well.

bad-tempered *adj* irritable, cross, crotchety, crabbed, crabby (*infml*), snappy, grumpy, querulous, petulant, fractious, stroppy (*infml*).
Ea good-tempered, genial, equable.

baffle *v* puzzle, perplex, mystify, bemuse, bewilder, confuse, confound, bamboozle (*infml*), flummox (*infml*), daze, upset, disconcert, foil, thwart, frustrate, hinder, check, defeat, stump (*infml*).
Ea enlighten, help.

bag *v* **1** CATCH, capture, trap, land, kill, shoot. **2** OBTAIN, acquire, get, gain, corner, take, grab, appropriate, commandeer, reserve.

➤ *n* container, sack, case, suitcase, grip, carrier, hold-all, handbag, shoulder-bag, satchel, rucksack, haversack, pack.

baggage *n* luggage, suitcases, bags, belongings, things, equipment, gear, paraphernalia, impedimenta (*fml*).

baggy *adj* loose, slack, roomy, ill-fitting, billowing, bulging, floppy, sagging, droopy.
Ea tight, firm.

bail *n* security, surety, pledge, bond, guarantee, warranty.
◇ **bail out**[1] help, aid, assist, relieve, rescue, finance.
◇ **bail out**[2], **bale out** withdraw, retreat, quit, back out, cop out (*sl*), escape.

bait *n* lure, incentive, inducement, bribe, temptation, enticement, allurement, attraction.
Ea disincentive.
➤ *v* tease, provoke, goad, irritate, annoy, irk, needle (*infml*), harass, persecute, torment.

balance *v* **1** STEADY, poise, stabilize, level, square, equalize, equate, match, counterbalance, counteract, neutralize, offset, adjust. **2** COMPARE, consider, weigh, estimate.
Ea 1 unbalance, overbalance.
➤ *n* **1** EQUILIBRIUM, steadiness, stability, evenness, symmetry, equality, parity, equity, equivalence, correspondence. **2** COMPOSURE, self-possession, poise, equanimity. **3** REMAINDER, rest, residue, surplus, difference.
Ea 1 imbalance, instability.

balcony *n* terrace, veranda, porch (*US*), gallery, upper circle, gods.

bald *adj* **1** BALD-HEADED, hairless, smooth, uncovered. **2** BARE, naked, unadorned, plain, simple, severe, stark, barren, treeless. **3** *a bald statement*: forthright, direct, straight, outright, downright, straightforward.
Ea 1 hairy, hirsute. **2** adorned.

bale *n* bundle, truss, pack, package, parcel.
◇ **bale out** *see* **bail out**[2].

balk, baulk *v* **1** FLINCH, recoil, shrink, jib, boggle, hesitate, refuse, resist, dodge, evade, shirk. **2** THWART, frustrate, foil, forestall, disconcert, baffle, hinder, obstruct, check, stall, bar, prevent, defeat, counteract.

ball[1] *n* sphere, globe, orb, globule, drop, conglomeration, pellet, pill, shot, bullet, slug (*infml*).

ball[2] *n* dance, dinner-dance, party, soirée, masquerade, carnival, assembly.

ballad *n* poem, song, folk song, shanty, carol, ditty.

ballet

> **Terms used in ballet include**: à pointe, arabesque, attitude, ballerina, prima ballerina, ballon, barre, battement, batterie, battu, bourrée, capriole, chassé, choreography, ciseaux, company, corps de ballet, coryphée, développé, divertissement, écarté, élévation, entrechat, fish dive, five positions, fouetté, fouetté en tournant, glissade, jeté, grand jeté, leotard, pas de deux, pas de seul, pirouette, plié, pointes, sur les pointes, port de bras, principal dancer, régisseur, répétiteur, ballet shoe, point shoe, splits, stulchak, tutu.

ballot *n* poll, polling, vote, voting, election, referendum, plebiscite.

ban *v* forbid, prohibit, disallow, proscribe, bar, exclude, ostracize, outlaw, banish, suppress, restrict.
F3 allow, permit, authorize.
➤ *n* prohibition, embargo, veto, boycott, stoppage, restriction, suppression, censorship, outlawry, proscription, condemnation, denunciation, curse, taboo.
F3 permission, dispensation.

banal *adj* trite, commonplace, ordinary, everyday, humdrum, boring, dull, unimaginative, hackneyed, clichéed, stock, stereotyped, corny (*infml*), stale, threadbare, tired, empty.
F3 original, fresh, imaginative.

band[1] *n* strip, belt, ribbon, tape, bandage, binding, tie, ligature, bond, strap, cord, chain.

band[2] *n* **1** TROOP, gang, crew, group, herd, flock, party, body, association, company, society, club, clique. **2** *the band played on*: group, orchestra, ensemble.
➤ *v* group, gather, join, unite, ally, collaborate, consolidate, amalgamate, merge, affiliate, federate.
F3 disband, disperse.

bandage *n* dressing, plaster, compress, ligature, tourniquet, swathe, swaddle.
➤ *v* bind, dress, cover, swathe, swaddle.

bandit *n* robber, thief, brigand, marauder, outlaw, highwayman, pirate, buccaneer, hijacker, cowboy, gunman, desperado, gangster.

bandy[1] *v* exchange, swap, trade, barter, interchange, reciprocate, pass, toss, throw.

bandy[2] *adj* bandy-legged, bow-legged, curved, bowed, bent, crooked.

bang *n* **1** BLOW, hit, knock, bump, crash, collision, smack, punch, thump, wallop (*infml*), stroke, whack (*infml*). **2** *a loud bang*: explosion, detonation, pop, boom, clap, peal, clang, clash, thud, thump, slam, noise, report, shot.
➤ *v* **1** STRIKE, hit, bash, knock, bump, rap, drum, hammer, pound, thump, stamp. **2** EXPLODE, burst, detonate, boom, echo, resound, crash, slam, clatter, clang, peal, thunder.
➤ *adv* straight, directly, headlong, right, precisely, slap, smack, hard, noisily, suddenly, abruptly.

banish *v* expel, eject, evict, deport, transport, exile, outlaw, ban, bar, debar, exclude, shut out, ostracize, excommunicate, dismiss, oust, dislodge, remove, get rid of, discard, dispel, eliminate, eradicate.
F3 recall, welcome.

banishment *n* expulsion, eviction, deportation, expatriation, transportation, exile, outlawry, ostracism, excommunication.
F3 return, recall, welcome.

bank¹ *n* accumulation, fund, pool, reservoir, depository, repository, treasury, savings, reserve, store, stock, stockpile, hoard, cache.
➤ *v* deposit, save, keep, store, accumulate, stockpile.
🔁 spend.

bank² *n* heap, pile, mass, mound, earthwork, ridge, rampart, embankment, side, slope, tilt, edge, shore.
➤ *v* 1 HEAP, pile, stack, mass, amass, accumulate, mound, drift. 2 SLOPE, incline, pitch, slant, tilt, tip.

bank³ *n* array, panel, bench, group, tier, rank, line, row, series, succession, sequence, train.

bankrupt *adj* insolvent, in liquidation, ruined, failed, beggared, destitute, impoverished, broke (*infml*), spent, exhausted, depleted, lacking.
🔁 solvent, wealthy.
➤ *n* insolvent, debtor, pauper.

banner *n* flag, standard, colours, ensign, pennant, streamer.

banquet *n* feast, dinner, meal, repast (*fml*), treat.

banter *n* joking, jesting, pleasantry, badinage, repartee, word play, chaff, chaffing, kidding (*infml*), ribbing (*sl*), derision, mockery, ridicule.

baptism *n* christening, dedication, beginning, initiation, introduction, debut, launch, launching, immersion, sprinkling, purification.

baptize *v* christen, name, call, term, style, title, introduce, initiate, enrol, recruit, immerse, sprinkle, purify, cleanse.

bar *n* 1 PUBLIC HOUSE, pub (*infml*), inn, tavern, saloon, lounge, counter. 2 SLAB, block, lump, chunk, wedge, ingot, nugget. 3 ROD, stick, shaft, pole, stake, stanchion, batten, cross-piece, rail, railing, paling, barricade. 4 OBSTACLE, impediment, hindrance, obstruction, barrier, stop, check, deterrent.
➤ *v* 1 EXCLUDE, debar, ban, forbid, prohibit, prevent, preclude, hinder, obstruct, restrain. 2 *bar the door*:

barricade, lock, bolt, latch, fasten, secure.

barbarian *n* savage, brute, ruffian, hooligan, vandal, lout, oaf, boor, philistine, ignoramus, illiterate.

barbaric *adj* barbarous, primitive, wild, savage, fierce, ferocious, cruel, inhuman, brutal, brutish, uncivilized, uncouth, vulgar, coarse, crude, rude.
🔁 humane, civilized, gracious.

barbarity *n* barbarousness, wildness, savagery, ferocity, viciousness, cruelty, inhumanity, brutality, brutishness, rudeness.
🔁 civilization, humanity, civility.

barbed *adj* 1 PRICKLY, spiny, thorny, spiked, pronged, hooked, jagged, toothed, pointed. 2 *a barbed remark*: cutting, caustic, acid, hurtful, unkind, nasty, snide, hostile, critical.

bare *adj* 1 NAKED, nude, unclothed, undressed, stripped, denuded, uncovered, exposed. 2 PLAIN, simple, unadorned, unfurnished, empty, barren, bald, stark, basic, essential.
🔁 1 clothed. 2 decorated, detailed.

barely *adv* hardly, scarcely, only just, just, almost.

bargain *n* 1 DEAL, transaction, contract, treaty, pact, pledge, promise, agreement, understanding, arrangement, negotiation. 2 DISCOUNT, reduction, snip, giveaway, special offer.
➤ *v* negotiate, haggle, deal, trade, traffic, barter, buy, sell, transact, contract, covenant, promise, agree.
◇ **bargain for** expect, anticipate, plan for, include, reckon on, look for, foresee, imagine, contemplate, consider.

barge *v* bump, hit, collide, impinge, shove, elbow, push (in), muscle in, butt in, interrupt, gatecrash, intrude, interfere.
➤ *n* canal boat, flatboat, narrow boat, houseboat, lighter.

bark *n* yap, woof, yelp, snap, snarl, growl, bay, howl.
➤ *v* yap, woof, yelp, snap, snarl, growl, bay, howl.

baroque *adj* elaborate, ornate, rococo, florid, flamboyant, exuberant, vigorous, bold, convoluted, decorated, overdecorated, overwrought, extravagant, OTT (*infml*), fanciful, fantastic, grotesque.
🖛 plain, simple.

barracks *n* garrison, camp, encampment, guardhouse, quarters, billet, lodging, accommodation.

barrage *n* bombardment, shelling, gunfire, cannonade, broadside, volley, salvo, burst, assault, attack, onset, onslaught, deluge, torrent, stream, storm, hail, rain, shower, mass, profusion.

barrel *n* cask, keg, tun, butt, water-butt.

barren *adj* **1** ARID, dry, desert, desolate, waste, empty. **2** INFERTILE, sterile, childless, unprolific, unbearing. **3** FLAT, dull, uninteresting, uninspiring, uninformative, uninstructive, unrewarding, unproductive, profitless, unfruitful, fruitless, pointless, useless, boring.
🖛 **1** productive, fruitful. **2** fertile. **3** useful.

barricade *n* blockade, obstruction, barrier, fence, stockade, bulwark, rampart, protection.
🖛 *v* block, obstruct, bar, fortify, defend, protect.

barrier *n* **1** WALL, fence, railing, barricade, blockade, boom, rampart, fortification, ditch, frontier, boundary, bar, check. **2** *a barrier to success*: obstacle, hurdle, stumbling-block, impediment, obstruction, hindrance, handicap, limitation, restriction, drawback, difficulty.

bartender *n* barman, barmaid, barkeeper, publican.

barter *v* exchange, swap, trade, traffic, deal, negotiate, bargain, haggle.

base *n* **1** *the base of the statue*: bottom, foot, pedestal, plinth, stand, rest, support, foundation, bed, groundwork. **2** BASIS, fundamental, essential, principal, key, heart, core, essence, root, origin, source. **3** HEADQUARTERS, centre, post, station, camp, settlement, home, starting point.
🖛 *v* establish, found, ground, locate, station, build, construct, derive, depend, hinge.

baseless *adj* groundless, unfounded, unsupported, unsubstantiated, unauthenticated, unconfirmed, unjustified, uncalled-for, gratuitous.
🖛 justifiable.

bashful *adj* shy, retiring, backward, reticent, reserved, unforthcoming, hesitant, shrinking, nervous, timid, coy, diffident, modest, inhibited, self-conscious, embarrassed, blushing, abashed, shamefaced, sheepish.
🖛 bold, confident, aggressive.

basic *adj* fundamental, elementary, primary, root, underlying, key, central, inherent, intrinsic, essential, indispensable, mission-critical (*infml*), vital, necessary, important.
🖛 inessential, minor, peripheral.

basically *adv* fundamentally, at bottom, at heart, inherently, intrinsically, essentially, principally, primarily.

basics *n* fundamentals, rudiments, principles, essentials, necessaries, practicalities, brass tacks (*infml*), grass roots, bedrock, rock bottom, core, facts.

basin *n* bowl, dish, sink, crater, cavity, hollow, depression, dip.

basis *n* base, bottom, footing, support, foundation, ground, groundwork, fundamental, premise, principle, essential, heart, core, thrust.

bask *v* sunbathe, lie, lounge, relax, laze, wallow, revel, delight in, enjoy, relish, savour.

basket *n* hamper, creel, pannier, punnet, bassinet.

bass *adj* deep, low, low-toned, grave, resonant.

bastion *n* stronghold, citadel, fortress, defence, bulwark, mainstay, support, prop, pillar, rock.

batch *n* lot, consignment, parcel, pack, bunch, set, assortment, collection, assemblage, group, contingent, amount, quantity.

bath *n* wash, scrub, soak, shower, douche, tub (*US*), Jacuzzi®.

➤ *v* bathe, wash, clean, soak, shower.

bathe *v* swim, wet, moisten, immerse, wash, cleanse, rinse, soak, steep, flood, cover, suffuse.

➤ *n* swim, dip, paddle, wash, rinse, soak.

battalion *n* army, force, brigade, regiment, squadron, company, platoon, division, contingent, legion, horde, multitude, throng, host, mass, herd.

batter *v* beat, pound, pummel, buffet, smash, dash, pelt, lash, thrash, wallop (*infml*), abuse, maltreat, ill-treat, manhandle, maul, assault, hurt, injure, bruise, disfigure, mangle, distress, crush, demolish, destroy, ruin, shatter.

battered *adj* beaten, abused, ill-treated, injured, bruised, weather-beaten, dilapidated, tumbledown, ramshackle, crumbling, damaged, crushed.

battle *n* war, warfare, hostilities, action, conflict, strife, combat, fight, engagement, encounter, attack, fray, skirmish, clash, struggle, contest, campaign, crusade, row, disagreement, dispute, debate, controversy.

➤ *v* fight, combat, war, feud, contend, struggle, strive, campaign, crusade, agitate, clamour, contest, argue, dispute.

battle-cry *n* war cry, war song, slogan, motto, watchword, catchword.

baulk *see* **balk**.

bay¹ *n* gulf, bight, arm, inlet, cove.

bay² *n* recess, alcove, niche, nook, opening, compartment, cubicle, booth, stall, carrel.

bay³ *v* howl, roar, bellow, bell, bawl, cry, holler (*infml*), bark.

bazaar *n* market, marketplace, mart, exchange, sale, fair, fête, bring-and-buy.

be *v* 1 EXIST, breathe, live, inhabit, reside, dwell. 2 STAY, remain, abide, last, endure, persist, continue, survive, stand, prevail, obtain. 3 HAPPEN, occur, arise, come about, take place, come to pass, befall, develop.

beach *n* sand, sands, shingle, shore, strand, seashore, seaside, water's edge, coast, seaboard.

beacon *n* signal, fire, watch fire, bonfire, light, beam, lighthouse, flare, rocket, sign.

bead *n* drop, droplet, drip, globule, glob (*infml*), blob, dot, bubble, pearl, jewel, pellet.

beaker *n* glass, tumbler, jar, cup, mug, tankard.

beam *n* 1 *a beam of light*: ray, shaft, gleam, glint, glimmer, glow. 2 PLANK, board, timber, rafter, joist, girder, spar, boom, bar, support.

➤ *v* 1 EMIT, broadcast, transmit, radiate, shine, glare, glitter, glow, glimmer. 2 SMILE, grin.

bean

> *Varieties of bean and pulse include*: adzuki bean, alfalfa, beansprout, black bean, black-eyed pea, borlotti bean, broad bean, butter bean, cannellini bean, carob bean, chick pea, chilli bean, dal, dwarf runner bean, fava bean, flageolet bean, French bean, garbanzo pea, green bean, haricot bean, kidney bean, lentil, lima bean (*US*), locust bean, mange tout, marrowfat pea, mung bean, navy bean (*US*), okra, pea, pinto bean (*US*), red kidney bean, runner bean, scarlet runner (*US*), snap bean, soya bean, split pea, string bean, sugar bean, tonka bean, wax bean (*US*).

bear *v* 1 CARRY, convey, transport, move, take, bring. 2 HOLD, support, shoulder, uphold, sustain, maintain, harbour, cherish. 3 *bear children*: give birth to, breed, propagate, beget, engender, produce, generate, develop, yield, bring forth, give up. 4 TOLERATE, stand, put up with, endure, abide, suffer, permit, allow, admit.

◇ **bear on** refer to, relate to, affect, concern, involve.

◇ **bear out** confirm, endorse, support, uphold, prove, demonstrate, corroborate, substantiate, vindicate, justify.

◇ **bear up** persevere, soldier on, carry on, suffer, endure, survive, withstand.

◇ **bear with** tolerate, put up with, endure, suffer, forbear, be patient with, make allowances for.

bearable *adj* tolerable, endurable, sufferable, supportable, sustainable, acceptable, manageable.
E3 unbearable, intolerable.

bearded *adj* unshaven, bristly, whiskered, tufted, hairy, hirsute, shaggy, bushy.
E3 beardless, clean-shaven, smooth.

bearer *n* carrier, conveyor, porter, courier, messenger, runner, holder, possessor.

bearing *n* **1** *have no bearing on the matter*: relevance, significance, connection, relation, reference. **2** DEMEANOUR, manner, mien, air, aspect, attitude, behaviour, comportment, poise, deportment, carriage, posture.

bearings *n* orientation, position, situation, location, whereabouts, course, track, way, direction, aim.

beast *n* animal, creature, brute, monster, savage, barbarian, pig, swine, devil, fiend.

beat *v* **1** WHIP, flog, lash, tan (*infml*), cane, strap, thrash, lay into, hit, punch, strike, swipe, knock, bang, wham, bash, pound, hammer, batter, buffet, pelt, bruise. **2** PULSATE, pulse, throb, thump, race, palpitate, flutter, vibrate, quiver, tremble, shake, quake. **3** DEFEAT, trounce, best, worst, hammer (*infml*), slaughter (*sl*), conquer, overcome, overwhelm, vanquish, subdue, surpass, excel, outdo, outstrip, outrun.

➤ *n* **1** PULSATION, pulse, stroke, throb, thump, palpitation, flutter. **2** RHYTHM, time, tempo, metre, measure, rhyme, stress, accent. **3** *a police officer's beat*:

round, rounds, territory, circuit, course, journey, way, path, route.

◇ **beat up** (*infml*) attack, assault, knock about, knock around, batter, do over (*infml*).

beaten *adj* **1** HAMMERED, stamped, forged, wrought, worked, formed, shaped, fashioned. **2** WHISKED, whipped, mixed, blended, frothy, foamy.

beating *n* **1** CORPORAL PUNISHMENT, chastisement, whipping, flogging, caning, thrashing. **2** DEFEAT, conquest, rout, ruin, downfall.

beautiful *adj* attractive, fair, pretty, lovely, good-looking, handsome, gorgeous, radiant, ravishing, stunning (*infml*), pleasing, appealing, alluring, charming, delightful, fine, exquisite.
E3 ugly, plain, hideous.

beautify *v* embellish, enhance, improve, grace, gild, garnish, decorate, ornament, deck, bedeck, adorn, array, glamorize, titivate (*infml*), tart up (*sl*).
E3 disfigure, spoil.

beauty *n* attractiveness, fairness, prettiness, loveliness, (good) looks, handsomeness, glamour, appeal, allure, charm, grace, elegance, symmetry, excellence.
E3 ugliness, repulsiveness.

because *conj* as, for, since, owing to, on account of, by reason of, thanks to.

beckon *v* summon, motion, gesture, signal, nod, wave, gesticulate, call, invite, attract, pull, draw, lure, allure, entice, tempt, coax.

become *v* **1** *become old-fashioned*: turn, grow, get, change into, develop into. **2** SUIT, befit, flatter, enhance, grace, embellish, ornament, set off, harmonize.

bed *n* **1** DIVAN, couch, bunk, berth, cot, mattress, pallet, sack (*sl*). **2** LAYER, stratum, substratum, matrix, base, bottom, foundation, groundwork, watercourse, channel. **3** *bed of flowers*: garden, border, patch, plot.

Kinds of bed include: bed settee, berth, box bed, bunk bed, camp-bed, chaise longue, cot, cradle, crib, day bed, divan bed, double bed, foldaway bed, folding bed, four-poster, futon, hammock, mattress, pallet, palliasse, Put-u-up®, put-you-up, single bed, sofa bed, trucklebed, trundlebed, twin bed, water bed, Z-bed.

bedclothes *n* bedding, bedlinen, covers.

Kinds of bedclothes include: mattress cover, pillow, pillow sham, bolster, pillowcase, pillowslip, sheet, fitted sheet, valanced sheet, valance, blanket, cellular blanket, electric blanket, quilt, patchwork quilt, duvet, quilt cover, duvet cover, eiderdown, bedspread, candlewick bedspread, throwover, counterpane, coverlet, comforter (*US*), bed canopy.

bedraggled *adj* untidy, unkempt, dishevelled, disordered, scruffy, slovenly, messy, dirty, muddy, muddied, soiled, wet, sodden, drenched.
ⓔ neat, tidy, clean.

before *adv* ahead, in front, in advance, sooner, earlier, formerly, previously.
ⓔ after, later.

beforehand *adv* in advance, preliminarily, already, before, previously, earlier, sooner.

befriend *v* help, aid, assist, succour, back, support, stand by, uphold, sustain, comfort, encourage, welcome, favour, benefit, take under one's wing, make friends with, get to know.
ⓔ neglect, oppose.

beg *v* request, require, desire, crave, beseech, plead, entreat, implore, pray, supplicate, petition, solicit, cadge, scrounge, sponge.

beggar *n* mendicant, supplicant, pauper, down-and-out, tramp, vagrant, cadger, scrounger, sponger.

begin *v* start, commence, set about, embark on, set in motion, activate, kick in (*infml*), originate, initiate, introduce,

found, institute, instigate, arise, spring, emerge, appear.
ⓔ end, finish, cease.

beginner *n* novice, tiro, starter, learner, trainee, apprentice, student, freshman, fresher, recruit, cub, tenderfoot, fledgling.
ⓔ veteran, old hand, expert.

beginning *n* start, commencement, onset, outset, opening, preface, prelude, introduction, initiation, establishment, inauguration, inception, starting point, birth, dawn, origin, source, fountainhead, root, seed, emergence, rise.
ⓔ end, finish.

begrudge *v* resent, grudge, mind, object to, envy, covet, stint.
ⓔ allow.

beguile *v* 1 CHARM, enchant, bewitch, captivate, amuse, entertain, divert, distract, occupy, engross. 2 DECEIVE, fool, hoodwink, dupe, trick, cheat, delude, mislead.

behalf *n* sake, account, good, interest, benefit, advantage, profit, name, authority, side, support.

behave *v* act, react, respond, work, function, run, operate, perform, conduct oneself, acquit oneself, comport oneself.

behaviour *n* conduct, comportment, manner, manners, actions, doings, dealings, ways, habits, action, reaction, response, functioning, operation, performance.

behead *v* decapitate, execute, guillotine.

behind *prep* 1 FOLLOWING, after, later than, causing, responsible for, instigating, initiating. 2 SUPPORTING, backing, for.
➤ *adv* after, following, next, subsequently, behindhand, late, overdue, in arrears, in debt.
➤ *n* rump, rear, posterior (*infml*), buttocks, seat, bottom, backside (*infml*), bum (*sl*), butt (*US infml*), arse (*sl*), ass (*US sl*), tail (*infml*).

beige adj buff, fawn, mushroom, camel, sandy, khaki, coffee, neutral.

being n **1** EXISTENCE, actuality, reality, life, animation, essence, substance, nature, soul, spirit. **2** CREATURE, animal, beast, human being, mortal, person, individual, thing, entity.

belated adj late, tardy, overdue, delayed, behindhand, unpunctual.
☒ punctual, timely.

belch v burp (*infml*), hiccup, emit, discharge, disgorge, spew.
➤ n burp (*infml*), hiccup.

beleaguered adj harassed, worried, pestered, badgered, bothered, vexed, plagued, persecuted, surrounded, beset, besieged.

belief n **1** CONVICTION, persuasion, credit, trust, reliance, confidence, assurance, certainty, sureness, presumption, expectation, feeling, intuition, impression, notion, theory, view, opinion, judgement. **2** IDEOLOGY, faith, creed, doctrine, dogma, tenet, principle.
☒ **1** disbelief.

believable adj credible, imaginable, conceivable, acceptable, plausible, possible, likely, probable, authoritative, reliable, trustworthy.
☒ unbelievable, incredible, unconvincing.

believe v accept, wear (*infml*), swallow (*infml*), credit, trust, count on, depend on, rely on, swear by, hold, maintain, postulate, assume, presume, gather, speculate, conjecture, guess, imagine, think, consider, reckon, suppose, deem, judge.
☒ disbelieve, doubt.

believer n convert, proselyte, disciple, follower, adherent, devotee, zealot, supporter, upholder.
☒ unbeliever, sceptic.

belittle v minimize, play down, dismiss, underrate, undervalue, underestimate, lessen, diminish, detract from, deprecate, decry, disparage, run down, deride, scorn, ridicule.
☒ exaggerate, praise.

belligerent adj aggressive, militant, argumentative, quarrelsome, contentious, combative, pugnacious, violent, bullying, antagonistic, warring, warlike, bellicose.
☒ peaceable.

bellow v roar, yell, shout, bawl, cry, scream, shriek, howl, clamour.

belong v fit, go with, be part of, attach to, link up with, tie up with, be connected with, relate to.

belongings n possessions, property, chattels, goods, effects, things, stuff (*infml*), gear (*infml*), paraphernalia.

beloved adj loved, adored, cherished, treasured, prized, precious, pet, favourite, dearest, dear, darling, admired, revered.

below adv beneath, under, underneath, down, lower, lower down.
☒ above.
➤ prep **1** UNDER, underneath, beneath. **2** INFERIOR TO, lesser than, subordinate to, subject to.
☒ above.

belt n **1** SASH, girdle, waistband, girth, strap. **2** STRIP, band, swathe, stretch, tract, area, region, district, zone, layer.

bemused adj confused, muddled, bewildered, puzzled, perplexed, dazed, befuddled, stupefied.
☒ clear-headed, clear, lucid.

bench n **1** SEAT, form, settle, pew, ledge, counter, table, stall, workbench, worktable. **2** COURT, courtroom, tribunal, judiciary, judicature, judge, magistrate.

bend v curve, turn, deflect, swerve, veer, diverge, twist, contort, flex, shape, mould, buckle, bow, incline, lean, stoop, crouch.
☒ straighten.
➤ n curvature, curve, arc, bow, loop, hook, crook, elbow, angle, corner, turn, twist, zigzag.

beneath adv below, under, underneath, lower, lower down.
➤ prep **1** UNDER, underneath, below, lower than. **2** UNWORTHY OF, unbefitting.

benefactor n philanthropist, patron, sponsor, angel (*infml*), backer, supporter, promoter, donor, contributor, subscriber, provider, helper, friend, well-wisher.
🔁 opponent, persecutor.

beneficial adj advantageous, favourable, useful, helpful, profitable, rewarding, valuable, improving, edifying, wholesome.
🔁 harmful, detrimental, useless.

beneficiary n payee, receiver, recipient, inheritor, legatee, heir, heiress, successor.

benefit n advantage, good, welfare, interest, favour, help, aid, assistance, service, use, avail, gain, profit, asset, blessing.
🔁 disadvantage, harm, damage.
➤ v help, aid, assist, serve, avail, advantage, profit, improve, enhance, better, further, advance, promote.
🔁 hinder, harm, undermine.

benevolent adj philanthropic, humanitarian, charitable, generous, liberal, munificent, altruistic, benign, humane, kind, kindly, well-disposed, compassionate, caring, considerate.
🔁 mean, selfish, malevolent.

benign adj 1 BENEVOLENT, good, gracious, gentle, kind, obliging, friendly, amiable, genial, sympathetic. 2 *a benign tumour*: curable, harmless. 3 FAVOURABLE, propitious (*fml*), beneficial, temperate, mild, warm, refreshing, restorative, wholesome.
🔁 1 hostile. 2 malignant. 3 harmful, unpleasant.

bent adj 1 ANGLED, curved, bowed, arched, folded, doubled, twisted, hunched, stooped. 2 (*infml*) DISHONEST, crooked (*infml*), illegal, criminal, corrupt, untrustworthy.
🔁 1 straight, upright. 2 honest.
➤ n tendency, inclination, leaning, preference, ability, capacity, faculty, aptitude, facility, gift, talent, knack, flair, forte.
◇ **bent on** determined, resolved, set, fixed, inclined, disposed.

bequeath v will, leave, bestow, gift, endow, grant, settle, hand down, pass on, impart, transmit, assign, entrust, commit.

bequest n legacy, inheritance, heritage, trust, bestowal, endowment, gift, donation, estate, devisal, settlement.

bereavement n loss, deprivation, dispossession, death.

bereft adj deprived, robbed, stripped, destitute, devoid, lacking, wanting, minus.

berserk adj mad, crazy, demented, insane, deranged, frantic, frenzied, wild, raging, furious, violent, rabid, raving.
🔁 sane, calm.

berth n 1 BED, bunk, hammock, billet. 2 MOORING, anchorage, quay, wharf, dock, harbour, port.

beside prep alongside, abreast of, next to, adjacent, abutting, bordering, neighbouring, next door to, close to, near, overlooking.

besides adv also, as well, too, in addition, additionally, further, furthermore, moreover.
➤ prep apart from, other than, in addition to, over and above.

besiege v 1 LAY SIEGE TO, blockade, surround, encircle, confine. 2 TROUBLE, bother, importune, assail, beset, beleaguer, harass, pester, badger, nag, hound, plague.

besotted adj infatuated, doting, obsessed, smitten, hypnotized, spellbound, intoxicated.
🔁 indifferent, disenchanted.

best adj optimum, optimal, premium, first, foremost, leading, unequalled, unsurpassed, matchless, incomparable, supreme, greatest, highest, largest, finest, excellent, outstanding, superlative, first-rate, first-class, top-drawer (*infml*), blue-chip (*infml*), perfect.
🔁 worst.
➤ adv greatly, extremely, exceptionally, excellently, superlatively.
🔁 worst.

➤ *n* finest, cream, prime, élite, top, first, pick, choice, favourite.
⊟ worst.

bestow *v* award, present, grant, confer, endow, bequeath, commit, entrust, impart, transmit, allot, apportion, accord, give, donate, lavish.
⊟ withhold, deprive.

bet *n* wager, flutter (*infml*), gamble, speculation, risk, venture, stake, ante, bid, pledge.
➤ *v* wager, gamble, punt, speculate, risk, hazard, chance, venture, lay, stake, bid, pledge.

betray *v* 1 *betray a friend*: inform on, shop (*sl*), sell (out), double-cross, desert, abandon, forsake. 2 DISCLOSE, give away, tell, divulge, expose, reveal, show, manifest.
⊟ 1 defend, protect. 2 conceal, hide.

betrayal *n* treachery, treason, sell-out, disloyalty, unfaithfulness, double-dealing, duplicity, deception, trickery, falseness.
⊟ loyalty, protection.

betrayer *n* traitor, Judas, informer, grass (*sl*), supergrass (*sl*), double-crosser, deceiver, conspirator, renegade, apostate.
⊟ protector, supporter.

better *adj* 1 SUPERIOR, bigger, larger, longer, greater, worthier, finer, surpassing, preferable. 2 IMPROVING, progressing, on the mend, recovering, fitter, healthier, stronger, recovered, restored.
⊟ 1 inferior. 2 worse.
➤ *v* 1 IMPROVE, ameliorate, enhance, raise, further, promote, forward, reform, mend, correct. 2 SURPASS, top, beat, outdo, outstrip, overtake.
⊟ 1 worsen, deteriorate.

between *prep* mid, amid, amidst, among, amongst.

beverage *n* drink, draught, liquor, liquid, refreshment.

bevy *n* gathering, band, company, troupe, group, flock, gaggle, pack, bunch, crowd, throng.

beware *v* watch out, look out, mind, take heed, steer clear of, avoid, shun, guard against.

bewilder *v* confuse, muddle, disconcert, confound, bamboozle (*infml*), baffle, puzzle, perplex, mystify, daze, stupefy, disorient.

bewildered *adj* confused, muddled, uncertain, disoriented, nonplussed, bamboozled (*infml*), baffled, puzzled, perplexed, mystified, bemused, surprised, stunned.
⊟ unperturbed, collected.

bewitch *v* charm, enchant, allure, beguile, spellbind, possess, captivate, enrapture, obsess, fascinate, entrance, hypnotize.

beyond *prep* past, further than, apart from, away from, remote from, out of range of, out of reach of, above, over, superior to.

bias *n* slant, angle, distortion, bent, leaning, inclination, tendency, propensity, partiality, favouritism, prejudice, one-sidedness, unfairness, bigotry, intolerance.
⊟ impartiality, fairness.

biased *adj* slanted, angled, distorted, warped, twisted, loaded, weighted, influenced, swayed, partial, predisposed, prejudiced, one-sided, unfair, bigoted, blinkered, jaundiced.
⊟ impartial, fair.

bicker *v* squabble, row, quarrel, wrangle, argue, scrap (*infml*), spar, fight, clash, disagree, dispute.
⊟ agree.

bicycle *n* cycle, bike (*infml*), two-wheeler, push-bike, racer, mountain-bike, tandem, penny-farthing.

Parts of a bicycle include: bell, brake, brake block, brake cable, brake caliper, brake lever, brake shoe, cable braking system, carrier, centre-pull brake cable, chain, chain guide, chain guard, chain link, chain stays, chain transmission, chain wheel, coaster brake, crank, crank lever, crankset, crossbar, derailleur gear, diamond frame, down tube, drum brake, dynamo, footrest, fork, frame, freewheel unit, gear, gear cable, gearwheel, handgrip, handlebars, handlebar stem, hub, hub gear, inner tube, kickstand, lamp, lamp bracket, mudguard, fender (*US*), pannier, pedal, prop stand, pulley, pump, reflector, rim brake, rim tape, rod braking system, roller chain, saddle, saddle spring, seat pillar, seat stays, seat tube, side-pull brake cable, speedometer, spokes, spoke nipples, sprocket (wheel), stabilizer, steering head, steering tube, stirrup guide, toe clip, tool bag, tyre or (*US*) tire; tyre valve, Presta® valve, Schrader® valve, Woods® valve; wheel bearing, wheel lock, wheel nut, wheel rim, wheel spindle.

bid *v* **1** ASK, request, desire, instruct, direct, command, enjoin, require, charge, call, summon, invite, solicit. **2** *he bid more than it was worth*: offer, proffer, tender, submit, propose.
➤ *n* **1** OFFER, tender, sum, amount, price, advance, submission, proposal. **2** ATTEMPT, effort, try, go (*infml*), endeavour, venture.

big *adj* **1** LARGE, great, sizable, considerable, substantial, huge, enormous, immense, massive, colossal, gigantic, mammoth, burly, bulky, extensive, spacious, vast, voluminous. **2** IMPORTANT, significant, momentous, serious, main, principal, eminent, prominent, influential. **3** *that's big of you*: generous, magnanimous, gracious, unselfish.
Fa **1** small, little. **2** insignificant, unknown.

bigot *n* chauvinist, sectarian, racist, sexist, dogmatist, fanatic, zealot.
Fa liberal, humanitarian.

bigoted *adj* prejudiced, biased, intolerant, illiberal, narrow-minded, narrow, blinkered, closed, dogmatic, opinionated, obstinate.
Fa tolerant, liberal, broad-minded, enlightened.

bigotry *n* prejudice, discrimination, bias, injustice, unfairness, intolerance, narrow-mindedness, chauvinism, jingoism, sectarianism, racism, racialism, sexism, dogmatism, fanaticism.
Fa tolerance.

bilious *adj* **1** IRRITABLE, choleric, cross, grumpy, crotchety, testy, grouchy, peevish. **2** SICK, queasy, nauseated, sickly, out of sorts (*infml*).

bill *n* **1** INVOICE, statement, account, charges, reckoning, tally, score. **2** CIRCULAR, leaflet, handout, bulletin, handbill, broadsheet, advertisement, notice, poster, placard, playbill, programme. **3** *parliamentary bill*: proposal, measure, legislation.
➤ *v* invoice, charge, debit.

billet *n* **1** ACCOMMODATION, quarters, barracks, lodging, housing, berth. **2** EMPLOYMENT, post, occupation.

billow *v* swell, expand, bulge, puff out, fill out, balloon, rise, heave, surge, roll, undulate.

bind *v* **1** ATTACH, fasten, secure, clamp, stick, tie, lash, truss, strap, bandage, cover, dress, wrap. **2** OBLIGE, force, compel, constrain, necessitate, restrict, confine, restrain, hamper.

binding *adj* obligatory, compulsory, mandatory, necessary, requisite, permanent, conclusive, irrevocable, unalterable, indissoluble, unbreakable, strict.
➤ *n* border, edging, trimming, tape, bandage, covering, wrapping.

biography *n* life story, life, history, autobiography, memoirs, recollections, curriculum vitae, account, record.

biology

Biological terms include:
bacteriology, biochemistry, biology, bionics, botany, cybernetics, cytology, Darwinism, neo-Darwinism, ecology, embryology, endocrinology, evolution, Haeckel's law, genetics, Mendelism, Lamarckism, marine biology, natural

history, palaeontology, pathology, physiology, systematics, taxonomy, zoology; amino acid, anatomy, animal behaviour, animal kingdom, bacillus, bacteria, biologist, botanist, cell, chromosome, class, clone, coccus, conservation, corpuscle, cultivar, cytoplasm, deoxyribonucleic acid (DNA), diffusion, ecosystem, ectoplasm, embryo, endoplasmic reticulum (ER), enzyme, evolution, excretion, extinction, flora and fauna, food chain, fossil, gene, genetic engineering, genetic fingerprinting, genetically modified (GM), population genetics, germ, Golgi apparatus, hereditary factor, homeostasis, living world, meiosis, membrane, metabolism, microorganism, microbe, mitosis, molecule, mutation, natural selection, nuclear membrane, nucleus, nutrition, order, organism, osmosis, parasitism, photosynthesis, pollution, protein, protoplasm, reproduction, respiration, reticulum, ribonucleic acid (RNA), ribosome, secretion, survival of the fittest, symbiosis, virus.

bird

Birds include: sparrow, thrush, starling, blackbird, bluetit, chaffinch, greenfinch, bullfinch, dunnock, robin, wagtail, swallow, tit, wren, martin, swift, crow, magpie, dove, pigeon, skylark, nightingale, linnet, warbler, jay, jackdaw, rook, raven, cuckoo, shrike, woodpecker, yellowhammer; duck, mallard, eider, teal, swan, goose, heron, stork, flamingo, pelican, kingfisher, moorhen, coot, lapwing, peewit, plover, curlew, snipe, avocet, seagull, guillemot, tern, petrel, crane, bittern, petrel, albatross, gannet, cormorant, auk, puffin, dipper; eagle, owl, hawk, sparrowhawk, falcon, kestrel, osprey, buzzard, vulture, condor; emu, ostrich, kiwi, peacock, penguin; chicken, grouse, partridge, pheasant, quail, turkey; canary, budgerigar, budgie (*infml*), cockatiel, cockatoo, lovebird, parakeet, parrot,

macaw, toucan, myna bird, mockingbird, kookaburra, bird of paradise.

birth *n* **1** CHILDBIRTH, parturition, confinement, delivery, nativity. **2** *of noble birth*: ancestry, family, parentage, descent, line, lineage, genealogy, pedigree, blood, stock, race, extraction, background, breeding. **3** BEGINNING, rise, emergence, origin, source, derivation.

birthplace *n* place of origin, native town, native country, fatherland, mother country, roots, provenance, source, fount.

bisect *v* halve, divide, separate, split, intersect, cross, fork, bifurcate.

bit *n* fragment, part, segment, piece, slice, crumb, morsel, scrap, atom, mite, whit, jot, iota, grain, speck.
◊ **bit by bit** gradually, little by little, step by step, piecemeal.
🔁 wholesale.

bitchy *adj* catty, snide, nasty, mean, spiteful, malicious, vindictive, backbiting, venomous, cruel, vicious.
🔁 kind.

bite *v* **1** CHEW, masticate, munch, gnaw, nibble, champ, crunch, crush. **2** *the dog bit her hand*: nip, pierce, wound, tear, rend. **3** SMART, sting, tingle. **4** GRIP, hold, seize, pinch, take effect.
➤ *n* **1** NIP, wound, sting, smarting, pinch. **2** *a bite to eat*: snack, refreshment, mouthful, morsel, taste. **3** PUNGENCY, piquancy, kick (*infml*), punch.

biting *adj* **1** COLD, freezing, bitter, harsh, severe. **2** CUTTING, incisive, piercing, penetrating, raw, stinging, sharp, tart, caustic, scathing, cynical, hurtful.
🔁 **1** mild. **2** bland.

bitter *adj* **1** SOUR, tart, sharp, acid, acid, vinegary, unsweetened. **2** RESENTFUL, embittered, jaundiced, cynical, rancorous, acrimonious, acerbic, hostile. **3** INTENSE, severe, harsh, fierce, cruel, savage, merciless,

painful, stinging, biting, freezing, raw.
F3 **1** sweet. **2** contented. **3** mild.

bizarre *adj* strange, odd, queer,
curious, weird, peculiar, eccentric, way-
out (*infml*), off-the-wall (*infml*), left-field
(*infml*), outlandish, ludicrous, ridiculous,
fantastic, extravagant, grotesque,
freakish, abnormal, deviant, unusual,
extraordinary.
F3 normal, ordinary.

black *adj* **1** JET-BLACK, coal-black, jet,
ebony, sable, inky, sooty, dusky, swarthy.
2 DARK, unlit, moonless, starless,
overcast, dingy, gloomy, sombre,
funereal. **3** FILTHY, dirty, soiled, grimy,
grubby.
F3 **1** white. **2** bright. **3** clean.
➤ *v* boycott, blacklist, ban, bar, taboo.
◇ **black out 1** FAINT, pass out, collapse,
flake out (*infml*). **2** DARKEN, eclipse,
cover up, conceal, suppress, withhold,
censor, gag.

blacken *v* **1** DARKEN, dirty, soil, smudge,
cloud. **2** DEFAME, malign, slander, libel,
vilify, revile, denigrate (*fml*), detract, smear,
besmirch, sully, stain, tarnish, taint, defile,
discredit, dishonour.
F3 **2** praise, enhance.

blackmail *n* extortion, chantage, hush
money (*infml*), intimidation, protection,
pay-off, ransom.
➤ *v* extort, bleed, milk, squeeze, hold to
ransom, threaten, lean on (*infml*), force,
compel, coerce, demand.

blackout *n* **1** *a news blackout*:
suppression, censorship, cover-up
(*infml*), concealment, secrecy. **2** FAINT,
coma, unconsciousness, oblivion.
3 POWER FAILURE, power cut.

blade *n* edge, knife, dagger, sword,
scalpel, razor, vane.

blame *n* censure, criticism, reproach,
reprimand, reproof, recrimination,
condemnation, accusation, charge,
rap (*sl*), incrimination, guilt, culpability,
fault, responsibility, accountability,
liability, onus.
➤ *v* accuse, charge, tax, reprimand,
chide, reprove, upbraid, reprehend,

admonish, rebuke, reproach, censure,
criticize, find fault with, disapprove,
condemn.
F3 exonerate, vindicate.

blameless *adj* innocent, guiltless,
clear, faultless, perfect, unblemished,
stainless, virtuous, sinless, upright,
above reproach, irreproachable,
unblamable, unimpeachable, squeaky
clean (*infml*).
F3 guilty, blameworthy.

blanch *v* blench, whiten, pale, fade,
bleach.
F3 colour, blush, redden.

bland *adj* boring, monotonous,
humdrum, tedious, dull, uninspiring,
uninteresting, unexciting, nondescript,
characterless, flat, insipid, tasteless,
weak, mild, smooth, soft, gentle, non-
irritant.
F3 lively, stimulating, sharp.

blank *adj* **1** *a blank page*: empty,
unfilled, void, clear, bare, unmarked,
plain, clean, white. **2** EXPRESSIONLESS,
deadpan, poker-faced, impassive,
apathetic, glazed, vacant,
uncomprehending.
➤ *n* space, gap, break, void, emptiness,
vacancy, vacuity, nothingness, vacuum.

blanket *n* covering, coating, coat,
layer, film, carpet, rug, cloak, mantle,
cover, sheet, envelope, wrapper,
wrapping.
➤ *v* cover, coat, eclipse, hide, conceal,
mask, cloak, surround, muffle, deaden,
obscure, cloud.

blare *v* trumpet, clamour, roar, blast,
boom, resound, ring, peal, clang, hoot,
toot, honk.

blasé *adj* nonchalant, offhand,
unimpressed, unmoved, unexcited,
jaded, weary, bored, uninterested,
uninspired, apathetic, indifferent, cool,
unconcerned.
F3 excited, enthusiastic.

blaspheme *v* profane, desecrate,
swear, curse, imprecate, damn,
execrate, revile, abuse.

blasphemous *adj* profane, impious,

sacrilegious, imprecatory, godless, ungodly, irreligious, irreverent.

blasphemy *n* profanity, curse, expletive, imprecation, cursing, swearing, execration, impiety, irreverence, sacrilege, desecration, violation, outrage.

blast *n* **1** EXPLOSION, detonation, bang, crash, clap, crack, volley, burst, outburst, discharge. **2** *a blast of cold air*: draught, gust, gale, squall, storm, tempest. **3** SOUND, blow, blare, roar, boom, peal, hoot, wail, scream, shriek.
➤ *v* **1** EXPLODE, blow up, burst, shatter, destroy, demolish, ruin, assail, attack.
2 SOUND, blare, roar, boom, peal, hoot, wail, scream, shriek.

blatant *adj* flagrant, brazen, barefaced, arrant, open, overt, undisguised, ostentatious, glaring, conspicuous, obtrusive, prominent, pronounced, obvious, sheer, outright, unmitigated.

blaze *n* fire, flames, conflagration, bonfire, flare-up, explosion, blast, burst, outburst, radiance, brilliance, glare, flash, gleam, glitter, glow, light, flame.
➤ *v* burn, flame, flare (up), erupt, explode, burst, fire, flash, gleam, glare, beam, shine, glow.

bleach *v* whiten, blanch, decolorize, fade, pale, lighten.

bleak *adj* **1** GLOOMY, sombre, leaden, grim, dreary, dismal, depressing, joyless, cheerless, comfortless, hopeless, discouraging, disheartening.
2 COLD, chilly, raw, weather-beaten, unsheltered, windy, windswept, exposed, open, barren, bare, empty, desolate, gaunt.
🖅 **1** bright, cheerful.

bleed *v* **1** HAEMORRHAGE, gush, spurt, flow, run, exude, weep, ooze, seep, trickle. **2** DRAIN, suck dry, exhaust, squeeze, milk, sap, reduce, deplete.

blemish *n* flaw, imperfection, defect, fault, deformity, disfigurement, mark, speck, smudge, blotch, blot, stain, taint, disgrace, dishonour.

Kinds of blemish include: acne, birthmark, blackhead, blister, boil, bump, bunion, callus, carbuncle, chilblain, corn, freckle, mole, naevus, pimple, pockmark, pustule, scab, scar, spot, strawberry mark, verruca, wart, whitehead, zit (*sl*).

➤ *v* flaw, deface, disfigure, spoil, mar, damage, impair, spot, mark, blot, blotch, stain, sully, taint, tarnish.

blend *v* **1** MERGE, amalgamate, coalesce, compound, synthesize, fuse, unite, combine, mix, mingle.
2 HARMONIZE, complement, fit, match.
🖅 **1** separate.
➤ *n* compound, composite, alloy, amalgam, amalgamation, synthesis, fusion, combination, union, mix, mixture, concoction.

bless *v* **1** ANOINT, sanctify, consecrate, hallow, dedicate, ordain. **2** PRAISE, extol, magnify, glorify, exalt, thank.
3 APPROVE, countenance, favour, grace, bestow, endow, provide.
🖅 **1** curse. **2** condemn.

blessed *adj* **1** HOLY, sacred, hallowed, sanctified, revered, adored, divine.
2 HAPPY, contented, glad, joyful, joyous, lucky, fortunate, prosperous, favoured, endowed.
🖅 **1** cursed.

blessing *n* **1** CONSECRATION, dedication, benediction, grace, thanksgiving, invocation. **2** BENEFIT, advantage, favour, godsend, windfall, gift, gain, profit, help, service. **3** *give a proposal one's blessing*: approval, concurrence, backing, support, authority, sanction, consent, permission, leave.
🖅 **2** curse, blight. **3** condemnation.

blight *n* curse, bane, evil, scourge, affliction, disease, cancer, canker, fungus, mildew, rot, decay, pollution, contamination, corruption, infestation.
🖅 blessing, boon.
➤ *v* spoil, mar, injure, undermine, ruin, wreck, crush, shatter, destroy,

annihilate, blast, wither, shrivel, frustrate, disappoint.
🖪 bless.

blind *adj* 1 SIGHTLESS, unsighted, unseeing, eyeless, purblind, partially sighted. 2 IMPETUOUS, impulsive, hasty, rash, reckless, wild, mad, senseless, indiscriminate, careless, heedless, mindless, unthinking, unreasoning, irrational. 3 *blind to their needs*: ignorant, oblivious, unaware, unconscious, unobservant, inattentive, neglectful, indifferent, insensitive, thoughtless, inconsiderate. 4 CLOSED, obstructed, hidden, concealed, obscured.
🖪 1 sighted. 2 careful, cautious. 3 aware, sensitive.

> *Ways of describing sight impairment include*: amaurotic, astigmatic, having cataracts, colour-blind, far-sighted, glaucomatous, hemeralopic, hypermetropic, long-sighted, myopic, near-sighted, night-blind, nyctalopic, presbyopic, sand-blind, short-sighted, snow-blind, stone-blind, trachomatous, visually handicapped, visually impaired, blind as a bat (*infml*).

➤ *n* screen, cover, cloak, mask, camouflage, masquerade, front, façade, distraction, smokescreen, cover-up (*infml*).

bliss *n* blissfulness, ecstasy, euphoria, rapture, joy, happiness, gladness, blessedness, paradise, heaven.
🖪 misery, hell, damnation.

blissful *adj* ecstatic, euphoric, elated, enraptured, rapturous, delighted, enchanted, joyful, joyous, happy.
🖪 miserable, wretched.

blister *n* sore, swelling, cyst, boil, abscess, ulcer, pustule, pimple, carbuncle.

blizzard *n* snowstorm, squall, storm, tempest.

bloated *adj* swollen, puffy, blown up, inflated, distended, dilated, expanded, enlarged, turgid, bombastic.
🖪 thin, shrunken, shrivelled.

blob *n* drop, droplet, globule, glob (*infml*), bead, pearl, bubble, dab, spot, gob, lump, mass, ball, pellet, pill.

block *n* 1 *a block of stone*: piece, lump, mass, chunk, hunk, square, cube, brick, bar. 2 OBSTACLE, barrier, bar, jam, blockage, stoppage, resistance, obstruction, impediment, hindrance, let, delay.
➤ *v* choke, clog, plug, stop up, dam up, close, bar, obstruct, impede, hinder, stonewall, stop, check, arrest, halt, thwart, scotch, deter.

blockade *n* barrier, barricade, siege, obstruction, restriction, stoppage, closure.

blockage *n* blocking, obstruction, stoppage, occlusion, block, clot, jam, log-jam, gridlock, congestion, hindrance, impediment.

blond, blonde *adj* fair, flaxen, golden, fair-haired, golden-haired, light-coloured, bleached.

blood *n* extraction, birth, descent, lineage, family, kindred, relations, ancestry, descendants, kinship, relationship.

bloodcurdling *adj* horrifying, chilling, spine-chilling, hair-raising, terrifying, frightening, scary, dreadful, fearful, horrible, horrid, horrendous.

bloodshed *n* killing, murder, slaughter, massacre, bloodbath, butchery, carnage, gore, bloodletting.

bloodthirsty *adj* murderous, homicidal, warlike, savage, barbaric, barbarous, brutal, ferocious, vicious, cruel, inhuman, ruthless.

bloody *adj* bleeding, bloodstained, gory, sanguinary, murderous, savage, brutal, ferocious, fierce, cruel.

bloom *n* 1 BLOSSOM, flower, bud. 2 PRIME, heyday, perfection, blush, flush, glow, rosiness, beauty, radiance, lustre, health, vigour, freshness.
➤ *v* bud, sprout, grow, wax, develop,

mature, blossom, flower, blow, open.
🖛 fade, wither.

blossom *n* bloom, flower, bud.
➤ *v* develop, mature, bloom, flower,
blow, flourish, thrive, prosper, succeed.
🖛 fade, wither.

blot *n* spot, stain, smudge, blotch,
smear, mark, speck, blemish, flaw, fault,
defect, taint, disgrace.
➤ *v* spot, mark, stain, smudge, blur,
sully, taint, tarnish, spoil, mar, disfigure,
disgrace.
◇ **blot out** obliterate, cancel, delete,
erase, expunge, darken, obscure,
shadow, eclipse.

blotch *n* patch, splodge, splotch, splash,
smudge, blot, spot, mark, stain, blemish.

blotchy *adj* spotty, spotted, patchy,
uneven, smeary, blemished, reddened,
inflamed.

blow¹ *v* **1** BREATHE, exhale, pant, puff,
waft, fan, flutter, float, flow, stream,
rush, whirl, whisk, sweep, fling, buffet,
drive, blast. **2** *blow a horn*: play, sound,
pipe, trumpet, toot, blare.
➤ *n* puff, draught, flurry, gust, blast,
wind, gale, squall, tempest.
◇ **blow over** die down, subside, end,
finish, cease, pass, vanish, disappear,
dissipate, fizzle out, peter out.
◇ **blow up 1** EXPLODE, go off, detonate,
burst, blast, bomb. **2** LOSE ONE'S
TEMPER, blow one's top (*infml*), erupt, hit
the roof (*infml*), rage, go mad (*infml*). **3**
INFLATE, pump up, swell, fill (out), puff up,
bloat, distend, dilate, expand, enlarge,
magnify, exaggerate, overstate.

blow² *n* **1** *a blow on the head*:
concussion, box, cuff, clip, clout, swipe,
biff (*infml*), bash, slap, smack, whack
(*infml*), wallop (*infml*), belt (*infml*),
buffet, bang, clap, knock, rap, stroke,
thump, punch. **2** MISFORTUNE, affliction,
reverse, setback, comedown,
disappointment, upset, whammy
(*infml*), jolt, shock, bombshell, calamity,
catastrophe, disaster.

blowy *adj* breezy, windy, fresh, blustery,
gusty, squally, stormy.

bludgeon *v* **1** BEAT, strike, club, batter,
cosh (*sl*), cudgel. **2** FORCE, coerce,
bulldoze, badger, hector, harass,
browbeat, bully, terrorize, intimidate.

blue *adj* **1** AZURE, sapphire, cobalt,
ultramarine, navy, indigo, aquamarine,
turquoise, cyan. **2** DEPRESSED, low, down
in the dumps (*infml*), dejected,
downcast, dispirited, downhearted,
despondent, gloomy, glum, dismal, sad,
unhappy, miserable, melancholy,
morose, fed up (*infml*). **3** *a blue joke*:
obscene, offensive, indecent, improper,
coarse, vulgar, lewd, X-rated (*infml*),
dirty, pornographic, bawdy, smutty, near
the bone, near the knuckle, risqué.
🖛 **2** cheerful, happy. **3** decent, clean.

blueprint *n* archetype, prototype,
model, pattern, design, outline, draft,
sketch, pilot, guide, plan, scheme, project.

bluff *v* lie, pretend, feign, sham, fake,
deceive, delude, mislead, hoodwink,
blind, bamboozle (*infml*), fool.
➤ *n* lie, idle boast, bravado, humbug,
pretence, show, sham, fake, fraud, trick,
scam (*infml*), subterfuge, deceit,
deception.

blunder *n* mistake, error, solecism,
howler (*infml*), bloomer (*infml*), clanger
(*infml*), inaccuracy, slip, boob (*infml*),
indiscretion, gaffe, faux pas, slip-up
(*infml*), oversight, fault, cock-up (*sl*).
➤ *v* stumble, flounder, bumble, err, slip
up (*infml*), miscalculate, misjudge,
bungle, botch, fluff (*infml*), mismanage,
cock up (*sl*).

blunt *adj* **1** UNSHARPENED, dull, worn,
pointless, rounded, stubbed. **2** FRANK,
candid, direct, forthright, straight,
unceremonious, explicit, plain-spoken,
honest, downright, outspoken, tactless,
insensitive, rude, impolite, uncivil,
brusque, curt, abrupt.
🖛 **1** sharp, pointed. **2** subtle, tactful.
➤ *v* dull, take the edge off, dampen,
soften, deaden, numb, anaesthetize,
alleviate, allay, abate, weaken.
🖛 sharpen, intensify.

blur *v* smear, smudge, mist, fog, befog,

cloud, becloud, blear, dim, darken, obscure, mask, conceal, soften.

➤ *n* smear, smudge, blotch, haze, mist, fog, cloudiness, fuzziness, indistinctness, muddle, confusion, dimness, obscurity.

blurred *adj* out of focus, fuzzy, unclear, indistinct, vague, ill-defined, faint, hazy, misty, foggy, cloudy, bleary, dim, obscure, confused.
🗷 clear, distinct.

blurt out exclaim, cry, gush, spout, utter, tell, reveal, disclose, divulge, blab (*infml*), let out, leak, let slip, spill the beans (*infml*).
🗷 bottle up, hush up.

blush *v* flush, redden, colour, glow.
🗷 blanch.

➤ *n* flush, reddening, rosiness, ruddiness, colour, glow.

blushing *adj* flushed, red, rosy, glowing, confused, embarrassed, ashamed, modest.
🗷 pale, white, composed.

bluster *v* boast, brag, crow, talk big (*infml*), swagger, strut, vaunt, show off, rant, roar, storm, bully, hector.
➤ *n* boasting, crowing, bravado, bluff, swagger.

blustery *adj* windy, gusty, squally, stormy, tempestuous, violent, wild, boisterous.
🗷 calm.

board *n* 1 *a wooden board*: sheet, panel, slab, plank, beam, timber, slat. 2 COMMITTEE, council, panel, jury, commission, directorate, directors, trustees, advisers. 3 MEALS, food, provisions, rations.
➤ *v* get on, embark, mount, enter, catch.

boast *v* brag, crow, swank (*infml*), claim, exaggerate, talk big (*infml*), bluster, trumpet, vaunt, strut, swagger, show off, exhibit, possess.
🗷 belittle, deprecate.

➤ *n* brag, swank (*infml*), claim, vaunt, pride, joy, gem, treasure.

boastful *adj* proud, conceited, vain,

swollen-headed, big-headed (*infml*), puffed up, bragging, crowing, swanky (*infml*), cocky, swaggering.
🗷 modest, self-effacing, humble.

boat

Types of boat or ship include: canoe, dinghy, lifeboat, rowing-boat, kayak, dugout, coracle, skiff, punt, sampan, dhow, gondola, pedalo, catamaran, trimaran, yacht; airboat, cabin-cruiser, motorboat, motor-launch, speedboat, swamp boat, trawler, barge, narrow boat, houseboat, dredger, junk, smack, lugger; hovercraft, hydrofoil; clipper, cutter, ketch, packet, brig, schooner, square-rigger, galleon; ferry, paddle-steamer, tug, freighter, liner, container ship, tanker; warship, battleship, destroyer, submarine, U-boat, frigate, aircraft carrier, cruiser, dreadnought, corvette, minesweeper, man-of-war. *see also* **sail**; **ship**.

---

bob *v* bounce, hop, skip, spring, jump, leap, twitch, jerk, jolt, shake, quiver, wobble, oscillate, nod, bow, curtsy.

◇ **bob up** appear, emerge, arrive, show up (*infml*), materialize, rise, surface, pop up, spring up, crop up, arise.

bodily *adj* physical, corporeal, carnal, fleshly, real, actual, tangible, substantial, concrete, material.
🗷 spiritual.

➤ *adv* altogether, en masse, collectively, as a whole, completely, fully, wholly, entirely, totally, in toto.
🗷 piecemeal.

body *n* 1 ANATOMY, physique, build, figure, trunk, torso. 2 CORPSE, cadaver, carcase, stiff (*sl*). 3 COMPANY, association, society, corporation, confederation, bloc, cartel, syndicate, congress, collection, group, band, crowd, throng, multitude, mob, mass. 4 CONSISTENCY, density, solidity, firmness, bulk, mass, substance, essence, fullness, richness.

bodyguard *n* guard, protector, minder (*infml*).

bog *n* marsh, swamp, fen, mire, quagmire, quag, slough, morass, quicksands, marshland, swampland, wetlands.

◇ **bog down** encumber, hinder, impede, overwhelm, deluge, sink, stick, slow down, slow up, delay, retard, halt, stall.

bogus *adj* false, fake, counterfeit, forged, fraudulent, phoney (*infml*), spurious, sham, pseudo, artificial, imitation, dummy.
🔁 genuine, true, real, valid.

bohemian *adj* artistic, arty (*infml*), unconventional, unorthodox, nonconformist, alternative, eccentric, offbeat, way-out (*sl*), bizarre, exotic.
🔁 bourgeois, conventional, orthodox.
➤ *n* beatnik, hippie, dropout, new-ager, nonconformist.
🔁 bourgeois, conformist.

boil¹ *v* **1** SIMMER, stew, seethe, brew, gurgle, bubble, fizz, effervesce, froth, foam, steam. **2** *boil with anger*: erupt, explode, rage, rave, storm, fulminate, fume.
◇ **boil down** reduce, concentrate, distil, condense, digest, abstract, summarize, abridge.

boil² *n* pustule, abscess, gumboil, ulcer, tumour, pimple, carbuncle, blister, inflammation.

boiling *adj* **1** *boiling water*: turbulent, gurgling, bubbling, steaming. **2** HOT, baking, roasting, scorching, blistering. **3** ANGRY, indignant, incensed, infuriated, enraged, furious, fuming, flaming.

boisterous *adj* exuberant, rumbustious (*infml*), rollicking, bouncy, turbulent, tumultuous, loud, noisy, clamorous, rowdy, rough, disorderly, riotous, wild, unrestrained, unruly, obstreperous.
🔁 quiet, calm, restrained.

bold *adj* **1** FEARLESS, dauntless, daring, audacious, brave, courageous, valiant, heroic, gallant, intrepid, adventurous, venturesome, enterprising, plucky,

spirited, confident, outgoing. **2** EYE-CATCHING, striking, conspicuous, prominent, strong, pronounced, bright, vivid, colourful, loud, flashy, showy, flamboyant. **3** BRAZEN, brash, forward, shameless, unabashed, cheeky, impudent, insolent.
🔁 **1** cautious, timid, shy. **2** faint, restrained.

bolt *n* bar, rod, shaft, pin, peg, rivet, fastener, latch, catch, lock.
➤ *v* **1** FASTEN, secure, bar, latch, lock. **2** ABSCOND, escape, flee, fly, run, sprint, rush, dash, hurtle. **3** *bolt one's food*: gulp, wolf, gobble, gorge, devour, cram, stuff.

bomb *n* atom bomb, petrol bomb, shell, bombshell, explosive, charge, grenade, mine, torpedo, rocket, missile, projectile. *see also* **weapon**.
➤ *v* bombard, shell, torpedo, attack, blow up, destroy.

bombard *v* attack, assault, assail, pelt, pound, strafe, blast, bomb, shell, blitz, besiege, hound, harass, pester.

bombardment *n* attack, assault, air-raid, bombing, shelling, blitz, barrage, cannonade, fusillade, salvo, fire, flak.

bombastic *adj* grandiloquent, magniloquent, grandiose, pompous, high-flown, inflated, bloated, windy, wordy, verbose.

bond *n* **1** CONNECTION, relation, link, tie, union, affiliation, attachment, affinity. **2** CONTRACT, covenant, agreement, pledge, promise, word, obligation. **3** FETTER, shackle, manacle, chain, cord, band, binding.
➤ *v* connect, fasten, bind, unite, fuse, glue, gum, paste, stick, seal.

bondage *n* imprisonment, incarceration, captivity, confinement, restraint, slavery, enslavement, serfdom, servitude, subservience, subjection, subjugation, yoke.
🔁 freedom, independence.

bone

Human bones include: carpal, clavicle (or collarbone), coccyx, femur (or thigh bone), fibula, hip bone, humerus (or funny bone), ilium, ischium, mandible, maxilla, metacarpal, metatarsal, patella (or kneecap), pelvic girdle, pelvis, phalange, pubis, radius, rib, sacrum, scapula (or shoulder blade), skull, sternum (or breastbone), tarsal, temporal, tibia, ulna, vertebra.

bonus *n* advantage, benefit, plus (*infml*), extra, perk (*infml*), perquisite, commission, dividend, premium, prize, reward, honorarium, tip, gratuity, gift, handout.
Ⓕ disadvantage, disincentive.

bony *adj* thin, lean, angular, lanky, gawky, gangling, skinny, scrawny, emaciated, rawboned, gaunt, drawn.
Ⓕ fat, plump.

book *n* volume, tome, publication, work, booklet, tract.

Types of book include: hardback, paperback, softback, audio book, e-book; fiction, novel, story; children's book, primer, picture book, annual; reference book, encyclopedia, dictionary, lexicon, thesaurus, concordance, anthology, compendium, omnibus, atlas, guidebook, gazetteer, directory, A to Z, anthology, pocket companion, handbook, manual, cookbook, yearbook, almanac, catalogue; notebook, exercise book, textbook, scrapbook, album, sketchbook, diary, journal, book of days, chapbook, jotter, pad, ledger, Filofax®; libretto, manuscript, hymn book, hymnal, prayer book, psalter, missal, lectionary. *see also* **literature**; **story**.

➤ *v* reserve, bag (*infml*), engage, charter, procure, order, arrange, organize, schedule, programme.
Ⓕ cancel.

bookbinding

Terms used in bookbinding include: adhesive binding, all edges gilt (aeg), backboard, backbone, back cornering, back lining, binder's board (*US*), binder's brass, binder's die (*US*), binding, blind blocking, blocking, boards, bolts, book block, buckram, case, casebound, casing-in, cloth-lined board, comb-binding, drawn-on, dust cover, embossing, endpaper, flyleaf, fore edge, front board, full bound, gather, half bound, hardback, head, headband, headcap, hinge, jacket, laminating, library binding, limp, lining, Linson®, loose-leaf, mechanical binding, millboard, morocco, notch binding, open-flat, paperback, pasteboard, perfect binding, quarter bound, raised band, ring binding, rounding and backing, saddle-stitch, sewing, shoulder, side-stitch, signature, smashing, soft-cover, spine, spiral binding, square-back, stab-stitch, stamping (*US*), strawboard, tail, tailband, thermoplastic binding, thread sewing, unsewn binding, varnishing, whole bound, wire binding, wire stitching, wiro binding, yapp.

boom *v* **1** BANG, crash, roar, thunder, roll, rumble, resound, reverberate, blast, explode. **2** FLOURISH, thrive, prosper, succeed, develop, grow, increase, gain, expand, swell, escalate, intensify, strengthen, explode.
Ⓕ 2 fail, collapse, slump.
➤ *n* **1** BANG, clap, crash, roar, thunder, rumble, reverberation, blast, explosion, burst. **2** INCREASE, growth, expansion, gain, upsurge, jump, spurt, boost, upturn, improvement, advance, escalation, explosion.
Ⓕ 2 failure, collapse, slump, recession, depression.

boon *n* blessing, advantage, benefit, godsend, windfall, favour, kindness, gift, present, grant, gratuity.
Ⓕ disadvantage, blight.

boorish *adj* uncouth, oafish, loutish, ill-mannered, rude, coarse, crude, vulgar, unrefined, uncivilized, uneducated, ignorant.
Ⓕ polite, refined, cultured.

boost *n* improvement, enhancement, expansion, increase, rise, jump, increment, addition, supplement, booster, lift, hoist, heave, push, thrust, help, advancement, promotion, praise, encouragement, fillip, ego-trip (*sl*).
F3 setback, blow.
➤ *v* raise, elevate, improve, enhance, develop, enlarge, expand, amplify, increase, augment, heighten, lift, hoist, jack up, heave, push, thrust, help, aid, assist, advance, further, promote, advertise, plug (*infml*), praise, talk up (*infml*), inspire, encourage, foster, support, sustain, bolster, supplement.
F3 hinder, undermine.

boot *n* gumboot, wellington, welly (*infml*), galosh, overshoe, walking-boot, riding-boot, top-boot.

booth *n* kiosk, stall, stand, hut, box, compartment, cubicle, carrel.

booty *n* loot, plunder, pillage, spoils, swag (*sl*), haul, gains, takings, pickings, winnings.

border *n* **1** BOUNDARY, frontier, bound, bounds, confine, confines, limit, demarcation, borderline, margin, fringe, periphery, surround, perimeter, circumference, edge, rim, brim, verge, brink. **2** TRIMMING, frill, valance, skirt, hem, frieze.
◇ **border on 1** ADJOIN, abut, touch, impinge, join, connect, communicate with. **2** RESEMBLE, approximate, approach, verge on.

bore¹ *v* drill, mine, pierce, perforate, penetrate, sink, burrow, tunnel, undermine, sap.

bore² *v* tire, weary, fatigue, jade, trouble, bother, worry, irritate, annoy, vex, irk.
F3 interest, excite.
➤ *n* (*infml*) nuisance, bother, bind, drag (*infml*), bummer (*sl*), pain (*infml*), headache (*infml*).
F3 pleasure, delight.

boredom *n* tedium, tediousness, monotony, flatness, dullness, apathy, listlessness, weariness, world-weariness.
F3 interest, excitement.

boring *adj* tedious, monotonous, routine, repetitious, uninteresting, unexciting, uneventful, dull, dreary, humdrum, commonplace, trite, unimaginative, uninspired, dry, stale, flat, insipid.
F3 interesting, exciting, stimulating, original.

borrow *v* steal, pilfer, filch, lift, plagiarize, crib, copy, imitate, mimic, echo, take, draw, derive, obtain, adopt, use, scrounge, cadge, sponge, appropriate, usurp.
F3 lend.

bosom *n* **1** BUST, breasts, chest, breast. **2** HEART, core, centre, midst, protection, shelter, sanctuary.

boss *n* employer, governor, master, owner, captain, head, chief, leader, supremo, administrator, executive, director, manager, foreman, gaffer, superintendent, overseer, supervisor.
◇ **boss around** order around, order about, domineer, tyrannize, bully, bulldoze, browbeat, push around, dominate.

bossy *adj* authoritarian, autocratic, tyrannical, despotic, dictatorial, domineering, overbearing, oppressive, lordly, high-handed, imperious, insistent, assertive, demanding, exacting.
F3 unassertive.

bother *v* disturb, inconvenience, harass, hassle (*infml*), pester, plague, nag, annoy, irritate, irk, molest, trouble, worry, concern, alarm, dismay, distress, upset, vex.
➤ *n* inconvenience, trouble, problem, difficulty, hassle (*infml*), fuss, bustle, flurry, nuisance, pest, annoyance, irritation, aggravation (*infml*), vexation, worry, strain.

bottle

Types of bottle include: ampulla, calabash, carafe, carboy, decanter, demijohn, flacon, flagon, flask, gourd, jack, phial, pitcher, vial; apothecary bottle, beer bottle, cruet, feeding bottle, hip flask, hot-water bottle, milk bottle, scent bottle, snuff bottle, Thermos® flask, vinegar bottle, wine bottle. *see also* **wine.**

◊ **bottle up** hide, conceal, restrain, curb, hold back, suppress, inhibit, restrict, enclose, contain.
🎜 unbosom, unburden.

bottleneck *n* hold-up, traffic jam, gridlock, snarl-up, congestion, clogging, blockage, obstruction, block, obstacle.

bottom *n* **1** UNDERSIDE, underneath, sole, base, foot, plinth, pedestal, support, foundation, substructure, ground, floor, bed, depths, nadir. **2** RUMP, rear, behind, posterior (*infml*), buttocks, seat, backside (*infml*), bum (*sl*), butt (*US infml*), arse (*sl*), ass (*US sl*), tail (*infml*).
🎜 **1** top.

bottomless *adj* deep, profound, fathomless, unfathomed, unplumbed, immeasurable, measureless, infinite, boundless, limitless, unlimited, inexhaustible.
🎜 shallow, limited.

bounce *v* spring, jump, leap, bound, bob, ricochet, rebound, recoil.
➤ *n* **1** SPRING, bound, springiness, elasticity, give, resilience, rebound, recoil. **2** EBULLIENCE, exuberance, vitality, vivacity, energy, vigour, go (*infml*), zip (*infml*), animation, liveliness.

bound[1] *adj* **1** FASTENED, secured, fixed, tied (up), chained, held, restricted, bandaged. **2** LIABLE, committed, duty-bound, obliged, required, forced, compelled, constrained, destined, fated, doomed, sure, certain.

bound[2] *v* jump, leap, vault, hurdle, spring, bounce, bob, hop, skip, frisk, gambol, frolic, caper, prance.
➤ *n* jump, leap, vault, spring, bounce, bob, hop, skip, gambol, frolic, caper, dance, prance.

boundary *n* border, frontier, barrier,

line, borderline, demarcation, bounds, confines, limits, margin, fringe, verge, brink, edge, perimeter, extremity, termination.

boundless *adj* unbounded, limitless, unlimited, unconfined, countless, untold, incalculable, vast, immense, measureless, immeasurable, infinite, endless, unending, interminable, inexhaustible, unflagging, indefatigable.
🎜 limited, restricted.

bounds *n* confines, limits, borders, marches, margins, fringes, periphery, circumference, edges, extremities.

bounty *n* **1** GENEROSITY, liberality, munificence, largesse, almsgiving, charity, philanthropy, beneficence, kindness. **2** REWARD, recompense, premium, bonus, gratuity, gift, present, donation, grant, allowance.

bouquet *n* **1** *bouquet of flowers*: bunch, posy, nosegay, spray, corsage, buttonhole, wreath, garland. **2** AROMA, smell, odour, scent, perfume, fragrance.

bourgeois *adj* middle-class, materialistic, conservative, traditional, conformist, conventional, hidebound, unadventurous, dull, humdrum, banal, commonplace, trite, unoriginal, unimaginative.
🎜 bohemian, unconventional, original.

bout *n* **1** FIGHT, battle, engagement, encounter, struggle, set-to, match, contest, competition, round, heat. **2** PERIOD, spell, time, stint, turn, go (*infml*), term, stretch, run, course, session, spree, attack, fit.

bow *v* **1** *bow one's head*: incline, bend, nod, bob, curtsy, genuflect (*fml*), kowtow, salaam, stoop. **2** YIELD, give in, consent, surrender, capitulate, submit, acquiesce, concede, accept, comply, defer. **3** SUBDUE, overpower, conquer, vanquish, crush, subjugate.
➤ *n* inclination, bending, nod, bob, curtsy, genuflexion (*fml*), kowtow, salaam, obeisance (*fml*), salutation, acknowledgement.

◊ **bow out** withdraw, pull out, desert,

abandon, defect, back out, chicken out (*infml*), retire, resign, quit, stand down, step down, give up.

bowels *n* **1** INTESTINES, viscera, entrails, guts, insides, innards (*infml*). **2** DEPTHS, interior, inside, middle, centre, core, heart.

bowl¹ *n* receptacle, container, vessel, dish, basin, sink.

bowl² *v* throw, hurl, fling, pitch, roll, spin, whirl, rotate, revolve.
◇ **bowl over** surprise, amaze, astound, astonish, stagger, stun, dumbfound, flabbergast (*infml*), floor (*infml*).

box¹ *n* container, receptacle, case, carton, packet, present, chest.

Types of box include: bin, caddy, canister, cartridge, casket, coffer, coffin, crate, locker, pack, package, punnet, sarcophagus, tea chest, tin, trunk; ballot box, black box, box file, cardboard box, cigarette box, collection box, coolbox, dispatch box, hatbox, jewellery box, knife box, matchbox, pencilbox, pillbox, pillar box, postbox, safe, sewing box, shoebox, snuffbox, strongbox, suggestion box, toolbox, trinket box.

➤ *v* case, encase, package, pack, wrap.
◇ **box in** enclose, surround, circumscribe, cordon off, hem in, corner, trap, confine, restrict, imprison, cage, coop up, contain.

box² *v* fight, spar, punch, hit, strike, slap, buffet, cuff, clout, sock (*sl*), wallop (*infml*), whack (*infml*).

boxer *n* pugilist (*fml*), fighter, prizefighter, sparring partner, flyweight, featherweight, lightweight, welterweight, middleweight, heavyweight.

boxing *n* pugilism (*fml*), prizefighting, fisticuffs, sparring.

Weight divisions in professional boxing: heavyweight, cruiserweight/ junior-heavyweight, light-heavyweight, super-middleweight, middleweight, light-middleweight/

junior-middleweight, welterweight, light-welterweight/junior-welterweight, lightweight, junior-lightweight/superfeatherweight, featherweight, super-bantamweight/ junior-featherweight, bantamweight, super-flyweight/junior-bantamweight, flyweight, light-flyweight/junior-flyweight, mini-flyweight/straw-weight/minimum weight.

boy *n* son, lad, youngster, kid (*infml*), nipper (*infml*), stripling, youth, fellow.

boycott *v* refuse, reject, embargo, black, ban, prohibit, disallow, bar, exclude, blacklist, outlaw, ostracize, cold-shoulder, ignore, spurn.
🢒 encourage, support.

boyfriend *n* young man, man, fellow (*infml*), bloke (*infml*), admirer, date, sweetheart, lover, fiancé, partner.

brace *n* pair, couple, twosome, duo.
➤ *v* strengthen, reinforce, fortify, bolster, buttress, prop, shore (up), support, steady, tighten, fasten, tie, strap, bind, bandage.

bracing *adj* fresh, crisp, refreshing, reviving, strengthening, fortifying, tonic, rousing, stimulating, exhilarating, invigorating, enlivening, energizing, brisk, energetic, vigorous.
🢒 weakening, debilitating.

braid *v* plait, interweave, interlace, intertwine, weave, lace, twine, entwine, ravel, twist, wind.
🢒 undo, unravel.

brain *n* **1** CEREBRUM, grey matter, head, mind, intellect, nous, brains (*infml*), intelligence, wit, reason, sense, common sense, shrewdness, understanding. **2** MASTERMIND, intellectual, highbrow, egghead (*infml*), scholar, expert, boffin, genius, prodigy.
🢒 **2** simpleton.

Parts of the brain include: brainstem, cerebellum, cerebral cortex (grey matter), cerebrum, corpus callosum, forebrain, frontal lobe, hindbrain, hypothalamus, medulla oblongata, mesencephalon, midbrain, occipital lobe, optic thalamus, parietal lobe, pineal body, pituitary gland, pons, spinal cord, temporal lobe, thalamus.

brainy (*infml*) *adj* intellectual, intelligent, clever, smart, bright, brilliant.
🠲 dull.

brake *n* check, curb, rein, restraint, control, restriction, constraint, drag.
➤ *v* slow, decelerate, retard, drag, slacken, moderate, check, halt, stop, pull up.
🠲 accelerate.

branch *n* 1 BOUGH, limb, sprig, shoot, offshoot, arm, wing, prong. 2 *a different branch of the company*: department, office, part, section, division, subsection, subdivision.
◊ **branch out** diversify, vary, develop, expand, enlarge, extend, broaden out, increase, multiply, proliferate, ramify.

brand *n* make, brand-name, tradename, trademark, logo, mark, symbol, sign, emblem, label, stamp, hallmark, grade, quality, class, kind, type, sort, line, variety, species.
➤ *v* mark, stamp, label, type, stigmatize, burn, scar, stain, taint, disgrace, discredit, denounce, censure.

brandish *v* wave, flourish, shake, raise, swing, wield, flash, flaunt, exhibit, display, parade.

brash *adj* 1 BRAZEN, forward, impertinent, impudent, insolent, rude, cocky, assured, bold, audacious, in-your-face (*infml*). 2 RECKLESS, rash, impetuous, impulsive, hasty, precipitate, foolhardy, incautious, indiscreet.
🠲 1 reserved. 2 cautious.

bravado *n* swagger, boasting, bragging, bluster, bombast, talk, boast, vaunting, showing off, parade, show, pretence.
🠲 modesty, restraint.

brave *adj* courageous, plucky, unafraid, fearless, dauntless, undaunted, bold, audacious, daring, intrepid, stalwart, hardy, stoical, resolute, stout-hearted, valiant, gallant, heroic, indomitable.
🠲 cowardly, afraid, timid.
➤ *v* face, confront, defy, challenge, dare, stand up to, face up to, suffer, endure, bear, withstand.
🠲 capitulate.

bravery *n* courage, pluck, guts (*infml*), fearlessness, dauntlessness, boldness, audacity, daring, intrepidity, stalwartness, hardiness, fortitude, resolution, stout-heartedness, valiance, valour, gallantry, heroism, grit, indomitability, mettle, spirit.
🠲 cowardice, faint-heartedness, timidity.

brawl *n* fight, punch-up (*infml*), scrap (*infml*), scuffle, dust-up (*infml*), mêlée, free-for-all, fray, affray, broil, fracas, rumpus, disorder, row, argument, quarrel, squabble, altercation, dispute, clash.
➤ *v* fight, scrap (*infml*), scuffle, wrestle, tussle, row, argue, quarrel, squabble, wrangle, dispute.

brawny *adj* muscular, sinewy, athletic, well-built, burly, beefy, hunky (*infml*), hefty, solid, bulky, hulking, massive, strapping, strong, powerful, vigorous, sturdy, robust, hardy, stalwart.
🠲 slight, frail.

brazen *adj* blatant, flagrant, brash, brassy, bold, forward, in-your-face (*infml*), saucy, pert, barefaced, impudent, insolent, defiant, shameless, unashamed, unabashed, immodest.
🠲 shy, shamefaced, modest.

breach *n* 1 *a breach of the rules*: violation, contravention, infringement, trespass, disobedience, offence, transgression, lapse, disruption.
2 QUARREL, disagreement, dissension, difference, variance, schism, rift, rupture, split, division, separation, parting, estrangement, alienation, disaffection, dissociation. 3 BREAK, crack, rift, rupture, fissure, cleft, crevice, opening, aperture, gap, space, hole, chasm.

bread *n* loaf, roll, food, provisions, diet, fare, nourishment, nutriment, sustenance, subsistence, necessities.

Types of bread and rolls include: bagel, baguette, brioche, challah, chapati, ciabatta, croissant, focaccia, granary, milk bread, naan, pitta, poori, pretzel, pumpernickel, roti, rye bread, soda bread, sourdough, tortilla, wholemeal, wholewheat.

breadth *n* width, broadness, wideness, latitude, thickness, size, magnitude, measure, scale, range, reach, scope, compass, span, sweep, extent, stretch, expanse, spread, comprehensiveness, extensiveness, vastness.

break *v* 1 FRACTURE, crack, snap, split, sever, separate, divide, rend, smash, disintegrate, splinter, shiver, shatter, ruin, destroy, demolish. 2 *break the law*: violate, contravene, infringe, breach, disobey, flout. 3 PAUSE, halt, stop, discontinue, interrupt, suspend, rest. 4 SUBDUE, tame, weaken, enfeeble, impair, undermine, demoralize. 5 *break the news*: tell, inform, impart, divulge, disclose, reveal, announce. 6 *break a record*: exceed, beat, better, excel, surpass, outdo, outstrip.

🔁 1 mend. 2 keep, observe, abide by. 4 strengthen.

➤ *n* 1 FRACTURE, crack, split, rift, rupture, schism, separation, tear, gash, fissure, cleft, crevice, opening, gap, hole, breach. 2 INTERVAL, intermission, interlude, interruption, pause, halt, lull, let-up (*infml*), respite, rest, breather (*infml*), time out, holiday. 3 OPPORTUNITY, chance, advantage, fortune, luck.

◇ **break away** separate, split, part company, detach, secede, leave, depart, quit, run away, escape, flee, fly.

◇ **break down** 1 *the van broke down*: fail, stop, pack up (*infml*), conk out (*sl*), seize up, give way, collapse, crack up (*infml*). 2 ANALYSE, dissect, separate, itemize, detail.

◇ **break in** 1 INTERRUPT, butt in, interpose, interject, intervene, intrude, encroach, impinge. 2 BURGLE, rob, raid, invade.

◇ **break off** 1 DETACH, snap off, sever, separate, part, divide, disconnect. 2 PAUSE, interrupt, suspend, discontinue, halt, stop, cease, end, finish, terminate.

◇ **break out** 1 START, begin, commence, arise, emerge, happen, occur, erupt, flare up, burst out. 2 ESCAPE, abscond, bolt, flee.

◇ **break up** 1 DISMANTLE, take apart, demolish, destroy, disintegrate, splinter, sever, divide, split, part, separate, divorce. 2 DISBAND, disperse, dissolve, adjourn, suspend, stop, finish, terminate.

breakable *adj* brittle, fragile, delicate, flimsy, insubstantial, frail.
🔁 unbreakable, durable, sturdy.

breakdown *n* 1 FAILURE, collapse, disintegration, malfunction, interruption, stoppage. 2 ANALYSIS, dissection, itemization, classification, categorization.

break-in *n* burglary, house-breaking, robbery, raid, invasion, intrusion, trespass.

breakthrough *n* discovery, find, finding, invention, innovation, advance, progress, headway, step, leap, development, improvement.

break-up *n* divorce, separation, parting, split, rift, finish, termination, dissolution, dispersal, disintegration, crumbling.

breakwater *n* groyne, mole, jetty, pier, quay, wharf, dock.

breath *n* 1 AIR, breathing, respiration, inhalation, exhalation, sigh, gasp, pant, gulp. 2 BREEZE, puff, waft, gust. 3 AROMA, smell, odour, whiff. 4 HINT, suggestion, suspicion, undertone, whisper, murmur.

breathe *v* 1 RESPIRE, inhale, exhale, expire, sigh, gasp, pant, puff. 2 SAY, utter, express, voice, articulate, murmur, whisper, impart, tell. **3** INSTIL, imbue, infuse, inject, inspire.

breathless *adj* **1** SHORT-WINDED, out of breath, panting, puffing, puffed (out), exhausted, winded, gasping, wheezing, choking. **2** *breathless anticipation*: expectant, impatient, eager, agog, excited, feverish, anxious.

breathtaking *adj* awe-inspiring, impressive, magnificent, overwhelming, amazing, astonishing, stunning, exciting, thrilling, stirring, moving.

breed *v* **1** REPRODUCE, procreate, multiply, propagate, hatch, bear, bring forth, rear, raise, bring up, educate, train, instruct. **2** PRODUCE, create, originate, arouse, cause, occasion, engender, generate, make, foster, nurture, nourish, cultivate, develop.
➤ *n* species, strain, variety, family, ilk, sort, kind, type, stamp, stock, race, progeny, line, lineage, pedigree.

breeding *n* **1** REPRODUCTION, procreation, nurture, development, rearing, raising, upbringing, education, training, background, ancestry, lineage, stock. **2** MANNERS, politeness, civility, gentility, urbanity, refinement, culture, polish.
2 vulgarity.

breeze *n* wind, gust, flurry, waft, puff, breath, draught, air.

breezy *adj* **1** WINDY, blowing, fresh, airy, gusty, blustery, squally. **2** ANIMATED, lively, vivacious, jaunty, buoyant, blithe, debonair, carefree, cheerful, easy-going (*infml*), casual, informal, light, bright, exhilarating.
1 still. **2** staid, serious.

brevity *n* briefness, shortness, terseness, conciseness, succinctness, pithiness, crispness, incisiveness, abruptness, curtness, impermanence, ephemerality, transience, transitoriness.
2 verbosity, permanence, longevity.

brew *v* **1** INFUSE, stew, boil, seethe, ferment, prepare, soak, steep, mix, cook. **2** PLOT, scheme, plan, project, devise, contrive, concoct, hatch, excite, foment,

build up, gather, develop.
➤ *n* infusion, drink, beverage, liquor, potion, broth, gruel, stew, mixture, blend, concoction, preparation, fermentation, distillation.

bribe *n* incentive, inducement, allurement, enticement, back-hander (*infml*), kickback, payola, refresher (*infml*), sweetener (*infml*), hush money (*infml*), protection money.
➤ *v* corrupt, suborn, buy off, reward.

bribery *n* corruption, graft (*sl*), palm-greasing, inducement, lubrication.

bric-à-brac *n* knick-knacks, ornaments, curios, antiques, trinkets, baubles.

bridal *adj* wedding, nuptial, marriage, matrimonial, marital, conjugal.

bridge *n* arch, span, causeway, link, connection, bond, tie.

Types of bridge include: suspension bridge, arch bridge, cantilever bridge, flying bridge, flyover, overpass, footbridge, railway bridge, viaduct, aqueduct, humpback bridge, toll bridge, pontoon bridge, Bailey bridge, rope bridge, drawbridge, swing bridge.

➤ *v* span, cross, traverse, fill, link, connect, couple, join, unite, bind.

bridle *v* check, curb, restrain, control, govern, master, subdue, moderate, repress, contain.

brief *adj* **1** SHORT, terse, succinct, concise, pithy, crisp, compressed, thumbnail, laconic, abrupt, sharp, brusque, blunt, curt, surly. **2** SHORT-LIVED, momentary, ephemeral, transient, fleeting, passing, transitory, temporary, limited, cursory, hasty, quick, swift, fast.
1 long. **2** lengthy.
➤ *n* **1** ORDERS, instructions, directions, remit, mandate, directive, advice, briefing, data, information. **2** OUTLINE, summary, précis, dossier, case, defence, argument.
➤ *v* instruct, direct, explain, guide, advise, prepare, prime, inform, fill in (*infml*), gen up (*sl*), bring up to speed (*infml*).

briefing *n* meeting, conference, preparation, priming, filling-in (*infml*), gen (*sl*), low-down (*sl*), information, advice, guidance, directions, instructions, orders.

bright *adj* 1 LUMINOUS, illuminated, radiant, shining, beaming, flashing, gleaming, glistening, glittering, sparkling, twinkling, shimmering, glowing, brilliant, resplendent, glorious, splendid, dazzling, glaring, blazing, intense, vivid. 2 HAPPY, cheerful, glad, joyful, merry, jolly, lively, vivacious, upbeat. 3 *the future looks bright*: promising, propitious (*fml*), auspicious, favourable, rosy, optimistic, hopeful, encouraging. 4 CLEVER, brainy (*infml*), smart, intelligent, quick-witted, quick, sharp, acute, keen, astute, perceptive. 5 CLEAR, transparent, translucent, lucid. 6 *a bright day*: fine, sunny, cloudless, unclouded.
F3 1 dull. 2 sad. 3 depressing. 4 stupid. 5 muddy. 6 dark.

brighten *v* 1 LIGHT UP, illuminate, lighten, clear up. 2 POLISH, burnish, rub up, shine, gleam, glow. 3 CHEER UP, gladden, hearten, encourage, enliven, perk up.
F3 1 darken. 2 dull, tarnish.

brilliance *n* 1 TALENT, virtuosity, genius, greatness, distinction, excellence, aptitude, cleverness. 2 RADIANCE, brightness, sparkle, dazzle, intensity, vividness, gloss, lustre, sheen, glamour, glory, magnificence, splendour.

brilliant *adj* 1 *a brilliant pianist*: gifted, talented, accomplished, expert, skilful, masterly, exceptional, outstanding, superb, illustrious, famous, celebrated. 2 SPARKLING, glittering, scintillating, dazzling, glaring, blazing, intense, vivid, bright, shining, glossy, showy, glorious, magnificent, splendid. 3 CLEVER, brainy (*infml*), intelligent, quick, astute.
F3 1 undistinguished. 2 dull. 3 stupid.

brim *n* rim, perimeter, circumference, lip, edge, margin, border, brink, verge, top, limit.

bring *v* 1 CARRY, bear, convey, transport, fetch, take, deliver, escort, accompany, usher, guide, conduct, lead. 2 CAUSE, produce, engender, create, prompt, provoke, force, attract, draw.
◇ **bring about** cause, occasion, create, produce, generate, effect, accomplish, achieve, fulfil, realize, manage, engineer, manoeuvre, manipulate.
◇ **bring in** earn, net, gross, produce, yield, fetch, return, accrue, realize.
◇ **bring off** achieve, accomplish, fulfil, execute, discharge, perform, succeed, win.
◇ **bring on** cause, occasion, induce, lead to, give rise to, generate, inspire, prompt, provoke, precipitate, expedite, accelerate, advance.
F3 inhibit.
◇ **bring out 1** EMPHASIZE, stress, highlight, enhance, draw out. 2 PUBLISH, print, issue, launch, introduce.
◇ **bring up 1** REAR, raise, foster, nurture, educate, teach, train, form. 2 *bring up a subject*: introduce, broach, mention, submit, propose. 3 VOMIT, regurgitate, throw up (*infml*).

brink *n* verge, threshold, edge, margin, fringe, border, boundary, limit, extremity, lip, rim, brim, bank.

brisk *adj* 1 ENERGETIC, vigorous, quick, snappy, lively, spirited, active, busy, bustling, agile, nimble, alert. 2 INVIGORATING, exhilarating, stimulating, bracing, refreshing, fresh, crisp.
F3 1 lazy, sluggish.

bristle *n* hair, whisker, stubble, spine, prickle, barb, thorn.

bristly *adj* hairy, whiskered, bearded, unshaven, stubbly, rough, spiny, prickly, spiky, thorny.
F3 clean-shaven, smooth.

brittle *adj* breakable, fragile, delicate, frail, crisp, crumbly, crumbling, friable, shattery, shivery.
F3 durable, resilient.

broad *adj* 1 WIDE, large, vast, roomy, spacious, capacious, ample, extensive,

widespread. **2** WIDE-RANGING, far-reaching, encyclopedic, catholic, eclectic, all-embracing, inclusive, comprehensive, general, sweeping, universal, unlimited.
🔁 **1** narrow. **2** restricted.

broadcast *v* air, show, transmit, beam, relay, televise, report, announce, publicize, advertise, publish, circulate, promulgate, disseminate, spread.
➤ *n* transmission, programme, show.

broaden *v* widen, thicken, swell, spread, enlarge, expand, extend, stretch, increase, augment, develop, open up, branch out, diversify.

broadminded *adj* liberal, tolerant, permissive, enlightened, free-thinking, open-minded, receptive, unbiased, unprejudiced.
🔁 narrow-minded, intolerant, biased.

brochure *n* leaflet, booklet, pamphlet, prospectus, broadsheet, handbill, circular, handout, flyer, folder.

broke (*infml*) *adj* insolvent, penniless, bankrupt, bust, ruined, impoverished, destitute.
🔁 solvent, rich, affluent.

broken *adj* **1** FRACTURED, burst, ruptured, severed, separated, faulty, defective, out of order, shattered, destroyed, demolished. **2** DISJOINTED, disconnected, fragmentary, discontinuous, interrupted, intermittent, spasmodic, erratic, hesitating, stammering, halting, imperfect. **3** *a broken man*: beaten, defeated, crushed, demoralized, down, weak, feeble, exhausted, tamed, subdued, oppressed.
🔁 **1** mended. **2** fluent.

broken-down *adj* dilapidated, worn-out, ruined, collapsed, decayed, inoperative, out of order.

broken-hearted *adj* heartbroken, inconsolable, devastated, grief-stricken, desolate, despairing, miserable, wretched, mournful, sorrowful, sad, unhappy, dejected, despondent, crestfallen, disappointed.

brooch *n* badge, pin, clip, clasp.

brood *v* ponder, ruminate, meditate, muse, mull over, go over, rehearse, dwell on, agonize, fret, mope.
➤ *n* clutch, chicks, hatch, litter, young, offspring, issue, progeny, children, family.

brook *n* stream, rivulet, beck, burn, watercourse, channel.

brother *n* sibling, relation, relative, comrade, friend, mate, partner, colleague, associate, fellow, companion, monk, friar.

brotherhood *n* fraternity, association, society, league, confederation, confederacy, alliance, union, guild, fellowship, community, clique.

browbeat *v* bully, coerce, dragoon, bulldoze, awe, cow, intimidate, threaten, tyrannize, domineer, overbear, oppress, hound.
🔁 coax.

brown *adj* mahogany, chocolate, coffee, hazel, bay, chestnut, umber, sepia, tan, tawny, russet, rust, rusty, brunette, dark, dusky, sunburnt, tanned, bronzed, browned, toasted.

browse *v* **1** LEAF THROUGH, flick through, dip into, skim, survey, scan, peruse. **2** GRAZE, pasture, feed, eat, nibble.

bruise *v* discolour, blacken, mark, blemish, pound, pulverize, crush, hurt, injure, insult, offend, grieve.
➤ *n* contusion, discoloration, black eye, shiner (*sl*), mark, blemish, injury.

brush[1] *n* broom, sweeper, besom.
➤ *v* **1** CLEAN, sweep, flick, burnish, polish, shine. **2** TOUCH, contact, graze, kiss, stroke, rub, scrape.
◇ **brush aside** dismiss, pooh-pooh (*infml*), belittle, disregard, ignore, flout, override.
◇ **brush off** disregard, ignore, slight, snub, cold-shoulder, rebuff, dismiss, spurn, reject, repulse, disown, repudiate (*fml*).
◇ **brush up 1** REVISE, relearn, improve, polish up, study, read up, swot (*infml*). **2** REFRESH, freshen up, clean, tidy.

brush² *n* scrub, thicket, bushes, shrubs, brushwood, undergrowth, ground cover.

brush³ *n* confrontation, encounter, clash, conflict, fight, scrap, skirmish, set-to, tussle, dust-up (*infml*), fracas.

brusque *adj* abrupt, sharp, short, terse, curt, gruff, surly, discourteous, impolite, uncivil, blunt, tactless, undiplomatic.
🔁 courteous, polite, tactful.

brutal *adj* animal, bestial, beastly, brutish, inhuman, savage, bloodthirsty, vicious, ferocious, cruel, inhumane, remorseless, pitiless, merciless, ruthless, callous, insensitive, unfeeling, heartless, harsh, gruff, rough, coarse, crude, rude, uncivilized, barbarous.
🔁 kindly, humane, civilized.

brutality *n* savagery, bloodthirstiness, viciousness, ferocity, cruelty, inhumanity, violence, atrocity, ruthlessness, callousness, roughness, coarseness, barbarism, barbarity.
🔁 gentleness, kindness.

brute *n* animal, beast, swine, creature, monster, ogre, devil, fiend, savage, sadist, bully, lout.

bubble *n* blister, vesicle, globule, ball, drop, droplet, bead.
➤ *v* effervesce, fizz, sparkle, froth, foam, seethe, boil, burble, gurgle.

bubbly *adj* 1 EFFERVESCENT, fizzy, sparkling, carbonated, frothy, foaming, sudsy. 2 LIVELY, bouncy, happy, merry, elated, excited, hyper (*infml*).
🔁 1 flat, still. 2 lethargic.

bucket *n* pail, can, bail, scuttle, vessel.

buckle *n* clasp, clip, catch, fastener.
➤ *v* 1 *buckle one's belt*: fasten, clasp, catch, hook, hitch, connect, close, secure. 2 BEND, warp, twist, distort, bulge, cave in, fold, wrinkle, crumple, collapse.

bud *n* shoot, sprout, germ, embryo.
➤ *v* shoot, sprout, burgeon, develop, grow.
🔁 wither, waste away.

budding *adj* potential, promising, embryonic, burgeoning, developing, growing, flowering.

budge *v* move, stir, shift, remove, dislodge, push, roll, slide, propel, sway, influence, persuade, convince, change, bend, yield, give (way).

budget *n* finances, funds, resources, means, allowance, allotment, allocation, estimate.
➤ *v* plan, estimate, alow, allot, allocate, apportion, ration.

buff¹ *adj* yellowish-brown, straw, sandy, fawn, khaki.
➤ *v* polish, burnish, shine, smooth, rub, brush.

buff² (*infml*) *n* expert, connoisseur, enthusiast, fan, admirer, devotee, addict, fiend, freak.

buffer *n* shock absorber, bumper, fender, pad, cushion, pillow, intermediary, screen, shield.

buffet¹ *n* snack-bar, counter, café, cafeteria.

buffet² *v* batter, hit, strike, knock, bang, bump, push, shove, pound, pummel, beat, thump, box, cuff, clout, slap.
➤ *n* blow, knock, bang, bump, jar, jolt, push, shove, thump, box, cuff, clout, slap, smack.

bug *n* 1 VIRUS, bacterium, germ, microbe, micro-organism, infection, disease. 2 FAULT, defect, flaw, blemish, imperfection, failing, error, gremlin (*infml*).
➤ *v* (*infml*) annoy, irritate, vex, irk, needle (*infml*), bother, disturb, harass, badger.

build *v* 1 ERECT, raise, construct, fabricate, make, form, constitute, assemble, knock together, develop, enlarge, extend, increase, augment, escalate, intensify. 2 BASE, found, establish, institute, inaugurate, initiate, begin.
🔁 1 destroy, demolish, knock down, lessen.

Types of building material include: aluminium, ashlar, asphalt, bitumen, breeze block, brick, building block, cast iron, cement, chipboard, clay, concrete, reinforced concrete, fixings, flagstone, girder, glass, glass fibre, gravel, granite, grout, gypsum, hardboard, hard core, insulation, foam insulation, loose-fill insulation, lagging, lintel, lumber (*US*), marble, mortar, paving stone, paviour, plaster, plasterboard, plastic, plywood, sand, sandstone, shingle, slate, stainless steel, steel, steel beam, stone, tarmac, thatch, tile, floor tile, roof tile, timber, wattle and daub, wood.

➤ *n* physique, figure, body, form, shape, size, frame, structure.

◇ **build up** strengthen, reinforce, fortify, extend, expand, develop, amplify, increase, escalate, intensify, heighten, boost, improve, enhance, publicize, advertise, promote, plug (*infml*), hype (*sl*), talk up (*infml*).
🔁 weaken, lessen.

building *n* edifice, dwelling, erection, construction, fabrication, structure, architecture.

Types of building include: house, bungalow, cottage, block of flats, cabin, farmhouse, villa, mansion, chateau, castle, palace; church, chapel, cathedral, abbey, monastery, temple, pagoda, mosque, synagogue, gurdwara, mandir; shop, store, garage, factory, warehouse, silo, office block, tower block, skyscraper, high-rise, low-rise, theatre, cinema, multiplex, gymnasium, sports hall, restaurant, café, hotel, pub (*infml*), public house, inn, school, college, museum, library, hospital, prison, power station, observatory; barracks, fort, fortress, monument, mausoleum; shed, barn, outhouse, stable, mill, lighthouse, pier, pavilion, boathouse, beach hut, summerhouse, gazebo, dovecote, windmill. *see also* **house**; **restaurant**; **shop**.

build-up *n* **1** ENLARGEMENT, expansion, development, increase, gain, growth,

escalation, publicity, promotion, plug (*infml*), hype (*sl*). **2** ACCUMULATION, mass, load, heap, stack, store, stockpile.
🔁 **1** reduction, decrease.

bulb

Plants grown from bulbs and corms include: acidanthera, allium, amaryllis, anemone, bluebell (endymion), chincherinchee, chionodoxa, crocosmia, crocus, autumn crocus (colchicum), cyclamen, daffodil, crown imperial (fritillaria), galtonia, garlic, gladiolus, grape hyacinth (muscari), hyacinth, iris, ixia, jonquil, lily, montbretia, narcissus, nerine, ranunculus, scilla, snowdrop (galanthus), sparaxis, tulip, winter aconite.

bulge *n* **1** SWELLING, bump, lump, hump, distension, protuberance, projection. **2** RISE, increase, surge, upsurge, intensification.
➤ *v* swell, puff out, bulb, hump, dilate, expand, enlarge, distend, protrude, project.

bulk *n* size, magnitude, dimensions, extent, amplitude, bigness, largeness, immensity, volume, mass, weight, substance, body, preponderance, majority, most.

bulky *adj* substantial, big, large, huge, enormous, immense, mammoth, massive, colossal, hulking, hefty, heavy, weighty, unmanageable, unwieldy, awkward, cumbersome.
🔁 insubstantial, small, handy.

bullet *n* shot, pellet, ball, slug (*infml*), missile, projectile.

bulletin *n* report, newsflash, dispatch, communiqué, statement, announcement, notification, communication, message.

bully *n* persecutor, tormentor, browbeater, intimidator, bully-boy, heavy (*sl*), ruffian, tough.
➤ *v* persecute, torment, terrorize, bulldoze, coerce, browbeat, bullyrag, intimidate, cow, tyrannize, domineer, overbear, oppress, push around.

bump *v* **1** HIT, strike, knock, bang, crash, collide (with). **2** JOLT, jerk, jar, jostle, rattle, shake, bounce.
➤ *n* **1** BLOW, hit, knock, bang, thump, thud, smash, crash, collision, impact, jolt, jar, shock. **2** LUMP, swelling, bulge, hump, protuberance.
◇ **bump into** meet, encounter, run into, chance upon, come across.
◇ **bump off** (*infml*) kill, murder, assassinate, eliminate (*sl*), liquidate (*sl*), do in (*sl*), top (*sl*).

bumper *adj* plentiful, abundant, large, great, enormous, massive, excellent, exceptional.
🔁 small.

bumptious *adj* self-important, pompous, officious, overbearing, pushy, assertive, over-confident, forward, presumptuous, impudent, arrogant, cocky, conceited, swaggering, boastful, full of oneself, egotistic.
🔁 humble, modest.

bumpy *adj* jerky, jolting, bouncy, choppy, rough, lumpy, knobbly, knobby, uneven, irregular.
🔁 smooth, even.

bunch *n* **1** BUNDLE, sheaf, tuft, clump, cluster, batch, lot, heap, pile, stack, mass, number, quantity, collection, assortment. **2** *bunch of flowers*: bouquet, posy, spray. **3** GANG, band, troop, crew, team, party, gathering, flock, swarm, crowd, mob, multitude.
➤ *v* group, bundle, cluster, collect, assemble, congregate, gather, flock, herd, crowd, mass, pack, huddle.
🔁 disperse, scatter, spread out.

bundle *n* bunch, sheaf, roll, bale, truss, parcel, package, packet, carton, box, bag, pack, batch, consignment, group, set, collection, assortment, quantity, mass, accumulation, pile, stack, heap.
➤ *v* pack, wrap, bale, truss, bind, tie, fasten.

bungle *v* mismanage, cock up (*sl*), screw up (*sl*), foul up (*infml*), mess up (*infml*), ruin, spoil, mar, botch, fudge, blunder.

buoy *n* float, marker, signal, beacon.
◇ **buoy up** support, sustain, raise, lift, boost, encourage, cheer, hearten.
🔁 depress, discourage.

buoyant *adj* **1** *in buoyant mood*: light-hearted, carefree, bright, cheerful, happy, joyful, lively, animated, bouncy. **2** FLOATABLE, floating, afloat, light, weightless.
🔁 **1** depressed, despairing. **2** heavy.

burden *n* cargo, load, weight, dead-weight, encumbrance, millstone, onus, responsibility, obligation, duty, strain, stress, worry, anxiety, care, trouble, trial, affliction, sorrow.
➤ *v* load, weigh down, encumber, handicap, bother, worry, tax, strain, overload, lie heavy on, oppress, overwhelm.
🔁 unburden, relieve.

bureau *n* service, agency, office, branch, department, division, counter, desk.

bureaucracy *n* administration, government, ministry, civil service, the authorities, the system, officialdom, red tape, regulations.

burglar *n* housebreaker, robber, thief, pilferer, trespasser.

burglary *n* housebreaking, break-in, robbery, theft, stealing, trespass.

burial *n* burying, interment, entombment, funeral, obsequies.

burly *adj* big, well-built, hulking, hunky (*infml*), hefty, heavy, stocky, sturdy, brawny, beefy, muscular, athletic, strapping, strong, powerful.
🔁 small, puny, thin, slim.

burn *v* **1** FLAME, blaze, flare, flash, glow, flicker, smoulder, smoke, fume, simmer, seethe. **2** IGNITE, light, kindle, incinerate, cremate, consume, corrode. **3** SCALD, scorch, parch, shrivel, singe, char, toast, brand, sear, smart, sting, bite, hurt, tingle.

burning *adj* **1** ABLAZE, aflame, afire, fiery, flaming, blazing, flashing, gleaming, glowing, smouldering, alight, lit, illuminated. **2** HOT, scalding, scorching, searing, piercing, acute, smarting, stinging, prickling, tingling, biting, caustic, pungent. **3** *burning desire*: ardent, fervent, eager, earnest, intense, vehement, passionate, impassioned, frantic, frenzied, consuming. **4** *burning issue*: urgent, pressing, important, significant, crucial, essential, vital.

◆ 2 cold. **3** apathetic. **4** unimportant.

burrow *n* warren, hole, earth, set, den, lair, retreat, shelter, tunnel.
➤ *v* tunnel, dig, delve, excavate, mine, undermine.

burst *v* puncture, rupture, tear, split, crack, break, fragment, shatter, shiver, disintegrate, explode, blow up, erupt, gush, spout, rush, run.
➤ *n* **1** PUNCTURE, blow-out (*infml*), rupture, split, crack, break, breach, explosion, blast, bang, eruption. **2** DISCHARGE, gush, spurt, surge, rush, spate, torrent, outpouring, outburst, outbreak, fit.

bury *v* **1** *bury the dead*: inter, entomb, lay to rest, shroud. **2** SINK, submerge, immerse, plant, implant, embed, conceal, hide, cover, enshroud, engulf, enclose, engross, occupy, engage, absorb.
◆ 1 disinter, exhume. **2** uncover.

bush *n* **1** SHRUB, hedge, thicket. **2** SCRUB, brush, scrubland, backwoods, wilds.

business *n* **1** TRADE, commerce, industry, manufacturing, dealings, transactions, bargaining, trading, buying, selling. **2** COMPANY, firm, corporation, establishment, organization, concern, enterprise, venture. **3** JOB, occupation, work, employment, trade, profession, line, calling, career, vocation, duty, task, responsibility. **4** AFFAIR, matter, issue, subject, topic, question, problem, point.

businesslike *adj* professional, efficient, thorough, systematic, methodical, organized, orderly,

well-ordered, practical, matter-of-fact, precise, correct, formal, impersonal.
◆ inefficient, disorganized.

businessman, businesswoman
n entrepreneur, industrialist, trader, merchant, tycoon, magnate, capitalist, financier, employer, executive.

bust *n* **1** SCULPTURE, head, torso, statue. **2** BOSOM, breasts, chest, breast.

bustle *v* dash, rush, scamper, scurry, hurry, hasten, scramble, fuss.
➤ *n* activity, stir, commotion, tumult, agitation, excitement, fuss, ado, flurry, hurry, haste.

busy *adj* occupied, engaged, tied up (*infml*), employed, working, slaving, stirring, restless, tireless, diligent, industrious, active, lively, energetic, strenuous, tiring, full, crowded, swarming, teeming, bustling, hectic, eventful.
◆ idle, lazy, quiet.
➤ *v* occupy, engage, employ, engross, absorb, immerse, interest, concern, bother.

busybody *n* meddler, nosey parker (*infml*), intruder, pry, gossip, eavesdropper, snoop, snooper, troublemaker.

butt[1] *n* stub, end, tip, tail, base, foot, shaft, stock, handle, haft.

butt[2] *n* target, mark, object, subject, victim, laughing stock, dupe.

butt[3] *v, n* hit, bump, knock, buffet, push, shove, ram, thrust, punch, jab, prod, poke.
◇ butt in interrupt, cut in, interpose, intrude, meddle, interfere.

butterfly

Types of butterfly include: red admiral, white admiral, apollo, brown argus, chalkhill blue, common blue, brimstone, meadow brown, wall brown, Camberwell beauty, Cleopatra, clouded yellow, comma, copper, Duke of Burgundy, fritillary, heath fritillary, marsh fritillary, gatekeeper, grayling, hairstreak, purple hairstreak, white letter hairstreak, heath, map, monarch, orange-tip, painted lady, peacock, purple emperor, ringlet, skipper, chequered skipper, grizzled skipper, swallowtail, tortoiseshell, wall, cabbage white.

Types of moth include: brown-tail, buff-tip, burnet, six-spot, carpet, cinnabar, clothes, emperor, garden tiger, gypsy, death's head hawkmoth, privet hawkmoth, Io, Kentish glory, lackey, lappet, leopard, lobster, magpie, meal, oak hook-tip, pale tussock, peach blossom, peppered, puss, red underwing, silkworm, silver-Y, swallowtail, turnip, wax, winter.

buttocks *n* rump, hindquarters, rear, posterior (*infml*), seat, bottom, behind, backside (*infml*), arse (*sl*), ass (*US sl*).

buttonhole *v* accost, waylay, catch, grab, nab, detain, importune.

buttress *n* support, prop, shore, stay, brace, pier, strut, stanchion, mainstay, reinforcement.

➤ *v* support, prop up, shore up, hold up, brace, strengthen, reinforce, bolster up, sustain.
🔹 undermine, weaken.

buy *v* purchase, invest in (*infml*), pay for, procure, acquire, obtain, get.
🔹 sell.
➤ *n* purchase, acquisition, bargain, deal.

buyer *n* purchaser, shopper, consumer, customer, vendee, emptor.
🔹 seller, vendor.

by *prep* near, next to, beside, along, over, through, via, past.
➤ *adv* near, close, handy, at hand, past, beyond, away, aside.

bypass *v* avoid, dodge, sidestep, skirt, circumvent, ignore, neglect, omit.
➤ *n* ring road, detour, diversion.

by-product *n* consequence, result, side-effect, fallout (*infml*), repercussion, after-effect.

bystander *n* spectator, onlooker, looker-on, watcher, observer, witness, eyewitness, passer-by.

Cc

cabin *n* **1** BERTH, quarters, compartment, room. **2** HUT, shack, shanty, lodge, chalet, cottage, shed, shelter.

cabinet *n* cupboard, closet, dresser, case, locker.

cable *n* line, rope, cord, chain, wire, flex, lead.

cadge *v* scrounge, sponge, beg, hitch.

café *n* coffee shop, tea shop, tea room, coffee bar, cafeteria, snackbar, bistro, brasserie, restaurant.

cage *v* encage, coop up, shut up, confine, restrain, fence in, imprison, impound, incarcerate, lock up.
🗷 release, let out, free.
➤ *n* aviary, coop, hutch, enclosure, pen, pound, corral.

cajole *v* coax, persuade, wheedle, flatter, sweet-talk (*infml*), butter up (*infml*), tempt, lure, seduce, entice, beguile, mislead, dupe.
🗷 bully, force, compel.

cake *v* coat, cover, encrust, dry, harden, solidify, consolidate, coagulate, congeal, thicken.
➤ *n* **1** *tea and cakes*: gâteau, fancy, madeleine, bun, pie, flan. **2** LUMP, mass, bar, slab, block, loaf.

Types of cake include: angel food cake, banana cake, birthday cake, Black Forest gâteau, carrot cake, chocolate cake, cream cake, Christmas cake, Dundee cake, fruit cake, genoa sponge, gingerbread, poppyseed cake, sponge cake, sultana cake, Victoria sponge, yeast cake; French cake, madeleine, muffin, queen cake.

---

calamitous *adj* disastrous, catastrophic, ruinous, devastating, deadly, fatal, dire, ghastly, dreadful, tragic, woeful, grievous.
🗷 good, fortunate, happy.

calamity *n* disaster, catastrophe, mishap, misadventure, mischance, misfortune, adversity, reverse, trial, tribulation, affliction, distress, tragedy, ruin, downfall.
🗷 blessing, godsend.

calculate *v* compute, work out, count, enumerate, reckon, figure, determine, weigh, rate, value, estimate, gauge, judge, consider, plan, intend, aim.

calculating *adj* crafty, cunning, sly, devious, scheming, designing, contriving, sharp, shrewd.
🗷 artless, naïve.

calculation *n* sum, computation, answer, result, reckoning, figuring, estimate, forecast, judgement, planning, deliberation.

calibre *n* **1** DIAMETER, bore, gauge, size, measure. **2** *candidates of the right calibre*: talent, gifts, strength, worth, merit, quality, character, ability, capacity, faculty, stature, distinction.

call *v* **1** NAME, christen, baptize, title, entitle, dub, style, term, label, designate. **2** SHOUT, yell, exclaim, cry. **3** SUMMON, invite, bid, convene, assemble. **4** TELEPHONE, phone, ring (up), contact.
➤ *n* **1** CRY, exclamation, shout, yell, scream. **2** VISIT, ring, summons, invitation. **3** *there's no call for it*: demand, need, occasion, cause, excuse, justification, reason, grounds, right. **4** APPEAL, request, plea, order, command, claim, announcement, signal.

◇ **call for 1** DEMAND, require, need, necessitate, involve, entail, occasion, suggest. **2** FETCH, collect, pick up.
◇ **call off** cancel, drop, abandon, discontinue, break off, withdraw.

calling n mission, vocation, career, profession, occupation, job, trade, business, line, work, employment, field, province, pursuit.

callous adj heartless, hard-hearted, cold, indifferent, uncaring, unsympathetic, unfeeling, insensitive, hardened, thick-skinned.
🖅 kind, caring, sympathetic, sensitive.

calm adj **1** COMPOSED, self-possessed, collected, cool, dispassionate, unemotional, impassive, unmoved, placid, sedate, imperturbable, unflappable, unexcitable, laid back (*infml*), relaxed, unexcited, unruffled, unflustered, unperturbed, undisturbed, untroubled, unapprehensive. **2** *calm waters*: smooth, still, windless, unclouded, mild, tranquil, serene, peaceful, quiet, uneventful, restful.
🖅 **1** excitable, worried, anxious.
2 rough, wild, stormy.
➤ v compose, soothe, relax, sedate, tranquillize, hush, quieten, placate, pacify.
🖅 excite, worry.
➤ n calmness, stillness, tranquillity, serenity, peacefulness, peace, quiet, hush, repose.
🖅 storminess, restlessness.

camera

Types of camera include: advanced photo system (APS), automatic, bellows, binocular, box Brownie®, camcorder, camera obscura, cine, cinematographic, compact, daguerreotype, digital, disc, disposable, film, Instamatic®, large-format, miniature, subminiature, panoramic, pinhole, plate, dry-plate, half-plate, quarter-plate, wet-plate, point-and-shoot, Polaroid®, press, reflex, folding reflex, single-lens reflex (SLR), twin-lens reflex (TLR), security, sliding box, sound, Steadicam®, still, stereo, Super 8®, surveillance, TV, video, view, Webcam. *see also* **photographic equipment**.

Parts of a camera include: accessory shoe, AF lenses, aperture, aperture setting control, autofocus (AF), autofocus sensor, automatic focusing system, battery chamber, blind, cable release, card door, card on/off key, card window, compact lens, compound lens, data panel/display, diaphragm, exposure meter, exposure mode button, film advance/transport, film gate, film holder, fisheye lens, flash contact, flash setting, focal plane shutter, focus control/setting, focusing hood, focusing ring, frame counter, function adjustment button, function selector key, iris diaphragm, leaf shutter, lens, lens cap, lens release, light control, long-focus lens, magazine, medium focal-length lens, meter cell, mirror, mirror lens, mirror shutter, object lens, pentaprism, program card, program reset button, rangefinder window, reflex viewer, registration pin, release button, rewind handle/crank, shutter, shutter release, shutter speed control, shutter/film speed indicator, spool, spool knob, take-up reel/spool, telephoto lens, viewfinder eyepiece, viewfinder, viewing lens, wide-angle lens, zoom lens.

camouflage n disguise, guise, masquerade, mask, cloak, screen, blind, front, cover, concealment, deception.
➤ v disguise, mask, cloak, veil, screen, cover, conceal, hide, obscure.
🖅 uncover, reveal.

campaign n crusade, movement, promotion, drive, push, offensive, attack, battle, expedition, operation.
➤ v crusade, promote, push, advocate, fight, battle.

cancel v call off, abort, abandon, drop, abolish, annul, quash, rescind, revoke, repeal, countermand, delete, erase, obliterate, eliminate, offset, compensate, redeem, neutralize, nullify.

cancer n 1 EVIL, blight, canker, pestilence, sickness, corruption, rot. 2 TUMOUR, growth, malignancy, carcinoma.

candid adj frank, open, truthful, honest, sincere, forthright, straightforward, ingenuous, guileless, simple, plain, clear, unequivocal, blunt, outspoken.
F3 guarded, evasive, devious.

candidate n applicant, aspirant, contender, contestant, competitor, entrant, runner, possibility, nominee, claimant, pretender, suitor.

candour n frankness, openness, truthfulness, honesty, plain-dealing, sincerity, straightforwardness, directness, ingenuousness, guilelessness, naïvety, artlessness, simplicity, plainness, bluntness, unequivocalness, outspokenness.
F3 evasiveness, deviousness.

canopy n awning, covering, shade, shelter, sunshade, umbrella.

cantankerous adj irritable, irascible, grumpy, grouchy, crusty, crotchety, crabbed, crabby, testy, bad-tempered, ill-humoured, cross, peevish, difficult, perverse, contrary, quarrelsome.
F3 good-natured, easy-going (infml).

canvass v 1 ELECTIONEER, agitate, campaign, solicit, ask for, seek, poll. 2 EXAMINE, inspect, scrutinize, study, scan, investigate, analyse, sift, discuss, debate.
➤ n poll, survey, examination, scrutiny, investigation, inquiry.

canyon n gorge, ravine, gully, valley.

cap n 1 HAT, skullcap, beret, tam-o'-shanter. 2 LID, top, cover.
➤ v exceed, surpass, transcend, better, beat, outdo, outstrip, eclipse, complete, finish, crown, top, cover.

capability n ability, capacity, faculty, power, potential, means, facility, competence, qualification, skill,

proficiency, talent.
F3 inability, incompetence.

capable adj able, competent, efficient, qualified, experienced, accomplished, skilful, proficient, gifted, talented, masterly, clever, intelligent, fitted, suited, apt, liable, disposed.
F3 incapable, incompetent, useless.

capacity n 1 VOLUME, space, room, size, dimensions, magnitude, extent, compass, range, scope. 2 CAPABILITY, ability, faculty, power, potential, competence, efficiency, skill, gift, talent, genius, cleverness, intelligence, aptitude, readiness. 3 in her capacity as president: role, function, position, office, post, appointment, job.

cape[1] n headland, head, promontory, point, ness, peninsula.

cape[2] n cloak, shawl, wrap, robe, poncho, coat.

capital n funds, finance, principal, money, cash, savings, investment(s), wealth, means, wherewithal, resources, assets, property, stock.

capitalize on profit from, take advantage of, exploit, cash in on.

capitulate v surrender, throw in the towel, yield, give in, relent, submit, succumb.
F3 fight on.

capsize v overturn, turn over, turn turtle, invert, keel over, upset.

capsule n pill, tablet, lozenge, receptacle, shell, sheath, pod, module.

captain n commander, master, skipper, pilot, head, chief, leader, boss, officer.

captivate v charm, enchant, bewitch, beguile, fascinate, enthral, hypnotize, mesmerize, lure, allure, seduce, win, attract, enamour, infatuate, enrapture, dazzle.
F3 repel, disgust, appal.

captive n prisoner, hostage, slave, detainee, internee, convict.
➤ adj imprisoned, caged, confined, restricted, secure, locked up, enchained,

enslaved, ensnared.
F3 free.

captivity *n* custody, detention, imprisonment, incarceration, internment, confinement, restraint, bondage, duress, slavery, servitude.
F3 freedom.

capture *v* catch, trap, snare, take, seize, arrest, apprehend, imprison, secure.
➤ *n* catching, trapping, taking, seizure, arrest, imprisonment.

car *n* automobile, motor car, motor, vehicle.

Types of car include: saloon, hatchback, fastback, estate, sports car, cabriolet, convertible, limousine, limo (*infml*), jalopy (*infml*), banger (*infml*), Mini, bubble-car, coupé, station wagon, shooting brake, veteran car, vintage car, Beetle (*infml*), four-wheel drive, all-roader, multi-purpose vehicle (or MPV or people carrier), sport-utility vehicle (or SUV), Jeep®, buggy, Land Rover, Range Rover, panda car, patrol car, taxi, cab.

carcase *n* body, corpse, cadaver, remains, relics, skeleton, shell, structure, framework, hulk.

care *n* **1** WORRY, anxiety, stress, strain, pressure, concern, trouble, distress, affliction, tribulation, vexation. **2** CAREFULNESS, caution, prudence, forethought, vigilance, watchfulness, pains, meticulousness, attention, heed, regard, consideration, interest. **3** *in their care*: keeping, custody, guardianship, protection, ward, charge, responsibility, control, supervision.
F3 2 carelessness, thoughtlessness, inattention, neglect.
➤ *v* worry, mind, bother.
◇ **care for 1** LOOK AFTER, nurse, tend, mind, watch over, protect, minister to, attend. **2** LIKE, be fond of, love, be keen on, enjoy, delight in, want, desire.

career *n* vocation, calling, life-work, occupation, pursuit, profession, trade,

job, employment, livelihood.
➤ *v* rush, dash, tear, hurtle, race, run, gallop, speed, shoot, bolt.

carefree *adj* unworried, untroubled, unconcerned, blithe, breezy, happy-go-lucky, cheery, light-hearted, cheerful, happy, easy-going (*infml*), laid back (*infml*).
F3 worried, anxious, despondent.

careful *adj* **1** CAUTIOUS, prudent, circumspect, judicious, wary, chary, vigilant, watchful, alert, attentive, mindful. **2** METICULOUS, painstaking, conscientious, scrupulous, thorough, detailed, punctilious, particular, accurate, precise, thoughtful.
F3 1 careless, inattentive, thoughtless, reckless. **2** careless.

careless *adj* **1** UNTHINKING, thoughtless, inconsiderate, uncaring, unconcerned, heedless, unmindful, forgetful, remiss, negligent, irresponsible, unguarded. **2** *careless work*: inaccurate, messy, untidy, disorderly, sloppy, neglectful, slipshod, slapdash, hasty, cursory, offhand, casual.
F3 1 thoughtful, prudent. **2** careful, accurate, meticulous.

caress *v* stroke, pet, fondle, cuddle, hug, embrace, kiss, touch, rub.
➤ *n* stroke, pat, fondle, cuddle, hug, embrace, kiss.

caretaker *n* janitor, porter, watchman, keeper, custodian, curator, warden, superintendent.

cargo *n* freight, load, payload, lading, tonnage, shipment, consignment, contents, goods, merchandise, baggage.

caricature *n* cartoon, parody, lampoon, burlesque, satire, send-up (*infml*), take-off (*infml*), imitation, representation, distortion, travesty.
➤ *v* parody, mock, ridicule, satirize, send up (*infml*), take off (*infml*), mimic, distort, exaggerate.

carnage *n* bloodshed, bloodbath, butchery, slaughter, killing, murder, massacre, holocaust.

carnival *n* festival, fiesta, gala,

jamboree, fête, fair, holiday, jubilee, celebration, merrymaking, revelry.

carriage *n* **1** COACH, wagon, car, vehicle. **2** DEPORTMENT, posture, bearing, air, manner, mien, demeanour, behaviour, conduct. **3** CARRYING, conveyance, transport, transportation, delivery, postage.

carry *v* **1** BRING, convey, transport, haul, move, transfer, relay, release, conduct, take, fetch. **2** BEAR, shoulder, support, underpin, maintain, uphold, sustain, suffer, stand.

◇ **carry on 1** CONTINUE, proceed, last, endure, maintain, keep on, persist, persevere. **2** *carry on a business*: operate, run, manage, administer.

1 stop, finish.

◇ **carry out** do, perform, undertake, discharge, conduct, execute, implement, fulfil, accomplish, achieve, realize, bring off.

cart *n* barrow, handcart, wheelbarrow, wagon, truck.

► *v* move, convey, transport, haul, lug (*infml*), hump (*infml*), bear, carry.

carton *n* box, packet, pack, case, container, package, parcel.

cartoon *n* comic strip, animation, sketch, drawing, caricature, parody.

cartridge *n* cassette, canister, cylinder, tube, container, case, capsule, shell, magazine, round, charge.

carve *v* cut, slice, hack, hew, chisel, chip, sculpt, sculpture, shape, form, fashion, mould, etch, engrave, incise, indent.

cascade *n* rush, gush, outpouring, flood, deluge, torrent, avalanche, cataract, waterfall, falls, fountain, shower.

1 trickle.

► *v* rush, gush, surge, flood, overflow, spill, tumble, fall, descend, shower, pour, plunge, pitch.

case¹ *n* container, receptacle, holder, suitcase, trunk, crate, box, carton, casket, chest, cabinet, showcase, casing, cartridge, shell, capsule, sheath, cover, jacket, wrapper.

case² *n* **1** CIRCUMSTANCES, context, state, condition, position, situation, contingency, occurrence, occasion, event, specimen, example, instance, illustration, point. **2** LAWSUIT, suit, trial, proceedings, action, process, cause, argument, dispute.

cash *n* money, hard money, ready money, banknotes, notes, coins, change, legal tender, currency, hard currency, bullion, funds, resources, wherewithal.

► *v* encash, exchange, realize, liquidate.

cashier *n* clerk, teller, treasurer, bursar, purser, banker, accountant.

cask *n* barrel, tun, hogshead, firkin, vat, tub, butt.

cast *v* **1** THROW, hurl, lob, pitch, fling, toss, sling, shy, launch, impel, drive, direct, project, shed, emit, diffuse, spread, scatter. **2** MOULD, shape, form, model, found.

► *n* **1** COMPANY, troupe, actors, players, performers, entertainers, characters, dramatis personae. **2** CASTING, mould, shape, form.

◇ **cast down** depress, discourage, dishearten, deject, sadden, crush, desolate.

1 cheer up, encourage.

castle *n* stronghold, fortress, citadel, keep, tower, château, palace, mansion, stately home, country house.

Parts of a castle include: approach, arrow-slit, bailey, barbican, bartizan, bastion, battlements, berm, brattice, buttress, chapel, corbel, courtyard, crenel, crenellation, crosslet, curtain wall, ditch, donjon, drawbridge, dungeon, embrasure, enclosure wall, fosse, gatehouse, inner wall, keep, loophole, merlon, moat, motte, mound, outer bailey, parados, parapet, portcullis, postern, rampart, scarp, stockade, tower, lookout tower, turret, wall walk, ward, watchtower.

casual *adj* **1** *a casual meeting*: chance, fortuitous, accidental, unintentional,

unpremeditated, unexpected, unforeseen, irregular, random, occasional, incidental, superficial, cursory. **2** NONCHALANT, blasé, lackadaisical, negligent, couldn't-care-less (*infml*), apathetic, indifferent, unconcerned, informal, offhand, relaxed, laid back (*infml*).
F3 1 deliberate, planned. **2** formal.

casualty *n* injury, loss, death, fatality, victim, sufferer, injured person, wounded person, dead person.

cat

> *Breeds of cat include*: Abyssinian, American shorthair, Balinese, Birman, Bombay, British shorthair, British longhair, Burmese, Carthusian, chinchilla, Cornish rex, Cymric, Devon rex, domestic tabby, Egyptian Mau, Exotic shorthair, Foreign Blue, Foreign spotted shorthair, Foreign White, Havana, Himalayan, Japanese Bobtail, Korat, Maine Coon, Manx, Norwegian Forest, Persian, rag-doll, rex, Russian Blue, Scottish Fold, Siamese, silver tabby, Singapura, Somali, Tiffany, Tonkinese, Tortoiseshell, Turkish Angora, Turkish Van.

catalogue *n* list, inventory, roll, register, roster, schedule, record, table, index, directory, gazetteer, brochure, prospectus.
➤ *v* list, register, record, index, classify, alphabetize, file.

catapult *v* hurl, fling, throw, pitch, toss, sling, launch, propel, shoot, fire.

cataract *n* waterfall, falls, rapids, force, cascade, downpour, torrent, deluge.

catastrophe *n* disaster, calamity, cataclysm, debacle, fiasco, failure, ruin, devastation, tragedy, blow, reverse, mischance, misfortune, adversity, affliction, trouble, upheaval.

catch *v* **1** SEIZE, grab, take, hold, grasp, grip, clutch, capture, trap, entrap, snare, ensnare, hook, net, arrest, apprehend. **2** HEAR, understand, perceive, recognize. **3** SURPRISE, expose,

unmask, find (out), discover, detect, discern. **4** *catch a cold*: contract, get, develop, go down with.
F3 1 drop, release, free. **2** miss.
➤ *n* **1** FASTENER, clip, hook, clasp, hasp, latch, bolt. **2** DISADVANTAGE, drawback, snag, hitch, obstacle, problem.
◇ **catch up** gain on, draw level with, overtake.

catching *adj* infectious, contagious, communicable, transmittable.

catchword *n* catchphrase, slogan, motto, watchword, byword, password.

catchy *adj* memorable, haunting, popular, melodic, tuneful, attractive, captivating.
F3 dull, boring.

categorical *adj* absolute, total, utter, unqualified, unreserved, unconditional, downright, positive, definite, emphatic, unequivocal, clear, explicit, express, direct.
F3 tentative, qualified, vague.

categorize *v* class, classify, group, sort, grade, rank, order, list.

category *n* class, classification, group, grouping, sort, type, section, division, department, chapter, head, heading, grade, rank, order, list.

cater *v* provision, victual, provide, supply, furnish, serve, indulge, pander.

catholic *adj* broad, wide, wide-ranging, universal, global, general, comprehensive, inclusive, all-inclusive, all-embracing, liberal, tolerant, broad-minded.
F3 narrow, limited, narrow-minded.

cattle *n* cows, bulls, oxen, livestock, stock, beasts.

> *Breeds of cattle include*: Aberdeen Angus, Africander, Alderney, Ankole, Ayrshire, Blonde d'Aquitaine, Brahman, Brown Swiss, cattabu, cattalo, Charolais, Chillingham, Devon, dexter, Durham, Friesian, Galloway, Guernsey, Hereford, Highland, Holstein, Jersey, Latvian, Limousin, Longhorn, Luing, Red Poll,

Romagnola, Santa Gertrudis, Shetland, Shorthorn, Simmenthaler, Teeswater, Ukrainian, Welsh Black.

cause *n* **1** SOURCE, origin, beginning, root, basis, spring, originator, creator, producer, maker, agent, agency. **2** REASON, motive, grounds, motivation, stimulus, incentive, inducement, impulse. **3** *a worthy cause*: object, purpose, end, ideal, belief, conviction, movement, undertaking, enterprise.
Fa 1 effect, result, consequence.
➤ *v* begin, give rise to, lead to, result in, occasion, bring about, effect, produce, generate, create, precipitate, motivate, stimulate, provoke, incite, induce, force, compel.
Fa stop, prevent.

caustic *adj* corrosive, acid, burning, stinging, biting, cutting, mordant, trenchant, keen, pungent, bitter, acrimonious, sarcastic, scathing, virulent, severe.
Fa soothing, mild.

caution *n* **1** CARE, carefulness, prudence, vigilance, watchfulness, alertness, heed, discretion, forethought, deliberation, wariness. **2** WARNING, caveat, injunction, admonition, advice, counsel.
Fa 1 carelessness, recklessness.
➤ *v* warn, admonish, advise, urge.

cautious *adj* careful, prudent, circumspect, judicious, vigilant, watchful, alert, heedful, discreet, tactful, chary, wary, cagey (*infml*), guarded, tentative, softly-softly, unadventurous.
Fa incautious, imprudent, heedless, reckless.

cavalcade *n* procession, parade, march-past, troop, array, retinue, train.

cavalier *n* horseman, equestrian, knight, gentleman, gallant, escort, partner.
➤ *adj* supercilious, condescending, lordly, haughty, lofty, arrogant, swaggering, insolent, scornful, disdainful, curt, offhand, free-and-easy.

cave *n* cavern, grotto, hole, pothole, hollow, cavity.
◇ **cave in** collapse, subside, give way, yield, fall, slip.

cavernous *adj* hollow, concave, gaping, yawning, echoing, resonant, deep, sunken.

cavity *n* hole, gap, dent, hollow, crater, pit, well, sinus, ventricle.

cavort *v* caper, frolic, gambol, prance, skip, dance, frisk, sport, romp.

cease *v* stop, desist, refrain, pack in (*sl*), halt, call a halt, break off, discontinue, finish, end, conclude, terminate, fail, die.
Fa begin, start, commence.

ceaseless *adj* endless, unending, never-ending, eternal, everlasting, continuous, non-stop, incessant, interminable, constant, perpetual, continual, persistent, untiring, unremitting.
Fa occasional, irregular.

cede *v* surrender, give up, resign, abdicate, renounce, abandon, yield, relinquish, convey, transfer, hand over, grant, allow, concede.

celebrate *v* commemorate, remember, observe, keep, rejoice, toast, drink to, honour, exalt, glorify, praise, extol, eulogize, commend, bless, solemnize.

celebrated *adj* famous, well-known, famed, renowned, illustrious, glorious, eminent, distinguished, notable, prominent, outstanding, popular, acclaimed, exalted, revered.
Fa unknown, obscure, forgotten.

celebration *n* commemoration, remembrance, observance, anniversary, jubilee, festival, gala, merrymaking, jollification, revelry, festivity, party, rave-up (*infml*).

Celebrations include: anniversary, banquet, baptism, bar mitzvah, bat mitzvah, birthday, centenary, christening, coming-of-age, commemoration, Confirmation, feast, fête, festival, gala, graduation, harvest festival, homecoming, Independence Day, jubilee, marriage, May Day, name-day, party, reception, remembrance, retirement, reunion, saint's day, thanksgiving, tribute, wedding. *see also* **anniversary**; **party**.

celebrity *n* celeb (*infml*), personage, dignitary, VIP (*infml*), luminary, worthy, personality, name, big name, star, superstar.
🔁 nobody, nonentity.

celibacy *n* singleness, bachelorhood, spinsterhood, virginity, chastity, purity, abstinence, continence.

cell *n* dungeon, prison, room, cubicle, chamber, compartment, cavity, unit.

cellar *n* basement, crypt, vault, storeroom, wine cellar.

cement *v* stick, bond, weld, solder, join, unite, bind, combine.
➤ *n* plaster, mortar, concrete.

cemetery *n* burial ground, graveyard, churchyard.

censor *v* cut, edit, blue-pencil, bowdlerize, expurgate.

censorious *adj* condemnatory, disapproving, disparaging, fault-finding, carping, cavilling, critical, hypercritical, severe.
🔁 complimentary, approving.

censure *n* condemnation, blame, disapproval, criticism, admonishment, admonition, reprehension, reproof, reproach, rebuke, reprimand, telling-off (*infml*).
🔁 praise, compliments, approval.
➤ *v* condemn, denounce, blame, criticize, castigate (*fml*), admonish, reprehend, reprove, upbraid, reproach, rebuke, reprimand, scold, tell off (*infml*).
🔁 praise, compliment, approve.

central *adj* middle, mid, inner, interior, focal, main, chief, key, principal, primary, fundamental, vital, essential, important.
🔁 peripheral, minor, secondary.

centre *n* middle, mid-point, bull's-eye, heart, core, nucleus, pivot, hub, focus, crux.
🔁 edge, periphery, outskirts.
➤ *v* focus, concentrate, converge, gravitate, revolve, pivot, hinge.

ceremonial *adj* formal, official, stately, solemn, ritual, ritualistic.
🔁 informal, casual.
➤ *n* ceremony, formality, protocol, solemnity, ritual, rite.

ceremonious *adj* stately, dignified, grand, solemn, ritual, civil, polite, courteous, deferential, courtly, formal, stiff, starchy, exact, precise, punctilious.
🔁 unceremonious, informal, relaxed.

ceremony *n* **1** *wedding ceremony*: service, rite, commemoration, observance, celebration, function, parade. **2** ETIQUETTE, protocol, decorum, propriety, formality, form, niceties, ceremonial, ritual, pomp, show.

certain *adj* **1** SURE, positive, assured, confident, convinced, undoubted, indubitable, unquestionable, incontrovertible, undeniable, irrefutable, plain, conclusive, absolute, convincing, true. **2** INEVITABLE, unavoidable, bound, destined, fated. **3** SPECIFIC, special, particular, individual, precise, express, fixed, established, settled, decided, definite. **4** DEPENDABLE, reliable, trustworthy, constant, steady, stable.
🔁 **1** uncertain, unsure, hesitant, doubtful. **2** unlikely. **4** unreliable.

certainly *adv* of course, naturally, definitely, for sure, undoubtedly, doubtlessly.

certainty *n* sureness, positiveness, assurance, confidence, conviction, faith, trust, truth, validity, fact, reality, inevitability.
🔁 uncertainty, doubt, hesitation.

certificate *n* document, award, diploma, qualification, credentials, testimonial, guarantee, endorsement, warrant, licence, authorization, pass, voucher.

certify *v* declare, attest (*fml*), aver, assure, guarantee, endorse, corroborate, confirm, vouch, testify, witness, verify, authenticate, validate, authorize, license.

chain *n* **1** FETTER, manacle, restraint, bond, link, coupling, union. **2** *chain of events*: sequence, succession, progression, string, train, series, set.
➤ *v* tether, fasten, secure, bind, restrain, confine, fetter, shackle, manacle, handcuff, enslave.
🔁 release, free.

chairman, chairwoman *n* chair, chairperson, president, convenor, organizer, director, master of ceremonies, MC, toastmaster, speaker.

challenge *v* **1** DARE, defy, throw down the gauntlet, confront, brave, accost, provoke, test, tax, try. **2** DISPUTE, question, query, protest, object to.
➤ *n* dare, defiance, confrontation, provocation, test, trial, hurdle, obstacle, question, ultimatum.

champion *n* winner, victor, conqueror, hero, guardian, protector, defender, vindicator, patron, backer, supporter, upholder, advocate.
➤ *v* defend, stand up for, back, support, maintain, uphold, espouse, advocate, promote.

chance *n* **1** ACCIDENT, fortuity, coincidence, fluke (*infml*), luck, fortune, providence, fate, destiny, risk, gamble, speculation, possibility, prospect, probability, likelihood, odds. **2** *a second chance*: opportunity, opening, occasion, time.
🔁 **1** certainty.
➤ *v* **1** RISK, hazard, gamble, wager, stake, try, venture. **2** HAPPEN, occur.
➤ *adj* fortuitous, casual, accidental, inadvertent, unintentional, unintended, unforeseen, unlooked-for, random, haphazard, incidental.
🔁 deliberate, intentional, foreseen, certain.

change *v* alter, modify, convert, reorganize, reform, remodel, restyle, transform, transfigure, metamorphose, mutate, vary, fluctuate, vacillate, shift, displace, swap, exchange, trade, switch, transpose, substitute, replace, alternate, interchange.
➤ *n* alteration, modification, conversion, transformation, metamorphosis, mutation, variation, fluctuation, shift, exchange, transposition, substitution, interchange, difference, diversion, novelty, innovation, variety, transition, revolution, upheaval.

changeable *adj* variable, mutable, fluid, kaleidoscopic, shifting, mobile, unsettled, uncertain, unpredictable, unreliable, erratic, irregular, inconstant, fickle, capricious, volatile, unstable, unsteady, wavering, vacillating.
🔁 constant, reliable.

channel *n* **1** DUCT, conduit, main, groove, furrow, trough, gutter, canal, flume, watercourse, waterway, strait, sound. **2** *channel of communication*: route, course, path, avenue, way, means, medium, approach, passage.
➤ *v* direct, guide, conduct, convey, send, transmit, force.

chant *n* plainsong, psalm, song, melody, chorus, refrain, slogan, war cry.
➤ *v* recite, intone, sing, chorus.

chaos *n* disorder, confusion, disorganization, anarchy, lawlessness, tumult, pandemonium, bedlam.
🔁 order.

chaotic *adj* disordered, confused, disorganized, topsy-turvy, deranged, anarchic, lawless, riotous, tumultuous, unruly, uncontrolled.
🔁 ordered, organized.

chap (*infml*) *n* fellow, bloke (*infml*), guy (*infml*), man, boy, person, individual, character, sort, type.

chapter *n* part, section, division, clause, topic, episode, period, phase, stage.

character *n* **1** PERSONALITY, nature, disposition, temperament, temper, constitution, make-up, individuality, peculiarity, features, attributes, quality, type, stamp, calibre, reputation, status, position, trait. **2** LETTER, figure, symbol, sign, mark, type, cipher, rune, hieroglyph, ideograph. **3** INDIVIDUAL, person, sort, type, role, part.

characteristic *adj* distinctive, distinguishing, individual, idiosyncratic, peculiar, specific, special, typical, representative, symbolic, symptomatic. ⊟ uncharacteristic, untypical.
➤ *n* peculiarity, idiosyncrasy, mannerism, feature, trait, attribute, property, quality, hallmark, mark, symptom.

characterize *v* typify, mark, stamp, brand, identify, distinguish, indicate, represent, portray.

charge *v* **1** *charge a high price*: ask, demand, levy, exact, debit. **2** ACCUSE, indict, impeach, incriminate, blame. **3** ATTACK, assail, storm, rush.
➤ *n* **1** PRICE, cost, fee, rate, amount, expense, expenditure, outlay, payment. **2** ACCUSATION, indictment, allegation, imputation. **3** ATTACK, assault, onslaught, sortie, rush. **4** *in your charge*: custody, keeping, care, safekeeping, guardianship, ward, trust, responsibility, duty.

charitable *adj* philanthropic, humanitarian, benevolent, benign, kind, compassionate, sympathetic, understanding, considerate, generous, magnanimous, liberal, tolerant, broad-minded, lenient, forgiving, indulgent, gracious.
⊟ uncharitable, inconsiderate, unforgiving.

charity *n* **1** GENEROSITY, bountifulness, alms-giving, beneficence, philanthropy, unselfishness, altruism, benevolence, benignness, kindness, goodness, humanity, compassion, tender-heartedness, love, affection, clemency, indulgence. **2** ALMS, gift, handout, aid, relief, assistance.
⊟ **1** selfishness, malice.

charm *v* please, delight, enrapture, captivate, fascinate, beguile, enchant, bewitch, mesmerize, attract, allure,
cajole, win, enamour.
⊟ repel.
➤ *n* **1** ATTRACTION, allure, magnetism, appeal, desirability, fascination, enchantment, spell, sorcery, magic. **2** *lucky charm*: trinket, talisman, amulet, fetish, idol.

charming *adj* pleasing, delightful, pleasant, lovely, captivating, enchanting, attractive, fetching, appealing, sweet, winsome, seductive, winning, irresistible.
⊟ ugly, unattractive, repulsive.

chart *n* diagram, table, graph, map, plan, blueprint.
➤ *v* map, map out, sketch, draw, draft, outline, delineate, mark, plot, place.

charter *n* right, privilege, prerogative, authorization, permit, licence, franchise, concession, contract, indenture, deed, bond, document.
➤ *v* hire, rent, lease, commission, engage, employ, authorize, sanction, license.

chase *v* pursue, follow, hunt, track, drive, expel, rush, hurry.

chasm *n* gap, opening, gulf, abyss, void, hollow, cavity, crater, breach, rift, split, cleft, fissure, crevasse, canyon, gorge, ravine.

chaste *adj* pure, virginal, unsullied, undefiled, immaculate, abstinent, continent, celibate, virtuous, moral, innocent, wholesome, modest, decent, plain, simple, austere.
⊟ corrupt, lewd, vulgar, indecorous.

chasten *v* humble, humiliate, tame, subdue, repress, curb, moderate, soften, discipline, punish, correct, chastise, castigate, reprove.

chastise *v* punish, discipline, correct, beat, flog, whip, lash, scourge, smack, spank, castigate, reprove, admonish, scold, upbraid, berate, censure.

chat *n* talk, conversation, natter (*infml*), gossip, chinwag (*infml*), tête-à-tête, heart-to-heart.
➤ *v* talk, crack, natter (*infml*), schmooze, gossip, chatter, rabbit (on) (*infml*).

chatter *v, n* prattle, babble, chat, natter (*infml*), gossip, tattle.

chatty *adj* talkative, gossipy, newsy, friendly, informal, colloquial, familiar.
🔁 quiet.

cheap *adj* 1 INEXPENSIVE, reasonable, dirt-cheap, bargain, reduced, cut-price, knock-down, budget, economy, economical. 2 TAWDRY, tatty, cheapo (*sl*), shoddy, inferior, second-rate, low-rent (*infml*), worthless, vulgar, common, poor, paltry, mean, contemptible, despicable, low.
🔁 1 expensive, costly. 2 superior, noble, admirable.

cheapen *v* devalue, degrade, lower, demean, depreciate, belittle, disparage, denigrate, downgrade.

cheat *v* defraud, swindle, diddle, short-change, do (*infml*), rip off (*sl*), fleece, con (*infml*), double-cross, mislead, deceive, dupe, fool, trick, hoodwink, bamboozle (*infml*), beguile.
➤ *n* cheater, dodger, fraud, swindler, shark (*infml*), con man (*infml*), extortioner, double-crosser, impostor, charlatan, deceiver, trickster, rogue.

check *v* 1 EXAMINE, inspect, scrutinize, give the once-over (*infml*), investigate, probe, test, monitor, study, research, compare, cross-check, confirm, verify.
2 *check an impulse*: curb, bridle, restrain, control, limit, repress, inhibit, damp, thwart, hinder, impede, obstruct, bar, retard, delay, stop, arrest, halt.
➤ *n* 1 EXAMINATION, inspection, scrutiny, once-over (*infml*), check-up, investigation, audit, test, research.
2 CURB, restraint, control, limitation, constraint, inhibition, damper, blow, disappointment, reverse, setback, frustration, hindrance, impediment, obstruction, stoppage.

cheek *n* impertinence, impudence, insolence, disrespect, effrontery, brazenness, temerity, audacity, nerve (*infml*), gall.

cheeky *adj* impertinent, impudent, insolent, disrespectful, forward, brazen,

pert, saucy (*infml*), audacious.
🔁 respectful, polite.

cheer *v* 1 ACCLAIM, hail, clap, applaud.
2 COMFORT, console, brighten, gladden, warm, uplift, elate, exhilarate, encourage, hearten.
🔁 1 boo, jeer. 2 dishearten.
➤ *n* acclamation, hurrah, bravo, applause, ovation.
◊ **cheer up** encourage, hearten, take heart, rally, buck up (*infml*), perk up (*infml*).

cheerful *adj* happy, glad, contented, joyful, joyous, blithe, carefree, light-hearted, cheery, good-humoured, sunny, optimistic, upbeat, enthusiastic, hearty, genial, jovial, jolly, merry, lively, animated, bright, chirpy, breezy, jaunty, buoyant, sparkling.
🔁 sad, dejected, depressed.

cheese

Varieties of cheese include:
Amsterdam, Bel Paese, Bleu d'Auvergne, Blue Cheshire, Blue Vinny, Boursin, Brie, Caboc, Caerphilly, Camembert, Carré, Cheddar, Cheshire, Churnton, cottage cheese, cream cheese, Crowdie, curd cheese, Danish blue, Derby, Dolcelatte, Dorset Blue, Double Gloucester, Dunlop, Edam, Emmental, Emmentaler, ewe cheese, Feta, fontina, fromage frais, goat cheese, Gloucester, Gorgonzola, Gouda, Gruyère, Huntsman, Jarlsberg®, Killarney, Lancashire, Leicester, Limburg(er), Lymeswold, mascarpone, Monterey Jack, mouse-trap, mozzarella, Neufchâtel, Orkney, Parmesan, pecorino, Petit Suisse, Pont-l'Évêque, Port Salut, processed cheese, provolone, quark, Red Leicester, Red Windsor, ricotta, Roquefort, sage Derby, Saint-Paulin, Stilton, stracchino, vegetarian cheese, Vacherin, Wensleydale.

chemical elements

The chemical elements (with their symbols) are: actinium (Ac), aluminium (Al), americium (Am), antimony (Sb), argon (Ar), arsenic (As), astatine (At), barium (Ba), berkelium (Bk), beryllium (Be), bismuth (Bi), boron (B), bromine (Br), cadmium (Cd), caesium (Cs), calcium (Ca), californium (Cf), carbon (C), cerium (Ce), chlorine (Cl), chromium (Cr), cobalt (Co), copper (Cu), curium (Cm), dubnium (Db), dysprosium (Dy), einsteinium (Es), erbium (Er), europium (Eu), fermium (Fm), fluorine (F), francium (Fr), gadolinium (Gd), gallium (Ga), germanium (Ge), gold (Au), hafnium (Hf), hahnium (Ha), helium (He), holmium (Ho), hydrogen (H), indium (In), iodine (I), iridium (Ir), iron (Fe), krypton (Kr), lanthanum (La), lawrencium (Lr), lead (Pb), lithium (Li), lutetium (Lu), magnesium (Mg), manganese (Mn), mendelevium (Md), mercury (Hg), molybdenum (Mo), neodymium (Nd), neon (Ne), neptunium (Np), nickel (Ni), niobium (Nb), nitrogen (N), nobelium (No), osmium (Os), oxygen (O), palladium (Pd), phosphorus (P), platinum (Pt), plutonium (Pu), polonium (Po), potassium (K), praseodymium (Pr), promethium (Pm), protactinium (Pa), radium (Ra), radon (Rn), rhenium (Re), rhodium (Rh), rubidium (Rb), ruthenium (Ru), rutherfordium (Rf), samarium (Sm), scandium (Sc), selenium (Se), silicon (Si), silver (Ag), sodium (Na), strontium (Sr), sulphur (S), tantalum (Ta), technetium (Tc), tellurium (Te), terbium (Tb), thallium (Tl), thorium (Th), thulium (Tm), tin (Sn), titanium (Ti), tungsten (W), uranium (U), vanadium (V), xenon (Xe), ytterbium (Yb), yttrium (Y), zinc (Zn), zirconium (Zr).

chemistry

Terms used in chemistry include: analytical chemistry, biochemistry, inorganic chemistry, organic chemistry, physical chemistry; acid, alkali, analysis, atom, atomic number, atomic structure, subatomic particles, base, bond, buffer, catalysis, catalyst, chain reaction, chemical bond, chemical compound, chemical element, chemical equation, chemical reaction, chemist, chlorination, combustion, compound, corrosion, covalent bond, crystal, cycle, decomposition, diffusion, dissociation, distillation, electrochemical cell, electrode, electron, electrolysis, emulsion, fermentation, fixation, formula, free radical, gas, halogen, hydrolysis, immiscible, indicator, inert gas, ion, ionic bond, isomer, isotope, lipid, liquid, litmus paper, litmus test, mass, matter, metallic bond, mixture, mole, molecule, neutron, noble gas, nucleus, oxidation, periodic table, pH, polymer, proton, radioactivity, reaction, reduction, respiration, salt, solids, solution, solvent, substance, suspension, symbol, synthesis, valency, zwitterion. *see also* **acid**; **atom**; **gas**; **mineral**.

cherish *v* foster, care for, look after, nurse, nurture, nourish, sustain, support, harbour, shelter, entertain, hold dear, value, prize, treasure.

chest *n* trunk, crate, box, case, casket, coffer, strongbox.

chew *v* masticate, gnaw, munch, champ, crunch, grind.

chief *adj* leading, foremost, uppermost, highest, supreme, grand, arch, premier, principal, main, key, central, prime, prevailing, predominant, pre-eminent, outstanding, vital, essential, primary, major.
🔳 minor, unimportant.
➤ *n* ruler, chieftain, lord, master, supremo, head, principal, leader, commander, captain, governor, boss, director, manager, superintendent, superior, ringleader.

chiefly *adv* mainly, mostly, for the most part, predominantly, principally, primarily, essentially, especially, generally, usually.

child *n* youngster, kid (*infml*), nipper (*infml*), brat (*infml*), baby, infant, toddler, rugrat (*sl*), ankle-biter (*sl*), sprog (*sl*), tot (*infml*), minor, juvenile, offspring, issue, progeny, descendant.

childhood *n* babyhood, infancy, boyhood, girlhood, schooldays, youth, adolescence, minority, immaturity.

childish *adj* babyish, boyish, girlish, infantile, puerile, juvenile, immature, silly, foolish, frivolous.
F3 mature, sensible.

childlike *adj* innocent, naïve, ingenuous, artless, guileless, credulous, trusting, trustful, simple, natural.

chill *v* **1** COOL, refrigerate, freeze, ice. **2** FRIGHTEN, terrify, dismay, dishearten, discourage, depress, dampen.
F3 **1** warm, heat.
➤ *n* coolness, cold, coldness, frigidity, rawness, bite, nip, crispness.
F3 warmth.

chilly *adj* **1** *chilly weather*: cold, fresh, brisk, crisp, nippy (*infml*), wintry. **2** *a chilly response*: cool, frigid, cold, unsympathetic, unwelcoming, aloof, stony, unfriendly, hostile.
F3 **1** warm. **2** friendly.

chime *v* sound, strike, toll, ring, peal, clang, dong, jingle, tinkle.

china *adj* porcelain, ceramic, pottery, earthenware, terracotta.

Chinese calendar

The animals representing the years in which people are born: rat, buffalo, tiger, rabbit (or hare), dragon, snake, horse, goat (or sheep), monkey, rooster, dog, pig.

chink *n* crack, rift, cleft, fissure, crevice, slot, opening, aperture, gap, space.

chip *n* **1** NOTCH, nick, scratch, dent, flaw. **2** FRAGMENT, scrap, wafer, sliver, flake, shaving, paring.
➤ *v* chisel, whittle, nick, notch, gash, damage.

chirp *v, n* chirrup, tweet, cheep, peep, twitter, warble, sing, pipe, whistle.

chivalrous *adj* gentlemanly, polite, courteous, gallant, heroic, valiant, brave, courageous, bold, noble, honourable.
F3 ungallant, cowardly.

chivalry *n* gentlemanliness, politeness, courtesy, gallantry, bravery, courage, boldness.

choice *n* option, alternative, selection, variety, pick, preference, say, decision, dilemma, election, discrimination, choosing, opting.
➤ *adj* best, superior, prime, plum, excellent, fine, exquisite, exclusive, select, hand-picked, special, prize, valuable, precious.
F3 inferior, poor.

choke *v* **1** THROTTLE, strangle, asphyxiate, suffocate, stifle, smother, suppress. **2** OBSTRUCT, constrict, congest, clog, block, dam, bar, close, stop. **3** COUGH, gag, retch.

choose *v* pick, select, single out, designate, predestine, opt for, plump for, vote for, settle on, fix on, adopt, elect, prefer, wish, desire, see fit.

choosy (*infml*) *adj* selective, discriminating, picky (*infml*), fussy, particular, finicky, fastidious, exacting.
F3 undemanding.

chop *v* cut, hack, hew, lop, sever, truncate, cleave, divide, split, slash.
◇ **chop up** cut (up), slice (up), divide, cube, dice, mince.

choppy *adj* rough, turbulent, tempestuous, stormy, squally, ruffled, wavy, uneven, broken.
F3 calm, still.

chore *n* task, job, errand, duty, burden.

chorus *n* **1** REFRAIN, burden, response, call, shout. **2** CHOIR, choristers, singers, vocalists, ensemble.

christen *v* baptize, name, call, dub, title, style, term, designate, inaugurate, use.

Christmas *n* Xmas, Noel, Yule, Yuletide.

chronic *adj* **1** INCURABLE, deep-seated, recurring, incessant, persistent, inveterate, confirmed, habitual, ingrained, deep-rooted. **2** (*infml*) *a chronic film*: awful, terrible, dreadful, appalling, atrocious.

🔁 **1** acute, temporary.

chronological *adj* historical, consecutive, sequential, progressive, ordered.

chubby *adj* plump, podgy, fleshy, flabby, stout, portly, rotund, round, tubby, paunchy.

🔁 slim, skinny.

chuckle *v* laugh, giggle, titter, snigger, chortle, snort, crow.

chunk *n* lump, hunk, mass, wodge (*infml*), wedge, block, slab, piece, portion.

church *n* chapel, house of God, cathedral, minster, abbey, temple.

> *Parts of a church or cathedral include*: aisle, almonry, altar, ambulatory, apse, arcade, arch, belfry, bell screen, bell tower, chancel, chapel, choir, clerestory, cloister, confessional, credence, crossing, crypt, fenestella, font, frontal, gallery, keystone, lectern, narthex, nave, parvis, pew, pinnacle, piscina, porch, portal, predella, presbytery, pulpit, reredos, rood, rood screen, sacristy, sanctuary, sedile, shrine, slype, spire, squint, stall, steeple, stoup, tomb, tower, transept, triforium, vault, vestry.

> *Names of church services include*: baptism, christening, Christingle, communion, Holy Communion, confirmation, dedication, Eucharist, evening service, evensong, funeral, Lord's Supper, marriage, Mass, High Mass, Vigil Mass, Midnight Mass, Nuptial Mass, Requiem Mass, Holy Matrimony, memorial service, morning prayers, morning service.

> *Names of canonical hours include*: compline, lauds, matins, none, prime, sext, terce, vespers.

cinema *n* **1** FILMS, pictures, movies (*infml*), flicks (*sl*), big screen. **2** PICTURE-HOUSE, picture-palace, fleapit (*infml*).

circle *n* group, band, company, crowd, set, clique, coterie, club, society, fellowship, fraternity.

> *Types of circle include*: annulus, ball, band, belt, circuit, circumference, coil, cordon, coronet, crown, curl, cycle, disc, discus, ellipse, girdle, globe, halo, hoop, lap, loop, orb, orbit, oval, perimeter, plate, revolution, ring, rotation, round, saucer, sphere, spiral, turn, tyre, wheel, wreath.

➤ *v* **1** RING, loop, encircle, surround, gird, encompass, enclose, envelop, hem in, circumscribe, circumnavigate. **2** ROTATE, revolve, pivot, gyrate, whirl, turn, coil, wind.

circuit *n* lap, orbit, revolution, tour, journey, course, route, track, round, beat, district, area, region, circumference, boundary, bounds, limit, range, compass, ambit.

circuitous *adj* roundabout, periphrastic, indirect, oblique, devious, tortuous, winding, meandering, rambling, labyrinthine.

🔁 direct, straight.

circular *adj* round, annular, ring-shaped, hoop-shaped, disc-shaped.
➤ *n* handbill, leaflet, pamphlet, notice, announcement, advertisement, letter.

circulate *v* **1** *circulate information*: spread, diffuse, broadcast, publicize, publish, issue, propagate, pass round, distribute. **2** GO ROUND, rotate, revolve, gyrate, whirl, swirl, flow.

circulation *n* **1** FLOW, blood-flow, motion, rotation, circling. **2** SPREAD, transmission, publication, dissemination, distribution.

circumference *n* circuit, perimeter, rim, edge, outline, boundary, border, bounds, limits, extremity, margin, verge, fringe, periphery.

circumstances *n* details, particulars, facts, items, elements, factors, conditions, state, state of affairs, situation, position, status, lifestyle, means, resources.

cistern n tank, reservoir, sink, basin, vat.

citadel n fortress, stronghold, bastion, castle, keep, tower, fortification, acropolis.

cite v quote, adduce, name, specify, enumerate, mention, refer to, advance, bring up.

citizen n city-dweller, townsman, townswoman, inhabitant, denizen, resident, householder, taxpayer, subject.

city n metropolis, town, municipality, conurbation, cosmopolis.

civic adj city, urban, municipal, borough, community, local, public, communal.

civil adj 1 POLITE, courteous, well-mannered, well-bred, courtly, refined, civilized, polished, urbane, affable, complaisant, obliging, accommodating. 2 civil affairs: domestic, home, national, internal, interior, state, municipal, civic.
🖙 1 uncivil, discourteous, rude. 2 international, military.

civility n politeness, courteousness, courtesy, breeding, refinement, urbanity, graciousness, affability, amenity.
🖙 discourtesy, rudeness.

civilization n progress, advancement, development, education, enlightenment, cultivation, culture, refinement, sophistication, urbanity.
🖙 barbarity, primitiveness.

civilize v tame, humanize, educate, enlighten, cultivate, refine, polish, sophisticate, improve, perfect.

civilized adj advanced, developed, educated, enlightened, cultured, refined, sophisticated, urbane, polite, sociable.
🖙 uncivilized, barbarous, primitive.

claim v 1 ALLEGE, pretend, profess, state, affirm, assert, maintain, contend,

hold, insist. 2 claim a refund: ask, request, require, need, demand, exact, take, collect.
➤ n 1 ALLEGATION, pretension, affirmation, assertion, contention, insistence. 2 APPLICATION, petition, request, requirement, demand, call, right, privilege.

clairvoyant adj psychic, prophetic, visionary, telepathic, extra-sensory.
➤ n psychic, fortune-teller, prophet, prophetess, visionary, seer, soothsayer, augur, oracle, diviner, telepath.

clammy adj damp, moist, sweaty, sweating, sticky, slimy, dank, muggy, heavy, close.

clamp n vice, grip, press, brace, bracket, fastener.
➤ v fasten, secure, fix, clinch, grip, brace.

clan n tribe, family, house, race, society, brotherhood, fraternity, confraternity, sect, faction, group, band, set, clique, coterie.

clap v 1 APPLAUD, acclaim, cheer. 2 SLAP, smack, pat, wallop (*infml*), whack (*infml*), bang.

clarify v 1 EXPLAIN, throw light on, illuminate, elucidate, gloss, define, simplify, resolve, clear up. 2 REFINE, purify, filter, clear.
🖙 1 obscure, confuse. 2 cloud.

clarity n clearness, transparency, lucidity, simplicity, intelligibility, comprehensibility, explicitness, unambiguousness, obviousness, definition, precision.
🖙 obscurity, vagueness, imprecision.

clash v 1 CRASH, bang, clank, clang, jangle, clatter, rattle, jar. 2 CONFLICT, disagree, quarrel, wrangle, grapple, fight, feud, war.
➤ n 1 CRASH, bang, jangle, clatter, noise. 2 a clash with the police: confrontation, showdown, conflict, disagreement, fight, brush.

clasp n 1 FASTENER, buckle, clip, pin, hasp, hook, catch. 2 HOLD, grip, grasp, embrace, hug.

➤ *v* **1** HOLD, grip, grasp, clutch, embrace, enfold, hug, squeeze, press. **2** FASTEN, connect, attach, grapple, hook, clip, pin.

class *n* **1** CATEGORY, classification, group, set, section, division, department, sphere, grouping, order, league, rank, status, caste, quality, grade, type, genre, sort, kind, species, genus, style. **2** *a French class*: lesson, lecture, seminar, tutorial, course.

Social classes/groups include: aristocracy, nobility, gentry, landed gentry, gentlefolk, élite, nob (*sl*), high society, top drawer (*infml*), upper class, Sloane Ranger (*sl*), ruling class, jet set, glitterati (*infml*), middle class, lower class, working class, bourgeoisie, proletariat, hoi-polloi, commoner, serf, plebeian, pleb (*infml*). *see also* **nobility**.

➤ *v* categorize, classify, group, sort, rank, grade, rate, designate, brand.

classic *adj* typical, characteristic, standard, regular, usual, traditional, time-honoured, established, archetypal, model, exemplary, ideal, best, finest, first-rate, consummate, definitive, masterly, excellent, ageless, immortal, undying, lasting, enduring, abiding.

☒ unrepresentative, second-rate.

➤ *n* standard, model, prototype, exemplar, masterwork, masterpiece, pièce de résistance.

classical *adj* elegant, refined, pure, traditional, excellent, well-proportioned, symmetrical, harmonious, restrained.

☒ modern, inferior.

classification *n* categorization, taxonomy, sorting, grading, arrangement, systematization, codification, tabulation, cataloguing.

classify *v* categorize, class, group, pigeonhole, sort, grade, rank, arrange, dispose, distribute, systematize, codify, tabulate, file, catalogue.

clause *n* article, item, part, section, subsection, paragraph, heading, chapter, passage, condition, proviso, provision, specification, point.

claw *n* talon, nail, pincer, nipper, gripper.

➤ *v* scratch, scrabble, scrape, graze, tear, rip, lacerate, maul, mangle.

clean *adj* **1** WASHED, laundered, sterile, aseptic, antiseptic, hygienic, sanitary, sterilized, decontaminated, purified, pure, unadulterated, fresh, unpolluted, uncontaminated, immaculate, spotless, unspotted, unstained, unsoiled, unsullied, perfect, faultless, flawless, unblemished. **2** *a clean life*: innocent, guiltless, virtuous, upright, moral, honest, honourable, respectable, decent, chaste. **3** SMOOTH, regular, straight, neat, tidy.

☒ **1** dirty, polluted. **2** dishonourable, indecent. **3** rough.

Ways to clean include: bath, bathe, bleach, brush, buff, cleanse, comb, decontaminate, deodorize, disinfect, distil, dry-clean, dust, filter, floss, flush, freshen, freshen up, fumigate, groom, hoover, launder, mop, muck out, pasteurize, pick, polish, purge, purify, refine, rinse, rub, sandblast, sanitize, scour, scrape, scrub, shampoo, shine, shower, soak, soap, sponge, spring-clean, spruce, spruce up, steep, sterilize, swab, sweep, swill, vacuum, valet, wash, wipe.

cleanser *n* soap, soap powder, detergent, cleaner, solvent, scourer, scouring powder, purifier, disinfectant.

clear *adj* **1** PLAIN, distinct, coherent, lucid, comprehensible, intelligible, explicit, precise, unambiguous, well-defined, apparent, evident, patent, obvious, manifest, conspicuous, unmistakable, unquestionable. **2** SURE, certain, positive, definite, convinced. **3** *clear water*: transparent, limpid, crystalline, glassy, see-through, clean, unclouded, colourless. **4** *a clear day*: cloudless, unclouded, fine, bright, sunny, light, luminous, undimmed. **5** UNOBSTRUCTED, unblocked, open, free,

empty, unhindered, unimpeded.
6 AUDIBLE, perceptible, pronounced,
distinct, recognizable.
🔁 **1** unclear, vague, ambiguous,
confusing. **2** unsure, muddled.
3 opaque, cloudy. **4** dull. **5** blocked.
6 inaudible, indistinct.
➤ v **1** UNBLOCK, unclog, decongest, free,
rid, extricate, disentangle, loosen.
2 CLEAN, wipe, erase, cleanse, refine,
filter, tidy, empty, unload. **3** ACQUIT,
exculpate, exonerate, absolve,
vindicate, excuse, justify, free, liberate,
release, let go.
🔁 **1** block. **2** dirty, defile. **3** condemn.
◇ **clear up 1** EXPLAIN, clarify, elucidate,
unravel, solve, resolve, answer. **2** TIDY,
order, sort, rearrange, remove.

clearance n **1** AUTHORIZATION,
sanction, endorsement, permission,
consent, leave, OK (*infml*), go-ahead,
green light (*infml*). **2** SPACE, gap,
headroom, margin, allowance.

clearing n space, gap, opening, glade,
dell.

clergy n clergymen, churchmen, clerics,
the church, the cloth, ministry,
priesthood.

clergyman n churchman, cleric,
ecclesiastic, divine, man of God,
minister, priest, reverend, father, vicar,
pastor, padre, parson, rector, canon,
dean, deacon, chaplain, curate,
presbyter, rabbi.

clerical adj **1** OFFICE, secretarial,
white-collar, official, administrative.
2 ECCLESIASTIC(AL), pastoral, ministerial,
priestly, episcopal, canonical,
sacerdotal.

Types of clerical vestment include:
alb, amice, biretta, cassock, chasuble,
chimere, clerical collar, dog collar
(*infml*), cope, cotta, cowl, dalmatic,
ephod, frock, Geneva bands, Geneva
gown, habit, hood, maniple, mantle,
mitre, mozzetta, pallium, rochet,
scapular, scarf, skullcap, soutane,
stole, surplice, tallith, tippet, tunicle,
wimple, yarmulka.

clever adj intelligent, brainy (*infml*),
bright, smart, witty, gifted, expert,
knowledgeable, adroit, apt, able,
capable, quick, quick-witted, sharp,
keen, shrewd, knowing, discerning,
cunning, ingenious, inventive,
resourceful, sensible, rational.
🔁 foolish, stupid, senseless, ignorant.

cliché n platitude, commonplace,
banality, truism, bromide, chestnut,
stereotype.

client n customer, patron, regular,
buyer, shopper, consumer, user, patient,
applicant.

cliff n bluff, face, rock face, scar, scarp,
escarpment, crag, overhang, precipice.

climate n weather, temperature,
setting, milieu, environment, ambience,
atmosphere, feeling, mood, temper,
disposition, tendency, trend.

climax n culmination, height, high
point, highlight, acme, zenith, peak,
summit, top, head.
🔁 nadir.

climb v ascend, scale, shin up, clamber,
mount, rise, soar, top.
◇ **climb down** retract, eat one's words,
back down, do a U-turn, retreat.

cling v clasp, clutch, grasp, grip, stick,
adhere, cleave, fasten, embrace, hug.

clip[1] v trim, snip, cut, prune, pare, shear,
crop, dock, poll, truncate, curtail,
shorten, abbreviate.

clip[2] v pin, staple, fasten, attach, fix,
hold.

clipping n cutting, snippet, quotation,
citation, passage, section, excerpt,
extract, clip.

clique n circle, set, coterie, group,
bunch, pack, gang, crowd, faction, clan.

cloak n cape, mantle, robe, wrap, coat,
cover, shield, mask, front, pretext.
➤ v cover, veil, mask, screen, hide,
conceal, obscure, disguise, camouflage.

clock n timepiece, chronometer.

Types of clock include: alarm clock,
digital clock, mantel clock, bracket

clock, carriage clock, cuckoo clock, longcase clock, grandfather clock, grandmother clock, speaking clock, Tim (*infml*), chronograph, sundial.

clog *v* block, choke, stop up, bung up, dam, congest, jam, obstruct, impede, hinder, hamper, burden.

EI unblock.

close¹ *v* **1** SHUT, fasten, secure, lock, bar, obstruct, block, clog, plug, cork, stop up, fill, seal, fuse, join, unite. **2** END, finish, complete, conclude, terminate, wind up, stop, cease.

EI 1 open, separate. **2** start.

➤ *n* end, finish, completion, conclusion, culmination, ending, finale, dénouement, termination, cessation, stop, pause.

close² *adj* **1** NEAR, nearby, at hand, neighbouring, adjacent, adjoining, impending, imminent. **2** INTIMATE, dear, familiar, attached, devoted, loving. **3** OPPRESSIVE, heavy, muggy, humid, sultry, sweltering, airless, stifling, suffocating, stuffy, unventilated. **4** MISERLY, mean, parsimonious, tight (*infml*), stingy, niggardly. **5** SECRETIVE, uncommunicative, taciturn, private, secret, confidential. **6** *a close translation*: exact, precise, accurate, strict, literal, faithful. **7** *pay close attention*: fixed, concentrated, intense, keen. **8** DENSE, solid, packed, cramped.

EI 1 far, distant. **2** cool, unfriendly. **3** fresh, airy. **4** generous. **5** open. **6** rough.

clot *n* lump, mass, thrombus, thrombosis, clotting, coagulation.

➤ *v* coalesce, curdle, coagulate, congeal, thicken, solidify, set, gel.

cloth *n* **1** FABRIC, material, stuff, textile. **2** RAG, face cloth, flannel, dishcloth, floorcloth, duster, towel.

clothe *v* dress, put on, robe, attire, deck, outfit, rig, vest, invest, drape, cover.

EI undress, strip, disrobe.

clothes *n* clothing, garments, wear, attire, garb, gear (*infml*), togs (*infml*), outfit, get-up (*infml*), dress, costume, wardrobe.

Clothes include: suit, trouser suit, dress suit, catsuit, jumpsuit, tracksuit, shell suit, wet suit; dress, frock, evening dress, shirtwaister, caftan, kimono, sari; skirt, mini skirt, dirndl, pencil skirt, pinafore skirt, divided skirt, culottes, kilt, sarong; cardigan, jumper, jersey, sweater, fleece, polo neck, turtleneck, guernsey, pullover, twin-set, shirt, dress shirt, sweatshirt, tee-shirt, T-shirt, waistcoat, blouse, smock, tabard, tunic; trousers, jeans, Levis®, denims, slacks, cords, cargo pants, combat trousers, flannels, drainpipes, bell-bottoms, dungarees, leggings, pedal-pushers, breeches, plus-fours, jodhpurs, Bermuda shorts, hot pants, shorts; bra, brassière, body stocking, camisole, liberty bodice, corset, girdle, garter, suspender belt, suspenders, shift, slip, petticoat, teddy, basque, bustier, briefs, pants, panties, thong, G-string, French knickers, camiknickers, pantihose, tights, stockings; underpants, boxer shorts, boxers (*infml*), Y-fronts, vest, string vest, singlet; swimsuit, bathing costume, bikini, swimming costume, swimming trunks, leotard, salopette; nightdress, nightie (*infml*), pyjamas, bedjacket, bedsocks, dressing-gown, housecoat, negligee; scarf, glove, mitten, muffler, earmuffs, legwarmers, sock, tie, bow tie, cravat, stole, shawl, belt, braces, cummerbund, veil, yashmak. *see also* **clerical**; **coat**; **footwear**; **hat**.

cloud *n* vapour, haze, mist, fog, gloom, darkness, obscurity.

➤ *v* mist, fog, blur, dull, dim, darken, shade, shadow, overshadow, eclipse, veil, shroud, obscure, muddle, confuse, obfuscate.

EI clear.

Types of cloud include: cirrus, cirrostratus, cirrocumulus, altocumulus, altostratus, cumulus, stratocumulus, nimbostratus, fractostratus, fractocumulus, cumulonimbus, stratus.

cloudy *adj* nebulous, hazy, misty, foggy, blurred, blurry, opaque, milky, muddy, dim, indistinct, obscure, dark, murky, sombre, leaden, lowering, overcast, dull, sunless.
☒ clear, bright, sunny, cloudless.

clown *n* buffoon, comic, comedian, joker, jester, fool, harlequin, pierrot.

club *n* **1** ASSOCIATION, society, company, league, guild, order, union, fraternity, group, set, circle, clique. **2** BAT, stick, mace, bludgeon, truncheon, cosh (*sl*), cudgel.
➤ *v* hit, strike, beat, bash, clout, clobber (*sl*), bludgeon, cosh (*sl*), batter, pummel.

clue *n* hint, tip, suggestion, idea, notion, lead, tip-off, pointer, sign, indication, evidence, trace, suspicion, inkling, intimation.

clump *n* cluster, bundle, bunch, mass, tuft, thicket.
➤ *v* tramp, clomp, stamp, stomp, plod, lumber, thump, thud.

clumsy *adj* **1** BUNGLING, ham-fisted, unhandy, unskilful, inept, bumbling, blundering, lumbering, gauche, ungainly, gawky (*infml*), unco-ordinated, awkward, ungraceful, uncouth. **2** ROUGH, crude, ill-made, shapeless, unwieldy, heavy, bulky, cumbersome, clunky (*infml*).
☒ **1** careful, graceful, elegant.

cluster *n* bunch, clump, batch, group, knot, mass, crowd, gathering, huddle, collection, assembly.
➤ *v* bunch, group, gather, collect, assemble, flock.

clutch *v* hold, clasp, grip, hang on to, grasp, seize, snatch, grab, catch, grapple, embrace.

clutter *n* litter, mess, jumble, untidiness, disorder, disarray, muddle, confusion.
➤ *v* litter, encumber, fill, cover, strew, scatter.

coach *n* trainer, instructor, tutor, teacher.
➤ *v* train, drill, instruct, teach, tutor, cram, prepare.

coagulate *v* clot, curdle, congeal, thicken, solidify, gel.
☒ melt.

coalition *n* merger, amalgamation, combination, integration, fusion, alliance, league, bloc, compact, federation, confederation, confederacy, association, affiliation, union.

coarse *adj* **1** ROUGH, unpolished, unfinished, uneven, lumpy, unpurified, unrefined, unprocessed. **2** *coarse humour*: bawdy, ribald, earthy, smutty, blue, vulgar, crude, offensive, foul-mouthed, boorish, loutish, rude, impolite, indelicate, improper, indecent, immodest.
☒ **1** smooth, fine. **2** refined, sophisticated, polite.

coast *n* coastline, seaboard, shore, beach, seaside.
➤ *v* free-wheel, glide, slide, sail, cruise, drift.

coat *n* **1** FUR, hair, fleece, pelt, hide, skin. **2** LAYER, coating, covering.

Types of coat include: overcoat, greatcoat, car coat, duffel coat, Afghan, blanket, frock coat, tailcoat, jacket, bomber jacket, dinner-jacket, donkey jacket, hacking jacket, reefer, shooting jacket, sports jacket, safari jacket, Eton jacket, matinee jacket, tuxedo, blazer, raincoat, trenchcoat, mackintosh, mac (*infml*), Burberry, parka, snorkel, anorak, cagoul, puffa jacket, windcheater, jerkin, blouson, cape, cloak, poncho.

➤ *v* cover, paint, spread, smear, plaster.

coating *n* covering, layer, dusting, wash, coat, blanket, sheet, membrane, film, glaze, varnish, finish, veneer, lamination, overlay.

coax *v* persuade, cajole, wheedle, sweet-talk (*infml*), soft-soap, flatter, beguile, allure, entice, tempt.

cocky *adj* arrogant, bumptious, self-important, conceited, vain, swollen-headed, egotistical, swaggering, brash, cocksure, self-assured, self-confident, overconfident.

🎦 humble, modest, shy.

code *n* 1 ETHICS, rules, regulations, principles, system, custom, convention, etiquette, manners. 2 *written in code*: cipher, secret language.

coerce *v* force, drive, compel, constrain, pressurize, bully, intimidate, browbeat, bludgeon, bulldoze, dragoon, press-gang.

coercion *n* force, duress, compulsion, constraint, pressure, bullying, intimidation, threats, browbeating, arm-twisting.

coffee

> *Types of coffee include*: black coffee, café noir, white coffee, café au lait, cappuccino, espresso, iced coffee, latte; Gaelic coffee, Irish coffee, Turkish coffee; Arabica, Blue Mountain, Columbian, Costa Rican, Java, Mocha, Kenyan; light roast, dark roast, French roast; filter, ground, instant, percolated; decaffeinated, decaf (*infml*).

coffer *n* casket, case, box, chest, trunk, strongbox, treasury, repository.

cognition *n* perception, awareness, knowledge, apprehension, discernment, insight, comprehension, understanding, intelligence, reasoning.

cohere *v* 1 STICK, adhere, cling, fuse, unite, bind, combine, coalesce, consolidate. 2 *the argument does not cohere*: agree, square, correspond, harmonize, hold, hang together.

🎦 1 separate.

coherent *adj* articulate, intelligible, comprehensible, meaningful, lucid, consistent, logical, reasoned, rational, sensible, orderly, systematic, organized.

🎦 incoherent, unintelligible, meaningless.

coil *v* wind, spiral, convolute, curl, loop, twist, writhe, snake, wreathe, twine, entwine.

➤ *n* roll, curl, loop, ring, convolution, spiral, corkscrew, helix, twist.

coin *v* invent, make up, think up, conceive, devise, formulate, originate, create, fabricate, produce, mint, forge.

➤ *n* piece, bit, money, cash, change, small change, loose change, silver, copper.

> *Types of coin include*: angel, bezant, bob (*infml*), copper, crown, dandiprat, denarius, dime, doubloon, ducat, farthing, florin, groat, guilder, guinea, half-crown, half guinea, halfpenny, half sovereign, ha'penny, krugerrand, louis d'or, moidore, napoleon, nickel, noble, obol, penny, pound, quid (*infml*), rap, real, sesterce, shilling, sixpence, solidus, sou, sovereign, spade guinea, stater, tanner (*infml*), thaler, threepenny bit.

coincide *v* coexist, synchronize, agree, concur, correspond, square, tally, accord, harmonize, match.

coincidence *n* 1 CHANCE, accident, eventuality, fluke (*infml*), luck, fortuity. 2 COEXISTENCE, conjunction, concurrence, correspondence, correlation.

coincidental *adj* 1 CHANCE, accidental, casual, unintentional, unplanned, flukey (*infml*), lucky, fortuitous. 2 COINCIDENT, coexistent, concurrent, simultaneous, synchronous.

🎦 1 deliberate, planned.

cold *adj* 1 UNHEATED, cool, chilled, chilly, chill, shivery, nippy, parky (*infml*), raw, biting, bitter, wintry, frosty, icy, glacial, freezing, frozen, arctic, polar. 2 UNSYMPATHETIC, unmoved, unfeeling, stony, frigid, unfriendly, distant, aloof, standoffish, reserved, undemonstrative, unresponsive, indifferent, lukewarm.

🎦 1 hot, warm. 2 friendly, responsive.

➤ *n* coldness, chill, chilliness, coolness, frigidity, iciness.

🎦 warmth.

cold-blooded *adj* cruel, inhuman, brutal, savage, barbaric, barbarous, merciless, pitiless, callous, unfeeling, heartless.
Ⓔ compassionate, merciful.

collaborate *v* conspire, collude, work together, co-operate, join forces, team up, participate.

collaboration *n* conspiring, collusion, association, alliance, partnership, teamwork, co-operation.

collaborator *n* co-worker, associate, partner, team-mate, colleague, assistant, accomplice, traitor, turncoat.

collapse *v* **1** *collapse with exhaustion*: faint, pass out, crumple. **2** FALL, sink, founder, fail, fold (*infml*), fall apart, disintegrate, crumble, subside, cave in.
➤ *n* failure, breakdown, flop, debacle, downfall, ruin, disintegration, subsidence, cave-in, faint, exhaustion.

colleague *n* workmate, co-worker, team-mate, partner, collaborator, ally, associate, confederate, confrère, comrade, companion, aide, helper, assistant, auxiliary.

collect *v* gather, assemble, congregate, convene, muster, rally, converge, cluster, aggregate, accumulate, amass, heap, hoard, stockpile, save, acquire, obtain, secure.
Ⓔ disperse, scatter.

collected *adj* composed, self-possessed, placid, serene, calm, unruffled, unperturbed, imperturbable, cool.
Ⓔ anxious, worried, agitated.

collection *n* **1** GATHERING, assembly, convocation, congregation, crowd, group, cluster, accumulation, conglomeration, mass, heap, pile, hoard, stockpile, store. **2** SET, assemblage, assortment, job-lot, anthology, compilation.

collective *adj* united, combined, concerted, co-operative, joint, common, shared, corporate, democratic, composite, aggregate, cumulative.
Ⓔ individual.

Collective nouns (by animal) include: shrewdness of *apes*, cete of *badgers*, sloth of *bears*, swarm of *bees*, obstinacy of *buffaloes*, clowder of *cats*, drove of *cattle*, brood of *chickens*, bask of *crocodiles*, murder of *crows*, herd of *deer*, pack of *dogs*, school of *dolphins*, dole of *doves*, team of *ducks*, parade of *elephants*, busyness of *ferrets*, charm of *finches*, shoal of *fish*, skulk of *foxes*, army of *frogs*, gaggle/skein of *geese*, tribe of *goats*, husk of *hares*, cast of *hawks*, brood of *hens*, bloat of *hippopotamuses*, string of *horses*, pack of *hounds*, troop of *kangaroos*, kindle of *kittens*, exaltation of *larks*, leap of *leopards*, pride of *lions*, swarm of *locusts*, tittering of *magpies*, troop of *monkeys*, watch of *nightingales*, family of *otters*, parliament of *owls*, pandemonium of *parrots*, covey of *partridges*, muster of *peacocks*, rookery of *penguins*, nye of *pheasants*, litter of *pigs*, school of *porpoises*, bury of *rabbits*, colony of *rats*, unkindness of *ravens*, crash of *rhinoceroses*, building of *rooks*, pod of *seals*, flock of *sheep*, murmuration of *starlings*, ambush of *tigers*, rafter of *turkeys*, turn of *turtles*, descent of *woodpeckers*, gam of *whales*, rout of *wolves*, zeal of *zebras*.

collector

Names of collectors and enthusiasts include: zoophile (*animals*), antiquary (*antiques*), tegestologist (*beer mats*), campanologist (*bell-ringing*), ornithologist (*birds*), bibliophile (*books*), audiophile (*broadcast and recorded sound*), lepidopterist (*butterflies*), cartophilist (*cigarette cards*), numismatist (*coins/medals*), gamer (*computer games*), conservationist (*countryside*), cruciverbalist (*crosswords*), environmentalist (*the environment*), xenophile (*foreigners*), gourmet (*good food and drink*), gastronome (*good food and drink*), discophile (*gramophone records*), chirographist (*handwriting*), hippophile (*horses*), entomologist (*insects*), phillumenist (*matches/matchboxes*), monarchist (*the monarchy*), deltiologist (*postcards*), arachnologist (*spiders/ arachnids*), philatelist (*stamps*), arctophile (*teddy bears*), etymologist (*words*).

collide *v* crash, bump, smash, clash, conflict, confront, meet.

collision *n* impact, crash, bump, smash, accident, pile-up, clash, conflict, confrontation, opposition.

colloquial *adj* conversational, informal, familiar, everyday, vernacular, idiomatic.
🔀 formal.

collude *v* conspire, plot, connive, collaborate, scheme, machinate, intrigue.

colonist *n* colonial, settler, immigrant, emigrant, pioneer.

colonize *v* settle, occupy, people, populate.

colony *n* settlement, outpost, dependency, dominion, possession, territory, province.

colossal *adj* huge, enormous, immense, vast, massive, gigantic, mega (*infml*), mammoth, monstrous, monumental.
🔀 tiny, minute.

colour *n* 1 HUE, shade, tinge, tone, tincture, tint, dye, paint, wash, pigment, pigmentation, coloration, complexion. 2 VIVIDNESS, brilliance, rosiness, ruddiness, glow, liveliness, animation.

The range of colours includes: red, crimson, scarlet, vermilion, cherry, cerise, magenta, maroon, burgundy, ruby, orange, tangerine, apricot, coral, salmon, peach, amber, brown, chestnut, mahogany, bronze, auburn, rust, copper, cinnamon, chocolate, tan, sepia, taupe, beige, fawn, yellow, lemon, canary, ochre, saffron, topaz, gold, chartreuse, green, eau de nil, emerald, jade, bottle, avocado, sage, khaki, turquoise, aquamarine, cobalt, blue, sapphire, gentian, indigo, navy, violet, purple, mauve, plum, lavender, lilac, pink, rose, magnolia, cream, ecru, milky, white, grey, silver, charcoal, ebony, jet, black.

➤ *v* 1 PAINT, crayon, dye, tint, stain, tinge. 2 BLUSH, flush, redden. 3 *colour one's judgement*: affect, bias, prejudice, distort, pervert, exaggerate, falsify.

colourful *adj* 1 MULTICOLOURED, kaleidoscopic, variegated, parti-coloured, vivid, bright, brilliant, rich, intense. 2 *a colourful description*: vivid, graphic, picturesque, lively, stimulating, exciting, interesting.
🔀 1 colourless, drab.

colourless *adj* 1 TRANSPARENT, neutral, bleached, washed out, faded, pale, ashen, sickly, anaemic. 2 INSIPID, lacklustre, dull, dreary, drab, plain, characterless, unmemorable, uninteresting, tame.
🔀 1 colourful. 2 bright, exciting.

column *n* 1 PILLAR, post, shaft, upright, support, obelisk. 2 LIST, line, row, rank, file, procession, queue, string.

comb *v* 1 *comb one's hair*: groom, neaten, tidy, untangle. 2 SEARCH, hunt, scour, sweep, sift, screen, rake, rummage, ransack.

combat *n* war, warfare, hostilities, action, battle, fight, skirmish, struggle, conflict, clash, encounter, engagement, contest, bout, duel.
➤ *v* fight, battle, strive, struggle, contend, contest, oppose, resist, withstand, defy.

combination *n* 1 BLEND, mix, mixture, composite, amalgam, synthesis, compound. 2 MERGER, amalgamation, unification, alliance, coalition, association, federation, confederation, confederacy, combine, consortium, syndicate, union, integration, fusion, coalescence, connection.

combine v merge, amalgamate, unify, blend, mix, integrate, incorporate, synthesize, compound, fuse, bond, bind, join, connect, link, marry, unite, pool, associate, co-operate.
🔃 divide, separate, detach.

come v advance, move towards, approach, near, draw near, reach, attain, arrive, enter, appear, materialize, happen, occur.
🔃 go, depart, leave.
◊ **come about** happen, occur, come to pass, transpire, result, arise.
◊ **come across** find, discover, chance upon, happen upon, bump into, meet, encounter, notice.
◊ **come along** arrive, happen, develop, improve, progress, rally, mend, recover, recuperate.
◊ **come apart** disintegrate, fall to bits, break, separate, split, tear.
◊ **come between** separate, part, divide, split up, disunite, estrange, alienate.
◊ **come down** descend, fall, reduce, decline, deteriorate, worsen, degenerate.
◊ **come in** enter, appear, show up (*infml*), arrive, finish.
◊ **come off** happen, occur, take place, succeed.
◊ **come on** begin, appear, advance, proceed, progress, develop, improve, thrive, succeed.
◊ **come out** result, end, conclude, terminate.
◊ **come out with** say, state, affirm, declare, exclaim, disclose, divulge.
◊ **come round 1** *come round from the anaesthetic*: recover, wake, awake. **2** YIELD, relent, concede, allow, grant, accede.
◊ **come through** endure, withstand, survive, prevail, triumph, succeed, accomplish, achieve.
◊ **come up** rise, arise, happen, occur, crop up.

comeback n return, reappearance, resurgence, revival, recovery.

comedian n comic, clown, humorist, wit, joker, wag.

comedown n anticlimax, let-down, disappointment, deflation, blow, reverse, decline, descent, demotion, humiliation, degradation.

comedy n farce, slapstick, clowning, hilarity, drollery, humour, wit, joking, jesting, facetiousness.

comfort v ease, soothe, relieve, alleviate, assuage, console, cheer, gladden, reassure, hearten, encourage, invigorate, strengthen, enliven, refresh.
➤ n **1** CONSOLATION, compensation, cheer, reassurance, encouragement, alleviation, relief, help, aid, support. **2** EASE, relaxation, luxury, snugness, cosiness, wellbeing, satisfaction, contentment, enjoyment.
🔃 **1** distress. **2** discomfort.

comfortable adj **1** SNUG, cosy, comfy (*infml*), relaxing, restful, easy, convenient, pleasant, agreeable, enjoyable, delightful. **2** AT EASE, relaxed, contented, happy. **3** AFFLUENT, well-off, well-to-do, prosperous.
🔃 **1** uncomfortable, unpleasant. **2** uneasy, nervous. **3** poor.

comic adj funny, hilarious, side-splitting, comical, droll, humorous, witty, amusing, entertaining, diverting, joking, facetious, light, farcical, ridiculous, ludicrous, absurd, laughable, priceless (*infml*), rich (*infml*).
🔃 tragic, serious.
➤ n comedian, gagster (*infml*), joker, jester, clown, buffoon, humorist, wit, wag.

coming adj next, forthcoming, impending, imminent, due, approaching, near, future, aspiring, rising, up-and-coming.
➤ n advent, approach, arrival, accession.

command v **1** ORDER, bid, charge, enjoin, direct, instruct, require, demand, compel. **2** LEAD, head, rule, reign, govern, control, dominate, manage, supervise.
➤ n **1** COMMANDMENT, decree, edict, precept, mandate, order, bidding, charge, injunction, directive, direction,

instruction, requirement. **2** *be in command*: power, authority, leadership, control, domination, dominion, rule, sway, government, management.

commander *n* leader, head, chief, boss, commander-in-chief, general, admiral, captain, commanding officer, officer.

commemorate *v* celebrate, solemnize, remember, memorialize, mark, honour, salute, immortalize, observe, keep.

commemoration *n* celebration, observance, remembrance, tribute, honouring, ceremony.

commence *v* begin, start, embark on, originate, initiate, inaugurate, open, launch.
🔁 finish, end, cease.

commend *v* **1** PRAISE, compliment, acclaim, extol, applaud, approve, recommend. **2** COMMIT, entrust, confide, consign, deliver, yield.
🔁 **1** criticize, censure.

comment *v* say, mention, interpose, interject, remark, observe, note, annotate, interpret, explain, elucidate, criticize.
➤ *n* statement, remark, observation, note, annotation, footnote, marginal note, explanation, elucidation, illustration, exposition, commentary, criticism.

commentary *n* narration, voice-over, analysis, description, review, critique, explanation, notes, treatise.

commentator *n* sportscaster, broadcaster, reporter, narrator, commenter, critic, annotator, interpreter.

commerce *n* trade, traffic, business, dealings, relations, dealing, trafficking, exchange, marketing, merchandising.

commercial *adj* trade, trading, business, sales, profit-making, profitable, sellable, saleable, popular, monetary, financial, mercenary, venal.

commission *n* **1** ASSIGNMENT, mission, errand, task, job, duty, function,

appointment, employment, mandate, warrant, authority, charge, trust. **2** COMMITTEE, board, delegation, deputation, representative. **3** *commission on a sale*: percentage, cut (*infml*), rake-off (*infml*), allowance, fee.
➤ *v* nominate, select, appoint, engage, employ, authorize, empower, delegate, depute, send, order, request, ask for.

commit *v* **1** *commit a crime*: do, perform, execute, enact, perpetrate. **2** ENTRUST, confide, commend, consign, deliver, hand over, give, deposit. **3** BIND, obligate, pledge, engage, involve.
◇ **commit oneself** decide, undertake, promise, pledge, bind oneself.

commitment *n* undertaking, guarantee, assurance, promise, word, pledge, vow, engagement, involvement, dedication, devotion, adherence, loyalty, tie, obligation, duty, responsibility, liability.
🔁 vacillation, wavering.

committee

Types of committee include: advisory committee, assembly, board, caucus, commission, congress, council, delegation, deputation, discussion group, focus group, group, jury, legation, mission, panel, quango, quorum, steering committee, steering group, sub-committee, synod, task force, team, think-tank (*infml*), user group, working party, workshop.

common *adj* **1** FAMILIAR, customary, habitual, usual, daily, everyday, routine, regular, frequent, widespread, prevalent, general, universal, standard, average, ordinary, plain, simple, workaday, run-of-the-mill, bog-standard (*infml*) undistinguished, unexceptional, conventional, accepted, popular, commonplace. **2** VULGAR, coarse, unrefined, crude, inferior, low, ill-bred, loutish, plebeian. **3** COMMUNAL, public, shared, mutual, joint, collective.
🔁 **1** uncommon, unusual, rare, noteworthy. **2** tasteful, refined.

commonplace *adj* ordinary, everyday, common, humdrum, pedestrian, banal, trite, widespread, frequent, hackneyed, stock, stale, obvious, worn out, boring, uninteresting, threadbare.
Ea memorable, exceptional.

commonsense *adj* commonsensical, matter-of-fact, sensible, level-headed, sane, sound, reasonable, practical, down-to-earth, pragmatic, hard-headed, realistic, shrewd, astute, prudent, judicious.
Ea foolish, unreasonable, unrealistic.

commotion *n* agitation, hurly-burly, turmoil, tumult, excitement, ferment, fuss, bustle, ado, to-do (*infml*), uproar, furore, ballyhoo (*infml*), hullabaloo (*infml*), racket, hubbub, rumpus, fracas, disturbance, bust-up (*infml*), disorder, riot.

communal *adj* public, community, shared, joint, collective, general, common.
Ea private, personal.

commune *n* collective, co-operative, kibbutz, community, fellowship, colony, settlement.
➤ *v* converse, discourse, communicate, make contact.

communicate *v* **1** ANNOUNCE, declare, proclaim, report, reveal, disclose, divulge, impart, inform, acquaint, intimate, notify, publish, disseminate, spread, diffuse, transmit, convey. **2** TALK, converse, commune, correspond, write, phone, telephone, email, contact.

communication *n* information, intelligence, intimation, disclosure, contact, connection, transmission, dissemination.

Forms of communication include: broadcasting, radio, wireless, television, TV, cable TV, digital TV, satellite, video, teletext; Internet, World Wide Web, webcast, website; newspaper, press, news, newsflash, magazine, journal, advertising, publicity, poster, leaflet, pamphlet, brochure, catalogue; post, dispatch, correspondence, letter, postcard, aerogram, telegram, Telemessage®, cable, wire (*infml*), chain letter, junk mail, mailshot; conversation, word, message, dialogue, speech, gossip, grapevine (*infml*); notice, bulletin, announcement, communiqué, circular, memo, note, report, statement, press release; SMS (or short message service), text message, telephone, intercom, call-conferencing, video-conferencing, answering machine, voice mail, walkie-talkie, bleeper, pager, tannoy, telex, teleprinter, facsimile, fax, computer, PDA (Personal Digital Assistant), email, word processor, typewriter, dictaphone, megaphone, loudhailer; radar, Morse code, semaphore, Braille, sign language. *see also* **telephone**.

communicative *adj* talkative, voluble, expansive, informative, chatty, sociable, friendly, forthcoming, outgoing, extrovert, unreserved, free, open, frank, candid.
Ea quiet, reserved, reticent, secretive.

community *n* district, locality, population, people, populace, public, residents, nation, state, colony, commune, kibbutz, society, association, fellowship, brotherhood, fraternity.

commute *v* **1** REDUCE, decrease, shorten, curtail, lighten, soften, mitigate, remit, adjust, modify, alter, change, exchange, alternate.
2 *commute by train*: travel, journey.

compact *adj* small, short, brief, terse, succinct, concise, condensed, compressed, close, dense, impenetrable, solid, firm.
Ea large, rambling, diffuse.

companion *n* fellow, comrade, friend, buddy (*infml*), crony (*infml*), intimate, confidant(e), ally, confederate, colleague, associate, partner, mate, consort, escort, chaperon(e), attendant, aide, assistant, accomplice, follower.

companionship n fellowship, comradeship, camaraderie, esprit de corps, support, friendship, company, togetherness, conviviality, sympathy, rapport.

company n 1 *a manufacturing company*: firm, business, concern, association, corporation, establishment, house, partnership, syndicate, cartel, consortium. 2 TROUPE, group, band, ensemble, set, circle, crowd, throng, body, troop, crew, party, assembly, gathering, community, society. 3 GUESTS, visitors, callers, society, companionship, fellowship, support, attendance, presence.

comparable adj similar, alike, related, akin, cognate, corresponding, analogous, equivalent, tantamount, proportionate, commensurate, parallel, equal.
Ea dissimilar, unlike, unequal.

compare v liken, equate, contrast, juxtapose, balance, weigh, correlate, resemble, match, equal, parallel.

comparison n juxtaposition, analogy, parallel, correlation, relationship, likeness, resemblance, similarity, comparability, contrast, distinction.

compartment n section, division, subdivision, category, pigeonhole, cubbyhole, niche, alcove, bay, area, stall, booth, cubicle, locker, carrel, cell, chamber, berth, carriage.

compassion n kindness, tenderness, fellow-feeling, humanity, mercy, pity, sympathy, commiseration, condolence, sorrow, concern, care.
Ea cruelty, indifference.

compassionate adj kind-hearted, kindly, tender-hearted, tender, caring, warm-hearted, benevolent, humanitarian, humane, merciful, clement, lenient, pitying, sympathetic, understanding, supportive.
Ea cruel, indifferent.

compatible adj harmonious, consistent, congruous, matching, consonant, accordant, suitable, reconcilable, adaptable, conformable, sympathetic, like-minded, well-matched, similar.
Ea incompatible, antagonistic, contradictory.

compel v force, make, constrain, oblige, necessitate, drive, urge, impel, coerce, pressurize, hustle, browbeat, bully, strongarm, bulldoze, press-gang, dragoon.

compelling adj forceful, coercive, imperative, urgent, pressing, irresistible, overriding, powerful, cogent, persuasive, convincing, conclusive, incontrovertible, irrefutable, gripping, enthralling, spellbinding, mesmeric, compulsive.
Ea weak, unconvincing, boring.

compensate v balance, counterbalance, cancel, neutralize, counteract, offset, redress, satisfy, requite, repay, refund, reimburse, indemnify, recompense, reward, remunerate, atone, redeem, make good, restore.

compensation n amends, redress, satisfaction, requital, repayment, refund, reimbursement, payback, indemnification, indemnity, damages, reparation, recompense, reward, payment, remuneration, return, restoration, restitution, consolation, comfort.

compete v vie, contest, fight, battle, struggle, strive, oppose, challenge, rival, emulate, contend, participate, take part.

competent adj capable, able, adept, efficient, trained, qualified, well-qualified, skilled, experienced, proficient, expert, masterly, equal, fit, suitable, appropriate, satisfactory, adequate, sufficient.
Ea incompetent, incapable, unable, inefficient.

competition n 1 CONTEST, championship, tournament, cup, event, race, match, game, quiz. 2 RIVALRY, opposition, challenge, contention,

conflict, struggle, strife, competitiveness, combativeness.
3 COMPETITORS, rivals, opponents, challengers, field.

competitive *adj* combative, contentious, antagonistic, aggressive, pushy, ambitious, keen, cut-throat.

competitor *n* contestant, contender, entrant, candidate, challenger, opponent, adversary, antagonist, rival, emulator, competition, opposition.

compile *v* compose, put together, collect, gather, garner, cull, accumulate, amass, assemble, marshal, organize, arrange.

complacent *adj* smug, self-satisfied, gloating, triumphant, proud, self-righteous, unconcerned, serene, self-assured, pleased, gratified, contented, satisfied.
E3 diffident, concerned, discontented.

complain *v* protest, grumble, grouse, gripe, beef, carp, kvetch (*US infml*), fuss, lament, bemoan, bewail, moan, whine, whinge (*infml*), groan, growl.

complaint *n* **1** PROTEST, objection, grumble, grouse, gripe, beef, moan, grievance, dissatisfaction, annoyance, fault-finding, criticism, censure, accusation, charge. **2** *a chest complaint*: ailment, illness, sickness, disease, malady, malaise, indisposition, affliction, disorder, trouble, upset.

complementary *adj* reciprocal, interdependent, correlative, interrelated, corresponding, matching, twin, fellow, companion.
E3 contradictory, incompatible.

complete *adj* **1** UTTER, total, absolute, downright, out-and-out, thorough, perfect. **2** FINISHED, ended, concluded, over, done, accomplished, achieved.
3 UNABRIDGED, unabbreviated, unedited, unexpurgated, integral, whole, entire, full, undivided, intact.
E3 1 partial. **2** incomplete. **3** abridged.
➤ *v* finish, end, close, conclude, wind up, terminate, finalize, settle, clinch, perform, discharge, execute, fulfil,

realize, accomplish, achieve, consummate, crown, perfect.

completion *n* finish, end, close, conclusion, termination, finalization, settlement, closure, discharge, fulfilment, realization, accomplishment, achievement, attainment, fruition, culmination, consummation, perfection.

complex *adj* complicated, intricate, elaborate, involved, convoluted, circuitous, tortuous, devious, mixed, varied, diverse, multiple, composite, compound, ramified.
E3 simple, easy.
➤ *n* **1** NETWORK, structure, system, scheme, organization, establishment, institute, development. **2** FIXATION, obsession, preoccupation, hang-up (*infml*), phobia.

complexion *n* **1** SKIN, colour, colouring, pigmentation. **2** LOOK, appearance, aspect, light, character, nature, type, kind.

complicate *v* compound, elaborate, involve, muddle, mix up, confuse, tangle, entangle.
E3 simplify.

complicated *adj* complex, intricate, elaborate, involved, convoluted, tortuous, difficult, problematic, puzzling, perplexing.
E3 simple, easy.

complication *n* difficulty, drawback, snag, obstacle, problem, ramification, repercussion, complexity, intricacy, elaboration, convolution, tangle, web, confusion, mixture.

compliment *n* flattery, admiration, favour, approval, congratulations, tribute, honour, accolade, bouquet, commendation, praise, eulogy.
E3 insult, criticism.
➤ *v* flatter, admire, commend, praise, extol, congratulate, applaud, salute.
E3 insult, condemn.

complimentary *adj* **1** FLATTERING, admiring, favourable, approving, appreciative, congratulatory,

commendatory, eulogistic.
2 *complimentary ticket*: free, gratis, honorary, courtesy.
F3 1 insulting, unflattering, critical.

comply *v* agree, consent, assent, accede, yield, submit, defer, respect, observe, obey, fall in, conform, follow, perform, discharge, fulfil, satisfy, meet, oblige, accommodate.
F3 defy, disobey.

component *n* part, constituent, ingredient, element, factor, item, unit, piece, bit, spare part.

compose *v* **1** CONSTITUTE, make up, form. **2** CREATE, invent, devise, write, arrange, produce, make, form, fashion, build, construct, frame. **3** CALM, soothe, quiet, still, settle, tranquillize, quell, pacify, control, regulate.

composed *adj* calm, tranquil, serene, relaxed, unworried, unruffled, level-headed, cool, collected, self-possessed, confident, imperturbable, unflappable, placid.
F3 agitated, worried, troubled.

composition *n* **1** MAKING, production, formation, creation, invention, design, formulation, writing, compilation, proportion.
2 CONSTITUTION, make-up, mixture, combination, form, structure, configuration, layout, arrangement, organization, harmony, consonance, balance, symmetry. **3** *a musical composition*: work, opus, piece, study, exercise.

composure *n* calm, tranquillity, serenity, ease, coolness, self-possession, confidence, assurance, self-assurance, aplomb, poise, dignity, imperturbability, placidity, equanimity, dispassion, impassivity.
F3 agitation, nervousness, discomposure.

compound *v* **1** COMBINE, amalgamate, unite, fuse, coalesce, synthesize, alloy, blend, mix, mingle, intermingle. **2** WORSEN, exacerbate, aggravate, complicate, intensify, heighten, magnify,

increase, augment.
➤ *n* alloy, blend, mixture, medley, composite, amalgam, synthesis, fusion, composition, amalgamation, combination.
➤ *adj* composite, mixed, multiple, complex, complicated, intricate.

comprehend *v* **1** UNDERSTAND, conceive, see, grasp, get it (*infml*), fathom, penetrate, tumble to (*infml*), realize, appreciate, know, apprehend, perceive, discern, take in, assimilate.
2 INCLUDE, comprise, encompass, embrace, cover.
F3 1 misunderstand.

comprehensible *adj* intelligible, understandable, coherent, explicit, clear, lucid, plain, straightforward, simple.
F3 incomprehensible, obscure.

comprehension *n* understanding, conception, grasp, realization, appreciation, knowledge, apprehension, perception, discernment, judgement, sense, intelligence.
F3 incomprehension, unawareness.

comprehensive *adj* thorough, exhaustive, full, complete, encyclopedic, compendious, broad, wide, extensive, sweeping, general, blanket, inclusive, all-inclusive, all-embracing, across-the-board.
F3 partial, incomplete, selective.

compress *v* press, squeeze, crush, squash, flatten, jam, wedge, cram, stuff, compact, concentrate, condense, contract, telescope, shorten, abbreviate, summarize.
F3 expand, diffuse.

comprise *v* consist of, include, contain, incorporate, embody, involve, encompass, embrace, cover.

compromise *v* **1** NEGOTIATE, bargain, arbitrate, settle, agree, concede, make concessions, meet halfway, adapt, adjust. **2** *compromise one's principles*: weaken, undermine, expose, endanger, imperil, jeopardize, risk, prejudice.
3 DISHONOUR, discredit, embarrass,

involve, implicate.

➤ *n* bargain, trade-off, settlement, agreement, concession, give and take, co-operation, accommodation, adjustment.

🔁 disagreement, intransigence.

compulsive *adj* 1 IRRESISTIBLE, overwhelming, overpowering, uncontrollable, compelling, driving, urgent. 2 *a compulsive gambler*: obsessive, hardened, incorrigible, irredeemable, incurable, hopeless.

compulsory *adj* obligatory, mandatory, imperative, forced, required, requisite, set, stipulated, binding, contractual.

🔁 optional, voluntary, discretionary.

computer *n* personal computer, PC, mainframe, processor, word processor, data processor, calculator, adding machine.

Computing terms include:
types of computer: mainframe, microcomputer, minicomputer, PC (personal computer), Apple Mac®, Mac (*infml*), iMac®, desktop, laptop, notebook, palmtop, handheld; *hardware*: chip, silicon chip, circuit board, motherboard, CPU (central processing unit), card, graphics card, sound card, video card, disk drive, floppy drive, hard drive, joystick, joypad, keyboard, light pen, microprocessor, modem, cable modem, monitor, mouse, pointer, printer, bubblejet printer, dot-matrix printer, inkjet printer, laser printer, screen, scanner, terminal, touchpad, trackball, VDU (visual display unit); *software*: program, application, abandonware, freeware, shareware; *types of memory*: backing storage, external memory, immediate access memory, internal memory, magnetic tape, RAM (Random Access Memory), ROM (Read Only Memory), CD-R (Compact Disc Recordable), CD-ROM (Compact Disc Read Only Memory), DVD-ROM (Digital Versatile Disc Read Only Memory);

types of disk: Compact Disc (CD), Digital Versatile Disc (DVD), magnetic disk, floppy disk, hard disk, optical disk, zip disk; *programming languages*: BASIC, C, C++, COBOL, Delphi, FORTRAN, Java, Pascal; *miscellaneous computing terms*: access, ASCII, autosave, backup, binary, BIOS (Basic Input/Output System), bitmap, boot, cold boot, reboot, warm boot, buffer, bug, bus, byte, gigabyte, kilobyte, megabyte, terabyte, cache, character, character code, client-server, compression, computer game, computer graphics, computer literate, computer simulation, cracking, cursor, data, databank, database, debugging, default, desktop publishing (DTP), digitizer, directory, DOS (disk operating system), editor, email (or e-mail), file, format, FTP (File Transfer Protocol), function, grammar checker, graphics, GUI (graphical user interface), hacking, icon, installation, interface, Internet, Linux, login, log off, log on, Mac OS (Macintosh® operating system), macro, menu, message box, metafile, MS-DOS (Microsoft® disk operating system), mouse mat, multimedia, network, output, P2P (peer-to-peer), package, password, peripheral, pixel, platform, port, parallel port, serial port, protocol, script, scripting language, scrolling, shell, shellscript, spellchecker, spreadsheet, sprite, subdirectory, template, toggle, toolbar, Unicode, Unix®, upgrade, user-friendly, user interface, utilities, video game, virtual reality (VR), virus, virus checker, window, Windows®, word processing, workstation, World Wide Web (WWW), worm, WYSIWYG (what you see is what you get). *see also* **Internet**.

con (*infml*) *v* trick, hoax, dupe, deceive, mislead, inveigle, hoodwink, bamboozle (*infml*), cheat, double-cross, swindle,

sting (*sl*), defraud, rip off (*sl*), rook.
➤ *n* confidence trick, trick, bluff, deception, swindle, sting (*sl*), fraud.

concave *adj* hollow, hollowed, cupped, scooped, excavated, sunken, depressed.
🔁 convex.

conceal *v* hide, obscure, disguise, camouflage, mask, screen, veil, cloak, cover, bury, submerge, smother, suppress, keep dark, keep quiet, hush up (*infml*).
🔁 reveal, disclose, uncover.

concede *v* 1 ADMIT, confess, acknowledge, recognize, own, grant, allow, accept. 2 YIELD, give up, surrender, relinquish, forfeit, sacrifice.
🔁 1 deny.

conceit *n* conceitedness, vanity, boastfulness, swagger, egotism, self-love, self-importance, cockiness, self-satisfaction, complacency, pride, arrogance.
🔁 modesty, diffidence.

conceited *adj* vain, boastful, swollen-headed, bigheaded (*infml*), egotistical, self-important, cocky, self-satisfied, complacent, smug, proud, arrogant, stuck-up (*infml*), toffee-nosed (*infml*).
🔁 modest, self-effacing, diffident, humble.

conceivable *adj* imaginable, credible, believable, thinkable, tenable, possible, likely, probable.
🔁 inconceivable, unimaginable.

conceive *v* 1 IMAGINE, envisage, visualize, see, grasp, understand, comprehend, realize, appreciate, believe, think, suppose. 2 INVENT, design, devise, formulate, create, originate, form, produce, develop.

concentrate *v* 1 FOCUS, converge, centre, cluster, crowd, congregate, gather, collect, accumulate. 2 APPLY ONESELF, think, pay attention, attend. 3 CONDENSE, evaporate, reduce, thicken, intensify.
🔁 1 disperse. 3 dilute.

concentrated *adj* 1 *concentrated liquid*: condensed, evaporated, reduced, thickened, dense, rich, strong, undiluted. 2 INTENSE, intensive, all-out, concerted, hard, deep.
🔁 1 diluted. 2 half-hearted.

concentration *n* 1 CONVERGENCE, centralization, cluster, crowd, grouping, collection, accumulation, agglomeration, conglomeration. 2 ATTENTION, heed, absorption, application, single-mindedness, intensity. 3 COMPRESSION, reduction, consolidation, denseness, thickness.
🔁 1 dispersal. 2 distraction. 3 dilution.

concept *n* idea, notion, plan, theory, hyphothesis, thought, abstraction, conception, conceptualization, visualization, image, picture, impression.

conception *n* 1 CONCEPT, idea, notion, thought. 2 KNOWLEDGE, understanding, appreciation, perception, visualization, image, picture, impression, inkling, clue. 3 INVENTION, design, birth, beginning, origin, outset, initiation, inauguration, formation. 4 *from conception to birth*: impregnation, insemination, fertilization.

concern *v* 1 UPSET, distress, trouble, disturb, bother, worry. 2 RELATE TO, refer to, regard, involve, interest, affect, touch.
➤ *n* 1 *a cause for concern*: anxiety, worry, unease, disquiet, care, sorrow, distress. 2 REGARD, consideration, attention, heed, thought. 3 *it's not my concern*: duty, responsibility, charge, job, task, field, business, affair, matter, problem, interest, involvement. 4 COMPANY, firm, business, corporation, establishment, enterprise, organization.
🔁 1 joy. 2 indifference.

concerned *adj* 1 ANXIOUS, worried, uneasy, apprehensive, upset, unhappy, distressed, troubled, disturbed, bothered, attentive, caring. 2 CONNECTED, related, involved, implicated, interested, affected.
🔁 1 unconcerned, indifferent, apathetic.

concerning *prep* about, regarding, with regard to, as regards, respecting, with reference to, relating to, in the matter of.

concerted *adj* combined, united, joint, collective, shared, collaborative, co-ordinated, organized, prearranged, planned.
E3 separate, unco-ordinated, disorganized.

concession *n* compromise, adjustment, grant, allowance, exception, privilege, favour, indulgence, permit, admission, acknowledgement.

concise *adj* short, brief, terse, succinct, pithy, compendious, compact, compressed, condensed, abridged, abbreviated, summary, synoptic.
E3 diffuse, wordy.

conclude *v* **1** INFER, deduce, assume, surmise, suppose, reckon, judge. **2** END, close, finish, complete, consummate, cease, terminate, culminate. **3** SETTLE, resolve, decide, establish, determine, clinch.
E3 **2** start, commence.

conclusion *n* **1** INFERENCE, deduction, assumption, opinion, conviction, judgement, verdict, decision, resolution, settlement, result, consequence, outcome, upshot, answer, solution. **2** END, close, finish, completion, consummation, termination, culmination, finale.

conclusive *adj* final, ultimate, definitive, decisive, clear, convincing, definite, undeniable, irrefutable, indisputable, incontrovertible, unarguable, unanswerable, clinching.
E3 inconclusive, questionable.

concoct *v* fabricate, invent, devise, contrive, formulate, plan, plot, hatch, brew, prepare, develop.

concoction *n* brew, potion, mixture, preparation, blend, mix, compound, creation, contrivance.

concrete *adj* real, actual, factual, solid, physical, material, substantial, tangible, touchable, perceptible, visible, firm, definite, specific, explicit.
E3 abstract, vague.

concurrent *adj* simultaneous, synchronous, contemporaneous, coinciding, coincident, concomitant, coexisting, coexistent.

condemn *v* disapprove, reprehend, reprove, upbraid, reproach, castigate (*fml*), blame, disparage, revile, denounce, censure, slam (*infml*), slate (*infml*), damn, doom, convict.
E3 praise, approve.

condemnation *n* disapproval, reproof, reproach, castigation (*fml*), blame, disparagement, denunciation, censure, thumbs-down (*infml*), damnation, conviction, sentence, judgement.
E3 praise, approval.

condensation *n* **1** *condensation of liquid*: distillation, liquefaction, precipitation, concentration, evaporation, reduction, consolidation. **2** ABRIDGEMENT, précis, synopsis, digest, contraction, compression, curtailment.

condense *v* **1** *condense a book*: shorten, curtail, abbreviate, abridge, précis, summarize, encapsulate, contract, compress, compact. **2** DISTIL, precipitate, concentrate, evaporate, reduce, thicken, solidify, coagulate.
E3 **1** expand. **2** dilute.

condescend *v* deign, see fit, stoop, bend, lower oneself, patronize, talk down.

condescending *adj* patronizing, disdainful, supercilious, snooty, snobbish, haughty, lofty, superior, lordly, imperious.
E3 gracious, humble.

condition *n* **1** CASE, state, lot, circumstances, position, situation, predicament, plight. **2** REQUIREMENT, obligation, prerequisite, terms, stipulation, proviso, qualification, limitation, restriction, rule. **3** *a heart condition*: disorder, defect, weakness, infirmity, problem, complaint, disease. **4** *out of condition*: fitness, health, state, shape, form, fettle, nick (*sl*).

➤ *v* indoctrinate, brainwash, influence, mould, educate, train, groom, equip, prepare, prime, accustom, season, temper, adapt, adjust, tune.

conditional *adj* provisional, qualified, limited, restricted, tied, relative, dependent, contingent.
🔁 unconditional, absolute.

conditions *n* surroundings, environment, milieu, setting, atmosphere, background, context, circumstances, situation, state.

condom *n* sheath, French letter (*sl*), johnnie (*sl*), rubber (*sl*), protective.

condone *v* forgive, pardon, excuse, overlook, ignore, disregard, tolerate, brook, allow.
🔁 condemn, censure.

conducive *adj* leading, tending, contributory, productive, advantageous, beneficial, favourable, helpful, encouraging.
🔁 detrimental, adverse, unfavourable.

conduct *n* 1 *good conduct*: behaviour, comportment, actions, ways, manners, bearing, attitude. 2 ADMINISTRATION, management, direction, running, organization, operation, control, supervision, leadership, guidance.
➤ *v* 1 ADMINISTER, manage, run, organize, orchestrate, chair, control, handle, regulate. 2 ACCOMPANY, escort, usher, lead, guide, direct, pilot, steer. 3 *conduct heat*: convey, carry, bear, transmit. 4 *conduct oneself*: behave, acquit, comport, act.

confer *v* 1 DISCUSS, debate, deliberate, consult, talk, converse. 2 BESTOW, award, present, give, grant, accord, impart, lend.

conference *n* meeting, convention, congress, convocation, symposium, assembly, forum, discussion, debate, consultation.

confess *v* admit, confide, own (up), come clean (*infml*), grant, concede, acknowledge, recognize, affirm, assert, profess, declare, disclose, divulge, expose.
🔁 deny, conceal.

confession *n* admission, acknowledgement, affirmation, assertion, profession, declaration, disclosure, divulgence, revelation, unburdening.
🔁 denial, concealment.

confide *v* confess, admit, reveal, disclose, divulge, whisper, breathe, tell, impart, unburden.
🔁 hide, suppress.

confidence *n* certainty, faith, credence, trust, reliance, dependence, assurance, composure, calmness, self-possession, self-confidence, self-reliance, self-assurance, boldness, courage.
🔁 distrust, diffidence.

confident *adj* sure, certain, positive, upbeat, convinced, assured, composed, self-possessed, cool, self-confident, self-reliant, self-assured, bold, fearless, dauntless, unabashed.
🔁 doubtful, diffident.

confidential *adj* secret, top secret, classified, restricted, hush-hush (*infml*), off-the-record, private, personal, intimate, privy.

confine *v* enclose, circumscribe, bound, limit, restrict, cramp, constrain, imprison, incarcerate, intern, cage, shut up, immure, bind, shackle, trammel, restrain, repress, inhibit.
🔁 free.

confinement *n* 1 IMPRISONMENT, incarceration, internment, custody, detention, house arrest. 2 CHILDBIRTH, birth, labour, delivery.
🔁 1 freedom, liberty.

confines *n* limits, bounds, border, boundary, frontier, circumference, perimeter, edge.

confirm *v* 1 ENDORSE, back, support, reinforce, strengthen, fortify, validate, verify, prove, evidence, authenticate, corroborate, substantiate. 2 ESTABLISH, fix, settle, clinch, ratify, sanction, approve.
🔁 1 refute, deny.

confirmation *n* ratification, sanction,

approval, assent, acceptance, agreement, endorsement, backing, support, validation, authentication, corroboration, substantiation, verification, proof, evidence, testimony.
▪ denial.

confirmed *adj* inveterate, fixed, entrenched, dyed-in-the-wool, rooted, established, long-established, long-standing, habitual, chronic, seasoned, hardened, incorrigible, incurable.

confiscate *v* seize, appropriate, expropriate, remove, take away, impound, sequester, commandeer.
▪ return, restore.

conflict *n* 1 DIFFERENCE, variance, discord, contention, disagreement, dissension, dispute, opposition, antagonism, hostility, friction, strife, unrest, confrontation. 2 BATTLE, war, warfare, combat, fight, contest, engagement, skirmish, set-to, fracas, brawl, quarrel, feud, encounter, clash.
▪ 1 agreement, harmony, concord.
➤ *v* differ, clash, collide, disagree, contradict, oppose, contest, fight, combat, battle, war, strive, struggle, contend.
▪ agree, harmonize.

conform *v* agree, accord, harmonize, match, correspond, tally, square, adapt, adjust, accommodate, comply, obey, follow.
▪ differ, conflict, rebel.

conformity *n* conventionality, orthodoxy, traditionalism, compliance, observance, allegiance, affinity, agreement, consonance, harmony, correspondence, congruity, likeness, similarity, resemblance.
▪ nonconformity, rebellion, difference.

confound *v* 1 CONFUSE, bewilder, baffle, perplex, mystify, bamboozle (*infml*), nonplus, surprise, amaze, astonish, astound, flabbergast (*infml*), dumbfound, stupefy. 2 *confound their plans*: thwart, upset, defeat, overwhelm, overthrow, destroy, demolish, ruin.

confront *v* face, meet, encounter, accost, address, oppose, challenge, defy, brave, beard.
▪ evade.

confrontation *n* encounter, clash, collision, showdown, conflict, fight, disagreement, battle, quarrel, set-to, engagement, contest.

confuse *v* 1 PUZZLE, baffle, perplex, mystify, confound, bewilder, disorient, disconcert, fluster, discompose, upset, embarrass, mortify. 2 MUDDLE, mix up, mistake, jumble, disarrange, disorder, tangle, entangle, involve, mingle.
▪ 1 enlighten, clarify.

confused *adj* 1 PUZZLED, baffled, confounded, perplexed, flummoxed (*infml*), nonplussed, bewildered, disorientated. 2 MUDDLED, jumbled, disarranged, disordered, untidy, disorderly, higgledy-piggledy (*infml*), chaotic, disorganized.
▪ 1 orderly.

confusion *n* 1 DISORDER, disarray, untidiness, mess, clutter, jumble, muddle, mix-up, disorganization, chaos, turmoil, commotion, upheaval.
2 MISUNDERSTANDING, puzzlement, perplexity, mystification, bewilderment.
▪ 1 order. 2 clarity.

congeal *v* clot, curdle, coalesce, coagulate, thicken, stiffen, harden, solidify, set, gel, freeze.
▪ dissolve, melt.

congested *adj* clogged, blocked, jammed, packed, stuffed, crammed, full, crowded, overcrowded, overflowing, teeming.
▪ clear.

congestion *n* clogging, blockage, overcrowding, jam, traffic jam, snarl-up, gridlock, bottleneck.

conglomeration *n* mass, agglomeration, aggregation, accumulation, collection, assemblage, composite, medley, hotchpotch.

congratulate *v* praise, felicitate, compliment, wish well.
▪ commiserate.

congregate v gather, assemble, collect, muster, rally, rendezvous, meet, convene, converge, flock, crowd, throng, mass, accumulate, cluster, clump, conglomerate.
🔁 disperse.

congregation n assembly, crowd, throng, multitude, host, flock, parishioners, parish, laity, fellowship.

conical adj cone-shaped, pyramidal, tapering, tapered, pointed.

conjecture v speculate, theorize, hypothesize, guess, estimate, reckon, suppose, surmise, assume, infer, imagine, suspect.
➤ n speculation, theory, hypothesis, notion, guesswork, guess, estimate, supposition, surmise, assumption, presumption, conclusion, inference, extrapolation, projection.

conjure v summon, invoke, rouse, raise, bewitch, charm, fascinate, compel.
◊ **conjure up** evoke, create, produce, excite, awaken, recollect, recall.

connect v join, link, unite, couple, combine, fasten, affix, attach, relate, associate, ally.
🔁 disconnect, cut off, detach.

connected adj joined, linked, united, coupled, combined, related, akin, associated, affiliated, allied.
🔁 disconnected, unconnected.

connection n junction, coupling, fastening, attachment, bond, tie, link, association, alliance, relation, relationship, interrelation, contact, communication, correlation, correspondence, relevance.
🔁 disconnection.

connoisseur n authority, specialist, expert, judge, devotee, buff (*infml*), gourmet, epicure.

connotation n implication, suggestion, hint, nuance, undertone, overtone, colouring, association.

conquer v **1** DEFEAT, beat, overthrow, vanquish, rout, overrun, best, worst, get the better of, overcome, surmount, win, succeed, triumph, prevail, overpower, master, crush, subdue, quell, subjugate, humble. **2** SEIZE, take, annex, occupy, possess, acquire, obtain.
🔁 **1** surrender, yield, give in.

conqueror n victor, winner, champion, champ (*infml*), hero, vanquisher, master, lord.

conquest n victory, triumph, defeat, overthrow, coup, rout, mastery, subjugation, subjection, invasion, occupation, capture, appropriation, annexation, acquisition.

conscience n principles, standards, morals, ethics, scruples, qualms.

conscientious adj diligent, hard-working, scrupulous, painstaking, thorough, meticulous, punctilious, particular, careful, attentive, responsible, upright, honest, faithful, dutiful.
🔁 careless, irresponsible, unreliable.

conscious adj **1** AWAKE, alive, responsive, sentient, sensible, rational, reasoning, alert. **2** AWARE, self-conscious, heedful, mindful, knowing, deliberate, intentional, calculated, premeditated, studied, wilful, voluntary.
🔁 **1** unconscious. **2** unaware.

consciousness n awareness, sentience, sensibility, knowledge, intuition, realization, recognition.
🔁 unconciousness.

consecrate v sanctify, hallow, bless, dedicate, devote, ordain, venerate, revere, exalt.

consecutive adj sequential, successive, continuous, unbroken, uninterrupted, following, succeeding, running.
🔁 discontinuous.

consent v agree, concur, accede, assent, approve, permit, allow, grant, admit, concede, acquiesce, yield, comply.
🔁 refuse, decline, oppose.
➤ n agreement, concurrence, assent, approval, permission, go-ahead, green

light (*infml*), sanction, concession, acquiescence, compliance.
🖪 disagreement, refusal, opposition.

consequence *n* **1** RESULT, outcome, issue, end, upshot, effect, side effect, repercussion. **2** *of no consequence*: importance, significance, concern, value, weight, note, eminence, distinction.
🖪 **1** cause. **2** unimportance, insignificance.

consequent *adj* resultant, resulting, ensuing, subsequent, following, successive, sequential.

conservation *n* keeping, safe-keeping, custody, saving, economy, husbandry, maintenance, upkeep, preservation, protection, safeguarding, ecology, environmentalism.
🖪 destruction.

conservative *adj* Tory, right-wing, hidebound, die-hard, reactionary, establishmentarian, unprogressive, conventional, traditional, moderate, middle-of-the-road, cautious, guarded, sober, button-down (*infml*).
🖪 left-wing, liberal, radical, innovative.
➤ *n* Tory, right-winger, die-hard, stick-in-the-mud, reactionary, traditionalist, moderate.
🖪 left-winger, liberal, radical.

conservatory *n* greenhouse, glasshouse, hothouse.

conserve *v* keep, save, store up, hoard, maintain, preserve, protect, guard, safeguard.
🖪 use, waste, squander.

consider *v* **1** PONDER, deliberate, reflect, contemplate, meditate, muse, mull over, chew over, examine, study, weigh, respect, remember, take into account. **2** *consider it an honour*: regard, deem, think, believe, judge, rate, count.

considerable *adj* great, large, big, sizable, substantial, tidy (*infml*), ample, plentiful, abundant, lavish, marked, noticeable, perceptible, appreciable, reasonable, tolerable, respectable,

important, significant, noteworthy, distinguished, influential.
🖪 small, slight, insignificant, unremarkable.

considerate *adj* kind, thoughtful, caring, attentive, obliging, helpful, charitable, unselfish, altruistic, gracious, sensitive, tactful, discreet.
🖪 inconsiderate, thoughtless, selfish.

consideration *n* **1** THOUGHT, deliberation, reflection, contemplation, meditation, examination, analysis, scrutiny, review, attention, notice, regard. **2** KINDNESS, thoughtfulness, care, attention, regard, respect.
🖪 **1** disregard. **2** thoughtlessness.

consign *v* entrust, commit, devote, hand over, transfer, deliver, convey, ship, banish, relegate.

consignment *n* cargo, shipment, load, batch, delivery, goods.

consist of comprise, be composed of, contain, include, incorporate, embody, embrace, involve, amount to.

consistency *n* **1** *of the consistency of porridge*: viscosity, thickness, density, firmness. **2** STEADINESS, regularity, evenness, uniformity, sameness, identity, constancy, steadfastness. **3** AGREEMENT, accordance, correspondence, congruity, compatibility, harmony.
🖪 **3** inconsistency.

consistent *adj* **1** STEADY, stable, regular, uniform, unchanging, undeviating, constant, persistent, unfailing, dependable. **2** AGREEING, accordant, consonant, congruous, compatible, harmonious, logical.
🖪 **1** irregular, erratic. **2** inconsistent.

console *v* comfort, cheer, hearten, encourage, relieve, soothe, calm.
🖪 upset, agitate.

consolidate *v* reinforce, strengthen, secure, stabilize, unify, unite, join, combine, amalgamate, fuse, cement, compact, condense, thicken, harden, solidify.

conspicuous *adj* apparent, visible, noticeable, marked, clear, obvious, evident, patent, manifest, prominent, striking, blatant, flagrant, glaring, ostentatious, showy, flashy, garish.
▪ inconspicuous, concealed, hidden.

conspiracy *n* plot, scheme, intrigue, machination, fix (*infml*), frame-up (*infml*), collusion, league, treason.

conspirator *n* conspirer, plotter, schemer, intriguer, traitor.

conspire *v* plot, scheme, intrigue, manoeuvre, connive, collude, hatch, devise.

constancy *n* **1** STABILITY, steadiness, permanence, firmness, regularity, uniformity, resolution, perseverance, tenacity. **2** LOYALTY, faithfulness, fidelity, devotion.
▪ **1** change, irregularity. **2** fickleness.

constant *adj* **1** CONTINUOUS, unbroken, never-ending, non-stop, endless, interminable, ceaseless, incessant, eternal, everlasting, perpetual, continual, unremitting, relentless, persistent, resolute, persevering, unflagging, unwavering, stable, steady, unchanging, unvarying, changeless, immutable, invariable, unalterable, fixed, permanent, firm, even, regular, uniform. **2** *a constant friend*: loyal, faithful, staunch, steadfast, dependable, trustworthy, true, devoted.
▪ **1** variable, irregular, fitful, occasional. **2** disloyal, fickle.

constellation

The constellations (with common English names) are: Andromeda, Antlia (Air Pump), Apus (Bird of Paradise), Aquarius (Water Bearer), Aquila (Eagle), Ara (Altar), Aries (Ram), Auriga (Charioteer), Boötes (Herdsman), Caelum (Chisel), Camelopardalis (Giraffe), Cancer (Crab), Canes Venatici (Hunting Dogs), Canis Major (Great Dog), Canis Minor (Little Dog), Capricornus (Sea Goat), Carina (Keel), Cassiopeia, Centaurus (Centaur), Cepheus, Cetus (Whale), Chamaeleon (Chameleon), Circinus (Compasses), Columba (Dove), Coma Berenices (Berenice's Hair), Corona Australis (Southern Crown), Corona Borealis (Northern Crown), Corvus (Crow), Crater (Cup), Crux (Southern Cross), Cygnus (Swan), Delphinus (Dolphin), Dorado (Swordfish), Draco (Dragon), Equuleus (Little Horse), Eridanus (River Eridanus), Fornax (Furnace), Gemini (Twins), Grus (Crane), Hercules, Horologium (Clock), Hydra (Sea Serpent), Hydrus (Water Snake), Indus (Indian), Lacerta (Lizard), Leo (Lion), Leo Minor (Little Lion), Lepus (Hare), Libra (Scales), Lupus (Wolf), Lynx, Lyra (Harp), Mensa (Table), Microscopium (Microscope), Monoceros (Unicorn), Musca (Fly), Norma (Level), Octans (Octant), Ophiuchus (Serpent Bearer), Orion, Pavo (Peacock), Pegasus (Winged Horse), Perseus, Phoenix, Pictor (Easel), Pisces (Fishes), Piscis Austrinus (Southern Fish), Puppis (Ship's Stern), Pyxis (Mariner's Compass), Reticulum (Net), Sagitta (Arrow), Sagittarius (Archer), Scorpius (Scorpion), Sculptor, Scutum (Shield), Serpens (Serpent), Sextans (Sextant), Taurus (Bull), Telescopium (Telescope), Triangulum (Triangle), Triangulum Australe (Southern Triangle), Tucana (Toucan), Ursa Major (Great Bear), Ursa Minor (Little Bear), Vela (Sails), Virgo (Virgin), Volans (Flying Fish), Vulpecula (Fox). *see also* **star**.

constituent *adj* component, integral, essential, basic, intrinsic, inherent.
➤ *n* ingredient, element, factor, principle, component, part, bit, section, unit.
▪ whole.

constitute *v* represent, make up, compose, comprise, form, create, establish, set up, found.

constrain *v* **1** FORCE, compel, oblige, necessitate, drive, impel, urge. **2** LIMIT, confine, constrict, restrain, check, curb, bind.

constrained *adj* uneasy,

embarrassed, inhibited, reticent, reserved, guarded, stiff, forced, unnatural.
F3 relaxed, free.

constraint n 1 FORCE, duress, compulsion, coercion, pressure, necessity, deterrent. 2 RESTRICTION, limitation, hindrance, restraint, check, curb, damper.

constrict v squeeze, compress, pinch, cramp, narrow, tighten, contract, shrink, choke, strangle, inhibit, limit, restrict.
F3 expand.

construct v build, erect, raise, elevate, make, manufacture, fabricate, assemble, put together, compose, form, shape, fashion, model, design, engineer, create, found, establish, formulate.
F3 demolish, destroy.

construction n building, edifice, erection, structure, fabric, form, shape, figure, model, manufacture, fabrication, assembly, composition, constitution, formation, creation.
F3 destruction.

constructive adj practical, productive, positive, helpful, useful, valuable, beneficial, advantageous.
F3 destructive, negative, unhelpful.

consult v refer to, ask, question, interrogate, confer, discuss, debate, deliberate.

consultant n adviser, expert, authority, specialist.

consultation n discussion, deliberation, dialogue, conference, meeting, hearing, interview, examination, appointment, session.

consume v 1 EAT, drink, swallow, devour, gobble. 2 USE, absorb, spend, expend, deplete, drain, exhaust, use up, dissipate, squander, waste. 3 DESTROY, demolish, annihilate, devastate, ravage.

consumer n user, end-user, customer, buyer, purchaser, shopper.

consumption n use, utilization, spending, expenditure, depletion, exhaustion, waste.

contact n touch, impact, juxtaposition, contiguity, communication, meeting, junction, union, connection, association.
➤ v approach, apply to, reach, get hold of, get in touch with, telephone, phone, ring, call, notify.

contagious adj infectious, catching, communicable, transmissible, spreading, epidemic.

contain v 1 INCLUDE, comprise, incorporate, embody, involve, embrace, enclose, hold, accommodate, seat. 2 contain one's feelings: repress, stifle, restrain, control, check, curb, limit.
F3 1 exclude.

container n receptacle, vessel, holder.

Types of container include: bag, barrel, basin, basket, bath, beaker, bin, bottle, bowl, box, bucket, can, canister, carton, case, cask, casket, cauldron, chest, churn, cistern, crate, crock, cup, cylinder, dish, drum, dustbin, glass, hamper, jar, jug, keg, kettle, locker, mug, pack, packet, pail, pan, pannier, pitcher, pot, punnet, sack, suitcase, tank, tea caddy, tea chest, teapot, tin, trough, trunk, tub, tube, tumbler, tureen, urn, vase, waste bin, waste-paper basket, water-butt, well. *see also* **box**.

---

contaminate v infect, pollute, adulterate, taint, soil, sully, defile, corrupt, deprave, debase, stain, tarnish.
F3 purify.

contemplate v 1 MEDITATE, reflect on, ponder, mull over, deliberate, consider, regard, view, survey, observe, study, examine, inspect, scrutinize. 2 EXPECT, foresee, envisage, plan, design, propose, intend, mean.

contemporary adj 1 MODERN, current, present, present-day, recent, latest, up to date, fashionable, up-to-the-minute, ultra-modern. 2 CONTEMPORANEOUS, coexistent, concurrent, synchronous, simultaneous.
F3 1 out of date, old-fashioned.

contempt *n* scorn, disdain, condescension, derision, ridicule, mockery, disrespect, dishonour, disregard, neglect, dislike, loathing, detestation.
⊟ admiration, regard.

contemptible *adj* despicable, shameful, ignominious, low, mean, vile, detestable, loathsome, abject, wretched, pitiful, paltry, worthless.
⊟ admirable, honourable.

contemptuous *adj* scornful, disdainful, sneering, supercilious, condescending, arrogant, haughty, high and mighty, cynical, derisive, insulting, disrespectful, insolent.
⊟ humble, respectful.

contend *v* 1 MAINTAIN, hold, argue, allege, assert, declare, affirm.
2 COMPETE, vie, contest, dispute, clash, wrestle, grapple, struggle, strive, cope.

content *v* satisfy, humour, indulge, gratify, please, delight, appease, pacify, placate.
⊟ displease.
➤ *n* 1 SUBSTANCE, matter, essence, gist, meaning, significance, text, subject matter, ideas, contents, load, burden.
2 CAPACITY, volume, size, measure.
➤ *adj* satisfied, fulfilled, contented, untroubled, pleased, happy, willing.
⊟ dissatisfied, troubled.

contented *adj* happy, glad, pleased, cheerful, comfortable, relaxed, content, satisfied.
⊟ discontented, unhappy, annoyed.

contentment *n* contentedness, happiness, gladness, pleasure, gratification, comfort, ease, complacency, peace, peacefulness, serenity, equanimity, content, satisfaction, fulfilment.
⊟ unhappiness, discontent, dissatisfaction.

contents *n* 1 *the contents of the package*: constituents, parts, elements, ingredients, content, load, items.
2 CHAPTERS, divisions, subjects, topics, themes.

contest *n* competition, game, match, tournament, encounter, fight, battle, set-to, combat, conflict, struggle, dispute, debate, controversy.
➤ *v* 1 DISPUTE, debate, question, doubt, challenge, oppose, argue against, litigate, deny, refute. 2 COMPETE, vie, contend, strive, fight.
⊟ 1 accept.

contestant *n* competitor, contender, player, participant, entrant, candidate, aspirant, rival, opponent.

context *n* background, setting, surroundings, framework, frame of reference, situation, position, circumstances, conditions.

continent *n* land mass, mainland, terra firma.

> *The continents of the world are*: Africa, Antarctica, Asia, Australia, Europe, North America, South America.

contingent *n* body, company, deputation, delegation, detachment, section, group, set, batch, quota, complement.

continual *adj* constant, perpetual, incessant, interminable, eternal, everlasting, regular, frequent, recurrent, repeated.
⊟ occasional, intermittent, temporary.

continuation *n* resumption, maintenance, prolongation, extension, development, furtherance, addition, supplement.
⊟ cessation, termination.

continue *v* resume, recommence, carry on, go on, proceed, persevere, stick at, persist, last, endure, survive, remain, abide, stay, rest, pursue, sustain, maintain, lengthen, prolong, extend, project.
⊟ discontinue, stop.

continuity *n* flow, progression, succession, sequence, linkage, interrelationship, connection, cohesion.
⊟ discontinuity.

continuous *adj* unbroken,

uninterrupted, consecutive, non-stop, endless, ceaseless, unending, unceasing, constant, unremitting, prolonged, extended, continued, lasting.

🔁 discontinuous, broken, sporadic.

contort v twist, distort, warp, wrench, disfigure, deform, misshape, convolute, gnarl, knot, writhe, squirm, wriggle.

contour n outline, silhouette, shape, form, figure, curve, relief, profile, character, aspect.

contract v **1** SHRINK, lessen, diminish, reduce, shorten, curtail, abbreviate, abridge, condense, compress, constrict, narrow, tighten, tense, shrivel, wrinkle. **2** contract pneumonia: catch, get, go down with, develop. **3** PLEDGE, promise, undertake, agree, stipulate, arrange, negotiate, bargain.

🔁 **1** expand, enlarge, lengthen.

➤ n bond, commitment, engagement, covenant, treaty, convention, pact, compact, agreement, transaction, deal, bargain, settlement, arrangement, understanding.

contradict v deny, disaffirm, confute, challenge, oppose, impugn (fml), dispute, counter, negate, gainsay.

🔁 agree, confirm, corroborate.

contradictory adj contrary, opposite, paradoxical, conflicting, discrepant, inconsistent, incompatible, antagonistic, irreconcilable, opposed, repugnant.

🔁 consistent.

contraption n contrivance, device, gadget, apparatus, rig, machine, mechanism.

contrary adj **1** OPPOSITE, counter, reverse, conflicting, antagonistic, opposed, adverse, hostile. **2** PERVERSE, awkward, disobliging, difficult, wayward, obstinate, intractable, cantankerous, stroppy (infml).

🔁 **1** like. **2** obliging.

➤ n opposite, converse, reverse.

contrast n difference, dissimilarity, disparity, divergence, distinction, differentiation, comparison, foil, antithesis, opposition.

🔁 similarity.

➤ v compare, differentiate, distinguish, discriminate, differ, oppose, clash, conflict.

contravene v infringe, violate, break, breach, disobey, defy, flout, transgress.

🔁 uphold, observe, obey.

contribute v donate, subscribe, chip in (infml), add, give, bestow, provide, supply, furnish, help, lead, conduce.

🔁 withhold.

contribution n donation, subscription, gift, gratuity, handout, grant, offering, input, addition.

contributor n **1** DONOR, subscriber, giver, patron, benefactor, sponsor, backer, supporter. **2** WRITER, journalist, reporter, correspondent, freelance.

contrite adj sorry, regretful, remorseful, repentant, penitent, conscience-stricken, chastened, humble, ashamed.

contrivance n **1** INVENTION, device, contraption, gadget, implement, appliance, machine, mechanism, apparatus, equipment, gear. **2** STRATAGEM, ploy, trick, dodge, ruse, expedient, plan, design, project, scheme, plot, intrigue, machination.

contrived adj unnatural, artificial, false, forced, strained, laboured, mannered, elaborate, overdone.

🔁 natural, genuine.

control v **1** LEAD, govern, rule, command, direct, manage, oversee, supervise, superintend, run, operate. **2** control the temperature: regulate, adjust, monitor, verify. **3** control one's temper: restrain, check, curb, subdue, repress, hold back, contain.

➤ n **1** POWER, charge, authority, command, mastery, government, rule, direction, management, oversight, supervision, superintendence, discipline, guidance. **2** RESTRAINT, check, curb, repression. **3** INSTRUMENT, dial, switch, button, knob, lever.

controversial adj contentious,

polemical, disputed, doubtful, questionable, debatable, disputable.

controversy n debate, discussion, war of words, polemic, dispute, disagreement, argument, quarrel, squabble, wrangle, strife, contention, dissension.
🔁 accord, agreement.

convenience n 1 ACCESSIBILITY, availability, handiness, usefulness, use, utility, serviceability, service, benefit, advantage, help, suitability, fitness.
2 all modern conveniences: facility, amenity, appliance.
🔁 **1** inconvenience.

convenient adj nearby, at hand, accessible, available, handy, useful, commodious, beneficial, helpful, labour-saving, adapted, fitted, suited, suitable, fit, appropriate, opportune, timely, well-timed.
🔁 inconvenient, awkward.

convention n 1 CUSTOM, tradition, practice, usage, protocol, etiquette, formality, matter of form, code.
2 ASSEMBLY, congress, conference, meeting, council, delegates, representatives.

conventional adj traditional, orthodox, formal, correct, proper, prevalent, prevailing, accepted, received, expected, unoriginal, ritual, routine, usual, customary, regular, standard, normal, ordinary, straight, stereotyped, hidebound, pedestrian, commonplace, common, run-of-the-mill.
🔁 unconventional, unusual, exotic.

converge v focus, concentrate, approach, merge, coincide, meet, join, combine, gather.
🔁 diverge, disperse.

convergence n concentration, approach, merging, confluence, blending, meeting, coincidence, junction, intersection, union.
🔁 divergence, separation.

conversation n talk, chat, gossip, discussion, discourse, dialogue, exchange, communication.

converse n opposite, reverse, contrary, antithesis, obverse.
➤ adj opposite, reverse, counter, contrary, reversed, transposed.

conversion n alteration, change, transformation, adaptation, modification, remodelling, reconstruction, reorganization, reformation, regeneration, rebirth.

convert v 1 ALTER, change, turn, transform, adapt, modify, remodel, restyle, revise, reorganize. **2** WIN OVER, convince, persuade, reform, proselytize.

convex adj rounded, bulging, protuberant.
🔁 concave.

convey v carry, bear, bring, fetch, move, transport, send, forward, deliver, transfer, conduct, guide, transmit, communicate, impart, tell, relate, reveal.

convict v condemn, sentence, imprison.
➤ n criminal, felon, culprit, prisoner.

conviction n assurance, confidence, fervour, earnestness, certainty, firmness, persuasion, view, opinion, belief, faith, creed, tenet, principle.

convince v assure, persuade, sway, win over, bring round, reassure, satisfy.

convincing adj persuasive, cogent, powerful, telling, impressive, credible, plausible, likely, probable, conclusive, incontrovertible.
🔁 unconvincing, improbable.

convoluted adj twisting, winding, meandering, tortuous, involved, complicated, complex, tangled.
🔁 straight, straightforward.

convoy n fleet, escort, guard, protection, attendance, train.

convulsion n 1 FIT, seizure, paroxysm, spasm, cramp, contraction, tic, tremor.
2 ERUPTION, outburst, furore, disturbance, commotion, tumult, agitation, turbulence, upheaval.

convulsive adj jerky, spasmodic, fitful, sporadic, uncontrolled, violent.

cook

Ways of cooking include: bake, barbecue, boil, braise, broil, casserole, chargrill, coddle, deep-fry, fry, grill, microwave, poach, pot-roast, roast, sauté, scramble, sear, simmer, spit-roast, steam, stew, stir-fry, toast; prepare, heat. *see also* **utensil**.

cookery

Terms used in cookery include: bake blind, bind, blend, bone, brown, caramelize, carve, chill, chop, cream, crumble, cure, defrost, deglaze, devil, drizzle, dust, fillet, flash fry, fold in, freeze, glaze, grate, grind, ice, joint, jug, knead, knock back, liquidize, marinate, mash, mince, mix, mull, peel, peppered, pickle, plate (up), potted, prep (*infml*), preserve, prove, purée, reduce, re-heat, rest, rise, sear, sieve, sift, skim, smoke, souse, stir, strain, stuff, sweat, thicken, truss, whisk.

Terms used in French cookery include: à la crème, à la Grècque, au gratin, au poivre, Bolognese, brûlée, cacciatore, chasseur, cordon bleu, coulis, en cocotte, en croute, farci, frappé, galette, gougère, haute cuisine, Lyonnaise, mornay, Niçoise, nouvelle cuisine, Provençal, roux, sur le plat.

Terms used in Indian cookery include: akhni, aloo, balti, bargar, bhajee or bhaji, bhindi or bindi, bhoona or bhuna, dhal, dhansak, dopiaza, dum, gosht, kalia, karahi, kofta, korma, madras, masala, Moglai, paneer, tandoori, tikka, vindaloo.

◇ **cook up** concoct, prepare, brew, invent, fabricate, contrive, devise, plan, plot, scheme.

cool *adj* **1** CHILLY, fresh, breezy, nippy, cold, chilled, iced, refreshing. **2** CALM, unruffled, unexcited, composed, self-possessed, level-headed, unemotional, quiet, relaxed, laid back (*infml*). **3** *a cool*

reception: unfriendly, unwelcoming, cold, frigid, chilly, lukewarm, half-hearted, unenthusiastic, apathetic, uninterested, unresponsive, uncommunicative, reserved, distant, aloof, standoffish.

🔁 **1** warm, hot. **2** excited, angry. **3** friendly, welcoming.

➤ *v* **1** CHILL, refrigerate, ice, freeze, fan. **2** MODERATE, lessen, temper, dampen, quiet, abate, calm, allay, assuage.

🔁 **1** warm, heat. **2** excite.

➤ *n* coolness, calmness, collectedness, composure, poise, self-possession, self-discipline, self-control, control, temper.

co-operate *v* collaborate, work together, play ball (*infml*), help, assist, aid, contribute, participate, combine, unite, conspire.

co-operation *n* helpfulness, assistance, participation, collaboration, teamwork, unity, co-ordination, give-and-take.

🔁 opposition, rivalry, competition.

co-operative *adj* **1** HELPFUL, supportive, obliging, accommodating, willing. **2** COLLECTIVE, joint, shared, combined, united, concerted, co-ordinated.

🔁 **1** unco-operative, rebellious.

co-ordinate *v* organize, arrange, systematize, tabulate, integrate, mesh, synchronize, harmonize, match, correlate, regulate.

cope *v* manage, carry on, survive, get by, make do.

◇ **cope with** deal with, encounter, contend with, struggle with, grapple with, wrestle with, handle, manage, weather.

copious *adj* abundant, plentiful, inexhaustible, overflowing, profuse, rich, lavish, bountiful, liberal, full, ample, generous, extensive, great, huge.

🔁 scarce, meagre.

copy *n* duplicate, carbon copy, photocopy, Photostat®, Xerox®, facsimile, reproduction, print, tracing, transcript, transcription, replica, clone, model, pattern, archetype,

representation, image, likeness, counterfeit, forgery, fake, imitation, borrowing, plagiarism, crib.
⊟ original.

➤ v duplicate, photocopy, reproduce, print, trace, transcribe, forge, counterfeit, simulate, imitate, impersonate, mimic, ape, parrot, repeat, echo, mirror, follow, emulate, borrow, plagiarize, crib.

cord n string, twine, rope, line, cable, flex, connection, link, bond, tie.

core n kernel, nucleus, heart, centre, middle, nub, crux, essence, gist, nitty-gritty (*infml*).
⊟ surface, exterior.

corner n 1 *round the corner*: angle, joint, crook, bend, turning. 2 NOOK, cranny, niche, recess, cavity, hole, hideout, hideaway, retreat.

corporation n council, authorities, association, society, organization, company, firm, combine, conglomerate.

corpse n body, stiff (*sl*), carcase, skeleton, remains.

correct v 1 *correct an error*: rectify, put right, right, emend, remedy, cure, debug, redress, adjust, regulate, improve, amend. 2 PUNISH, discipline, reprimand, reprove, reform.
➤ adj 1 *the correct answer*: right, accurate, precise, exact, strict, true, truthful, word-perfect, faultless, flawless. 2 PROPER, acceptable, OK (*infml*), standard, regular, just, appropriate, fitting.
⊟ 1 incorrect, wrong, inaccurate.

correction n rectification, emendation, adjustment, alteration, modification, amendment, improvement.

correspond v 1 MATCH, fit, answer, conform, tally, square, agree, concur, coincide, correlate, accord, harmonize, dovetail, complement. 2 COMMUNICATE, write.

correspondence n 1 LETTERS, communication, writing, post, mail. 2 CONFORMITY, agreement, concurrence, coincidence, correlation, relation, analogy, comparison, comparability, similarity, resemblance, congruity, equivalence, harmony, match.
⊟ 2 divergence, incongruity.

correspondent n journalist, reporter, contributor, writer.

corresponding adj matching, complementary, reciprocal, interrelated, analogous, equivalent, similar, identical.

corridor n aisle, passageway, passage, hallway, hall, lobby.

corroborate v confirm, prove, bear out, support, endorse, ratify, substantiate, validate, authenticate, document, underpin, sustain.
⊟ contradict.

corrode v erode, wear away, eat away, consume, waste, rust, oxidize, tarnish, impair, deteriorate, crumble, disintegrate.

corrosive adj corroding, acid, caustic, cutting, abrasive, erosive, wearing, consuming, wasting.

corrugated adj ridged, fluted, grooved, channelled, furrowed, wrinkled, crinkled, rumpled, creased.

corrupt adj rotten, unscrupulous, unprincipled, unethical, immoral, fraudulent, shady (*infml*), dishonest, bent (*infml*), crooked (*infml*), untrustworthy, depraved, degenerate, dissolute.
⊟ ethical, virtuous, upright, honest, trustworthy.
➤ v contaminate, pollute, adulterate, taint, defile, debase, pervert, deprave, lead astray, lure, bribe, suborn.
⊟ purify.

corruption n unscrupulousness, immorality, impurity, depravity, degeneration, degradation, perversion, distortion, dishonesty, crookedness (*infml*), fraud, shadiness (*infml*), bribery, extortion, vice, wickedness, iniquity, evil.
⊟ honesty, virtue.

cosmetic adj superficial, surface.
⊟ essential.

cosmetics *n* make-up, grease paint.

Cosmetics include: blusher, cleanser, eyebrow pencil, eyelash dye, eyeliner, eye shadow, face cream, face mask, face pack, face powder, false eyelashes, foundation, kohl pencil, lip gloss, lip liner, lipstick, loose powder, mascara, moisturizer, nail polish, nail varnish, panstick, pressed powder, rouge, toner.

cosmopolitan *adj* worldly, worldly-wise, well-travelled, sophisticated, urbane, international, universal.
🔁 insular, parochial, rustic.

cosset *v* coddle, mollycoddle, baby, pamper, indulge, spoil, pet, fondle, cuddle, cherish.

cost *n* **1** EXPENSE, outlay, payment, disbursement, expenditure, charge, price, rate, amount, figure, worth. **2** DETRIMENT, harm, injury, hurt, loss, deprivation, sacrifice, penalty, price.

costly *adj* **1** EXPENSIVE, dear, pricey (*infml*), exorbitant, excessive, lavish, rich, splendid, valuable, precious, priceless. **2** HARMFUL, damaging, disastrous, catastrophic, loss-making.
🔁 **1** cheap, inexpensive.

costume *n* outfit, uniform, livery, robes, vestments, dress, clothing, get-up (*infml*), fancy dress.

cosy *adj* snug, comfortable, comfy (*infml*), warm, sheltered, secure, homely, intimate.
🔁 uncomfortable, cold.

cottage *n* lodge, chalet, bungalow, hut, cabin, shack.

couch *n* sofa, settee, chesterfield, chaise-longue, ottoman, divan, bed.

council *n* committee, panel, board, cabinet, ministry, parliament, congress, assembly, convention, conference.

counsel *n* **1** ADVICE, suggestion, recommendation, guidance, direction, information, consultation, deliberation, consideration, forethought. **2** *counsel for the defence*: lawyer, advocate,

solicitor, attorney, barrister.
➤ *v* advise, warn, caution, suggest, recommend, advocate, urge, exhort, guide, direct, instruct.

count *v* **1** NUMBER, enumerate, list, include, reckon, calculate, compute, tell, check, add, total, tot up, score. **2** MATTER, signify, qualify. **3** *count yourself lucky*: consider, regard, deem, judge, think, reckon, hold.
➤ *n* numbering, enumeration, poll, reckoning, calculation, computation, sum, total, tally.
◇ **count on** depend on, rely on, bank on, reckon on, expect, believe, trust.

counter *adv* against, in opposition, conversely.
➤ *adj* contrary, opposite, opposing, conflicting, contradictory, contrasting, opposed, against, adverse.
➤ *v* parry, resist, offset, answer, respond, retaliate, retort, return, meet.

counteract *v* neutralize, offset, counterbalance, countervail, act against, oppose, resist, hinder, check, thwart, frustrate, foil, defeat, undo, negate, annul, invalidate.
🔁 support, assist.

counterfeit *v* fake, forge, fabricate, copy, imitate, impersonate, pretend, feign, simulate, sham.
➤ *adj* fake, false, phoney (*infml*), forged, copied, fraudulent, bogus, pseudo, sham, spurious, imitation, artificial, simulated, feigned, pretended.
🔁 genuine, authentic, real.
➤ *n* fake, forgery, copy, reproduction, imitation, fraud, sham.

counterpart *n* equivalent, opposite number, complement, supplement, match, fellow, mate, twin, duplicate, copy.

countless *adj* innumerable, myriad, numberless, unnumbered, untold, incalculable, infinite, endless, immeasurable, measureless, limitless.
🔁 finite, limited.

country *n* **1** STATE, nation, people, kingdom, realm, principality. **2** COUNTRYSIDE, green belt, farmland,

provinces, sticks (*infml*), boondocks (*US infml*), backwoods, wilds. **3** TERRAIN, land, territory, region, area, district.
🖛 2 town, city.
➤ *adj* rural, provincial, agrarian, agricultural, pastoral, rustic, bucolic, landed.
🖛 urban.

countryside *n* landscape, scenery, country, green belt, farmland, outdoors.

county *n* shire, province, region, area, district.

couple *n* pair, brace, twosome, duo.
➤ *v* pair, match, marry, wed, unite, join, link, connect, fasten, hitch, clasp, buckle, yoke.

coupon *n* voucher, token, slip, check, ticket, certificate.

courage *n* bravery, pluck, guts (*infml*), fearlessness, dauntlessness, heroism, gallantry, valour, boldness, audacity, nerve, daring, resolution, fortitude, spirit, mettle.
🖛 cowardice, fear.

courageous *adj* brave, plucky, fearless, dauntless, indomitable, heroic, gallant, valiant, lion-hearted, hardy, bold, audacious, daring, intrepid, resolute.
🖛 cowardly, afraid.

course *n* **1** CURRICULUM, syllabus, classes, lessons, lectures, studies.
2 FLOW, movement, advance, progress, development, furtherance, order, sequence, series, succession, progression. **3** DURATION, time, period, term, passage. **4** DIRECTION, way, path, track, road, route, channel, trail, line, circuit, orbit, trajectory, flight path.
5 *course of action*: plan, schedule, programme, policy, procedure, method, mode.

court *n* **1** LAWCOURT, bench, bar, tribunal, trial, session. **2** COURTYARD, yard, quadrangle, square, cloister, forecourt, enclosure. **3** ENTOURAGE, attendants, retinue, suite, train, cortège.

Types of lawcourt include: Admiralty

Division, assizes, Central Criminal Court, Chancery Division, children's court, circuit court, civil court, coroner's court, county court, court-martial, court of appeals, court of claims, Court of Common Pleas, Court of Exchequer, court of justice, Court of Protection, Court of Session, criminal court, crown court, district court, divorce court, European Court of Justice, family court, federal court, High Court, High Court of Justiciary, House of Lords, industrial tribunal, International Court of Justice, juvenile court, Lord Chancellor's Court, magistrates' court, municipal court, Old Bailey, police court, Privy Council, sheriff court, small claims court, Supreme Court.

courteous *adj* polite, civil, respectful, well-mannered, well-bred, ladylike, gentlemanly, gracious, obliging, considerate, attentive, gallant, courtly, urbane, debonair, refined, polished.
🖛 discourteous, impolite, rude.

courtesy *n* politeness, civility, respect, manners, breeding, graciousness, consideration, attention, gallantry, urbanity.
🖛 discourtesy, rudeness.

courtier *n* noble, nobleman, lord, lady, steward, page, attendant, follower, flatterer, sycophant, toady.

courtyard *n* yard, quadrangle, quad (*infml*), area, enclosure, court.

cove *n* bay, bight, inlet, estuary, firth, fiord, creek.

cover *v* **1** HIDE, conceal, obscure, shroud, veil, screen, mask, disguise, camouflage. **2** *covered with mud*: coat, spread, daub, plaster, encase, wrap, envelop, clothe, dress. **3** SHELTER, protect, shield, guard, defend. **4** *cover a topic*: deal with, treat, consider, examine, investigate, encompass, embrace, incorporate, embody, involve, include, contain, comprise.
🖛 1 uncover. **2** strip. **3** expose.
4 exclude.

➤ *n* **1** COATING, covering, top, lid, cup, veil, screen, mask, front, façade, jacket, wrapper, case, envelope, clothing, dress, bedspread, canopy. **2** SHELTER, refuge, protection, shield, guard, defence, concealment, disguise, camouflage.
◇ **cover up** (*infml*) conceal, hide, whitewash, dissemble, suppress, hush up, keep dark, repress.
🔁 disclose, reveal.

covering *n* layer, coat, coating, blanket, film, veneer, skin, crust, shell, casing, housing, wrapping, clothing, protection, mask, overlay, cover, top, shelter, roof.

cover-up (*infml*) *n* concealment, whitewash, smokescreen, front, façade, pretence, conspiracy, complicity.

covet *v* envy, begrudge, crave, long for, yearn for, hanker for, want, desire, fancy (*infml*), lust after.

coward *n* craven, faint-heart, chicken (*infml*), scaredy-cat (*infml*), yellow-belly (*sl*), wimp (*infml*), wuss (*sl*), renegade, deserter.
🔁 hero.

cowardice *n* cowardliness, faint-heartedness, timorousness, spinelessness.
🔁 courage, valour.

cowardly *adj* faint-hearted, craven, fearful, timorous, scared, unheroic, chicken-hearted, chicken-livered, chicken (*infml*), yellow-bellied (*sl*), yellow (*sl*), spineless, weak, weak-kneed, soft, wimpish (*infml*).
🔁 brave, courageous, bold.

cower *v* crouch, grovel, skulk, shrink, flinch, cringe, quail, tremble, shake, shiver.

coy *adj* modest, demure, prudish, diffident, shy, bashful, timid, shrinking, backward, retiring, self-effacing, reserved, evasive, arch, flirtatious, coquettish, skittish, kittenish.
🔁 bold, forward.

crack *v* **1** SPLIT, burst, fracture, break, snap, shatter, splinter, chip. **2** EXPLODE, burst, pop, crackle, snap, crash, clap, slap, whack (*infml*). **3** *crack a code*: decipher, work out, solve.
➤ *n* **1** BREAK, fracture, split, rift, gap, crevice, fissure, chink, line, flaw, chip. **2** EXPLOSION, burst, pop, snap, crash, clap, blow, smack, slap, whack (*infml*). **3** JOKE, quip, witticism, gag (*infml*), wisecrack, gibe, dig.
➤ *adj* (*infml*) first-class, first-rate, top-notch (*infml*), excellent, superior, choice, hand-picked.
◇ **crack down on** clamp down on, end, stop, put a stop to, crush, suppress, check, repress, act against.
◇ **crack up** go mad, go to pieces, break down, collapse.

cradle *n* **1** COT, crib, bed. **2** SOURCE, origin, spring, wellspring, fount, fountainhead, birthplace, beginning.
➤ *v* hold, support, rock, lull, nurse, nurture, tend.

craft *n* **1** SKILL, expertise, mastery, talent, knack, ability, aptitude, dexterity, cleverness, art, handicraft, handiwork. **2** TRADE, business, calling, vocation, job, occupation, work, employment. **3** VESSEL, boat, ship, aircraft, spacecraft, spaceship.

craftsman, craftswoman *n* artisan, technician, master, maker, wright, smith.

craftsmanship *n* artistry, workmanship, technique, dexterity, expertise, mastery.

crafty *adj* sly, cunning, artful, wily, devious, subtle, scheming, calculating, designing, deceitful, fraudulent, sharp, shrewd, astute, canny.
🔁 artless, naïve.

cram *v* stuff, jam, ram, force, press, squeeze, crush, compress, pack, crowd, overfill, glut, gorge.

cramp¹ *v* hinder, hamper, obstruct, impede, inhibit, handicap, thwart, frustrate, check, restrict, confine, shackle, tie.

cramp² *n* pain, ache, twinge, pang, contraction, convulsion, spasm, crick, stitch, pins and needles, stiffness.

cramped *adj* narrow, tight, uncomfortable, restricted, confined, crowded, packed, squashed, squeezed, overcrowded, jam-packed, congested.
Ea spacious.

crash *n* **1** *car crash*: accident, collision, bump, smash, pile-up, smash-up (*infml*), wreck. **2** BANG, clash, clatter, clang, thud, thump, boom, thunder, racket, din. **3** *stock-market crash*: collapse, failure, ruin, downfall, bankruptcy, depression.
➤ *v* **1** COLLIDE, hit, knock, bump, bang. **2** BREAK, fracture, smash, dash, shatter, splinter, shiver, fragment, disintegrate. **3** FALL, topple, pitch, plunge, collapse, fail, fold (up), go under, go bust (*infml*).

crate *n* container, box, case, tea-chest, packing-box, packing-case.

crave *v* hunger for, thirst for, long for, yearn for, pine for, hanker after, fancy (*infml*), desire, want, need, require.
Ea dislike.

craving *n* appetite, hunger, thirst, longing, yearning, hankering, lust, desire, urge.
Ea dislike, distaste.

crawl *v* **1** CREEP, inch, edge, slither, wriggle. **2** GROVEL, cringe, toady, fawn, flatter, suck up (*sl*).

craze *n* fad, novelty, fashion, vogue, mode, trend, rage (*infml*), thing (*infml*), obsession, preoccupation, mania, frenzy, passion, infatuation, enthusiasm.

crazy *adj* **1** MAD, insane, lunatic, unbalanced, deranged, demented, crazed, potty (*infml*), barmy (*infml*), daft (*infml*), silly, foolish, idiotic, senseless, unwise, imprudent, nonsensical, absurd, ludicrous, ridiculous, preposterous, outrageous, half-baked, impracticable, irresponsible, wild, berserk. **2** (*infml*) *crazy about golf*: enthusiastic, fanatical, zealous, ardent, passionate, infatuated, enamoured, smitten, mad, wild.
Ea 1 sane, sensible. **2** indifferent.

creak *v* squeak, groan, grate, scrape, rasp, scratch, grind, squeal, screech.

cream *n* **1** PASTE, emulsion, oil, lotion, ointment, salve, cosmetic. **2** BEST, pick, élite, prime.

creamy *adj* **1** CREAM-COLOURED, off-white, yellowish-white. **2** MILKY, buttery, oily, smooth, velvety, rich, thick.

crease *v* fold, pleat, wrinkle, pucker, crumple, rumple, crinkle, crimp, corrugate, ridge.
➤ *n* fold, line, pleat, tuck, wrinkle, pucker, ruck, crinkle, corrugation, ridge, groove.

create *v* invent, coin, formulate, compose, design, devise, concoct, hatch, originate, initiate, found, establish, set up, institute, cause, occasion, produce, generate, engender, make, form, appoint, install, invest, ordain.
Ea destroy.

creation *n* **1** MAKING, formation, constitution, invention, concoction, origination, foundation, establishment, institution, production, generation, procreation, conception, birth. **2** INVENTION, brainchild, concept, product, handiwork, chef d'oeuvre, masterwork, masterpiece, achievement.
Ea 1 destruction.

creative *adj* artistic, inventive, original, imaginative, inspired, visionary, talented, gifted, clever, ingenious, resourceful, fertile, productive.
Ea unimaginative.

creator *n* maker, inventor, designer, architect, author, originator, initiator.

creature *n* animal, beast, bird, fish, organism, being, mortal, individual, person, man, woman, body, soul.

credentials *n* diploma, certificate, reference, testimonial, credit, recommendation, accreditation, authorization, warrant, licence, permit, passport, identity card, papers, documents, deed, title.

credibility *n* integrity, reliability, trustworthiness, plausibility, probability.
Ea implausibility.

credible *adj* believable, imaginable,

conceivable, thinkable, tenable, plausible, likely, probable, possible, reasonable, persuasive, convincing, sincere, honest, trustworthy, reliable, dependable.

🠳 incredible, unbelievable, implausible, unreliable.

credit *n* acknowledgement, thanks, approval, recognition, commendation, praise, acclaim, tribute, glory, fame, prestige, distinction, honour, reputation, esteem, estimation.
🠳 discredit, shame.
➤ *v* believe, swallow (*infml*), accept, subscribe to, trust, rely on.
🠳 disbelieve.

creditable *adj* honourable, reputable, respectable, estimable, admirable, commendable, praiseworthy, good, excellent, exemplary, worthy, deserving.
🠳 shameful, blameworthy.

credulous *adj* naïve, gullible, wide-eyed, trusting, unsuspecting, uncritical.
🠳 sceptical, suspicious.

creed *n* belief, faith, persuasion, credo, catechism, doctrine, principles, tenets, articles, canon, dogma.

creek *n* inlet, estuary, cove, bay, bight.

creep *v* inch, edge, tiptoe, steal, sneak, slink, crawl, slither, worm, wriggle, squirm, grovel, writhe.

creepy *adj* eerie, spooky, sinister, threatening, frightening, scary, terrifying, hair-raising, nightmarish, macabre, gruesome, horrible, unpleasant, disturbing.

crest *n* **1** *the crest of the hill*: ridge, crown, top, peak, summit, pinnacle, apex, head. **2** TUFT, tassel, plume, comb, mane. **3** INSIGNIA, device, symbol, emblem, badge.

crevice *n* crack, fissure, split, rift, cleft, slit, chink, cranny, gap, hole, opening, break.

crew *n* team, party, squad, troop, corps, company, gang, band, bunch, crowd, mob, set, lot.

crime *n* law-breaking, lawlessness, delinquency, offence, felony, misdemeanour, misdeed, wrongdoing, misconduct, transgression, violation, sin, iniquity, vice, villainy, wickedness, atrocity, outrage.

Crimes include: theft, robbery, burglary, larceny, pilfering, mugging, poaching; assault, rape, grievous bodily harm, GBH (*infml*), battery, manslaughter, homicide, murder, assassination; fraud, bribery, corruption, embezzlement, extortion, blackmail; arson, treason, terrorism, hijack, piracy, kidnapping, sabotage, vandalism, hooliganism, drug smuggling, forgery, counterfeiting, perjury, joyriding, drink-driving, drunk and disorderly.

criminal *n* law-breaker, felon, delinquent, offender, wrongdoer, miscreant, culprit, convict, prisoner.

Types of criminal include: armed robber, arsonist, assassin, bandit, batterer, bigamist, blackmailer, bootlegger, brigand, buccaneer, burglar, car thief, cat burglar, counterfeiter, cracksman, crook, dope pusher, drink-driver, drug smuggler, embezzler, extortionist, fire-raiser, forger, gangster, gunman, highwayman, hijacker, hood (*sl*), hoodlum, housebreaker, joyrider, kerb-crawler, kidnapper, killer, lag (*sl*), larcenist, mobster (*US*), mugger, murderer, perjurer, pickpocket, pirate, poacher, racketeer, ram-raider, rapist, receiver, robber, rustler, saboteur, safecracker, sexual abuser, shoplifter, smuggler, strangler, swindler, terrorist, thief, thug, trespasser, vandal, war criminal.

➤ *adj* illegal, unlawful, illicit, lawless, wrong, culpable, indictable, crooked (*infml*), bent (*infml*), dishonest, corrupt, wicked, scandalous, deplorable.
🠳 legal, lawful, honest, upright.

cringe *v* shrink, recoil, shy, start, flinch, wince, quail, tremble, quiver, cower, crouch, bend, bow, stoop, grovel, crawl, creep.

cripple v lame, paralyse, disable, handicap, injure, maim, mutilate, damage, impair, spoil, ruin, destroy, sabotage, incapacitate, weaken, debilitate.

crippled *adj* lame, paralysed, disabled, handicapped, incapacitated.

crisis n emergency, extremity, crunch (*infml*), catastrophe, disaster, calamity, dilemma, quandary, predicament, difficulty, trouble, problem.

crisp *adj* 1 *a crisp biscuit*: crispy, crunchy, brittle, crumbly, firm, hard. 2 BRACING, invigorating, refreshing, fresh, brisk. 3 TERSE, pithy, snappy, brief, short, clear, incisive.
E 1 soggy, limp, flabby. 2 muggy. 3 wordy, vague.

criterion n standard, norm, touchstone, benchmark, yardstick, measure, gauge, rule, principle, canon, test.

critic n reviewer, commentator, analyst, pundit, authority, expert, judge, censor, carper, fault-finder, attacker, knocker (*infml*).

critical *adj* 1 *at the critical moment*: crucial, vital, essential, all-important, momentous, decisive, urgent, pressing, serious, grave, dangerous, perilous. 2 ANALYTICAL, diagnostic, penetrating, probing, discerning, perceptive. 3 UNCOMPLIMENTARY, derogatory, disparaging, disapproving, censorious, carping, fault-finding, cavilling, nit-picking (*infml*).
E 1 unimportant. 3 complimentary, appreciative.

criticism n 1 CONDEMNATION, disapproval, disparagement, fault-finding, censure, blame, brickbat, flak (*infml*). 2 REVIEW, critique, assessment, evaluation, appraisal, judgement, analysis, commentary, appreciation.
E 1 praise, commendation.

criticize v 1 CONDEMN, slate (*infml*),

slam (*infml*), knock (*infml*), disparage, carp, find fault, censure, blame. 2 REVIEW, assess, evaluate, appraise, judge, analyse.
E 1 praise, commend.

crockery n dishes, tableware, china, porcelain, earthenware, stoneware, pottery.

Items of crockery include: cup, saucer, coffee cup, mug, beaker, plate, side plate, dinner plate, bowl, cereal bowl, soup bowl, salad bowl, sugar bowl, jug, milk jug, basin, pot, teapot, coffee pot, percolator, cafetière, cakestand, meat dish, butter dish, tureen, gravy boat, cruet, teaset, dinner service.

crook n criminal, thief, robber, swindler, cheat, shark (*infml*), rogue, villain.

crooked *adj* 1 ASKEW, skew-whiff (*infml*), awry, lopsided, asymmetric, irregular, uneven, off-centre, tilted, slanting, bent, angled, hooked, curved, bowed, warped, distorted, misshapen, deformed, twisted, tortuous, winding, zigzag. 2 (*infml*) ILLEGAL, unlawful, illicit, criminal, nefarious, dishonest, deceitful, bent (*infml*), corrupt, fraudulent, shady (*infml*), shifty, underhand, treacherous, unscrupulous, unprincipled, unethical.
E 1 straight. 2 honest.

crop n growth, yield, produce, fruits, harvest, vintage, gathering.

Types of arable crop include: alfalfa (*US*), barley, bean, mung bean, soya bean, corn, popcorn, sweetcorn, fodder beet, mangel wurzel, sugar beet, cassava, kale, lucerne, linseed, millet, oats, oilseed rape, pea, potato, sweet potato, yam, rice, rye, sorghum, swede, turnip, wheat.

➤ v cut, snip, clip, shear, trim, pare, prune, lop, shorten, curtail.
◇ **crop up** arise, emerge, appear, arrive, occur, happen.

cross *adj* 1 IRRITABLE, annoyed, angry, vexed, shirty (*infml*), bad-tempered, ill-tempered, crotchety, grumpy, grouchy,

irascible, crabby, short, snappy, snappish, surly, sullen, fractious, fretful, impatient. **2** TRANSVERSE, crosswise, oblique, diagonal, intersecting, opposite, reciprocal.
▣ 1 placid, pleasant.
➤ v **1** *cross the river*: go across, traverse, ford, bridge, span.
2 INTERSECT, meet, criss-cross, lace, intertwine. **3** CROSSBREED, interbreed, mongrelize, hybridize, cross-fertilize, cross-pollinate, blend, mix. **4** THWART, frustrate, foil, hinder, impede, obstruct, block, oppose.
➤ n **1** BURDEN, load, affliction, misfortune, trouble, worry, trial, tribulation, grief, misery, woe.
2 CROSSBREED, hybrid, mongrel, blend, mixture, amalgam, combination.

Types of cross include: ankh, Avelian, botoné, Calvary, capital, cardinal, Celtic, Constantinian, Cornish, crosslet, crucifix, encolpion, fleury, fylfot, Geneva, Greek, Jerusalem, Latin, Lorraine, Maltese, moline, papal, patriarchal, potent, quadrate, rood, Russian, saltire, St Andrew's, St Anthony's, St George's, St Peter's, swastika, tau, Y-cross.

---

crouch v squat, kneel, stoop, bend, bow, hunch, duck, cower, cringe.

crowd n **1** THRONG, multitude, host, mob, masses, populace, people, public, riff-raff, rabble, horde, swarm, flock, herd, pack, press, crush, squash, assembly, company, group, bunch, lot, set, circle, clique. **2** SPECTATORS, gate, attendance, audience.
➤ v gather, congregate, muster, huddle, mass, throng, swarm, flock, surge, stream, push, shove, elbow, jostle, press, squeeze, bundle, pile, pack, congest, cram, compress.

crowded adj full, filled, packed, jammed, jam-packed, congested, cramped, overcrowded, overpopulated, busy, teeming, swarming, overflowing.
▣ empty, deserted.

crown n **1** CORONET, diadem, tiara, circlet, wreath, garland. **2** PRIZE, trophy,

reward, honour, laurels. **3** SOVEREIGN, monarch, king, queen, ruler, sovereignty, monarchy, royalty. **4** TOP, tip, apex, crest, summit, pinnacle, peak, acme.
➤ v **1** ENTHRONE, anoint, adorn, festoon, honour, dignify, reward. **2** TOP, cap, complete, fulfil, consummate, perfect.

crucial adj urgent, pressing, vital, essential, key, pivotal, central, important, momentous, decisive, critical, trying, testing, searching.
▣ unimportant, trivial.

crude adj **1** RAW, unprocessed, unrefined, rough, unfinished, unpolished, natural, primitive. **2** *a crude remark*: VULGAR, coarse, rude, indecent, obscene, gross, dirty, lewd.
▣ 1 refined, finished. **2** polite, decent.

cruel adj fierce, ferocious, vicious, savage, barbarous, bloodthirsty, murderous, cold-blooded, sadistic, brutal, inhuman, inhumane, unkind, malevolent, spiteful, callous, heartless, unfeeling, merciless, pitiless, flinty, hard-hearted, stony-hearted, implacable, ruthless, remorseless, relentless, unrelenting, inexorable, grim, hellish, atrocious, bitter, harsh, severe, cutting, painful, excruciating.
▣ kind, compassionate, merciful.

cruelty n ferocity, viciousness, savagery, barbarity, bloodthirstiness, murderousness, violence, sadism, brutality, bestiality, inhumanity, spite, venom, callousness, heartlessness, hard-heartedness, mercilessness, ruthlessness, tyranny, harshness, severity.
▣ kindness, compassion, mercy.

crumble v fragment, break up, decompose, disintegrate, decay, degenerate, deteriorate, collapse, crush, pound, grind, powder, pulverize.

crumple v crush, wrinkle, pucker, crinkle, rumple, crease, fold, collapse.

crunch v munch, chomp, champ, masticate, grind, crush.

crusade n campaign, drive, push, movement, cause, undertaking, expedition, holy war, jihad.

crush v 1 SQUASH, compress, squeeze, press, pulp, break, smash, pound, pulverize, grind, crumble, crumple, wrinkle. 2 *the rebels were crushed*: conquer, vanquish, demolish, devastate, overpower, overwhelm, overcome, quash, quell, subdue, put down, humiliate, shame, abash.

crust n surface, exterior, outside, covering, coat, coating, layer, film, skin, rind, shell, scab, incrustation, caking, concretion.

crux n nub, heart, core, essence.

cry v 1 WEEP, sob, blubber, wail, bawl, whimper, snivel. 2 SHOUT, call, exclaim, roar, bellow, yell, scream, shriek, screech.
➤ n 1 WEEP, sob, blubber, wail, bawl, whimper, snivel. 2 SHOUT, call, plea, exclamation, roar, bellow, yell, scream, shriek.

cryptic adj enigmatic, ambiguous, equivocal, puzzling, perplexing, mysterious, strange, bizarre, secret, hidden, veiled, obscure, abstruse, esoteric, dark, occult.
☒ straightforward, clear, obvious.

cuddle v hug, embrace, clasp, hold, nurse, nestle, snuggle, pet, fondle, caress.

cuddly adj cuddlesome, lovable, huggable, plump, soft, warm, cosy.

cue n signal, sign, nod, hint, suggestion, reminder, prompt, incentive, stimulus.

cuff v hit, thump, box, clip, knock, biff (*infml*), buffet, slap, smack, strike, clout (*infml*), clobber (*sl*), belt (*infml*), beat, whack (*infml*).

culminate v climax, end (up), terminate, close, conclude, finish, consummate.
☒ start, begin.

culmination n climax, height, peak, pinnacle, summit, top, crown, perfection, consummation, finale, conclusion, completion.
☒ start, beginning.

culprit n guilty party, offender,

wrongdoer, miscreant, law-breaker, criminal, felon, delinquent.

cult n 1 SECT, denomination, school, movement, party, faction. 2 CRAZE, fad, fashion, vogue, trend.

cultivate v 1 FARM, till, work, plough, grow, sow, plant, tend, harvest.
2 FOSTER, nurture, cherish, help, aid, support, encourage, promote, further, work on, develop, train, prepare, polish, refine, improve, enrich.
☒ 2 neglect.

cultural adj artistic, aesthetic, liberal, civilizing, humanizing, enlightening, educational, edifying, improving, enriching, elevating.

culture n 1 CIVILIZATION, society, lifestyle, way of life, customs, mores, the arts. 2 CULTIVATION, taste, education, enlightenment, breeding, gentility, refinement, politeness, urbanity.

cultured adj cultivated, civilized, advanced, enlightened, educated, well-read, well-informed, scholarly, highbrow, well-bred, refined, polished, genteel, urbane.
☒ uncultured, uneducated, ignorant.

cumbersome adj awkward, inconvenient, bulky, unwieldy, clunky (*infml*), unmanageable, burdensome, onerous, heavy, weighty.
☒ convenient, manageable.

cunning adj crafty, sly, artful, wily, tricky, devious, subtle, deceitful, guileful, sharp, shrewd, astute, canny, knowing, deep, imaginative, ingenious, skilful, deft, dexterous.
☒ naïve, ingenuous, gullible.
➤ n craftiness, slyness, artfulness, trickery, deviousness, subtlety, deceitfulness, guile, sharpness, shrewdness, astuteness, ingenuity, cleverness, adroitness.

cup n mug, tankard, beaker, goblet, chalice, trophy.

cupboard n cabinet, locker, closet, wardrobe.

curb v restrain, constrain, restrict,

contain, control, check, moderate, bridle, muzzle, suppress, subdue, repress, inhibit, hinder, impede, hamper, retard. ▄ encourage, foster.

curdle *v* coagulate, congeal, clot, thicken, turn, sour, ferment.

cure *v* **1** HEAL, remedy, correct, restore, repair, mend, relieve, ease, alleviate, help. **2** PRESERVE, dry, smoke, salt, pickle, kipper.
➤ *n* remedy, antidote, panacea, medicine, specific, corrective, restorative, healing, treatment, therapy, alleviation, recovery.

curiosity *n* **1** INQUISITIVENESS, nosiness, prying, snooping, interest. **2** CURIO, objet d'art, antique, bygone, novelty, trinket, knick-knack. **3** ODDITY, rarity, freak, phenomenon, spectacle.

curious *adj* **1** INQUISITIVE, nosey, prying, meddlesome, questioning, inquiring, interested. **2** *a curious sight*: ODD, queer, funny (*infml*), strange, peculiar, bizarre, mysterious, puzzling, extraordinary, unusual, rare, unique, novel, exotic, unconventional, unorthodox, quaint.
▄ **1** uninterested, indifferent. **2** ordinary, usual, normal.

curl *v* crimp, frizz, wave, ripple, bend, curve, meander, loop, turn, twist, wind, wreathe, twine, coil, spiral, corkscrew, scroll.
▄ uncurl.
➤ *n* wave, kink, swirl, twist, ringlet, coil, spiral, whorl.

curly *adj* wavy, kinky, curling, spiralled, corkscrew, curled, crimped, permed, frizzy, fuzzy.
▄ straight.

currency *n* **1** MONEY, legal tender, coinage, coins, notes, bills. **2** ACCEPTANCE, publicity, popularity, vogue, circulation, prevalence, exposure.

Currencies of the world include: baht (*Thailand*), bolivar (*Venezuela*), cent (*US, Canada, Australia, NZ, S Africa, etc*), centavo (*Brazil, Mexico, etc*), centime (*Algeria, Andorra, etc*), dinar (*Iraq, Jordan, etc*), dirham (*Morocco*), dollar (*US, Canada, Australia, NZ, etc*), dong (*Vietnam*), euro (*EU*), fils (*Iraq, Jordan, etc*), franc (*Switzerland*), hryvnia (*Ukraine*), kopeck (*Russia*), koruna (*Czech Republic, Slovakia*), krona (*Sweden*), króna (*Iceland*), krone (*Denmark, Norway*), kyat (*Myanmar*), lek (*Albania*), leu (*Romania*), lev (*Bulgaria*), pence (*UK*), peso (*Mexico, Chile, etc*), piastre (*Egypt, Syria, etc*), pound (*UK, Egypt, etc*), rand (*S Africa*), real (*Brazil*), renminbi (*China*), rial (*Iran*), riyal (*Saudi Arabia*), rouble (*Russia*), rupee (*India, Pakistan, etc*), shekel (*Israel*), shilling (*Kenya, Uganda, etc*), sterling (*UK*), sucre (*Ecuador*), sum (*Uzbekistan*), tolar (*Slovenia*), won (*N Korea, S Korea*), yen (*Japan*), yuan (*China*), zloty (*Poland*).

current *adj* present, ongoing, existing, contemporary, present-day, modern, fashionable, up to date, up-to-the-minute, trendy (*infml*), popular, widespread, prevalent, common, general, prevailing, reigning, accepted. ▄ obsolete, old-fashioned.
➤ *n* draught, stream, jet, flow, drift, tide, course, trend, tendency, undercurrent, mood, feeling.

curse *n* **1** SWEAR-WORD, oath, expletive, obscenity, profanity, blasphemy. **2** JINX, anathema, bane, evil, plague, scourge, affliction, trouble, torment, ordeal, calamity, disaster.
▄ **2** blessing, advantage.
➤ *v* **1** SWEAR, blaspheme, damn, condemn, denounce, fulminate. **2** BLIGHT, plague, scourge, afflict, trouble, torment.
▄ **2** bless.

curtain *n* blind, screen, backdrop, hanging, drapery, tapestry.

curve *v* bend, arch, arc, bow, bulge, hook, crook, turn, twist, spiral, coil.
➤ *n* bend, turn, arc, trajectory, loop, camber, curvature.

curved *adj* bent, arched, bowed, rounded, humped, convex, concave, crooked, twisted, sinuous, serpentine. ◨ straight.

cushion n pad, buffer, shock absorber, bolster, pillow, headrest, hassock.
➤ v soften, deaden, dampen, absorb, muffle, stifle, suppress, lessen, mitigate, protect, bolster, buttress, support.

custody n 1 KEEPING, possession, charge, care, safekeeping, protection, preservation, custodianship, trusteeship, guardianship, supervision. 2 DETENTION, confinement, imprisonment, incarceration.

custom n tradition, usage, use, habit, routine, procedure, practice, policy, way, manner, style, form, convention, etiquette, formality, observance, ritual.

customary adj traditional, conventional, accepted, established, habitual, routine, regular, usual, normal, ordinary, everyday, familiar, common, general, popular, fashionable, prevailing. ◨ unusual, rare.

customer n client, patron, regular, punter (*infml*), consumer, shopper, buyer, purchaser, prospect.

cut v 1 CLIP, trim, crop, shear, mow, shave, pare, chop, hack, hew, slice, carve, divide, part, split, bisect, dock, lop, sever, prune, excise, incise, penetrate, pierce, stab, wound, nick, gash, slit, slash, lacerate, score, engrave, chisel, sculpt. 2 REDUCE, decrease, lower, shorten, curtail, abbreviate, abridge, condense, précis, edit, delete.
➤ n 1 INCISION, wound, nick, gash, slit, slash, rip, laceration. 2 *spending cuts*: REDUCTION, decrease, lowering, cutback, saving, economy.
◇ **cut down 1** *cut down a tree*: fell, hew, lop, level, raze. **2** REDUCE, decrease, lower, lessen, diminish.
◇ **cut in** interrupt, butt in, interject, interpose, intervene, intrude.
◇ **cut off 1** SEVER, amputate, separate, isolate, disconnect, block, obstruct, intercept. **2** STOP, end, halt, suspend, discontinue, disown, disinherit.
◇ **cut up** chop, dice, mince, dissect,

divide, carve, slice, slash.

cutback n cut, saving, economy, retrenchment, reduction, downsizing, decrease, lowering, lessening.

cutlery

Items of cutlery include: knife, butter knife, carving knife, fish knife, steak knife, cheese knife, breadknife, vegetable knife, fork, fish fork, carving fork, pickle fork, corn holders, spoon, dessertspoon, tablespoon, teaspoon, soup spoon, caddy spoon, salt spoon, apostle spoon, ladle, salad servers, fish slice, cake server, sugar tongs, chopsticks, canteen of cutlery. *see also* **kitchen**.

cutter

Types of cutter include: axe, billhook, blade, chisel, chopper, clippers, guillotine, hedgetrimmer, knife, flick knife, penknife, pocket knife, Stanley knife®, Swiss army knife, lopper, machete, mower, lawnmower, plane, razor, saw, chainsaw, fretsaw, hacksaw, jigsaw, scalpel, scissors, scythe, secateurs, shears, pinking shears, sickle, Strimmer®, sword. *see also* **cutlery**; **saw**; **weapon**.

cutting adj sharp, keen, pointed, trenchant, incisive, penetrating, piercing, wounding, stinging, biting, mordant, caustic, acid, scathing, sarcastic, malicious, bitter, raw, chill.
➤ n clipping, extract, piece.

cycle n circle, round, rotation, revolution, series, sequence, phase, period, era, age, epoch, aeon.

cynic n sceptic, doubter, pessimist, killjoy, spoilsport (*infml*), knocker (*infml*).

cynical adj sceptical, doubtful, distrustful, pessimistic, negative, scornful, derisive, contemptuous, sneering, sarcastic, sardonic, ironic.

cynicism n scepticism, doubt, disbelief, distrust, pessimism, scorn, sarcasm, irony.

Dd

dab *v* pat, tap, daub, swab, wipe.
➤ *n* **1** BIT, dollop (*infml*), drop, speck, spot, trace, smear, smudge, fleck.
2 TOUCH, pat, stroke, tap.

dabble *v* **1** TRIFLE, tinker, toy, dally, potter. **2** PADDLE, moisten, wet, sprinkle, splash.

dabbler *n* amateur, dilettante, trifler.
E3 professional, expert.

daft *adj* **1** FOOLISH, crazy, silly, stupid, absurd, dotty (*infml*), idiotic, inane.
2 INSANE, mad, lunatic, simple, crazy, mental. **3** (*infml*) INFATUATED.
E3 **1** sensible. **2** sane.

daily *adj* **1** REGULAR, routine, everyday, customary, common, commonplace, ordinary. **2** EVERYDAY, diurnal (*fml*).

dainty *adj* **1** DELICATE, elegant, exquisite, refined, fine, graceful, neat, charming, delectable. **2** FASTIDIOUS, fussy, particular, scrupulous, nice (*fml*).
E3 **1** gross, clumsy.

dam *n* barrier, barrage, embankment, blockage, obstruction, hindrance.
➤ *v* block, confine, restrict, check, barricade, staunch, stem, obstruct.

damage *n* harm, injury, hurt, destruction, devastation, loss, suffering, mischief, mutilation, impairment, detriment.
E3 repair.
➤ *v* harm, injure, hurt, spoil, ruin, impair, mar, wreck, deface, mutilate, weaken, tamper with, play havoc with, incapacitate.
E3 mend, repair, fix.

damn *v* **1** CURSE, swear, blast, imprecate, blaspheme. **2** ABUSE, revile, denounce, criticise, censure, slate (*infml*), denunciate, execrate, castigate,
slam (*infml*). **3** CONDEMN, doom, sentence.
E3 **1** bless.

damnation *n* condemnation, doom, denunciation, perdition, excommunication, anathema.

damp *n* dampness, moisture, clamminess, dankness, humidity, wet, dew, drizzle, fog, mist, vapour.
E3 dryness.
➤ *adj* moist, wet, clammy, dank, humid, dewy, muggy, drizzly, misty, soggy.
E3 dry, arid.

dampen *v* **1** MOISTEN, wet, spray. **2** DISCOURAGE, dishearten, deter, dash, dull, deaden, restrain, check, depress, dismay, reduce, lessen, moderate, decrease, diminish, muffle, stifle, smother.
E3 **1** dry. **2** encourage.

dance *n* ball, hop (*infml*), knees-up (*infml*), social, shindig (*infml*).

> *Dances include*: waltz, quickstep, foxtrot, tango, polka, one-step, military two-step, valeta, Lancers, rumba, samba, mambo, bossanova, beguine, fandango, flamenco, mazurka, bolero, paso doble, salsa, macarena, merengue, can-can; rock 'n' roll, jive, twist, stomp, bop, jitterbug, mashed potato, ceroc; black bottom, Charleston, cha-cha, turkey-trot, kazachoc; Circassian circle, Paul Jones, jig, reel, quadrille, Highland fling, morris dance, clog dance, hoe-down, hokey-cokey, Lambeth Walk, conga, hora, belly dance; galliard, gavotte, minuet.

> *Types of dancing include*: ballet, tap, ballroom, old-time, disco, folk, country, set dancing, step dancing,

Irish, Highland, Latin-American, clog dancing, morris dancing, limbo dancing, line dancing, break-dancing, robotics. *see also* **ballet**.

Dance functions include: disco, dance, social, tea dance, barn dance, ball, fancy dress ball, charity ball, hunt ball, hop (*infml*), knees-up (*infml*), shindig (*infml*), rave (*infml*), prom (*US*), ceilidh.

danger *n* **1** *in danger of falling*: insecurity, endangerment, jeopardy, precariousness, liability, vulnerability. **2** *the dangers of smoking*: risk, threat, peril, hazard, menace.
₹₃ 1 safety, security. **2** safety.

dangerous *adj* unsafe, insecure, risky, threatening, breakneck, hairy (*infml*), hazardous, perilous, precarious, reckless, treacherous, vulnerable, menacing, exposed, alarming, critical, severe, serious, grave, daring, nasty.
₹₃ safe, secure, harmless.

dangle *v* **1** HANG, droop, swing, sway, flap, trail. **2** TEMPT, entice, flaunt, flourish, lure, tantalize.

dank *adj* damp, moist, clammy, dewy, slimy, soggy.
₹₃ dry.

dappled *adj* speckled, mottled, spotted, stippled, dotted, flecked, freckled, variegated, bespeckled, piebald, checkered.

dare *v* **1** RISK, venture, brave, hazard, adventure, endanger, stake, gamble. **2** CHALLENGE, goad, provoke, taunt. **3** DEFY, presume.
➤ *n* challenge, provocation, taunt, gauntlet.

daredevil *n* adventurer, desperado, madcap.
₹₃ coward.

daring *adj* bold, adventurous, intrepid, fearless, brave, plucky, audacious, dauntless, reckless, rash, impulsive, valiant.
₹₃ cautious, timid, afraid.
➤ *n* boldness, fearlessness, courage,

bravery, nerve, audacity, guts (*infml*), intrepidity, defiance, pluck, rashness, spirit, grit, gall, prowess.
₹₃ caution, timidity, cowardice.

dark *adj* **1** *a dark room*: unlit, overcast, black, dim, unilluminated, shadowy, murky, cloudy, dusky, dingy. **2** *a dark manner*: gloomy, grim, cheerless, dismal, bleak, forbidding, sombre, sinister, mournful, ominous, menacing, drab. **3** *dark secrets*: hidden, mysterious, obscure, secret, unintelligible, enigmatic, cryptic, abstruse.
₹₃ 1 light. **2** bright, cheerful.
3 comprehensible.
➤ *n* **1** DARKNESS, dimness, night, night-time, nightfall, gloom, dusk, twilight, murkiness. **2** CONCEALMENT, secrecy, obscurity.
₹₃ 1 light. **2** openness.

darken *v* **1** DIM, obscure, blacken, cloud (over), shadow, overshadow, eclipse. **2** DEPRESS, sadden.
₹₃ 1 lighten. **2** brighten.

darling *n* beloved, dear, dearest, favourite, sweetheart, love, pet.
➤ *adj* dear, beloved, adored, cherished, precious, treasured.

dart *v* **1** DASH, bound, sprint, flit, flash, fly, rush, run, race, spring, tear. **2** THROW, hurl, fling, shoot, sling, launch, propel, send.
➤ *n* bolt, arrow, barb, shaft.

dash *v* **1** RUSH, dart, hurry, race, sprint, run, bolt, tear. **2** FLING, throw, crash, hurl. **3** DISCOURAGE, disappoint, dampen, confound, blight, ruin, destroy, spoil, frustrate, smash, shatter.
➤ *n* **1** DROP, pinch, touch, flavour, soupçon, suggestion, hint, bit, little. **2** SPRINT, dart, bolt, rush, spurt, race, run.

dashing *adj* **1** LIVELY, vigorous, spirited, gallant, daring, bold, plucky, exuberant. **2** SMART, stylish, elegant, debonair, showy, flamboyant.
₹₃ 1 lethargic. **2** dowdy.

data *n* information, documents, facts, input, statistics, figures, details, gen (*infml*), materials.

date *n* **1** TIME, age, period, era, stage, epoch. **2** APPOINTMENT, engagement, assignation, meeting, rendezvous. **3** ESCORT, steady (*infml*), partner, friend.
◇ **out of date** *adj* old-fashioned, unfashionable, outdated, obsolete, dated, outmoded, antiquated, passé.
◄ fashionable, modern.
◇ **up to date** *adj* fashionable, modern, current, contemporary.
◄ old-fashioned, dated.

daunt *v* **1** DISCOURAGE, dishearten, put off, dispirit, deter. **2** INTIMIDATE, overawe, unnerve, alarm, dismay, frighten, scare.
◄ **1** encourage.

dauntless *adj* fearless, undaunted, resolute, brave, courageous, bold, intrepid, daring, plucky, valiant.
◄ discouraged, disheartened.

dawdle *v* delay, loiter, lag, hang about, dally, trail, potter, dilly-dally (*infml*).
◄ hurry.

dawn *n* **1** SUNRISE, daybreak, morning, daylight. **2** BEGINNING, start, emergence, onset, origin, birth, advent.
◄ **1** dusk. **2** end.
➤ *v* **1** BREAK, brighten, lighten, gleam, glimmer. **2** BEGIN, appear, emerge, open, develop, originate, rise.

day *n* **1** DAYTIME, daylight. **2** AGE, period, time, date, era, generation, epoch.
◄ **1** night.
◇ **day after day** regularly, continually, endlessly, persistently, monotonously, perpetually, relentlessly.
◇ **day by day** gradually, progressively, slowly but surely, steadily.

daydream *n* fantasy, imagining, reverie, castles in the air, pipe dream, vision, musing, wish, dream, figment.
➤ *v* fantasize, imagine, muse, fancy, dream.

daze *v* **1** STUN, stupefy, shock. **2** DAZZLE, bewilder, blind, confuse, baffle, dumbfound, amaze, surprise, startle, perplex, astonish, flabbergast (*infml*), astound, stagger.
➤ *n* bewilderment, confusion, stupor, trance, shock, distraction.

dazzle *v* **1** DAZE, blind, confuse, blur. **2** SPARKLE, fascinate, impress, overwhelm, awe, overawe, scintillate, bedazzle, amaze, astonish, bewitch, stupefy.
➤ *n* sparkle, brilliance, magnificence, splendour, scintillation, glitter, glare.

dead *adj* **1** LIFELESS, deceased, inanimate, defunct, departed, late, gone. **2** UNRESPONSIVE, apathetic, dull, indifferent, insensitive, numb, cold, frigid, lukewarm, torpid. **3** EXHAUSTED, tired, worn out, dead-beat (*infml*). **4** EXACT, absolute, perfect, unqualified, utter, outright, complete, entire, total, downright.
◄ **1** alive. **2** lively. **3** refreshed.

deaden *v* reduce, blunt, muffle, lessen, quieten, suppress, weaken, numb, diminish, stifle, alleviate, anaesthetize, desensitize, smother, check, abate, allay, dampen, hush, mute, paralyse.
◄ heighten.

deadlock *n* standstill, stalemate, impasse, halt.

deadly *adj* **1** *deadly poison*: lethal, fatal, dangerous, venomous, destructive, pernicious, malignant, murderous, mortal. **2** *a deadly lecture*: dull, boring, uninteresting, tedious, monotonous. **3** *deadly aim*: unerring, effective, true.
◄ **1** harmless. **2** exciting.

deaf *adj* **1** HARD OF HEARING, stone-deaf. **2** UNCONCERNED, indifferent, unmoved, oblivious, heedless, unmindful.
◄ **2** aware, conscious.

deafening *adj* piercing, ear-splitting, booming, resounding, thunderous, ringing, roaring.
◄ quiet.

deal *v* **1** APPORTION, distribute, share, dole out, divide, allot, dispense, assign, mete out, give, bestow. **2** TRADE, negotiate, traffic, bargain, treat.
➤ *n* **1** QUANTITY, amount, extent, degree,

portion, share. **2** AGREEMENT, contract, understanding, pact, transaction, bargain, buy. **3** ROUND, hand, distribution.

◇ **deal with** attend to, concern, see to, manage, handle, cope with, treat, consider, oversee.

dealer *n* trader, merchant, wholesaler, marketer, merchandiser.

dear *adj* **1** LOVED, beloved, treasured, valued, cherished, precious, favourite, esteemed, intimate, close, darling, familiar. **2** EXPENSIVE, high-priced, costly, overpriced, pricey (*infml*).
1 disliked, hated. **2** cheap.
➤ *n* beloved, loved one, precious, darling, treasure.

dearly *adv* **1** *he loves her dearly*: fondly, affectionately, lovingly, devotedly, tenderly. **2** *I wish it dearly*: greatly, extremely, profoundly.

dearth *n* scarcity, shortage, insufficiency, inadequacy, deficiency, lack, want, absence, scantiness, sparsity, need, paucity, poverty, famine.
excess, abundance.

death *n* **1** DECEASE, end, finish, loss, demise, departure, fatality, cessation, passing, expiration, dissolution. **2** DESTRUCTION, ruin, undoing, annihilation, downfall, extermination, extinction, obliteration, eradication.
1 life, birth.

deathly *adj* **1** ASHEN, grim, haggard, pale, pallid, ghastly, wan. **2** FATAL, deadly, mortal, intense.

debase *v* **1** DEGRADE, demean, devalue, disgrace, dishonour, shame, humble, humiliate, lower, reduce, abase, defile. **2** CONTAMINATE, pollute, corrupt, adulterate, taint.
1 elevate. **2** purify.

debatable *adj* questionable, uncertain, disputable, contestable, controversial, arguable, open to question, doubtful, contentious, undecided, unsettled, problematical, dubious, moot.
unquestionable, certain, incontrovertible.

debate *v* **1** DISPUTE, argue, discuss, contend, wrangle. **2** CONSIDER, deliberate, ponder, reflect, meditate on, mull over, weigh.
➤ *n* discussion, argument, controversy, disputation, deliberation, forum, consideration, contention, dispute, reflection, polemic.

debauchery *n* depravity, intemperance, overindulgence, dissipation, licentiousness, dissoluteness, excess, decadence, wantonness, lewdness, carousal, orgy, revel, lust, riot.
restraint, temperance.

debilitate *v* weaken, enervate, undermine, sap, incapacitate, wear out, exhaust, impair.
strengthen, invigorate, energize.

debris *n* remains, ruins, rubbish, waste, wreck, wreckage, litter, fragments, rubble, trash, pieces, bits, sweepings, drift.

debt *n* indebtedness, obligation, debit, arrears, due, liability, duty, bill, commitment, claim, score.
credit, asset.

debtor *n* borrower, bankrupt, insolvent, defaulter, mortgagor.
creditor.

debunk *v* expose, deflate, show up, ridicule, mock, explode, lampoon.

debut *n* introduction, launching, beginning, entrance, presentation, inauguration, première, appearance, initiation.

decadent *adj* **1** CORRUPT, debased, debauched, depraved, dissolute, immoral, degenerate, degraded, self-indulgent. **2** DECAYING, declining.
1 moral.

decay *v* **1** ROT, go bad, putrefy, decompose, spoil, perish, mortify. **2** DECLINE, deteriorate, disintegrate, corrode, crumble, waste away, degenerate, wear away, dwindle, shrivel, wither, sink.
2 flourish, grow.
➤ *n* **1** ROT, decomposition, rotting,

perishing. **2** DECLINE, deterioration, disintegration, degeneration, collapse, decadence, wasting, failing, withering, fading.

decease *n* death, dying, demise, departure, passing, dissolution.

deceased *adj* dead, departed, former, late, lost, defunct, expired, gone, finished, extinct.
➤ *n* dead, departed.

deceit *n* deception, pretence, cheating, misrepresentation, fraud, duplicity, trickery, fraudulence, double-dealing, underhandedness, fake, guile, sham, subterfuge, swindle, treachery, hypocrisy, artifice, ruse, cunning, slyness, craftiness, stratagem, wile, imposition, feint, shift, abuse.
✷ honesty, openness, frankness.

deceitful *adj* dishonest, deceptive, deceiving, false, insincere, untrustworthy, double-dealing, fraudulent, two-faced (*infml*), treacherous, duplicitous, guileful, tricky (*infml*), underhand, sneaky, counterfeit, crafty, hypocritical, designing, illusory, knavish.
✷ honest, open.

deceive *v* mislead, delude, cheat, betray, fool, take in (*infml*), trick, dissemble, hoax, con (*infml*), have on (*infml*), take for a ride (*infml*), double-cross (*infml*), dupe, kid (*infml*), swindle, impose upon, bamboozle (*infml*), two-time (*infml*), lead on, outwit, hoodwink, beguile, ensnare, camouflage, abuse, befool, gull.

decency *n* propriety, courtesy, modesty, decorum, respectability, civility, correctness, fitness, etiquette, helpfulness.
✷ impropriety, discourtesy.

decent *adj* **1** RESPECTABLE, proper, fitting, decorous, chaste, seemly, suitable, modest, appropriate, presentable, pure, fit, becoming, befitting, nice. **2** KIND, obliging, courteous, helpful, generous, polite, gracious. **3** ADEQUATE, acceptable,

satisfactory, reasonable, sufficient, tolerable, competent.
✷ **1** indecent. **2** disobliging.

deception *n* deceit, pretence, trick, cheat, fraud, imposture, lie, dissembling, deceptiveness, insincerity, con (*infml*), sham, subterfuge, artifice, hypocrisy, bluff, treachery, hoax, fraudulence, duplicity, ruse, snare, stratagem, leg-pull (*infml*), illusion, wile, guile, craftiness, cunning.
✷ openness, honesty.

deceptive *adj* dishonest, false, fraudulent, misleading, unreliable, illusive, fake, illusory, spurious, mock, fallacious, ambiguous, specious.
✷ genuine, artless, open.

decide *v* choose, determine, resolve, reach a decision, settle, elect, opt, judge, adjudicate, conclude, fix, purpose, decree.

decided *adj* **1** DEFINITE, certain, undeniable, indisputable, absolute, clear-cut, undisputed, unmistakable, unquestionable, positive, unambiguous, categorical, distinct, emphatic. **2** RESOLUTE, decisive, determined, firm, unhesitating, deliberate, forthright.
✷ **1** inconclusive. **2** irresolute.

decipher *v* decode, unscramble, crack, construe, interpret, make out (*infml*), figure out (*infml*), understand, transliterate.
✷ encode.

decision *n* **1** RESULT, conclusion, outcome, verdict, finding, settlement, judgement, arbitration, ruling. **2** DETERMINATION, decisiveness, firmness, resolve, purpose.

decisive *adj* **1** CONCLUSIVE, definite, definitive, absolute, final. **2** DETERMINED, resolute, decided, positive, firm, forceful, forthright, strong-minded. **3** SIGNIFICANT, critical, crucial, influential, momentous, fateful.
✷ **1** inconclusive. **2** indecisive. **3** insignificant.

declaration *n* **1** AFFIRMATION,

acknowledgement, assertion, statement, testimony, attestation, disclosure, profession, revelation. **2** ANNOUNCEMENT, notification, pronouncement, proclamation, edict, manifesto, promulgation.

declare v **1** AFFIRM, assert, claim, profess, maintain, state, attest, certify, confess, confirm, disclose, reveal, show, aver, swear, testify, witness, validate. **2** ANNOUNCE, proclaim, pronounce, decree, broadcast.

decline v **1** REFUSE, reject, deny, forgo, avoid, balk. **2** DIMINISH, decrease, dwindle, lessen, fall, sink, wane. **3** DECAY, deteriorate, worsen, degenerate. **4** DESCEND, sink, slope, dip, slant.
◼ **3** improve. **4** rise.
➤ n **1** DETERIORATION, dwindling, lessening, decay, degeneration, weakening, worsening, failing, downturn, diminution, falling-off, recession, slump, abatement. **2** DESCENT, dip, declivity, declination, hill, slope, incline, divergence, deviation.
◼ **1** improvement. **2** rise.

decode v decipher, interpret, unscramble, translate, transliterate, uncipher.
◼ encode.

decompose v disintegrate, rot, decay, putrefy, break down, break up, crumble, spoil, dissolve, separate, fester.

décor n decoration, furnishings, colour scheme, ornamentation, scenery.

decorate v **1** ORNAMENT, adorn, beautify, embellish, trim, deck, tart up (sl), grace, enrich, prettify, trick out. **2** RENOVATE, do up (infml), paint, paper, colour, refurbish. **3** HONOUR, crown, cite, garland, bemedal.

decoration n **1** ORNAMENT, adornment, ornamentation, trimming, embellishment, beautification, garnish, flourish, enrichment, elaboration, frill, scroll, bauble. **2** AWARD, medal, order, badge, garland, crown, colours, ribbon, laurel, star, emblem.

decorative adj ornamental, fancy,

adorning, beautifying, embellishing, non-functional, pretty, ornate, enhancing.
◼ plain.

decorum n propriety, seemliness, etiquette, good manners, respectability, protocol, behaviour, decency, dignity, deportment, restraint, politeness, modesty, grace, breeding.
◼ impropriety, indecorum, bad manners.

decoy n lure, trap, enticement, inducement, ensnarement, pretence, attraction, bait.
➤ v bait, lure, entrap, entice, ensnare, allure, tempt, deceive, attract, seduce, lead, draw.

decrease v lessen, lower, diminish, dwindle, decline, fall off, reduce, subside, abate, cut down, contract, drop, ease, shrink, taper, wane, slim, slacken, peter out, curtail.
◼ increase.
➤ n lessening, reduction, decline, falling-off, dwindling, loss, diminution, abatement, cutback, contraction, downturn, ebb, shrinkage, subsidence, step-down.
◼ increase.

decree n order, command, law, ordinance, regulation, ruling, statute, act, enactment, edict, proclamation, mandate, precept, interlocution.
➤ v order, command, rule, lay down, dictate, decide, determine, ordain, prescribe, proclaim, pronounce, enact.

decrepit adj dilapidated, run-down, rickety, broken-down, worn-out, tumbledown.

dedicate v **1** DEVOTE, commit, assign, give over to, pledge, present, offer, sacrifice, surrender. **2** CONSECRATE, bless, sanctify, set apart, hallow. **3** dedicate a book: inscribe, address.

dedicated adj devoted, committed, enthusiastic, single-minded, wholehearted, single-hearted, zealous, given over to, purposeful.
◼ uncommitted, apathetic.

dedication n 1 COMMITMENT, devotion, single-mindedness, wholeheartedness, allegiance, attachment, adherence, faithfulness, loyalty, self-sacrifice. 2 CONSECRATION, hallowing, presentation. 3 INSCRIPTION, address.
⊞ 1 apathy.

deduce v derive, infer, gather, conclude, reason, surmise, understand, draw, glean.

deduct v subtract, take away, remove, reduce by, decrease by, knock off (*infml*), withdraw.
⊞ add.

deduction n 1 INFERENCE, reasoning, finding, conclusion, corollary, assumption, result. 2 SUBTRACTION, reduction, decrease, diminution, abatement, withdrawal, discount, allowance.
⊞ 2 addition, increase.

deed n 1 ACTION, act, achievement, performance, exploit, feat, fact, truth, reality. 2 DOCUMENT, contract, record, title, transaction, indenture (*fml*).

deep adj 1 PROFOUND, bottomless, unplumbed, fathomless, yawning, immersed. 2 OBSCURE, mysterious, difficult, recondite, abstruse, esoteric. 3 WISE, perceptive, discerning, profound, learned, astute. 4 INTENSE, serious, earnest, extreme. 5 LOW, bass, resonant, booming.
⊞ 1 shallow, open. 2 clear, plain, open. 3 superficial. 4 light. 5 high.

deepen v 1 INTENSIFY, grow, increase, strengthen, reinforce, magnify. 2 HOLLOW, scoop out.

deep-seated adj ingrained, entrenched, deep-rooted, fixed, confirmed, deep, settled.
⊞ eradicable, temporary.

deface v damage, spoil, disfigure, blemish, impair, mutilate, mar, sully, tarnish, vandalize, deform, obliterate, injure, destroy.
⊞ repair.

defamation n vilification (*fml*),

aspersion (*fml*), slander, libel, disparagement, slur, smear, innuendo, scandal.
⊞ commendation, praise.

defamatory adj vilifying (*fml*), slanderous, libellous, denigrating (*fml*), disparaging, pejorative, insulting, injurious, derogatory.
⊞ complimentary, appreciative.

default n failure, absence, neglect, non-payment, omission, deficiency, lapse, fault, want, lack, defect.
➤ v fail, evade, defraud, neglect, dodge, swindle, backslide.

defaulter n non-payer, offender.

defeat v 1 CONQUER, beat, overpower, subdue, overthrow, worst, repel, subjugate, overwhelm, rout, ruin, thump (*infml*), quell, vanquish (*fml*). 2 FRUSTRATE, confound, balk, get the better of, disappoint, foil, thwart, baffle, checkmate.
➤ n 1 CONQUEST, beating, overthrow, rout, subjugation, vanquishment (*fml*). 2 FRUSTRATION, failure, setback, reverse, disappointment, checkmate.

defeatist n pessimist, quitter, prophet of doom.
⊞ optimist.
➤ adj pessimistic, resigned, fatalistic, despondent, helpless, hopeless, despairing, gloomy.
⊞ optimistic.

defect n imperfection, fault, flaw, deficiency, failing, mistake, inadequacy, blemish, error, bug (*infml*), shortcoming, want, weakness, frailty, lack, spot, absence, taint.
➤ v desert, break faith, rebel, apostatize (*fml*), revolt, renegue.

defective adj faulty, imperfect, shoddy, out of order, flawed, deficient, broken, abnormal.
⊞ in order, operative.

defence n 1 PROTECTION, resistance, security, fortification, cover, safeguard, shelter, guard, shield, deterrence, barricade, bastion, immunity, bulwark, rampart, buttress. 2 JUSTIFICATION, explanation, excuse, argument, exoneration, plea, vindication, apologia (*fml*), pleading, alibi, case.

🔁 **1** attack, assault. **2** accusation.

defenceless *adj* unprotected, undefended, unarmed, unguarded, vulnerable, exposed, helpless, powerless.

🔁 protected, guarded.

defend *v* **1** PROTECT, guard, safeguard, shelter, fortify, secure, shield, screen, cover, contest. **2** SUPPORT, stand up for, stand by, uphold, endorse, vindicate, champion, argue for, speak up for, justify, plead.

🔁 **1** attack. **2** accuse.

defendant *n* accused, offender, prisoner, respondent.

defender *n* **1** PROTECTOR, guard, bodyguard. **2** SUPPORTER, advocate, vindicator, champion, patron, sponsor, counsel.

🔁 **1** attacker. **2** accuser.

defensive *adj* **1** PROTECTIVE, defending, safeguarding, wary, opposing, cautious, watchful. **2** SELF-JUSTIFYING, apologetic.

defer[1] *v* delay, postpone, put off, adjourn, hold over, shelve, suspend, procrastinate, prorogue (*fml*), protract, waive.

defer[2] *v* yield, give way, comply, submit, accede, capitulate, respect, bow.

deference *n* **1** SUBMISSION, submissiveness, compliance, acquiescence, obedience, yielding. **2** RESPECT, regard, honour, esteem, reverence, courtesy, civility, politeness, consideration.

🔁 **1** resistance. **2** contempt.

defiance *n* opposition, confrontation, resistance, challenge, disobedience, rebelliousness, contempt, disregard, insubordination, insolence.

🔁 compliance, acquiescence, submissiveness.

defiant *adj* challenging, resistant,

antagonistic, aggressive, rebellious, insubordinate, disobedient, intransigent, bold, contumacious (*fml*), insolent, obstinate, unco-operative, provocative.

🔁 compliant, acquiescent, submissive.

deficiency *n* **1** SHORTAGE, lack, inadequacy, scarcity, insufficiency, dearth, want, scantiness, absence, deficit. **2** IMPERFECTION, shortcoming, weakness, fault, defect, flaw, failing, frailty.

🔁 **1** excess, surfeit. **2** perfection.

deficient *adj* **1** INADEQUATE, insufficient, scarce, short, lacking, wanting, meagre, scanty, skimpy, incomplete. **2** IMPERFECT, impaired, flawed, faulty, defective, shoddy, unsatisfactory, inferior, weak.

🔁 **1** excessive. **2** perfect.

deficit *n* shortage, shortfall, deficiency, loss, arrears, lack, default.

🔁 excess.

defile *v* pollute, violate, contaminate, degrade, dishonour, desecrate, debase, soil, stain, sully, tarnish, taint, profane, corrupt, disgrace.

define *v* **1** *define the boundaries*: bound, limit, delimit, demarcate, mark out. **2** *define the meaning*: explain, characterize, describe, interpret, expound, determine, designate, specify, spell out, detail.

definite *adj* **1** CERTAIN, settled, sure, positive, fixed, decided, determined, assured, guaranteed. **2** CLEAR, clear-cut, exact, precise, specific, explicit, particular, obvious, marked.

🔁 **1** indefinite. **2** vague.

definitely *adv* positively, surely, unquestionably, absolutely, certainly, categorically, undeniably, clearly, doubtless, unmistakably, plainly, obviously, indeed, easily.

definition *n* **1** DELINEATION, demarcation, delimitation. **2** EXPLANATION, description, interpretation, exposition, clarification, elucidation, determination. **3**

DISTINCTNESS, clarity, precision, clearness, focus, contrast, sharpness.

definitive adj decisive, conclusive, final, authoritative, standard, correct, ultimate, reliable, exhaustive, perfect, exact, absolute, complete.
➤ interim.

deflate v 1 FLATTEN, puncture, collapse, exhaust, squash, empty, contract, void, shrink, squeeze. 2 DEBUNK, humiliate, put down (*infml*), dash, dispirit, humble, mortify, disconcert. 3 DECREASE, devalue, reduce, lessen, lower, diminish, depreciate, depress.
➤ 1 inflate. 2 boost. 3 increase.

deflect v deviate, diverge, turn (aside), swerve, veer, sidetrack, twist, avert, wind, glance off, bend, ricochet.

deform v distort, contort, disfigure, warp, mar, pervert, ruin, spoil, twist.

deformed adj distorted, misshapen, contorted, disfigured, crippled, crooked, bent, twisted, warped, buckled, defaced, mangled, maimed, marred, ruined, mutilated, perverted, corrupted.

deformity n distortion, contortion, misshapenness, malformation, disfigurement, abnormality, irregularity, misproportion, defect, ugliness, monstrosity, corruption.

defraud v cheat, swindle, dupe, fleece, sting (*sl*), rip off (*sl*), do (*infml*), diddle (*infml*), rob, trick, con (*infml*), rook, deceive, delude, embezzle, beguile.

deft adj adept, handy, dexterous, nimble, skilful, adroit, agile, expert, nifty, proficient, able, neat, clever.
➤ clumsy, awkward.

defunct adj 1 DEAD, deceased, departed, gone, expired, extinct. 2 OBSOLETE, invalid, inoperative, expired.
➤ 1 alive, live. 2 operative.

defy v 1 *defy the authorities*: challenge, confront, resist, dare, brave, face, repel, spurn, beard, flout, withstand, disregard, scorn, despise, defeat, provoke, thwart. 2 *her writings defy categorization*: elude, frustrate, baffle, foil.
➤ 1 obey. 2 permit.

degenerate adj dissolute, debauched, depraved, degraded, debased, base, low, decadent, corrupt, fallen, immoral, mean, degenerated, perverted, deteriorated.
➤ moral, upright.
➤ v decline, deteriorate, sink, decay, rot, slip, worsen, regress, fall off, lapse, decrease.
➤ improve.

degradation n 1 DETERIORATION, degeneration, decline, downgrading, demotion. 2 ABASEMENT, humiliation, mortification, dishonour, disgrace, shame, ignominy, decadence.
➤ 1 virtue. 2 enhancement.

degrade v 1 DISHONOUR, disgrace, debase, abase, shame, humiliate, humble, discredit, demean, lower, weaken, impair, deteriorate, cheapen, adulterate, corrupt. 2 DEMOTE, depose, downgrade, deprive, cashier.
➤ 1 exalt. 2 promote.

degree n 1 GRADE, class, rank, order, position, standing, status. 2 EXTENT, measure, range, stage, step, level, intensity, standard. 3 LEVEL, limit, unit, mark.

deify v exalt, elevate, worship, glorify, idolize, extol, venerate, immortalize, ennoble, idealize.

deign v condescend, stoop, lower oneself, consent, demean oneself.

deity n god, goddess, divinity, godhead, idol, demigod, demigoddess, power, immortal.

dejected adj downcast, despondent, depressed, downhearted, disheartened, down, low, melancholy, disconsolate, sad, miserable, cast down, gloomy, glum, crestfallen, dismal, wretched, doleful, morose, spiritless.
➤ cheerful, high-spirited, happy.

delay v 1 OBSTRUCT, hinder, impede, hold up, check, hold back, set back,

stop, halt, detain. **2** DEFER, put off, postpone, procrastinate, suspend, shelve, hold over, stall. **3** DAWDLE, linger, lag, loiter, dilly-dally (*infml*), tarry.
🔁 **1** accelerate. **2** bring forward. **3** hurry.

➤ *n* **1** OBSTRUCTION, hindrance, impediment, hold-up, check, setback, stay, stoppage. **2** DEFERMENT, postponement, procrastination, suspension. **3** DAWDLING, lingering, tarrying. **4** INTERRUPTION, lull, interval, wait.
🔁 **1** hastening. **3** hurry. **4** continuation.

delegate *n* representative, agent, envoy, messenger, deputy, ambassador, commissioner.

➤ *v* authorize, appoint, depute, charge, commission, assign, empower, entrust, devolve, consign, designate, nominate, name, hand over.

delegation *n* **1** DEPUTATION, commission, legation, mission, contingent, embassy. **2** AUTHORIZATION, commissioning, assignment.

delete *v* erase, remove, cross out, cancel, rub out, strike (out), obliterate, edit (out), blot out, efface.
🔁 add, insert.

deliberate *v* consider, ponder, reflect, think, cogitate, meditate, mull over, debate, discuss, weigh, consult.

➤ *adj* **1** INTENTIONAL, planned, calculated, prearranged, premeditated, willed, conscious, designed, considered, advised. **2** CAREFUL, unhurried, thoughtful, methodical, cautious, circumspect, studied, prudent, slow, ponderous, measured, heedful.
🔁 **1** unintentional, accidental. **2** hasty.

deliberation *n* **1** CONSIDERATION, reflection, thought, calculation, forethought, meditation, rumination, study, debate, discussion, consultation, speculation. **2** CARE, carefulness, caution, circumspection, prudence.

delicacy *n* **1** DAINTINESS, fineness, elegance, exquisiteness, lightness, precision. **2** REFINEMENT, sensitivity,

subtlety, finesse, discrimination, tact, niceness. **3** TITBIT, dainty, taste, sweetmeat, savoury, relish.
🔁 **1** coarseness, roughness. **2** tactlessness.

delicate *adj* **1** FINE, fragile, dainty, exquisite, flimsy, elegant, graceful. **2** FRAIL, weak, ailing, faint. **3** SENSITIVE, scrupulous, discriminating, careful, accurate, precise. **4** SUBTLE, muted, pastel, soft.
🔁 **1** coarse, clumsy. **2** healthy.

delicious *adj* **1** ENJOYABLE, pleasant, agreeable, delightful. **2** APPETIZING, palatable, tasty, delectable, scrumptious (*infml*), yummy (*infml*), mouth-watering, succulent, savoury.
🔁 **1** unpleasant. **2** unpalatable.

delight *n* bliss, happiness, joy, pleasure, ecstasy, enjoyment, gladness, rapture, transport, gratification, jubilation.
🔁 disgust, displeasure.

➤ *v* please, charm, gratify, enchant, tickle, thrill, ravish.
🔁 displease, dismay.

◇ **delight in** enjoy, relish, like, love, appreciate, revel in, take pride in, glory in, savour.
🔁 dislike, hate.

delighted *adj* charmed, elated, happy, pleased, enchanted, captivated, ecstatic, thrilled, overjoyed, jubilant, joyous.
🔁 disappointed, dismayed.

delightful *adj* charming, enchanting, captivating, enjoyable, pleasant, thrilling, agreeable, pleasurable, engaging, attractive, pleasing, gratifying, entertaining, fascinating.
🔁 nasty, unpleasant.

delinquency *n* crime, offence, wrongdoing, misbehaviour, misconduct, law-breaking, misdemeanour, criminality.

delinquent *n* offender, criminal, wrongdoer, law-breaker, hooligan, culprit, miscreant (*fml*).

delirious *adj* demented, raving,

incoherent, beside oneself, deranged, frenzied, light-headed, wild, mad, frantic, insane, crazy, ecstatic.
🗷 sane.

deliver v 1 *deliver a parcel*: convey, bring, send, give, carry, supply. 2 SURRENDER, hand over, relinquish, yield, transfer, grant, entrust, commit. 3 UTTER, speak, proclaim, pronounce. 4 ADMINISTER, inflict, direct. 5 SET FREE, liberate, release, emancipate.

delivery n 1 CONVEYANCE, consignment, dispatch, transmission, transfer, surrender. 2 ARTICULATION, enunciation, speech, utterance, intonation, elocution. 3 CHILDBIRTH, labour, confinement.

delude v deceive, mislead, beguile, dupe, take in, trick, hoodwink, hoax, cheat, misinform.

deluge n flood, inundation, downpour, torrent, spate, rush.
➤ v flood, inundate, drench, drown, overwhelm, soak, swamp, engulf, submerge.

delusion n illusion, hallucination, fancy, misconception, misapprehension, deception, misbelief, fallacy.

demand v 1 ASK, request, call for, insist on, solicit, claim, exact, inquire, question, interrogate. 2 NECESSITATE, need, require, involve.
➤ n 1 REQUEST, question, claim, order, inquiry, desire, interrogation. 2 NEED, necessity, call.

demanding adj hard, difficult, challenging, exacting, taxing, tough, exhausting, wearing, back-breaking, insistent, pressing, urgent, trying.
🗷 easy, undemanding, easy-going.

demean v lower, humble, degrade, humiliate, debase, abase, descend, stoop, condescend.
🗷 exalt, enhance.

demeanour n bearing, manner, deportment, conduct, behaviour, air.

demented adj mad, insane, lunatic, out of one's mind, crazy, loony (*sl*),

deranged, unbalanced, frenzied.
🗷 sane.

demise n 1 DEATH, decease, end, passing, departure, termination, expiration. 2 DOWNFALL, fall, collapse, failure, ruin. 3 TRANSFER, conveyance, inheritance, transmission, alienation.

democracy n self-government, commonwealth, autonomy, republic.

democratic adj self-governing, representative, egalitarian, autonomous, popular, populist.

demolish v 1 DESTROY, dismantle, knock down, pull down, flatten, bulldoze, raze, tear down, level. 2 RUIN, defeat, destroy, annihilate, wreck, overturn, overthrow.
🗷 1 build up.

demolition n destruction, dismantling, levelling, razing.

demon n 1 DEVIL, fiend, evil spirit, fallen angel, imp. 2 VILLAIN, devil, rogue, monster.

demonstrable adj verifiable, provable, arguable, attestable, self-evident, obvious, evident, certain, clear, positive.
🗷 unverifiable.

demonstrate v 1 SHOW, display, prove, establish, exhibit, substantiate, manifest, testify to, indicate. 2 EXPLAIN, illustrate, describe, teach. 3 PROTEST, march, parade, rally, picket, sit in.

demonstration n 1 DISPLAY, exhibition, manifestation, proof, confirmation, affirmation, substantiation, validation, evidence, testimony, expression. 2 EXPLANATION, illustration, description, exposition, presentation, test, trial. 3 PROTEST, march, demo (*infml*), rally, picket, sit-in, parade.

demonstrative adj affectionate, expressive, expansive, emotional, open, loving.
🗷 reserved, cold, restrained.

demoralize v 1 DISCOURAGE, dishearten, dispirit, undermine,

depress, deject, crush, lower, disconcert. **2** CORRUPT, deprave, debase.
F₃ 1 encourage. **2** improve.

demote v downgrade, degrade, relegate, reduce, cashier.
F₃ promote, upgrade.

demur v disagree, dissent, object, take exception, refuse, protest, dispute, balk, scruple, doubt, hesitate.

demure adj modest, reserved, reticent, prim, coy, shy, retiring, prissy, grave, prudish, sober, strait-laced, staid.
F₃ wanton, forward.

den n lair, hideout, hole, retreat, study, hideaway, shelter, sanctuary, haunt.

denial n **1** CONTRADICTION, negation, dissent, repudiation, disavowal, disclaimer, dismissal, renunciation. **2** REFUSAL, rebuff, rejection, prohibition, veto.

denigrate v disparage, run down, slander, revile, defame, malign, vilify, decry, besmirch, impugn, belittle, abuse, assail, criticize.
F₃ praise, acclaim.

denomination n **1** CLASSIFICATION, category, class, kind, sort. **2** RELIGION, persuasion, sect, belief, faith, creed, communion, school.

denote v indicate, stand for, signify, represent, symbolize, mean, express, designate, typify, mark, show, imply.

dénouement n climax, culmination, conclusion, outcome, upshot, pay-off (*infml*), finale, resolution, finish, solution, close.

denounce v condemn, censure, accuse, revile, decry, attack, inform against, betray, impugn, vilify, fulminate.
F₃ acclaim, praise.

dense adj **1** COMPACT, thick, close, close-knit, compressed, condensed, heavy, solid, opaque, impenetrable, packed, crowded. **2** STUPID, thick (*infml*), crass, dull, slow, slow-witted.
F₃ 1 thin, sparse. **2** quick-witted, clever.

dent n hollow, depression, dip, concavity, indentation, crater, dimple, dint, pit.
➤ v depress, gouge, push in, indent.

denude v strip, divest, expose, uncover, bare, deforest.
F₃ cover, clothe.

denunciation n condemnation, denouncement, censure, accusation, incrimination, invective, criticism.
F₃ praise.

deny v **1** *deny God's existence*: contradict, oppose, refute, disagree with, disaffirm, disprove. **2** *deny one's parentage*: disown, disclaim, renounce, repudiate, recant. **3** *deny their human rights*: refuse, turn down, forbid, reject, withhold, rebuff, veto.
F₃ 1 admit. **3** allow.

depart v **1** GO, leave, withdraw, exit, make off, quit, decamp, take one's leave, absent oneself, set off, remove, retreat, migrate, escape, disappear, retire, vanish. **2** DEVIATE, digress, differ, diverge, swerve, veer.
F₃ 1 arrive, return. **2** keep to.

departed adj dead, deceased, gone, late, expired.

department n **1** DIVISION, branch, subdivision, section, sector, office, station, unit, region, district. **2** SPHERE, realm, province, domain, field, area, concern, responsibility, speciality, line.

departure n **1** EXIT, going, leave-taking, removal, withdrawal, retirement, exodus. **2** DEVIATION, digression, divergence, variation, innovation, branching (out), difference, change, shift, veering.
F₃ 1 arrival, return.

depend on 1 RELY UPON, count on, bank on (*infml*), calculate on, reckon on (*infml*), build upon, trust in, lean on, expect. **2** HINGE ON, rest on, revolve around, be contingent upon, hang on.

dependable adj reliable, trustworthy, steady, trusty, responsible, faithful, unfailing, sure, honest, conscientious, certain.
F₃ unreliable, fickle.

dependence n 1 RELIANCE, confidence, faith, trust, need, expectation. 2 SUBORDINATION, attachment, subservience, helplessness, addiction.
🔁 2 independence.

dependent adj 1 RELIANT, helpless, weak, immature, subject, subordinate, vulnerable. 2 CONTINGENT, conditional, determined by, relative.
🔁 1 independent.

depict v portray, illustrate, delineate, sketch, outline, draw, picture, paint, trace, describe, characterize, detail.

deplete v empty, drain, exhaust, evacuate, use up, expend, run down, reduce, lessen, decrease.

deplorable adj 1 GRIEVOUS, lamentable, pitiable, regrettable, unfortunate, wretched, distressing, sad, miserable, heartbreaking, melancholy, disastrous, dire, appalling. 2 REPREHENSIBLE, disgraceful, scandalous, shameful, dishonourable, disreputable.
🔁 1 excellent. 2 commendable.

deplore v 1 GRIEVE FOR, lament, mourn, regret, bemoan, rue. 2 CENSURE, condemn, denounce, deprecate.
🔁 2 extol.

deploy v dispose, arrange, position, station, use, utilize, distribute.

deport v expel, banish, exile, extradite, transport, expatriate, oust, ostracize.

depose v demote, dethrone, downgrade, dismiss, unseat, topple, disestablish, displace, oust.

deposit v 1 LAY, drop, place, put, settle, dump (*infml*), park, precipitate, sit, locate. 2 SAVE, store, hoard, bank, amass, consign, entrust, lodge, file.
➤ n 1 SEDIMENT, accumulation, dregs, precipitate, lees, silt. 2 SECURITY, stake, down payment, pledge, retainer, instalment, part payment, money.

depot n 1 *military depot*: storehouse, store, warehouse, depository, repository, arsenal. 2 *bus depot*: station, garage, terminus.

deprave v corrupt, debauch, debase, degrade, pervert, subvert, infect, demoralize, seduce.
🔁 improve, reform.

depraved adj corrupt, debauched, degenerate, perverted, debased, dissolute, immoral, base, shameless, licentious, wicked, sinful, vile, evil.
🔁 moral, upright.

deprecate v deplore, condemn, censure, disapprove of, object to, protest at, reject.
🔁 approve, commend.

depreciate v 1 DEVALUE, deflate, downgrade, decrease, reduce, lower, drop, fall, lessen, decline, slump. 2 DISPARAGE, belittle, undervalue, underestimate, underrate, slight.
🔁 1 appreciate. 2 overrate.

depreciation n 1 DEVALUATION, deflation, depression, slump, fall. 2 DISPARAGEMENT, belittlement, underestimation.

depress v 1 DEJECT, sadden, dispirit, dishearten, discourage, oppress, upset, daunt, burden, overburden. 2 WEAKEN, undermine, sap, tire, drain, exhaust, weary, impair, reduce, lessen, press, lower, level. 3 DEVALUE, bring down, lower.
🔁 1 cheer. 2 fortify. 3 increase, raise.

depressed adj 1 DEJECTED, low-spirited, melancholy, dispirited, sad, unhappy, low, down, downcast, disheartened, fed up (*infml*), miserable, moody, cast down, discouraged, glum, downhearted, distressed, despondent, morose, crestfallen, pessimistic. 2 POOR, disadvantaged, deprived, destitute. 3 SUNKEN, recessed, concave, hollow, indented, dented.
🔁 1 cheerful. 2 affluent. 3 convex, protuberant.

depressing adj dejecting, dismal, bleak, gloomy, saddening, cheerless, dreary, disheartening, sad, melancholy, sombre, grey, black, daunting, discouraging, heartbreaking, distressing, hopeless.
🔁 cheerful, encouraging.

depression n 1 DEJECTION, despair, despondency, melancholy, low spirits, sadness, gloominess, doldrums, blues (*infml*), glumness, dumps (*infml*), hopelessness. 2 RECESSION, slump, stagnation, hard times, decline, inactivity. 3 INDENTATION, hollow, dip, concavity, dent, dimple, valley, pit, sink, dint, bowl, cavity, basin, impression, dish, excavation.
Fa 1 cheerfulness. 2 prosperity, boom. 3 convexity, protuberance.

deprive v 1 DISPOSSESS, strip, divest, denude, bereave, expropriate, rob. 2 DENY, withhold, refuse.
Fa 1 endow. 2 provide.

deprived adj poor, needy, underprivileged, disadvantaged, impoverished, destitute, lacking, bereft.
Fa prosperous.

depth n 1 DEEPNESS, profoundness, extent, measure, drop. 2 MIDDLE, midst, abyss, deep, gulf. 3 WISDOM, insight, discernment, penetration. 4 INTENSITY, strength.
Fa 1 shallowness. 2 surface.

deputation n commission, delegation, embassy, mission, representatives, legation.

deputize v 1 REPRESENT, stand in for, substitute, replace, understudy, double. 2 DELEGATE, commission.

deputy n representative, agent, delegate, proxy, substitute, second-in-command, ambassador, commissioner, lieutenant, surrogate, subordinate, assistant, locum.

deranged adj disordered, demented, crazy, mad, lunatic, insane, unbalanced, disturbed, confused, frantic, delirious, distraught, berserk.
Fa sane, calm.

derelict adj abandoned, neglected, deserted, forsaken, desolate, discarded, dilapidated, ruined.

deride v ridicule, mock, scoff, scorn, jeer, sneer, satirize, knock (*infml*), gibe, disparage, insult, belittle, disdain, taunt.
Fa respect, praise.

derision n ridicule, mockery, scorn, contempt, scoffing, satire, sneering, disrespect, insult, disparagement, disdain.
Fa respect, praise.

derisive adj mocking, scornful, contemptuous, disrespectful, irreverent, jeering, disdainful, taunting.
Fa respectful, flattering.

derivation n source, origin, root, beginning, etymology, extraction, foundation, genealogy, ancestry, basis, descent, deduction, inference.

derivative adj unoriginal, acquired, copied, borrowed, derived, imitative, obtained, second-hand, secondary, plagiarized, cribbed (*infml*), hackneyed, trite.
➤ n derivation, offshoot, by-product, development, branch, outgrowth, spin-off, product, descendant.

derive v 1 GAIN, obtain, get, draw, extract, receive, procure, acquire, borrow. 2 ORIGINATE, arise, spring, flow, emanate, descend, proceed, stem, issue, follow, develop. 3 INFER, deduce, trace, gather, glean.

derogatory adj insulting, pejorative, offensive, disparaging, depreciative, critical, defamatory, injurious.
Fa flattering.

descend v 1 DROP, go down, fall, plummet, plunge, tumble, swoop, sink, arrive, alight, dismount, dip, slope, subside. 2 DEGENERATE, deteriorate. 3 CONDESCEND, deign, stoop. 4 ORIGINATE, proceed, spring, stem.
Fa 1 ascend, rise.

descendants n offspring, children, issue, progeny (*fml*), successors, lineage, line, seed (*fml*).

descent n 1 FALL, drop, plunge, dip, decline, incline, slope. 2 COMEDOWN, debasement, degradation. 3 ANCESTRY, parentage, heredity, family tree, genealogy, lineage, extraction, origin.
Fa 1 ascent, rise.

describe v portray, depict, delineate, illustrate, characterize, specify, draw, define, detail, explain, express, tell, narrate, outline, relate, recount, present, report, sketch, mark out, trace.

description *n* **1** PORTRAYAL, representation, characterization, account, delineation, depiction, sketch, presentation, report, outline, explanation, exposition, narration. **2** SORT, type, kind, variety, specification, order.

descriptive *adj* illustrative, explanatory, expressive, detailed, graphic, colourful, pictorial, vivid.

desert[1] *n* wasteland, wilderness, wilds, void.

> *Deserts of the world, with locations, include*: Sahara, N Africa; Arabian, SW Asia; Gobi, Mongolia and NE China; Patagonian, Argentina; Great Basin, SW USA; Chihuahuan, Mexico; Great Sandy, NW Australia; Nubian, Sudan; Great Victoria, SW Australia; Thar, India/Pakistan; Sonoran, SW USA; Kara Kum, Turkmenistan; Kyzyl-Kum, Kazakhstan; Takla Makan, N China; Kalahari, SW Africa.

➤ *adj* bare, barren, waste, wild, uninhabited, uncultivated, dry, arid, infertile, desolate, sterile, solitary.

desert[2] *v* abandon, forsake, leave, maroon, strand, decamp, defect, give up, renounce, relinquish, jilt, abscond, quit.
🔁 stand by, support.

desert[3] *n* **1** DUE, right, reward, deserts, return, retribution, come-uppance (*infml*), payment, recompense, remuneration. **2** WORTH, merit, virtue.

deserted *adj* abandoned, forsaken, empty, derelict, desolate, godforsaken, neglected, underpopulated, stranded, isolated, bereft, vacant, betrayed, lonely, solitary, unoccupied.
🔁 populous.

deserter *n* runaway, absconder, escapee, truant, renegade, defector, rat (*infml*), traitor, fugitive, betrayer, apostate, backslider, delinquent.

deserve *v* earn, be worthy of, merit, be

entitled to, warrant, justify, win, rate, incur.

deserved *adj* due, earned, merited, justifiable, warranted, right, rightful, well-earned, suitable, proper, fitting, fair, just, appropriate, apt, legitimate, apposite, meet (*fml*).
🔁 gratuitous, undeserved.

deserving *adj* worthy, estimable, exemplary, praiseworthy, admirable, commendable, laudable, righteous.
🔁 undeserving, unworthy.

design *n* **1** BLUEPRINT, draft, pattern, plan, prototype, sketch, drawing, outline, model, guide. **2** STYLE, shape, form, figure, structure, organization, arrangement, composition, construction, motif. **3** AIM, intention, goal, purpose, plan, end, object, objective, scheme, plot, project, meaning, target, undertaking.
➤ *v* **1** PLAN, plot, intend, devise, purpose, aim, scheme, shape, project, propose, tailor, mean. **2** SKETCH, draft, outline, draw (up). **3** INVENT, originate, conceive, create, think up, develop, construct, fashion, form, model, fabricate, make.

designation *n* **1** NAME, title, label, epithet, nickname. **2** INDICATION, specification, description, definition, classification, category. **3** NOMINATION, appointment, selection.

designer *n* deviser, originator, maker, stylist, inventor, creator, contriver, fashioner, architect, author.

designing *adj* artful, crafty, scheming, conspiring, devious, intriguing, plotting, tricky, wily, sly, deceitful, cunning, guileful, underhand, sharp, shrewd.
🔁 artless, naïve.

desirable *adj* **1** ADVANTAGEOUS, profitable, worthwhile, advisable, appropriate, expedient, beneficial, preferable, sensible, eligible, good, pleasing. **2** ATTRACTIVE, alluring, sexy (*infml*), seductive, fetching, tempting.
🔁 **1** undesirable. **2** unattractive.

desire *v* **1** ASK, request, petition,

solicit. **2** WANT, wish for, covet, long for, need, crave, hunger for, yearn for, fancy (*infml*), hanker after.
➤ *n* **1** WANT, longing, wish, need, yearning, craving, hankering, appetite, aspiration. **2** LUST, passion, concupiscence (*fml*), ardour. **3** REQUEST, petition, appeal, supplication.

desist *v* stop, cease, leave off, refrain, discontinue, end, break off, give up, halt, abstain, suspend, pause, peter out, remit, forbear (*fml*).
🖅 continue, resume.

desolate *adj* **1** DESERTED, uninhabited, abandoned, unfrequented, barren, bare, arid, bleak, gloomy, dismal, dreary, lonely, godforsaken, forsaken, waste, depressing. **2** FORLORN, bereft, depressed, dejected, forsaken, despondent, distressed, melancholy, miserable, lonely, gloomy, disheartened, dismal, downcast, solitary, wretched.
🖅 **1** populous. **2** cheerful.
➤ *v* devastate, lay waste, destroy, despoil, spoil, wreck, denude, depopulate, ruin, waste, ravage, plunder, pillage.

desolation *n* **1** DESTRUCTION, ruin, devastation, ravages. **2** DEJECTION, despair, despondency, gloom, misery, sadness, melancholy, sorrow, unhappiness, anguish, grief, distress, wretchedness. **3** BARRENNESS, bleakness, emptiness, forlornness, loneliness, isolation, solitude, wildness.

despair *v* lose heart, lose hope, give up, give in, collapse, surrender.
🖅 hope.
➤ *n* despondency, gloom, hopelessness, desperation, anguish, misery, inconsolableness, melancholy, wretchedness.
🖅 cheerfulness, resilience.

despairing *adj* despondent, distraught, inconsolable, desolate, desperate, heartbroken, suicidal, grief-stricken, hopeless, disheartened, dejected, miserable, wretched, sorrowful, dismayed, downcast.
🖅 cheerful, hopeful.

despatch *see* **dispatch**.

desperado *n* bandit, criminal, brigand, gangster, hoodlum (*infml*), outlaw, ruffian, thug, cut-throat, law-breaker.

desperate *adj* **1** HOPELESS, inconsolable, wretched, despondent, abandoned. **2** RECKLESS, rash, impetuous, audacious, daring, dangerous, do-or-die, foolhardy, risky, hazardous, hasty, precipitate, wild, violent, frantic, frenzied, determined. **3** CRITICAL, acute, serious, severe, extreme, urgent.
🖅 **1** hopeful. **2** cautious.

desperately *adv* dangerously, critically, gravely, hopelessly, seriously, severely, badly, dreadfully, fearfully, frightfully.

desperation *n* **1** DESPAIR, despondency, anguish, hopelessness, misery, agony, distress, pain, sorrow, trouble, worry, anxiety. **2** RECKLESSNESS, rashness, frenzy, madness, hastiness.

despicable *adj* contemptible, vile, worthless, detestable, disgusting, mean, wretched, disgraceful, disreputable, shameful, reprobate.
🖅 admirable, noble.

despise *v* scorn, deride, look down on, hold in contempt, disdain, condemn, spurn, undervalue, slight, revile, deplore, dislike, detest, loathe.
🖅 admire.

despite *prep* in spite of, regardless of, notwithstanding, in the face of, undeterred by, against, defying.

despondent *adj* depressed, dejected, disheartened, downcast, down, low, gloomy, glum, discouraged, miserable, melancholy, sad, sorrowful, doleful, despairing, heartbroken, inconsolable, mournful, wretched.
🖅 cheerful, heartened, hopeful.

despot *n* autocrat, tyrant, dictator, oppressor, absolutist, boss.

despotic *adj* autocratic, tyrannical, imperious, oppressive, dictatorial,

authoritarian, domineering, absolute, overbearing, arbitrary, arrogant.
◼ democratic, egalitarian, liberal, tolerant.

despotism *n* autocracy, totalitarianism, tyranny, dictatorship, absolutism, oppression, repression.
◼ democracy, egalitarianism, liberalism, tolerance.

destination *n* **1** GOAL, aim, objective, object, purpose, target, end, intention, aspiration, design, ambition.
2 JOURNEY'S END, terminus, station, stop.

destined *adj* **1** FATED, doomed, inevitable, predetermined, ordained, certain, foreordained, meant, unavoidable, inescapable, intended, designed, appointed. **2** BOUND, directed, en route, headed, heading, scheduled, assigned, booked.

destiny *n* fate, doom, fortune, karma, lot, portion, predestiny, kismet.

destitute *adj* **1** LACKING, needy, wanting, devoid of, bereft, innocent of, deprived, deficient, depleted. **2** POOR, penniless, poverty-stricken, impoverished, down and out (*infml*), distressed, bankrupt.
◼ **2** prosperous, rich.

destroy *v* **1** DEMOLISH, ruin, shatter, wreck, devastate, smash, break, crush, overthrow, sabotage, undo, dismantle, thwart, undermine, waste, gut, level, ravage, raze, torpedo, unshape. **2** KILL, annihilate, eliminate, extinguish, eradicate, dispatch, slay (*fml*), nullify.
◼ **1** build up. **2** create.

destruction *n* **1** RUIN, devastation, shattering, crushing, wreckage, demolition, defeat, downfall, overthrow, ruination, desolation, undoing, wastage, havoc, ravagement. **2** ANNIHILATION, extermination, eradication, elimination, extinction, slaughter, massacre, end, liquidation, nullification.
◼ **2** creation.

destructive *adj* **1** *destructive storms*:

devastating, damaging, catastrophic, disastrous, deadly, harmful, fatal, disruptive, lethal, ruinous, detrimental, hurtful, malignant, mischievous, nullifying, slaughterous. **2** *destructive criticism*: adverse, hostile, negative, discouraging, disparaging, contrary, undermining, subversive, vicious.
◼ **1** creative. **2** constructive.

desultory *adj* random, erratic, aimless, disorderly, haphazard, irregular, spasmodic, inconsistent, undirected, unco-ordinated, unsystematic, unmethodical, fitful, disconnected, loose, capricious.
◼ systematic, methodical.

detach *v* separate, disconnect, unfasten, disjoin, cut off, disengage, remove, undo, uncouple, sever, dissociate, isolate, loosen, free, unfix, unhitch, segregate, divide, disentangle, estrange.
◼ attach.

detached *adj* **1** SEPARATE, disconnected, dissociated, severed, free, loose, divided, discrete. **2** ALOOF, dispassionate, impersonal, neutral, impartial, independent, disinterested, objective.
◼ **1** connected. **2** involved.

detachment *n* **1** ALOOFNESS, remoteness, coolness, unconcern, indifference, impassivity, disinterestedness, neutrality, impartiality, objectivity, fairness.
2 SEPARATION, disconnection, disunion, disengagement. **3** SQUAD, unit, force, corps, brigade, patrol, task force.

detail *n* particular, item, factor, element, aspect, component, feature, point, specific, ingredient, attribute, count, respect, technicality, complication, intricacy, triviality, fact, thoroughness, elaboration, meticulousness, refinement, nicety.
► *v* **1** LIST, enumerate, itemize, specify, catalogue, recount, relate. **2** ASSIGN, appoint, charge, delegate, commission.

detailed *adj* comprehensive, exhaustive, full, blow-by-blow (*infml*), thorough, minute, exact, specific, particular, itemized, intricate, elaborate, complex, complicated, meticulous, descriptive.

🔁 cursory, general.

detain v 1 DELAY, hold (up), hinder, impede, check, retard, slow, stay, stop. 2 CONFINE, arrest, intern, hold, restrain, keep.

🔁 2 release.

detect v 1 NOTICE, ascertain, note, observe, perceive, recognize, discern, distinguish, identify, sight, spot, spy. 2 UNCOVER, catch, discover, disclose, expose, find, track down, unmask, reveal.

detective n investigator, private eye (*infml*), sleuth (*infml*), sleuth-hound (*infml*), gumshoe (*US sl*).

detention n 1 DETAINMENT, custody, confinement, imprisonment, restraint, incarceration, constraint, quarantine. 2 DELAY, hindrance, holding back.

🔁 1 release.

deter v discourage, put off, inhibit, intimidate, dissuade, daunt, turn off (*infml*), check, caution, warn, restrain, hinder, frighten, disincline, prevent, prohibit, stop.

🔁 encourage.

deteriorate v 1 WORSEN, decline, degenerate, depreciate, go downhill (*infml*), fail, fall off, lapse, slide, relapse, slip. 2 DECAY, disintegrate, decompose, weaken, fade.

🔁 1 improve. 2 progress.

determination n 1 RESOLUTENESS, tenacity, firmness, will-power, perseverance, persistence, purpose, backbone, guts (*infml*), grit (*infml*), steadfastness, single-mindedness, will, insistence, conviction, dedication, drive, fortitude. 2 DECISION, judgement, settlement, resolution, conclusion.

🔁 1 irresolution.

determine v 1 DECIDE, settle, resolve, make up one's mind, choose, conclude, fix on, elect, clinch, finish. 2 DISCOVER, establish, find out, ascertain, identify,

check, detect, verify. 3 AFFECT, influence, govern, control, dictate, direct, guide, regulate, ordain.

determined adj resolute, firm, purposeful, strong-willed, single-minded, persevering, persistent, strong-minded, steadfast, tenacious, dogged, insistent, intent, fixed, convinced, decided, unflinching.

🔁 irresolute, wavering.

deterrent n hindrance, impediment, obstacle, repellent, check, bar, discouragement, obstruction, curb, restraint, difficulty.

🔁 incentive, encouragement.

detest v hate, abhor, loathe, abominate, execrate (*fml*), dislike, recoil from, deplore, despise.

🔁 adore, love.

detestable adj hateful, loathsome, abhorrent, abominable, repellent, obnoxious, execrable (*fml*), despicable, revolting, repulsive, repugnant, offensive, vile, disgusting, accursed (*fml*), heinous, shocking, sordid.

🔁 adorable, admirable.

detour n deviation, diversion, indirect route, circuitous route, roundabout route, digression, byroad, byway, bypath, bypass.

detract (from) v diminish, subtract from, take away from, reduce, lessen, lower, devaluate, depreciate, belittle, disparage.

🔁 add to, enhance, praise.

detriment n damage, harm, hurt, disadvantage, loss, ill, injury, disservice, evil, mischief, prejudice.

🔁 advantage, benefit.

detrimental adj damaging, harmful, hurtful, adverse, disadvantageous, injurious, prejudicial, mischievous, destructive.

🔁 advantageous, favourable, beneficial.

devastate v 1 DESTROY, desolate, lay waste, demolish, spoil, despoil, wreck, ruin, ravage, waste, ransack, plunder, level, raze, pillage, sack. 2 DISCONCERT, overwhelm, take aback, confound, shatter (*infml*), floor (*infml*), nonplus, discomfit.

devastating *adj* 1 *devastating storms*: destructive, disastrous. 2 *a devastating argument*: effective, incisive, overwhelming, stunning.

devastation *n* destruction, desolation, havoc, ruin, wreckage, ravages, demolition, annihilation, pillage, plunder, spoliation.

develop *v* 1 ADVANCE, evolve, expand, progress, foster, flourish, mature, prosper, branch out. 2 ELABORATE, amplify, argument, enhance, unfold. 3 ACQUIRE, contract, begin, generate, create, invent. 4 RESULT, come about, grow, ensue, arise, follow, happen.

development *n* 1 GROWTH, evolution, advance, blossoming, elaboration, furtherance, progress, unfolding, expansion, extension, spread, increase, improvement, maturity, promotion, refinement, issue. 2 OCCURRENCE, happening, event, change, outcome, situation, result, phenomenon.

deviate *v* diverge, veer, turn (aside), digress, swerve, vary, differ, depart, stray, yaw, wander, err, go astray, go off the rails (*infml*), drift, part.

deviation *n* divergence, aberration, departure, abnormality, irregularity, variance, variation, digression, eccentricity, anomaly, deflection, alteration, disparity, discrepancy, detour, fluctuation, change, quirk, shift, freak.
🔁 conformity, regularity.

device *n* 1 TOOL, implement, appliance, gadget, contrivance, contraption (*infml*), apparatus, utensil, instrument, machine. 2 SCHEME, ruse, strategy, plan, plot, gambit, manoeuvre, wile, trick, dodge (*infml*), machination. 3 EMBLEM, symbol, motif, logo, design, insignia, crest, badge, shield.

devil *n* 1 DEMON, Satan, fiend, evil spirit, arch-fiend, Lucifer, imp, Evil One, Prince of Darkness, Adversary, Beelzebub, Mephistopheles, Old Nick

(*infml*), Old Harry (*infml*). 2 BRUTE, rogue, monster, ogre.

devious *adj* 1 UNDERHAND, deceitful, dishonest, disingenuous, double-dealing, scheming, tricky (*infml*), insidious, insincere, calculating, cunning, evasive, wily, sly, slippery (*infml*), surreptitious, treacherous, misleading. 2 INDIRECT, circuitous, rambling, roundabout, wandering, winding, tortuous, erratic.
🔁 straightforward.

devise *v* invent, contrive, plan, plot, design, conceive, arrange, formulate, imagine, scheme, construct, concoct, forge, frame, project, shape, form.

devoid *adj* lacking, wanting, without, free, bereft, destitute, deficient, deprived, barren, empty, vacant, void.
🔁 endowed.

devote *v* dedicate, consecrate, commit, give oneself, set apart, set aside, reserve, apply, allocate, allot, sacrifice, enshrine, assign, appropriate, surrender, pledge.

devoted *adj* dedicated, ardent, committed, loyal, faithful, devout, loving, staunch, steadfast, true, constant, fond, unswerving, tireless, concerned, attentive, caring.
🔁 indifferent, disloyal.

devotee *n* enthusiast, fan, fanatic, addict, aficionado, follower, supporter, zealot, adherent, admirer, disciple, buff (*infml*), freak (*infml*), merchant (*infml*), fiend (*infml*), hound.

devotion *n* 1 DEDICATION, commitment, consecration, ardour, loyalty, allegiance, adherence, zeal, support, love, passion, fervour, fondness, attachment, adoration, affection, faithfulness, reverence, steadfastness, regard, earnestness. 2 DEVOUTNESS, piety, godliness, faith, holiness, spirituality. 3 PRAYER, worship.
🔁 1 inconstancy. 2 irreverence.

devour *v* 1 EAT, consume, guzzle, gulp, gorge, gobble, bolt, wolf down, swallow, stuff (*infml*), cram, polish off (*infml*), snarf (*infml*), gormandize, feast on, relish, revel in. **2** DESTROY, consume, absorb, engulf, ravage, dispatch.

devout adj **1** SINCERE, earnest, devoted, fervent, genuine, staunch, steadfast, ardent, passionate, serious, wholehearted, constant, faithful, intense, heartfelt, zealous, unswerving, deep, profound. **2** PIOUS, godly, religious, reverent, prayerful, saintly, holy, orthodox.
₣ 1 insincere. **2** irreligious.

dexterous adj deft, adroit, agile, able, nimble, proficient, skilful, clever, expert, nifty, nippy, handy, facile, nimble-fingered, neat-handed.
₣ clumsy, inept, awkward.

diabolical adj devilish, fiendish, demonic, hellish, damnable, evil, infernal, wicked, vile, dreadful, outrageous, shocking, disastrous, excruciating, atrocious.

diagnose v identify, determine, recognize, pinpoint, distinguish, analyse, explain, isolate, interpret, investigate.

diagnosis n identification, verdict, explanation, conclusion, answer, interpretation, analysis, opinion, investigation, examination, scrutiny.

diagonal adj oblique, slanting, cross, crosswise, sloping, crooked, angled, cornerways.

diagram n plan, sketch, chart, drawing, figure, representation, schema, illustration, outline, graph, picture, layout, table.

dial n circle, disc, face, clock, control.
➤ v phone, ring, call (up).

dialect n idiom, language, regionalism, patois, provincialism, vernacular, argot, jargon, accent, lingo (**infml**), speech, diction.

dialectic adj dialectical, logical, rational, argumentative, analytical, rationalistic, logistic, polemical, inductive, deductive.
➤ n dialectics, logic, reasoning, rationale, disputation, analysis, debate,

argumentation, contention, discussion, polemics, induction, deduction.

dialogue n **1** CONVERSATION, interchange, discourse, talk, exchange, communication, discussion, converse, debate, conference. **2** LINES, script.

diametric adj diametrical, opposed, opposite, contrary, counter, contrasting, antithetical.

diary n journal, daybook, logbook, chronicle, yearbook, appointment book, engagement book.

diatribe n tirade, invective, abuse, harangue, attack, onslaught, denunciation, criticism, insult, reviling, upbraiding.
₣ praise, eulogy.

dicey (**infml**) adj risky, chancy, unpredictable, tricky, problematic, dangerous, difficult, iffy (**infml**), dubious, hairy (**infml**).
₣ certain.

dictate v **1** SAY, speak, utter, announce, pronounce, transmit. **2** COMMAND, order, direct, decree, instruct, rule.
➤ n command, decree, precept, principle, rule, direction, injunction, edict, order, ruling, statute, requirement, ordinance, law, bidding, mandate, ultimatum, word.

dictator n despot, autocrat, tyrant, supremo, Big Brother (**infml**).

dictatorial adj tyrannical, despotic, totalitarian, authoritarian, autocratic, oppressive, imperious, domineering, bossy (**infml**), absolute, repressive, overbearing, arbitrary, dogmatic.
₣ democratic, egalitarian, liberal.

diction n speech, articulation, language, elocution, enunciation, intonation, pronunciation, inflection, fluency, delivery, expression, phrasing.

dictionary n lexicon, glossary, thesaurus, vocabulary, wordbook, encyclopaedia, concordance.

dictum n pronouncement, ruling, maxim, decree, dictate, edict, fiat (**fml**), precept, axiom, command, order, utterance.

didactic *adj* instructive, educational, educative, pedagogic, prescriptive, pedantic, moralizing, moral.

die *v* **1** DECEASE, perish, pass away, expire, depart, breathe one's last, peg out (*infml*), snuff it (*sl*), bite the dust (*infml*), kick the bucket (*sl*), flatline (*sl*). **2** DWINDLE, fade, ebb, sink, wane, wilt, wither, peter out, decline, decay, finish, lapse, end, disappear, vanish, subside.
🔁 **1** live.

diehard *n* reactionary, intransigent, hardliner, blimp (*infml*), ultra-conservative, old fogey (*infml*), stick-in-the-mud (*infml*), rightist, fanatic.

diet *n* **1** FOOD, nutrition, provisions, sustenance, rations, foodstuffs, subsistence. **2** FAST, abstinence, regimen.
➤ *v* lose weight, slim, fast, reduce, abstain, weight-watch (*infml*).

differ *v* **1** VARY, diverge, deviate, depart from, contradict, contrast. **2** DISAGREE, argue, conflict, oppose, dispute, dissent, be at odds with, clash, quarrel, fall out, debate, contend, take issue.
🔁 **1** conform. **2** agree.

difference *n* **1** DISSIMILARITY, unlikeness, discrepancy, divergence, diversity, variation, variety, distinctness, distinction, deviation, differentiation, contrast, disparity, singularity, exception. **2** DISAGREEMENT, clash, dispute, conflict, contention, controversy. **3** REMAINDER, rest.
🔁 **1** conformity. **2** agreement.

different *adj* **1** DISSIMILAR, unlike, contrasting, divergent, inconsistent, deviating, at odds, clashing, opposed. **2** VARIED, various, diverse, miscellaneous, assorted, disparate, many, numerous, several, sundry, other. **3** UNUSUAL, unconventional, unique, distinct, distinctive, extraordinary, individual, original, special, strange, separate, peculiar, rare, bizarre, anomalous.
🔁 **1** similar. **2** same. **3** conventional.

differentiate *v* distinguish, tell

apart, discriminate, contrast, separate, mark off, individualize, particularize.

difficult *adj* **1** HARD, laborious, demanding, arduous, strenuous, tough, wearisome, uphill, formidable. **2** COMPLEX, complicated, intricate, involved, abstruse, obscure, dark, knotty, thorny, problematical, perplexing, abstract, baffling, intractable. **3** UNMANAGEABLE, perverse, troublesome, trying, unco-operative, tiresome, stubborn, obstinate, intractable.
🔁 **1** easy. **2** straightforward. **3** manageable.

difficulty *n* **1** HARDSHIP, trouble, labour, arduousness, painfulness, trial, tribulation, awkwardness. **2** PROBLEM, predicament, dilemma, quandary, perplexity, embarrassment, plight, distress, fix (*infml*), mess (*infml*), jam (*infml*), spot (*infml*), hiccup (*infml*), hang-up. **3** OBSTACLE, hindrance, hurdle, impediment, objection, opposition, block, complication, pitfall, protest, stumbling-block.
🔁 **1** ease.

diffidence *n* unassertiveness, modesty, shyness, self-consciousness, self-effacement, timidity, insecurity, reserve, bashfulness, humility, inhibition, meekness, self-distrust, self-doubt, hesitancy, reluctance, backwardness.
🔁 confidence.

diffident *adj* unassertive, modest, shy, timid, self-conscious, self-effacing, insecure, bashful, abashed, meek, reserved, withdrawn, tentative, shrinking, inhibited, hesitant, reluctant, unsure, shamefaced.
🔁 assertive, confident.

diffuse *adj* **1** *diffuse outbreaks of rain*: scattered, unconcentrated, diffused, dispersed, disconnected. **2** *a diffuse prose style*: verbose, imprecise, wordy, rambling, long-winded, waffling (*infml*), vague, discursive.
🔁 **1** concentrated. **2** succinct.
➤ *v* spread, scatter, disperse, distribute,

propagate, dispense, disseminate, circulate, dissipate.
🔄 concentrate.

dig v 1 EXCAVATE, penetrate, burrow, mine, quarry, scoop, tunnel, till, gouge, delve, pierce. 2 POKE, prod. 3 INVESTIGATE, probe, go into, research, search.
➤ n gibe, jeer, sneer, taunt, crack, insinuation, insult, wisecrack.
🔄 compliment.
◇ **dig up** discover, unearth, uncover, disinter, expose, extricate, exhume, find, retrieve, track down.
🔄 bury, obscure.

digest v 1 ABSORB, assimilate, incorporate, process, dissolve. 2 TAKE IN, absorb, understand, assimilate, grasp, study, consider, contemplate, meditate, ponder. 3 SHORTEN, summarize, condense, compress, reduce.
➤ n summary, abridgement, abstract, précis, synopsis, résumé, reduction, abbreviation, compression, compendium.

dignified adj stately, solemn, imposing, majestic, noble, august, lordly, lofty, exalted, formal, distinguished, grave, impressive, reserved, honourable.
🔄 undignified, lowly.

dignitary n worthy, notable, VIP (*infml*), high-up, personage, bigwig (*infml*).

dignity n stateliness, propriety, solemnity, decorum, courtliness, grandeur, loftiness, majesty, honour, eminence, importance, nobility, self-respect, self-esteem, standing, poise, respectability, greatness, status, pride.

digress v diverge, deviate, stray, wander, go off at a tangent, drift, depart, ramble.

dilapidated adj ramshackle, shabby, broken-down, neglected, tumbledown, uncared-for, rickety, decrepit, crumbling, run-down, worn-out, ruined, decayed, decaying.

dilate v distend, enlarge, expand, spread, broaden, widen, increase, extend, stretch, swell.
🔄 contract.

dilatory adj delaying, procrastinating, slow, tardy, tarrying, sluggish, lingering, lackadaisical, slack.
🔄 prompt.

dilemma n quandary, conflict, predicament, problem, catch-22 (*infml*), difficulty, puzzle, embarrassment, perplexity, plight.

diligent adj assiduous, industrious, hard-working, conscientious, painstaking, busy, attentive, tireless, careful, meticulous, persevering, persistent, studious.
🔄 negligent, lazy.

dilute v adulterate, water down, thin (out), attenuate, weaken, diffuse, diminish, decrease, lessen, reduce, temper, mitigate.
🔄 concentrate.

dim adj 1 DARK, dull, dusky, cloudy, shadowy, gloomy, sombre, dingy, lack-lustre, feeble, imperfect. 2 INDISTINCT, blurred, hazy, ill-defined, obscure, misty, unclear, foggy, fuzzy, vague, faint, weak. 3 STUPID, dense, obtuse, thick (*infml*), doltish.
🔄 1 bright. 2 distinct. 3 bright, intelligent.
➤ v darken, dull, obscure, cloud, blur, fade, tarnish, shade.
🔄 brighten, illuminate.

dimension(s) n extent, size, measurement, measure, scope, magnitude, largeness, capacity, mass, scale, range, bulk, importance, greatness.

diminish v 1 DECREASE, lessen, reduce, lower, contract, decline, dwindle, shrink, recede, taper off, wane, weaken, abate, fade, sink, subside, ebb, slacken, cut. 2 BELITTLE, disparage, deprecate, devalue.
🔄 1 increase. 2 exaggerate.

diminutive adj undersized, small, tiny, little, miniature, minute,

infinitesimal, wee, petite, midget, mini (*infml*), teeny (*infml*), teeny-weeny (*infml*), Lilliputian, dinky (*infml*), pint-size(d) (*infml*), pocket(-sized), pygmy.
🖛 big, large, oversized.

din *n* noise, row, racket, clash, clatter, clamour, pandemonium, uproar, commotion, crash, hullabaloo (*infml*), hubbub, outcry, shout, babble.
🖛 quiet, calm.

dine *v* eat, feast, sup, lunch, banquet, feed.

dingy *adj* dark, drab, grimy, murky, faded, dull, dim, shabby, soiled, discoloured, dirty, dreary, gloomy, seedy, sombre, obscure, run-down, colourless, dusky, worn.
🖛 bright, clean.

dinner *n* meal, supper, tea (*infml*), banquet, feast, spread, repast (*fml*).

dinosaur

Dinosaurs include: Ornithischia, Saurischia; Allosaurus, Ankylosaurus, Apatosaurus, Barosaurus, Brachiosaurus, Brontosaurus, Camptosaurus, Coelophysis, Compsognathus, Corythosaurus, Deinonychus, Diplodocus, Heterodontosaurus, Iguanodon, Ophiacodon, Ornithomimus, Pachycephalosaurus, Parasaurolophus, Plateosaurus, Stegosaurus, Styracosaurus, Triceratops, Tyrannosaurus.

dip *v* 1 PLUNGE, immerse, submerge, duck, dunk, bathe, douse, sink.
2 DESCEND, decline, drop, fall, subside, slump, sink, lower.
➤ *n* 1 HOLLOW, basin, decline, hole, concavity, incline, depression, fall, slope, slump, lowering. 2 BATHE, immersion, plunge, soaking, ducking, swim, drenching, infusion, dive.

diplomacy *n* 1 TACT, tactfulness, finesse, delicacy, discretion, savoir-faire, subtlety, skill, craft. 2 STATECRAFT, statesmanship, politics, negotiation, manoeuvring.

diplomat *n* go-between, mediator, negotiator, ambassador, envoy, conciliator, peacemaker, moderator, politician.

diplomatic *adj* tactful, politic, discreet, judicious, subtle, sensitive, prudent, discreet.
🖛 tactless.

dire *adj* 1 DISASTROUS, dreadful, awful, appalling, calamitous, catastrophic.
2 DESPERATE, urgent, grave, drastic, crucial, extreme, alarming, ominous.

direct *v* 1 CONTROL, manage, run, administer, organize, lead, govern, regulate, superintend, supervise. 2 INSTRUCT, command, order, charge.
3 GUIDE, lead, conduct, point. 4 AIM, point, focus, turn.
➤ *adj* 1 STRAIGHT, undeviating, through, uninterrupted. 2 STRAIGHTFORWARD, outspoken, blunt, frank, unequivocal, sincere, candid, honest, explicit.
3 IMMEDIATE, first-hand, face-to-face, personal.
🖛 1 circuitous. 2 equivocal. 3 indirect.

direction *n* 1 CONTROL, administration, management, government, supervision, guidance, leadership. 2 ROUTE, way, line, road.

directions *n* instructions, guidelines, orders, briefing, guidance, recommendations, indication, plan.

directive *n* command, instruction, order, regulation, ruling, imperative, dictate, decree, charge, mandate, injunction, ordinance, edict, fiat (*fml*), notice.

directly *adv* 1 IMMEDIATELY, instantly, promptly, right away, speedily, forthwith, instantaneously, quickly, soon, presently, straightaway, straight.
2 FRANKLY, bluntly, candidly, honestly.

director *n* manager, head, boss, chief, controller, executive, principal, governor, leader, organizer, supervisor, administrator, producer, conductor.

dirt *n* 1 EARTH, soil, clay, dust, mud.
2 FILTH, grime, muck, mire, excrement, stain, smudge, slime, tarnish.

3 INDECENCY, impurity, obscenity, pornography.

dirty adj **1** FILTHY, grimy, grubby, mucky, soiled, unwashed, foul, messy, muddy, polluted, squalid, dull, miry, scruffy, shabby, sullied, clouded, dark.
2 INDECENT, obscene, filthy, smutty, sordid, salacious, vulgar, pornographic, x-rated (*infml*), corrupt.
1 clean. **2** decent.
➤ v pollute, soil, stain, foul, mess up, defile, smear, smirch, spoil, smudge, sully, muddy, blacken.
clean, cleanse.

disability n handicap, impairment, disablement, disorder, inability, incapacity, infirmity, defect, unfitness, disqualification, affliction, ailment, complaint, weakness.

disable v cripple, lame, incapacitate, damage, handicap, impair, debilitate, disqualify, weaken, immobilize, invalidate, paralyse, prostrate.

disabled adj handicapped, incapacitated, impaired, infirm, crippled, lame, immobilized, maimed, weak, weakened, paralysed, wrecked.
able, able-bodied.

disadvantage n **1** HARM, damage, detriment, hurt, injury, loss, prejudice.
2 DRAWBACK, snag, hindrance, handicap, impediment, inconvenience, flaw, nuisance, weakness, trouble.
2 advantage, benefit.

disadvantaged adj deprived, underprivileged, poor, handicapped, impoverished, struggling.
privileged.

disadvantageous adj harmful, detrimental, inopportune, unfavourable, prejudicial, adverse, damaging, hurtful, injurious, inconvenient, ill-timed.
advantageous, auspicious.

disaffected adj disloyal, hostile, estranged, alienated, antagonistic, rebellious, dissatisfied, disgruntled, discontented.
loyal.

disaffection n disloyalty, hostility, alienation, discontentment, resentment, ill-will, dissatisfaction, animosity, coolness, unfriendliness, antagonism, disharmony, discord, disagreement, aversion, dislike.
loyalty, contentment.

disagree v **1** DISSENT, oppose, quarrel, argue, bicker, fall out (*infml*), wrangle, fight, squabble, contend, dispute, contest, object. **2** CONFLICT, clash, diverge, contradict, counter, differ, deviate, depart, run counter to, vary.
1 agree. **2** correspond.

disagreeable adj **1** *disagreeable old man*: bad-tempered, ill-humoured, difficult, peevish, rude, surly, churlish, irritable, contrary, cross, brusque. **2** *a disagreeable taste*: disgusting, offensive, repulsive, repellent, obnoxious, unsavoury, objectionable, nasty.
1 amiable, pleasant. **2** agreeable.

disagreement n **1** DISPUTE, argument, conflict, altercation (*fml*), quarrel, clash, dissent, falling-out, contention, strife, misunderstanding, squabble, tiff (*infml*), wrangle.
2 DIFFERENCE, variance, unlikeness, disparity, discrepancy, deviation, discord, dissimilarity, incompatibility, divergence, diversity, incongruity.
1 agreement, harmony. **2** similarity.

disappear v **1** VANISH, wane, recede, fade, evaporate, dissolve, ebb. **2** GO, depart, withdraw, retire, flee, fly, escape, scarper (*infml*), hide. **3** END, expire, perish, pass.
1 appear. **3** emerge.

disappearance n vanishing, fading, evaporation, departure, loss, going, passing, melting, desertion, flight.
appearance, manifestation.

disappoint v fail, dissatisfy, let down, disillusion, dash, dismay, disenchant, sadden, thwart, vex, frustrate, foil, dishearten, disgruntle, disconcert, hamper, hinder, deceive, defeat, delude.
satisfy, please, delight.

disappointed *adj* let down, frustrated, thwarted, disillusioned, dissatisfied, miffed (*infml*), upset, discouraged, disgruntled, disheartened, distressed, downhearted, saddened, despondent, depressed.
🔁 pleased, satisfied.

disappointment *n* **1** FRUSTRATION, dissatisfaction, failure, disenchantment, disillusionment, displeasure, discouragement, distress, regret. **2** FAILURE, let-down, setback, comedown, blow, misfortune, fiasco, disaster, calamity, washout (*infml*), damp squib (*infml*), swiz (*infml*), swizzle (*infml*).
🔁 **1** pleasure, satisfaction, delight. **2** success.

disapproval *n* censure, disapprobation (*fml*), condemnation, criticism, displeasure, reproach, objection, dissatisfaction, denunciation, dislike.
🔁 approbation (*fml*), approval.

disapprove of censure, condemn, blame, take exception to, object to, deplore, denounce, disparage, dislike, reject, spurn.
🔁 approve of.

disarm *v* **1** DISABLE, unarm, demilitarize, demobilize, deactivate, disband. **2** APPEASE, conciliate, win, mollify, persuade.
🔁 **1** arm.

disarray *n* disorder, confusion, chaos, mess, muddle, shambles (*infml*), disorganization, clutter, untidiness, unruliness, jumble, indiscipline, tangle, upset.
🔁 order.

disaster *n* calamity, catastrophe, misfortune, reverse, tragedy, blow, accident, act of God, cataclysm, debacle, mishap, failure, flop (*infml*), fiasco, ruin, stroke, trouble, mischance, ruination.
🔁 success, triumph.

disastrous *adj* calamitous, catastrophic, cataclysmic, devastating, ruinous, tragic, unfortunate, dreadful, dire, terrible, destructive, ill-fated, fatal, miserable.
🔁 successful, auspicious.

disband *v* disperse, break up, scatter, dismiss, demobilize, part company, separate, dissolve.
🔁 assemble, muster.

disbelief *n* unbelief, incredulity, doubt, scepticism, suspicion, distrust, mistrust, rejection.
🔁 belief.

disbelieve *v* discount, discredit, repudiate, reject, mistrust, suspect.
🔁 believe, trust.

disc *n* **1** CIRCLE, face, plate, ring. **2** RECORD, album, LP, CD, MiniDisc. **3** DISK, diskette, hard disk, floppy disk, CD-ROM, DVD.

discard *v* reject, abandon, dispose of, get rid of, jettison, dispense with, cast aside, ditch (*infml*), dump (*infml*), drop, scrap, shed, remove, relinquish.
🔁 retain, adopt.

discern *v* **1** PERCEIVE, make out, observe, detect, recognize, see, ascertain, notice, determine, discover, descry. **2** DISCRIMINATE, distinguish, differentiate, judge.

discernible *adj* perceptible, noticeable, detectable, appreciable, distinct, observable, recognizable, visible, apparent, clear, obvious, plain, patent, manifest, discoverable.
🔁 imperceptible.

discerning *adj* discriminating, perceptive, astute, clear-sighted, sensitive, shrewd, wise, sharp, subtle, sagacious, penetrating, acute, piercing, critical, eagle-eyed.
🔁 dull, obtuse.

discharge *v* **1** LIBERATE, free, pardon, release, clear, absolve, exonerate, acquit, relieve, dismiss. **2** EXECUTE, carry out, perform, fulfil, dispense. **3** FIRE, shoot, let off, detonate, explode. **4** EMIT, sack (*infml*), remove, fire (*infml*), expel, oust, eject.
🔁 **1** detain. **2** neglect. **4** appoint.

➤ n **1** LIBERATION, release, acquittal, exoneration. **2** EMISSION, secretion, ejection. **3** EXECUTION, accomplishment, fulfilment.
🔁 **1** confinement, detention. **2** absorption. **3** neglect.

disciple n follower, convert, proselyte, adherent, believer, devotee, supporter, learner, pupil, student.

disciplinarian n authoritarian, taskmaster, autocrat, stickler, despot, tyrant.

discipline n **1** TRAINING, exercise, drill, practice. **2** PUNISHMENT, chastisement, correction. **3** STRICTNESS, restraint, regulation, self-control, orderliness.
🔁 **3** indiscipline.
➤ v **1** TRAIN, instruct, drill, educate, exercise, break in. **2** CHECK, control, correct, restrain, govern. **3** PUNISH, chastize, chasten, penalize, reprimand, castigate.

disclaim v deny, disown, repudiate, abandon, renounce, reject, abjure (fml).
🔁 accept, confess.

disclose v **1** DIVULGE, make known, reveal, tell, confess, let slip, relate, publish, communicate, impart, leak (infml). **2** EXPOSE, reveal, uncover, lay bare, unveil, discover.
🔁 conceal.

disclosure n divulgence, exposure, exposé, revelation, uncovering, publication, leak (infml), discovery, admission, acknowledgement, announcement, declaration.

discomfort n ache, pain, uneasiness, malaise, trouble, distress, disquiet, hardship, vexation, irritation, annoyance.
🔁 comfort, ease.

disconcerting adj disturbing, confusing, upsetting, unnerving, alarming, bewildering, off-putting (infml), distracting, embarrassing, awkward, baffling, perplexing, dismaying, bothersome.

disconnect v cut off, disengage,

uncouple, sever, separate, detach, unplug, unhook, part, divide.
🔁 attach, connect.

disconnected adj confused, incoherent, rambling, unco-ordinated, unintelligible, loose, irrational, disjointed, illogical, jumbled.
🔁 coherent, connected.

disconsolate adj desolate, dejected, dispirited, sad, melancholy, unhappy, wretched, miserable, gloomy, forlorn, inconsolable, crushed, heavy-hearted, hopeless.
🔁 cheerful, joyful.

discontent n uneasiness, dissatisfaction, disquiet, restlessness, fretfulness, unrest, impatience, vexation, regret.
🔁 content.

discontented adj dissatisfied, fed up (infml), disgruntled, unhappy, browned off (infml), cheesed off (infml), pissed off (sl), irritated, disaffected, miserable, exasperated, complaining.
🔁 contented, satisfied.

discontinue v stop, end, finish, cease, break off, terminate, halt, drop, suspend, abandon, cancel, interrupt.
🔁 continue.

discord n **1** DISSENSION, disagreement, discordance, clashing, disunity, incompatibility, conflict, difference, dispute, contention, friction, division, opposition, strife, split, wrangling. **2** DISSONANCE, disharmony, cacophony (fml), jangle, jarring, harshness.
🔁 **1** concord, agreement. **2** harmony.

discordant adj **1** DISAGREEING, conflicting, at odds, clashing, contradictory, incongruous, incompatible, inconsistent. **2** DISSONANT, cacophonous (fml), grating, jangling, jarring, harsh.
🔁 **1** harmonious. **2** harmonious.

discount[1] v **1** DISREGARD, ignore, overlook, disbelieve, gloss over. **2** REDUCE, deduct, mark down, knock off (infml).

discount[2] n reduction, rebate,

allowance, cut, concession, deduction, mark-down.

discourage v **1** DISHEARTEN, dampen, dispirit, depress, demoralize, dismay, unnerve, deject, disappoint. **2** DETER, dissuade, hinder, put off, restrain, prevent.
 1 hearten. **2** encourage.

discouragement n
1 DOWNHEARTEDNESS, despondency, pessimism, dismay, depression, dejection, despair, disappointment. **2** DETERRENT, damper, setback, impediment, obstacle, opposition, hindrance, restraint, rebuff.
 1 encouragement. **2** incentive.

discourse n **1** CONVERSATION, dialogue, chat, communication, talk, converse, discussion. **2** SPEECH, address, oration (*fml*), lecture, sermon, essay, treatise, dissertation, homily.
➤ v converse, talk, discuss, debate, confer, lecture.

discourteous adj rude, bad-mannered, ill-mannered, impolite, boorish, disrespectful, ill-bred, uncivil, unceremonious, insolent, offhand, curt, brusque, abrupt.
 courteous, polite.

discover v **1** FIND, uncover, unearth, dig up, disclose, reveal, light on, locate. **2** ASCERTAIN, determine, realize, notice, recognize, perceive, see, find out, spot, discern, learn, detect. **3** ORIGINATE, invent, pioneer.
 1 miss. **2** conceal, cover (up).

discovery n **1** BREAKTHROUGH, find, origination, introduction, innovation, invention, exploration. **2** DISCLOSURE, detection, revelation, location.

discredit v **1** DISBELIEVE, distrust, doubt, question, mistrust, challenge. **2** DISPARAGE, dishonour, degrade, defame, disgrace, slander, slur, smear, reproach, vilify.
 1 believe. **2** honour.
➤ n **1** DISBELIEF, distrust, doubt, mistrust, scepticism, suspicion. **2** DISHONOUR, disrepute, censure,

aspersion, disgrace, blame, shame, reproach, slur, smear, scandal.
 1 belief. **2** credit.

discreditable adj dishonourable, disreputable, disgraceful, reprehensible, scandalous, blameworthy, shameful, infamous, degrading, improper.
 creditable.

discreet adj tactful, careful, diplomatic, politic, prudent, cautious, delicate, judicious, reserved, wary, sensible.
 tactless, indiscreet.

discrepancy n difference, disparity, variance, variation, inconsistency, dissimilarity, discordance, divergence, disagreement, conflict, inequality.

discretion n **1** TACT, diplomacy, judiciousness, caution, prudence, wisdom, circumspection, discernment, judgement, care, carefulness, consideration, wariness. **2** CHOICE, freedom, preference, will, wish.
 1 indiscretion.

discriminate v distinguish, differentiate, discern, tell apart, make a distinction, segregate, separate.
 confuse, confound.
◇ **discriminate (against)** be prejudiced, be biased, victimize.

discriminating adj discerning, fastidious, selective, critical, perceptive, particular, tasteful, astute, sensitive, cultivated.

discrimination n **1** BIAS, prejudice, intolerance, unfairness, bigotry, favouritism, inequity, racism, sexism. **2** DISCERNMENT, judgement, acumen, perception, acuteness, insight, penetration, subtlety, keenness, refinement, taste.

discursive adj rambling, digressing, wandering, long-winded, meandering, wide-ranging, circuitous.
 terse.

discuss v debate, talk about, confer, argue, consider, deliberate, converse, consult, examine.

discussion *n* debate, conference, argument, conversation, dialogue, exchange, consultation, discourse, deliberation, consideration, analysis, review, examination, scrutiny, seminar, symposium.

disdain *n* scorn, contempt, arrogance, haughtiness, derision, sneering, dislike, snobbishness.
🔁 admiration, respect.

disdainful *adj* scornful, derisive, contemptuous, haughty, aloof, arrogant, supercilious, sneering, superior, proud, insolent.
🔁 respectful.

disease *n* illness, sickness, ill-health, infirmity, complaint, disorder, ailment, indisposition, malady, condition, affliction, infection, epidemic.
🔁 health.

Diseases and disorders include:
Addison's disease, AIDS, alopecia, Alzheimer's disease, anaemia, angina, anorexia nervosa, anthrax, arthritis, asbestosis, asthma, athlete's foot, autism, Bell's Palsy, beriberi, Black Death, botulism, Bright's disease, bronchitis, brucellosis, bubonic plague, bulimia, cancer, cerebral palsy, chickenpox, cholera, cirrhosis, coeliac disease, common cold, consumption, croup, cystic fibrosis, diabetes, diphtheria, dropsy, dysentery, eclampsia, emphysema, encephalitis, endometriosis, enteritis, farmer's lung, flu (*infml*), foot-and-mouth disease, gangrene, German measles, gingivitis, glandular fever, glaucoma, gonorrhoea, haemophilia, herpes, hepatitis, Hodgkin's disease, Huntington's chorea, hydrophobia, impetigo, influenza, Lassa fever, Legionnaires' disease, leprosy, leukaemia, lockjaw, malaria, mastoiditis, measles, meningitis, motor neurone disease, multiple sclerosis (MS), mumps, muscular dystrophy, myalgic encephalomyelitis (ME), nephritis, osteomyelitis, osteoporosis, Paget's disease, Parkinson's disease, peritonitis, pneumonia, poliomyelitis, psittacosis, psoriasis, pyorrhoea, rabies, rheumatic fever, rheumatoid arthritis, rickets, ringworm, rubella, scabies, scarlet fever, schistosomiasis, schizophrenia, scurvy, septicaemia, shingles, silicosis, smallpox, syphilis, tapeworm, tetanus, thrombosis, thrush, tinnitus, tuberculosis (TB), typhoid, typhus, vertigo, whooping cough, yellow fever.

diseased *adj* sick, ill, unhealthy, ailing, unsound, contaminated, infected.
🔁 healthy.

disembark *v* land, arrive, alight, debark.
🔁 embark.

disembodied *adj* bodiless, incorporeal (*fml*), ghostly, phantom, spiritual, immaterial, intangible.

disengage *v* disconnect, detach, loosen, free, extricate, undo, release, liberate, separate, disentangle, untie, withdraw.
🔁 connect, engage.

disentangle *v* 1 LOOSE, free, extricate, disconnect, untangle, disengage, detach, unravel, separate, unfold. 2 RESOLVE, clarify, simplify.
🔁 1 entangle.

disfigure *v* deface, blemish, mutilate, scar, mar, deform, distort, damage, spoil.
🔁 adorn, embellish.

disgrace *n* shame, ignominy, disrepute, dishonour, disfavour, humiliation, defamation, discredit, scandal, reproach, slur, stain.
🔁 honour, esteem.
➤ *v* shame, dishonour, abase, defame, humiliate, disfavour, stain, discredit, reproach, slur, sully, taint, stigmatize.
🔁 honour, respect.

disgraceful *adj* shameful, dishonourable, disreputable, ignominious, scandalous, shocking, unworthy, dreadful, appalling.
🔁 honourable, respectable.

disguise v 1 CONCEAL, cover, camouflage, mask, hide, dress up, cloak, screen, veil, shroud. 2 FALSIFY, deceive, dissemble, misrepresent, fake, fudge.
🔁 1 reveal, expose.
➤ n concealment, camouflage, cloak, cover, costume, mask, front, façade, masquerade, deception, pretence, travesty, screen, veil.

disgust v offend, displease, nauseate, revolt, sicken, repel, outrage, put off.
🔁 delight, please.
➤ n revulsion, repulsion, repugnance, distaste, aversion, abhorrence, nausea, loathing, detestation, hatred.

disgusted adj repelled, repulsed, revolted, offended, appalled, outraged.
🔁 attracted, delighted.

disgusting adj repugnant, repellent, revolting, offensive, sickening, nauseating, odious, foul, unappetizing, unpleasant, vile, obscene, abominable, detestable, objectionable, nasty.
🔁 delightful, pleasant.

dish n plate, bowl, platter, food, recipe.
◇ **dish out** distribute, give out, hand out, hand round, dole out, allocate, mete out, inflict.
◇ **dish up** serve, present, ladle, spoon, dispense, scoop.

dishearten v discourage, dispirit, dampen, cast down, depress, dismay, dash, disappoint, deject, daunt, crush, deter.
🔁 encourage, hearten.

dishevelled adj tousled, unkempt, uncombed, untidy, bedraggled, messy, ruffled, slovenly, disordered.
🔁 neat, tidy.

dishonest adj untruthful, fraudulent, deceitful, false, lying, deceptive, double-dealing, cheating, crooked (*infml*), treacherous, unprincipled, swindling, shady (*infml*), corrupt, disreputable.
🔁 honest, trustworthy, scrupulous.

dishonesty n deceit, falsehood, falsity, fraudulence, fraud, criminality, insincerity, treachery, cheating,

crookedness (*infml*), corruption, unscrupulousness, trickery.
🔁 honesty, truthfulness.

dishonour v disgrace, shame, humiliate, debase, defile, degrade, defame, discredit, demean, debauch.
🔁 honour.
➤ n disgrace, abasement, humiliation, shame, degradation, discredit, disrepute, indignity, ignominy, reproach, slight, slur, scandal, insult, disfavour, outrage, aspersion, abuse, discourtesy.
🔁 honour.

disillusioned adj disenchanted, disabused, undeceived, disappointed.

disinclined adj averse, reluctant, resistant, indisposed, loath, opposed, hesitant.
🔁 inclined, willing.

disinfect v sterilize, fumigate, sanitize, decontaminate, cleanse, purify, purge, clean.
🔁 contaminate, infect.

disinfectant n sterilizer, antiseptic, sanitizer.

disintegrate v break up, decompose, fall apart, crumble, rot, moulder, separate, splinter.

disinterest n disinterestedness, impartiality, neutrality, detachment, unbiasedness, dispassionateness, fairness.

disinterested adj unbiased, neutral, impartial, unprejudiced, dispassionate, detached, uninvolved, open-minded, equitable, even-handed, unselfish.
🔁 biased, concerned.

disjointed adj 1 DISCONNECTED, dislocated, divided, separated, disunited, displaced, broken, fitful, split, disarticulated. 2 INCOHERENT, aimless, confused, disordered, loose, unconnected, bitty, rambling, spasmodic.
🔁 2 coherent.

dislike n aversion, hatred, repugnance, hostility, distaste, disinclination, disapproval, disapprobation,

displeasure, animosity, antagonism, enmity, detestation, disgust, loathing.
Ea liking, predilection.
➤ *v* hate, detest, object to, loathe, abhor, abominate, disapprove, shun, despise, scorn.
Ea like, favour.

dislocate *v* disjoint, displace, misplace, disengage, put out (*infml*), disorder, shift, disconnect, disrupt, disunite.

dislodge *v* displace, eject, remove, oust, extricate, shift, move, uproot.

disloyal *adj* treacherous, faithless, false, traitorous, two-faced (*infml*), unfaithful, apostate, unpatriotic.
Ea loyal, trustworthy.

dismal *adj* dreary, gloomy, depressing, bleak, cheerless, dull, drab, low-spirited, melancholy, sad, sombre, lugubrious, forlorn, despondent, dark, sorrowful, long-faced (*infml*), hopeless, discouraging.
Ea cheerful, bright.

dismantle *v* demolish, take apart, disassemble, strip.
Ea assemble, put together.

dismay *v* alarm, daunt, frighten, unnerve, unsettle, scare, put off, dispirit, distress, disconcert, dishearten, discourage, disillusion, depress, horrify, disappoint.
Ea encourage, hearten.
➤ *n* consternation, alarm, distress, apprehension, agitation, dread, fear, trepidation, fright, horror, terror, discouragement, disappointment.
Ea boldness, encouragement.

dismember *v* disjoint, amputate, dissect, dislocate, divide, mutilate, sever.
Ea assemble, join.

dismiss *v* **1** *the class was dismissed*: discharge, free, let go, release, send away, remove, drop, discord, banish. **2** *dismiss employees*: sack (*infml*), make redundant, lay off, fire (*infml*), relegate. **3** *dismiss it from your mind*: discount, disregard, reject, repudiate,

set aside, shelve, spurn.
Ea 1 retain. **2** appoint. **3** accept.

disobey *v* contravene, infringe, violate, transgress, flout, disregard, defy, ignore, resist, rebel.
Ea obey.

disorder *n* **1** CONFUSION, chaos, muddle, disarray, mess, untidiness, shambles (*infml*), clutter, jumble, disorganization. **2** DISTURBANCE, tumult, riot, confusion, commotion, uproar, fracas, brawl, fight, clamour, quarrel. **3** ILLNESS, complaint, disease, sickness, disability, ailment, malady, affliction. *see panel at* **disease**.
Ea 1 neatness, order. **2** law and order, peace.
➤ *v* disturb, mess up, disarrange, mix up, muddle, upset, disorganize, confuse, confound, clutter, jumble, discompose, scatter, unsettle.
Ea arrange, organize.

disorderly *adj* **1** DISORGANIZED, confused, chaotic, irregular, messy, untidy. **2** UNRULY, undisciplined, unmanageable, obstreperous, rowdy, turbulent, rebellious, lawless.
Ea 1 neat, tidy. **2** well-behaved.

disorganize *v* disorder, disrupt, disturb, disarrange, muddle, upset, confuse, discompose, jumble, play havoc with, unsettle, break up, destroy.
Ea organize.

disown *v* repudiate, renounce, disclaim, deny, cast off, disallow, reject, abandon.
Ea accept, acknowledge.

disparaging *adj* derisive, derogatory, mocking, scornful, critical, insulting, snide.
Ea flattering, praising.

dispassionate *adj* detached, objective, impartial, neutral, disinterested, impersonal, fair, cool, calm, composed.
Ea biased, emotional.

dispatch, despatch *v* **1** SEND, express, transmit, forward, consign, expedite, accelerate. **2** DISPOSE OF, finish, perform, discharge, conclude.

3 KILL, murder, execute.
☰ 1 receive.
➤ *n* **1** COMMUNICATION, message, report, bulletin, communiqué, news, letter, account. **2** PROMPTNESS, speed, alacrity, expedition, celerity, haste, rapidity, swiftness.
☰ 2 slowness.

dispense *v* **1** DISTRIBUTE, give out, apportion, allot, allocate, assign, share, mete out. **2** ADMINISTER, apply, implement, enforce, discharge, execute, operate.
◇ dispense with dispose of, get rid of, abolish, discard, omit, disregard, cancel, forgo, ignore, waive.

disperse *v* scatter, dispel, spread, distribute, diffuse, dissolve, break up, dismiss, separate.
☰ gather.

displace *v* **1** DISLODGE, move, shift, misplace, disturb, dislocate. **2** DEPOSE, oust, remove, replace, dismiss, discharge, supplant, eject, evict, succeed, supersede.

display *v* **1** SHOW, present, exhibit, demonstrate. **2** BETRAY, disclose, reveal, show, expose. **3** SHOW OFF, flourish, parade, flaunt.
☰ 1 conceal. **2** disguise.
➤ *n* show, exhibition, demonstration, presentation, parade, spectacle, revelation.

displease *v* offend, annoy, irritate, piss off (*sl*), anger, upset, put out (*infml*), infuriate, exasperate, incense.
☰ please.

displeasure *n* offence, annoyance, disapproval, irritation, resentment, disfavour, anger, indignation, wrath.
☰ pleasure.

disposal *n* **1** ARRANGEMENT, grouping, order. **2** CONTROL, direction, command. **3** REMOVAL, riddance, discarding, jettisoning.

dispose of **1** DEAL WITH, decide, settle. **2** GET RID OF, discard, scrap, destroy, dump (*infml*), ditch (*infml*), jettison.
☰ 2 keep.

disposed *adj* liable, inclined, predisposed, prone, likely, apt, minded, subject, ready, willing.
☰ disinclined.

disposition *n* character, nature, temperament, inclination, make-up, bent, leaning, predisposition, constitution, habit, spirit, tendency, proneness.

disproportionate *adj* unequal, uneven, incommensurate, excessive, unreasonable.
☰ balanced.

disprove *v* refute, rebut, confute, discredit, invalidate, contradict, expose.
☰ confirm, prove.

dispute *v* argue, debate, question, contend, challenge, discuss, doubt, contest, contradict, deny, quarrel, clash, wrangle, squabble.
☰ agree.
➤ *n* argument, debate, disagreement, controversy, conflict, contention, quarrel, wrangle, feud, strife, squabble.
☰ agreement, settlement.

disqualify *v* **1** INCAPACITATE, disable, invalidate. **2** DEBAR, preclude, rule out, disentitle, eliminate, prohibit.
☰ 2 qualify, accept.

disquiet *n* anxiety, worry, concern, nervousness, uneasiness, restlessness, alarm, distress, fretfulness, fear, disturbance, trouble.
☰ calm, reassurance.

disregard *v* **1** IGNORE, overlook, discount, neglect, pass over, disobey, make light of, turn a blind eye to (*infml*), brush aside. **2** SLIGHT, snub, despise, disdain, disparage.
☰ 1 heed, pay attention to. **2** respect.
➤ *n* neglect, negligence, inattention, oversight, indifference, disrespect, contempt, disdain, brush-off (*infml*).
☰ attention, heed.

disrepair *n* dilapidation, deterioration, decay, collapse, ruin, shabbiness.
☰ good repair.

disreputable *adj* **1** DISGRACEFUL, discreditable, dishonourable,

unrespectable, notorious, scandalous, shameful, shady, base, contemptible, low, mean, shocking. **2** SCRUFFY, shabby, seedy, unkempt.
F₃ 1 respectable. **2** smart.

disrespectful *adj* rude, discourteous, impertinent, impolite, impudent, insolent, uncivil, unmannerly, cheeky, insulting, irreverent, contemptuous.
F₃ polite, respectful.

disrupt *v* disturb, disorganize, confuse, interrupt, break up, unsettle, intrude, upset.

dissatisfaction *n* discontent, displeasure, dislike, discomfort, disappointment, frustration, annoyance, irritation, exasperation, regret, resentment.
F₃ satisfaction.

dissect *v* **1** DISMEMBER, anatomize. **2** ANALYSE, investigate, scrutinize, examine, inspect, pore over.

dissension *n* disagreement, discord, dissent, dispute, contention, conflict, strife, friction, quarrel.
F₃ agreement.

dissent *v* disagree, differ, protest, object, refuse, quibble.
F₃ assent.
➤ *n* disagreement, difference, dissension, discord, resistance, opposition, objection.
F₃ agreement, conformity.

disservice *n* disfavour, injury, wrong, bad turn, harm, unkindness, injustice.
F₃ favour.

dissident *adj* disagreeing, differing, dissenting, discordant, nonconformist, heterodox (*fml*).
F₃ acquiescent, orthodox.
➤ *n* dissenter, protestor, noncomformist, rebel, agitator, revolutionary, schismatic, recusant.
F₃ assenter.

dissimilar *adj* unlike, different, divergent, disparate, unrelated, incompatible, mismatched, diverse, various, heterogeneous.
F₃ similar, like.

dissipate *v* **1** *he dissipated his inheritance*: spend, waste, squander, expend, consume, deplete, fritter away, burn up. **2** *the clouds dissipated*: disperse, vanish, disappear, dispel, diffuse, evaporate, dissolve.
F₃ 1 accumulate. **2** appear.

dissociate *v* separate, detach, break off, disunite, disengage, disconnect, cut off, disband, divorce, disrupt, isolate, segregate.
F₃ associate, join.

dissolute *adj* dissipated, debauched, degenerate, depraved, wanton, abandoned, corrupt, immoral, licentious, lewd, wild.
F₃ restrained, virtuous.

dissolution *n* **1** DISINTEGRATION, decomposition, separation, resolution, division. **2** ENDING, termination, conclusion, finish, discontinuation, divorce, dismissal, dispersal, destruction, overthrow. **3** EVAPORATION, disappearance.

dissolve *v* **1** EVAPORATE, disintegrate, liquefy, melt. **2** DECOMPOSE, disintegrate, disperse, break up, disappear, crumble. **3** END, terminate, separate, sever, divorce.

dissuade *v* deter, discourage, put off, disincline.
F₃ persuade.

distance *n* **1** SPACE, interval, gap, extent, range, reach, length, width. **2** ALOOFNESS, reserve, coolness, coldness, remoteness.
F₃ 1 closeness. **2** approachability.

distant *adj* **1** FAR, faraway, far-flung, out-of-the-way, remote, outlying, abroad, dispersed. **2** ALOOF, cool, reserved, standoffish, formal, cold, restrained, stiff.
F₃ 1 close. **2** approachable.

distaste *n* dislike, aversion, repugnance, disgust, revulsion, loathing, abhorrence.
F₃ liking.

distasteful *adj* disagreeable, offensive, unpleasant, objectionable,

repulsive, obnoxious, repugnant, unsavoury, loathsome, abhorrent.
🔳 pleasing.

distinct *adj* 1 SEPARATE, different, detached, individual, dissimilar.
2 CLEAR, plain, evident, obvious, apparent, marked, definite, noticeable, recognizable.
🔳 2 indistinct, vague.

distinction *n* 1 DIFFERENTIATION, discrimination, discernment, separation, difference, dissimilarity, contrast. 2 CHARACTERISTIC, peculiarity, individuality, feature, quality, mark.
3 RENOWN, fame, celebrity, prominence, eminence, importance, reputation, greatness, honour, prestige, repute, superiority, worth, merit, excellence, quality.
🔳 3 unimportance, obscurity.

distinctive *adj* characteristic, distinguishing, individual, peculiar, different, unique, singular, special, original, extraordinary, idiosyncratic.
🔳 ordinary, common.

distinguish *v* 1 DIFFERENTIATE, tell apart, discriminate, determine, categorize, characterize, classify.
2 DISCERN, perceive, identify, ascertain, make out, recognize, see, discriminate.

distinguished *adj* famous, eminent, celebrated, well-known, acclaimed, illustrious, notable, noted, renowned, famed, honoured, outstanding, striking, marked, extraordinary, conspicuous.
🔳 insignificant, obscure, unimpressive.

distort *v* 1 DEFORM, contort, bend, misshape, disfigure, twist, warp.
2 FALSIFY, misrepresent, pervert, slant, colour, garble.

distract *v* 1 DIVERT, sidetrack, deflect.
2 CONFUSE, disconcert, bewilder, confound, disturb, perplex, puzzle.
3 AMUSE, occupy, divert, engross.

distraught *adj* agitated, anxious, overwrought, upset, distressed, distracted, beside oneself, worked up, frantic, hysterical, raving, mad, wild, crazy.
🔳 calm, untroubled.

distress *n* 1 ANGUISH, grief, misery, sorrow, heartache, affliction, suffering, torment, wretchedness, sadness, worry, anxiety, desolation, pain, agony.
2 ADVERSITY, hardship, poverty, need, privation, destitution, misfortune, trouble, difficulties, trial.
🔳 1 content. 2 comfort, ease.
➤ *v* upset, afflict, grieve, disturb, trouble, sadden, worry, torment, harass, harrow, pain, agonize, bother.
🔳 comfort.

distribute *v* 1 DISPENSE, allocate, dole out, dish out, share, deal, divide, apportion. 2 DELIVER, hand out, spread, issue, circulate, diffuse, disperse, scatter.
🔳 2 collect.

distribution *n* 1 ALLOCATION, apportionment, division, sharing.
2 CIRCULATION, spreading, scattering, delivery, dissemination, supply, dealing, handling. 3 ARRANGEMENT, grouping, classification, organization.
🔳 2 collection.

district *n* region, area, quarter, neighbourhood, locality, sector, precinct, parish, locale, community, vicinity, ward.

distrust *v* mistrust, doubt, disbelieve, suspect, question.
🔳 trust.
➤ *n* mistrust, doubt, disbelief, suspicion, misgiving, wariness, scepticism, question, qualm.
🔳 trust.

disturb *v* 1 DISRUPT, interrupt, distract.
2 AGITATE, unsettle, upset, distress, worry, fluster, annoy, bother.
3 DISARRANGE, disorder, confuse, upset.
🔳 2 reassure. 3 order.

disturbance *n* 1 DISRUPTION, agitation, interruption, intrusion, upheaval, upset, confusion, annoyance, bother, trouble, hindrance. 2 DISORDER, uproar, commotion, tumult, turmoil, fracas, fray, brawl, riot.
🔳 1 peace. 2 order.

disuse *n* neglect, desuetude (*fml*),

abandonment, discontinuance, decay.
🔁 use.

ditch n trench, dyke, channel, gully, furrow, moat, drain, level, watercourse.

dither v hesitate, shilly-shally (*infml*), waver, vacillate.

dive v plunge, plummet, dip, submerge, jump, leap, nose-dive, fall, drop, swoop, descend, pitch.
➤ n 1 PLUNGE, lunge, header, jump, leap, nosedive, swoop, dash, spring. 2 (*infml*) BAR, club, saloon.

diverge v 1 DIVIDE, branch, fork, separate, spread, split. 2 DEVIATE, digress, stray, wander. 3 DIFFER, vary, disagree, dissent, conflict.
🔁 1 converge. 3 agree.

diverse adj various, varied, varying, sundry, different, differing, assorted, dissimilar, miscellaneous, discrete, separate, several, distinct.
🔁 similar, identical.

diversify v vary, change, expand, branch out, spread out, alter, mix, assort.

diversion n 1 DEVIATION, detour. 2 AMUSEMENT, entertainment, distraction, pastime, recreation, relaxation, play, game. 3 ALTERATION, change.

diversity n variety, dissimilarity, difference, variance, assortment, range, medley.
🔁 similarity, likeness.

divert v 1 DEFLECT, redirect, reroute, sidetrack, avert, distract, switch. 2 AMUSE, entertain, occupy, distract, interest.

divide v 1 SPLIT, separate, part, cut, break up, detach, bisect, disconnect. 2 DISTRIBUTE, share, allocate, deal out, allot, apportion. 3 DISUNITE, separate, estrange, alienate. 4 CLASSIFY, group, sort, grade, segregate.
🔁 1 join. 2 collect. 3 unite.

divine adj 1 GODLIKE, superhuman, supernatural, celestial, heavenly, angelic, spiritual. 2 HOLY, sacred, sanctified, consecrated, transcendent,

exalted, glorious, religious, supreme.
🔁 1 human. 2 mundane.

divinity n god, goddess, deity, godliness, holiness, sanctity, godhead, spirit.

division n 1 SEPARATION, detaching, parting, cutting, disunion. 2 BREACH, rupture, split, schism, disunion, estrangement, disagreement, feud. 3 DISTRIBUTION, sharing, allotment, apportionment. 4 SECTION, sector, segment, part, department, category, class, compartment, branch.
🔁 1 union. 2 unity. 3 collection. 4 whole.

divorce n dissolution, annulment, break-up, split-up, rupture, separation, breach, disunion.
➤ v separate, part, annul, split up, sever, dissolve, divide, dissociate.
🔁 marry, unite.

divulge v disclose, reveal, tell, leak (*infml*), communicate, impart, confess, betray, uncover, let slip, expose, publish, proclaim.

dizzy adj 1 GIDDY, faint, light-headed, woozy (*infml*), shaky, reeling. 2 CONFUSED, bewildered, dazed, muddled.

do v 1 PERFORM, carry out, execute, accomplish, achieve, fulfil, implement, complete, undertake, work, put on, present, conclude, end, finish. 2 BEHAVE, act, conduct oneself. 3 FIX, prepare, organize, arrange, deal with, look after, manage, produce, make, create, cause, proceed. 4 SUFFICE, satisfy, serve.
➤ n (*infml*) function, affair, event, gathering, party, occasion.
◇ **do away with** get rid of, dispose of, exterminate, eliminate, abolish, discontinue, remove, destroy, discard, kill, murder.
◇ **do up 1** FASTEN, tie, lace, pack. 2 RENOVATE, restore, decorate, redecorate, modernize, repair.
◇ **do without** dispense with, abstain from, forgo, give up, relinquish.

docile adj tractable, co-operative,

manageable, submissive, obedient, amenable, controlled, obliging.
🔁 truculent, unco-operative.

dock[1] *n* harbour, wharf, quay, boat-yard, pier, waterfront, marina.
➤ *v* anchor, moor, drop anchor, land, berth, put in, tie up.

dock[2] *v* crop, clip, cut, shorten, curtail, deduct, reduce, lessen, withhold, decrease, subtract, diminish.

doctor *n* physician, general practitioner, GP, medic (*infml*), medical officer, consultant, clinician, doc (*infml*), bones (*infml*), quack (*infml*).

> *Types of medical doctor include*: general practitioner, GP, family doctor, family practitioner, locum, hospital doctor, houseman, intern, resident, registrar, consultant, medical officer (MO), dentist, veterinary surgeon, vet (*infml*). *see also* **medical**; **surgeon**.

➤ *v* **1** ALTER, tamper with, falsify, misrepresent, pervert, adulterate, change, disguise, dilute. **2** REPAIR, fix, patch up.

doctrine *n* dogma, creed, belief, tenet, principle, teaching, precept, conviction, opinion, canon.

document *n* paper, certificate, deed, record, report, form, instrument (*fml*).
➤ *v* **1** RECORD, report, chronicle, list, detail, cite. **2** SUPPORT, prove, verify, corroborate.

dodge *v* avoid, elude, evade, swerve, side-step, shirk, shift.
➤ *n* trick, ruse, ploy, wile, scheme, stratagem, machination, manoeuvre.

dog *n* hound, cur, mongrel, canine, puppy, pup, bitch, mutt (*infml*), pooch (*infml*).

> *Breeds of dog include*: Afghan hound, alsatian, Australian terrier, basset hound, beagle, Border collie, borzoi, bull mastiff, bulldog, bull terrier, cairn terrier, chihuahua, chow, cocker spaniel, collie, corgi, dachshund, Dalmatian, Doberman pinscher,

English terrrier, foxhound, fox terrier, German Shepherd, golden retriever, Great Dane, greyhound, husky, Irish setter, Irish wolfhound, Jack Russell, King Charles spaniel, komondor, Labrador, lhasa apso, lurcher, Maltese, Old English sheepdog, Pekingese, pit bull terrier, pointer, poodle, pug, Rottweiler, saluki, sausage dog (*infml*), schnauzer, Scottie (*infml*), Scottish terrier, Sealyham, setter, sheltie, shih tzu, springer spaniel, Staffordshire terrier, St Bernard, terrier, whippet, West Highland terrier, Westie (*infml*), wolfhound, Yorkshire terrier.

➤ *v* pursue, follow, trail, track, tail, hound, shadow, plague, harry, haunt, trouble, worry.

dogged *adj* determined, resolute, persistent, persevering, intent, tenacious, firm, steadfast, staunch, single-minded, indefatigable, steady, unshakable, stubborn, obstinate, relentless, unyielding.
🔁 irresolute, apathetic.

dogma *n* doctrine, creed, belief, precept, principle, article (of faith), credo, tenet, conviction, teaching, opinion.

dogmatic *adj* opinionated, assertive, authoritative, positive, doctrinaire, dictatorial, doctrinal, categorical, emphatic, overbearing, arbitrary.

dole out distribute, allocate, hand out, dish out, apportion, allot, mete out, share, divide, deal, issue, ration, dispense, administer, assign.

domain *n* **1** DOMINION, kingdom, realm, territory, region, empire, lands, province. **2** FIELD, area, speciality, concern, department, sphere, discipline, jurisdiction.

domestic *adj* **1** HOME, family, household, home-loving, stay-at-home, homely, house-trained, tame, pet, private. **2** INTERNAL, indigenous, native.
➤ *n* servant, maid, charwoman, char, daily help, daily, au pair.

domesticate *v* tame, house-train, break, train, accustom, familiarize.

dominant *adj* **1** AUTHORITATIVE, controlling, governing, ruling, powerful, assertive, influential. **2** PRINCIPAL, main, outstanding, chief, important, predominant, primary, prominent, leading, pre-eminent, prevailing, prevalent, commanding.
F3 **1** submissive. **2** subordinate.

dominate *v* **1** CONTROL, domineer, govern, rule, direct, monopolize, master, lead, overrule, prevail, overbear, tyrannize. **2** OVERSHADOW, eclipse, dwarf.

domineering *adj* overbearing, authoritarian, imperious, autocratic, bossy (*infml*), dictatorial, despotic, masterful, high-handed, oppressive, tyrannical, arrogant.
F3 meek, servile.

dominion *n* **1** POWER, authority, domination, command, control, rule, sway, jurisdiction, government, lordship, mastery, supremacy, sovereignty. **2** DOMAIN, country, territory, province, colony, realm, kingdom, empire.

donate *v* give, contribute, present, bequeath, cough up (*infml*), fork out (*infml*), bestow (*fml*), confer (*fml*), subscribe.
F3 receive.

donation *n* gift, present, offering, grant, gratuity, largess(e), contribution, presentation, subscription, alms, benefaction (*fml*), bequest.

done *adj* **1** FINISHED, over, accomplished, completed, ended, concluded, settled, realized, executed. **2** CONVENTIONAL, acceptable, proper. **3** COOKED, ready.

donor *n* giver, donator, benefactor, contributor, philanthropist, provider, fairy godmother (*infml*).
F3 beneficiary.

doom *n* **1** FATE, fortune, destiny, portion, lot. **2** DESTRUCTION, catastrophe, downfall, ruin, death, death-knell. **3** CONDEMNATION,

judgement, sentence, verdict.
➤ *v* condemn, damn, consign, judge, sentence, destine.

doomed *adj* condemned, damned, fated, ill-fated, ill-omened, cursed, destined, hopeless, luckless, ill-starred.

door *n* opening, entrance, entry, exit, doorway, portal, hatch.

dope (*infml*) *n* **1** NARCOTIC, drugs, marijuana, cannabis, opiate, hallucinogen. **2** FOOL, dolt, idiot, half-wit (*infml*), dimwit (*infml*), dunce, simpleton, clot (*infml*), blockhead. **3** INFORMATION, facts, low-down (*infml*), gen (*infml*), SP (*infml*), details.
➤ *v* drug, sedate, anaesthetize, stupefy, medicate, narcotize, inject, doctor.

dormant *adj* **1** INACTIVE, asleep, sleeping, inert, resting, slumbering, sluggish, torpid, hibernating, fallow, comatose. **2** LATENT, unrealized; potential, undeveloped, undisclosed.
F3 **1** active, awake. **2** realized, developed.

dose *n* measure, dosage, amount, portion, quantity, draught, potion, prescription, shot.
➤ *v* medicate, administer, prescribe, dispense, treat.

dot *n* point, spot, speck, mark, fleck, circle, pinpoint, atom, decimal point, full stop, iota, jot.
➤ *v* spot, sprinkle, stud, dab, punctuate.

dote on adore, idolize, treasure, admire, indulge.

double *adj* dual, twofold, twice, duplicate, twin, paired, doubled, coupled.
F3 single, half.
➤ *v* duplicate, enlarge, increase, repeat, multiply, fold, magnify.
➤ *n* twin, duplicate, copy, clone, replica, doppelgänger, lookalike, spitting image (*infml*), ringer (*infml*), image, counterpart, impersonator.
◇ **at the double** immediately, at once, quickly, without delay.

double-cross *v* cheat, swindle,

defraud, trick, con (*infml*), hoodwink, betray, two-time (*infml*), mislead.

doubt *v* 1 DISTRUST, mistrust, query, question, suspect, fear. 2 BE UNCERTAIN, be dubious, hesitate, vacillate, waver.
🖛 1 believe, trust.
➤ *n* 1 DISTRUST, suspicion, mistrust, scepticism, reservation, misgiving, incredulity, apprehension, hesitation. 2 UNCERTAINTY, difficulty, confusion, ambiguity, problem, indecision, perplexity, dilemma, quandary.
🖛 1 trust, faith. 2 certainty, belief.

doubtful *adj* 1 *doubtful about his future*: uncertain, unsure, undecided, suspicious, irresolute, wavering, hesitant, vacillating, tentative, sceptical. 2 *writing of doubtful origin*: dubious, questionable, unclear, ambiguous, vague, obscure, debatable.
🖛 1 certain, decided. 2 definite, settled.

doubtless *adv* 1 CERTAINLY, without doubt, undoubtedly, unquestionably, indisputably, no doubt, clearly, surely, of course, truly, precisely. 2 PROBABLY, presumably, most likely, seemingly, supposedly.

dour *adj* 1 GLOOMY, dismal, forbidding, grim, morose, unfriendly, dreary, austere, sour, sullen. 2 HARD, inflexible, unyielding, rigid, severe, rigorous, strict, obstinate.
🖛 1 cheerful, bright. 2 easy-going.

douse, dowse *v* 1 SOAK, saturate, steep, submerge, immerse, immerge, dip, duck, drench, dunk, plunge. 2 EXTINGUISH, put out, blow out, smother, snuff.

dowdy *adj* unfashionable, ill-dressed, frumpish, drab, shabby, tatty (*infml*), frowsy, tacky (*infml*), dingy, old-fashioned, slovenly.
🖛 fashionable, smart.

down *v* 1 KNOCK DOWN, fell, floor, prostrate, throw, topple. 2 SWALLOW, drink, gulp, swig (*infml*), knock back (*infml*).
◇ **down and out** destitute,

impoverished, penniless, derelict, ruined, bankrupt.

downcast *adj* dejected, depressed, despondent, sad, unhappy, miserable, down, low, disheartened, dispirited, blue (*infml*), fed up (*infml*), discouraged, disappointed, crestfallen, dismayed.
🖛 cheerful, happy, elated.

downfall *n* fall, ruin, failure, collapse, destruction, disgrace, debacle, undoing, overthrow.

downgrade *v* 1 DEGRADE, demote, lower, humble. 2 DISPARAGE, denigrate, belittle, run down, decry.
🖛 1 upgrade, improve. 2 praise.

downhearted *adj* depressed, dejected, despondent, sad, downcast, discouraged, disheartened, low-spirited, unhappy, gloomy, glum, dismayed.
🖛 cheerful, enthusiastic.

downpour *n* cloudburst, deluge, rainstorm, flood, inundation, torrent.

downright *adj, adv* absolute(ly), outright, plain(ly), utter(ly), clear(ly), complete(ly), out-and-out, frank(ly), explicit(ly).

downtrodden *adj* oppressed, subjugated, subservient, exploited, trampled on, abused, tyrannized, victimized, helpless.

downward *adj* descending, declining, downhill, sliding, slipping.
🖛 upward.

dowse *see* **douse**.

doze *v* sleep, nod off, drop off, snooze, kip (*sl*), zizz (*sl*).
➤ *n* nap, catnap, siesta, snooze, forty winks (*infml*), kip (*sl*), shut-eye (*infml*), zizz (*sl*).

drab *adj* dull, dingy, dreary, dismal, gloomy, flat, grey, lacklustre, cheerless, sombre, shabby.
🖛 bright, cheerful.

draft[1] *v* draw (up), outline, sketch, plan, design, formulate, compose.
➤ *n* outline, sketch, plan, delineation, abstract, rough, blueprint, protocol.

draft[2] *n* bill of exchange, cheque, money order, letter of credit, postal order.

drag *v* 1 DRAW, pull, haul, lug, tug, trail, tow. 2 GO SLOWLY, creep, crawl, lag.
➤ *n* (*infml*) bore, annoyance, nuisance, pain (*infml*), bother.

drain *v* 1 EMPTY, remove, evacuate, draw off, strain, dry, milk, bleed.
2 DISCHARGE, trickle, flow out, leak, ooze. 3 EXHAUST, consume, sap, use up, deplete, drink up, swallow.
🖪 1 fill.
➤ *n* 1 CHANNEL, conduit, culvert, duct, outlet, trench, ditch, pipe, sewer.
2 DEPLETION, exhaustion, sap, strain.

drama *n* 1 PLAY, acting, theatre, show, spectacle, stagecraft, scene, melodrama. 2 EXCITEMENT, crisis, turmoil.

dramatic *adj* 1 EXCITING, striking, stirring, thrilling, marked, significant, expressive, impressive. 2 HISTRIONIC, exaggerated, melodramatic, flamboyant.

dramatize *v* 1 STAGE, put on, adapt.
2 ACT, play-act, exaggerate, overdo, overstate.

drape *v* cover, wrap, hang, fold, drop, suspend.

drastic *adj* extreme, radical, strong, forceful, severe, harsh, far-reaching, desperate, dire.
🖪 moderate, cautious.

draught *n* 1 PUFF, current, influx, flow.
2 DRINK, potion, quantity. 3 PULLING, traction.

draw *v* 1 ATTRACT, allure, entice, bring in, influence, persuade, elicit. 2 PULL, drag, haul, tow, tug. 3 DELINEATE, map out, sketch, portray, trace, pencil, depict, design. 4 TIE, be equal, be even.
🖪 1 repel. 2 push.
➤ *n* 1 ATTRACTION, enticement, lure, appeal, bait, interest. 2 TIE, stalemate, dead heat.
◇ **draw out** protract, extend, prolong, drag out, spin out, elongate, stretch, lengthen, string out.
🖪 shorten.

◇ **draw up** 1 DRAFT, compose, formulate, prepare, frame, write out.
2 PULL UP, stop, halt, run in.

drawback *n* disadvantage, snag, hitch, obstacle, impediment, hindrance, difficulty, flaw, fault, fly in the ointment (*infml*), catch, stumbling block, nuisance, trouble, defect, handicap, deficiency, imperfection.
🖪 advantage, benefit.

drawing *n* sketch, picture, outline, representation, delineation, portrayal, illustration, cartoon, graphic, portrait.

dread *v* fear, shrink from, quail, cringe at, flinch, shy, shudder, tremble.
➤ *n* fear, apprehension, misgiving, trepidation, dismay, alarm, horror, terror, fright, disquiet, worry, quietly, qualm.
🖪 confidence, security.

dreadful *adj* awful, terrible, frightful, horrible, appalling, dire, shocking, ghastly, horrendous, tragic, grievous, hideous, tremendous.
🖪 wonderful, comforting.

dream *n* 1 VISION, illusion, reverie, trance, fantasy, daydream, nightmare, hallucination, delusion, imagination.
2 ASPIRATION, wish, hope, ambition, desire, pipe-dream, ideal, goal, design, speculation.
➤ *v* imagine, envisage, fancy, fantasize, daydream, hallucinate, conceive, visualize, conjure up, muse.
◇ **dream up** invent, devise, conceive, think up, imagine, concoct, hatch, create, spin, contrive.

dreamer *n* idealist, visionary, fantasizes, romancer, daydreamer, star-gazer, theorizer.
🖪 realist, pragmatist.

dreamy *adj* 1 FANTASTIC, unreal, imaginary, shadowy, vague, misty.
2 IMPRACTICAL, fanciful, daydreaming, romantic, visionary, faraway, absent, musing, pensive.
🖪 1 real. 2 practical, down-to-earth.

dreary *adj* 1 *a dreary job*: boring, tedious, uneventful, dull, humdrum, routine, monotonous, wearisome, commonplace, colourless, lifeless. **2** *a dreary landscape*: gloomy, depressing, drab, dismal, bleak, sombre, sad, mournful.

🔁 **1** interesting. **2** cheerful.

dregs *n* **1** SEDIMENT, deposit, residue, lees, grounds, scum, dross, trash, waste. **2** OUTCASTS, rabble, riff-raff, scum, down-and-outs.

drench *v* soak, saturate, steep, wet, douse, souse, immerse, inundate, duck, flood, imbue, drown.

dress *n* **1** FROCK, gown, robe. **2** CLOTHES, clothing, garment(s), outfit, costume, garb, get-up (*infml*), gear (*infml*), togs (*infml*).

➤ *v* **1** CLOTHE, put on, garb, rig, robe, wear, don, decorate, deck, garnish, trim, adorn, fit, drape. **2** ARRANGE, adjust, dispose, prepare, groom, straighten. **3** BANDAGE, tend, treat.

🔁 **1** strip, undress.

◊ **dress up** beautify, adorn, embellish, improve, deck, doll up, tart up (*infml*), gild, disguise.

dribble *v* **1** TRICKLE, drip, leak, run, seep, drop, ooze. **2** DROOL, slaver, slobber, drivel.

drift *v* **1** WANDER, waft, stray, float, freewheel, coast. **2** GATHER, bank, accumulate, pile up, drive.

➤ *n* **1** ACCUMULATION, mound, pile, bank, mass, heap. **2** TREND, tendency, course, direction, flow, movement, current, rush, sweep. **3** MEANING, intention, implication, gist, tenor, thrust, significance, aim, design, scope.

drill *v* **1** TEACH, train, instruct, coach, practise, school, rehearse, exercise, discipline. **2** BORE, pierce, penetrate, puncture, perforate.

➤ *n* **1** INSTRUCTION, training, practice, coaching, exercise, repetition, tuition, preparation, discipline. **2** BORER, awl, bit, gimlet.

drink *v* **1** IMBIBE, swallow, sip, drain, down, gulp, swig (*infml*), knock back (*infml*), sup, quaff, absorb, guzzle,

partake of (*fml*), swill. **2** GET DRUNK, booze (*infml*), tipple (*infml*), indulge, carouse, revel, tank up (*infml*).

➤ *n* **1** BEVERAGE, liquid, refreshment, draught, sip, swallow, swig (*infml*), gulp.

Types of non-alcoholic drink include: tea, coffee, cocoa, hot chocolate, Horlicks®, Ovaltine®, milk, milk shake, float (*US*); fizzy drink, pop (*infml*), cherryade, Coca Cola®, coke (*infml*), cream soda, ginger beer, lemonade, limeade, Pepsi®, root beer, sarsaparilla, cordial, squash, barley water, Ribena®, fruit juice, mixer, bitter lemon, Canada Dry®, ginger ale, soda water, tonic water, mineral water, Perrier®, seltzer, Vichy water, Lucozade®, Wincarnis®, beef tea. *see also* **coffee**; **tea**.

2 ALCOHOL, spirits, booze (*infml*), liquor, tipple (*infml*), tot, the bottle (*infml*), stiffener (*infml*).

Alcoholic drinks include: ale, beer, cider, lager, shandy, stout, Guinness®; aquavit, Armagnac, bourbon, brandy, Calvados, Cognac, gin, gin and tonic, pink gin, sloe gin, rum, grog, rye, vodka, whisky, Scotch and soda, hot toddy; wine, red wine, vin rouge, vin rosé, white wine, vin blanc, champagne, bubbly (*infml*), mead, perry; absinthe, advocaat, alcopop, Benedictine, Chartreuse, black velvet, bloody Mary, Buck's fizz, Campari, cherry brandy, cocktail, Cointreau®, crème de menthe, daiquiri, eggnog, Galliano, ginger wine, kirsch, Marsala, Martini®, ouzo, Pernod®, piña colada, port, punch, retsina, sake, sangria, schnapps, sherry, snowball, tequila, Tom Collins, vermouth. *see also* **wine**.

drip *v* drop, dribble, trickle, plop, percolate, drizzle, splash, sprinkle, weep.

➤ *n* **1** DROP, trickle, dribble, leak, bead, tear. **2** (*infml*) WEAKLING, wimp (*infml*), softy (*infml*), bore, wet (*infml*), wuss (*sl*), ninny (*infml*).

drive *v* **1** DIRECT, control, manage,

operate, run, handle, motivate. **2** FORCE, compel, impel, coerce, constrain, press, push, urge, dragoon, goad, guide, oblige. **3** STEER, motor, propel, ride, travel.

➤ *n* **1** ENERGY, enterprise, ambition, initiative, get-up-and-go (*infml*), vigour, motivation, determination. **2** CAMPAIGN, crusade, appeal, effort, action. **3** EXCURSION, outing, journey, ride, spin, trip, jaunt. **4** URGE, instinct, impulse, need, desire.

◇ **drive at** imply, allude to, intimate, mean, suggest, hint, get at, intend, refer to, signify, insinuate, indicate.

driving *adj* compelling, forceful, vigorous, dynamic, energetic, forthright, heavy, violent, sweeping.

drizzle *n* mist, mizzle, rain, spray, shower.

➤ *v* spit, spray, sprinkle, rain, spot, shower.

droop *v* **1** HANG (DOWN), dangle, sag, bend. **2** LANGUISH, decline, flag, falter, slump, lose heart, wilt, wither, drop, faint, fall down, fade, slouch. **3** SINK.

E3 1 straighten. **2** flourish, rise.

drop *n* **1** DROPLET, bead, tear, drip, bubble, globule, trickle. **2** DASH, pinch, spot, sip, trace, dab. **3** FALL, decline, falling-off, lowering, downturn, decrease, reduction, slump, plunge, deterioration. **4** DESCENT, precipice, slope, chasm, abyss.

➤ *v* **1** FALL, sink, decline, plunge, plummet, tumble, dive, descend, lower, droop, depress, diminish. **2** ABANDON, forsake, desert, give up, relinquish, reject, jilt, ditch (*infml*), leave, renounce, throw over, repudiate, cease, discontinue, quit.

E3 1 rise.

◇ **drop off 1** NOD OFF, doze, snooze, have forty winks (*infml*). **2** DECLINE, fall off, decrease, dwindle, lessen, diminish, slacken. **3** DELIVER, set down, leave.

E3 1 wake up. **2** increase. **3** pick up.

◇ **drop out** back out, abandon, cry off, withdraw, forsake, leave, quit.

drought *n* dryness, aridity,

parchedness, dehydration, desiccation, shortage, want.

drove *n* herd, horde, gathering, crowd, multitude, swarm, throng, flock, mob, company, press.

drown *v* **1** SUBMERGE, immerse, inundate, go under, flood, sink, deluge, engulf, drench. **2** OVERWHELM, overpower, overcome, swamp, wipe out, extinguish.

drowsy *adj* sleepy, tired, lethargic, nodding, dreamy, dozy, somnolent (*fml*).

E3 alert, awake.

drudge *n* toiler, menial, dogsbody (*infml*), hack, servant, slave, factotum, worker, skivvy (*infml*), galley-slave, lackey.

➤ *v* plod, toil, work, slave, plug away (*infml*), grind (*infml*), labour, beaver (*infml*).

E3 idle, laze.

drudgery *n* labour, donkey work (*infml*), hack-work, slog (*infml*), grind (*infml*), slavery, sweat, sweated labour, toil, skivvying, chore.

drug *n* medication, medicine, remedy, potion.

Types of drug include: anaesthetic, analgesic, antibiotic, antidepressant, antihistamine, barbiturate, narcotic, opiate, hallucinogenic, sedative, steroid, stimulant, tranquillizer; chloroform, aspirin, codeine, paracetamol, morphine, penicillin, diazepam, temazepam, Valium®, Prozac®, Viagra®, cortisone, insulin, digitalis, laudanum, quinine, progesterone, oestrogen, cannabis, marijuana, smack, LSD, acid, ecstasy, E (*sl*), heroin, opium, cocaine, crack, dope (*infml*). *see also* **medicine**.

➤ *v* medicate, sedate, tranquillize, dope (*infml*), anaesthetize, dose, knock out (*infml*), stupefy, deaden, numb.

drum *v* beat, pulsate, tap, throb, thrum, tattoo, reverberate, rap.

◇ **drum up** obtain, round up, collect, gather, solicit, canvass, petition, attract.

drunk *adj* inebriated (*fml*), intoxicated, under the influence, drunken, stoned (*sl*), legless (*sl*), paralytic (*infml*), sloshed (*infml*), merry (*infml*), tight (*infml*), tipsy (*infml*), tanked up (*sl*), tiddly (*infml*), plastered (*sl*), loaded (*infml*), lit up (*infml*), sozzled (*infml*), well-oiled (*infml*), canned (*sl*), blotto (*sl*). ☒ sober, temperate, abstinent, teetotal.

drunkard *n* drunk, inebriate (*fml*), alcoholic, dipsomaniac, boozer (*infml*), wino (*infml*), tippler (*infml*), soak (*infml*), lush (*infml*), sot (*infml*).

dry *adj* 1 ARID, parched, thirsty, dehydrated, desiccated, barren. 2 BORING, dull, dreary, tedious, monotonous. 3 *dry humour*: ironic, cynical, droll, deadpan, sarcastic, cutting.
☒ 1 wet. 2 interesting.
➤ *v* dehydrate, parch, desiccate, drain, shrivel, wither.
☒ soak.

dual *adj* double, twofold, duplicate, duplex, binary, combined, paired, twin, matched.

dubious *adj* 1 DOUBTFUL, uncertain, undecided, unsure, wavering, unsettled, suspicious, sceptical, hesitant.
2 QUESTIONABLE, debatable, unreliable, ambiguous, suspect, obscure, fishy (*infml*), shady (*infml*).
☒ 1 certain. 2 trustworthy.

duck *v* 1 CROUCH, stoop, bob, bend. 2 AVOID, dodge, evade, shirk, sidestep.
3 DIP, immerse, plunge, dunk, dive, submerge, douse, souse, wet, lower.

due *adj* 1 OWED, owing, payable, unpaid, outstanding, in arrears.
2 RIGHTFUL, fitting, appropriate, proper, merited, deserved, justified, suitable.
3 ADEQUATE, enough, sufficient, ample, plenty of. 4 EXPECTED, scheduled.
☒ 1 paid. 3 inadequate.
➤ *adv* exactly, direct(ly), precisely, straight, dead (*infml*).

duel *n* affair of honour, combat, contest, fight, clash, competition, rivalry, encounter.

dull *adj* 1 BORING, uninteresting,

unexciting, flat, dreary, monotonous, tedious, uneventful, humdrum, unimaginative, dismal, lifeless, plain, insipid, heavy. 2 DARK, gloomy, drab, murky, indistinct, grey, cloudy, lack-lustre, opaque, dim, overcast.
3 UNINTELLIGENT, dense, dim, dimwitted (*infml*), thick (*infml*), stupid, slow.
☒ 1 interesting, exciting. 2 bright.
3 intelligent, clever.
➤ *v* 1 BLUNT, alleviate, mitigate, moderate, lessen, relieve, soften.
2 DEADEN, numb, paralyse. 3 DISCOURAGE, dampen, subdue, sadden.
4 DIM, obscure, fade.

dumb *adj* silent, mute, soundless, speechless, tongue-tied, inarticulate, mum (*infml*).

dumbfounded *adj* astonished, amazed, astounded, overwhelmed, speechless, taken aback, thrown (*infml*), startled, overcome, confounded, flabbergasted (*infml*), staggered, confused, bowled over, dumb, floored (*infml*), paralysed.

dummy *n* 1 COPY, duplicate, imitation, counterfeit, substitute. 2 MODEL, lay-figure, mannequin, figure, form. 3 TEAT, pacifier.
➤ *adj* 1 ARTIFICIAL, fake, imitation, false, bogus, mock, sham, phoney.
2 SIMULATED, practice, trial.

dump *v* 1 DEPOSIT, drop, offload, throw down, let fall, unload, empty out, discharge, park. 2 GET RID OF, scrap, throw away, dispose of, ditch, tip, jettison.
➤ *n* 1 RUBBISH TIP, junkyard, rubbish-heap, tip. 2 HOVEL, slum, shack, shanty, hole (*infml*), joint (*infml*), pigsty, mess.

dungeon *n* cell, prison, jail, gaol, cage, lock-up, keep, oubliette, vault.

dupe *n* victim, sucker (*infml*), fool, gull, mug (*infml*), pushover (*infml*), fall guy (*infml*), pawn, puppet, instrument, stooge (*infml*), simpleton.
➤ *v* deceive, delude, fool, trick, outwit, con (*infml*), cheat, hoax, swindle, rip off (*sl*), take in, hoodwink, defraud, bamboozle (*infml*).

duplicate *adj* identical, matching, twin, twofold, corresponding, matched.
➤ *n* copy, replica, clone, reproduction, photocopy, carbon (copy), match, facsimile.
➤ *v* copy, reproduce, repeat, photocopy, double, clone, echo.

durable *adj* lasting, enduring, long-lasting, abiding, hard-wearing, strong, sturdy, tough, unfading, substantial, sound, reliable, dependable, stable, resistant, persistent, constant, permanent, firm, fixed, fast.
🔁 perishable, weak, fragile.

duress *n* constraint, coercion, compulsion, pressure, restraint, threat, force.

dusk *n* twilight, sunset, nightfall, evening, sundown, gloaming, darkness, dark, gloom, shadows, shade.
🔁 dawn, brightness.

dust *n* powder, particles, dirt, earth, soil, ground, grit, grime.

dusty *adj* 1 DIRTY, grubby, filthy. 2 POWDERY, granular, crumbly, chalky, sandy.
🔁 1 clean. 2 solid, hard.

dutiful *adj* obedient, respectful, conscientious, devoted, filial, reverential, submissive.

duty *n* 1 OBLIGATION, responsibility, assignment, calling, charge, role, task, job, business, function, work, office, service. 2 OBEDIENCE, respect, loyalty. 3 TAX, toll, tariff, levy, customs, excise.
◇ **on duty** at work, engaged, busy.

dwarf *n* 1 PERSON OF RESTRICTED GROWTH, midget, pygmy, Tom Thumb, Lilliputian. 2 GNOME, goblin.
➤ *adj* miniature, small, tiny, pocket, mini (*infml*), diminutive, petite, Lilliputian, baby.
🔁 large.
➤ *v* 1 STUNT, retard, check.
2 OVERSHADOW, tower over, dominate.

dwell *v* live, inhabit, reside, stay, settle, populate, people, lodge, rest, abide (*fml*).

dwindle *v* diminish, decrease, decline, lessen, subside, ebb, fade, weaken, taper off, tail off, shrink, peter out, fall, wane, waste away, die out, wither, shrivel, disappear.
🔁 increase, grow.

dye *n* colour, colouring, stain, pigment, tint, tinge.
➤ *v* colour, tint, stain, pigment, tinge, imbue.

dying *adj* moribund, passing, final, going, mortal, not long for this world, perishing, failing, fading, vanishing.
◇ **dying for** longing for, pining for, yearning for
🔁 reviving.

dynamic *adj* forceful, powerful, energetic, vigorous, go-ahead, high-powered, driving, self-starting, spirited, vital, lively, active.
🔁 inactive, apathetic.

dynasty *n* house, line, succession, dominion, regime, government, rule, empire, sovereignty.

Ee

eager *adj* **1** KEEN, enthusiastic, fervent, intent, earnest, zealous. **2** LONGING, yearning.

☒ **1** unenthusiastic, indifferent.

ear *n* **1** ATTENTION, heed, notice, regard. **2** *an ear for language*: perception, sensitivity, discrimination, appreciation, hearing, skill, ability.

> *Parts of the ear include*: anvil (incus), auditory canal, auditory nerve, auricle, cochlea, concha, eardrum, eustachian tube, hammer (malleus), helix, labyrinth, lobe, oval window, pinna, round window, semicircular canal, stirrup (stapes), tragus, tympanum, vestibular nerve, vestibule.

early *adj* **1** *early symptoms*: forward, advanced, premature, untimely, undeveloped. **2** *early theatre*: primitive, ancient, primeval.

➤ *adv* ahead of time, in good time, beforehand, in advance, prematurely.

☒ late.

earn *v* **1** *earn a good salary*: receive, obtain, make, get, draw, bring in (*infml*), gain, realize, gross, reap. **2** *earn one's reputation*: deserve, merit, warrant, win, rate.

☒ **1** spend, lose.

earnest *adj* **1** RESOLUTE, devoted, ardent, conscientious, intent, keen, fervent, firm, fixed, eager, enthusiastic, steady. **2** SERIOUS, sincere, solemn, grave, heartfelt.

☒ **1** apathetic. **2** frivolous, flippant.

earnings *n* pay, income, salary, wages, profits, gain, proceeds, reward, receipts, return, revenue, remuneration, stipend.

☒ expenditure, outgoings.

earth *n* **1** WORLD, planet, globe, sphere. **2** LAND, ground, soil, clay, loam, sod, humus.

earthenware *n* pottery, ceramics, crockery, pots.

earthly *adj* **1** *our earthly life*: material, physical, human, worldly, mortal, mundane, fleshly, secular, sensual, profane, temporal. **2** *no earthly explanation*: possible, likely, conceivable, slightest.

☒ **1** spiritual, heavenly.

earthy *adj* crude, coarse, vulgar, bawdy, rough, raunchy (*infml*), down-to-earth, ribald, robust.

☒ refined, modest.

ease *n* **1** FACILITY, effortlessness, skilfulness, deftness, dexterity, naturalness, cleverness. **2** COMFORT, contentment, peace, affluence, repose, leisure, relaxation, rest, quiet, happiness.

☒ **1** difficulty. **2** discomfort.

➤ *v* **1** *ease the pain*: alleviate, moderate, lessen, lighten, relieve, mitigate, abate, relent, allay, assuage, relax, comfort, calm, soothe, facilitate, smooth. **2** *ease it into position*: inch, steer, slide, still.

☒ **1** aggravate, intensify, worsen.

easily *adv* **1** EFFORTLESSLY, comfortably, readily, simply. **2** BY FAR, undoubtedly, indisputably, definitely, certainly, doubtlessly, clearly, far and away, undeniably, simply, surely, probably, well.

☒ **1** laboriously.

easy *adj* **1** EFFORTLESS, simple, uncomplicated, undemanding, straightforward, manageable, cushy (*infml*). **2** RELAXED, carefree, easy-going

(*infml*), laid-back (*infml*), comfortable, informal, calm, natural, leisurely.
F3 1 difficult, demanding, exacting.
2 tense, uneasy.

easy-going (*infml*) *adj* relaxed, tolerant, laid back (*infml*), amenable, happy-go-lucky (*infml*), carefree, calm, even-tempered, serene.
F3 strict, intolerant, critical.

eat *v* **1** CONSUME, feed, swallow, devour, chew, scoff (*infml*), munch, dine.
2 CORRODE, erode, wear away, decay, rot, crumble, dissolve.

eatable *adj* edible, palatable, good, wholesome, digestible, comestible (*fml*), harmless.
F3 inedible, unpalatable.

eavesdrop *v* listen in, spy, overhear, snoop (*infml*), tap (*infml*), bug (*infml*), monitor.

eccentric *adj* odd, peculiar, abnormal, unconventional, strange, quirky, weird, way-out (*infml*), queer, outlandish, left-field (*infml*), idiosyncratic, bizarre, freakish, erratic, singular, dotty.
F3 conventional, orthodox, normal.
➤ *n* nonconformist, oddball (*infml*), oddity, crank (*infml*), freak (*infml*), character (*infml*).

eccentricity *n* unconventionality, strangeness, peculiarity, nonconformity, abnormality, oddity, weirdness, idiosyncrasy, singularity, quirk, freakishness, aberration, anomaly, capriciousness.
F3 conventionality, ordinariness.

ecclesiastical *adj* church, churchly, religious, clerical, priestly, divine, spiritual.

echo *v* **1** REVERBERATE, resound, repeat, reflect, reiterate, ring. **2** IMITATE, copy, reproduce, mirror, resemble, mimic.
➤ *n* **1** REVERBERATION, reiteration, repetition, reflection. **2** IMITATION, copy, reproduction, mirror image, image, parallel.

eclipse *v* **1** BLOT OUT, obscure, cloud, veil, darken, dim. **2** OUTDO, overshadow, outshine, surpass, transcend.

➤ *n* **1** OBSCURATION, overshadowing, darkening, shading, dimming.
2 DECLINE, failure, fall, loss.

economic *adj* **1** COMMERCIAL, business, industrial. **2** FINANCIAL, budgetary, fiscal, monetary.
3 PROFITABLE, profit-making, money-making, productive, cost-effective, viable.

economical *adj* **1** THRIFTY, careful, prudent, saving, sparing, frugal.
2 CHEAP, inexpensive, low-priced, reasonable, cost-effective, modest, efficient.
F3 1 wasteful. **2** expensive, uneconomical.

economize *v* save, cut back, tighten one's belt (*infml*), budget, cut costs.
F3 waste, squander.

economy *n* thrift, saving, restraint, prudence, frugality, parsimony, providence, husbandry.
F3 extravagance.

ecstasy *n* delight, rapture, bliss, elation, joy, euphoria, frenzy, exaltation, fervour.
F3 misery, torment.

ecstatic *adj* elated, blissful, joyful, rapturous, overjoyed, euphoric, delirious, frenzied, fervent.
F3 downcast.

eddy *n* whirlpool, swirl, vortex, twist.
➤ *v* swirl, whirl.

edge *n* **1** BORDER, rim, boundary, limit, brim, threshold, brink, fringe, margin, outline, side, verge, line, perimeter, periphery, lip. **2** ADVANTAGE, superiority, force. **3** SHARPNESS, acuteness, keenness, incisiveness, pungency, zest.
➤ *v* creep, inch, ease, sidle.

edgy *adj* on edge, nervous, tense, anxious, ill at ease, keyed-up, touchy (*infml*), irritable.
F3 calm.

edible *adj* eatable, palatable, digestible, wholesome, good, harmless.
F3 inedible.

edict *n* command, order, proclamation, law, decree, regulation, pronouncement, ruling, mandate, statute, injunction, manifesto.

edifice *n* building, construction, structure, erection.

edify *v* instruct, improve, enlighten, inform, guide, educate, nurture, teach.

edit *v* correct, emend, revise, rewrite, reorder, rearrange, adapt, check, compile, rephrase, select, polish, annotate, censor.

edition *n* copy, volume, impression, printing, issue, version, number.

educate *v* teach, train, instruct, tutor, coach, school, inform, cultivate, edify, drill, improve, discipline, develop.

educated *adj* learned, taught, schooled, trained, knowledgeable, informed, instructed, lettered, cultured, civilized, tutored, refined, well-bred. ▣ uneducated, uncultured.

education *n* teaching, training, schooling, tuition, tutoring, coaching, guidance, instruction, cultivation, culture, scholarship, improvement, enlightenment, knowledge, nurture, development.

Educational establishments include: kindergarten, nursery school, infant school, primary school, middle school, combined school, secondary school, secondary modern, upper school, high school, grammar school, community school, foundation school, voluntary school, preparatory school, public school, private school, boarding school, college, sixth form college, city technical college, CTC, technical college, university, adult education centre, academy, seminary, finishing school, business school, secretarial college, Sunday school, convent school, summer-school.

Educational terms include: adult education, assisted places scheme, A-level, (international) baccalaureate, board of governors, break time, bursar, campus, catchment area, certificate, classroom, coeducation,

common entrance, course, course of studies, curriculum, degree, diploma, discipline, double-first, educational programme, eleven-plus, enrolment, examination, exercise book, final exam, finals, further education, GCSE (General Certificate of Secondary Education), governor, graduation, half-term, head boy, head girl, head teacher, higher education, Higher Grade, homework, intake, invigilator, lecture, literacy, matriculation, matron, mixed-ability teaching, modular course, module, national curriculum, newly qualified teacher, NVQ (national vocational qualification), numeracy, O-level, opting out, parent governor, PTA (parent teacher association), playground, playtime, prefect, primary education, proctor, professor, pupil, quadrangle, qualification, refresher course, register, report, scholarship, school term, secondary education, special education, Standard Grade, statemented, streaming, student, student grant, student loan, study, subject, syllabus, teacher, teacher training, test paper, textbook, thesis, timetable, truancy, university entrance, work experience.

eerie *adj* weird, strange, uncanny, spooky (*infml*), creepy, frightening, scary, spine-chilling.

effect *n* **1** OUTCOME, result, conclusion, consequence, upshot, aftermath, issue. **2** POWER, force, impact, efficacy, impression, strength. **3** MEANING, significance, import.

➤ *v* cause, execute, create, achieve, accomplish, perform, produce, make, initiate, fulfil, complete.

◇ **in effect** in fact, actually, really, in reality, to all intents and purposes, for all practical purposes, essentially, effectively, virtually.

◇ **take effect** be effective, become operative, come into force, come into operation, be implemented, begin, work, kick in (*infml*).

effective *adj* **1** EFFICIENT, efficacious, productive, adequate, capable, useful. **2** OPERATIVE, in force, functioning, current, active. **3** STRIKING, impressive, forceful, cogent, powerful, persuasive, convincing, telling.
F3 1 ineffective, powerless.

effects *n* belongings, possessions, property, goods, gear (*infml*), movables, chattels (*fml*), things, trappings.

effeminate *adj* unmanly, womanly, womanish, feminine, sissy (*infml*), delicate.
F3 manly.

effervescent *adj* **1** BUBBLY, sparkling, fizzy, frothy, carbonated, foaming. **2** LIVELY, ebullient, vivacious, animated, buoyant, exhilarated, enthusiastic, exuberant, excited, vital.
F3 1 flat. **2** dull.

efficiency *n* effectiveness, competence, proficiency, skill, expertise, skilfulness, capability, ability, productivity.
F3 inefficiency, incompetence.

efficient *adj* effective, competent, proficient, skilful, capable, able, productive, well-organized, businesslike, powerful, well-conducted.
F3 inefficient, incompetent.

effort *n* **1** EXERTION, strain, application, struggle, trouble, energy, toil, striving, pains, travail (*fml*). **2** ATTEMPT, try, go (*infml*), endeavour, shot (*infml*), stab (*infml*). **3** ACHIEVEMENT, accomplishment, feat, exploit, production, creation, deed, product, work.

effortless *adj* easy, simple, undemanding, facile, painless, smooth.
F3 difficult.

effrontery *n* audacity, impertinence, insolence, cheek, impudence, temerity, boldness, brazenness, cheekiness, gall, nerve, presumption, disrespect, arrogance, brashness.
F3 respect, timidity.

effusive *adj* fulsome, gushing, unrestrained, expansive, ebullient, demonstrative, profuse, overflowing,
enthusiastic, exuberant, extravagant, lavish, talkative, voluble.
F3 reserved, restrained.

egotism *n* egoism, egomania, self-centredness, self-importance, conceitedness, self-regard, self-love, self-conceit, narcissism, self-admiration, vanity, bigheadedness (*infml*).
F3 humility.

egotistic *adj* egoistic, egocentric, self-centred, self-important, conceited, vain, swollen-headed (*infml*), bigheaded (*infml*), boasting, bragging.
F3 humble.

ejaculate *v* **1** DISCHARGE, eject, spurt, emit. **2** EXCLAIM, call, blurt (out), cry, shout, yell, utter, scream.

eject *v* **1** EMIT, expel, discharge, spout, spew, evacuate, vomit. **2** OUST, evict, throw out, drive out, turn out, expel, remove, banish, deport, dismiss, exile, kick out, fire (*infml*), sack (*infml*).

elaborate *adj* **1** *elaborate plans*: detailed, careful, thorough, exact, extensive, painstaking, precise, perfected, minute, laboured, studied. **2** *elaborate design*: intricate, complex, complicated, involved, ornamental, ornate, fancy, decorated, ostentatious, showy, fussy.
F3 2 simple, plain.
➤ *v* amplify, develop, enlarge, expand, flesh out, polish, improve, refine, devise, explain.
F3 précis, simplify.

elapse *v* pass, lapse, go by, slip away.

elastic *adj* **1** PLIABLE, flexible, stretchable, supple, resilient, yielding, springy, rubbery, pliant, plastic, bouncy, buoyant. **2** ADAPTABLE, flexible, accommodating, tolerant, adjustable.
F3 1 rigid. **2** inflexible.

elasticity *n* **1** PLIABILITY, flexibility, resilience, stretch, springiness, suppleness, give, plasticity, bounce, buoyancy. **2** ADAPTABILITY, flexibility, tolerance, adjustability.
F3 1 rigidity. **2** inflexibility.

elated *adj* exhilarated, excited, euphoric, ecstatic, exultant, jubilant, overjoyed, joyful.
 despondent, downcast.

elbow *v* jostle, nudge, push, shove, bump, crowd, knock, shoulder.

elder *adj* older, senior, first-born, ancient.
 younger.

elderly *adj* aging, aged, old, hoary, senile.
 young, youthful.

elect *v* choose, pick, opt for, select, vote for, prefer, adopt, designate, appoint, determine.
 ➤ *adj* choice, elite, chosen, designated, designate, picked, prospective, selected, to be, preferred, hand-picked.

election *n* choice, selection, voting, ballot, poll, appointment, determination, decision, preference.

elector *n* selector, voter, constituent.

electric *adj* electrifying, exciting, stimulating, thrilling, charged, dynamic, stirring, tense, rousing.
 unexciting, flat.

electrical

> *Types of electrical component and device include*: adaptor, ammeter, armature, battery, bayonet fitting, cable, ceiling rose, circuit breaker, conduit, continuity tester, copper conductor, dimmer switch, dry-cell battery, earthed plug, electrical screwdriver, electricity meter, extension lead, fluorescent tube, fuse, fusebox, fuse carrier, high voltage tester, insulating tape, lampholder, lightbulb, multimeter, neon lamp, socket, test lamp, three-core cable, three-pin plug, transducer, transformer, two-pin plug, universal test meter, voltage doubler, wire strippers.

electricity

> *Electricity and electronics terms include*: alternating current (AC), alternator, amp, ampere, amplifier, analogue signal, anode, bandpass filter, battery, bioelectricity, capacitance, capacitor, cathode, cathode-ray tube, cell, commutator, condenser, conductivity, coulomb, digital signal, diode, direct current (DC), Dolby® (system), dynamo, eddy current, electrode, electrolyte, electromagnet, electron tube, farad, Faraday cage, Foucault current, frequency modulation, galvanic, galvanometer, generator, grid system, henry, impedance, induced current, inductance, integrated circuit, isoelectric, isoelectronic, logic gate, loudspeaker, microchip, mutual induction, NICAM®, ohm, optoelectronics, oscillator, oscilloscope, piezoelectricity, polarity, power station, reactance, resistance, resistor, rheostat, semiconductor, siemens, silicon chip, solenoid, solid state circuit, static electricity, stepdown transformer, superconductivity, switch, thermionics, thermistor, thyristor, transformer, transistor, triode, truth table, turboalternator, tweeter, valve, volt, voltaic, voltage amplifier, watt, Wheatstone bridge, woofer.

electrify *v* thrill, excite, shock, invigorate, animate, stimulate, stir, rouse, fire, jolt, galvanize, amaze, astonish, astound, stagger.
 bore.

elegant *adj* stylish, chic, fashionable, modish, smart, refined, polished, genteel, smooth, tasteful, fine, exquisite, beautiful, graceful, handsome, delicate, neat, artistic.
 inelegant, unrefined, unfashionable.

elegy *n* dirge, lament, requiem, plaint.

element *n* factor, component, constituent, ingredient, member, part, piece, fragment, feature, trace.
 whole.

elementary *adj* basic, fundamental, rudimentary, principal, primary, clear,

easy, introductory, straightforward, uncomplicated, simple.
🔁 advanced.

elements *n* basics, fundamentals, foundations, principles, rudiments, essentials.

elevate *v* **1** LIFT, raise, hoist, heighten, intensify, magnify. **2** EXALT, advance, promote, aggrandize, upgrade. **3** UPLIFT, rouse, boost, brighten.
🔁 **1** lower. **2** downgrade.

elevated *adj* raised, lofty, exalted, high, grand, noble, dignified, sublime.
🔁 base.

elevation *n* **1** RISE, promotion, advancement, preferment, aggrandizement. **2** EXALTATION, loftiness, grandeur, eminence, nobility. **3** HEIGHT, altitude, hill, rise.
🔁 **1** demotion. **2** dip.

elicit *v* evoke, draw out, derive, extract, obtain, exact, extort, cause.

eligible *adj* qualified, fit, appropriate, suitable, acceptable, worthy, proper, desirable.
🔁 ineligible.

eliminate *v* remove, get rid of, cut out, take out, exclude, delete, dispense with, rub out, omit, reject, disregard, dispose of, drop, do away with, eradicate, expel, extinguish, stamp out, exterminate, knock out, kill, murder.
🔁 include, accept.

elite *n* best, elect, aristocracy, upper classes, nobility, gentry, crème de la crème, establishment, high society.
➤ *adj* choice, best, exclusive, selected, first-class, aristocratic, noble, upper-class.

elocution *n* delivery, articulation, diction, enunciation, pronunciation, oratory, rhetoric, speech, utterance.

elongated *adj* lengthened, extended, prolonged, protracted, stretched, long.

elope *v* run off, run away, decamp, bolt, abscond, do a bunk (*infml*), escape, steal away, leave, disappear.

eloquent *adj* articulate, fluent,

well-expressed, glib, expressive, vocal, voluble, persuasive, moving, forceful, graceful, plausible, stirring, vivid.
🔁 inarticulate, tongue-tied.

elucidate *v* explain, clarify, clear up, interpret, spell out, illustrate, unfold.
🔁 confuse.

elude *v* **1** AVOID, escape, evade, dodge, shirk, duck (*infml*), flee. **2** PUZZLE, frustrate, baffle, confound, thwart, stump, foil.

elusive *adj* **1** INDEFINABLE, intangible, unanalysable, subtle, puzzling, baffling, transient, transitory. **2** EVASIVE, shifty, slippery, tricky.

emaciated *adj* thin, gaunt, lean, haggard, wasted, scrawny, skeletal, pinched, attenuated, meagre, lank.
🔁 plump, well-fed.

emanate *v* **1** ORIGINATE, proceed, arise, derive, issue, spring, stem, flow, come, emerge. **2** DISCHARGE, send out, emit, give out, give off, radiate.

emancipate *v* free, liberate, release, set free, enfranchise, deliver, discharge, loose, unchain, unshackle, unfetter.
🔁 enslave.

embankment *n* causeway, dam, rampart, levee, earthwork.

embargo *n* restriction, ban, prohibition, restraint, proscription, bar, barrier, interdiction (*fml*), impediment, check, hindrance, blockage, stoppage, seizure.

embark *v* board (ship), go aboard, take ship.
🔁 disembark.
◇ **embark on** begin, start, commence, set about, launch, undertake, enter, initiate, engage.
🔁 complete, finish.

embarrass *v* disconcert, mortify, show up, discompose, fluster, humiliate, shame, distress.

embarrassment *n*
1 DISCOMPOSURE, self-consciousness, chagrin, mortification, humiliation, shame, awkwardness, confusion,

bashfulness. **2** DIFFICULTY, constraint, predicament, distress, discomfort.

embellish v adorn, ornament, decorate, deck, dress up, beautify, gild, garnish, festoon, elaborate, embroider, enrich, exaggerate, enhance, varnish, grace.
🔁 simplify, denude.

embellishment n adornment, ornament, ornamentation, decoration, elaboration, garnish, trimming, gilding, enrichment, enhancement, embroidery, exaggeration.

embezzle v appropriate, misappropriate, steal, pilfer, filch, pinch (*infml*).

embezzlement n appropriation, misappropriation, pilfering, fraud, stealing, theft, filching.

embittered adj bitter, disaffected, sour, disillusioned.

emblem n symbol, sign, token, representation, logo, insignia, device, crest, mark, badge, figure.

embodiment n incarnation, personification, exemplification, expression, epitome, example, incorporation, realization, representation, manifestation, concentration.

embody v **1** PERSONIFY, exemplify, represent, stand for, symbolize, incorporate, express, manifest. **2** INCLUDE, contain, integrate.

embrace v **1** HUG, clasp, cuddle, hold, grasp, squeeze. **2** INCLUDE, encompass, incorporate, contain, comprise, cover, involve. **3** ACCEPT, take up, welcome.
➤ n hug, cuddle, clasp, clinch (*infml*).

embroidery

Types of embroidery stitch include: backstitch, blanket, bullion, chain, chevron, cross, feather, fishbone, French knot, half-cross, herringbone, lazy-daisy, longstitch, long-and-short, moss, Oriental couching, Romanian couching, running, satin, stem, straight, Swiss darning, tent.

embroil v involve, implicate, entangle, enmesh, mix up, incriminate.

embryo n nucleus, germ, beginning, root.

embryonic adj undeveloped, rudimentary, immature, early, germinal, primary.
🔁 developed.

emerge v **1** ARISE, rise, surface, appear, develop, crop up (*infml*), transpire, turn up, materialize. **2** EMANATE, issue, proceed.
🔁 **1** disappear.

emergence n appearance, rise, advent, coming, dawn, development, arrival, disclosure, issue.
🔁 disappearance.

emergency n crisis, danger, difficulty, exigency (*fml*), predicament, plight, pinch, strait, quandary.

emigrate v migrate, relocate, move, depart.

eminence n distinction, fame, pre-eminence, prominence, renown, reputation, greatness, importance, esteem, note, prestige, rank.

eminent adj distinguished, famous, prominent, illustrious, outstanding, notable, pre-eminent, prestigious, celebrated, renowned, noteworthy, conspicuous, esteemed, important, well-known, elevated, respected, great, high-ranking, grand, superior.
🔁 unknown, obscure, unimportant.

emissary n ambassador, agent, envoy, messenger, delegate, herald, courier, representative, scout, deputy, spy.

emission n discharge, issue, ejection, emanation, ejaculation, diffusion, transmission, exhalation, radiation, release, exudation, vent.

emit v discharge, issue, eject, emanate, exude, give out, give off, diffuse, radiate, release, shed, vent.
🔁 absorb.

emotion n feeling, passion, sensation, sentiment, ardour, fervour, warmth, reaction, vehemence, excitement.

emotional *adj* **1** FEELING, passionate, sensitive, responsive, ardent, tender, warm, roused, demonstrative, excitable, enthusiastic, fervent, impassioned, moved, sentimental, zealous, hot-blooded, heated, tempestuous, overcharged, temperamental, fiery. **2** EMOTIVE, moving, poignant, thrilling, touching, stirring, heart-warming, exciting, pathetic.
F3 1 unemotional, cold, detached, calm.

emphasis *n* stress, weight, significance, importance, priority, underscoring, accent, force, power, prominence, pre-eminence, attention, intensity, strength, urgency, positiveness, insistence, mark, moment.

emphasize *v* stress, accentuate, underline, highlight, accent, feature, dwell on, weight, point up, spotlight, play up, insist on, press home, intensify, strengthen, punctuate.
F3 play down, understate.

emphatic *adj* forceful, positive, insistent, certain, definite, decided, unequivocal, absolute, categorical, earnest, marked, pronounced, significant, strong, striking, vigorous, distinct, energetic, forcible, important, impressive, momentous, powerful, punctuated, telling, vivid, graphic, direct.
F3 tentative, hesitant, understated.

empire *n* **1** SUPREMACY, sovereignty, rule, authority, command, government, jurisdiction, control, power, sway. **2** DOMAIN, dominion, kingdom, realm, commonwealth, territory.

employ *v* **1** ENGAGE, hire, take on, recruit, enlist, commission, retain, fill, occupy, take up. **2** USE, utilize, make use of, apply, bring to bear, ply, exercise.

employee *n* worker, member of staff, job-holder, hand, wage-earner.

employer *n* boss (*infml*), proprietor, owner, manager, gaffer (*infml*), management, company, firm, business, establishment.

employment *n* **1** JOB, work, occupation, situation, business, calling, profession, line, vocation, trade, pursuit, craft. **2** ENLISTMENT, employ, engagement, hire.
F3 1 unemployment.

empower *v* authorize, warrant, enable, license, sanction, permit, entitle, commission, delegate, qualify.

emptiness *n* **1** VACUUM, vacantness, void, hollowness, hunger, bareness, barrenness, desolation. **2** FUTILITY, meaninglessness, worthlessness, aimlessness, ineffectiveness, unreality.
F3 1 fullness.

empty *adj* **1** VACANT, void, unoccupied, uninhabited, unfilled, deserted, bare, hollow, desolate, blank, clear. **2** FUTILE, aimless, meaningless, senseless, trivial, vain, worthless, useless, insubstantial, ineffective, insincere. **3** VACUOUS, inane, expressionless, blank, vacant.
F3 1 full. **2** meaningful.
➤ *v* drain, exhaust, discharge, clear, evacuate, vacate, pour out, unload, void, gut.
F3 fill.

empty-headed *adj* inane, silly, frivolous, scatter-brained (*infml*), feather-brained (*infml*), air-headed (*infml*).

emulate *v* match, copy, mimic, follow, imitate, echo, compete with, contend with, rival, vie with.

enable *v* equip, qualify, empower, authorize, sanction, warrant, allow, permit, prepare, fit, facilitate, license, commission, endue.
F3 prevent, inhibit, forbid.

enact *v* **1** DECREE, ordain, order, authorize, command, legislate, sanction, ratify, pass, establish. **2** ACT (OUT), perform, play, portray, represent, depict.
F3 1 repeal, rescind.

enamoured *adj* charmed, infatuated, in love with, enchanted, captivated, entranced, smitten, keen, taken, fascinated, fond.

enchant v **1** CAPTIVATE, charm, fascinate, enrapture, attract, allure, appeal, delight, thrill. **2** ENTRANCE, enthral, bewitch, spellbind, hypnotize, mesmerize.
🗷 **1** repel.

enclose v encircle, encompass, surround, fence, hedge, hem in, bound, encase, embrace, envelop, confine, hold, shut in, close in, wrap, pen, cover, circumscribe, incorporate, include, insert, contain, comprehend.

enclosure n pen, pound, compound, paddock, fold, stockade, sty, arena, corral, court, ring, cloister.

encompass v **1** ENCIRCLE, circle, ring, surround, gird, envelop, circumscribe, hem in, enclose, hold. **2** INCLUDE, cover, embrace, contain, comprise, admit, incorporate, involve, embody, comprehend.

encounter v **1** MEET, come across, run into (*infml*), happen on, chance upon, run across, confront, face, experience. **2** FIGHT, clash with, combat, cross swords with (*infml*), engage, grapple with, struggle, strive, contend.
➤ n **1** MEETING, brush, confrontation. **2** CLASH, fight, combat, conflict, contest, battle, set-to (*infml*), dispute, action, engagement, skirmish, run-in, fray, collision.

encourage v **1** HEARTEN, exhort, stimulate, spur, reassure, rally, inspire, incite, egg on (*infml*), buoy up, cheer, urge, rouse, comfort, console. **2** PROMOTE, advance, aid, boost, forward, further, foster, support, help, strengthen.
🗷 **1** discourage, depress. **2** discourage.

encouragement n **1** REASSURANCE, inspiration, cheer, exhortation, incitement, pep talk (*infml*), urging, stimulation, consolation, succour (*fml*). **2** PROMOTION, help, aid, boost, shot in the arm (*infml*), incentive, support, stimulus.
🗷 **1** discouragement, disapproval.

encouraging adj heartening, promising, hopeful, reassuring, stimulating, uplifting, auspicious, cheering, comforting, bright, rosy, cheerful, satisfactory.
🗷 discouraging.

encroach v intrude, invade, impinge, trespass, infringe, usurp, overstep, make inroads, muscle in (*infml*).

encumber v burden, overload, weigh down, saddle, oppress, handicap, hamper, hinder, impede, slow down, obstruct, inconvenience, prevent, retard, cramp.

encumbrance n burden, cumbrance, load, cross, millstone, albatross, difficulty, handicap, impediment, obstruction, obstacle, inconvenience, hindrance, liability.

end n **1** FINISH, conclusion, termination, close, completion, cessation, finale, culmination, dénouement. **2** EXTREMITY, boundary, edge, limit, tip. **3** REMAINDER, tip, butt, leftover, remnant, stub, scrap, fragment. **4** AIM, object, objective, purpose, intention, goal, point, reason, design. **5** RESULT, outcome, upshot, consequence. **6** DEATH, demise, destruction, extermination, downfall, doom, ruin, dissolution.
🗷 **1** beginning, start. **6** birth.
➤ v **1** FINISH, close, cease, conclude, stop, terminate, complete, culminate, wind up. **2** DESTROY, annihilate, exterminate, extinguish, ruin, abolish, dissolve.
🗷 **1** begin, start.

endanger v imperil, hazard, jeopardize, risk, expose, threaten, compromise.
🗷 protect.

endearing adj lovable, charming, appealing, attractive, winsome, delightful, enchanting.

endeavour n attempt, effort, go (*infml*), try, shot (*infml*), stab (*infml*), undertaking, enterprise, aim, venture.
➤ v attempt, try, strive, aim, aspire, undertake, venture, struggle, labour, take pains.

ending n end, close, finish, completion, termination, conclusion, culmination,

climax, resolution, consummation, dénouement, finale, epilogue.
‡ beginning, start.

endless *adj* **1** INFINITE, boundless, unlimited, measureless. **2** EVERLASTING, ceaseless, perpetual, constant, continual, continuous, undying, eternal, interminable, monotonous.
‡ **1** finite, limited. **2** temporary.

endorse *v* **1** APPROVE, sanction, authorize, support, back, affirm, ratify, confirm, vouch for, advocate, warrant, recommend, subscribe to, sustain, adopt. **2** SIGN, countersign.

endorsement *n* **1** APPROVAL, sanction, authorization, support, backing, affirmation, ratification, confirmation, advocacy, warrant, recommendation, commendation, seal of approval, testimonial, OK (*infml*). **2** SIGNATURE, countersignature.

endow *v* bestow, bequeath, leave, will, give, donate, endue (*fml*), confer, grant, present, award, finance, fund, support, make over, furnish, provide, supply.

endowment *n* **1** BEQUEST, legacy, award, grant, fund, gift, provision, settlement, donation, bestowal, benefaction, dowry, income, revenue. **2** TALENT, attribute, faculty, gift, ability, quality, flair, genius, qualification.

endurance *n* fortitude, patience, staying power, stamina, resignation, stoicism, tenacity, perseverance, resolution, stability, persistence, strength, toleration.

endure *v* **1** *endure hardship*: bear, stand, put up with, tolerate, weather, brave, cope with, face, go through, experience, submit to, suffer, sustain, swallow, undergo, withstand, stick, stomach, allow, permit, support. **2** *a peace that will endure for ever*: last, abide (*fml*), remain, live, survive, stay, persist, hold, prevail.

enemy *n* adversary, opponent, foe (*fml*), rival, antagonist, the opposition, competitor, opposer, other side.
‡ friend, ally.

energetic *adj* lively, vigorous, active, animated, dynamic, spirited, tireless, zestful, brisk, strong, forceful, potent, powerful, strenuous, high-powered.
‡ lethargic, sluggish, inactive, idle.

energy *n* liveliness, vigour, activity, animation, drive, dynamism, get-up-and-go (*infml*), life, spirit, verve, vivacity, vitality, zest, zeal, ardour, fire, efficiency, force, forcefulness, zip (*infml*), strength, power, intensity, exertion, stamina.
‡ lethargy, inertia, weakness.

enforce *v* impose, administer, implement, apply, execute, discharge, insist on, compel, oblige, urge, carry out, constrain, require, coerce, prosecute, reinforce.

engage *v* **1** PARTICIPATE, take part, embark on, take up, practise, involve. **2** ATTRACT, allure, draw, captivate, charm, catch. **3** OCCUPY, engross, absorb, busy, tie up, grip. **4** EMPLOY, hire, appoint, take on, enlist, enrol, commission, recruit, contract. **5** INTERLOCK, mesh, interconnect, join, interact, attach. **6** FIGHT, battle with, attack, take on, encounter, assail, combat.
‡ **2** repel. **4** dismiss, discharge. **5** disengage.

engaged *adj* **1** *engaged in his work*: occupied, busy, engrossed, immersed, absorbed, preoccupied, involved, employed. **2** *engaged to be married*: promised, betrothed (*fml*), pledged, spoken for, committed. **3** *the phone is engaged*: busy, tied up, unavailable.

engagement *n* **1** APPOINTMENT, meeting, date, arrangement, assignation, fixture, rendezvous. **2** PROMISE, pledge, betrothal (*fml*), commitment, obligation, assurance, vow, troth (*fml*). **3** FIGHT, battle, combat, conflict, action, encounter, contest, confrontation.

engaging *adj* charming, attractive, appealing, sexy (*infml*), captivating, pleasing, delightful, winsome, lovable, likable, pleasant, fetching, fascinating, agreeable.
‡ repulsive, repellent.

engine *n* motor, machine, mechanism, appliance, contraption, apparatus, device, instrument, tool, locomotive, dynamo.

> *Types of engine include*: diesel, donkey, fuel-injection, internal-combustion, jet, petrol, steam, turbine, turbojet, turboprop, V-engine.

> *Parts of an automotive engine and its ancillaries include*: air filter, alternator, camshaft, camshaft cover, carburettor, choke, connecting rod, con-rod (*infml*), cooling fan, crankshaft pulley, cylinder block, cylinder head, drive belt, exhaust manifold, exhaust valve, fan belt, flywheel, fuel and ignition ECU (electronic control unit), fuel injector, gasket, ignition coil, ignition distributor, inlet manifold, inlet valve, oil filter, oil pump, oil seal, petrol pump, piston, piston ring, power-steering pump, push-rod, radiator, rocker arm, rocker cover, rotor arm, spark plug, starter motor, sump, tappet, thermostat, timing belt, timing pulley, turbocharger.

engineer *n* **1** MECHANIC, technician, engine driver. **2** DESIGNER, originator, planner, inventor, deviser, mastermind, architect.
➤ *v* plan, contrive, devise, manoeuvre, cause, manipulate, control, bring about, mastermind, originate, orchestrate, effect, plot, scheme, manage, create, rig.

engrave *v* **1** INSCRIBE, cut, carve, chisel, etch, chase. **2** *engraved on her mind*: imprint, impress, fix, stamp, lodge, ingrain.

engraving *n* print, impression, inscription, carving, etching, woodcut, plate, block, cutting, chiselling, mark.

engross *v* absorb, occupy, engage, grip, hold, preoccupy, rivet, fascinate, captivate, enthral, arrest, involve, intrigue.
🔁 bore.

enhance *v* heighten, intensify, increase, improve, elevate, magnify, swell, exalt, raise, lift, boost, strengthen, reinforce, embellish.
🔁 reduce, minimize.

enigma *n* mystery, riddle, puzzle, conundrum, problem, poser (*infml*), brain-teaser.

enigmatic *adj* mysterious, puzzling, cryptic, obscure, strange, perplexing.
🔁 simple, straightforward.

enjoy *v* take pleasure in, delight in, appreciate, like, relish, revel in, rejoice in, savour.
🔁 dislike, hate.
◇ **enjoy oneself** have a good time, have fun, make merry, have it large (*sl*).

enjoyable *adj* pleasant, agreeable, delightful, pleasing, gratifying, entertaining, amusing, fun, delicious, good, satisfying.
🔁 disagreeable.

enjoyment *n* **1** PLEASURE, delight, amusement, gratification, entertainment, relish, joy, fun, happiness, diversion, indulgence, recreation, zest, satisfaction.
2 POSSESSION, use, advantage, benefit.
🔁 **1** displeasure.

enlarge *v* increase, expand, augment, add to, grow, extend, magnify, inflate, swell, wax, stretch, multiply, develop, amplify, blow up, widen, broaden, lengthen, heighten, elaborate.
🔁 diminish, shrink.

enlighten *v* instruct, edify, educate, inform, illuminate, teach, counsel, apprise, advise.
🔁 confuse.

enlightened *adj* informed, aware, knowledgeable, educated, civilized, cultivated, refined, sophisticated, conversant, wise, reasonable, liberal, open-minded, literate.
🔁 ignorant, confused.

enlist *v* engage, enrol, register, sign up, recruit, conscript, employ, volunteer, join (up), gather, muster, secure, obtain, procure, enter.

enmity *n* animosity, hostility, antagonism, discord, strife, feud, antipathy, acrimony, bitterness, hatred, aversion, ill-will, bad blood, rancour, malevolence, malice, venom.
🔁 friendship.

enormity *n* atrocity, outrage, iniquity, horror, evil, crime, abomination, monstrosity, wickedness, vileness, depravity, atrociousness, viciousness.

enormous *adj* huge, immense, vast, gigantic, massive, colossal, mega (*infml*), gross, gargantuan, monstrous, mammoth, jumbo (*infml*), tremendous, prodigious.
🔁 small, tiny.

enough *adj* sufficient, adequate, ample, plenty, abundant.
➤ *n* sufficiency, adequacy, plenty, abundance.
➤ *adv* sufficiently, adequately, reasonably, tolerably, passably, moderately, fairly, satisfactorily, amply.

enquire *see* **inquire**.

enquiry *see* **inquiry**.

enrage *v* incense, infuriate, anger, madden, provoke, incite, inflame, exasperate, irritate, rile.
🔁 calm, placate.

enrich *v* **1** ENDOW, enhance, improve, refine, develop, cultivate, augment. **2** ADORN, ornament, beautify, embellish, decorate, grace.
🔁 **1** impoverish.

enrol *v* **1** REGISTER, enlist, sign on, sign up, join up, recruit, engage, admit. **2** RECORD, list, note, inscribe.

enrolment *n* registration, recruitment, enlistment, admission, acceptance.

ensemble *n* **1** WHOLE, total, entirety, sum, aggregate, set, collection. **2** OUTFIT, costume, apparel (*fml*), get-up (*infml*), rig-out (*infml*). **3** GROUP, band, company, troupe, chorus.

ensign *n* banner, standard, flag, colours, pennant, jack, badge.

enslave *v* subjugate, subject, dominate, bind, enchain, yoke.
🔁 free, emancipate.

ensue *v* follow, issue, proceed, succeed, result, arise, happen, turn out, befall, flow, derive, stem.
🔁 precede.

ensure *v* **1** CERTIFY, guarantee, warrant. **2** PROTECT, guard, safeguard, secure.

entail *v* involve, necessitate, occasion, require, demand, cause, give rise to, lead to, result in.

entangle *v* enmesh, ensnare, embroil, involve, implicate, snare, tangle, entrap, trap, catch, mix up, knot, ravel, muddle.
🔁 disentangle.

enter *v* **1** COME IN, go in, arrive, insert, introduce, board, penetrate. **2** RECORD, log, note, register, take down, inscribe. **3** JOIN, embark upon, enrol, enlist, set about, sign up, participate, commence, start, begin.
🔁 **1** depart. **2** delete.

enterprise *n* **1** UNDERTAKING, venture, project, plan, effort, operation, programme, endeavour. **2** INITIATIVE, resourcefulness, drive, vitality, adventurousness, boldness, get-up-and-go (*infml*), push, energy, enthusiasm, spirit. **3** BUSINESS, firm, company, establishment, concern.
🔁 **2** apathy.

enterprising *adj* venturesome, adventurous, bold, daring, go-ahead, imaginative, resourceful, self-reliant, enthusiastic, energetic, keen, ambitious, aspiring, spirited, active.
🔁 unenterprising, lethargic.

entertain *v* **1** AMUSE, divert, please, delight, cheer. **2** RECEIVE, have guests, accommodate, put up, treat. **3** HARBOUR, countenance, contemplate, consider, imagine, conceive.
🔁 **1** bore. **3** reject.

entertainer

Entertainers include: acrobat, actor, actress, busker, chat show host, clown, comedian, comic, conjuror, dancer, disc jockey, DJ (*infml*), escapologist, game show host, hypnotist, ice-skater, impressionist, jester, juggler, magician, mimic, mind-reader, minstrel, musician, presenter, singer, song-and-dance act, stand-up comic, striptease artist, stripper (*infml*), trapeze artist, tightrope walker, ventriloquist; performer, artiste *see also* **musician**; **singer**.

entertaining *adj* amusing, diverting, fun, delightful, interesting, pleasant, pleasing, humorous, witty.
🗉 boring.

entertainment *n* **1** AMUSEMENT, diversion, recreation, enjoyment, play, pastime, fun, sport, distraction, pleasure. **2** SHOW, spectacle, performance, extravaganza.

Forms of entertainment include: cinema, cartoon show, video, DVD, radio, television, theatre, pantomime; documentary, docusoap, chat show, game show, reality television, sitcom, soap opera; dance, disco, club, discothèque, concert, recital, musical, opera, variety show, music hall, revue, karaoke, cabaret, nightclub, casino; magic show, puppet show, Punch and Judy show, circus, gymkhana, waxworks, laser light show, zoo, rodeo, carnival, pageant, fête, festival, firework party, barbecue. *see also* **performance**; **theatrical**.

enthral *v* captivate, entrance, enchant, fascinate, charm, beguile, thrill, intrigue, hypnotize, mesmerize, engross.
🗉 bore.

enthusiasm *n* zeal, ardour, fervour, passion, keenness, eagerness, vehemence, warmth, frenzy, excitement, earnestness, relish, spirit, devotion, craze, mania, rage.
🗉 apathy.

enthusiast *n* devotee, zealot, admirer, fan, supporter, follower, buff (*infml*), freak (*infml*), fanatic, fiend (*infml*), lover.

enthusiastic *adj* keen, ardent, eager,

fervent, vehement, passionate, warm, wholehearted, zealous, vigorous, spirited, earnest, devoted, avid, excited, exuberant.
🗉 unenthusiastic, apathetic.

entice *v* tempt, lure, attract, seduce, lead on, draw, coax, persuade, induce, sweet-talk (*infml*).

entire *adj* complete, whole, total, full, intact, perfect.
🗉 incomplete, partial.

entirely *adv* completely, wholly, totally, fully, utterly, unreservedly, absolutely, in toto, thoroughly, altogether, perfectly, solely, exclusively, every inch.
🗉 partially.

entitle *v* **1** AUTHORIZE, qualify, empower, enable, allow, permit, license, warrant. **2** NAME, call, term, title, style, christen, dub, label, designate.

entity *n* being, existence, thing, body, creature, individual, organism, substance.

entrance[1] *n* **1** ACCESS, admission, admittance, entry, entrée. **2** ARRIVAL, appearance, debut, initiation, introduction, start. **3** OPENING, way in, door, doorway, gate.
🗉 **2** departure. **3** exit.

entrance[2] *v* charm, enchant, enrapture, captivate, bewitch, spellbind, fascinate, delight, ravish, transport, hypnotize, mesmerize.
🗉 repel.

entrant *n* **1** NOVICE, beginner, newcomer, initiate, convert, probationer. **2** COMPETITOR, candidate, contestant, contender, entry, participant, player.

entreat *v* beg, implore, plead with, beseech, crave, supplicate (*fml*), pray, invoke, ask, petition, request, appeal to.

entreaty *n* appeal, plea, prayer, petition, supplication (*fml*), suit, invocation, cry, solicitation, request.

entrench *v* establish, fix, embed, dig in, ensconce, install, lodge, root, ingrain,

settle, seat, plant, anchor, set.
🔁 dislodge.

entrust v trust, commit, confide, consign, authorize, charge, assign, turn over, commend, depute, invest, delegate, deliver.

entry n 1 ENTRANCE, appearance, admittance, admission, access, entrée, introduction. 2 OPENING, entrance, door, doorway, access, threshold, way in, passage, gate. 3 RECORD, item, minute, note, memorandum, statement, account. 4 ENTRANT, competitor, contestant, candidate, participant, player.
🔁 2 exit.

enumerate v list, name, itemize, cite, detail, specify, count, number, relate, recount, spell out, tell, mention, calculate, quote, recite, reckon.

enunciate v 1 ARTICULATE, pronounce, vocalize, voice, express, say, speak, utter, sound. 2 STATE, declare, proclaim, announce, propound.

envelop v wrap, enfold, enwrap, encase, cover, swathe, shroud, engulf, enclose, encircle, encompass, surround, cloak, veil, blanket, conceal, obscure, hide.

envelope n wrapper, wrapping, cover, case, casing, sheath, covering, shell, skin, jacket, coating.

enviable adj desirable, privileged, favoured, blessed, fortunate, lucky, advantageous, sought-after, excellent, fine.
🔁 unenviable.

envious adj covetous, jealous, resentful, green (with envy), dissatisfied, grudging, jaundiced, green-eyed (*infml*).

environment n surroundings, conditions, circumstances, milieu, atmosphere, habitat, situation, element, medium, background, ambience, setting, context, territory, domain.

envisage v visualize, imagine, picture, envision, conceive of, preconceive,

predict, anticipate, foresee, image, see, contemplate.

envoy n agent, representative, ambassador, diplomat, messenger, legate, emissary, minister, delegate, deputy, courier, intermediary.

envy n covetousness, jealousy, resentfulness, resentment, grudge, ill-will, malice, spite, dissatisfaction.
➤ v covet, resent, begrudge, grudge, crave.

epidemic adj widespread, prevalent, rife, rampant, pandemic, sweeping, wide-ranging, prevailing.
➤ n plague, outbreak, spread, rash, upsurge, wave.

epilogue n afterword, postscript, coda, conclusion.
🔁 foreword, prologue, preface.

episode n 1 INCIDENT, event, occurrence, happening, occasion, circumstance, experience, adventure, matter, business. 2 INSTALMENT, part, chapter, passage, section, scene.

epitome n 1 PERSONIFICATION, embodiment, representation, model, archetype, type, essence. 2 SUMMARY, abstract, abridgement, digest.

epoch n age, era, period, time, date.

equable adj 1 *an equable person*: even-tempered, placid, calm, serene, unexcitable, tranquil, unflappable, composed, level-headed, easy-going. 2 *an equable climate*: uniform, even, consistent, constant, regular, temperate, unvarying, steady, stable, smooth.
🔁 1 excitable. 2 variable.

equal adj 1 IDENTICAL, the same, alike, like, equivalent, corresponding, commensurate, comparable. 2 EVEN, uniform, regular, unvarying, balanced, matched. 3 COMPETENT, able, adequate, fit, capable, suitable.
🔁 1 different. 2 unequal. 3 unsuitable.
➤ n peer, counterpart, equivalent, coequal, match, parallel, twin, fellow.
➤ v match, parallel, correspond to,

balance, square with, tally with, equalize, equate, rival, level, even.

equality n 1 UNIFORMITY, evenness, equivalence, correspondence, balance, parity, par, symmetry, proportion, identity, sameness, likeness.
2 IMPARTIALITY, fairness, justice, egalitarianism.
🖃 2 inequality.

equalize v level, even up, match, equal, equate, draw level, balance, square, standardize, compensate, smooth.

equate v compare, liken, match, pair, correspond to, correspond with, balance, parallel, equalize, offset, square, agree, tally, juxtapose.

equation n equality, correspondence, equivalence, balancing, agreement, parallel, pairing, comparison, match, likeness, juxtaposition.

equilibrium n 1 BALANCE, poise, symmetry, evenness, stability.
2 EQUANIMITY, self-possession, composure, calmness, coolness, serenity.
🖃 1 imbalance.

equip v provide, fit out, supply, furnish, prepare, arm, fit up, kit out, stock, endow, rig, dress, array, deck out.

equipment n apparatus, gear (*infml*), supplies, tackle, rig-out (*infml*), tools, material, furnishings, baggage, outfit, paraphernalia, stuff, things, accessories, furniture.

equivalence n identity, parity, correspondence, agreement, likeness, interchangeability, similarity, substitutability, correlation, parallel, conformity, sameness.
🖃 unlikeness, dissimilarity.

equivalent adj equal, same, similar, substitutable, corresponding, alike, comparable, interchangeable, even, tantamount, twin.
🖃 unlike, different.

equivocal adj ambiguous, uncertain, obscure, vague, evasive, oblique, misleading, dubious, confusing, indefinite.
🖃 unequivocal, clear.

equivocate v prevaricate, evade, dodge, fence, beat about the bush (*infml*), hedge, mislead.

era n age, epoch, period, date, day, days, time, aeon, stage, century.

eradicate v eliminate, annihilate, get rid of, remove, root out, suppress, destroy, exterminate, extinguish, weed out, stamp out, abolish, erase, obliterate.

erase v obliterate, rub out, expunge (*fml*), delete, blot out, cancel, efface, get rid of, remove, eradicate.

erect adj upright, straight, vertical, upstanding, standing, raised, rigid, stiff.
➤ v build, construct, put up, establish, set up, elevate, assemble, found, form, institute, initiate, raise, rear, lift, mount, pitch, create.

erode v wear away, eat away, wear down, corrode, abrade, consume, grind down, disintegrate, deteriorate, spoil.

erosion n wear, corrosion, abrasion, attrition, denudation, disintegration, deterioration, destruction, undermining.

erotic adj aphrodisiac, seductive, sexy, sensual, titillating, pornographic, lascivious, stimulating, suggestive, amorous, amatory, venereal, carnal, lustful, voluptuous.

err v 1 MAKE A MISTAKE, be wrong, miscalculate, mistake, misjudge, slip up, blunder, misunderstand. 2 DO WRONG, sin, misbehave, go astray, offend, transgress, deviate.

errand n commission, charge, mission, assignment, message, task, job, duty.

erratic adj changeable, variable, fitful, fluctuating, inconsistent, irregular, unstable, shifting, inconstant, unpredictable, unreliable, aberrant, abnormal, eccentric, desultory, meandering.
🖃 steady, consistent, stable.

erroneous *adj* incorrect, wrong, mistaken, false, untrue, inaccurate, inexact, invalid, illogical, unfounded, faulty, flawed.
F3 correct, right.

error *n* mistake, inaccuracy, slip, slip-up, blunder, howler (*infml*), gaffe, faux pas, solecism, lapse, miscalculation, misunderstanding, misconception, misapprehension, misprint, oversight, omission, fallacy, flaw, fault, wrong.

erudite *adj* learned, scholarly, well-educated, knowledgeable, lettered, educated, well-read, literate, academic, cultured, wise, highbrow, profound.
F3 illiterate, ignorant.

erupt *v* break out, explode, belch, discharge, burst, gush, spew, spout, eject, expel, emit, flare up, vomit, break.

eruption *n* 1 OUTBURST, discharge, ejection, emission, explosion, flare-up. 2 RASH, outbreak, inflammation.

escalate *v* increase, intensify, grow, accelerate, rise, step up, heighten, raise, spiral, magnify, enlarge, expand, extend, mount, ascend, climb, amplify.
F3 decrease, diminish.

escapade *n* adventure, exploit, fling, prank, caper, romp, spree, lark (*infml*), antic, stunt, trick.

escape *v* 1 GET AWAY, break free, run away, bolt, abscond, flee, fly, decamp, break loose, break out, do a bunk (*infml*), flit, slip away, shake off, slip. 2 AVOID, evade, elude, dodge, skip, shun. 3 LEAK, seep, flow, drain, gush, issue, discharge, ooze, trickle, pour forth, pass.
➤ *n* 1 GETAWAY, flight, bolt, flit, breakout, decampment, jailbreak. 2 AVOIDANCE, evasion. 3 LEAK, seepage, leakage, outflow, gush, drain, discharge, emission, spurt, outpour, emanation. 4 ESCAPISM, diversion, distraction, recreation, relaxation, pastime, safety-valve.

escapist *n* dreamer, daydreamer, fantasizer, wishful thinker, non-realist, ostrich (*infml*).
F3 realist.

escort *n* 1 COMPANION, chaperon(e), partner, attendant, aide, squire, guide, bodyguard, protector. 2 ENTOURAGE, company, retinue, suite, train, guard, convoy, cortège.
➤ *v* accompany, partner, chaperone, guide, lead, usher, conduct, guard, protect.

esoteric *adj* recondite, obscure, abstruse, cryptic, inscrutable, mysterious, mystic, mystical, occult, hidden, secret, confidential, private, inside.
F3 well-known, familiar.

especially *adv* 1 CHIEFLY, mainly, principally, primarily, pre-eminently, above all. 2 PARTICULARLY, specially, markedly, notably, exceptionally, outstandingly, expressly, supremely, uniquely, unusually, strikingly, very.

essay *n* composition, dissertation, paper, article, assignment, thesis, piece, commentary, critique, discourse, treatise, review, leader, tract.

essence *n* 1 NATURE, being, quintessence, substance, soul, spirit, core, centre, heart, meaning, quality, significance, life, entity, crux, kernel, marrow, pith, character, characteristics, attributes, principle. 2 CONCENTRATE, extract, distillation, spirits.

essential *adj* 1 FUNDAMENTAL, basic, intrinsic, inherent, principal, main, key, characteristic, definitive, typical, constituent. 2 CRUCIAL, indispensable, necessary, vital, mission-critical (*infml*), requisite, required, needed, important.
F3 1 incidental. 2 dispensable, inessential.
➤ *n* necessity, prerequisite, must, requisite, sine qua non (*fml*), requirement, basic, fundamental, necessary, principle.
F3 inessential.

establish *v* 1 SET UP, found, start, form, institute, create, organize, inaugurate, introduce, install, plant, settle, secure, lodge, base. 2 PROVE, substantiate, demonstrate, authenticate, ratify, verify, validate, certify, confirm, affirm.
F3 1 uproot. 2 refute.

establishment n 1 FORMATION, setting up, founding, creation, foundation, installation, institution, inauguration. 2 BUSINESS, company, firm, institute, organization, concern, institution, enterprise. 3 RULING CLASS, the system, the authorities, the powers that be.

estate n 1 POSSESSIONS, effects, assets, belongings, holdings, property, goods, lands. 2 AREA, development, land, manor. 3 (fml) STATUS, standing, situation, position, class, place, condition, state, rank.

estimate v assess, reckon, evaluate, calculate, gauge, guess, value, conjecture, consider, judge, think, number, count, compute, believe.
➤ n reckoning, valuation, judgement, guess, approximation, assessment, estimation, evaluation, computation, opinion.

estimation n 1 JUDGEMENT, opinion, belief, consideration, estimate, view, evaluation, assessment, reckoning, conception, calculation, computation. 2 RESPECT, regard, appreciation, esteem, credit.

estranged adj divided, separate, alienated, disaffected, antagonized.
🖪 reconciled, united.

estuary n inlet, mouth, firth, fjord, creek, arm, sea loch.

eternal adj 1 eternal bliss: unending, endless, ceaseless, everlasting, never-ending, infinite, limitless, immortal, undying, imperishable. 2 eternal truths: unchanging, timeless, enduring, lasting, perennial, abiding. 3 (infml) eternal quarrelling: constant, continuous, perpetual, incessant, interminable.
🖪 1 ephemeral, temporary.
2 changeable.

eternity n 1 EVERLASTINGNESS, endlessness, everlasting, imperishability, infinity, timelessness, perpetuity, immutability, ages, age, aeon. 2 AFTERLIFE, hereafter, immortality, heaven, paradise, next world, world to come.

ethical adj moral, principled, just, right, proper, virtuous, honourable, fair, upright, righteous, seemly, honest, good, correct, commendable, fitting, noble, meet (fml).
🖪 unethical.

ethics n moral values, morality, principles, standards, code, moral philosophy, rules, beliefs, propriety, conscience, equity.

ethnic adj racial, native, indigenous, traditional, tribal, folk, cultural, national, aboriginal.

ethos n attitude, beliefs, standards, manners, ethics, morality, code, principles, spirit, tenor, rationale, character, disposition.

etiquette n code, formalities, standards, correctness, conventions, customs, protocol (fml), rules, manners, politeness, courtesy, civility, decorum, ceremony, decency.

euphemism n evasion, polite term, substitution, genteelism, politeness, understatement.

euphoria n elation, ecstasy, bliss, rapture, high spirits, well-being, high (infml), exhilaration, exultation, joy, intoxication, jubilation, transport, glee, exaltation, enthusiasm, cheerfulness.
🖪 depression, despondency.

evacuate v 1 LEAVE, depart, withdraw, quit, remove, retire from, clear (out) (infml), abandon, desert, forsake, vacate, decamp, relinquish. 2 EMPTY, eject, void, expel, discharge, eliminate, defecate, purge.

evacuation n 1 DEPARTURE, withdrawal, retreat, exodus, removal, quitting, desertion, abandonment, clearance, relinquishment, retirement, vacation. 2 EMPTYING, expulsion, ejection, discharge, elimination, defecation, urination.

evade v 1 evade one's duties: elude, avoid, escape, dodge, shirk, steer clear

of, shun, sidestep, duck (*infml*), balk, skive (*infml*), fend off, chicken out (*infml*), cop out (*infml*). **2** *evade a question*: prevaricate, equivocate, fence, fudge, parry, quibble, hedge.
F3 **1** confront, face.

evaluate *v* value, assess, appraise, estimate, reckon, calculate, gauge, judge, rate, size up, weigh, compute, rank.

evaluation *n* valuation, appraisal, assessment, estimation, estimate, judgement, reckoning, calculation, opinion, computation.

evaporate *v* **1** DISAPPEAR, dematerialize, vanish, melt (away), dissolve, disperse, dispel, dissipate, fade. **2** VAPORIZE, dry, dehydrate, exhale.

evasion *n* avoidance, escape, dodge, equivocation, excuse, prevarication, put-off, trickery, subterfuge, shirking.
F3 frankness, directness.

evasive *adj* equivocating, indirect, prevaricating, devious, shifty (*infml*), unforthcoming, slippery (*infml*), misleading, deceitful, deceptive, cagey (*infml*), oblique, secretive, tricky, cunning.
F3 direct, frank.

eve *n* day before, verge, brink, edge, threshold.

even *adj* **1** LEVEL, flat, smooth, horizontal, flush, parallel, plane. **2** STEADY, unvarying, constant, regular, uniform. **3** EQUAL, balanced, matching, same, similar, like, symmetrical, fifty-fifty, level, side by side, neck and neck. **4** EVEN-TEMPERED, calm, placid, serene, tranquil, composed, unruffled. **5** EVEN-HANDED, balanced, equitable, fair, impartial.
F3 **1** uneven. **3** unequal.
➤ *v* smooth, flatten, level, match, regularize, balance, equalize, align, square, stabilize, steady, straighten.

evening *n* nightfall, dusk, eve, eventide, twilight, sunset, sundown.

event *n* **1** HAPPENING, occurrence,

incident, occasion, affair, circumstance, episode, eventuality, experience, matter, case, adventure, business, fact, possibility, milestone. **2** CONSEQUENCE, result, outcome, conclusion, end, effect, issue, termination. **3** GAME, match, competition, contest, tournament, engagement.

even-tempered *adj* calm, level-headed, placid, stable, tranquil, serene, composed, cool, steady, peaceful, peaceable.
F3 excitable, erratic.

eventful *adj* busy, exciting, lively, active, full, interesting, remarkable, significant, memorable, momentous, notable, noteworthy, unforgettable.
F3 dull, ordinary.

eventual *adj* final, ultimate, resulting, concluding, ensuing, future, later, subsequent, prospective, projected, planned, impending.

eventually *adv* finally, ultimately, at last, in the end, at length, subsequently, after all, sooner or later.

ever *adv* **1** ALWAYS, evermore, for ever, perpetually, constantly, at all times, continually, endlessly. **2** AT ANY TIME, in any case, in any circumstances, at all, on any account.
F3 **1** never.

everlasting *adj* eternal, undying, never-ending, endless, immortal, infinite, imperishable, constant, permanent, perpetual, indestructible, timeless.
F3 temporary, transient.

everyday *adj* ordinary, common, commonplace, day-to-day, familiar, run-of-the-mill, regular, plain, routine, usual, workaday, common-or-garden, bog-standard (*infml*), normal, customary, stock, accustomed, conventional, daily, habitual, monotonous, frequent, simple, informal.
F3 unusual, exceptional, special.

everyone *n* everybody, one and all, each one, all and sundry, the whole world.

everywhere *adv* all around, all over, throughout, far and near, far and wide, high and low, ubiquitous, left, right and centre (*infml*).

evict *v* expel, eject, dispossess, put out, turn out, turf out (*infml*), kick out (*infml*), force out, remove, cast out, chuck out (*infml*), oust, dislodge, expropriate.

evidence *n* 1 PROOF, verification, confirmation, affirmation, grounds, substantiation, documentation, data. 2 TESTIMONY, declaration. 3 INDICATION, manifestation, suggestion, sign, mark, hint, demonstration, token.

evident *adj* clear, obvious, manifest, apparent, plain, patent, visible, conspicuous, noticeable, clear-cut, unmistakable, perceptible, distinct, discernible, tangible, incontestable, indisputable, incontrovertible.

evidently *adv* clearly, apparently, plainly, patently, manifestly, obviously, seemingly, undoubtedly, doubtless(ly), indisputably.

evil *adj* 1 WICKED, wrong, sinful, bad, immoral, vicious, vile, malevolent, iniquitous, cruel, base, corrupt, heinous, malicious, malignant, devilish, depraved, mischievous. 2 HARMFUL, pernicious, destructive, deadly, detrimental, hurtful, poisonous. 3 DISASTROUS, ruinous, calamitous, catastrophic, adverse, dire, inauspicious. 4 OFFENSIVE, noxious, foul.
➤ *n* 1 WICKEDNESS, wrongdoing, wrong, immorality, badness, sin, sinfulness, vice, viciousness, iniquity, depravity, baseness, corruption, malignity, mischief, heinousness. 2 ADVERSITY, affliction, calamity, disaster, misfortune, suffering, sorrow, ruin, catastrophe, blow, curse, distress, hurt, harm, ill, injury, misery, woe.

evoke *v* summon (up), call, elicit, invoke, arouse, stir, raise, stimulate, call forth, call up, conjure up, awaken, provoke, excite, recall.
☒ suppress.

evolution *n* development, growth, progression, progress, expansion, increase, ripening, derivation, descent.

evolve *v* develop, grow, increase, mature, progress, unravel, expand, enlarge, emerge, descend, derive, result, elaborate.

exact *adj* 1 PRECISE, accurate, correct, faithful, literal, flawless, faultless, right, true, veracious, definite, explicit, detailed, specific, strict, unerring, close, factual, identical, express, word-perfect, blow-by-blow (*infml*). 2 CAREFUL, scrupulous, particular, rigorous, methodical, meticulous, orderly, painstaking.
☒ 1 inexact, imprecise.
➤ *v* extort, extract, claim, insist on, wrest, wring, compel, demand, command, force, impose, require, squeeze, milk (*infml*).

exacting *adj* demanding, difficult, hard, laborious, arduous, rigorous, taxing, tough, harsh, painstaking, severe, strict, unsparing.
☒ easy.

exactly *adv* 1 PRECISELY, accurately, literally, faithfully, correctly, specifically, rigorously, scrupulously, veraciously, verbatim, carefully, faultlessly, unerringly, strictly, to the letter, particularly, methodically, explicitly, expressly, dead (*infml*). 2 ABSOLUTELY, definitely, precisely, indeed, certainly, truly, quite, just, unequivocally.
☒ 1 inaccurately, roughly.

exaggerate *v* overstate, overdo, magnify, overemphasize, emphasize, embellish, embroider, enlarge, amplify, oversell, pile it on (*infml*).
☒ understate.

examination *n* 1 INSPECTION, enquiry, scrutiny, study, survey, search, analysis, exploration, investigation, probe, appraisal, observation, research, review, scan, once-over (*infml*), perusal, check, check-up, audit, critique. 2 TEST, exam, quiz, questioning, cross-examination, cross-questioning, trial, inquisition, interrogation, viva.

examine v 1 INSPECT, investigate, scrutinize, study, survey, analyse, explore, enquire, consider, probe, review, scan, check (out), ponder, pore over, sift, vet, weigh up, appraise, assay, audit, peruse, case (*sl*). 2 TEST, quiz, question, cross-examine, cross-question, interrogate, grill (*infml*), catechize (*fml*).

example n instance, case, case in point, illustration, exemplification, sample, specimen, model, pattern, ideal, archetype, prototype, standard, type, lesson, citation.

exasperate v infuriate, annoy, anger, incense, irritate, madden, provoke, get on someone's nerves, enrage, irk, rile, rankle, rouse, get to (*infml*), goad, vex.
🖪 appease, pacify.

excavate v dig (out), dig up, hollow, burrow, tunnel, delve, unearth, mine, quarry, disinter, gouge, scoop, exhume, uncover.

excavation n hole, hollow, pit, quarry, mine, dugout, dig, diggings, burrow, cavity, crater, trench, trough, shaft, ditch, cutting.

exceed v surpass, outdo, outstrip, beat, better, pass, overtake, top, outshine, eclipse, outreach, outrun, transcend, cap, overdo, overstep.

excel v 1 SURPASS, outdo, beat, outclass, outperform, outrank, eclipse, better. 2 BE EXCELLENT, succeed, shine, stand out, predominate.

excellence n superiority, eminence, pre-eminence, distinction, merit, supremacy, quality, worth, fineness, eminence, goodness, greatness, virtue, perfection, purity.

excellent adj superior, first-class, first-rate, prime, premium, superlative, unequalled, outstanding, surpassing, remarkable, distinguished, great, good, exemplary, select, superb, admirable, commendable, top-drawer (*infml*), top-notch (*infml*), blue chip (*infml*), splendid, boffo (*infml*), noteworthy, notable, fine, wonderful, worthy.
🖪 inferior, second-rate.

except prep excepting, but, apart from, other than, save, omitting, not counting, leaving out, excluding, except for, besides, bar, minus, less.
➤ v leave out, omit, bar, exclude, reject, rule out.

exception n oddity, anomaly, deviation, abnormality, irregularity, peculiarity, inconsistency, rarity, special case, quirk.

exceptional adj 1 ABNORMAL, unusual, anomalous, strange, odd, irregular, extraordinary, peculiar, special, rare, uncommon.
2 OUTSTANDING, remarkable, phenomenal, prodigious, notable, noteworthy, superior, unequalled, marvellous.
🖪 1 normal. 2 mediocre.

excerpt n extract, passage, portion, section, selection, quote, quotation, part, citation, scrap, fragment.

excess n 1 SURFEIT, overabundance, glut, plethora, superfluity, superabundance, surplus, overflow, overkill, remainder, leftover.
2 OVERINDULGENCE, dissipation, immoderateness, intemperance, extravagance, unrestraint, debauchery.
🖪 1 deficiency. 2 restraint.
➤ adj extra, surplus, spare, redundant, remaining, residual, left-over, additional, superfluous, supernumerary.
🖪 inadequate.

excessive adj immoderate, inordinate, extreme, undue, uncalled-for, disproportionate, unnecessary, unneeded, superfluous, unreasonable, exorbitant, extravagant, steep (*infml*).
🖪 insufficient.

exchange v barter, change, trade, swap, switch, replace, interchange, convert, commute, substitute, reciprocate, bargain, bandy.
➤ n 1 CONVERSATION, discussion, chat.
2 TRADE, commerce, dealing, market, traffic, barter, bargain. 3 INTERCHANGE, swap, switch, replacement, substitution, reciprocity.

excitable *adj* temperamental, volatile, passionate, emotional, highly-strung, fiery, hot-headed, hasty, nervous, hot-tempered, irascible, quick-tempered, sensitive, susceptible.
🖅 calm, stable.

excite *v* 1 MOVE, agitate, disturb, upset, touch, stir up, thrill, elate, impress. 2 AROUSE, rouse, animate, awaken, fire, inflame, kindle, motivate, stimulate, turn on (*sl*), engender, inspire, instigate, incite, induce, ignite, galvanize, generate, provoke, sway, quicken, evoke.
🖅 1 calm.

excited *adj* aroused, roused, stimulated, stirred, thrilled, elated, enthusiastic, eager, moved, high (*infml*), hyper (*infml*), worked up, wrought-up, overwrought, restless, frantic, frenzied, wild.
🖅 calm, apathetic.

excitement *n* 1 UNREST, ado, action, activity, commotion, fuss, tumult, flurry, furore, adventure. 2 DISCOMPOSURE, agitation, passion, thrill, animation, elation, enthusiasm, restlessness, kicks (*infml*), ferment, fever, eagerness, stimulation.
🖅 1 calm. 2 apathy.

exciting *adj* stimulating, stirring, intoxicating, exhilarating, thrilling, action-packed, high-octane (*infml*), rousing, moving, enthralling, electrifying, nail-biting (*infml*), white-knuckle (*infml*), cliff-hanging (*infml*), striking, sexy (*infml*), sensational, provocative, inspiring, interesting.
🖅 dull, unexciting.

exclaim *v* cry (out), declare, blurt (out), call, yell, shout, proclaim, utter.

exclamation *n* cry, call, yell, shout, expletive, interjection, ejaculation, outcry, utterance.

exclude *v* 1 BAN, bar, prohibit, disallow, veto, proscribe, forbid, blacklist. 2 OMIT, leave out, keep out, refuse, reject, ignore, shut out, rule out, ostracize, eliminate. 3 EXPEL, eject,

evict, excommunicate.
🖅 1 admit. 2 include.

exclusive *adj* 1 SOLE, single, unique, only, undivided, unshared, whole, total, peculiar. 2 RESTRICTED, limited, closed, private, narrow, restrictive, choice, select, discriminative, cliquey, chic, classy (*infml*), elegant, fashionable, posh (*infml*), snobbish.

excruciating *adj* agonizing, painful, severe, tormenting, unbearable, insufferable, acute, intolerable, intense, sharp, piercing, extreme, atrocious, racking, harrowing, savage, burning, bitter.

excursion *n* outing, trip, jaunt, expedition, day trip, journey, tour, airing, breather, junket (*infml*), ride, drive, walk, ramble.

excuse *v* 1 FORGIVE, pardon, overlook, absolve, acquit, exonerate, tolerate, ignore, indulge. 2 RELEASE, free, discharge, liberate, let off, relieve, spare, exempt. 3 CONDONE, explain, mitigate, justify, vindicate, defend, apologize for.
🖅 1 criticize. 2 punish.
➤ *n* justification, explanation, grounds, defence, plea, alibi, reason, apology, pretext, pretence, exoneration, evasion, cop-out (*infml*), shift, substitute.

execute *v* 1 PUT TO DEATH, kill, liquidate, hang, electrocute, shoot, guillotine, decapitate, behead. 2 CARRY OUT, perform, do, accomplish, achieve, fulfil, complete, discharge, effect, enact, deliver, enforce, finish, implement, administer, consummate, realize, dispatch, expedite, validate, serve, render, sign.

execution *n* 1 DEATH PENALTY, capital punishment, killing, firing squad. 2 ACCOMPLISHMENT, operation, performance, completion, achievement, administration, effect, enactment, implementation, realization, discharge, dispatch, consummation, enforcement. 3 STYLE, technique, rendition, delivery, performance, manner, mode.

Means of execution include:
beheading, burning, crucifixion,

decapitation, electrocution, garrotting, gassing, guillotining, hanging, lethal injection, lynching, shooting, stoning, stringing up (*infml*).

executive *n* 1 ADMINISTRATION, management, government, leadership, hierarchy. 2 ADMINISTRATOR, manager, organizer, leader, controller, director, governor, official.
➤ *adj* administrative, managerial, controlling, supervisory, regulating, decision-making, governing, organizing, directing, directorial, organizational, leading, guiding.

exemplary *adj* 1 MODEL, ideal, perfect, admirable, excellent, faultless, flawless, correct, good, commendable, praiseworthy, worthy, laudable, estimable, honourable. 2 CAUTIONARY, warning.
E 1 imperfect, unworthy.

exemplify *v* illustrate, demonstrate, show, instance, represent, typify, manifest, embody, epitomize, exhibit, depict, display.

exempt *v* excuse, release, relieve, let off, free, absolve, discharge, dismiss, liberate, spare.
➤ *adj* excused, not liable, immune, released, spared, absolved, discharged, excluded, free, liberated, clear.
E liable.

exercise *v* 1 USE, utilize, employ, apply, exert, practise, wield, try, discharge. 2 TRAIN, drill, practise, work out (*infml*), keep fit. 3 WORRY, disturb, trouble, upset, burden, distress, vex, annoy, agitate, afflict.
➤ *n* 1 TRAINING, drill, practice, effort, exertion, task, lesson, work, discipline, activity, physical jerks (*infml*), work-out (*infml*), aerobics, labour. 2 USE, utilization, employment, application, implementation, practice, operation, discharge, assignment, fulfilment, accomplishment.

exert *v* use, utilize, employ, apply, exercise, bring to bear, wield, expend.
◇ **exert oneself** strive, struggle,

strain, make every effort, take pains, toil, labour, work, sweat (*infml*), endeavour, apply oneself.

exertion *n* 1 EFFORT, industry, labour, toil, work, struggle, diligence, assiduousness, perseverance, pains, endeavour, attempt, strain, travail (*fml*), trial. 2 USE, utilization, employment, application, exercise, operation, action.
E 1 idleness, rest.

exhaust *v* 1 CONSUME, empty, deplete, drain, sap, spend, waste, squander, dissipate, impoverish, use up, finish, dry, bankrupt. 2 TIRE (OUT), weary, fatigue, tax, strain, weaken, overwork, wear out.
E 1 renew. 2 refresh.
➤ *n* emission, exhalation, discharge, fumes.

exhausted *adj* 1 EMPTY, finished, depleted, spent, used up, drained, dry, worn out, void. 2 TIRED (OUT), dead tired, dead-beat (*infml*), all in (*infml*), done (in) (*infml*), fatigued, weak, washed-out, whacked (*infml*), knackered (*infml*), jaded.
E 1 fresh. 2 vigorous.

exhausting *adj* tiring, strenuous, taxing, gruelling, arduous, hard, laborious, backbreaking, draining, severe, testing, punishing, formidable, debilitating.
E refreshing.

exhaustion *n* fatigue, tiredness, weariness, debility, feebleness, jet-lag.
E freshness, liveliness.

exhaustive *adj* comprehensive, all-embracing, all-inclusive, far-reaching, complete, extensive, encyclopedic, full-scale, thorough, full, in-depth, intensive, detailed, definitive, all-out, sweeping.
E incomplete, restricted.

exhibit *v* display, show, present, demonstrate, manifest, expose, parade, reveal, express, disclose, indicate, air, flaunt, offer.
E conceal.
➤ *n* display, exhibition, show, illustration, model.

exhibition *n* display, show,

demonstration, demo (*infml*), exhibit, presentation, manifestation, spectacle, exposition, expo, showing, fair, performance, airing, representation, showcase.

exhilarate *v* thrill, excite, elate, animate, enliven, invigorate, vitalize, stimulate.
☒ bore.

exile *n* **1** BANISHMENT, deportation, expatriation, expulsion, ostracism, transportation. **2** EXPATRIATE, refugee, émigré, deportee, outcast.
➤ *v* banish, expel, deport, expatriate, drive out, ostracize, oust.

exist *v* **1** BE, live, abide, continue, endure, have one's being, breathe, prevail. **2** SUBSIST, survive. **3** BE PRESENT, occur, happen, be available, remain.

existence *n* **1** BEING, life, reality, actuality, continuance, continuation, endurance, survival, breath, subsistence. **2** CREATION, the world. **3** (*fml*) ENTITY, creature, thing.
☒ **1** death, non-existence.

exit *n* **1** DEPARTURE, going, retreat, withdrawal, leave-taking, retirement, farewell, exodus. **2** DOOR, way out, doorway, gate, vent.
☒ **1** entrance, arrival. **2** entrance.
➤ *v* depart, leave, go, retire, withdraw, take one's leave, retreat, issue.
☒ arrive, enter.

exonerate *v* **1** ABSOLVE, acquit, clear, vindicate, exculpate (*fml*), justify, pardon, discharge. **2** EXEMPT, excuse, spare, let off, release, relieve.
☒ **1** incriminate.

exorbitant *adj* excessive, unreasonable, unwarranted, undue, inordinate, immoderate, extravagant, extortionate, enormous, preposterous.
☒ reasonable, moderate.

exotic *adj* **1** FOREIGN, alien, imported, introduced. **2** UNUSUAL, striking, different, unfamiliar, extraordinary, bizarre, curious, strange, fascinating, colourful, peculiar, outlandish.
☒ **1** native. **2** ordinary.

expand *v* **1** STRETCH, swell, widen, lengthen, thicken, magnify, multiply, inflate, broaden, blow up, open out, fill out, fatten. **2** INCREASE, grow, extend, enlarge, develop, amplify, spread, branch out, diversify, elaborate.
☒ **1** contract.

expanse *n* extent, space, area, breadth, range, stretch, sweep, field, plain, tract.

expansive *adj* **1** FRIENDLY, genial, outgoing, open, affable, sociable, talkative, warm, communicative, effusive. **2** EXTENSIVE, broad, comprehensive, wide-ranging, all-embracing, thorough.
☒ **1** reserved, cold. **2** restricted, narrow.

expect *v* **1** *expect the money soon*: anticipate, await, look forward to, hope for, look for, bank on, bargain for, envisage, predict, forecast, foresee, contemplate, project. **2** *expect you to comply*: require, want, wish, insist on, demand, rely on, count on. **3** *expect you're right*: suppose, surmise, assume, believe, think, presume, imagine, reckon, guess (*infml*), trust.

expectant *adj* **1** AWAITING, anticipating, hopeful, in suspense, ready, apprehensive, anxious, watchful, eager, curious. **2** PREGNANT, expecting (*infml*), with child (*fml*).

expedition *n* **1** JOURNEY, excursion, trip, voyage, tour, exploration, trek, safari, hike, sail, ramble, raid, quest, pilgrimage, mission, crusade. **2** (*fml*) PROMPTNESS, speed, alacrity, haste.

expel *v* **1** DRIVE OUT, eject, evict, banish, throw out, ban, bar, oust, exile, expatriate. **2** DISCHARGE, evacuate, void, cast out.
☒ **1** welcome.

expend *v* **1** SPEND, pay, disburse (*fml*), fork out (*infml*). **2** CONSUME, use (up), dissipate, exhaust, employ.
☒ **1** save. **2** conserve.

expenditure *n* spending, expense, cost, outlay, outgoings, disbursement

(*fml*), payment, output.
▨ income.

expense *n* spending, expenditure, disbursement (*fml*), outlay, payment, loss, cost, charge.

expensive *adj* dear, high-priced, costly, exorbitant, extortionate, steep (*infml*), extravagant, lavish.
▨ cheap, inexpensive.

experience *n* 1 KNOWLEDGE, familiarity, know-how, involvement, participation, practice, understanding. 2 INCIDENT, event, episode, happening, encounter, occurrence, adventure.
▨ 1 inexperience.
➤ *v* undergo, go through, live through, suffer, feel, endure, encounter, face, meet, know, try, perceive, sustain.

experienced *adj* 1 PRACTISED, knowledgeable, familiar, capable, competent, well-versed, expert, accomplished, qualified, skilled, tried, trained, professional. 2 MATURE, seasoned, wise, veteran.
▨ 1 inexperienced, unskilled.

experiment *n* trial, test, investigation, experimentation, research, examination, trial run, venture, trial and error, attempt, procedure, proof.
➤ *v* try, test, investigate, examine, research, sample, verify.

experimental *adj* trial, test, exploratory, empirical (*fml*), tentative, provisional, speculative, pilot, preliminary, trial-and-error.

expert *n* specialist, connoisseur, authority, professional, pro (*infml*), dab hand (*infml*), maestro, virtuoso.
➤ *adj* proficient, adept, skilled, skilful, knowledgeable, experienced, able, practised, professional, masterly, specialist, qualified, virtuoso.
▨ amateurish, novice.

expertise *n* expertness, proficiency, skill, skilfulness, know-how, knack (*infml*), knowledge, mastery, dexterity, virtuosity.
▨ inexperience.

expire *v* end, cease, finish, stop, close, terminate, conclude, discontinue, run out, lapse, die, depart, decease, perish.
▨ begin.

explain *v* 1 INTERPRET, clarify, describe, define, make clear, elucidate, simplify, resolve, solve, spell out, translate, unfold, unravel, untangle, illustrate, demonstrate, disclose, expound, teach. 2 JUSTIFY, excuse, account for, rationalize.
▨ 1 obscure, confound.

explanation *n* 1 INTERPRETATION, clarification, definition, elucidation, illustration, demonstration, account, description, exegesis (*fml*). 2 JUSTIFICATION, excuse, warrant, rationalization. 3 ANSWER, meaning, motive, reason, key, sense, significance.

explanatory *adj* descriptive, interpretive, explicative, demonstrative, expository (*fml*), justifying.

explicit *adj* 1 CLEAR, distinct, exact, categorical, absolute, certain, positive, precise, specific, unambiguous, express, definite, declared, detailed, stated. 2 OPEN, direct, frank, outspoken, straightforward, unreserved, plain.
▨ 1 implicit, unspoken, vague.

explode *v* 1 BLOW UP, burst, go off, set off, detonate, discharge, blast, erupt. 2 DISCREDIT, disprove, give the lie to, debunk, invalidate, refute, rebut, repudiate.
▨ 2 prove, confirm.

exploit *n* deed, feat, adventure, achievement, accomplishment, attainment, stunt.
➤ *v* 1 USE, utilize, capitalize on, profit by, turn to account, take advantage of, cash in on, make capital out of. 2 MISUSE, abuse, oppress, ill-treat, impose on, manipulate, rip off (*sl*), fleece (*infml*).

exploration *n* 1 INVESTIGATION, examination, enquiry, research, scrutiny, study, inspection, analysis, probe. 2 EXPEDITION, survey, reconnaissance, search, trip, tour, voyage, travel, safari.

explore v 1 INVESTIGATE, examine, inspect, research, scrutinize, probe, analyse. 2 TRAVEL, tour, search, reconnoitre, prospect, scout, survey.

explosion n detonation, blast, burst, outburst, discharge, eruption, bang, outbreak, clap, crack, fit, report.

explosive adj unstable, volatile, sensitive, tense, fraught, charged, touchy, overwrought, dangerous, hazardous, perilous, stormy.
☒ stable, calm.

expose v 1 REVEAL, show, exhibit, display, disclose, uncover, bring to light, present, manifest, detect, divulge, unveil, unmask, denounce. 2 ENDANGER, jeopardize, imperil, risk, hazard.
☒ 1 conceal. 2 cover up.

exposed adj bare, open, revealed, laid bare, unprotected, vulnerable, exhibited, on display, on show, on view, shown, susceptible.
☒ covered, sheltered.

exposure n 1 REVELATION, uncovering, disclosure, exposé, showing, unmasking, unveiling, display, airing, exhibition, presentation, publicity, manifestation, discovery, divulgence. 2 FAMILIARITY, experience, knowledge, contact. 3 JEOPARDY, danger, hazard, risk, vulnerability.

express v 1 ARTICULATE, verbalize, utter, voice, say, speak, state, communicate, pronounce, tell, assert, declare, put across, formulate, intimate, testify, convey. 2 SHOW, manifest, exhibit, disclose, divulge, reveal, indicate, denote, depict, embody. 3 SYMBOLIZE, stand for, represent, signify, designate.
➤ adj 1 SPECIFIC, explicit, exact, definite, clear, categorical, precise, distinct, clear-cut, certain, plain, manifest, particular, stated, unambiguous. 2 FAST, speedy, rapid, quick, high-speed, non-stop.
☒ 1 vague.

expression n 1 LOOK, air, aspect, countenance, appearance, mien (fml).

2 REPRESENTATION, manifestation, demonstration, indication, exhibition, embodiment, show, sign, symbol, style. 3 UTTERANCE, verbalization, communication, articulation, statement, assertion, announcement, declaration, pronouncement, speech. 4 TONE, intonation, delivery, diction, enunciation, modulation, wording. 5 PHRASE, term, turn of phrase, saying, set phrase, idiom.

expressionless adj dull, blank, deadpan, impassive, straight-faced, poker-faced (infml), inscrutable, empty, vacuous, glassy.
☒ expressive.

expressive adj eloquent, meaningful, forceful, telling, revealing, informative, indicative, communicative, emphatic, demonstrative, moving, poignant, lively, striking, suggestive, significant, thoughtful, vivid, sympathetic.

expulsion n ejection, eviction, exile, banishment, removal, discharge, exclusion, dismissal.

exquisite adj 1 BEAUTIFUL, attractive, dainty, delicate, charming, elegant, delightful, lovely, pleasing. 2 PERFECT, flawless, fine, excellent, choice, precious, rare, outstanding. 3 REFINED, discriminating, meticulous, sensitive, impeccable. 4 INTENSE, keen, sharp, poignant.
☒ 1 ugly. 2 flawed. 3 unrefined.

extend v 1 SPREAD, stretch, reach, continue. 2 ENLARGE, increase, expand, develop, amplify, lengthen, widen, elongate, draw out, protract, prolong, spin out, unwind. 3 OFFER, give, grant, hold out, impart, present, bestow, confer.
☒ 2 contract, shorten. 3 withhold.

extension n 1 ENLARGEMENT, increase, stretching, broadening, widening, lengthening, expansion, elongation, development, enhancement, protraction, continuation. 2 ADDITION, supplement, appendix, annexe, addendum (fml). 3 DELAY, postponement.

extensive *adj* **1** BROAD, comprehensive, far-reaching, large-scale, thorough, widespread, universal, extended, all-inclusive, general, pervasive, prevalent. **2** LARGE, huge, roomy, spacious, vast, voluminous, long, lengthy, wide.
Ea 1 restricted, narrow. **2** small.

extent *n* **1** DIMENSION(S), amount, magnitude, expanse, size, area, bulk, degree, breadth, quantity, spread, stretch, volume, width, measure, duration, term, time. **2** LIMIT, bounds, lengths, range, reach, scope, compass, sphere, play, sweep.

exterior *n* outside, surface, covering, coating, face, façade, shell, skin, finish, externals, appearance.
Ea inside, interior.
➤ *adj* outer, outside, outermost, surface, external, superficial, surrounding, outward, peripheral, extrinsic.
Ea inside, interior.

exterminate *v* annihilate, eradicate, destroy, eliminate, massacre, abolish, wipe out.

external *adj* outer, surface, outside, exterior, superficial, outward, outermost, apparent, visible, extraneous, extrinsic, extramural, independent.
Ea internal.

extinct *adj* **1** DEFUNCT, dead, gone, obsolete, ended, exterminated, terminated, vanished, lost, abolished. **2** EXTINGUISHED, quenched, inactive, out.
Ea 1 living.

extinction *n* annihilation, extermination, death, eradication, obliteration, destruction, abolition, excision.

extinguish *v* **1** PUT OUT, blow out, snuff out, stifle, smother, douse, quench. **2** ANNIHILATE, exterminate, eliminate, destroy, kill, eradicate, erase, expunge, abolish, remove, end, suppress.

extort *v* extract, wring, exact, coerce, force, milk (*infml*), blackmail, squeeze, bleed (*infml*), bully.

extortionate *adj* exorbitant, excessive, grasping, exacting, immoderate, rapacious, unreasonable, oppressive, blood-sucking (*infml*), rigorous, severe, hard, harsh, inordinate.

extra *adj* **1** ADDITIONAL, added, auxiliary, supplementary, new, more, further, ancillary, fresh, other. **2** EXCESS, spare, superfluous, supernumerary, surplus, unused, unneeded, leftover, reserve, redundant.
Ea 1 integral. **2** essential.
➤ *n* addition, supplement, extension, accessory, appendage, bonus, complement, adjunct, addendum (*fml*), attachment.
➤ *adv* especially, exceptionally, extraordinarily, particularly, unusually, remarkably, extremely.

extract *v* **1** REMOVE, take out, draw out, exact, uproot, withdraw. **2** DERIVE, draw, distil, obtain, get, gather, glean, wrest, wring, elicit. **3** CHOOSE, select, cull, abstract, cite, quote.
Ea 1 insert.
➤ *n* **1** DISTILLATION, essence, juice. **2** EXCERPT, passage, selection, clip, cutting, quotation, abstract, citation.

extraordinary *adj* remarkable, unusual, exceptional, notable, noteworthy, outstanding, unique, special, strange, peculiar, rare, surprising, amazing, wonderful, unprecedented, marvellous, fantastic, significant, particular.
Ea commonplace, ordinary.

extravagance *n* **1** OVERSPENDING, profligacy, squandering, waste. **2** EXCESS, immoderation, recklessness, profusion, outrageousness, folly.
Ea 1 thrift. **2** moderation.

extravagant *adj* **1** PROFLIGATE, prodigal, spendthrift, thriftless, wasteful, reckless. **2** IMMODERATE, flamboyant, preposterous, outrageous, ostentatious, pretentious, lavish,

ornate, flashy (*infml*), fanciful, fantastic, wild. **3** OVERPRICED, exorbitant, expensive, excessive, costly.
⊟ 1 thrifty. **2** moderate. **3** reasonable.

extreme *adj* **1** INTENSE, great, immoderate, inordinate, utmost, utter, out-and-out, full-on (*infml*), maximum, acute, downright, extraordinary, exceptional, greatest, highest, unreasonable, remarkable. **2** FARTHEST, far-off, faraway, distant, endmost, outermost, remotest, uttermost, final, last, terminal, ultimate. **3** RADICAL, zealous, extremist, fanatical. **4** DRASTIC, dire, uncompromising, stern, strict, rigid, severe, harsh.
⊟ 1 mild. **3** moderate.
➤ *n* extremity, limit, maximum, ultimate, utmost, excess, top, pinnacle, peak, height, end, climax, depth, edge, termination.

extremity *n* **1** EXTREME, limit, boundary, brink, verge, bound, border, apex, height, tip, top, edge, excess, end, acme, termination, peak, pinnacle, margin, terminal, terminus, ultimate, pole, maximum, minimum, frontier, depth. **2** CRISIS, danger, emergency, plight, hardship.

extricate *v* disentangle, clear, disengage, free, deliver, liberate, release, rescue, relieve, remove, withdraw.
⊟ involve.

extroverted *adj* outgoing, friendly, sociable, amicable, amiable, exuberant.
⊟ introverted.

exuberant *adj* **1** LIVELY, vivacious, spirited, zestful, high-spirited, effervescent, ebullient, enthusiastic, sparkling, excited, exhilarated, effusive, cheerful, fulsome. **2** PLENTIFUL, lavish, overflowing, plenteous.
⊟ 1 apathetic. **2** scarce.

exult *v* rejoice, revel, delight, glory, celebrate, relish, crow, gloat, triumph.

eye *n* **1** APPRECIATION, discrimination, discernment, perception, recognition. **2** VIEWPOINT, opinion, judgement, mind. **3** WATCH, observation, lookout.

Parts of the eye include: anterior chamber, aqueous humour, blind spot, choroid, ciliary body, cone, conjunctiva, cornea, eyelash, fovea, iris, lacrimal duct, lens, lower eyelid, ocular muscle, optic nerve, papilla, pupil, posterior chamber, retina, rod, sclera, suspension ligament, upper eyelid, vitreous humour.

➤ *v* look at, watch, regard, observe, stare at, gaze at, glance at, view, scrutinize, scan, examine, peruse, study, survey, inspect, contemplate.

eyesight *n* vision, sight, perception, observation, view.

eyesore *n* ugliness, blemish, monstrosity, blot on the landscape, disfigurement, horror, blight, atrocity, mess.

eyewitness *n* witness, observer, spectator, looker-on, onlooker, bystander, viewer, passer-by.

Ff

fable *n* allegory, parable, story, tale, yarn, myth, legend, fiction, fabrication, invention, lie, untruth, falsehood, tall story, old wives' tale.

fabric *n* **1** CLOTH, material, textile, stuff, web, texture. **2** STRUCTURE, framework, construction, make-up, constitution, organization, infrastructure, foundations.

Fabrics include: alpaca, angora, astrakhan, barathea, bouclé, cashmere, chenille, duffel, felt, flannel, fleece, Harris tweed®, mohair, paisley, pashmina, serge, sheepskin, Shetland wool, tweed, vicuña, wool, worsted; buckram, calico, cambric, candlewick, canvas, chambray, cheesecloth, chino, chintz, cord, corduroy, cotton, crêpe, denim, drill, jean, flannelette, gaberdine, gingham, jersey, lawn, linen, lisle, madras, moleskin, muslin, needlecord, piqué, poplin, sateen, seersucker, terry towelling, ticking, Viyella®, webbing, winceyette; brocade, grosgrain, damask, lace, Brussels lace, Chantilly, chiffon, georgette, gossamer, voile, organza, organdie, tulle, net, crêpe de Chine, silk, taffeta, shantung, satin, velvet, velour; polycotton, polyester, rayon, nylon, Crimplene®, Terylene®, Lurex®, Lycra®, elastane, lamé; hessian, horsehair, chamois, kid, leather, leather-cloth, sharkskin, suede.

fabricate *v* **1** FAKE, falsify, forge, invent, make up, trump up, concoct. **2** MAKE, manufacture, construct, assemble, build, erect, form, shape, fashion, create, devise.
🔁 **2** demolish, destroy.

fabulous *adj* **1** WONDERFUL, marvellous, fantastic, superb, breathtaking, spectacular, phenomenal, amazing, astounding, unbelievable, incredible, inconceivable. **2** *a fabulous beast*: mythical, legendary, fabled, fantastic, fictitious, invented, imaginary.
🔁 **2** real.

face *n* **1** FEATURES, countenance, visage, physiognomy. **2** EXPRESSION, look, appearance, air. **3** *pull a face*: grimace, frown, scowl, pout. **4** EXTERIOR, outside, surface, cover, front, façade, aspect, side.
➤ *v* **1** BE OPPOSITE, give on to, front, overlook. **2** CONFRONT, face up to, deal with, cope with, tackle, brave, defy, oppose, encounter, meet, experience. **3** COVER, coat, dress, clad, overlay, veneer.
◇ **face to face** opposite, eye to eye, eyeball to eyeball, in confrontation.
◇ **face up to** accept, come to terms with, acknowledge, recognize, cope with, deal with, confront, meet head-on, stand up to.

facet *n* surface, plane, side, face, aspect, angle, point, feature, characteristic.

facetious *adj* flippant, frivolous, playful, jocular, jesting, tongue-in-cheek, funny, amusing, humorous, comical, witty.
🔁 serious.

facile *adj* easy, simple, simplistic, ready, quick, hasty, glib, fluent, smooth, slick, plausible, shallow, superficial.
🔁 complicated, profound.

facilitate *v* ease, help, assist, further, promote, forward, expedite, speed up.

facilities *n* amenities, services,

conveniences, resources, prerequisites, equipment, mod cons (*infml*), means, opportunities.

facility *n* ease, effortlessness, readiness, quickness, fluency, proficiency, skill, skilfulness, talent, gift, knack, ability.

fact *n* **1** *facts and figures*: information, datum, detail, particular, specific, point, item, circumstance, event, incident, occurrence, happening, act, deed, fait accompli. **2** REALITY, actuality, truth.
🖾 **2** fiction.
◇ **in fact** actually, in actual fact, in point of fact, as a matter of fact, in reality, really, indeed.

faction *n* splinter group, ginger group, minority, division, section, contingent, party, camp, set, clique, coterie, cabal, junta, lobby, pressure group.

factor *n* cause, influence, circumstance, contingency, consideration, element, ingredient, component, part, point, aspect, fact, item, detail.

factory *n* works, plant, mill, shop floor, assembly line, assembly shop, manufactory.

factual *adj* true, historical, actual, real, genuine, authentic, correct, accurate, precise, exact, literal, faithful, close, detailed, unbiased, objective.
🖾 false, fictitious, imaginary, fictional.

faculties *n* wits, senses, intelligence, reason, powers, capabilities.

faculty *n* ability, capability, capacity, power, facility, knack, gift, talent, skill, aptitude, bent.

fad *n* craze, rage (*infml*), mania, fashion, mode, vogue, trend, whim, fancy, affectation.

fade *v* **1** DISCOLOUR, bleach, blanch, blench, pale, whiten, dim, dull.
2 DECLINE, fall, diminish, dwindle, ebb, wane, disappear, vanish, flag, weaken, droop, wilt, wither, shrivel, perish, die.

fail *v* **1** GO WRONG, miscarry, misfire, flop, miss, flunk (*sl*), fall through, come to grief, collapse, fold (*infml*), go

bankrupt, go bust, go under, founder, sink, decline, fall, weaken, dwindle, fade, wane, peter out, cease, die. **2** *fail to pay a bill*: omit, neglect, forget. **3** LET DOWN, disappoint, leave, desert, abandon, forsake.
🖾 **1** succeed, prosper.

failing *n* weakness, foible, fault, defect, imperfection, flaw, blemish, drawback, deficiency, shortcoming, failure, lapse, error.
🖾 strength, advantage.

failure *n* **1** MISCARRIAGE, flop, washout (*infml*), fiasco, disappointment, loss, defeat, downfall, decline, decay, deterioration, ruin, bankruptcy, crash, collapse, breakdown, stoppage.
2 OMISSION, slip-up (*infml*), neglect, negligence, failing, shortcoming, deficiency.
🖾 **1** success, prosperity.

faint *adj* **1** SLIGHT, weak, feeble, soft, low, hushed, muffled, subdued, faded, bleached, light, pale, dull, dim, hazy, indistinct, vague. **2** *I feel faint*: dizzy, giddy, woozy (*infml*), light-headed, weak, feeble, exhausted.
🖾 **1** strong, clear.
➤ *v* black out, pass out, swoon, collapse, flake out (*infml*), keel over (*infml*), drop.
➤ *n* blackout, swoon, collapse, unconsciousness.

fair¹ *adj* **1** JUST, equitable, square, even-handed, dispassionate, impartial, objective, disinterested, unbiased, unprejudiced, right, proper, lawful, legitimate, honest, trustworthy, upright, honourable. **2** FAIR-HAIRED, fair-headed, blond(e), light. **3** *fair weather*: fine, dry, sunny, bright, clear, cloudless, unclouded. **4** AVERAGE, moderate, middling, not bad, all right, OK (*infml*), satisfactory, adequate, acceptable, tolerable, reasonable, passable, mediocre, so-so (*infml*).
🖾 **1** unfair. **2** dark. **3** inclement, cloudy. **4** excellent, poor.

fair² *n* show, exhibition, exposition, expo, market, bazaar, fête, festival, carnival, gala.

faith n 1 BELIEF, credit, trust, reliance, dependence, conviction, confidence, assurance. 2 RELIGION, denomination, persuasion, church, creed, dogma. 3 FAITHFULNESS, fidelity, loyalty, allegiance, honour, sincerity, honesty, truthfulness.
E3 1 mistrust. 3 unfaithfulness, treachery.

faithful adj 1 LOYAL, devoted, staunch, steadfast, constant, trusty, reliable, dependable, true. 2 a faithful description: accurate, precise, exact, strict, close, true, truthful.
E3 1 disloyal, treacherous. 2 inaccurate, vague.

fake v forge, fabricate, counterfeit, copy, imitate, simulate, feign, sham, pretend, put on, affect, assume.
➤ n forgery, copy, reproduction, replica, imitation, simulation, sham, hoax, fraud, phoney (*infml*), impostor, charlatan.
➤ adj forged, counterfeit, false, spurious, phoney (*infml*), pseudo, bogus, assumed, affected, sham, artificial, simulated, mock, imitation, faux, reproduction.
E3 genuine.

fall v 1 TUMBLE, stumble, trip, topple, keel over, collapse, slump, crash. 2 DESCEND, go down, drop, slope, incline, slide, sink, dive, plunge, plummet, nose-dive, pitch. 3 DECREASE, lessen, decline, diminish, dwindle, fall off, subside.
E3 2 rise. 3 increase.
➤ n 1 TUMBLE, descent, slope, incline, dive, plunge, decrease, reduction, lessening, drop, decline, dwindling, slump, crash. 2 the fall of Rome: defeat, conquest, overthrow, downfall, collapse, surrender, capitulation.
◇ **fall apart** break, go to pieces, shatter, disintegrate, crumble, decompose, decay, rot.
◇ **fall asleep** drop off, doze off, nod off (*infml*).
◇ **fall back on** resort to, have recourse to, use, turn to, look to.
◇ **fall behind** lag, trail, drop back.

◇ **fall in** cave in, come down, collapse, give way, subside, sink.
◇ **fall in with** agree with, assent to, go along with, accept, comply with, co-operate with.
◇ **fall off** decrease, lessen, drop, slump, decline, deteriorate, worsen, slow, slacken.
◇ **fall out** quarrel, argue, squabble, bicker, fight, clash, disagree, differ.
E3 agree.
◇ **fall through** come to nothing, fail, miscarry, founder, collapse.
E3 come off, succeed.

fallacy n misconception, delusion, mistake, error, flaw, inconsistency, falsehood.
E3 truth.

fallow adj uncultivated, unplanted, unsown, undeveloped, unused, idle, inactive, dormant, resting.

false adj 1 WRONG, incorrect, mistaken, erroneous, inaccurate, inexact, misleading, faulty, fallacious, invalid. 2 UNREAL, artificial, synthetic, imitation, simulated, mock, fake, counterfeit, forged, feigned, pretended, sham, bogus, assumed, fictitious. 3 false friends: disloyal, unfaithful, faithless, lying, deceitful, insincere, hypocritical, two-faced, double-dealing, treacherous, unreliable.
E3 1 true, right. 2 real, genuine. 3 faithful, reliable.

falsehood n untruth, lie, fib, story, fiction, fabrication, perjury, untruthfulness, deceit, deception, dishonesty.
E3 truth, truthfulness.

falsify v alter, cook (*infml*), tamper with, doctor, distort, pervert, misrepresent, misstate, forge, counterfeit, fake.

falter v totter, stumble, stammer, stutter, hesitate, waver, vacillate, flinch, quail, shake, tremble, flag, fail.

fame n renown, celebrity, stardom, prominence, eminence, illustriousness, glory, honour, esteem, reputation, name.

familiar *adj* 1 EVERYDAY, routine, household, common, ordinary, well-known, recognizable. 2 INTIMATE, close, confidential, friendly, informal, free, free-and-easy, relaxed. 3 *familiar with the procedure*: aware, acquainted, abreast, knowledgeable, versed, conversant.
E3 1 unfamiliar, strange. 2 formal, reserved. 3 unfamiliar, ignorant.

familiarity *n* 1 INTIMACY, liberty, closeness, friendliness, sociability, openness, naturalness, informality. 2 AWARENESS, acquaintance, experience, knowledge, understanding, grasp.

familiarize *v* accustom, acclimatize, school, train, coach, instruct, prime, brief.

family *n* 1 RELATIVES, relations, kin, kindred, kinsmen, people, folk (*infml*), ancestors, forebears, children, offspring, issue, progeny, descendants. 2 CLAN, tribe, race, dynasty, house, pedigree, ancestry, parentage, descent, line, lineage, extraction, blood, stock, birth. 3 CLASS, group, classification.
◇ **family tree** ancestry, pedigree, genealogy, line, lineage, extraction.

> *Members of a family include*: ancestor, forebear, forefather, descendant, offspring, heir; husband, wife, spouse, parent, father, dad (*infml*), daddy (*infml*), old man (*infml*), mother, mum (*infml*), mummy (*infml*), mom (*US infml*), grandparent, grandfather, grandmother, granny (*infml*), nanny (*infml*), grandchild, son, daughter, brother, half-brother, sister, half-sister, sibling, uncle, aunt, nephew, niece, cousin, godfather, godmother, godchild, stepfather, stepmother, foster-parent, foster-child.

famine *n* starvation, hunger, destitution, want, scarcity, death.
E3 plenty.

famous *adj* well-known, famed, renowned, celebrated, noted, great, distinguished, illustrious, eminent, honoured, acclaimed, glorious, legendary, remarkable, notable, prominent, signal.
E3 unheard-of, unknown, obscure.

fan[1] *v* 1 COOL, ventilate, air, air-condition, air-cool, blow, refresh. 2 INCREASE, provoke, stimulate, rouse, arouse, excite, agitate, stir up, work up, whip up.
➤ *n* extractor fan, ventilator, air-conditioner, blower, propeller, vane.

fan[2] *n* enthusiast, admirer, supporter, follower, adherent, devotee, lover, buff (*infml*), fiend, freak.

fanatic *n* zealot, devotee, enthusiast, addict, fiend, freak, maniac, visionary, bigot, extremist, militant, activist.

fanatical *adj* overenthusiastic, extreme, passionate, zealous, fervent, burning, mad, wild, frenzied, rabid, obsessive, single-minded, bigoted, visionary.
E3 moderate, unenthusiastic.

fanaticism *n* extremism, monomania, single-mindedness, obsessiveness, madness, infatuation, bigotry, zeal, fervour, enthusiasm, dedication.
E3 moderation.

fanciful *adj* imaginary, mythical, fabulous, fantastic, visionary, romantic, fairy-tale, airy-fairy, vaporous, whimsical, wild, extravagant, curious.
E3 real, ordinary.

fancy *v* 1 LIKE, be attracted to, take a liking to, take to, go for, prefer, favour, desire, wish for, long for, yearn for. 2 THINK, conceive, imagine, dream of, picture, conjecture, believe, suppose, reckon, guess.
E3 1 dislike.
➤ *n* 1 DESIRE, craving, hankering, urge, liking, fondness, inclination, preference. 2 NOTION, thought, impression, imagination, dream, fantasy.
E3 1 dislike, aversion. 2 fact, reality.
➤ *adj* elaborate, ornate, decorated, ornamented, rococo, baroque, elegant, extravagant, fantastic, fanciful, far-fetched.
E3 plain.

fantastic adj 1 WONDERFUL, marvellous, sensational, superb, excellent, first-rate, tremendous, terrific, great, incredible, unbelievable, overwhelming, enormous, extreme. 2 STRANGE, weird, odd, exotic, outlandish, fanciful, fabulous, imaginative, visionary.
 1 ordinary. 2 real.

fantasy n dream, daydream, reverie, pipe-dream, nightmare, vision, hallucination, illusion, mirage, apparition, invention, fancy, flight of fancy, delusion, misconception, imagination, unreality.
 reality.

far adv a long way, a good way, miles (infml), much, greatly, considerably, extremely, decidedly, incomparably.
 near, close.
➤ adj distant, far-off, faraway, far-flung, outlying, remote, out of the way, godforsaken, removed, far-removed, further, opposite, other.
 nearby, close.

farce n 1 COMEDY, slapstick, buffoonery, satire, burlesque. 2 TRAVESTY, sham, parody, joke, mockery, ridiculousness, absurdity, nonsense.

fare n 1 pay one's fare: charge, cost, price, fee, passage. 2 FOOD, eatables (infml), provisions, rations, sustenance, meals, diet, menu, board, table.

far-fetched adj implausible, improbable, unlikely, dubious, incredible, unbelievable, fantastic, preposterous, crazy, unrealistic.
 plausible.

farm n ranch, farmstead, grange, homestead, station, land, holding, acreage, acres.

> *Types of farm include*: arable farm, cattle ranch, dairy farm, fish farm, free-range farm, mixed farm, organic farm, ostrich farm, pig farm, sheep station, croft, smallholding, estate, plantation, wind farm.

➤ v cultivate, till, work the land, plant, operate.

farmer n agriculturist, crofter, smallholder, husbandman, yeoman.

farming n agriculture, cultivation, husbandry, crofting.

far-reaching adj broad, extensive, widespread, sweeping, important, significant, momentous.
 insignificant.

fascinate v absorb, engross, intrigue, delight, charm, captivate, spellbind, enthral, rivet, transfix, hypnotize, mesmerize.
 bore, repel.

fascination n interest, attraction, lure, magnetism, pull, charm, enchantment, spell, sorcery, magic.
 boredom, repulsion.

fashion n 1 MANNER, way, method, mode, style, shape, form, pattern, line, cut, look, appearance, type, sort, kind. 2 VOGUE, trend, mode, style, fad, craze, rage (infml), latest (infml), custom, convention.
➤ v create, form, shape, mould, model, design, fit, tailor, alter, adjust, adapt, suit.

fashionable adj chic, smart, elegant, stylish, modish, à la mode, in vogue, trendy (infml), in, all the rage (infml), popular, prevailing, current, latest, up to the minute, contemporary, modern, up to date.
 unfashionable.

fast[1] adj 1 QUICK, swift, rapid, brisk, accelerated, speedy, nippy (infml), hasty, hurried, flying. 2 FASTENED, secure, fixed, immovable, immobile, firm, tight.
 1 slow, unhurried. 2 loose.
➤ adv quickly, swiftly, rapidly, speedily, like a flash, like a shot, hastily, hurriedly, apace, presto.
 slowly, gradually.

fast[2] v go hungry, diet, starve, abstain.
➤ n fasting, diet, starvation, abstinence.
 gluttony, self-indulgence.

fasten v fix, attach, clamp, grip, anchor, rivet, nail, seal, close, shut, lock, bolt, secure, tie, bind, chain, link, interlock, connect, join, unite, do up, button, lace, buckle.

F3 unfasten, untie.

fastener

Types of fastener include: button, catch, clasp, clip, collar stud, cotter, cufflink, eyelet, frog, hasp, hinge, hook, hook-and-eye, knot, lace, loop, nail, paperclip, press stud, rivet, screw, shoelace, split pin, staple, stitch, stud, tie, toggle, treasury tag, Velcro®, zip, zipper (*US*).

fat *adj* plump, obese, tubby, stout, corpulent (*fml*), portly, round, rotund, paunchy, pot-bellied, overweight, heavy, beefy, solid, chubby, podgy, fleshy, flabby, gross.

F3 thin, slim, poor.

➤ *n* fatness, obesity, overweight, corpulence (*fml*), paunch, pot (belly), blubber, flab (*infml*).

fatal *adj* deadly, lethal, mortal, killing, incurable, malignant, terminal, final, destructive, calamitous, catastrophic, disastrous.

F3 harmless.

fatality *n* death, mortality, loss, casualty, deadliness, lethality, disaster.

fate *n* destiny, providence, chance, future, fortune, horoscope, stars, lot, doom, end, outcome, ruin, destruction, death.

fated *adj* destined, predestined, preordained, foreordained, doomed, unavoidable, inevitable, inescapable, certain, sure.

F3 avoidable.

fateful *adj* crucial, critical, decisive, important, momentous, significant, fatal, lethal, disastrous.

F3 unimportant.

father *n* **1** PARENT, begetter, procreator, progenitor, sire (*fml*), papa, dad (*infml*), daddy (*infml*), old man (*infml*), patriarch, elder, forefather, ancestor, forebear, predecessor. **2** FOUNDER, creator, originator, inventor, maker, architect, author, patron, leader, prime

mover. **3** PRIEST, padre, abbé, curé.

➤ *v* beget, procreate, sire, produce.

fathom *v* **1** MEASURE, gauge, plumb, sound, probe, penetrate. **2** UNDERSTAND, comprehend, grasp, see, work out, get to the bottom of, interpret.

fatigue *n* tiredness, weariness, exhaustion, lethargy, listlessness, lassitude, weakness, debility.

F3 energy.

➤ *v* tire, wear out, weary, exhaust, drain, weaken, debilitate.

fatten *v* feed, nourish, build up, overfeed, cram, stuff, bloat, swell, fill out, spread, expand, thicken.

fatty *adj* fat, greasy, oily.

fault *n* **1** DEFECT, flaw, blemish, imperfection, deficiency, shortcoming, weakness, failing, foible, negligence, omission, oversight. **2** ERROR, mistake, blunder, slip-up (*infml*), slip, lapse, misdeed, offence, wrong, sin. **3** *it's your fault*: responsibility, accountability, liability, culpability (*fml*).

➤ *v* find fault with, pick holes in, criticize, knock (*infml*), impugn (*fml*), censure, blame, call to account.

F3 praise.

◇ **at fault** (in the) wrong, blameworthy, to blame, responsible, guilty, culpable (*fml*).

faultless *adj* perfect, flawless, unblemished, spotless, immaculate, unsullied, pure, blameless, exemplary, model, correct, accurate.

F3 faulty, imperfect, flawed.

faulty *adj* imperfect, defective, shoddy, flawed, blemished, damaged, impaired, out of order, broken, wrong.

F3 faultless.

favour *n* **1** APPROVAL, esteem, support, backing, sympathy, goodwill, patronage, favouritism, preference, partiality. **2** *he did me a favour*: kindness, service, good turn, courtesy.

F3 **1** disapproval.

➤ *v* **1** PREFER, choose, opt for, like, approve, support, back, advocate,

champion. **2** HELP, assist, aid, benefit, promote, encourage, pamper, spoil.
⊟ 1 dislike. **2** mistreat.
◇ **in favour of** for, supporting, on the side of.
⊟ against.

favourable adj beneficial, advantageous, helpful, fit, suitable, convenient, timely, opportune, good, fair, promising, auspicious, hopeful, positive, encouraging, complimentary, enthusiastic, friendly, amicable, well-disposed, kind, sympathetic, understanding, reassuring.
⊟ unfavourable, unhelpful, negative.

favourite adj preferred, favoured, pet, best-loved, dearest, beloved, esteemed, chosen.
⊟ hated.
➤ n preference, choice, pick, pet, blue-eyed boy, teacher's pet, the apple of one's eye, darling, idol.
⊟ bête noire, pet hate.

favouritism n nepotism, preferential treatment, preference, partiality, one-sidedness, partisanship, bias, injustice.
⊟ impartiality.

fear n alarm, fright, terror, horror, panic, agitation, worry, anxiety, consternation, concern, dismay, distress, uneasiness, qualms, misgivings, apprehension, trepidation, dread, foreboding, awe, phobia, nightmare.
⊟ courage, bravery, confidence.
➤ v take fright, shrink from, dread, shudder at, tremble, worry, suspect, anticipate, expect, foresee, respect, venerate.

fearful adj **1** FRIGHTENED, afraid, scared, alarmed, nervous, anxious, tense, uneasy, apprehensive, hesitant, nervy, panicky. **2** TERRIBLE, fearsome, dreadful, awful, frightful, atrocious, shocking, appalling, monstrous, gruesome, hideous, ghastly, horrible.
⊟ 1 brave, courageous, fearless.
2 wonderful, delightful.

feasible adj practicable, practical, workable, achievable, attainable, realizable, viable, reasonable, possible, likely.
⊟ impossible.

feast n **1** BANQUET, dinner, spread, blow-out (sl), binge (infml), beano (infml), junket. **2** FESTIVAL, holiday, gala, fête, celebration, revels.
➤ v gorge, binge (infml), pig out (sl), eat one's fill, wine and dine, treat, entertain.

feat n exploit, deed, act, accomplishment, achievement, attainment, performance.

feature n **1** ASPECT, facet, point, factor, attribute, quality, property, trait, lineament, characteristic, peculiarity, mark, hallmark, speciality, highlight.
2 a magazine feature: column, article, report, story, piece, item, comment.
➤ v **1** EMPHASIZE, highlight, spotlight, play up, promote, show, present.
2 APPEAR, figure, participate, act, perform, star.

fee n charge, terms, bill, account, pay, remuneration, payment, retainer, subscription, reward, recompense, hire, toll.

feeble adj **1** WEAK, faint, exhausted, frail, delicate, puny, sickly, infirm, powerless, helpless. **2** INADEQUATE, lame, poor, thin, flimsy, ineffective, incompetent, indecisive.
⊟ 1 strong, powerful.

feed v nourish, cater for, provide for, supply, sustain, suckle, nurture, foster, strengthen, fuel, graze, pasture, eat, dine.
➤ n food, fodder, forage, pasture, silage.
◇ **feed on** eat, consume, devour, live on, exist on.

feel v **1** EXPERIENCE, go through, undergo, suffer, endure, enjoy. **2** TOUCH, finger, handle, manipulate, hold, stroke, caress, fondle, paw, fumble, grope. **3** feel soft: seem, appear. **4** THINK, believe, consider, reckon, judge. **5** SENSE, perceive, notice, observe, know.
➤ n texture, surface, finish, touch, knack, sense, impression, feeling, quality.

◇ **feel for** pity, sympathize (with), empathize (with), commiserate (with), be sorry for.

◇ **feel like** fancy, want, desire.

feeling *n* 1 SENSATION, perception, sense, instinct, hunch, suspicion, inkling, impression, idea, notion, opinion, view, point of view. 2 EMOTION, passion, intensity, warmth, compassion, sympathy, understanding, pity, concern, affection, fondness, sentiment, sentimentality, susceptibility, sensibility, sensitivity, appreciation. 3 AIR, aura, atmosphere, mood, quality.

fell *v* cut down, hew, knock down, strike down, floor, level, flatten, raze, demolish.

fellow *n* 1 PERSON, man, boy, chap (*infml*), bloke (*infml*), guy (*infml*), individual, character. 2 PEER, compeer, equal, partner, associate, colleague, co-worker, companion, comrade, friend, counterpart, match, mate, twin, double.
➤ *adj* co-, associate, associated, related, like, similar.

fellowship *n* 1 COMPANIONSHIP, camaraderie, communion, familiarity, intimacy. 2 ASSOCIATION, league, guild, society, club, fraternity, brotherhood, sisterhood, order.

female *adj* feminine, she-, girlish, womanly.
▣ male.

Female terms include: girl, lass, maiden, woman, lady, daughter, sister, girlfriend, fiancée, bride, wife, mother, aunt, niece, grandmother, matriarch, godmother, widow, dowager, dame, madam, mistress, virgin, spinster, old maid, bird (*sl*), chick (*sl*), lesbian, bitch (*sl*), prostitute, whore, harlot; cow, heifer, bitch, doe, ewe, hen, mare, filly, nanny-goat, sow, tigress, vixen.

feminine *adj* 1 FEMALE, womanly, ladylike, graceful, gentle, tender. 2 EFFEMINATE, unmanly, womanish, girlish, girly, sissy.
▣ 1 masculine. 2 manly.

feminism *n* women's movement, women's lib(eration), female emancipation, women's rights.

fence *n* barrier, railing, paling, wall, hedge, windbreak, guard, defence, barricade, stockade, rampart.
➤ *v* 1 SURROUND, encircle, bound, hedge, wall, enclose, pen, coop, confine, restrict, separate, protect, guard, defend, fortify. 2 PARRY, dodge, evade, hedge, equivocate, quibble, pussyfoot, stonewall.

fencing

Fencing terms include: appel, attack, balestra, barrage, coquille, disengage, en garde, épée, feint, flèche, foible, foil, forte, hit, lunge, on guard, parry, counter-parry, pink, piste, plastron, remise, reprise, riposte, counter-riposte, sabre, tac-au-tac, thrust, touch, touché, volt.

fend for look after, take care of, shift for, support, maintain, sustain, provide for.

fend off ward off, beat off, parry, deflect, avert, resist, repel, repulse, hold at bay, keep off, shut out.

ferment *v* 1 BUBBLE, effervesce, froth, foam, boil, seethe, smoulder, fester, brew, rise. 2 ROUSE, stir up, excite, work up, agitate, foment, incite, provoke, inflame, heat.
➤ *n* unrest, agitation, turbulence, stir, excitement, turmoil, disruption, commotion, tumult, hubbub, uproar, furore, frenzy, fever, glow.
▣ calm.

ferocious *adj* vicious, savage, fierce, wild, barbarous, barbaric, brutal, inhuman, cruel, sadistic, murderous, bloodthirsty, violent, merciless, pitiless, ruthless.
▣ gentle, mild, tame.

ferocity *n* viciousness, savagery, fierceness, wildness, barbarity, brutality, inhumanity, cruelty, sadism, violence, bloodthirstiness, ruthlessness.
▣ gentleness, mildness.

ferry *n* ferry boat, car ferry, ship, boat, vessel.
➤ *v* transport, ship, convey, carry, take, shuttle, taxi, drive, run, move, shift.

fertile *adj* fruitful, productive, generative, yielding, prolific, teeming, abundant, plentiful, rich, lush, luxuriant, fat.
☒ infertile, barren, sterile, unproductive.

fertilize *v* **1** IMPREGNATE, inseminate, pollinate. **2** *fertilize land*: enrich, feed, dress, compost, manure, dung.

fertilizer *n* dressing, compost, manure, dung.

fervent *adj* ardent, earnest, eager, enthusiastic, wholehearted, excited, energetic, vigorous, fiery, spirited, intense, vehement, passionate, full-blooded, zealous, devout, heartfelt, impassioned, emotional, warm.
☒ cool, indifferent, apathetic.

fervour *n* ardour, eagerness, enthusiasm, excitement, animation, energy, vigour, spirit, verve, intensity, vehemence, passion, zeal, warmth.
☒ apathy.

fester *v* ulcerate, gather, suppurate, discharge, putrefy, rot, decay, rankle, smoulder.

festival *n* celebration, anniversary, commemoration, jubilee, holiday, feast, gala, fête, carnival, fiesta, party, merrymaking, entertainment, festivities.

festive *adj* celebratory, festal, holiday, gala, carnival, happy, joyful, merry, hearty, cheery, jolly, jovial, cordial, convivial.
☒ gloomy, sombre, sober.

festivity *n* celebration, jubilation, feasting, banqueting, fun, enjoyment, pleasure, entertainment, sport, amusement, merriment, merrymaking, revelry, jollity, joviality, conviviality.

festoon *v* adorn, deck, bedeck, garland, wreathe, drape, hang, swathe, decorate, garnish.

fetch *v* **1** *fetch a bucket*: get, collect, bring, carry, transport, deliver, escort. **2** SELL FOR, go for, bring in, yield, realize, make, earn.

fetching *adj* attractive, pretty, sweet, cute, charming, enchanting, fascinating, captivating.
☒ repellent.

fête *n* fair, bazaar, sale of work, garden party, gala, carnival, festival.
➤ *v* entertain, treat, regale, welcome, honour, lionize.

feud *n* vendetta, quarrel, row, argument, disagreement, dispute, conflict, strife, discord, animosity, ill will, bitterness, enmity, hostility, antagonism, rivalry.
☒ agreement, peace.

fever *n* **1** FEVERISHNESS, (high) temperature, delirium. **2** EXCITEMENT, agitation, turmoil, unrest, restlessness, heat, passion, ecstasy.

feverish *adj* **1** DELIRIOUS, hot, burning, flushed. **2** EXCITED, impatient, agitated, restless, nervous, overwrought, frenzied, frantic, hectic, hasty, hurried.
☒ **1** cool. **2** calm.

few *adj* scarce, rare, uncommon, sporadic, infrequent, sparse, thin, scant, scanty, meagre, inconsiderable, inadequate, insufficient, in short supply.
☒ many.
➤ *pron* not many, hardly any, one or two, a couple, scattering, sprinkling, handful, some.
☒ many.

fibre *n* **1** FILAMENT, strand, thread, nerve, sinew, pile, texture. **2** *moral fibre*: character, calibre, backbone, strength, stamina, toughness, courage, resolution, determination.

fickle *adj* inconstant, disloyal, unfaithful, faithless, treacherous, unreliable, unpredictable, changeable, capricious, mercurial, irresolute, vacillating.
☒ constant, steady, stable.

fiction *n* **1** FANTASY, fancy, imagination, figment, invention, fabrication,

concoction, improvisation, story-telling.
2 NOVEL, romance, story, tale, yarn, fable,
parable, legend, myth, lie.
F3 2 non-fiction, fact, truth.

fictional *adj* literary, invented, made-
up, imaginary, make-believe, legendary,
mythical, mythological, fabulous, non-
existent, unreal.
F3 factual, real.

fictitious *adj* false, untrue, invented,
made-up, fabricated, apocryphal,
imaginary, non-existent, bogus,
counterfeit, spurious, assumed,
supposed.
F3 true, genuine.

fiddle *v* **1** *fiddling with her necklace*:
play, tinker, toy, trifle, tamper, mess
around, meddle, interfere, fidget.
2 CHEAT, swindle, diddle, cook the books
(*infml*), juggle, manoeuvre, racketeer,
graft (*sl*).
➤ *n* swindle, con (*infml*), scam (*infml*),
rip-off (*sl*), fraud, racket, sharp practice,
graft (*sl*).

fiddling *adj* trifling, petty, trivial,
insignificant, negligible, paltry.
F3 important, significant.

fidelity *n* **1** FAITHFULNESS, loyalty,
allegiance, devotion, constancy,
reliability. **2** ACCURACY, exactness,
precision, closeness, adherence.
F3 1 infidelity, inconstancy, treachery.
2 inaccuracy.

fidget *v* squirm, wriggle, shuffle, twitch,
jerk, jump, fret, fuss, bustle, fiddle, mess
about, play around.

fidgety *adj* restless, impatient, uneasy,
nervous, agitated, jittery, jumpy, twitchy,
on edge.
F3 still.

field *n* **1** GRASSLAND, meadow, pasture,
paddock, playing-field, ground, pitch,
green, lawn. **2** RANGE, scope, bounds,
limits, confines, territory, area, province,
domain, sphere, environment,
department, discipline, speciality, line,
forte. **3** PARTICIPANTS, entrants,
contestants, competitors, contenders,
runners, candidates, applicants,

opponents, opposition, competition.

fiend *n* **1** EVIL SPIRIT, demon, devil,
monster. **2** *a health fiend*: enthusiast,
fanatic, addict, devotee, freak (*infml*),
nut (*infml*).

fiendish *adj* devilish, diabolical,
infernal, wicked, malevolent, cunning,
cruel, inhuman, savage, monstrous,
unspeakable.

fierce *adj* ferocious, vicious, savage,
cruel, brutal, merciless, aggressive,
dangerous, murderous, frightening,
menacing, threatening, stern, grim,
relentless, raging, wild, passionate,
intense, strong, powerful.
F3 gentle, kind, calm.

fiery *adj* **1** BURNING, afire, flaming,
aflame, blazing, ablaze, red-hot,
glowing, aglow, flushed, hot, torrid,
sultry. **2** PASSIONATE, inflamed, ardent,
fervent, impatient, excitable,
impetuous, impulsive, hot-headed,
fierce, violent, heated.
F3 1 cold. **2** impassive.

fight *v* **1** WRESTLE, box, fence, joust,
brawl, scrap, scuffle, tussle, skirmish,
combat, battle, do battle, war, wage war,
clash, cross swords, engage, grapple,
struggle, strive, contend. **2** QUARREL,
argue, dispute, squabble, bicker,
wrangle. **3** OPPOSE, contest, campaign
against, resist, withstand, defy, stand up
to.
➤ *n* **1** BOUT, contest, duel, combat,
action, battle, war, hostilities, brawl,
scrap, scuffle, tussle, struggle, skirmish,
set-to (*infml*), clash, engagement,
brush, encounter, conflict, fray, free-for-
all, fracas, riot. **2** QUARREL, row,
argument, dispute, dissension.
◇ **fight back 1** RETALIATE, defend
oneself, resist, put up a fight, retort,
reply. **2** *fight back the tears*: hold back,
restrain, curb, control, repress, bottle
up, contain, suppress.
◇ **fight off** hold off, keep at bay, ward
off, stave off, resist, repel, rebuff, beat
off, rout, put to flight.

fighter *n* combatant, contestant,
contender, disputant, boxer, wrestler,

pugilist, prizefighter, soldier, trouper, mercenary, warrior, man-at-arms, swordsman, gladiator.

figurative adj metaphorical, symbolic, emblematic, representative, allegorical, parabolic, descriptive, pictorial.
☒ literal.

figure n 1 NUMBER, numeral, digit, integer, sum, amount. 2 SHAPE, form, outline, silhouette, body, frame, build, physique. 3 *public figure*: dignitary, celebrity, personality, character, person. 4 DIAGRAM, illustration, picture, drawing, sketch, image, representation, symbol.
➤ v 1 RECKON, guess, estimate, judge, think, believe. 2 FEATURE, appear, crop up.
◊ **figure out** work out, calculate, compute, reckon, puzzle out, resolve, fathom, understand, see, make out, decipher.

figurehead n mouthpiece, front man, name, dummy, puppet.

filament n fibre, strand, thread, hair, whisker, wire, string, pile.

file¹ v rub (down), sand, abrade, scour, scrape, grate, rasp, hone, whet, shave, plane, smooth, polish.

file² n folder, dossier, portfolio, binder, case, record, documents, data, information.
➤ v record, register, note, enter, process, store, classify, categorize, pigeonhole, catalogue.

file³ n line, queue, column, row, procession, cortège, train, string, stream, trail.
➤ v march, troop, parade, stream, trail.

fill v 1 REPLENISH, stock, supply, furnish, satisfy, pack, crowd, cram, stuff, congest, block, clog, plug, bung, cork, stop, close, seal. 2 PERVADE, imbue, permeate, soak, impregnate. 3 *fill a post*: take up, hold, occupy, discharge, fulfil.
☒ 1 empty, drain.
◊ **fill in 1** *fill in a form*: complete, fill out,

answer. 2 (*infml*) STAND IN, deputize, understudy, substitute, replace, represent, act for. 3 (*infml*) BRIEF, inform, advise, acquaint, bring up to date, bring up to speed (*infml*).

filling n contents, inside, stuffing, padding, wadding, filler.
➤ adj satisfying, nutritious, square, solid, substantial, heavy, large, big, generous, ample.
☒ insubstantial.

film n 1 MOTION PICTURE, picture, movie (*infml*), video, feature film, short, documentary. 2 LAYER, covering, dusting, coat, coating, glaze, skin, membrane, tissue, sheet, veil, screen, cloud, mist, haze.

Kinds of film include: action, adult, adventure, animated, art-house, auteur, avant-garde, biopic, B-movie, black comedy, blaxploitation, blockbuster, blue (*infml*), Bollywood, buddy, burlesque, Carry-on, cartoon, Charlie Chaplin, cinéma-vérité, classic, cliff-hanger, comedy, comedy thriller, courtroom drama, cowboy and Indian, crime, cult, detective, disaster, Disney, documentary, dogme, Ealing comedy, epic, erotic, escapist, ethnographic, exploitation, expressionist, family, fantasy, farce, film à clef, film noir, flashback, gangster, gaveller (*infml*), historical romance, Hitchcock, Hollywood, horror, James Bond, kitchen sink, love story, low-budget, medieval, melodrama, multiple-story, murder, murder mystery, musical, newsreel, new wave, nouvelle vague, period epic, police, police thriller, political, pornographic, psychological thriller, realist, remake, rites of passage, road movie, robbery, romantic, romantic comedy, rom-com (*infml*), satirical, science-fiction, screwball comedy, serial, sexploitation, short, silent, slasher, snuff, social comedy, social problem, space-age, space exploration, spaghetti western, spoof, spy, surrealist, tear-jerker (*infml*), thriller, tragedy, tragicomedy, travelogue, underground, war, western, whodunnit.

➤ *v* photograph, shoot, video, videotape.

filter *v* strain, sieve, sift, screen, refine, purify, clarify, percolate, ooze, seep, leak, trickle, dribble.
➤ *n* strainer, sieve, sifter, colander, mesh, gauze, membrane.

filth *n* 1 DIRT, grime, muck, dung, excrement, faeces, sewage, refuse, rubbish, garbage, trash, slime, sludge, effluent, pollution, contamination, corruption, impurity, uncleanness, foulness, sordidness, squalor.
2 OBSCENITY, pornography, smut, indecency, vulgarity, coarseness.
🔁 1 cleanness, cleanliness, purity.

filthy *adj* 1 DIRTY, soiled, unwashed, grimy, grubby, mucky, muddy, slimy, sooty, unclean, impure, foul, gross, sordid, squalid, vile, low, mean, base, contemptible, despicable. 2 OBSCENE, pornographic, X-rated (*infml*), smutty, bawdy, suggestive, indecent, offensive, foul-mouthed, vulgar, coarse, corrupt, depraved.
🔁 1 clean, pure. 2 decent.

final *adj* last, latest, closing, concluding, finishing, end, ultimate, terminal, dying, last-minute, eventual, conclusive, definitive, decisive, definite, incontrovertible.
🔁 first, initial.

finale *n* climax, dénouement, culmination, crowning glory, end, conclusion, close, curtain, epilogue.

finalize *v* conclude, finish, complete, round off, resolve, settle, agree, decide, close, clinch, sew up (*infml*), wrap up (*infml*).

finally *adv* lastly, in conclusion, ultimately, eventually, at last, at length, in the end, conclusively, once and for all, for ever, irreversibly, irrevocably, definitely.

finance *n* economics, money

management, accounting, banking, investment, stock market, business, commerce, trade, money, funding, sponsorship, subsidy.
➤ *v* pay for, fund, sponsor, back, support, underwrite, guarantee, subsidize, capitalize, float, set up.

finances *n* accounts, affairs, budget, bank account, income, revenue, liquidity, resources, assets, capital, wealth, money, cash, funds, wherewithal. *see panel at* **account.**

financial *adj* monetary, money, pecuniary, economic, fiscal, budgetary, commercial.

financier *n* financialist, banker, stockbroker, money-maker, investor, speculator, venture capitalist.

find *v* 1 DISCOVER, locate, track down, trace, retrieve, recover, unearth, uncover, expose, reveal, come across, chance on, stumble on, meet, encounter, detect, recognize, notice, observe, perceive, realize, learn.
2 ATTAIN, achieve, win, reach, gain, obtain, get. 3 *find it difficult*: consider, think, judge, declare.
🔁 1 lose.
◇ **find out** 1 LEARN, ascertain, discover, detect, note, observe, perceive, realize.
2 UNMASK, expose, show up, uncover, reveal, disclose, catch, suss out (*sl*), rumble (*sl*), tumble to (*infml*).

finding *n* 1 FIND, discovery, breakthrough. 2 DECISION, conclusion, judgement, verdict, pronouncement, decree, recommendation, award.

fine[1] *adj* 1 EXCELLENT, outstanding, exceptional, superior, exquisite, splendid, magnificent, brilliant, beautiful, handsome, attractive, elegant, lovely, nice, good. 2 THIN, slender, sheer, gauzy, powdery, flimsy, fragile, delicate, dainty. 3 SATISFACTORY, acceptable, all right, OK (*infml*). 4 *fine weather*: bright, sunny, clear, cloudless, dry, fair.
🔁 1 mediocre. 2 thick, coarse.
4 cloudy.

fine[2] *n* penalty, punishment, forfeit, forfeiture, damages.

finger *v* touch, handle, manipulate, feel, stroke, caress, fondle, paw, fiddle with, toy with, play about with, meddle with.

finicky *adj* **1** PARTICULAR, finickety, pernickety, fussy, choosy (*infml*), fastidious, meticulous, scrupulous, critical, hypercritical, nit-picking. **2** FIDDLY, intricate, tricky, difficult, delicate.
E3 1 easy-going. **2** easy.

finish *v* **1** END, terminate, stop, cease, complete, accomplish, achieve, fulfil, discharge, deal with, do, conclude, close, wind up, settle, round off, culminate, perfect. **2** DESTROY, ruin, exterminate, get rid of, annihilate, defeat, overcome, rout, overthrow. **3** USE (UP), consume, devour, eat, drink, exhaust, drain, empty.
E3 1 begin, start.
> *n* **1** END, termination, completion, conclusion, close, ending, finale, culmination. **2** SURFACE, appearance, texture, grain, polish, shine, gloss, lustre, smoothness.
E3 1 beginning, start, commencement.

finite *adj* limited, restricted, bounded, demarcated, terminable, definable, fixed, measurable, calculable, countable, numbered.
E3 infinite.

fire *n* **1** FLAMES, blaze, bonfire, conflagration, inferno, burning, combustion. **2** PASSION, feeling, excitement, enthusiasm, spirit, intensity, heat, radiance, sparkle.
> *v* **1** IGNITE, light, kindle, set fire to, set on fire, set alight, torch (*infml*). **2** *fire a missile*: shoot, launch, set off, let off, detonate, explode. **3** DISMISS, discharge, sack (*infml*), eject. **4** EXCITE, whet, enliven, galvanize, electrify, stir, arouse, rouse, stimulate, inspire, incite, spark off, trigger off.
◇ on fire burning, alight, ignited, flaming, in flames, aflame, blazing, ablaze, fiery.

fireplace

Types of fireplace include: backboiler, boiler, bonfire, brazier, campfire, electric fire, firebox, forge, furnace, gas fire, grate, hearth, incinerator, kiln, open fire, oven, stove, paraffin stove, wood burning stove.

firework

Types of firework include: banger, Catherine wheel, cracker, Chinese cracker, firecracker, fountain, golden rain, indoor firework, jumping-jack, pinwheel, rocket, roman candle, skyrocket, sparkler, squib.

firm[1] *adj* **1** *firm ground*: dense, compressed, compact, concentrated, set, solid, hard, unyielding, stiff, rigid, inflexible. **2** FIXED, embedded, fast, tight, secure, fastened, anchored, immovable, motionless, stationary, steady, stable, sturdy, strong. **3** ADAMANT, unshakable, resolute, determined, dogged, unwavering, strict, constant, steadfast, staunch, dependable, true, sure, convinced, definite, settled, committed.
E3 1 soft, flabby. **2** unsteady. **3** hesitant.

firm[2] *n* company, corporation, business, enterprise, concern, house, establishment, institution, organization, association, partnership, syndicate, conglomerate.

first *adj* **1** INITIAL, opening, introductory, preliminary, elementary, primary, basic, fundamental. **2** ORIGINAL, earliest, earlier, prior, primitive, primeval, oldest, eldest, senior. **3** CHIEF, main, key, cardinal, principal, head, leading, ruling, sovereign, highest, uppermost, paramount, primary, prime, predominant, pre-eminent.
E3 1 last, final.
> *adv* initially, to begin with, to start with, at the outset, beforehand, originally, in preference, rather, sooner.
◇ first name forename, Christian name, baptismal name, given name.

first-rate *adj* first-class, A1, second-to-none, matchless, peerless, top, top-notch (*infml*), top-flight, leading, supreme, superior, prime, excellent, outstanding, superlative, exceptional, splendid, superb, fine, admirable.
🖃 inferior.

fish

Types of fish include: bloater, brisling, cod, coley, Dover sole, flounder, haddock, hake, halibut, herring, hoki, jellied eel, kipper, ling, mackerel, pilchard, plaice, rainbow trout, salmon, sardine, sole, sprat, trout, tuna, turbot, whitebait; bass, Bombay duck, bream, brill, carp, catfish, chub, conger eel, cuttlefish, dab, dace, dogfish, dory, eel, goldfish, guppy, marlin, minnow, monkfish, mullet, octopus, perch, pike, piranha, pollock, ray, roach, roughy, shark, skate, snapper, squid, stickleback, stingray, sturgeon, swordfish, tench, whiting; clam, cockle, crab, crayfish, crawfish (*US*), king prawn, lobster, mussel, oyster, prawn, scallop, shrimp, whelk. *see also* **shark**.

➤ *v* angle, trawl, delve, hunt, seek, invite, solicit.
◇ **fish out** produce, take out, extract, find, come up with, dredge up, haul up.

fishing *n* angling, trawling.

fit[1] *adj* **1** SUITABLE, appropriate, apt, fitting, correct, right, proper, ready, prepared, able, capable, competent, qualified, eligible, worthy. **2** HEALTHY, well, able-bodied, in good form, in good shape, sound, sturdy, strong, robust, hale and hearty.
🖃 **1** unsuitable, unworthy. **2** unfit.
➤ *v* **1** MATCH, correspond, conform, follow, agree, concur, tally, suit, harmonize, go, belong, dovetail, interlock, join, meet, arrange, place, position, accommodate. **2** ALTER, modify, change, adjust, adapt, tailor, shape, fashion.
◇ **fit out** equip, rig out, kit out, outfit, provide, supply, furnish, prepare, arm.

fit[2] *n* seizure, convulsion, spasm, paroxysm, attack, outbreak, bout, spell, burst, surge, outburst, eruption, explosion.

fitful *adj* sporadic, intermittent, occasional, spasmodic, erratic, irregular, uneven, broken, disturbed.
🖃 steady, regular.

fitted *adj* **1** *fitted wardrobe*: built-in, permanent. **2** EQUIPPED, rigged out, provided, furnished, appointed, prepared, armed. **3** SUITED, right, suitable, fit, qualified.

fitting *adj* apt, appropriate, suitable, fit, correct, right, proper, seemly, meet (*fml*), desirable, deserved.
🖃 unsuitable, improper.
➤ *n* connection, attachment, accessory, part, component, piece, unit, fitment.

fittings *n* equipment, furnishings, furniture, fixtures, installations, fitments, accessories, extras.

fix *v* **1** FASTEN, secure, tie, bind, attach, join, connect, link, couple, anchor, pin, nail, rivet, stick, glue, cement, set, harden, solidify, stiffen, stabilize, plant, root, implant, embed, establish, install, place, locate, position. **2** *fix a date*: arrange, set, specify, define, agree on, decide, determine, settle, resolve, finalize. **3** MEND, repair, correct, rectify, adjust, restore.
🖃 **1** move, shift. **3** damage.
➤ *n* (*infml*) dilemma, quandary, predicament, plight, difficulty, hole (*infml*), corner, spot (*infml*), mess, muddle.
◇ **fix up** arrange, organize, plan, lay on, provide, supply, furnish, equip, settle, sort out, produce, bring about.

fixation *n* preoccupation, obsession, mania, fetish, thing (*infml*), infatuation, compulsion, hang-up (*infml*), complex.

fixed *adj* decided, settled, established, definite, arranged, planned, set, firm, rigid, inflexible, steady, secure, fast, rooted, permanent.
🖃 variable.

fizz *v* effervesce, sparkle, bubble, froth,

foam, fizzle, hiss, sizzle, sputter, spit.

fizzy *adj* effervescent, sparkling, aerated, carbonated, gassy, bubbly, bubbling, frothy, foaming.

flabbergasted (*infml*) *adj* amazed, confounded, astonished, astounded, staggered, dumbfounded, speechless, stunned, dazed, overcome, overawed, overwhelmed, bowled over.

flabby *adj* fleshy, soft, yielding, flaccid, limp, floppy, drooping, hanging, sagging, slack, loose, lax, weak, feeble.
Ea firm, strong.

flag[1] *v* lessen, diminish, decline, fall (off), abate, subside, sink, slump, dwindle, peter out, fade, fail, weaken, slow, falter, tire, weary, wilt, droop, sag, flop, faint, die.
Ea revive.

flag[2] *n* ensign, jack, pennant, colours, standard, banner, streamer.

Types of flag include: banner, bunting, burgee, colours, cornet, gonfalon, jack, oriflamme, pennant, pilot flag, signal flag, standard, streamer, swallow tail.

Names of flags include: Blue Ensign, Blue Peter, Crescent, Hammer and Sickle, Jolly Roger, Old Glory, Olympic Flag, Red Crescent, Red Cross, Red Ensign, Rising Sun, Saltire, Skull and Crossbones, Star Spangled Banner, Stars and Stripes, Tricolour, Union Jack, White Ensign, Yellow Jack.

➤ *v* 1 SIGNAL, wave, salute, motion. 2 MARK, indicate, label, tag, note.

flail *v* thresh, thrash, beat, whip.

flair *n* skill, ability, aptitude, faculty, gift, talent, facility, knack, mastery, genius, feel, taste, discernment, acumen, style, elegance, stylishness, panache.
Ea inability, ineptitude.

flake *n* scale, peeling, paring, shaving, sliver, wafer, chip, splinter.
➤ *v* scale, peel, chip, splinter.

flamboyant *adj* showy, ostentatious,

flashy, gaudy, colourful, brilliant, dazzling, striking, extravagant, rich, elaborate, ornate, florid, OTT (*infml*).
Ea modest, restrained.

flame *v* burn, flare, blaze, glare, flash, beam, shine, glow, radiate.
➤ *n* 1 FIRE, blaze, light, brightness, heat, warmth. 2 PASSION, ardour, fervour, enthusiasm, zeal, intensity, radiance.

flaming *adj* 1 *a flaming torch*: burning, alight, aflame, blazing, fiery, brilliant, scintillating, red-hot, glowing, smouldering. 2 INTENSE, vivid, aroused, impassioned, hot, raging, frenzied.

flammable *adj* inflammable, ignitable, combustible.
Ea non-flammable, incombustible, flameproof, fire-resistant.

flank *n* side, edge, quarter, wing, loin, hip, thigh.
➤ *v* edge, fringe, skirt, line, border, bound, confine, wall, screen.

flap *v* flutter, vibrate, wave, agitate, shake, wag, swing, swish, thrash, beat.
➤ *n* 1 FOLD, fly, lapel, tab, lug, tag, tail, skirt, aileron. 2 (*infml*) PANIC, state (*infml*), fuss, commotion, fluster, agitation, flutter, dither, tizzy (*infml*).

flare *v* 1 FLAME, burn, blaze, glare, flash, flicker, burst, explode, erupt. 2 BROADEN, widen, flare out, spread out, splay.
➤ *n* 1 FLAME, blaze, glare, flash, flicker, burst. 2 BROADENING, widening, splay.
◇ **flare up** erupt, break out, explode, blow up.

flash *v* 1 BEAM, shine, light up, flare, blaze, glare, gleam, glint, flicker, twinkle, sparkle, glitter, shimmer. 2 *the train flashed past*: streak, fly, dart, race, dash.
➤ *n* beam, ray, shaft, spark, blaze, flare, burst, streak, gleam, glint, flicker, twinkle, sparkle, shimmer.

flashy *adj* showy, ostentatious, flamboyant, glamorous, bold, loud, garish, gaudy, jazzy, flash, tawdry, cheap, vulgar, tasteless.
Ea plain, tasteful.

flat¹ *adj* **1** LEVEL, plane, even, smooth, uniform, unbroken, horizontal, outstretched, prostrate, prone, recumbent, reclining, low. **2** DULL, boring, monotonous, tedious, uninteresting, unexciting, stale, lifeless, dead, spiritless, lacklustre, vapid, insipid, weak, watery, empty, pointless. **3** *a flat refusal*: absolute, utter, total, unequivocal, categorical, positive, unconditional, unqualified, point-blank, direct, straight, explicit, plain, final. **4** *a flat tyre*: punctured, burst, deflated, collapsed.
⊟ 1 bumpy, vertical. **2** exciting, full. **3** equivocal.
◇ **flat out** at top speed, at full speed, all out, for all one is worth.

flat² *n* apartment, penthouse, maisonette, tenement, flatlet, rooms, suite, bedsit(ter).

flatten *v* **1** SMOOTH, iron, press, roll, crush, squash, compress, level, even out. **2** KNOCK DOWN, prostrate, floor, fell, demolish, raze, overwhelm, subdue.

flatter *v* praise, compliment, sweet-talk (*infml*), adulate, fawn, butter up (*infml*), wheedle, humour, play up to, court, pay court to, curry favour with.
⊟ criticize.

flattery *n* adulation, eulogy, sweet talk (*infml*), soft soap (*infml*), flannel (*infml*), blarney, cajolery, fawning, toadyism, sycophancy, ingratiation, servility.
⊟ criticism.

flavour *n* **1** TASTE, tang, smack, savour, relish, zest, zing (*infml*), aroma, odour. **2** QUALITY, property, character, style, aspect, feeling, feel, atmosphere. **3** HINT, suggestion, touch, tinge, tone.
➤ *v* season, spice, ginger up, infuse, imbue.

flavouring *n* seasoning, zest, essence, extract, additive.

flaw *n* defect, imperfection, fault, blemish, spot, mark, speck, crack, crevice, fissure, cleft, split, rift, break, fracture, weakness, shortcoming, failing, fallacy, lapse, slip, error, mistake.

flawed *adj* imperfect, defective, faulty, blemished, marked, damaged, spoilt, marred, cracked, chipped, broken, unsound, fallacious, erroneous.
⊟ flawless, perfect.

flawless *adj* perfect, faultless, unblemished, spotless, immaculate, stainless, sound, intact, whole, unbroken, undamaged.
⊟ flawed, imperfect.

fleck *v* dot, spot, mark, speckle, dapple, mottle, streak, sprinkle, dust.
➤ *n* dot, point, spot, mark, speck, speckle, streak.

flee *v* run away, bolt, fly, take flight, take off, make off, cut and run, escape, get away, decamp, abscond, leave, depart, withdraw, retreat, vanish, disappear.
⊟ stay.

fleet *n* flotilla, armada, navy, task force, squadron.

fleeting *adj* short, brief, flying, short-lived, momentary, ephemeral, transient, transitory, passing, temporary.
⊟ lasting, permanent.

flesh *n* body, tissue, fat, muscle, brawn, skin, meat, pulp, substance, matter, physicality.

flex *v* bend, bow, curve, angle, ply, double up, tighten, contract.
⊟ straighten, extend.
➤ *n* cable, wire, lead, cord.

flexible *adj* **1** BENDABLE, bendy (*infml*), pliable, pliant, plastic, malleable, mouldable, elastic, stretchy, springy, yielding, supple, lithe, limber, double-jointed, mobile. **2** ADAPTABLE, adjustable, amenable, accommodating, variable, open.
⊟ 1 inflexible, rigid.

flick *v* hit, strike, rap, tap, touch, dab, flip, jerk, whip, lash.
➤ *n* rap, tap, touch, dab, flip, jerk, click.
◇ **flick through** flip through, thumb through, leaf through, glance at, skim, scan.

flicker *v* flash, blink, wink, twinkle, sparkle, glimmer, shimmer, gutter,

flutter, vibrate, quiver, waver.
➤ *n* flash, gleam, glint, twinkle, glimmer, spark, trace, drop, iota, atom, indication.

flight[1] *n* **1** FLYING, aviation, aeronautics, air transport, air travel. **2** JOURNEY, trip, voyage.

flight[2] *n* fleeing, escape, getaway, breakaway, exit, departure, exodus, retreat.

flimsy *adj* thin, fine, light, slight, insubstantial, ethereal, fragile, delicate, shaky, rickety, makeshift, weak, feeble, meagre, inadequate, shallow, superficial, trivial, poor, unconvincing, implausible.
🖾 sturdy.

flinch *v* wince, start, cringe, cower, quail, tremble, shake, quake, shudder, shiver, shrink, recoil, draw back, balk, shy away, duck, shirk, withdraw, retreat, flee.

fling *v* throw, hurl, pitch, lob, toss, chuck (*infml*), cast, sling, catapult, launch, propel, send, let fly, heave, jerk.

flip *v* flick, spin, twirl, twist, turn, toss, throw, cast, pitch, jerk, flap.
➤ *n* flick, spin, twirl, twist, turn, toss, jerk, flap.

flippant *adj* facetious, light-hearted, frivolous, superficial, offhand, flip, glib, pert, saucy (*infml*), cheeky, impudent, impertinent, rude, disrespectful, irreverent.
🖾 serious, respectful.

flirt *v* chat up, make up to, lead on, philander, dally.
◇ **flirt with** consider, entertain, toy with, play with, trifle with, dabble in, try.

flit *v* dart, speed, flash, fly, wing, flutter, whisk, skim, slip, pass, bob, dance.

float *v* **1** GLIDE, sail, swim, bob, drift, waft, hover, hang. **2** LAUNCH, initiate, set up, promote.
🖾 **1** sink.

floating *adj* **1** AFLOAT, buoyant, unsinkable, sailing, swimming, bobbing, drifting. **2** VARIABLE, fluctuating, movable, migratory, transitory, wandering, unattached, free, uncommitted.
🖾 **1** sinking. **2** fixed.

flock *v* herd, swarm, troop, converge, mass, bunch, cluster, huddle, crowd, throng, group, gather, collect, congregate.
➤ *n* herd, pack, crowd, throng, multitude, mass, bunch, cluster, group, gathering, assembly, congregation.

flog *v* beat, whip, lash, flagellate, scourge, birch, cane, flay, drub, thrash, whack (*infml*), chastise, punish.

flogging *n* beating, whipping, lashing, flagellation, scourging, birching, caning, flaying, thrashing, hiding.

flood *v* **1** DELUGE, inundate, soak, drench, saturate, fill, overflow, immerse, submerge, engulf, swamp, overwhelm, drown. **2** FLOW, pour, stream, rush, surge, gush.
➤ *n* deluge, inundation, downpour, torrent, flow, tide, stream, rush, spate, outpouring, overflow, glut, excess, abundance, profusion.
🖾 drought, trickle, dearth.

floor *n* **1** FLOORING, ground, base, basis. **2** *on the third floor*: storey, level, stage, landing, deck, tier.
➤ *v* (*infml*) defeat, overwhelm, beat, stump (*infml*), frustrate, confound, perplex, baffle, puzzle, bewilder, disconcert, throw.

flop *v* **1** DROOP, hang, dangle, sag, drop, fall, topple, tumble, slump, collapse. **2** FAIL, misfire, fall flat, founder, fold.
➤ *n* failure, non-starter, fiasco, debacle, wash-out (*infml*), disaster.

floppy *adj* droopy, hanging, dangling, sagging, limp, loose, baggy, soft, flabby.
🖾 firm.

florid *adj* **1** FLOWERY, ornate, elaborate, fussy, overelaborate, OTT (*infml*), baroque, rococo, flamboyant, grandiloquent. **2** *a florid complexion*: ruddy, red, purple.
🖾 **1** plain, simple. **2** pale.

flotsam *n* jetsam, wreckage, debris, rubbish, junk, oddments.

flounder v wallow, struggle, grope, fumble, blunder, stagger, stumble, falter.

flourish v 1 THRIVE, grow, wax, increase, flower, blossom, bloom, develop, progress, get on, do well, prosper, succeed, boom. 2 BRANDISH, wave, shake, twirl, swing, display, wield, flaunt, parade, vaunt.

▪ 1 decline, languish, fail.

➤ n display, parade, show, gesture, wave, sweep, fanfare, ornament, decoration, panache, pizzazz (*infml*).

flourishing adj thriving, blooming, prosperous, successful, booming.

flout v defy, disobey, violate, break, disregard, spurn, reject, scorn, jeer at, scoff at, mock, ridicule.

▪ obey, respect, regard.

flow v 1 CIRCULATE, ooze, trickle, ripple, bubble, well, spurt, squirt, gush, spill, run, pour, cascade, rush, stream, teem, flood, overflow, surge, sweep, move, drift, slip, slide, glide, roll, swirl. 2 ORIGINATE, derive, arise, spring, emerge, issue, result, proceed, emanate.

➤ n course, flux, tide, current, drift, outpouring, stream, deluge, cascade, spurt, gush, flood, spate, abundance, plenty.

flower n 1 BLOOM, blossom, bud, floret. 2 BEST, cream, pick, choice, elite.

Flowers include: African violet, alyssum, anemone, aster, aubrietia, azalea, begonia, bluebell, busy lizzie (impatiens), calendula, candytuft, carnation, chrysanthemum, cornflower, cowslip, crocus, cyclamen, daffodil, dahlia, daisy, delphinium, forget-me-not, foxglove (digitalis), freesia, fuchsia, gardenia, geranium, gladioli, hollyhock, hyacinth, iris (flag), lily, lily-of-the-valley, lobelia, lupin, marigold, narcissus, nasturtium, nemesia, nicotiana, night-scented stock, orchid, pansy, petunia, pink (dianthus), phlox, poinsettia, polyanthus, poppy, primrose, primula, rose, salvia, snapdragon (antirrhinum), snowdrop, stock, sunflower, sweet pea, sweet william, tulip, verbena, viola, violet, wallflower, zinnia. *see also* **bulb**; **plant**; **shrub**; **wild flower**.

Parts of a flower include: anther, calyx, capitulum, carpel, corolla, corymb, dichasium, filament, gynoecium, monochasium, nectary, ovary, ovule, panicle, pedicel, petal, pistil, raceme, receptacle, sepal, spadix, spike, stalk, stamen, stigma, style, thalamus, torus, umbel.

➤ v bud, burgeon, bloom, blossom, open, come out.

flowery adj florid, ornate, elaborate, fancy, baroque, rhetorical.

▪ plain, simple.

fluctuate v vary, change, alter, shift, rise and fall, seesaw, ebb and flow, alternate, swing, sway, oscillate, vacillate, waver.

fluent adj flowing, smooth, easy, effortless, articulate, eloquent, voluble, glib, ready.

▪ broken, inarticulate, tongue-tied.

fluff n down, nap, pile, fuzz, floss, lint, dust.

fluffy adj furry, fuzzy, downy, feathery, fleecy, woolly, hairy, shaggy, velvety, silky, soft.

fluid adj 1 LIQUID, liquefied, aqueous, watery, running, runny, melted, molten. 2 *a fluid situation*: variable, changeable, unstable, inconstant, shifting, mobile, adjustable, adaptable, flexible, open. 3 *fluid movements*: flowing, smooth, graceful.

▪ 1 solid. 2 stable.

➤ n liquid, solution, liquor, juice, gas, vapour.

flurry n 1 BURST, outbreak, spell, spurt, gust, blast, squall. 2 BUSTLE, hurry, fluster, fuss, to-do, commotion, tumult, whirl, disturbance, stir, flap (*infml*).

flush[1] v 1 BLUSH, go red, redden,

crimson, colour, burn, glow, suffuse.
2 CLEANSE, wash, rinse, hose, swab, clear, empty, evacuate.
➤ *adj* **1** ABUNDANT, lavish, generous, full, overflowing, rich, wealthy, moneyed, prosperous, well-off, well-heeled, well-to-do. **2** LEVEL, even, smooth, flat, plane, square, true.

flush² *v* start, rouse, disturb, drive out, force out, expel, eject, run to earth, discover, uncover.

fluster *v* bother, upset, embarrass, disturb, perturb, agitate, ruffle, discompose, confuse, confound, unnerve, disconcert, rattle (*infml*), put off, distract.
◨ calm.
➤ *n* flurry, bustle, commotion, upset, disturbance, turmoil, state (*infml*), agitation, embarrassment, flap (*infml*), dither, tizzy (*infml*).
◨ calm.

fluted *adj* grooved, furrowed, channelled, corrugated, ribbed, ridged.

flutter *v* flap, wave, beat, bat, flicker, vibrate, palpitate, agitate, shake, tremble, quiver, shiver, ruffle, ripple, twitch, toss, waver, fluctuate.
➤ *n* flapping, beat, flicker, vibration, palpitation, tremble, tremor, quiver, shiver, shudder, twitch.

flux *n* fluctuation, instability, change, alteration, modification, fluidity, flow, movement, motion, transition, development.
◨ stability, rest.

fly *v* **1** TAKE OFF, rise, ascend, mount, soar, glide, float, hover, flit, wing.
2 RACE, sprint, dash, tear, rush, hurry, speed, zoom, shoot, dart, career.
◇ **fly at** attack, go for, fall upon.

foam *n* froth, lather, suds, head, bubbles, effervescence.
➤ *v* froth, lather, bubble, effervesce, fizz, boil, seethe.

fob off foist, pass off, palm off (*infml*), get rid of, dump, unload, inflict, impose, deceive, put off.

focus *n* focal point, target, centre,

heart, core, nucleus, kernel, crux, hub, axis, linchpin, pivot, hinge.
➤ *v* converge, meet, join, centre, concentrate, aim, direct, fix, spotlight, home in, zoom in, zero in (*infml*).

fog *n* **1** MIST, haze, cloud, gloom, murkiness, smog, pea-souper.
2 PERPLEXITY, puzzlement, confusion, bewilderment, daze, trance, vagueness, obscurity.
➤ *v* mist, steam up, cloud, dull, dim, darken, obscure, blur, confuse, muddle.

foggy *adj* misty, hazy, smoggy, cloudy, murky, dark, shadowy, dim, indistinct, obscure.
◨ clear.

foil¹ *v* defeat, outwit, frustrate, thwart, baffle, counter, nullify, stop, check, obstruct, block, circumvent, elude.
◨ abet.

foil² *n* setting, background, relief, contrast, complement, balance.

fold *v* **1** BEND, ply, double, overlap, tuck, pleat, crease, crumple, crimp, crinkle.
2 (*infml*) *the business folded*: fail, go bust, shut down, collapse, crash.
3 ENFOLD, embrace, hug, clasp, envelop, wrap (up), enclose, entwine, intertwine.
➤ *n* bend, turn, layer, ply, overlap, tuck, pleat, crease, knife-edge, line, wrinkle, furrow, corrugation.

folder *n* file, binder, folio, portfolio, envelope, holder.

folk *n* people, society, nation, race, tribe, clan, family, kin, kindred.
➤ *adj* ethnic, national, traditional, native, indigenous, tribal, ancestral.

follow *v* **1** *night follows day*: come after, succeed, come next, replace, supersede, supplant. **2** CHASE, pursue, go after, hunt, track, trail, shadow, tail, hound, catch.
3 ACCOMPANY, go (along) with, escort, attend. **4** RESULT, ensue, develop, emanate, arise. **5** OBEY, comply with, adhere to, heed, mind, observe, conform to, carry out, practise. **6** GRASP, understand, comprehend, fathom.
◨ **1** precede. **3** abandon, desert.
5 disobey.

◇ **follow through** continue, pursue, see through, finish, complete, conclude, fulfil, implement.

◇ **follow up** investigate, check out, continue, pursue, reinforce, consolidate.

follower *n* attendant, retainer, helper, companion, sidekick (*infml*), apostle, disciple, pupil, imitator, emulator, adherent, hanger-on, believer, convert, backer, supporter, admirer, fan, devotee, freak (*infml*), buff (*infml*). ☲ leader, opponent.

following *adj* subsequent, next, succeeding, successive, resulting, ensuing, consequent, later. ☲ previous.

➤ *n* followers, suite, retinue, entourage, circle, fans, supporters, support, backing, patronage, clientèle, audience, public.

folly *n* foolishness, stupidity, senselessness, rashness, recklessness, irresponsibility, indiscretion, craziness, madness, lunacy, insanity, idiocy, imbecility, silliness, absurdity, nonsense. ☲ wisdom, prudence, sanity.

fond *adj* affectionate, warm, tender, caring, loving, adoring, devoted, doting, indulgent.

◇ **fond of** partial to, attached to, enamoured of, keen on, addicted to, hooked on.

fondle *v* caress, stroke, pat, pet, cuddle.

food *n* foodstuffs, comestibles (*fml*), eatables, victuals, provisions, stores, rations, eats (*infml*), grub (*sl*), nosh (*sl*), refreshment, sustenance, nourishment, nutrition, nutriment, subsistence, feed, fodder, diet, fare, cooking, cuisine, menu, board, table, larder.

Kinds of food include: soup, broth, minestrone, bouillabaisse, borsch, chowder, consommé, gazpacho, vichyssoise; chips, French fries, ratatouille, sauerkraut, bubble-and-squeak, nut cutlet, cauliflower cheese, chilladas, hummus, macaroni cheese;

pasta, cannelloni, fettuccine, ravioli, spaghetti bolognese, tortellini, lasagne; fish and chips, fishcake, fish-finger, fisherman's pie, kedgeree, gefilte fish, kipper, pickled herring, scampi, calamari, prawn cocktail, caviar; meat, casserole, cassoulet, goulash, hotpot, shepherd's pie, cottage pie, chilli con carne, balti, biriyani, chop suey, burrito, empanada, enchilada, fajita, taco, moussaka, paella, samosa, pizza, ragout, risotto, tandoori, vindaloo, Wiener schnitzel, smöga[an]sbord, stroganoff, Scotch woodcock, welsh rarebit, faggot, haggis, sausage, salami, chorizo, frankfurter, hot dog, fritter, hamburger, McDonald's®, Big Mac®, Wimpy®, bacon, egg, omelette, frittata, quiche, tofu, Quorn®, Yorkshire pudding, toad-in-the-hole; ice cream, charlotte russe, cheesecake, crème caramel, egg custard, fruit salad, fruit cocktail, ganache, gateau, kulfi, millefeuilles, pavlova, profiterole, Sachertorte, soufflé, summer pudding, Bakewell tart, banoffee pie, trifle, yogurt, sundae, syllabub, queen of puddings, Christmas pudding, tapioca, rice pudding, roly-poly pudding, spotted dick, tiramisu, zabaglione; doughnut, Chelsea bun, Eccles cake, éclair, flapjack, fruitcake, Danish pastry, Genoa cake, Battenburg cake, Madeira cake, lardy cake, hot-cross-bun, brownie, muffin, ginger nut, gingerbread, shortbread, ginger snap, macaroon, Garibaldi biscuit; bread, French bread, French toast, pumpernickel, cottage loaf, croissant; gravy, fondue, salad cream, mayonnaise, French dressing, olive oil, balsamic vinegar; dip, guacamole, salsa, hummus, taramasalata; *sauces*: tartare, Worcestershire, bechamel, white, barbecue, tomato ketchup, hollandaise, Tabasco®, apple, mint, cranberry, horseradish, pesto. *see also* **bread**; **cake**; **cheese**; **fish**; **fruit**; **meat**; **nut**;

pasta; pastry; sugar; sweets; vegetable; vegetable dishes.

fool n blockhead, fat-head, nincompoop (*infml*), ass (*infml*), chump (*infml*), ninny (*infml*), clot (*infml*), dope (*infml*), wally (*sl*), divvy (*sl*), dork (*sl*), twit (*infml*), nitwit (*infml*), nit (*infml*), dunce, dimwit, simpleton, halfwit, idiot, imbecile, moron, dupe, sucker (*infml*), mug (*infml*), stooge, clown, buffoon, jester.
➤ v deceive, take in, delude, mislead, dupe, gull, hoodwink, put one over on, trick, hoax, con (*infml*), cheat, swindle, diddle (*infml*), string along (*infml*), have on (*infml*), kid (*infml*), tease, joke, jest.
◇ **fool about** lark about, horse around (*sl*), play about, mess about (*infml*), mess around (*infml*).

foolhardy adj rash, reckless, imprudent, ill-advised, irresponsible.
Ea cautious, prudent.

foolish adj stupid, senseless, unwise, ill-advised, ill-considered, short-sighted, half-baked, daft (*infml*), crazy, mad, insane, idiotic, moronic, harebrained, half-witted, simple-minded, simple, unintelligent, inept, inane, silly, absurd, ridiculous, ludicrous, nonsensical.
Ea wise, prudent.

foolproof adj idiot-proof, infallible, fail-safe, sure, certain, sure-fire (*infml*), guaranteed.
Ea unreliable.

footing n base, foundation, basis, ground, relations, relationship, terms, conditions, state, standing, status, grade, rank, position, balance, foothold, purchase.

footprint n footmark, track, trail, trace, vestige.

footwear

Types of footwear include: shoe, court shoe, brogue, casual, lace-up (*infml*), slip-on (*infml*), slingback, sandal, espadrille, jelly, stiletto heel, kitten heel, platform heel, moccasin, Doc Martens®, slipper, mule, flip-flop (*infml*), thong, boot, bootee, Chelsea boot, wellington boot, welly (*infml*), galosh, gumboot, football boot, rugby boot, tennis shoe, plimsoll, pump, sneaker, trainer, ballet shoe, clog, sabot, snowshoe, beetle-crusher (*sl*), brothel creeper (*sl*).

forage n fodder, pasturage, feed, food, foodstuffs.
➤ v rummage, search, cast about, scour, hunt, scavenge, ransack, plunder, raid.

forbid v prohibit, disallow, ban, proscribe, interdict, veto, refuse, deny, outlaw, debar, exclude, rule out, preclude, prevent, block, hinder, inhibit.
Ea allow, permit, approve.

forbidden adj prohibited, banned, proscribed, taboo, vetoed, outlawed, out of bounds.

forbidding adj stern, formidable, awesome, daunting, off-putting, uninviting, menacing, threatening, ominous, sinister, frightening.
Ea approachable, congenial.

force n 1 COMPULSION, impulse, influence, coercion, constraint, pressure, duress, violence, aggression. 2 POWER, might, strength, intensity, effort, energy, vigour, drive, dynamism, stress, emphasis. 3 ARMY, troop, body, corps, regiment, squadron, battalion, division, unit, detachment, patrol.
Ea 2 weakness.
➤ v 1 COMPEL, make, oblige, necessitate, urge, coerce, constrain, press, pressurize, lean on (*infml*), press-gang, bulldoze, drive, propel, push, thrust. 2 PRISE, wrench, wrest, extort, exact, wring.

forced adj unnatural, stiff, wooden, stilted, laboured, strained, false, artificial, contrived, feigned, affected, insincere.
Ea spontaneous, sincere.

forceful adj strong, mighty, powerful, potent, effective, compelling, convincing, persuasive, cogent, telling,

weighty, urgent, emphatic, vehement, forcible, dynamic, energetic, vigorous.
🔁 weak, feeble.

forebear *n* ancestor, forefather, father, predecessor, forerunner, antecedent.
🔁 descendant.

foreboding *n* misgiving, anxiety, worry, apprehension, dread, fear, omen, sign, token, premonition, warning, prediction, prognostication, intuition, feeling.

forecast *v* predict, prophesy, foretell, foresee, anticipate, expect, estimate, calculate.
➤ *n* prediction, prophecy, expectation, prognosis, outlook, projection, guess, guesstimate (*infml*).

forefront *n* front, front line, firing line, van, vanguard, lead, fore, avant-garde.
🔁 rear.

foregoing *adj* preceding, antecedent, above, previous, earlier, former, prior.
🔁 following.

foreign *adj* alien, immigrant, imported, international, external, outside, overseas, exotic, faraway, distant, remote, strange, unfamiliar, unknown, uncharacteristic, incongruous, extraneous, borrowed.
🔁 native, indigenous.

foreigner *n* alien, immigrant, incomer, stranger, newcomer, visitor.
🔁 native.

foremost *adj* first, leading, front, chief, main, principal, primary, cardinal, paramount, central, highest, uppermost, supreme, premium, prime, pre-eminent.

forerunner *n* predecessor, ancestor, antecedent, precursor, harbinger, herald, envoy, sign, token.
🔁 successor, follower.

foresee *v* envisage, anticipate, expect, forecast, predict, prophesy, prognosticate, foretell, forebode, divine.

foreshadow *v* prefigure, presage,

augur, predict, prophesy, signal, indicate, promise.

foresight *n* anticipation, planning, forethought, far-sightedness, vision, caution, prudence, circumspection, care, readiness, preparedness, provision, precaution.
🔁 improvidence.

forestall *v* pre-empt, anticipate, preclude, obviate, avert, head off, ward off, parry, balk, frustrate, thwart, hinder, prevent.

foretaste *n* preview, trailer, sample, specimen, example, whiff, indication, warning, premonition.

foretell *v* prophesy, forecast, predict, prognosticate, augur, presage, signify, foreshadow, forewarn.

forethought *n* preparation, planning, forward planning, provision, precaution, anticipation, foresight, far-sightedness, circumspection, prudence, caution.
🔁 improvidence, carelessness.

forever *adv* continually, constantly, persistently, incessantly, perpetually, endlessly, eternally, always, evermore, for all time, permanently.

foreword *n* preface, introduction, prologue.
🔁 appendix, postscript, epilogue.

forfeit *n* loss, surrender, confiscation, sequestration, penalty, fine, damages.
➤ *v* lose, give up, surrender, relinquish, sacrifice, forgo, renounce, abandon.

forge *v* 1 MAKE, mould, cast, shape, form, fashion, beat out, hammer out, work, create, invent. **2** *forge a document*: fake, counterfeit, falsify, copy, imitate, simulate, feign.

forgery *n* fake, counterfeit, copy, replica, reproduction, imitation, dud (*infml*), phoney (*infml*), sham, fraud.
🔁 original.

forget *v* omit, fail, neglect, let slip, overlook, disregard, ignore, lose sight of, dismiss, think no more of, unlearn.
🔁 remember, recall, recollect.

forgetful *adj* absent-minded, dreamy,

inattentive, oblivious, negligent, lax, heedless.

☒ attentive, heedful.

forgive v pardon, absolve, excuse, exonerate, exculpate, acquit, remit, let off, overlook, condone.

☒ punish, censure.

forgiveness n pardon, absolution, exoneration, acquittal, remission, amnesty, mercy, clemency, leniency.

☒ punishment, censure, blame.

forgiving adj merciful, clement, lenient, tolerant, forbearing, indulgent, kind, humane, compassionate, soft-hearted, mild.

☒ merciless, censorious, harsh.

forgo v give up, yield, surrender, relinquish, sacrifice, forfeit, waive, renounce, abandon, resign, pass up, do without, abstain from, refrain from.

☒ claim, indulge in.

fork v split, divide, part, separate, diverge, branch (off).

forlorn adj deserted, abandoned, forsaken, forgotten, bereft, friendless, lonely, lost, homeless, destitute, desolate, hopeless, unhappy, miserable, wretched, helpless, pathetic, pitiable.

☒ cheerful.

form v 1 SHAPE, mould, model, fashion, make, manufacture, produce, create, found, establish, build, construct, assemble, put together, arrange, organize. 2 COMPRISE, constitute, make up, compose. 3 APPEAR, take shape, materialize, crystallize, grow, develop.

➤ n 1 APPEARANCE, shape, mould, cast, cut, outline, silhouette, figure, build, frame, structure, format, model, pattern, design, arrangement, organization, system. 2 a form of punishment: type, kind, sort, order, species, variety, genre, style, manner, nature, character, description. 3 CLASS, year, grade, stream. 4 on top form: health, fitness, fettle, condition, spirits. 5 ETIQUETTE, protocol, custom, convention, ritual, behaviour, manners. 6 QUESTIONNAIRE, document, paper, sheet.

formal adj 1 OFFICIAL, ceremonial, stately, solemn, conventional, orthodox, correct, fixed, set, regular. 2 PRIM, starchy, stiff, strict, rigid, precise, exact, punctilious, ceremonious, stilted, reserved.

☒ 2 informal, casual.

formality n custom, convention, ceremony, ritual, procedure, matter of form, bureaucracy, red tape, protocol, etiquette, form, correctness, propriety, decorum, politeness.

☒ informality.

formation n 1 STRUCTURE, construction, composition, constitution, configuration, format, organization, arrangement, grouping, pattern, design, figure. 2 CREATION, generation, production, manufacture, appearance, development, establishment.

former adj past, ex-, one-time, sometime, late, departed, old, old-time, ancient, bygone, earlier, prior, previous, preceding, antecedent, foregoing, above.

☒ current, present, future, following.

formerly adv once, previously, earlier, before, at one time, lately.

☒ currently, now, later.

formidable adj daunting, challenging, intimidating, threatening, frightening, terrifying, terrific, frightful, fearful, great, huge, tremendous, prodigious, impressive, awesome, overwhelming, staggering.

formula n recipe, prescription, proposal, blueprint, code, wording, rubric, rule, principle, form, procedure, technique, method, way.

formulate v create, invent, originate, found, form, devise, work out, plan, design, draw up, frame, define, express, state, specify, detail, develop, evolve.

forsake v desert, abandon, jilt, throw over, discard, jettison, reject, disown, leave, quit, give up, surrender, relinquish, renounce, forgo.

fort n fortress, castle, tower, citadel,

stronghold, fortification, garrison, station, camp.

forthcoming *adj* **1** *their forthcoming wedding*: impending, imminent, approaching, coming, future, prospective, projected, expected. **2** COMMUNICATIVE, talkative, chatty, conversational, sociable, informative, expansive, open, frank, direct.
🔁 **2** reticent, reserved.

forthright *adj* direct, straightforward, blunt, frank, candid, plain, open, bold, outspoken.
🔁 devious, secretive.

fortify *v* **1** STRENGTHEN, reinforce, brace, shore up, buttress, garrison, defend, protect, secure. **2** INVIGORATE, sustain, support, boost, encourage, hearten, cheer, reassure.
🔁 **1** weaken.

fortitude *n* courage, bravery, valour, grit, pluck, resolution, determination, perseverance, firmness, strength of mind, willpower, hardihood, endurance, stoicism.
🔁 cowardice, fear.

fortuitous *adj* accidental, chance, random, arbitrary, casual, incidental, unforeseen, lucky, fortunate, providential.
🔁 intentional, planned.

fortunate *adj* lucky, providential, happy, felicitous, prosperous, successful, well-off, timely, well-timed, opportune, convenient, propitious, advantageous, favourable, auspicious.
🔁 unlucky, unfortunate, unhappy.

fortune *n* **1** WEALTH, riches, treasure, mint (*infml*), pile (*infml*), income, means, assets, estate, property, possessions, affluence, prosperity, success. **2** LUCK, chance, accident, providence, fate, destiny, doom, lot, portion, life, history, future.

forward *adj* **1** FIRST, head, front, fore, foremost, leading, onward, progressive, go-ahead, forward-looking, far-sighted, enterprising. **2** CONFIDENT, assertive, pushy, bold, audacious, brazen, brash, barefaced, cocky, cheeky, impudent,

impertinent, fresh (*sl*), familiar, presumptuous. **3** EARLY, advance, precocious, premature, advanced, well-advanced, well-developed.
🔁 **1** backward, retrograde. **2** shy, modest. **3** late, retarded.
➤ *adv* forwards, ahead, on, onward, out, into view.
➤ *v* advance, promote, further, foster, encourage, support, back, favour, help, assist, aid, facilitate, accelerate, speed, hurry, hasten, expedite, dispatch, send (on), post, transport, ship.
🔁 impede, obstruct, hinder, slow.

foster *v* raise, rear, bring up, nurse, care for, take care of, nourish, feed, sustain, support, promote, advance, encourage, stimulate, cultivate, nurture, cherish, entertain, harbour.
🔁 neglect, discourage.

foul *adj* **1** DIRTY, filthy, unclean, tainted, polluted, contaminated, rank, fetid, stinking, smelly, putrid, rotten, odious, nauseating, offensive, repulsive, revolting, disgusting, squalid. **2** *foul language*: obscene, lewd, smutty, indecent, coarse, vulgar, gross, blasphemous, abusive. **3** NASTY, disagreeable, wicked, vicious, vile, base, abhorrent, disgraceful, shameful. **4** *foul weather*: bad, unpleasant, rainy, wet, stormy, rough.
🔁 **1** clean. **4** fine.
➤ *v* **1** DIRTY, soil, stain, sully, defile, taint, pollute, contaminate. **2** BLOCK, obstruct, clog, choke, foul up. **3** ENTANGLE, catch, snarl, twist, ensnare.
🔁 **1** clean. **2** clear. **3** disentangle.

found *v* **1** START, originate, create, initiate, institute, inaugurate, set up, establish, endow, organize. **2** BASE, ground, bottom, rest, settle, fix, plant, raise, build, erect, construct.

foundation *n* **1** BASE, foot, bottom, ground, bedrock, substance, basis, footing. **2** SETTING UP, establishment, institution, inauguration, endowment, organization, groundwork.

founder[1] *n* originator, initiator, father, mother, benefactor, creator, author, architect, designer, inventor, maker, builder, constructor, organizer.

founder² v sink, go down, submerge, subside, collapse, break down, fall, come to grief, fail, misfire, miscarry, abort, fall through, come to nothing.

fountain n 1 SPRAY, jet, spout, spring, well, wellspring, reservoir, waterworks. 2 SOURCE, origin, fount, font, fountainhead, wellhead.

fracture n break, crack, fissure, cleft, rupture, split, rift, rent, schism, breach, gap, opening.
➤ v break, crack, rupture, split, splinter, chip.
🔁 join.

fragile adj brittle, breakable, frail, delicate, flimsy, dainty, fine, slight, insubstantial, weak, feeble, infirm.
🔁 robust, tough, durable.

fragment n piece, bit, part, portion, fraction, particle, crumb, morsel, scrap, remnant, shred, chip, splinter, shiver, sliver, shard.
➤ v break, shatter, splinter, shiver, crumble, disintegrate, come to pieces, come apart, break up, divide, split (up), disunite.
🔁 hold together, join.

fragmentary adj bitty, piecemeal, scrappy, broken, disjointed, disconnected, separate, scattered, sketchy, partial, incomplete.
🔁 whole, complete.

fragrance n perfume, scent, smell, odour, aroma, bouquet.

fragrant adj perfumed, scented, sweet-smelling, sweet, balmy, aromatic, odorous.
🔁 unscented.

frail adj delicate, brittle, breakable, fragile, flimsy, insubstantial, slight, puny, weak, feeble, infirm, vulnerable.
🔁 robust, tough, strong.

frailty n weakness, foible, failing, deficiency, shortcoming, fault, defect, flaw, blemish, imperfection, fallibility, susceptibility.

🔁 strength, robustness, toughness.

frame v 1 COMPOSE, formulate, conceive, devise, contrive, concoct, cook up, plan, map out, sketch, draw up, draft, shape, form, model, fashion, mould, forge, assemble, put together, build, construct, fabricate, make. 2 SURROUND, enclose, box in, case, mount. 3 *I've been framed*: set up, fit up (*sl*), trap.
➤ n 1 STRUCTURE, fabric, framework, skeleton, carcase, shell, casing, chassis, construction, bodywork, body, build, form. 2 MOUNT, mounting, setting, surround, border, edge.
◇ **frame of mind** state of mind, mindset, mood, humour, temper, disposition, spirit, outlook, attitude.

framework n structure, fabric, bare bones, skeleton, shell, frame, outline, plan, foundation, groundwork.

franchise n concession, licence, charter, authorization, privilege, right, suffrage, liberty, freedom, immunity, exemption.

frank adj honest, truthful, sincere, candid, blunt, open, free, plain, direct, forthright, straight, straightforward, downright, outspoken.
🔁 insincere, evasive.

frankly adv to be frank, to be honest, in truth, honestly, candidly, bluntly, openly, freely, plainly, directly, straight.
🔁 insincerely, evasively.

frantic adj agitated, overwrought, fraught, desperate, beside oneself, furious, raging, mad, wild, raving, frenzied, berserk, hectic.
🔁 calm, composed.

fraternize v mix, mingle, socialize, consort, associate, affiliate, unite, sympathize.
🔁 shun, ignore.

fraud n 1 DECEIT, deception, guile, cheating, swindling, double-dealing, sharp practice, fake, counterfeit, forgery, sham, hoax, trick, scam (*infml*). 2 (*infml*) CHARLATAN, impostor, pretender, phoney (*infml*), bluffer, hoaxer, cheat, swindler, double-dealer, con man (*infml*).

fraudulent *adj* dishonest, crooked (*infml*), criminal, deceitful, deceptive, false, bogus, phoney (*infml*), sham, counterfeit, swindling, double-dealing.
F3 honest, genuine.

fray *n* brawl, scuffle, dust-up (*infml*), free-for-all, set-to, clash, conflict, fight, combat, battle, quarrel, row, rumpus, disturbance, riot.

frayed *adj* ragged, tattered, worn, threadbare, unravelled.

freak *n* 1 MONSTER, mutant, mutation, monstrosity, malformation, deformity, irregularity, anomaly, abnormality, aberration, oddity, curiosity, quirk, caprice, vagary, twist, turn. 2 ENTHUSIAST, fanatic, addict, devotee, fan, buff (*infml*), fiend (*infml*), nut (*infml*).
➤ *adj* abnormal, atypical, unusual, exceptional, odd, queer, bizarre, aberrant, capricious, erratic, unpredictable, unexpected, surprise, chance, fortuitous, flukey.
F3 normal, common.

free *adj* 1 AT LIBERTY, at large, loose, unattached, unrestrained, liberated, emancipated, independent, self-ruling, democratic, self-governing. 2 *free time*: spare, available, idle, unemployed, unoccupied, vacant, empty. 3 *free tickets*: gratis, without charge, free of charge, complimentary, on the house. 4 CLEAR, unobstructed, unimpeded, open. 5 GENEROUS, liberal, open-handed, lavish, charitable, hospitable.
F3 1 imprisoned, confined, restricted. 2 busy, occupied.
➤ *v* release, let go, loose, turn loose, set free, untie, unbind, unchain, unleash, liberate, emancipate, rescue, deliver, save, ransom, disentangle, disengage, extricate, clear, rid, relieve, unburden, exempt, absolve, acquit.
F3 imprison, confine.
◊ **free of** lacking, devoid of, without, unaffected by, immune to, exempt from, safe from.

freedom *n* 1 LIBERTY, emancipation, deliverance, release, exemption, immunity, impunity. 2 INDEPENDENCE, autonomy, self-government, home rule. 3 RANGE, scope, play, leeway, latitude, licence, privilege, power, free rein, free hand, opportunity, informality.
F3 1 captivity, confinement. 3 restriction.

freely *adv* 1 READILY, willingly, voluntarily, spontaneously, easily. 2 *give freely*: generously, liberally, lavishly, extravagantly, amply, abundantly. 3 *speak freely*: frankly, candidly, unreservedly, openly, plainly.
F3 2 grudgingly. 3 evasively, cautiously.

freeze *v* 1 ICE OVER, ice up, glaciate, congeal, solidify, harden, stiffen. 2 DEEP-FREEZE, ice, refrigerate, chill, cool. 3 STOP, suspend, fix, immobilize, hold.
➤ *n* 1 FROST, freeze-up. 2 STOPPAGE, halt, standstill, shutdown, suspension, interruption, postponement, stay, embargo, moratorium.

freezing *adj* icy, frosty, glacial, arctic, polar, Siberian, wintry, raw, bitter, biting, cutting, penetrating, numbing, cold, chilly.
F3 hot, warm.

freight *n* cargo, load, lading, payload, contents, goods, merchandise, consignment, shipment, transportation, conveyance, carriage, haulage.

frenzied *adj* frantic, frenetic, hectic, feverish, desperate, furious, wild, uncontrolled, mad, demented, hysterical.
F3 calm, composed.

frenzy *n* 1 TURMOIL, agitation, distraction, derangement, madness, lunacy, mania, hysteria, delirium, fever. 2 BURST, fit, spasm, paroxysm, convulsion, seizure, outburst, transport, passion, rage, fury.
F3 1 calm, composure.

frequent *adj* 1 NUMEROUS, countless, incessant, constant, continual, persistent, repeated, recurring, regular. 2 COMMON, commonplace, everyday, familiar, usual, customary.

⚖ **1** infrequent.

➤ *v* visit, patronize, attend, haunt, hang out at (*infml*), associate with, hang about with (*infml*), hang out with (*infml*).

fresh *adj* **1** ADDITIONAL, supplementary, extra, more, further, other. **2** NEW, novel, innovative, original, different, unconventional, modern, up to date, recent, latest. **3** REFRESHING, bracing, invigorating, brisk, crisp, keen, cool, fair, bright, clear, pure. **4** *fresh fruit*: raw, natural, unprocessed, crude. **5** REFRESHED, revived, restored, renewed, rested, invigorated, energetic, vigorous, lively, alert. **6** PERT, saucy (*infml*), cheeky, disrespectful, impudent, insolent, bold, brazen, forward, familiar, presumptuous.

⚖ **2** old, hackneyed. **3** stale. **4** processed. **5** tired.

freshen *v* **1** AIR, ventilate, purify. **2** REFRESH, restore, revitalize, reinvigorate, liven, enliven, spruce up, tart up (*infml*).

⚖ **2** tire.

fret *v* **1** WORRY, agonize, brood, pine. **2** VEX, irritate, nettle, bother, trouble, torment.

friction *n* **1** DISAGREEMENT, dissension, dispute, disharmony, conflict, antagonism, hostility, opposition, rivalry, animosity, ill feeling, bad blood, resentment. **2** RUBBING, chafing, irritation, abrasion, scraping, grating, rasping, erosion, wearing away, resistance.

friend *n* mate (*infml*), pal (*infml*), chum (*infml*), buddy (*infml*), crony (*infml*), intimate, confidant(e), bosom friend, soul mate, comrade, ally, partner, associate, companion, playmate, pen-friend, acquaintance, well-wisher, supporter.

⚖ enemy, opponent.

friendly *adj* **1** AMIABLE, affable, genial, kind, kindly, neighbourly, helpful, sympathetic, fond, affectionate, familiar, intimate, close, matey (*infml*), pally (*infml*), chummy (*infml*), companionable, sociable, outgoing,

approachable, receptive, comradely, amicable, peaceable, well-disposed, favourable. **2** *a friendly atmosphere*: convivial, congenial, cordial, welcoming, warm.

⚖ **1** hostile, unsociable. **2** cold.

friendship *n* closeness, intimacy, familiarity, affinity, rapport, attachment, affection, fondness, love, harmony, concord, goodwill, friendliness, alliance, fellowship, comradeship.

⚖ enmity, animosity.

fright *n* shock, scare, alarm, consternation, dismay, dread, apprehension, trepidation, fear, terror, horror, panic.

frighten *v* alarm, daunt, unnerve, dismay, intimidate, terrorize, scare, startle, scare stiff, terrify, petrify, horrify, appal, shock.

⚖ reassure, calm.

frightening *adj* alarming, daunting, formidable, fearsome, scary, terrifying, hair-raising, bloodcurdling, spine-chilling, white-knuckle (*infml*), petrifying, traumatic.

frightful *adj* unpleasant, disagreeable, awful, dreadful, fearful, terrible, appalling, shocking, harrowing, unspeakable, dire, grim, ghastly, hideous, horrible, horrid, grisly, macabre, gruesome.

⚖ pleasant, agreeable.

frigid *adj* **1** UNFEELING, unresponsive, passionless, unloving, cool, aloof, passive, lifeless. **2** FROZEN, icy, frosty, glacial, arctic, cold, chill, chilly, wintry.

⚖ **1** responsive. **2** hot.

frilly *adj* ruffled, crimped, gathered, frilled, trimmed, lacy, fancy, ornate.

⚖ plain.

fringe *n* **1** MARGIN, periphery, outskirts, edge, perimeter, limits, borderline. **2** BORDER, edging, trimming, tassel, frill, valance.

➤ *adj* unconventional, unorthodox, unofficial, alternative, avant-garde.

⚖ conventional, mainstream.

frisk *v* jump, leap, skip, hop, bounce,

caper, dance, gambol, frolic, romp, play, sport.

frisky *adj* lively, spirited, high-spirited, frolicsome, playful, ludic, romping, rollicking, bouncy.
🔄 quiet.

fritter *v* waste, squander, dissipate, idle, misspend, blow (*sl*).

frivolity *n* fun, gaiety, flippancy, facetiousness, jest, light-heartedness, levity, triviality, superficiality, silliness, folly, nonsense.
🔄 seriousness.

frivolous *adj* trifling, trivial, unimportant, shallow, superficial, light, flippant, jocular, light-hearted, juvenile, puerile, foolish, silly, idle, vain, pointless.
🔄 serious, sensible.

frolic *v* gambol, caper, romp, play, lark around, rollick, make merry, frisk, prance, cavort, dance.
➤ *n* fun, amusement, sport, gaiety, jollity, merriment, revel, romp, prank, lark, caper, high jinks, antics.

front *n* **1** *at the front*: face, aspect, frontage, façade, outside, exterior, facing, cover, obverse, top, head, lead, vanguard, forefront, front line, foreground, forepart, bow. **2** PRETENCE, show, air, appearance, look, expression, manner, façade, cover, mask, disguise, pretext, cover-up.
🔄 **1** back, rear.
➤ *adj* fore, leading, foremost, head, first.
🔄 back, rear, last.
◇ **in front** ahead, leading, first, in advance, before, preceding.
🔄 behind.

frontier *n* border, boundary, borderline, limit, edge, perimeter, confines, marches, bounds, verge.

frosty *adj* **1** ICY, frozen, freezing, frigid, wintry, cold, chilly. **2** UNFRIENDLY, unwelcoming, cool, aloof, standoffish, stiff, discouraging.
🔄 warm.

froth *n* bubbles, effervescence, foam, lather, suds, head, scum.

➤ *v* foam, lather, ferment, fizz, effervesce, bubble.

frown *v* scowl, glower, lour, glare, grimace.
➤ *n* scowl, glower, dirty look (*infml*), glare, grimace.
◇ **frown on** disapprove of, object to, dislike, discourage.
🔄 approve of.

frozen *adj* iced, chilled, icy, icebound, ice-covered, arctic, ice-cold, frigid, freezing, numb, solidified, stiff, rigid, fixed.
🔄 warm.

frugal *adj* thrifty, penny-wise, parsimonious, careful, provident, saving, economical, sparing, meagre.
🔄 wasteful, generous.

fruit

Varieties of fruit include: apple, Bramley, Cox's Orange Pippin, Golden Delicious, Granny Smith, crab apple; pear, William, Conference, Asian pear; orange, Jaffa, mandarin, mineola, clementine, satsuma, tangerine, kumquat, Seville; apricot, peach, plum, persimmon, sharon fruit, nectarine, cherry, sloe, damson, greengage, grape, gooseberry, goosegog (*infml*), physalis, rhubarb, tomato; banana, pineapple, olive, lemon, lime, ugli fruit, star fruit, lychee, date, fig, grapefruit, kiwi fruit, mango, papaya, pawpaw, guava, passion fruit, avocado; melon, honeydew, cantaloupe, casaba, Galia, watermelon; strawberry, raspberry, blackberry, bilberry, loganberry, elderberry, blueberry, boysenberry, cranberry; redcurrant, blackcurrant.

fruitful *adj* **1** FERTILE, rich, teeming, plentiful, abundant, prolific, productive. **2** REWARDING, profitable, effective, advantageous, beneficial, worthwhile, well-spent, useful, successful.
🔄 **1** barren. **2** fruitless.

fruition *n* realization, fulfilment, attainment, achievement, completion, maturity, ripeness, consummation, perfection, success, enjoyment.

fruitless *adj* unsuccessful, abortive, useless, futile, pointless, vain, idle, hopeless, barren, sterile.
ᴇᴈ fruitful, successful, profitable.

frustrate *v* **1** THWART, foil, balk, baffle, block, check, spike, defeat, circumvent, forestall, counter, nullify, neutralize, inhibit. **2** DISAPPOINT, discourage, dishearten, depress.
ᴇᴈ **1** further, promote. **2** encourage.

fuel *n* **1** *a tax on fuel*: combustible, propellant, motive power.
2 PROVOCATION, incitement, encouragement, ammunition, material.

> *Fuels include*: gas, Calor gas®, propane, butane, methane, acetylene, electricity, coal, coke, anthracite, charcoal, oil, petrol, gasoline, diesel, derv, paraffin, kerosine, methylated spirit, wood, logs, peat, nuclear power.

➤ *v* incite, inflame, fire, encourage, fan, feed, nourish, sustain, stoke up.
ᴇᴈ discourage, damp down.

fugitive *n* escapee, runaway, deserter, refugee.
➤ *adj* fleeting, transient, transitory, passing, short, brief, flying, temporary, ephemeral, elusive.
ᴇᴈ permanent.

fulfil *v* complete, finish, conclude, consummate, perfect, realize, achieve, accomplish, perform, execute, discharge, implement, carry out, comply with, observe, keep, obey, conform to, satisfy, fill, answer.
ᴇᴈ fail, break.

fulfilment *n* completion, perfection, consummation, realization, success, achievement, accomplishment, performance, execution, discharge, implementation, observance, satisfaction.
ᴇᴈ failure.

full *adj* **1** FILLED, loaded, packed, crowded, crammed, stuffed, jammed. **2** ENTIRE, whole, intact, total, complete,

unabridged, unexpurgated. **3** THOROUGH, comprehensive, exhaustive, all-inclusive, broad, vast, extensive, ample, generous, abundant, plentiful, copious, profuse. **4** *a full sound*: rich, resonant, loud, deep, clear, distinct. **5** *at full speed*: maximum, top, highest, greatest, utmost.
ᴇᴈ **1** empty. **2** partial, incomplete. **3** superficial.

full-grown *adj* adult, grown-up, of age, mature, ripe, developed, full-blown, full-scale.
ᴇᴈ young, undeveloped.

fully *adv* completely, totally, utterly, wholly, entirely, thoroughly, altogether, quite, positively, without reserve, perfectly.
ᴇᴈ partly.

fumble *v* grope, feel, bungle, botch, mishandle, mismanage.

fume *v* **1** SMOKE, smoulder, boil, steam. **2** RAGE, storm, rant, rave, seethe.

fumes *n* exhaust, smoke, gas, vapour, haze, fog, smog, pollution.

fumigate *v* deodorize, disinfect, sterilize, purify, cleanse.

fun *n* enjoyment, pleasure, amusement, entertainment, diversion, distraction, recreation, play, sport, game, foolery, tomfoolery, horseplay, skylarking, romp, merrymaking, mirth, jollity, jocularity, joking, jesting.
◇ **make fun of** rag, jeer at, ridicule, laugh at, mock, taunt, tease, rib (*sl*).

function *n* **1** ROLE, part, office, duty, charge, responsibility, concern, job, task, occupation, business, activity, purpose, use. **2** RECEPTION, party, gathering, affair, do (*infml*), dinner, luncheon.
➤ *v* work, operate, run, go, serve, act, perform, behave.

functional *adj* working, operational, practical, useful, utilitarian, utility, plain, hard-wearing.
ᴇᴈ useless, decorative.

fund *n* pool, kitty, treasury, repository,

storehouse, store, reserve, stock, hoard, cache, stack, mine, well, source, supply.

➤ *v* finance, capitalize, endow, subsidize, underwrite, sponsor, back, support, promote, float.

fundamental *adj* basic, primary, first, rudimentary, elementary, underlying, integral, central, principal, cardinal, prime, main, key, essential, mission-critical (*infml*), indispensable, vital, necessary, crucial, important.

funds *n* money, finance, backing, capital, resources, savings, wealth, cash.

funeral *n* burial, interment, entombment, cremation, obsequies, wake.

fungus

> *Types of fungus include*: black spot, blight, botritis, brown rot, candida, downy mildew, ergot, grey mould, mushroom, orange-peel fungus, penicillium, potato blight, powdery mildew, rust, scab, smut, sooty mould, toadstool, yeast, brewer's yeast. *see also* **mushroom**.

funnel *v* channel, direct, convey, move, transfer, pass, pour, siphon, filter.

funny *adj* **1** HUMOROUS, amusing, entertaining, comic, comical, hilarious, witty, facetious, droll, farcical, laughable, ridiculous, absurd, silly.
2 ODD, strange, peculiar, curious, queer, weird, unusual, remarkable, puzzling, perplexing, mysterious, suspicious, dubious.
🖃 **1** serious, solemn, sad. **2** normal, ordinary, usual.

furious *adj* **1** ANGRY, mad (*infml*), up in arms (*infml*), livid, enraged, infuriated, incensed, raging, fuming, boiling.
2 VIOLENT, wild, fierce, intense, vehement, vigorous, frantic, boisterous, stormy, tempestuous.
🖃 **1** calm, pleased.

furnish *v* equip, fit out, decorate, rig, stock, provide, supply, afford,

grant, give, offer, present.
🖃 divest.

furniture *n* equipment, appliances, furnishings, fittings, fitments, household goods, movables, possessions, effects, things.

> *Types of furniture include*: table, dining table, gateleg table, refectory table, lowboy, side table, coffee table, card table; chair, easy chair, armchair, rocking chair, recliner, dining chair, carver, kitchen chair, stool, swivel chair, high chair, suite, settee, sofa, couch, studio couch, chesterfield, pouffe, footstool, bean bag; bed, four-poster, chaise longue, daybed, bed settee, futon, divan, camp-bed, bunk, water bed, cot, cradle; desk, bureau, secretaire, bookcase, cupboard, cabinet, china cabinet, Welsh dresser, sideboard, buffet, butcher's cabinet, dumb waiter, fireplace, overmantel, fender, firescreen, hallstand, umbrella stand, mirror, magazine rack; wardrobe, armoire, dressing-table, vanity unit, washstand, chest of drawers, tallboy, chiffonier, commode, ottoman, chest, coffer, blanket box.

> *Styles of furniture include*: Adam, Anglo-Colonial, Anglo-Indian, Art Deco, Art Nouveau, Baroque, Beidermeier, boulle, buhl, Charles II, Chippendale, Colonial, Continental Empire, Cromwellian, Dutch Colonial, Dutch Neoclassical, Edwardian, Empire, French Provincial, French Second Empire, Gainsborough, Georgian, Gothic, Hepplewhite, Louis Philippe, Louis-Quatorze, Louis-Quinze, provincial, Queen Anne, Regency, Restauration, rococo, Sheraton, Shibayama, Transitional, Vernis Martin, Victorian, William and Mary, William IV, Windsor.

furrow *n* groove, channel, trench, hollow, rut, track, line, crease, wrinkle.
➤ *v* seam, flute, corrugate, groove, crease, wrinkle, draw together, knit.

further *adj* more, additional, supplementary, extra, fresh, new, other.
➤ *v* advance, forward, promote, champion, push, encourage, foster, help, aid, assist, ease, facilitate, speed, hasten, accelerate, expedite.
▣ stop, frustrate.

furthermore *adv* moreover, what's more (*infml*), in addition, further, besides, also, too, as well, additionally.

furthest *adj* farthest, furthermost, remotest, outermost, outmost, extreme, ultimate, utmost, uttermost.
▣ nearest.

furtive *adj* surreptitious, sly, stealthy, secretive, underhand, hidden, covert, secret.
▣ open.

fury *n* anger, rage, wrath, frenzy, madness, passion, vehemence, fierceness, ferocity, violence, wildness, turbulence, power.
▣ calm, peacefulness.

fusion *n* melting, smelting, welding, union, synthesis, blending, coalescence, amalgamation, integration, merger, federation.

fuss *n* bother, trouble, hassle (*infml*), palaver, to-do (*infml*), hoo-ha (*infml*), furore, squabble, row, commotion, stir, fluster, confusion, upset, worry, agitation, flap (*infml*), excitement, bustle, flurry, hurry.
▣ calm.

➤ *v* complain, grumble, fret, worry, flap (*infml*), take pains, bother, bustle, fidget.

fussy *adj* 1 PARTICULAR, fastidious, scrupulous, finicky, pernickety, difficult, hard to please, choosy (*infml*), discriminating. 2 FANCY, elaborate, ornate, cluttered.
▣ 1 casual, uncritical. 2 plain.

futile *adj* pointless, useless, worthless, vain, idle, wasted, fruitless, profitless, unavailing, unsuccessful, abortive, unprofitable, unproductive, barren, empty, hollow, forlorn.
▣ fruitful, profitable.

futility *n* pointlessness, uselessness, worthlessness, vanity, emptiness, hollowness, aimlessness.
▣ use, purpose.

future *n* hereafter, tomorrow, outlook, prospects, expectations.
▣ past.

➤ *adj* prospective, designate, to be, fated, destined, to come, forthcoming, in the offing, impending, coming, approaching, expected, planned, unborn, later, subsequent, eventual.
▣ past.

fuzzy *adj* 1 FRIZZY, fluffy, furry, woolly, fleecy, downy, velvety, napped. 2 BLURRED, unfocused, ill-defined, unclear, vague, faint, hazy, shadowy, woolly, muffled, distorted.
▣ 2 clear, distinct.

Gg

gadget *n* tool, appliance, device, contrivance, contraption, thing, thingumajig (*infml*), invention, novelty, gimmick.

gag[1] muffle, muzzle, silence, quiet, stifle, throttle, suppress, curb, check, still.

gag[2] (*infml*) joke, jest, quip, crack, wisecrack, one-liner, pun, witticism, funny (*infml*).

gaiety *n* happiness, glee, cheerfulness, joie de vivre, jollity, merriment, mirth, hilarity, fun, merrymaking, revelry, festivity, celebration, joviality, good humour, high spirits, light-heartedness, liveliness, brightness, brilliance, sparkle, colour, colourfulness, show, showiness.
Fa sadness, drabness.

gaily *adv* happily, joyfully, merrily, blithely, brightly, brilliantly, colourfully, flamboyantly.
Fa sadly, dully.

gain *v* **1** EARN, make, produce, gross, net, clear, profit, yield, bring in, reap, harvest, win, capture, secure, net, obtain, acquire, procure. **2** REACH, arrive at, come to, get to, attain, achieve, realize. **3** *gain speed*: increase, pick up, gather, collect, advance, progress, improve.
Fa 1 lose. **3** lose.
➤ *n* earnings, proceeds, income, revenue, winnings, profit, return, yield, dividend, growth, increase, increment, rise, advance, progress, headway, improvement, advantage, benefit, attainment, achievement, acquisition.
Fa loss.
◇ **gain on** close with, narrow the gap, approach, catch up, level with, overtake, outdistance, leave behind.

gala *n* festivity, celebration, festival, carnival, jubilee, jamboree, fête, fair, pageant, procession.

gale *n* **1** WIND, squall, storm, hurricane, tornado, typhoon, cyclone. **2** BURST, outburst, outbreak, fit, eruption, explosion, blast.

gallant *adj* chivalrous, gentlemanly, courteous, polite, gracious, courtly, noble, dashing, heroic, valiant, brave, courageous, fearless, dauntless, bold, daring.
Fa ungentlemanly, cowardly.

gallery *n* art gallery, museum, arcade, passage, walk, balcony, circle, gods (*infml*), spectators.

gallop *v* bolt, run, sprint, race, career, fly, dash, tear, speed, zoom, shoot, dart, rush, hurry, hasten.
Fa amble.

galvanize *v* electrify, shock, jolt, prod, spur, provoke, stimulate, stir, move, arouse, excite, fire, invigorate, vitalize.

gamble *v* bet, wager, have a flutter (*infml*), try one's luck, punt, play, game, stake, chance, take a chance, risk, hazard, venture, speculate, back.
➤ *n* bet, wager, flutter (*infml*), punt, lottery, chance, risk, venture, speculation.

gambler *n* better, punter.

gambol *v* caper, frolic, frisk, skip, jump, bound, hop, bounce.

game[1] *n* **1** RECREATION, play, sport, pastime, diversion, distraction, entertainment, amusement, fun, frolic, romp, joke, jest.

Types of indoor game include: board game, backgammon, checkers (*US*), chess, Cluedo®, draughts, halma, Jenga®, ludo, mah-jong, Monopoly®, nine men's morris, Pictionary®, Scrabble®, snakes and ladders, Trivial Pursuit®; card game, baccarat, beggar-my-neighbour, bezique, blackjack, brag, bridge, canasta, chemin de fer, crib (*infml*), cribbage, faro, gin rummy, rummy, happy families, nap (*infml*), napoleon, newmarket, old maid, patience, Pelmanism, picquet, poker, draw poker, stud poker, pontoon, vingt-et-un, snap, solitaire, twenty-one, whist, partner whist, solo whist; bagatelle, pinball, billiards, pool, snooker, bowling, ten-pin bowling, bowls, darts, dice, craps, dominoes, roulette, shove ha'penny, table tennis, ping pong.

Types of children's game include: battleships, blind man's buff, charades, Chinese whispers, consequences, fivestones, forfeits, hangman, hide-and-seek, I-spy, jacks, jackstraws, musical chairs, noughts and crosses, pass the parcel, piggy-in-the-middle, pin the tail on the donkey, postman's knock, sardines, Simon says, spillikins, spin the bottle, tiddlywinks.

2 COMPETITION, contest, match, round, tournament, event, meeting. **3** GAME BIRDS, animals, meat, flesh, prey, quarry, bag, spoils.

Types of game (killed for sport) include: antelope, badger, bear, blackcock, boar, wild boar, caribou, deer, fallow deer, red deer, roe deer, duck, elk, fox, grouse, hazel grouse, wood grouse, hare, lion, moose, mountain lion, partridge, pheasant, quail, rabbit, snipe, squirrel, stag, tiger, waterfowl.

game² adj (*infml*) **1** *game for anything*: willing, inclined, ready, prepared, eager. **2** BOLD, daring, intrepid, brave, courageous, fearless, resolute, spirited.
E₃ **1** unwilling. **2** cowardly.

gamut n scale, series, range, sweep, scope, compass, spectrum, field, area.

gang n group, band, ring, pack, herd, mob, crowd, circle, clique, coterie, set, lot, team, crew, squad, shift, party.

gangster n mobster (*US infml*), goodfella (*US infml*), goombah (*US sl*), desperado, hoodlum, ruffian, rough, tough, thug, heavy (*sl*), racketeer, bandit, brigand, robber, criminal, crook (*infml*).

gaol *see* **jail**.

gaoler *see* **jailer**.

gap n **1** SPACE, blank, void, hole, opening, crack, chink, crevice, cleft, breach, rift, divide, divergence, difference. **2** INTERRUPTION, break, recess, pause, lull, interlude, intermission, interval.

gape v **1** STARE, gaze, gawp (*infml*), goggle, gawk (*infml*). **2** OPEN, yawn, part, split, crack.

gaping adj open, yawning, broad, wide, vast, cavernous.
E₃ tiny.

garage n lock-up, petrol station, gas station (*US*), service station.

garble v confuse, muddle, jumble, scramble, mix up, twist, distort, pervert, slant, misrepresent, falsify.
E₃ decipher.

garden n yard, backyard, plot, park.

Types of garden include: allotment, alpine garden, arboretum, arbour, beer garden, border, botanical garden, bottle garden, cottage garden, fruit garden, garden of rest, hanging garden, herb garden, herbaceous border, hop garden, indoor garden, Japanese garden, kitchen garden, knot garden, lawn, market garden, ornamental garden, orchard, raised bed, rock garden, rockery, rose arbour, rose bed, rose garden, shrubbery, sink garden, sunken garden, tea garden, terrarium, vegetable plot, walled garden, water garden, window box, winter garden.

garish *adj* gaudy, lurid, loud, glaring, flashy, showy, tawdry, vulgar, tasteless.
🔁 quiet, tasteful.

garland *n* wreath, festoon, decoration, flowers, laurels, honours.
➤ *v* wreathe, festoon, deck, adorn, crown.

garments *n* clothes, clothing, wear, attire, gear (*infml*), togs (*infml*), outfit, get-up (*infml*), dress, costume, uniform.

garnish *v* decorate, adorn, ornament, trim, embellish, enhance, grace, set off.
🔁 divest.
➤ *n* decoration, ornament, trimming, embellishment, enhancement, relish.

gas

> *Types of gas include*: acetylene, ammonia, black damp, butane, carbon dioxide, carbon monoxide, chloroform, choke damp, CS gas, cyanogen, ether, ethylene, fire damp, helium, hydrogen sulphide, ketene, krypton, laughing gas, marsh gas, methane, mustard gas, natural gas, neon, nerve gas, niton, nitrous oxide, ozone, propane, radon, tear gas, town gas, xenon.

gash *v* cut, wound, slash, slit, incise, lacerate, tear, rend, split, score, gouge.
➤ *n* cut, wound, slash, slit, incision, laceration, tear, rent, split, score, gouge.

gasp *v* pant, puff, blow, breathe, wheeze, choke, gulp.
➤ *n* pant, puff, blow, breath, gulp, exclamation.

gate *n* barrier, door, doorway, gateway, opening, entrance, exit, access, passage.

gather *v* **1** CONGREGATE, convene, muster, rally, round up, assemble, collect, group, amass, accumulate, hoard, stockpile, heap, pile up, build. **2** INFER, deduce, conclude, surmise, assume, understand, learn, hear. **3** FOLD, pleat, tuck, pucker. **4** *gather flowers*: pick, pluck, cull, select, reap, harvest, glean.
🔁 **1** scatter, dissipate.

gathering *n* assembly, convocation, convention, meeting, round-up, rally, get-together, jamboree, party, group, company, congregation, mass, crowd, throng, turnout.

gaudy *adj* bright, brilliant, glaring, garish, loud, flashy, showy, ostentatious, tinselly, glitzy (*infml*), tawdry, vulgar, tasteless.
🔁 drab, plain.

gauge *v* estimate, guess, judge, assess, evaluate, value, rate, reckon, figure, calculate, compute, count, measure, weigh, determine, ascertain.
➤ *n* **1** STANDARD, norm, criterion, benchmark, yardstick, rule, guideline, indicator, measure, meter, test, sample, example, model, pattern. **2** SIZE, magnitude, measure, capacity, bore, calibre, thickness, width, span, extent, scope, height, depth, degree.

> *Gauges include*: cutting gauge, drill gauge, feeler gauge, gauge glass, gauge rod, gauge wheel, marking gauge, mortise gauge, paper gauge, pressure gauge, radius gauge, rain gauge, ring gauge, snap gauge, steam gauge, strain gauge, taper gauge, tide gauge, vacuum gauge, water gauge.
> *see also* **measure**.

gaunt *adj* **1** HAGGARD, hollow-eyed, angular, bony, thin, lean, lank, skinny, scraggy, scrawny, skeletal, emaciated, wasted. **2** BLEAK, stark, bare, desolate, forlorn, dismal, dreary, grim, harsh.
🔁 **1** plump.

gawky *adj* awkward, clumsy, maladroit, gauche, inept, oafish, ungainly, gangling, unco-ordinated, graceless.
🔁 graceful.

gay *adj* **1** HAPPY, joyful, jolly, merry, cheerful, blithe, sunny, carefree, debonair, fun-loving, pleasure-seeking, vivacious, lively, animated, playful, light-hearted. **2** *gay colours*: vivid, rich, bright, brilliant, sparkling, festive, colourful, gaudy, garish, flashy, showy, flamboyant. **3** HOMOSEXUAL, lesbian, queer (*sl*), pink (*infml*).

🔳 **1** sad, gloomy. **3** heterosexual, straight (*sl*).
➤ *n* homosexual, homo (*sl*), queer (*sl*), poof (*sl*), lesbian, dike (*sl*).
🔳 heterosexual.

gaze *v* stare, contemplate, regard, watch, view, look, gape, wonder.
➤ *n* stare, look.

gear *n* **1** EQUIPMENT, kit, outfit, tackle, apparatus, tools, instruments, accessories. **2** GEARWHEEL, cogwheel, cog, gearing, mechanism, machinery, works. **3** (*infml*) BELONGINGS, possessions, things, stuff, baggage, luggage, paraphernalia. **4** (*infml*) CLOTHES, clothing, garments, attire, dress, garb (*infml*), togs (*infml*), get-up (*infml*).

gel, jell *v* set, congeal, coagulate, crystallize, harden, thicken, solidify, materialize, come together, finalize, form, take shape.

gelatinous *adj* jelly-like, jellied, congealed, rubbery, glutinous, gummy, gluey, gooey (*infml*), sticky, viscous.

gem *n* gemstone, precious stone, stone, jewel, treasure, prize, masterpiece, pièce de rêsistance.

> *Gems and gemstones include*:
> diamond, white sapphire, zircon, cubic zirconia, marcasite, rhinestone, pearl, moonstone, onyx, opal, mother-of-pearl, amber, citrine, fire opal, topaz, agate, tiger's eye, jasper, morganite, ruby, garnet, rose quartz, beryl, cornelian, coral, amethyst, sapphire, turquoise, lapis lazuli, emerald, aquamarine, bloodstone, jade, peridot, tourmaline, jet.

genealogy *n* family tree, pedigree, lineage, ancestry, descent, derivation, extraction, family, line.

general *adj* **1** *a general statement*: broad, sweeping, blanket, all-inclusive, comprehensive, universal, global, total, across-the-board, widespread, prevalent, extensive, overall, panoramic. **2** VAGUE, ill-defined, indefinite, imprecise, inexact, approximate, loose, unspecific. **3** USUAL, regular, normal, typical, ordinary, everyday, customary, conventional, common, public.
🔳 **1** particular, limited. **2** specific. **3** rare.

generally *adv* usually, normally, as a rule, by and large, on the whole, mostly, mainly, chiefly, broadly, commonly, universally.

generate *v* produce, engender, whip up, arouse, cause, bring about, give rise to, create, originate, initiate, make, form, breed, propagate.
🔳 prevent.

generation *n* **1** AGE GROUP, age, era, epoch, period, time. **2** PRODUCTION, creation, origination, formation, genesis, procreation, reproduction, propagation, breeding.

generosity *n* liberality, munificence, open-handedness, bounty, charity, magnanimity, philanthropy, kindness, big-heartedness, benevolence, goodness.
🔳 meanness, selfishness.

generous *adj* **1** LIBERAL, free, bountiful, open-handed, unstinting, unsparing, lavish. **2** MAGNANIMOUS, charitable, philanthropic, public-spirited, unselfish, kind, big-hearted, benevolent, good, high-minded, noble. **3** AMPLE, full, plentiful, abundant, copious, overflowing.
🔳 **1** mean, miserly. **2** selfish. **3** meagre.

genial *adj* affable, amiable, friendly, convivial, cordial, kindly, kind, warm-hearted, warm, hearty, jovial, jolly, cheerful, happy, good-natured, easy-going (*infml*), agreeable, pleasant.
🔳 cold.

genius *n* **1** VIRTUOSO, maestro, master, past master, expert, adept, egghead (*infml*), intellectual, mastermind, brain, intellect. **2** INTELLIGENCE, brightness, brilliance, ability, aptitude, gift, talent, flair, knack, bent, inclination, propensity, capacity, faculty.

gentle *adj* **1** KIND, kindly, amiable, tender, soft-hearted, compassionate, sympathetic, merciful, mild, placid, calm, tranquil. **2** *a gentle slope*: gradual, slow, easy, smooth, moderate, slight, light, imperceptible. **3** SOOTHING, peaceful, serene, quiet, soft, balmy.
F3 1 unkind, rough, harsh, wild.

genuine *adj* real, actual, natural, pure, original, authentic, veritable, true, bona fide, legitimate, honest, sincere, frank, candid, earnest.
F3 artificial, false, insincere.

germ *n* **1** MICRO-ORGANISM, microbe, bacterium, bacillus, virus, bug (*infml*). **2** BEGINNING, start, origin, source, cause, spark, rudiment, nucleus, root, seed, embryo, bud, sprout.

germinate *v* bud, sprout, shoot, develop, grow, swell.

gesticulate *v* wave, signal, gesture, indicate, sign.

gesture *n* act, action, movement, motion, indication, sign, signal, wave, gesticulation.
➤ *v* indicate, sign, motion, beckon, point, signal, wave, gesticulate.

get *v* **1** OBTAIN, acquire, procure, come by, receive, earn, gain, win, secure, achieve, realize. **2** *it's getting dark*: become, turn, go, grow. **3** *get him to help*: persuade, coax, induce, urge, influence, sway. **4** MOVE, go, come, reach, arrive. **5** FETCH, collect, pick up, take, catch, capture, seize, grab. **6** CONTRACT, catch, pick up, develop, come down with.
F3 1 lose. **4** leave.
◊ **get across** communicate, transmit, convey, impart, put across, bring home to.
◊ **get ahead** advance, progress, get on, go places (*infml*), thrive, flourish, prosper, succeed, make good, make it, get there (*infml*).
F3 fall behind, fail.
◊ **get along 1** COPE, manage, get by, survive, fare, progress, develop. **2** AGREE, harmonize, get on, hit it off.
◊ **get at 1** REACH, attain, find, discover.

2 (*infml*) BRIBE, suborn, corrupt, influence. **3** (*infml*) MEAN, intend, imply, insinuate, hint, suggest. **4** (*infml*) CRITICIZE, find fault with, pick on, attack, make fun of.
◊ **get away** escape, get out, break out, break away, run away, flee, depart, leave.
◊ **get back** recover, regain, recoup, repossess, retrieve.
◊ **get down 1** DEPRESS, sadden, dishearten, dispirit. **2** DESCEND, dismount, disembark, alight, get off.
F3 1 encourage. **2** board.
◊ **get in** enter, penetrate, infiltrate, arrive, come, land, embark.
◊ **get off 1** *get off a train*: alight, disembark, dismount, descend. **2** REMOVE, detach, separate, shed, get down.
F3 1 get on. **2** put on.
◊ **get on 1** BOARD, embark, mount, ascend. **2** COPE, manage, fare, get along, make out, prosper, succeed. **3** CONTINUE, proceed, press on, advance, progress.
F3 1 get off.
◊ **get out 1** ESCAPE, flee, break out, extricate oneself, free oneself, leave, quit (*infml*), vacate, evacuate, clear out, clear off (*infml*). **2** *she got out a pen*: take out, produce.
◊ **get over 1** RECOVER FROM, shake off, survive. **2** SURMOUNT, overcome, defeat, deal with. **3** COMMUNICATE, get across, convey, put over, impart, explain.
◊ **get round 1** CIRCUMVENT, bypass, evade, avoid. **2** PERSUADE, win over, talk round, coax, prevail upon.
◊ **get together** assemble, collect, gather, congregate, rally, meet, join, unite, collaborate.
◊ **get up** stand (up), arise, rise, ascend, climb, mount, scale.

ghastly *adj* awful, dreadful, frightful, terrible, grim, gruesome, hideous, horrible, horrid, loathsome, repellent, shocking, appalling.
F3 delightful, attractive.

ghost *n* spectre, phantom, spook (*infml*), apparition, visitant, spirit, wraith, soul, shade, shadow.

ghostly *adj* eerie, spooky (*infml*), creepy, supernatural, unearthly, ghostlike, spectral, wraith-like, phantom, illusory.

giant *n* monster, titan, colossus, Goliath, Hercules.
➤ *adj* gigantic, colossal, titanic, mammoth, jumbo (*infml*), king-size, huge, enormous, immense, vast, large.

gibe, jibe *n* jeer, sneer, mockery, ridicule, taunt, derision, scoff, dig (*infml*), crack (*infml*), poke, quip.

giddy *adj* 1 DIZZY, faint, light-headed, unsteady, reeling, vertiginous. 2 SILLY, flighty, wild.

gift *n* 1 PRESENT, offering, donation, contribution, bounty, largess, gratuity, tip, bonus, freebie (*sl*), legacy, bequest, endowment. 2 TALENT, genius, flair, aptitude, bent, knack, power, faculty, attribute, ability, capability, capacity.

gifted *adj* talented, adept, skilful, expert, masterly, skilled, accomplished, able, capable, clever, intelligent, bright, brilliant.

gigantic *adj* huge, enormous, vast, immense, giant, colossal, mega (*infml*), titanic, mammoth, gargantuan, Brobdingnagian.
🔁 tiny, Lilliputian.

giggle *v, n* titter, snigger, chuckle, chortle, laugh.

gilded *adj* gilt, gold, golden, gold-plated.

gimmick *n* attraction, ploy, stratagem, ruse, scheme, trick, stunt, dodge, device, contrivance, gadget.

gingerly *adv* tentatively, hesitantly, warily, cautiously, carefully, delicately.
🔁 boldly, carelessly.

gipsy *see* gypsy.

girdle *n* belt, sash, band, waistband, corset.

girl *n* lass, young woman, daughter.

girlfriend *n* young lady, girl, lass (*infml*), bird (*sl*), date, sweetheart, lover, fiancée, partner.

girth *n* circumference, perimeter, measure, size, bulk, strap, band.

gist *n* pith, essence, marrow, substance, matter, meaning, significance, import, sense, idea, drift, direction, point, nub, core, quintessence.

give *v* 1 PRESENT, award, confer, offer, lend, donate, contribute, provide, supply, furnish, grant, bestow, endow, gift, make over, hand over, deliver, entrust, commit, devote. 2 *give news*: communicate, transmit, impart, utter, announce, declare, pronounce, publish, set forth. 3 CONCEDE, allow, admit, yield, give way, surrender. 4 *give trouble*: cause, occasion, make, produce, do, perform. 5 SINK, yield, bend, give way, break, collapse, fall.
🔁 1 take, withhold. 5 withstand.
◇ **give away** betray, inform on, expose, uncover, divulge, let slip, disclose, reveal, leak, let out.
◇ **give in** surrender, capitulate, submit, yield, give way, concede, give up, quit.
🔁 hold out.
◇ **give off** emit, discharge, release, give out, send out, throw out, pour out, exhale, exude, produce.
◇ **give out** 1 DISTRIBUTE, hand out, dole out, deal. 2 ANNOUNCE, declare, broadcast, publish, disseminate, communicate, transmit, impart, notify, advertise.
◇ **give up** 1 STOP, cease, quit, resign, abandon, renounce, relinquish, waive. 2 SURRENDER, capitulate, give in.
🔁 1 start. 2 hold out.

given *adj* 1 *a given number*: specified, particular, definite. 2 INCLINED, disposed, likely, liable, prone.

glad *adj* 1 PLEASED, delighted, gratified, contented, happy, joyful, merry, cheerful, cheery, bright. 2 WILLING, eager, keen, ready, inclined, disposed.
🔁 1 sad, unhappy. 2 unwilling, reluctant.

glamorous *adj* smart, elegant, attractive, beautiful, gorgeous, enchanting, captivating, alluring, appealing, fascinating, exciting, dazzling, glossy, colourful.
🔁 plain, drab, boring.

glamour *n* attraction, allure, appeal, fascination, charm, magic, beauty, elegance, glitter, prestige.

glance *v* peep, peek, glimpse, view, look, scan, skim, leaf, flip, thumb, dip, browse.
➤ *n* peep, peek, glimpse, look.

gland

> *Types of gland include*: adrenal, cortex medulla, apocrine, eccrine, endocrine, exocrine, holocrine, lachrymal, lymph, lymph node, mammary, merocrine, ovary, pancreas, parathyroid, parotid, pineal, pituitary, prostate, sebaceous, testicle, thymus, thyroid.

glare *v* 1 GLOWER, look daggers, frown, scowl, stare. 2 DAZZLE, blaze, flame, flare, shine, reflect.
➤ *n* 1 BLACK LOOK, dirty look (*infml*), frown, scowl, stare, look. 2 BRIGHTNESS, brilliance, blaze, flame, dazzle, spotlight.

glaring *adj* blatant, flagrant, open, conspicuous, manifest, patent, obvious, outrageous, gross.
🔁 hidden, concealed, minor.

glassy *adj* 1 GLASSLIKE, smooth, slippery, icy, shiny, glossy, transparent, clear. 2 *a glassy stare*: expressionless, blank, empty, vacant, dazed, fixed, glazed, cold, lifeless, dull.

glaze *v* coat, enamel, gloss, varnish, lacquer, polish, burnish.
➤ *n* coat, coating, finish, enamel, varnish, lacquer, polish, shine, lustre, gloss.

gleam *n* glint, flash, beam, ray, flicker, glimmer, shimmer, sparkle, glitter, gloss, glow.
➤ *v* glint, flash, glance, flare, shine, glisten, glimmer, glitter, sparkle, shimmer, glow.

glib *adj* fluent, easy, facile, quick, ready, talkative, plausible, insincere, smooth, slick, suave, smooth-tongued.
🔁 tongue-tied, implausible.

glide *v* slide, slip, skate, skim, fly, float, drift, sail, coast, roll, run, flow.

glimmer *v* glow, shimmer, glisten, glitter, sparkle, twinkle, wink, blink, flicker, gleam, shine.
➤ *n* 1 GLOW, shimmer, sparkle, twinkle, flicker, glint, gleam. 2 TRACE, hint, suggestion, grain.

glimpse *n* peep, peek, squint, glance, look, sight, sighting, view.
➤ *v* spy, espy, spot, catch sight of, sight, view.

glint *v* flash, gleam, shine, reflect, glitter, sparkle, twinkle, glimmer.
➤ *n* flash, gleam, shine, reflection, glitter, sparkle, twinkle, glimmer.

glisten *v* shine, gleam, glint, glitter, sparkle, twinkle, glimmer, shimmer.

glitter *v* sparkle, spangle, scintillate, twinkle, shimmer, glimmer, glisten, glint, gleam, flash, shine.
➤ *n* sparkle, coruscation, scintillation, twinkle, shimmer, glimmer, glint, gleam, flash, shine, lustre, sheen, brightness, radiance, brilliance, splendour, showiness, glamour, tinsel.

gloat *v* triumph, glory, exult, rejoice, revel in, relish, crow, boast, vaunt, rub it in (*infml*).

global *adj* universal, worldwide, international, general, all-encompassing, total, thorough, exhaustive, comprehensive, all-inclusive, encylopedic, wide-ranging.
🔁 parochial, limited.

globe *n* world, earth, planet, sphere, ball, orb, round.

gloom *n* 1 DEPRESSION, low spirits, despondency, dejection, sadness, unhappiness, glumness, melancholy, misery, desolation, despair. 2 DARK, darkness, shade, shadow, dusk, twilight, dimness, obscurity, cloud, cloudiness, dullness.
🔁 1 cheerfulness, happiness.
2 brightness.

gloomy *adj* 1 DEPRESSED, down, low, despondent, dejected, downcast, dispirited, downhearted, sad, miserable, glum, morose, pessimistic, cheerless, dismal, depressing. 2 DARK,

sombre, shadowy, dim, obscure, overcast, dull, dreary.
🔄 **1** cheerful. **2** bright.

glorious *adj* **1** ILLUSTRIOUS, eminent, distinguished, famous, renowned, noted, great, noble, splendid, magnificent, grand, majestic, triumphant. **2** FINE, bright, radiant, shining, brilliant, dazzling, beautiful, gorgeous, superb, excellent, wonderful, marvellous, delightful, heavenly.
🔄 **1** unknown.

glory *n* **1** FAME, renown, celebrity, illustriousness, greatness, eminence, distinction, honour, prestige, kudos, triumph. **2** PRAISE, homage, tribute, worship, veneration, adoration, exaltation, blessing, thanksgiving, gratitude. **3** BRIGHTNESS, radiance, brilliance, beauty, splendour, resplendence, magnificence, grandeur, majesty, dignity.

gloss¹ *n* polish, varnish, lustre, sheen, shine, brightness, brilliance, show, appearance, semblance, surface, front, façade, veneer, window-dressing.
◊ **gloss over** conceal, hide, veil, mask, disguise, camouflage, cover up, whitewash, explain away.

gloss² *n* annotation, note, footnote, explanation, elucidation, definition, interpretation, translation, comment, commentary.
➤ *v* annotate, define, explain, elucidate, interpret, construe, translate, comment.

glossy *adj* shiny, sheeny, lustrous, sleek, silky, smooth, glassy, polished, burnished, glazed, enamelled, bright, shining, brilliant.
🔄 matt.

glow *n* **1** LIGHT, gleam, glimmer, radiance, luminosity, brightness, vividness, brilliance, splendour. **2** ARDOUR, fervour, intensity, warmth, passion, enthusiasm, excitement. **3** FLUSH, blush, rosiness, redness, burning.
➤ *v* **1** SHINE, radiate, gleam, glimmer, burn, smoulder. **2** *their faces glowed*:

flush, blush, colour, redden.

glower *v* glare, look daggers, frown, scowl.
➤ *n* glare, black look, dirty look (*infml*), frown, scowl, stare, look.

glowing *adj* **1** BRIGHT, luminous, vivid, vibrant, rich, warm, flushed, red, flaming. **2** *a glowing review*: complimentary, enthusiastic, ecstatic, rhapsodic, rave (*infml*).
🔄 **1** dull, colourless. **2** restrained.

glue *n* adhesive, gum, paste, size, cement.
➤ *v* stick, affix, gum, paste, seal, bond, cement, fix.

glut *n* surplus, excess, surfeit, superfluity, overabundance, superabundance, saturation, overflow.
🔄 scarcity, lack.

glutton *n* gourmand, gormandizer, guzzler, gorger, gobbler, pig.
🔄 ascetic.

gluttony *n* gourmandise, gourmandism, greed, greediness, voracity, insatiability, piggishness.
🔄 abstinence, asceticism.

gnarled *adj* gnarly, knotted, knotty, twisted, contorted, distorted, rough, rugged, weather-beaten.

gnaw *v* **1** BITE, nibble, munch, chew, eat, devour, consume, erode, wear. **2** WORRY, niggle, fret, trouble, plague, nag, prey, haunt.

go *v* **1** MOVE, pass, advance, progress, proceed, make for, travel, journey, start, begin, depart, leave, take one's leave, retreat, withdraw, disappear, vanish. **2** OPERATE, function, work, run, act, perform. **3** EXTEND, spread, stretch, reach, span, continue, unfold. **4** *time goes quickly*: pass, elapse, lapse, roll on.
🔄 **2** break down, fail.
➤ *n* (*infml*) **1** *have a go*: attempt, try, shot (*infml*), bash (*infml*), stab (*infml*), turn. **2** ENERGY, get-up-and-go (*infml*), vitality, life, spirit, dynamism, effort.
◊ **go about** approach, begin, set about, address, tackle, attend to,

undertake, engage in, perform.

◇ **go ahead** begin, proceed, carry on, continue, advance, progress, move.

◇ **go away** depart, leave, clear off (*infml*), withdraw, retreat, disappear, vanish.

◇ **go back** return, revert, backslide, retreat.

◇ **go by 1** PASS, elapse, flow. **2** *go by the rules*: observe, follow, comply with, heed.

◇ **go down** descend, sink, set, fall, drop, decrease, decline, deteriorate, degenerate, fail, founder, go under, collapse, fold (*infml*).

◇ **go for 1** (*infml*) CHOOSE, prefer, favour, like, admire, enjoy. **2** ATTACK, assail, set about, lunge at.

◇ **go in for** enter, take part in, participate in, engage in, take up, embrace, adopt, undertake, practise, pursue, follow.

◇ **go into** discuss, consider, review, examine, study, scrutinize, investigate, inquire into, check out, probe, delve into, analyse, dissect.

◇ **go off 1** DEPART, leave, quit, abscond, vanish, disappear. **2** EXPLODE, blow up, detonate. **3** *the milk has gone off*: deteriorate, turn, sour, go bad, rot.

◇ **go on 1** CONTINUE, carry on, proceed, persist, stay, endure, last. **2** CHATTER, rabbit (*infml*), witter (*infml*), ramble on. **3** HAPPEN, occur, take place.

◇ **go out** exit, depart, leave.

◇ **go over** examine, peruse, study, revise, scan, read, inspect, check, review, repeat, rehearse, list.

◇ **go through 1** SUFFER, undergo, experience, bear, tolerate, endure, withstand. **2** INVESTIGATE, check, examine, look, search, hunt, explore. **3** USE, consume, exhaust, spend, squander.

◇ **go together** match, harmonize, accord, fit.

◇ **go with 1** MATCH, harmonize, co-ordinate, blend, complement, suit, fit, correspond. **2** ACCOMPANY, escort, take, usher.
₤ 1 clash.

◇ **go without** abstain, forgo, do without, manage without, lack, want.

goad *v* prod, prick, spur, impel, push, drive, provoke, incite, instigate, arouse, stimulate, prompt, urge, nag, hound, harass, annoy, irritate, vex.

go-ahead *n* permission, consent, authorization, clearance, green light (*infml*), sanction, assent, OK (*infml*), agreement.
₤ ban, veto, embargo.
➤ *adj* enterprising, pioneering, progressive, ambitious, up-and-coming, dynamic, energetic.
₤ unenterprising, sluggish.

goal *n* target, mark, objective, aim, intention, object, purpose, end, ambition, aspiration.

gobble *v* bolt, guzzle, gorge, cram, stuff, devour, consume, put away (*infml*), scoff (*infml*), swallow, gulp.

go-between *n* intermediary, mediator, liaison, contact, middleman, broker, dealer, agent, messenger, medium.

God *n* Supreme Being, Creator, Providence, Lord, Almighty, Holy One, Jehovah, Yahweh, Allah, Brahma, Zeus.

god, goddess *n* deity, divinity, idol, spirit, power.

godforsaken *adj* remote, isolated, lonely, bleak, desolate, abandoned, deserted, forlorn, dismal, dreary, gloomy, miserable, wretched.

godless *adj* ungodly, atheistic, heathen, pagan, irreligious, unholy, impious, sacrilegious, profane, irreverent, bad, evil, wicked.
₤ godly, pious.

godly *adj* religious, holy, pious, devout, God-fearing, righteous, good, virtuous, pure, innocent.
₤ godless, impious.

godsend *n* blessing, boon, stroke of luck, windfall, miracle.
₤ blow, setback.

golden *adj* **1** GOLD, gilded, gilt, yellow, blond(e), fair, bright, shining, lustrous, resplendent. **2** PROSPEROUS, successful, glorious, excellent, happy, joyful, favourable, auspicious, promising, rosy.

golf

> *Types of golf club include*: driver, brassie, spoon, wood, metal wood, iron, driving iron, midiron, midmashie, mashie iron, mashie, spade mashie, mashie niblick, pitching niblick, putter, pitching wedge, sand wedge, lob wedge.

good *adj* **1** ACCEPTABLE, satisfactory, pleasant, agreeable, nice, enjoyable, pleasing, commendable, excellent, great (*infml*), super (*infml*), first-class, first-rate, superior, advantageous, beneficial, favourable, auspicious, helpful, useful, worthwhile, profitable, appropriate, suitable, fitting. **2** *good at her job*: competent, proficient, skilled, expert, accomplished, professional, skilful, clever, talented, gifted, fit, able, capable, dependable, reliable. **3** KIND, considerate, gracious, benevolent, charitable, philanthropic. **4** VIRTUOUS, exemplary, moral, upright, honest, trustworthy, worthy, righteous. **5** WELL-BEHAVED, obedient, well-mannered. **6** THOROUGH, complete, whole, substantial, considerable.
F3 **1** bad, poor. **2** incompetent. **3** unkind, inconsiderate. **4** wicked, immoral. **5** naughty, disobedient.
➤ *n* **1** VIRTUE, morality, goodness, righteousness, right. **2** USE, purpose, avail, advantage, profit, gain, worth, merit, usefulness, service. **3** *for your own good*: welfare, wellbeing, interest, sake, behalf, benefit, convenience.

goodbye *n* farewell, adieu, au revoir, valediction, leave-taking, parting.

good-humoured *adj* cheerful, happy, jovial, genial, affable, amiable, friendly, congenial, pleasant, good-tempered, approachable.
F3 ill-humoured.

good-looking *adj* attractive, handsome, beautiful, fair, pretty,

personable, presentable.
F3 ugly, plain.

good-natured *adj* kind, kindly, kind-hearted, sympathetic, benevolent, helpful, neighbourly, gentle, good-tempered, approachable, friendly, tolerant, patient.
F3 ill-natured.

goodness *n* virtue, uprightness, rectitude, honesty, probity, kindness, compassion, graciousness, goodwill, benevolence, unselfishness, generosity, friendliness, helpfulness.
F3 badness, wickedness.

goods *n* **1** PROPERTY, chattels, possessions, effects, belongings, paraphernalia, stuff, things, gear (*infml*). **2** MERCHANDISE, wares, commodities, stock, freight.

goodwill *n* benevolence, kindness, generosity, favour, friendliness, friendship, zeal.
F3 ill-will.

gore *v* pierce, penetrate, stab, spear, stick, impale, wound.

gorge *n* canyon, ravine, gully, defile, chasm, abyss, cleft, fissure, gap, pass.
➤ *v* feed, guzzle, gobble, devour, bolt, wolf, gulp, swallow, cram, stuff, fill, sate, surfeit, glut, overeat.
F3 fast.

gorgeous *adj* magnificent, splendid, grand, glorious, superb, fine, rich, sumptuous, luxurious, brilliant, dazzling, showy, glamorous, attractive, beautiful, handsome, good-looking, delightful, pleasing, lovely, enjoyable, good.
F3 dull, plain.

gory *adj* bloody, sanguinary, bloodstained, blood-soaked, grisly, brutal, savage, murderous.

gossip *n* **1** IDLE TALK, prattle, chitchat, tittle-tattle, rumour, hearsay, report, scandal. **2** GOSSIPMONGER, scandalmonger, whisperer, prattler, babbler, chatterbox, nosey parker (*infml*), busybody, talebearer, tell-tale, tattler.

➤ *v* talk, chat, natter, chatter, gabble, prattle, tattle, tell tales, whisper, rumour.

gouge *v* chisel, cut, hack, incise, score, groove, scratch, claw, gash, slash, dig, scoop, hollow, extract.

gourmet *n* gastronome, epicure, epicurean, connoisseur, bon vivant.

govern *v* **1** RULE, reign, direct, manage, superintend, supervise, oversee, preside, lead, head, command, influence, guide, conduct, steer, pilot. **2** *govern one's temper*: dominate, master, control, regulate, curb, check, restrain, contain, quell, subdue, tame, discipline.

government *n* **1** *blame the government*: administration, executive, ministry, Establishment, authorities, powers that be, state, régime. **2** RULE, sovereignty, sway, direction, management, superintendence, supervision, surveillance, command, charge, authority, guidance, conduct, domination, dominion, control, regulation, restraint.

Government systems include: absolutism, autocracy, commonwealth, communism, democracy, despotism, dictatorship, empire, federation, hierocracy, junta, kingdom, monarchy, plutocracy, puppet government, republic, theocracy, triumvirate. *see also* **parliament**.

governor *n* ruler, commissioner, administrator, executive, director, manager, leader, head, chief, commander, superintendent, supervisor, overseer, controller, boss.

gown *n* robe, dress, frock, dressing-gown, habit, costume.

grab *v* seize, snatch, take, nab (*infml*), pluck, snap up, catch hold of, grasp, clutch, grip, catch, bag, capture, collar (*infml*), commandeer, appropriate, usurp, annex.

grace *n* **1** GRACEFULNESS, poise, beauty,

attractiveness, loveliness, shapeliness, elegance, tastefulness, refinement, polish, breeding, manners, etiquette, decorum, decency, courtesy, charm. **2** KINDNESS, kindliness, compassion, consideration, goodness, virtue, generosity, charity, benevolence, goodwill, favour, forgiveness, indulgence, mercy, leniency, pardon, reprieve. **3** *say grace*: blessing, benediction, thanksgiving, prayer. **F2** cruelty, harshness.
➤ *v* favour, honour, dignify, distinguish, embellish, enhance, set off, trim, garnish, decorate, ornament, adorn. **F3** spoil, detract from.

graceful *adj* easy, flowing, smooth, supple, agile, deft, natural, slender, fine, tasteful, elegant, beautiful, charming, suave. **F3** graceless, awkward, clumsy, ungainly.

gracious *adj* elegant, refined, polite, courteous, well-mannered, considerate, sweet, obliging, accommodating, kind, compassionate, kindly, benevolent, generous, magnanimous, charitable, hospitable, forgiving, indulgent, lenient, mild, clement, merciful. **F3** ungracious.

grade *n* rank, status, standing, station, place, position, level, stage, degree, step, rung, notch, mark, brand, quality, standard, condition, size, order, group, class, category.
➤ *v* sort, arrange, categorize, order, group, class, rate, size, rank, range, classify, evaluate, assess, value, mark, brand, label, pigeonhole, type.

gradient *n* slope, incline, hill, bank, rise, declivity.

gradual *adj* slow, leisurely, unhurried, easy, gentle, moderate, regular, even, measured, steady, continuous, progressive, step-by-step. **F3** sudden, precipitate.

gradually *adv* little by little, bit by bit, imperceptibly, inch by inch, step by step, progressively, by degrees, piecemeal, slowly, gently, cautiously, gingerly, moderately, evenly, steadily.

graduate v 1 *graduate from medical school*: pass, qualify. 2 CALIBRATE, mark off, measure out, proportion, grade, arrange, range, order, rank, sort, group, classify.

graft n implant, implantation, transplant, splice, bud, sprout, shoot, scion.
➤ v engraft, implant, insert, transplant, join, splice.

grain n 1 BIT, piece, fragment, scrap, morsel, crumb, granule, particle, molecule, atom, jot, iota, mite, speck, modicum, trace. 2 SEED, kernel, corn, cereals. 3 TEXTURE, fibre, weave, pattern, marking, surface.

grand adj 1 MAJESTIC, regal, stately, splendid, magnificent, glorious, superb, sublime, fine, excellent, outstanding, first-rate, impressive, imposing, striking, monumental, large, noble, lordly, lofty, pompous, pretentious, grandiose, ambitious. 2 SUPREME, pre-eminent, leading, head, chief, arch, highest, senior, great, illustrious.
🖅 1 humble, common, poor.

grandeur n majesty, stateliness, pomp, state, dignity, splendour, magnificence, nobility, greatness, illustriousness, importance.
🖅 humbleness, lowliness, simplicity.

grandiose adj pompous, pretentious, high-flown, lofty, ambitious, extravagant, ostentatious, showy, flamboyant, grand, majestic, stately, magnificent, impressive, imposing, monumental.
🖅 unpretentious.

grant v 1 GIVE, donate, present, award, confer, bestow, impart, transmit, dispense, apportion, assign, allot, allocate, provide, supply. 2 ADMIT, acknowledge, concede, allow, permit, consent to, agree to, accede to.
🖅 1 withhold. 2 deny.
➤ n allowance, subsidy, concession, award, bursary, scholarship, gift, donation, endowment, bequest, annuity, pension, honorarium.

granular adj grainy, granulated, gritty, sandy, lumpy, rough, crumbly, friable.

graph n diagram, chart, table, grid.

graphic adj vivid, descriptive, expressive, striking, telling, lively, realistic, explicit, clear, lucid, specific, detailed, blow-by-blow, visual, pictorial, diagrammatic, illustrative.
🖅 vague, impressionistic.

grapple v seize, grasp, snatch, grab, grip, clutch, clasp, hold, wrestle, tussle, struggle, contend, fight, combat, clash, engage, encounter, face, confront, tackle, deal with, cope with.
🖅 release, avoid, evade.

grasp v 1 HOLD, clasp, clutch, grip, grapple, seize, snatch, grab, catch. 2 *grasp a concept*: understand, comprehend, get (*infml*), follow, see, realize.
➤ n 1 GRIP, clasp, hold, embrace, clutches, possession, control, power, rule. 2 UNDERSTANDING, comprehension, apprehension, mastery, familiarity, knowledge.

grasping adj avaricious, greedy, rapacious, acquisitive, mercenary, mean, selfish, miserly, close-fisted, tight-fisted, parsimonious.
🖅 generous.

grass n turf, lawn, green, grassland, field, meadow, pasture, prairie, pampas, savanna, steppe.

Types of grass include: bamboo, barley, beard grass, bent, buckwheat, cane, cocksfoot, corn, couch grass, English ryegrass, esparto, fescue, Italian ryegrass, Kentucky bluegrass, kangaroo grass, knot grass, maize, marijuana, marram grass, meadow foxtail, meadow grass, millet, oats, paddy, pampas grass, papyrus, rattan, reed, rice, rye, ryegrass, sorghum, squirrel-tail grass, sugar cane, switch grass, twitch grass, wheat, wild oat.

grate v 1 GRIND, shred, mince, pulverize, rub, rasp, scrape. 2 JAR, set one's teeth on edge, annoy, irritate, aggravate (*infml*), get on one's nerves, vex, irk, exasperate.

grateful *adj* thankful, appreciative, indebted, obliged, obligated, beholden.
🔁 ungrateful.

gratify *v* satisfy, fulfil, indulge, pander to, humour, favour, please, gladden, delight, thrill.
🔁 frustrate, thwart.

grating[1] *adj* harsh, rasping, scraping, squeaky, strident, discordant, jarring, annoying, irritating, unpleasant, disagreeable.
🔁 harmonious, pleasing.

grating[2] *n* grate, grill, grid, lattice, trellis.

gratitude *n* gratefulness, thankfulness, thanks, appreciation, acknowledgement, recognition, indebtedness, obligation.
🔁 ingratitude, ungratefulness.

gratuitous *adj* wanton, unnecessary, needless, superfluous, unwarranted, unjustified, groundless, undeserved, unprovoked, uncalled-for, unasked-for, unsolicited, voluntary, free, gratis, complimentary.
🔁 justified, provoked.

gratuity *n* tip, bonus, perk (*infml*), gift, present, donation, reward, recompense.

grave[1] *n* burial-place, tomb, vault, crypt, sepulchre, mausoleum, pit, barrow, tumulus, cairn.

grave[2] *adj* 1 *a grave mistake*: important, significant, weighty, momentous, serious, critical, vital, crucial, urgent, acute, severe, dangerous, hazardous. 2 SOLEMN, dignified, sober, sedate, serious, thoughtful, pensive, grim, long-faced, quiet, reserved, subdued, restrained.
🔁 1 trivial, light, slight. 2 cheerful.

graveyard *n* cemetery, burial ground, churchyard.

gravity *n* 1 IMPORTANCE, significance, seriousness, urgency, acuteness, severity, danger. 2 SOLEMNITY, dignity,

sobriety, seriousness, thoughtfulness, sombreness, reserve, restraint. 3 GRAVITATION, attraction, pull, weight, heaviness.
🔁 1 triviality. 2 levity.

graze *v* scratch, scrape, skin, abrade, rub, chafe, shave, brush, skim, touch.
➤ *n* scratch, scrape, abrasion.

grease *n* oil, lubrication, fat, lard, dripping, tallow.

greasy *adj* oily, fatty, lardy, buttery, smeary, slimy, slippery, smooth, waxy.

great *adj* 1 LARGE, big, huge, vast, enormous, massive, colossal, gigantic, mammoth, immense, impressive. 2 *with great care*: considerable, pronounced, extreme, excessive, inordinate. 3 FAMOUS, renowned, celebrated, illustrious, eminent, distinguished, prominent, noteworthy, notable, remarkable, outstanding, grand, glorious, fine. 4 IMPORTANT, significant, serious, major, principal, primary, main, chief, leading. 5 (*infml*) EXCELLENT, first-rate, superb, wonderful, marvellous, tremendous, terrific, fantastic, fabulous.
🔁 1 small. 2 slight. 3 unknown. 4 unimportant, insignificant.

greed *n* 1 HUNGER, ravenousness, gluttony, gourmandism, voracity, insatiability. 2 ACQUISITIVENESS, covetousness, desire, craving, longing, eagerness, avarice, selfishness.
🔁 1 abstemiousness, self-restraint.

greedy *adj* 1 HUNGRY, starving, ravenous, gluttonous, gormandizing, voracious, insatiable. 2 ACQUISITIVE, covetous, desirous, craving, eager, impatient, avaricious, grasping, selfish.
🔁 1 abstemious.

green *adj* 1 GRASSY, leafy, verdant, unripe, unseasoned, tender, fresh, budding, blooming, flourishing. 2 *green with envy*: envious, covetous, jealous, resentful. 3 IMMATURE, naïve, unsophisticated, ignorant, untrained, inexperienced, raw, new, recent, young. 4 ECOLOGICAL, environmental,

eco-friendly, environmentally aware.
➤ *n* common, lawn, grass, turf.

greenhouse *n* glasshouse, hothouse, conservatory, pavilion, vinery, orangery.

greet *v* hail, salute, acknowledge, address, accost, meet, receive, welcome.
🖃 ignore.

greeting *n* salutation, wave, hallo, acknowledgement, the time of day, address, reception, welcome.

greetings *n* regards, respects, compliments, salutations, best wishes, good wishes, love.

gregarious *adj* sociable, outgoing, extrovert, friendly, affable, social, convivial, cordial, warm.
🖃 unsociable.

grey *adj* **1** NEUTRAL, colourless, pale, ashen, leaden, dull, cloudy, overcast, dim, dark, murky. **2** GLOOMY, dismal, cheerless, depressing, dreary, bleak.

grief *n* sorrow, sadness, unhappiness, depression, dejection, desolation, distress, misery, woe, heartbreak, mourning, bereavement, heartache, anguish, agony, pain, suffering, affliction, trouble, regret, remorse.
🖃 happiness, delight.

grievance *n* complaint, moan (*infml*), grumble (*infml*), resentment, objection, protest, charge, wrong, injustice, injury, damage, trouble, affliction, hardship, trial, tribulation.

grieve *v* **1** SORROW, mope, lament, mourn, wail, cry, weep. **2** SADDEN, upset, dismay, distress, afflict, pain, hurt, wound.
🖃 **1** rejoice. **2** please, gladden.

grim *adj* **1** UNPLEASANT, horrible, horrid, ghastly, gruesome, grisly, sinister, frightening, fearsome, terrible, shocking. **2** STERN, severe, harsh, dour, forbidding, surly, sullen, morose, gloomy, depressing, unattractive.
🖃 **1** pleasant. **2** attractive.

grimace *n* frown, scowl, pout, smirk, sneer, face.

➤ *v* make a face, pull a face, frown, scowl, pout, smirk, sneer.

grime *n* dirt, muck, filth, soot, dust.

grimy *adj* dirty, mucky, grubby, soiled, filthy, sooty, smutty, dusty, smudgy.
🖃 clean.

grind *v* crush, pound, pulverize, powder, mill, grate, scrape, gnash, rut, abrade, sand, file, smooth, polish, sharpen, whet.

grip *n* hold, grasp, clasp, embrace, clutches, control, power.
➤ *v* **1** HOLD, grasp, clasp, clutch, seize, grab, catch. **2** FASCINATE, thrill, enthral, spellbind, mesmerize, hypnotize, rivet, engross, absorb, involve, engage, compel.

grisly *adj* gruesome, gory, grim, macabre, horrid, horrible, ghastly, awful, frightful, terrible, dreadful, abominable, appalling, shocking.
🖃 delightful.

grit *n* gravel, pebbles, shingle, sand, dust.
➤ *v* clench, gnash, grate, grind.

groan *n* moan, sigh, cry, whine, wail, lament, complaint, objection, protest, outcry.
🖃 cheer.
➤ *v* moan, sigh, cry, whine, wail, lament, complain, object, protest.
🖃 cheer.

groom *v* **1** SMARTEN, neaten, tidy, spruce up, clean, brush, curry, preen, dress. **2** *groomed for her new post*: PREPARE, train, school, educate, drill.

groove *n* furrow, rut, track, slot, channel, gutter, trench, hollow, indentation, score.
🖃 ridge.

grope *v* feel, fumble, scrabble, flounder, cast about, fish, search, probe.

gross *adj* **1** *gross misconduct*: serious, grievous, blatant, flagrant, glaring, obvious, plain, sheer, utter, outright, shameful, shocking. **2** OBSCENE, lewd, improper, indecent, offensive, rude, coarse, crude, vulgar, tasteless. **3** FAT,

obese, overweight, big, large, huge, colossal, hulking, bulky, heavy. **4** *gross earnings*: inclusive, all-inclusive, total, aggregate, entire, complete, whole.
F3 3 slight. **4** net.

grotesque *adj* bizarre, odd, weird, unnatural, freakish, monstrous, hideous, ugly, unsightly, misshapen, deformed, distorted, twisted, fantastic, fanciful, extravagant, absurd, surreal, macabre.
F3 normal, graceful.

ground *n* **1** BOTTOM, foundation, surface, land, terrain, dry land, terra firma, earth, soil, clay, loam, dirt, dust. **2** *football ground*: field, pitch, stadium, arena, park.
➤ *v* **1** BASE, found, establish, set, fix, settle. **2** PREPARE, introduce, initiate, familiarize with, acquaint with, inform, instruct, teach, train, drill, coach, tutor.

groundless *adj* baseless, unfounded, unsubstantiated, unsupported, empty, imaginary, false, unjustified, unwarranted, unprovoked, uncalled-for.
F3 well-founded, reasonable, justified.

grounds¹ *n* land, terrain, holding, estate, property, territory, domain, gardens, park, campus, surroundings, fields, acres.

grounds² *n* base, foundation, justification, excuse, vindication, reason, motive, inducement, cause, occasion, call, score, account, argument, principle, basis.

group *n* band, gang, pack, team, crew, troop, squad, detachment, party, faction, set, circle, clique, club, society, association, organization, company, gathering, congregation, crowd, collection, bunch, clump, cluster, conglomeration, constellation, batch, lot, combination, formation, grouping, class, classification, category, genus, species.
➤ *v* **1** GATHER, collect, assemble, congregate, mass, cluster, clump, bunch. **2** *group them according to size*: sort, range, arrange, marshal, organize, order, class, classify, categorize, band, link, associate.

grovel *v* crawl, creep, suck up (*sl*), ingratiate oneself, toady, flatter, fawn, cringe, cower, kowtow, defer, demean oneself.

grow *v* **1** INCREASE, rise, expand, enlarge, swell, spread, extend, stretch, develop, proliferate, mushroom. **2** ORIGINATE, arise, issue, spring, germinate, shoot, sprout, bud, flower, mature, develop, progress, thrive, flourish, prosper. **3** CULTIVATE, farm, produce, propagate, breed, raise. **4** *grow cold*: become, get, go, turn.
F3 1 decrease, shrink.

growl *v* snarl, snap, yap, rumble, roar.

grown-up *adj* adult, mature, of age, full-grown, fully-fledged.
F3 young, immature.
➤ *n* adult, man, woman.
F3 child.

growth *n* **1** INCREASE, rise, extension, enlargement, expansion, spread, proliferation, development, evolution, progress, advance, improvement, success, prosperity. **2** TUMOUR, lump, swelling, protuberance, outgrowth.
F3 1 decrease, decline, failure.

grub *v* dig, burrow, delve, probe, root, rummage, forage, ferret, hunt, search, scour, explore.
➤ *n* maggot, worm, larva, pupa, caterpillar, chrysalis.

grubby *adj* dirty, soiled, unwashed, mucky, grimy, filthy, squalid, seedy, scruffy.
F3 clean.

grudge *n* resentment, bitterness, envy, jealousy, spite, malice, enmity, antagonism, hate, dislike, animosity, ill-will, hard feelings, grievance.
F3 favour.
➤ *v* begrudge, resent, envy, covet, dislike, take exception to, object to, mind.

grudging *adj* reluctant, unwilling, hesitant, half-hearted, unenthusiastic, resentful, envious, jealous.

gruelling *adj* hard, difficult, taxing, demanding, tiring, exhausting, laborious,

arduous, strenuous, backbreaking, harsh, severe, tough, punishing.
F3 easy.

gruesome *adj* horrible, disgusting, repellent, repugnant, repulsive, hideous, grisly, macabre, grim, ghastly, awful, terrible, horrific, shocking, monstrous, abominable.
F3 pleasant.

gruff *adj* **1** CURT, brusque, abrupt, blunt, rude, surly, sullen, grumpy, bad-tempered. **2** *a gruff voice*: rough, harsh, rasping, guttural, throaty, husky, hoarse.
F3 **1** friendly, courteous.

grumble *v* complain, moan, whine, bleat, grouch, gripe, mutter, murmur, carp, kvetch (*US sl*), find fault.

grumpy *adj* bad-tempered, ill-tempered, crotchety, crabbed, cantankerous, cross, irritable, surly, sullen, sulky, grouchy, discontented.
F3 contented.

guarantee *n* warranty, insurance, assurance, promise, word of honour, pledge, oath, bond, security, collateral, surety, endorsement, testimonial.
➤ *v* assure, promise, pledge, swear, vouch for, answer for, warrant, certify, underwrite, endorse, secure, protect, insure, ensure, make sure, make certain.

guard *v* protect, safeguard, save, preserve, shield, screen, shelter, cover, defend, patrol, police, escort, supervise, oversee, watch, look out, mind, beware.
➤ *n* **1** PROTECTOR, defender, custodian, warder, escort, bodyguard, minder (*infml*), watchman, lookout, sentry, picket, patrol, security. **2** PROTECTION, safeguard, defence, wall, barrier, screen, shield, bumper, buffer, pad.

guarded *adj* cautious, wary, careful, watchful, discreet, non-committal, reticent, reserved, secretive, cagey (*infml*).
F3 communicative, frank.

guardian *n* trustee, curator, custodian, keeper, warden, protector, preserver, defender, champion, guard, warder, escort, attendant.

guess *v* speculate, conjecture, predict, estimate, judge, reckon, work out, suppose, assume, surmise, think, believe, imagine, fancy, feel, suspect.
➤ *n* prediction, estimate, speculation, conjecture, supposition, assumption, belief, fancy, idea, notion, theory, hypothesis, opinion, feeling, suspicion, intuition.

guesswork *n* speculation, conjecture, estimation, reckoning, supposition, assumption, surmise, intuition.

guest *n* visitor, caller, boarder, lodger, resident, patron, regular.

guidance *n* leadership, direction, management, control, teaching, instruction, advice, counsel, counselling, help, instructions, directions, guidelines, indications, pointers, recommendations.

guide *v* lead, conduct, direct, navigate, point, steer, pilot, manoeuvre, usher, escort, accompany, attend, control, govern, manage, oversee, supervise, superintend, advise, counsel, influence, educate, teach, instruct, train.
➤ *n* **1** LEADER, courier, navigator, pilot, helmsman, steersman, usher, escort, chaperon, attendant, companion, adviser, counsellor, mentor, guru, teacher, instructor. **2** MANUAL, handbook, guidebook, user guide, catalogue, directory. **3** GUIDELINE, example, model, standard, criterion, indication, pointer, signpost, sign, marker.

guilt *n* **1** *he confessed his guilt*: culpability, responsibility, blame, disgrace, dishonour. **2** *a feeling of guilt*: guilty conscience, conscience, shame, self-condemnation, self-reproach, regret, remorse, contrition.
F3 **1** innocence, righteousness.
2 shamelessness.

guilty *adj* **1** CULPABLE, responsible, blamable, blameworthy, offending, wrong, sinful, wicked, criminal, convicted. **2** CONSCIENCE-STRICKEN, ashamed, shamefaced, sheepish, sorry, regretful, remorseful, contrite,

penitent, repentant.
☒ **1** innocent, guiltless, blameless.
2 shameless.

gulf *n* bay, bight, basin, gap, opening, separation, rift, split, breach, cleft, chasm, gorge, abyss, void.

gullible *adj* credulous, suggestible, impressionable, trusting, unsuspecting, foolish, naïve, green, unsophisticated, innocent.
☒ astute.

gully *n* channel, watercourse, gutter, ditch, ravine.

gulp *v* swallow, swig, swill, knock back (*infml*), bolt, wolf (*infml*), gobble, guzzle, devour, stuff (*infml*).
☒ sip, nibble.
➤ *n* swallow, swig, draught, mouthful.

gum *n* adhesive, glue, paste, cement.
➤ *v* stick, glue, paste, fix, cement, seal, clog.

gun *n* firearm, handgun, pistol, revolver, shooter (*sl*), shooting iron (*sl*), rifle, shotgun, bazooka, howitzer, cannon. *see also* **weapon**.

gurgle *v* bubble, babble, burble, murmur, ripple, lap, splash, crow.
➤ *n* babble, murmur, ripple.

gush *v* **1** FLOW, run, pour, stream, cascade, flood, rush, burst, spurt,

spout, jet. **2** ENTHUSE, chatter, babble, jabber, go on (*infml*), drivel.
➤ *n* flow, outflow, stream, torrent, cascade, flood, tide, rush, burst, outburst, spurt, spout, jet.

gust *n* blast, burst, rush, flurry, blow, puff, breeze, wind, gale, squall.

gusto *n* zest, relish, appreciation, enjoyment, pleasure, delight, enthusiasm, exuberance, élan, verve, zeal.
☒ distaste, apathy.

gut *v* **1** *gut fish*: disembowel, draw, clean (out). **2** STRIP, clear, empty, rifle, ransack, plunder, loot, sack, ravage.

guts *n* **1** INTESTINES, bowels, viscera, entrails, insides, innards (*infml*), belly, stomach. **2** (*infml*) COURAGE, bravery, pluck, grit, nerve, mettle.

gutter *n* drain, sluice, ditch, trench, trough, channel, duct, conduit, passage, pipe, tube.

guy (*infml*) *n* fellow, bloke (*infml*), chap (*infml*), man, boy, youth, person, individual.

gypsy, gipsy *n* Romany, traveller, wanderer, nomad, tinker.

gyrate *v* turn, revolve, rotate, twirl, pirouette, spin, whirl, wheel, circle, spiral.

Hh

habit *n* custom, usage, practice, routine, rule, second nature, way, manner, mode, wont, inclination, tendency, bent, mannerism, quirk, addiction, dependence, fixation, obsession, weakness.

habitat *n* home, abode, domain, element, environment, surroundings, locality, territory, terrain.

habitual *adj* 1 CUSTOMARY, traditional, wonted, routine, usual, ordinary, common, natural, normal, standard, regular, recurrent, fixed, established, familiar. 2 *habitual drinker*: confirmed, inveterate, hardened, addicted, dependent, persistent.
🖪 1 occasional, infrequent.

hack¹ *v* cut, chop, hew, notch, gash, slash, lacerate, mutilate, mangle.

hack² *n* scribbler, journalist, drudge, slave.

hackneyed *adj* stale, overworked, tired, worn-out, time-worn, threadbare, unoriginal, corny (*infml*), clichéed, stereotyped, stock, banal, trite, commonplace, common, pedestrian, uninspired.
🖪 original, new, fresh.

hag *n* crone, witch, battle-axe (*infml*), shrew, termagant, vixen.

haggard *adj* drawn, gaunt, careworn, thin, wasted, shrunken, pinched, pale, wan, ghastly.
🖪 hale.

haggle *v* bargain, negotiate, barter, wrangle, squabble, bicker, quarrel, dispute.

hail¹ *n* barrage, bombardment, volley, torrent, shower, rain, storm.
➤ *v* pelt, bombard, barrage, volley,

shower, rain, batter, attack, assail.

hail² *v* greet, address, acknowledge, salute, wave, signal to, flag down, shout, call, acclaim, cheer, applaud, honour, welcome.

hair *n* locks, tresses, shock, mop, mane.

hairdresser *n* hairstylist, stylist, barber, coiffeur, coiffeuse.

hairless *adj* bald, bald-headed, shorn, tonsured, shaven, clean-shaven, beardless.
🖪 hairy, hirsute.

hair-raising *adj* frightening, scary, terrifying, horrifying, shocking, bloodcurdling, spine-chilling, white-knuckle (*infml*), eerie, alarming, startling, thrilling.

hairstyle *n* style, coiffure, hairdo (*infml*), cut, haircut, set, perm (*infml*).

Hairstyles include: Afro, backcombed, bangs, beehive, bob, bouffant, braid, bun, chignon, combover, corn rows, cowlick, crewcut, crimped, crop, curled, dreadlocks, Eton crop, flat top, French plait, fringe, frizette, marcel wave, mohican, mullet, pageboy, perm, pigtail, plait, pompadour, ponytail, pouffe, quiff, ringlets, shed, shingle, short back and sides, sideboards, sideburns, skinhead, tonsure, topknot, undercut; hair-piece, rug (*infml*), toupee, wig.

---

hairy *adj* hirsute, bearded, shaggy, bushy, fuzzy, furry, woolly.
🖪 bald, clean-shaven.

half *n* fifty per cent, bisection, hemisphere, semicircle, section, segment, portion, share, fraction.
➤ *adj* semi-, halved, divided, fractional,

part, partial, incomplete, moderate, limited.
Ea whole.

➤ *adv* partly, partially, incompletely, moderately, slightly.
Ea completely.

half-hearted *adj* lukewarm, cool, weak, feeble, passive, apathetic, uninterested, indifferent, neutral.
Ea wholehearted, enthusiastic.

halfway *adv* midway, in the middle, centrally.

➤ *adj* middle, central, equidistant, mid, midway, intermediate.

hall *n* hallway, corridor, passage, passageway, entrance hall, foyer, vestibule, lobby, concert hall, auditorium, chamber, assembly room.

hallmark *n* stamp, mark, trademark, brand-name, sign, indication, symbol, emblem, device, badge.

hallucinate *v* dream, imagine, see things, daydream, fantasize, freak out (*sl*), trip (*sl*).

hallucination *n* illusion, mirage, vision, apparition, dream, daydream, fantasy, figment, delusion, freak-out (*sl*), trip (*sl*).

halt *v* stop, draw up, pull up, pause, wait, rest, break off, discontinue, cease, desist, quit, end, terminate, check, stem, curb, obstruct, impede.
Ea start, continue.

➤ *n* stop, stoppage, arrest, interruption, break, pause, rest, standstill, end, close, termination.
Ea start, continuation.

halting *adj* hesitant, stuttering, stammering, faltering, stumbling, broken, imperfect, laboured, awkward.
Ea fluent.

halve *v* bisect, cut in half, split in two, divide, split, share, cut down, reduce, lessen.

hammer *v* hit, strike, beat, drum, bang, bash, pound, batter, knock, drive, shape, form, make.

➤ *n* mallet, gavel.

◇ **hammer out** settle, sort out, negotiate, thrash out, produce, bring about, accomplish, complete, finish.

hamper *v* hinder, impede, obstruct, slow down, hold up, frustrate, thwart, prevent, handicap, hamstring, shackle, cramp, restrict, curb, restrain.
Ea aid, facilitate.

hand *n* **1** FIST, palm, paw (*infml*), mitt (*infml*). **2** *give me a hand*: help, aid, assistance, support, participation, part, influence. **3** WORKER, employee, operative, workman, labourer, farm-hand, hireling.

➤ *v* give, pass, offer, submit, present, yield, deliver, transmit, conduct, convey.
◇ **at hand** near, close, to hand, handy, accessible, available, ready, imminent.
◇ **hand down** bequeath, will, pass on, transfer, give, grant.
◇ **hand out** distribute, deal out, give out, share out, dish out (*infml*), mete out, dispense.
◇ **hand over** yield, relinquish, surrender, turn over, deliver, release, give, donate, present.
Ea keep, retain.

handbook *n* manual, instruction book, guide, guidebook, user guide, companion.

handful *n* few, sprinkling, scattering, smattering.
Ea a lot, many.

handicap *n* obstacle, block, barrier, impediment, stumbling block, hindrance, drawback, disadvantage, restriction, limitation, penalty, disability, impairment, defect, shortcoming.
Ea assistance, advantage.

➤ *v* impede, hinder, disadvantage, hold back, retard, hamper, burden, encumber, restrict, limit, disable.
Ea help, assist.

handicraft *n* craft, art, craftwork, handwork, handiwork.

handiwork *n* work, doing, responsibility, achievement, product, result, design, invention, creation, production, skill, workmanship, craftsmanship, artisanship.

handle *n* grip, handgrip, knob, stock, shaft, hilt.

➤ *v* **1** TOUCH, finger, feel, fondle, pick up, hold, grasp. **2** *handle a situation*: tackle, treat, deal with, manage, cope with, control, supervise.

handout *n* **1** CHARITY, alms, dole, largess(e), share, issue, free sample, freebie (*sl*). **2** LEAFLET, flyer, circular, bulletin, statement, press release, literature.

hands *n* care, custody, possession, charge, authority, command, power, control, supervision.

handsome *adj* **1** GOOD-LOOKING, attractive, fair, personable, elegant. **2** GENEROUS, liberal, large, considerable, ample.
◨ **1** ugly, unattractive. **2** mean.

handwriting *n* writing, script, hand, fist (*infml*), penmanship, calligraphy.

handy *adj* **1** AVAILABLE, to hand, ready, at hand, near, accessible, convenient, practical, useful, helpful. **2** SKILFUL, proficient, expert, skilled, clever, practical.
◨ **1** inconvenient. **2** clumsy.

hang *v* **1** SUSPEND, dangle, swing, drape, drop, flop, droop, sag, trail. **2** FASTEN, attach, fix, stick. **3** *hang in the air*: float, drift, hover, linger, remain, cling.
◇ **hang about** hang around, linger, loiter, dawdle, waste time, associate with, frequent, haunt.
◇ **hang back** hold back, demur, hesitate, shy away, recoil.
◇ **hang on 1** WAIT, hold on, remain, hold out, endure, continue, carry on, persevere, persist. **2** GRIP, grasp, hold fast. **3** DEPEND ON, hinge on, turn on.
◨ **1** give up.

hanger-on *n* follower, minion, lackey, toady, sycophant, parasite, sponger, dependant.

hang-up (*infml*) *n* inhibition, difficulty, problem, obsession, preoccupation, thing (*infml*), block, mental block.

hanker for hanker after, crave, hunger for, thirst for, want, wish for, desire, covet, yearn for, long for, pine for, itch for.

hankering *n* craving, hunger, thirst, wish, desire, yearning, longing, itch, urge.

haphazard *adj* random, chance, casual, arbitrary, hit-or-miss, unsystematic, disorganized, disorderly, careless, slapdash, slipshod.
◨ methodical, orderly.

happen *v* occur, take place, arise, crop up, develop, materialize, come about, result, ensue, follow, turn out, transpire.

happening *n* occurrence, event, phenomenon, incident, episode, occasion, adventure, experience, accident, chance, circumstance, case, affair.

happiness *n* joy, joyfulness, gladness, cheerfulness, contentment, pleasure, delight, glee, elation, bliss, ecstasy, euphoria.
◨ unhappiness, sadness.

happy *adj* **1** JOYFUL, jolly, merry, cheerful, glad, pleased, delighted, thrilled, elated, satisfied, content, contented. **2** *a happy coincidence*: lucky, fortunate, felicitous, favourable, appropriate, apt, fitting.
◨ **1** unhappy, sad, discontented. **2** unfortunate, inappropriate.

harangue *n* diatribe, tirade, lecture, speech, address.
➤ *v* lecture, preach, hold forth, spout (*infml*), declaim, address.

harass *v* pester, badger, harry, plague, bug (*infml*), torment, persecute, exasperate, vex, annoy, irritate, bother, disturb, hassle (*infml*), trouble, worry, stress, tire, wear out, exhaust, fatigue.

harbour *n* port, dock, quay, wharf, marina, mooring, anchorage, haven, shelter.
➤ *v* **1** HIDE, conceal, protect, shelter. **2** *harbour a feeling*: hold, retain, cling to, entertain, foster, nurse, nurture, cherish, believe, imagine.

hard *adj* **1** SOLID, firm, unyielding, tough, strong, dense, impenetrable, stiff, rigid, inflexible. **2** DIFFICULT, arduous, strenuous, laborious, tiring, exhausting, backbreaking, complex, complicated, involved, knotty, baffling, puzzling, perplexing. **3** HARSH, severe, strict, stern, callous, unfeeling, unsympathetic, cruel, pitiless, merciless, ruthless, unrelenting, distressing, painful, unpleasant.
F3 **1** soft, yielding. **2** easy, simple. **3** kind, pleasant.
➤ *adv* industriously, diligently, assiduously, doggedly, steadily, laboriously, strenuously, earnestly, keenly, intently, strongly, violently, intensely, energetically, vigorously.
◇ **hard up** poor, broke (*infml*), penniless, impoverished, in the red, bankrupt, bust, short, lacking.
F3 rich.

harden *v* solidify, set, freeze, bake, cake, stiffen, strengthen, reinforce, fortify, buttress, brace, steel, nerve, toughen, season, accustom, train.
F3 soften, weaken.

hard-headed *adj* shrewd, astute, businesslike, level-headed, clear-thinking, sensible, realistic, pragmatic, practical, hard-boiled, tough, unsentimental.
F3 unrealistic.

hard-hearted *adj* callous, unfeeling, cold, hard, stony, heartless, cruel, unsympathetic, inhuman, pitiless, merciless.
F3 soft-hearted, kind, merciful.

hard-hitting *adj* condemnatory, critical, unsparing, no-holds-barred, vigorous, forceful, tough.
F3 mild.

hardly *adv* barely, scarcely, just, only just, not quite, not at all, by no means.

hardship *n* misfortune, adversity, trouble, difficulty, affliction, distress, suffering, trial, tribulation, want, need, privation, austerity, poverty, destitution, misery.
F3 ease, comfort, prosperity.

hard-wearing *adj* durable, lasting, strong, tough, sturdy, stout, rugged, resilient.
F3 delicate.

hard-working *adj* industrious, diligent, assiduous, conscientious, zealous, busy, energetic.
F3 idle, lazy.

hardy *adj* strong, tough, sturdy, robust, vigorous, fit, sound, healthy.
F3 weak, unhealthy.

harm *n* damage, loss, injury, hurt, detriment, ill, misfortune, wrong, abuse.
F3 benefit.
➤ *v* damage, impair, blemish, spoil, mar, ruin, hurt, injure, wound, ill-treat, maltreat, abuse, misuse.
F3 benefit, improve.

harmful *adj* damaging, detrimental, pernicious, noxious, unhealthy, unwholesome, injurious, dangerous, hazardous, poisonous, toxic, destructive.
F3 harmless.

harmless *adj* safe, innocuous, non-toxic, inoffensive, gentle, innocent.
F3 harmful, dangerous, destructive.

harmonious *adj* **1** MELODIOUS, tuneful, musical, sweet-sounding. **2** MATCHING, co-ordinated, balanced, compatible, like-minded, agreeable, cordial, amicable, friendly, sympathetic.
F3 **1** discordant.

harmonize *v* match, co-ordinate, balance, fit in, suit, tone, blend, correspond, agree, reconcile, accommodate, adapt, arrange, compose.
F3 clash.

harmony *n* **1** TUNEFULNESS, tune, melody, euphony. **2** *live in harmony*: agreement, unanimity, accord (*fml*), concord (*fml*), unity, compatibility, like-mindedness, peace, goodwill, rapport, sympathy, understanding, amicability, friendliness, co-operation, co-ordination, balance, symmetry, correspondence, conformity.
F3 **1** discord. **2** conflict.

harness *n* tackle, gear, equipment, reins, straps, tack.

> *Parts of a horse's harness include*: backband, bellyband, bit, blinders (*US*), blinkers, breeching, bridle, collar, crupper, girth, hackamore, halter, hames, headstall (*US*), martingale, noseband, reins, saddle, saddlepad, stirrup, throatlatch/throatlash (*US*), traces.

➤ *v* control, channel, use, utilize, exploit, make use of, employ, mobilize, apply.

harrowing *adj* distressing, upsetting, heart-rending, disturbing, alarming, frightening, terrifying, nerve-racking, traumatic, agonizing, excruciating.

harry *v* badger, pester, nag, chivvy, harass, plague, torment, persecute, annoy, vex, worry, trouble, bother, hassle (*infml*), disturb, molest.

harsh *adj* **1** SEVERE, strict, Draconian, unfeeling, cruel, hard, pitiless, austere, Spartan, bleak, grim, comfortless. **2** *a harsh sound*: rough, coarse, rasping, croaking, guttural, grating, jarring, discordant, strident, raucous, sharp, shrill, unpleasant. **3** BRIGHT, dazzling, glaring, gaudy, lurid.
▣ **1** lenient. **2** soft.

harvest *n* **1** HARVEST-TIME, ingathering, reaping, collection. **2** CROP, yield, return, produce, fruits, result, consequence.
➤ *v* reap, mow, pick, gather, collect, accumulate, amass.

hash *n* mess, botch, muddle, mix-up, jumble, confusion, hotchpotch, mishmash.

haste *n* hurry, rush, hustle, bustle, speed, velocity, rapidity, swiftness, quickness, briskness, urgency, rashness, recklessness, impetuosity.
▣ slowness.

hasten *v* hurry, rush, make haste, run, sprint, dash, tear, race, fly, bolt, accelerate, speed (up), quicken, expedite, dispatch, precipitate, urge, press, advance, step up.
▣ dawdle, delay.

hasty *adj* hurried, rushed, impatient, headlong, rash, reckless, heedless, thoughtless, impetuous, impulsive, hot-headed, fast, quick, rapid, swift, speedy, brisk, prompt, short, brief, cursory.
▣ slow, careful, deliberate.

hat

> *Hats include*: trilby, bowler, fedora, top hat, Homburg, derby (*US*), pork-pie hat, flat cap, beret, bonnet, Tam o' Shanter, tammy, deerstalker, hunting-cap, stovepipe hat, Stetson®, ten-gallon hat, boater, sunhat, panama, straw hat, picture hat, pillbox, cloche, beanie, Bronx hat, poke-bonnet, mob cap, turban, fez, sombrero, sou'wester, glengarry, bearskin, busby, peaked cap, sailor hat, baseball cap, jockey cap, balaclava, hood, snood, toque, helmet, mortarboard, skullcap, yarmulka, mitre, biretta.

hatch *v* **1** INCUBATE, brood, breed. **2** CONCOCT, formulate, originate, think up, dream up, conceive, devise, contrive, plot, scheme, design, plan, project.

hate *v* dislike, despise, detest, loathe, abhor, abominate, execrate.
▣ like, love.
➤ *n* hatred, aversion, dislike, loathing, abhorrence, abomination.
▣ liking, love.

hatred *n* hate, aversion, dislike, detestation, loathing, repugnance, revulsion, abhorrence, abomination, execration, animosity, ill-will, antagonism, hostility, enmity, antipathy.
▣ liking, love.

haughty *adj* lofty, imperious, high and mighty, supercilious, cavalier, snooty (*infml*), contemptuous, disdainful, scornful, superior, snobbish, arrogant, proud, stuck-up (*infml*), conceited.
▣ humble, modest.

haul *v* pull, heave, tug, draw, tow, drag, trail, move, transport, convey, carry, cart, lug, hump (*infml*).
▣ push.
➤ *n* loot, booty, plunder, swag (*sl*),

spoils, takings, gain, yield, find.

haunt v 1 FREQUENT, patronize, visit.
2 *memories haunted her*: plague,
torment, trouble, disturb, recur, prey on,
beset, obsess, possess.
➤ n resort, hangout (*infml*), stamping-
ground, den, meeting place,
rendezvous.

haunting adj memorable,
unforgettable, persistent, recurrent,
evocative, nostalgic, poignant.
✍ unmemorable.

have v 1 OWN, possess, get, obtain,
gain, acquire, procure, secure, receive,
accept, keep, hold. 2 FEEL, experience,
enjoy, suffer, undergo, endure, put up
with. 3 CONTAIN, include, comprise,
incorporate, consist of. 4 *have a baby*:
give birth to, bear.
✍ 1 lack.
◇ **have to** must, be forced, be
compelled, be obliged, be required,
ought, should.

haven n harbour, port, anchorage,
shelter, refuge, sanctuary, asylum,
retreat.

havoc n chaos, confusion, disorder,
disruption, damage, destruction, ruin,
wreck, rack and ruin, devastation,
waste, desolation.

haywire (*infml*) adj wrong, tangled,
out of control, crazy, mad, wild, chaotic,
confused, disordered, disorganized,
topsy-turvy.

hazard n risk, danger, peril, jeopardy,
threat, death-trap, accident, chance.
✍ safety.
➤ v 1 RISK, endanger, jeopardize,
expose. 2 CHANCE, gamble, stake,
venture, suggest, speculate.

hazardous adj risky, dangerous,
unsafe, perilous, precarious, insecure,
chancy, difficult, tricky.
✍ safe, secure.

haze n mist, fog, cloud, steam, vapour,
film, mistiness, smokiness, dimness,
obscurity.

hazy adj misty, foggy, smoky, clouded,

cloudy, milky, fuzzy, blurred, ill-defined,
veiled, obscure, dim, faint, unclear,
indistinct, vague, indefinite, uncertain.
✍ clear, bright, definite.

head n 1 SKULL, cranium, brain, mind,
mentality, brains (*infml*), intellect,
intelligence, understanding, thought.
2 TOP, peak, summit, crown, tip, apex,
height, climax, front, fore, lead.
3 LEADER, chief, captain, commander,
boss (*infml*), director, manager,
superintendent, principal, head teacher,
ruler.
✍ 1 foot, tail. 2 base, foot.
3 subordinate.
➤ adj leading, front, foremost, first,
chief, main, prime, principal, top,
highest, supreme, premier, dominant,
pre-eminent.
➤ v lead, rule, govern, command, direct,
manage, run, superintend, oversee,
supervise, control, guide, steer.
◇ **head for** make for, go towards, direct
towards, aim for, point to, turn for, steer
for.
◇ **head off** forestall, intercept,
intervene, interpose, deflect, divert,
fend off, ward off, avert, prevent, stop.

heading n title, name, headline, rubric,
caption, section, division, category,
class.

headland n promontory, cape, head,
point, foreland.

headlong adj hasty, precipitate,
impetuous, impulsive, rash, reckless,
dangerous, breakneck, head-first.
➤ adv head first, hurriedly, hastily,
precipitately, rashly, recklessly,
heedlessly, thoughtlessly, wildly.

headquarters n HQ, base (camp),
head office, nerve centre.

headstrong adj stubborn, obstinate,
intractable, pigheaded, wilful, self-
willed, perverse, contrary.
✍ tractable, docile.

headway n advance, progress, way,
improvement.

heady adj intoxicating, strong,
stimulating, exhilarating, thrilling, exciting.

heal v cure, remedy, mend, restore, treat, soothe, salve, settle, reconcile, patch up.

health n fitness, constitution, form, shape, trim, fettle, condition, tone, state, healthiness, good condition, wellbeing, welfare, soundness, robustness, strength, vigour.
▣ illness, infirmity.

healthy adj 1 WELL, fit, good, fine, in condition, in good shape, in fine fettle, sound, sturdy, robust, strong, vigorous, hale and hearty, blooming, flourishing, thriving. 2 healthy food: wholesome, nutritious, nourishing, bracing, invigorating, healthful.
▣ 1 ill, sick, infirm.

heap n pile, stack, mound, mountain, lot, mass, accumulation, collection, hoard, stockpile, store.
➤ v pile, stack, mound, bank, build, amass, accumulate, collect, gather, hoard, stockpile, store, load, burden, shower, lavish.

hear v 1 LISTEN, catch, pick up, overhear, eavesdrop, heed, pay attention. 2 LEARN, find out, discover, ascertain, understand, gather. 3 JUDGE, try, examine, investigate.

hearing n 1 EARSHOT, sound, range, reach, ear, perception. 2 TRIAL, inquiry, investigation, inquest, audition, interview, audience.

hearsay n rumour, word of mouth, talk, gossip, tittle-tattle, report, buzz (*infml*).

heart n 1 SOUL, mind, character, disposition, nature, temperament, feeling, emotion, sentiment, love, tenderness, compassion, sympathy, pity. 2 lose heart: courage, bravery, boldness, spirit, resolution, determination. 3 CENTRE, middle, core, kernel, nucleus, nub, crux, essence.
▣ 2 cowardice. 3 periphery.

Parts of the heart include: aortic valve, ascending aorta, bicuspid valve, carotid artery, descending thoracic aorta, inferior vena cava, left atrium, left pulmonary artery, left pulmonary veins, left ventricle, mitral valve, myocardium, papillary muscle, pulmonary valve, right atrium, right pulmonary artery, right pulmonary veins, right ventricle, superior vena cava, tricuspid valve, ventricular septum.

◇ **by heart** by rote, parrot-fashion, pat, off pat, word for word, verbatim.

heartbreaking adj distressing, sad, tragic, harrowing, heart-rending, pitiful, agonizing, painful, grievous, bitter, disappointing.
▣ heartwarming, heartening.

heartbroken adj broken-hearted, desolate, sad, miserable, dejected, despondent, downcast, crestfallen, disappointed, dispirited, grieved, crushed.
▣ delighted, elated.

hearten v comfort, console, reassure, cheer (up), buck up (*infml*), encourage, boost, inspire, stimulate, rouse, pep up (*infml*).
▣ dishearten, depress, dismay.

heartfelt adj deep, profound, sincere, honest, genuine, earnest, ardent, fervent, wholehearted, warm.
▣ insincere, false.

heartless adj unfeeling, uncaring, cold, hard, hard-hearted, callous, unkind, cruel, inhuman, brutal, pitiless, merciless.
▣ kind, considerate, sympathetic, merciful.

heart-rending adj harrowing, heartbreaking, agonizing, pitiful, piteous, pathetic, tragic, sad, distressing, moving, affecting, poignant.

heartwarming adj pleasing, gratifying, satisfying, cheering, heartening, encouraging, touching, moving, affecting.
▣ heartbreaking.

hearty adj 1 ENTHUSIASTIC, wholehearted, unreserved, heartfelt, sincere, genuine, warm, friendly, cordial, jovial, cheerful, ebullient, exuberant, boisterous, energetic, vigorous. 2 a

hearty breakfast: large, sizable, substantial, filling, ample, generous.
F3 1 half-hearted, cool, cold.

heat *n* **1** HOTNESS, warmth, sultriness, closeness, high temperature, fever. **2** ARDOUR, fervour, fieriness, passion, intensity, vehemence, fury, excitement, impetuosity, earnestness, zeal.
F3 1 cold(ness). **2** coolness.
➤ *v* warm, boil, toast, cook, bake, roast, reheat, warm up, inflame, excite, animate, rouse, stimulate, flush, glow.
F3 cool, chill.

heated *adj* angry, furious, raging, passionate, fiery, stormy, tempestuous, bitter, fierce, intense, vehement, violent, frenzied.
F3 calm.

heave *v* **1** PULL, haul, drag, tug, raise, lift, hitch, hoist, lever, rise, surge. **2** THROW, fling, hurl, cast, toss, chuck, let fly. **3** RETCH, vomit, throw up (*infml*), spew.

heaven *n* sky, firmament, next world, hereafter, afterlife, paradise, utopia, ecstasy, rapture, bliss, happiness, joy.
F3 hell.

heavenly *adj* **1** BLISSFUL, wonderful, glorious, beautiful, lovely, delightful, out of this world. **2** CELESTIAL, unearthly, supernatural, spiritual, divine, godlike, angelic, immortal, sublime, blessed.
F3 1 hellish. **2** infernal.

heavy *adj* **1** WEIGHTY, hefty, ponderous, burdensome, massive, large, bulky, solid, dense, stodgy. **2** *heavy work*: hard, difficult, tough, arduous, laborious, strenuous, demanding, taxing, harsh, severe. **3** OPPRESSIVE, intense, serious, dull, tedious.
F3 1 light. **2** easy.

heavy-handed *adj* clumsy, awkward, unsubtle, tactless, insensitive, thoughtless, oppressive, overbearing, domineering, autocratic.

hectic *adj* busy, frantic, frenetic, chaotic, fast, feverish, excited, heated, furious, wild.
F3 leisurely.

hedge *n* hedgerow, screen, windbreak, barrier, fence, dike, boundary.
➤ *v* **1** SURROUND, enclose, hem in, confine, restrict, fortify, guard, shield, protect, safeguard, cover. **2** STALL, temporize, equivocate, dodge, sidestep, evade, duck.

heed *v* listen, pay attention, mind, note, regard, observe, follow, obey.
F3 ignore, disregard.

heedless *adj* oblivious, unthinking, careless, negligent, rash, reckless, inattentive, unobservant, thoughtless, unconcerned.
F3 heedful, mindful, attentive.

hefty *adj* heavy, weighty, big, large, burly, hulking, beefy, brawny, strong, powerful, vigorous, robust, strapping, solid, substantial, massive, colossal, bulky, unwieldy.
F3 slight, small.

height *n* **1** HIGHNESS, altitude, elevation, tallness, loftiness, stature. **2** TOP, summit, peak, pinnacle, apex, crest, crown, zenith, apogee, culmination, climax, extremity, maximum, limit, ceiling.
F3 1 depth.

heighten *v* raise, elevate, increase, add to, magnify, intensify, strengthen, sharpen, improve, enhance.
F3 lower, decrease, diminish.

hell *n* **1** *heaven and hell*: underworld, Hades, inferno, lower regions, nether world, abyss. **2** SUFFERING, anguish, agony, torment, ordeal, nightmare, misery.
F3 1 heaven.

hellish *adj* infernal, devilish, diabolical, fiendish, accursed, damnable, monstrous, abominable, atrocious, dreadful.
F3 heavenly.

helm *n* tiller, wheel, driving seat, reins, saddle, command, control, leadership, direction.

help *v* **1** AID, assist, lend a hand, serve, be of use, collaborate, co-operate, back, stand by, support. **2** IMPROVE, ameliorate, relieve, alleviate, mitigate, ease, facilitate.

🔁 **1** hinder. **2** worsen.

➤ *n* aid, assistance, collaboration, co-operation, support, advice, guidance, service, use, utility, avail, benefit.

🔁 hindrance.

helper *n* assistant, deputy, auxiliary, subsidiary, attendant, right-hand man, PA, mate, partner, associate, colleague, collaborator, accomplice, ally, supporter, second.

helpful *adj* **1** USEFUL, practical, constructive, worthwhile, valuable, beneficial, advantageous. **2** *a helpful person*: co-operative, obliging, neighbourly, friendly, caring, considerate, kind, sympathetic, supportive.

🔁 **1** useless, futile.

helping *n* serving, portion, share, ration, amount, plateful, piece, dollop (*infml*).

helpless *adj* weak, feeble, powerless, dependent, vulnerable, exposed, unprotected, defenceless, abandoned, friendless, destitute, forlorn, incapable, incompetent, infirm, disabled, paralysed.

🔁 strong, independent, competent.

hem *n* edge, border, margin, fringe, trimming.

◇ **hem in** surround, enclose, box in, confine, restrict.

henpecked *adj* dominated, subjugated, browbeaten, bullied, intimidated, meek, timid.

🔁 dominant.

herald *n* messenger, courier, harbinger, forerunner, precursor, omen, token, signal, sign, indication.

➤ *v* announce, proclaim, broadcast, advertise, publicize, trumpet, pave the way, precede, usher in, show, indicate, promise.

heraldry

Heraldic terms include: shield, crest, mantling, helmet, supporters, field, charge, compartment, motto, dexter, centre, sinister, annulet, fleur-de-lis, martlet, mullet, rampant, passant, sejant, caboched, statant, displayed, couchant, dormant, urinant, volant, chevron, pile, pall, saltire, quarter, orle, bordure, gyronny, lozenge, impale, escutcheon, antelope, camelopard, cockatrice, eagle, griffin, lion, phoenix, unicorn, wivern, addorsed, bezant, blazon, canton, cinquefoil, quatrefoil, roundel, semé, tierced, undee, urdé.

herb

Herbs and spices include: angelica, anise, basil, bay, bergamot, borage, camomile, catmint, chervil, chives, cohosh, comfrey, cumin, dill, echinacea, fennel, gaillardia, garlic, hyssop, lavender, lemon balm, lovage, marjoram, mint, oregano, parsley, rosemary, sage, savory, sorrel, St John's wort (or hypericum), tarragon, thyme; allspice, caper, caraway seeds, cardamon, cayenne pepper, chilli, cinnamon, cloves, coriander, curry, ginger, mace, mustard, nutmeg, paprika, pepper, saffron, sesame, turmeric, vanilla.

herd *n* drove, flock, swarm, pack, press, crush, mass, horde, throng, multitude, crowd, mob, the masses, rabble.

➤ *v* **1** FLOCK, congregate, gather, collect, assemble, rally. **2** LEAD, guide, shepherd, round up, drive, force.

hereditary *adj* inherited, bequeathed, handed down, family, ancestral, inborn, inbred, innate, natural, congenital, genetic.

heresy *n* heterodoxy, unorthodoxy, free-thinking, apostasy, dissidence, schism, blasphemy.

🔁 orthodoxy.

heretic *n* free-thinker, nonconformist, apostate, dissident, dissenter, revisionist, separatist, schismatic, sectarian, renegade.

🔁 conformist.

heretical *adj* heterodox, unorthodox, free-thinking, rationalistic, schismatic, impious, irreverent, iconoclastic, blasphemous.
🔁 orthodox, conventional, conformist.

heritage *n* **1** INHERITANCE, legacy, bequest, endowment, lot, portion, share, birthright, due. **2** HISTORY, past, tradition, culture.

hermit *n* recluse, solitary, monk, ascetic, anchorite.

hero *n* protagonist, lead, celebrity, star, superstar, idol, paragon, goody (*infml*), champion, conqueror.

heroic *adj* brave, courageous, fearless, dauntless, undaunted, lion-hearted, stout-hearted, valiant, bold, daring, intrepid, adventurous, gallant, chivalrous, noble, selfless.
🔁 cowardly, timid.

heroism *n* bravery, courage, valour, boldness, daring, intrepidity, gallantry, prowess, selflessness.
🔁 cowardice, timidity.

hesitant *adj* hesitating, reluctant, half-hearted, uncertain, unsure, indecisive, irresolute, vacillating, wavering, tentative, wary, shy, timid, halting, stammering, stuttering.
🔁 decisive, resolute, confident, fluent.

hesitate *v* pause, delay, wait, be reluctant, be unwilling, think twice, hold back, shrink from, scruple, boggle, demur, vacillate, waver, be uncertain, dither, shilly-shally, falter, stumble, halt, stammer, stutter.
🔁 decide.

hesitation *n* pause, delay, reluctance, unwillingness, hesitance, scruple(s), qualm(s), misgivings, doubt, second thoughts, vacillation, uncertainty, indecision, irresolution, faltering, stumbling, stammering, stuttering.
🔁 eagerness, assurance.

hew *v* cut, fell, axe, lop, chop, hack, sever, split, carve, sculpt, sculpture, fashion, model, form, shape, make.

heyday *n* peak, prime, flush, bloom,
flowering, golden age, boom time.

hidden *adj* **1** *a hidden door*: concealed, covered, shrouded, veiled, disguised, camouflaged, unseen, secret. **2** OBSCURE, dark, occult, secret, covert, close, cryptic, mysterious, abstruse, mystical, latent, ulterior.
🔁 **1** showing, apparent. **2** obvious.

hide¹ *v* **1** CONCEAL, cover, cloak, shroud, veil, screen, mask, camouflage, disguise, obscure, shadow, eclipse, bury, stash (*infml*), secrete, withhold, keep dark, suppress. **2** TAKE COVER, shelter, lie low, go to ground, hole up (*infml*).
🔁 **1** reveal, show, display.

hide² *n* skin, pelt, fell, fur, leather.

hidebound *adj* set, rigid, entrenched, narrow-minded, strait-laced, conventional, ultra-conservative.
🔁 liberal, progressive.

hideous *adj* ugly, repulsive, grotesque, monstrous, horrid, ghastly, awful, dreadful, frightful, terrible, grim, gruesome, macabre, terrifying, shocking, appalling, disgusting, revolting, horrible.
🔁 beautiful, attractive.

hiding¹ *n* beating, flogging, whipping, caning, spanking, thrashing, walloping (*infml*).

hiding² *n* concealment, cover, veiling, screening, disguise, camouflage.

hiding-place *n* hideaway, hideout, lair, den, hole, hide, cover, refuge, haven, sanctuary, retreat.

hierarchy *n* pecking order, ranking, grading, scale, series, ladder, echelons, strata.

high *adj* **1** TALL, lofty, elevated, soaring, towering. **2** GREAT, strong, intense, extreme. **3** IMPORTANT, influential, powerful, eminent, distinguished, prominent, chief, leading, senior. **4** HIGH-PITCHED, soprano, treble, sharp, shrill, piercing. **5** *a high price*: expensive, dear, costly, exorbitant, excessive.
🔁 **1** low, short. **3** lowly. **4** deep.
5 cheap.

high-born *adj* noble, aristocratic, blue-blooded, thoroughbred.
🔁 low-born.

highbrow *n* intellectual, egghead (*infml*), scholar, academic.
➤ *adj* intellectual, sophisticated, cultured, cultivated, academic, bookish, brainy (*infml*), deep, serious, classical.
🔁 low-brow.

high-class *adj* upper-class, posh (*infml*), classy (*infml*), top-class, top-flight, high-quality, quality, de luxe, superior, excellent, first-rate, choice, select, exclusive.
🔁 ordinary, mediocre.

high-flown *adj* florid, extravagant, exaggerated, elaborate, flamboyant, ostentatious, pretentious, high-standing, grandiose, pompous, bombastic, turgid, artificial, stilted, affected, lofty, highfalutin, la-di-da (*infml*), supercilious.

high-handed *adj* overbearing, domineering, bossy (*infml*), imperious, dictatorial, autocratic, despotic, tyrannical, oppressive, arbitrary.

highlight *n* high point, high spot, peak, climax, best, cream.
➤ *v* underline, emphasize, stress, accentuate, play up, point up, spotlight, illuminate, show up, set off, focus on, feature.

highly *adv* very, greatly, considerably, decidedly, extremely, immensely, tremendously, exceptionally, extraordinarily, enthusiastically, warmly, well.

highly-strung *adj* sensitive, neurotic, nervy, jumpy, edgy, temperamental, excitable, restless, nervous, tense.
🔁 calm.

high-minded *adj* lofty, noble, moral, ethical, principled, idealistic, virtuous, upright, righteous, honourable, worthy.
🔁 immoral, unscrupulous.

high-powered *adj* powerful, forceful, driving, aggressive, dynamic, go-ahead, enterprising, energetic, vigorous.

high-spirited *adj* boisterous, bouncy, exuberant, effervescent, frolicsome, ebullient, sparkling, vibrant, vivacious, lively, energetic, spirited, dashing, bold, daring.
🔁 quiet, sedate.

hijack *v* commandeer, expropriate, skyjack, seize, take over.

hike *v* ramble, walk, trek, tramp, trudge, plod.
➤ *n* ramble, walk, trek, tramp, march.

hilarious *adj* funny, amusing, comical, side-splitting, hysterical (*infml*), uproarious, noisy, rollicking, merry, jolly, jovial.
🔁 serious, grave.

hilarity *n* mirth, laughter, fun, amusement, levity, frivolity, merriment, jollity, conviviality, high spirits, boisterousness, exuberance, exhilaration.
🔁 seriousness, gravity.

hill *n* **1** HILLOCK, knoll, mound, prominence, eminence, elevation, foothill, down, fell, mountain, height. **2** *a steep hill*: slope, incline, gradient, ramp, rise, ascent, acclivity, drop, descent, declivity.

hinder *v* hamper, obstruct, impede, encumber, handicap, hamstring, hold up, delay, retard, slow down, hold back, check, curb, stop, prevent, frustrate, thwart, oppose.
🔁 help, aid, assist.

hindrance *n* obstruction, impediment, handicap, encumbrance, obstacle, stumbling block, barrier, bar, check, restraint, restriction, limitation, difficulty, drag, snag, hitch, drawback, disadvantage, inconvenience, deterrent.
🔁 help, aid, assistance.

hinge *v* centre, turn, revolve, pivot, hang, depend, rest.

hint *n* **1** TIP, advice, suggestion, help, clue, inkling, suspicion, tip-off, reminder, indication, sign, pointer, mention, allusion, intimation, insinuation, implication, innuendo. **2** *a hint of garlic*: touch, trace, tinge, taste, dash, soupçon, speck.

➤ *v* suggest, prompt, tip off, indicate, imply, insinuate, intimate, allude, mention.

hire *v* rent, let, lease, charter, commission, book, reserve, employ, take on, sign up, engage, appoint, retain.

◾ dismiss, fire.

➤ *n* rent, rental, fee, charge, cost, price.

hiss *v* **1** WHISTLE, shrill, whizz, sizzle. **2** JEER, mock, ridicule, deride, boo, hoot.

historic *adj* momentous, consequential, important, significant, epoch-making, notable, remarkable, outstanding, extraordinary, celebrated, renowned, famed, famous.

◾ unimportant, insignificant, unknown.

historical *adj* real, actual, authentic, factual, documented, recorded, attested, verifiable.

◾ legendary, fictional.

history *n* **1** PAST, olden days, days of old, antiquity. **2** CHRONICLE, record, annals, archives, chronology, account, narrative, story, tale, saga, biography, life, autobiography, memoirs.

hit *v* **1** STRIKE, knock, tap, smack, slap, thrash, whack (*infml*), bash, thump, clout (*infml*), punch, belt (*infml*), wallop (*infml*), beat, batter. **2** BUMP, collide with, bang, crash, smash, damage, harm.

➤ *n* **1** STROKE, shot, blow, knock, tap, slap, smack, bash, bump, collision, impact, crash, smash. **2** SUCCESS, triumph, winner (*sl*).

◾ **2** failure.

◇ **hit back** retaliate, reciprocate, counter-attack, strike back.

◇ **hit on** chance on, stumble on, light on, discover, invent, realize, arrive at, guess.

◇ **hit out** lash out, assail, attack, rail, denounce, condemn, criticize.

hitch *v* **1** FASTEN, attach, tie, harness, yoke, couple, connect, join, unite. **2** PULL, heave, yank (*infml*), tug, jerk,

hoist, hike (up) (*infml*).

◾ **1** unhitch, unfasten.

➤ *n* delay, hold-up, trouble, problem, difficulty, mishap, setback, hiccup, drawback, snag, catch, impediment, hindrance.

hoard *n* collection, accumulation, mass, heap, pile, fund, reservoir, supply, reserve, store, stash (*infml*), stockpile, cache, treasure-trove.

➤ *v* collect, gather, amass, accumulate, save, put by, lay up, store, stash away (*infml*), stockpile, keep, treasure.

◾ use, spend, squander.

hoarse *adj* husky, croaky, throaty, guttural, gravelly, gruff, growling, rough, harsh, rasping, grating, raucous, discordant.

◾ clear, smooth.

hoax *n* trick, prank, practical joke, put-on, joke, leg-pull (*infml*), spoof, fake, fraud, deception, bluff, humbug, cheat, swindle, con (*infml*).

➤ *v* trick, deceive, take in, fool, dupe, gull, delude, have on (*infml*), pull someone's leg (*infml*), con (*infml*), swindle, take for a ride (*infml*), cheat, hoodwink, bamboozle (*infml*), bluff.

hobble *v* limp, stumble, falter, stagger, totter, dodder, shuffle.

hobby *n* pastime, diversion, recreation, relaxation, pursuit, sideline.

Hobbies include: aerobics, astronomy, ballet, ballroom dancing, beekeeping, birdwatching, board games, bridge, bungee jumping, camping, chess, climbing, collecting, computer games, cooking, crochet, crosswords, darts, diving, DIY, extreme sports, gardening, hillwalking, horseriding, jigsaws, kite-flying, knitting, martial arts, model railways, orienteering, origami, paintball, patchwork, photography, pottery, quilting, rollerblading, skateboarding, snooker, sports, wargaming, winetasting, woodwork, yoga. *see also* **collector**; **dance**; **martial arts**; **sport**.

hoist *v* lift, elevate, raise, erect, jack up, winch up, heave, rear, uplift.
➤ *n* jack, winch, crane, tackle, lift, elevator.

hold *v* **1** GRIP, grasp, clutch, clasp, embrace, have, own, possess, keep, retain. **2** *hold a meeting*: conduct, carry on, continue, call, summon, convene, assemble. **3** CONSIDER, regard, deem, judge, reckon, think, believe, maintain. **4** BEAR, support, sustain, carry, comprise, contain, accommodate. **5** IMPRISON, detain, stop, arrest, check, curb, restrain. **6** CLING, stick, adhere, stay.
▣ **1** drop. **5** release, free, liberate.
➤ *n* **1** GRIP, grasp, clasp, embrace. **2** INFLUENCE, power, sway, mastery, dominance, authority, control, leverage.
◇ **hold back 1** CONTROL, curb, check, restrain, suppress, stifle, retain, withhold, repress, inhibit. **2** HESITATE, delay, desist, refrain, shrink, refuse.
▣ **1** release.
◇ **hold forth** speak, talk, lecture, discourse, orate (*fml*), preach, declaim.
◇ **hold off 1** FEND OFF, ward off, stave off, keep off, repel, rebuff. **2** PUT OFF, postpone, defer, delay, wait.
◇ **hold out 1** OFFER, give, present, extend. **2** LAST, continue, persist, endure, persevere, stand fast, hang on.
▣ **2** give in, yield.
◇ **hold up 1** SUPPORT, sustain, brace, shore up, lift, raise. **2** DELAY, detain, retard, slow, hinder, impede.
◇ **hold with** agree with, go along with, approve of, countenance, support, subscribe to, accept.

holder *n* **1** *holders of British passports*: bearer, owner, possessor, proprietor, keeper, custodian, occupant, incumbent. **2** CONTAINER, receptacle, case, housing, cover, sheath, rest, stand.

hold-up *n* **1** DELAY, wait, hitch, setback, snag, difficulty, trouble, obstruction, stoppage, (traffic) jam, bottleneck. **2** ROBBERY, heist (*sl*), stick-up (*sl*).

hole *n* aperture, opening, orifice, pore, puncture, perforation, eyelet, tear, split, vent, outlet, shaft, slot, gap, breach, break, crack, fissure, fault, defect, flaw, dent, dimple, depression, hollow, cavity, crater, pit, excavation, cavern, cave, chamber, pocket, niche, recess, burrow, nest, lair, retreat.

holiday *n* vacation, recess, leave, time off, day off, break, rest, half-term, bank holiday, feast day, festival, celebration, anniversary.

holiness *n* sacredness, sanctity, spirituality, divinity, piety, devoutness, godliness, saintliness, virtuousness, righteousness, purity.
▣ impiety.

hollow *adj* **1** CONCAVE, indented, depressed, sunken, deep, cavernous, empty, vacant, unfilled. **2** FALSE, artificial, deceptive, insincere, meaningless, empty, vain, futile, fruitless, worthless.
▣ **1** solid. **2** real.
➤ *n* hole, pit, well, cavity, crater, excavation, cavern, cave, depression, concavity, basin, bowl, cup, dimple, dent, indentation, groove, channel, trough, valley.
➤ *v* dig, excavate, burrow, tunnel, scoop, gouge, channel, groove, furrow, pit, dent, indent.

holy *adj* **1** *holy ground*: sacred, hallowed, consecrated, sanctified, dedicated, blessed, venerated, revered, spiritual, divine, evangelical. **2** PIOUS, religious, devout, godly, God-fearing, saintly, virtuous, good, righteous, faithful, pure, perfect.
▣ **1** unsanctified. **2** impious, irreligious.

homage *n* recognition, tribute, acknowledgement, honour, praise, adulation, admiration, regard, esteem, respect, deference, reverence, adoration, awe, veneration, worship, devotion.

home *n* residence, domicile, dwelling-place, abode, base, house, pied-à-terre, hearth, fireside, birthplace, home town, home ground, territory, habitat, element.

➤ *adj* domestic, household, family, internal, local, national, inland.
✖ foreign, international.

◇ **at home 1** COMFORTABLE, relaxed, at ease. **2** FAMILIAR, knowledgeable, experienced, skilled.

homeland *n* native land, native country, fatherland, motherland.

homeless *adj* itinerant, travelling, nomadic, wandering, vagrant, rootless, unsettled, displaced, dispossessed, evicted, exiled, outcast, abandoned, forsaken, destitute, down-and-out.
➤ *n* travellers, vagabonds, vagrants, tramps, down-and-outs, dossers (*sl*), squatters.

homely *adj* homelike, homey, comfortable, cosy, snug, relaxed, informal, friendly, intimate, familiar, everyday, ordinary, domestic, natural, plain, simple, modest, unassuming, unpretentious, unsophisticated, folksy, homespun.
✖ grand, formal.

homicide *n* murder, manslaughter, assassination, killing, bloodshed.

homogeneous *adj* uniform, consistent, unvarying, identical, similar, alike, akin, kindred, analogous, comparable, harmonious, compatible.
✖ different.

homosexual *n* gay, queer (*sl*), poof (*sl*), lesbian, dike (*sl*).
✖ heterosexual, straight (*sl*).
➤ *adj* gay, queer (*sl*), lesbian.

hone *v* sharpen, whet, point, edge, grind, file, polish.

honest *adj* **1** TRUTHFUL, sincere, frank, candid, blunt, outspoken, direct, straight, outright, forthright, straightforward, plain, simple, open, above-board, legitimate, legal, lawful, on the level (*infml*), fair, just, impartial, objective. **2** LAW-ABIDING, virtuous, upright, ethical, moral, high-minded, scrupulous, honourable, reputable, respectable, reliable, trustworthy, true, genuine, real.
✖ **1** dishonest. **2** dishonourable.

honestly *adv* truly, really, truthfully,

sincerely, frankly, directly, outright, plainly, openly, legitimately, legally, lawfully, on the level, fairly, justly, objectively, honourably, in good faith.
✖ dishonestly, dishonourably.

honesty *n* **1** TRUTHFULNESS, sincerity, frankness, candour, bluntness, outspokenness, straightforwardness, plain-speaking, explicitness, openness, legitimacy, legality, equity, fairness, justness, objectivity, even-handedness. **2** VIRTUE, uprightness, honour, integrity, decency, morality, scrupulousness, trustworthiness, genuineness, veracity.
✖ **1** dishonesty.

honorary *adj* unpaid, unofficial, titular, nominal, in name only, honorific, formal.
✖ paid.

honour *n* **1** REPUTATION, good name, repute, renown, distinction, esteem, regard, respect, credit, dignity, self-respect, pride, integrity, morality, decency, rectitude, probity. **2** AWARD, accolade, commendation, tribute, acknowledgement, recognition, privilege. **3** PRAISE, acclaim, homage, admiration, reverence, worship, adoration.
✖ **1** dishonour, disgrace.
➤ *v* **1** PRAISE, acclaim, exalt, glorify, pay homage to, decorate, crown, celebrate, commemorate, remember, admire, esteem, respect, revere, worship, prize, value. **2** *honour a promise*: keep, observe, respect, fulfil, carry out, discharge, execute, perform.
✖ **1** dishonour, disgrace.

honourable *adj* great, eminent, distinguished, renowned, respected, worthy, prestigious, trusty, reputable, respectable, virtuous, upright, upstanding, straight, honest, trustworthy, true, sincere, noble, high-minded, principled, moral, ethical, fair, just, right, proper, decent.
✖ dishonourable, unworthy, dishonest.

hoodwink *v* deceive, dupe, fool, take in, delude, bamboozle (*infml*), have on (*infml*), mislead, hoax, trick, cheat, con (*infml*), rook, gull, swindle.

hook *n* crook, sickle, peg, barb, trap, snare, catch, fastener, clasp, hasp.
➤ *v* **1** BEND, crook, curve, curl. **2** CATCH, capture, bag, grab, trap, snare, ensnare, entangle. **3** FASTEN, clasp, hitch, fix, secure.

hooligan *n* ruffian, rowdy, hoodlum, mobster, bovver boy (*sl*), thug, tough, lout, yob (*sl*), vandal, delinquent.

hoop *n* ring, circle, round, loop, wheel, band, girdle, circlet.

hoot *n*, *v* call, cry, shout, shriek, whoop, toot, beep, whistle, boo, jeer, laugh, howl.

hop *v* jump, leap, spring, bound, vault, skip, dance, prance, frisk, limp, hobble.
➤ *n* jump, leap, spring, bound, vault, bounce, step, skip, dance.

hope *n* hopefulness, optimism, ambition, aspiration, wish, desire, longing, dream, expectation, anticipation, prospect, promise, belief, confidence, assurance, conviction, faith.
ᚱ pessimism, despair.
➤ *v* aspire, wish, desire, long, expect, await, look forward, anticipate, contemplate, foresee, believe, trust, rely, reckon on, assume.
ᚱ despair.

hopeful *adj* **1** OPTIMISTIC, bullish (*infml*), confident, assured, expectant, sanguine, cheerful, buoyant. **2** *a hopeful sign*: encouraging, heartening, reassuring, favourable, auspicious, promising, rosy, bright.
ᚱ **1** pessimistic, despairing. **2** discouraging.

hopeless *adj* **1** PESSIMISTIC, defeatist, negative, despairing, demoralized, downhearted, dejected, despondent, forlorn, wretched. **2** UNATTAINABLE, unachievable, impracticable, impossible, vain, foolish, futile, useless, pointless, worthless, poor, helpless, lost, irremediable, irreparable, incurable.
ᚱ **1** hopeful, optimistic. **2** curable.

horde *n* band, gang, pack, herd, drove, flock, swarm, crowd, mob, throng, multitude, host.

horizon *n* skyline, vista, prospect, compass, range, scope, perspective.

horrible *adj* unpleasant, disagreeable, nasty, unkind, horrid, disgusting, revolting, offensive, repulsive, hideous, grim, ghastly, awful, dreadful, frightful, fearful, terrible, abominable, shocking, appalling, horrific.
ᚱ pleasant, agreeable, lovely, attractive.

horrific *adj* horrifying, shocking, appalling, awful, dreadful, ghastly, gruesome, terrifying, frightening, scary, harrowing, bloodcurdling.

horrify *v* shock, outrage, scandalize, appal, disgust, sicken, dismay, alarm, startle, scare, frighten, terrify.
ᚱ please, delight.

horror *n* **1** *recoil in horror*: shock, outrage, disgust, revulsion, repugnance, abhorrence, loathing, consternation, dismay, alarm, fright, fear, terror, panic, dread, apprehension. **2** GHASTLINESS, awfulness, frightfulness, hideousness.
ᚱ **1** approval, delight.

horse

Breeds of horse include: Akhal-Tekē, Alter-Réal, American Quarter Horse, American Saddle Horse, American Trotter, Andalusian, Anglo-Arab, Anglo-Norman, Appaloosa, Arab, Ardennias, Auxois, Barb, Bavarian Warmblood, Boulonnais, Brabançon, Breton, British Warmblood, Brumby, Budyonny, Calabrese, Charollais Halfbred, Cleveland Bay, Clydesdale, Comtois, Criollo, Danubian, Døle Gudbrandsdal, Døle Trotter, Don, Dutch Draught, East Bulgarian, East Friesian, Einsiedler, Finnish, Frederiksborg, Freiberger, French Saddle Horse, French Trotter, Friesian, Furioso, Gelderland, German Trotter, Groningen, Hanoverian, Hispano, Holstein, Iomud, Irish Draught, Irish Hunter, Italian Heavy Draught, Jutland, Kabardin, Karabair, Karabakh, Kladruber, Knabstrup,

Kustanair, Latvian Harness Horse, Limousin Halfbred, Lipizzaner, Lithuanian Heavy Draught, Lokai, Lusitano, Mangalarga, Maremmana, Masuren, Mecklenburg, Metis Trotter, Morgan, Muraköz, Murgese, Mustang, New Kirgiz, Nonius, North Swedish, Oldenburg, Orlov Trotter, Palomino, Paso Fino, Percheron, Peruvian Stepping Horse, Pinto, Pinzgauer Noriker, Plateau Persian, Poitevin, Rhineland Heavy Draught, Russian Heavy Draught, Salerno, Sardinian, Shagya Arab, Shire, Suffolk Punch, Swedish Halfbred, Tchenaran, Tennessee Walking Horse, Tersky, Thoroughbred, Toric, Trait du Nord, Trakehner, Vladimir Heavy Draught, Waler, Welsh Cob, Württemberg.

Breeds of pony include: Connemara, Dales, Dartmoor, Exmoor, Falabella, Fell, Hackney, Highland, New Forest, Przewalski's Horse, Shetland, Welsh Mountain Pony, Welsh Pony.

The points of a horse are: back, breast, cannon, chestnut, crest of the neck, croup/crupper/rump, ear, elbow, eye, face, fetlock, forearm, forefoot, forehead, forelock, gaskin, haunch, head, hind leg, hip, hock, hoof, knee, loins, lower jaw, lower/under lip, mane, mouth, neck, nose, nostril, pastern, root/dock of the tail, shoulder, spur vein, stifle (joint), tail, throat, upper lip, withers.

horseman, horsewoman *n* equestrian, rider, jockey, cavalryman, hussar.

horseplay *n* clowning, buffoonery, foolery, tomfoolery, skylarking, pranks, capers, high jinks, fun and games, rough-and-tumble.

hospitable *adj* friendly, sociable, welcoming, receptive, cordial, amicable, congenial, convivial, genial, kind, gracious, generous, liberal.
🗪 inhospitable, unfriendly, hostile.

hospitality *n* friendliness, sociability, welcome, accommodation, entertainment, conviviality, warmth, cheer, generosity, open-handedness.
🗪 unfriendliness.

host[1] *n* **1** COMPÈRE, master of ceremonies, presenter, announcer, anchorman, anchorwoman, linkman. **2** PUBLICAN, innkeeper, landlord, proprietor.
➤ *v* present, introduce, compère.

host[2] *n* multitude, myriad, array, army, horde, crowd, throng, swarm, pack, band.

hostage *n* prisoner, captive, pawn, surety, security, pledge.

hostel *n* youth hostel, residence, dosshouse (*sl*), boarding-house, guest house, hotel, inn.

hostile *adj* belligerent, warlike, ill-disposed, unsympathetic, unfriendly, inhospitable, inimical, antagonistic, opposed, adverse, unfavourable, contrary, opposite.
🗪 friendly, welcoming, favourable.

hostilities *n* war, warfare, battle, fighting, conflict, strife, bloodshed.

hostility *n* opposition, aggression, belligerence, enmity, estrangement, antagonism, animosity, ill-will, malice, resentment, hate, hatred, dislike, aversion, abhorrence.
🗪 friendliness, friendship.

hot *adj* **1** WARM, heated, fiery, burning, scalding, blistering, scorching, roasting, baking, boiling, steaming, sizzling, sweltering, sultry, torrid, tropical. **2** SPICY, peppery, piquant, sharp, pungent, strong.
🗪 **1** cold, cool. **2** mild.

hotchpotch *n* mishmash, medley, miscellany, collection, mix, mixture, jumble, confusion, mess.

hotel *n* boarding-house, guest house, pension, motel, inn, public house, pub (*infml*), hostel.

hotheaded *adj* headstrong, impetuous, impulsive, hasty, rash, reckless, fiery, volatile, hot-tempered, quick-tempered.

Ea cool, calm.

hothouse n greenhouse, glasshouse, conservatory, orangery, vinery.

hound v chase, pursue, hunt (down), drive, goad, prod, chivvy, nag, pester, badger, harry, harass, persecute.

house n 1 BUILDING, dwelling, residence, home. 2 DYNASTY, family, clan, tribe.

Types of house include: semi-detached, semi (*infml*), detached, terraced, town house, council house, cottage, thatched cottage, prefab (*infml*), pied-à-terre, bungalow, chalet bungalow; flat, bedsit, apartment, studio, maisonette, penthouse, granny flat, duplex (*US*), condominium (*US*); manor, hall, lodge, grange, villa, mansion, rectory, vicarage, parsonage, manse, croft, farmhouse, homestead, ranchhouse, chalet, log cabin, shack, shanty, hut, igloo, hacienda.

➤ v 1 LODGE, quarter, billet, board, accommodate, put up, take in, shelter, harbour. 2 HOLD, contain, protect, cover, sheathe, place, keep, store.

household n family, family circle, house, home, ménage, establishment, set-up.

➤ adj domestic, home, family, ordinary, plain, everyday, common, familiar, well-known, established.

householder n resident, tenant, occupier, occupant, owner, landlady, freeholder, leaseholder, proprietor, landlord, homeowner, head of the household.

housing n 1 ACCOMMODATION, houses, homes, dwellings, habitation, shelter. 2 CASING, case, container, holder, covering, cover, sheath, protection.

hovel n shack, shanty, cabin, hut, shed, dump, hole (*infml*).

hover v 1 HANG, poise, float, drift, fly,
flutter, flap. 2 *he hovered by the door*: pause, linger, hang about, hesitate, waver, fluctuate, seesaw.

however conj nevertheless, nonetheless, still, yet, even so, notwithstanding (*fml*), though, anyhow.

howl n, v wail, cry, shriek, scream, shout, yell, roar, bellow, bay, yelp, hoot, moan, groan.

hub n centre, middle, focus, focal point, axis, pivot, linchpin, nerve centre, core, heart.

hubbub n noise, racket, din, clamour, commotion, disturbance, riot, uproar, hullabaloo, rumpus, confusion, disorder, tumult, hurly-burly, chaos, pandemonium.

Ea peace, quiet.

huddle n 1 CLUSTER, clump, knot, mass, crowd, muddle, jumble. 2 CONCLAVE, conference, meeting.

➤ v cluster, gravitate, converge, meet, gather, congregate, crowd, flock, throng, press, cuddle, snuggle, nestle, curl up, crouch, hunch.

Ea disperse.

hue n colour, shade, tint, dye, tinge, nuance, tone, complexion, aspect, light.

huff n pique, sulks, mood, bad mood, anger, rage, passion.

hug v embrace, cuddle, squeeze, enfold, hold, clasp, clutch, grip, cling to, enclose.

➤ n embrace, cuddle, squeeze, clasp, hold, clinch.

huge adj immense, vast, enormous, massive, mega (*infml*), colossal, titanic, giant, gigantic, mammoth, monstrous, monumental, seismic (*infml*), tremendous, great, big, large, bulky, unwieldy.

Ea tiny, minute.

hulking adj massive, heavy, unwieldy, bulky, awkward, ungainly.

Ea small, delicate.

hull n body, frame, framework, structure, casing, covering.

hullabaloo n fuss, palaver, to-do

(*infml*), outcry, furore, hue and cry, uproar, pandemonium, rumpus, disturbance, commotion, hubbub.
€ calm, peace.

hum *v* buzz, whirr, purr, drone, thrum, croon, sing, murmur, mumble, throb, pulse, vibrate.
➤ *n* buzz, whirr, purring, drone, murmur, mumble, throb, pulsation, vibration.

human *adj* 1 MORTAL, fallible, susceptible, reasonable, rational. 2 KIND, considerate, understanding, humane, compassionate.
€ 2 inhuman.
➤ *n* human being, mortal, homo sapiens, man, woman, child, person, individual, body, soul.

humane *adj* kind, compassionate, sympathetic, understanding, kind-hearted, good-natured, gentle, tender, loving, mild, lenient, merciful, forgiving, forbearing, kindly, benevolent, charitable, humanitarian, good.
€ inhumane, cruel.

humanitarian *adj* benevolent, charitable, philanthropic, public-spirited, compassionate, humane, altruistic, unselfish.
€ selfish, self-seeking.
➤ *n* philanthropist, benefactor, good Samaritan, do-gooder, altruist.
€ egoist, self-seeker.

humanity *n* 1 HUMAN RACE, humankind, mankind, womankind, mortality, people. 2 HUMANENESS, kindness, compassion, fellow-feeling, understanding, tenderness, benevolence, generosity, goodwill.
€ 2 inhumanity.

humanize *v* domesticate, tame, civilize, cultivate, educate, enlighten, edify, improve, better, polish, refine.

humble *adj* 1 MEEK, submissive, unassertive, self-effacing, polite, respectful, deferential, servile, subservient, sycophantic, obsequious. 2 LOWLY, low, mean, insignificant, unimportant, common, commonplace,

ordinary, plain, simple, modest, unassuming, unpretentious, unostentatious.
€ 1 proud, assertive. 2 important, pretentious.
➤ *v* bring down, lower, bring low, abase, demean, sink, discredit, disgrace, shame, humiliate, mortify, chasten, crush, deflate, subdue.
€ exalt.

humbug *n* 1 DECEPTION, pretence, sham, found, swindle, trick, hoax, deceit, trickery. 2 NONSENSE, rubbish, baloney (*sl*), bunkum (*infml*), claptrap (*infml*), eye-wash (*infml*), bluff, cant, hypocrisy.

humdrum *adj* boring, tedious, monotonous, routine, dull, dreary, uninteresting, uneventful, ordinary, mundane, everyday, commonplace.
€ lively, unusual, exceptional.

humid *adj* damp, moist, dank, clammy, sticky, muggy, sultry, steamy.
€ dry.

humiliate *v* mortify, embarrass, confound, crush, break, deflate, chasten, shame, disgrace, discredit, degrade, demean, humble, bring low.
€ dignify, exalt.

humiliation *n* mortification, embarrassment, shame, disgrace, dishonour, ignominy, abasement, deflation, put-down (*infml*), snub, rebuff, affront.
€ gratification, triumph.

humility *n* meekness, submissiveness, deference, self-abasement, servility, humbleness, lowliness, modesty, unpretentiousness.
€ pride, arrogance, assertiveness.

humorist *n* wit, satirist, comedian, comic, joker, wag, jester, clown.

humorous *adj* funny, amusing, comic, entertaining, witty, satirical, jocular, facetious, playful, waggish, droll, whimsical, comical, farcical, zany (*infml*), ludicrous, absurd, hilarious, side-splitting.
€ serious, humourless.

humour n 1 WIT, drollery, jokes, jesting, badinage, repartee, facetiousness, satire, comedy, farce, fun, amusement. 2 *in a bad humour*: mood, temper, frame of mind, spirits, disposition, temperament.

➤ v go along with, comply with, accommodate, gratify, indulge, pamper, spoil, favour, please, mollify, flatter.

humourless adj boring, tedious, dull, dry, solemn, serious, glum, morose.
F3 humorous, witty.

hump n hunch, lump, knob, bump, projection, protuberance, bulge, swelling, mound, prominence.

hunch n premonition, presentiment, intuition, suspicion, feeling, impression, idea, guess.

➤ v hump, bend, curve, arch, stoop, crouch, squat, huddle, draw in, curl up.

hunger n 1 HUNGRINESS, emptiness, starvation, malnutrition, famine, appetite, ravenousness, voracity, greed, greediness. 2 *hunger for power*: desire, craving, longing, yearning, itch, thirst.

➤ v starve, want, wish, desire, crave, hanker, long, yearn, pine, ache, itch, thirst.

hungry adj 1 STARVING, underfed, undernourished, peckish (*infml*), empty, hollow, famished, ravenous, greedy. 2 *hungry for knowledge*: desirous, craving, longing, aching, thirsty, eager, avid.
F3 1 satisfied, full.

hunk n chunk, lump, piece, block, slab, wedge, mass, clod.

hunt v 1 CHASE, pursue, hound, dog, stalk, track, trail. 2 SEEK, look for, search, scour, rummage, forage, investigate.

➤ n chase, pursuit, search, quest, investigation.

hurdle n jump, fence, wall, hedge, barrier, barricade, obstacle, obstruction, stumbling block, hindrance, impediment, handicap, problem, snag, difficulty, complication.

hurl v throw, toss, fling, sling, catapult,

project, propel, fire, launch, send.

hurricane n gale, tornado, typhoon, cyclone, whirlwind, squall, storm, tempest.

hurried adj rushed, hectic, hasty, precipitate, speedy, quick, swift, rapid, passing, brief, short, cursory, superficial, shallow, careless, slapdash.
F3 leisurely.

hurry v rush, dash, fly, get a move on (*infml*), hasten, quicken, speed up, hustle, push.
F3 slow down, delay.

➤ n rush, haste, quickness, speed, urgency, hustle, bustle, flurry, commotion.
F3 leisureliness, calm.

hurt v 1 *my leg hurts*: ache, pain, throb, sting. 2 INJURE, wound, maltreat, ill-treat, bruise, cut, burn, torture, maim, disable. 3 DAMAGE, impair, harm, mar, spoil. 4 UPSET, sadden, grieve, distress, afflict, offend, annoy.

➤ n pain, soreness, discomfort, suffering, injury, wound, damage, harm, distress, sorrow.

➤ adj 1 INJURED, wounded, bruised, grazed, cut, scarred, maimed. 2 UPSET, sad, saddened, distressed, aggrieved, annoyed, offended, affronted.

hurtful adj 1 UPSETTING, wounding, vicious, cruel, mean, unkind, nasty, malicious, spiteful, catty, derogatory, scathing, cutting. 2 HARMFUL, damaging, injurious, pernicious, destructive.
F3 1 kind.

hurtle v dash, tear, race, fly, shoot, speed, rush, charge, plunge, dive, crash, rattle.

husband n spouse, partner, mate, better half, hubby (*infml*), groom, married man.

hush v quieten, silence, still, settle, compose, calm, soothe, subdue.
F3 disturb, rouse.

➤ n quietness, silence, peace, stillness,

repose, calm, calmness, tranquillity, serenity.
▰ noise, clamour.
➤ *interj* quiet, hold your tongue, shut up, not another word.
◇ **hush up** keep dark, suppress, conceal, cover up, stifle, gag.
▰ publicize.

hush-hush *adj* secret, confidential, classified, restricted, under wraps (*infml*), top-secret.
▰ open, public.

husk *n* covering, case, shell, pod, hull, rind, bran, chaff.

husky *adj* hoarse, croaky, croaking, low, throaty, guttural, gruff, rasping, rough, harsh.

hustle *v* hasten, rush, hurry, bustle, force, push, shove, thrust, bundle, elbow, jostle.

hut *n* cabin, shack, shanty, booth, shed, lean-to, shelter, den.

hybrid *n* cross, crossbreed, half-breed, mongrel, composite, combination, mixture, amalgam, compound.
➤ *adj* crossbred, mongrel, composite, combined, mixed, heterogeneous, compound.
▰ pure-bred.

hygiene *n* sanitariness, sanitation, sterility, disinfection, cleanliness, purity, wholesomeness.
▰ insanitariness.

hygienic *adj* sanitary, sterile, aseptic, germ-free, disinfected, clean, pure, salubrious, healthy, wholesome.
▰ unhygienic, insanitary.

hyperbole *n* overstatement,

exaggeration, magnification, extravagance.
▰ understatement.

hypnotic *adj* mesmerizing, soporific, sleep-inducing, spellbinding, fascinating, compelling, irresistible, magnetic.

hypnotism *n* hypnosis, mesmerism, suggestion.

hypnotize *v* mesmerize, spellbind, bewitch, enchant, entrance, fascinate, captivate, magnetize.

hypocrisy *n* insincerity, double-talk, double-dealing, falsity, deceit, deception, pretence.
▰ sincerity.

hypocritical *adj* insincere, two-faced, self-righteous, double-dealing, false, hollow, deceptive, spurious, deceitful, dissembling, pharisaic(al).
▰ sincere, genuine.

hypothesis *n* theory, thesis, premise, postulate, proposition, supposition, conjecture, speculation.

hypothetical *adj* theoretical, imaginary, supposed, assumed, proposed, conjectural, speculative.
▰ real, actual.

hysteria *n* agitation, frenzy, panic, hysterics, neurosis, mania, madness.
▰ calm, composure.

hysterical *adj* **1** FRANTIC, frenzied, berserk, uncontrollable, mad, raving, crazed, demented, overwrought, neurotic, hyper (*infml*). **2** (*infml*) HILARIOUS, uproarious, side-splitting, priceless (*infml*), rich (*infml*).
▰ **1** calm, composed, self-possessed.

Ii

ice _n_ frost, rime, icicle, glacier, iciness, frostiness, coldness, chill.
➤ _v_ freeze, refrigerate, chill, cool, frost, glaze.

icon _n_ idol, portrait, image, symbol, representation.

icy _adj_ **1** ICE-COLD, arctic, polar, glacial, freezing, frozen, raw, bitter, biting, cold, chill, chilly. **2** _icy roads_: frosty, slippery, glassy, frozen, icebound, frostbound. **3** HOSTILE, cold, stony, cool, indifferent, aloof, distant, formal.
🔁 **1** hot. **3** friendly, warm.

idea _n_ **1** THOUGHT, concept, notion, theory, hypothesis, guess, conjecture, belief, opinion, view, viewpoint, judgement, conception, vision, image, impression, perception, interpretation, understanding, inkling, suspicion, clue. **2** _a good idea_: brainwave, suggestion, proposal, proposition, motion, recommendation, plan, scheme, design. **3** AIM, intention, purpose, reason, point, object.

ideal _n_ perfection, epitome, acme, paragon, exemplar, example, model, pattern, archetype, prototype, type, image, criterion, standard.
➤ _adj_ **1** PERFECT, dream, utopian, best, optimum, optimal, supreme, highest, model, archetypal. **2** UNREAL, imaginary, theoretical, hypothetical, unattainable, impractical, idealistic.

idealist _n_ perfectionist, romantic, visionary, dreamer, optimist.
🔁 realist, pragmatist.

idealistic _adj_ perfectionist, utopian, visionary, romantic, quixotic, starry-eyed, optimistic, unrealistic, impractical, impracticable.
🔁 realistic, pragmatic.

idealize _v_ utopianize, romanticize, glamorize, glorify, exalt, worship, idolize.
🔁 caricature.

identical _adj_ same, self-same, indistinguishable, interchangeable, twin, duplicate, like, alike, corresponding, matching, equal, equivalent.
🔁 different.

identification _n_ **1** RECOGNITION, detection, diagnosis, naming, labelling, classification. **2** EMPATHY, association, involvement, rapport, relationship, sympathy, fellow-feeling. **3** IDENTITY CARD, documents, papers, credentials.

identify _v_ recognize, know, pick out, single out, distinguish, perceive, make out, discern, notice, detect, diagnose, name, label, tag, specify, pinpoint, place, catalogue, classify.
◇ **identify with** empathize with, relate to, sympathize with, associate with, respond to, feel for.

identity _n_ **1** INDIVIDUALITY, particularity, singularity, uniqueness, self, personality, character, existence. **2** SAMENESS, likeness.

ideology _n_ philosophy, world-view, ideas, principles, tenets, doctrine(s), convictions, belief(s), faith, creed, dogma.

idiocy _n_ folly, stupidity, silliness, senselessness, lunacy.
🔁 wisdom, sanity.

idiom _n_ phrase, expression, colloquialism, language, turn of phrase, phraseology, style, usage, jargon, vernacular.

idiosyncrasy _n_ characteristic, peculiarity, singularity, oddity, eccentricity, freak, quirk, habit, mannerism, trait, feature.

idiosyncratic *adj* personal, individual, characteristic, distinctive, peculiar, singular, odd, eccentric, quirky.
E3 general, common.

idiot *n* fool, blockhead, ass (*infml*), nitwit (*infml*), dimwit, halfwit, imbecile, moron, cretin (*infml*), simpleton, dunce, divvy (*sl*), dork (*sl*), ignoramus.

idiotic *adj* foolish, stupid, silly, absurd, senseless, daft (*infml*), lunatic, insane, foolhardy, harebrained, halfwitted, moronic, cretinous, crazy.
E3 sensible, sane.

idle *adj* 1 INACTIVE, inoperative, unused, unoccupied, unemployed, jobless, redundant. 2 LAZY, work-shy, indolent. 3 *idle talk*: empty, trivial, casual, futile, vain, pointless, unproductive.
E3 1 active. 2 busy.
➤ *v* do nothing, laze, lounge, take it easy, kill time, potter, loiter, dawdle, fritter, waste, loaf, slack, skive (*infml*).
E3 work.

idol *n* icon, effigy, image, graven image, god, deity, fetish, favourite, darling, hero, heroine, pin-up.

idolize *v* hero-worship, lionize, exalt, glorify, worship, venerate, revere, admire, adore, love, dote on.
E3 despise.

idyllic *adj* perfect, idealized, heavenly, delightful, charming, picturesque, pastoral, rustic, unspoiled, peaceful, happy.
E3 unpleasant.

ignite *v* set fire to, set alight, catch fire, flare up, burn, conflagrate, fire, kindle, touch off, spark off.
E3 quench.

ignoble *adj* low, mean, petty, base, vulgar, wretched, contemptible, despicable, vile, heinous, infamous, disgraceful, dishonourable, shameless.
E3 noble, worthy, honourable.

ignominious *adj* humiliating, mortifying, degrading, undignified,

shameful, dishonourable, disreputable, disgraceful, despicable, scandalous.
E3 triumphant, honourable.

ignorance *n* unintelligence, illiteracy, unawareness, unconsciousness, oblivion, unfamiliarity, inexperience, innocence, naïvety.
E3 knowledge, wisdom.

ignorant *adj* uneducated, illiterate, unread, untaught, untrained, inexperienced, stupid, clueless (*infml*), uninitiated, unenlightened, uninformed, ill-informed, unwitting, unaware, unconscious, oblivious.
E3 educated, knowledgeable, clever, wise.

ignore *v* disregard, take no notice of, shut one's eyes to, overlook, pass over, neglect, omit, reject, snub, cold-shoulder, blank (*sl*).
E3 notice, observe.

ill *adj* 1 SICK, poorly, unwell, indisposed, laid up, ailing, off-colour, out of sorts (*infml*), under the weather (*infml*), seedy, queasy, diseased, unhealthy, infirm, frail. 2 *an ill omen*: bad, evil, damaging, harmful, injurious, detrimental, ruinous, adverse, unfavourable, inauspicious, unpromising, sinister, ominous, threatening, unlucky, unfortunate, difficult, harsh, severe, unkind, unfriendly, antagonistic.
E3 1 well. 2 good, favourable, fortunate.

ill-advised *adj* imprudent, injudicious, unwise, foolish, ill-considered, thoughtless, reckless, hasty, rash, short-sighted, misguided, inappropriate.
E3 wise, sensible, well-advised.

ill-bred *adj* bad-mannered, ill-mannered, discourteous, impolite, rude, coarse, indelicate.
E3 well-bred, polite.

illegal *adj* unlawful, illicit, criminal, wrong, forbidden, prohibited, banned, outlawed, unauthorized, under-the-counter, black-market, wrongful, unconstitutional.
E3 legal, lawful.

illegible *adj* unreadable, hard to read, indecipherable, scrawled, obscure, faint, indistinct.
🗷 legible.

illegitimate *adj* **1** *an illegitimate child*: natural, bastard, born out of wedlock (*fml*). **2** ILLEGAL, unlawful, illicit, unauthorized, unwarranted, improper, incorrect, inadmissible, spurious, invalid, unsound.
🗷 **1** legitimate. **2** legal.

ill-fated *adj* doomed, ill-starred, ill-omened, unfortunate, unlucky, luckless, unhappy.
🗷 lucky.

illicit *adj* illegal, unlawful, criminal, wrong, illegitimate, improper, forbidden, prohibited, unauthorized, unlicensed, black-market, contraband, ill-gotten, under-the-counter, furtive, clandestine.
🗷 legal, permissible.

illness *n* disease, disorder, complaint, ailment, sickness, ill health, ill-being, indisposition, infirmity, disability, affliction. *see panel at* **disease**.

illogical *adj* irrational, unreasonable, unscientific, invalid, unsound, faulty, fallacious, specious, sophistical, inconsistent, senseless, meaningless, absurd.
🗷 logical.

ill-treat *v* maltreat, abuse, injure, harm, damage, neglect, mistreat, mishandle, misuse, wrong, oppress.

illuminate *v* **1** LIGHT, light up, brighten, decorate. **2** ENLIGHTEN, edify, instruct, elucidate, illustrate, explain, clarify, clear up.
🗷 **1** darken. **2** mystify.

illumination *n* light, lights, lighting, beam, ray, brightness, radiance, decoration, ornamentation.
🗷 darkness.

illusion *n* apparition, mirage, hallucination, figment, fantasy, fancy, delusion, misapprehension, misconception, error, fallacy.
🗷 reality, truth.

illusory *adj* illusive, deceptive, misleading, apparent, seeming, deluding, delusive, unreal, unsubstantial, sham, false, fallacious, untrue, mistaken.
🗷 real.

illustrate *v* draw, sketch, depict, picture, show, exhibit, demonstrate, exemplify, explain, interpret, clarify, elucidate, illuminate, decorate, ornament, adorn.

illustration *n* **1** PICTURE, plate, half-tone, photograph, drawing, sketch, figure, representation, decoration. **2** EXAMPLE, specimen, instance, case, analogy, demonstration, explanation, interpretation.

illustrious *adj* great, noble, eminent, distinguished, celebrated, famous, famed, renowned, noted, prominent, outstanding, remarkable, notable, brilliant, excellent, splendid, magnificent, glorious, exalted.
🗷 ignoble, inglorious.

ill-will *n* hostility, antagonism, bad blood, enmity, unfriendliness, malevolence, malice, spite, animosity, ill-feeling, resentment, hard feelings, grudge, dislike, aversion, hatred.
🗷 goodwill, friendship.

image *n* **1** IDEA, notion, concept, impression, perception. **2** REPRESENTATION, likeness, picture, portrait, icon, effigy, figure, statue, idol, replica, reflection.

imaginable *adj* conceivable, thinkable, believable, credible, plausible, likely, possible.
🗷 unimaginable.

imaginary *adj* imagined, fanciful, illusory, hallucinatory, visionary, pretend, make-believe, unreal, non-existent, fictional, fabulous, legendary, mythological, made-up, invented, fictitious, assumed, supposed, hypothetical.
🗷 real.

imagination *n* imaginativeness, creativity, inventiveness, originality, inspiration, insight, ingenuity, resourcefulness, enterprise, wit, vision, mind's eye, fancy, illusion.

🔄 unimaginativeness, reality.

imaginative *adj* creative, inventive, innovative, original, inspired, visionary, ingenious, clever, resourceful, enterprising, fanciful, fantastic, vivid.

🔄 unimaginative.

imagine *v* **1** PICTURE, visualize, envisage, conceive, fancy, fantasize, pretend, make believe, conjure up, dream up, think up, invent, devise, create, plan, project. **2** *I imagine so*: think, believe, judge, suppose, guess, conjecture, assume, take it, gather.

imbalance *n* unevenness, inequality, disparity, disproportion, unfairness, partiality, bias.

🔄 balance, parity.

imbecile *n* idiot, halfwit, simpleton, moron, cretin (*infml*), fool, blockhead, bungler.

imbue *v* permeate, impregnate, pervade, suffuse, fill, saturate, steep, inculcate (*fml*), instil, tinge, tint.

imitate *v* copy, emulate, follow, ape, mimic, impersonate, take off (*infml*), caricature, parody, send up (*infml*), spoof, mock, parrot, repeat, echo, mirror, duplicate, reproduce, simulate, counterfeit, forge.

imitation *n* **1** MIMICRY, impersonation, impression, take-off (*infml*), caricature, parody, send-up (*infml*), spoof, mockery, travesty. **2** COPY, duplicate, replica, reproduction, simulation, counterfeit, fake, forgery, sham, likeness, resemblance, reflection, dummy. ➤ *adj* artificial, synthetic, faux, man-made, ersatz, fake, phoney (*infml*), mock, pseudo, reproduction, simulated, sham, dummy.

🔄 genuine.

imitative *adj* copying, mimicking, parrot-like, unoriginal, derivative, plagiarized, second-hand, simulated, mock.

imitator *n* mimic, impersonator,

impressionist, parrot, copycat (*infml*), copier, emulator, follower.

immaculate *adj* perfect, unblemished, flawless, faultless, impeccable, spotless, clean, spick and span, pure, unsullied, undefiled, untainted, stainless, blameless, innocent.

🔄 blemished, stained, contaminated.

immaterial *adj* irrelevant, insignificant, unimportant, minor, trivial, trifling, inconsequential.

🔄 relevant, important.

immature *adj* young, under-age, adolescent, juvenile, childish, puerile, infantile, babyish, raw, crude, callow, inexperienced, green, unripe, undeveloped.

🔄 mature.

immeasurable *adj* vast, immense, infinite, limitless, unlimited, boundless, unbounded, endless, bottomless, inexhaustible, incalculable, inestimable.

🔄 limited.

immediate *adj* **1** INSTANT, instantaneous, direct, prompt, swift, current, present, existing, urgent, pressing. **2** NEAREST, next, adjacent, near, close, recent.

🔄 **1** delayed. **2** distant.

immediately *adv* now, straight away, right away, at once, instantly, directly, forthwith, without delay, promptly, unhesitatingly.

🔄 eventually, never.

immense *adj* vast, great, huge, enormous, massive, giant, gigantic, tremendous, monumental.

🔄 tiny, minute.

immensity *n* magnitude, bulk, expanse, vastness, greatness, hugeness, enormousness, massiveness.

🔄 minuteness.

immerse *v* plunge, submerge, submerse, sink, duck, dip, douse, bathe.

immigrant *n* incomer, settler, newcomer, alien.

🔄 emigrant.

imminent *adj* impending, forthcoming, in the offing, approaching, coming, near, close, looming, menacing, threatening, brewing, in the air.
🔄 remote, far-off.

immobile *adj* stationary, motionless, unmoving, still, stock-still, static, immovable, rooted, fixed, frozen, rigid, stiff.
🔄 mobile, moving.

immobilize *v* stop, halt, fix, freeze, transfix, paralyse, cripple, disable.
🔄 mobilize.

immodest *adj* indecent, revealing, shameless, forward, improper, immoral, obscene, lewd, coarse, risqué.

immoral *adj* unethical, wrong, bad, sinful, evil, wicked, unscrupulous, unprincipled, dishonest, corrupt, depraved, degenerate, dissolute, lewd, indecent, pornographic, obscene, impure.
🔄 moral, right, good.

immortal *adj* undying, imperishable, eternal, everlasting, perpetual, endless, ceaseless, lasting, enduring, abiding, timeless, ageless.
🔄 mortal.

immortalize *v* celebrate, commemorate, memorialize, perpetuate, enshrine.

immovable *adj* fixed, rooted, immobile, stuck, fast, secure, stable, constant, firm, set, determined, resolute, adamant, unshakable, obstinate, unyielding.
🔄 movable.

immune *adj* invulnerable, unsusceptible, resistant, proof, protected, safe, exempt, free, clear.
🔄 susceptible.

The immune system's components and responses include: antibody, antigen (or antibody generator), commensals, complement system, cytotoxic cells, histamine, immunoglobulins, interferon, leucocyte, lymphocyte, B-lymphocytes, T-cells, T-lymphocytes, killer T-cells, helper T-cells, memory T-cells, lysosome, lysozyme, phagocyte, plasma cells, receptor (binding) site; acquired immunity, artificially acquired immunity (immunization), naturally acquired immunity, passive immunity, cell-mediated immunity, cellular response, humoral immunity/response, adaptive immune system, innate immune system, non-specific immune response, specific immune response, autoimmune response, primary response, secondary response, inflammatory response, immunosurveillance, allergy, phagocyte action (adherence/ingestion/digestion), phagocytosis, sneeze reflex, tissue rejection.

immunity *n* resistance, protection, exemption, indemnity, impunity, exoneration, freedom, liberty, licence, franchise, privilege, right.
🔄 susceptibility.

immunize *v* vaccinate, inoculate, inject, protect, safeguard.

impact *n* **1** *the impact of the reforms*: effect, consequences, repercussions, impression, power, influence, significance, meaning. **2** COLLISION, crash, smash, bang, bump, blow, knock, contact, jolt, shock, brunt.

impair *v* damage, harm, injure, hinder, mar, spoil, worsen, undermine, weaken, reduce, lessen, diminish, blunt.
🔄 improve, enhance.

impale *v* pierce, puncture, perforate, run through, spear, lance, spike, skewer, spit, stick, transfix.

impart *v* tell, relate, communicate, make known, disclose, divulge, reveal, convey, pass on, give, grant, confer, offer, contribute, lend.
🔄 withhold.

impartial *adj* objective, detached, dispassionate, disinterested, neutral, non-partisan, unbiased, unprejudiced, open-minded, fair, just, equitable, even-handed, equal.
🔄 biased, prejudiced.

impasse *n* deadlock, stalemate, dead end, cul-de-sac, blind alley, halt, standstill.

impassive *adj* expressionless, calm, composed, unruffled, unconcerned, cool, unfeeling, unemotional, unmoved, imperturbable, unexcitable, stoical, indifferent, dispassionate.
F₃ responsive, moved.

impatience *n* eagerness, keenness, restlessness, agitation, anxiety, nervousness, irritability, intolerance, shortness, brusqueness, haste, rashness.
F₃ patience.

impatient *adj* eager, keen, restless, fidgety, fretful, edgy, irritable, snappy, hot-tempered, quick-tempered, intolerant, brusque, abrupt, impetuous, hasty, precipitate, headlong.
F₃ patient.

impeach *v* accuse, charge, indict, arraign (*fml*), denounce, impugn (*fml*), disparage, criticize, censure, blame.

impeccable *adj* perfect, faultless, precise, exact, flawless, unblemished, stainless, immaculate, pure, irreproachable, blameless, innocent.
F₃ faulty, flawed, corrupt.

impede *v* hinder, hamper, obstruct, block, clog, slow, retard, hold up, delay, check, curb, restrain, thwart, disrupt, stop, bar.
F₃ aid, promote, further.

impediment *n* hindrance, obstacle, obstruction, barrier, bar, block, stumbling block, snag, difficulty, handicap, check, curb, restraint, restriction.
F₃ aid.

impel *v* urge, force, oblige, compel, constrain, drive, propel, push, spur, goad, prompt, stimulate, excite, instigate, motivate, inspire, move.
F₃ deter, dissuade.

impending *adj* imminent, forthcoming, approaching, coming, close, near, looming, menacing, threatening.
F₃ remote.

impenetrable *adj* 1 *impenetrable jungle*: solid, thick, dense, impassable. 2 UNINTELLIGIBLE, incomprehensible, unfathomable, baffling, mysterious, cryptic, enigmatic, obscure, dark, inscrutable.
F₃ 2 accessible, understandable.

imperative *adj* compulsory, obligatory, essential, vital, crucial, pressing, urgent.
F₃ optional, unimportant.

imperceptible *adj* inappreciable, indiscernible, inaudible, faint, slight, negligible, infinitesimal, microscopic, minute, tiny, small, fine, subtle, gradual.
F₃ perceptible.

imperfect *adj* faulty, flawed, defective, damaged, broken, chipped, deficient, incomplete.
F₃ perfect.

imperfection *n* fault, flaw, defect, blemish, deficiency, shortcoming, weakness, failing.
F₃ perfection.

imperial *adj* sovereign, supreme, royal, regal, majestic, grand, magnificent, great, noble.

imperil *v* endanger, jeopardize, risk, hazard, expose, compromise, threaten.

imperious *adj* overbearing, domineering, autocratic, despotic, tyrannical, dictatorial, high-handed, commanding, arrogant, haughty.
F₃ humble.

impersonal *adj* formal, official, businesslike, bureaucratic, faceless, aloof, remote, distant, detached, neutral, objective, dispassionate, cold, frosty, glassy.
F₃ informal, friendly.

impersonate *v* imitate, mimic, take off (*infml*), parody, caricature, mock, masquerade as, pose as, act, portray.

impertinence *n* rudeness, impoliteness, disrespect, insolence, impudence, cheek, brass (*sl*), effrontery, nerve (*infml*), audacity, boldness, brazenness, forwardness, presumption.
F₃ politeness, respect.

impertinent *adj* rude, impolite, ill-mannered, discourteous, disrespectful, insolent, impudent, cheeky, saucy (*infml*), pert, bold, brazen, forward, presumptuous, fresh.
⊟ polite, respectful.

imperturbable *adj* unexcitable, unflappable (*infml*), calm, tranquil, composed, collected, self-possessed, cool, unmoved, unruffled.

impervious *adj* **1** IMPERMEABLE, waterproof, damp-proof, watertight, hermetic, closed, sealed, impenetrable. **2** *impervious to criticism*: immune, invulnerable, untouched, unaffected, unmoved, resistant.
⊟ **1** porous, pervious. **2** responsive, vulnerable.

impetuous *adj* impulsive, spontaneous, unplanned, unpremeditated, hasty, precipitate, rash, reckless, thoughtless, unthinking.
⊟ cautious, wary, circumspect.

impetus *n* impulse, momentum, force, energy, power, drive, boost, push, spur, stimulus, incentive, motivation.

impinge *v* hit, touch (on), affect, influence, encroach, infringe, intrude, trespass, invade.

implacable *adj* inexorable, relentless, remorseless, merciless, pitiless, cruel, ruthless, intransigent, inflexible.
⊟ compassionate.

implant *v* graft, engraft, embed, sow, plant, fix, root, insert, instil, inculcate (*fml*).

implausible *adj* improbable, unlikely, far-fetched, dubious, suspect, unconvincing, weak, flimsy, thin, transparent.
⊟ plausible, likely, reasonable.

implement *n* tool, instrument, utensil, gadget, device, apparatus, appliance.
➤ *v* enforce, effect, bring about, carry out, execute, discharge, perform, do, fulfil, complete, accomplish, realize.

implicate *v* involve, embroil, entangle, incriminate, stitch up (*sl*), compromise, include, concern, connect, associate.
⊟ exonerate.

implication *n* **1** INFERENCE, insinuation, suggestion, meaning, significance, ramification, repercusssion. **2** INVOLVEMENT, entanglement, incrimination, connection, association.

implicit *adj* **1** IMPLIED, inferred, insinuated, indirect, unsaid, unspoken, tacit, understood. **2** *implicit belief*: unquestioning, utter, total, full, complete, absolute, unqualified, unreserved, wholehearted.
⊟ **1** explicit. **2** half-hearted.

imply *v* suggest, insinuate, hint, intimate, mean, signify, point to, indicate, involve, require.
⊟ state.

impolite *adj* rude, discourteous, bad-mannered, ill-mannered, ill-bred, disrespectful, insolent, rough, coarse, vulgar, abrupt.
⊟ polite, courteous.

importance *n* momentousness, significance, consequence, substance, matter, concern, interest, usefulness, value, worth, weight, influence, mark, prominence, eminence, distinction, esteem, prestige, status, standing.
⊟ unimportance.

important *adj* **1** MOMENTOUS, noteworthy, significant, meaningful, relevant, material, salient, urgent, vital, essential, mission-critical (*infml*), key, primary, major, substantial, valuable, seminal, weighty, serious, grave, far-reaching. **2** LEADING, foremost, high-level, high-ranking, influential, powerful, pre-eminent, prominent, outstanding, eminent, noted.
⊟ **1** unimportant, insignificant, trivial.

impose *v* **1** INTRODUCE, institute, enforce, promulgate, exact, levy, set, fix, put, place, lay, inflict, burden, encumber, saddle. **2** INTRUDE, butt in, encroach, trespass, obtrude, force oneself, presume, take liberties.

imposing *adj* impressive, striking, grand, stately, majestic, dignified.
🖪 unimposing, modest.

imposition *n* 1 INTRODUCTION, infliction, exaction, levying.
2 INTRUSION, encroachment, liberty, burden, constraint, charge, duty, task, punishment.

impossible *adj* hopeless, impracticable, unworkable, unattainable, unachievable, out (*infml*), unobtainable, insoluble, unreasonable, unacceptable, inconceivable, out of the question, unthinkable, preposterous, absurd, ludicrous, ridiculous.
🖪 possible.

impostor *n* fraud, fake, phoney (*infml*), quack, charlatan, impersonator, pretender, con man (*infml*), swindler, cheat, rogue.

impotent *adj* powerless, helpless, unable, incapable, ineffective, incompetent, inadequate, weak, feeble, frail, infirm, disabled, incapacitated, paralysed.
🖪 potent, strong.

impoverished *adj* poor, needy, impecunious, poverty-stricken, destitute, bankrupt, ruined.
🖪 rich.

impracticable *adj* unworkable, unfeasible, unattainable, unachievable, impossible, unviable, useless, unserviceable, inoperable.
🖪 practicable.

impractical *adj* unrealistic, idealistic, romantic, starry-eyed, impracticable, unworkable, impossible, awkward, inconvenient.
🖪 practical, realistic, sensible.

imprecise *adj* inexact, inaccurate, approximate, estimated, rough, loose, indefinite, vague, woolly, hazy, ill-defined, sloppy, ambiguous, equivocal.
🖪 precise, exact.

impregnable *adj* impenetrable, unconquerable, invincible, unbeatable, unassailable, indestructible, fortified,

strong, solid, secure, safe, invulnerable.
🖪 vulnerable.

impregnate *v* 1 SOAK, steep, saturate, fill, permeate, pervade, suffuse, imbue. 2 INSEMINATE, fertilize.

impress *v* 1 *I'm not impressed*: strike, move, touch, affect, influence, stir, inspire, excite, grab (*sl*). 2 STAMP, imprint, mark, indent, instil, inculcate.

impression *n* 1 FEELING, awareness, consciousness, sense, illusion, idea, notion, opinion, belief, conviction, suspicion, hunch, memory, recollection.
2 STAMP, mark, print, dent, outline.
3 IMPERSONATION, imitation, take-off (*infml*), parody, send-up (*infml*). 4 *make a good impression*: effect, impact, influence.

impressionable *adj* naïve, gullible, susceptible, vulnerable, sensitive, responsive, open, receptive.

impressive *adj* striking, imposing, grand, powerful, effective, stirring, exciting, moving, touching.
🖪 unimpressive, uninspiring.

imprint *n* print, mark, stamp, impression, sign, logo.
➤ *v* print, mark, brand, stamp, impress, engrave, etch.

imprison *v* jail, incarcerate, intern, detain, send down (*infml*), put away (*infml*), lock up, cage, confine, shut in.
🖪 release, free.

imprisonment *n* incarceration, internment, detention, custody, confinement.
🖪 freedom, liberty.

improbable *adj* uncertain, questionable, doubtful, unlikely, dubious, implausible, unconvincing, far-fetched, preposterous, unbelievable, incredible.
🖪 probable, likely, convincing.

impromptu *adj* improvised, extempore, ad-lib, off-the-cuff, unscripted, unrehearsed, unprepared, spontaneous.
🖪 rehearsed.

➤ *adv* extempore, ad lib, off the cuff, off the top of one's head, spontaneously, on the spur of the moment.

improper *adj* wrong, incorrect, irregular, unsuitable, inappropriate, inopportune, incongruous, out of place, indecent, rude, vulgar, unseemly (*fml*), unbecoming, shocking.
🔁 proper, appropriate, decent.

improve *v* better, ameliorate, enhance, polish, touch up, mend, rectify, correct, amend, reform, upgrade, increase, rise, pick up, develop, look up, advance, progress, get better, recover, rally, recuperate, perk up, mend one's ways, turn over a new leaf.
🔁 worsen, deteriorate, decline.

improvement *n* betterment, amelioration, enhancement, rectification, correction, amendment, reformation, increase, rise, upswing, gain, development, advance, progress, furtherance, recovery, rally.
🔁 deterioration, decline.

improvise *v* 1 CONTRIVE, devise, concoct, invent, throw together, make do. 2 EXTEMPORIZE, ad-lib, play by ear, vamp.

imprudent *adj* unwise, ill-advised, foolish, short-sighted, rash, reckless, hasty, irresponsible, careless, heedless, impolitic, indiscreet.
🔁 prudent, wise, cautious.

impudence *n* impertinence, cheek, effrontery, nerve (*infml*), face (*infml*), boldness, insolence, rudeness, presumption.
🔁 politeness.

impudent *adj* impertinent, cheeky, saucy (*infml*), bold, forward, shameless, cocky, insolent, rude, presumptuous, fresh.
🔁 polite.

impulse *n* 1 URGE, wish, desire, inclination, whim, notion, instinct, feeling, passion. 2 IMPETUS, momentum, force, pressure, drive, thrust, push, incitement, stimulus, motive.

impulsive *adj* impetuous, rash, reckless, hasty, quick, spontaneous,

automatic, instinctive, intuitive.
🔁 cautious, premeditated.

impure *adj* 1 UNREFINED, adulterated, diluted, contaminated, polluted, tainted, infected, corrupt, debased, unclean, dirty, foul. 2 OBSCENE, indecent, immodest.
🔁 1 pure. 2 chaste, decent.

impurity *n* adulteration, contamination, pollution, infection, corruption, dirtiness, contaminant, dirt, filth, foreign body, mark, spot.
🔁 purity.

inability *n* incapability, incapacity, powerlessness, impotence, inadequacy, weakness, handicap, disability.
🔁 ability.

inaccessible *adj* isolated, remote, unfrequented, unapproachable, unreachable, unget-at-able (*infml*), unattainable.
🔁 accessible.

inaccuracy *n* mistake, error, miscalculation, slip, blunder, fault, defect, imprecision, inexactness, unreliability.
🔁 accuracy, precision.

inaccurate *adj* incorrect, wrong, erroneous, mistaken, faulty, flawed, defective, imprecise, inexact, loose, unreliable, unfaithful, untrue.
🔁 accurate, correct.

inaction *n* inactivity, immobility, inertia, rest, idleness, lethargy, torpor, stagnation.
🔁 action.

inactive *adj* immobile, inert, idle, unused, inoperative, dormant, passive, sedentary, lazy, lethargic, sluggish, torpid, sleepy.
🔁 active, working, busy.

inadequacy *n* 1 INSUFFICIENCY, lack, shortage, dearth, want, deficiency, scantiness, meagreness, defectiveness, ineffectiveness, inability, incompetence. 2 *the inadequacies of the system*: fault, defect, imperfection, weakness, failing, shortcoming.
🔁 1 adequacy.

inadequate *adj* **1** INSUFFICIENT, short, wanting, deficient, scanty, sparse, meagre, niggardly. **2** INCOMPETENT, incapable, unequal, unqualified, ineffective, faulty, defective, imperfect, unsatisfactory.
F₃ 1 adequate. **2** satisfactory.

inadmissible *adj* unacceptable, irrelevant, immaterial, inappropriate, disallowed, prohibited.
F₃ admissible.

inadvertent *adj* accidental, chance, unintentional, unintended, unplanned, unpremeditated, careless.
F₃ deliberate, conscious, careful.

inadvisable *adj* unwise, imprudent, injudicious, foolish, silly, ill-advised, misguided, indiscreet.
F₃ advisable, wise.

inane *adj* senseless, foolish, stupid, unintelligent, silly, idiotic, fatuous, frivolous, trifling, puerile, mindless, vapid, empty, vacuous, vain, worthless, futile.
F₃ sensible.

inanimate *adj* lifeless, dead, defunct, extinct, unconscious, inactive, inert, dormant, immobile, stagnant, spiritless, dull.
F₃ animate, living, alive.

inappropriate *adj* unsuitable, inapt, ill-suited, ill-fitted, irrelevant, incongruous, out of place, untimely, ill-timed, tactless, improper, unseemly, unbecoming, unfitting.
F₃ appropriate, suitable.

inarticulate *adj* incoherent, unintelligible, incomprehensible, unclear, indistinct, hesitant, faltering, halting, tongue-tied, speechless, dumb, mute.
F₃ articulate.

inattention *n* carelessness, negligence, disregard, absent-mindedness, forgetfulness, daydreaming, preoccupation.

inattentive *adj* distracted, dreamy, daydreaming, preoccupied, absent-minded, unmindful, heedless, regardless, careless, negligent.
F₃ attentive.

inaudible *adj* silent, noiseless, imperceptible, faint, indistinct, muffled, muted, low, mumbled.
F₃ audible, loud.

inaugural *adj* opening, introductory, first, initial.

inaugurate *v* institute, originate, begin, commence (*fml*), start, set up, open, launch, introduce, usher in, initiate, induct, ordain, invest, install, commission, dedicate, consecrate.

inauspicious *adj* unfavourable, bad, unlucky, unfortunate, unpromising, discouraging, threatening, ominous, black.
F₃ auspicious, promising.

inborn *adj* innate, inherent, natural, native, congenital, inbred, hereditary, inherited, ingrained, instinctive, intuitive.
F₃ learned.

incalculable *adj* countless, untold, inestimable, limitless, unlimited, immense, vast.
F₃ limited, restricted.

incapable *adj* unable, powerless, impotent, helpless, weak, feeble, unfit, unsuited, unqualified, incompetent, inept, inadequate, ineffective.
F₃ capable.

incapacitate *v* disable, cripple, paralyse, immobilize, disqualify, put out of action, lay up, scupper (*infml*).

incapacity *n* incapability, inability, disability, powerlessness, impotence, ineffectiveness, weakness, feebleness, inadequacy, incompetency.
F₃ capability.

incarnation *n* personification, embodiment, manifestation, impersonation.

incautious *adj* careless, imprudent, injudicious, ill-judged, unthinking, thoughtless, inconsiderate, rash, reckless, hasty, impulsive.
F₃ cautious, careful.

incense v anger, enrage, infuriate, madden, exasperate, irritate, rile, provoke, excite.
ᴇ calm.

incentive n bait, lure, enticement, carrot (*infml*), sweetener (*infml*), reward, encouragement, inducement, reason, motive, impetus, spur, stimulus, motivation.
ᴇ disincentive, discouragement, deterrent.

incessant adj ceaseless, unceasing, endless, never-ending, interminable, continual, persistent, constant, perpetual, eternal, everlasting, continuous, unbroken, unremitting, non-stop.
ᴇ intermittent, sporadic, periodic, temporary.

incidence n frequency, commonness, prevalence, extent, range, amount, degree, rate, occurrence.

incident n 1 OCCURRENCE, happening, event, episode, adventure, affair, occasion, instance. 2 CONFRONTATION, clash, fight, skirmish, commotion, disturbance, scene, upset, mishap.

incidental adj accidental, chance, random, minor, non-essential, secondary, subordinate, subsidiary, ancillary, supplementary, accompanying, attendant, related, contributory.
ᴇ important, essential.

incinerate v burn, cremate, reduce to ashes.

incision n cut, opening, slit, gash, notch.

incisive adj cutting, keen, sharp, acute, trenchant, piercing, penetrating, biting, caustic, acid, astute, perceptive.
ᴇ vague.

incite v prompt, instigate, rouse, foment, stir up, whip up, work up, excite, animate, provoke, stimulate, spur, goad, impel, drive, urge, encourage, egg on (*infml*).
ᴇ restrain.

incitement n prompting, instigation, agitation, provocation, spur, goad, impetus, stimulus, motivation, encouragement, inducement, incentive.
ᴇ discouragement.

inclement adj intemperate, harsh, severe, stormy, tempestuous, rough.
ᴇ fine.

inclination n 1 LIKING, fondness, taste, predilection (*fml*), preference, partiality, bias, tendency, trend, disposition, propensity, leaning. 2 *an inclination of 45 degrees*: angle, slope, gradient, incline, pitch, slant, tilt, bend, bow, nod.
ᴇ 1 disinclination, dislike.

incline v 1 DISPOSE, influence, persuade, affect, bias, prejudice.
2 LEAN, slope, slant, tilt, tip, bend, bow, tend, veer.
➤ n slope, gradient, ramp, hill, rise, ascent, acclivity, dip, descent, declivity.

inclined adj liable, likely, given, apt, disposed, of a mind, willing.

include v comprise, incorporate, embody, comprehend, contain, enclose, embrace, encompass, cover, subsume, take in, add, allow for, take into account, involve, rope in.
ᴇ exclude, omit, eliminate.

inclusion n incorporation, involvement, addition, insertion.
ᴇ exclusion.

inclusive adj comprehensive, full, all-in, all-inclusive, all-embracing, blanket, across-the-board, general, catch-all, overall, sweeping.
ᴇ exclusive, narrow.

incognito adj in disguise, disguised, masked, veiled, unmarked, unidentified, unrecognizable, unknown.
ᴇ undisguised.

incoherent adj unintelligible, incomprehensible, inarticulate, rambling, stammering, stuttering, unconnected, disconnected, broken, garbled, scrambled, confused, muddled, jumbled, disordered.
ᴇ coherent, intelligible.

income *n* revenue, returns, proceeds, gains, profits, interest, takings, receipts, earnings, pay, salary, wages, means.
⊞ expenditure, expenses.

incoming *adj* arriving, entering, approaching, coming, homeward, returning, ensuing, succeeding, next, new.
⊞ outgoing.

incomparable *adj* matchless, unmatched, unequalled, unparalleled, unrivalled, peerless, supreme, superlative, superb, brilliant.
⊞ ordinary, run-of-the-mill, poor.

incompatible *adj* irreconcilable, contradictory, conflicting, at variance, inconsistent, clashing, mismatched, unsuited.
⊞ compatible.

incompetent *adj* incapable, unable, unfit, inefficient, inexpert, unskilful, bungling, stupid, useless, ineffective.
⊞ competent, able.

incomplete *adj* deficient, lacking, short, unfinished, abridged, partial, part, fragmentary, broken, imperfect, defective.
⊞ complete, exhaustive.

incomprehensible *adj* unintelligible, impenetrable, unfathomable, above one's head, puzzling, perplexing, baffling, mysterious, inscrutable, obscure, opaque.
⊞ comprehensible, intelligible.

inconceivable *adj* unthinkable, unimaginable, mind-boggling (*infml*), staggering, unheard-of, unbelievable, incredible, implausible.
⊞ conceivable.

inconclusive *adj* unsettled, undecided, open, uncertain, indecisive, ambiguous, vague, unconvincing, unsatisfying.
⊞ conclusive.

incongruous *adj* inappropriate, unsuitable, out of place, out of keeping, inconsistent, conflicting, incompatible, irreconcilable, contradictory, contrary.

⊞ consistent, compatible.

inconsequential *adj* minor, trivial, trifling, unimportant, insignificant, immaterial.
⊞ important.

inconsiderable *adj* small, slight, negligible, trivial, petty, minor, unimportant, insignificant.
⊞ considerable, large.

inconsiderate *adj* unkind, uncaring, unconcerned, selfish, self-centred, intolerant, insensitive, tactless, rude, thoughtless, unthinking, careless, heedless.
⊞ considerate.

inconsistent *adj* **1** CONFLICTING, at variance, at odds, incompatible, contradictory, contrary, incongruous, discordant. **2** CHANGEABLE, variable, irregular, unpredictable, varying, unstable, unsteady, inconstant, fickle.
⊞ **2** constant.

inconsolable *adj* heartbroken, brokenhearted, devastated, desolate, despairing, wretched.

inconspicuous *adj* hidden, concealed, camouflaged, plain, ordinary, unobtrusive, discreet, low-key, modest, unassuming, quiet, retiring, insignificant.
⊞ conspicuous, noticeable, obtrusive.

incontrovertible *adj* indisputable, unquestionable, irrefutable, undeniable, certain, clear, self-evident.
⊞ questionable, uncertain.

inconvenience *n* awkwardness, difficulty, annoyance, nuisance, hindrance, drawback, bother, trouble, fuss, upset, disturbance, disruption.
⊞ convenience.
➤ *v* bother, disturb, disrupt, put out, trouble, upset, irk.
⊞ convenience.

inconvenient *adj* awkward, ill-timed, untimely, inopportune, unsuitable, difficult, embarrassing, annoying, troublesome, unwieldy, unmanageable.
⊞ convenient.

incorporate v include, embody, contain, subsume, take in, absorb, assimilate, integrate, combine, unite, merge, blend, mix, fuse, coalesce, consolidate.
🔁 separate.

incorrect adj wrong, mistaken, erroneous, inaccurate, imprecise, inexact, false, untrue, faulty, ungrammatical, improper, illegitimate, inappropriate, unsuitable.
🔁 correct.

incorrigible adj irredeemable, incurable, inveterate, hardened, hopeless.

incorruptible adj honest, straight, upright, moral, honourable, trustworthy, unbribable, just.
🔁 corruptible.

increase v raise, boost, add to, improve, enhance, advance, step up, intensify, strengthen, heighten, grow, develop, build up, wax, enlarge, extend, prolong, expand, spread, swell, magnify, multiply, proliferate, rise, mount, soar, escalate.
🔁 decrease, reduce, decline.
➤ n rise, surge, upsurge, upturn, gain, boost, addition, increment, advance, step-up, intensification, growth, development, enlargement, extension, expansion, spread, proliferation, escalation.
🔁 decrease, reduction, decline.

incredible adj unbelievable, improbable, implausible, far-fetched, preposterous, absurd, crazy, impossible, inconceivable, unthinkable, unimaginable, extraordinary, amazing, astonishing, astounding.
🔁 credible, believable.

incredulity n unbelief, disbelief, scepticism, doubt, distrust, mistrust.
🔁 credulity.

incredulous adj unbelieving, disbelieving, unconvinced, sceptical, doubting, distrustful, suspicious, dubious, doubtful, uncertain.
🔁 credulous.

incriminate v inculpate (fml), implicate, stitch up (sl), involve, accuse, charge, impeach, indict, point the finger at, blame.
🔁 exonerate.

incur v suffer, sustain, provoke, arouse, bring upon oneself, expose oneself to, meet with, run up, gain, earn.

incurable adj 1 an incurable disease: terminal, fatal, untreatable, inoperable, hopeless. 2 INCORRIGIBLE, inveterate, hardened, dyed-in-the-wool.
🔁 1 curable.

indebted adj obliged, grateful, thankful.

indecency n immodesty, indecorum, impurity, obscenity, pornography, lewdness, vulgarity, coarseness, crudity, foulness, grossness.
🔁 decency, modesty.

indecent adj improper, immodest, impure, indelicate, offensive, obscene, pornographic, X-rated (infml), lewd, licentious, vulgar, coarse, crude, dirty, filthy, foul, gross, outrageous, shocking.
🔁 decent, modest.

indecision n indecisiveness, irresolution, vacillation, wavering, hesitation, hesitancy, ambivalence, uncertainty, doubt.
🔁 decisiveness, resolution.

indecisive adj undecided, irresolute, undetermined, vacillating, wavering, in two minds, hesitating, faltering, tentative, uncertain, unsure, doubtful, inconclusive, indefinite, indeterminate, unclear.
🔁 decisive.

indeed adv really, actually, in fact, certainly, positively, truly, undeniably, undoubtedly, to be sure.

indefensible adj unjustifiable, inexcusable, unforgivable, unpardonable, insupportable, untenable, wrong, faulty.
🔁 defensible, excusable.

indefinite adj unknown, uncertain, unsettled, unresolved, undecided,

undetermined, undefined, unspecified, unlimited, ill-defined, vague, indistinct, unclear, obscure, ambiguous, imprecise, inexact, loose, general.
🔹 definite, limited, clear.

indefinitely *adv* for ever, eternally, endlessly, continually, ad infinitum.

indelible *adj* lasting, enduring, permanent, fast, ineffaceable, ingrained, indestructible.
🔹 erasable.

indemnity *n* compensation, reimbursement, remuneration, reparation, insurance, guarantee, security, protection, immunity, amnesty.

indentation *n* notch, nick, cut, serration, dent, groove, furrow, depression, dip, hollow, pit, dimple.

independence *n* autonomy, self-government, self-determination, self-rule, home rule, sovereignty, freedom, liberty, individualism, separation.
🔹 dependence.

independent *adj* 1 AUTONOMOUS, self-governing, self-determining, sovereign, absolute, non-aligned, neutral, impartial, unbiased. 2 FREE, free-thinking, liberated, unconstrained, individualistic, unconventional, self-sufficient, self-supporting, self-reliant, unaided. 3 INDIVIDUAL, self-contained, separate, unconnected, unrelated.
🔹 1 dependent.

indescribable *adj* indefinable, ineffable (*fml*), inexpressible, unutterable, unspeakable.
🔹 describable.

indestructible *adj* unbreakable, durable, tough, strong, lasting, enduring, abiding, permanent, eternal, everlasting, immortal, imperishable.
🔹 breakable, mortal.

indeterminate *adj* unspecified, unstated, undefined, unfixed, imprecise, inexact, indefinite, vague, open-ended, undecided, undetermined, uncertain.
🔹 known, specified, fixed.

index *n* 1 *index of names*: table, key, list, catalogue, directory, guide.
2 INDICATOR, pointer, needle, hand, sign, token, mark, indication, clue.

indicate *v* register, record, show, reveal, display, manifest, point to, designate, specify, point out, mark, signify, mean, denote, express, suggest, imply.

indication *n* mark, sign, evidence, manifestation, symptom, signal, warning, omen, intimation, suggestion, hint, clue, note, explanation.

indicator *n* pointer, needle, marker, sign, symbol, token, signal, display, dial, gauge, meter, index, guide, signpost.

indict *v* charge, accuse, arraign, impeach, summon, summons, prosecute, incriminate.
🔹 exonerate.

indifference *n* apathy, unconcern, coldness, coolness, inattention, disregard, negligence, neutrality, disinterestedness.
🔹 interest, concern.

indifferent *adj* 1 UNINTERESTED, unenthusiastic, unexcited, apathetic, unconcerned, unmoved, uncaring, unsympathetic, cold, cool, distant, aloof, detached, uninvolved, neutral, disinterested. 2 MEDIOCRE, average, middling, passable, moderate, fair, ordinary.
🔹 1 interested, caring. 2 excellent.

indigenous *adj* native, aboriginal, original, local, home-grown.
🔹 foreign, non-indigenous.

indignant *adj* annoyed, angry, irate, heated, fuming, livid, furious, incensed, infuriated, exasperated, outraged.
🔹 pleased, delighted.

indignation *n* annoyance, anger, ire, wrath, rage, fury, exasperation, outrage, scorn, contempt.
🔹 pleasure, delight.

indirect *adj* 1 ROUNDABOUT, circuitous, wandering, rambling, winding, meandering, zigzag, tortuous. 2 *an*

indirect effect: secondary, incidental, unintended, subsidiary, ancillary.
🔁 **1** direct. **2** primary.

indiscreet *adj* tactless, undiplomatic, impolitic, injudicious, imprudent, unwise, foolish, rash, reckless, hasty, careless, heedless, unthinking.
🔁 discreet, cautious.

indiscretion *n* mistake, error, slip, boob (*infml*), faux pas, gaffe, tactlessness, rashness, recklessness, foolishness, folly.

indiscriminate *adj* general, sweeping, wholesale, random, haphazard, hit-or-miss, aimless, unsystematic, unmethodical, mixed, motley, miscellaneous.
🔁 selective, specific, precise.

indispensable *adj* vital, essential, mission-critical (*infml*), basic, key, crucial, imperative, required, requisite, needed, necessary.
🔁 dispensable, unnecessary.

indisposed *adj* ill, sick, unwell, poorly, ailing, laid up.
🔁 well.

indisputable *adj* incontrovertible, unquestionable, irrefutable, undeniable, absolute, undisputed, definite, positive, certain, sure.
🔁 doubtful.

indistinct *adj* unclear, ill-defined, blurred, fuzzy, misty, hazy, shadowy, obscure, dim, faint, muffled, confused, unintelligible, vague, woolly, ambiguous, indefinite.
🔁 distinct, clear.

individual *n* person, being, creature, party, body, soul, character, fellow.
➤ *adj* distinctive, characteristic, idiosyncratic, peculiar, singular, unique, exclusive, special, personal, own, proper, respective, several, separate, distinct, specific, personalized, particular, single.
🔁 collective, shared, general.

individuality *n* character, personality, distinctiveness, peculiarity, singularity, uniqueness, separateness, distinction.
🔁 sameness.

indoctrinate *v* brainwash, teach, instruct, school, ground, train, drill.

induce *v* **1** CAUSE, effect, bring about, occasion, give rise to, lead to, incite, instigate, prompt, provoke, produce, generate. **2** COAX, prevail upon, encourage, press, persuade, talk into, move, influence, draw, tempt.
🔁 **2** discourage, deter.

inducement *n* lure, bait, attraction, enticement, encouragement, incentive, reward, spur, stimulus, motive, reason.
🔁 disincentive.

indulge *v* gratify, satisfy, humour, pander to, go along with, give in to, yield to, favour, pet, cosset, mollycoddle, pamper, spoil, treat, regale.

indulgence *n* extravagance, luxury, excess, immoderation, intemperance, favour, tolerance.

indulgent *adj* tolerant, easy-going (*infml*), lenient, permissive, generous, liberal, kind, fond, tender, patient, understanding.
🔁 strict, harsh.

industrialist *n* manufacturer, producer, magnate, tycoon, baron, captain of industry, capitalist, financier.

industrious *adj* busy, productive, hard-working, diligent, assiduous, conscientious, zealous, active, energetic, tireless, persistent, persevering.
🔁 lazy, idle.

industry *n* **1** *the steel industry*: business, trade, commerce, manufacturing, production. **2** INDUSTRIOUSNESS, diligence, application, effort, labour, toil, persistence, perseverance, determination.

inebriated *adj* drunk, intoxicated, tipsy, merry.
🔁 sober.

inedible *adj* uneatable, unpalatable, indigestible, harmful, noxious, poisonous, deadly.
🔁 edible.

ineffective *adj* useless, worthless, vain, idle, futile, unavailing, fruitless, unproductive, unsuccessful, powerless, impotent, ineffectual, inadequate, weak, feeble, inept, incompetent.
F3 effective, effectual.

inefficient *adj* uneconomic, wasteful, money-wasting, time-wasting, incompetent, inexpert, unworkmanlike, slipshod, sloppy, careless, negligent.
F3 efficient.

inelegant *adj* graceless, ungraceful, clumsy, awkward, clunky (*infml*), laboured, ugly, unrefined, crude, unpolished, rough, unsophisticated, uncultivated, uncouth.
F3 elegant.

ineligible *adj* disqualified, ruled out, unacceptable, undesirable, unworthy, unsuitable, unfit, unqualified, unequipped.
F3 eligible.

inept *adj* awkward, clumsy, bungling, incompetent, unskilful, inexpert, foolish, stupid.
F3 competent, skilful.

inequality *n* unequalness, difference, diversity, dissimilarity, disparity, unevenness, disproportion, bias, prejudice.
F3 equality.

inert *adj* immobile, motionless, unmoving, still, inactive, inanimate, lifeless, dead, passive, unresponsive, apathetic, dormant, idle, lazy, lethargic, sluggish, torpid, sleepy.
F3 lively, animated.

inertia *n* immobility, stillness, inactivity, passivity, unresponsiveness, apathy, idleness, laziness, lethargy, torpor.
F3 activity, liveliness.

inescapable *adj* inevitable, unavoidable, destined, fated, certain, sure, irrevocable, unalterable.
F3 escapable.

inevitable *adj* unavoidable, inescapable, necessary, definite, certain, sure, decreed, ordained, destined, fated, automatic, assured, fixed, unalterable, irrevocable, inexorable.
F3 avoidable, uncertain, alterable.

inexcusable *adj* indefensible, unforgivable, unpardonable, intolerable, unacceptable, outrageous, shameful, blameworthy, reprehensible.
F3 excusable, justifiable.

inexhaustible *adj* 1 *an inexhaustible supply*: unlimited, limitless, boundless, unbounded, infinite, endless, never-ending, abundant. 2 INDEFATIGABLE, tireless, untiring, unflagging, unwearied, unwearying.
F3 1 limited.

inexpensive *adj* cheap, low-priced, reasonable, modest, bargain, budget, low-cost, economical.
F3 expensive, dear.

inexperience *n* inexpertness, ignorance, unfamiliarity, strangeness, newness, rawness, naïveness, innocence.
F3 experience.

inexperienced *adj* inexpert, untrained, unskilled, amateur, probationary, apprentice, unacquainted, unfamiliar, unaccustomed, new, fresh, raw, callow, young, immature, green, naïve, unsophisticated, innocent.
F3 experienced, mature.

inexplicable *adj* unexplainable, unaccountable, strange, mystifying, puzzling, baffling, mysterious, enigmatic, unfathomable, incomprehensible, incredible, unbelievable, miraculous.
F3 explicable.

inexpressive *adj* unexpressive, expressionless, deadpan, inscrutable, blank, vacant, empty, emotionless, impassive.
F3 expressive.

infallible *adj* accurate, unerring, unfailing, foolproof, fail-safe, sure-fire (*infml*), certain, sure, reliable, dependable, trustworthy, sound,

perfect, faultless, impeccable.
🔁 fallible.

infamous adj notorious, ill-famed, disreputable, disgraceful, shameful, shocking, outrageous, scandalous, wicked, iniquitous.
🔁 illustrious, glorious.

infamy n notoriety, disrepute, disgrace, shame, dishonour, discredit, ignominy, wickedness.
🔁 glory.

infancy n 1 BABYHOOD, childhood, youth. 2 BEGINNING, start, commencement, inception, outset, birth, dawn, genesis, emergence, origins, early stages.
🔁 1 adulthood.

infant n baby, toddler, tot (*infml*), rugrat (*sl*), ankle-biter (*sl*), child, babe (*fml*), babe in arms (*fml*).
🔁 adult.
➤ adj newborn, baby, young, youthful, juvenile, immature, growing, developing, rudimentary, early, initial, new.
🔁 adult, mature.

infantile adj babyish, childish, puerile, juvenile, young, youthful, adolescent, immature.
🔁 adult, mature.

infatuated adj besotted, obsessed, enamoured, smitten (*infml*), crazy (*infml*), spellbound, mesmerized, captivated, fascinated, enraptured, ravished.
🔁 indifferent, disenchanted.

infatuation n besottedness, obsession, fixation, passion, crush (*sl*), love, fondness, fascination.
🔁 indifference, disenchantment.

infect v contaminate, pollute, defile, taint, blight, poison, corrupt, pervert, influence, affect, touch, inspire.

infection n illness, disease, virus, epidemic, contagion, pestilence, contamination, pollution, defilement, taint, blight, poison, corruption, influence.

infectious adj contagious, infective, communicable, transmissible, catching, spreading, epidemic, virulent, deadly, contaminating, polluting, defiling, corrupting.

infer v derive, extrapolate, deduce, conclude, assume, presume, surmise, gather, understand.

inference n deduction, conclusion, corollary, consequence, assumption, presumption, surmise, conjecture, extrapolation, construction, interpretation, reading.

inferior adj 1 LOWER, lesser, minor, secondary, junior, subordinate, subsidiary, second-class, low, humble, menial. 2 *inferior work*: substandard, second-rate, mediocre, bad, poor, unsatisfactory, slipshod, shoddy.
🔁 1 superior. 2 excellent.
➤ n subordinate, junior, underling (*infml*), minion, vassal, menial.
🔁 superior.

inferiority n 1 SUBORDINATION, subservience, humbleness, lowliness, meanness, insignificance. 2 MEDIOCRITY, imperfection, inadequacy, slovenliness, shoddiness.
🔁 1 superiority. 2 excellence.

infernal adj hellish, satanic, devilish, diabolical, fiendish, accursed, damned.
🔁 heavenly.

infertile adj barren, sterile, childless, unproductive, unfruitful, arid, parched, dried-up.
🔁 fertile, fruitful.

infest v swarm, teem, throng, flood, overrun, invade, infiltrate, penetrate, permeate, pervade, ravage.

infidelity n adultery, unfaithfulness, faithlessness, disloyalty, duplicity, treachery, betrayal, cheating, falseness.
🔁 fidelity, faithfulness.

infiltrate v penetrate, enter, creep into, insinuate, intrude, pervade, permeate, filter, percolate.

infinite adj limitless, unlimited, boundless, unbounded, endless,

never-ending, inexhaustible, bottomless, innumerable, numberless, uncountable, countless, untold, incalculable, inestimable, immeasurable, unfathomable, vast, immense, enormous, huge, absolute, total.
🔁 finite, limited.

infinitesimal *adj* tiny, minute, microscopic, minuscule, inconsiderable, insignificant, negligible, inappreciable, imperceptible.
🔁 great, large, enormous.

infinity *n* eternity, perpetuity, limitlessness, boundlessness, endlessness, inexhaustibility, countlessness, immeasurableness, vastness, immensity.
🔁 finiteness, limitation.

infirm *adj* weak, feeble, frail, ill, unwell, poorly, sickly, failing, faltering, unsteady, shaky, wobbly, doddery, lame.
🔁 healthy, strong.

inflame *v* anger, enrage, infuriate, incense, exasperate, madden, provoke, stimulate, excite, rouse, arouse, agitate, foment, kindle, ignite, fire, heat, fan, fuel, increase, intensify, worsen, aggravate.
🔁 cool, quench.

inflamed *adj* sore, swollen, septic, infected, poisoned, red, hot, heated, fevered, feverish.

inflammable *adj* flammable, combustible, burnable.
🔁 non-flammable, incombustible, flameproof.

inflammation *n* soreness, painfulness, tenderness, swelling, abscess, infection, redness, heat, rash, sore, irritation.

inflate *v* blow up, pump up, blow out, puff out, swell, distend, bloat, expand, enlarge, increase, boost, exaggerate.
🔁 deflate.

inflation *n* expansion, increase, rise, escalation, hyperinflation.
🔁 deflation.

inflexible *adj* rigid, stiff, hard, solid, set, fixed, fast, immovable, firm, strict, stringent, unbending, unyielding, adamant, resolute, relentless, implacable, uncompromising, stubborn, obstinate, intransigent, entrenched, dyed-in-the-wool.
🔁 flexible, yielding, adaptable.

inflict *v* impose, enforce, perpetrate, wreak, administer, apply, deliver, deal, mete out, lay, burden, exact, levy.

influence *n* power, sway, rule, authority, domination, mastery, hold, control, direction, guidance, bias, prejudice, pull, pressure, effect, impact, weight, importance, prestige, standing.
➤ *v* dominate, control, manipulate, direct, guide, manoeuvre, change, alter, modify, affect, impress, move, stir, arouse, rouse, sway, persuade, induce, incite, instigate, prompt, motivate, dispose, incline, bias, prejudice, predispose.

influential *adj* dominant, controlling, leading, authoritative, charismatic, persuasive, convincing, compelling, inspiring, moving, powerful, potent, effective, telling, strong, weighty, momentous, important, significant, instrumental, guiding.
🔁 ineffective, unimportant.

influx *n* inflow, inrush, invasion, arrival, stream, flow, rush, flood, inundation.

inform *v* tell, advise, notify, communicate, impart, leak, tip off, acquaint, fill in (*infml*), brief, instruct, enlighten, illuminate.
◊ **inform on** betray, incriminate, shop (*sl*), tell on (*infml*), squeal (*sl*), blab, grass (*sl*), denounce.

informal *adj* unofficial, casual, unceremonious, relaxed, easy, free, natural, simple, unpretentious, familiar, colloquial.
🔁 formal, solemn.

information *n* facts, data, input, gen (*infml*), SP (*infml*), bumf (*sl*), intelligence, news, report, bulletin, communiqué, message, word, advice, notice, briefing, instruction, knowledge, dossier, database, databank, clues, evidence.

informative *adj* educational, instructive, edifying, enlightening, illuminating, revealing, forthcoming, communicative, chatty, gossipy, newsy, helpful, useful, constructive.
🠪 uninformative.

informed *adj* **1** *we'll keep you informed*: familiar, conversant, acquainted, enlightened, briefed, primed, posted, up to date, up to speed (*infml*), abreast, au fait, in the know (*infml*). **2** *an informed opinion*: well-informed, authoritative, expert, versed, well-read, erudite, learned, knowledgeable, well-researched.
🠪 **1** ignorant, unaware.

informer *n* informant, grass (*sl*), supergrass (*sl*), betrayer, traitor, Judas, tell-tale, sneak, spy, mole (*infml*).

infringe *v* **1** BREAK, violate, contravene, transgress, overstep, disobey, defy, flout, ignore. **2** INTRUDE, encroach, trespass, invade.

infuriate *v* anger, vex, enrage, incense, exasperate, madden, provoke, rouse, annoy, irritate, rile, antagonize.
🠪 calm, pacify.

ingenious *adj* clever, shrewd, cunning, crafty, skilful, masterly, imaginative, creative, inventive, resourceful, original, innovative.
🠪 unimaginative.

ingenuous *adj* artless, guileless, innocent, honest, sincere, frank, open, plain, simple, unsophisticated, naïve, trusting.
🠪 artful, sly.

ingrained *adj* fixed, rooted, deep-rooted, deep-seated, entrenched, immovable, ineradicable, permanent, inbuilt, inborn, inbred.

ingratiate *v* curry favour, flatter, creep, crawl, grovel, fawn, get in with.

ingratitude *n* ungratefulness, thanklessness, unappreciativeness, ungraciousness.

🠪 gratitude, thankfulness.

ingredient *n* constituent, element, factor, component, part.

inhabit *v* live, dwell, reside, occupy, possess, colonize, settle, people, populate, stay.

inhabitant *n* resident, dweller, citizen, native, occupier, occupant, inmate, tenant, lodger.

inherent *adj* inborn, inbred, innate, inherited, hereditary, native, natural, inbuilt, built-in, intrinsic, ingrained, essential, fundamental, basic.

inherit *v* succeed to, accede to, assume, come into, be left, receive.

inheritance *n* legacy, bequest, heritage, birthright, heredity, descent, succession.

inheritor *n* heir, heiress, successor, beneficiary, recipient.

inhibit *v* discourage, repress, hold back, suppress, curb, check, restrain, hinder, impede, obstruct, interfere with, frustrate, thwart, prevent, stop, stanch, stem.
🠪 encourage, assist.

inhibited *adj* repressed, self-conscious, shy, reticent, withdrawn, reserved, guarded, subdued.
🠪 uninhibited, open, relaxed.

inhibition *n* repression, hang-up (*infml*), self-consciousness, shyness, reticence, reserve, restraint, curb, check, hindrance, impediment, obstruction, bar.
🠪 freedom.

inhuman *adj* barbaric, barbarous, animal, bestial, vicious, savage, sadistic, cold-blooded, brutal, cruel, inhumane.
🠪 human.

inhumane *adj* unkind, insensitive, callous, unfeeling, heartless, cold-hearted, hard-hearted, pitiless, ruthless, cruel, brutal, inhuman.
🠪 humane, kind, compassionate.

initial *adj* first, beginning, opening, introductory, inaugural, original, primary, early, formative.
🠪 final, last.

initially *adv* at first, at the beginning, to begin with, to start with, originally, first, firstly, first of all.
🔁 finally, in the end.

initiate *v* begin, start, commence, originate, pioneer, institute, set up, introduce, launch, open, inaugurate, instigate, activate, trigger, prompt, stimulate, cause.

initiation *n* admission, reception, entrance, entry, debut, introduction, enrolment, induction, investiture, installation, inauguration, inception.

initiative *n* 1 ENERGY, drive, dynamism, get-up-and-go (*infml*), ambition, enterprise, resourcefulness, inventiveness, originality, innovativeness. 2 SUGGESTION, recommendation, action, lead, first move, first step.

inject *v* 1 *inject drugs*: inoculate, vaccinate, shoot (*sl*). 2 INTRODUCE, insert, add, bring, infuse, instil.

injection *n* inoculation, vaccination, jab (*infml*), shot (*infml*), fix (*sl*), dose, insertion, introduction.

injunction *n* command, order, directive, ruling, mandate, direction, instruction, precept.

injure *v* hurt, harm, damage, impair, spoil, mar, ruin, disfigure, deface, mutilate, wound, cut, break, fracture, maim, disable, cripple, lame, ill-treat, maltreat, abuse, offend, wrong, upset, put out.

injury *n* 1 WOUND, cut, lesion, fracture, trauma, hurt, mischief, ill, harm, damage, impairment, ruin, disfigurement, mutilation. 2 ILL-TREATMENT, abuse, insult, offence, wrong, injustice.

injustice *n* unfairness, inequality, disparity, discrimination, oppression, bias, prejudice, one-sidedness, partisanship, partiality, favouritism, wrong, iniquity.
🔁 justice, fairness.

inkling *n* suspicion, idea, notion,

faintest (*infml*), glimmering, clue, hint, intimation, suggestion, allusion, indication, sign, pointer.

inlet *n* bay, cove, creek, fiord, opening, entrance, passage.

inn *n* public house, pub (*infml*), local (*infml*), tavern, hostelry, hotel.

innate *adj* inborn, inbred, inherent, intrinsic, native, natural, instinctive, intuitive.
🔁 acquired, learnt.

inner *adj* internal, interior, inside, inward, innermost, central, middle, concealed, hidden, secret, private, personal, intimate, mental, psychological, spiritual, emotional.
🔁 outer, outward.

innocence *n* 1 GUILTLESSNESS, blamelessness, honesty, virtue, righteousness, purity, chastity, virginity, incorruptibility, harmlessness, innocuousness. 2 ARTLESSNESS, guilelessness, naïvety, inexperience, ignorance, naturalness, simplicity, unsophistication, unworldliness, credulity, gullibility, trustfulness.
🔁 1 guilt. 2 experience.

innocent *adj* 1 GUILTLESS, blameless, irreproachable, unimpeachable, honest, upright, virtuous, righteous, sinless, faultless, impeccable, stainless, spotless, squeaky clean (*infml*), immaculate, unsullied, untainted, uncontaminated, pure, chaste, virginal, incorrupt, inoffensive, harmless, innocuous. 2 ARTLESS, guileless, ingenuous, naïve, green, inexperienced, fresh, natural, simple, unsophisticated, unworldly, childlike, credulous, gullible, trusting.
🔁 1 guilty. 2 experienced.

innocuous *adj* harmless, safe, inoffensive, unobjectionable, innocent.
🔁 harmful.

innovation *n* newness, novelty, neologism, modernization, progress, reform, change, alteration, variation, departure.

innovative *adj* new, fresh, original,

ground-breaking, creative, imaginative, inventive, resourceful, enterprising, go-ahead, progressive, reforming, bold, daring, adventurous.
🔁 conservative, unimaginative.

innuendo *n* insinuation, aspersion, slur, whisper, hint, intimation, suggestion, implication.

innumerable *adj* numberless, unnumbered, countless, uncountable, untold, incalculable, infinite, numerous, many.

inoculation *n* vaccination, immunization, protection, injection, shot (*infml*), jab (*infml*).

inoffensive *adj* harmless, innocuous, innocent, peaceable, mild, unobtrusive, unassertive, quiet, retiring.
🔁 offensive, harmful, provocative.

inordinate *adj* excessive, immoderate, unwarranted, undue, unreasonable, disproportionate, great.
🔁 moderate, reasonable.

inquire, enquire *v* ask, question, quiz, query, investigate, look into, probe, examine, inspect, scrutinize, search, explore.

inquiry, enquiry *n* question, query, investigation, inquest, hearing, inquisition, examination, inspection, scrutiny, study, survey, poll, search, probe, exploration.

inquisitive *adj* curious, questioning, probing, searching, prying, peeping, snooping, nosey, interfering, meddlesome, intrusive.

insane *adj* **1** MAD, crazy, mentally ill, lunatic, mental (*sl*), demented, deranged, unhinged, disturbed. **2** FOOLISH, stupid, senseless, impractical.
🔁 **1** sane. **2** sensible.

insanity *n* madness, craziness, lunacy, mental illness, neurosis, psychosis, mania, dementia, derangement, folly, stupidity, senselessness, irrationality, irresponsibility.
🔁 sanity.

insatiable *adj* unquenchable,

unsatisfiable, ravenous, voracious, immoderate, inordinate.

inscribe *v* engrave, etch, carve, cut, incise, imprint, impress, stamp, print, write, sign, autograph, dedicate.

inscription *n* engraving, epitaph, caption, legend, lettering, words, writing, signature, autograph, dedication.

inscrutable *adj* incomprehensible, unfathomable, impenetrable, deep, inexplicable, unexplainable, baffling, mysterious, enigmatic, cryptic, hidden.
🔁 comprehensible, expressive.

insect

Insects include: fly, gnat, midge, mosquito, tsetse fly, locust, dragonfly, cranefly, daddy longlegs (*infml*), horsefly, onion fly, mayfly, butterfly, red admiral, cabbage white, moth, tiger moth, bee, bumblebee, wasp, hornet, aphid, blackfly, greenfly, whitefly, froghopper, ladybird, ladybug (*US*), water boatman, lacewing; beetle, cockroach, roach (*US*), earwig, stick insect, grasshopper, cricket, cicada, flea, louse, nit, leatherjacket, termite, glowworm, woodworm, weevil, woodlouse. *see also* **butterfly**.

Arachnids include: spider, black widow, tarantula, scorpion, mite, tick.

insecure *adj* **1** ANXIOUS, worried, nervous, uncertain, unsure, afraid. **2** UNSAFE, dangerous, hazardous, perilous, precarious, unsteady, shaky, loose, unprotected, defenceless, exposed, vulnerable.
🔁 **1** confident, self-assured. **2** secure, safe.

insensible *adj* numb, anaesthetized, dead, cold, insensitive, unresponsive, blind, deaf, unconscious, unaware, oblivious, unmindful.
🔁 conscious.

insensitive *adj* hardened, tough, resistant, impenetrable, impervious, immune, unsusceptible, thick-skinned,

unfeeling, impassive, indifferent, unaffected, unmoved, untouched, uncaring, unconcerned, callous, thoughtless, tactless, crass.
🔄 sensitive.

inseparable *adj* indivisible, indissoluble, inextricable, close, intimate, bosom, devoted.
🔄 separable.

insert *v* put, place, put in, stick in, push in, introduce, implant, embed, engraft, set, inset, let in, interleave, intercalate (*fml*), interpolate (*fml*), interpose (*fml*).
➤ *n* insertion, enclosure, inset, notice, advertisement, supplement, addition.

inside *n* interior, content, contents, middle, centre, heart, core.
🔄 outside.
➤ *adv* within, indoors, internally, inwardly, secretly, privately.
🔄 outside.
➤ *adj* interior, internal, inner, innermost, inward, secret, classified, confidential, private.

insides *n* entrails, guts, intestines, bowels, innards (*infml*), organs, viscera, belly, stomach.

insidious *adj* subtle, sly, crafty, cunning, wily, deceptive, devious, stealthy, surreptitious, furtive, sneaking, treacherous.
🔄 direct, straightforward.

insight *n* awareness, knowledge, comprehension, understanding, grasp, apprehension, perception, intuition, sensitivity, discernment, judgement, acumen, penetration, observation, vision, wisdom, intelligence.

insignificant *adj* unimportant, irrelevant, meaningless, immaterial, inconsequential, minor, trivial, trifling, petty, paltry, small, tiny, insubstantial, inconsiderable, negligible, non-essential.
🔄 significant, important.

insincere *adj* hypocritical, two-faced, double-dealing, lying, untruthful, dishonest, deceitful, devious, unfaithful, faithless, untrue, false, feigned, pretended, phoney (*infml*), hollow.
🔄 sincere.

insinuate *v* imply, suggest, allude, hint, intimate, get at (*infml*), indicate.

insipid *adj* tasteless, flavourless, unsavoury, unappetizing, watery, weak, bland, wishy-washy (*infml*), colourless, drab, dull, monotonous, boring, uninteresting, tame, flat, lifeless, spiritless, characterless, trite, unimaginative, dry.
🔄 tasty, spicy, piquant, appetizing.

insist *v* demand, require, urge, stress, emphasize, repeat, reiterate, dwell on, harp on, assert, maintain, claim, contend, hold, vow, swear, persist, stand firm.

insistence *n* demand, entreaty, exhortation (*fml*), urging, stress, emphasis, repetition, reiteration, assertion, claim, contention, persistence, determination, resolution, firmness.

insistent *adj* demanding, importunate, emphatic, forceful, pressing, urgent, dogged, tenacious, persistent, persevering, relentless, unrelenting, unremitting, incessant.

insolent *adj* rude, abusive, insulting, disrespectful, cheeky, impertinent, impudent, saucy (*infml*), bold, forward, fresh, presumptuous, arrogant, defiant, insubordinate.
🔄 polite, respectful.

insoluble *adj* unsolvable, unexplainable, inexplicable, incomprehensible, unfathomable, impenetrable, obscure, mystifying, puzzling, perplexing, baffling.
🔄 explicable.

insolvent *adj* bankrupt, bust, failed, ruined, broke (*infml*), penniless, destitute.
🔄 solvent.

inspect *v* check, vet, look over, examine, search, investigate, scrutinize, study, scan, survey, superintend, supervise, oversee, visit.

inspection n check, check-up, examination, scrutiny, scan, study, survey, review, search, investigation, supervision, visit.

inspector n supervisor, superintendent, overseer, surveyor, controller, scrutineer, checker, tester, examiner, investigator, reviewer, critic.

inspiration n 1 CREATIVITY, imagination, genius, muse, influence, encouragement, stimulation, motivation, spur, stimulus. 2 IDEA, brainwave, insight, illumination, revelation, awakening.

inspire v encourage, hearten, influence, impress, animate, enliven, quicken, galvanize, fire, kindle, stir, arouse, trigger, spark off, prompt, spur, motivate, provoke, stimulate, excite, exhilarate, thrill, enthral, enthuse, imbue, infuse.

inspiring adj encouraging, heartening, uplifting, invigorating, stirring, rousing, stimulating, exciting, exhilarating, thrilling, enthralling, moving, affecting, memorable, impressive.
🔁 uninspiring, dull.

instability n unsteadiness, shakiness, vacillation, wavering, irresolution, uncertainty, unpredictability, changeableness, variability, fluctuation, volatility, capriciousness, fickleness, inconstancy, unreliability, insecurity, unsafeness, unsoundness.
🔁 stability.

install v fix, fit, lay, put, place, position, locate, site, situate, station, plant, settle, establish, set up, introduce, institute, inaugurate, invest, induct, ordain.

instalment n 1 *pay in instalments*: payment, repayment, portion. 2 EPISODE, chapter, part, section, division.

instant n flash, twinkling, trice, moment, tick (*infml*), split second, second, minute, time, occasion.
➤ adj instantaneous, immediate,

on-the-spot, direct, prompt, urgent, unhesitating, quick, fast, rapid, swift.
🔁 slow.

instead adv alternatively, preferably, rather.
◇ **instead of** in place of, in lieu of, on behalf of, in preference to, rather than.

instigate v initiate, set on, start, begin, cause, generate, inspire, move, influence, encourage, urge, spur, prompt, provoke, stimulate, incite, stir up, whip up, foment, rouse, excite.

instil v infuse, imbue, insinuate, introduce, inject, implant, inculcate (*fml*), impress, din into (*infml*).

instinct n intuition, sixth sense, gut reaction (*infml*), impulse, urge, feeling, hunch, flair, knack, gift, talent, feel, faculty, ability, aptitude, predisposition, tendency.

instinctive adj natural, native, inborn, innate, inherent, intuitive, impulsive, involuntary, automatic, knee-jerk (*infml*), mechanical, reflex, spontaneous, immediate, unthinking, unpremeditated, gut (*infml*), visceral.
🔁 conscious, voluntary, deliberate.

institute v originate, initiate, introduce, enact, begin, start, commence, create, establish, set up, organize, found, inaugurate, open, launch, appoint, install, invest, induct, ordain.
🔁 cancel, discontinue, abolish.
➤ n school, college, academy, conservatory, foundation, institution.

institution n 1 CUSTOM, tradition, usage, practice, ritual, convention, rule, law. 2 ORGANIZATION, association, society, guild, concern, corporation, foundation, establishment, institute, hospital, home. 3 INITIATION, introduction, enactment, inception, creation, establishment, formation, founding, foundation, installation.

instruct v 1 TEACH, educate, tutor, coach, train, drill, ground, school, discipline. 2 ORDER, command, direct, mandate, tell, inform, notify, advise, counsel, guide.

instruction n 1 *follow the instructions*: direction, briefing, recommendation, advice, guidance, information, order, command, injunction, mandate, directive, ruling. 2 EDUCATION, schooling, lesson(s), tuition, teaching, training, coaching, drilling, grounding, preparation.

instructive adj informative, educational, edifying, enlightening, illuminating, helpful, useful.
🔁 unenlightening.

instructor n teacher, master, mistress, tutor, coach, trainer, demonstrator, exponent, adviser, mentor, guide, guru.

instrument n 1 TOOL, implement, utensil, appliance, gadget, contraption, device, contrivance, apparatus, mechanism. 2 AGENT, agency, vehicle, organ, medium, factor, channel, way, means.

instrumental adj active, involved, contributory, conducive, influential, useful, helpful, auxiliary, subsidiary.
🔁 obstructive, unhelpful.

insufferable adj intolerable, unbearable, detestable, loathsome, dreadful, impossible.
🔁 pleasant, tolerable.

insufficiency n inadequacy, shortage, deficiency, lack, scarcity, dearth, want, need, poverty.
🔁 sufficiency, excess.

insufficient adj inadequate, short, deficient, lacking, sparse, scanty, scarce.
🔁 sufficient, excessive.

insular adj parochial, provincial, cut off, detached, isolated, remote, withdrawn, inward-looking, blinkered, closed, narrow-minded, narrow, limited, petty.

insulate v cushion, pad, lag, cocoon, protect, shield, shelter, isolate, separate, cut off.

insult v abuse, call names, disparage, revile, libel, slander, slight, snub, injure, affront, offend, outrage.

🔁 compliment, praise.
➤ n abuse, rudeness, insolence, defamation, libel, slander, slight, snub, affront, indignity, offence, outrage.
🔁 compliment, praise.

insurance n cover, protection, safeguard, security, provision, assurance, indemnity, guarantee, warranty, policy, premium.

insure v cover, protect, assure, underwrite, indemnify, guarantee, warrant.

insurmountable adj insuperable, unconquerable, invincible, overwhelming, hopeless, impossible.
🔁 surmountable.

insurrection n rising, uprising, insurgence, riot, rebellion, mutiny, revolt, revolution, coup, putsch.

intact adj unbroken, in one piece, whole, complete, integral, entire, perfect, sound, undamaged, unhurt, uninjured.
🔁 broken, incomplete, damaged.

intangible adj insubstantial, imponderable, elusive, fleeting, airy, shadowy, vague, indefinite, abstract, unreal, invisible.
🔁 tangible, real.

integral adj 1 *an integral part*: intrinsic, constituent, elemental, basic, fundamental, necessary, essential, indispensable. 2 COMPLETE, entire, full, whole, undivided.
🔁 1 extra, additional, unnecessary.

integrate v assimilate, merge, join, unite, combine, amalgamate, incorporate, coalesce, fuse, knit, mesh, mix, blend, harmonize.
🔁 divide, separate.

integrity n 1 HONESTY, uprightness, probity, incorruptibility, purity, morality, principle, honour, virtue, goodness, righteousness. 2 COMPLETENESS, wholeness, unity, coherence, cohesion.
🔁 1 dishonesty. 2 incompleteness.

intellect n mind, brain(s) (*infml*), brainpower, intelligence, genius, reason,

understanding, sense, wisdom, judgement.
▪ stupidity.

intellectual *adj* academic, scholarly, intelligent, studious, thoughtful, cerebral, mental, highbrow, cultural.
▪ low-brow.

➤ *n* thinker, academic, highbrow, egghead (*infml*), mastermind, genius.
▪ low-brow.

intelligence *n* **1** INTELLECT, reason, wit(s), brain(s) (*infml*), brainpower, cleverness, brightness, aptitude, quickness, alertness, discernment, perception, understanding, comprehension. **2** INFORMATION, facts, data, low-down (*sl*), knowledge, findings, news, report, warning, tip-off.
▪ **1** stupidity, foolishness.

intelligent *adj* clever, bright, smart, brainy (*infml*), quick, alert, quick-witted, sharp, acute, knowing, knowledgeable, well-informed, thinking, rational, sensible.
▪ unintelligent, stupid, foolish.

intend *v* aim, have a mind, contemplate, mean, propose, plan, project, scheme, plot, design, purpose, resolve, determine, destine, mark out, earmark, set apart.

intense *adj* great, deep, profound, strong, powerful, forceful, full-on (*infml*), fierce, harsh, severe, acute, sharp, keen, eager, earnest, ardent, fervent, fervid, passionate, vehement, energetic, violent, intensive, concentrated, heightened.
▪ moderate, mild, weak.

intensify *v* increase, step up, escalate, heighten, hot up (*infml*), fire, boost, fuel, aggravate, add to, strengthen, reinforce, sharpen, whet, quicken, deepen, concentrate, emphasize, enhance.
▪ reduce, weaken.

intensive *adj* concentrated, thorough, exhaustive, comprehensive, detailed, in-depth, thoroughgoing, all-out, intense.
▪ superficial.

intent *adj* determined, resolved, resolute, set, bent, concentrated, eager, earnest, committed, steadfast, fixed, alert, attentive, concentrating, preoccupied, engrossed, wrapped up, absorbed, occupied.
▪ absent-minded, distracted.

intention *n* aim, purpose, object, end, point, target, goal, objective, idea, plan, design, view, intent, meaning.

intentional *adj* designed, wilful, conscious, planned, deliberate, prearranged, premeditated, calculated, studied, intended, meant.
▪ unintentional, accidental.

intercede *v* mediate, arbitrate, intervene, plead, entreat, beseech, speak.

intercept *v* head off, ambush, interrupt, cut off, stop, arrest, catch, take, seize, check, block, obstruct, delay, frustrate, thwart.

interchangeable *adj* reciprocal, equivalent, similar, identical, the same, synonymous, standard.
▪ different.

interest *n* **1** CURIOSITY, care, attention, notice, concern, involvement, participation. **2** IMPORTANCE, significance, consequence, relevance, note. **3** *leisure interests*: activity, pursuit, pastime, hobby, diversion, amusement. **4** *earn interest*: dividend, return, benefit, profit, gain, credits.
▪ **1** boredom.

➤ *v* **1** ATTRACT, move, occupy, engage, absorb, engross, fascinate, intrigue. **2** CONCERN, involve, affect, touch.
▪ bore.

interested *adj* **1** ATTENTIVE, curious, absorbed, engrossed, fascinated, enthusiastic, keen, attracted. **2** CONCERNED, involved, affected.
▪ **1** uninterested, indifferent, apathetic. **2** disinterested, unaffected.

interesting *adj* attractive, appealing, entertaining, engaging, absorbing, engrossing, fascinating, intriguing, compelling, gripping, stimulating,

thought-provoking, curious, unusual.
🔄 uninteresting, boring, monotonous, tedious.

interfere *v* **1** INTRUDE, poke one's nose in, pry, butt in, interrupt, intervene, meddle, tamper. **2** HINDER, hamper, obstruct, block, impede, handicap, cramp, inhibit, conflict, clash.
🔄 **2** assist.

interference *n* **1** INTRUSION, prying, interruption, intervention, meddling. **2** OBSTRUCTION, opposition, conflict, clashing.
🔄 **2** assistance.

interim *adj* temporary, provisional, stopgap, makeshift, improvised, stand-in, acting, caretaker.
➤ *n* meantime, meanwhile, interval.

interior *adj* **1** INTERNAL, inside, inner, central, inward, mental, spiritual, private, secret, hidden. **2** HOME, domestic. **3** INLAND, up-country, remote.
🔄 **1** exterior, external.
➤ *n* inside, centre, middle, core, heart, depths.
🔄 exterior, outside.

interjection *n* exclamation, ejaculation, cry, shout, call, interpolation.

intermediary *n* mediator, go-between, middleman, broker, agent.

intermediate *adj* midway, halfway, in-between, middle, mid, median, mean, intermediary, intervening, transitional.
🔄 extreme.

interminable *adj* endless, never-ending, ceaseless, perpetual, limitless, unlimited, long, long-winded, long-drawn-out, dragging, wearisome.
🔄 limited, brief.

intermission *n* interval, entr'acte, interlude, break, recess, rest, respite, breather (*infml*), breathing space, pause, lull, let-up (*infml*), remission, suspension, interruption, halt, stop, stoppage, cessation.

intermittent *adj* occasional, periodic, sporadic, spasmodic, fitful,

erratic, irregular, broken.
🔄 continuous, constant.

internal *adj* inside, inner, interior, inward, intimate, private, personal, domestic, in-house.
🔄 external.

international *adj* global, worldwide, intercontinental, cosmopolitan, universal, general.
🔄 national, local, parochial.

Internet

Internet terms include: account, address, ADSL (Asynchronous Digital Subscriber Line), alias, anonymous FTP, applet, ASP (Active Server Page), attachment, authoring, backbone, bandwidth, banner, BBS (Bulletin Board System), bookmark, bot, bps (bits per second), broadband, browser, cable modem, cache, cancelbot, CGI (Common Gateway Interface), chatroom, cookie, cybercafé, cyberspace, dialer, dialup connection, decryption, dedicated line, denial of service, digital signing, DNS (Domain Name Server/System), domain name, dotcom, download, e-business, e-commerce, email (or e-mail), emoticon, encryption, extranet, FAQ (Frequently Asked Questions), favorites, firewall, flame, forum, FTP (File Transfer Protocol), frame, gateway, GIF (Graphical Interchange Format), helper application, hit, hit counter, homepage, honeypot, host, host name, HTML (HyperText Markup Language), DHTML (Dynamic HTML), HTTP or http (HyperText Transfer Protocol), hyperlink, hypertext, IMAP (Internet Message Access Protocol), intelligent agent, Internet access provider (IAP), Internet Protocol (IP), Internet Relay Chat (IRC), Internet service provider (ISP), intranet, ISDN (Integrated Services Digital Network), Javascript, JPEG (Joint Photographics Experts Group), junk mail, kill file, link, lurk, mailbox, mailing list, mail server, main menu, message board, Microsoft Internet Explorer®, MIME

(Multipurpose Internet Mail
Extensions), mirror site, moderator,
modem, MP3, MPEG (Moving Picture
Experts Group), navigation bar,
newbie, newsgroup, newsreader,
NNTP (Network News Transfer
Protocol), node, offline, online, online
service, packet, pane, Perl, pingstorm,
plain text, plugin, PNG (Portable
Network Graphic), POP (Point of
Presence), POP3 (Post Office
Protocol), popup, portal, post,
postmaster, PPP (Point to Point
Protocol), protocol, remote access,
rollover, router, scrollbar, search
engine, server, set-top box, signature
file, site map, smiley, snail mail, spam,
spider, SSI (Server Side Includes),
stylesheet, cascading stylesheet
(CSS), surf, TCP/IP (Transmission
Control Protocol/Internet Protocol),
timeout, troll, upload, uptime, URL
(Uniform or Universal Resource
Locator), Usenet, username, viral
email, virus, W3C (World Wide Web
Consortium), WAN (wide area
network), WAP (Wireless Application
Protocol), web bug, Webcam, webcast,
webmaster, web page, website, World
Wide Web (WWW or www), XML
(Extensible Markup Language), XSL
(Extensible Style Language).

interplay *n* exchange, interchange,
interaction, reciprocation, give-and-
take (*infml*).

interpose *v* insert, introduce,
interject, interpolate, put in, thrust in,
interrupt, intrude, interfere, come
between, intervene, step in, mediate.

interpret *v* explain, expound,
elucidate, clarify, throw light on, define,
paraphrase, translate, render, decode,
decipher, solve, make sense of,
understand, construe, read, take.

interpretation *n* explanation,
clarification, analysis, translation,
rendering, version, performance,
reading, understanding, take (*infml*),
sense, meaning.

interrogate *v* question, quiz,
examine, cross-examine, grill (*infml*),
give the third degree (*infml*), pump,
debrief.

interrogation *n* questioning, cross-
questioning, examination, cross-
examination, grilling (*infml*), third
degree (*infml*), inquisition, inquiry,
inquest.

interrupt *v* intrude, barge in (*infml*),
butt in (*infml*), interject, break in, heckle,
disturb, disrupt, interfere, obstruct,
check, hinder, hold up, stop, halt,
suspend, discontinue, cut off,
disconnect, punctuate, separate,
divide, cut, break.

interruption *n* intrusion,
interjection, disturbance, disruption,
obstruction, impediment, obstacle,
hitch, pause, break, halt, stop,
stoppage, suspension, discontinuance,
disconnection, separation, division.

intersect *v* cross, criss-cross, cut
across, bisect, divide, meet, converge.

intersection *n* junction, interchange,
crossroads, crossing.

intertwine *v* entwine, interweave,
interlace, interlink, twist, twine, cross,
weave.

interval *n* interlude, intermission,
break, rest, pause, delay, wait, interim,
meantime, meanwhile, gap, opening,
space, distance, period, spell, time,
season.

intervene *v* 1 STEP IN, mediate,
arbitrate, interfere, interrupt, intrude.
2 OCCUR, happen, elapse, pass.

intervention *n* involvement,
interference, intrusion, mediation,
agency, intercession.

interview *n* audience, consultation,
talk, dialogue, meeting, conference,
press conference, oral examination,
viva.
➤ *v* question, interrogate, examine, vet.

intestines *n* bowels, guts, entrails,
insides, innards (*infml*), offal, viscera,
vitals.

intimacy *n* friendship, closeness, familiarity, confidence, confidentiality, privacy.
🔁 distance.

intimate[1] *v* hint, insinuate, imply, suggest, indicate, communicate, impart, tell, state, declare, announce.

intimate[2] *adj* friendly, informal, familiar, cosy, warm, affectionate, dear, bosom, close, near, confidential, secret, private, personal, internal, innermost, deep, penetrating, detailed, exhaustive.
🔁 unfriendly, cold, distant.
➤ *n* friend, bosom friend, confidant(e), associate.
🔁 stranger.

intimidate *v* daunt, cow, overawe, appal, dismay, alarm, scare, frighten, terrify, threaten, menace, terrorize, bully, browbeat, bulldoze, coerce, pressure, pressurize, lean on (*infml*).

intolerable *adj* unbearable, unendurable, insupportable, unacceptable, insufferable, impossible.
🔁 tolerable.

intolerant *adj* impatient, prejudiced, bigoted, narrow-minded, small-minded, opinionated, dogmatic, illiberal, uncharitable.
🔁 tolerant, liberal.

intonation *n* modulation, tone, accentuation, inflection.

intoxicated *adj* 1 DRUNK, drunken, inebriated, tipsy. 2 EXCITED, elated, exhilarated, thrilled.
🔁 1 sober.

intoxicating *adj* 1 *intoxicating liquor*: alcoholic, strong. 2 EXCITING, stimulating, heady, exhilarating, thrilling.
🔁 1 sobering.

intoxication *n* 1 DRUNKENNESS, inebriation, tipsiness. 2 EXCITEMENT, elation, exhilaration, euphoria.
🔁 1 sobriety.

intrepid *adj* bold, daring, brave, courageous, plucky, valiant, lion-hearted, fearless, dauntless, undaunted, stout-hearted, stalwart, gallant, heroic.
🔁 cowardly, timid.

intricate *adj* elaborate, fancy, ornate, rococo, complicated, complex, sophisticated, involved, convoluted, tortuous, tangled, entangled, knotty, perplexing, difficult.
🔁 simple, plain, straightforward.

intrigue *n* 1 PLOT, scheme, conspiracy, collusion, machination, manoeuvre, stratagem, ruse, wile, trickery, double-dealing, sharp practice. 2 ROMANCE, liaison, affair, amour, intimacy.
➤ *v* 1 FASCINATE, rivet, puzzle, tantalize, attract, charm, captivate. 2 PLOT, scheme, conspire, connive, machinate, manoeuvre.
🔁 1 bore.

introduce *v* 1 INSTITUTE, begin, start, .commence, establish, found, inaugurate, launch, open, bring in, announce, present, acquaint, familiarize, initiate. 2 PUT FORWARD, advance, submit, offer, propose, suggest.
🔁 1 end, conclude. 2 remove, take away.

introduction *n* 1 INSTITUTION, beginning, start, commencement, establishment, inauguration, launch, presentation, debut, initiation.
2 FOREWORD, preface, preamble, prologue, preliminaries, overture, prelude, lead-in, opening.
🔁 1 removal, withdrawal. 2 appendix, conclusion.

introductory *adj* preliminary, preparatory, opening, inaugural, first, initial, early, elementary, basic.

introspective *adj* inward-looking, contemplative, meditative, pensive, thoughtful, brooding, introverted, self-centred, reserved, withdrawn.
🔁 outward-looking.

introverted *adj* introspective, inward-looking, self-centred, withdrawn, shy, reserved, quiet.
🔁 extroverted.

intrude *v* interrupt, butt in, meddle,

interfere, violate, infringe, encroach, trespass.
🔳 withdraw, stand back.

intruder *n* trespasser, prowler, burglar, raider, invader, infiltrator, interloper, gatecrasher.

intrusion *n* interruption, interference, violation, infringement, encroachment, trespass, invasion, incursion.
🔳 withdrawal.

intuition *n* instinct, sixth sense, perception, discernment, insight, hunch, feeling, gut feeling (*infml*).
🔳 reasoning.

intuitive *adj* instinctive, spontaneous, involuntary, innate, untaught.
🔳 reasoned.

inundate *v* flood, deluge, swamp, engulf, submerge, immerse, drown, bury, overwhelm, overrun.

invade *v* enter, penetrate, infiltrate, burst in, descend on, attack, raid, seize, occupy, overrun, swarm over, infest, pervade, encroach, infringe, violate.
🔳 withdraw, evacuate.

invalid¹ *adj* sick, ill, poorly, ailing, sickly, weak, feeble, frail, infirm, disabled, bedridden.
🔳 healthy.
➤ *n* patient, convalescent.

invalid² *adj* **1** FALSE, fallacious, unsound, ill-founded, unfounded, baseless, groundless, illogical, irrational, unscientific, wrong, incorrect. **2** ILLEGAL, null, void, worthless.
🔳 **1** valid. **2** legal.

invaluable *adj* priceless, inestimable, incalculable, precious, valuable, useful.
🔳 worthless, cheap.

invariable *adj* fixed, set, unvarying, unchanging, unchangeable, permanent, constant, steady, unwavering, uniform, rigid, inflexible, habitual, regular.
🔳 variable.

invariably *adv* always, without exception, without fail, unfailingly, consistently, regularly, habitually.
🔳 never.

invasion *n* attack, offensive, onslaught, raid, incursion, foray, breach, penetration, infiltration, intrusion, encroachment, infringement, violation.
🔳 withdrawal, evacuation.

invent *v* conceive, think up, design, discover, create, originate, formulate, frame, devise, contrive, improvise, fabricate, make up, concoct, cook up, trump up, imagine, dream up.

invention *n* **1** *her latest invention*: design, creation, brainchild, discovery, development, device, gadget. **2** LIE, falsehood, deceit, fabrication, fiction, tall story, fantasy, figment. **3** INVENTIVENESS, imagination, creativity, innovation, originality, ingenuity, inspiration, genius.
🔳 **2** truth.

inventive *adj* imaginative, creative, innovative, original, ingenious, resourceful, fertile, inspired, gifted, clever.

inventor *n* designer, discoverer, creator, originator, author, architect, maker, scientist, engineer.

inverse *adj* inverted, upside down, transposed, reversed, opposite, contrary, reverse, converse.

invert *v* upturn, turn upside down, overturn, capsize, upset, transpose, reverse.
🔳 right.

invertebrate

> *Invertebrates include*:
> *sponges*: calcareous, glass, horny;
> *jellyfish, corals and sea anemones*: Portuguese man-of-war, box jellyfish, sea wasp, dead-men's fingers, sea pansy, sea gooseberry, Venus's girdle;
> *echinoderms*: sea lily, feather star, starfish, crown-of-thorns, brittle star, sea urchin, sand dollar, sea cucumber;
> *worms*: annelid worm, arrow worm, blood fluke, bristle worm, earthworm, eelworm, flatworm, fluke, hookworm, leech, liver fluke, lugworm, peanut worm, pinworm, ragworm, ribbonworm, roundworm, sea mouse,

tapeworm, threadworm;
crustaceans: acorn barnacle,
barnacle, brine shrimp, crayfish,
daphnia, fairy shrimp, fiddler crab, fish
louse, goose barnacle, hermit crab,
krill, lobster, mantis shrimp, mussel
shrimp, pill bug, prawn, sandhopper,
seed shrimp, spider crab, spiny
lobster, tadpole shrimp, water flea,
whale louse, woodlouse; centipede,
millipede, velvet worm. *see also*
butterfly; **insect**; **mollusc**.

invest *v* 1 SPEND, lay out, put in, sink.
2 PROVIDE, supply, endow, vest,
empower, authorize, sanction.

investigate *v* inquire into, look into,
consider, examine, study, inspect,
scrutinize, analyse, go into, probe,
explore, search, sift.

investigation *n* inquiry, inquest,
hearing, examination, study, research,
survey, review, inspection, scrutiny,
analysis, probe, exploration, search.

investigator *n* examiner, researcher,
detective, sleuth (*infml*), private
detective, private eye (*infml*).

investment *n* asset, speculation,
venture, stake, contribution, outlay,
expenditure, transaction.

invigorate *v* vitalize, energize,
animate, enliven, liven up, quicken,
strengthen, fortify, brace, stimulate,
inspire, exhilarate, perk up, refresh,
freshen, revitalize, rejuvenate.
☒ tire, weary, dishearten.

invincible *adj* unbeatable,
unconquerable, insuperable,
unsurmountable, indomitable,
unassailable, impregnable,
impenetrable, invulnerable,
indestructible.
☒ beatable.

invisible *adj* unseen, out of sight,
hidden, concealed, disguised,
inconspicuous, indiscernible,
imperceptible, infinitesimal,
microscopic, imaginary, non-existent.
☒ visible.

invitation *n* request, solicitation, call,
summons, temptation, enticement,
allurement, come-on (*infml*),
encouragement, inducement,
provocation, incitement, challenge.

invite *v* ask, call, summon, welcome,
encourage, lead, draw, attract, tempt,
entice, allure, bring on, provoke, ask for,
request, solicit, seek.

inviting *adj* welcoming, appealing,
attractive, tempting, seductive,
enticing, alluring, pleasing, delightful,
captivating, fascinating, intriguing,
tantalizing.
☒ uninviting, unappealing.

invoke *v* call upon, conjure, appeal to,
petition, solicit, implore, entreat, beg,
beseech, supplicate, pray.

involuntary *adj* spontaneous,
unconscious, automatic, mechanical,
reflex, instinctive, conditioned, knee-
jerk (*infml*), impulsive, unthinking, blind,
uncontrolled, unintentional.
☒ deliberate, intentional.

involve *v* 1 REQUIRE, necessitate,
mean, imply, entail, include,
incorporate, embrace, cover, take in,
affect, concern. 2 IMPLICATE,
incriminate, inculpate, draw in, mix up,
embroil, associate. 3 ENGAGE, occupy,
absorb, engross, preoccupy, hold, grip,
rivet.
☒ 1 exclude.

involved *adj* 1 CONCERNED, implicated,
mixed up, caught up, in on (*sl*),
participating. 2 *an involved
explanation*: complicated, complex,
intricate, elaborate, tangled, knotty,
tortuous, confusing.
☒ 1 uninvolved. 2 simple.

involvement *n* concern, interest,
responsibility, association, connection,
participation, implication, entanglement.

invulnerable *adj* safe, secure,
unassailable, impenetrable, invincible,
indestructible.
☒ vulnerable.

inward *adj* incoming, entering, inside,
interior, internal, inner, innermost,

inmost, personal, private, secret, confidential.
🔁 outward, external.

iota *n* scrap, bit, mite, jot, speck, trace, hint, grain, particle, atom.

irate *adj* annoyed, irritated, indignant, up in arms, angry, enraged, mad (*infml*), furious, infuriated, incensed, worked up, fuming, livid, exasperated.
🔁 calm, composed.

iron *adj* rigid, inflexible, adamant, determined, hard, steely, tough, strong.
🔁 pliable, weak.
➤ *v* press, smooth, flatten.
◇ **iron out** resolve, settle, sort out, straighten out, clear up, put right, reconcile, deal with, get rid of, eradicate, eliminate.

ironic *adj* ironical, sarcastic, sardonic, scornful, contemptuous, derisive, sneering, scoffing, mocking, satirical, wry, paradoxical.

irony *n* sarcasm, mockery, satire, paradox, contrariness, incongruity.

irrational *adj* unreasonable, unsound, illogical, absurd, crazy, wild, foolish, silly, senseless, unwise.
🔁 rational.

irreconcilable *adj* incompatible, opposed, conflicting, clashing, contradictory, inconsistent.
🔁 reconcilable.

irrefutable *adj* undeniable, incontrovertible, indisputable, incontestable, unquestionable, unanswerable, certain, sure.

irregular *adj* **1** ROUGH, bumpy, uneven, crooked. **2** VARIABLE, fluctuating, wavering, erratic, fitful, intermittent, sporadic, spasmodic, occasional, random, haphazard, disorderly, unsystematic. **3** ABNORMAL, unconventional, unorthodox, improper, unusual, exceptional, anomalous.
🔁 **1** smooth, level. **2** regular.
3 conventional.

irrelevant *adj* immaterial, beside the point, inapplicable, inappropriate,

unrelated, unconnected, inconsequent, peripheral, tangential.
🔁 relevant.

irreplaceable *adj* indispensable, essential, vital, unique, priceless, peerless, matchless, unmatched.
🔁 replaceable.

irrepressible *adj* ebullient, bubbly, uninhibited, buoyant, resilient, boisterous, uncontrollable, ungovernable, unstoppable.

irreproachable *adj* irreprehensible, blameless, unimpeachable, faultless, impeccable, perfect, unblemished, immaculate, stainless, spotless, pure.
🔁 blameworthy, culpable.

irresistible *adj* overwhelming, overpowering, unavoidable, inevitable, inescapable, uncontrollable, potent, compelling, imperative, pressing, urgent, tempting, seductive, ravishing, enchanting, charming, fascinating.
🔁 resistible, avoidable.

irresponsible *adj* unreliable, untrustworthy, careless, negligent, thoughtless, heedless, ill-considered, rash, reckless, wild, carefree, light-hearted, immature.
🔁 responsible, cautious.

irreverent *adj* **1** IMPIOUS, godless, irreligious, profane, sacrilegious, blasphemous. **2** DISRESPECTFUL, discourteous, rude, impudent, impertinent, mocking, flippant.
🔁 **1** reverent. **2** respectful.

irreversible *adj* irrevocable, unalterable, final, permanent, lasting, irreparable, irremediable, irretrievable, incurable, hopeless.
🔁 reversible, remediable, curable.

irrevocable *adj* unalterable, unchangeable, changeless, invariable, immutable, final, fixed, settled, predetermined, irreversible, irretrievable.
🔁 alterable, flexible, reversible.

irrigate *v* water, flood, inundate, wet, moisten, dampen.

irritable *adj* cross, bad-tempered, ill-tempered, crotchety, crusty, cantankerous, crabby (*infml*), testy, short-tempered, snappish, snappy, short, impatient, touchy (*infml*), edgy, thin-skinned, hypersensitive, prickly, peevish, fretful, fractious.
🔁 good-tempered, cheerful.

irritate *v* **1** ANNOY, get on one's nerves, aggravate (*infml*), bother, harass, bug (*infml*), rouse, provoke, rile, anger, enrage, infuriate, incense, exasperate, peeve (*infml*), put out. **2** INFLAME, chafe, rub, tickle, itch.
🔁 **1** please, gratify.

irritation *n* displeasure, annoyance, dissatisfaction, aggravation (*infml*), provocation, anger, vexation, indignation, fury, exasperation, irritability, crossness, testiness, snappiness, impatience.
🔁 pleasure, satisfaction, delight.

island *n* isle, islet, atoll, archipelago.

> *The world's largest islands include*: Australia, Greenland, New Guinea, Borneo, Madagascar, Sumatra, Baffin (Canada), Honshu (Japan), Great Britain, Victoria (Canada).

isolate *v* set apart, sequester, seclude, keep apart, segregate, quarantine, insulate, cut off, detach, remove, disconnect, separate, divorce, alienate, shut out, ostracize, exclude.
🔁 assimilate, incorporate.

isolated *adj* **1** REMOTE, out-of-the-way, outlying, godforsaken, deserted, unfrequented, secluded, detached, cut off, lonely, solitary, single. **2** *an isolated occurrence*: unique, special, exceptional, atypical, unusual, freak, abnormal, anomalous.

🔁 **1** populous. **2** typical.

isolation *n* quarantine, solitude, solitariness, loneliness, remoteness, seclusion, retirement, withdrawal, exile, segregation, insulation, separation, detachment, disconnection, dissociation, alienation.

issue *n* **1** MATTER, affair, concern, problem, point, subject, topic, question, debate, argument, dispute, controversy. **2** PUBLICATION, release, distribution, supply, delivery, circulation, promulgation, broadcast, announcement. **3** *last week's issue*: copy, number, instalment, edition, impression, printing.
➤ *v* **1** PUBLISH, release, distribute, supply, deliver, give out, deal out, circulate, promulgate, broadcast, announce, put out, emit, produce.
2 ORIGINATE, stem, spring, rise, emerge, burst forth, gush, flow, proceed, emanate, arise.

itch *v* tickle, irritate, tingle, prickle, crawl.
➤ *n* **1** ITCHINESS, tickle, irritation, prickling. **2** EAGERNESS, keenness, desire, longing, yearning, hankering, craving.

item *n* **1** OBJECT, article, thing, piece, component, ingredient, element, factor, point, detail, particular, aspect, feature, consideration, matter. **2** *an item in the local paper*: article, piece, report, account, notice, entry, paragraph.

itinerant *adj* travelling, peripatetic, roving, roaming, wandering, rambling, nomadic, migratory, rootless, unsettled.
🔁 stationary, settled.

itinerary *n* route, course, journey, tour, circuit, plan, programme, schedule.

Jj

jab *v* poke, prod, dig, nudge, stab, push, elbow, lunge, punch, tap, thrust.

jackpot *n* prize, winnings, kitty, pool, pot, reward, award, big time (*infml*), bonanza, stakes.

jaded *adj* fatigued, exhausted, dulled, played-out, tired, tired out, weary, spent, bored, fagged (*infml*).
Ea fresh, refreshed.

jagged *adj* uneven, irregular, notched, indented, rough, serrated, saw-edged, toothed, ragged, pointed, ridged, craggy, barbed, broken.
Ea even, smooth.

jail, gaol *n* prison, jailhouse, custody, lock-up, penitentiary, pen (*US sl*), guardhouse, inside (*infml*), nick (*sl*), clink (*sl*), slammer (*sl*).
➤ *v* imprison, incarcerate, lock up, put away, send down, confine, detain, intern, impound, immure.

jailer, gaoler *n* prison officer, warden, warder, guard, screw (*sl*), keeper, captor.

jam¹ *v* **1** CRAM, pack, wedge, squash, squeeze, press, crush, crowd, congest, ram, stuff, confine, force. **2** BLOCK, clog, obstruct, stall, stick.
➤ *n* **1** CRUSH, crowd, press, congestion, pack, mob, throng, bottleneck, traffic jam, gridlock. **2** PREDICAMENT, trouble, quandary, plight, fix (*infml*).

jam² *n* conserve, preserve, jelly, spread, marmalade.

jangle *v* clank, clash, jar, clatter, jingle, chime, rattle, vibrate.
➤ *n* clang, clash, rattle, jar, cacophony, dissonance, din, discord, racket, reverberation.
Ea euphony.

jar¹ *n* pot, container, vessel, receptacle, crock, pitcher, urn, vase, flagon, jug, mug.

jar² *v* **1** JOLT, agitate, rattle, shake, vibrate, jangle, rock, disturb, discompose. **2** ANNOY, irritate, grate, nettle (*infml*), offend, upset, irk. **3** BICKER, quarrel, clash, disagree.

jargon *n* **1** PARLANCE, cant, argot, vernacular, idiom. **2** NONSENSE, gobbledygook (*infml*), mumbo-jumbo (*infml*), gibberish.

jarring *adj* discordant, jangling, harsh, grating, irritating, cacophonous, rasping, strident, upsetting, disturbing, jolting.

jaundiced *adj* **1** BITTER, cynical, pessimistic, sceptical, distrustful, disbelieving, envious, jealous, hostile, jaded, suspicious, resentful. **2** DISTORTED, biased, prejudiced, preconceived.

jaunty *adj* sprightly, lively, perky, breezy, buoyant, high-spirited, self-confident, carefree, airy, cheeky, debonair, dapper, smart, showy, spruce.
Ea depressed, dowdy.

jaw (*infml*) *v* chat, chatter, gossip, natter (*infml*), talk, rabbit (on) (*infml*), gabble, babble.
➤ *n* talk, gossip, chat, conversation, discussion, chinwag, natter (*infml*).

jealous *adj* **1** ENVIOUS, covetous, grudging, resentful, green (*infml*), green-eyed (*infml*). **2** SUSPICIOUS, wary, distrustful, anxious, possessive, protective.
Ea **1** contented, satisfied.

jealousy *n* **1** ENVY, covetousness, grudge, resentment, spite, ill-will. **2** SUSPICION, distrust, mistrust, possessiveness.

jeer v mock, scoff, taunt, jibe, ridicule, sneer, deride, make fun of, chaff, barrack, twit, knock (*infml*), heckle, banter.
➤ n mockery, derision, ridicule, taunt, jibe, sneer, scoff, abuse, catcall, dig (*infml*), hiss, hoot.

jell *see* gel.

jeopardize v endanger, imperil, risk, hazard, venture, gamble, chance, threaten, menace, expose, stake.
F3 protect, safeguard.

jeopardy n danger, peril, risk, hazard, endangerment, venture, vulnerability, precariousness, insecurity, exposure, liability.
F3 safety, security.

jerk n jolt, tug, twitch, jar, jog, yank, wrench, pull, pluck, lurch, throw, thrust, shrug.
➤ v jolt, tug, twitch, jog, yank, wrench, pull, jiggle, lurch, pluck, thrust, shrug, throw, bounce.

jerky adj fitful, twitchy, spasmodic, jumpy, fidgety, jolting, convulsive, disconnected, bumpy, bouncy, shaky, rough, unco-ordinated, uncontrolled, incoherent.
F3 smooth.

jest n joke, quip, wisecrack (*infml*), witticism, crack (*infml*), banter, fooling, gag (*infml*), prank, kidding (*infml*), leg-pull (*infml*), trick, hoax.
➤ v joke, quip, fool, kid (*infml*), tease, mock, jeer.

jet¹ n gush, spurt, spout, spray, spring, sprinkler, sprayer, fountain, flow, stream, squirt.

jet² adj black, pitch-black, ebony, sable, sooty.

jetty n breakwater, pier, dock, groyne, quay, wharf.

jewel n 1 GEM, precious stone, gemstone, ornament, rock (*sl*).
2 TREASURE, find, prize, rarity, paragon, pearl.

jewellery

Types of jewellery include: bangle, bracelet, charm bracelet, power beads, anklet, cufflink, tiepin, hatpin, lapel pin, brooch, cameo, earring, nose-ring, toe ring, ring, signet ring, solitaire ring, necklace, necklet, choker, pendant, locket, chain, beads, amulet, torque, tiara, coronet, diadem, body jewel, nail jewel, tooth jewel, bindi.

Jewish calendar

The Jewish calendar and its Gregorian equivalents: Tishri (September-October), Hesshvan (October-November), Kislev (November-December), Tevet (December-January), Shevat (January-February), Adar (February-March), Adar Sheni (leap years only), Nisan (March-April), Iyar (April-May), Sivan (May-June), Tammuz (June-July), Av (July-August), Elul (August-September).

jibe *see* gibe.

jig v jerk, prance, caper, hop, jump, twitch, skip, bounce, bob, wiggle, shake, wobble.

jilt v abandon, reject, desert, discard, brush off, ditch (*infml*), drop, spurn, betray.

jingle v clink, tinkle, ring, chime, chink, jangle, clatter, rattle.
➤ n 1 CLINK, tinkle, ringing, clang, rattle, clangour. 2 RHYME, verse, song, tune, ditty, doggerel, melody, poem, chant, chorus.

jingoism n chauvinism, flag-waving, patriotism, nationalism, imperialism, warmongering, insularity.

jinx (*infml*) n spell, curse, evil eye, hex, voodoo, hoodoo, black magic, gremlin (*infml*), charm, plague.
➤ v curse, bewitch, bedevil, doom, plague.

job n 1 she has a good job: work, employment, occupation, position, post, situation, profession, career, calling, vocation, trade, métier, capacity, business, livelihood. **2** *it's a difficult job*: task, chore, duty, responsibility, charge, commission, mission, activity, affair, concern, proceeding, project, enterprise, office, pursuit, role, undertaking, venture, province, part, place, share, errand, function, contribution, stint, assignment, consignment.

jobless *adj* unemployed, out of work, laid off, on the dole, inactive, redundant.
🔁 employed.

jocular *adj* joking, jesting, funny, jocose (*fml*), humorous, jovial, amusing, comical, entertaining, facetious, droll, whimsical, teasing, witty.
🔁 serious.

jog *v* **1** JOLT, jar, bump, jostle, jerk, joggle, nudge, poke, shake, prod, bounce, push, rock. **2** PROMPT, remind, stir, arouse, activate, stimulate. **3** RUN, trot.
➤ *n* **1** JOLT, bump, jerk, nudge, shove, push, poke, prod, shake. **2** RUN, trot.

join *v* **1** UNITE, connect, combine, conjoin, attach, link, amalgamate, fasten, merge, marry, couple, yoke, tie, splice, knit, cement, add, adhere, annex. **2** ABUT, adjoin, border (on), verge on, touch, meet, coincide, march with. **3** ASSOCIATE, affiliate, accompany, ally, enlist, enrol, enter, sign up, opt in, team.
🔁 **1** divide, separate. **3** leave.

joint *n* junction, connection, union, juncture, intersection, hinge, knot, articulation, seam.
➤ *adj* combined, common, communal, joined, shared, united, collective, amalgamated, mutual, co-operative, co-ordinated, consolidated, concerted.

joke *n* **1** JEST, quip, crack (*infml*), gag (*infml*), witticism, wisecrack (*infml*), one-liner (*infml*), pun, hoot, whimsy, yarn. **2** TRICK, jape, lark, prank, spoof, fun.
➤ *v* jest, quip, clown, fool, pun, wisecrack (*infml*), kid (*infml*), tease, banter, mock, laugh, frolic, gambol.

joker *n* comedian, comic, wit, humorist, jester, trickster, wag, clown, buffoon, kidder, droll, card (*infml*), character, sport.

jolly *adj* jovial, merry, cheerful, playful, hearty, happy, exuberant.
🔁 sad.

jolt *v* **1** JAR, jerk, jog, bump, jostle, knock, bounce, shake, push. **2** UPSET, startle, shock, surprise, stun, discompose, disconcert, disturb.
➤ *n* **1** JAR, jerk, jog, bump, blow, impact, lurch, shake. **2** SHOCK, surprise, reversal, setback, start.

jostle *v* push, shove, jog, bump, elbow, hustle, jolt, crowd, shoulder, joggle, shake, squeeze, throng.

jot down write down, take down, note, list, record, scribble, register, enter.

journal *n* newspaper, periodical, magazine, fanzine, e-zine, paper, publication, review, weekly, monthly, register, chronicle, diary, gazette, daybook, log, record.

journalist *n* reporter, news writer, hack, correspondent, editor, columnist, feature writer, commentator, broadcaster, contributor.

journey *n* voyage, trip, travel, expedition, passage, trek, tour, ramble, outing, wanderings, safari, progress.
➤ *v* travel, voyage, go, trek, tour, roam, rove, proceed, wander, tramp, ramble, range, gallivant.

jovial *adj* jolly, cheery, merry, affable, cordial, genial.
🔁 gloomy.

joy *n* happiness, gladness, delight, pleasure, bliss, ecstasy, elation, joyfulness, exultation, gratification, rapture.
🔁 despair, grief.

joyful *adj* happy, pleased, delighted, glad, elated, ecstatic, triumphant.
🔁 sorrowful.

jubilant *adj* joyful, rejoicing, overjoyed, delighted, elated, triumphant, exuberant, excited, euphoric, thrilled.

jubilee *n* celebration, anniversary,

commemoration, festival, festivity, gala, fête, carnival.

judge *n* **1** JUSTICE, Law Lord, magistrate, arbiter, adjudicator, arbitrator, mediator, moderator, referee, umpire, beak (*sl*). **2** CONNOISSEUR, authority, expert, evaluator, assessor, critic.

➤ *v* **1** ADJUDICATE, arbitrate, try, referee, umpire, decree, mediate, examine, sentence, review, rule, find. **2** ASCERTAIN, determine, decide, assess, appraise, evaluate, estimate, value, distinguish, discern, reckon, believe, think, consider, conclude, rate. **3** CONDEMN, criticize, doom.

judgement *n* **1** VERDICT, sentence, ruling, decree, conclusion, decision, arbitration, finding, result, mediation, order. **2** DISCERNMENT, discrimination, understanding, wisdom, prudence, common sense, sense, intelligence, taste, shrewdness, penetration, enlightenment. **3** ASSESSMENT, evaluation, appraisal, estimate, opinion, view, belief, diagnosis. **4** CONVICTION, damnation, punishment, retribution, doom, fate, misfortune.

judicial *adj* legal, judiciary, magistral, forensic, official, discriminating, critical, impartial.

judicious *adj* wise, prudent, careful, cautious, astute, discerning, informed, shrewd, thoughtful, reasonable, sensible, sound, well-judged, well-advised, considered.
🔁 injudicious.

jug *n* pitcher, carafe, ewer, flagon, urn, jar, vessel, container.

juggle *v* alter, change, manipulate, falsify, rearrange, rig, doctor (*infml*), cook (*infml*), disguise.

juice *n* liquid, fluid, extract, essence, sap, secretion, nectar, liquor.

juicy *adj* **1** SUCCULENT, moist, lush, watery. **2** (*infml*) INTERESTING, colourful, sensational, racy, risqué, suggestive, lurid.
🔁 **1** dry.

jumble *v* disarrange, confuse, disorganize, mix (up), muddle, shuffle, tangle.
🔁 order.

➤ *n* disorder, disarray, confusion, mess, chaos, mix-up, muddle, clutter, mixture, hotch-potch, mishmash (*infml*), medley.

jump *v* **1** LEAP, spring, bound, vault, clear, bounce, skip, hop, prance, frolic, gambol. **2** START, flinch, jerk, recoil, jump out of one's skin (*infml*), wince, quail. **3** OMIT, leave out, miss, skip, pass over, bypass, disregard, ignore, avoid, digress. **4** RISE, increase, gain, appreciate, ascend, escalate, mount, advance, surge, spiral.

➤ *n* **1** LEAP, spring, bound, vault, hop, skip, bounce, prance, frisk, frolic, pounce. **2** START, jerk, jolt, jar, lurch, shock, spasm, quiver, shiver, twitch. **3** BREAK, gap, interruption, lapse, omission, interval, breach, switch. **4** RISE, increase, escalation, boost, advance, increment, upsurge, upturn, mounting. **5** HURDLE, fence, gate, hedge, barricade, obstacle.

jumpy *adj* nervous, anxious, agitated, apprehensive, jittery, tense, edgy, fidgety, shaky.
🔁 calm, composed.

junction *n* joint, join, joining, connection, juncture, union, intersection, linking, coupling, meeting-point, confluence.

junior *adj* younger, minor, lesser, lower, subordinate, secondary, subsidiary, inferior.
🔁 senior.

junk *n* rubbish, refuse, trash, debris, garbage, waste, scrap, litter, clutter, oddments, rummage, dregs, wreckage.

jurisdiction *n* power, authority, control, influence, dominion, province, sovereignty, command, domination, rule, prerogative (*fml*), sway, orbit, bounds, area, field, scope, range, reach, sphere, zone.

just adj 1 a just ruler: fair, equitable, impartial, unbiased, unprejudiced, fair-minded, even-handed, objective, righteous, upright, virtuous, ethical, honourable, good, honest, upstanding, irreproachable. 2 a just punishment: deserved, merited, fitting, well-deserved, appropriate, suitable, due, proper, reasonable, rightful, lawful, legitimate.
🔁 1 unjust. 2 undeserved.

justice n 1 FAIRNESS, equity, impartiality, objectivity, equitableness, justness, legitimacy, honesty, right, rightfulness, rightness, justifiableness, reasonableness, rectitude. 2 LEGALITY, law, penalty, recompense, reparation, satisfaction. 3 JUDGE, Justice of the Peace, JP, magistrate.
🔁 1 injustice, unfairness.

justifiable adj defensible, excusable, warranted, reasonable, justified, lawful, legitimate, acceptable, explainable, forgivable, pardonable, understandable, valid, well-founded, right, proper,

explicable, fit, tenable.
🔁 unjustifiable.

justification n defence, plea, mitigation, apology, explanation, excuse, vindication, warrant, rationalization, reason, grounds.

justify v vindicate, exonerate, warrant, substantiate, defend, acquit, absolve, excuse, forgive, explain, pardon, validate, uphold, sustain, support, maintain, establish.

jut (out) v project, protrude, stick out, overhang, extend.
🔁 recede.

juvenile n child, youth, minor, young person, youngster, adolescent, teenager, boy, girl, kid (*infml*), infant.
➤ adj young, youthful, immature, childish, puerile, infantile, adolescent, babyish, unsophisticated.
🔁 mature.

juxtaposition n contiguity, proximity, nearness, closeness, contact, vicinity, immediacy.

Kk

karate

> *Shotokan karate belts include*:
> *junior grades (Kyu)*: white belt
> (beginner), orange belt (9th Kyu), red
> belt (8th Kyu), yellow belt (7th Kyu),
> green belt (6th Kyu), purple belt (5th-
> 4th Kyu), brown belt (3rd-1st Kyu);
> *senior grades (Dans)*: black belts (1st-
> 8th Dan).

keel over 1 OVERTURN, capsize,
founder, collapse, upset. **2** FAINT, pass
out, swoon, fall, drop, stagger, topple
over.

keen *adj* **1** EAGER, avid, fervent,
enthusiastic, earnest, devoted, diligent,
industrious. **2** ASTUTE, shrewd, clever,
perceptive, wise, discerning, quick, deep,
sensitive. **3** SHARP, piercing, penetrating,
incisive, acute, pointed, intense, pungent,
trenchant.

1 apathetic. **2** superficial. **3** dull.

keep *v* **1** RETAIN, hold, preserve, hold on
to, hang on to, store, stock, possess,
amass, accumulate, collect, stack,
conserve, deposit, heap, pile, place,
maintain, furnish. **2** CARRY ON, keep on,
continue, persist, remain. **3** LOOK
AFTER, tend, care for, have charge of,
have custody of, maintain, provide for,
subsidize, support, sustain, be
responsible for, foster, mind, protect,
shelter, guard, defend, watch (over),
shield, safeguard, feed, nurture,
manage. **4** DETAIN, delay, retard, check,
hinder, hold (up), impede, obstruct,
prevent, block, curb, interfere with,
restrain, limit, inhibit, deter, hamper,
keep back, control, constrain, arrest,
withhold. **5** OBSERVE, comply with,
respect, obey, fulfil, adhere to,

recognize, keep up, keep faith with,
commemorate, celebrate, hold,
maintain, perform, perpetuate, mark,
honour.

➤ *n* **1** SUBSISTENCE, board, livelihood,
living, maintenance, support, upkeep,
means, food, nourishment, nurture. **2**
FORT, fortress, tower, castle, citadel,
stronghold, dungeon.

◇ **keep back 1** RESTRAIN, check,
constrain, curb, impede, limit, prohibit,
retard, stop, control, delay. **2** HOLD
BACK, restrict, suppress, withhold,
conceal, censor, hide, hush up, stifle,
reserve, retain.

◇ **keep in 1** REPRESS, keep back, inhibit,
bottle up, conceal, stifle, suppress, hide,
control, restrain, quell, stop up. **2**
CONFINE, detain, shut in, coop up.

1 declare. **2** release.

◇ **keep on** continue, carry on, endure,
persevere, persist, keep at it, last,
remain, stay, stay the course, soldier on
(*infml*), hold on, retain, maintain.

◇ **keep up** keep pace, equal, contend,
compete, vie, rival, match, emulate,
continue, maintain, persevere, support,
sustain, preserve.

keeper *n* guard, custodian, curator,
caretaker, attendant, guardian,
overseer, steward, warder, jailer, gaoler,
warden, supervisor, minder, inspector,
conservator (*fml*), defender, governor,
superintendent, surveyor.

keepsake *n* memento, souvenir,
remembrance, relic, reminder, token,
pledge, emblem.

kernel *n* core, grain, seed, nucleus,
heart, nub, essence, germ, marrow,
substance, nitty-gritty (*infml*), gist.

key *n* **1** CLUE, cue, indicator, pointer,

explanation, sign, answer, solution, interpretation, means, secret. **2** GUIDE, glossary, translation, legend, code, table, index.

➤ *adj* important, essential, vital, crucial, mission-critical (*infml*), necessary, principal, decisive, central, chief, main, major, leading, basic, fundamental.

keynote *n* core, centre, heart, substance, theme, gist, essence, emphasis, accent, stress.

keystone *n* cornerstone, core, crux, base, basis, foundation, ground, linchpin, principle, root, mainspring, source, spring, motive.

kick *v* **1** BOOT, hit, strike, jolt. **2** (*infml*) GIVE UP, quit, stop, leave off, abandon, desist from, break.

➤ *n* **1** BLOW, recoil, jolt, striking. **2** (*infml*) STIMULATION, thrill, excitement.

◇ **kick off** begin, commence (*fml*), start, open, get under way, open the proceedings, set the ball rolling, introduce, inaugurate, initiate.

◇ **kick out** eject, evict, expel, oust, remove, chuck out (*infml*), discharge, dismiss, get rid of, sack (*infml*), throw out, reject.

kid¹ *n* child, youngster, youth, juvenile, infant, girl, boy, teenager, lad, nipper (*infml*), tot (*infml*).

kid² *v* tease, joke, have on (*infml*), hoax, fool, pull someone's leg (*infml*), pretend, trick, delude, dupe, con (*infml*), jest, hoodwink, humbug, bamboozle.

kidnap *v* abduct, capture, seize, hold to ransom, snatch, run away with (*infml*), hijack, steal.

kill *v* **1** SLAUGHTER, murder, slay (*fml*), put to death, exterminate, assassinate, do to death, do in (*infml*), bump off (*infml*), finish off, massacre, smite (*fml*), execute, eliminate (*sl*), destroy, dispatch (*infml*), do away with, butcher, annihilate, liquidate (*sl*), knock off (*sl*), rub out (*sl*). **2** STIFLE, deaden, smother, quash, quell, suppress.

killer *n* murderer, assassin, executioner, destroyer, slaughterer,

exterminator, butcher (*infml*), cut-throat, gunman, hatchet man (*sl*), hitman (*sl*).

killing *n* **1** SLAUGHTER, murder, massacre, homicide, assassination, execution, slaying, manslaughter, extermination, carnage, bloodshed, elimination, fatality, liquidation. **2** (*infml*) GAIN, fortune, windfall, profit, lucky break, coup, clean-up (*infml*), success, stroke of luck, bonanza (*infml*), hit, big hit.

➤ *adj* (*infml*) **1** FUNNY, hilarious, comical, amusing, side-splitting (*infml*), ludicrous. **2** EXHAUSTING, hard, taxing, arduous.

kind *n* sort, type, class, category, set, variety, character, genus, genre, style, brand, family, breed, race, nature, persuasion, description, species, stamp, temperament, manner.

➤ *adj* benevolent, kind-hearted, kindly, good-hearted, good-natured, helpful, obliging, humane, generous, compassionate, charitable, amiable, friendly, congenial, soft-hearted, thoughtful, warm, warm-hearted, considerate, courteous, sympathetic, tender-hearted, understanding, lenient, mild, hospitable, gentle, indulgent, neighbourly, tactful, giving, good, loving, gracious.

◪ cruel, inconsiderate, unhelpful.

kindle *v* **1** IGNITE, light, set alight, set on fire. **2** INFLAME, fire, stir, thrill, stimulate, rouse, arouse, awaken, excite, fan, incite, inspire, induce, provoke.

kindly *adj* benevolent, kind, compassionate, charitable, good-natured, helpful, warm, generous, cordial, favourable, giving, indulgent, pleasant, sympathetic, tender, gentle, mild, patient, polite.

◪ cruel, uncharitable.

kindness *n* **1** BENEVOLENCE, kindliness, charity, magnanimity, compassion, generosity, hospitality, humanity, loving-kindness (*fml*), courtesy, friendliness, good will, goodness, grace, indulgence, tolerance, understanding, gentleness.

2 FAVOUR, good turn, assistance, help, service.

Fa 1 cruelty, inhumanity. **2** disservice.

king *n* monarch, ruler, sovereign, majesty, emperor, chief, chieftain, prince, supremo, leading light (*infml*).

kingdom *n* monarchy, sovereignty, reign, realm, empire, dominion, commonwealth, nation, principality, state, country, domain, dynasty, province, sphere, territory, land, division.

kink *n* **1** CURL, twist, bend, dent, indentation, knot, loop, crimp, coil, tangle, wrinkle. **2** QUIRK, eccentricity, idiosyncrasy, foible, perversion.

kinship *n* **1** KIN, blood, relation. **2** AFFINITY, similarity, association, alliance, connection, correspondence, relationship, tie, community, conformity.

kiosk *n* booth, stall, stand, news-stand, bookstall, cabin, box, counter.

kiss *v* **1** CARESS, osculate (*fml*), peck (*infml*), smooch (*infml*), neck (*infml*), snog (*sl*). **2** TOUCH, graze, glance, brush, lick, scrape, fan.
➤ *n* osculation (*fml*), peck (*infml*), smack (*infml*), smacker (*sl*).

kit *n* equipment, gear, apparatus, supplies, tackle, provisions, outfit, implements, set, tools, trappings, rig, instruments, paraphernalia, utensils, effects, luggage, baggage.
◇ **kit out** equip, fit out, outfit, supply, fix up, furnish, prepare, arm, deck out, dress.

knack *n* flair, faculty, facility, hang (*infml*), bent, skill, talent, genius, gift, trick, propensity, ability, expertise, skilfulness, forte, capacity, handiness, dexterity, quickness, turn.

knapsack *n* bag, pack, haversack, rucksack, backpack.

knead *v* manipulate, press, massage, work, ply, squeeze, shape, rub, form, mould, knuckle.

knell *n* toll, ringing, chime, peal, knoll.

knick-knack *n* trinket, trifle, bauble, gewgaw, gimcrack, bric-à-brac, plaything.

knife *n* blade, cutter, carver, dagger, penknife, pocket knife, switchblade, jack-knife, flick-knife, machete. *see also* **utensil, weapon**.
➤ *v* cut, rip, slash, stab, pierce, wound.

knit *v* **1** JOIN, unite, secure, connect, tie, fasten, link, mend, interlace, intertwine. **2** KNOT, loop, crotchet, weave. **3** WRINKLE, furrow.

knock *v* hit, strike, rap, thump, pound, slap, smack.
➤ *n* blow, box, rap, thump, cuff, clip, pounding, hammering, slap, smack.
◇ **knock about 1** WANDER, travel, roam, rove, saunter, traipse, ramble, range. **2** ASSOCIATE, go around. **3** BEAT UP, batter, abuse, mistreat, hurt, hit, bash, damage, maltreat, manhandle, bruise, buffet.
◇ **knock down** demolish, destroy, fell, floor, level, wreck, raze, pound, batter, clout (*infml*), smash, wallop.
◇ **knock off 1** (*infml*) FINISH, cease, stop, pack (it) in (*infml*), clock off, clock out, terminate. **2** (*infml*) STEAL, rob, pilfer, pinch (*infml*), nick (*infml*), filch. **3** DEDUCT, take away. **4** (*sl*) KILL, murder, slay (*fml*), assassinate, do away with, bump off (*infml*), do in (*infml*), waste (*sl*).

knockout (*infml*) *n* success, triumph, sensation, hit, smash (*infml*), smash-hit (*infml*), winner (*sl*), stunner (*infml*).
Fa flop, loser.

knot *v* tie, secure, bind, entangle, tangle, knit, entwine, ravel, weave.
➤ *n* **1** TIE, bond, joint, fastening, loop, splice, hitch. **2** BUNCH, cluster, clump, group.

Types of knot include: bend, Blackwall hitch, blood knot, bow, bowline, running bowline, carrick bend, clove hitch, common whipping, double-overhang, Englishman's tie (or knot), figure of eight, fisherman's bend, fisherman's knot, flat knot, granny knot, half hitch, highwayman's hitch, hitch, Hunter's bend, loop knot, overhand knot (or thumb knot), reef knot or square knot, rolling hitch, round turn and two half hitches, seizing, sheepshank, sheet bend (or common bend or swab hitch), slipknot, spade-end knot, surgeon's knot, tie, timber hitch, Turk's head, turle knot, wall knot, weaver's knot, Windsor knot.

know v 1 *know French*: understand, comprehend, apprehend, perceive, notice, be aware, fathom, experience, realize, see, undergo. 2 *I know George*: be acquainted with, be familiar with, recognize, identify. 3 *know a good wine*: distinguish, discriminate, discern, differentiate, make out, tell.

knowledge n 1 LEARNING, scholarship, erudition, education, schooling, instruction, tuition, information, enlightenment, know-how.
2 ACQUAINTANCE, familiarity, awareness, cognizance, intimacy, consciousness.
3 UNDERSTANDING, comprehension, cognition, apprehension, recognition, judgement, discernment, ability, grasp, wisdom, intelligence.
Ⅎ 1 ignorance. 2 unawareness.

knowledgeable adj 1 EDUCATED, scholarly, learned, well-informed, lettered, intelligent. 2 AWARE, acquainted, conscious, familiar, au fait, in the know (*infml*), sussed (*infml*), conversant, experienced.
Ⅎ 1 ignorant.

known adj acknowledged, recognized, well-known, noted, obvious, patent, plain, admitted, familiar, avowed, commonplace, published, confessed, celebrated, famous.

kowtow v defer, cringe, fawn, grovel, pander, suck up (*infml*), brown-nose (*sl*), toady, flatter, kneel.

Ll

label *n* **1** TAG, ticket, docket, mark, marker, sticker, trademark. **2** DESCRIPTION, categorization, identification, characterization, classification, badge, brand.

➤ *v* **1** TAG, mark, stamp. **2** DEFINE, describe, classify, categorize, characterize, identify, class, designate, brand, call, dub, name.

laboratory

> *Laboratory apparatus includes*: autoclave, beaker, bell jar, boiling tube, Büchner funnel, Bunsen burner, burette, centrifuge, clamp, condenser, conical flask, crucible, cylinder, desiccator, distillation apparatus, dropper, evaporating dish, filter flask, filter paper, flask, fume cupboard, funnel, glove box, Kipp's apparatus, Liebig condenser, measuring cylinder, microscope, mortar, pestle, Petri dish, pipette, retort, separating funnel, slide, spatula, stand, still, stirrer, stop clock, test tube, test tube rack, thermometer, top-pan balance, tripod, trough, U-tube, volumetric flask, Woulfe bottle.

laborious *adj* **1** HARD, arduous, difficult, strenuous, tough, backbreaking, wearisome, exhausting, tiring, tiresome, uphill, onerous, heavy, toilsome. **2** HARD-WORKING, industrious, painstaking, indefatigable, diligent.
🔁 **1** easy, effortless. **2** lazy.

labour *n* **1** WORK, task, job, chore, toil, effort, exertion, drudgery, grind (*infml*), slog (*infml*), sweat (*infml*). **2** WORKERS, employees, workforce, labourers. **3** CHILDBIRTH, birth, delivery, labour pains, contractions.

🔁 **1** ease, leisure. **2** management.

➤ *v* **1** WORK, toil, drudge, slave, strive, endeavour, struggle, grind (*infml*), sweat (*infml*), plod, travail (*fml*). **2** OVERDO, overemphasize, dwell on, elaborate, overstress, strain.
🔁 **1** laze, idle, lounge.

labourer *n* manual worker, blue-collar worker, navvy, hand, worker, drudge, hireling.

labyrinth *n* maze, complexity, intricacy, complication, puzzle, riddle, windings, tangle, jungle.

lace *n* **1** NETTING, meshwork, openwork, tatting, crochet. **2** STRING, cord, thong, tie, shoelace, bootlace.

➤ *v* **1** TIE, do up, fasten, thread, close, bind, attach, string, intertwine, interweave. **2** ADD TO, mix in, spike (*infml*), fortify.

lacerate *v* tear, rip, rend, cut, gash, slash, wound, claw, mangle, maim, torture, torment, distress, afflict.

lack *n* need, want, scarcity, shortage, insufficiency, dearth, deficiency, absence, scantiness, vacancy, void, privation, deprivation, destitution, emptiness.
🔁 abundance, profusion.

➤ *v* need, want, require, miss.

lacking *adj* needing, wanting, without, short of, missing, minus, inadequate, deficient, defective, flawed.

lacklustre *adj* drab, dull, flat, boring, uninteresting, unexciting, leaden, lifeless, unimaginative, dim.
🔁 brilliant, inspired.

laconic *adj* terse, succinct, pithy, concise, crisp, taciturn, short, curt, brief.
🔁 verbose, wordy.

lad *n* boy, youth, youngster, kid (*infml*), schoolboy, chap, guy (*infml*), fellow.

ladder

> *Types of ladder include*:
> accommodation ladder, companion ladder, étrier, extension ladder, folding ladder, fruit-picking ladder, gangway ladder, hook ladder, loft ladder, multipurpose ladder, platform ladder, quarter ladder, ratline, rolling ladder, roof ladder, rope ladder, scale, side ladder, stepladder, stepstool, stern ladder, stile, straight ladder, tower scaffold.

lag *v* dawdle, loiter, hang back, linger, straggle, trail, saunter, delay, shuffle, tarry, idle.
☒ hurry, lead.

lair *n* den, burrow, hole, nest, earth, form, roost, retreat, hideout, refuge, sanctuary, stronghold.

> *Lairs and homes of creatures include*:
> sett (*badger*); den (*bear*); lodge (*beaver*); hive (*bee*); nest (*bird*); byre (*cow*); eyrie (*eagle*); coop (*fowl*); earth (*fox*); form (*hare*); den (*lion*); fortress (*mole*); hole, nest (*mouse*); holt (*otter*); sty (*pig*); dovecote (*pigeon*); burrow, warren (*rabbit*); pen, fold (*sheep*); shell (*snail*); drey (*squirrel*); nest, vespiary (*wasp*).

lake *n* lagoon, reservoir, loch, mere, tarn.

lame *adj* **1** DISABLED, handicapped, crippled, limping, hobbling. **2** WEAK, feeble, flimsy, inadequate, poor, unsatisfactory.
☒ **1** able-bodied. **2** convincing.

lament *v* mourn, bewail, bemoan, grieve, sorrow, weep, wail, complain, deplore, regret.
☒ rejoice, celebrate.
➤ *n* lamentation, dirge, elegy, requiem, threnody (*fml*), complaint, moan, wail.

lamentable *adj* **1** DEPLORABLE, regrettable, mournful, distressing, tragic, unfortunate, sorrowful. **2**

MEAGRE, low, inadequate, insufficient, mean, unsatisfactory, pitiful, miserable, poor, disappointing.

lampoon *n* satire, skit, caricature, parody, send-up (*infml*), spoof, take-off (*infml*), burlesque.
➤ *v* satirize, caricature, parody, send up (*infml*), take off (*infml*), spoof, make fun of, ridicule, mock, burlesque.

land *n* **1** EARTH, ground, soil, terra firma. **2** PROPERTY, grounds, estate, real estate, country, countryside, farmland, tract. **3** COUNTRY, nation, region, territory, province.
➤ *v* **1** ALIGHT, disembark, dock, berth, touch down, come to rest, arrive, deposit, wind up, end up, drop, settle, turn up. **2** OBTAIN, secure, gain, get, acquire, net, capture, achieve, win.

landlord *n* owner, proprietor, host, publican, innkeeper, hotelier, hotel-keeper, restaurateur, freeholder.
☒ tenant.

landmark *n* **1** FEATURE, monument, signpost, milestone, beacon, cairn. **2** TURNING-POINT, watershed, crisis.

landscape *n* scene, scenery, view, panorama, outlook, vista, prospect, countryside, aspect.

landslide *n* landslip, earthfall, rock-fall, avalanche.
➤ *adj* overwhelming, decisive, emphatic, runaway.

language *n* **1** SPEECH, vocabulary, terminology, parlance. **2** TALK, conversation, discourse. **3** WORDING, style, phraseology, phrasing, expression, utterance, diction.

> *Language terms include*: brogue, dialect, idiom, patois, tongue, pidgin, creole, lingua franca, vernacular, argot, cant, jargon, doublespeak, gobbledygook, buzzword, journalese, lingo (*infml*), patter, slang, cockney rhyming slang; etymology, lexicography, linguistics, phonetics, semantics, syntax, usage, grammar, orthography, sociolinguistics; language engineering, natural

language processing (NLP), machine translation, automatic speech recognition (ASR).

Languages of the world include: Aborigine, Afghan, Afrikaans, Arabic, Balinese, Bantu, Basque, Bengali, Burmese, Belorussian, Catalan, Celtic, Chinese, Cornish, Czech, Danish, Dutch, Ebonics, English, Esperanto, Estonian, Ethiopian, Farsi, Finnish, Flemish, French, Gaelic, German, Greek, Haitian, Hawaiian, Hebrew, Hindi, Hindustani, Hottentot, Hungarian, Icelandic, Indonesian, Inuit, Iranian, Iraqi, Irish, Italian, Japanese, Kurdish, Lapp, Latin, Latvian, Lithuanian, Magyar, Malay, Maltese, Mandarin, Manx, Maori, Nahuatl, Navajo, Norwegian, Persian, Polish, Portuguese, Punjabi, Quechua, Romanian, Romany, Russian, Sanskrit, Scots, Serbo-Croat, Siamese, Sinhalese, Slavonic, Slovak, Slovenian, Somali, Spanish, Swahili, Swedish, Swiss, Tamil, Thai, Tibetan, Tupī, Turkish, Ukrainian, Urdu, Vietnamese, Volapük, Welsh, Yiddish, Zulu.

---

languish *v* **1** WILT, droop, fade, fail, flag, wither, waste away, weaken, sink, faint, decline, mope, waste, grieve, sorrow, sigh, sicken. **2** PINE, yearn, want, long, desire, hanker, hunger.
F₃ **1** flourish.

lanky *adj* gaunt, gangling, scrawny, tall, thin, scraggy, weedy.
F₃ short, squat.

lap¹ *v* drink, sip, sup, lick.

lap² *n* circuit, round, orbit, tour, loop, course, circle, distance.
➤ *v* wrap, fold, envelop, enfold, swathe, surround, cover, swaddle, overlap.

lapse *n* **1** ERROR, slip, mistake, negligence, omission, oversight, fault, failing, indiscretion, aberration, backsliding, relapse. **2** FALL, descent, decline, drop, deterioration. **3** BREAK, gap, interval, lull, interruption,

intermission, pause.
➤ *v* **1** DECLINE, fall, sink, drop, deteriorate, slide, slip, fail, worsen, degenerate, backslide. **2** EXPIRE, run out, end, stop, terminate, cease, discontinue.

large *adj* **1** BIG, huge, immense, massive, colossal, vast, sizable, great, giant, gigantic, bulky, enormous, king-sized, broad, considerable, titanic, monumental, mega (*infml*), substantial. **2** FULL, extensive, generous, liberal, roomy, plentiful, spacious, grand, sweeping, grandiose.
F₃ **1** small, tiny.
◊ **at large** free, at liberty, on the loose, on the run, independent.

largely *adv* mainly, principally, chiefly, generally, primarily, predominantly, mostly, considerably, by and large, widely, extensively, greatly.

lark *n* escapade, antic, fling, prank, romp, skylark (*infml*), revel, mischief, frolic, caper, game.

lash¹ *n* blow, whip, stroke, swipe, hit.
➤ *v* **1** WHIP, flog, beat, hit, thrash, strike, scourge. **2** ATTACK, criticize, lay into, scold.

lash² *v* tie, bind, fasten, secure, make fast, join, affix, rope, tether, strap.

last¹ *adj* final, ultimate, closing, latest, rearmost, terminal, furthest, remotest, concluding, utmost, extreme, conclusive, definitive.
F₃ first, initial.
➤ *adv* finally, ultimately, behind, after.
F₃ first, firstly.
◊ **at last** eventually, finally, in the end, in due course, at length.

last² *v* continue, endure, remain, persist, keep (on), survive, hold out, carry on, wear, stay, hold on, stand up, abide.
F₃ cease, stop, fade.

lasting *adj* enduring, unchanging, unceasing, unending, continuing, permanent, perpetual, lifelong, long-standing, long-term.
F₃ brief, fleeting, short-lived.

latch *n* fastening, catch, bar, bolt, lock, hook, hasp.

late *adj* **1** OVERDUE, behind, behindhand, slow, unpunctual, delayed, lastminute. **2** FORMER, previous, departed, dead, deceased, past, preceding, old. **3** RECENT, up to date, current, fresh, new. **Ea 1** early, punctual.

lately *adv* recently, of late, latterly.

latent *adj* potential, dormant, undeveloped, unrealized, lurking, unexpressed, unseen, secret, concealed, hidden, invisible, underlying, veiled. **Ea** active, conspicuous.

later *adv* next, afterwards, subsequently, after, successively. **Ea** earlier.

lateral *adj* sideways, side, oblique, sideward, edgeways, marginal, flanking.

lather *n* **1** FOAM, suds, soap-suds, froth, bubbles, soap, shampoo. **2** AGITATION, fluster, fuss, dither, state (*infml*), flutter, flap (*infml*), fever.
➤ *v* foam, froth, soap, shampoo, whip up.

latitude *n* **1** SCOPE, range, room, space, play, clearance, breadth, width, spread, sweep, reach, span, field, extent. **2** FREEDOM, liberty, licence, leeway, indulgence.

latter *adj* last-mentioned, last, later, closing, concluding, ensuing, succeeding, successive, second. **Ea** former.

laugh *v* chuckle, giggle, guffaw, snigger, titter, chortle, split one's sides, fall about (*infml*), crease up (*infml*).
➤ *n* giggle, chuckle, snigger, titter, guffaw, chortle, lark, scream (*infml*), hoot (*infml*), joke.
◇ **laugh at** mock, ridicule, deride, jeer, make fun of, scoff at, scorn, taunt.

laughable *adj* **1** FUNNY, amusing, comical, humorous, hilarious, droll, farcical, diverting. **2** RIDICULOUS, absurd, ludicrous, preposterous, nonsensical, derisory, derisive. **Ea 1** serious.

laughing stock figure of fun, butt, victim, target, Aunt Sally, fair game.

laughter *n* laughing, giggling, chuckling, chortling, guffawing, tittering, hilarity, amusement, merriment, mirth, glee, convulsions.

launch *v* **1** PROPEL, dispatch, discharge, send off, project, float, set in motion, throw, fire. **2** BEGIN, commence, start, embark on, establish, found, open, initiate, inaugurate, introduce, instigate, kick off (*infml*).

lavatory *n* toilet, loo (*infml*), WC, bathroom, cloakroom, washroom, restroom (*US*), water closet, public convenience, Ladies (*infml*), Gents (*infml*), bog (*sl*), can (*sl*), john (*US sl*), urinal, powder room.

lavish *adj* **1** ABUNDANT, lush, luxuriant, plentiful, profuse, unlimited, prolific. **2** GENEROUS, liberal, open-handed, extravagant, thriftless, prodigal, immoderate, intemperate, unstinting, fulsome. **Ea 1** scant. **2** frugal, thrifty.

law *n* **1** RULE, act, decree, edict, order, statute, regulation, command, ordinance, charter, constitution, enactment. **2** PRINCIPLE, axiom, criterion, standard, precept, formula, code, canon. **3** JURISPRUDENCE, legislation, litigation.

law-abiding *adj* obedient, upright, orderly, lawful, honest, honourable, decent, good. **Ea** lawless.

lawful *adj* legal, legitimate, permissible, legalized, authorized, allowable, warranted, valid, proper, rightful. **Ea** illegal, unlawful, illicit.

lawless *adj* disorderly, rebellious, anarchic(al), unruly, riotous, mutinous, unrestrained, chaotic, wild, reckless. **Ea** law-abiding.

lawsuit *n* litigation, suit, action, proceedings, case, prosecution, dispute, process, trial, argument, contest, cause.

lawyer *n* solicitor, barrister, advocate, attorney, counsel, QC.

lax *adj* **1** CASUAL, careless, easy-going, slack, lenient, negligent, remiss. **2** IMPRECISE, inexact, indefinite, loose.
F3 1 strict. **2** exact.

lay[1] *v* **1** PUT, place, deposit, set down, settle, lodge, plant, set, establish, leave. **2** ARRANGE, position, set out, locate, work out, devise, prepare, present, submit. **3** ATTRIBUTE, ascribe, assign, charge.
◇ **lay in** store (up), stock up, amass, accumulate, hoard, stockpile, gather, collect, build up, glean.
◇ **lay into** (*infml*) attack, assail, pitch into, set about, tear into, let fly at.
◇ **lay off 1** DISMISS, discharge, make redundant, sack (*infml*), pay off, let go. **2** (*infml*) GIVE UP, drop, stop, quit, cease, desist, leave off, leave alone, let up.
◇ **lay on** provide, supply, cater, furnish, give, set up.
◇ **lay out 1** DISPLAY, set out, spread out, exhibit, arrange, plan, design. **2** (*infml*) KNOCK OUT, fell, flatten, demolish. **3** (*infml*) SPEND, pay, shell out (*infml*), fork out (*infml*), give, invest.
◇ **lay up** store up, hoard, accumulate, amass, keep, save, put away.

lay[2] *adj* **1** LAIC, secular. **2** AMATEUR, non-professional, non-specialist.
F3 1 clergy. **2** expert.

layer *n* **1** COVER, coating, coat, covering, film, blanket, mantle, sheet, lamina. **2** STRATUM, seam, thickness, tier, bed, plate, row, ply.

layman *n* **1** LAYPERSON, parishioner. **2** AMATEUR, outsider.
F3 1 clergyman. **2** expert.

layout *n* arrangement, design, outline, plan, sketch, draft, map.

laze *v* idle, loaf (*infml*), lounge, sit around, lie around, loll.

lazy *adj* idle, slothful, slack, workshy, inactive, lethargic.
F3 industrious.

lead *v* **1** GUIDE, conduct, escort, steer, pilot, usher. **2** RULE, govern, head,
preside over, direct, supervise. **3** INFLUENCE, persuade, incline. **4** SURPASS, outdo, excel, outstrip, transcend. **5** PASS, spend, live, undergo.
F3 1 follow.
➤ *n* **1** PRIORITY, precedence, first place, start, van, vanguard, advantage, edge, margin. **2** LEADERSHIP, guidance, direction, example, model. **3** CLUE, hint, indication, guide, tip, suggestion. **4** TITLE ROLE, starring part, principal.
◇ **lead off** begin, commence, open, get going, start (off), inaugurate, initiate, kick off (*infml*), start the ball rolling.
◇ **lead on** entice, lure, seduce, tempt, draw on, beguile, persuade, string along, deceive, trick.
◇ **lead to** cause, result in, produce, bring about, bring on, contribute to, tend towards.
◇ **lead up to** prepare (the way) for, approach, introduce, make overtures, pave the way.

leader *n* head, chief, director, ruler, principal, commander, captain, boss (*infml*), superior, chieftain, ringleader, guide, conductor.
F3 follower.

leadership *n* direction, control, command, management, authority, guidance, domination, pre-eminence, premiership, administration, sway, directorship.

leading *adj* main, principal, chief, primary, first, supreme, outstanding, foremost, dominant, ruling, superior, greatest, highest, governing, pre-eminent, number one, blue-chip (*infml*).
F3 subordinate.

leaf

Leaf parts include: axillary bud, blade, chloroplasts, epidermis, leaf axil, leaf cells, margin, midrib, petiole, sheath, stipule, stomata, tip, vein.

Leaf shapes include: abruptly pinnate, acerose, ciliate, cordate, crenate, dentate, digitate, doubly dentate, elliptic, entire, falcate, hastate, lanceolate, linear, lobed, lyrate, obovate, orbicular, ovate, palmate, peltate, pinnate, pinnatifid, reniform, runcinate, sagittate, spathulate, subulate, ternate, trifoliate.

leaflet *n* pamphlet, booklet, brochure, circular, handout, flyer.

league *n* 1 ASSOCIATION, union, confederation, alliance, federation, confederacy, coalition, combination, band, syndicate, guild, consortium, cartel, combine, partnership, fellowship, compact. 2 CATEGORY, class, level, group.
◇ **in league** allied, collaborating, conspiring.

leak *n* 1 CRACK, hole, opening, puncture, crevice, chink. 2 LEAKAGE, leaking, seepage, drip, oozing, percolation. 3 DISCLOSURE, divulgence.
➤ *v* 1 SEEP, drip, ooze, escape, spill, trickle, percolate, exude, discharge. 2 DIVULGE, disclose, reveal, let slip, make known, make public, tell, give away, pass on.

leaky *adj* leaking, holey, perforated, punctured, split, cracked, porous, permeable.

lean¹ *v* 1 SLANT, slope, bend, incline, tilt, list, tend. 2 RECLINE, prop, rest. 3 INCLINE, favour, prefer.

lean² *adj* 1 THIN, skinny, bony, gaunt, lank, angular, slim, scraggy, scrawny, emaciated. 2 SCANTY, inadequate, bare, barren.
➤ 1 fat.

leaning *n* tendency, inclination, propensity (*fml*), partiality, liking, bent, bias, disposition, aptitude.

leap *v* 1 JUMP (OVER), bound, spring, vault, clear, skip, hop, bounce, prance, caper, gambol. 2 SOAR, surge, increase, rocket, escalate, rise.
➤ 2 drop, fall.
➤ *n* 1 JUMP, bound, spring, vault, hop, skip, caper. 2 INCREASE, upsurge, upswing, surge, rise, escalation.

learn *v* 1 GRASP, comprehend, understand, master, acquire, pick up, gather, assimilate, discern. 2 MEMORIZE, learn by heart. 3 DISCOVER, find out, ascertain, hear, detect, determine.

learned *adj* scholarly, erudite (*fml*), well-informed, well-read, cultured, academic, lettered, literate, intellectual, versed.
➤ uneducated, illiterate.

learner *n* novice, beginner, student, trainee, pupil, scholar, apprentice.

learning *n* scholarship, erudition (*fml*), education, schooling, knowledge, information, letters, study, wisdom, tuition, culture, edification, research.

lease *v* let, loan, rent, hire, sublet, charter.

least *adj* smallest, lowest, minimum, fewest, slightest, poorest.
➤ most.

leave¹ *v* 1 DEPART, go, go away, set out, take off, decamp, exit, move, retire, withdraw, quit (*infml*), disappear, do a bunk (*infml*). 2 ABANDON, desert, forsake, give up, drop, relinquish, renounce, pull out, surrender, desist, cease. 3 ASSIGN, commit, entrust, consign, bequeath, will, hand down, leave behind, give over, transmit.
➤ 1 arrive. 3 receive.
◇ **leave off** stop, cease, discontinue, desist (*fml*), abstain, refrain, lay off, quit (*infml*), terminate, break off, end, halt, give over.
◇ **leave out** omit, exclude, overlook, ignore, except, disregard, pass over, count out, cut (out), eliminate, neglect, reject, cast aside, bar.

leave² *n* 1 PERMISSION, authorization, consent, allowance, sanction, concession, dispensation, indulgence, liberty, freedom. 2 HOLIDAY, time off, vacation, sabbatical, furlough.
➤ 1 refusal, rejection.

lecture *n* 1 DISCOURSE, address, lesson, speech, talk, instruction. 2 REPRIMAND, rebuke, reproof, scolding, harangue, censure, chiding, telling-off

(*infml*), talking-to (*infml*), dressing-down (*infml*).
➤ *v* **1** TALK, teach, hold forth, speak, expound, address. **2** REPRIMAND, reprove, scold, upbraid, admonish, harangue, chide, censure, tell off (*infml*).

ledge *n* shelf, sill, mantle, ridge, projection, step.

leeway *n* space, room, latitude, elbow-room, play, scope.

left *adj* **1** LEFT-HAND, port, sinistral. **2** LEFT-WING, socialist, radical, progressive, revolutionary, liberal, communist, red (*infml*).
🗷 **1** right. **2** right-wing.

leftovers *n* leavings, remainder, remains, remnants, residue, surplus, scraps, sweepings, refuse, dregs, excess.

leg *n* **1** LIMB, member, shank, pin (*infml*), stump (*infml*). **2** SUPPORT, prop, upright, brace. **3** STAGE, part, section, portion, stretch, segment, lap.

legacy *n* bequest, endowment, gift, heritage, heritance, inheritance, birthright, estate, heirloom.

legal *adj* **1** LAWFUL, legitimate, permissible, sanctioned, allowed, authorized, allowable, legalized, constitutional, valid, warranted, above-board, proper, rightful. **2** JUDICIAL, forensic. **3** JUDICIARY.
🗷 **1** illegal.

Legal terms include:
courts: county court, courthouse, courtroom, Court of Appeal, Court of Protection, Court of Session, Crown Court, European Court of Human Rights, European Court of Justice, High Court of Justice, House of Lords, International Court of Justice, juvenile court, magistrates' court, Old Bailey, sheriff court, small claims court, Supreme Court (*US*);
criminal law: acquittal, age of consent, alibi, arrest, bail, caution, charge, confession, contempt of court, dock, fine, guilty, indictment, innocent, malice aforethought, pardon, parole,

plead guilty, plead not guilty, prisoner, probation, remand, reprieve, sentence;
marriage and divorce: adultery, alimony, annulment, bigamy, decree absolute, decree nisi, divorce, maintenance, settlement;
people: accessory, accomplice, accused, advocate, Attorney General, barrister, brief (*infml*), clerk of the court, client, commissioner for oaths, convict, coroner, criminal, defendant, Director of Public Prosecutions, DPP, executor, felon, judge, jury, justice of the peace, JP, juvenile, Law Lord, lawyer, Lord Advocate, Lord Chancellor, Lord Chief Justice, liquidator, magistrate, notary public, offender, plaintiff, procurator fiscal, receiver, Queen's Counsel, QC, sheriff, solicitor, witness, young offender;
property or ownership: asset, conveyance, copyright, deed, easement, endowment, estate, exchange of contracts, fee simple, foreclosure, freehold, inheritance, intestacy, lease, leasehold, legacy, local search, mortgage, patent, tenancy, title, trademark, will;
miscellaneous: act of God, Act of Parliament, adjournment, affidavit, agreement, allegation, amnesty, appeal, arbitration, bar, Bill of Rights, bench, brief, by-law, charter, civil law, claim, codicil, common law, constitution, contract covenant, cross-examine, courtcase, court martial, custody, damages, defence, demand, equity, eviction, evidence, extradition, grant, hearing, hung jury, indemnity, injunction, inquest, inquiry, judgment, judiciary, lawsuit, legal aid, liability, mandate, misadventure, miscarriage of justice, oath, party, penalty, power of attorney, precedent, probate, proceedings, proof, proxy, public inquiry, repeal, sanction, settlement, statute, subpoena, sue, summons, testimony, trial, tribunal, verdict, waiver, ward of court, warrant, will, writ. *see also* **court**; **crime**.

legalize v legitimize, license, permit, sanction, allow, authorize, warrant, validate, approve.

legend n 1 MYTH, story, tale, folk tale, fable, fiction, narrative. 2 INSCRIPTION, caption, key, motto.

legendary adj 1 MYTHICAL, fabulous, storybook, fictitious, traditional. 2 FAMOUS, celebrated, renowned, well-known, illustrious.

legible adj readable, intelligible, decipherable, clear, distinct, neat.
Ɛ illegible.

legislate v enact, ordain, authorize, codify, constitutionalize, prescribe, establish.

legislation n 1 LAW, statute, regulation, bill, act, charter, authorization, ruling, measure. 2 LAW-MAKING, enactment, codification.

legislative adj law-making, law-giving, judicial, parliamentary, congressional, senatorial.

legislator n law-maker, law-giver, member of parliament, parliamentarian.

legislature n assembly, chamber, house, parliament, congress, senate.

legitimate adj 1 LEGAL, lawful, authorized, statutory, rightful, proper, correct, real, acknowledged. 2 REASONABLE, sensible, admissible, acceptable, justifiable, warranted, well-founded, valid, true.
Ɛ 1 illegal. 2 invalid.

leisure n relaxation, rest, spare time, time off, ease, freedom, liberty, recreation, retirement, holiday, vacation.
Ɛ work.

leisurely adj unhurried, slow, relaxed, comfortable, easy, unhasty, tranquil, restful, gentle, carefree, laid-back (*infml*), lazy, loose.
Ɛ rushed, hectic.

lend v 1 LOAN, advance. 2 GIVE, grant, bestow, provide, furnish, confer, supply, impart, contribute.
Ɛ 1 borrow.

length n 1 EXTENT, distance, measure, reach. 2 PIECE, portion, section, segment. 3 DURATION, period, term, stretch, space, span.

lengthen v stretch, extend, elongate, draw out, prolong, protract, spin out, eke (out), pad out, increase, expand, continue.
Ɛ reduce, shorten.

lengthy adj long, prolonged, protracted, extended, lengthened, overlong, long-drawn-out, long-winded, rambling, diffuse, verbose, drawn-out, interminable.
Ɛ brief, concise.

lenient adj tolerant, forbearing, sparing, indulgent, merciful, forgiving, soft-hearted, kind, mild, gentle, compassionate.
Ɛ strict, severe.

lessen v decrease, reduce, diminish, lower, ease, abate (*fml*), contract, die down, dwindle, lighten, slow down, weaken, shrink, abridge, de-escalate, erode, minimize, narrow, moderate, slack, flag, fail, deaden, impair.
Ɛ grow, increase.

lesser adj lower, secondary, inferior, smaller, subordinate, slighter, minor.
Ɛ greater.

lesson n 1 CLASS, period, instruction, lecture, tutorial, teaching, coaching. 2 ASSIGNMENT, exercise, homework, practice, task, drill. 3 EXAMPLE, model, warning, deterrent.

let v 1 PERMIT, allow, give leave, give permission, authorize, consent to, agree to, sanction, grant, OK (*infml*), enable, tolerate. 2 LEASE, hire, rent.
Ɛ 1 prohibit, forbid.
◇ **let in** admit, accept, receive, take in, include, incorporate, welcome.
Ɛ prohibit, bar, forbid.
◇ **let off** 1 EXCUSE, absolve, pardon, exempt, forgive, acquit, exonerate, spare, ignore, liberate, release. 2 DISCHARGE, detonate, fire, explode, emit.
Ɛ 1 punish.
◇ **let out** 1 FREE, release, let go,

discharge. **2** REVEAL, disclose, make known, utter, betray, let slip, leak.
▣ **1** keep in.
◇ **let up** abate (*fml*), subside, ease (up), moderate, slacken, diminish, decrease, stop, end, cease, halt.
▣ continue.

let-down *n* anticlimax, comedown, disappointment, disillusionment, setback, betrayal, desertion, wash-out (*infml*).

lethal *adj* fatal, deadly, deathly, mortal, dangerous, poisonous, noxious, destructive, devastating.
▣ harmless, safe.

lethargy *n* lassitude, listlessness, sluggishness, torpor, dullness, inertia, slowness, apathy, inaction, indifference, sleepiness, drowsiness, stupor.
▣ liveliness.

letter *n* **1** NOTE, message, line, missive, epistle (*fml*), dispatch, communication, chit, acknowledgement. **2** CHARACTER, symbol, sign, grapheme.

level *adj* **1** FLAT, smooth, even, flush, horizontal, aligned, plane. **2** EQUAL, balanced, even, on a par, neck and neck, matching, uniform.
▣ **1** uneven. **2** unequal.
➤ *v* **1** DEMOLISH, destroy, devastate, flatten, knock down, raze, pull down, bulldoze, tear down, lay low. **2** EVEN OUT, flush, plane, smooth, equalize. **3** DIRECT, point.
➤ *n* **1** HEIGHT, elevation, altitude. **2** POSITION, rank, status, class, degree, grade, standard, standing, plane, echelon, layer, stratum, storey, stage, zone.

level-headed *adj* calm, balanced, even-tempered, sensible, steady, reasonable, composed, cool, unflappable (*infml*), sane, self-possessed, dependable.

lever *n* bar, crowbar, jemmy, joystick, handle.
➤ *v* force, prise, pry, raise, dislodge, jemmy, shift, move, heave.

levity *n* light-heartedness, frivolity,

facetiousness, flippancy, irreverence, triviality, silliness.
▣ seriousness.

levy *v* tax, impose, exact, demand, charge.
➤ *n* tax, toll, subscription, contribution, duty, fee, tariff, collection.

lewd *adj* obscene, smutty, X-rated (*infml*), indecent, bawdy, pornographic, salacious, licentious, lascivious, impure, vulgar, unchaste, lustful.
▣ decent, chaste.

liability *n* **1** ACCOUNTABILITY, duty, obligation, responsibility, onus. **2** DEBT, arrears, indebtedness. **3** DRAWBACK, disadvantage, hindrance, impediment, drag (*infml*).

liable *adj* **1** INCLINED, likely, apt, disposed, prone, tending, susceptible. **2** RESPONSIBLE, answerable, accountable, amenable.

liaison *n* **1** CONTACT, connection, go-between, link. **2** LOVE AFFAIR, affair, romance, fling (*infml*), intrigue, amour, entanglement.

liar *n* falsifier, perjurer, deceiver, fibber (*infml*).

libel *n* defamation, slur, smear, slander, vilification (*fml*), aspersion (*fml*), calumny.
➤ *v* defame, slur, smear, slander, vilify (*fml*), malign.

libellous *adj* defamatory, vilifying (*fml*), slanderous, derogatory, maligning, injurious, scurrilous, untrue.

liberal *adj* **1** BROAD-MINDED, open-minded, tolerant, lenient. **2** PROGRESSIVE, reformist, moderate. **3** GENEROUS, ample, bountiful, lavish, plentiful, handsome.
▣ **1** narrow-minded. **2** conservative. **3** mean, miserly.

liberate *v* free, emancipate, release, let loose, let go, let out, set free, deliver, unchain, discharge, rescue, ransom.
▣ imprison, enslave.

liberty *n* **1** FREEDOM, emancipation, release, independence, autonomy.

2 LICENCE, permission, sanction, right, authorization, dispensation, franchise. **3** FAMILIARITY, disrespect, overfamiliarity, presumption, impertinence, impudence.

Ea 1 imprisonment. **3** respect.

◇ **at liberty** free, unconstrained, unrestricted, not confined.

licence *n* **1** PERMISSION, permit, leave, warrant, authorization, authority, certificate, charter, right, imprimatur, entitlement, privilege, dispensation, carte blanche, freedom, liberty, exemption, independence. **2** ABANDON, dissipation, excess, immoderation, indulgence, lawlessness, unruliness, anarchy, disorder, debauchery, dissoluteness, impropriety, irresponsibility.

Ea 1 prohibition, restriction.
2 decorum, moderation.

license *v* permit, allow, authorize, certify, warrant, entitle, empower, sanction, commission, accredit.
Ea ban, prohibit.

licentious *adj* debauched, dissolute, profligate, lascivious, immoral, abandoned, lewd, promiscuous, libertine, impure, lax, lustful, disorderly, wanton, unchaste.
Ea modest, chaste.

lick *v* tongue, touch, wash, lap, taste, dart, flick, flicker, play over, smear, brush.

lie¹ *v* perjure, misrepresent, fabricate, falsify, fib (*infml*), invent, equivocate, prevaricate, forswear oneself (*fml*).
➤ *n* falsehood, untruth, falsification, fabrication, invention, fiction, deceit, fib (*infml*), falsity, white lie, prevarication, whopper (*infml*), porkie (*infml*).
Ea truth.

lie² *v* be, exist, dwell, belong, extend, remain.
◇ **lie down** repose, rest, recline, stretch out, lounge, couch, laze.

life *n* **1** BEING, existence, animation, breath, viability, entity, soul.
2 DURATION, course, span, career.

3 LIVELINESS, vigour, vitality, vivacity, verve, zest, energy, élan, spirit, sparkle, activity.

lifeless *adj* **1** DEAD, deceased, defunct, cold, unconscious, inanimate, insensible, stiff. **2** LETHARGIC, listless, sluggish, dull, apathetic, passive, insipid, colourless, slow. **3** BARREN, bare, empty, desolate, arid.
Ea 1 alive. **2** lively.

lifelike *adj* realistic, true-to-life, real, true, vivid, natural, authentic, faithful, exact, graphic.
Ea unrealistic, unnatural.

lifelong *adj* lifetime, long-lasting, long-standing, persistent, lasting, enduring, abiding, permanent, constant.
Ea impermanent, temporary.

lift *v* **1** *she lifted the chair*: raise, elevate, hoist, upraise. **2** *he lifted their spirits*: uplift, exalt, buoy up, boost. **3** *the ban has been lifted*: revoke, repeal, cancel, relax.
Ea 1 drop. **2** lower.

light¹ *n* **1** ILLUMINATION, brightness, brilliance, luminescence, radiance, glow, ray, shine, glare, gleam, glint, lustre, flash, blaze. **2** LAMP, lantern, lighter, match, torch, candle, bulb, beacon. **3** DAY, daybreak, daylight, daytime, dawn, sunrise. **4** ENLIGHTENMENT, explanation, elucidation, understanding.
Ea 1 darkness. **3** night.

Sources of light include:
natural light: aurora borealis, daylight, lightning, moonlight, starlight, sunlight; infrared, ultraviolet;
electric light: Belisha beacon, brake light, chandelier, courtesy light, fairy light, flashgun, floodlight, fluorescent light, fog lamp, footlight, halogen light, headlight, indicator light, laser, light bulb, light buoy, lighthouse, navigation light, neon light, night light, pedestrian light, range light, runway light, searchlight, spotlight, standard lamp, streetlight, strip light, strobe light,

sunlamp, tail-light, torch, traffic light; *fire light*: bonfire, candlelight, fire, firework, flare, gaslight, hurricane lamp, lighter, match, oil lamp, pilot light.

➤ *v* **1** IGNITE, fire, set alight, set fire to, kindle. **2** ILLUMINATE, light up, lighten, brighten, animate, cheer, switch on, turn on, put on.
🔁 **1** extinguish. **2** darken.

➤ *adj* **1** ILLUMINATED, bright, brilliant, luminous, glowing, shining, well-lit, sunny. **2** PALE, pastel, fair, blond, blonde, bleached, faded, faint.
🔁 **1** dark. **2** black.

light² *adj* **1** WEIGHTLESS, insubstantial, delicate, airy, buoyant, flimsy, feathery, slight. **2** TRIVIAL, inconsiderable, trifling, inconsequential, worthless. **3** CHEERFUL, cheery, carefree, lively, merry, blithe. **4** ENTERTAINING, amusing, funny, humorous, frivolous, witty, pleasing.
🔁 **1** heavy, weighty. **2** important, serious. **3** solemn. **4** serious.

lighten¹ *v* illuminate, illumine, brighten, light up, shine.
🔁 darken.

lighten² *v* **1** EASE, lessen, unload, lift, relieve, reduce, mitigate, alleviate. **2** BRIGHTEN, cheer, encourage, hearten, inspirit, uplift, gladden, revive, elate, buoy up, inspire.
🔁 **1** burden. **2** depress.

light-headed *adj* **1** FAINT, giddy, dizzy, woozy (*infml*), delirious. **2** FLIGHTY, scatterbrained (*infml*), foolish, frivolous, silly, superficial, shallow, feather-brained (*infml*), flippant, vacuous, air-headed (*infml*), trifling.
🔁 **2** level-headed, solemn.

light-hearted *adj* cheerful, joyful, jolly, happy-go-lucky, bright, carefree, untroubled, merry, sunny, glad, elated, jovial, playful.
🔁 sad, unhappy, serious.

likable *adj* loveable, pleasing, appealing, agreeable, charming, engaging, winsome, pleasant, amiable, congenial, attractive, sympathetic.

🔁 unpleasant, disagreeable.

like¹ *adj* similar, resembling, alike, same, identical, equivalent, akin, corresponding, related, relating, parallel, allied, analogous, approximating.
🔁 unlike, dissimilar.

like² *v* **1** ENJOY, delight in, care for, admire, appreciate, love, adore, hold dear, esteem, cherish, prize, relish, revel in, approve, take (kindly) to. **2** PREFER, choose, select, feel inclined, go for (*infml*), desire, want, wish.
🔁 **1** dislike. **2** reject.

likelihood *n* likeliness, probability, possibility, chance, prospect, liability.
🔁 improbability, unlikeliness.

likely *adj* **1** PROBABLE, possible, anticipated, expected, liable, prone, tending, predictable, odds-on (*infml*), inclined, foreseeable. **2** CREDIBLE, believable, plausible, feasible, reasonable. **3** PROMISING, hopeful, pleasing, appropriate, proper, suitable.
🔁 **1** unlikely. **3** unsuitable.

➤ *adv* probably, presumably, like as not, in all probability, no doubt, doubtlessly.

liken *v* compare, equate, match, parallel, relate, juxtapose, associate, set beside.

likeness *n* **1** SIMILARITY, resemblance, affinity, correspondence. **2** REPRESENTATION, image, copy, reproduction, replica, facsimile, effigy, picture, portrait, photograph, counterpart. **3** SEMBLANCE, guise, appearance, form.
🔁 **1** dissimilarity, unlikeness.

likewise *adv* moreover, furthermore, in addition, similarly, also, further, besides, by the same token, too.

liking *n* fondness, love, affection, preference, partiality, affinity, predilection (*fml*), penchant, taste, attraction, appreciation, proneness, propensity (*fml*), inclination, tendency, bias, desire, weakness, fancy, soft spot (*infml*).
🔁 dislike, aversion, hatred.

limb *n* arm, leg, member, appendage, branch, projection, offshoot, wing, fork, extension, part, spur, extremity, bough.

limber up loosen up, warm up, work out, exercise, prepare.

limelight *n* fame, celebrity, spotlight, stardom, recognition, renown, glory, attention, notoriety, prominence, publicity, public eye.

limit *n* **1** BOUNDARY, bound, border, frontier, confines, edge, brink, threshold, verge, brim, end, perimeter, rim, compass, termination, ultimate, utmost, terminus, extent. **2** CHECK, curb, restraint, restriction, limitation, ceiling, maximum, cut-off point, saturation point, deadline.
➤ *v* check, curb, restrict, restrain, constrain, confine, demarcate, delimit, bound, hem in, ration, specify, hinder.

limitation *n* **1** CHECK, restriction, curb, control, constraint, restraint, delimitation, demarcation, block. **2** INADEQUACY, shortcoming, disadvantage, drawback, condition, qualification, reservation.
Fa **1** extension.

limited *adj* restricted, circumscribed, constrained, controlled, confined, checked, defined, finite, fixed, minimal, narrow, inadequate, insufficient.
Fa limitless.

limitless *adj* unlimited, unbounded, boundless, illimited, undefined, immeasurable, incalculable, infinite, countless, endless, never-ending, unending, inexhaustible, untold, vast.
Fa limited.

limp[1] *v* hobble, falter, stumble, hop, dodder, shuffle, shamble.

limp[2] *adj* **1** FLABBY, drooping, flaccid, floppy, loose, slack, relaxed, lax, soft, flexible, pliable, limber. **2** TIRED, weary, exhausted, spent, weak, worn out, lethargic, debilitated, enervated.
Fa **1** stiff. **2** vigorous.

line[1] *n* **1** STROKE, band, bar, stripe, mark, strip, rule, dash, strand, streak, underline, score, scratch. **2** ROW, rank, queue, file, column, sequence, series, procession, chain, trail. **3** LIMIT, boundary, border, borderline, edge, frontier, demarcation. **4** STRING, rope, cord, cable, thread, filament, wire. **5** PROFILE, contour, outline, silhouette, figure, formation, configuration. **6** CREASE, wrinkle, furrow, groove, corrugation. **7** COURSE, path, direction, track, route, axis. **8** APPROACH, avenue, course (of action), belief, ideology, policy, system, position, practice, procedure, method, scheme. **9** OCCUPATION, business, trade, profession, vocation, job, activity, interest, employment, department, calling, field, province, forte, area, pursuit, specialization, specialty, specialism, speciality. **10** ANCESTRY, family, descent, extraction, lineage, pedigree, stock, race, breed, ancestors, forebears.
◇ **line up 1** ALIGN, range, straighten, marshal, order, regiment, queue up, form ranks, fall in, array, assemble. **2** ORGANIZE, lay on, arrange, prepare, produce, procure, secure, obtain.

line[2] *v* encase, cover, fill, pad, stuff, reinforce.

lineage *n* ancestry, descent, extraction, genealogy, family, line, pedigree, race, stock, birth, breed, house, heredity, ancestors, forebears, descendants, offspring, succession.

lined *adj* **1** RULED, feint. **2** WRINKLED, furrowed, wizened, worn.
Fa **1** unlined. **2** smooth.

line-up *n* array, arrangement, queue, row, selection, cast, team, bill.

linger *v* **1** LOITER, delay, dally, tarry, wait, remain, stay, hang on, lag, procrastinate, dawdle, dilly-dally (*infml*), idle, stop. **2** ENDURE, hold out, last, persist, survive.
Fa **1** leave, rush.

lining *n* inlay, interfacing, padding, backing, encasement, stiffening.

link *n* **1** CONNECTION, bond, tie, association, joint, relationship, tie-up, union, knot, liaison, attachment, communication. **2** PART, piece, element, member, constituent, component, division.

➤ *v* connect, join, couple, tie, fasten, unite, bind, amalgamate, merge, ally, associate, bracket, identify, relate, yoke, attach, hook up, join forces, team up.
F₃ separate, unfasten.

lip *n* edge, brim, border, brink, rim, margin, verge.

liquid *n* liquor, fluid, juice, drink, sap, solution, lotion.

➤ *adj* fluid, flowing, liquefied, watery, wet, runny, melted, molten, thawed, clear, smooth.
F₃ solid.

liquidate *v (sl)* **1** ANNIHILATE, terminate, do away with, dissolve, kill, murder, massacre, assassinate, destroy, dispatch, abolish, eliminate *(sl)*, exterminate, remove, finish off, rub out *(sl)*. **2** PAY (OFF), close down, clear, discharge, wind up, sell.

liquor *n* alcohol, intoxicant, strong drink, spirits, drink, hard stuff *(infml)*, booze *(infml)*.

list¹ *n* catalogue, roll, inventory, register, enumeration, schedule, index, listing, record, file, directory, table, tabulation, tally, series, syllabus, invoice.

➤ *v* enumerate, register, itemize, catalogue, index, tabulate, record, file, enrol, enter, note, bill, book, set down, write down.

list² *v* lean, incline, tilt, slope, heel (over), tip.

listen *v* hark, attend, pay attention, hear, heed, hearken, hang on (someone's) words, prick up one's ears, take notice, lend an ear, eavesdrop, overhear, give ear.

listless *adj* sluggish, lethargic, languid, torpid, enervated, spiritless, limp, lifeless, inert, inactive, impassive, indifferent, uninterested, vacant, apathetic, indolent, depressed, bored, heavy.
F₃ energetic, enthusiastic.

literal *adj* **1** VERBATIM, word-for-word, strict, close, actual, precise, faithful, exact, accurate, factual, true, genuine, unexaggerated. **2** PROSAIC, dull, unimaginative, uninspired, matter-of-fact, down-to-earth, humdrum.
F₃ **1** imprecise, loose. **2** imaginative.

literary *adj* educated, well-read, bookish, learned, erudite *(fml)*, scholarly, lettered, literate, cultured, cultivated, refined, formal.
F₃ ignorant, illiterate.

literature *n* **1** WRITINGS, letters, paper(s). **2** INFORMATION, leaflet(s), pamphlet(s), circular(s), brochure(s), handout(s), bumf *(infml)*.

Types of literature include: allegory, anti-novel, autobiography, belles-lettres *(fml)*, Bildungsroman, biography, classic novel, crime fiction, criticism, drama, epic, epistle, essay, fiction, Gothic novel, interactive fiction, lampoon, libretto, magnum opus, non-fiction, novel, novella, parody, pastiche, penny dreadful *(infml)*, picaresque novel, poetry, polemic, postil, prose, pulp fiction, roman à clef, roman novel, saga, satire, science fiction, thesis, tragedy, treatise, triad, trilogy, verse. *see also* **poem**; **story**.

litigation *n* lawsuit, action, suit, case, prosecution, process, contention.

litter *n* **1** RUBBISH, debris, refuse, waste, mess, disorder, clutter, confusion, disarray, untidiness, junk *(infml)*, muck, jumble, fragments, shreds. **2** OFFSPRING, young, progeny *(fml)*, brood, family.

➤ *v* strew, scatter, mess up, disorder, clutter.
F₃ tidy.

little *adj* **1** SMALL, short, tiny, wee *(infml)*, minute, teeny *(infml)*, diminutive, miniature, infinitesimal, mini *(infml)*, microscopic, petite, pint-size(d) *(infml)*, slender. **2** SHORT-LIVED, brief, fleeting, passing, transient.
3 INSUFFICIENT, sparse, scant, meagre, paltry, skimpy. **4** INSIGNIFICANT,

inconsiderable, negligible, trivial, petty, trifling, unimportant.
Ea 1 big. **2** lengthy. **3** ample. **4** considerable.

➤ *adv* barely, hardly, scarcely, rarely, seldom, infrequently, not much.
Ea frequently.

➤ *n* bit, dash, pinch, spot, trace, drop, dab, speck, touch, taste, particle, hint, fragment, modicum, trifle, tad.
Ea lot.

live[1] *v* **1** BE, exist, breathe, draw breath. **2** LAST, endure, continue, remain, persist, survive. **3** DWELL, inhabit, reside, lodge, abide. **4** PASS, spend, lead.
Ea 1 die. **2** cease.

live[2] *adj* **1** ALIVE, living, existent. **2** LIVELY, vital, active, energetic, dynamic, alert, vigorous. **3** BURNING, glowing, blazing, ignited. **4** RELEVANT, current, topical, pertinent, controversial.
Ea 1 dead. **2** apathetic.

livelihood *n* occupation, job, employment, living, means, income, maintenance, work, support, subsistence, sustenance.

lively *adj* **1** ANIMATED, alert, active, energetic, spirited. feisty, vivacious, vigorous, sprightly, spry, agile, nimble, quick, keen. **2** CHEERFUL, blithe, merry, frisky, perky, breezy, chirpy (*infml*), frolicsome. **3** BUSY, bustling, brisk, crowded, eventful, exciting, buzzing. **4** VIVID, bright, colourful, stimulating, stirring, invigorating, racy, refreshing, sparkling.
Ea 1 apathetic, moribund. **3** inactive.

liven (up) *v* enliven, vitalize, put life into, rouse, invigorate, animate, energize, brighten, stir (up), buck up (*infml*), pep up (*infml*), perk up (*infml*), hot up (*infml*).
Ea dishearten.

livery *n* uniform, costume, regalia, dress, clothes, clothing, apparel (*fml*), attire, vestments, suit, garb, habit.

livid *adj* **1** LEADEN, black-and-blue,

bruised, discoloured, greyish, purple. **2** PALE, pallid, ashen, blanched, bloodless, wan, waxy, pasty. **3** (*infml*) ANGRY, furious, infuriated, irate, outraged, enraged, raging, fuming, indignant, incensed, exasperated, mad (*infml*).
Ea 3 calm.

living *adj* alive, breathing, existing, live, current, extant, operative, strong, vigorous, active, lively, vital, animated.
Ea dead, sluggish.

➤ *n* **1** BEING, life, animation, existence. **2** LIVELIHOOD, maintenance, support, income, subsistence, sustenance, work, job, occupation, profession, benefice, way of life.

load *n* **1** BURDEN, onus, encumbrance, weight, pressure, oppression, millstone. **2** CARGO, consignment, shipment, goods, lading, freight.

➤ *v* **1** BURDEN, weigh down, encumber, overburden, oppress, trouble, weight, saddle with. **2** PACK, pile, heap, freight, fill, stack.

loaded *adj* burdened, charged, laden, full, weighted.

loafer *n* (*infml*) idler, layabout (*infml*), shirker, skiver (*infml*), sluggard, wastrel, lounger, ne'er-do-well, lazybones (*infml*), couch potato (*infml*).

loan *n* advance, credit, mortgage, allowance.

➤ *v* lend, advance, credit, allow.

loathe *v* hate, detest, abominate, abhor, despise, dislike.
Ea adore, love.

loathing *n* hatred, detestation, abhorrence, abomination, repugnance, revulsion, repulsion, dislike, disgust, aversion, horror.
Ea affection, love.

loathsome *adj* detestable, abhorrent, odious, repulsive, abominable, hateful, repugnant, repellent, offensive, horrible, disgusting, vile, revolting, nasty.

lobby *v* campaign for, press for, demand, persuade, call for, urge, push for, influence, solicit, pressure, promote.

➤ *n* **1** VESTIBULE, foyer, porch, anteroom, hall, hallway, waiting-room, entrance hall, corridor, passage. **2** PRESSURE GROUP, campaign, ginger group.

local *adj* regional, provincial, community, district, neighbourhood, parochial, vernacular, small-town, limited, narrow, restricted, parish-pump.

🗷 national.

➤ *n* **1** INHABITANT, citizen, resident, native. **2** (*infml*) PUB.

locality *n* neighbourhood, vicinity, district, area, locale, region, position, place, site, spot, scene, setting.

locate *v* **1** FIND, discover, unearth, run to earth (*infml*), track down, detect, lay one's hands on (*infml*), pinpoint, identify. **2** SITUATE, settle, fix, establish, place, put, set, seat.

location *n* position, situation, place, locus, whereabouts, venue, site, locale, bearings, spot, point.

lock *n* fastening, bolt, clasp, padlock.

Parts of a lock include: barrel, bolt, cylinder, cylinder hole, dead bolt, escutcheon, face plate, hasp, key, key card, keyhole, keyway, knob, latch, latch bolt, latch follower, latch lever, mortise lock, pin, push button, rose, sash, sash bolt, spindle, spindle hole, spring, strike plate, staple.

➤ *v* **1** FASTEN, secure, bolt, latch, seal, shut. **2** JOIN, unite, engage, link, mesh, entangle, entwine, clench. **3** CLASP, hug, embrace, grasp, encircle, enclose, clutch, grapple.

🗷 unlock.

◇ **lock out** shut out, refuse admittance to, keep out, exclude, bar, debar.

◇ **lock up** imprison, jail, confine, shut in, shut up, incarcerate, secure, cage, pen, detain, close up.

🗷 free.

lodge *n* hut, cabin, cottage, chalet, shelter, retreat, den, gatehouse, house, hunting-lodge, meeting-place, club, haunt.

➤ *v* **1** ACCOMMODATE, put up (*infml*), quarter, board, billet, shelter. **2** LIVE, stray, reside. **3** FIX, embed, implant, get stuck. **4** DEPOSIT, place, put, submit, register.

lodger *n* boarder, paying guest, resident, tenant, roomer, inmate, guest.

lodgings *n* accommodation, digs (*infml*), dwelling, quarters, billet, abode, boarding-house, rooms, pad (*infml*), residence.

log *n* **1** TIMBER, trunk, block, chunk. **2** RECORD, diary, journal, logbook, daybook, account, tally.

➤ *v* record, register, write up, note, book, chart, tally.

logic *n* reasoning, reason, sense, deduction, rationale, argumentation.

logical *adj* reasonable, rational, reasoned, coherent, consistent, valid, sound, well-founded, clear, sensible, deducible, methodical, well-organized.

🗷 illogical, irrational.

loiter *v* dawdle, hang about, idle, linger, dally, dilly-dally (*infml*), delay, mooch, lag, saunter.

lone *adj* single, sole, one, only, isolated, solitary, separate, separated, alone, unattached, unaccompanied, unattended.

🗷 accompanied.

loneliness *n* aloneness, isolation, lonesomeness, solitariness, solitude, seclusion, desolation.

lonely *adj* **1** ALONE, friendless, lonesome, solitary, abandoned, forsaken, companionless, unaccompanied, destitute. **2** ISOLATED, uninhabited, remote, out-of-the-way, unfrequented, secluded, abandoned, deserted, forsaken, desolate.

🗷 **1** popular. **2** crowded, populous.

long *adj* lengthy, extensive, extended, expanded, prolonged, protracted, stretched, spread out, sustained, expansive, far-reaching, long-drawn-out, interminable, slow.

🗷 brief, short, fleeting, abbreviated.

◇ **long for** yearn for, crave, want, wish, desire, dream of, hanker for, pine, thirst for, lust after, covet, itch for, yen for (*infml*).

longing *n* craving, desire, yearning, hungering, hankering, yen, thirst, wish, urge, coveting, aspiration, ambition.

long-lasting *adj* permanent, imperishable, enduring, unchanging, unfading, continuing, abiding, long-standing, prolonged, protracted.
ⴲ short-lived, ephemeral, transient.

long-standing *adj* established, long-established, long-lived, long-lasting, enduring, abiding, time-honoured, traditional.

long-suffering *adj* uncomplaining, forbearing, forgiving, tolerant, patient, stoical.

long-winded *adj* lengthy, overlong, prolonged, diffuse, verbose, wordy, voluble, long-drawn-out, discursive, repetitious, rambling, tedious.
ⴲ brief, terse.

look *v* 1 WATCH, see, observe, view, survey, regard, gaze, study, stare, examine, inspect, scrutinize, glance, contemplate, scan, peep, peer, gawp (*infml*). 2 SEEM, appear, show, exhibit, display.
➤ *n* 1 VIEW, survey, inspection, examination, observation, sight, review, once-over (*infml*), glance, glimpse, gaze, peek. 2 APPEARANCE, aspect, manner, semblance, mien, expression, bearing, face, complexion.

◇ **look after** take care of, mind, care for, attend to, take charge of, tend, keep an eye on, watch over, protect, supervise, guard.
ⴲ neglect.

◇ **look down on** despise, scorn, sneer at, hold in contempt, disdain, look down one's nose at (*infml*), turn one's nose up at (*infml*).
ⴲ esteem, approve.

◇ **look forward to** anticipate, await, expect, hope for, long for, envisage, envision, count on, wait for, look for.

◇ **look into** investigate, probe, research, study, go into, examine,

enquire about, explore, check out, inspect, scrutinize, look over, plumb, fathom.

◇ **look out** pay attention, watch out, beware, be careful, keep an eye out.

◇ **look over** inspect, examine, check, give a once-over (*infml*), cast an eye over, look through, scan, view.

◇ **look up 1** SEARCH FOR, research, hunt for, find, track down. **2** VISIT, call on, drop in on, look in on, pay a visit to, stop by, drop by. **3** IMPROVE, get better, pick up, progress, come on.

◇ **look up to** admire, esteem, respect, revere, honour, have a high opinion of.

lookalike *n* double, replica, twin, spitting image (*infml*), living image, clone, spit (*infml*), ringer (*infml*), doppelgänger.

lookout *n* 1 GUARD, sentry, watch, watch-tower, watchman, sentinel, tower, post. **2** (*infml*) CONCERN, responsibility, worry, affair, business, problem.

loom *v* appear, emerge, take shape, menace, threaten, impend, hang over, dominate, tower, overhang, rise, soar, overshadow, overtop.

loop *n* hoop, ring, circle, noose, coil, eyelet, loophole, spiral, curve, curl, kink, twist, whorl, twirl, turn, bend.
➤ *v* coil, encircle, roll, bend, circle, curve round, turn, twist, spiral, connect, join, knot, fold, braid.

loophole *n* let-out, escape, evasion, excuse, pretext, plea, pretence.

loose *adj* 1 FREE, unfastened, untied, movable, unattached, insecure, wobbly. **2** SLACK, lax, baggy, hanging. **3** IMPRECISE, vague, inexact, ill-defined, indefinite, inaccurate, indistinct.
ⴲ 1 firm, secure. 2 tight. 3 precise.

loosen *v* 1 EASE, relax, loose, slacken, undo, unbind, untie, unfasten. **2** FREE, set free, release, let go, let out, deliver.
ⴲ 1 tighten.

loot *n* spoils, booty, plunder, haul, swag (*infml*), prize.
➤ *v* plunder, pillage, rob, sack, rifle, raid, maraud, ransack, ravage.

lopsided *adj* asymmetrical, unbalanced, askew, off balance, uneven.
🔄 balanced, symmetrical.

lord *n* **1** PEER, noble, earl, duke, count, baron. **2** MASTER, ruler, superior, overlord, leader, commander, governor, king.

lordly *adj* **1** NOBLE, dignified, aristocratic. **2** PROUD, arrogant, disdainful, haughty, imperious, condescending, high-handed, domineering, overbearing.
🔄 **1** low(ly). **2** humble.

lore *n* knowledge, wisdom, learning, erudition, scholarship, traditions, teaching, beliefs, sayings.

lose *v* **1** MISLAY, misplace, forget, miss, forfeit. **2** WASTE, squander, dissipate, use up, exhaust, expend, drain. **3** FAIL, fall short, suffer defeat.
🔄 **1** gain. **2** make. **3** win.

loser *n* failure, also-ran, runner-up, flop (*infml*), no-hoper.
🔄 winner.

loss *n* **1** DEPRIVATION, disadvantage, defeat, failure, losing, bereavement, damage, destruction, ruin, hurt. **2** WASTE, depletion, disappearance, deficiency, deficit.
🔄 **1** gain.

lost *adj* **1** MISLAID, missing, vanished, disappeared, misplaced, astray. **2** CONFUSED, disoriented, bewildered, puzzled, baffled, perplexed, nonplussed, flummoxed (*infml*), preoccupied. **3** WASTED, squandered, ruined, destroyed.
🔄 **1** found.

lot *n* **1** COLLECTION, batch, assortment, quantity, group, set, crowd. **2** SHARE, portion, allowance, ration, quota, part, piece, parcel.

lotion *n* ointment, balm, cream, salve.

lottery *n* **1** DRAW, raffle, sweepstake. **2** SPECULATION, venture, risk, gamble.

loud *adj* **1** NOISY, deafening, booming, resounding, ear-piercing, ear-splitting, piercing, thundering, roaring, blaring, clamorous, vociferous. **2** GARISH, gaudy, glaring, flashy, brash, showy, ostentatious, tasteless.
🔄 **1** quiet. **2** subdued.

lounge *v* relax, loll, idle, laze, waste time, kill time, lie about, take it easy, sprawl, recline, lie back, slump.
➤ *n* sitting-room, living room, drawing-room, day room, parlour.

lovable *adj* adorable, endearing, winsome, captivating, charming, engaging, attractive, fetching, sweet, lovely, pleasing, delightful.
🔄 detestable, hateful.

love *v* **1** *he loves his wife*: adore, cherish, dote on, treasure, hold dear, idolize, worship. **2** *I love macaroons*: like, take pleasure in, enjoy, delight in, appreciate, desire, fancy.
🔄 detest, hate.
➤ *n* adoration, affection, fondness, attachment, care, regard, liking, amorousness, ardour, devotion, adulation, passion, rapture, tenderness, warmth, inclination, infatuation, delight, enjoyment, soft spot (*infml*), weakness, taste, friendship.
🔄 detestation, hate, loathing.
◇ **love affair** *n* affair, romance, fling (*infml*), liaison, relationship, love, passion.

lovely *adj* beautiful, charming, delightful, attractive, enchanting, pleasing, pleasant, pretty, adorable, agreeable, enjoyable, sweet, winning, exquisite.
🔄 ugly, hideous.

lover *n* beloved, admirer, boyfriend, girlfriend, sweetheart, suitor, mistress, fiancé(e), flame (*infml*).

loving *adj* amorous, affectionate, devoted, doting, fond, ardent, passionate, warm, warm-hearted, tender.

low *adj* **1** SHORT, small, squat, stunted, little, shallow, deep, depressed, sunken. **2** INADEQUATE, deficient, poor, sparse, meagre, paltry, scant, insignificant. **3** UNHAPPY, depressed, downcast,

gloomy. **4** BASE, coarse, vulgar, mean, contemptible. **5** CHEAP, inexpensive, reasonable. **6** SUBDUED, muted, soft.
🔁 **1** high, raised. **2** high. **3** cheerful. **4** honourable. **5** expensive, exorbitant. **6** loud.

lower *adj* inferior, lesser, subordinate, secondary, minor, second-class, low-level, lowly, junior.
🔁 higher.
➤ *v* **1** DROP, depress, sink, descend, let down. **2** REDUCE, decrease, cut, lessen, diminish.
🔁 **1** raise. **2** increase.

lowly *adj* humble, low-born, obscure, poor, plebeian, plain, simple, modest, ordinary, inferior, meek, mild, mean, submissive, subordinate.
🔁 lofty, noble.

low-spirited *adj* depressed, gloomy, heavy-hearted, low, glum, down, downhearted, despondent, fed up (*infml*), sad, unhappy, miserable, moody.
🔁 high-spirited, cheerful.

loyal *adj* true, faithful, steadfast, staunch, devoted, trustworthy, sincere, patriotic.
🔁 disloyal, treacherous.

loyalty *n* allegiance, faithfulness, fidelity, devotion, steadfastness, constancy, trustworthiness, reliability, patriotism.
🔁 disloyalty, treachery.

lubricate *v* oil, grease, smear, wax, lard.

luck *n* **1** CHANCE, fortune, accident, fate, fortuity (*fml*), fluke (*infml*), destiny. **2** GOOD FORTUNE, success, break (*infml*), godsend.
🔁 **1** design. **2** misfortune.

luckily *adv* fortunately, happily, providentially.
🔁 unfortunately.

lucky *adj* fortunate, favoured, auspicious, successful, prosperous, timely.
🔁 unlucky.

lucrative *adj* profitable, well-paid, remunerative, advantageous.
🔁 unprofitable.

ludicrous *adj* absurd, ridiculous, preposterous, nonsensical, laughable, farcical, silly, comical, funny, outlandish, crazy (*infml*), mad.
🔁 serious.

lug *v* pull, drag, haul, carry, tow, heave, hump.

luggage

> *Types of luggage include*: case, suitcase, vanity case, bag, holdall, portmanteau, valise, overnight bag, kit bag, flight bag, hand luggage, tote bag, travel bag, Gladstone bag, grip, rucksack, knapsack, haversack, backpack, bumbag, moneybelt, briefcase, attaché case, portfolio, satchel, basket, hamper, trunk, chest, box.

lukewarm *adj* cool, half-hearted, apathetic, tepid, indifferent, unenthusiastic, uninterested, unresponsive, unconcerned.

lull *v* soothe, subdue, calm, hush, pacify, quieten down, quiet, quell, compose.
🔁 agitate.
➤ *n* calm, peace, quiet, tranquillity, stillness, let-up, pause, hush, silence.
🔁 agitation.

lumber[1] *n* clutter, jumble, rubbish, bits and pieces, odds and ends, junk.

lumber[2] *v* clump, shamble, plod, shuffle, stump, trundle.

luminous *adj* glowing, illuminated, lit, lighted, radiant, shining, fluorescent, brilliant, lustrous, bright.

lump *n* **1** MASS, cluster, clump, clod, ball, bunch, piece, chunk, cake, hunk, nugget, wedge. **2** SWELLING, growth, bulge, bump, protuberance, protrusion, tumour.
➤ *v* collect, mass, gather, cluster, combine, coalesce, group, consolidate, unite.

lunacy *n* madness, insanity, aberration,

derangement, mania, craziness (*infml*), idiocy, imbecility, folly, absurdity, stupidity. **Ⓕ** sanity.

lunatic *n* psychotic, psychopath, madman, maniac, loony (*sl*), nutcase (*sl*), nutter (*sl*), fruitcake (*infml*). ➤ *adj* mad, insane, deranged, psychotic, irrational, crazy (*infml*), bonkers (*infml*). **Ⓕ** sane.

lunge *v* thrust, jab, stab, pounce, plunge, pitch into, charge, dart, dash, dive, poke, strike (at), fall upon, grab (at), hit (at), leap. ➤ *n* thrust, stab, pounce, charge, jab, pass, cut, spring.

lurch *v* roll, rock, pitch, sway, stagger, reel, list.

lure *v* tempt, entice, draw, attract, allure, seduce, ensnare, lead on. ➤ *n* temptation, enticement, attraction, bait, inducement.

lurid *adj* 1 SENSATIONAL, shocking, startling, graphic, exaggerated. 2 MACABRE, gruesome, gory, ghastly, grisly. 3 BRIGHTLY COLOURED, garish, glaring, loud, vivid.

lurk *v* skulk, prowl, lie in wait, crouch, lie low, hide, snoop.

luscious *adj* delicious, juicy, succulent, appetizing, mouth-watering, sweet, tasty, savoury, desirable.

lush *adj* 1 FLOURISHING, luxuriant, abundant, prolific, overgrown, green, verdant. 2 SUMPTUOUS, opulent, ornate, plush, rich.

lust *n* 1 SENSUALITY, libido, lechery, licentiousness, lewdness. 2 CRAVING, desire, appetite, longing, passion, greed, covetousness. ◇ **lust after** desire, crave, yearn for, want, need, hunger for, thirst for.

lustre *n* 1 SHINE, gloss, sheen, gleam, glow, brilliance, brightness, radiance, sparkle, resplendence, burnish, glitter, glint. 2 GLORY, honour, prestige, illustriousness.

lusty *adj* robust, strong, sturdy, vigorous, hale, hearty, healthy, gutsy (*infml*), energetic, strapping, rugged, powerful.

luxurious *adj* sumptuous, opulent, lavish, de luxe, plush (*infml*), posh (*infml*), magnificent, splendid, expensive, costly, self-indulgent, pampered. **Ⓕ** austere, spartan.

luxury *n* sumptuousness, opulence, hedonism, splendour, affluence, richness, magnificence, pleasure, indulgence, gratification, comfort, extravagance, satisfaction. **Ⓕ** austerity.

lying *adj* deceitful, dishonest, false, untruthful, double-dealing, two-faced (*infml*), duplicitous. **Ⓕ** honest, truthful. ➤ *n* dishonesty, untruthfulness, deceit, falsity, fibbing (*infml*), perjury, duplicity, fabrication, double-dealing. **Ⓕ** honesty, truthfulness.

Mm

macabre *adj* gruesome, grisly, grim, horrible, frightful, dreadful, ghostly, eerie.

machine *n* 1 INSTRUMENT, device, contrivance, tool, mechanism, engine, apparatus, appliance. 2 AGENCY, organization, structure, system.

machinery *n* 1 INSTRUMENTS, mechanism, tools, apparatus, equipment, tackle, gear. 2 ORGANIZATION, channels, structure, system, procedure.

> *Types of heavy machinery include*: all-terrain forklift, bulldozer, caterpillar tractor, combine harvester, concrete mixer, concrete pump, crane, crawler crane, crawler tractor, digger, dragline excavator, dredger, dumper, dump truck, dustcart, excavator, fertilizer spreader, fire appliance, forklift truck, gantry crane, grader, grapple, gritter, hydraulic bale loader, hydraulic shovel, JCB®, muck spreader, pick-up loader, piledriver, platform hoist, riding mower, road roller, road-sweeping lorry, Rotovator®, silage harvester, snowplough, straw baler, threshing machine, tower crane, tracklayer, tractor, tractor-scraper, truck crane, wheel loader.

mad *adj* 1 INSANE, lunatic, unbalanced, psychotic, deranged, demented, out of one's mind, crazy (*infml*), nuts (*infml*), barmy (*infml*), bonkers (*infml*). 2 (*infml*) ANGRY, furious, enraged, infuriated, incensed, livid (*infml*). 3 IRRATIONAL, illogical, unreasonable, absurd, preposterous, foolish. 4 FANATICAL, enthusiastic, eager, infatuated, ardent.

F3 1 sane. 2 calm. 3 sensible. 4 apathetic.

madden *v* anger, enrage, infuriate, incense, exasperate, provoke, rile, annoy, irritate, aggravate (*infml*).
F3 calm, pacify.

madly *adv* 1 *he rolled his eyes madly*: insanely, dementedly, hysterically, wildly. 2 *madly cleaning up*: excitedly, frantically, furiously, recklessly, violently, energetically, rapidly, hastily, hurriedly. 3 *madly in love*: intensely, extremely, exceedingly, fervently, devotedly.

madman, madwoman *n* lunatic, psychotic, psychopath, maniac, loony (*sl*), nutter (*sl*), nutcase (*sl*), fruitcake (*infml*).

magazine *n* 1 JOURNAL, periodical, paper, weekly, monthly, quarterly. 2 ARSENAL, storehouse, ammunition dump, depot, ordnance.

magic *n* 1 SORCERY, enchantment, occultism, black art, witchcraft, wicca, spell. 2 CONJURING, illusion, sleight of hand, trickery. 3 CHARM, fascination, glamour, allure.
➤ *adj* charming, enchanting, bewitching, fascinating, spellbinding.

magician *n* sorcerer, miracle-worker, conjuror, enchanter, wizard, witch, warlock, spellbinder, wonder-worker.

magnanimous *adj* generous, liberal, open-handed, benevolent, selfless, charitable, big-hearted, kind, noble, unselfish, ungrudging.
F3 mean.

magnate *n* tycoon, captain of industry, industrialist, mogul, entrepreneur, plutocrat, baron, personage, notable.

magnetic *adj* attractive, alluring, fascinating, charming, mesmerizing, seductive, irresistible, entrancing,

captivating, gripping, absorbing, charismatic.
🔄 repellent, repulsive.

magnetism n attraction, allure, fascination, charm, lure, appeal, drawing power, draw, pull, hypnotism, mesmerism, charisma, grip, magic, power, spell.

magnificent adj splendid, grand, imposing, impressive, glorious, gorgeous, brilliant, excellent, majestic, superb, sumptuous, noble, elegant, fine, rich.
🔄 modest, humble, poor.

magnify v enlarge, amplify, increase, expand, intensify, boost, enhance, greaten, heighten, deepen, build up, talk up (*infml*), exaggerate, dramatize, overemphasize, overplay, overstate, overdo, blow up (*infml*).
🔄 belittle, play down.

magnitude n 1 SIZE, extent, measure, amount, expanse, dimensions, mass, proportions, quantity, volume, bulk, largeness, space, strength, amplitude. 2 IMPORTANCE, consequence, significance, weight, greatness, moment, intensity.

maiden n girl, virgin, lass, lassie, damsel (*fml*), miss.

mail n post, letters, correspondence, packages, parcels, delivery.
➤ v post, send, dispatch, forward.

maim v mutilate, wound, incapacitate, injure, disable, hurt, impair, cripple, lame.

main adj principal, chief, leading, first, foremost, predominant, pre-eminent, primary, prime, supreme, paramount, central, cardinal, outstanding, essential, critical, crucial, necessary, vital.
🔄 minor, unimportant, insignificant.
➤ n pipe, duct, conduit, channel, cable, line.

mainly adv primarily, principally, chiefly, in the main, mostly, on the whole, for the most part, generally, in general, especially, as a rule, above all, largely, overall.

mainstay n support, buttress, bulwark, linchpin, prop, pillar, backbone, foundation.

maintain v 1 CARRY ON, continue, keep (up), sustain, retain. 2 CARE FOR, conserve, look after, take care of, preserve, support, finance, supply. 3 ASSERT, affirm, claim, contend, declare, hold, state, insist, believe, fight for.
🔄 2 neglect. 3 deny.

maintenance n 1 CONTINUATION, continuance, perpetuation. 2 CARE, conservation, preservation, support, repairs, protection, upkeep, running. 3 KEEP, subsistence, living, livelihood, allowance, alimony.
🔄 2 neglect.

majestic adj magnificent, grand, dignified, noble, royal, stately, splendid, imperial, impressive, exalted, imposing, regal, sublime, superb, lofty, monumental, pompous.
🔄 lowly, unimpressive, unimposing.

majesty n grandeur, glory, dignity, magnificence, nobility, royalty, resplendence, splendour, stateliness, pomp, exaltedness, impressiveness, loftiness.

major adj greater, chief, main, larger, bigger, higher, leading, outstanding, notable, supreme, uppermost, primary, paramount, significant, crucial, important, key, keynote, great, senior, older, superior, pre-eminent, vital, weighty.
🔄 minor, unimportant, trivial.

majority n 1 BULK, mass, preponderance, most, greater part. 2 ADULTHOOD, maturity, manhood, womanhood, years of discretion.
🔄 1 minority.

make v 1 CREATE, manufacture, fabricate, construct, build, produce, put together, originate, compose, form, shape. 2 CAUSE, bring about, effect, accomplish, occasion, give rise to, generate, engender, render, perform. 3 COERCE, force, oblige, constrain, compel, prevail upon, pressurize, press, require. **4** APPOINT, elect, designate, nominate, ordain, install. **5** EARN, gain, net, obtain, acquire. **6** CONSTITUTE, compose, comprise, add up to, amount to.

 1 dismantle. **5** spend.

➤ *n* brand, sort, type, style, variety, manufacture, model, mark, kind, form, structure.

◊ **make off** run off, run away, depart, bolt, leave, fly, cut and run (*infml*), beat a hasty retreat (*infml*), clear off (*infml*).

◊ **make out 1** DISCERN, perceive, decipher, distinguish, recognize, see, detect, discover, understand, work out, grasp, follow, fathom. **2** DRAW UP, complete, fill in, write out. **3** MAINTAIN, imply, claim, assert, describe, demonstrate, prove. **4** MANAGE, get on, progress, succeed, fare (*fml*).

◊ **make up 1** CREATE, invent, devise, fabricate, construct, originate, formulate, dream up, compose. **2** COMPLETE, fill, supply, meet, supplement. **3** COMPRISE, constitute, compose, form. **4** BE RECONCILED, make peace, settle differences, bury the hatchet (*infml*), forgive and forget, call it quits (*infml*).

◊ **make up for** compensate for, make good, make amends for, redress, recompense, redeem, atone for.

make-believe *n* pretence, imagination, fantasy, unreality, play-acting, role-play, dream, charade.
 reality.

maker *n* creator, manufacturer, constructor, builder, producer, director, architect, author.

makeshift *adj* temporary, improvised, rough and ready, provisional, substitute, stop-gap, expedient, make-do.
 permanent.

make-up *n* **1** COSMETICS, paint, powder, maquillage, war paint (*infml*), slap (*sl*). **2** CONSTITUTION, nature, composition, character, construction, form, format, formation, arrangement, organization, style, structure, assembly.

maladjusted *adj* disturbed, unstable, confused, alienated, neurotic, estranged.
 well-adjusted.

male *adj* masculine, manly, virile, boyish, laddish (*infml*), he-.
 female.

Male terms include: boy, lad, youth, man, gentleman, gent (*infml*), bachelor, chap (*infml*), bloke (*infml*), guy (*infml*), son, brother, boyfriend, beau, toy boy (*sl*), fiancé, bridegroom, husband, father, uncle, nephew, grandfather, patriarch, godfather, widower, sugar daddy (*sl*), hunk (*sl*), gigolo, homosexual, gay, rent boy, male chauvinist pig (MCP) (*sl*); bull, dog, buck, tup, cock, cockerel, stallion, billy-goat, boar, dog fox, stag, ram, tom cat, drake, gander.

malevolent *adj* malicious, malign, spiteful, vindictive, ill-natured, hostile, vicious, venomous, evil-minded.
 benevolent, kind.

malformation *n* irregularity, deformity, distortion, warp.

malformed *adj* misshapen, irregular, deformed, distorted, twisted, warped, crooked, bent.
 perfect.

malfunction *n* fault, defect, failure, breakdown.

➤ *v* break down, go wrong, fail.

malice *n* malevolence, enmity, animosity, ill-will, hatred, hate, spite, vindictiveness, bitterness.
 love.

malicious *adj* malevolent, ill-natured, malign, spiteful, venomous, vicious, vengeful, evil-minded, bitter, resentful.
 kind, friendly.

malign *adj* malignant, malevolent, bad, evil, harmful, hurtful, injurious, destructive, hostile.
 benign.

➤ *v* defame, slander, libel, disparage, abuse, run down (*infml*), harm, injure.
 praise.

malignant *adj* **1** MALEVOLENT, malicious, spiteful, evil, hostile, vicious, venomous, destructive, harmful, hurtful, pernicious. **2** FATAL, deadly, incurable, terminal, dangerous, cancerous, uncontrollable, virulent.
E3 1 kind. **2** benign.

malpractice *n* misconduct, mismanagement, negligence, impropriety, dereliction of duty (*fml*), abuse, misdeed.

maltreat *v* ill-treat, mistreat, misuse, abuse, injure, harm, damage, hurt.
E3 care for.

mammal

> *Mammals include*: aardvark, African black rhinoceros, African elephant, anteater, antelope, armadillo, baboon, Bactrian camel, badger, bat, bear, beaver, bushbaby, cat, chimpanzee, chipmunk, cow, deer, dog, dolphin, duck-billed platypus, dugong, echidna, flying lemur, fox, gerbil, gibbon, giraffe, goat, gorilla, guinea pig, hamster, hare, hedgehog, hippopotamus, horse, human being, hyena, Indian elephant, kangaroo, koala, lemming, leopard, lion, manatee, marmoset, marmot, marsupial mouse, mole, mouse, opossum, orang utan, otter, pig, porcupine, porpoise, rabbit, raccoon, rat, sea cow, seal, sea lion, sheep, shrew, sloth, squirrel, tamarin, tapir, tiger, vole, wallaby, walrus, weasel, whale, wolf, zebra. *see also* **cat**; **cattle**; **dog**; **horse**; **marsupial**; **monkey**; **rodent**.

mammoth *adj* enormous, huge, vast, colossal, gigantic, giant, massive, immense, monumental, mighty.
E3 tiny, minute.

man *n* **1** MALE, gentleman, fellow, bloke (*infml*), chap (*infml*), guy (*infml*).
2 HUMAN BEING, person, individual, adult, human. **3** HUMANITY, humankind, mankind, human race, people, Homo sapiens, mortals. **4** MANSERVANT, servant, worker, employee, hand, soldier, valet, houseman, houseboy.
➤ *v* staff, crew, take charge of, operate, occupy.

manacle *v* handcuff, shackle, restrain, fetter, chain, put in chains, bind, curb, check, hamper, inhibit.
E3 free, unshackle.

manage *v* **1** ACCOMPLISH, succeed, bring about, bring off, effect.
2 ADMINISTER, direct, run, command, control, govern, preside over, rule, superintend, supervise, officiate, oversee, conduct. **3** CONTROL, influence, deal with, handle, operate, manipulate, guide. **4** COPE, fare, survive, get by, get along, get on, make do.
E3 1 fail. **2** mismanage.

manageable *adj* tractable, governable, controllable, amenable, submissive, docile.
E3 unmanageable.

management *n* **1** ADMINISTRATION, direction, control, government, command, running, superintendence, supervision, charge, care, handling.
2 MANAGERS, directors, directorate, executive, executives, governors, board, bosses (*infml*), supervisors.
E3 1 mismanagement. **2** workers.

manager *n* director, executive, administrator, controller, superintendent, supervisor, overseer, governor, organizer, head, boss (*infml*).

mandate *n* order, command, decree, edict, injunction, charge, directive, warrant, authorization, authority, instruction, commission, sanction.

mandatory *adj* obligatory, compulsory, binding, required, necessary, requisite, essential.
E3 optional.

mangle *v* mutilate, disfigure, mar, maim, spoil, butcher, destroy, deform, wreck, twist, maul, distort, crush, cut, hack, tear, rend.

mangy *adj* seedy, shabby, scruffy, scabby, tatty (*infml*), shoddy, moth-eaten, dirty, mean.

manhandle v 1 *the porters manhandled the baggage*: haul, heave, hump, pull, push, shove, tug. 2 *the police manhandled the demonstrators*: maul, mistreat, maltreat, misuse, abuse, knock about (*infml*), rough up (*infml*).

manhood n 1 ADULTHOOD, maturity. 2 MASCULINITY, virility, manliness, manfulness, machismo (*infml*).

mania n 1 MADNESS, insanity, lunacy, psychosis, derangement, disorder, aberration, craziness (*infml*), frenzy. 2 PASSION, craze, rage, obsession, compulsion, enthusiasm, fad (*infml*), infatuation, fixation, craving.

Manias (by name of disorder) include: dipsomania (*alcohol*), bibliomania (*books*), ailuromania (*cats*), demomania (*crowds*), necromania (*dead bodies*), thanatomania (*death*), cynomania (*dogs*), narcomania (*drugs*), pyromania (*fire-raising*), anthomania (*flowers*), hippomania (*horses*), mythomania (*lying and exaggerating*), egomania (*oneself*), ablutomania (*personal cleanliness*), hedonomania (*pleasure*), megalomania (*power*), theomania (*religion*), nymphomania (*sex*), monomania (*single idea or thing*), kleptomania (*stealing*), tomomania (*surgery*), logomania (*talking*), ergomania (*work*). *see also* **phobia** and supplement **Words Grouped by Ending**.

---

maniac n 1 LUNATIC, madman, madwoman, psychotic, psychopath, nutcase (*sl*), nutter (*sl*), loony (*sl*). 2 ENTHUSIAST, fan (*infml*), fanatic, fiend (*infml*), freak (*infml*).

manifest adj obvious, evident, clear, apparent, plain, open, patent, distinct, noticeable, conspicuous, unmistakable, visible, unconcealed.
🖪 unclear.
➤ v show, exhibit, display, demonstrate, reveal, set forth, expose, prove, illustrate, establish.
🖪 conceal.

manifestation n display, exhibition, demonstration, show, revelation, exposure, disclosure, appearance, expression, sign, indication.

manifesto n statement, declaration, policies, platform.

manifold adj (*fml*) many, numerous, varied, various, diverse, multiple, kaleidoscopic, abundant, copious.

manipulate v 1 HANDLE, control, wield, operate, use, manoeuvre, influence, engineer, guide, direct, steer, negotiate, work. 2 FALSIFY, rig, juggle with, doctor (*infml*), cook (*infml*), fiddle (*infml*).

mankind n humankind, humanity, human race, man, Homo sapiens, people.

manly adj masculine, male, virile, manful, macho (*infml*), robust.

man-made adj synthetic, manufactured, simulated, imitation, artificial.
🖪 natural.

manner n 1 WAY, method, means, fashion, style, procedure, process, form. 2 BEHAVIOUR, conduct, bearing, comportment (*fml*), demeanour, air, appearance, look, character.

mannerism n idiosyncrasy, peculiarity, characteristic, quirk, trait, feature, foible, habit.

manners n behaviour, conduct, comportment (*fml*), demeanour, etiquette, politeness, bearing, courtesy, formalities, social graces, p's and q's.

manoeuvre n move, movement, operation, action, exercise, plan, ploy, plot, ruse, stratagem, machination, gambit, tactic, trick, scheme, dodge (*infml*).
➤ v 1 MOVE, manipulate, handle, guide, pilot, steer, navigate, jockey, direct, drive, exercise. 2 CONTRIVE, engineer, plot, scheme, wangle (*infml*), pull strings (*infml*), manipulate, manage, plan, devise, negotiate.

mantle n cloak, cover, covering, cape,

hood, blanket, shawl, veil, wrap, shroud, screen.

manual *n* handbook, guide, A to Z, guidebook, instructions, Bible, vade mecum, directions.
➤ *adj* hand-operated, by hand, physical, human.

manufacture *v* 1 MAKE, produce, construct, build, fabricate, create, assemble, put together, mass-produce, turn out, process, forge, form. 2 INVENT, make up, concoct, fabricate, think up.
➤ *n* production, making, construction, fabrication, mass-production, assembly, creation, formation.

manufacturer *n* maker, producer, industrialist, constructor, factory-owner, builder, creator.

manure *n* fertilizer, compost, muck, dung.

many *adj* numerous, countless, lots of (*infml*), manifold (*fml*), various, varied, sundry, diverse, umpteen (*infml*).
🖪 few.

map *n* chart, plan, street plan, atlas, graph, plot.

mar *v* spoil, impair, harm, hurt, damage, deface, disfigure, mutilate, injure, maim, scar, detract from, mangle, ruin, wreck, tarnish.
🖪 enhance.

marauder *n* bandit, brigand, robber, raider, plunderer, pillager, pirate, buccaneer, outlaw, ravager, predator.

march *v* walk, stride, parade, pace, file, tread, stalk.
➤ *n* 1 STEP, pace, stride. 2 WALK, trek, hike, footslog (*infml*). 3 PROCESSION, parade, demonstration, demo (*infml*). 4 ADVANCE, development, progress, evolution, passage.

margin *n* 1 BORDER, edge, boundary, bound, periphery, perimeter, rim, brink, limit, confine, verge, side, skirt.
2 ALLOWANCE, play, leeway, latitude, scope, room, space, surplus, extra.

marginal *adj* borderline, peripheral, negligible, minimal, insignificant, minor, slight, doubtful, low, small.
🖪 central, core.

marine *adj* sea, maritime, naval, nautical, seafaring, sea-going, ocean-going, salt-water.

mariner *n* sailor, seaman, seafarer, deckhand, navigator, tar (*infml*), sea-dog (*infml*), salt (*infml*).

marital *adj* conjugal (*fml*), matrimonial, married, wedded, nuptial (*fml*), connubial (*fml*).

maritime *adj* marine, nautical, naval, seafaring, sea, seaside, oceanic, coastal.

mark *n* 1 SPOT, stain, blemish, blot, blotch, smudge, dent, impression, scar, scratch, bruise, line. 2 SYMBOL, sign, indication, emblem, brand, stamp, token, characteristic, feature, proof, evidence, badge. 3 TARGET, goal, aim, objective, purpose.
➤ *v* 1 STAIN, blemish, blot, smudge, dent, scar, scratch, bruise. 2 BRAND, label, stamp, characterize, identify, distinguish. 3 EVALUATE, assess, correct, grade. 4 HEED, listen, note, observe, regard, notice, take to heart.

marked *adj* 1 NOTICEABLE, obvious, conspicuous, evident, pronounced, distinct, decided, emphatic, considerable, remarkable, apparent, glaring. 2 SUSPECTED, watched, doomed.
🖪 1 unnoticeable, slight.

market *n* mart, marketplace, bazaar, fair, exchange, outlet.
➤ *v* sell, retail, deal in, hawk, peddle.
🖪 buy.

marketing

Terms used in marketing include: above-the-line advertising, account executive (AE), ACORN (A Classification of Residential Neighbourhoods), adopter, after-sales service, AIDA (attention, interest, desire, action), aided or prompted recall, area sampling, articles of ostentation, ASA (Advertising Standards Authority), attitude research, audience research, below-the-line advertising, blanket coverage, blind advertisement, BOGO(F)F (buy one get one (for) free), brand awareness, brand image, brand leader, brand loyalty, buyers' market, buying motives, call rate, campaign, cannibalism, canvass, captive audience, captive market, classified advertising, cluster sampling, cold call, commando salesman, commercial, comparative advertising, competitive market, concentrated marketing, concept testing, consumer panel, consumer research, consumer sovereignty, co-operative advertising, corner a market, corporate identity, corporate image, coverage, credibility gap, customer orientation, customer profile, DAGMAR (Defining Advertising Goals for Measured Advertising Results), dealer brand, demarketing, early adopter, elasticity of demand, face-to-face selling, family brand, family life cycle, field selling, filter question, flash pack, FMCGs (fast moving consumer goods), focus group survey, four p's (product, price, promotion and place), free gift/ sample, frequency, Gallup poll, gap analysis, generic, geographical concentration, Giffen good, gimmick, give-away, group discussion, growth-share matrix, cash cow, dog, star, problem children (or wildcats), halo effect, hard sell, harvesting strategy, heavy user, heterogeneous products, hierarchy of effects, hierarchy of needs, high-involvement products, high-pressure selling, hit rate, horizontal marketing, homogeneous products, house-to-house, impulse buying, incentive marketing, industrial advertising, inertia selling, institutional advertising, international marketing, island display, jingle, journey planning, key prospects, launch, leading question, loss leader, low-involvement products, low-pressure selling, loyalty card, macro marketing, mailshot, market demand, market leader, market orientation, market penetration, market potential, market profile, market research, market segmentation, market share, marketing audit, marketing board, marketing concept, marketing intelligence, marketing mix, matched sample, media buyer, media independent, media planner, media research, merchandising, micro marketing, missionary selling, mock-up, motivation research, multi-brand strategy, necessity good, Nielsen index, normal good, observation, opportunity to see, opinion leaders, outdoor advertising, own label, paired comparisons, party selling, perceptual map, perfect competition, personal selling, personality promotion, piggy-back promotion, predatory pricing, product differentiation/orientation/ positioning, promotion, psychographic measurement, pyramid selling, random sampling, recognition, reference group, response rate, retail audit, rolling launch, sales aid, sales campaign, sales drive, saturation point, shout, skimming pricing, slogan, social marketing, socio-economic groups, solus position, static market, subliminal advertising, tachistoscope, target audience, Target Group Index, telephone selling, test marketing, unaided recall, undifferentiated marketing, unprompted response, up-market, USP (unique selling proposition), vertical marketing, viral marketing, visualizer.

maroon *v* abandon, cast away, desert, put ashore, strand, leave, isolate.

marriage *n* **1** MATRIMONY, wedlock, wedding, nuptials (*fml*). **2** UNION, alliance, merger, coupling, amalgamation, link, association, confederation.

E3 1 divorce. **2** separation.

marrow *n* essence, heart, nub, kernel, core, soul, spirit, substance, matter, quick, stuff, gist.

marry v **1** WED, join in matrimony, tie the knot (*infml*), get hitched (*infml*), get spliced (*infml*), lead up the aisle (*infml*). **2** UNITE, ally, join, merge, match, link, knit.
E3 **1** divorce. **2** separate.

marsh n marshland, bog, swamp, fen, morass, quagmire, slough.

marshal v **1** ARRANGE, dispose, order, line up, align, array, rank, organize, assemble, gather, muster, group, collect, draw up, deploy. **2** GUIDE, lead, escort, conduct, usher.

marsupial

> *Marsupials include*: bandicoot, cuscus, kangaroo, rat kangaroo, tree kangaroo, wallaroo, koala, marsupial anteater, marsupial mouse, marsupial mole, marsupial rat, opossum, pademelon, phalanger, Tasmanian Devil, Tasmanian wolf, wallaby, rock wallaby, wombat.

martial adj warlike, military, belligerent, soldierly, militant, heroic, brave.

martial arts

> *Martial arts include*:
> *unarmed*: aikido, capoeira, judo, jujitsu, karate, kempo, kickboxing, kung fu, tae kwon do, t'ai chi, wushu; *weapons*: bandesh, bojutsu, jojutsu, kendo, kenjutsu, kumdo, kyodo.

marvel n wonder, miracle, phenomenon, prodigy, spectacle, sensation, genius.
➤ v wonder, gape, gaze, be amazed at.

marvellous adj **1** WONDERFUL, excellent, splendid, superb, magnificent, terrific (*infml*), super, fantastic (*infml*). **2** EXTRAORDINARY, amazing, astonishing, astounding, miraculous, remarkable, surprising, unbelievable, incredible, glorious.
E3 **1** terrible, awful. **2** ordinary, run-of-the-mill.

masculine adj **1** MALE, manlike, manly, mannish, virile, macho (*infml*), laddish (*infml*). **2** VIGOROUS, strong, strapping, robust, powerful, muscular, red-blooded, bold, brave, gallant, resolute, stout-hearted.
E3 **1** feminine.

mash v crush, pulp, beat, pound, pulverize, pummel, grind, smash.

mask n disguise, camouflage, façade, front, concealment, cover-up, cover, guise, pretence, semblance, cloak, veil, blind, show, veneer, visor.
➤ v disguise, camouflage, cover, conceal, cloak, veil, hide, obscure, screen, shield.
E3 expose, uncover.

masquerade n **1** MASQUE, masked ball, costume ball, fancy dress party. **2** DISGUISE, counterfeit, cover-up, cover, deception, front, pose, pretence, guise, cloak.
➤ v disguise, impersonate, pose, pass oneself off, mask, play, pretend, profess, dissimulate.

mass n **1** HEAP, pile, load, stack, collection, accumulation, aggregate, conglomeration, combination, entirety, whole, totality, sum, lot, group, batch, bunch. **2** QUANTITY, multitude, throng, troop, crowd, band, horde, mob. **3** MAJORITY, body, bulk. **4** SIZE, dimension, magnitude, immensity. **5** LUMP, piece, chunk, block, hunk.
➤ adj widespread, large-scale, extensive, comprehensive, general, indiscriminate, popular, across-the-board, sweeping, wholesale, blanket.
E3 limited, small-scale.
➤ v collect, gather, assemble, congregate, crowd, rally, cluster, muster, swarm, throng.
E3 separate.

massacre n slaughter, murder, extermination, carnage, butchery, holocaust, blood bath, annihilation, killing.
➤ v slaughter, butcher, murder, mow down, wipe out, exterminate, annihilate, kill, decimate.

massage n manipulation, kneading, rubbing, rub-down.

➤ v manipulate, knead, rub (down).

massive adj huge, immense, enormous, vast, colossal, gigantic, mega (*infml*), big, bulky, monumental, solid, substantial, heavy, large-scale, extensive, seismic (*infml*).
🖪 tiny, small.

master n 1 RULER, chief, governor, head, lord, captain, boss (*infml*), employer, commander, controller, director, manager, superintendent, overseer, principal, overlord, owner. 2 EXPERT, genius, virtuoso, past master, maestro, dab hand (*infml*), ace (*infml*), pro (*infml*). 3 TEACHER, tutor, instructor, schoolmaster, guide, guru, preceptor (*fml*).
🖪 1 servant, underling. 2 amateur. 3 learner, pupil.

➤ adj 1 CHIEF, principal, main, leading, foremost, prime, predominant, controlling, great, grand. 2 EXPERT, masterly, skilled, skilful, proficient.
🖪 1 subordinate. 2 inept.

➤ v 1 CONQUER, defeat, subdue, subjugate, vanquish, triumph over, overcome, quell, rule, control. 2 LEARN, grasp, acquire, get the hang of (*infml*), manage.

masterful adj 1 ARROGANT, authoritative, domineering, high-handed, overbearing, despotic, dictatorial, autocratic, bossy (*infml*), tyrannical, powerful. 2 EXPERT, masterly, skilful, skilled, dexterous, first-rate, professional.
🖪 1 humble. 2 inept, unskilful.

masterly adj expert, skilled, skilful, dexterous, adept, adroit, first-rate, ace (*infml*), excellent, superb, superior, supreme.
🖪 inept, clumsy.

masterpiece n masterwork, magnum opus, pièce de résistance, chef d'oeuvre, jewel.

mastery n 1 PROFICIENCY, skill, ability, command, expertise, virtuosity, knowledge, know-how, dexterity, familiarity, grasp. 2 CONTROL, command, domination, supremacy, upper hand, dominion, authority, charge.
🖪 1 incompetence. 2 subjugation.

match n 1 CONTEST, competition, bout, game, test, trial. 2 EQUAL, equivalent, peer, counterpart, fellow, mate, rival, copy, double, replica, lookalike, twin, duplicate. 3 MARRIAGE, alliance, union, partnership, affiliation.

➤ v 1 EQUAL, compare, measure up to, rival, compete, oppose, contend, vie, pit against. 2 FIT, go with, accord, agree, suit, correspond, harmonize, tally, co-ordinate, blend, adapt, go together, relate, tone with, accompany. 3 JOIN, marry, unite, mate, link, couple, combine, ally, pair, yoke, team.
🖪 2 clash. 3 separate.

matching adj corresponding, comparable, equivalent, like, identical, co-ordinating, similar, duplicate, same, twin.
🖪 clashing.

matchless adj unequalled, peerless, incomparable, unmatched, unrivalled, unparalleled, unsurpassed, inimitable, unique.

mate n 1 FRIEND, companion, comrade, pal (*infml*), chum (*infml*), colleague, partner, fellow-worker, co-worker, associate. 2 SPOUSE, husband, wife. 3 ASSISTANT, helper, subordinate. 4 MATCH, fellow, twin.

➤ v 1 COUPLE, pair, breed, copulate. 2 JOIN, match, marry, wed.

material n 1 STUFF, substance, body, matter. 2 FABRIC, textile, cloth. 3 INFORMATION, facts, data, evidence, constituents, work, notes.

➤ adj 1 PHYSICAL, concrete, tangible, substantial. 2 RELEVANT, significant, important, meaningful, pertinent, essential, vital, indispensable, serious.
🖪 1 abstract. 2 irrelevant.

materialize v appear, arise, take shape, turn up, happen, occur.
🖪 disappear.

mathematics

Mathematical terms include: acute angle, addition, algebra, algorithm, analysis, angle, apex, approximate, arc, area, argument, arithmetic, arithmetic progression, asymmetrical, average, axis, axis of symmetry, bar chart, bar graph, base, bearing, binary, binomial, breadth, calculus, capacity, cardinal number, Cartesian co-ordinates, chance, chaos, chord, circumference, coefficient, combination, commutative operation, complement, complementary angle, complex number, concave, concentric circles, congruent, conjugate angles, constant, continuous distribution, converse, convex, co-ordinate, correlation, cosine, covariance, cross section, cube, cube root, curve, decimal, degree, denominator, depth, derivative, determinant, diagonal, diameter, differentiation, directed number, distribution, dividend, division, divisor, edge, equal, equation, equidistant, even number, exponent, exponential, face, factor, factorial, Fibonacci sequence, formula, fraction, function, geometric progression, geometry, gradient, graph, greater than, group, harmonic progression, height, helix, histogram, horizontal, hyperbola, hypotenuse, identity, infinity, integer, integration, irrational number, latitude, length, less than, linear, line, locus, logarithm, longitude, magic square, matrix, maximum, mean, measure, median, minimum, minus, mirror image, mirror symmetry, Möbius strip, mode, modulus, multiple, multiplication, natural logarithm, natural number, negative number, number, numerator, oblique, obtuse angle, odd number, operation, ordinal number, origin, parabola, parallel lines, parallel planes, parameter, percentage, percentile, perimeter, permutation, perpendicular, pi, pie chart, place value, plane figure, plus, point, positive number, prime number, probability, product, proportion, protractor, Pythagoras's theorem, quadrant, quadratic equation, quadrilateral, quartile, quotient, radian, radius, random sample, ratio, rational number, real numbers, reciprocal, recurring decimal, reflection, reflex angle, regression, remainder, right-angle, right-angled triangle, root, rotation, rotational symmetry, sample, scalar segment, secant, sector, set, side, simultaneous equation, sine, speed, spiral, square, square root, standard deviation, straight line, subset, subtractor, supplementary angles, symmetry, tangent, three-dimensional, total, transcendental number, triangulation, trigonometry, unit, universal set, variable, variance, vector, velocity, Venn diagram, vertex, vertical, volume, whole number, width, zero. *see also* **shape**.

matrimonial *adj* marital, nuptial (*fml*), marriage, wedding, married, wedded, conjugal (*fml*).

matter *n* **1** SUBJECT, issue, topic, question, affair, business, concern, event, episode, incident. **2** IMPORTANCE, significance, consequence, note. **3** TROUBLE, problem, difficulty, worry. **4** SUBSTANCE, stuff, material, body, content.

➤ *v* count, be important, make a difference, mean something.

matter-of-fact *adj* unemotional, prosaic, emotionless, straightforward, sober, unimaginative, flat, deadpan (*infml*).

🔢 emotional.

mature *adj* **1** ADULT, senior, grown-up, grown, full-grown, fully grown, fully fledged, developed, complete, perfect, perfected, well-thought-out. **2** RIPE, ripened, seasoned, mellow, ready.

🔢 **1** childish. **2** immature.

➤ *v* grow up, come of age, develop, mellow, ripen, perfect, age, bloom, fall due.

maturity *n* **1** ADULTHOOD, majority, womanhood, manhood, wisdom, experience. **2** RIPENESS, readiness, mellowness, perfection.
Ea 1 childishness. **2** immaturity.

maul *v* abuse, ill-treat, manhandle, maltreat, molest, paw, beat (up), knock about, rough up, claw, lacerate, batter.

maxim *n* saying, proverb, adage, axiom, aphorism, epigram, motto, byword, precept, rule.

maximum *adj* greatest, highest, largest, biggest, most, utmost, supreme, optimum.
Ea minimum.
➤ *n* most, top (point), utmost, upper limit, peak, pinnacle, summit, height, ceiling, extremity, zenith (*fml*).
Ea mimimum.

maybe *adv* perhaps, possibly, perchance (*fml*).
Ea definitely.

maze *n* labyrinth, network, tangle, web, complex, confusion, puzzle, intricacy.

meadow *n* field, grassland, pasture, lea.

meagre *adj* **1** SCANTY, sparse, inadequate, deficient, skimpy, paltry, negligible, poor. **2** THIN, puny, insubstantial, bony, emaciated, scrawny, slight.
Ea 1 ample. **2** fat.

meal

Meals include: breakfast, wedding breakfast, elevenses (*infml*), brunch, lunch, luncheon, tea, tea break, tea party, tiffin, afternoon tea, cream tea, high tea, evening meal, dinner, TV dinner, supper, harvest supper, fork supper, banquet, feast, blow-out (*sl*), barbecue, barbie (*infml*), buffet, cold table, spread, picnic, snack, takeaway.
---

mean[1] *adj* **1** MISERLY, niggardly, parsimonious, selfish, tight (*infml*), tight-fisted, stingy (*infml*), penny-pinching (*infml*). **2** UNKIND, unpleasant, nasty, bad-tempered, cruel, spiteful,

malicious. **3** LOWLY, base, poor, humble, wretched.
Ea 1 generous. **2** kind. **3** splendid.

mean[2] *v* **1** SIGNIFY, represent, denote, stand for, symbolize, suggest, indicate, imply. **2** INTEND, aim, propose, design. **3** CAUSE, give rise to, involve, entail.

mean[3] *adj* average, intermediate, middle, halfway, median, normal.
Ea extreme.
➤ *n* average, middle, mid-point, norm, median, compromise, middle course, middle way, happy medium, golden mean.
Ea extreme.

meander *v* **1** WIND, zigzag, turn, twist, snake, curve. **2** WANDER, stray, amble, ramble, stroll.

meaning *n* **1** SIGNIFICANCE, sense, import, implication, gist, trend, explanation, interpretation. **2** AIM, intention, purpose, object, idea. **3** VALUE, worth, point.

meaningful *adj* **1** IMPORTANT, significant, relevant, valid, useful, worthwhile, material, purposeful, serious. **2** EXPRESSIVE, speaking, suggestive, warning, pointed.
Ea 1 unimportant, worthless.

meaningless *adj* **1** SENSELESS, pointless, purposeless, useless, insignificant, aimless, futile, insubstantial, trifling, trivial. **2** EMPTY, hollow, vacuous, vain, worthless, nonsensical, absurd.
Ea 1 important, meaningful.
2 worthwhile.

means *n* **1** METHOD, mode, way, medium, course, agency, process, instrument, channel, vehicle.
2 RESOURCES, funds, money, income, wealth, riches, substance, wherewithal, fortune, affluence.

measure *n* **1** PORTION, ration, share, allocation, quota. **2** SIZE, quantity, magnitude, amount, degree, extent, range, scope, proportion. **3** RULE, gauge, scale, standard, criterion, norm, touchstone, yardstick, test, meter.

4 STEP, course, action, deed, procedure, method, act, bill, statute.

➤ *v* quantify, evaluate, assess, weigh, value, gauge, judge, sound, fathom, determine, calculate, estimate, plumb, survey, compute, measure out, measure off.

> *Measuring instruments include*: altimeter, ammeter, anemometer, audiometer, balance, barometer, bathometer, Breathalyser®, burette, callipers, calorimeter, chronometer, clinometer, colorimeter, cyclometer, densitometer, galvanometer, Geiger counter, gravimeter, hourglass, hydrometer, hygrometer, hypsometer, manometer, measuring cylinder, meter, micrometer, multimeter, octant, optometer, pedometer, photometer, pipette, planimeter, plumb line, protractor, psychrometer, pyranometer, pyrometer, quadrant, radiosonde, rheometer, rule, saccharometer, salinometer, seismograph, sextant, speedometer, spherometer, sphygmomanometer, steelyard, stopwatch, tachometer, tachymeter, tape measure, tensiometer, theodolite, thermometer, vinometer, voltmeter, weightbridge, Wheatstone bridge. *see also* **gauge**.

◇ **measure up to** equal, meet, match, compare with, touch, rival, make the grade.

measured *adj* deliberate, planned, reasoned, slow, unhurried, steady, studied, well-thought-out, calculated, careful, considered, precise.

measurement *n* **1** DIMENSION, size, extent, amount, magnitude, area, capacity, height, depth, length, width, weight, volume. **2** ASSESSMENT, evaluation, estimation, computation, calculation, calibration, gauging, judgement, appraisal, appreciation, survey.

> *SI (Système International d'Unités) base units include*: ampere, candela, kelvin, kilogram, metre, mole, second; *SI derivatives and other measurements include*: acre, angstrom, atmosphere, bar, barrel, becquerel, bushel, cable, calorie, centimetre, century, chain, coulomb, cubic centimetre, cubic foot, cubic inch, cubic metre, cubic yard, day, decade, decibel, degree, dyne, erg, farad, fathom, fluid ounce, fresnel, foot, foot-pound, furlong, gallon, gill, gram, hand, hectare, hertz, horsepower, hour, hundredweight, inch, joule, kilolitre, kilometre, knot, league, litre, lumen, micrometre, mile, millennium, millibar, millilitre, minute, month, nautical mile, newton, ohm, ounce, pascal, peak, pint, pound, pound per square inch, radian, rod, siemens, span, square centimetre, square foot, square inch, square kilometre, square metre, square mile, square yard, steradian, stone, therm, ton, tonne, volt, watt, week, yard, year.

meat *n* **1** FLESH. **2** (*infml*) FOOD, rations, provisions, nourishment, sustenance, subsistence, eats (*infml*).

> *Kinds of meat include*: beef, pork, lamb, mutton, ham, bacon, gammon, chicken, turkey, goose, duck, rabbit, hare, venison, pheasant, grouse, partridge, pigeon, quail; offal, liver, heart, tongue, kidney, brains, brawn, pig's knuckle, trotters, oxtail, sweetbread, tripe; steak, minced beef, sausage, rissole, faggot, beefburger, hamburger, black pudding, pâté.

> *Cuts of meat include*: shoulder, collar, hand, loin, hock, leg, chop, shin, knuckle, rib, spare-rib, breast, brisket, chine, cutlet, fillet, rump, scrag, silverside, topside, sirloin, flank, escalope, neck, saddle.

mechanical *adj* automatic, involuntary, instinctive, routine, habitual, impersonal, emotionless, cold, matter-of-fact, unfeeling, lifeless, dead, dull.

◨ conscious.

mechanism *n* **1** MACHINE, machinery, engine, appliance, instrument, tool, motor, works, workings, gadget, device, apparatus, contrivance, gears, components. **2** MEANS, method, agency, process, procedure, system, technique, medium, structure, operation, functioning, performance.

meddle *v* interfere, intervene, pry, snoop (*infml*), intrude, butt in, tamper.

meddlesome *adj* interfering, meddling, prying, snooping (*infml*), intrusive, intruding, mischievous.

mediate *v* arbitrate, conciliate, intervene, referee, umpire, intercede, moderate, reconcile, negotiate, resolve, settle, step in.

mediator *n* arbitrator, referee, umpire, intermediary, negotiator, go-between, interceder, judge, moderator, intercessor, conciliator, peacemaker, Ombudsman.

medical

Medical and surgical equipment includes: aspirator, audiometer, aural spectrum, auriscope, autoclave, body scanner, bronchoscope, cannula, catheter, CAT scanner, clamp, curette, defibrillator, disposable enema pack, ear syringe, ECG (electrocardiograph), electroencephalograph, endoscope, first aid kit, forceps, haemodialysis unit, hypodermic needle, hypodermic syringe, incubator, inhaler, instrument table, iron lung, isolator tent, kidney dish, laparoscope, laryngoscope, microscope, nebulizer, obstetrical forceps, oesophagoscope, operating table, ophthalmoscope, oxygen cylinder, oxygen mask, rectoscope, respirator, resuscitator, retractor, rhinoscope, scales, scalpel, sliding-weight scales, specimen glass, speculum, sphygmomanometer, sterile donor-pack, sterilizer, stethoscope, stomach pump, surgical

mask, surgical suture materials, swabs, syringe, thermometer, tracheostomy tube, traction apparatus, tweezers, ultrasound scanner, urethroscope, vaginal speculum, X-ray unit.

Medical specialists include: anaesthetist, bacteriologist, cardiologist, chiropodist, chiropractor, dentist, dermatologist, dietician, doctor, embryologist, endocrinologist, forensic pathologist, gastroenterologist, geriatrician, gerontologist, gynaecologist, haematologist, homeopath, immunologist, microbiologist, neurologist, obstetrician, oncologist, ophthalmologist, optician (or optometrist), orthodontist, orthopaedist, orthoptist, paediatrician, pathologist, pharmacist, pharmacologist, physiotherapist, psychiatrist, psychologist, rheumatologist, toxicologist, vaccinologist. *see also* **doctor**; **nurse**; **surgeon**.

Medical terms include: abortion, allergy, amniocentesis, amputation, analgesic, antibiotics, antiseptic, assisted conception, bandage, barium meal, biopsy, blood bank, blood count, blood donor, blood group, blood pressure, blood test, caesarean, cardiopulmonary resuscitation (CPR), case history, casualty, cauterization, cervical smear, check-up, childbirth, circulation, circumcision, clinic, complication, compress, consultant, consultation, contraception, convulsion, cure, diagnosis, dialysis, dislocate, dissection, doctor, donor, dressings, enema, examination, gene, genetic counselling, health screening, home visit, hormone replacement therapy (HRT), hospice, hospital, immunization, implantation, incubation, infection, inflammation, injection, injury, inoculation, intensive care, in-vitro fertilization (IVF), keyhole surgery, labour, laser treatment, microsurgery, miscarriage, mouth-to-mouth, nurse, ointment, operation, paraplegia, post-mortem, pregnancy, prescription, prognosis, prosthesis, psychosomatic, quarantine, radiotherapy, recovery, rehabilitation, relapse, remission, respiration, resuscitation, scan, side effect, sling, smear test, specimen, splint, sterilization, steroid, surgery, suture, symptom, syndrome, therapy, tourniquet, tranquillizer, transfusion, transplant, trauma, treatment, tumour, ultrasound scanning, vaccination, vaccine, virus, X-ray.

medicinal *adj* therapeutic, healing, remedial, curative, restorative, medical.

medicine *n* medication, drug, cure, remedy, medicament, prescription, pharmaceutical, panacea.

Types of medicine include: tablet, capsule, pill, painkiller, lozenge, pastille, gargle, linctus, tonic, laxative, suppository, antacid, ointment, arnica, eye drops, ear drops, nasal spray, inhaler, Ventolin, antibiotic, penicillin, emetic, gripe water, paregoric. *see also* **drug**.

Forms of alternative medicine include: acupressure, acupuncture, aromatherapy, Ayurveda, Chinese medicine, chiropractic, craniosacral therapy, herbal medicine, homeopathy, hypnotherapy, iridology, naturopathy, osteopathy, reflexology, reiki, rolfing, shiatsu.

mediocre *adj* ordinary, average, middling, medium, indifferent, unexceptional, undistinguished, so-so (*infml*), run-of-the-mill, bog-standard (*infml*), commonplace, insignificant, second-rate, inferior, uninspired.
Ex exceptional, extraordinary, distinctive.

mediocrity *n* **1** ORDINARINESS, unimportance, insignificance, poorness,

inferiority, indifference. **2** NONENTITY, nobody, cipher.

meditate *v* **1** REFLECT, ponder, ruminate, contemplate, muse, brood, think. **2** THINK OVER, consider, deliberate, mull over, study, speculate, scheme, plan, devise, intend.

medium *adj* average, middle, median, mean, medial, intermediate, middling, midway, standard, fair.
➤ *n* **1** AVERAGE, middle, mid-point, middle ground, compromise, centre, happy medium, golden mean. **2** MEANS, agency, channel, vehicle, instrument, way, mode, form, avenue, organ. **3** PSYCHIC, spiritualist, spiritist, clairvoyant.

medley *n* assortment, mixture, miscellany, potpourri, hotchpotch, hodge-podge, collection, jumble.

meek *adj* modest, long-suffering, forbearing, humble, docile, patient, unassuming, unpretentious, resigned, gentle, peaceful, tame, timid, submissive, spiritless.
Ex arrogant, assertive, rebellious.

meet *v* **1** ENCOUNTER, come across, run across, run into, chance on, bump into (*infml*). **2** EXPERIENCE, encounter, face, go through, undergo, endure. **3** GATHER, collect, assemble, congregate, convene, come together. **4** FULFIL, satisfy, match, answer, measure up to, equal, discharge, perform. **5** JOIN, converge, come together, connect, cross, intersect, touch, abut, unite.
Ex **3** scatter. **5** diverge.

meeting *n* **1** ENCOUNTER, confrontation, rendezvous, date, engagement, assignation, introduction, tryst (*fml*). **2** ASSEMBLY, gathering, convention, forum, conclave, session. **3** CONVERGENCE, confluence, junction, intersection, union.

Types of meeting include: assembly, assignation, audience, audition, board, briefing, cabinet, committee, conference, congregation, congress, consultation, convention, council, debate, get-together (*infml*), interview, party, rally, rendezvous, reunion, seminar, service, social, soirée, symposium. *see also* **committee**.

melancholy *adj* depressed, dejected, downcast, down, downhearted, gloomy, low, low-spirited, heavy-hearted, sad, unhappy, despondent, dispirited, miserable, mournful, dismal, sorrowful, moody.
◾ cheerful, elated, joyful.
➤ *n* depression, dejection, gloom, despondency, low spirits, blues (*infml*), sadness, unhappiness, sorrow.
◾ elation, joy.

mellow *adj* **1** MATURE, ripe, juicy, full-flavoured, sweet, tender, mild. **2** GENIAL, cordial, affable, pleasant, relaxed, placid, serene, tranquil, cheerful, happy, jolly. **3** SMOOTH, melodious, rich, rounded, soft.
◾ **1** unripe. **2** cold. **3** harsh.
➤ *v* mature, ripen, improve, sweeten, soften, temper, season, perfect.

melodious *adj* tuneful, musical, melodic, harmonious, dulcet, sweet-sounding, euphonious (*fml*), silvery.
◾ discordant, grating, harsh.

melodramatic *adj* histrionic, theatrical, overdramatic, exaggerated, overdone, over-the-top, OTT (*infml*), overemotional, sensational, hammy (*infml*).

melody *n* tune, music, song, refrain, harmony, theme, air, strain.

melt *v* liquefy, dissolve, thaw, fuse, deliquesce (*fml*).
◾ freeze, solidify.
◇ **melt away** disappear, vanish, fade, evaporate, dissolve, disperse.

member *n* adherent, associate, subscriber, representative, comrade, fellow.

memento *n* souvenir, keepsake, remembrance, reminder, token, memorial, record, relic.

memoirs *n* reminiscences, recollections, autobiography, life story, diary, chronicles, annals, journals, records, confessions, experiences.

memorable *adj* unforgettable, remarkable, significant, impressive, notable, noteworthy, extraordinary, important, outstanding, momentous.
◾ forgettable, trivial, unimportant.

memorial *n* remembrance, monument, souvenir, memento, record, stone, plaque, mausoleum.
➤ *adj* commemorative, celebratory.

memorize *v* learn, learn by heart, commit to memory, remember.
◾ forget.

memory *n* recall, retention, recollection, remembrance, reminiscence, commemoration.
◾ forgetfulness.

menace *v* threaten, frighten, alarm, intimidate, terrorize, loom.
➤ *n* **1** INTIMIDATION, threat, terrorism, warning. **2** DANGER, peril, hazard, jeopardy, risk. **3** NUISANCE, annoyance, pest.

mend *v* **1** REPAIR, renovate, restore, refit, fix, patch, cobble, darn, heal.
2 RECOVER, get better, improve.
3 REMEDY, correct, rectify, reform, revise.
◾ **1** break. **2** deteriorate. **3** destroy.

menial *adj* low, lowly, humble, base, dull, humdrum, routine, degrading, demeaning, ignominious, unskilled, subservient, servile, slavish.
➤ *n* servant, domestic, labourer, minion, attendant, drudge, slave, underling, skivvy (*infml*), dogsbody (*infml*).

mental *adj* **1** INTELLECTUAL, abstract, conceptual, cognitive, cerebral, theoretical, rational. **2** (*infml*) MAD, insane, lunatic, crazy, unbalanced, deranged, psychotic, disturbed, loony (*infml*), flaky (*US infml*).
◾ **1** physical. **2** sane.

mentality *n* **1** INTELLECT, brains, understanding, faculty, rationality.
2 FRAME OF MIND, character, disposition, personality, psychology, outlook.

mention v refer to, speak of, allude to, touch on, name, cite, acknowledge, bring up, report, make known, impart, declare, communicate, broach, divulge, disclose, intimate, point out, reveal, state, hint at, quote.
➤ n reference, allusion, citation, observation, recognition, remark, acknowledgement, announcement, notification, tribute, indication.

mercenary adj 1 GREEDY, avaricious, covetous, grasping, acquisitive, materialistic. 2 HIRED, paid, venal.

merchandise n goods, commodities, stock, produce, products, wares, cargo, freight, shipment.

merchant n trader, dealer, broker, trafficker, wholesaler, retailer, seller, shopkeeper, vendor.

merciful adj compassionate, forgiving, forbearing, humane, lenient, sparing, tender-hearted, pitying, gracious, humanitarian, kind, liberal, sympathetic, generous, mild.
🔁 hard-hearted, merciless.

merciless adj pitiless, relentless, unmerciful, ruthless, hard-hearted, hard, heartless, implacable, inhumane, unforgiving, remorseless, unpitying, unsparing, severe, cruel, callous, inhuman.
🔁 compassionate, merciful.

mercy n 1 COMPASSION, clemency, forgiveness, forbearance, leniency, pity, humanitarianism, kindness, grace. 2 BLESSING, godsend, good luck, relief.
🔁 1 cruelty, harshness.

mere adj sheer, plain, simple, bare, utter, pure, absolute, complete, stark, unadulterated, common, paltry, petty.

merge v join, unite, combine, converge, amalgamate, blend, coalesce, mix, intermix, mingle, melt into, fuse, meet, meld, incorporate, consolidate.

merger n amalgamation, union, fusion, combination, coalition, consolidation, confederation, incorporation.

merit n worth, worthiness, excellence, value, quality, good, goodness, virtue, asset, credit, benefit, advantage, strong point, talent, justification, due, claim.
🔁 fault.
➤ v deserve, be worthy of, earn, justify, warrant.

merriment n fun, jollity, mirth, hilarity, laughter, conviviality, festivity, amusement, revelry, frolic, liveliness, joviality.
🔁 gloom, seriousness.

merry adj jolly, light-hearted, mirthful, joyful, happy, convivial, festive, cheerful, glad.
🔁 gloomy, melancholy, sober.

mesh n meshwork, net, network, netting, lattice, web, tangle, entanglement, snare, trap.
➤ v engage, interlock, dovetail, fit, connect, harmonize, co-ordinate, combine, come together.

mess n 1 CHAOS, untidiness, disorder, disarray, confusion, muddle, jumble, clutter, disorganization, mix-up, shambles (infml). 2 DIFFICULTY, trouble, predicament, fix (infml).
🔁 1 order, tidiness.
◇ **mess about** mess around, fool around, play, play around, play about, muck about (infml), interfere, tamper, trifle.
◇ **mess up 1** DISARRANGE, jumble, muddle, tangle, dishevel, disrupt. 2 BOTCH, bungle, spoil, muck up (infml), screw up (sl).

message n 1 COMMUNICATION, bulletin, dispatch, communiqué, report, missive (fml), errand, letter, memo, memorandum, note, notice. 2 MEANING, idea, point, theme, moral.

messenger n courier, emissary (fml), envoy, go-between, herald, runner, carrier, bearer, harbinger, agent, ambassador.

messy adj untidy, unkempt, dishevelled, disorganized, chaotic, sloppy, slovenly, confused, dirty, grubby, muddled, cluttered.
🔁 neat, ordered, tidy.

metamorphosis *n* change, alteration, transformation, rebirth, regeneration, transfiguration, conversion, modification, changeover.

metaphor *n* figure of speech, allegory, analogy, symbol, picture, image.

metaphorical *adj* figurative, allegorical, symbolic.

mete out allot, apportion, deal out, dole out, hand out, measure out, share out, ration out, portion, distribute, dispense, divide out, assign, administer.

meteoric *adj* rapid, speedy, swift, sudden, overnight, instantaneous, momentary, brief, spectacular, brilliant, dazzling.

method *n* **1** WAY, approach, means, course, manner, mode, fashion, process, procedure, route, technique, style, plan, scheme, programme. **2** ORGANIZATION, order, structure, system, pattern, form, planning, regularity, routine.

methodical *adj* systematic, structured, organized, ordered, orderly, tidy, regular, planned, efficient, disciplined, businesslike, deliberate, neat, scrupulous, precise, meticulous, painstaking.
F∃ chaotic, irregular, confused.

meticulous *adj* precise, scrupulous, exact, punctilious, fussy, detailed, accurate, thorough, fastidious, painstaking, strict.
F∃ careless, slapdash.

metropolis *n* capital, municipality, city, megalopolis, cosmopolis.

mettle *n* **1** CHARACTER, temperament, disposition. **2** SPIRIT, courage, vigour, nerve (*infml*), boldness, daring, indomitability, pluck, resolve, valour, bravery, fortitude.

microbe *n* micro-organism, bacterium, bacillus, germ, virus, pathogen, bug (*infml*).

microscopic *adj* minute, tiny, minuscule, infinitesimal, indiscernible, imperceptible, negligible.
F∃ huge, enormous.

middle *adj* central, halfway, mean, median, intermediate, inner, inside, intervening.
➤ *n* centre, halfway point, mid-point, mean, heart, core, midst, inside, bull's eye.
F∃ extreme, end, edge, beginning, border.

middling *adj* mediocre, medium, ordinary, moderate, average, unexceptional, unremarkable, run-of-the-mill, indifferent, modest, passable, tolerable, so-so (*infml*), OK (*infml*).

midget *n* person of restricted growth, pygmy, dwarf, Tom Thumb, gnome.
F∃ giant.
➤ *adj* tiny, small, miniature, little, pocket, pocket-sized, pint-sized (*infml*).
F∃ giant.

midst *n* middle, centre, mid-point, heart, hub, interior.

migrant *n* traveller, wanderer, itinerant, emigrant, immigrant, rover, nomad, globe-trotter, drifter, gypsy, tinker, vagrant.

migrate *v* move, resettle, relocate, wander, roam, rove, journey, emigrate, travel, voyage, trek, drift.

mild *adj* **1** *mild manners*: gentle, calm, peaceable, placid, tender, soft, good-natured, kind, amiable, lenient, compassionate. **2** *mild weather*: calm, temperate, warm, balmy, clement, fair, pleasant. **3** *mild coffee*: bland, mellow, smooth, subtle, soothing.
F∃ 1 harsh, fierce. **2** stormy. **3** strong.

militant *adj* aggressive, belligerent, vigorous, fighting, warring.
F∃ pacifist, peaceful.
➤ *n* activist, combatant, fighter, struggler, warrior, aggressor, belligerent.

military *adj* martial, armed, soldierly, warlike, service.

Military terms include: about turn, absent without leave (AWOL), action, action stations, adjutant, aide-de-camp (ADC), air cover, air-drop,

Airborne Warning and Control System (AWACS), allies, ambush, arm, armed forces, armistice, army, arsenal, artillery, assault course, atomic warfare, attack, attention, barracks, base, battalion, battery, battle, battle fatigue, beachhead, billet, bivouac, blockade, bomb, bombardment, brevet, bridgehead, briefing, brigade, bugle call, call up, camoflage, camp, campaign, canteen, carpet bombing, ceasefire, charge, citation, collateral damage, colours, combat, command, commission, company, conquest, conscript, conscription, corps, counter-attack, court-martial, crossfire, debriefing, decamp, decoration, defeat, defence, demilitarize, demob (*infml*), demotion, depot, desertion, detachment, detail, disarmament, discharge, dispatches, division, draft, drill, duty, encampment, enemy, enlist, ensign, epaulette, evacuation, excursion, expedition, fallout, fatigues, firing line, first post, flank, fleet, flight, flotilla, foe, foray, forced march, friendly fire, front line, fusillade, garrison, guard, incursion, infantry, insignia, inspection, installation, insubordination, intelligence, invasion, kit bag, landing, last post, latrine, leave, left wheel, liaison, lines, logistics, manoeuvres, march, marching orders, march past, married quarters, martinet, minefield, mission, mobilize, munitions, muster, mutiny, national service, navy, Navy, Army and Air Force Institutes (NAAFI), observation post, offensive, operational command, operational fleet, operations, orders, ordnance, outpost, padre, parade, parade ground, parley, parole, patrol, pincer movement, platoon, posting, prisoner of war (POW), quartermaster, quarters, quick march, radar, range, rank, ration, rearguard, recce (*infml*), recruit, regiment, reinforcements, requisition, retreat, reveille, rifle range, roll call, rout, route march, salute,

sentry, shell, shell-shock, signal, skirmish, slow march, sniper, sortie, squad, squadron, square-bashing (*sl*), standard, stores, strategy, supplies, surrender, tactics, tank, target, taskforce, tattoo, the front, training, trench, troop, truce, unit, vanguard, victory, wing. *see also* **army**; **rank**; **sailor**; **soldier**.

➤ *n* army, armed forces, soldiers, forces, services.

militate against oppose, counter, counteract, count against, tell against, weigh against, contend, resist.

milk *v* drain, bleed, tap, extract, draw off, exploit, use, express, press, pump, siphon, squeeze, wring.

milky *adj* white, milk-white, chalky, opaque, clouded, cloudy.

mill *n* 1 FACTORY, plant, works, workshop, foundry. 2 GRINDER, crusher, quern, roller.
➤ *v* grind, pulverize, powder, pound, crush, roll, press, grate.

mime *n* dumb show, pantomime, charade, gesture, mimicry.
➤ *v* gesture, signal, act out, represent, simulate, impersonate, mimic.

mimic *v* imitate, parody, caricature, take off (*infml*), send up (*infml*), ape, parrot, impersonate, echo, mirror, simulate, look like.
➤ *n* imitator, impersonator, impressionist, caricaturist, copy-cat (*infml*), copy.

mimicry *n* imitation, imitating, impersonation, copying, parody, impression, caricature, take-off (*infml*), burlesque.

mince *v* 1 CHOP, cut, hash, dice, grind, crumble. 2 DIMINISH, suppress, play down, tone down, hold back, moderate, weaken, soften, spare.

mind *n* 1 INTELLIGENCE, intellect, brains, reason, sense, understanding, wits, mentality, thinking, thoughts, grey matter (*infml*), head, genius, concentration, attention, spirit, psyche.

2 MEMORY, remembrance, recollection.
3 OPINION, view, point of view, belief,
attitude, mindset, judgement, feeling,
sentiment. **4** INCLINATION, disposition,
tendency, will, wish, intention, desire.
➤ *v* **1** CARE, object, take offence, resent,
disapprove, dislike. **2** REGARD, heed, pay
attention, pay heed to, note, obey, listen
to, comply with, follow, observe, be
careful, watch. **3** LOOK AFTER, take care
of, watch over, guard, have charge of,
keep an eye on (*infml*).
◊ **bear in mind** consider, remember,
note.
◊ **make up one's mind** decide,
choose, determine, settle, resolve.

mindful *adj* aware, conscious, alive
(to), alert, attentive, careful, watchful,
wary.
🔁 heedless, inattentive.

mindless *adj* **1** THOUGHTLESS,
senseless, illogical, irrational, stupid,
foolish, gratuitous, negligent.
2 MECHANICAL, automatic, tedious.
🔁 **1** thoughtful, intelligent.

mine *n* **1** PIT, colliery, coalfield,
excavation, vein, seam, shaft, trench,
deposit. **2** SUPPLY, source, stock,
store, reserve, fund, hoard, treasury,
wealth.

Parts of a coalmine include: air lock;
bord-and-pillar, long-wall, long-wall
face, retreat long-wall; bunker, cage,
cage-winding system, capping,
charging conveyor, coal seam, coal-
bearing rock; coal-cutter, jib coal-
cutter, plough coal-cutter, scraper
chain, pan, shearer loader; fan drift,
fault line, gallery, goaf/gob/waste,
overburden; pit prop, hydraulic pit
prop, powered support; pithead
frame, pithead gear; shaft, main shaft,
staple shaft, lateral; skip winding
system, spoil, sump/sink, tunnelling
machine, ventilation shaft, winding
engine.

➤ *v* excavate, dig for, dig up, delve,
quarry, extract, unearth, tunnel, remove,
undermine.

mineral

Minerals include: alabaster, albite,
anhydrite, asbestos, aventurine,
azurite, bentonite, blacklead,
bloodstone, blue john, borax,
cairngorm, calamine, calcite, calcspar,
cassiterite, chalcedony, chlorite,
chrysoberyl, cinnabar, corundum,
dolomite, emery, feldspar, fluorite,
fluorspar, fool's gold, French chalk,
galena, graphite, gypsum, haematite,
halite, haüyne, hornblende, hyacinth,
idocrase, jacinth, jargoon, jet, kandite,
kaolinite, lapis lazuli, lazurite,
magnetite, malachite, meerschaum,
mica, microcline, montmorillonite,
orthoclase, plumbago, pyrites, quartz,
rock salt, rutile, saltpetre, sanidine,
silica, smithsonite, sodalite, spar,
sphalerite, spinel, talc, uralite, uranite,
vesuvianite, wurtzite, zircon.

---

mingle *v* **1** MIX, intermingle, intermix,
combine, blend, merge, unite, alloy,
coalesce, join, compound. **2** ASSOCIATE,
socialize, circulate, hobnob (*infml*), rub
shoulders (*infml*), schmooze.

miniature *adj* tiny, small, scaled-
down, minute, diminutive, baby, pocket-
sized, pint-sized (*infml*), little, mini
(*infml*).
🔁 giant.

minimal *adj* least, smallest, minimum,
slightest, littlest, negligible, minute,
token.

minimize *v* **1** REDUCE, decrease,
diminish. **2** BELITTLE, make light of, make
little of, disparage, deprecate, discount,
play down, underestimate, underrate.
🔁 **1** maximize.

minimum *n* least, lowest point,
slightest, bottom.
🔁 maximum.
➤ *adj* minimal, least, lowest, slightest,
smallest, littlest, tiniest.
🔁 maximum.

minion *n* **1** ATTENDANT, follower,
underling, lackey, hireling. **2** DEPENDANT,
hanger-on, favourite, darling,

sycophant, toady, yes-man (*infml*), bootlicker (*infml*).

minister *n* **1** OFFICIAL, office-holder, politician, dignitary, diplomat, ambassador, delegate, envoy, consul, cabinet minister, agent, aide, administrator, executive. **2** MEMBER OF THE CLERGY, clergyman, clergywoman, churchman, churchwoman, cleric, parson, priest, pastor, vicar, preacher, ecclesiastic (*fml*), divine.
➤ *v* attend, serve, tend, take care of, wait on, cater to, accommodate, nurse.

ministry *n* **1** GOVERNMENT, cabinet, department, office, bureau, administration. **2** THE CHURCH, holy orders, the priesthood.

minor *adj* lesser, secondary, smaller, inferior, subordinate, subsidiary, junior, younger, insignificant, inconsiderable, negligible, petty, trivial, trifling, second-class, unclassified, slight, light.
F∃ major, significant, important.

mint *v* coin, stamp, strike, cast, forge, punch, make, manufacture, produce, construct, devise, fashion, invent, make up.
➤ *adj* perfect, brand-new, fresh, immaculate, unblemished, excellent, first-class.

minute[1] *n* moment, mo (*infml*), second, instant, flash, jiffy (*infml*), tick (*infml*).

minute[2] *adj* **1** TINY, infinitesimal, minuscule, microscopic, miniature, inconsiderable, negligible, small. **2** DETAILED, precise, meticulous, painstaking, close, critical, exhaustive.
F∃ 1 gigantic, huge. **2** cursory, superficial.

minutes *n* proceedings, record(s), notes, memorandum, transcript, transactions, details, tapes.

miracle *n* wonder, marvel, prodigy, phenomenon.

miraculous *adj* wonderful, marvellous, phenomenal, extraordinary, amazing, astounding, astonishing, unbelievable, supernatural, incredible, inexplicable, unaccountable, superhuman.
F∃ natural, normal.

mirage *n* illusion, optical illusion, trick of the light, hallucination, fantasy, phantasm.

mirror *n* **1** GLASS, looking-glass, reflector. **2** REFLECTION, likeness, image, double, copy.
➤ *v* reflect, echo, imitate, copy, represent, show, depict, mimic.

mirth *n* merriment, hilarity, gaiety, fun, laughter, jollity, jocularity, amusement, revelry, glee, cheerfulness.
F∃ gloom, melancholy.

misapprehension *n* misunderstanding, misconception, misinterpretation, misreading, error, mistake, fallacy, delusion.

misappropriate *v* steal, embezzle, peculate, pocket, swindle (*infml*), diddle (*infml*), misspend, misuse, misapply, abuse, pervert.

misbehave *v* offend, transgress, trespass, get up to mischief, mess about, muck about (*infml*), play up, act up (*infml*).

misbehaviour *n* misconduct, misdemeanour, impropriety, disobedience, naughtiness, insubordination.

miscalculate *v* misjudge, get wrong, slip up, blunder, boob (*infml*), miscount, overestimate, underestimate.

miscarriage *n* failure, breakdown, abortion, mishap, mismanagement, error, disappointment.
F∃ success.

miscarry *v* fail, abort, come to nothing, fall through, misfire, founder, come to grief.
F∃ succeed.

miscellaneous *adj* mixed, varied, various, assorted, diverse, diversified, sundry, motley, jumbled, indiscriminate.

miscellany *n* mixture, variety, assortment, collection, anthology, medley, mixed bag, potpourri, hotch-potch, jumble, diversity.

mischief *n* **1** TROUBLE, harm, evil, damage, injury, disruption. **2** MISBEHAVIOUR, naughtiness, impishness, pranks.

mischievous *adj* **1** MALICIOUS, evil, spiteful, vicious, wicked, pernicious, destructive, injurious. **2** NAUGHTY, impish, rascally, roguish, playful, ludic (*fml*), teasing.
🔁 **1** kind. **2** well-behaved, good.

misconception *n* misapprehension, misunderstanding, misreading, error, mistake, fallacy, delusion, the wrong end of the stick (*infml*).

misconduct *n* misbehaviour, impropriety, misdemeanour, malpractice, mismanagement, wrong-doing.

miser *n* niggard, skinflint, penny-pincher (*infml*), Scrooge.
🔁 spendthrift.

miserable *adj* **1** UNHAPPY, sad, dejected, despondent, downcast, heartbroken, wretched, distressed, crushed. **2** CHEERLESS, depressing, dreary, impoverished, shabby, gloomy, dismal, forlorn, joyless, squalid. **3** CONTEMPTIBLE, despicable, ignominious, detestable, disgraceful, deplorable, shameful. **4** MEAGRE, paltry, niggardly, worthless, pathetic (*infml*), pitiful.
🔁 **1** cheerful, happy. **2** pleasant. **4** generous.

miserly *adj* mean, niggardly, tight (*infml*), stingy (*infml*), sparing, parsimonious, cheeseparing, beggarly, penny-pinching (*infml*), mingy (*infml*).
🔁 generous, spendthrift.

misery *n* **1** UNHAPPINESS, sadness, suffering, distress, depression, despair, gloom, grief, wretchedness, affliction. **2** PRIVATION, hardship, deprivation, poverty, want, oppression, destitution. **3** (*infml*) SPOILSPORT, pessimist, killjoy, wet blanket (*infml*), party pooper (*infml*).
🔁 **1** contentment. **2** comfort.

misfire *v* miscarry, go wrong, abort, fail, fall through, flop (*infml*), founder, fizzle out, come to grief.
🔁 succeed.

misfit *n* individualist, nonconformist, eccentric, maverick, dropout, loner, lone wolf.
🔁 conformist.

misfortune *n* bad luck, mischance, mishap, ill-luck, setback, reverse, calamity, catastrophe, disaster, blow, accident, tragedy, trouble, hardship, trial, tribulation.
🔁 luck, success.

misgiving *n* doubt, uncertainty, hesitation, qualm, reservation, apprehension, scruple, suspicion, second thoughts, niggle, anxiety, worry, fear.
🔁 confidence.

misguided *adj* misled, misconceived, ill-considered, ill-advised, ill-judged, imprudent, rash, misplaced, deluded, foolish, erroneous, mistaken.
🔁 sensible, wise.

mishap *n* misfortune, ill-fortune, misadventure, accident, setback, whammy (*infml*), calamity, disaster, adversity.

misinterpret *v* misconstrue, misread, misunderstand, mistake, misapprehend, distort, garble.

misjudge *v* miscalculate, mistake, misinterpret, misconstrue, misunderstand, overestimate, underestimate.

mislay *v* lose, misplace, miss, lose sight of.

mislead *v* misinform, misdirect, deceive, delude, lead astray, fool, trick.

misleading *adj* deceptive, confusing, unreliable, ambiguous, biased, loaded, evasive, tricky (*infml*).
🔁 unequivocal, authoritative, informative.

mismanage *v* mishandle, botch, bungle, make a mess of, mess up, misrule, misspend, misjudge, foul up, mar, waste.

misprint *n* mistake, error, erratum, literal, typo (*infml*).

misrepresent *v* distort, falsify, slant, pervert, twist, garble, misquote, exaggerate, minimize, misconstrue, misinterpret.

miss *v* 1 FAIL, miscarry, lose, let slip, let go, omit, overlook, pass over, slip, leave out, mistake, trip, misunderstand, err. 2 AVOID, escape, evade, dodge, forego, skip, bypass, circumvent. 3 PINE FOR, long for, yearn for, regret, grieve for, mourn, sorrow for, want, wish, need, lament.
➤ *n* failure, error, blunder, mistake, omission, oversight, fault, flop (*infml*), fiasco.

misshapen *adj* deformed, distorted, twisted, malformed, warped, contorted, crooked, crippled, grotesque, ugly, monstrous.
🎝 regular, shapely.

missile *n* projectile, shot, guided missile, arrow, shaft, dart, rocket, bomb, shell, flying bomb, grenade, torpedo, weapon.

missing *adj* absent, lost, lacking, gone, mislaid, unaccounted-for, wanting, disappeared, astray, strayed, misplaced.
🎝 found, present.

mission *n* 1 TASK, undertaking, assignment, operation, campaign, crusade, business, errand. 2 CALLING, duty, purpose, vocation, raison d'être, aim, charge, office, job, work. 3 COMMISSION, ministry, delegation, deputation, legation, embassy.

missionary *n* evangelist, campaigner, preacher, proselytizer, apostle, crusader, propagandist, champion, promoter, emissary, envoy, ambassador.

mist *n* haze, fog, vapour, smog, cloud, condensation, film, spray, drizzle, dew, steam, veil, dimness.
◊ **mist over** cloud over, fog, dim, blur, steam up, obscure, veil.
🎝 clear.

mistake *n* error, inaccuracy, slip, slip-up, oversight, lapse, blunder, clanger (*infml*), boob (*infml*), gaffe, fault, faux pas, solecism (*fml*), indiscretion, misjudgement, miscalculation, misunderstanding, misprint, misspelling, misreading, mispronunciation, howler (*infml*).
➤ *v* misunderstand, misapprehend, misconstrue, misjudge, misread, miscalculate, confound, confuse, slip up, blunder, err, boob (*infml*).

mistaken *adj* wrong, incorrect, erroneous, inaccurate, inexact, untrue, inappropriate, ill-judged, inauthentic, false, deceived, deluded, misinformed, misled, faulty.
🎝 correct, right.

mistreat *v* abuse, ill-treat, ill-use, maltreat, harm, hurt, batter, injure, knock about, molest.

mistress *n* 1 LOVER, live-in lover, kept woman, concubine, courtesan, girlfriend, paramour, woman, lady-love. 2 TEACHER, governess, tutor.

mistrust *n* distrust, doubt, suspicion, wariness, misgiving, reservations, qualm, hesitancy, chariness, caution, uncertainty, scepticism, apprehension.
🎝 trust.
➤ *v* distrust, doubt, suspect, be wary of, beware, have reservations, fear.
🎝 trust.

misty *adj* hazy, foggy, cloudy, blurred, fuzzy, murky, smoky, unclear, dim, indistinct, obscure, opaque, vague, veiled.
🎝 clear.

misunderstand *v* misapprehend, misconstrue, misinterpret, misjudge, mistake, get wrong, miss the point, mishear, get hold of the wrong end of the stick (*infml*).
🎝 understand.

misunderstanding *n* 1 MISTAKE, error, fallacy, misapprehension, misconception, misjudgement, misinterpretation, misreading, mix-up. 2 DISAGREEMENT, argument, dispute,

conflict, clash, difference, breach, quarrel, discord, rift.
E3 1 understanding. **2** agreement.

misuse *n* mistreatment, maltreatment, abuse, harm, ill-treatment, misapplication, misappropriation, waste, perversion, corruption, exploitation.

➤ *v* abuse, misapply, misemploy, ill-use, ill-treat, harm, mistreat, wrong, distort, injure, corrupt, pervert, waste, squander, misappropriate, exploit, dissipate.

mitigating *adj* extenuating, justifying, vindicating, modifying, qualifying.

mix *v* **1** COMBINE, blend, mingle, intermingle, intermix, amalgamate, compound, homogenize, synthesize, merge, join, unite, coalesce, fuse, incorporate, fold in. **2** ASSOCIATE, consort, fraternize, socialize, mingle, join, hobnob (*infml*), schmooze.
E3 1 divide, separate.

➤ *n* mixture, blend, assortment, combination, conglomerate, amalgam, compound, fusion, synthesis, medley, composite, mishmash (*infml*).
◇ **mix up** confuse, bewilder, muddle, perplex, puzzle, confound, mix, jumble, complicate, garble, involve, implicate, disturb, upset, snarl up.

mixed *adj* **1** *mixed race*: combined, hybrid, mingled, crossbred, mongrel, blended, composite, compound, incorporated, united, alloyed, amalgamated, fused. **2** *mixed biscuits*: assorted, varied, miscellaneous, diverse, diversified, motley. **3** *mixed feelings*: ambivalent, equivocal, conflicting, contradicting, uncertain.

mixture *n* mix, blend, combination, amalgamation, amalgam, compound, conglomeration, composite, coalescence, alloy, brew, synthesis, union, fusion, concoction, cross, hybrid, assortment, variety, miscellany, medley, mélange, mixed bag, potpourri, jumble, hotchpotch.

moan *n* lament, lamentation, sob, wail,

howl, whimper, whine, grumble, complaint, grievance, groan.
➤ *v* **1** LAMENT, wail, sob, weep, howl, groan, whimper, mourn, grieve.
2 (*infml*) COMPLAIN, grumble, whine, whinge (*infml*), gripe (*infml*), kvetch (*US sl*), carp.
E3 1 rejoice.

mob *n* **1** CROWD, mass, throng, multitude, horde, host, swarm, gathering, group, collection, flock, herd, pack, set, tribe, troop, company, crew, gang. **2** POPULACE, rabble, masses, hoi polloi, plebs (*infml*), riff-raff (*infml*).
➤ *v* crowd, crowd round, surround, swarm round, jostle, overrun, set upon, besiege, descend on, throng, pack, pester, charge.

mobile *adj* **1** MOVING, movable, portable, peripatetic, travelling, roaming, roving, itinerant, wandering, migrant. **2** FLEXIBLE, agile, active, energetic, nimble. **3** CHANGING, changeable, ever-changing, expressive, lively.
E3 1 immobile.

mobilize *v* assemble, marshal, rally, conscript, muster, call up, enlist, activate, galvanize, organize, prepare, ready, summon, animate.

mock *v* **1** RIDICULE, jeer, make fun of, laugh at, disparage, deride, scoff, sneer, taunt, scorn, tease. **2** IMITATE, simulate, mimic, ape, caricature, satirize.
➤ *adj* imitation, counterfeit, artificial, sham, simulated, synthetic, false, faux, fake, forged, fraudulent, bogus, phoney (*infml*), pseudo, spurious, feigned, faked, pretended, dummy.

mockery *n* **1** RIDICULE, jeering, scoffing, scorn, derision, contempt, disdain, disrespect, sarcasm. **2** PARODY, satire, sham, travesty.

mocking *adj* scornful, derisive, contemptuous, sarcastic, satirical, taunting, scoffing, sardonic, snide (*infml*), insulting, irreverent, impudent, disrespectful, disdainful, cynical.

model *n* **1** COPY, replica, duplicate,

representation, facsimile, imitation, mock-up. **2** EXAMPLE, exemplar, pattern, standard, ideal, mould, prototype, template. **3** DESIGN, style, type, version, mark. **4** MANNEQUIN, dummy, sitter, subject, poser.

➤ *adj* exemplary, perfect, typical, ideal.

➤ *v* **1** MAKE, form, fashion, mould, sculpt, carve, cast, shape, work, create, design, plan. **2** DISPLAY, wear, show off.

moderate *adj* **1** MEDIOCRE, medium, ordinary, fair, indifferent, average, middle-of-the-road. **2** REASONABLE, restrained, sensible, calm, controlled, cool, mild, well-regulated.

☒ **1** exceptional. **2** immoderate.

➤ *v* control, regulate, decrease, lessen, soften, restrain, tone down, play down, diminish, ease, curb, calm, check, modulate, repress, subdue, soft-pedal, tame, subside, pacify, mitigate, allay, alleviate, abate, dwindle.

moderately *adv* somewhat, quite, rather, fairly, slightly, reasonably, passably, to some extent.

☒ extremely.

moderation *n* **1** DECREASE, reduction. **2** RESTRAINT, self-control, caution, control, composure, sobriety, abstemiousness, temperance, reasonableness.

modern *adj* current, contemporary, up to date, new, fresh, latest, late, novel, present, present-day, recent, up-to-the-minute, newfangled (*infml*), advanced, avant-garde, progressive, modernistic, innovative, inventive, state-of-the-art, go-ahead, fashionable, stylish, in vogue, in style, modish, trendy (*infml*).

☒ old-fashioned, old, out of date, antiquated.

modernize *v* renovate, refurbish, rejuvenate, regenerate, streamline, revamp, renew, update, improve, do up, redesign, reform, remake, remodel, refresh, transform, modify, progress.

☒ regress.

modest *adj* **1** UNASSUMING, humble, self-effacing, self-deprecating, quiet,

reserved, retiring, unpretentious, discreet, bashful, shy. **2** MODERATE, ordinary, unexceptional, fair, reasonable, limited, small.

☒ **1** immodest, conceited. **2** exceptional, excessive.

modesty *n* humility, humbleness, self-effacement, reticence, reserve, quietness, decency, propriety, demureness, shyness, bashfulness, coyness.

☒ immodesty, vanity, conceit.

modify *v* **1** CHANGE, alter, redesign, revise, vary, adapt, adjust, tweak (*infml*), transform, reform, convert, improve, reorganize. **2** MODERATE, reduce, temper, tone down, limit, soften, qualify.

modulate *v* modify, adjust, balance, alter, soften, lower, regulate, vary, harmonize, inflect, tune.

moist *adj* damp, clammy, humid, wet, dewy, rainy, muggy, marshy, drizzly, watery, soggy.

☒ dry, arid.

moisten *v* moisturize, dampen, damp, wet, water, lick, irrigate.

☒ dry.

moisture *n* water, liquid, wetness, wateriness, damp, dampness, dankness, humidity, vapour, dew, mugginess, condensation, steam, spray.

☒ dryness.

molest *v* **1** ANNOY, disturb, bother, harass, irritate, persecute, pester, plague, tease, torment, hound, upset, worry, trouble, badger. **2** ATTACK, accost, assail, hurt, ill-treat, maltreat, mistreat, abuse, harm, injure.

mollusc

Molluscs include: abalone, conch, cowrie, cuttlefish, clam, cockle, limpet, mussel, nautilus, nudibranch, octopus, oyster, periwinkle, scallop, sea slug, slug, freshwater snail, land snail, marine snail, squid, tusk shell, whelk.

moment *n* second, instant, mo (*infml*), minute, split second, trice, jiffy (*infml*), tick (*infml*).

momentary *adj* brief, short-lived, temporary, transient, transitory, fleeting, ephemeral, hasty, quick, passing.
🖃 lasting, permanent.

momentous *adj* significant, important, critical, crucial, decisive, weighty, grave, serious, vital, fateful, historic, earth-shaking, seismic (*infml*), epoch-making, eventful, major.
🖃 insignificant, unimportant, trivial.

momentum *n* impetus, force, energy, impulse, drive, power, thrust, speed, velocity, impact, incentive, stimulus, urge, strength, push.

monarch *n* sovereign, crowned head, ruler, king, queen, emperor, empress, prince, princess, tsar, potentate.

monarchy *n* 1 KINGDOM, empire, principality, realm, domain, dominion. 2 ROYALISM, sovereignty, autocracy, monocracy, absolutism, despotism, tyranny.

monastery *n* friary, priory, abbey, cloister, charterhouse.

monastic *adj* reclusive, withdrawn, secluded, cloistered, austere, ascetic, celibate, contemplative.
🖃 secular, worldly.

monetary *adj* financial, fiscal, pecuniary (*fml*), budgetary, economic, capital, cash.

money *n* currency, cash, legal tender, banknotes, coin, funds, capital, dough (*infml*), dosh (*infml*), spondulicks (*sl*), riches, wealth.

mongrel *n* cross, crossbreed, hybrid, half-breed.
➤ *adj* crossbred, hybrid, half-breed, bastard, mixed, ill-defined.
🖃 pure-bred, pedigree.

monitor *n* 1 SCREEN, display, VDU, recorder, scanner. 2 SUPERVISOR, watchdog, overseer, invigilator, adviser, prefect.
➤ *v* check, watch, keep track of, keep under surveillance, keep an eye on, follow, track, supervise, observe, note, survey, trace, scan, record, plot, detect.

monkey *n* 1 PRIMATE, simian, ape. 2 (*infml*) SCAMP, imp, urchin, brat, rogue, scallywag (*infml*), rascal.

> *Monkeys include*: ape, baboon, capuchin, colobus monkey, drill and mandrill, guenon, guereza, howler monkey, langur, leaf monkey, macaque, mangabey, marmoset, night monkey (or douroucouli), proboscis monkey, rhesus monkey, saki, spider monkey, squirrel monkey, tamarin, titi, toque, uakari (or cacajou), woolly monkey.

monopolize *v* dominate, take over, appropriate, corner, control, hog (*infml*), engross, occupy, preoccupy, take up, tie up.
🖃 share.

monotonous *adj* boring, dull, tedious, uninteresting, tiresome, wearisome, unchanging, uneventful, unvaried, uniform, toneless, flat, colourless, repetitive, routine, plodding, humdrum, soul-destroying.
🖃 lively, varied, colourful.

monotony *n* tedium, dullness, boredom, sameness, tiresomeness, uneventfulness, flatness, wearisomeness, uniformity, routine, repetitiveness.
🖃 liveliness, colour.

monster *n* 1 BEAST, fiend, brute, barbarian, savage, villain, giant, ogre, troll, mammoth. 2 FREAK, monstrosity, mutant.
➤ *adj* huge, gigantic, giant, gargantuan, colossal, enormous, immense, massive, monstrous, jumbo, mammoth, vast, tremendous.
🖃 tiny, minute.

monstrous *adj* 1 WICKED, evil, vicious, cruel, criminal, heinous, outrageous, scandalous, disgraceful, atrocious, abhorrent, dreadful, frightful, horrible, horrifying, terrible. 2 UNNATURAL, inhuman, freakish, grotesque, hideous, deformed, malformed, misshapen.

3 HUGE, enormous, colossal, gigantic, vast, immense, massive, mammoth.

monument *n* memorial, cenotaph, headstone, gravestone, tombstone, shrine, mausoleum, cairn, barrow, cross, marker, obelisk, pillar, statue, relic, remembrance, commemoration, testament, reminder, record, memento, evidence, token.

monumental *adj* **1** IMPRESSIVE, imposing, awe-inspiring, awesome, overwhelming, significant, important, epoch-making, historic, magnificent, majestic, memorable, notable, outstanding, abiding, immortal, lasting, classic. **2** HUGE, immense, enormous, colossal, vast, tremendous, massive, great. **3** COMMEMORATIVE, memorial.
EX 1 insignificant, unimportant.

mood *n* **1** DISPOSITION, frame of mind, state of mind, temper, humour, spirit, tenor, whim. **2** BAD TEMPER, sulk, the sulks, pique, melancholy, depression, blues (*infml*), doldrums, dumps (*infml*).

moody *adj* changeable, volatile, temperamental, unpredictable, capricious, irritable, short-tempered, crabby (*infml*), crotchety, crusty (*infml*), testy, touchy, morose, angry, broody, mopy, sulky, sullen, gloomy, melancholy, miserable, downcast, doleful, glum, impulsive, fickle, flighty.
EX equable, cheerful.

moon *v* idle, loaf, mooch, languish, pine, mope, brood, daydream, dream, fantasize.

moor¹ *v* fasten, secure, tie up, drop anchor, anchor, berth, dock, make fast, fix, hitch, bind.
EX loose.

moor² *n* moorland, heath, fell, upland.

mop *n* head of hair, shock, mane, tangle, thatch, mass.
➤ *v* swab, sponge, wipe, clean, wash, absorb, soak.

mope *v* brood, fret, sulk, pine, languish, droop, despair, grieve, idle.

moral *adj* ethical, virtuous, good, right, principled, honourable, decent, upright, upstanding, straight, righteous, high-minded, honest, incorruptible, proper, blameless, chaste, clean-living, squeaky-clean (*infml*), pure, just, noble.
EX immoral.
➤ *n* lesson, message, teaching, dictum, meaning, maxim, adage, precept, saying, proverb, aphorism, epigram.

morale *n* confidence, spirits, esprit de corps, self-esteem, state of mind, heart, mood.

morality *n* ethics, morals, ideals, principles, standards, virtue, rectitude, righteousness, decency, goodness, honesty, integrity, justice, uprightness, propriety, conduct, manners.
EX immorality.

morals *n* morality, ethics, principles, standards, ideals, integrity, scruples, behaviour, conduct, habits, manners.

morbid *adj* **1** GHOULISH, ghastly, gruesome, macabre, hideous, horrid, grim. **2** GLOOMY, dark, pessimistic, melancholy, sombre. **3** SICK, unhealthy, unwholesome, insalubrious.

more *adj* further, extra, additional, added, new, fresh, increased, other, supplementary, repeated, alternative, spare.
EX less.
➤ *adv* further, longer, again, besides, moreover, better.
EX less.

moreover *adv* furthermore, further, besides, in addition, as well, also, additionally, what is more.

morning *n* daybreak, daylight, dawn, sunrise, break of day, before noon.

morose *adj* ill-tempered, bad-tempered, moody, sullen, sulky, surly, gloomy, grim, gruff, sour, taciturn, glum, grouchy (*infml*), crabby (*infml*), crotchety, saturnine.
EX cheerful, communicative.

morsel *n* bit, scrap, piece, fragment, crumb, bite, mouthful, nibble, taste, soupçon, titbit, slice, fraction, modicum, grain, atom, part.

mortal *adj* **1** WORLDLY, earthly, bodily, human, perishable, temporal. **2** FATAL, lethal, deadly. **3** EXTREME, great, severe, intense, grave, awful.
🔳 **1** immortal.
➤ *n* human being, human, individual, person, being, body, creature.
🔳 immortal, god.

mortality *n* **1** HUMANITY, death, impermanence, perishability. **2** FATALITY, death rate.
🔳 **1** immortality.

mortified *adj* humiliated, shamed, ashamed, humbled, embarrassed, crushed.

mostly *adv* mainly, on the whole, principally, chiefly, generally, usually, largely, for the most part, as a rule.

moth *see panel at* **butterfly**.

mother *n* **1** PARENT, procreator (*fml*), progenitress (*fml*), birth mother, dam, mamma, mum (*infml*), mummy (*infml*), matriarch, ancestor, matron, old woman (*infml*). **2** ORIGIN, source.
➤ *v* **1** BEAR, produce, nurture, raise, rear, nurse, care for, cherish. **2** PAMPER, spoil, baby, indulge, overprotect, fuss over.

motherly *adj* maternal, caring, comforting, affectionate, kind, loving, protective, warm, tender, gentle, fond.
🔳 neglectful, uncaring.

motif *n* theme, idea, topic, concept, pattern, design, figure, form, logo, shape, device, ornament, decoration.

motion *n* **1** MOVEMENT, action, mobility, moving, activity, locomotion, travel, transit, passage, passing, progress, change, flow, inclination. **2** GESTURE, gesticulation, signal, sign, wave, nod. **3** PROPOSAL, suggestion, plan, recommendation, proposition.
➤ *v* signal, gesture, gesticulate, sign, wave, nod, beckon, direct, usher.

motionless *adj* unmoving, still, stationary, static, immobile, at a standstill, fixed, halted, at rest, resting, standing, paralysed, inanimate, lifeless, frozen, rigid, stagnant.
🔳 active, moving.

motivate *v* prompt, incite, impel, spur, provoke, stimulate, drive, lead, stir, urge, push, propel, persuade, move, inspire, encourage, cause, trigger, induce, kindle, draw, arouse, bring.
🔳 deter, discourage.

motive *n* grounds, cause, reason, purpose, motivation, object, intention, influence, rationale, thinking, incentive, impulse, stimulus, inspiration, incitement, urge, encouragement, design, desire, consideration.
🔳 deterrent, disincentive.

motor vehicle *see* **car**; **vehicle**.

Parts of a motor vehicle include: ABS (anti-lock braking system), accelerator, airbag, air brake, air-conditioner, air inlet, antidazzle mirror, antiglare switch, anti-roll bar, antitheft device, ashtray, axle, backup light (*US*), battery, bench seat, bezel, bodywork, bonnet, boot, brake drum, brake light, brake pad, brake shoe, bull bars, bumper, car phone, car radio, catalytic converter, central locking, centre console, chassis, child-safety seat, cigarette lighter, clock, clutch, courtesy light, crankcase, cruise control, dashboard, differential gear, dimmer, disk brake, door, door-lock, drive shaft, drum brake, electric window, emergency light, engine, exhaust pipe, fender (*US*), filler cap, flasher switch, fog lamp, folding seat, four-wheel drive, fuel gauge, gas tank (*US*), gear, gearbox, gear lever (or gear stick), glove compartment, grille, handbrake, hazard warning light, headlight, headrest, heated rear window, heater, hood (*US*), horn, hubcap, hydraulic brake, hydraulic suspension, ignition, ignition key, indicator, instrument panel, jack, jump lead, kingpin, license plate (*US*), lift plate (*US*), monocoque, number plate, oil gauge, overrider, parcel shelf, parking light, petrol tank, pneumatic tyre, power brake, prop shaft, quarterlight, rack and pinion, radial-ply tyre, rear light, rear-view mirror, reclining seat, reflector, rev counter (*infml*), reversing light, roof rack, screen-washer bottle, seat belt, shaft, shock absorber, sidelight, side-impact bar, side mirror, silencer, sill, solenoid, spare tyre, speedometer, spoiler, steering column, steering-wheel, stick shift (*US*), stoplight, sunroof, sun visor, suspension, temperature gauge, towbar, track rod, transmission, trunk (*US*), tyre, vent, windscreen-washer, windscreen wiper, windshield (*US*), wing, wing mirror. *see also* **engine**.

mottled *adj* speckled, dappled, blotchy, flecked, piebald, stippled, streaked, tabby, spotted, freckled, variegated.

Ea monochrome, uniform.

motto *n* saying, slogan, maxim, watchword, catchword, byword, precept, proverb, adage, formula, rule, golden rule, dictum.

mould[1] *n* **1** CAST, form, die, template, pattern, matrix. **2** SHAPE, form, format, pattern, structure, style, type, build, construction, cut, design, kind, model, sort, stamp, arrangement, brand, frame, character, nature, quality, line, make.

➤ *v* **1** FORGE, cast, shape, stamp, make, form, create, design, construct, sculpt, model, work. **2** INFLUENCE, direct, control.

mould[2] *n* mildew, fungus, mouldiness, mustiness, blight.

mouldy *adj* mildewed, blighted, musty, decaying, corrupt, rotten, fusty, putrid, bad, spoiled, stale.

Ea fresh, wholesome.

mound *n* **1** HILL, hillock, hummock, rise, knoll, bank, dune, elevation, ridge, embankment, earthwork. **2** HEAP, pile, stack.

mount *v* **1** PRODUCE, put on, set up, prepare, stage, exhibit, display, launch. **2** INCREASE, grow, accumulate, multiply, rise, intensify, soar, swell. **3** CLIMB, ascend, get up, go up, get on, clamber up, scale, get astride.

Ea **2** decrease, descend. **3** descend, dismount, go down.

➤ *n* horse, steed, support, mounting.

mountain *n* **1** HEIGHT, elevation, mount, peak, mound, alp, tor, massif. **2** HEAP, pile, stack, mass, abundance, backlog.

The highest mountains of the world include:
Asia: Everest (Himalaya-Nepal/Tibet), K2 (Pakistan/India), Kangchenjunga (Himalaya-Nepal/India), Makalu (Himalaya-Nepal/Tibet), Dhaulagiri (Himalaya-Nepal), Nanga Parbat (Himalaya-India), Annapurna (Himalaya-Nepal);
South America: Aconcagua (Andes-Argentina);
North America: McKinley (Alaska Range);
Africa: Kilimanjaro (Tanzania);
Europe: Elbruz (Caucasus), Mount Blanc (Alps-France);
Antarctica: Vinson Massif;
Australasia: Jaja (New Guinea).

---

mountaineering

Mountaineering and climbing terms include: abseiling, abseil station, adze, adz (*US*), Alpinism, arête, ascender, ascent, avalanche; axe, ax (*US*), ice axe, hammer axe; base camp; belay, belayer, non-belayer, self-belaying; bivouac; bolting, debolting; bouldering, cam, carabiner (or karabiner), chalk bag, chalk cliff climbing, chimney, chock, chockstone, cleft, climbing wall, col, cornice, corrie, crag, crampon, crevasse, descender, descent, Dülfer seat, étrier, fissure, glacier, gully; harness, climbing harness, sit harness; hand hold, helmet, helmet lamp, hut, ice climbing, ice ridge, ice screw, ice slope, ice step, Munro; nut, wallnut; overhang, pick, piolet, pitch; piton, abseil piton, corkscrew piton, drive-in ice piton, ice piton, ringed piton; prusik knot, prusik loop, rapelling, ridge, rock, rock face, rock spike, rock wall; rope, dynamic rope, kernmantel rope, standing rope, on the rope, unrope; saddle, scree, sérac, Sherpa, shunt; sling, abseil sling, rope sling, sling seat, wrist sling; solo ascent, snow bridge, snow cornice, snow gaiters, snow goggles, spike, sport climbing, spur; stack, sea stack; summit, top out, trad route, traverse, tying in.

mountainous *adj* 1 CRAGGY, rocky, hilly, high, highland, upland, alpine, soaring, steep. 2 HUGE, towering, enormous, immense.
🔁 1 flat. 2 tiny.

mourn *v* grieve, lament, sorrow, bemoan, miss, regret, deplore, weep, wail.
🔁 rejoice.

mournful *adj* sorrowful, sad, unhappy, desolate, grief-stricken, heavy-hearted, heartbroken, broken-hearted, cast-down, downcast, miserable, tragic, woeful, melancholy, sombre, depressed, dejected, gloomy, dismal, dark.
🔁 joyful.

mourning *n* bereavement, grief, grieving, lamentation, sadness, sorrow, desolation, weeping.
🔁 rejoicing.

mouth *n* 1 LIPS, jaws, trap (*infml*), gob (*sl*), bazoo (*US sl*). 2 OPENING, aperture, orifice, cavity, entrance, gateway, inlet, estuary.

Parts of the mouth include: alveolar ridge, gum, hard palate, inferior dental arch, isthmus of fauces, labial commissure, lower lip, palatoglossal arch, palato-pharyngeal arch, soft palate, superior dental arch, tongue, tonsil, upper lip, uvula. *see also* **tooth**.

➤ *v* enunciate, articulate, utter, pronounce, whisper, form.

movable *adj* mobile, portable, transportable, changeable, alterable, adjustable, flexible, transferable.
🔁 fixed, immovable.

move *v* 1 STIR, go, advance, budge, change, proceed, progress, make strides. 2 TRANSPORT, carry, transfer. 3 DEPART, go away, leave, decamp, migrate, remove, move house, relocate. 4 PROMPT, stimulate, urge, impel, drive, propel, motivate, incite, provoke, persuade, induce, inspire. 5 AFFECT, touch, agitate, stir, impress, excite.
➤ *n* 1 MOVEMENT, motion, step, manoeuvre, action, device, stratagem. 2 REMOVAL, relocation, migration, transfer.

movement *n* 1 REPOSITIONING, move, moving, relocation, activity, act, action, agitation, stirring, transfer, passage. 2 CHANGE, development, advance, evolution, current, drift, flow, shift, progress, progression, trend, tendency. 3 CAMPAIGN, crusade, drive, group, organization, party, faction.

moving *adj* 1 MOBILE, active, in motion. 2 TOUCHING, affecting, poignant, impressive, emotive, arousing, stirring, inspiring, inspirational, exciting, thrilling, persuasive, stimulating.
🔁 1 immobile. 2 unemotional.

mow *v* cut, trim, crop, clip, shear, scythe.

much *adv* greatly, considerably, a lot, frequently, often.
➤ *adj* copious, plentiful, ample, considerable, a lot, abundant, great, substantial.
➤ *n* plenty, a lot, lots (*infml*), loads (*infml*), heaps (*infml*), lashings (*infml*).
🔁 little.

muck *n* dirt, dung, manure, mire, filth, mud, sewage, slime, gunge (*infml*), ordure, scum, sludge.
◇ **muck up** ruin, wreck, spoil, mess up, make a mess of, botch, bungle, cock up (*sl*), screw up (*sl*).

mud *n* clay, mire, ooze, dirt, sludge, silt.

muddle *v* 1 DISORGANIZE, disorder, mix up, mess up, jumble, scramble, tangle. 2 CONFUSE, bewilder, bemuse, perplex.
➤ *n* chaos, confusion, disorder, mess, mix-up, jumble, clutter, tangle.

muddy *adj* 1 DIRTY, foul, miry, mucky, marshy, boggy, swampy, quaggy, grimy. 2 CLOUDY, indistinct, obscure, opaque, murky, hazy, blurred, fuzzy, dull.
🖪 1 clean. 2 clear.

muffle *v* 1 WRAP, envelop, cloak, swathe, cover. 2 DEADEN, dull, quieten, silence, stifle, dampen, muzzle, suppress.
🖪 2 amplify.

mug[1] *n* cup, beaker, pot, tankard.

mug[2] *v* set upon, attack, assault, waylay, steal from, rob, beat up, jump (on).

muggy *adj* humid, sticky, stuffy, sultry, close, clammy, oppressive, sweltering, moist, damp.
🖪 dry.

mull over *v* reflect on, ponder, contemplate, think over, think about, ruminate, consider, weigh up, chew over, meditate, study, examine, deliberate.

multiple *adj* many, numerous, manifold, various, several, sundry, collective.

multiply *v* increase, proliferate, expand, spread, reproduce, propagate, breed, accumulate, intensify, extend, build up, augment, boost.
🖪 decrease, lessen.

multitude *n* crowd, throng, horde, swarm, mob, mass, herd, congregation, host, lot, lots, legion, public, people, populace.
🖪 few, scattering.

munch *v* eat, chew, crunch, masticate (*fml*), chomp (*infml*).

mundane *adj* banal, ordinary, everyday, commonplace, prosaic, humdrum, workaday, routine.
🖪 extraordinary.

municipal *adj* civic, city, town, urban, borough, community, public.

murder *n* homicide, killing, slaying, manslaughter, assassination, massacre, bloodshed.
➤ *v* kill, slaughter, slay, assassinate, butcher, massacre.

murderer *n* killer, homicide, slayer, slaughterer, assassin, butcher, cut-throat.

murderous *adj* 1 HOMICIDAL, brutal, barbarous, bloodthirsty, bloody, cut-throat, killing, lethal, cruel, savage, ferocious, deadly. 2 (*infml*) DIFFICULT, exhausting, strenuous, unpleasant, dangerous.

murky *adj* dark, dismal, gloomy, dull, overcast, misty, foggy, dim, cloudy, obscure, shadowy, veiled, grey.
🖪 bright, clear.

murmur *n* mumble, muttering, whisper, undertone, humming, rumble, drone, grumble.
➤ *v* mutter, mumble, whisper, buzz, hum, rumble, purr, burble.

muscular *adj* brawny, beefy (*infml*), sinewy, athletic, powerfully built, strapping, hefty, powerful, husky, robust, stalwart, vigorous, strong.
🖪 puny, flabby, weak.

mushroom

Types of mushroom and toadstool include:
edible: beefsteak fungus, blewits, boletus, chestnut boletus, button mushroom, cep, champignon, chanterelle, clouded agaric, common morel, cramp ball, cultivated mushroom, dingy agaric, elf cup, fairy ring, the goat's lip, gypsy mushroom, honey fungus, horn of plenty, horse mushroom, lawyer's wig, man on horseback, march mushroom, meadow mushroom, oyster mushroom, parasol mushroom, penny bun, porcini, saffron milk cap, shaggy parasol, slippery jack, sweetbread mushroom, truffle, trumpet agaric, velvet shank, winter mushroom, wood hedgehog;
inedible/poisonous: amanita, common ink cap, copper trumpet, death cap, destroying angel, devil's boletus, earth ball, false morel, fly agaric, mower's mushroom, panther cap, purple boletus, satan's

mushroom, shaggy milk cap, stinking parasol, sulphur tuft, verdigris agaric, woolly milk cap, yellow-staining mushroom.

music

Types of music include: acid house, acid jazz, adult-orientated rock (AOR), ambient, ballet, ballroom, bebop, Big Beat, bluegrass, blues, boogie-woogie, cajun, calypso, chamber, choral, classical, country and western, dance, disco, Dixieland, doo-wop, drum and bass, easy listening, electronic, folk, folk rock, funk, fusion, gamelan, gangsta, garage, glam rock, gospel, grunge, hardcore, hard rock, heavy metal, hip-hop, honky-tonk, house, incidental, instrumental, jazz, jazz-funk, jazz-pop, jazz-rock, jive, jungle, karaoke, middle-of-the-road, nu-metal, operatic, orchestral, pop, punk rock, ragtime, rap, reggae, rhythm and blues (R & B), rock, rock and roll, sacred, salsa, samba, ska, skiffle, soft rock, soul, swing, techno, thrash metal, trance, trip-hop.

musical *adj* tuneful, melodious, melodic, harmonious, dulcet, sweet-sounding, lyrical.
🔁 discordant, unmusical.

Musical compositions include: arabesque, aubade, bagatelle, bourrée, canon, capriccio, cavatina, chaconne, concerto, concerto grosso, divertimento, étude, extravaganza, fanfare, fantasia, fugue, gavotte, humoresque, impromptu, intermezzo, march, minuet, nocturne, opus, overture, partita, pastorale, polonaise, prelude, requiem, rhapsody, rondo, round, scherzo, serenade, sinfonietta, sonata, sonatina, suite, symphony, toccata, voluntary. *see also* **song**.

Musical instruments include: balalaika, banjo, cello, clarsach, double-bass, erhu, guitar, harp,

hurdy-gurdy, lute, lyre, mandolin, oud, sitar, spinet, ukulele, viola, violin, fiddle (*infml*), zither; accordion, concertina, squeeze-box (*infml*), clavichord, harmonium, harpsichord, keyboard, mbira, melodeon, organ, Wurlitzer®, piano, grand piano, Pianola®, player-piano, synthesizer, virginals; bagpipes, bassoon, bugle, clarinet, cor anglais, cornet, didgeridoo, euphonium, fife, flugelhorn, flute, French horn, gaita, harmonica, horn, kazoo, mouth organ, oboe, Pan-pipes, piccolo, recorder, saxophone, sousaphone, trombone, trumpet, tuba, uillean pipes; castanets, cymbal, glockenspiel, maracas, marimba, rainstick, tambourine, triangle, tubular bells, xylophone; bass drum, bodhran, bongo, kettle drum, snare drum, steel pan, tabla, tenor drum, timpani, tom-tom.

Musical terms include: accelerando, acciaccatura, accidental, accompaniment, acoustic, adagio, ad lib, a due, affettuoso, agitato, al fine, al segno, alla breve, alla cappella, allargando, allegretto, allegro, al segno, alto, amoroso, andante, animato, appoggiatura, arco, arpeggio, arrangement, a tempo, attacca, bar, bar line, double bar line, baritone, bass, beat, bis, breve, buffo, cadence, cantabile, cantilena, chord, chromatic, clef, alto clef, bass clef, tenor clef, treble clef, coda, col canto, con brio, concert, con fuoco, con moto, consonance, contralto, counterpoint, crescendo, crotchet, cross-fingering, cue, da capo, decrescendo, demisemiquaver, descant, diatonic, diminuendo, dissonance, dolce, doloroso, dominant, dotted note, dotted rest, downbeat, drone, duplet, triplet, quadruplet, quintuplet, sextuplet, encore, ensemble, expression, finale, fine, fingerboard, flat, double flat, forte, fortissimo, fret, glissando, grave, harmonics, harmony, hemidemisemiquaver, hold, imitation, improvisation, interval, augmented interval, diminished interval, second interval, third interval, fourth interval, fifth interval, sixth interval, seventh interval, major interval, minor interval, perfect interval, intonation, key, key signature, langsam, larghetto, largo, leading note, ledger line, legato, lento, lyric, maestoso, major, manual, marcato, mediant, medley, melody, metre, mezza voce, mezzo forte, microtone, middle C, minim, minor, moderato, mode, modulation, molto, mordent, movement, mute, natural, non troppo, note, obbligato, octave, orchestra, ostinato, part, pause, pedal point, pentatonic, perdendo, phrase, pianissimo, piano, piece, pitch, pizzicato, presto, quarter tone, quaver, rallentando, recital, refrain, resolution, rest, rhythm, ritenuto, root, scale, score, semibreve, semiquaver, semitone, semplice, sempre, senza, sequence, sforzando, shake, sharp, double sharp, slur, smorzando, solo, soprano, sostenuto, sotto voce, spiritoso, staccato, staff, stave, subdominant, subito, submediant, sul ponticello, supertonic, swell, syncopation, tablature, tacet, tanto, tempo, tenor, tenuto, theme, tie, timbre, time signature, compound time, simple time, two-two time, three-four time, four-four time, six-eight time, tone, tonic sol-fa, transposition, treble, tremolo, triad, trill, double trill, tune, tuning, turn, tutti, upbeat, unison, vibrato, vigoroso, virtuoso, vivace.

musician

Musicians include: instrumentalist, accompanist, performer, player; bugler, busker, cellist, clarinettist, clarsair, drummer, flautist, fiddler, guitarist, harpist, lutenist, oboist, organist, percussionist, pianist, piper, soloist, trombonist, trumpeter, violinist; singer, vocalist, balladeer, diva, prima donna; conductor,

maestro; band, orchestra, group, backing group, ensemble, chamber orchestra, choir, duo, duet, trio, quartet, quintet, sextet, octet, nonet.

muster *v* assemble, convene, gather, call together, mobilize, round up, marshal, come together, congregate, collect, group, meet, rally, mass, throng, call up, summon, enrol.

musty *adj* mouldy, mildewy, stale, stuffy, fusty, dank, airless, decayed, smelly.

mutation *n* change, alteration, variation, modification, transformation, deviation, anomaly, evolution.

mute *adj* silent, dumb, voiceless, wordless, speechless, mum (*infml*), unspoken, noiseless, unexpressed, unpronounced.
🔁 vocal, talkative.
➤ *v* tone down, subdue, muffle, lower, moderate, dampen, deaden, soften, silence.

mutilate *v* 1 MAIM, injure, wound, dismember, disable, disfigure, lame, mangle, cut to pieces, cut up, butcher. 2 SPOIL, mar, damage, cut, censor.

mutinous *adj* rebellious, insurgent, insubordinate, disobedient, seditious, revolutionary, riotous, subversive, bolshie (*infml*), unruly.
🔁 obedient, compliant.

mutiny *n* rebellion, insurrection, revolution, revolt, rising, uprising, insubordination, disobedience, defiance, resistance, riot, strike.
➤ *v* rebel, revolt, rise up, resist, protest, disobey, strike.

mutter *v* 1 MUMBLE, murmur, rumble. 2 COMPLAIN, grumble, carp, grouse (*infml*), gripe.

mutual *adj* reciprocal, shared, common, joint, interchangeable, interchanged, exchanged, complementary.

muzzle *v* restrain, stifle, suppress, gag, mute, silence, censor, choke.

mysterious *adj* enigmatic, cryptic, mystifying, inexplicable, puzzling, perplexing, incomprehensible, obscure, strange, unfathomable, unsearchable, mystical, baffling, curious, hidden, insoluble, secret, weird, secretive, veiled, dark, furtive.
🔁 straightforward, comprehensible.

mystery *n* 1 ENIGMA, puzzle, secret, riddle, conundrum, question.
2 OBSCURITY, secrecy, ambiguity.

mystical *adj* occult, arcane, mystic, esoteric, supernatural, paranormal, transcendental, metaphysical, hidden, mysterious.

mystify *v* puzzle, bewilder, baffle, flummox (*infml*), perplex, nonplus, confound, confuse.

myth *n* legend, fable, fairytale, allegory, parable, saga, story, fiction, tradition, fancy, fantasy, superstition.

mythical *adj* 1 MYTHOLOGICAL, legendary, fabled, fairytale.
2 FICTITIOUS, imaginary, made-up, invented, make-believe, non-existent, unreal, pretended, fanciful.
🔁 1 historical. 2 actual, real.

mythology *n* legend, myths, lore, tradition(s), folklore, folk tales, tales.

Mythological creatures and spirits include: abominable snowman (or yeti), afrit, basilisk, Bigfoot, brownie, bunyip, centaur, Cerberus, Chimera, cockatrice, Cyclops, dragon, dryad, dwarf, Echidna, elf, Erinyes (or Furies), Fafnir, fairy, faun, Frankenstein's monster, genie, Geryon, giant, gnome, goblin, golem, Gorgon, griffin, hamadryad, Harpies, hippocampus, hippogriff, hobgoblin, imp, kelpie, kraken, lamia, leprechaun, Lilith, Loch Ness monster, mermaid, merman, Minotaur, naiad, nereid, nymph, ogre, ogress, orc, oread, Pegasus, phoenix, pixie, roc, salamander, sasquatch, satyr, sea serpent, selkie, Siren, Sphinx, sylph, troll, Typhoeus, unicorn, vampire, werewolf, wivern, yaksha.

Nn

nag *v* scold, berate, irritate, annoy, pester, badger, plague, torment, harass, earbash (*infml*), henpeck (*infml*), harry, vex, upbraid, goad.

nail *v* fasten, attach, secure, pin, tack, fix, join.
➤ *n* 1 FASTENER, pin, tack, spike, skewer. 2 TALON, claw.

naïve *adj* unsophisticated, ingenuous, innocent, green (*infml*), unaffected, artless, guileless, simple, natural, childlike, open, trusting, unsuspecting, gullible, credulous, wide-eyed.
🔁 experienced, sophisticated.

naïvety *n* ingenuousness, innocence, inexperience, naturalness, simplicity, openness, frankness, gullibility, credulity.
🔁 experience, sophistication.

naked *adj* 1 NUDE, bare, undressed, unclothed, uncovered, stripped, stark-naked, disrobed, denuded, in the altogether (*infml*). 2 OPEN, unadorned, undisguised, unqualified, plain, stark, overt, blatant, barefaced, exposed.
🔁 1 clothed, covered. 2 concealed.

name *n* 1 TITLE, appellation (*fml*), designation, label, term, moniker (*sl*), epithet, handle (*infml*). 2 REPUTATION, character, repute, renown, esteem, eminence, fame, honour, distinction, note.

Kinds of name include: full name, first name, given name, Christian name, baptismal name, second name, middle name; surname, family name, last name; maiden name; nickname, sobriquet, agnomen, pet name, term of endearment, diminutive; false name, pseudonym, alias, stage-name, nom-de-plume, assumed name, pen-name; proper name; place name; brand name, trademark; code name.

➤ *v* 1 CALL, christen, baptize, term, title, entitle, dub, label, style. 2 DESIGNATE, nominate, cite, choose, select, specify, classify, commission, appoint.

nameless *adj* 1 UNNAMED, unknown, anonymous, unidentified, obscure. 2 INEXPRESSIBLE, indescribable, unutterable, unspeakable, unmentionable, unheard-of.
🔁 1 named.

namely *adv* that is, ie, specifically, viz, that is to say.

nap *v* doze, sleep, snooze, nod (off), drop off, rest, kip (*infml*).
➤ *n* rest, sleep, siesta, catnap, snooze, forty winks (*infml*), kip (*infml*).

narcotic *n* drug, opiate, sedative, tranquillizer, painkiller.
➤ *adj* soporific, hypnotic, sedative, analgesic, painkilling, numbing, dulling, calming, stupefying.

narrate *v* tell, relate, report, recount, describe, unfold, recite, state, detail.

narrative *n* story, tale, chronicle, account, history, report, detail, statement.

narrator *n* storyteller, chronicler, reporter, raconteur, commentator, writer.

narrow *adj* 1 TIGHT, confined, constricted, cramped, slim, slender, thin, fine, tapering, close. 2 LIMITED, restricted, circumscribed. 3 NARROW-MINDED, biased, bigoted, intolerant, exclusive, dogmatic.
🔁 1 wide. 2 broad. 3 broad-minded, tolerant.

➤ *v* constrict, limit, tighten, reduce, diminish, simplify.
◨ broaden, widen, increase.

narrow-minded *adj* illiberal, biased, bigoted, prejudiced, reactionary, small-minded, conservative, intolerant, insular, exclusive, petty.
◨ broad-minded.

nasty *adj* 1 UNPLEASANT, repellent, repugnant, repulsive, objectionable, offensive, disgusting, sickening, horrible, filthy, foul, polluted, obscene. 2 MALICIOUS, mean, spiteful, wicked, vicious, malevolent.
◨ 1 agreeable, pleasant, decent. 2 benevolent, kind.

nation *n* country, people, race, state, realm, population, community, society.

national *adj* countrywide, civil, domestic, nationwide, state, internal, general, governmental, public, widespread, social.
➤ *n* citizen, native, subject, inhabitant, resident.

nationalism *n* patriotism, allegiance, loyalty, chauvinism, xenophobia, jingoism.

nationality *n* race, nation, ethnic group, birth, tribe, clan.

native *adj* 1 LOCAL, indigenous, domestic, vernacular, home, aboriginal, autochthonous (*fml*), mother, original. 2 INBORN, inherent, innate, inbred, hereditary, inherited, congenital, instinctive, natural, intrinsic, natal.
➤ *n* inhabitant, resident, national, citizen, dweller, aborigine, autochthon (*fml*).
◨ foreigner, outsider, stranger.

natural *adj* 1 ORDINARY, normal, common, regular, standard, usual, typical. 2 INNATE, inborn, instinctive, intuitive, inherent, congenital, native, indigenous. 3 GENUINE, pure, authentic, unrefined, unprocessed, unmixed, real. 4 SINCERE, unaffected, genuine, artless, ingenuous, guileless, simple, unsophisticated, open, candid, spontaneous.

◨ 1 unnatural. 2 acquired. 3 artificial. 4 affected, disingenuous.

naturalistic *adj* natural, realistic, true-to-life, representational, lifelike, graphic, real-life, photographic.

naturally *adv* 1 OF COURSE, as a matter of course, simply, obviously, logically, typically, certainly, absolutely. 2 NORMALLY, genuinely, instinctively, spontaneously.

nature *n* 1 ESSENCE, quality, character, features, disposition, attributes, personality, make-up, constitution, temperament, mood, outlook, temper. 2 KIND, sort, type, description, category, variety, style, species. 3 UNIVERSE, world, creation, earth, environment. 4 COUNTRYSIDE, country, landscape, scenery, natural history.

naughty *adj* 1 BAD, badly behaved, mischievous, disobedient, wayward, exasperating, playful, roguish. 2 INDECENT, obscene, bawdy, risqué, smutty.
◨ 1 good, well-behaved. 2 decent.

nausea *n* 1 VOMITING, sickness, retching, queasiness, biliousness. 2 DISGUST, revulsion, loathing, repugnance.

nauseate *v* sicken, disgust, revolt, repel, offend, turn one's stomach (*infml*).

nautical *adj* naval, marine, maritime, sea-going, seafaring, sailing, oceanic, boating.

Nautical terms include: afloat, aft, air-sea rescue, amidships, ballast, beam, bear away, beat, bow-wave, breeches buoy, broach, capsize, cargo, cast off, chandler, circumnavigate, coastguard, compass bearing, convoy, course, cruise, current, Davy Jones's locker, dead reckoning, deadweight, disembark, dock, dockyard, dry dock, ebb tide, embark, ferry, fleet, float, flotilla, flotsam, foghorn, fore, foreshore, go about, gybe, harbour, harbour-bar, harbour dues, harbour-master, haven, heave to, head to wind, heavy swell, heel, helm, high tide, inflatable life-raft, jetsam, jetty, knot, launch, lay a course, lay up, lee, leeward, lee shore, life buoy, life-jacket, life-rocket, list, low tide, make fast, marina, marine, maroon, mayday, moor, mooring, mutiny, navigation, neap tide, on board, pitch and toss, plane, put in, put to sea, quay, reach, reef, refit, ride out, riptide, roll, row, run, run aground, run before the wind, salvage, seafaring, sea lane, sea legs, seamanship, seasick, seaworthy, set sail, sheet in, shipping, shipping lane, ship's company, ship water, shipyard, shipwreck, shore leave, sink, slip anchor, slipway, stevedore, stowaway, tack, tide, trim, voyage, wake, wash, watch, wave, weather, weight anchor, wharf, wreck. *see also* **sail**.

navigate *v* steer, drive, direct, pilot, guide, handle, manoeuvre, cruise, sail, skipper, voyage, journey, cross, helm, plot, plan.

navigation *n* sailing, steering, cruising, voyaging, seamanship, helmsmanship.

Navigational aids include:
astronavigation, bell buoy, channel-marker buoy, chart, chronometer, conical buoy, Decca® navigator system, depth gauge, dividers, echosounder, flux-gate compass, Global Positioning System (GPS), gyrocompass, lighthouse, lightship, log, loran (long-range radio navigation), magnetic compass, marker buoy, nautical table, parallel ruler, pilot, radar, sectored leading-light, sextant, VHF radio.

navy *n* fleet, ships, flotilla, armada, warships.

near *adj* **1** NEARBY, close, bordering, adjacent, adjoining, alongside, neighbouring. **2** IMMINENT, impending, forthcoming, coming, approaching. **3** DEAR, familiar, close, related, intimate, akin.
F3 **1** far. **2** distant. **3** remote.

nearby *adj* near, neighbouring, adjoining, adjacent, accessible, convenient, handy.
F3 faraway.
➤ *adv* near, within reach, at close quarters, close at hand, at close range, not far away.

nearly *adv* almost, practically, virtually, closely, approximately, more or less, as good as, just about, roughly, well-nigh.
F3 completely, totally.

neat *adj* **1** TIDY, orderly, smart, spruce, trim, clean, spick-and-span (*infml*), shipshape. **2** DEFT, clever, adroit, skilful, expert. **3** UNDILUTED, unmixed, unadulterated, straight, pure.
F3 **1** untidy. **2** clumsy. **3** diluted.

nebulous *adj* vague, hazy, imprecise, indefinite, indistinct, cloudy, misty, obscure, uncertain, unclear, dim, ambiguous, confused, fuzzy, shapeless, amorphous.
F3 clear.

necessary *adj* needed, required, essential, compulsory, indispensable, vital, mission-critical (*infml*), imperative, mandatory, obligatory, needful, unavoidable, inevitable, inescapable, inexorable, certain.
F3 unnecessary, inessential, unimportant.

necessitate *v* require, involve, entail, call for, demand, oblige, force, constrain, compel.

necessity *n* **1** REQUIREMENT, obligation, prerequisite, essential, fundamental, need, want, compulsion, demand. **2** INDISPENSABILITY, inevitability, needfulness. **3** POVERTY, destitution, hardship.

need *v* miss, lack, want, require, demand, call for, necessitate, have need of, have to, crave.
➤ *n* **1** *a need for caution*: call, demand, obligation, requirement. **2** *the country's needs*: essential, necessity, requisite, prerequisite, desideratum. **3** *a need for equipment*: want, lack, insufficiency, inadequacy, neediness, shortage.

needless *adj* unnecessary, gratuitous, uncalled-for, unwanted, redundant, superfluous, useless, pointless, purposeless.
☒ necessary, essential.

needy *adj* poor, destitute, impoverished, penniless, disadvantaged, deprived, poverty-stricken, underprivileged.
☒ affluent, wealthy, well-off.

negate *v* 1 NULLIFY, annul, cancel, invalidate, undo, countermand, abrogate (*fml*), neutralize, quash, retract, reverse, revoke, rescind, wipe out, void, repeal. 2 DENY, contradict, oppose, disprove, refute, repudiate.
☒ 2 affirm.

negative *adj* 1 CONTRADICTORY, contrary, denying, opposing, invalidating, neutralizing, nullifying, annulling. 2 UNCO-OPERATIVE, cynical, pessimistic, gloomy, unenthusiastic, uninterested, unwilling, defeatist.
☒ 1 affirmative, positive.
2 constructive, positive.
➤ *n* contradiction, denial, opposite, refusal.

neglect *v* 1 DISREGARD, ignore, leave alone, abandon, pass by, rebuff, scorn, disdain, slight, spurn. 2 FORGET, fail (in), omit, overlook, let slide, shirk, skimp.
☒ 1 cherish, appreciate. 2 remember.
➤ *n* negligence, disregard, carelessness, failure, inattention, indifference, slackness, dereliction of duty, forgetfulness, heedlessness, oversight, slight, disrespect.
☒ care, attention, concern.

negligence *n* inattentiveness, carelessness, laxity, neglect, slackness, thoughtlessness, forgetfulness, indifference, omission, oversight, disregard, failure, default.
☒ attentiveness, care, regard.

negligent *adj* neglectful, inattentive, remiss, thoughtless, casual, lax, careless, indifferent, offhand, nonchalant, slack, uncaring, forgetful.
☒ attentive, careful, scrupulous.

negligible *adj* unimportant, insignificant, small, imperceptible, trifling, trivial, minor, minute.
☒ significant.

negotiate *v* 1 CONFER, deal, mediate, arbitrate, bargain, arrange, transact, work out, manage, settle, consult, contract. 2 GET ROUND, cross, surmount, traverse, pass.

negotiation *n* mediation, arbitration, debate, discussion, diplomacy, bargaining, transaction.

negotiator *n* arbitrator, go-between, mediator, intermediary, moderator, intercessor, adjudicator, broker, ambassador, diplomat.

neighbourhood *n* district, locality, vicinity, community, locale, environs, confines, surroundings, region, proximity.

neighbouring *adj* adjacent, bordering, near, nearby, adjoining, connecting, next, surrounding.
☒ distant, remote.

neighbourly *adj* sociable, friendly, amiable, kind, helpful, genial, hospitable, obliging, considerate, companionable.

nerve *n* 1 COURAGE, bravery, mettle, pluck, guts (*infml*), spunk (*infml*), spirit, vigour, intrepidity, daring, fearlessness, firmness, resolution, fortitude, steadfastness, will, determination, endurance, force. 2 (*infml*) AUDACITY, impudence, cheek, effrontery, brazenness, boldness, chutzpah (*infml*), impertinence, insolence.
☒ 1 weakness. 2 timidity.

nerve-racking *adj* harrowing, distressing, trying, stressful, tense, maddening, worrying, difficult, frightening.

nerves *n* nervousness, tension, stress, anxiety, worry, strain, fretfulness.

nervous *adj* highly-strung, excitable, hyper (*infml*), anxious, agitated, nervy (*infml*), on edge, edgy, jumpy (*infml*), jittery (*infml*), tense, fidgety,

apprehensive, neurotic, shaky, uneasy, worried, flustered, fearful.
🔁 calm, relaxed.

nest *n* **1** BREEDING-GROUND, den, roost, eyrie, lair. **2** RETREAT, refuge, haunt, hideaway.

nestle *v* snuggle, huddle, cuddle, curl up.

net[1] *n* mesh, meshwork, web, network, netting, openwork, lattice, lace.
➤ *v* catch, trap, capture, bag, ensnare, entangle, nab (*infml*).

net[2] *adj* nett, clear, after tax, final, lowest.
➤ *v* bring in, clear, earn, make, realize, receive, gain, obtain, accumulate.

network *n* system, organization, arrangement, structure, complex, interconnections, grid, net, maze, mesh, labyrinth, channels, circuitry, convolution, grill, tracks.

neurosis *n* disorder, affliction, abnormality, disturbance, imbalance, derangement, deviation, obsession, mania, phobia.

neurotic *adj* disturbed, maladjusted, anxious, nervous, overwrought, unstable, unhealthy, deviant, abnormal, compulsive, obsessive, phobic.

neuter *v* castrate, emasculate, doctor, geld, spay.

neutral *adj* **1** IMPARTIAL, uncommitted, unbia(s)sed, non-aligned, disinterested, unprejudiced, undecided, non-partisan, non-committal, objective, indifferent, dispassionate, even-handed. **2** DULL, nondescript, colourless, drab, expressionless, indistinct.
🔁 **1** biased, partisan. **2** colourful.

neutralize *v* counteract, offset, counterbalance, negate, cancel, nullify, invalidate, undo, frustrate.

never-ending *adj* everlasting, eternal, non-stop, perpetual, unceasing, uninterrupted, unremitting, interminable, incessant, unbroken, permanent, persistent, unchanging, relentless.
🔁 fleeting, transitory.

nevertheless *adv* nonetheless, notwithstanding (*fml*), still, anyway, even so, yet, however, anyhow, but, regardless.

new *adj* **1** NOVEL, original, fresh, different, unfamiliar, unusual, ground-breaking, brand-new, mint, unknown, unused, virgin, newborn. **2** MODERN, contemporary, current, latest, recent, up to date, up-to-the-minute, topical, trendy (*infml*), ultra-modern, advanced, newfangled (*infml*). **3** CHANGED, altered, modernized, improved, renewed, restored, redesigned. **4** ADDED, extra, additional, more, supplementary.
🔁 **1** usual. **2** outdated, out of date. **3** old, former.

newcomer *n* immigrant, alien, foreigner, incomer, colonist, settler, arrival, outsider, stranger, novice, beginner.

news *n* report, account, information, intelligence, dispatch, communiqué, bulletin, gossip, hearsay, rumour, statement, story, word, tidings, latest, release, scandal, revelation, lowdown (*infml*), exposé, disclosure, gen (*infml*), SP (*infml*), advice.

next *adj* **1** ADJACENT, adjoining, neighbouring, nearest, closest. **2** FOLLOWING, subsequent, succeeding, ensuing, later.
🔁 **2** previous, preceding.
➤ *adv* afterwards, subsequently, later, then.

nibble *n* bite, morsel, taste, titbit, bit, crumb, snack, piece.
➤ *v* bite, eat, peck, pick at, nosh (*sl*), munch, gnaw.

nice *adj* **1** PLEASANT, agreeable, delightful, charming, likable, attractive, good, kind, friendly, well-mannered, polite, respectable. **2** SUBTLE, delicate, fine, fastidious, discriminating, scrupulous, precise, exact, accurate, careful, strict.
🔁 **1** nasty, disagreeable, unpleasant.
2 careless.

nicety *n* **1** DELICACY, refinement, subtlety, distinction, nuance.

2 PRECISION, accuracy, meticulousness, scrupulousness, minuteness, finesse.

niche _n_ **1** RECESS, alcove, hollow, nook, cubby-hole, corner, opening.
2 POSITION, place, vocation, calling, métier, slot.

nick _n_ **1** NOTCH, indentation, chip, cut, groove, dent, scar, scratch, mark. **2** (_sl_) PRISON, jail, police station.
➤ _v_ **1** NOTCH, cut, dent, indent, chip, score, scratch, scar, mark, damage, snick. **2** (_sl_) STEAL, pilfer, knock off (_infml_), pinch (_infml_), nab (_infml_).

nickname _n_ pet name, moniker (_sl_), sobriquet, epithet, diminutive.

night _n_ night-time, darkness, dark, dead of night.
🔁 day, daytime.

nightfall _n_ sunset, dusk, twilight, evening, gloaming.
🔁 dawn, sunrise.

nightmare _n_ **1** BAD DREAM, night terror, hallucination. **2** ORDEAL, horror, torment, trial.

nil _n_ nothing, zero, none, nought, naught, cipher, love, duck, zilch (_sl_).

nimble _adj_ agile, active, lively, sprightly, spry, smart, quick, brisk, nippy (_infml_), deft, alert, light-footed, prompt, ready, swift, quick-witted, sharp.
🔁 clumsy, slow.

nip¹ _v_ bite, pinch, squeeze, snip, clip, tweak, catch, grip, nibble.

nip² _n_ dram, draught, shot, swallow, mouthful, drop, sip, taste, portion.

nobility _n_ **1** NOBLENESS, dignity, grandeur, illustriousness, stateliness, majesty, magnificence, eminence, excellence, superiority, uprightness, honour, virtue, worthiness. **2** ARISTOCRACY, peerage, nobles, gentry, élite, lords, high society.
🔁 **1** baseness. **2** proletariat.

Titles of the nobility include:
aristocrat, baron, baroness, baronet, count, countess, dame, dowager, duchess, duke, earl, grand duchess, grand duke, governor, knight, lady, laird, liege, liege lord, life peer, lord, marchioness, marquess, marquis, noble, nobleman, noblewoman, peer, peeress, ruler, seigneur, squire, thane, viscount, viscountess.

noble _n_ aristocrat, peer, lord, lady, nobleman, noblewoman.
🔁 commoner.
➤ _adj_ **1** ARISTOCRATIC, high-born, titled, high-ranking, patrician, blue-blooded (_infml_). **2** MAGNIFICENT, magnanimous, splendid, stately, generous, dignified, distinguished, eminent, grand, great, honoured, honourable, imposing, impressive, majestic, virtuous, worthy, excellent, elevated, fine, gentle.
🔁 **1** low-born. **2** ignoble, base, contemptible.

nobody _n_ no-one, nothing, nonentity, menial, cipher.
🔁 somebody.

nod _v_ **1** GESTURE, indicate, sign, signal, salute, acknowledge. **2** AGREE, assent. **3** SLEEP, doze, drowse, nap.
➤ _n_ gesture, indication, sign, signal, salute, greeting, beck, acknowledgement.

noise _n_ sound, din, racket, row, clamour, clash, clatter, commotion, outcry, hubbub, uproar, cry, blare, talk, pandemonium, tumult, babble.
🔁 quiet, silence.
➤ _v_ report, rumour, publicize, announce, circulate.

noiseless _adj_ silent, inaudible, soundless, quiet, mute, still, hushed.
🔁 loud, noisy.

noisy _adj_ loud, deafening, ear-splitting, clamorous, piercing, vocal, vociferous, tumultuous, boisterous, obstreperous.
🔁 quiet, silent, peaceful.

nomad _n_ traveller, wanderer, itinerant, gypsy, rambler, roamer, rover, migrant.

nominal _adj_ **1** TITULAR, supposed, purported, professed, ostensible, so-called, theoretical, self-styled, puppet, symbolic. **2** TOKEN, minimal, trifling, trivial, insignificant, small.
🔁 **1** actual, genuine, real.

nominate *v* propose, choose, select, name, designate, submit, suggest, recommend, put up, present, elect, appoint, assign, commission, elevate, term.

nomination *n* proposal, choice, selection, submission, suggestion, recommendation, designation, election, appointment.

nominee *n* candidate, entrant, contestant, appointee, runner, assignee.

nonchalant *adj* unconcerned, detached, dispassionate, offhand, blasé, indifferent, casual, cool, collected, apathetic, careless, insouciant.
🖙 concerned, careful.

non-committal *adj* guarded, unrevealing, cautious, wary, reserved, ambiguous, discreet, equivocal, evasive, circumspect, careful, neutral, indefinite, politic, tactful, tentative, vague.

nonconformist *n* dissenter, rebel, individualist, dissident, radical, protester, heretic, iconoclast, eccentric, maverick, secessionist.
🖙 conformist.

nondescript *adj* featureless, indeterminate, undistinctive, undistinguished, unexceptional, ordinary, run-of-the-mill, commonplace, plain, dull, uninspiring, uninteresting, unclassified.
🖙 distinctive, remarkable.

none *pron* no-one, not any, not one, nobody, nil, zero.

nonplussed *adj* disconcerted, confounded, taken aback, stunned, bewildered, astonished, astounded, dumbfounded, perplexed, stumped, flabbergasted, flummoxed (*infml*), puzzled, baffled, dismayed, embarrassed.

nonsense *n* rubbish, trash, drivel, balderdash, gibberish, gobbledygook, senselessness, stupidity, silliness, foolishness, folly, rot (*infml*), blather, twaddle, ridiculousness, claptrap (*infml*), cobblers (*sl*).
🖙 sense, wisdom.

nonsensical *adj* ridiculous, meaningless, senseless, foolish, inane, irrational, silly, incomprehensible, ludicrous, absurd, fatuous, crazy (*infml*).
🖙 reasonable, sensible, logical.

non-stop *adj* never-ending, uninterrupted, continuous, incessant, constant, endless, interminable, unending, unbroken, round-the-clock, ongoing.
🖙 intermittent, occasional.

nook *n* recess, alcove, corner, cranny, niche, cubby-hole, hideout, retreat, shelter, cavity.

norm *n* average, mean, standard, rule, pattern, criterion, model, yardstick, benchmark, measure, reference.

normal *adj* usual, standard, general, common, ordinary, conventional, average, regular, routine, typical, mainstream, natural, accustomed, well-adjusted, straight, rational, reasonable.
🖙 abnormal, irregular, peculiar.

normality *n* usualness, commonness, ordinariness, regularity, routine, conventionality, balance, adjustment, typicality, naturalness, reason, rationality.
🖙 abnormality, irregularity, peculiarity.

normally *adv* ordinarily, usually, as a rule, typically, commonly, routinely, characteristically.
🖙 abnormally, exceptionally.

nosegay *n* bouquet, posy, spray, bunch.

nosey (*infml*) *adj* inquisitive, meddlesome, prying, interfering, snooping, curious, eavesdropping.

nostalgia *n* yearning, longing, regretfulness, remembrance, reminiscence, homesickness, pining.

nostalgic *adj* yearning, longing, wistful, emotional, regretful, sentimental, homesick.

notable *adj* noteworthy, remarkable, noticeable, striking, extraordinary, impressive, outstanding, marked, unusual, celebrated, distinguished,

famous, eminent, well-known, notorious, renowned, rare.
🖪 ordinary, commonplace, usual.
➤ *n* celebrity, notability, VIP, personage, somebody, dignitary, luminary, worthy.
🖪 nobody, nonentity.

notably *adv* markedly, noticeably, particularly, remarkably, strikingly, conspicuously, distinctly, especially, impressively, outstandingly, eminently.

notation *n* symbols, characters, code, signs, alphabet, system, script, noting, record, shorthand.

notch *n* cut, nick, indentation, incision, score, groove, cleft, mark, snip, degree, grade, step.
➤ *v* cut, nick, score, scratch, indent, mark.

note *n* **1** COMMUNICATION, letter, message, memorandum, reminder, memo (*infml*), line, jotting, record. **2** ANNOTATION, comment, gloss, remark. **3** INDICATION, signal, token, mark, symbol. **4** EMINENCE, distinction, consequence, fame, renown, repute, reputation. **5** HEED, attention, regard, notice, observation.
➤ *v* **1** NOTICE, observe, perceive, heed, detect, mark, remark, mention, see, witness. **2** RECORD, register, write down, enter.

noted *adj* famous, well-known, renowned, notable, celebrated, eminent, prominent, great, acclaimed, illustrious, distinguished, respected, recognized.
🖪 obscure, unknown.

notes *n* jottings, record, impressions, report, sketch, outline, synopsis, draft.

noteworthy *adj* remarkable, significant, important, notable, memorable, exceptional, extraordinary, unusual, outstanding.
🖪 commonplace, unexceptional, ordinary.

nothing *n* nought, zero, cipher, nothingness, zilch (*sl*), nullity, non-existence, emptiness, void, nobody, nonentity.
🖪 something.

notice *v* note, remark, perceive, observe, mind, see, discern, distinguish, make out, mark, detect, heed, spot.
🖪 ignore, overlook.
➤ *n* **1** NOTIFICATION, announcement, information, declaration, memorandum, communication, intelligence, news, warning, instruction. **2** ADVERTISEMENT, poster, sign, bill. **3** REVIEW, comment, criticism. **4** ATTENTION, observation, awareness, note, regard, consideration, heed.

noticeable *adj* perceptible, observable, appreciable, unmistakable, conspicuous, evident, manifest, clear, distinct, significant, striking, plain, obvious, measurable.
🖪 inconspicuous, unnoticeable.

notification *n* announcement, information, notice, declaration, advice, warning, intelligence, message, publication, statement, bulletin, communication.

notify *v* inform, tell, advise, announce, declare, warn, acquaint, alert, publish, disclose, reveal.

notion *n* **1** IDEA, thought, concept, conception, belief, impression, view, opinion, understanding, apprehension. **2** INCLINATION, wish, whim, fancy, caprice.

notoriety *n* infamy, disrepute, dishonour, disgrace, scandal.

notorious *adj* infamous, ill-famed, disreputable, scandalous, dishonourable, disgraceful, ignominious, flagrant, well-known.

nought *n* zero, nil, zilch (*sl*), cipher, naught, nothing, nothingness.

nourish *v* **1** NURTURE, feed, foster, care for, provide for, sustain, support, tend, nurse, maintain, cherish. **2** STRENGTHEN, encourage, promote, cultivate, stimulate.

nourishment *n* nutrition, food, sustenance, diet.

novel *adj* new, original, fresh, ground-breaking, innovative, unfamiliar,

unusual, uncommon, different, imaginative, unconventional, strange.
🔁 hackneyed, familiar, ordinary.
➤ *n* fiction, story, tale, narrative, romance.

novelty *n* **1** NEWNESS, originality, freshness, innovation, unfamiliarity, uniqueness, difference, strangeness. **2** GIMMICK, gadget, trifle, memento, knick-knack, curiosity, souvenir, trinket, bauble, gimcrack.

novice *n* beginner, tiro, learner, pupil, trainee, probationer, apprentice, neophyte (*fml*), amateur, newcomer.
🔁 expert.

now *adv* **1** IMMEDIATELY, at once, directly, instantly, straight away, promptly, next. **2** AT PRESENT, nowadays, these days.

noxious *adj* harmful, poisonous, pernicious, toxic, injurious, unhealthy, deadly, destructive, noisome, foul.
🔁 innocuous, wholesome.

nuance *n* subtlety, suggestion, shade, hint, suspicion, gradation, distinction, overtone, refinement, touch, trace, tinge, degree, nicety.

nub *n* centre, heart, core, middle, nucleus, kernel, crux, gist, pith, point, essence.

nucleus *n* centre, heart, nub, core, focus, kernel, pivot, basis, crux.

nude *adj* naked, bare, undressed, unclothed, stripped, stark-naked, uncovered, starkers (*infml*), in one's birthday suit (*infml*).
🔁 clothed, dressed.

nudge *v*, *n* poke, prod, shove, dig, jog, prompt, push, elbow, bump.

nuisance *n* annoyance, inconvenience, bother, irritation, pest, pain (*infml*), drag (*infml*), bore, problem, trial, trouble, drawback.

null *adj* void, invalid, ineffectual, useless, vain, worthless, powerless, inoperative.
🔁 valid.

nullify *v* annul, revoke, cancel,

invalidate, abrogate (*fml*), abolish, negate, rescind, quash, repeal, counteract.
🔁 validate.

numb *adj* benumbed, insensible, unfeeling, deadened, insensitive, frozen, immobilized.
🔁 sensitive.
➤ *v* deaden, anaesthetize, freeze, immobilize, paralyse, dull, stun.
🔁 sensitize.

number *n* **1** FIGURE, numeral, digit, integer, unit. **2** TOTAL, sum, aggregate, collection, amount, quantity, several, many, company, crowd, multitude, throng, horde. **3** COPY, issue, edition, impression, volume, printing.
➤ *v* count, calculate, enumerate, reckon, total, add, compute, include.

numerous *adj* many, abundant, several, plentiful, copious, profuse, sundry.
🔁 few.

nurse *v* **1** TEND, care for, look after, treat. **2** BREAST-FEED, feed, suckle, nurture, nourish. **3** PRESERVE, sustain, support, cherish, encourage, keep, foster, promote.

> *Nurses include*: charge nurse, children's nurse, dental nurse, district nurse, healthcare assistant, health visitor, home nurse, Iain Rennie nurse, locality manager, Macmillan nurse, matron, midwife, nanny, night nurse, night sister, nurse consultant, nursemaid, nursery nurse, nurse tutor, occupational health nurse, psychiatric nurse, Registered General Nurse (RGN), school nurse, sister, staff nurse, State Enrolled Nurse (SEN), State Registered Nurse (SRN), theatre sister, ward sister.

nurture *n* **1** FOOD, nourishment. **2** REARING, upbringing, training, care, cultivation, development, education, discipline.
➤ *v* **1** FEED, nourish, nurse, tend, care for, foster, support, sustain. **2** BRING UP, rear,

cultivate, develop, educate, instruct, train, school, discipline.

nut

Varieties of nut include: almond, beech nut, brazil nut, cashew, chestnut, cobnut, coconut, filbert, hazelnut, macadamia, monkey nut, peanut, pecan, pine nut, pistachio, walnut.

nutrition *n* food, nourishment, sustenance.

nutritious *adj* nourishing, nutritive, alimentary, wholesome, healthful, health-giving, good, beneficial, strengthening, substantial, invigorating. ✗ bad, unwholesome.

Oo

oasis *n* **1** SPRING, watering-hole. **2** REFUGE, haven, island, sanctuary, retreat.

oath *n* **1** VOW, pledge, promise, word, affirmation, assurance, word of honour. **2** CURSE, imprecation, swear-word, profanity, expletive, blasphemy.

obedient *adj* compliant, docile, acquiescent, submissive, tractable, yielding, dutiful, law-abiding, deferential, respectful, subservient, observant.
☒ disobedient, rebellious, wilful.

obesity *n* fatness, overweight, corpulence, stoutness, grossness, plumpness, portliness, bulk.
☒ thinness, slenderness, skinniness.

obey *v* **1** COMPLY, submit, surrender, yield, be ruled by, bow to, take orders from, defer (to), give way, follow, observe, abide by, adhere to, conform, heed, keep, mind. **2** CARRY OUT, discharge, execute, act upon, fulfil, perform.
☒ **1** disobey.

object[1] *n* **1** THING, entity, article, body. **2** AIM, objective, purpose, goal, target, intention, motive, end, reason, point, design. **3** TARGET, recipient, butt, victim.

object[2] *v* protest, oppose, demur, take exception, disapprove, refuse, complain, rebut, repudiate.
☒ agree, acquiesce.

objection *n* protest, dissent, disapproval, opposition, demur, complaint, challenge, scruple.
☒ agreement, assent.

objectionable *adj* unacceptable, displeasing, unpleasant, offensive, obnoxious, repellent, repugnant, disgusting, disagreeable, abhorrent, detestable, deplorable, despicable.
☒ acceptable.

objective *adj* impartial, unbiased, detached, unprejudiced, unbiased, non-partisan, open-minded, equitable, dispassionate, even-handed, neutral, disinterested, just, fair.
☒ subjective.
➤ *n* object, aim, goal, end, purpose, ambition, mark, target, intention, design.

obligation *n* duty, responsibility, onus, charge, commitment, liability, requirement, bond, contract, debt, burden, trust.

obligatory *adj* compulsory, mandatory, statutory, required, binding, essential, necessary, enforced.
☒ optional.

oblige *v* **1** COMPEL, constrain, coerce, require, make, necessitate, force, bind. **2** HELP, assist, accommodate, do a favour, serve, gratify, please.

obliging *adj* accommodating, co-operative, helpful, considerate, agreeable, friendly, kind, civil.
☒ unhelpful.

oblique *adj* slanting, sloping, inclined, angled, tilted.

obliterate *v* eradicate, destroy, annihilate, delete, blot out, wipe out, erase.

oblivion *n* obscurity, nothingness, unconsciousness, void, limbo.
☒ awareness.

oblivious *adj* unaware, unconscious, inattentive, careless, heedless, unmindful, blind, deaf, insensible, negligent.
☒ aware.

obnoxious *adj* unpleasant, disagreeable, disgusting, loathsome, nasty, horrid, odious, repulsive, revolting, repugnant, sickening, nauseating.
▣ pleasant.

obscene *adj* indecent, improper, immoral, impure, filthy, dirty, bawdy, lewd, licentious, pornographic, X-rated (*infml*), scurrilous, suggestive, foul, disgusting, shocking, shameless, offensive.
▣ decent, wholesome.

obscenity *n* 1 INDECENCY, immodesty, impurity, impropriety, lewdness, licentiousness, suggestiveness, pornography, dirtiness, filthiness, foulness, grossness, indelicacy, coarseness. 2 ATROCITY, evil, outrage, offence. 3 PROFANITY, expletive, swear-word, four-letter word.

obscure *adj* 1 UNKNOWN, unimportant, little-known, unheard-of, undistinguished, nameless, inconspicuous, humble, minor. 2 INCOMPREHENSIBLE, enigmatic, cryptic, recondite, esoteric, arcane, mysterious, deep, abstruse, confusing. 3 INDISTINCT, unclear, indefinite, shadowy, blurred, loudy, faint, hazy, dim, misty, shady, vague, murky, gloomy, dusky.
▣ 1 famous, renowned. 2 intelligible, straightforward. 3 clear, definite.
➤ *v* conceal, cloud, obfuscate, hide, cover, blur, disguise, mask, overshadow, shadow, shade, cloak, veil, shroud, darken, dim, eclipse, screen, block out.
▣ clarify, illuminate.

obsequious *adj* servile, ingratiating, grovelling, fawning, toadying, sycophantic, cringing, deferential, flattering, smarmy (*infml*), unctuous, oily, submissive, subservient, slavish.

observance *n* 1 ADHERENCE, compliance, observation, performance, obedience, fulfilment, honouring, notice, attention. 2 RITUAL, custom, ceremony, practice, celebration.

observant *adj* attentive, alert, vigilant, watchful, perceptive, eagle-eyed, wide-awake, heedful.
▣ unobservant.

observation *n* 1 ATTENTION, notice, examination, inspection, scrutiny, monitoring, study, watching, consideration, discernment. 2 REMARK, comment, utterance, thought, statement, pronouncement, reflection, opinion, finding, note.

observe *v* 1 WATCH, see, study, notice, contemplate, keep an eye on, perceive. 2 REMARK, comment, say, mention. 3 ABIDE BY, comply with, adhere to, honour, keep, fulfil, celebrate, perform.
▣ 1 miss. 3 break, violate.

observer *n* watcher, spectator, viewer, witness, looker-on, onlooker, eyewitness, commentator, bystander, beholder.

obsess *v* preoccupy, dominate, rule, monopolize, haunt, grip, plague, prey on, possess.

obsession *n* preoccupation, fixation, ideé fixe, ruling passion, compulsion, fetish, hang-up (*infml*), infatuation, mania, enthusiasm.

obsessive *adj* consuming, gripping, compulsive, fixed, haunting, nagging, tormenting, maddening.

obsolete *adj* outmoded, disused, out of date, old-fashioned, passé, dated, outworn, old, antiquated, antique, dead, extinct.
▣ modern, current, up to date.

obstacle *n* barrier, bar, obstruction, impediment, hurdle, hindrance, check, snag, stumbling block, drawback, difficulty, hitch, catch, stop, interference, interruption.
▣ advantage, help.

obstinate *adj* stubborn, inflexible, immovable, intractable (*fml*), pig-headed (*infml*), unyielding, intransigent (*fml*), persistent, dogged, headstrong, bloody-minded (*sl*), strong-minded, self-willed, steadfast, firm, determined, wilful.
▣ flexible, tractable.

obstruct *v* block, impede, hinder, prevent, check, frustrate, hamper, clog, choke, bar, barricade, stop, stall, retard, restrict, thwart, inhibit, hold up, curb, arrest, slow down, interrupt, interfere with, shut off, cut off, obscure.
ea assist, further.

obstruction *n* barrier, blockage, jam, log-jam, bar, barricade, hindrance, impediment, check, stop, stoppage, difficulty.
ea help.

obstructive *adj* hindering, delaying, blocking, stalling, unhelpful, awkward, difficult, restrictive, inhibiting.
ea co-operative, helpful.

obtain *v* **1** ACQUIRE, get, gain, come by, attain, procure, secure, earn, achieve. **2** PREVAIL, exist, hold, be in force, be the case, stand, reign, rule, be prevalent.

obtrusive *adj* **1** PROMINENT, protruding, noticeable, obvious, blatant, forward. **2** INTRUSIVE, interfering, prying, meddling, nosey (*infml*), pushy (*infml*).
ea **1** unobtrusive.

obtuse *adj* slow, stupid, thick (*infml*), dull, dense, crass, dumb (*infml*), stolid, dull-witted, thick-skinned.
ea bright, sharp.

obvious *adj* evident, self-evident, manifest, patent, clear, plain, distinct, transparent, undeniable, unmistakable, conspicuous, glaring, apparent, open, unconcealed, visible, noticeable, perceptible, pronounced, recognizable, self-explanatory, straightforward, prominent.
ea unclear, indistinct, obscure.

obviously *adv* plainly, clearly, evidently, manifestly, undeniably, unmistakably, without doubt, certainly, distinctly, of course.

occasion *n* **1** EVENT, occurrence, incident, time, instance, chance, case, opportunity. **2** REASON, cause, excuse, justification, grounds. **3** CELEBRATION, function, affair, party, do (*infml*).

occasional *adj* periodic, intermittent, irregular, sporadic, infrequent, uncommon, incidental, odd, rare, casual.
ea frequent, regular, constant.

occasionally *adv* sometimes, on occasion, from time to time, at times, at intervals, now and then, now and again, irregularly, periodically, every so often, once in a while, off and on, infrequently.
ea frequently, often, always.

occult *adj* mystical, supernatural, magical, esoteric, mysterious, concealed, arcane, recondite, obscure, secret, hidden, veiled.

Terms associated with the occult include: amulet, astral projection, astrology, astrologer, bewitch, black cat, black magic, black mass, cabbala, charm, chiromancer, chiromancy, clairvoyance, clairvoyant, conjure, coven, crystal ball, curse, déjà vu, divination, diviner, divining-rod, dream, ectoplasm, evil eye, evil spirit, exorcism, exorcist, extrasensory perception (ESP), familiar, fetish, fortune-teller, garlic, Hallowe'en, hallucination, hoodoo, horoscope, horseshoe, hydromancer, hydromancy, illusion, incantation, jinx, juju, magic, magician, mascot, medium, necromancer, necromancy, obi, omen, oneiromancer, oneiromancy, Ouija board®, palmist, palmistry, paranormal, pentagram, planchette, poltergeist, possession, prediction, premonition, psychic, rabbit's foot, relic, rune, satanic, Satanism, Satanist, séance, second sight, shaman, shamrock, sixth sense, sorcerer, sorcery, spell, spirit, spiritualism, spiritualist, supernatural, superstition, talisman, tarot card, tarot reading, telepathist, telepathy, totem, trance, vision, voodoo, Walpurgis Night, warlock, white magic, wicca, witch, witchcraft, witch doctor, witch's broomstick, witch's sabbath.

occupant *n* occupier, holder, inhabitant, resident, householder, tenant, user, lessee, squatter, inmate.

occupation *n* 1 JOB, profession, work, vocation, employment, trade, post, calling, business, line, pursuit, craft, walk of life, activity. 2 INVASION, seizure, conquest, control, takeover. 3 OCCUPANCY, possession, holding, tenancy, tenure, residence, habitation, use.

occupy *v* 1 INHABIT, live in, possess, reside in, stay in, take possession of, own. 2 ABSORB, take up, engross, engage, hold, involve, preoccupy, amuse, busy, interest. 3 INVADE, seize, capture, overrun, take over. 4 FILL, take up, use.

occur *v* happen, come about, take place, transpire, chance, come to pass, materialize, befall, develop, crop up, arise, appear, turn up, obtain, result, exist, be present, be found.

occurrence *n* 1 INCIDENT, event, happening, affair, circumstance, episode, instance, case, development, action. 2 INCIDENCE, existence, appearance, manifestation.

odd *adj* 1 UNUSUAL, strange, uncommon, peculiar, abnormal, exceptional, curious, atypical, different, queer, bizarre, left-field, eccentric, remarkable, unconventional, weird, irregular, extraordinary, outlandish, rare. 2 OCCASIONAL, incidental, irregular, random, casual. 3 UNMATCHED, unpaired, single, spare, surplus, left-over, remaining, sundry, various, miscellaneous.
⊟ 1 normal, usual. 2 regular.

oddity *n* 1 ABNORMALITY, peculiarity, rarity, eccentricity, idiosyncrasy, phenomenon, quirk. 2 CURIOSITY, character, freak, misfit.

oddment *n* bit, scrap, leftover, fragment, offcut, end, remnant, shred, snippet, patch.

odds *n* 1 LIKELIHOOD, probability, chances. 2 ADVANTAGE, edge, lead, superiority.

odious *adj* offensive, loathsome, unpleasant, obnoxious, disgusting, hateful, repulsive, repellent, revolting, repugnant, foul, execrable, detestable, abhorrent, horrible, horrid, abominable, despicable.
⊟ pleasant.

odour *n* smell, scent, fragrance, aroma, perfume, redolence, stench, stink (*infml*).

off *adj* 1 ROTTEN, bad, sour, turned, rancid, mouldy, decomposed. 2 CANCELLED, postponed. 3 AWAY, absent, gone. 4 SUBSTANDARD, below par, disappointing, unsatisfactory, slack.
➤ *adv* away, elsewhere, out, at a distance, apart, aside.

off-colour *adj* indisposed, off form, under the weather (*infml*), unwell, sick, out of sorts (*infml*), ill, poorly.

offence *n* 1 MISDEMEANOUR, transgression, violation, wrong, wrongdoing, infringement, crime, misdeed, sin, trespass (*fml*). 2 AFFRONT, insult, injury, snub. 3 RESENTMENT, indignation, pique, umbrage, outrage, hurt, hard feelings.

offend *v* 1 HURT, insult, injure, affront, wrong, wound, displease, snub, upset, annoy, outrage. 2 DISGUST, repel, sicken, nauseate. 3 TRANSGRESS, sin, violate, err.
⊟ 1 please.

offender *n* transgressor, wrongdoer, culprit, criminal, miscreant, guilty party, law-breaker, delinquent.

offensive *adj* 1 DISAGREEABLE, unpleasant, objectionable, displeasing, disgusting, odious, obnoxious, repellent, repugnant, revolting, loathsome, vile, nauseating, nasty, detestable, abominable. 2 INSOLENT, abusive, rude, insulting, disrespectful, impertinent.
⊟ 1 pleasant. 2 polite.
➤ *n* attack, assault, onslaught, invasion, raid, sortie.

offer *v* 1 PRESENT, make available, advance, extend, put forward, submit, suggest, hold out, provide, sell. 2 PROFFER, propose, bid, tender. 3

VOLUNTEER, come forward, present oneself, show willing (*infml*).

➤ *n* proposal, bid, submission, tender, suggestion, proposition, overture, approach, attempt, presentation.

offering *n* present, gift, donation, contribution, subscription.

offhand *adj* casual, unconcerned, uninterested, take-it-or-leave-it (*infml*), brusque, abrupt, perfunctory, informal, cavalier, careless.

➤ *adv* impromptu, off the cuff, extempore (*fml*), off the top of one's head, immediately.

🔳 calculated, planned.

office *n* **1** RESPONSIBILITY, duty, obligation, charge, commission, occupation, situation, post, employment, function, appointment, business, role, service. **2** WORKPLACE, workroom, bureau.

Office equipment includes: acoustic hood, adhesive binder, answering machine, calculator, cash box, collating machine, comb binder, computer, copy holder, data cartridge, date-stamp, desk organizer, desk-top display calculator, Dictaphone®, dictation machine, disk storage system, diskette mailer, duplicator, dust cover, electric typewriter, electronic organizer, electronic typewriter, facsimile machine (or fax), flip chart easel, guillotine, hole puncher, information board, inkpad, intercom, keyboard, laminator, laptop computer, letter-folding machine, letter opener, letter scales, letter tray, message board, microcassette, microcassette recorder, microfiche reader, monitor, monitor arm, mouse, mouse mat, notice board, overhead projector (OHP), paper-folding machine, paper punch, parcel scales, photocopier, plan file, planner, planning board, printer, printwheel, projection screen, reference book, rotary filing system, scanner, screen, screen filter, share certificate book, shredder, slide projector, stapler, staple remover, switchboard, tacker, telephone, telephone directory, telephone index, telex machine, terminal trolley, textphone, thermal binder, time clock, trimmer, typewriter, visitors' book, visual display unit (VDU), wages book, waste paper bin, white board, wire bindings, wire binding machine, word processor.

Office furniture includes: boardroom table, computer desk, conference table, desk, desk lamp, display cabinet, draughtsman's chair, drawing-board, executive chair, executive desk, filing cabinet, filing cupboard, filing trolley, fire cupboard, fire extinguisher, fire safe, lectern, partition, plan chest, printer stand, reception chair, safe, secretarial desk, stationery cupboard, stepstool, storage unit, swivel chair, typist's chair, work station, work table. *see also* **computer**; **stationery**.

officer *n* official, office-holder, public servant, functionary, dignitary, bureaucrat, administrator, representative, executive, agent, appointee.

official *adj* authorized, authoritative, legitimate, formal, licensed, accredited, certified, approved, authenticated, authentic, bona fide, proper.

🔳 unofficial.

➤ *n* office-bearer, officer, functionary, bureaucrat, executive, agent, representative.

Officials include: agent, ambassador, bailiff, bureaucrat, captain, chairman, chairwoman, chairperson, chancellor, chief, clerk, commander, commissar, commissioner, congressman, congresswoman, consul, coroner, councillor, delegate, diplomat, director, elder, envoy, equerry, Eurocrat, executive, Euro-MP, gauleiter, governor, hakim, inspector, justice of the peace (JP), magistrate, manager, mandarin, marshal, mayor, mayoress, member of parliament, minister, monitor, notary, ombudsman, overseer, prefect, president, principal, proctor, proprietor, public prosecutor, registrar, senator (*US*), sheriff, steward, superintendent, supervisor, usher.

officiate *v* preside, superintend, conduct, chair, manage, oversee, run.

officious *adj* obtrusive, dictatorial, intrusive, bossy (*infml*), interfering, meddlesome, over-zealous, self-important, pushy (*infml*), forward, bustling, importunate (*fml*).

offload *v* unburden, unload, jettison, dump, drop, deposit, get rid of, discharge.

off-putting *adj* intimidating, daunting, disconcerting, discouraging, disheartening, formidable, unnerving, unsettling, demoralizing, disturbing.

offset *v* counterbalance, compensate for, cancel out, counteract, make up for, balance out, neutralize.

offshoot *n* branch, outgrowth, limb, arm, development, spin-off, by-product, appendage.

offspring *n* child, children, young, issue, progeny (*fml*), brood, heirs, successors, descendants.
Ⓔ parent(s).

often *adv* frequently, repeatedly, regularly, generally, again and again, time after time, time and again, much.
Ⓔ rarely, seldom, never.

ogre *n* giant, monster, fiend, bogeyman, demon, devil, troll.

oil *v* grease, lubricate, anoint.

oily *adj* **1** GREASY, fatty. **2** UNCTUOUS, smooth, obsequious, ingratiating, smarmy (*infml*), glib, flattering.

ointment *n* salve, balm, cream, lotion, liniment, embrocation.

OK (*infml*) *adj* acceptable, all right, fine, permitted, in order, fair, satisfactory, reasonable, tolerable, passable, not bad, good, adequate, convenient, correct, accurate.

➤ *n* authorization, approval, go-ahead, endorsement, permission, green light, consent, agreement.
➤ *v* approve, authorize, pass, give the go-ahead to, give the green light to (*infml*), rubber-stamp, agree to.
➤ *interj* all right, fine, very well, agreed, right, yes.

old *adj* **1** AGED, elderly, senior, advanced in years, grey, senile. **2** ANCIENT, original, primitive, antiquated, mature. **3** LONG-STANDING, long-established, time-honoured, traditional. **4** OBSOLETE, old-fashioned, out of date, worn-out, decayed, decrepit. **5** FORMER, previous, earlier, one-time, ex-.
Ⓔ **1** young. **2** new. **4** modern. **5** current.

old-fashioned *adj* outmoded, out of date, outdated, dated, unfashionable, obsolete, behind the times, fusty, antiquated, oldfangled, archaic, passé, obsolescent.
Ⓔ modern, up to date.

omen *n* portent, sign, warning, premonition, foreboding, augury, indication.

ominous *adj* portentous, inauspicious, foreboding, menacing, sinister, fateful, unpromising, threatening.
Ⓔ auspicious, favourable.

omission *n* exclusion, gap, oversight, failure, lack, neglect, default, avoidance.

omit *v* leave out, exclude, miss out, pass over, overlook, drop, skip, eliminate, forget, neglect, leave undone, fail, disregard, edit out.
Ⓔ include.

once *adv* formerly, previously, in the past, at one time, long ago, in times past, once upon a time, in the old days.
◇ **at once 1** IMMEDIATELY, instantly, directly, right away, straight away, without delay, now, promptly, forthwith. **2** SIMULTANEOUSLY, together, at the same time.

oncoming *adj* approaching, advancing, upcoming, looming, onrushing, gathering.

one *adj* **1** SINGLE, solitary, lone,

individual, only. **2** UNITED, harmonious, like-minded, whole, entire, complete, equal, identical, alike.

onerous (*fml*) *adj* oppressive, burdensome, demanding, laborious, hard, taxing, difficult, troublesome, exacting, exhausting, heavy, weighty.
Ⅎ easy, light.

one-sided *adj* **1** UNBALANCED, unequal, lopsided. **2** UNFAIR, unjust, prejudiced, biased, partial, partisan. **3** UNILATERAL, independent.
Ⅎ 1 balanced. **2** impartial. **3** bilateral, multilateral.

ongoing *adj* **1** CONTINUING, continuous, non-stop, unceasing, unbroken, uninterrupted, constant. **2** DEVELOPING, evolving, progressing, growing, in progress, unfinished, unfolding.

onlooker *n* bystander, observer, spectator, looker-on, eyewitness, witness, watcher, viewer.

only *adv* just, at most, merely, simply, purely, barely, exclusively, solely.
➤ *adj* sole, single, solitary, lone, unique, exclusive, individual.

onset *n* **1** BEGINNING, start, commencement, inception, outset, outbreak. **2** ASSAULT, attack, onslaught, onrush.
Ⅎ 1 end, finish.

onslaught *n* attack, assault, offensive, charge, bombardment, blitz.

onus *n* burden, responsibility, load, obligation, duty, liability, task.

onward(s) *adv* forward, on, ahead, in front, beyond, forth.
Ⅎ backward(s).

ooze *v* seep, exude, leak, percolate, escape, dribble, drip, drop, discharge, bleed, secrete, emit, overflow with, filter, drain.

opaque *adj* **1** CLOUDY, clouded, murky, dull, dim, hazy, muddied, muddy, turbid. **2** OBSCURE, unclear, impenetrable, incomprehensible, unintelligible, enigmatic, difficult.

Ⅎ 1 transparent. **2** clear, obvious.

open *adj* **1** UNCLOSED, ajar, gaping, uncovered, unfastened, unlocked, unsealed, yawning, lidless. **2** UNRESTRICTED, free, unobstructed, clear, accessible, exposed, unprotected, unsheltered, vacant, wide, available. **3** OVERT, obvious, plain, evident, manifest, noticeable, flagrant, conspicuous. **4** UNDECIDED, unresolved, unsettled, debatable, problematic, moot. **5** FRANK, candid, honest, guileless, natural, ingenuous, unreserved.
Ⅎ 1 shut. **2** restricted. **3** hidden. **4** decided. **5** reserved.
➤ *v* **1** UNFASTEN, undo, unlock, uncover, unseal, unblock, uncork, clear, expose. **2** EXPLAIN, divulge, disclose, lay bare. **3** EXTEND, spread (out), unfold, separate, split. **4** BEGIN, start, commence, inaugurate, initiate, set in motion, launch.
Ⅎ 1 close, shut. **2** hide. **4** end, finish.

open-air *adj* outdoor, alfresco.
Ⅎ indoor.

opening *n* **1** APERTURE, breach, gap, orifice, break, chink, crack, fissure, cleft, chasm, hole, split, vent, rupture. **2** START, onset, beginning, inauguration, inception, birth, dawn, launch. **3** OPPORTUNITY, chance, occasion, break (*infml*), place, vacancy.
Ⅎ 2 close, end.
➤ *adj* beginning, commencing, starting, first, inaugural, introductory, initial, early, primary.
Ⅎ closing.

openly *adv* overtly, frankly, candidly, blatantly, flagrantly, unashamedly, unreservedly, plainly, glaringly, in public, in full view, shamelessly.
Ⅎ secretly, slyly.

operate *v* **1** *it operates on batteries*: function, act, perform, run, work, go. **2** *she can operate that machine*: control, handle, manage, use, utilize, manoeuvre.

operation *n* **1** FUNCTIONING, action, running, motion, movement, performance, working. **2** INFLUENCE, manipulation, handling, management, use, utilization. **3** UNDERTAKING, enterprise, affair, procedure, proceeding, process, business, deal, transaction, effort. **4** CAMPAIGN, action, task, manoeuvre, exercise.

operational *adj* working, in working order, usable, functional, going, viable, workable, ready, prepared, in service.
🖪 out of order.

operative *adj* **1** OPERATIONAL, in operation, in force, functioning, active, effective, efficient, in action, workable, viable, serviceable, functional. **2** KEY, crucial, important, relevant, significant.
🖪 **1** inoperative, out of service.

opinion *n* belief, judgement, view, point of view, idea, perception, stance, theory, impression, feeling, sentiment, estimation, assessment, conception, mind, notion, way of thinking, persuasion, attitude.

opinionated *adj* dogmatic, doctrinaire, dictatorial, arrogant, inflexible, obstinate, stubborn, uncompromising, single-minded, prejudiced, biased, bigoted.
🖪 open-minded.

opponent *n* adversary, enemy, antagonist, foe, competitor, contestant, challenger, opposer, opposition, rival, objector, dissident.
🖪 ally.

opportunity *n* chance, opening, break (*infml*), occasion, possibility, hour, moment.

oppose *v* **1** RESIST, withstand, counter, attack, combat, contest, stand up to, take a stand against, take issue with, confront, defy, face, fight, fly in the face of, hinder, obstruct, bar, check, prevent, thwart. **2** COMPARE, contrast, match, offset, counterbalance, play off.
🖪 **1** defend, support.

opposed *adj* in opposition, against, hostile, conflicting, opposing, opposite, antagonistic, clashing, contrary, incompatible, anti.
🖪 in favour.

opposite *adj* **1** FACING, fronting, corresponding. **2** OPPOSED, antagonistic, conflicting, contrary, hostile, adverse, contradictory, antithetical, irreconcilable, unlike, reverse, inconsistent, different, contrasted, differing.
🖪 **2** same.
➤ *n* reverse, converse, contrary, antithesis, contradiction, inverse.
🖪 same.

opposition *n* **1** ANTAGONISM, hostility, resistance, obstructiveness, unfriendliness, disapproval. **2** OPPONENT, antagonist, rival, foe, other side.
🖪 **1** co-operation, support. **2** ally, supporter.

oppress *v* **1** BURDEN, afflict, lie heavy on, harass, depress, sadden, torment, vex. **2** SUBJUGATE, suppress, subdue, overpower, overwhelm, crush, trample, tyrannize, persecute, maltreat, abuse.

oppression *n* tyranny, subjugation, subjection, repression, despotism, suppression, injustice, cruelty, brutality, abuse, persecution, maltreatment, harshness, hardship.

oppressive *adj* **1** AIRLESS, stuffy, close, stifling, suffocating, sultry, muggy, heavy. **2** TYRANNICAL, despotic, overbearing, overwhelming, repressive, harsh, unjust, inhuman, cruel, brutal, burdensome, onerous, intolerable.
🖪 **1** airy. **2** just, gentle.

oppressor *n* tyrant, bully, taskmaster, slave-driver, despot, dictator, persecutor, tormentor, intimidator, autocrat.

optical

> *Optical instruments and devices include*: astronomical telescope, binoculars, camera, compound microscope, endoscope, field glasses, film projector, laser, magnifying glass, opera glass, periscope, photomicroscope, reflecting telescope, refracting telescope, sextant, simple microscope, slide

projector, spyglass, stereocamera, telescope, telescopic sight, theodolite. *see also* **spectacles**.

optimistic *adj* confident, assured, sanguine, hopeful, positive, upbeat, cheerful, buoyant, bright, idealistic, expectant.
F3 pessimistic.

optimum *adj* best, ideal, perfect, optimal, superlative, top, top-drawer (*infml*), choice, premium.
F3 worst.

option *n* choice, alternative, preference, possibility, selection.

optional *adj* voluntary, discretionary, elective, free, unforced.
F3 compulsory.

oral *adj* verbal, spoken, unwritten, vocal.
F3 written.

orbit *n* **1** CIRCUIT, cycle, circle, course, path, trajectory, track, revolution, rotation. **2** RANGE, scope, domain, influence, sphere of influence, compass.
➤ *v* revolve, circle, encircle, circumnavigate.

ordeal *n* trial, test, tribulation(s), affliction, trouble(s), suffering, anguish, agony, pain, persecution, torture, nightmare.

order *n* **1** COMMAND, directive, decree, injunction, instruction, direction, edict, ordinance, mandate, regulation, rule, precept, law. **2** REQUISITION, request, booking, commission, reservation, application, demand. **3** ARRANGEMENT, organization, grouping, disposition, sequence, categorization, classification, method, pattern, plan, system, array, layout, line-up, structure. **4** PEACE, quiet, calm, tranquillity, harmony, law and order, discipline. **5** ASSOCIATION, society, community, fraternity, brotherhood, sisterhood, lodge, guild, company, organization, denomination, sect, union. **6** CLASS, kind, sort, type, rank, species, hierarchy, family.

F3 **3** confusion, disorder. **4** anarchy.
➤ *v* **1** COMMAND, instruct, direct, bid, decree, require, authorize. **2** REQUEST, reserve, book, apply for, requisition. **3** ARRANGE, organize, dispose, classify, group, marshal, sort out, lay out, manage, control, catalogue.
◇ **out of order 1** BROKEN, broken down, not working, inoperative. **2** DISORDERED, disorganized, out of sequence. **3** UNSEEMLY, improper, uncalled-for, incorrect, wrong.

orderly *adj* **1** ORDERED, systematic, neat, tidy, regular, methodical, in order, well-organized, well-regulated. **2** WELL-BEHAVED, controlled, disciplined, law-abiding.
F3 **1** chaotic. **2** disorderly.

ordinary *adj* common, commonplace, regular, routine, standard, average, everyday, run-of-the-mill, bog-standard (*infml*), usual, unexceptional, unremarkable, vanilla (*infml*), typical, normal, customary, common-or-garden, plain, familiar, habitual, simple, conventional, modest, mediocre, indifferent, pedestrian, prosaic, undistinguished.
F3 extraordinary, unusual.

organ *n* **1** DEVICE, instrument, tool, implement, element, process, structure, unit, member. **2** MEDIUM, agency, forum, vehicle, mouthpiece, voice, publication, newspaper, periodical, journal.

organic *adj* natural, biological, living, animate.

organization *n* **1** ASSOCIATION, institution, society, company, firm, corporation, federation, group, league, club, confederation, consortium. **2** ARRANGEMENT, system, classification, methodology, order, formation, grouping, method, plan, structure, pattern, composition, configuration, design.

organize *v* **1** STRUCTURE, co-ordinate, arrange, order, group, marshal, classify, systematize, tabulate, catalogue. **2** ESTABLISH, found, set up, develop,

form, frame, construct, shape, run.
■ 1 disorganize.

orgy *n* debauch, carousal, revelry, bout, bacchanalia, indulgence, excess, spree.

orientation *n* 1 SITUATION, bearings, location, direction, position, alignment, placement, attitude. 2 INITIATION, training, acclimatization, familiarization, adaptation, adjustment, settling in.

origin *n* 1 SOURCE, spring, fount, foundation, base, cause, derivation, provenance, roots, wellspring. 2 BEGINNING, commencement, start, inauguration, launch, dawning, creation, emergence, genesis. 3 ANCESTRY, descent, extraction, heritage, family, lineage, parentage, pedigree, birth, paternity, stock.
■ 2 end, termination.

original *adj* 1 FIRST, early, earliest, initial, primary, archetypal, rudimentary, embryonic, starting, opening, commencing, first-hand. 2 NOVEL, innovative, ground-breaking, new, creative, fresh, imaginative, inventive, unconventional, unusual, unique.
■ 1 latest. 2 hackneyed, unoriginal.
➤ *n* prototype, master, paradigm, model, pattern, archetype, standard, type.

originate *v* 1 RISE, arise, spring, stem, issue, flow, proceed, derive, come, evolve, emerge, be born. 2 CREATE, invent, inaugurate, introduce, give birth to, develop, discover, establish, begin, commence, start, set up, launch, pioneer, conceive, form, produce, generate.
■ 1 end, terminate.

ornament *n* decoration, adornment, embellishment, garnish, trimming, accessory, frill, trinket, bauble, jewel.
➤ *v* decorate, adorn, embellish, garnish, trim, beautify, brighten, dress up, deck, gild.

ornamental *adj* decorative, embellishing, adorning, attractive, showy.

ornate *adj* elaborate, ornamented,

fancy, decorated, baroque, rococo, florid, flowery, fussy, busy, sumptuous.
■ plain.

orthodox *adj* conformist, conventional, accepted, official, traditional, usual, well-established, established, received, customary, conservative, recognized, authoritative.
■ nonconformist, unorthodox.

ostensible *adj* alleged, apparent, presumed, seeming, supposed, so-called, professed, outward, pretended, superficial.
■ real.

ostentatious *adj* showy, flashy, pretentious, vulgar, loud, garish, gaudy, flash, flamboyant, conspicuous, extravagant.
■ restrained.

ostracize *v* exclude, banish, exile, expel, excommunicate, reject, blacklist, blackball, segregate, send to Coventry, shun, snub, boycott, avoid, cold-shoulder (*infml*), cut.
■ accept, welcome.

other *adj* 1 DIFFERENT, dissimilar, unlike, separate, distinct, contrasting. 2 MORE, further, extra, additional, supplementary, spare, alternative.

oust *v* expel, eject, depose, displace, turn out, throw out, overthrow, evict, drive out, unseat, dispossess, disinherit, replace, topple.
■ install, settle.

out *adj* 1 AWAY, absent, elsewhere, not at home, gone, outside, abroad. 2 REVEALED, exposed, disclosed, public, evident, manifest. 3 FORBIDDEN, unacceptable, impossible, disallowed, excluded. 4 OUT OF DATE, unfashionable, old-fashioned, dated, antiquated, passé. 5 EXTINGUISHED, finished, expired, dead, used up.
■ 1 in. 2 concealed. 3 allowed. 4 up to date.

outbreak *n* eruption, outburst, explosion, flare-up, upsurge, flash, rash, burst, epidemic.

outburst *n* outbreak, eruption,

explosion, flare-up, outpouring, burst, fit, gush, surge, storm, spasm, seizure, gale, attack, fit of temper.

outcast *n* castaway, exile, pariah, outsider, untouchable, refugee, reject, persona non grata.

outcome *n* result, consequence, upshot, conclusion, effect, end result.

outcry *n* protest, complaint, protestation, objection, dissent, indignation, uproar, cry, exclamation, clamour, row, commotion, noise, hue and cry, hullaballoo (*infml*), outburst.

outdated *adj* out of date, old-fashioned, dated, unfashionable, outmoded, behind the times, obsolete, obsolescent, antiquated, archaic.
F3 fashionable, modern.

outdo *v* surpass, exceed, beat, excel, outstrip, outshine, get the better of, overcome, outclass, outdistance.

outdoor *adj* out-of-door(s), outside, open-air.
F3 indoor.

outer *adj* **1** EXTERNAL, exterior, outside, outward, surface, superficial, peripheral. **2** OUTLYING, distant, remote, further.
F3 1 internal. **2** inner.

outfit *n* **1** CLOTHES, costume, apparel (*fml*), ensemble, get-up (*infml*), togs (*infml*), garb. **2** EQUIPMENT, gear (*infml*), kit, rig, trappings, paraphernalia. **3** (*infml*) ORGANIZATION, firm, business, corporation, company, group, team, unit, set, set-up, crew, gang, squad.

outgoing *adj* **1** SOCIABLE, friendly, unreserved, amiable, warm, approachable, expansive, open, extrovert, cordial, easy-going, communicative, demonstrative, sympathetic. **2** DEPARTING, retiring, former, last, past, ex-.
F3 1 reserved. **2** incoming.

outing *n* excursion, expedition, jaunt, pleasure trip, trip, spin, picnic.

outlandish *adj* unconventional,

unfamiliar, bizarre, left-field, strange, odd, weird, eccentric, alien, exotic, barbarous, foreign, extraordinary.
F3 familiar, ordinary.

outlaw *n* bandit, brigand, robber, desperado, highwayman, criminal, marauder, pirate, fugitive.
➤ *v* ban, disallow, forbid, prohibit, exclude, embargo, bar, debar, banish, condemn.
F3 allow, legalize.

outlay *n* expenditure, expenses, outgoings, disbursement (*fml*), cost, spending.
F3 income.

outlet *n* **1** EXIT, way out, vent, egress, escape, opening, release, safety valve, channel. **2** RETAILER, shop, store, market.
F3 1 entry, inlet.

outline *n* **1** SUMMARY, synopsis, précis, bare facts, sketch, thumbnail sketch, abstract. **2** PROFILE, form, contour, silhouette, shape.
➤ *v* sketch, summarize, draft, trace, rough out.

outlook *n* **1** VIEW, viewpoint, point of view, attitude, perspective, frame of mind, mindset, angle, slant, standpoint, opinion. **2** EXPECTATIONS, future, forecast, prospect, prognosis.

outlying *adj* distant, remote, far-off, faraway, far-flung, outer, provincial.
F3 inner.

out-of-the-way *adj* remote, isolated, far-flung, far-off, faraway, distant, inaccessible, little-known, obscure, unfrequented.

output *n* production, productivity, product, yield, manufacture, achievement.

outrage *n* **1** ANGER, fury, rage, indignation, shock, affront, horror. **2** ATROCITY, offence, injury, enormity, barbarism, crime, violation, evil, scandal.
➤ *v* anger, infuriate, affront, incense, enrage, madden, disgust, injure, offend, shock, scandalize.

outrageous *adj* **1** ATROCIOUS, abominable, shocking, scandalous, offensive, disgraceful, monstrous, heinous, unspeakable, horrible. **2** EXCESSIVE, exorbitant, immoderate, unreasonable, extortionate, inordinate, preposterous.
2 acceptable, reasonable.

outright *adj* total, utter, absolute, complete, downright, out-and-out, unqualified, unconditional, perfect, pure, thorough, direct, definite, categorical, straightforward.
ambiguous, indefinite.
➤ *adv* **1** TOTALLY, absolutely, completely, utterly, thoroughly, openly, without restraint, straightforwardly, positively, directly, explicitly. **2** *killed outright*: instantaneously, at once, there and then, instantly, immediately.

outset *n* start, beginning, opening, inception, commencement, inauguration, kick-off (*infml*).
end, conclusion.

outside *adj* **1** EXTERNAL, exterior, outer, surface, superficial, outward, extraneous, outdoor, outermost, extreme. **2** *an outside chance*: remote, marginal, distant, faint, slight, slim, negligible.
1 inside.
➤ *n* exterior, façade, front, surface, face, appearance, cover.
inside.

outsider *n* stranger, intruder, alien, non-member, non-resident, foreigner, newcomer, visitor, intruder, interloper, misfit, odd man out.

outskirts *n* suburbs, vicinity, periphery, fringes, borders, boundary, edge, margin.
centre.

outspoken *adj* candid, frank, forthright, blunt, unreserved, plain-spoken, direct, explicit.
diplomatic, reserved.

outstanding *adj* **1** EXCELLENT, distinguished, eminent, pre-eminent, celebrated, exceptional, superior, remarkable, prominent, superb, great, notable, impressive, striking, superlative, important, noteworthy, memorable, special, extraordinary. **2** OWING, unpaid, due, unsettled, unresolved, uncollected, pending, payable, remaining, ongoing, left-over.
1 ordinary, unexceptional. **2** paid, settled.

outstrip *v* surpass, exceed, better, outdo, beat, top, transcend, outshine, pass, gain on, leave behind, leave standing, outrun, outdistance, overtake, eclipse.

outward *adj* external, exterior, outer, outside, surface, superficial, visible, apparent, observable, evident, supposed, professed, public, obvious, ostensible.
inner, private.

outwardly *adv* apparently, externally, to all appearances, visibly, superficially, supposedly, seemingly, on the surface, at first sight.

outweigh *v* override, prevail over, overcome, take precedence over, cancel out, make up for, compensate for, predominate.

outwit *v* outsmart, outthink, get the better of, trick, better, beat, dupe, cheat, deceive, defraud, swindle.

outworn *adj* outdated, out of date, outmoded, stale, discredited, defunct, old-fashioned, hackneyed, rejected, obsolete, disused, exhausted.
fresh, new.

oval *adj* egg-shaped, elliptical, ovoid, ovate.

ovation *n* applause, acclaim, acclamation, praises, plaudits (*fml*), tribute, clapping, cheering, bravos.
abuse, catcalls.

over *adj* finished, ended, done with, concluded, past, gone, completed, closed, in the past, settled, up, forgotten, accomplished.
➤ *adv* **1** ABOVE, beyond, overhead, on high. **2** EXTRA, remaining, surplus, superfluous, left, unclaimed, unused,

unwanted, in excess, in addition.
➤ *prep* **1** ABOVE, on, on top of, upon, in charge of, in command of. **2** EXCEEDING, more than, in excess of.

overact *v* overplay, exaggerate, overdo, ham (*infml*).
▣ underact, underplay.

overall *adj* total, all-inclusive, all-embracing, comprehensive, inclusive, general, universal, global, broad, blanket, complete, all-over.
▣ narrow, specific.
➤ *adv* in general, on the whole, by and large, broadly, generally speaking.

overbearing *adj* imperious, domineering, arrogant, dictatorial, tyrannical, high-handed, haughty, bossy (*infml*), cavalier, autocratic, oppressive.
▣ meek, unassertive.

overcast *adj* cloudy, grey, dull, dark, sombre, sunless, hazy, lowering.
▣ bright, clear.

overcharge *v* surcharge, short-change, cheat, extort, rip off (*sl*), sting (*sl*), do (*infml*), diddle (*infml*).
▣ undercharge.

overcome *v* conquer, defeat, beat, surmount, triumph over, vanquish, rise above, master, overpower, overwhelm, overthrow, subdue.

overcrowded *adj* congested, packed (out), jam-packed, crammed full, chock-full, chock-a-block, chocker (*infml*), overpopulated, overloaded, swarming.
▣ deserted, empty.

overdo *v* exaggerate, go too far, carry to excess, go overboard (*infml*), lay it on thick (*infml*), overindulge, overstate, overact, overplay, overwork.

overdue *adj* late, behindhand, behind schedule, delayed, owing, unpunctual, slow.
▣ early.

overeat *v* gorge, binge, overindulge, guzzle, stuff oneself, make a pig of oneself, pig out (*infml*), gormandize.
▣ abstain, starve.

overflow *v* spill, overrun, run over,

pour over, well over, brim over, bubble over, surge, flood, inundate, deluge, shower, submerge, soak, swamp, teem.
➤ *n* overspill, spill, inundation, flood, overabundance, surplus.

overhang *v* jut, project, bulge, protrude, stick out, extend.

overhaul *v* **1** RENOVATE, repair, service, recondition, mend, examine, inspect, check, survey, re-examine, fix. **2** OVERTAKE, pull ahead of, outpace, outstrip, gain on, pass.
➤ *n* reconditioning, repair, renovation, check, service, examination, inspection, going-over (*infml*).

overhead *adv* above, up above, on high, upward.
▣ below, underfoot.
➤ *adj* elevated, aerial, overhanging, raised.

overjoyed *adj* delighted, elated, euphoric, ecstatic, in raptures, enraptured, thrilled, jubilant, over the moon (*infml*).
▣ sad, disappointed.

overload *v* burden, oppress, strain, tax, weigh down, bog down, overcharge, encumber.

overlook *v* **1** FRONT ON TO, face, look on to, look over, command a view of. **2** MISS, disregard, ignore, omit, neglect, pass over, let pass, let ride, slight, snub. **3** EXCUSE, forgive, pardon, condone, wink at, turn a blind eye to.
▣ **2** notice. **3** penalize.

overpower *v* overcome, conquer, overwhelm, vanquish, defeat, beat, subdue, overthrow, quell, master, crush, immobilize, floor.

overpowering *adj* overwhelming, powerful, strong, forceful, irresistible, uncontrollable, compelling, extreme, oppressive, suffocating, unbearable, nauseating, sickening.

overrate *v* overestimate, overvalue, overpraise, magnify, blow up, make too much of.
▣ underrate.

overrule v overturn, override, countermand, revoke, reject, rescind (*fml*), reverse, invalidate, cancel, vote down.

overrun v 1 INVADE, occupy, infest, overwhelm, inundate, run riot, spread over, swamp, swarm over, surge over, ravage, overgrow. 2 EXCEED, overshoot, overstep, overreach.

overseer n supervisor, boss (*infml*), chief, foreman, forewoman, manager, superintendent.

overshadow v 1 OBSCURE, cloud, darken, dim, spoil, veil. 2 OUTSHINE, eclipse, excel, surpass, dominate, dwarf, put in the shade, rise above, tower above.

oversight n 1 LAPSE, omission, fault, error, slip-up, mistake, blunder, carelessness, neglect. 2 SUPERVISION, responsibility, care, charge, control, custody, keeping, administration, management, direction.

overt adj open, manifest, plain, evident, observable, obvious, apparent, public, professed, unconcealed. ◨ covert, secret.

overtake v 1 PASS, catch up with, outdistance, outstrip, draw level with, pull ahead of, overhaul. 2 COME UPON, befall, happen, strike, engulf.

overthrow v depose, oust, bring down, topple, unseat, displace, dethrone, conquer, vanquish, beat, defeat, crush, overcome, overpower, overturn, overwhelm, subdue, master, abolish, upset. ◨ install, protect, reinstate, restore. ➤ n ousting, unseating, defeat, deposition, dethronement, fall, rout, undoing, suppression, downfall, end, humiliation, destruction, ruin.

overtone n suggestion, intimation, nuance, hint, undercurrent, insinuation, connotation, association, feeling, implication, sense, flavour.

overture n 1 APPROACH, advance, offer, invitation, proposal, proposition, suggestion, signal, move, motion. 2 PRELUDE, opening, introduction, opening move, (opening) gambit.

overturn v 1 CAPSIZE, upset, upturn, tip over, topple, overbalance, keel over, knock over, spill. 2 OVERTHROW, repeal, rescind, reverse, annul, abolish, destroy, quash, set aside.

overwhelm v 1 OVERCOME, overpower, master, conquer, destroy, defeat, crush, rout, devastate. 2 OVERRUN, inundate, snow under, submerge, swamp, engulf. 3 CONFUSE, bowl over, stagger, floor.

overwork v overstrain, overload, exploit, exhaust, overuse, overtax, strain, wear out, weigh down, bog down, oppress, burden, weary.

overwrought adj tense, agitated, keyed up, on edge, worked up, wound up, frantic, overcharged, overexcited, excited, hyper (*infml*), beside oneself, uptight (*infml*). ◨ calm.

owing adj unpaid, due, owed, in arrears, outstanding, payable, unsettled, overdue. ◇ **owing to** because of, as a result of, on account of, thanks to.

own adj personal, individual, private, particular, idiosyncratic. ➤ v possess, have, hold, retain, keep, enjoy. ◇ **own up** admit, confess, come clean (*infml*), tell the truth, acknowledge.

owner n possessor, holder, landlord, landlady, proprietor, proprietress, master, mistress, freeholder.

Pp

pace *n* step, stride, walk, gait, tread, movement, motion, progress, rate, speed, velocity, celerity, quickness, rapidity, tempo, measure.
➤ *v* step, stride, walk, march, tramp, pound, patrol, mark out, measure.

pacifist *n* peace-lover, pacificist, conscientious objector, peacemaker, peacemonger, dove.
🔁 warmonger, hawk.

pacify *v* appease, conciliate, placate, mollify, calm, compose, soothe, assuage, allay, moderate, soften, lull, still, quiet, silence, quell, crush, put down, tame, subdue.
🔁 anger.

pack *n* 1 PACKET, box, carton, parcel, package, bundle, burden, load, backpack, rucksack, haversack, knapsack, kitbag. 2 GROUP, company, troop, herd, flock, band, crowd, gang, mob.
➤ *v* 1 WRAP, parcel, package, bundle, stow, store. 2 FILL, load, charge, cram, stuff, crowd, throng, press, ram, wedge, compact, compress.

package *n* parcel, pack, packet, box, carton, bale, consignment.
➤ *v* parcel (up), wrap (up), pack (up), box, batch.

packed *adj* filled, full, jam-packed, chock-a-block, chock-full, chocker (*infml*), crammed, crowded, congested.
🔁 empty, deserted.

packet *n* pack, carton, box, bag, package, parcel, case, container, wrapper, wrapping, packing.

pact *n* treaty, convention, covenant, bond, alliance, cartel, contract, deal, bargain, compact, agreement, arrangement, understanding.
🔁 disagreement, quarrel.

pad *n* 1 CUSHION, pillow, wad, buffer, padding, protection. 2 WRITING PAD, notepad, jotter, block.
➤ *v* fill, stuff, wad, pack, wrap, line, cushion, protect.
◇ **pad out** expand, inflate, fill out, augment, amplify, elaborate, flesh out, lengthen, stretch, protract, spin out.

padding *n* 1 FILLING, stuffing, wadding, packing, protection. 2 VERBIAGE, verbosity, wordiness, waffle (*infml*), bombast, hot air.

paddle[1] *n* oar, scull.
➤ *v* row, oar, scull, propel, steer.

paddle[2] *v* wade, splash, slop, dabble.

pagan *n* heathen, atheist, unbeliever, infidel, idolater.
🔁 believer.
➤ *adj* heathen, irreligious, atheistic, godless, infidel, idolatrous.

page[1] *n* leaf, sheet, folio, side.

page[2] *n* page-boy, attendant, messenger, bell-boy, footman, servant.
➤ *v* call, send for, summon, bid, announce.

pageant *n* procession, parade, show, display, tableau, scene, play, spectacle, extravaganza.

pageantry *n* pomp, ceremony, grandeur, magnificence, splendour, glamour, glitter, spectacle, parade, display, show, extravagance, theatricality, drama, melodrama.

pain *n* 1 HURT, ache, throb, cramp, spasm, twinge, pang, stab, sting, smart, soreness, tenderness, discomfort, distress, suffering, affliction, trouble,

anguish, agony, torment, torture. **2**
(*infml*) NUISANCE, bother, bore (*infml*),
bummer (*sl*), annoyance, vexation,
burden, headache (*infml*).
➤ *v* hurt, afflict, torment, torture,
agonize, distress, upset, sadden, grieve.
◨ please, delight, gratify.

pained *adj* hurt, injured, wounded,
stung, offended, aggrieved, reproachful,
distressed, upset, saddened, grieved.
◨ pleased, gratified.

painful *adj* **1** SORE, tender, aching,
throbbing, smarting, stabbing,
agonizing, excruciating. **2** *a painful
experience*: unpleasant, disagreeable,
distressing, upsetting, saddening,
harrowing, traumatic. **3** HARD, difficult,
laborious, tedious.
◨ **1** painless, soothing. **2** pleasant,
agreeable. **3** easy.

painkiller *n* analgesic, anodyne,
anaesthetic, palliative, sedative, drug,
remedy.

painless *adj* pain-free, trouble-free,
effortless, easy, simple, undemanding.
◨ painful, difficult.

pains *n* trouble, bother, effort, travail
(*fml*), labour, care, diligence.

painstaking *adj* careful, meticulous,
scrupulous, thorough, conscientious,
diligent, assiduous, industrious,
hardworking, dedicated, devoted,
persevering.
◨ careless, negligent.

paint *n* colour, colouring, pigment, dye,
tint, stain.

Paints include: acrylic paint,
colourwash, distemper, eggshell,
emulsion, enamel, gloss paint,
gouache, glaze, lacquer, masonry
paint, matt paint, oil paint, oils, pastel,
poster paint, primer, stencil paint,
undercoat, varnish, watercolour,
whitewash.

➤ *v* **1** COLOUR, dye, tint, stain, lacquer,
varnish, glaze, apply, daub, coat, cover,
decorate. **2** PORTRAY, depict, describe,
recount, picture, represent.

painting *n* oil painting, watercolour,
picture, portrait, landscape, still life,
miniature, illustration, fresco, mural.

Painting terms include: abstract, alla
prima, aquarelle, aquatint, art gallery,
bleeding, bloom, brush, filbert brush,
flat brush, round brush, rigger, sable
brush, brush strokes, canvas, canvas
board, capriccio, cartoon, charcoal,
chiaroscuro, collage, composition,
craquelure, diptych, easel, encaustic,
facture, fête champêtre, fête galante,
figurative, foreshortening, fresco,
frieze, frottage, gallery, genre painting,
gesso, gouache, grisaille, grotesque,
hard edge, illustration, icon, impasto,
landscape, mahlstick, miniature,
monochrome, montage, mural, oil
painting, paint, palette, palette knife,
pastels, pastoral, paysage, pencil
sketch, pentimento, perspective,
picture, pietà, pigment, pochade box,
pointillism, portrait, primer, scumble,
secco, sfumato, sgraffito, silhouette,
sketch, still life, stipple, tempera,
thinners, tint, tondo, tone, triptych,
trompe l'œil, turpentine,
underpainting, vignette, wash,
watercolour. *see also* **art**; **paint**;
picture.

pair *n* couple, brace, twosome, duo,
partnership, twins, two of a kind.
➤ *v* match (up), twin, team, mate, marry,
wed, splice, join, couple, link, bracket,
put together.
◨ separate, part.

palace *n* castle, château, mansion,
stately home, basilica, dome.

palatable *adj* tasty, appetizing,
eatable, edible, acceptable,
satisfactory, pleasant, agreeable,
enjoyable, attractive.
◨ unpalatable, unacceptable,
unpleasant, disagreeable.

palate *n* taste, appreciation, liking,
relish, enjoyment, appetite, stomach,
heart.

palatial *adj* grand, magnificent,
splendid, majestic, regal, stately,

grandiose, imposing, luxurious, de luxe, sumptuous, opulent, plush (*infml*), spacious.

pale *adj* **1** PALLID, livid, ashen, ashy, white, chalky, pasty, pasty-faced, waxen, waxy, wan, sallow, anaemic. **2** *pale blue*: light, pastel, faded, washed-out, bleached, colourless, insipid, vapid, weak, feeble, faint, dim.
⊟ **1** ruddy. **2** dark.
➤ *v* whiten, blanch, bleach, fade, dim.
⊟ colour, blush.

pall[1] *n* shroud, veil, mantle, cloak, cloud, shadow, gloom, damper.

pall[2] *v* tire, weary, jade, sate, satiate, cloy, sicken.

palm *n* hand, paw (*infml*), mitt (*sl*).
➤ *v* take, grab, snatch, appropriate.
◇ **palm off** foist, impose, fob off, offload, unload, pass off.

palpable *adj* solid, substantial, material, real, touchable, tangible, visible, apparent, clear, plain, obvious, evident, manifest, conspicuous, blatant, unmistakable.
⊟ impalpable, imperceptible, intangible, elusive.

palpitate *v* flutter, quiver, tremble, shiver, vibrate, beat, pulsate, pound, thump, throb.

paltry *adj* meagre, derisory, contemptible, mean, low, miserable, wretched, poor, sorry, small, slight, trifling, inconsiderable, negligible, trivial, minor, petty, unimportant, insignificant, worthless.
⊟ substantial, significant, valuable.

pamper *v* cosset, coddle, mollycoddle, humour, gratify, indulge, overindulge, spoil, pet, fondle.
⊟ neglect, ill-treat.

pamphlet *n* leaflet, brochure, booklet, folder, circular, handout, flyer, notice.

pan *n* saucepan, frying-pan, pot, casserole, container, vessel.

panache *n* flourish, flamboyance, ostentation, style, flair, élan, dash, spirit, enthusiasm, zest, energy, vigour, verve.

pandemonium *n* chaos, disorder, confusion, commotion, rumpus, turmoil, turbulence, tumult, uproar, din, bedlam, hubbub, hullaballoo, hue and cry, to-do (*infml*).
⊟ order, calm, peace.

pander to humour, indulge, pamper, please, gratify, satisfy, fulfil, provide, cater to.

panel *n* board, committee, jury, team.

pang *n* pain, ache, twinge, stab, sting, prick, jag, stitch, gripe, spasm, throe, agony, anguish, discomfort, distress.

panic *n* agitation, flap (*infml*), alarm, distress, dismay, consternation, fright, fear, horror, terror, frenzy, hysteria.
⊟ calmness, confidence.
➤ *v* lose one's nerve, lose one's head, lose the place (*infml*), go to pieces (*infml*), flap (*infml*), overreact.
⊟ relax.

panic-stricken *adj* alarmed, frightened, horrified, terrified, petrified, scared stiff, in a cold sweat, panicky, frantic, frenzied, hysterical.
⊟ relaxed, confident.

panorama *n* view, vista, prospect, scenery, landscape, scene, spectacle, perspective, overview, survey.

panoramic *adj* scenic, wide, sweeping, extensive, far-reaching, widespread, overall, general, universal.
⊟ narrow, restricted, limited.

pant *v* puff, blow, gasp, wheeze, breathe, sigh, heave, throb, palpitate.

pants *n* **1** UNDERPANTS, drawers, panties, briefs, knickers (*infml*), Y-fronts, boxer shorts, boxers (*infml*), trunks, shorts. **2** TROUSERS, slacks, jeans.

paper *n* **1** NEWSPAPER, daily, broadsheet, tabloid, rag (*sl*), blatt (*sl*), journal, organ. **2** DOCUMENT, credential, authorization, identification, certificate, deed. **3** *a paper on alternative medicine*: essay, composition, dissertation, thesis, treatise, article, report.

Types of paper include: acid-free paper, art paper, bank, blotting paper, bond, carbon paper, cartridge paper, crêpe paper, greaseproof paper, graph paper, handmade paper, manila, notepaper, parchment, rag paper, recycled paper, rice paper, silver paper, sugar paper, tissue paper, toilet paper, tracing paper, vellum, wallpaper, wrapping paper, writing paper; card, cardboard, pasteboard; A3, A4, A5, foolscap, legal (*US*), letter (*US*), quarto, atlas, crown.

parable *n* fable, allegory, lesson, moral tale, story.

parade *n* procession, cavalcade, motorcade, march, column, file, train, review, ceremony, spectacle, pageant, show, display, exhibition.
➤ *v* **1** MARCH, process, file past. **2** SHOW, display, exhibit, show off, vaunt, flaunt, brandish.

paradise *n* heaven, Utopia, Shangri-La, Elysium, Eden, bliss, delight.
🖪 hell, Hades.

paradox *n* contradiction, inconsistency, incongruity, absurdity, oddity, anomaly, mystery, enigma, riddle, puzzle.

paradoxical *adj* self-contradictory, contradictory, conflicting, inconsistent, incongruous, absurd, illogical, improbable, impossible, mysterious, enigmatic, puzzling, baffling.

paragon *n* ideal, exemplar, epitome, quintessence, model, pattern, archetype, prototype, standard, criterion.

paragraph *n* passage, section, part, portion, subsection, subdivision, clause, item.

parallel *adj* equidistant, aligned, coextensive, alongside, analogous, equivalent, corresponding, matching, like, similar, resembling.
🖪 divergent, different.
➤ *n* **1** MATCH, equal, twin, duplicate, analogue, equivalent, counterpart.
2 SIMILARITY, resemblance, likeness,

correspondence, correlation, equivalence, analogy, comparison.
➤ *v* match, echo, conform, agree, correspond, correlate, compare, liken.
🖪 diverge, differ.

paralyse *v* cripple, lame, disable, incapacitate, immobilize, anaesthetize, numb, deaden, freeze, transfix, halt, stop.

paralysed *adj* paralytic, paraplegic, quadriplegic, crippled, lame, disabled, incapacitated, immobilized, numb.
🖪 able-bodied.

paralysis *n* paraplegia, quadriplegia, palsy, numbness, deadness, immobility, halt, standstill, stoppage, shutdown.

parameter *n* variable, guideline, indication, criterion, specification, limitation, restriction, limit, boundary.

paramount *adj* supreme, highest, topmost, predominant, pre-eminent, prime, premier, principal, main, chief, cardinal, primary, first, foremost.
🖪 lowest, last.

paraphernalia *n* equipment, gear, tackle, apparatus, accessories, trappings, bits and pieces, odds and ends, belongings, effects, stuff, things, baggage.

paraphrase *n* rewording, rephrasing, restatement, version, interpretation, rendering, translation.
➤ *v* reword, rephrase, restate, interpret, render, translate.

parasite *n* sponger (*infml*), scrounger (*infml*), cadger (*infml*), hanger-on, freeloader, leech, bloodsucker.

parcel *n* package, packet, pack, box, carton, bundle.
➤ *v* package, pack, wrap, bundle, tie up.
◇ **parcel out** divide, carve up, apportion, allocate, allot, share out, distribute, dispense, dole out, deal out, give out, mete out.

parch *v* dry (up), desiccate, dehydrate, bake, burn, scorch, sear, blister, wither, wizen, shrivel.

parched *adj* **1** ARID, waterless, dry, dried up, dehydrated, scorched, withered, shrivelled. **2** (*infml*) THIRSTY, gasping (*infml*).

pardon *v* forgive, condone, overlook, excuse, vindicate, acquit, absolve, remit, let off, reprieve, free, liberate, release.
Ea punish, discipline.
➤ *n* forgiveness, mercy, clemency, indulgence, amnesty, excuse, acquittal, absolution, reprieve, release, discharge.
Ea punishment, condemnation.

pardonable *adj* forgivable, excusable, justifiable, warrantable, understandable, allowable, permissible, minor, venial.
Ea inexcusable.

pare *v* peel, skin, shear, clip, trim, crop, cut, dock, lop, prune, cut back, reduce, decrease.

parent *n* father, mother, dam, sire, progenitor, begetter, procreator, guardian.

parish *n* district, community, parishioners, church, churchgoers, congregation, flock, fold.

park *n* grounds, gardens, woodland.

> *Types of park include*: amusement park, arboretum, botanical garden, country park, estate, game reserve, municipal park, national park, parkland, pleasance, pleasure garden, pleasure ground, recreation ground, reserve, safari park, theme park, wildlife park.

➤ *v* put, position, deposit, leave.

parliament *n* legislature, senate, congress, house, assembly, convocation, council, diet.

parliament

> *Names of parliaments and political assemblies include*: House of Representatives, Senate (*Australia*); Nationalrat, Bundesrat (*Austria*); Narodno Sobraniye (*Bulgaria*); House of Commons, Senate (*Canada*); National People's Congress (*China*); Folketing (*Denmark*); People's Assembly (*Egypt*); Eduskunta (*Finland*); National Assembly, Senate (*France*); Bundesrat, Bundestag, Landtag (*Germany*); Althing (*Iceland*); Lok Sabha, Rajya Sabha (*India*); Majlis (*Iran*); Dáil, Seanad (*Republic of Ireland*); Knesset (*Israel*); Camera del Deputati, Senato (*Italy*); Diet (*Japan*); Staten-Generaal (*Netherlands*); House of Representatives (*New Zealand*); Northern Irish Assembly (*Northern Ireland*); Storting (*Norway*); Sejm (*Poland*); Cortes (*Portugal*); State Duma, Federation Council (*Russia*); Scottish Parliament (*Scotland*); House of Assembly (*South Africa*); Cortes (*Spain*); Riksdag (*Sweden*); Nationalrat, Ständerat, Bundesrat (*Switzerland*); Porte (*Turkey*); House of Commons, House of Lords (*UK*); House of Representatives, Senate (*US*); National Assembly (*Vietnam*); Welsh Assembly (*Wales*).

parliamentary *adj* governmental, senatorial, congressional, legislative, law-making.

parochial *adj* insular, provincial, parish-pump, petty, small-minded, narrow-minded, inward-looking, blinkered, limited, restricted, confined.
Ea national, international.

parody *n* caricature, lampoon, burlesque, satire, send-up (*infml*), spoof, skit, mimicry, imitation, take-off (*infml*), travesty, distortion.
➤ *v* caricature, lampoon, burlesque, satirize, send up (*infml*), spoof, mimic, imitate, ape, take off (*infml*).

paroxysm *n* fit, seizure, spasm, convulsion, attack, outbreak, outburst, explosion.

parry *v* ward off, fend off, repel, repulse, field, deflect, block, avert, avoid, evade, duck, dodge, sidestep, shun.

parson *n* vicar, rector, priest, minister, pastor, preacher, clergyman, clergywoman, reverend, cleric, churchman, churchwoman.

part n **1** COMPONENT, constituent, element, factor, piece, bit, particle, fragment, scrap, segment, fraction, portion, share, section, division, department, branch, sector, district, region, territory. **2** ROLE, character, duty, task, responsibility, office, function, capacity.
F **1** whole, totality.
➤ v separate, detach, disconnect, sever, split, tear, break, break up, take apart, dismantle, come apart, split up, divide, disunite, part company, disband, disperse, scatter, leave, depart, withdraw, go away.
◇ **part with** relinquish, let go of, give up, yield, surrender, renounce, forgo, abandon, discard, jettison.

partial adj **1** a partial victory: incomplete, limited, restricted, imperfect, fragmentary, unfinished. **2** BIASED, prejudiced, partisan, one-sided, discriminatory, unfair, unjust, predisposed, coloured, affected.
F **1** complete, total. **2** impartial, disinterested, unbiased, fair.
◇ **partial to** fond of, keen on, crazy about (**infml**), mad about (**infml**).

partiality n liking, fondness, penchant, predilection (**fml**), proclivity (**fml**), inclination, preference, predisposition (**fml**).

participant n entrant, contributor, participator, member, party, co-operator, helper, worker.

participate v take part, join in, contribute, engage, be involved, enter, share, partake, co-operate, help, assist.

participation n involvement, sharing, partnership, co-operation, contribution, assistance.

particle n bit, piece, fragment, scrap, shred, sliver, speck, morsel, crumb, iota, whit, jot, tittle, atom, grain, drop. see panel at **atom**.

particular adj **1** on that particular day: specific, precise, exact, distinct, special, peculiar. **2** EXCEPTIONAL, remarkable, notable, marked, thorough, unusual, uncommon. **3** FUSSY, discriminating, choosy (**infml**), finicky, fastidious.
F **1** general.
➤ n detail, specific, point, feature, item, fact, circumstance.

particularly adv especially, exceptionally, remarkably, notably, extraordinarily, unusually, uncommonly, surprisingly, in particular, specifically, explicitly, distinctly.

parting n **1** DEPARTURE, going, leave-taking, farewell, goodbye, adieu. **2** DIVERGENCE, separation, division, partition, rift, split, rupture, breaking.
F **1** meeting. **2** convergence.
➤ adj departing, farewell, last, dying, final, closing, concluding.
F first.

partisan n devotee, adherent, follower, disciple, backer, supporter, champion, stalwart, guerrilla, irregular.
➤ adj biased, prejudiced, partial, predisposed, discriminatory, one-sided, factional, sectarian.
F impartial.

partition n **1** DIVIDER, barrier, wall, panel, screen, room-divider. **2** DIVISION, break-up, splitting, separation, parting, severance.
➤ v **1** SEPARATE, divide, subdivide, wall off, fence off, screen. **2** SHARE, divide, split up, parcel out.

partly adv somewhat, to some extent, to a certain extent, up to a point, slightly, fractionally, moderately, relatively, in part, partially, incompletely.
F completely, totally.

partner n associate, ally, confederate, colleague, team-mate, collaborator, accomplice, helper, mate, sidekick (**infml**), opposite number (**infml**), companion, comrade, consort, spouse, husband, wife.

partnership n **1** ALLIANCE, confederation, affiliation, combination, union, syndicate, co-operative, association, society, corporation, company, firm, fellowship, fraternity, brotherhood, sisterhood. **2** COLLABORATION, co-operation, participation, sharing.

party *n* **1** CELEBRATION, festivity, social, do (*infml*), knees-up (*sl*), rave-up (*sl*), get-together, gathering, reunion, function, reception, at-home, housewarming. **2** *a search party*: team, squad, crew, gang, band, group, company, detachment. **3** *a political party*: faction, side, league, cabal, alliance, association, grouping, combination. **4** PERSON, individual, litigant, plaintiff, defendant.

> *Types of party include*: acid house party, baby shower (*US*), barbecue, bash (*sl*), beanfeast (*infml*), beano (*infml*), birthday party, bridal shower (*US*), bunfight (*infml*), ceilidh, dinner party, disco, discotheque, do (*infml*), flatwarming, garden party, gathering of the clan (*infml*), Hallowe'en party, hen party, hooley, hootenanny (*US infml*), housewarming, orgy, picnic, potluck supper (*US*), pyjama party, rave, rave-up (*sl*), slumber party, social, soirée, stag night, stag party, supper party, tea party, thrash (*infml*), toga party, welcoming party, wrap party.

pass[1] *v* **1** SURPASS, exceed, go beyond, outdo, outstrip, overtake, leave behind. **2** *pass time*: spend, while away, fill, occupy. **3** GO PAST, go by, elapse, lapse, proceed, roll, flow, run, move, go, disappear, vanish. **4** GIVE, hand, transfer, transmit. **5** ENACT, ratify, validate, adopt, authorize, sanction, approve. **6** *pass an exam*: succeed, get through, qualify, graduate.

➤ *n* **1** THROW, kick, move, lunge, swing. **2** PERMIT, passport, identification, ticket, licence, authorization, warrant, permission.

◇ **pass away** die, pass on, expire, decease, give up the ghost.

◇ **pass off 1** FEIGN, counterfeit, fake, palm off. **2** HAPPEN, occur, take place, go off.

◇ **pass out 1** FAINT, black out, lose consciousness, collapse, flake out, keel over (*infml*), drop. **2** GIVE OUT, hand out, dole out, distribute, deal out, share out.

◇ **pass over** disregard, ignore, overlook, miss, omit, leave, neglect.

pass[2] *n* col, defile, gorge, ravine, canyon, gap, passage.

passable *adj* **1** SATISFACTORY, acceptable, allowable, tolerable, average, ordinary, unexceptional, moderate, fair, adequate, all right, OK (*infml*), mediocre. **2** CLEAR, unobstructed, unblocked, open, navigable.

☒ **1** unacceptable, excellent. **2** obstructed, blocked, impassable.

passage *n* **1** PASSAGEWAY, aisle, corridor, hall, hallway, lobby, vestibule, doorway, opening, entrance, exit. **2** THOROUGHFARE, way, route, road, avenue, path, lane, alley. **3** EXTRACT, excerpt, quotation, text, paragraph, section, piece, clause, verse. **4** JOURNEY, voyage, trip, crossing.

passenger *n* traveller, voyager, commuter, rider, fare, hitch-hiker.

passer-by *n* bystander, witness, looker-on, onlooker, spectator.

passing *adj* ephemeral, transient, short-lived, temporary, momentary, fleeting, brief, short, cursory, hasty, quick, slight, superficial, shallow, casual, incidental.

☒ lasting, permanent.

passion *n* feeling, emotion, love, adoration, infatuation, fondness, affection, lust, itch, desire, craving, fancy, mania, obsession, craze, eagerness, keenness, avidity, zest, enthusiasm, fanaticism, zeal, ardour, fervour, warmth, heat, fire, spirit, intensity, vehemence, anger, indignation, fury, rage, outburst.

☒ coolness, indifference, self-possession.

passionate *adj* **1** ARDENT, fervent, eager, keen, avid, enthusiastic, fanatical, zealous, warm, hot, fiery,

inflamed, aroused, excited, impassioned, intense, strong, fierce, vehement, violent, tempestuous, stormy, wild, frenzied. **2** EMOTIONAL, excitable, hot-headed, impetuous, impulsive, quick-tempered, irritable. **3** LOVING, affectionate, lustful, erotic, sexy, sensual, sultry.
⊟ 1 phlegmatic, laid-back (*infml*). **3** frigid.

passive *adj* receptive, unassertive, submissive, docile, unresisting, non-violent, patient, resigned, indifferent, long-suffering, apathetic, lifeless, inert, inactive, non-participating.
⊟ active, lively, responsive, involved.

past *adj* **1** OVER, ended, finished, completed, done, over and done with. **2** FORMER, previous, preceding, foregoing, late, recent. **3** ANCIENT, bygone, olden, early, gone, no more, extinct, defunct, forgotten.
⊟ 2 future.
➤ *n* **1** *in the past*: history, former times, olden days, antiquity. **2** LIFE, experience, background, track record.
⊟ 1 future.

pasta

Forms and shapes of pasta include: agnolotti, anelli, angel's hair, bombolotti, bucatini, cannelloni, cappelletti, casarecci, conchiglie, crescioni, ditali, elbow macaroni, farfalle, farfalline, fedelini, fettuccine, fiochetti, fusilli, gnocchi, lasagne, lasagne verde, linguini, lumache, macaroni, mafalde, manicotti, maruzze, mezzani, noodle, noodle farfel, penne, pennine, ravioli, rigatoni, ruoti, spaghetti, stelline, tagliatelle, taglierini, tortellini, trofie, vermicelli, ziti.

paste *n* adhesive, glue, gum, mastic, putty, cement.
➤ *v* stick, glue, gum, cement, fix.

pastel *adj* delicate, soft, soft-hued, light, pale, subdued, faint.

pastime *n* hobby, activity, game, sport,

recreation, play, fun, amusement, entertainment, diversion, distraction, relaxation.
⊟ work, employment.

pastoral *adj* **1** RURAL, country, rustic, bucolic, agricultural, agrarian, idyllic. **2** ECCLESIASTICAL, clerical, priestly, ministerial.
⊟ 1 urban.

pastry

Types of pastry include: American crust pastry, biscuit-crumb pastry, cheese pastry, choux, Danish pastry, filo pastry, flaky pastry, flan pastry, hot-water crust pastry, one-stage pastry, pâte à savarin, pâte brisée, pâte frolle, pâte sablée, pâte sucrée, plain pastry, pork-pie pastry, puff pastry, rich shortcrust pastry, rough-puff pastry, short pastry, shortcrust pastry, suetcrust pastry, sweet pastry, wholewheat pastry.

pasture *n* grass, grassland, meadow, field, paddock, pasturage, grazing.

pasty *adj* pale, pallid, wan, anaemic, pasty-faced, sickly, unhealthy.
⊟ ruddy, healthy.

pat *v* tap, dab, slap, touch, stroke, caress, fondle, pet.
➤ *n* tap, dab, slap, touch, stroke, caress.
➤ *adv* precisely, exactly, perfectly, flawlessly, faultlessly, fluently.
⊟ imprecisely, inaccurately, wrongly.
➤ *adj* glib, fluent, smooth, slick, ready, easy, facile, simplistic.

patch *n* piece, bit, scrap, spot, area, stretch, tract, plot, lot, parcel.
➤ *v* mend, repair, fix, cover, reinforce.

patchy *adj* uneven, irregular, inconsistent, variable, random, fitful, erratic, sketchy, bitty, spotty, blotchy.
⊟ even, uniform, regular, consistent.

patent *adj* obvious, evident, conspicuous, manifest, clear, transparent, apparent, visible, palpable, unequivocal, open, overt, blatant, flagrant, glaring.
⊟ hidden, opaque.

path *n* route, course, direction, way, passage, road, avenue, lane, footpath, bridleway, trail, track, walk.

pathetic *adj* **1** PITIABLE, poor, sorry, lamentable, miserable, sad, distressing, moving, touching, poignant, plaintive, heart-rending, heartbreaking. **2** (*infml*) CONTEMPTIBLE, derisory, deplorable, useless, worthless, inadequate, meagre, feeble, sad (*infml*).
F3 1 cheerful. **2** admirable, excellent, valuable.

patience *n* calmness, composure, self-control, restraint, tolerance, endurance, forbearance, fortitude, long-suffering, submission, resignation, acceptance, stoicism, persistence, perseverance, diligence.
F3 impatience, intolerance, exasperation.

patient *adj* calm, composed, self-possessed, self-controlled, restrained, even-tempered, mild, lenient, indulgent, understanding, forgiving, tolerant, accommodating, forbearing, long-suffering, uncomplaining, submissive, resigned, philosophical, stoical, persistent, persevering.
F3 impatient, restless, intolerant, exasperated.
➤ *n* invalid, sufferer, case, client.

patriotic *adj* nationalistic, chauvinistic, jingoistic, loyal, flag-waving.

patrol *n* **1** GUARD, sentry, sentinel, watchman. **2** *on patrol*: watch, surveillance, policing, protection, defence.
➤ *v* police, guard, protect, defend, go the rounds, tour, inspect.

patron *n* **1** BENEFACTOR, donor, philanthropist, sponsor, backer, supporter, sympathizer, advocate, champion, defender, protector, guardian, helper. **2** CUSTOMER, client, frequenter, regular, shopper, buyer, purchaser, subscriber.

Occupations with a patron saint include:

Accountants (*Matthew*), Actors (*Genesius; Vitus*), Advertisers (*Bernardino of Siena*), Architects (*Thomas, Apostle*), Artists (*Luke; Angelico*), Astronauts (*Joseph of Cupertino*), Astronomers (*Dominic*), Athletes (*Sebastian*), Authors (*Francis de Sales*), Aviators (*Our Lady of Loreto*), Bakers (*Honoratus*), Bankers (*Bernardino* (*Feltre*)), Barbers (*Cosmas and Damian*), Blacksmiths (*Eligius*), Bookkeepers (*Matthew*), Book trade (*John of God*), Brewers (*Amand; Wenceslaus*), Builders (*Barbara; Thomas, Apostle*), Butchers (*Luke*), Carpenters (*Joseph*), Chemists (*Cosmas and Damian*), Comedians (*Vitus*), Cooks (*Lawrence; Martha*), Dancers (*Vitus*), Dentists (*Apollonia*), Doctors (*Cosmas and Damian; Luke*), Editors (*Francis de Sales*), Farmers (*Isidore*), Firemen (*Florian*), Fishermen (*Andrew; Peter*), Florists (*Dorothy; Thérèse of Lisieux*), Gardeners (*Adam; Fiacre*), Glassworkers (*Luke; Lucy*), Gravediggers (*Joseph of Arimathea*), Grocers (*Michael*), Hotelkeepers (*Amand; Julian the Hospitaler*), Housewives (*Martha*), Jewellers (*Eligius*), Journalists (*Francis de Sales*), Labourers (*James; John Bosco*), Lawyers (*Ivo; Thomas More*), Librarians (*Jerome; Catherine of Alexandria*), Merchants (*Francis of Assisi*), Messengers (*Gabriel*), Metalworkers (*Eligius*), Midwives (*Raymond Nonnatus*), Miners (*Anne; Barbara*), Motorists (*Christopher*), Musicians (*Cecilia; Gregory the Great*), Nurses (*Camillus de Lellis; John of God*), Philosophers (*Thomas Aquinas; Catherine of Alexandria*), Poets (*Cecilia; David*), Police (*Michael*), Postal workers (*Gabriel*), Priests (*Jean-Baptiste Vianney*), Printers (*John of God*), Prisoners (*Leonard*), Radio workers (*Gabriel*), Sailors (*Christopher; Erasmus; Francis of Paola*), Scholars (*Thomas Aquinas*), Scientists (*Albert the Great*), Sculptors (*Luke; Louis*), Secretaries (*Genesius*),

Servants (*Martha; Zita*), Shoemakers (*Crispin; Crispinian*), Singers (*Cecilia; Gregory*), Soldiers (*George; Joan of Arc; Martin of Tours; Sebastian*), Students (*Thomas Aquinas*), Surgeons (*Luke; Cosmas and Damian*), Tailors (*Homobonus*), Tax collectors (*Matthew*), Taxi drivers (*Fiacre*), Teachers (*Gregory the Great; John Baptist de la Salle*), Theologians (*Augustine; Alphonsus Liguori; Thomas Aquinas*), Television workers (*Gabriel*), Undertakers (*Dismas; Joseph of Arimathea*), Waiters (*Martha*), Writers (*Lucy*).

patronage *n* custom, business, trade, sponsorship, backing, support.

patronize *v* **1** SPONSOR, fund, back, support, maintain, help, assist, promote, foster, encourage. **2** FREQUENT, shop at, buy from, deal with.

patronizing *adj* condescending, stooping, overbearing, high-handed, haughty, superior, snobbish, supercilious, disdainful.
☒ humble, lowly.

patter *v* tap, pat, pitter-patter, beat, pelt, scuttle, scurry.
➤ *n* **1** PATTERING, tapping, pitter-patter, beating. **2** *a salesman's patter*: chatter, gabble, jabber, line, pitch, spiel (*sl*), jargon, lingo (*infml*).

pattern *n* **1** SYSTEM, method, order, plan. **2** DECORATION, ornamentation, ornament, figure, motif, design, style. **3** MODEL, template, stencil, guide, original, prototype, standard, norm.

patterned *adj* decorated, ornamented, figured, printed.
☒ plain.

paunch *n* abdomen, belly, pot-belly, beer-belly, corporation (*infml*).

pause *v* halt, stop, cease, discontinue, break off, interrupt, take a break, rest, wait, delay, hesitate.
➤ *n* halt, stoppage, interruption, break, rest, breather (*infml*), lull, let-up (*infml*), respite, gap, interval, interlude, intermission, wait, delay, hesitation.

pave *v* flag, tile, floor, surface, cover, asphalt, tarmac, concrete.

paw *v* maul, manhandle, mishandle, molest.
➤ *n* foot, pad, forefoot, hand.

pawn[1] *n* dupe, puppet, instrument, tool, toy, plaything.

pawn[2] *v* deposit, pledge, stake, mortgage, hock (*sl*), pop (*sl*).

pay *v* **1** REMIT, settle, discharge, reward, remunerate, recompense, reimburse, repay, refund, spend, pay out. **2** BENEFIT, profit, pay off, bring in, yield, return. **3** ATONE, make amends, compensate, answer, suffer.
➤ *n* remuneration, wages, salary, earnings, income, fee, stipend, honorarium, emoluments, payment, reward, recompense, compensation, reimbursement.
◇ **pay back 1** REPAY, refund, reimburse, recompense, settle, square. **2** RETALIATE, get one's own back, take revenge, get even with, reciprocate, counter-attack.
◇ **pay off 1** DISCHARGE, settle, square, clear. **2** DISMISS, fire, sack (*infml*), lay off. **3** *the preparations paid off*: succeed, work.
◇ **pay out** spend, disburse, hand over, fork out (*infml*), shell out (*infml*), lay out.

payable *adj* owed, owing, unpaid, outstanding, in arrears, due, mature.

payment *n* remittance, settlement, discharge, premium, outlay, advance, deposit, instalment, contribution, donation, allowance, reward, remuneration, pay, fee, hire, fare, toll.

peace *n* **1** SILENCE, quiet, hush, stillness, rest, relaxation, tranquillity, calm, calmness, composure, contentment. **2** ARMISTICE, truce, ceasefire, conciliation, concord, harmony, agreement, treaty.
☒ **1** noise, disturbance. **2** war, disagreement.

peaceable *adj* pacific, peace-loving, unwarlike, non-violent, conciliatory, friendly, amicable, inoffensive, gentle,

placid, easy-going (*infml*), mild, serene.
⊟ belligerent, aggressive.

peaceful *adj* quiet, still, restful,
relaxing, tranquil, serene, calm, placid,
unruffled, undisturbed, untroubled,
friendly, amicable, peaceable, pacific,
gentle.
⊟ noisy, disturbed, troubled, violent.

peacemaker *n* appeaser, conciliator,
mediator, arbitrator, intercessor,
peacemonger, pacifist, dove.

peak *n* top, summit, pinnacle, crest,
crown, zenith, height, maximum, climax,
culmination, apex, tip, point.
⊟ nadir, trough.
➤ *v* climax, culminate, come to a head.

peal *n* chime, carillon, toll, knell, ring,
clang, ringing, reverberation, rumble,
roar, crash, clap.
➤ *v* chime, toll, ring, clang, resonate,
reverberate, resound, rumble, roll, roar,
crash.

peasant *n* rustic, provincial, yokel,
bumpkin, oaf, boor, lout.

peculiar *adj* **1** *a peculiar sound*:
strange, odd, curious, funny, weird,
bizarre, extraordinary, unusual,
abnormal, exceptional, unconventional,
offbeat, eccentric, way-out (*sl*),
outlandish, left-field, exotic. **2**
CHARACTERISTIC, distinctive, specific,
particular, special, individual, personal,
idiosyncratic, unique, singular.
⊟ **1** ordinary, normal. **2** general.

peculiarity *n* oddity, bizarreness,
abnormality, exception, eccentricity,
quirk, mannerism, feature, trait, mark,
quality, attribute, characteristic,
distinctiveness, particularity,
idiosyncrasy.

pedantic *adj* stilted, fussy, particular,
precise, exact, punctilious, hair-splitting
(*infml*), nit-picking (*infml*), finical,
academic, bookish, erudite.
⊟ imprecise, informal, casual.

peddle *v* sell, vend, flog (*infml*), hawk,
tout, push, trade, traffic, market, deal in.

pedestal *n* plinth, stand, support,

mounting, foot, base, foundation,
platform, podium.

pedestrian *n* walker, foot-traveller.
➤ *adj* dull, boring, flat, uninspired,
banal, mundane, run-of-the-mill,
commonplace, ordinary, mediocre,
indifferent, prosaic, stodgy, plodding.
⊟ exciting, imaginative.

pedigree *n* genealogy, family tree,
lineage, ancestry, descent, line, family,
parentage, derivation, extraction, race,
breed, stock, blood.

peel *v* pare, skin, strip, scale, flake (off).
➤ *n* skin, rind, zest, peeling.

peep *v* look, peek, glimpse, spy, squint,
peer, emerge, issue, appear.
➤ *n* look, peek, glimpse, glance, squint.

peephole *n* spyhole, keyhole, pinhole,
hole, opening, aperture, slit, chink,
crack, fissure, cleft, crevice.

peer[1] *v* look, gaze, scan, scrutinize,
examine, inspect, spy, snoop, peep,
squint.

peer[2] *n* **1** ARISTOCRAT, noble, nobleman,
lord, duke, marquess, marquis, earl,
count, viscount, baron. **2** EQUAL,
counterpart, equivalent, match, fellow.

peerage *n* aristocracy, nobility, upper
crust.

peeress *n* aristocrat, noble,
noblewoman, lady, dame, duchess,
marchioness, countess, viscountess,
baroness.

peevish *adj* petulant, querulous,
fractious, fretful, touchy, irritable, cross,
grumpy, ratty (*infml*), crotchety, ill-
tempered, crabbed, cantankerous,
crusty, snappy, short-tempered, surly,
sullen, sulky.
⊟ good-tempered.

peg *v* **1** FASTEN, secure, fix, attach, join,
mark. **2** *peg prices*: control, stabilize,
limit, freeze, fix, set.
➤ *n* pin, dowel, hook, knob, marker,
post, stake.

pejorative *adj* derogatory,
disparaging, belittling, slighting,
unflattering, uncomplimentary,

unpleasant, bad, negative.
🔁 complimentary.

pelt v **1** THROW, hurl, bombard, shower, assail, batter, beat, hit, strike. **2** POUR, teem, rain cats and dogs (*infml*). **3** RUSH, hurry, charge, belt (*infml*), tear, dash, speed, career.

pen[1] n fountain pen, ballpoint, Biro®, rollerball, felt-tip pen, light pen, mouse pen.
➤ v write, compose, draft, scribble, jot down.

pen[2] n enclosure, fold, stall, sty, coop, cage, hutch.
➤ v enclose, fence, hedge, hem in, confine, cage, coop, shut up.

penalize v punish, discipline, correct, fine, handicap.
🔁 reward.

penalty n punishment, retribution, fine, forfeit, handicap, disadvantage.
🔁 reward.

penance n atonement, reparation, punishment, penalty, mortification.

pendant n medallion, locket, necklace.

pending adj impending, in the offing, forthcoming, imminent, undecided, in the balance.
🔁 finished, settled.

penetrate v pierce, stab, prick, jab, jag, puncture, probe, sink, bore, enter, infiltrate, permeate, seep, pervade, suffuse.

penetrating adj piercing, stinging, biting, incisive, sharp, keen, acute, shrewd, discerning, perceptive, observant, profound, deep, searching, probing.
🔁 blunt.

penitence n repentance, contrition, remorse, regret, shame, self-reproach.

penitent adj repentant, contrite, sorry, apologetic, remorseful, regretful, conscience-stricken, shamefaced, humble.
🔁 unrepentant, hard-hearted, callous.

penniless adj poor, poverty-stricken, impoverished, destitute, bankrupt, ruined, bust, broke (*infml*), stony-broke (*sl*), skint (*sl*).
🔁 rich, wealthy, affluent.

pension n annuity, superannuation, allowance, benefit, grant.

pensive adj thoughtful, reflective, contemplative, meditative, ruminative, absorbed, preoccupied, absent-minded, wistful, solemn, serious, sober.
🔁 carefree.

pent-up adj repressed, inhibited, restrained, bottled-up, suppressed, stifled.

people n persons, individuals, humans, human beings, mankind, humanity, folk, public, general public, populace, rank and file, population, inhabitants, citizens, community, society, race, nation.
➤ v populate, inhabit, occupy, settle, colonize.

pep (*infml*) n energy, vigour, verve, spirit, vitality, liveliness, joie de vivre, get-up-and-go (*infml*), exuberance, high spirits.
◇ **pep up** (*infml*) invigorate, vitalize, liven up, quicken, stimulate, excite, exhilarate, inspire.
🔁 tone down.

perceive v **1** SEE, discern, make out, detect, discover, spot, catch sight of, notice, observe, view, remark, note, distinguish, recognize. **2** SENSE, feel, apprehend, learn, realize, appreciate, be aware of, know, grasp, understand, gather, deduce, conclude.

perceptible adj perceivable, discernible, detectable, appreciable, distinguishable, observable, noticeable, obvious, evident, conspicuous, clear, plain, apparent, visible.
🔁 imperceptible, inconspicuous.

perception n sense, feeling, impression, idea, conception, apprehension, awareness, consciousness, observation, recognition, grasp, understanding, insight, discernment, taste.

perceptive *adj* discerning, observant, sensitive, responsive, aware, alert, quick, quick-witted, sharp, astute, shrewd. ⊟ unobservant.

perch *v* land, alight, settle, sit, roost, balance, rest.

percolate *v* filter, strain, seep, ooze, leak, drip, penetrate, permeate, pervade.

peremptory *adj* imperious, commanding, dictatorial, autocratic, authoritative, assertive, high-handed, overbearing, domineering, bossy (*infml*), abrupt, curt, summary, arbitrary.

perennial *adj* lasting, enduring, everlasting, eternal, immortal, undying, imperishable, unceasing, incessant, never-ending, constant, continual, uninterrupted, perpetual, persistent, unfailing.

perfect *adj* **1** FAULTLESS, impeccable, flawless, immaculate, unblemished, spotless, blameless, pure, superb, excellent, matchless, incomparable. **2** EXACT, precise, accurate, right, correct, true. **3** IDEAL, model, exemplary, ultimate, consummate, expert, accomplished, experienced, skilful. **4** *perfect strangers*: utter, absolute, sheer, complete, entire, total.
⊟ **1** imperfect, flawed, blemished. **2** inaccurate, wrong. **3** inexperienced, unskilled.
➤ *v* fulfil, consummate, complete, finish, polish, refine, elaborate.
⊟ spoil, mar.

perfection *n* faultlessness, flawlessness, excellence, superiority, ideal, model, paragon, crown, pinnacle, acme, consummation, completion.
⊟ imperfection, flaw.

perfectionist *n* idealist, purist, pedant, stickler.

perfectly *adv* **1** UTTERLY, absolutely, quite, thoroughly, completely, entirely, wholly, totally, fully. **2** FAULTLESSLY, flawlessly, impeccably, ideally, exactly, correctly.
⊟ **1** partially. **2** imperfectly, badly.

perforate *v* hole, punch, drill, bore, pierce, prick, stab, puncture, penetrate.

perforation *n* hole, bore, prick, puncture, dotted line.

perform *v* **1** DO, carry out, execute, discharge, fulfil, satisfy, complete, achieve, accomplish, bring off, pull off, effect, bring about. **2** *perform a play*: stage, put on, present, enact, represent, act, play, appear as. **3** FUNCTION, work, operate, behave, produce.

performance *n* **1** SHOW, act, play, appearance, gig (*sl*), presentation, production, interpretation, rendition, representation, portrayal, acting. **2** ACTION, deed, doing, carrying out, execution, implementation, discharge, fulfilment, completion, achievement, accomplishment. **3** FUNCTIONING, operation, behaviour, conduct.

Types of performance include: act, audition, benefit, box-office hit, bomb (*infml*), charity concert, command performance, concert, début, dress rehearsal, dry run, encore, entertainment, exhibition, farewell performance, first house, first night, flop (*infml*), full house, gala night, gig, last night, last night at the Proms, matinée, one-night stand, opening night, play, pop concert, première, preview, production, read-through, recital, rehearsal, rendition, run-through, second house, sell-out, short run, show, sketch, smash hit (*infml*), sneak preview, theatre, turn. *see also* **theatrical**.

performer *n* actor, actress, player, artiste, entertainer.

perfume *n* scent, fragrance, smell, odour, aroma, bouquet, sweetness, balm, essence, cologne, toilet water, incense.

perhaps *adv* maybe, possibly, conceivably, feasibly.

peril *n* danger, hazard, risk, jeopardy, uncertainty, insecurity, threat, menace.
⊟ safety, security.

perilous *adj* dangerous, unsafe, hazardous, risky, chancy, precarious, insecure, unsure, vulnerable, exposed, menacing, threatening, dire.
Ea safe, secure.

perimeter *n* circumference, edge, border, boundary, frontier, limit, bounds, confines, fringe, margin, periphery.
Ea middle, centre, heart.

period *n* era, epoch, age, generation, date, years, time, term, season, stage, phase, stretch, turn, session, interval, space, span, spell, cycle.

periodic *adj* occasional, infrequent, sporadic, intermittent, recurrent, repeated, regular, periodical, seasonal.

periodical *n* magazine, journal, publication, weekly, monthly, quarterly.

peripheral *adj* **1** MINOR, secondary, incidental, unimportant, irrelevant, unnecessary, marginal, borderline, surface, superficial. **2** OUTLYING, outer, outermost.
Ea 1 major, crucial. **2** central.

perish *v* rot, decay, decompose, disintegrate, crumble, collapse, fall, die, expire, pass away.

perishable *adj* destructible, biodegradable, decomposable, short-lived.
Ea imperishable, durable.

perk (*infml*) *n* perquisite, fringe benefit, benefit, bonus, dividend, gratuity, tip, extra, plus (*infml*).
◇ **perk up** (*infml*) brighten, cheer up, buck up (*infml*), revive, liven up, pep up (*infml*), rally, recover, improve, look up.

permanence *n* fixedness, stability, imperishability, perpetuity, constancy, endurance, durability.
Ea impermanence, transience.

permanent *adj* fixed, stable, unchanging, imperishable, indestructible, unfading, eternal, everlasting, lifelong, perpetual, constant, steadfast, perennial, long-lasting, lasting, enduring, durable.

Ea temporary, ephemeral, fleeting.

permeable *adj* porous, absorbent, absorptive, penetrable.
Ea impermeable, watertight.

permeate *v* pass through, soak through, filter through, seep through, penetrate, infiltrate, pervade, imbue, saturate, impregnate, fill.

permissible *adj* permitted, allowable, allowed, admissible, all right, acceptable, proper, authorized, sanctioned, lawful, legal, legitimate.
Ea prohibited, banned, forbidden.

permission *n* consent, assent, agreement, approval, go-ahead, green light (*infml*), authorization, sanction, leave, warrant, permit, licence, dispensation, freedom, liberty.
Ea prohibition.

permissive *adj* liberal, broad-minded, open-minded, tolerant, forbearing, lenient, easy-going (*infml*), indulgent, overindulgent, lax, free.
Ea strict, rigid.

permit *v* allow, let, consent, agree, admit, grant, green-light (*infml*), authorize, sanction, warrant, license.
Ea prohibit, forbid.
➤ *n* pass, passport, visa, licence, warrant, authorization, sanction, permission.
Ea prohibition.

perpendicular *adj* vertical, upright, erect, straight, sheer, plumb.
Ea horizontal.

perpetrate *v* commit, carry out, execute, do, enact, perform, inflict, wreak.

perpetual *adj* eternal, everlasting, infinite, endless, unending, never-ending, interminable, ceaseless, unceasing, incessant, continuous, uninterrupted, constant, persistent, continual, repeated, recurrent, perennial, permanent, lasting, enduring, abiding, unchanging.
Ea intermittent, temporary, ephemeral, transient.

perpetuate v continue, keep up, maintain, preserve, keep alive, immortalize, commemorate.

perplex v puzzle, baffle, mystify, stump (*infml*), confuse, muddle, confound, bewilder, dumbfound.

persecute v hound, pursue, hunt, bother, worry, annoy, pester, harass, molest, abuse, ill-treat, maltreat, oppress, tyrannize, victimize, martyr, distress, afflict, torment, torture, crucify.
🔁 pamper, spoil.

persecution n harassment, molestation, abuse, maltreatment, discrimination, oppression, subjugation, suppression, tyranny, punishment, torture, martyrdom.

perseverance n persistence, determination, resolution, doggedness, tenacity, diligence, assiduity, dedication, commitment, constancy, steadfastness, stamina, endurance, indefatigability.

persevere v continue, carry on, stick at it (*infml*), keep going, soldier on, persist, plug away (*infml*), remain, stand firm, stand fast, hold on, hang on.
🔁 give up, quit, stop, discontinue.

persist v remain, linger, last, endure, abide, continue, carry on, keep at it, persevere, insist.
🔁 desist, stop.

persistent adj 1 INCESSANT, endless, never-ending, interminable, continuous, unrelenting, relentless, unremitting, constant, steady, continual, repeated, perpetual, lasting, enduring. 2 *persistent effort*: persevering, determined, resolute, tenacious, dogged, stubborn, obstinate, staunch, steadfast, zealous, tireless, unflagging, indefatigable.

person n individual, being, human being, human, man, woman, body, soul, character, type.

personal adj own, private, secret, confidential, intimate, special, particular, individual, exclusive, idiosyncratic, distinctive.
🔁 public, general, universal.

personality n 1 CHARACTER, nature, disposition, temperament, individuality, psyche, traits, make-up, charm, charisma, magnetism. 2 CELEBRITY, celeb (*infml*), notable, personage, public figure, VIP (*infml*), star.

personify v embody, epitomize, typify, exemplify, symbolize, represent, mirror.

personnel n staff, workforce, workers, employees, crew, human resources, manpower, people, members.

perspective n aspect, angle, slant, attitude, mindset, standpoint, viewpoint, point of view, view, vista, scene, prospect, outlook, proportion, relation.

perspiration n sweat, secretion, moisture, wetness.

perspire v sweat, exude (*fml*), secrete, swelter, drip.

persuade v coax, prevail upon, lean on, cajole, wheedle, sweet-talk (*infml*), inveigle, talk into, induce, bring round, win over, convince, convert, sway, influence, lead on, incite, prompt, urge, encourage, entice.
🔁 dissuade, deter, discourage.

persuasion n 1 COAXING, cajolery, wheedling, sweet talk (*infml*), inducement, enticement, pull, power, influence, conviction, conversion. 2 OPINION, school (of thought), party, faction, side, conviction, faith, belief, denomination, sect.

persuasive adj convincing, plausible, cogent, sound, valid, influential, forceful, weighty, effective, telling, potent, compelling, moving, touching.
🔁 unconvincing.

pertinent adj appropriate, suitable, fitting, apt, apposite, relevant, to the point, material, applicable.
🔁 inappropriate, unsuitable, irrelevant.

perturb v disturb, bother, trouble, upset, distress, worry, alarm, unsettle, disconcert, discompose, ruffle, fluster, agitate, vex.
🔁 reassure, compose.

peruse v study, pore over, read, browse, look through, scan, scrutinize, examine, inspect, check.

pervade v affect, penetrate, permeate, percolate, charge, fill, imbue, infuse, suffuse, saturate, impregnate.

pervasive adj prevalent, common, extensive, widespread, general, universal, inescapable, omnipresent, ubiquitous.

perverse adj contrary, wayward, wrong-headed, wilful, headstrong, stubborn, obstinate, unyielding, intransigent, disobedient, rebellious, troublesome, unmanageable, ill-tempered, cantankerous, unreasonable, incorrect, improper.
E3 obliging, co-operative, reasonable.

perversion n 1 CORRUPTION, sleaze, depravity, debauchery, immorality, vice, wickedness, deviance, kinkiness (*infml*), abnormality. 2 TWISTING, distortion, misrepresentation, travesty, misinterpretation, aberration, deviation, misuse, misapplication.

pervert v 1 *pervert the truth*: twist, warp, distort, misrepresent, falsify, garble, misinterpret.
2 CORRUPT, lead astray, deprave, debauch, debase, degrade, abuse, misuse, misapply.
➤ n deviant, debauchee, degenerate, weirdo (*infml*), perv (*sl*).

perverted adj twisted, warped, distorted, deviant, kinky (*infml*), pervy (*sl*), unnatural, abnormal, unhealthy, corrupt, depraved, debauched, debased, immoral, evil, wicked.
E3 natural, normal.

pessimistic adj negative, cynical, fatalistic, defeatist, resigned, hopeless, despairing, despondent, dejected, downhearted, glum, morose, melancholy, depressed, dismal, gloomy, bleak.
E3 optimistic.

pest n nuisance, bother, annoyance, irritation, vexation, trial, curse, scourge, bane, blight, bug.

pester v nag, badger, hound, hassle (*infml*), harass, plague, torment, provoke, worry, bother, disturb, annoy, irritate, pick on, get at (*infml*).

pet n favourite, darling, idol, treasure, jewel.
➤ adj favourite, favoured, preferred, dearest, cherished, special, particular, personal.
➤ v stroke, caress, fondle, cuddle, kiss, neck (*infml*), snog (*sl*).

peter out dwindle, taper off, fade, wane, ebb, fail, cease, stop.

petition n appeal, round robin, application, request, solicitation, plea, entreaty, prayer, supplication, invocation.
➤ v appeal, call upon, ask, crave, solicit, bid, urge, press, implore, beg, plead, entreat, beseech, supplicate, pray.

petrify v terrify, horrify, appal, paralyse, numb, stun, dumbfound.

petty adj 1 MINOR, unimportant, insignificant, trivial, secondary, lesser, small, little, slight, trifling, paltry, inconsiderable, negligible. 2 SMALL-MINDED, mean, ungenerous, grudging, spiteful.
E3 1 important, significant. 2 generous.

petulant adj fretful, peevish, cross, irritable, snappish, bad-tempered, ill-humoured, moody, sullen, sulky, sour, ungracious.

phantom n ghost, spectre, spirit, apparition, vision, hallucination, illusion, figment.

phase n stage, step, time, period, spell, season, chapter, position, point, aspect, state, condition.
◇ **phase out** wind down, run down, ease off, taper off, eliminate, dispose of, get rid of, remove, withdraw, close, terminate.

phenomenal adj marvellous, sensational, stupendous, amazing, remarkable, extraordinary, exceptional, unusual, unbelievable, incredible, astounding, awesome (*infml*).

phenomenon *n* 1 OCCURRENCE, happening, event, incident, episode, fact, appearance, sight. 2 WONDER, marvel, miracle, prodigy, rarity, curiosity, spectacle, sensation.

philanthropic *adj* humanitarian, public-spirited, altruistic, unselfish, benevolent, kind, charitable, alms-giving, generous, liberal, open-handed.
🔁 misanthropic.

philanthropist *n* humanitarian, benefactor, patron, sponsor, giver, donor, contributor, altruist.
🔁 misanthrope.

philanthropy *n* humanitarianism, public-spiritedness, altruism, unselfishness, benevolence, kind-heartedness, charity, alms-giving, patronage, generosity, liberality, open-handedness.
🔁 misanthropy.

philosophical *adj* 1 *a philosophical discussion*: metaphysical, abstract, theoretical, analytical, rational, logical, erudite, learned, wise, thoughtful. 2 RESIGNED, patient, stoical, unruffled, calm, composed.

philosophy *n* metaphysics, rationalism, reason, logic, thought, thinking, wisdom, knowledge, ideology, world-view, doctrine, beliefs, convictions, values, principles, attitude, viewpoint.

> *Philosophical schools of thought include*: absolutism, aesthetics, agnosticism, altruism, antinomianism, a posteriori, a priori, ascetism, atheism, atomism, behaviourism, deduction, deism, deontology, determinism, dialectical materialism, dogmatism, dualism, egoism, empiricism, entailment, Epicureanism, epistemology, ethics, existentialism, fatalism, hedonism, historicism, humanism, idealism, identity, induction, instrumentalism, interactionism, intuition, jurisprudence, libertarianism, logic, logical positivism, materialism, metaphysics, monism, naturalism, nihilism, nominalism, objectivism, ontology, pantheism, phenomenalism, phenomenology, positivism, pragmatism, prescriptivism, rationalism, realism, reductionism, relativism, scepticism, scholasticism, sensationalism, sense data, solipsism, stoicism, structuralism, subjectivism, substance, syllogism, teleology, theism, transcendentalism, utilitarianism.

phlegmatic *adj* placid, stolid, impassive, unemotional, unconcerned, indifferent, matter-of-fact, stoical, philosophical.
🔁 emotional, passionate.

phobia *n* fear, terror, dread, anxiety, neurosis, obsession, mania, hang-up (*infml*), thing (*infml*), aversion, dislike, hatred, horror, loathing, revulsion, repulsion.
🔁 love, liking.

> *Phobias (by name of fear) include*: zoophobia (*animals*), apiphobia (*bees*), ailurophobia (*cats*), necrophobia (*corpses*), scotophobia (*darkness*), cynophobia (*dogs*), claustrophobia (*enclosed places*), panphobia (*everything*), pyrophobia (*fire*), xenophobia (*foreigners*), phasmophobia (*ghosts*), acrophobia (*high places*), hippophobia (*horses*), entomophobia (*insects*), astraphobia (*lightning*), autophobia (*loneliness*), agoraphobia (*open spaces*), toxicophobia (*poison*), herpetophobia (*reptiles*), ophiophobia (*snakes*), tachophobia (*speed*), arachnophobia (*spiders*), triskaidekaphobia (*thirteen*), brontophobia (*thunder*), hydrophobia (*water*). *see also* supplement **Words Grouped by Ending**.

phone *v* telephone, ring (up), call (up), dial, contact, get in touch, give a buzz (*infml*), give a tinkle (*infml*).

phoney (*infml*) *adj* fake, counterfeit,

forged, bogus, trick, false, spurious, assumed, affected, put-on, sham, pseudo, imitation, faux.
🔁 real, genuine.

photocopy *v* copy, duplicate, Photostat, Xerox, print, run off.
➤ *n* copy, duplicate, Photostat, Xerox.

photograph *n* photo, snap, snapshot, print, shot, slide, transparency, picture, image, likeness.
➤ *v* snap, take, film, shoot, video, record.

Photographic equipment includes:
camera, stand, tripod, flash umbrella, boom arm; developer bath, developing tank, dry mounting press, easel, enlarger, enlarger timer, film-drying cabinet, fixing bath, focus magnifier, light-box, negative carrier, print washer, contact printer, photo printer, print-drying rack, paper drier, safelight, stop bath, Vertoscope®, viewer; slide viewer, slide projector, film projector, screen.

Photographic accessories include:
air-shutter release, battery, cable release, camera bag, eye-cup, eyepiece magnifier, film, cartridge film, cassette film, disc film, film pack, filter, colour filter, heat filter, polarizing filter, skylight filter, flashbulb, flash card, flashcube, flashgun, flash unit, hot shoe, lens, afocal lens, auxiliary lens, close-up lens, fish-eye lens, macro lens, supplementary lens, telephoto lens, teleconverter, wide-angle lens, zoom lens, lens cap, lens hood, lens shield, memory card, memory reader, light meter, exposure meter, spot meter, diffuser, barn doors, honeycomb diffuser, parabolic reflector, snoot, slide mount, viewfinder, right-angle finder; camcorder battery discharger/charger/tester, cassette adaptor, remote control, tele-cine converter, video editor, video light, video mixer.
see also **camera**.

---

phrase *n* construction, clause, idiom, expression, saying, utterance, remark.
➤ *v* word, formulate, frame, couch, present, put, express, say, utter, pronounce.

physical *adj* bodily, corporeal, fleshy, incarnate, mortal, earthly, material, concrete, solid, substantial, tangible, visible, real, actual.
🔁 mental, spiritual.

physics

Terms used in physics include:
absolute zero, acceleration, acoustics, alpha particles, analogue signal, applied physics, Archimedes principle, area, atom, beta particles, Big Bang theory, boiling point, bubble-chamber, capillary action, centre of gravity, centre of mass, centrifugal force, chain reaction, chaos, charge, charged particle, circuit, circuit breaker, couple, critical mass, cryogenics, density, diffraction, digital, dynamics, efficiency, elasticity, electric current, electric discharge, electricity, electrodynamics, electromagnetic spectrum, electromagnetic waves, electron, energy, engine, entropy, equation, equilibrium, evaporation, field, flash point, force, formula, freezing point, frequency, friction, fundamental constant, gamma ray, gas, gate, grand unified theory (GUT), gravity, half-life, heat, heavy water, hydraulics, hydrodynamics, hydrostatics, incandescence, indeterminacy principle, inertia, infrared, interference, ion, kinetic energy, kinetic theory, Kelvin effect, laser (light amplification by stimulated emission of radiation), latent heat, law, laws of motion, laws of reflection, laws of refraction, laws of thermodynamics, lens, lever, light, light emission, light intensity, light source, liquid, longitudinal wave, luminescence, Mach number, magnetic field, magnetism, mass, mechanics, microwaves, mirror, Mohs scale, molecule, moment, momentum, motion, neutron, nuclear, nuclear

fission, nuclear fusion, nuclear physics, nucleus, optical centre, optics, oscillation, parallel motion, particle, periodic law, perpetual motion, phonon, photon, photosensitivity, polarity, potential energy, power, pressure, principle, process, proton, quantum chromodynamics (QCD), quantum electrodynamics (QED), quantum mechanics, quantum theory, quark, radiation, radioactive element, radioactivity, radioisotope, radio wave, ratio, reflection, refraction, relativity, resistance, resonance, rule, semiconductor, sensitivity, separation, SI unit, sound, sound wave, specific gravity, specific heat capacity, spectroscopy, spectrum, speed, states of matter, statics, substance, superstring theory, supersymmetry, surface tension, temperature, tension, theory, theory of relativity, thermodynamics, Thomson effect, transverse wave, ultrasound, ultraviolet, uncertainty principle, velocity, visible spectrum, viscosity, volume, wave, wave property, weight, white heat, work, X-ray. *see also* **atom**; **electricity**; **particle**.

physician *n* doctor, medical practitioner, medic (*infml*), general practitioner, GP, houseman, intern, registrar, consultant, specialist, healer.

physique *n* body, figure, shape, form, build, frame, structure, constitution, make-up.

pick *v* **1** SELECT, choose, opt for, decide on, settle on, single out. **2** GATHER, collect, pluck, harvest, cull.

➤ *n* **1** CHOICE, selection, option, decision, preference. **2** BEST, cream, flower, élite, elect.

◇ **pick on** bully, torment, persecute, nag, get at (*infml*), needle (*infml*), bait.

◇ **pick out** spot, notice, perceive, recognize, distinguish, tell apart, separate, single out, hand-pick, choose, select.

◇ **pick up 1** LIFT, raise, hoist. **2** *I'll pick you up at eight*: call for, fetch, collect. **3**

LEARN, master, grasp, gather. **4** IMPROVE, rally, recover, perk up (*infml*). **5** BUY, purchase. **6** OBTAIN, acquire, gain. **7** *pick up an infection*: catch, contract, get.

picket *n* picketer, protester, demonstrator, striker.

➤ *v* protest, demonstrate, boycott, blockade, enclose, surround.

pickle *v* preserve, conserve, souse, marinade, steep, cure, salt.

pictorial *adj* graphic, diagrammatic, schematic, representational, vivid, striking, expressive, illustrated, picturesque, scenic.

picture *n* **1** DEPICTION, portrayal, description, account, report, impression, image, representation. **2** *the picture of health*: embodiment, personification, epitome, archetype, essence. **3** FILM, movie (*infml*), motion picture.

Kinds of picture include: abstract, cameo, caricature, cartoon, collage, design, doodle, drawing, effigy, engraving, etching, fresco, graffiti, graphics, icon, identikit, illustration, image, kakemono, landscape, likeness, miniature, montage, mosaic, mugshot (*infml*), mural, negative, oil-painting, old master, painting, passport photo, Photofit, photograph, photogravure, pin-up, plate, portrait, print, representation, reproduction, self-portrait, silhouette, sketch, slide, snap (*infml*), snapshot, still life, tableau, tapestry, tracing, transfer, transparency, triptych, trompe l'oeil, vignette, watercolour.

➤ *v* **1** IMAGINE, envisage, envision, conceive, visualize, see. **2** DEPICT, describe, represent, show, portray, draw, sketch, paint, photograph, illustrate.

picturesque *adj* **1** ATTRACTIVE, beautiful, pretty, charming, quaint, idyllic, scenic. **2** DESCRIPTIVE, graphic, vivid, colourful, striking.

🔁 **1** unattractive. **2** dull.

piece *n* **1** FRAGMENT, bit, scrap, morsel,

mouthful, bite, lump, chunk, slice, sliver, snippet, shred, offcut, sample, element, component, constituent, part, segment, section, division, fraction, share, portion, quantity. **2** ARTICLE, item, feature, study, work, composition, creation, specimen, example.

pier *n* **1** JETTY, breakwater, landing-stage, quay, wharf. **2** SUPPORT, upright, pillar, post.

pierce *v* penetrate, enter, stick into, puncture, drill, bore, probe, perforate, punch, prick, jab, jag, stab, lance, bayonet, run through, spear, skewer, spike, impale, transfix.

piercing *adj* **1** *a piercing cry*: shrill, high-pitched, loud, ear-splitting, sharp. **2** PENETRATING, probing, searching, incisive. **3** COLD, bitter, raw, biting, keen, fierce, severe, wintry, frosty, freezing. **4** PAINFUL, agonizing, excruciating, stabbing, lacerating.

piety *n* piousness, devoutness, godliness, saintliness, holiness, sanctity, religion, faith, devotion, reverence.
🔁 impiety, irreligion.

pig *n* swine, hog, sow, boar, animal, beast, brute, glutton, gourmand.

pigeonhole *n* compartment, niche, slot, cubby-hole, cubicle, locker, box, place, section, class, category, classification.
➤ *v* compartmentalize, label, classify, sort, file, catalogue, alphabetize, shelve, defer.

pigment *n* colour, hue, tint, dye, stain, paint, colouring, tincture.

pile[1] *n* stack, heap, mound, mountain, mass, accumulation, collection, assortment, hoard, stockpile.
➤ *v* stack, heap, mass, amass, gather, accumulate, build up, assemble, collect, hoard, stockpile, store, load, pack, jam, crush, crowd, flock, flood, stream, rush, charge.

pile[2] *n* post, column, upright, support, bar, beam, foundation.

pile[3] *n* nap, shag, plush, fur, hair, fuzz, down.

pilfer *v* steal, pinch (*infml*), nick (*sl*), nab (*infml*), knock off (*sl*), filch, lift, shoplift, rob, thieve.

pilgrim *n* crusader, traveller, wanderer.

pilgrimage *n* crusade, mission, expedition, journey, trip, tour.

pill *n* tablet, capsule, pellet.

pillar *n* column, shaft, post, mast, pier, upright, pile, support, prop, mainstay, bastion, tower of strength.

pilot *n* **1** FLYER, aviator, airman. **2** NAVIGATOR, steersman, helmsman, coxswain, captain, leader, director, guide.
➤ *v* fly, drive, steer, direct, control, handle, manage, operate, run, conduct, lead, guide, navigate.
➤ *adj* experimental, trial, test, model.

pimple *n* spot, zit (*sl*), blackhead, boil, swelling, lump.

pin *v* tack, nail, fix, affix, attach, join, staple, clip, fasten, secure, hold down, restrain, immobilize.
➤ *n* tack, nail, screw, spike, rivet, bolt, peg, fastener, clip, staple, brooch.
◇ **pin down 1** PINPOINT, identify, determine, specify. **2** FORCE, make, press, pressurize.

pinch *v* **1** SQUEEZE, compress, crush, press, tweak, nip, hurt, grip, grasp. **2** (*infml*) STEAL, nick, pilfer, filch, snatch.
➤ *n* **1** SQUEEZE, tweak, nip. **2** DASH, dab, soupçon, taste, bit, speck, jot, mite, tad. **3** EMERGENCY, crisis, predicament, difficulty, hardship, pressure, stress.

pine *v* long, yearn, ache, sigh, grieve, mourn, wish, desire, crave, hanker, hunger, thirst.

pinnacle *n* **1** PEAK, summit, top, cap, crown, crest, apex, vertex, acme, zenith, height, eminence. **2** SPIRE, steeple, turret, pyramid, cone, obelisk, needle.

pinpoint *v* identify, spot, distinguish, locate, place, home in on, zero in on (*infml*), pin down, determine, specify, define.

pioneer *n* colonist, settler, frontiersman, frontierswoman, explorer, developer, pathfinder, trailblazer, leader, innovator, inventor, discoverer, founder.

➤ *v* invent, discover, originate, create, initiate, instigate, begin, start, launch, institute, found, establish, set up, develop, open up.

pious *adj* **1** DEVOUT, godly, saintly, holy, spiritual, religious, reverent, good, virtuous, righteous, moral. **2** SANCTIMONIOUS, holier-than-thou, self-righteous, goody-goody (*infml*), hypocritical.

🔁 **1** impious, irreligious, irreverent.

pipe *n* tube, hose, piping, tubing, pipeline, line, main, flue, duct, conduit, channel, passage, conveyor.

➤ *v* **1** CHANNEL, funnel, siphon, carry, convey, conduct, transmit, supply, deliver. **2** WHISTLE, chirp, tweet, cheep, peep, twitter, sing, warble, trill, play, sound.

piquant *adj* **1** *piquant sauce*: spicy, tangy, savoury, salty, peppery, pungent, sharp, biting, stinging, nippy (*infml*). **2** LIVELY, spirited, stimulating, provocative, interesting, sparkling.

🔁 **1** bland, insipid. **2** dull, banal.

pique *n* annoyance, irritation, vexation, displeasure, offence, huff (*infml*), resentment, grudge.

piqued *adj* annoyed, irritated, vexed, riled, angry, displeased, offended, wounded, miffed (*infml*), peeved (*infml*), put out, resentful.

pit *n* mine, coalmine, excavation, trench, ditch, hollow, depression, indentation, dent, hole, cavity, crater, pothole, gulf, chasm, abyss.

pitch *v* **1** THROW, fling, toss, chuck (*infml*), lob, bowl, hurl, heave, sling, fire, launch, aim, direct. **2** PLUNGE, dive, plummet, drop, fall headlong, tumble, lurch, roll, wallow. **3** *pitch camp*: erect, put up, set up, place, station, settle, plant, fix.

➤ *n* **1** *cricket pitch*: ground, field,

playing-field, arena, stadium. **2** SOUND, tone, timbre, modulation, frequency, level. **3** GRADIENT, incline, slope, tilt, angle, degree, steepness.

piteous *adj* poignant, moving, touching, distressing, heart-rending, plaintive, mournful, sad, sorrowful, woeful, wretched, pitiful, pitiable, pathetic.

pitfall *n* danger, peril, hazard, trap, snare, stumbling block, catch, snag, drawback, difficulty.

pith *n* importance, significance, moment, weight, value, consequence, substance, matter, marrow, meat, gist, essence, crux, nub, heart, core, kernel.

pithy *adj* succinct, concise, compact, terse, short, brief, pointed, trenchant, forceful, cogent, telling.

🔁 wordy, verbose.

pitiful *adj* **1** CONTEMPTIBLE, despicable, low, mean, vile, shabby, deplorable, lamentable, woeful, inadequate, hopeless, pathetic (*infml*), sad (*infml*), insignificant, paltry, worthless. **2** PITEOUS, doleful, mournful, distressing, heart-rending, pathetic, pitiable, sad, miserable, wretched, poor, sorry.

pitiless *adj* merciless, cold-hearted, unsympathetic, unfeeling, uncaring, hard-hearted, callous, cruel, inhuman, brutal, cold-blooded, ruthless, relentless, unremitting, inexorable, harsh.

🔁 merciful, compassionate, kind, gentle.

pittance *n* modicum, crumb, drop (in the ocean), chicken-feed (*infml*), peanuts (*sl*), buttons (*sl*), trifle.

pitted *adj* dented, holey, potholed, pockmarked, blemished, scarred, marked, notched, indented, rough.

pity *n* **1** SYMPATHY, commiseration, regret, understanding, fellow-feeling, empathy, compassion, kindness, tenderness, mercy, forbearance. **2** *what a pity!*: shame, misfortune, bad luck.

🔁 **1** cruelty, anger, scorn.

> *v* feel sorry for, feel for, sympathize with, commiserate with, grieve for, weep for.

pivot *n* axis, hinge, axle, spindle, kingpin, linchpin, swivel, hub, focal point, centre, heart.

> *v* **1** SWIVEL, turn, spin, revolve, rotate, swing. **2** DEPEND, rely, hinge, hang, lie.

placard *n* poster, bill, notice, sign, advertisement.

placate *v* appease, pacify, conciliate, mollify, calm, assuage, soothe, lull, quiet.

🔁 anger, enrage, incense, infuriate.

place *n* **1** SITE, locale, venue, location, situation, spot, point, position, seat, space, room. **2** CITY, town, village, locality, neighbourhood, district, area, region. **3** BUILDING, property, dwelling, residence, house, flat, apartment, pad (*infml*), home.

> *v* put, set, plant, fix, position, locate, situate, rest, settle, lay, stand, deposit, leave.

◊ **in place of** instead of, in lieu of, as a replacement for, as a substitute for, as an alternative to.

◊ **out of place** inappropriate, unsuitable, unfitting, unbecoming, unseemly.

◊ **take place** happen, occur, come about, arise.

placid *adj* calm, composed, unruffled, untroubled, cool, self-possessed, level-headed, imperturbable, mild, gentle, equable, even-tempered, serene, tranquil, still, quiet, peaceful, restful.

🔁 excitable, agitated, disturbed.

plagiarize *v* crib (*infml*), copy, reproduce, imitate, counterfeit, pirate, infringe copyright, poach, steal, lift (*infml*), appropriate (*fml*), borrow.

plague *n* **1** PESTILENCE, epidemic, disease, infection, contagion, infestation. **2** NUISANCE, annoyance, curse, scourge, trial, affliction, torment, calamity.

> *v* annoy, vex, bother, disturb, trouble, distress, upset, pester, harass, hound, haunt, bedevil, afflict, torment, torture, persecute.

plain *adj* **1** *plain cookery*: ordinary, basic, simple, unpretentious, modest, unadorned, unelaborate, restrained. **2** OBVIOUS, evident, patent, clear, manifest, understandable, apparent, visible, unmistakable. **3** FRANK, candid, blunt, outspoken, direct, forthright, straightforward, unambiguous, plain-spoken, open, honest, truthful. **4** UNATTRACTIVE, ugly, unprepossessing, unlovely. **5** *plain fabric*: unpatterned, unvariegated, uncoloured, self-coloured.

🔁 **1** fancy, elaborate. **2** unclear, obscure. **3** devious, deceitful. **4** attractive, good-looking. **5** patterned.

> *n* grassland, prairie, steppe, lowland, flat, plateau, tableland.

plaintive *adj* doleful, mournful, melancholy, wistful, sad, sorrowful, grief-stricken, piteous, heart-rending.

plan *n* **1** BLUEPRINT, layout, diagram, chart, map, drawing, sketch, design, representation. **2** IDEA, suggestion, proposal, proposition, project, scheme, plot, system, method, procedure, strategy, programme, schedule, scenario.

> *v* **1** PLOT, scheme, design, invent, devise, contrive, formulate, frame, draft, outline, prepare, organize, arrange. **2** AIM, intend, propose, contemplate, envisage, foresee.

planet

> *Planets within the Earth's solar system (nearest the sun shown first) are*: Mercury, Venus, Earth, Mars, Jupiter, Saturn, Uranus, Neptune, Pluto.

plant

> *Plants include*: annual, biennial, perennial, herbaceous plant, evergreen, succulent, cultivar, hybrid, house plant, pot plant; flower, herb, shrub, bush, tree, vegetable, grass, vine, weed, cereal, wild flower, air plant, water plant, cactus, fern, moss,

algae, lichen, fungus; bulb, corm, seedling, sapling, bush, climber. *see also* **algae**; **bulb**; **flower**; **grass**; **leaf**; **poisonous**; **shrub**; **weed**; **wild flower**.

n factory, works, foundry, mill, shop, yard, workshop, machinery, apparatus, equipment, gear.

➤ *v* 1 SOW, seed, bury, transplant. 2 INSERT, put, place, set, fix, lodge, root, settle, found, establish.

plaster *n* 1 STICKING-PLASTER, dressing, bandage. 2 PLASTER OF PARIS, mortar, stucco.

➤ *v* daub, smear, coat, cover, spread.

plastic *adj* soft, pliable, flexible, supple, malleable, mouldable, ductile, receptive, impressionable, manageable. ◨ rigid, inflexible.

Types of plastic include: Bakelite®, Biopol®, celluloid®, epoxy resin, Perspex®, phenolic resin, plexiglass, polyester, polyethylene, polymethyl methacrylate, polynorbornene, polypropylene, polystyrene, polythene, polyurethane, PTFE (polytetrafluoroethylene), PVC (polyvinyl chloride), uPVC, silicone, Teflon®, transpolyisoprene, urea formaldehyde, vinyl.

plate *n* 1 DISH, platter, salver, helping, serving, portion. 2 ILLUSTRATION, picture, print, lithograph.

➤ *v* coat, cover, overlay, veneer, laminate, electroplate, anodize, galvanize, platinize, gild, silver, tin.

platform *n* 1 STAGE, podium, dais, rostrum, stand. 2 POLICY, party line, principles, tenets, manifesto, programme, objectives.

platitude *n* banality, commonplace, truism, bromide, cliché, chestnut.

plausible *adj* credible, believable, reasonable, logical, likely, possible, probable, convincing, persuasive, smooth-talking, glib. ◨ implausible, unlikely, improbable.

play *v* 1 AMUSE ONESELF, have fun, enjoy oneself, revel, sport, romp, frolic, caper. 2 PARTICIPATE, take part, join in, enter, compete. 3 *France played Italy*: oppose, vie with, challenge, take on. 4 ACT, perform, portray, represent, impersonate.
◨ 1 work. 2 drop out.

➤ *n* 1 FUN, amusement, entertainment, diversion, recreation, sport, game, hobby, pastime. 2 DRAMA, tragedy, comedy, farce, show, performance, production. 3 MOVEMENT, action, flexibility, give, leeway, latitude, margin, scope, range, room, space.
◨ 1 work.

◇ **play down** minimize, make light of, gloss over, underplay, understate, undervalue, underestimate.
◨ exaggerate.

◇ **play on** exploit, take advantage of, turn to account, profit by, trade on, capitalize on.

◇ **play up** 1 EXAGGERATE, highlight, spotlight, accentuate, emphasize, stress. 2 MISBEHAVE, malfunction, trouble, bother, annoy, hurt.

playboy *n* philanderer, womanizer, ladies' man, rake, libertine.

player *n* 1 CONTESTANT, competitor, participant, sportsman, sportswoman. 2 PERFORMER, entertainer, artiste, actor, actress, musician, instrumentalist.

playful *adj* sportive, frolicsome, ludic (*fml*), lively, spirited, mischievous, roguish, impish, puckish, kittenish, good-natured, jesting, teasing, humorous, tongue-in-cheek.
◨ serious.

playwright *n* dramatist, writer, scriptwriter, screenwriter.

plea *n* 1 APPEAL, petition, request, entreaty, supplication, prayer, invocation. 2 DEFENCE, justification, excuse, explanation, claim.

plead *v* 1 BEG, implore, beseech, entreat, appeal, petition, ask, request. 2 *plead ignorance*: assert, maintain, claim, allege.

pleasant *adj* agreeable, nice, fine, lovely, delightful, charming, likable, amiable, friendly, affable, good-humoured, cheerful, congenial, enjoyable, amusing, pleasing, gratifying, satisfying, acceptable, welcome, refreshing.
🖃 unpleasant, nasty, unfriendly.

please *v* 1 DELIGHT, charm, captivate, entertain, amuse, cheer, gladden, humour, indulge, gratify, satisfy, content, suit. 2 WANT, will, wish, desire, like, prefer, choose, think fit.
🖃 1 displease, annoy, anger, sadden.

pleased *adj* contented, satisfied, gratified, glad, happy, delighted, thrilled, euphoric.
🖃 displeased, annoyed.

pleasing *adj* gratifying, satisfying, acceptable, good, pleasant, agreeable, nice, delightful, charming, attractive, engaging, winning.
🖃 unpleasant, disagreeable.

pleasure *n* amusement, entertainment, diversion, recreation, fun, enjoyment, gratification, satisfaction, contentment, happiness, joy, delight, comfort, solace.
🖃 sorrow, pain, trouble, displeasure.

pleat *v* tuck, fold, crease, flute, crimp, gather, pucker.

pledge *n* 1 PROMISE, vow, word of honour, oath, bond, covenant, guarantee, warrant, assurance, undertaking. 2 DEPOSIT, security, surety, bail.
➤ *v* promise, vow, swear, contract, engage, undertake, vouch, guarantee, secure.

plentiful *adj* ample, abundant, profuse, copious, overflowing, lavish, generous, liberal, bountiful, fruitful, productive.
🖃 scarce, scanty, rare.

plenty *n* abundance, profusion, plethora, lots (*infml*), loads (*infml*), masses (*infml*), heaps (*infml*), piles (*infml*), stacks (*infml*), enough, sufficiency, quantity, mass,

volume, fund, mine, store.
🖃 scarcity, lack, want, need.

pliable *adj* pliant, flexible, bendable, bendy (*infml*), supple, lithe, malleable, plastic, yielding, adaptable, accommodating, manageable, tractable, docile, compliant, biddable, persuadable, responsive, receptive, impressionable, susceptible.
🖃 rigid, inflexible, headstrong.

plight *n* predicament, quandary, spot (*infml*), dilemma, extremity, trouble, difficulty, straits, state, condition, situation, circumstances, case.

plod *v* 1 TRUDGE, tramp, stump, clump, lumber, plough through. 2 DRUDGE, labour, toil, grind, slog, persevere, soldier on.

plot *n* 1 CONSPIRACY, intrigue, machination, scheme, stratagem, plan. 2 STORY, narrative, subject, theme, storyline, thread, outline, scenario. 3 *plot of land*: patch, tract, area, allotment, lot, parcel.
➤ *v* 1 CONSPIRE, intrigue, machinate, scheme, hatch, lay, cook up, devise, contrive, plan, project, design, draft. 2 CHART, map, mark, locate, draw, calculate.

plotter *n* conspirator, intriguer, machinator, schemer.

ploy *n* manoeuvre, stratagem, tactic, move, device, contrivance, scheme, game, trick, artifice, dodge, wile, ruse, subterfuge.

pluck *n* courage, bravery, spirit, mettle, nerve (*infml*), guts (*infml*), grit, backbone, fortitude, resolution, determination.
🖃 cowardice.
➤ *v* 1 PULL, draw, tug, snatch, pull off, remove, pick, collect, gather, harvest. 2 *pluck a guitar*: pick, twang, strum.

plucky *adj* brave, courageous, bold, daring, intrepid, heroic, valiant, spirited, feisty.
🖃 cowardly, weak, feeble.

plug *n* 1 STOPPER, bung, cork, spigot. 2 (*infml*) ADVERTISEMENT, publicity, mention, puff.

➤ *v* **1** STOP (UP), bung, cork, block, choke, close, seal, fill, pack, stuff. **2** (*infml*) ADVERTISE, publicize, hype (*sl*), promote, push, talk up (*infml*), mention.

plumb *adv* **1** VERTICALLY, perpendicularly. **2** PRECISELY, exactly, dead, slap (*infml*), bang (*infml*).
➤ *v* sound, fathom, measure, gauge, penetrate, probe, search, explore.

plumbing

Plumbing materials and equipment include: auger, back boiler, ball valve, ballcock, basin, basin spanner, bath, bend, bidet, blowtorch, boiler, bowl, ceiling joint, cistern, compression fitting, copper pipe, copper tube, coupler, cylinder, draincock, elbow joint, electric water heater, expansion (or header) tank, faucet (*US*), flare joint, float, flux, gas water heater, gasket, gate valve, geyser, hose, immersion heater, joint, jointing compound, lavatory, lavatory chain, lever tap, lockshield valve, mains pipe, mixer tap, monkey wrench, motorized zone valve, nipple, nipple key, overflow bend, pan, pedestal, pipe, pipe clip, pipe coupling, pipe wrench, plug, plunger, programmer, P-trap, pump, radiator, septic tank, shower, shower attachment, shower head, sink, siphon washer, soil vent, solder, stopcock, Stillson wrench, sump pump, tank, tap, tee, thermostat, thermostatic valve, toilet, trap, tube cutter, tube flaring tool, U-bend, union, urinal, washer, waste disposal unit, waste pipe, water closet, WC, Y-branch.

plummet *v* plunge, dive, nose-dive, descend, drop, fall, tumble.
ⁿ⁳ soar.

plump *adj* fat, obese, dumpy, tubby, stout, round, rotund (*fml*), portly, chubby, podgy, fleshy, flabby, full, ample, buxom.
ⁿ⁳ thin, skinny.

plump for opt for, choose, select, favour, back, support.

plunder *v* loot, pillage, ravage, devastate, sack, raid, ransack, rifle, steal, rob, strip.
➤ *n* loot, pillage, booty, swag (*sl*), spoils, pickings, ill-gotten gains, prize.

plunge *v* **1** DIVE, jump, nosedive, swoop, dive-bomb, plummet, descend, go down, sink, drop, fall, pitch, tumble, hurtle, career, charge, dash, rush, tear. **2** IMMERSE, submerge, dip.
➤ *n* dive, jump, swoop, descent, drop, fall, tumble, immersion, submersion.

ply *n* layer, fold, thickness, strand, sheet, leaf.

poach *v* steal, pilfer, appropriate, trespass, encroach, infringe.

pocket *n* pouch, bag, envelope, receptacle, compartment, hollow, cavity.
➤ *adj* small, little, mini (*infml*), concise, compact, portable, miniature.
➤ *v* take, appropriate, help oneself to, lift, pilfer, filch, steal, nick (*sl*), pinch (*infml*).

pod *n* shell, husk, case, hull.

poem

Types of poem include: ballad, elegy, epic, haiku, idyll, lay, limerick, lyric, madrigal, nursery rhyme, ode, pastoral, roundelay, sonnet, tanka.

poet *n* versifier, rhymer, rhymester, lyricist, bard, minstrel.

poetic *adj* poetical, lyrical, moving, artistic, graceful, flowing, metrical, rhythmical, rhyming.
ⁿ⁳ prosaic.

poignant *adj* moving, touching, affecting, tender, distressing, upsetting, heartbreaking, heart-rending, piteous, pathetic, sad, painful, agonizing.

point *n* **1** FEATURE, attribute, aspect, facet, detail, particular, item, subject, topic. **2** *what's the point?*: use, purpose, motive, reason, object, intention, aim, end, goal, objective. **3** ESSENCE, crux, core, pith, gist, thrust, meaning, drift. **4** PLACE, position, situation, location, site, spot. **5** MOMENT, instant, juncture, stage, time, period. **6** DOT, spot, mark, speck, full stop.

➤ *v* **1** *point a gun*: aim, direct, train, level. **2** INDICATE, signal, show, signify, denote, designate.

◇ **point of view** opinion, view, belief, judgement, attitude, position, standpoint, viewpoint, outlook, perspective, approach, angle, slant.

◇ **point out** show, indicate, draw attention to, point to, reveal, identify, specify, mention, bring up, allude to, remind.

point-blank *adj* direct, forthright, straightforward, plain, explicit, open, unreserved, blunt, frank, candid.

➤ *adv* directly, forthrightly, straightforwardly, plainly, explicitly, openly, bluntly, frankly, candidly.

pointed *adj* sharp, keen, edged, barbed, cutting, incisive, trenchant, biting, penetrating, telling.

pointer *n* **1** ARROW, indicator, needle, hand. **2** TIP, recommendation, suggestion, hint, guide, indication, advice, warning, caution.

pointless *adj* useless, futile, vain, fruitless, unproductive, unprofitable, worthless, senseless, absurd, meaningless, aimless.

🔁 useful, profitable, meaningful.

poise *n* calmness, composure, self-possession, presence of mind, coolness, cool (*infml*), equanimity, aplomb, assurance, dignity, elegance, grace, balance, equilibrium.

➤ *v* balance, position, hover, hang, suspend.

poised *adj* **1** DIGNIFIED, graceful, calm, composed, unruffled, collected, self-possessed, cool, level-headed, self-confident, assured. **2** *poised for action*: prepared, ready, set, waiting, expectant.

poison *n* toxin, venom, bane, blight, cancer, malignancy, contagion, contamination, corruption.

➤ *v* infect, envenomate (*fml*), contaminate, pollute, taint, adulterate, corrupt, deprave, pervert, warp.

poisonous *adj* toxic, venomous, lethal, deadly, fatal, mortal, noxious, pernicious, malicious.

Poisonous plants include: aconite, amanita, anemone, banewort, belladonna, black nightshade, castor oil plant, common nightshade, cowbane, cuckoo pint, deadly nightshade, digitalis, dwale, foxglove, giant hockweed, helmet flower, hemlock, hemlock water, dropwort, Jimsonweed, laburnum, latana, lords-and-ladies, meadow saffron, monkshood, naked boys, naked lady, oleander, poison ivy, stinkweed, stramonium, thorn apple, wake-robin, wild arum, windflower, wolfsbane. *see also* **mushroom**.

poke *v* prod, stab, jab, stick, thrust, push, shove, nudge, elbow, dig, butt, hit, punch.

➤ *n* prod, jab, thrust, shove, nudge, dig, butt, punch.

pole[1] *n* bar, rod, stick, shaft, spar, upright, post, stake, mast, staff.

pole[2] *n* antipode, extremity, extreme, limit.

◇ **poles apart** irreconcilable, worlds apart, incompatible, like chalk and cheese.

police *n* police force, constabulary, the Law (*infml*), the Bill (*sl*), the fuzz (*sl*).

➤ *v* check, control, regulate, monitor, watch, observe, supervise, oversee, patrol, guard, protect, defend, keep the peace.

policeman, policewoman *n* officer, constable, PC, cop (*sl*), copper (*infml*), bobby (*infml*).

policy *n* **1** CODE OF PRACTICE, rules, guidelines, procedure, method, practice, custom, protocol. **2** COURSE OF ACTION, line, course, plan, programme, scheme, stance, position.

polish *v* **1** SHINE, brighten, smooth,

rub, buff, burnish, clean, wax. **2** IMPROVE, enhance, brush up, touch up, finish, perfect, refine, cultivate.
F3 1 tarnish, dull.
➤ *n* **1** *a tin of polish*: wax, varnish. **2** SHINE, gloss, sheen, lustre, brightness, brilliance, sparkle, smoothness, finish, glaze, veneer. **3** REFINEMENT, cultivation, class, breeding, sophistication, finesse, style, elegance, grace, poise.
F3 2 dullness. **3** clumsiness.

polished *adj* **1** SHINING, shiny, glossy, lustrous, gleaming, burnished, smooth, glassy, slippery. **2** FAULTLESS, flawless, impeccable, perfect, outstanding, superlative, masterly, expert, professional, skilful, accomplished, perfected. **3** REFINED, cultivated, civilized, genteel, well-bred, polite, civil, sophisticated, urbane, suave, elegant, graceful.
F3 1 tarnished. **2** inexpert. **3** gauche.

polite *adj* courteous, well-mannered, respectful, civil, well-bred, refined, cultured, gentlemanly, ladylike, gracious, obliging, thoughtful, considerate, tactful, diplomatic.
F3 impolite, discourteous, rude.

political *adj* governmental, parliamentary, constitutional, ministerial, civil, public.

Political ideologies include: absolutism, anarchism, authoritarianism, Bolshevism, Christian democracy, collectivism, communism, conservatism, democracy, egalitarianism, fascism, federalism, holism, imperialism, individualism, liberalism, Maoism, Marxism, nationalism, Nazism, neocolonialism, neo-fascism, neo-nazism, pluralism, republicanism, social democracy, socialism, syndicalism, Thatcherism, theocracy, totalitarianism, unilateralism, Trotskyism, Whiggism. *see also* **government**; **parliament**.

Political parties include: Alliance, Co-operative, Communist, Conservative and Unionist, Democratic, Democratic Left, Democratic Unionist, Fianna Fáil, Fine Gael, Green, Labour, Liberal, Liberal Democratic, Militant Labour, National Front, Parliamentary, Parliamentary Labour, Plaid Cymru, Progressive Democrats, Republican, Scottish Conservative and Unionist, Scottish Liberal Democratic, Scottish National, Sinn Féin, Social and Liberal Democratic, Social Democratic and Labour, Ulster Democratic Unionist, Ulster Popular Unionist, Ulster Unionist, Welsh Liberal Democratic.

politician *n* Member of Parliament, MP, minister, statesman, stateswoman, legislator, representative.

People in politics include: activist, ambassador, Black Rod, capitalist, Communist, commie (*infml*), comrade, congressman, congresswoman, Conservative, councillor, Democrat, Deputy Speaker, dictator, dissident, dry (*infml*), Euro-sceptic, extremist, first minister, Green, high commissioner, independent, lefty (*infml*), Liberal, Liberal Democrat, loyalist, Marxist, Marxist-Leninist, member of parliament, minister, moderate, MP, MSP (Member of the Scottish Parliament), party chairman, party member, party worker, pinko (*infml*), politician, premier, president, presiding officer, prime minister, radical, red (*infml*), Republican, revolutionary, secretary of state, senator, Social Democrat, Socialist, speaker, spin doctor, Tory, Trotskyite, true-blue, wet (*infml*), Whig.

politics *n* public affairs, civics, affairs of state, statecraft, government, diplomacy, statesmanship, political science.

Terms used in politics include: alliance, apartheid, ballot, bill, blockade, cabinet, campaign, civil service, coalition, constitution, council, coup d'état, détente, election, electoral register, ethnic cleansing, focus group, general election, glasnost, go to the country, government, green paper, Hansard, judiciary, left wing, lobby, local government, majority, mandate, manifesto, nationalization, parliament, party, party line, perestroika, prime minister's question time, privatization, propaganda, proportional representation, rainbow coalition, referendum, right wing, sanction, shadow cabinet, sovereignty, state, summit, summit conference, term of office, trade union, veto, vote, welfare state, whip, three-line whip, white paper.

poll *n* ballot, vote, voting, plebiscite, referendum, straw-poll, sampling, canvass, opinion poll, survey, census, count, tally.

pollute *v* contaminate, infect, poison, taint, adulterate, debase, corrupt, dirty, foul, soil, defile, sully, stain, mar, spoil.

pollution *n* impurity, contamination, infection, adulteration, corruption, taint, dirtiness, foulness, defilement.
ⓔ purification, purity, cleanness.

pomp *n* ceremony, ceremonial, ritual, solemnity, formality, ceremoniousness, state, grandeur, magnificence, splendour, pageantry, show, display, parade, ostentation, flourish.
ⓔ austerity, simplicity.

pompous *adj* self-important, haughty, arrogant, grandiose, supercilious, overbearing, imperious, magisterial, bombastic, high-flown, overblown, windy, affected, pretentious, ostentatious.
ⓔ unassuming, modest, simple, unaffected.

pony *see* **horse**.

pool[1] *n* puddle, pond, lake, mere, tarn, watering hole, paddling pool, swimming pool.

pool[2] *n* **1** FUND, reserve, store, accumulation, bank, kitty, purse, pot,

jackpot. **2** SYNDICATE, cartel, ring, combine, consortium, collective, group, team.
➤ *v* contribute, chip in (*infml*), combine, amalgamate, merge, share, muck in (*infml*).

poor *adj* **1** IMPOVERISHED, poverty-stricken, badly off, hard-up, broke (*infml*), stony-broke (*sl*), skint (*sl*), bankrupt, penniless, destitute, miserable, wretched, distressed, straitened, needy, lacking, deficient, insufficient, scanty, skimpy, meagre, sparse, depleted, exhausted. **2** BAD, substandard, unsatisfactory, inferior, mediocre, below par (*infml*), low-grade, second-rate, third-rate, low-rent (*sl*), shoddy, imperfect, faulty, weak, feeble, pathetic (*infml*), sorry, worthless, fruitless. **3** UNFORTUNATE, unlucky, luckless, ill-fated, unhappy, miserable, pathetic, pitiable, pitiful.
ⓔ **1** rich, wealthy, affluent. **2** superior, impressive. **3** fortunate, lucky.

poorly *adj* ill, sick, unwell, indisposed, ailing, sickly, off-colour, below par (*infml*), out of sorts (*infml*), under the weather (*infml*), seedy, groggy, rotten (*infml*).
ⓔ well, healthy.

pop *v* burst, explode, go off, bang, crack, snap.
➤ *n* bang, crack, snap, burst, explosion.

popular *adj* well-liked, favourite, liked, favoured, approved, in demand, sought-after, fashionable, modish, in (*infml*), trendy (*infml*), prevailing, current, accepted, conventional, standard, stock, common, prevalent, widespread, universal, general, household, famous, well-known, celebrated, idolized.
ⓔ unpopular.

popularize *v* spread, propagate, universalize, democratize, simplify.

popularly *adv* commonly, widely, universally, generally, usually, customarily, conventionally, traditionally.

populate *v* people, occupy, settle,

colonize, inhabit, live in, overrun.

population *n* inhabitants, natives, residents, citizens, occupants, community, society, people, folk.

populous *adj* crowded, packed, swarming, teeming, crawling, overpopulated.
≠ deserted.

porcelain

> *Types of porcelain include*: biscuit, bisque, blue and white, bone china, Canton, Capodimonte, chinoiserie, Compagnie des Indes, copper red, eggshell, faïence, famille-rose, famille-verte, Firs Period Worcester, hard paste, Imari, Kakiemon, Kraak, nankeen, Parian, saltglazed, soapstone paste, soft paste, Yingqing.

> *Famous makes of porcelain include*: Arita, Belleek, Bow, Bristol, Caughley, Chantilly, Chelsea, Coalport, Copeland, Derby, Dresden, Limoges, Meissen, Ming, Minton, Nanking, Rockingham, Royal Doulton, Royal Worcester, Satsuma, Sèvres, Vienna, Wedgewood, Worcester.

pornographic *adj* obscene, X-rated (*infml*), indecent, dirty, filthy, blue, risqué, bawdy, coarse, gross, lewd, erotic, titillating.

porous *adj* permeable, pervious, penetrable, absorbent, spongy, honeycombed, pitted.
≠ impermeable, impervious.

portable *adj* movable, transportable, compact, lightweight, manageable, handy, convenient.
≠ fixed, immovable.

porter[1] *n* bearer, carrier, baggage attendant, baggage handler.

porter[2] *n* doorman, commissionaire, doorkeeper, gatekeeper, janitor, caretaker, concierge.

portion *n* share, allocation, allotment, parcel, allowance, ration, quota, measure, part, section, division, fraction,

percentage, bit, fragment, morsel, piece, segment, slice, serving, helping.

portly *adj* stout, corpulent (*fml*), rotund (*fml*), round, fat, plump, fleshy, flabby, obese, overweight, heavy, large, big.
≠ slim, thin, slight.

portrait *n* picture, painting, drawing, sketch, caricature, miniature, icon, photograph, likeness, image, representation, vignette, profile, characterization, description, depiction, portrayal.

portray *v* draw, sketch, paint, illustrate, picture, represent, depict, describe, evoke, play, impersonate, characterize, personify.

portrayal *n* representation, characterization, depiction, description, evocation, presentation, performance, interpretation, rendering.

pose *v* **1** MODEL, sit, position. **2** PRETEND, feign, affect, put on an act, masquerade, pass oneself off, impersonate. **3** *pose a question*: set, put forward, submit, present.
➤ *n* **1** POSITION, stance, air, bearing, posture, attitude. **2** PRETENCE, sham, affectation, façade, front, masquerade, role, act, charade.

poser[1] *n* puzzle, riddle, conundrum, brain-teaser, mystery, enigma, problem, vexed question.

poser[2] *n* poseur, poseuse, posturer, attitudinizer, exhibitionist, show-off, pseud (*infml*), phoney (*infml*).

posh (*infml*) *adj* smart, stylish, fashionable, high-class, upper-class, la-di-da (*sl*), grand, luxurious, lavish, swanky (*infml*), luxury, de luxe, up-market, exclusive, select, classy (*infml*), swish (*infml*).
≠ inferior, cheap.

position *n* **1** PLACE, situation, location, site, spot, point. **2** POSTURE, stance, pose, arrangement, disposition. **3** JOB, post, occupation, employment, office, duty, function, role. **4** RANK, grade, level, status, standing. **5** OPINION, point of view, belief, view, outlook, viewpoint, standpoint, stand.

➤ *v* put, place, set, fix, stand, arrange, dispose, lay out, deploy, station, locate, situate, site.

positive *adj* 1 SURE, certain, convinced, confident, assured, upbeat. 2 *positive criticism*: helpful, practical, constructive, useful, optimistic, hopeful, promising. 3 DEFINITE, decisive, conclusive, clear, unmistakable, explicit, unequivocal, express, firm, emphatic, categorical, undeniable, irrefutable, indisputable, incontrovertible. 4 ABSOLUTE, utter, sheer, complete, perfect.
▱ 1 uncertain. 2 negative, destructive. 3 indefinite, vague.

possess *v* 1 OWN, have, hold, enjoy, be endowed with. 2 SEIZE, take, obtain, acquire, take over, occupy, control, dominate, bewitch, haunt.

possession *n* ownership, title, tenure, occupation, custody, control, hold, grip.

possessions *n* belongings, property, things, gear (*infml*), paraphernalia, effects, goods, chattels, movables, assets, estate, wealth, riches.

possessive *adj* selfish, clinging, clingy (*infml*), overprotective, domineering, dominating, jealous, covetous, acquisitive, grasping.
▱ unselfish, sharing.

possibility *n* likelihood, probability, odds, chance, risk, danger, hope, prospect, potentiality, conceivability, practicability, feasibility.
▱ impossibility, impracticability.

possible *adj* potential, promising, likely, probable, imaginable, conceivable, practicable, feasible, viable, tenable, workable, achievable, attainable, accomplishable, realizable.
▱ impossible, unthinkable, impracticable, unattainable.

possibly *adv* perhaps, maybe, hopefully (*infml*), by any means, at all, by any chance.

post¹ *n* pole, stake, picket, pale, pillar,

column, shaft, support, baluster, upright, stanchion, strut, leg.

➤ *v* display, stick up, pin up, advertise, publicize, announce, make known, report, publish.

post² *n* office, job, employment, position, situation, place, vacancy, appointment, assignment, station, beat.

➤ *v* station, locate, situate, position, place, put, appoint, assign, second, transfer, move, send.

post³ *n* mail, letters, dispatch, collection, delivery.

➤ *v* mail, send, dispatch, transmit.

poster *n* notice, bill, sign, placard, sticker, advertisement, announcement.

posterity *n* descendants, successors, progeny (*fml*), issue, offspring, children.

postpone *v* put off, defer, put back, hold over, delay, adjourn, suspend, shelve, pigeonhole, freeze, put on ice.
▱ advance, forward.

postscript *n* PS (*infml*), addition, supplement, afterthought, addendum, codicil, appendix, afterword, epilogue.
▱ introduction, prologue.

postulate *v* theorize, hypothesize, suppose, assume, propose, advance, lay down, stipulate.

posture *n* position, stance, pose, attitude, disposition, bearing, carriage, deportment.

posy *n* bouquet, spray, buttonhole, corsage.

pot *n* receptacle, vessel, teapot, coffee pot, urn, jar, vase, bowl, basin, pan, cauldron, crucible.

potent *adj* powerful, mighty, strong, intoxicating, pungent, effective, impressive, cogent, convincing, persuasive, compelling, forceful, dynamic, vigorous, authoritative, commanding, dominant, influential, overpowering.
▱ impotent, weak.

potential *adj* possible, likely, probable, prospective, future, aspiring,

would-be, promising, up-and-coming, budding, embryonic, undeveloped, dormant, latent, hidden, concealed, unrealized.
➤ *n* possibility, ability, capability, capacity, aptitude, talent, powers, resources.

potion *n* mixture, concoction, brew, beverage, drink, draught, dose, medicine, tonic, elixir.

potpourri *n* medley, mixture, mix, jumble, hotchpotch, hodge-podge, miscellany, collection.

potter *v* tinker, fiddle, mess about (*infml*), dabble, loiter, fritter.

pottery *n* earthenware, stoneware, terracotta, ceramics, crockery, china, porcelain.

Terms used in pottery include: armorial, art pottery, basalt, blanc-de-chine, bronzing, celadon, ceramic, china clay, cloisonné, crackleware, crazing, creamware, delft, earthenware, enamel, faïence, fairing, figure, firing, flambé, flatback, glaze, grotesque, ground, ironstone, jasper, kiln, lustre, maiolica, majolica, maker's mark, mandarin palette, model, monogram, overglaze, porcelain, raku, sagger, scratch blue, sgraffito, slip, slip-cast, spongeware, Staffordshire, stoneware, terracotta, tin-glazed earthenware, transfer printing, underglaze, Willow pattern. *see also* **porcelain**.

pounce *v* fall, dive, swoop, drop, attack, strike, ambush, spring, jump, leap, snatch, grab.

pound[1] *v* **1** STRIKE, thump, beat, drum, pelt, pummel, hammer, batter, bang, bash, wallop (*infml*), smash. **2** PULVERIZE, powder, grind, mash, crush. **3** *his heart was pounding*: throb, pulsate, palpitate, thump, thud.

pound[2] *n* enclosure, compound, corral, yard, pen, fold.

pour *v* **1** *pour a drink*: serve, decant, tip. **2** SPILL, issue, discharge, flow, stream, run, rush, spout, spew, gush, cascade, crowd, throng, swarm.

pout *v* scowl, glower, grimace, pull a face, sulk, mope.
🔁 grin, smile.
➤ *n* scowl, glower, grimace, moue, long face.
🔁 grin, smile.

poverty *n* poorness, impoverishment, insolvency, bankruptcy, pennilessness, penury, destitution, distress, hardship, privation, need, necessity, want, lack, deficiency, shortage, inadequacy, insufficiency, depletion, scarcity, meagreness, paucity, dearth.
🔁 wealth, richness, affluence, plenty.

powdery *adj* dusty, sandy, grainy, granular, powdered, pulverized, ground, fine, loose, dry, crumbly, friable, chalky.

power *n* **1** COMMAND, authority, sovereignty, rule, dominion, control, influence. **2** RIGHT, privilege, prerogative, authorization, warrant, sanction. **3** POTENCY, strength, intensity, force, vigour, energy, stamina. **4** ABILITY, capability, capacity, potential, faculty, competence.
🔁 **1** subjection. **3** weakness. **4** inability.

powerful *adj* dominant, prevailing, leading, influential, high-powered, authoritative, commanding, potent, effective, strong, mighty, robust, muscular, energetic, forceful, telling, impressive, convincing, persuasive, compelling, winning, overwhelming.
🔁 impotent, ineffective, weak.

powerless *adj* impotent, incapable, ineffective, weak, feeble, frail, infirm, incapacitated, disabled, paralysed, helpless, vulnerable, defenceless, unarmed.
🔁 powerful, potent, able.

practicable *adj* possible, feasible, performable, achievable, attainable, viable, workable, practical, realistic.
🔁 impracticable.

practical *adj* **1** REALISTIC, sensible, commonsense, practicable, workable, feasible, down-to-earth, matter-of-fact, pragmatic, hardnosed (*infml*),

hard-headed, businesslike, experienced, trained, qualified, skilled, proficient, accomplished, hands on, applied. **2** USEFUL, handy, serviceable, utilitarian, functional, working, everyday, ordinary.
🖅 **1** impractical, unskilled, theoretical.

practically *adv* **1** ALMOST, nearly, well-nigh, virtually, pretty well, all but, just about, in principle, in effect, essentially, fundamentally, to all intents and purposes. **2** REALISTICALLY, sensibly, reasonably, rationally, pragmatically.

practice *n* **1** CUSTOM, tradition, convention, usage, habit, routine, way, method, system, procedure, policy. **2** REHEARSAL, run-through, dry run, dummy run, try-out, training, drill, exercise, work-out, study, experience. **3** *in practice*: effect, reality, actuality, action, operation, performance, use, application.
🖅 **3** theory, principle.

practise *v* **1** DO, perform, execute, implement, carry out, apply, put into practice, follow, pursue, engage in, undertake. **2** REHEARSE, run through, repeat, drill, exercise, train, study, perfect.

practised *adj* experienced, seasoned, veteran, trained, qualified, skilled, accomplished, versed, knowledgeable, able, proficient, expert, masterly, consummate, finished.
🖅 unpractised, inexperienced, inexpert.

pragmatic *adj* practical, realistic, sensible, matter-of-fact, businesslike, efficient, hard-headed, hardnosed (*infml*), unsentimental.
🖅 unrealistic, idealistic, romantic.

praise *n* approval, admiration, commendation, congratulation, compliment, flattery, adulation, eulogy, applause, ovation, cheering, acclaim, recognition, testimonial, tribute, accolade, homage, honour, glory, worship, adoration, devotion, thanksgiving.
🖅 criticism, revilement.
➤ *v* commend, congratulate, admire,

compliment, flatter, talk up (*infml*), eulogize, wax lyrical, rave over (*infml*), extol, promote, applaud, cheer, acclaim, hail, recognize, acknowledge, pay tribute to, honour, laud, glorify, magnify, exalt, worship, adore, bless.
🖅 criticize, revile.

praiseworthy *adj* commendable, fine, excellent, admirable, worthy, deserving, honourable, reputable, estimable, sterling.
🖅 blameworthy, dishonourable, ignoble.

prank *n* trick, practical joke, joke, jape, stunt, caper, frolic, lark, antic, escapade.

pray *v* invoke, call on, supplicate (*fml*), entreat, implore, plead, beg, beseech, petition, ask, request, crave, solicit.

prayer *n* collect, litany, devotion, communion, invocation, supplication, entreaty, plea, appeal, petition, request.

preach *v* address, lecture, harangue, pontificate, sermonize, evangelize, moralize, exhort, urge, advocate.

precarious *adj* unsafe, dangerous, treacherous, risky, hazardous, chancy, uncertain, unsure, dubious, doubtful, unpredictable, unreliable, unsteady, unstable, shaky, wobbly, insecure, vulnerable.
🖅 safe, certain, stable, secure.

precaution *n* safeguard, security, protection, insurance, providence, forethought, caution, prudence, foresight, anticipation, preparation, provision.

precautionary *adj* safety, protective, preventive, provident, cautious, prudent, judicious, preparatory, preliminary.

precede *v* come before, lead, come first, go before, take precedence, introduce, herald, usher in.
🖅 follow, succeed.

precedence *n* priority, preference, pride of place, superiority, supremacy, pre-eminence, lead, first place, seniority, rank.

precedent *n* example, instance, pattern, model, standard, criterion.

precinct *n* **1** ZONE, area, district, quarter, sector, division, section. **2** BOUNDARY, limit, bound, confine, edge.

precious *adj* **1** VALUED, treasured, prized, cherished, beloved, dearest, darling, favourite, loved, adored, idolized. **2** VALUABLE, expensive, costly, dear, priceless, inestimable, rare, choice, fine.

precipitate *v* hasten, hurry, speed, accelerate, quicken, expedite, advance, further, bring on, induce, trigger, cause, occasion.
➤ *adj* sudden, unexpected, abrupt, quick, swift, rapid, brief, hasty, hurried, headlong, breakneck, frantic, violent, impatient, hot-headed, impetuous, impulsive, rash, reckless, heedless, indiscreet.
◨ cautious, careful.

precipitation

Types of precipitation include: dew, downpour, drizzle, fog, hail, hailstone, mist, rain, raindrop, rainfall, rainstorm, shower, sleet, snow, snowfall, snowflake.

precipitous *adj* steep, sheer, perpendicular, vertical, high.
◨ gradual.

precise *adj* exact, accurate, right, punctilious, correct, factual, faithful, authentic, literal, word-for-word, express, definite, explicit, unequivocal, unambiguous, clear-cut, distinct, detailed, blow-by-blow, minute, nice, particular, specific, fixed, rigid, strict, careful, meticulous, scrupulous, fastidious.
◨ imprecise, inexact, ambiguous, careless.

precisely *adv* exactly, absolutely, just so, accurately, correctly, literally, verbatim, word for word, strictly, minutely, clearly, distinctly.

precision *n* exactness, accuracy, correctness, faithfulness, fidelity, explicitness, distinctness, detail, particularity, rigour, care, carefulness, meticulousness, scrupulousness, neatness.
◨ imprecision, inaccuracy.

precocious *adj* forward, ahead, advanced, early, premature, mature, developed, gifted, clever, bright, smart, quick, fast.
◨ backward.

preconceive *v* presuppose, presume, assume, anticipate, project, imagine, conceive, envisage, expect, visualize, picture.

preconception *n* presupposition, presumption, assumption, conjecture, anticipation, expectation, prejudgement, bias, prejudice.

precondition *n* condition, stipulation, requirement, prerequisite, essential, necessity, must.

precursor *n* antecedent, forerunner, sign, indication, herald, harbinger, messenger, usher, pioneer, trail-blazer.
◨ follower, successor.

predecessor *n* ancestor, forefather, forebear, antecedent, forerunner, precursor.
◨ successor, descendant.

predestination *n* destiny, fate, lot, fortune, doom, predetermination, foreordination.

predetermined *adj* **1** PREDESTINED, destined, fated, doomed, ordained, foreordained. **2** PREARRANGED, arranged, agreed, fixed, set.

predicament *n* situation, plight, trouble, mess, fix, spot (*infml*), quandary, dilemma, impasse, crisis, emergency.

predict *v* foretell, prophesy, foresee, forecast, prognosticate, project.

predictable *adj* foreseeable, expected, anticipated, likely, probable, imaginable, foreseen, foregone, certain, sure, reliable, dependable.
◨ unpredictable, uncertain.

prediction n prophecy, forecast, prognosis, augury, divination, fortune-telling, soothsaying.

predispose v dispose, incline, prompt, induce, make, sway, influence, affect, bias, prejudice.

predominant adj dominant, prevailing, preponderant, chief, main, principal, primary, capital, paramount, supreme, sovereign, ruling, controlling, leading, powerful, potent, prime, important, influential, forceful, strong.
F3 minor, lesser, weak.

pre-eminent adj supreme, unsurpassed, unrivalled, unequalled, unmatched, matchless, incomparable, inimitable, chief, foremost, leading, eminent, distinguished, renowned, famous, prominent, outstanding, exceptional, excellent, superlative, transcendent, superior.
F3 inferior, unknown.

preface n foreword, introduction, preamble, prologue, prelude, preliminaries.
F3 epilogue, postscript.
➤ v precede, prefix, lead up to, introduce, launch, open, begin, start.
F3 end, finish, complete.

prefer v favour, like better, would rather, would sooner, want, wish, desire, choose, select, pick, opt for, go for, plump for, single out, advocate, recommend, back, support, fancy, elect, adopt.
F3 reject.

preferable adj better, superior, nicer, preferred, favoured, chosen, desirable, advantageous, recommended, advisable.
F3 inferior, undesirable.

preference n 1 FAVOURITE, first choice, choice, pick, selection, option, wish, desire. 2 LIKING, fancy, inclination, predilection, partiality, favouritism, preferential treatment.

preferential adj better, superior, favoured, privileged, special, favourable, advantageous.
F3 equal.

pregnant adj 1 a pregnant woman: expectant, expecting, with child (fml), gravid (fml), in the club (sl). 2 a pregnant pause: meaningful, significant, eloquent, expressive, suggestive, charged, loaded, full.

prejudice n 1 BIAS, partiality, partisanship, discrimination, unfairness, injustice, intolerance, narrow-mindedness, bigotry, chauvinism, racism, sexism. 2 HARM, damage, impairment, hurt, injury, detriment, disadvantage, loss, ruin.
F3 1 fairness, tolerance. 2 benefit, advantage.
➤ v 1 BIAS, predispose, incline, sway, influence, condition, colour, slant, distort, load, weight. 2 HARM, damage, impair, hinder, undermine, hurt, injure, mar, spoil, ruin, wreck.
F3 2 benefit, help, advance.

prejudiced adj biased, partial, predisposed, subjective, partisan, one-sided, discriminatory, unfair, unjust, loaded, weighted, intolerant, narrow-minded, blinkered, bigoted, chauvinist, racist, sexist, jaundiced, distorted, warped, influenced, conditioned.
F3 impartial, fair, tolerant.

prejudicial adj harmful, damaging, hurtful, injurious, detrimental, disadvantageous, unfavourable, inimical.
F3 beneficial, advantageous.

preliminaries n preparation, groundwork, foundations, basics, rudiments, formalities, introduction, preface, prelude, opening, beginning, start.

preliminary adj preparatory, prior, advance, exploratory, experimental, trial, test, pilot, early, earliest, first, initial, primary, qualifying, inaugural, introductory, opening.
F3 final, closing.

prelude n overture, introduction, preface, foreword, preamble, prologue, opening, opener, preliminary, preparation, beginning, start, commencement, precursor, curtain raiser.

▣ finale, epilogue.

premature *adj* early, immature, green, unripe, embryonic, half-formed, incomplete, undeveloped, abortive, hasty, ill-considered, rash, untimely, inopportune, ill-timed.

▣ late, tardy.

premeditated *adj* planned, intended, intentional, deliberate, wilful, conscious, cold-blooded, calculated, considered, contrived, preplanned, prearranged, predetermined.

▣ unpremeditated, spontaneous.

première *n* first performance, opening, opening night, first night, début.

premise *n* proposition, statement, assertion, postulate, thesis, argument, basis, supposition, hypothesis, presupposition, assumption.

premises *n* building, property, establishment, office, grounds, estate, site, place.

premonition *n* presentiment, feeling, intuition, hunch, idea, suspicion, foreboding, misgiving, apprehension, fear, anxiety, worry, warning, omen, sign.

preoccupation *n* **1** OBSESSION, fixation, mania, hang-up (*infml*), concern, interest, enthusiasm, hobby-horse. **2** DISTRACTION, absent-mindedness, reverie, daydreaming, obliviousness, oblivion.

preoccupied *adj* **1** OBSESSED, intent, immersed, engrossed, engaged, taken up, wrapped up, involved. **2** DISTRACTED, abstracted, absent-minded, daydreaming, absorbed, faraway, heedless, oblivious, pensive.

preparation *n* **1** READINESS, provision, precaution, safeguard, foundation, groundwork, spadework, basics, rudiments, preliminaries, plans, arrangements. **2** MIXTURE, compound, concoction, potion, medicine, lotion, application.

preparatory *adj* preliminary, introductory, opening, initial, primary, basic, fundamental, rudimentary, elementary.

prepare *v* **1** GET READY, warm up, train, coach, study, make ready, adapt, adjust, plan, organize, arrange, pave the way. **2** *prepare a meal*: make, produce, create, construct, assemble, concoct, contrive, devise, draft, draw up, compose. **3** PROVIDE, supply, equip, fit out, rig out.

◇ **prepare oneself** brace oneself, steel oneself, gird oneself, fortify oneself.

prepared *adj* ready, waiting, set, fit, inclined, disposed, willing, planned, organized, arranged.

▣ unprepared, unready.

preponderant *adj* greater, larger, superior, predominant, prevailing, overriding, overruling, controlling, foremost, important, significant.

preposterous *adj* incredible, unbelievable, absurd, ridiculous, ludicrous, foolish, crazy, nonsensical, unreasonable, monstrous, shocking, outrageous, intolerable, unthinkable, impossible.

▣ sensible, reasonable, acceptable.

prerequisite *n* precondition, condition, proviso, qualification, requisite, requirement, imperative, necessity, essential, must.

▣ extra.

prescribe *v* ordain, decree, dictate, rule, command, order, require, direct, assign, specify, stipulate, lay down, set, appoint, impose, fix, define, limit.

prescription *n* **1** INSTRUCTION, direction, formula. **2** MEDICINE, drug, preparation, mixture, remedy, treatment.

presence *n* **1** ATTENDANCE, company, occupancy, residence, existence. **2** AURA, air, demeanour, bearing, comportment, carriage, appearance, poise, self-assurance, personality, charisma. **3** NEARNESS, closeness, proximity, vicinity.

F **1** absence. **3** remoteness.

present¹ *adj* **1** ATTENDING, here, there, near, at hand, to hand, available, ready. **2** *at the present time*: current, existent, existing, contemporary, present-day, immediate, instant.
F **1** absent. **2** past, out of date.

present² *v* **1** SHOW, display, exhibit, demonstrate, mount, stage, put on, introduce, announce. **2** AWARD, confer, bestow, grant, give, donate, hand over, entrust, extend, hold out, offer, tender, submit.

present³ *n* gift, prezzie (*infml*), offering, donation, grant, endowment, benefaction, bounty, largesse, gratuity, tip, favour.

presentable *adj* neat, tidy, clean, respectable, decent, proper, suitable, acceptable, satisfactory, tolerable.
F unpresentable, untidy, shabby.

presentation *n* **1** SHOW, performance, production, staging, representation, portrayal, display, exhibition, demonstration, talk, delivery, appearance, arrangement. **2** AWARD, conferral, bestowal, investiture.

present-day *adj* current, present, existent, existing, living, contemporary, modern, up-to-date, fashionable.
F past, future.

presently *adv* **1** SOON, shortly, in a minute, before long, by and by. **2** CURRENTLY, at present, now.

preserve *v* **1** PROTECT, safeguard, guard, defend, shield, shelter, care for, maintain, uphold, sustain, continue, perpetuate, keep, retain, conserve, save, store. **2** *preserve food*: bottle, tin, can, pickle, salt, cure, dry.
F **1** destroy, ruin.
➤ *n* **1** *home-made preserves*: conserve, jam, marmalade, jelly, pickle. **2** DOMAIN, realm, sphere, area, field, speciality. **3** RESERVATION, sanctuary, nature reserve, game reserve, safari park.

preside *v* chair, officiate, conduct, direct, manage, administer, control, run, head, lead, govern, rule.

press *v* **1** CRUSH, squash, squeeze, compress, stuff, cram, crowd, push, depress. **2** *press clothes*: iron, smooth, flatten. **3** HUG, embrace, clasp, squeeze. **4** URGE, plead, petition, campaign, demand, insist on, compel, constrain, force, pressure, pressurize, harass, harry.
➤ *n* **1** CROWD, throng, multitude, mob, horde, swarm, pack, crush, push. **2** JOURNALISTS, reporters, hacks (*infml*), correspondents, the media, newspapers, papers, Fleet Street, fourth estate, paparazzi.

pressing *adj* urgent, high-priority, burning, crucial, vital, essential, imperative, serious, important.
F unimportant, trivial.

pressure *n* **1** FORCE, power, load, burden, weight, heaviness, compression, squeezing, stress, strain. **2** DIFFICULTY, problem, demand, constraint, obligation, urgency.

pressurize *v* force, compel, constrain, oblige, drive, bulldoze, coerce, press, pressure, lean on (*infml*), browbeat, bully.

prestige *n* status, reputation, standing, stature, eminence, distinction, esteem, regard, importance, authority, influence, fame, renown, kudos, credit, honour.
F humbleness, unimportance.

prestigious *adj* esteemed, respected, reputable, important, influential, great, eminent, prominent, illustrious, renowned, celebrated, exalted, imposing, impressive, up-market.
F humble, modest.

presume *v* **1** ASSUME, take it, think, believe, suppose, surmise, infer, presuppose, take for granted, count on, rely on, depend on, bank on, trust. **2** *presume to criticize*: dare, make so bold, go so far, venture, undertake.

presumption *n* **1** ASSUMPTION, belief, opinion, hypothesis, supposition, presupposition, surmise, conjecture, guess, likelihood, probability. **2** PRESUMPTUOUSNESS, boldness, audacity, impertinence, cheek, nerve (*infml*), impudence, insolence, forwardness, assurance.

₪ 2 humility.

presumptuous *adj* bold, audacious, impertinent, impudent, insolent, over-familiar, forward, pushy, arrogant, over-confident, conceited.

₪ humble, modest.

pretence *n* show, display, appearance, cover, front, façade, veneer, cloak, veil, mask, guise, sham, feigning, faking, simulation, deception, trickery, wile, ruse, excuse, pretext, bluff, falsehood, deceit, fabrication, invention, make-believe, charade, acting, play-acting, posturing, posing, affectation, pretension, pretentiousness.

₪ honesty, openness.

pretend *v* **1** AFFECT, put on, assume, feign, sham, counterfeit, fake, simulate, bluff, impersonate, pass oneself off, act, play-act, mime, go through the motions. **2** CLAIM, allege, profess, purport. **3** IMAGINE, make believe, suppose.

pretender *n* claimant, aspirant, candidate.

pretension *n* **1** PRETENTIOUSNESS, pomposity, self-importance, airs, conceit, vanity, snobbishness, affectation, pretence, show, showiness, ostentation. **2** CLAIM, profession, demand, aspiration, ambition.

₪ 1 modesty, humility, simplicity.

pretentious *adj* pompous, self-important, conceited, immodest, snobbish, affected, mannered, showy, ostentatious, extravagant, over-the-top, OTT (*infml*), exaggerated, magniloquent, high-sounding, inflated, grandiose, ambitious, overambitious.

₪ modest, humble, simple, straightforward.

pretext *n* excuse, ploy, ruse, cover, cloak, mask, guise, semblance, appearance, pretence, show.

pretty *adj* attractive, good-looking,

beautiful, fair, lovely, bonny, cute, winsome, appealing, charming, dainty, graceful, elegant, fine, delicate, nice.

₪ plain, unattractive, ugly.

➤ *adv* fairly, somewhat, rather, quite, reasonably, moderately, tolerably.

prevail *v* **1** PREDOMINATE, dominate, preponderate, abound. **2** WIN, triumph, succeed, overcome, overrule, reign, rule.

₪ 2 lose.

◇ **prevail upon** persuade, talk into, prompt, induce, incline, sway, influence, convince, win over.

prevailing *adj* predominant, preponderant, main, principal, dominant, controlling, powerful, compelling, influential, reigning, ruling, current, fashionable, popular, mainstream, accepted, established, set, usual, customary, common, prevalent, widespread.

₪ minor, subordinate.

prevalent *adj* widespread, extensive, rampant, rife, frequent, general, customary, usual, universal, ubiquitous, common, everyday, popular, current, prevailing.

₪ uncommon, rare.

prevaricate *v* hedge, equivocate, quibble, cavil, dodge, evade, shift, shuffle, lie, deceive.

prevent *v* stop, avert, avoid, head off, ward off, stave off, intercept, forestall, anticipate, frustrate, thwart, check, restrain, inhibit, hinder, hamper, impede, obstruct, block, bar.

₪ cause, help, foster, encourage, allow.

prevention *n* avoidance, frustration, check, hindrance, impediment, obstruction, obstacle, bar, elimination, precaution, safeguard, deterrence.

₪ cause, help.

preventive *adj* preventative, anticipatory, pre-emptive, inhibitory, obstructive, precautionary, protective, counteractive, deterrent.

₪ causative.

previous *adj* preceding, foregoing,

earlier, prior, past, former, ex-, one-time, sometime, erstwhile.

▪ following, subsequent, later.

previously *adv* formerly, once, earlier, before, beforehand.

▪ later.

prey *n* quarry, victim, game, kill.

◇ **prey on 1** HUNT, kill, devour, feed on, live off, exploit. **2** *prey on one's mind*: haunt, trouble, distress, worry, burden, weigh down, oppress.

price *n* value, worth, cost, expense, outlay, expenditure, fee, charge, levy, toll, rate, bill, assessment, valuation, estimate, quotation, figure, amount, sum, payment, reward, penalty, forfeit, sacrifice, consequences.

➤ *v* value, rate, cost, evaluate, assess, estimate.

priceless *adj* **1** INVALUABLE, inestimable, incalculable, expensive, costly, dear, precious, valuable, prized, treasured, irreplaceable. **2** (*infml*) FUNNY, amusing, comic, hilarious, riotous, side-splitting, killing (*infml*), rich (*infml*).

▪ **1** cheap, run-of-the-mill.

prick *v* pierce, puncture, perforate, punch, jab, stab, sting, bite, jag, prickle, itch, tingle.

➤ *n* puncture, perforation, pinhole, jab, stab, pang, twinge, sting, bite.

prickle *n* thorn, spine, barb, spur, point, spike, needle.

➤ *v* tingle, itch, smart, sting, prick.

prickly *adj* **1** THORNY, brambly, spiny, barbed, spiky, bristly, rough, scratchy. **2** IRRITABLE, edgy, touchy, grumpy, grouchy, short-tempered.

▪ **1** smooth. **2** relaxed, easy-going (*infml*), laid-back (*infml*).

pride *n* **1** CONCEIT, vanity, egotism, bigheadedness, boastfulness, smugness, arrogance, self-importance, presumption, haughtiness, superciliousness, snobbery, pretentiousness. **2** DIGNITY, self-respect, self-esteem, honour. **3** SATISFACTION, gratification, pleasure, delight.

▪ **1** humility, modesty. **2** shame.

priest *n* minister, vicar, padre, father, man of God, woman of God, man of the cloth, clergyman, clergywoman, churchman, churchwoman.

priggish *adj* smug, self-righteous, goody-goody (*infml*), sanctimonious, holier-than-thou, puritanical, prim, prudish, narrow-minded.

▪ broad-minded.

prim *adj* prudish, strait-laced, formal, demure, proper, priggish, prissy, fussy, particular, precise, fastidious.

▪ informal, relaxed, easy-going (*infml*).

primarily *adv* chiefly, principally, mainly, mostly, basically, fundamentally, especially, particularly, essentially.

primary *adj* **1** FIRST, earliest, original, initial, introductory, beginning, basic, fundamental, essential, radical, rudimentary, elementary, simple. **2** CHIEF, principal, main, dominant, leading, foremost, prime, premier, supreme, cardinal, capital, paramount, greatest, highest, ultimate.

▪ **2** secondary, subsidiary, minor.

prime *adj* best, choice, select, quality, first-class, first-rate, premium, optimum, excellent, top, supreme, pre-eminent, superior, senior, leading, ruling, chief, principal, predominant, main, primary, premier.

▪ second-rate, secondary.

➤ *n* height, peak, zenith, heyday, flower, bloom, maturity, perfection.

primeval *adj* earliest, first, original, primordial, early, old, ancient, prehistoric, primitive, instinctive.

▪ modern.

primitive *adj* **1** CRUDE, rough, unsophisticated, uncivilized, barbarian, savage. **2** EARLY, elementary, rudimentary, primary, first, original, earliest.

▪ **1** advanced, sophisticated, civilized.

princely *adj* **1** SOVEREIGN, imperial, royal, regal, majestic, stately, grand, noble. **2** *princely sum*: generous, liberal, lavish, sumptuous, magnificent, handsome.

principal *adj* main, chief, key, essential, cardinal, primary, first, foremost, leading, dominant, prime, paramount, pre-eminent, supreme, highest.

🔁 minor, subsidiary, lesser, least.

➤ *n* head, head teacher, headmaster, headmistress, chief, leader, boss (*infml*), director, manager, superintendent.

principally *adv* mainly, mostly, chiefly, primarily, predominantly, above all, particularly, especially.

principle *n* **1** RULE, formula, law, canon, axiom, dictum, precept, maxim, truth, tenet, doctrine, creed, dogma, code, standard, criterion, proposition, fundamental, essential. **2** *a man of principle*: HONOUR, integrity, rectitude, uprightness, virtue, decency, morality, morals, ethics, standards, scruples, conscience.

print *v* mark, stamp, imprint, impress, engrave, copy, reproduce, run off, publish, issue.

➤ *n* **1** LETTERS, characters, lettering, type, typescript, typeface, fount. **2** MARK, impression, fingerprint, footprint. **3** COPY, reproduction, picture, engraving, lithograph, photograph, photo.

Printing methods include: bubblejet printing, collotype, colour-process printing, computer-to-plate (CTP), copper engraving, die-stamping, duplicating, electrostatic printing, engraving, etching, flexography, gravure, inkjet printing, intaglio, laser printing, letterpress, lino blocking, litho, lithography, offset lithography, offset printing, photoengraving, rotary press, screen printing, silk-screen printing, stencilling, thermography, twin-etching, xerography.

Printing terms include: anodized plate, author's proof, back margin, backing-up, bad break, base alignment, batter, bi-directional printing, black printer, blanket-to-blanket press, bold face, bromide,

camera-ready copy, carding, caret, cast-off, catchword, centre, character set, chase, cliché, cold composition, collograph, colour control bar, colour separation, column inch/centimetre, compose, composing room, composition size, compositor, condensed, copy, cylinder press, dampers, dot-etching, dot gain, drum printer, electrotype, em, en, end even, expanded type, feathering, finishing, first proof, flat-bed press, flong, font, forme, galley, gutter, hard hyphen, hot-metal typesetting, image printing, imposition, impression, indent, initial caps, inking roller, Intertype, italic, justification, keep standing, kern, kiss impression, large print, leaders, leading, letterset, line printer, Linotype, literal, logotype, lower-case, machine composition, machine proof, mackle, makeready, manuscript, margin, matrix, misprint, moiré, Monophoto, Monotype, mottling, newsprint, non-image area, non-impact printing, offprint, orphan, overprint, Ozalid, perfecting, phototypesetting, planographic, printing press, progressive proofs, proof, quoin, ragged right/left, registration, relief printing, reprint, roman, run-around, running head, running text, sans serif, see-through, signature, small capitals, soft hyphen, specimen page, spoilage, stereotype, stet, strike-on, strip in, take in, take over, text, thermal printer, tint, trim marks, type, typeface, type scale, typescript, typesetting, type spec, typo, typographer (*US*), upper-case, web-fed, web offset, widow, woodcut, wood engraving, zinco.

prior *adj* earlier, preceding, foregoing, previous, former.

🔁 later.

◇ **prior to** before, preceding, earlier than.

🔁 after, following.

priority *n* right of way, precedence, seniority, rank, superiority, supremacy, pre-eminence, the lead, first place, urgency.

☒ inferiority.

prison n jail, nick (*sl*), clink (*sl*), cooler (*sl*), slammer (*sl*), penitentiary, cell, lock-up, cage, dungeon, imprisonment, confinement, detention, custody.

prisoner n captive, hostage, convict, con (*sl*), jail-bird (*infml*), inmate, internee, detainee.

privacy n secrecy, confidentiality, independence, solitude, isolation, seclusion, concealment, retirement, retreat.

private adj secret, classified, hush-hush (*infml*), off the record, unofficial, confidential, intimate, personal, individual, own, exclusive, particular, special, separate, independent, solitary, isolated, secluded, hidden, concealed, reserved, withdrawn.

☒ public, open.

◇ **in private** privately, in confidence, secretly, in secret, behind closed doors, in camera.

☒ publicly, openly.

privilege n advantage, benefit, concession, birthright, title, due, right, prerogative, entitlement, freedom, liberty, franchise, licence, sanction, authority, immunity, exemption.

☒ disadvantage.

privileged adj advantaged, favoured, special, sanctioned, authorized, immune, exempt, élite, honoured, ruling, powerful.

☒ disadvantaged, under-privileged.

prize n reward, trophy, medal, award, winnings, jackpot, purse, premium, stake(s), honour, accolade.

➤ adj best, top, first-rate, excellent, outstanding, champion, winning, prize-winning, award-winning.

☒ second-rate.

➤ v treasure, value, appreciate, esteem, revere, cherish, hold dear.

☒ despise.

probability n likelihood, odds,

chances, expectation, prospect, chance, possibility.

☒ improbability.

probable adj 1 LIKELY, odds-on, predictable, expected, anticipated. 2 BELIEVABLE, credible, plausible, feasible, possible, apparent, seeming.

☒ improbable, unlikely.

probation n apprenticeship, trial period, trial, test.

probe v prod, poke, pierce, penetrate, sound, plumb, explore, examine, scrutinize, investigate, go into, look into, search, sift, test.

➤ n 1 BORE, drill. 2 INQUIRY, inquest, investigation, exploration, examination, test, scrutiny, study, research.

problem n 1 TROUBLE, worry, predicament, spot (*infml*), quandary, dilemma, difficulty, complication, snag. 2 QUESTION, poser, puzzle, brain-teaser, conundrum, riddle, enigma.

➤ adj difficult, unmanageable, uncontrollable, unruly, delinquent.

☒ well-behaved, manageable.

procedure n routine, process, method, system, technique, custom, practice, policy, formula, course, scheme, strategy, plan of action, move, step, action, conduct, operation, performance.

proceed v 1 *the permission to proceed*: advance, go ahead, move on, progress, continue, carry on, press on. 2 ORIGINATE, derive, flow, start, stem, spring, arise, issue, result, ensue, follow, come.

☒ 1 stop, retreat.

proceedings n 1 MATTERS, affairs, business, dealings, transactions, report, account, minutes, records, archives, annals. 2 EVENTS, happenings, deeds, doings, moves, steps, measures, action, course of action.

proceeds n revenue, income, returns, receipts, takings, earnings, gain, profit, yield, produce.

☒ expenditure, outlay.

process n 1 PROCEDURE, operation,

practice, method, system, technique, means, manner, mode, way, stage, step. **2** COURSE, progression, advance, progress, development, evolution, formation, growth, movement, action, proceeding.

➤ *v* deal with, handle, treat, prepare, refine, transform, convert, change, alter.

procession *n* march, parade, cavalcade, motorcade, cortège, file, column, train, succession, series, sequence, course, run.

proclaim *v* announce, declare, state, pronounce, affirm, give out, publish, advertise, make known, profess, testify, show, indicate.

proclamation *n* announcement, declaration, pronouncement, affirmation, publication, promulgation (*fml*), notice, notification, manifesto, decree, edict.

procrastinate *v* defer, put off, postpone, delay, retard, stall, temporize, play for time, dally, dilly-dally (*infml*), drag one's feet, prolong, protract.

🔁 advance, proceed.

procure *v* acquire, buy, purchase, get, obtain, find, come by, pick up, lay hands on, earn, gain, win, secure, appropriate, requisition.

🔁 lose.

prod *v* poke, jab, stab, dig, elbow, nudge, push, shove, goad, spur, urge, egg on (*infml*), prompt, stimulate, motivate.

➤ *n* poke, jab, stab, dig, elbow, nudge, push, shove, prompt, reminder, stimulus, motivation.

prodigy *n* genius, virtuoso, wonder, marvel, miracle, phenomenon, sensation, freak, curiosity, rarity, child genius, wonder child, whizz kid (*infml*).

produce *v* **1** CAUSE, occasion, give rise to, provoke, bring about, result in, effect, create, originate, invent, fashion, make, manufacture, fabricate, construct, compose, generate, yield, bear, deliver. **2** ADVANCE, put forward, present, offer,

give, supply, provide, furnish, bring out, bring forth, show, exhibit, demonstrate. **3** *produce a play*: direct, stage, mount, put on.

➤ *n* crop, harvest, yield, output, product.

product *n* **1** COMMODITY, merchandise, goods, end-product, artefact, work, creation, invention, production, output, yield, produce, fruit, return. **2** RESULT, consequence, outcome, issue, upshot, offshoot, spin-off, by-product, legacy.

🔁 **2** cause.

production *n* **1** MAKING, manufacture, fabrication, construction, assembly, creation, origination, preparation, formation. **2** *an amateur production*: staging, presentation, direction, management.

🔁 **1** consumption.

productive *adj* fruitful, profitable, rewarding, valuable, worthwhile, useful, constructive, creative, inventive, fertile, rich, teeming, busy, energetic, vigorous, efficient, effective.

🔁 unproductive, fruitless, useless.

productivity *n* productiveness, yield, output, work rate, efficiency.

profane *adj* secular, temporal, lay, unconsecrated, unhallowed, unsanctified, unholy, irreligious, impious, sacrilegious, blasphemous, ungodly, irreverent, disrespectful, abusive, crude, coarse, foul, filthy, unclean.

🔁 sacred, religious, respectful.

➤ *v* desecrate, pollute, contaminate, defile, debase, pervert, abuse, misuse.

🔁 revere, honour.

profess *v* admit, confess, avow (*fml*), acknowledge, own, confirm, certify, testify, declare, announce, proclaim, state, assert, affirm, maintain, claim, allege, make out, pretend.

profession *n* **1** CAREER, job, occupation, employment, business, line (of work), trade, vocation, calling, métier, craft, office, position. **2** ADMISSION, acknowledgement, confession, declaration, statement, announcement, testimony, assertion, affirmation, claim.

professional *adj* qualified, licensed, trained, experienced, practised, skilled, expert, masterly, proficient, competent, businesslike, efficient.
▣ amateur, unprofessional.
➤ *n* expert, authority, specialist, pro (*infml*), master, virtuoso, dab hand (*infml*).
▣ amateur.

proficiency *n* skill, skilfulness, expertise, mastery, talent, knack, dexterity, finesse, aptitude, ability, competence.
▣ incompetence.

proficient *adj* able, capable, skilled, qualified, trained, experienced, accomplished, expert, masterly, gifted, talented, clever, skilful, competent, efficient.
▣ unskilled, incompetent.

profile *n* **1** SIDE VIEW, outline, contour, silhouette, shape, form, figure, sketch, drawing, diagram, chart, graph. **2** BIOGRAPHY, curriculum vitae, CV, thumbnail sketch, vignette, portrait, study, analysis, examination, survey, review.

profit *n* gain, surplus, excess, bottom line, revenue, return, yield, proceeds, receipts, takings, earnings, winnings, interest, advantage, benefit, use, avail, value, worth.
▣ loss.
➤ *v* gain, make money, pay, serve, avail, benefit.
▣ lose.
◇ **profit by, profit from** exploit, take advantage of, use, utilize, turn to advantage, capitalize on, cash in on, reap the benefit of.

profitable *adj* cost-effective, economic, commercial, money-making, lucrative, remunerative, paying, rewarding, successful, fruitful, productive, advantageous, beneficial, useful, valuable, worthwhile.
▣ unprofitable, loss-making, non-profit-making.

profound *adj* **1** DEEP, great, intense, extreme, heartfelt, marked, far-reaching, extensive, exhaustive. **2** *a profound remark*: serious, weighty, deep, penetrating, thoughtful, philosophical, wise, learned, erudite (*fml*), abstruse.
▣ **1** shallow, slight, mild.

profuse *adj* ample, abundant, plentiful, copious, generous, liberal, lavish, rich, luxuriant, excessive, immoderate, extravagant, overabundant, superabundant, overflowing.
▣ inadequate, sparse.

profusion *n* abundance, plenty, wealth, multitude, plethora, glut, excess, surplus, superfluity, extravagance.
▣ inadequacy, scarcity.

programme *n* **1** SCHEDULE, timetable, agenda, calendar, order of events, listing, line-up, plan, scheme, project, syllabus, curriculum. **2** *radio programme*: broadcast, transmission, show, performance, production, presentation.

progress *n* movement, progression, passage, journey, way, advance, headway, step forward, breakthrough, development, evolution, growth, increase, improvement, betterment, promotion.
▣ recession, deterioration, decline.
➤ *v* proceed, advance, go forward, forge ahead, make progress, make headway, come on, develop, grow, mature, blossom, improve, better, prosper, increase.
▣ deteriorate, decline.

progression *n* cycle, chain, string, succession, series, sequence, order, course, advance, headway, progress, development.

progressive *adj* **1** MODERN, avant-garde, advanced, forward-looking, enlightened, liberal, radical, revolutionary, reformist, dynamic, enterprising, go-ahead, up-and-coming. **2** ADVANCING, continuing, developing, growing, increasing, intensifying.

▣ 1 regressive.

prohibit *v* forbid, ban, bar, veto, proscribe, outlaw, rule out, preclude, prevent, stop, hinder, hamper, impede, obstruct, restrict.

▣ permit, allow, authorize.

project *n* assignment, contract, task, job, work, occupation, activity, enterprise, undertaking, venture, plan, scheme, programme, design, proposal, idea, conception.

➤ *v* 1 PREDICT, forecast, extrapolate, estimate, reckon, calculate. 2 THROW, fling, hurl, launch, propel. 3 PROTRUDE, stick out, bulge, jut out, overhang.

projection *n* 1 PROTUBERANCE, bulge, overhang, ledge, sill, shelf, ridge. 2 PREDICTION, forecast, extrapolation, estimate, reckoning, calculation, computation.

proliferate *v* multiply, reproduce, breed, increase, build up, intensify, escalate, mushroom, snowball, spread, expand, flourish, thrive.

▣ dwindle.

prolific *adj* productive, fruitful, fertile, profuse, copious, abundant.

▣ unproductive.

prolong *v* lengthen, extend, stretch, protract, draw out, spin out, drag out, delay, continue, perpetuate.

▣ shorten.

prominence *n* 1 FAME, celebrity, renown, eminence, distinction, greatness, importance, reputation, name, standing, rank, prestige. 2 BULGE, protuberance, bump, hump, lump, mound, rise, elevation, projection, process, headland, promontory, cliff, crag.

▣ 1 unimportance, insignificance.

prominent *adj* 1 NOTICEABLE, conspicuous, obvious, unmistakable, striking, eye-catching. 2 BULGING, protuberant, projecting, jutting, protruding, obtrusive. 3 *a prominent writer*: famous, well-known, celebrated, renowned, noted, eminent, illustrious, distinguished, respected, leading, foremost, chief, main, important, popular, outstanding.

▣ 1 inconspicuous. 3 unknown, unimportant, insignificant.

promiscuity *n* looseness, laxity, permissiveness, wantonness, immorality, licentiousness, debauchery, depravity.

▣ chastity, morality.

promiscuous *adj* loose, immoral, licentious, dissolute, casual, random, haphazard, indiscriminate.

▣ chaste, moral.

promise *v* 1 VOW, pledge, swear, take an oath, contract, undertake, give one's word, vouch, warrant, guarantee, assure. 2 AUGUR, presage, indicate, suggest, hint at.

➤ *n* 1 VOW, pledge, oath, word of honour, bond, pact, compact, covenant, guarantee, assurance, undertaking, engagement, commitment. 2 POTENTIAL, ability, capability, aptitude, talent.

promising *adj* auspicious (*fml*), propitious (*fml*), favourable, rosy, bright, encouraging, hopeful, talented, gifted, budding, up-and-coming.

▣ unpromising, inauspicious, discouraging.

promote *v* 1 ADVERTISE, plug (*infml*), publicize, hype (*sl*), popularize, market, sell, push, talk up (*infml*), recommend, advocate, champion, endorse, sponsor, support, back, help, aid, assist, foster, nurture, further, forward, encourage, boost, stimulate, urge. 2 UPGRADE, advance, move up, raise, elevate, exalt, honour.

▣ 1 disparage, hinder. 2 demote.

promotion *n* 1 ADVANCEMENT, upgrading, rise, preferment, elevation, exaltation. 2 ADVERTISING, plugging (*infml*), publicity, hype (*sl*), campaign, propaganda, marketing, pushing, support, backing, furtherance, development, encouragement, boosting.

▣ **1** demotion. **2** disparagement, obstruction.

prompt[1] *adj* punctual, on time, immediate, instantaneous, instant, direct, quick, swift, rapid, speedy, unhesitating, willing, ready, alert, responsive, timely, early.
▣ slow, hesitant, late.
➤ *adv* promptly, punctually, exactly, on the dot, to the minute, sharp.

prompt[2] *v* cause, give rise to, result in, occasion, produce, instigate, call forth, elicit, provoke, incite, urge, encourage, inspire, move, stimulate, motivate, spur, prod, remind.
▣ deter, dissuade.
➤ *n* reminder, cue, hint, help, jolt, prod, spur, stimulus.

prone *adj* **1** LIKELY, given, inclined, disposed, predisposed, bent, apt, liable, subject, susceptible, vulnerable. **2** *she lay prone*: face down, prostrate, flat, horizontal, full-length, stretched, recumbent.
▣ **1** unlikely, immune. **2** upright, supine.

pronounce *v* **1** SAY, utter, speak, express, voice, vocalize, sound, enunciate, articulate, stress. **2** DECLARE, announce, proclaim, decree, judge, affirm, assert, state.

pronounced *adj* clear, distinct, definite, positive, decided, marked, noticeable, conspicuous, evident, obvious, striking, unmistakable, strong, broad.
▣ faint, vague.

pronunciation *n* speech, diction, elocution, enunciation, articulation, delivery, accent, stress, inflection, intonation, modulation.

proof *n* evidence, documentation, demonstration, verification, confirmation, corroboration, substantiation.

prop *v* **1** SUPPORT, sustain, uphold, maintain, shore, stay, buttress, bolster, underpin, set. **2** *propped against the wall*: lean, rest, stand.
➤ *n* support, stay, mainstay, strut, buttress, brace, truss.

propaganda *n* advertising, publicity, hype (*sl*), indoctrination, brainwashing, disinformation, spin (*infml*).

propagate *v* **1** SPREAD, transmit, broadcast, diffuse, disseminate, circulate, publish, promulgate, publicize, promote. **2** INCREASE, multiply, proliferate, generate, engender, produce, breed, beget, spawn, procreate, reproduce.

propel *v* move, drive, impel, force, thrust, push, shove, launch, shoot, send.
▣ stop.

proper *adj* **1** RIGHT, correct, accurate, exact, precise, true, genuine, real, actual. **2** ACCEPTED, correct, suitable, appropriate, fitting, meet (*fml*), decent, respectable, polite, formal.
▣ **1** wrong. **2** improper, indecent.

property *n* **1** ESTATE, land, real estate, acres, premises, buildings, house(s), wealth, riches, resources, means, capital, assets, holding(s), belongings, possessions, effects, goods, chattels. **2** FEATURE, trait, quality, attribute, characteristic, idiosyncrasy, peculiarity, mark.

prophecy *n* prediction, augury, forecast, prognosis.

prophesy *v* predict, foresee, augur, foretell, forewarn, forecast.

prophet *n* seer, soothsayer, foreteller, forecaster, oracle, clairvoyant, fortune-teller.

proportion *n* **1** PERCENTAGE, fraction, part, division, share, quota, amount. **2** RATIO, relationship, correspondence, symmetry, balance, distribution.
▣ **2** disproportion, imbalance.

proportional *adj* proportionate, relative, commensurate, consistent, corresponding, analogous, comparable, equitable, even.
▣ disproportionate.

proportions *n* dimensions, measurements, size, magnitude, volume, capacity.

proposal *n* proposition, suggestion,

recommendation, motion, plan, scheme, project, design, programme, manifesto, presentation, bid, offer, tender, terms.

propose v 1 SUGGEST, recommend, move, advance, put forward, proffer, introduce, bring up, table, submit, present, offer, tender. 2 INTEND, mean, aim, purpose, plan, design. 3 NAME, nominate, put up, recommend.
🔁 1 withdraw.

proprietor, proprietress n landlord, landlady, title-holder, freeholder, leaseholder, landowner, owner, possessor.

prosecute v accuse, indict, sue, charge, prefer charges, take to court, litigate, summon, put on trial, try.
🔁 defend.

prosody

Forms of prosody include: abstract verse, Alcaic verse, alexandrine, alliteration, amphibrach, amphimacer, Anacreontic verse, anacrusis, analysed rhyme, anapaest, antibacchius, antispast, Archilochian verse, asclepiad, assonance, asynartete, ballade, blank verse, broken rhyme, bouts rimés, caesura, canto, catalexis, choliamb, choree, choriamb, cinquain, couplet, dactyl, decastich, dipody, dispondee, distich, ditrochee, dizain, dochmius, elision, enjambment, envoy, epitrite, epode, eye rhyme, false quantity, feminine caesura, feminine ending, feminine rhyme, foot, free verse, galliambic, glyconic, half-rhyme, heptameter, heptapody, heroic couplet, hexameter, hexastich, hypermetrical, iamb, ictus, Ionic, kyrielle, laisse, Leonine rhyme, linked verse, long-measure, macaronic, masculine ending, masculine rhyme, metre, miurus, monometer, monorhyme, paeon, pantoum, pentameter, pentastich, Petrarchan sonnet, Pherecratean, Pindaric, poulters' measure, pyrrhic, Pythian verse, quatorzain, quatrain, reported verses, rhopalic, rhyme royal, rime riche, rime suffisante, rondeau,

rondel, rove-over, Sapphic, senarius, septenarius, sonnet, Spencerian stanza, spondee, sprung rhythm, strophe, substituion, synaphea, tetrameter, tetrapody, tetrastich, tribrach, trimeter, triolet, tripody, triseme, trochee, villanelle, virelay.

prospect n chance, odds, probability, likelihood, possibility, expectation, hope, anticipation, outlook, future.
🔁 unlikelihood.

prospective adj future, -to-be, intended, designate, elect, nominated, destined, forthcoming, approaching, coming, imminent, awaited, expected, anticipated, likely, possible, probable, potential, aspiring, would-be.
🔁 current.

prospectus n plan, scheme, programme, syllabus, manifesto, outline, synopsis, pamphlet, leaflet, brochure, catalogue, list.

prosper v boom, thrive, flourish, flower, bloom, succeed, get on, advance, progress, grow rich.
🔁 fail.

prosperity n boom, plenty, affluence, wealth, riches, fortune, well-being, luxury, the good life, success, good fortune.
🔁 adversity, poverty.

prosperous adj booming, thriving, flourishing, blooming, successful, fortunate, lucky, rich, wealthy, affluent, well-off, well-to-do.
🔁 unfortunate, poor.

prostrate adj flat, horizontal, prone, fallen, floored, overcome, overwhelmed, crushed, paralysed, powerless, helpless, defenceless.
🔁 triumphant.
➤ v lay low, overcome, overwhelm, crush, overthrow, floor, tire, wear out, fatigue, exhaust, drain, ruin.
🔁 strengthen.
◇ **prostrate oneself** bow down, kneel, kowtow, submit, grovel, cringe, abase oneself.

protagonist n hero, heroine, lead, principal, leader, prime mover, champion, advocate, supporter, proponent, exponent.

protect v safeguard, defend, guard, escort, cover, screen, shield, secure, watch over, look after, care for, support, shelter, harbour, keep, conserve, preserve, save.
☒ attack, neglect.

protection n 1 *protection of the environment*: care, custody, charge, guardianship, safekeeping, conservation, preservation, safety, safeguard. 2 BARRIER, buffer, bulwark, defence, guard, shield, armour, screen, cover, shelter, refuge, security, insurance.
☒ 1 neglect, attack.

protective adj 1 POSSESSIVE, defensive, motherly, maternal, fatherly, paternal, watchful, vigilant, careful. 2 *protective clothing*: waterproof, fireproof, windproof, Gore-tex®, insulating.
☒ 1 aggressive, threatening.

protest n objection, disapproval, opposition, dissent, complaint, protestation, outcry, appeal, demonstration, demo (*infml*).
☒ acceptance.
➤ v 1 OBJECT, take exception, complain, appeal, demonstrate, oppose, disapprove, disagree, argue. 2 *protest one's innocence*: assert, maintain, contend, argue, insist, profess.
☒ 1 accept.

protester n demonstrator, agitator, rebel, dissident, dissenter.

protocol n procedure, formalities, convention, custom, etiquette, manners, good form, propriety.

protracted adj long, lengthy, prolonged, extended, drawn-out, long-drawn-out, overlong, interminable.
☒ brief, shortened.

protrude v stick out, poke out, come through, bulge, jut out, project, extend, stand out, obtrude.

proud adj 1 CONCEITED, vain, egotistical, bigheaded, boastful, smug, complacent, arrogant, self-important, cocky, presumptuous, haughty, high and mighty, overbearing, supercilious, snooty (*infml*), snobbish, toffee-nosed (*infml*), stuck-up (*infml*). 2 SATISFIED, contented, gratified, pleased, delighted, honoured. 3 DIGNIFIED, noble, honourable, worthy, self-respecting.
☒ 1 humble, modest, unassuming. 2 ashamed. 3 deferential, ignoble.

prove v show, demonstrate, attest, verify, confirm, corroborate (*fml*), substantiate (*fml*), bear out, document, certify, authenticate, validate, justify, establish, determine, ascertain, try, test, check, examine, analyse.
☒ disprove, discredit, falsify.

proverb n saying, adage, aphorism, maxim, byword, dictum, precept.

proverbial adj axiomatic, accepted, conventional, traditional, customary, time-honoured, famous, well-known, legendary, notorious, typical, archetypal.

provide v 1 SUPPLY, furnish, stock, equip, outfit, prepare for, cater, serve, present, give, contribute, yield, lend, add, bring. 2 PLAN FOR, allow, make provision, accommodate, arrange for, take precautions. 3 STATE, specify, stipulate, lay down, require.
☒ 1 take, remove.

providence n 1 FATE, destiny, divine intervention, God's will, fortune, luck, karma, kismet. 2 PRUDENCE, far-sightedness, foresight, shrewdness, caution, care, carefulness, thrift.
☒ 2 improvidence.

provident adj prudent, far-sighted, judicious, shrewd, cautious, careful, thrifty, economical, frugal.
☒ improvident.

providential adj timely, opportune, convenient, fortunate, lucky, happy, welcome, heaven-sent.
☒ untimely.

providing conj provided, with the

proviso, given, as long as, on condition, on the understanding.

province n 1 REGION, area, district, zone, county, shire, department, territory, colony, dependency. 2 RESPONSIBILITY, concern, duty, office, role, function, field, sphere, domain, department, line.

provincial adj regional, local, rural, rustic, country, home-grown, small-town, parish-pump, parochial, insular, inward-looking, blinkered, limited, narrow, narrow-minded, small-minded.
national, cosmopolitan, urban, sophisticated.

provision n 1 PLAN, arrangement, preparation, measure, precaution. 2 STIPULATION, specification, proviso, condition, term, requirement.

provisional adj temporary, interim, transitional, stopgap, makeshift, conditional, tentative.
permanent, fixed, definite.

provisions n food, foodstuff, groceries, eatables (*infml*), victuals, sustenance, rations, supplies, stocks, stores.

proviso n condition, term, requirement, stipulation, qualification, reservation, restriction, limitation, provision, clause, rider.

provocation n cause, grounds, justification, reason, motive, stimulus, motivation, incitement, instigation, annoyance, aggravation (*infml*), vexation, grievance, offence, insult, affront, injury, taunt, challenge, dare.

provocative adj 1 ANNOYING, aggravating (*infml*), galling, outrageous, offensive, insulting, abusive. 2 STIMULATING, exciting, challenging. 3 EROTIC, titillating, arousing, sexy, seductive, alluring, tempting, inviting, tantalizing, teasing, suggestive.
1 conciliatory.

provoke v 1 ANNOY, irritate, rile, aggravate (*infml*), offend, insult, anger, enrage, infuriate, incense, madden, exasperate, tease, taunt. 2 CAUSE,

occasion, give rise to, produce, generate, engender, induce, elicit, evoke, excite, inspire, move, stir, prompt, stimulate, motivate, incite, instigate.
1 please, pacify. 2 result.

prowess n accomplishment, attainment, ability, aptitude, skill, expertise, mastery, command, talent, genius.

proximity n closeness, nearness, vicinity, neighbourhood, adjacency, juxtaposition.
remoteness.

proxy n agent, factor, deputy, stand-in, substitute, representative, delegate, attorney.

prudent adj wise, sensible, politic, judicious, shrewd, discerning, careful, cautious, wary, vigilant, circumspect, discreet, provident, far-sighted, thrifty.
imprudent, unwise, careless, rash.

pry v meddle, interfere, poke one's nose in, intrude, peep, peer, snoop, nose, ferret, dig, delve.
mind one's own business.

pseudonym n false name, assumed name, alias, incognito, pen name, nom de plume, stage name, moniker (*sl*).

psychic adj spiritual, supernatural, occult, mystic(al), clairvoyant, extra-sensory, telepathic, mental, psychological, intellectual, cognitive.

psychological adj mental, cerebral, intellectual, cognitive, emotional, subjective, subconscious, unconscious, psychosomatic, irrational, unreal.
physical, real.

puberty n pubescence, adolescence, teens, youth, growing up, maturity.
childhood, immaturity, old age.

public adj 1 *public buildings*: state, national, civil, community, social, collective, communal, common, general, universal, open, unrestricted. 2 KNOWN, well-known, recognized, acknowledged, overt, open, exposed, published.

◼ 1 private, personal. **2** secret.

➤ *n* people, nation, country, population, populace, masses, hoi-polloi, citizens, society, community, voters, electorate, followers, supporters, fans, audience, patrons, clientèle, customers, buyers, consumers.

◇ **public house** pub (*infml*), local (*infml*), bar, saloon, inn, tavern.

publication *n* **1** BOOK, newspaper, magazine, periodical, ezine, fanzine, booklet, leaflet, pamphlet, handbill, flyer. **2** ANNOUNCEMENT, declaration, notification, disclosure, release, issue, printing, publishing.

publicity *n* advertising, plug (*infml*), hype (*sl*), promotion, build-up, boost, attention, limelight, splash.

publicize *v* advertise, plug (*infml*), hype (*sl*), promote, push, spotlight, broadcast, make known, blaze.

publish *v* **1** ANNOUNCE, declare, communicate, make known, divulge, disclose, reveal, release, publicize, advertise. **2** *publish a book*: produce, print, issue, bring out, distribute, circulate, spread, diffuse.

pucker *v* gather, ruffle, wrinkle, shrivel, crinkle, crumple, crease, furrow, purse, screw up, contract, compress.

puerile *adj* childish, babyish, infantile, juvenile, immature, irresponsible, silly, foolish, inane, trivial.
◼ mature.

puff *n* **1** BREATH, waft, whiff, draught, flurry, gust, blast. **2** *a puff on a cigarette*: pull, drag, draw.

➤ *v* **1** BREATHE, pant, gasp, gulp, wheeze, blow, waft, inflate, expand, swell, balloon. **2** *puff a cigarette*: smoke, pull, drag, draw, suck.

puffy *adj* puffed up, inflated, swollen, bloated, distended, enlarged.

pugnacious *adj* hostile, aggressive, belligerent, contentious, disputatious, argumentative, quarrelsome, hot-tempered.
◼ peaceable.

pull *v* **1** TOW, drag, haul, draw, tug, jerk, yank (*infml*). **2** REMOVE, take out, extract, pull out, pluck, uproot, pull up, rip, tear. **3** ATTRACT, draw, lure, allure, entice, tempt, magnetize. **4** DISLOCATE, sprain, wrench, strain.
◼ 1 push, press. **3** repel, deter, discourage.

➤ *n* **1** TOW, drag, tug, jerk, yank (*infml*). **2** ATTRACTION, lure, allurement, drawing power, magnetism, influence, weight.

◇ **pull apart** separate, part, dismember, dismantle, take to pieces.
◼ join.

◇ **pull down** destroy, demolish, knock down, bulldoze.
◼ build, erect, put up.

◇ **pull off 1** ACCOMPLISH, achieve, bring off, succeed, manage, carry out. **2** DETACH, remove.
◼ 1 fail. **2** attach.

◇ **pull out** retreat, withdraw, leave, depart, quit, move out, evacuate, desert, abandon.
◼ join, arrive.

◇ **pull through** recover, rally, recuperate, survive, weather.

◇ **pull together** co-operate, work together, collaborate, team up.
◼ fight.

◇ **pull up 1** STOP, halt, park, draw up, pull in, pull over, brake. **2** REPRIMAND, tell off (*infml*), tick off (*infml*), take to task, rebuke, criticize.

pulp *n* flesh, marrow, paste, purée, mash, mush, pap.

➤ *v* crush, squash, pulverize, mash, purée, liquidize.

pulsate *v* pulse, beat, throb, pound, hammer, drum, thud, thump, vibrate, oscillate, quiver.

pulse *n* beat, stroke, rhythm, throb, pulsation, beating, pounding, drumming, vibration, oscillation.

pulverize *v* **1** CRUSH, pound, grind, mill, powder. **2** DEFEAT, destroy, demolish, annihilate.

pump *v* push, drive, force, inject, siphon, draw, drain.

◇ **pump up** blow up, inflate, puff up, fill.

pun *n* play on words, double entendre, witticism, quip.

punch[1] *v* hit, strike, pummel, jab, bash, clout, cuff, box, thump, sock (*sl*), wallop (*infml*), whack (*infml*).
➤ *n* **1** BLOW, jab, bash, clout, thump, wallop (*infml*), whack (*infml*). **2** FORCE, impact, effectiveness, drive, vigour, verve, panache.

punch[2] *v* perforate, pierce, puncture, prick, bore, drill, stamp, cut.

punctilious *adj* scrupulous, conscientious, meticulous, careful, exact, precise, strict, formal, proper, particular, finicky, fussy.
🔁 lax, informal.

punctual *adj* prompt, on time, on the dot, exact, precise, early, in good time.
🔁 unpunctual, late.

punctuation

> *Punctuation marks include*: comma, full stop, period, ellipsis, colon, semicolon, brackets, parentheses, square brackets, inverted commas, speech marks, quotation marks, quotes (*infml*), exclamation mark, question mark, apostrophe, asterisk, star, hyphen, dash, oblique stroke, solidus, backslash.

puncture *n* **1** FLAT TYRE, flat (*infml*), blow-out. **2** LEAK, hole, perforation, cut, nick.
➤ *v* prick, pierce, penetrate, perforate, hole, cut, nick, burst, rupture, flatten, deflate.

pungent *adj* strong, hot, peppery, spicy, aromatic, tangy, piquant, sharp, keen, acute, sour, bitter, acrid, caustic, stinging, biting, cutting, incisive, pointed, piercing, penetrating, sarcastic, scathing.
🔁 mild, bland, tasteless.

punish *v* penalize, discipline, correct, chastise, castigate, scold, beat, flog, lash, cane, spank, fine, imprison.
🔁 reward.

punishment *n* discipline, correction, chastisement, beating, flogging, penalty, fine, imprisonment, sentence, deserts, retribution, revenge.
🔁 reward.

> *Forms of punishment include*: banging up (*sl*), banishment, beating, belting, the birch, borstal, the cane, capital punishment, cashiering, chain gang, confinement, confiscation, corporal punishment, defrocking, demotion, deportation, detention, dressing-down, excommunication, execution, exclusion, exile, expulsion, fine, flaying, flogging, gaol, gating, grounding, hiding (*infml*), hitting, horsewhipping, house arrest, imprisonment, incarceration, internment, jail, jankers, keelhauling, larruping (*infml*), lashing, leathering, lines, penal colony, prison, probation, being put away (*infml*), the rack, rap across the knuckles, scourging, being sent down (*infml*), being sent to Coventry, sequestration, slapping, the slipper, smacking, spanking, the stocks, suspension, tanning someone's hide (*infml*), tarring and feathering, thrashing, torturing, transportation, unfrocking, walking the plank, walloping, whipping. *see also* **execution**.

punitive *adj* penal, disciplinary, retributive, retaliatory, vindictive, punishing.

puny *adj* weak, feeble, frail, sickly, undeveloped, underdeveloped, stunted, undersized, diminutive, little, tiny, insignificant.
🔁 strong, sturdy, large, important.

pupil *n* student, scholar, schoolboy, schoolgirl, learner, apprentice, beginner, novice, disciple, protégé(e).
🔁 teacher.

purchase *v* buy, pay for, invest in (*infml*), procure, acquire, obtain, get, secure, gain, earn, win.
🔁 sell.
➤ *n* acquisition, buy (*infml*), investment, asset, possession, property.
🔁 sale.

purchaser *n* buyer, consumer, shopper, customer, client.
🖪 seller, vendor.

pure *adj* 1 *pure gold*: unadulterated, unalloyed, unmixed, undiluted, neat, solid, simple, natural, real, authentic, genuine, true. 2 STERILE, germ-free, uncontaminated, unpolluted, aseptic, antiseptic, disinfected, sterilized, hygienic, sanitary, clean, immaculate, spotless, clear. 3 SHEER, utter, complete, total, thorough, absolute, perfect, unqualified. 4 CHASTE, virginal, undefiled, unsullied, moral, upright, virtuous, blameless, innocent, squeaky-clean (*infml*). 5 *pure mathematics*: theoretical, abstract, conjectural, speculative, academic.
🖪 1 impure, adulterated. 2 polluted, contaminated. 4 immoral. 5 applied.

purely *adv* 1 UTTERLY, completely, totally, entirely, wholly, thoroughly, absolutely. 2 ONLY, simply, merely, just, solely, exclusively.

purge *v* 1 PURIFY, cleanse, clean out, scour, clear, absolve. 2 OUST, remove, get rid of, eject, expel, root out, eradicate, exterminate, wipe out, kill.
➤ *n* removal, ejection, expulsion, witch hunt, eradication, extermination.

purify *v* refine, filter, clarify, clean, cleanse, decontaminate, sanitize, disinfect, sterilize, fumigate, deodorize.
🖪 contaminate, pollute, defile.

purist *n* pedant, literalist, formalist, stickler, quibbler, nit-picker (*infml*), perfectionist.

puritanical *adj* puritan, moralistic, disciplinarian, ascetic, abstemious, austere, severe, stern, strict, strait-laced, prim, proper, prudish, stuffy, disapproving, stiff, rigid, narrow-minded, bigoted, fanatical, zealous.
🖪 hedonistic, liberal, indulgent, broad-minded.

purity *n* 1 CLEARNESS, clarity, cleanness, cleanliness, untaintedness, wholesomeness. 2 SIMPLICITY, authenticity, genuineness, truth. 3

CHASTITY, decency, morality, integrity, rectitude, uprightness, virtue, innocence, blamelessness.
🖪 1 impurity. 3 immorality.

purpose *n* 1 INTENTION, aim, objective, end, goal, target, plan, design, vision, idea, point, object, reason, motive, rationale, principle, result, outcome. 2 DETERMINATION, resolve, resolution, drive, single-mindedness, dedication, devotion, constancy, steadfastness, persistence, tenacity, zeal. 3 USE, function, application, good, advantage, benefit, value.
◇ **on purpose** purposely, deliberately, intentionally, consciously, knowingly, wittingly, wilfully.
🖪 accidentally, impulsively, spontaneously.

purposeful *adj* determined, decided, resolved, resolute, single-minded, constant, steadfast, persistent, persevering, tenacious, strong-willed, positive, firm, deliberate.
🖪 purposeless, aimless.

purse *n* 1 MONEY-BAG, wallet, pouch, pocketbook (*US*). 2 MONEY, means, resources, finances, funds, coffers, treasury, exchequer. 3 REWARD, award, prize.
➤ *v* pucker, wrinkle, gather, draw together, close, tighten, contract, compress.

pursue *v* 1 *pursue an activity*: perform, engage in, practise, conduct, carry on, continue, keep on, keep up, maintain, persevere in, persist in, hold to, aspire to, aim for, strive for, try for. 2 CHASE, go after, follow, track, trail, shadow, tail, dog, harass, harry, hound, hunt, seek, search for, investigate, inquire into.

pursuit *n* 1 CHASE, hue and cry, tracking, stalking, trail, hunt, quest, search, investigation. 2 ACTIVITY, interest, hobby, pastime, occupation, trade, craft, line, speciality, vocation.

push *v* 1 PROPEL, thrust, ram, shove, jostle, elbow, prod, poke, press, depress, squeeze, squash, drive, force,

constrain. **2** PROMOTE, advertise, publicize, hype (*sl*), boost, encourage, urge, egg on (*infml*), incite, spur, influence, persuade, pressurize, bully.
F3 1 pull. **2** discourage, dissuade.
➤ *n* **1** KNOCK, shove, nudge, jolt, prod, poke, thrust. **2** ENERGY, vigour, vitality, vim, go (*infml*), drive, effort, dynamism, enterprise, initiative, ambition, determination.

pushy *adj* assertive, self-assertive, ambitious, forceful, aggressive, over-confident, forward, bold, brash, in-your-face (*infml*), arrogant, presumptuous, assuming, bossy (*infml*).
F3 unassertive, unassuming.

put *v* **1** PLACE, lay, deposit, plonk (*infml*), set, fix, settle, establish, stand, position, dispose, situate, station, post. **2** APPLY, impose, inflict, levy, assign, subject. **3** WORD, phrase, formulate, frame, couch, express, voice, utter, state. **4** *put a suggestion*: submit, present, offer, suggest, propose.
◇ **put across** put over, communicate, convey, express, explain, spell out, bring home to, get through to.
◇ **put aside** put by, set aside, keep, retain, save, reserve, store, stow, stockpile, stash (*infml*), hoard, salt away.
◇ **put away** (*infml*) **1** CONSUME, devour, gobble (up) (*infml*), eat, drink. **2** IMPRISON, jail, lock up, commit, certify.
◇ **put back 1** DELAY, defer, postpone, reschedule. **2** REPLACE, return.
F3 1 bring forward.
◇ **put down 1** WRITE DOWN, transcribe, enter, log, register, record, note. **2** CRUSH, quash, suppress, defeat, quell, silence, snub, slight, squash, deflate, humble, take down a peg, shame, humiliate, mortify. **3** *put down a sick dog*: kill, put to sleep. **4** ASCRIBE, attribute, blame, charge.
◇ **put forward** advance, suggest, recommend, nominate, propose, move, table, introduce, present, submit, offer, tender, proffer.
◇ **put in** insert, enter, input, submit, install, fit.

◇ **put off 1** DELAY, defer, postpone, reschedule. **2** DETER, dissuade, discourage, dishearten, demoralize, daunt, dismay, intimidate, disconcert, confuse, distract.
F3 2 encourage.
◇ **put on 1** ATTACH, affix, apply, place, add, impose. **2** PRETEND, feign, sham, fake, simulate, affect, assume. **3** STAGE, mount, produce, present, do, perform.
◇ **put out 1** PUBLISH, announce, broadcast, circulate. **2** EXTINGUISH, quench, douse, smother, switch off, turn off. **3** INCONVENIENCE, impose on, bother, disturb, trouble, upset, hurt, offend, annoy, irritate, irk, anger, exasperate.
F3 2 light.
◇ **put up 1** ERECT, build, construct, assemble. **2** ACCOMMODATE, house, lodge, shelter. **3** *put up prices*: raise, increase.
◇ **put up with** stand, bear, abide, stomach, endure, suffer, tolerate, allow, accept, stand for, take, take lying down.
F3 object to, reject.

putrid *adj* rotten, decayed, decomposed, mouldy, off, bad, rancid, addled, corrupt, contaminated, tainted, polluted, foul, rank, fetid, stinking.
F3 fresh, wholesome.

puzzle *v* **1** BAFFLE, mystify, perplex, confound, stump (*infml*), floor (*infml*), confuse, bewilder, nonplus, flummox (*infml*). **2** THINK, ponder, meditate, consider, mull over, deliberate, cogitate, ruminate, figure, rack one's brains.
➤ *n* question, poser, brain-teaser, mind-bender, crossword, rebus, anagram, riddle, conundrum, mystery, enigma, paradox.
◇ **puzzle out** solve, work out, figure out, decipher, decode, crack, unravel, untangle, sort out, resolve, clear up.

puzzled *adj* baffled, mystified, perplexed, confounded, at a loss, beaten, stumped (*infml*), confused, bewildered, nonplussed, lost, at sea, flummoxed (*infml*).
F3 clear.

Qq

quagmire *n* bog, marsh, quag, fen, swamp, morass, mire, quicksand.

quail *v* recoil, back away, shy away, shrink, flinch, cringe, cower, tremble, quake, shudder, falter.

quaint *adj* picturesque, charming, twee (*infml*), old-fashioned, antiquated, old-world, olde-worlde (*infml*), unusual, strange, odd, curious, bizarre, fanciful, whimsical.
E3 modern.

quake *v* shake, tremble, shudder, quiver, shiver, quail, vibrate, wobble, rock, sway, move, convulse, heave.

qualification *n* **1** CERTIFICATE, diploma, training, skill, competence, ability, capability, capacity, aptitude, suitability, fitness, eligibility. **2** RESTRICTION, limitation, reservation, exception, exemption, condition, caveat, provision, proviso, stipulation, modification.

qualified *adj* **1** CERTIFIED, chartered, licensed, professional, trained, experienced, practised, skilled, accomplished, expert, knowledgeable, skilful, talented, proficient, competent, efficient, able, capable, fit, eligible. **2** *qualified praise*: reserved, guarded, cautious, restricted, limited, bounded, contingent, conditional, provisional, equivocal.
E3 1 unqualified. **2** unconditional, wholehearted.

qualify *v* **1** TRAIN, prepare, equip, fit, pass, graduate, certify, empower, entitle, authorize, sanction, permit. **2** MODERATE, reduce, lessen, diminish, temper, soften, weaken, mitigate, ease, adjust, modify, restrain, restrict, limit, delimit, define, classify.
E3 1 disqualify.

quality *n* **1** PROPERTY, characteristic, peculiarity, attribute, aspect, feature, trait, mark. **2** *of poor quality*: standard, grade, class, kind, sort, nature, character, calibre, status, rank, value, worth, merit, condition.
3 EXCELLENCE, superiority, pre-eminence, distinction, refinement.

qualm *n* misgiving, apprehension, fear, anxiety, worry, disquiet, uneasiness, scruple, hesitation, reluctance, uncertainty, doubt.

quandary *n* dilemma, predicament, impasse, perplexity, bewilderment, confusion, mess, fix, hole (*infml*), spot (*infml*), problem, difficulty.

quantity *n* amount, number, sum, total, aggregate, mass, lot, share, portion, quota, allotment, measure, dose, proportion, part, content, capacity, volume, weight, bulk, size, magnitude, expanse, extent, length, breadth.

quarrel *n* row, argument, slanging match (*infml*), wrangle, squabble, tiff, misunderstanding, disagreement, dispute, dissension, controversy, difference, conflict, clash, contention, strife, fight, scrap, brawl, feud, vendetta, schism.
E3 agreement, harmony.
➤ *v* row, argue, bicker, squabble, wrangle, be at loggerheads, fall out, disagree, dispute, dissent, differ, be at variance, clash, contend, fight, scrap, feud.
E3 agree.

quarrelsome *adj* argumentative, disputatious, contentious, belligerent, ill-tempered, irritable.
E3 peaceable, placid.

quarry *n* prey, victim, object, goal, target, game, kill, prize.

quarter *n* district, sector, zone, neighbourhood, locality, vicinity, area, region, province, territory, division, section, part, place, spot, point, direction, side.
➤ *v* station, post, billet, accommodate, put up, lodge, board, house, shelter.

quarters *n* accommodation, lodgings, billet, digs (*infml*), residence, dwelling, habitation, domicile, rooms, barracks, station, post.

quash *v* annul, revoke, rescind, overrule, cancel, nullify (*fml*), void, invalidate, reverse, set aside, squash, crush, quell, suppress, subdue, defeat, overthrow.
🔄 confirm, vindicate, reinstate.

quaver *v* shake, tremble, quake, shudder, quiver, vibrate, pulsate, oscillate, flutter, flicker, trill, warble.

quay *n* wharf, pier, jetty, dock, harbour.

queasy *adj* sick, ill, unwell, queer, groggy, green, nauseated, sickened, bilious, squeamish, faint, dizzy, giddy.

queen *n* **1** MONARCH, sovereign, ruler, majesty, princess, empress, consort. **2** BEAUTY, belle.

queer *adj* **1** ODD, mysterious, strange, unusual, uncommon, weird, unnatural, bizarre, eccentric, peculiar, funny, puzzling, curious, remarkable. **2** *I feel queer*: unwell, ill, sick, queasy, lightheaded, faint, giddy, dizzy. **3** SUSPECT, suspicious, shifty, dubious, shady (*infml*). **4** (*sl*) HOMOSEXUAL, gay, lesbian.
🔄 **1** ordinary, usual, common. **2** well.

quell *v* subdue, quash, crush, squash, suppress, put down, overcome, conquer, defeat, overpower, moderate, mitigate, allay, alleviate, soothe, calm, pacify, hush, quiet, silence, stifle, extinguish.

quench *v* **1** *quench one's thirst*: slake, satisfy, sate, cool. **2** EXTINGUISH, douse, put out, snuff out.

querulous *adj* peevish, fretful, fractious, cantankerous, cross, irritable, complaining, grumbling, discontented, dissatisfied, critical, carping, captious, fault-finding, fussy.
🔄 placid, uncomplaining, contented.

query *v* ask, inquire, question, challenge, dispute, quarrel with, doubt, suspect, distrust, mistrust, disbelieve.
🔄 accept.
➤ *n* question, inquiry, problem, uncertainty, doubt, suspicion, scepticism, reservation, hesitation.

quest *n* search, hunt, pursuit, investigation, inquiry, mission, crusade, enterprise, undertaking, venture, journey, voyage, expedition, exploration, adventure.

question *v* interrogate, quiz, grill, pump, interview, examine, cross-examine, debrief, ask, inquire, investigate, probe, query, challenge, dispute, doubt, disbelieve.
➤ *n* **1** QUERY, inquiry, poser, problem, difficulty. **2** ISSUE, matter, subject, topic, point, proposal, proposition, motion, debate, dispute, controversy.

questionable *adj* debatable, disputable, unsettled, undetermined, unproven, uncertain, arguable, controversial, vexed, doubtful, dubious, suspicious, suspect, shady (*infml*), fishy (*infml*), iffy (*sl*).
🔄 unquestionable, indisputable, certain.

questionnaire *n* quiz, test, survey, opinion poll.

queue *n* line, tailback, file, crocodile, procession, train, string, succession, series, sequence, order.

quibble *v* carp, cavil, split hairs (*infml*), nit-pick (*infml*), equivocate, prevaricate.
➤ *n* complaint, objection, criticism, query.

quick *adj* **1** FAST, swift, rapid, speedy, express, hurried, hasty, cursory, fleeting, brief, prompt, ready, immediate, instant, instantaneous, sudden, brisk, nimble, sprightly, agile. **2** CLEVER,

intelligent, quick-witted, smart, sharp, keen, shrewd, astute, discerning, perceptive, responsive, receptive.
E3 1 slow, sluggish, lethargic. **2** unintelligent, dull.

quicken v **1** ACCELERATE, speed, hurry, hasten, precipitate, expedite, dispatch, advance. **2** ANIMATE, enliven, invigorate, energize, galvanize, activate, rouse, arouse, stimulate, excite, inspire, revive, refresh, reinvigorate, reactivate.
E3 1 slow, retard. **2** dull.

quiet adj **1** SILENT, noiseless, inaudible, hushed, soft, low. **2** PEACEFUL, still, tranquil, serene, calm, composed, undisturbed, untroubled, placid. **3** SHY, reserved, reticent, uncommunicative, taciturn, unforthcoming, retiring, withdrawn, thoughtful, subdued, meek. **4** a quiet spot: isolated, unfrequented, lonely, secluded, private.
E3 1 noisy, loud. **2** excitable. **3** extrovert.
➤ n quietness, silence, hush, peace, lull, stillness, tranquillity, serenity, calm, rest, repose.
E3 noise, loudness, disturbance, bustle.

quieten v **1** SILENCE, hush, mute, soften, lower, diminish, reduce, stifle, muffle, deaden, dull. **2** SUBDUE, pacify, quell, quiet, still, smooth, calm, soothe, compose, sober.
E3 2 disturb, agitate.

quilt n bedcover, coverlet, bedspread, counterpane, eiderdown, duvet.

quip n joke, jest, jape, crack, gag (infml), witticism, riposte, retort, gibe.

quirk n freak, eccentricity, curiosity, oddity, peculiarity, idiosyncrasy,

mannerism, habit, trait, foible, whim, caprice, turn, twist.

quit v **1** LEAVE, depart, go, exit, decamp, desert, forsake, abandon, renounce, relinquish, surrender, give up, resign, retire, withdraw. **2** quit smoking: stop, cease, end, discontinue, desist, drop, give up, pack in (sl).

quite adv **1** MODERATELY, rather, somewhat, fairly, relatively, comparatively. **2** UTTERLY, absolutely, totally, completely, entirely, wholly, fully, perfectly, exactly, precisely.

quiver v shake, tremble, shudder, shiver, quake, quaver, vibrate, palpitate, flutter, flicker, oscillate, wobble.
➤ n shake, tremble, shudder, shiver, tremor, vibration, palpitation, flutter, flicker, oscillation, wobble.

quiz n questionnaire, test, examination, competition.
➤ v question, interrogate, grill, pump, examine, cross-examine.

quizzical adj questioning, inquiring, curious, amused, humorous, teasing, mocking, satirical, sardonic, sceptical.

quota n ration, allowance, allocation, assignment, share, portion, part, slice, cut (infml), percentage, proportion.

quotation n **1** CITATION, quote (infml), extract, excerpt, passage, piece, cutting, reference. **2** ESTIMATE, quote (infml), tender, figure, price, cost, charge, rate.

quote v cite, refer to, mention, name, reproduce, echo, repeat, recite, recall, recollect.

Rr

rabble *n* crowd, throng, horde, herd, mob, masses, populace, riff-raff (*infml*).

rabble-rouser *n* agitator, troublemaker, incendiary, demagogue, ringleader.

race[1] *n* sprint, steeplechase, marathon, scramble, regatta, competition, contest, contention, rivalry, chase, pursuit, quest.

Types of race and famous races include: cycle race, cyclo-cross, road race, time trial, Milk Race, Tour de France; greyhound race, Greyhound Derby; horse race, Cheltenham Gold Cup, the Classics (Derby, Oaks, One Thousand Guineas, Two Thousand Guineas), Grand National, Kentucky Derby, Melbourne Cup, Prix de l'Arc de Triomphe, steeplechase, trotting race, harness race; motorcycle race, motocross, scramble, speedway, Isle of Man Tourist Trophy (TT); motor-race, GrandPrix, Indianapolis 500, Le Mans, Monte Carlo rally, RAC Rally, stock car race; rowing, regatta, Boat Race; running, cross-country, dash (*US*), hurdles, marathon, London Marathon, relay, sprint, steeplechase, track event; ski race, downhill, slalom; swimming race; walking race, walkathon; yacht race, Admiral's Cup, America's Cup; egg-and-spoon race, pancake race, sack race, wheelbarrow race.

➤ *v* run, sprint, dash, tear, fly, gallop, speed, career, dart, zoom, rush, hurry, hasten.

race[2] *n* nation, people, tribe, clan, house, dynasty, family, kindred, ancestry, lineage, line, blood, stock, genus, species, breed.

racecourse *n* racetrack, course, track, circuit, lap, turf, speedway.

racial *adj* national, tribal, ethnic, folk, genealogical, ancestral, inherited, genetic.

racism *n* racialism, xenophobia, chauvinism, jingoism, discrimination, bigotry, prejudice, bias.

rack *n* shelf, stand, support, structure, frame, framework.

racket *n* 1 NOISE, din, uproar, row, fuss, outcry, clamour, commotion, disturbance, pandemonium, hurly-burly, hubbub. 2 SWINDLE, con (*infml*), scam (*infml*), fraud, fiddle, deception, trick, dodge, scheme, business, game.

racy *adj* 1 RIBALD, bawdy, risqué, naughty, indecent, indelicate, suggestive, saucy (*infml*). 2 LIVELY, animated, spirited, energetic, dynamic, buoyant, boisterous.

radiance *n* light, luminosity, incandescence, radiation, brightness, brilliance, shine, lustre, gleam, glow, glitter, resplendence, splendour, happiness, joy, pleasure, delight, rapture.

radiant *adj* 1 BRIGHT, luminous, shining, gleaming, glowing, beaming, glittering, sparkling, brilliant, resplendent, splendid, glorious. 2 HAPPY, joyful, delighted, ecstatic.
🔄 1 dull. 2 miserable.

radiate *v* shine, gleam, glow, beam, shed, pour, give off, emit, emanate, diffuse, issue, disseminate, scatter, spread (out), diverge, branch.

radical *adj* 1 BASIC, fundamental, primary, essential, natural, native, innate, intrinsic, deep-seated, profound.

2 *radical changes*: drastic, comprehensive, thorough, sweeping, far-reaching, thoroughgoing, complete, total, entire. **3** FANATICAL, militant, extreme, extremist, revolutionary. **⊟ 1** superficial. **3** moderate.
➤ *n* fanatic, militant, extremist, revolutionary, reformer, reformist, fundamentalist.

raffle *n* draw, lottery, sweepstake, sweep, tombola.

rage *n* **1** ANGER, wrath, fury, frenzy, tantrum, temper. **2** (*infml*) *all the rage*: craze, mania (*infml*), fad, in-thing (*infml*), thing (*infml*), fashion, vogue, style, passion, enthusiasm, obsession.
➤ *v* fume, seethe, rant, rave, storm, thunder, explode, rampage.

ragged *adj* **1** *ragged clothes*: frayed, torn, ripped, tattered, worn-out, threadbare, tatty, shabby, scruffy, unkempt, down-at-heel. **2** JAGGED, serrated, indented, notched, rough, uneven, irregular, fragmented, erratic, disorganized.

raid *n* attack, onset, onslaught, invasion, inroad, incursion, foray, sortie, strike, blitz, swoop, bust (*sl*), robbery, break-in, hold-up.
➤ *v* loot, pillage, plunder, ransack, rifle, maraud, attack, descend on, invade, storm.

raider *n* attacker, invader, looter, plunderer, ransacker, marauder, robber, thief, brigand, pirate.

railing *n* fence, paling, barrier, parapet, rail, balustrade.

railway *n* track, line, rails, railroad (*US*).

Types of railway include: branch line, broad gauge, cable railway, cutting, electric railway, elevated railway, express, feeder line, freight, funicular railway, garden railway, goods line, high-speed line, light railway, main line, marshalling yard, metro, model railway, monorail, mountain railway, narrow gauge, passenger line, rack-and-pinion railway, rack railway, rapid transit system, siding, standard gauge, subway (*US*), tramway, trunk line, tube, underground.

rain *n* rainfall, precipitation, raindrops, drizzle, shower, cloudburst, downpour, deluge, torrent, storm, thunderstorm, squall.
➤ *v* spit, drizzle, shower, pour, teem, pelt, bucket (*infml*), deluge.

rainy *adj* wet, damp, showery, drizzly.
⊟ dry.

raise *v* **1** LIFT, elevate, hoist, jack up, erect, build, construct. **2** INCREASE, augment, escalate, magnify, heighten, strengthen, intensify, amplify, boost, enhance. **3** *raise funds*: get, obtain, collect, gather, assemble, rally, muster, recruit. **4** BRING UP, rear, breed, propagate, grow, cultivate, develop. **5** *raise a subject*: bring up, broach, introduce, present, put forward, moot, suggest.
⊟ 1 lower. **2** decrease, reduce. **5** suppress.

rake *v* hoe, scratch, scrape, graze, comb, scour, search, hunt, ransack, gather, collect, amass, accumulate.

rally *v* **1** GATHER, collect, assemble, congregate, convene, come together, muster, summon, round up, unite, marshal, organize, mobilize, reassemble, regroup, reorganize. **2** RECOVER, recuperate, revive, improve, pick up.
➤ *n* **1** GATHERING, assembly, convention, convocation, conference, meeting, jamboree, reunion, march, demonstration. **2** RECOVERY, recuperation, revival, comeback, improvement, resurgence, renewal.

ram *v* **1** HIT, strike, butt, hammer, pound, drum, crash, smash, slam. **2** FORCE, drive, thrust, cram, stuff, pack, crowd, jam, wedge.

ramble *v* **1** WALK, hike, trek, tramp, traipse, stroll, amble, saunter, straggle, wander, roam, rove, meander, wind, zigzag. **2** CHATTER, babble, rabbit (on) (*infml*), witter (on) (*infml*), expatiate, digress, drift.

➤ *n* walk, hike, trek, tramp, stroll, saunter, tour, trip, excursion.

rambler *n* hiker, walker, stroller, rover, roamer, wanderer, wayfarer.

rambling *adj* 1 SPREADING, sprawling, straggling, trailing. 2 CIRCUITOUS, roundabout, digressive, wordy, long-winded, long-drawn-out, disconnected, incoherent.
🗲 2 direct.

ramification *n* branch, offshoot, development, complication, result, consequence, upshot, implication.

ramp *n* slope, incline, gradient, rise.

rampage *v* run wild, run amok, run riot, rush, tear, storm, rage, rant, rave.
➤ *n* rage, fury, frenzy, storm, uproar, violence, destruction, havoc.
◇ **on the rampage** wild, amok, berserk, violent, out of control.

rampant *adj* unrestrained, uncontrolled, unbridled, unchecked, wanton, excessive, fierce, violent, raging, wild, riotous, rank, profuse, rife, widespread, prevalent.

ramshackle *adj* dilapidated, tumbledown, broken-down, crumbling, ruined, derelict, jerry-built, unsafe, rickety, shaky, unsteady, tottering, decrepit.
🗲 solid, stable.

rancid *adj* sour, off, bad, musty, stale, rank, foul, fetid, putrid, rotten.
🗲 sweet.

random *adj* arbitrary, chance, fortuitous, casual, incidental, haphazard, irregular, unsystematic, unplanned, accidental, aimless, purposeless, indiscriminate, stray.
🗲 systematic, deliberate.

range *n* 1 SCOPE, compass, scale, gamut, spectrum, sweep, spread, extent, distance, reach, span, limits, bounds, parameters, area, field, domain, province, sphere, orbit. 2 *a range of fittings*: variety, diversity, assortment, selection, sort, kind, class, order, series, string, chain.

➤ *v* 1 EXTEND, stretch, reach, spread, vary, fluctuate. 2 ALIGN, arrange, order, rank, classify, catalogue.

rank[1] *n* 1 GRADE, degree, class, caste, status, standing, position, station, condition, estate, echelon, level, stratum, tier, classification, sort, type, group, division. 2 ROW, line, range, column, file, series, order, formation.

Ranks in the armed services include:
air force: aircraftsman, aircraftswoman, corporal, sergeant, warrant officer, pilot officer, flying officer, flight lieutenant, squadron-leader, wing commander, group-captain, air-commodore, air-vice-marshal, air-marshal, air-chief-marshal, marshal of the Royal Air Force;
army: private, lance-corporal, corporal, sergeant, warrant officer, lieutenant, captain, major, lieutenant-colonel, colonel, brigadier, major general, lieutenant-general, general, field marshal;
navy: able seaman, rating, petty officer, chief petty officer, sublieutenant, lieutenant, lieutenant-commander, commander, captain, commodore, rear admiral, vice-admiral, admiral, admiral of the fleet.
see also **army**; **soldier**.

➤ *v* grade, class, rate, place, position, range, sort, classify, categorize, order, arrange, organize, marshal.

rank[2] *adj* 1 UTTER, total, complete, absolute, unmitigated, thorough, sheer, downright, out-and-out, arrant, gross, flagrant, glaring, outrageous. 2 FOUL, repulsive, disgusting, revolting, stinking, fetid, putrid, rancid, stale.

rankle *v* annoy, irritate, rile, nettle, gall, irk, anger, rouse.

ransack *v* search, scour, comb, rummage, rifle, raid, sack, strip, despoil (*fml*), ravage, loot, plunder, pillage.

ransom *n* price, money, payment, pay-off, redemption, deliverance,

rescue, liberation, release.
➤ *v* buy off, redeem, deliver, rescue,
liberate, free, release.

rant *v* shout, cry, yell, roar, bellow,
declaim, bluster, rave.

rap *v* **1** KNOCK, hit, strike, tap, thump.
2 (*sl*) REPROVE, reprimand, criticize,
censure, carpet (*infml*).
➤ *n* **1** KNOCK, blow, tap, thump. **2** (*sl*)
REBUKE, reprimand, censure, blame,
punishment.

rape *n* violation, assault, abuse,
maltreatment.
➤ *v* violate, assault, abuse, maltreat.

rapid *adj* swift, speedy, quick, fast,
express, lightning, prompt, brisk,
hurried, hasty, precipitate, headlong.
🖪 slow, leisurely, sluggish.

rapport *n* bond, link, affinity,
relationship, empathy, sympathy,
understanding, harmony.

rapt *adj* engrossed, absorbed,
preoccupied, intent, gripped,
spellbound, enthralled, captivated,
fascinated, entranced, charmed,
enchanted, delighted, ravished,
enraptured, transported.

rapture *n* delight, happiness, joy, bliss,
ecstasy, euphoria, exaltation.

rare *adj* **1** UNCOMMON, unusual, scarce,
sparse, sporadic, infrequent. **2**
EXQUISITE, superb, excellent, superlative,
incomparable, exceptional, remarkable,
precious.
🖪 **1** common, abundant, frequent.

rarefied *adj* exclusive, select, private,
esoteric, refined, high, noble, sublime.

rarely *adv* seldom, hardly ever,
infrequently, little.
🖪 often, frequently.

raring *adj* eager, keen, enthusiastic,
ready, willing, impatient, longing,
itching, desperate.

rarity *n* **1** CURIOSITY, curio, gem, pearl,
treasure, find. **2** UNCOMMONNESS,
unusualness, strangeness, scarcity,
shortage, sparseness, infrequency.
🖪 **2** commonness, frequency.

rascal *n* rogue, scoundrel, scamp,
scallywag, imp, devil, villain, good-for-
nothing, wastrel.

rash[1] *adj* reckless, ill-considered,
unwise, foolhardy, ill-advised, madcap,
hare-brained, hot-headed, headstrong,
impulsive, impetuous, hasty, headlong,
unguarded, unwary, indiscreet,
imprudent, careless, heedless,
unthinking.
🖪 cautious, wary, careful.

rash[2] *n* eruption, outbreak, epidemic,
plague.

rasp *n* grating, scrape, grinding,
scratch, harshness, hoarseness, croak.
➤ *v* grate, scrape, grind, file, sand, scour,
abrade, rub.

rate *n* **1** SPEED, velocity, tempo, time,
ratio, proportion, relation, degree,
grade, rank, rating, standard, basis,
measure, scale. **2** CHARGE, fee, hire, toll,
tariff, price, cost, value, worth, tax, duty,
amount, figure, percentage.
➤ *v* **1** JUDGE, regard, consider, deem,
count, reckon, figure, estimate,
evaluate, assess, weigh, measure,
grade, rank, class, classify. **2** ADMIRE,
respect, esteem, value, prize. **3**
DESERVE, merit.

rather *adv* **1** MODERATELY, relatively,
slightly, a bit, somewhat, fairly, quite,
pretty, noticeably, significantly, very.
2 PREFERABLY, sooner, instead.

ratify *v* approve, uphold, endorse, sign,
legalize, sanction, authorize, establish,
affirm, confirm, certify, validate,
authenticate.
🖪 repudiate, reject.

rating *n* class, rank, degree, status,
standing, position, placing, order,
grade, mark, evaluation, assessment,
classification, category.

ratio *n* percentage, fraction,
proportion, relation, relationship,
correspondence, correlation.

ration *n* quota, allowance, allocation,
allotment, share, portion, helping, part,
measure, amount.
➤ *v* apportion, allot, allocate, share,

deal out, distribute, dole out, mete out, dispense, supply, issue, control, restrict, limit, conserve, save.

rational *adj* logical, reasonable, sound, well-founded, realistic, practical, sensible, clear-headed, judicious, wise, sane, normal, balanced, lucid, reasoning, thinking, intelligent, enlightened.

⊟ irrational, illogical, insane, crazy.

rationale *n* logic, reasoning, philosophy, principle, basis, grounds, explanation, reason, motive, motivation, theory.

rationalize *v* 1 JUSTIFY, excuse, vindicate, explain, account for. 2 REORGANIZE, streamline.

rations *n* food, provisions, supplies, stores.

rattle *v* clatter, jingle, jangle, clank, shake, vibrate, jolt, jar, bounce, bump.
◊ **rattle off** reel off, list, run through, recite, repeat.

raucous *adj* harsh, rough, hoarse, husky, rasping, grating, jarring, strident, noisy, loud.

ravage *v* destroy, devastate, lay waste, demolish, raze, wreck, ruin, spoil, damage, loot, pillage, plunder, sack, despoil (*fml*).
➤ *n* destruction, devastation, havoc, damage, ruin, desolation, wreckage, pillage, plunder.

rave *v* rage, storm, thunder, roar, rant, ramble, babble, splutter.
➤ *adj* (*infml*) enthusiastic, rapturous, favourable, excellent, wonderful.

ravenous *adj* hungry, starving, starved, famished, greedy, voracious, insatiable.

ravine *n* canyon, gorge, gully, pass.

raving *adj* mad, insane, crazy, deranged, hysterical, delirious, wild, frenzied, furious, berserk.

ravish *v* enrapture, delight, overjoy, enchant, charm, captivate, entrance, fascinate, spellbind.

ravishing *adj* delightful, enchanting, charming, lovely, beautiful, gorgeous, stunning, radiant, dazzling, alluring, seductive.

raw *adj* 1 *raw vegetables*: uncooked, fresh. 2 UNPROCESSED, unrefined, untreated, crude, natural. 3 PLAIN, bare, naked, basic, harsh, brutal, realistic. 4 SCRATCHED, grazed, scraped, open, bloody, sore, tender, sensitive. 5 COLD, chilly, bitter, biting, piercing, freezing, bleak. 6 *a raw recruit*: new, green, immature, callow, inexperienced, untrained, unskilled.
⊟ 1 cooked, done. 2 processed, refined. 5 warm. 6 experienced, skilled.

ray *n* beam, shaft, flash, gleam, flicker, glimmer, glint, spark, trace, hint, indication.

raze *v* demolish, pull down, tear down, bulldoze, flatten, level, destroy.

razor

Types of razor include: battery shaver, cut-throat, disposable razor, double-edged razor, electric razor, razor blade, rechargeable razor, safety razor, shaver, wet razor, wet-and-dry shaver.

re *prep* about, concerning, regarding, with regard to, with reference to.

reach *v* arrive at, get to, attain, achieve, make, amount to, hit, strike, touch, contact, stretch, extend, grasp.
➤ *n* range, scope, compass, distance, spread, extent, stretch, grasp, jurisdiction, command, power, influence.

react *v* respond, retaliate, reciprocate, reply, answer, acknowledge, act, behave.

reaction *n* response, effect, reply, answer, acknowledgement, feedback, counteraction, reflex, recoil, reciprocation, retaliation.

reactionary *adj* conservative, right-wing, rightist, diehard, counter-revolutionary.
⊟ progressive, revolutionary.
➤ *n* conservative, right-winger, rightist,

diehard, counter-revolutionary.
Fa progressive, revolutionary.

read v 1 STUDY, peruse, pore over, scan,
skim, decipher, decode, interpret,
construe, understand, comprehend.
2 RECITE, declaim, deliver, speak, utter. 3
the gauge read zero: indicate, show,
display, register, record.

readable adj 1 LEGIBLE, decipherable,
intelligible, clear, understandable,
comprehensible. 2 INTERESTING,
enjoyable, entertaining, gripping,
unputdownable (*infml*).
Fa 1 illegible. 2 unreadable.

readily adv willingly, unhesitatingly,
gladly, happily, eagerly, promptly,
quickly, freely, smoothly, easily,
effortlessly.
Fa unwillingly, reluctantly.

reading n 1 STUDY, perusal, scrutiny,
examination, inspection, interpretation,
understanding, take (*infml*), rendering,
version, rendition, recital. 2 *a reading
from the Bible*: passage, lesson.

ready adj 1 *ready to go*: prepared,
waiting, set, fit, arranged, organized,
completed, finished. 2 WILLING, inclined,
disposed, happy, game (*infml*), eager,
keen. 3 AVAILABLE, to hand, present,
near, accessible, convenient, handy.
4 PROMPT, immediate, quick, sharp,
astute, perceptive, alert.
Fa 1 unprepared, disorganized.
2 unwilling, reluctant, disinclined.
3 unavailable, inaccessible. 4 slow.

real adj actual, existing, physical,
material, substantial, tangible,
genuine, authentic, bona fide,
official, rightful, legitimate, valid,
true, factual, certain, sure,
positive, veritable, honest, sincere,
heartfelt, unfeigned, unaffected.
Fa unreal, imaginary, false.

realistic adj 1 PRACTICAL, down-to-
earth, commonsense, sensible, level-
headed, clear-sighted, businesslike,
hard-headed, pragmatic, matter-of-
fact, rational, logical, objective,
detached, unsentimental, unromantic.

2 LIFELIKE, faithful, truthful, true,
genuine, authentic, natural, real, real-
life, graphic, representational.
Fa 1 unrealistic, impractical, irrational,
idealistic.

reality n truth, fact, certainty, realism,
actuality, existence, materiality,
tangibility, genuineness, authenticity,
validity.

realize v 1 UNDERSTAND, comprehend,
grasp, catch on, cotton on (*infml*), get
(*infml*), recognize, accept, appreciate. 2
ACHIEVE, accomplish, fulfil, complete,
implement, perform. 3 SELL FOR, fetch,
make, earn, produce, net, clear.

really adv actually, truly, honestly,
sincerely, genuinely, positively, certainly,
absolutely, categorically, definitely, very,
indeed.

realm n kingdom, monarchy,
principality, empire, country, state, land,
territory, area, region, province, domain,
sphere, orbit, field, department.

rear n back, stern, end, tail, rump,
buttocks, posterior, behind, bottom,
backside (*infml*).
Fa front.
➤ adj back, hind, hindmost, rearmost,
last.
Fa front.
➤ v 1 *rear a child*: bring up, raise, breed,
grow, cultivate, foster, nurse, nurture,
train, educate. 2 RISE, tower, soar, raise,
lift, elevate.

reason n 1 CAUSE, motive, incentive,
rationale, explanation, excuse,
justification, defence, warrant, ground,
basis, case, argument, aim, intention,
purpose, object, end, goal. 2 SENSE,
logic, reasoning, rationality, sanity,
mind, wit, brain, intellect, wisdom,
understanding, judgement, common
sense, gumption, nous (*sl*).
➤ v work out, solve, resolve, conclude,
deduce, infer, think.
◇ **reason with** urge, persuade, move,
remonstrate with, argue with, debate
with, discuss with.

reasonable adj 1 SENSIBLE, wise,

well-advised, sane, intelligent, rational, logical, practical, sound, reasoned, well-thought-out, realistic, plausible, credible, possible, viable. **2** *a reasonable price*: acceptable, satisfactory, tolerable, moderate, average, fair, just, modest, inexpensive. ☒ **1** irrational. **2** exorbitant.

reasoning *n* logic, thinking, thought, analysis, interpretation, deduction, supposition, hypothesis, argument, case, proof.

reassure *v* comfort, cheer, encourage, hearten, inspirit (*fml*), brace, bolster. ☒ alarm.

rebate *n* refund, repayment, reduction, discount, deduction, allowance.

rebel *v* revolt, mutiny, rise up, run riot, dissent, disobey, defy, resist, recoil, shrink. ☒ conform.
➤ *n* revolutionary, insurrectionary, mutineer, dissenter, nonconformist, schismatic, heretic.

rebellion *n* revolt, revolution, rising, uprising, insurrection, insurgence, mutiny, coup, resistance, opposition, defiance, disobedience, dissent, insubordination, heresy.

rebellious *adj* revolutionary, insurrectionary, insurgent, seditious, mutinous, resistant, defiant, disobedient, insubordinate, unruly, disorderly, ungovernable, unmanageable, intractable, obstinate. ☒ obedient, submissive.

rebirth *n* reincarnation, resurrection, renaissance, regeneration, renewal, restoration, revival, revitalization, rejuvenation.

rebound *v* recoil, backfire, return, bounce, ricochet, boomerang.

rebuff *v* spurn, reject, refuse, decline, turn down, repulse, discourage, snub, slight, cut, cold-shoulder.
➤ *n* rejection, refusal, repulse, check, discouragement, snub, brush-off (*infml*), slight, put-down, cold shoulder.

rebuke *v* reprove, castigate, chide, scold, tell off (*infml*), admonish, tick off (*infml*), reprimand, upbraid, rate, censure, blame, reproach. ☒ praise, compliment.
➤ *n* reproach, reproof, reprimand, lecture, dressing-down (*infml*), telling-off (*infml*), ticking-off (*infml*), admonition, censure, blame. ☒ praise, commendation.

recall *v* remember, recollect, cast one's mind back, evoke, bring back.

recapitulate *v* recap (*infml*), summarize, review, repeat, reiterate, restate, recount.

recede *v* go back, return, retire, withdraw, retreat, ebb, wane, sink, decline, diminish, dwindle, decrease, lessen, shrink, slacken, subside, abate. ☒ advance.

receipt *n* **1** VOUCHER, ticket, slip, counterfoil, stub, acknowledgement. **2** RECEIVING, reception, acceptance, delivery.

receipts *n* takings, income, proceeds, profits, gains, return.

receive *v* **1** TAKE, accept, get, obtain, derive, acquire, pick up, collect, inherit. **2** *receive guests*: admit, let in, greet, welcome, entertain, accommodate. **3** EXPERIENCE, undergo, suffer, sustain, meet with, encounter. **4** REACT TO, respond to, hear, perceive, apprehend. ☒ **1** give, donate.

recent *adj* late, latest, current, present-day, contemporary, modern, up to date, new, novel, fresh, young. ☒ old, out of date.

recently *adv* lately, newly, freshly.

receptacle *n* container, vessel, holder.

reception *n* **1** ACCEPTANCE, admission, greeting, recognition, welcome, treatment, response, reaction, acknowledgement, receipt. **2** PARTY, function, do (*infml*), entertainment.

receptive *adj* open-minded, amenable, accommodating, suggestible, susceptible, sensitive, responsive, open, accessible, approachable, friendly, hospitable, welcoming, sympathetic, favourable, interested.

Fa narrow-minded, resistant, unresponsive.

recess n 1 BREAK, interval, intermission, rest, respite, holiday, vacation. 2 ALCOVE, niche, nook, corner, bay, cavity, hollow, depression, indentation.

recession n slump, depression, downturn, decline.

Fa boom, upturn.

recipe n formula, prescription, ingredients, instructions, directions, method, system, procedure, technique.

reciprocal adj mutual, common, shared, joint, give-and-take, alternating, complementary, corresponding, equivalent, interchangeable.

reciprocate v respond, reply, requite, return, exchange, swap, trade, match, equal, correspond, interchange, alternate.

recital n performance, concert, recitation, reading, narration, account, rendition, rendering, interpretation, repetition.

recitation n passage, piece, party piece, poem, monologue, narration, story, tale, recital, telling.

recite v repeat, tell, narrate, relate, recount, speak, deliver, articulate, declaim, perform, reel off, itemize, enumerate.

reckless adj heedless, thoughtless, mindless, careless, negligent, irresponsible, imprudent, ill-advised, unwise, indiscreet, rash, hasty, foolhardy, daredevil, wild.

Fa cautious, wary, careful, prudent.

reckon v 1 CALCULATE, compute, figure out, work out, add up, total, tally, count, number, enumerate. 2 DEEM, regard, consider, esteem, value, rate, judge, evaluate, assess, estimate, gauge. 3 THINK, believe, imagine, fancy, suppose,

surmise, assume, guess, conjecture.

◇ **reckon on** rely on, depend on, bank on, count on, trust in, hope for, expect, anticipate, foresee, plan for, bargain for, figure on, take into account, face.

reckoning n 1 by my reckoning: calculation, computation, estimate. 2 BILL, account, charge, due, score, settlement. 3 JUDGEMENT, retribution, doom.

reclaim v recover, regain, recapture, retrieve, salvage, rescue, redeem, restore, reinstate, regenerate.

recline v rest, repose, lean back, lie, lounge, loll, sprawl, stretch out.

recognition n 1 IDENTIFICATION, detection, discovery, recollection, recall, remembrance, awareness, perception, realization, understanding. 2 CONFESSION, admission, acceptance, acknowledgement, gratitude, appreciation, honour, respect, greeting, salute.

recognize v 1 IDENTIFY, know, remember, recollect, recall, place, see, notice, spot, perceive. 2 CONFESS, own, acknowledge, accept, admit, grant, concede, allow, appreciate, understand, realize.

recollect v recall, remember, cast one's mind back, reminisce.

recollection n recall, remembrance, memory, souvenir, reminiscence, impression.

recommend v advocate, urge, exhort, advise, counsel, suggest, propose, put forward, advance, praise, commend, plug (infml), endorse, approve, vouch for.

Fa disapprove.

recommendation n advice, counsel, suggestion, proposal, advocacy, endorsement, approval, sanction, blessing, praise, commendation, plug (infml), reference, testimonial.

Fa disapproval.

recompense n compensation, indemnification, damages, reparation, restitution, amends, requital, repayment, reward, payment, remuneration, pay, wages.

reconcile *v* reunite, conciliate, pacify, appease, placate, propitiate, accord, harmonize, accommodate, adjust, resolve, settle, square.
◨ estrange, alienate.

reconciliation *n* reunion, conciliation, pacification, appeasement, propitiation, rapprochement, détente, settlement, agreement, peace, harmony, accommodation, adjustment, compromise.
◨ estrangement, separation.

reconnoitre *v* explore, survey, scan, spy out, recce (*sl*), inspect, examine, scrutinize, investigate, patrol.

reconstruct *v* remake, rebuild, reassemble, re-establish, refashion, remodel, reform, reorganize, recreate, restore, renovate, regenerate.

record *n* **1** REGISTER, log, report, account, minutes, memorandum, note, entry, document, file, dossier, diary, journal, memoir, history, annals, archives, documentation, evidence, testimony, trace. **2** RECORDING, disc, single, CD, compact disc, DVD, album, release, LP. **3** *break the record*: fastest time, best performance, personal best, world record. **4** BACKGROUND, track record, curriculum vitae, career.
➤ *v* **1** NOTE, enter, inscribe, write down, transcribe, register, log, put down, enrol, report, minute, chronicle, document, keep, preserve. **2** TAPE-RECORD, tape, videotape, video, cut, burn.

recording *n* release, performance, record, disc, CD, DVD, cassette, tape, DAT, video.

Types of recording include: album, audiotape, cassette, CD, compact disc, DAT (digital audio tape), digital recording, disc, DVD (digital versatile or video disk), EP (extended play), 45, gramophone record, long-playing record, LP, magnetic tape, MiniDisc,

mono recording, MP3, record, 78, single, stereo recording, tape, tape-recording, tele-recording, video, videocassette, video disc, videotape, vinyl (*infml*).

recount *v* tell, relate, impart, communicate, report, narrate, describe, depict, portray, detail, repeat, rehearse, recite.

recoup *v* recover, retrieve, regain, get back, make good, repay, refund, reimburse, compensate.

recover *v* **1** *recover from illness*: get better, improve, pick up, rally, mend, heal, pull through, get over, recuperate, revive, convalesce, come round. **2** REGAIN, get back, recoup, retrieve, salvage, save, retake, recapture, repossess, reclaim, restore.
◨ **1** worsen. **2** lose, forfeit.

recovery *n* **1** RECUPERATION, convalescence, rehabilitation, mending, healing, improvement, upturn, rally, revival, restoration. **2** RETRIEVAL, salvage, reclamation, repossession, recapture.
◨ **1** worsening. **2** loss, forfeit.

recreation *n* fun, enjoyment, pleasure, amusement, diversion, distraction, entertainment, hobby, pastime, game, sport, play, leisure, relaxation, refreshment.

recrimination *n* countercharge, accusation, counter-attack, retaliation, reprisal, retort, quarrel, bickering.

recruit *v* enlist, draft, conscript, enrol, sign up, engage, take on, mobilize, raise, gather, obtain, procure.
➤ *n* beginner, novice, initiate, learner, trainee, apprentice, conscript, convert.

rectify *v* correct, put right, right, remedy, cure, repair, fix, mend, improve, amend, adjust, reform.

recuperate *v* recover, get better, improve, pick up, rally, revive, mend, convalesce.
◨ worsen.

recur *v* repeat, persist, return, reappear.

recurrent *adj* recurring, chronic, persistent, repeated, repetitive, regular, periodic, frequent, intermittent.

recycle *v* reuse, reprocess, reclaim, recover, salvage, save.

red *adj* 1 SCARLET, vermilion, cherry, ruby, crimson, maroon, pink, reddish, bloodshot, inflamed. 2 RUDDY, florid, glowing, rosy, apple-cheeked, flushed, blushing, embarrassed, shamefaced. 3 *red hair*: ginger, carroty, auburn, chestnut, Titian.

redden *v* blush, flush, colour, go red, crimson.

redeem *v* 1 BUY BACK, repurchase, cash (in), exchange, change, trade, ransom, reclaim, regain, repossess, recoup, recover, recuperate, retrieve, salvage. 2 COMPENSATE FOR, make up for, offset, outweigh, atone for, expiate, absolve, acquit, discharge, release, liberate, emancipate, free, deliver, rescue, save.

reduce *v* 1 LESSEN, decrease, contract, shrink, slim, shorten, curtail, trim, cut, slash, discount, rebate, lower, moderate, weaken, diminish, impair. 2 DRIVE, force, degrade, downgrade, demote, humble, humiliate, impoverish, subdue, overpower, master, vanquish.
▪ 1 increase, raise, boost.

reduction *n* decrease, drop, fall, decline, lessening, moderation, weakening, diminution, contraction, compression, shrinkage, narrowing, shortening, curtailment, restriction, limitation, cutback, cut, discount, rebate, devaluation, depreciation, deduction, subtraction, loss.
▪ increase, rise, enlargement.

redundant *adj* 1 UNEMPLOYED, out of work, laid off, paid off, dismissed. 2 SUPERFLUOUS, surplus, excess, extra, supernumerary, unneeded, unnecessary, unwanted. 3 WORDY, verbose, repetitious, reiterative, tautological.
▪ 2 necessary, essential. 3 concise, pithy.

reel *v* stagger, totter, wobble, rock, sway, waver, falter, stumble, lurch, pitch, roll, revolve, gyrate, spin, wheel, twirl, whirl, swirl.

refer *v* 1 SEND, direct, point, guide, pass on, transfer, commit, deliver. 2 *refer to a catalogue*: consult, look up, turn to, resort to. 3 ALLUDE, mention, touch on, speak of, recommend, bring up, cite, quote, name. 4 APPLY, concern, relate, belong, pertain.

referee *n* umpire, judge, adjudicator, arbitrator, mediator, ref (*infml*).
➤ *v* umpire, judge, adjudicate, arbitrate.

reference *n* 1 ALLUSION, remark, mention, citation, quotation, illustration, instance, note. 2 TESTIMONIAL, recommendation, endorsement, character. 3 RELATION, regard, respect, connection, bearing.

refine *v* process, treat, purify, clarify, filter, distil, polish, hone, improve, perfect, elevate, exalt.

refined *adj* civilized, cultured, cultivated, polished, sophisticated, urbane, genteel, gentlemanly, ladylike, well-bred, well-mannered, polite, civil, elegant, fine, delicate, subtle, precise, exact, sensitive, discriminating.
▪ coarse, vulgar, rude.

refinement *n* 1 MODIFICATION, alteration, amendment, improvement. 2 CULTIVATION, sophistication, urbanity, gentility, breeding, style, elegance, taste, discrimination, subtlety, finesse.
▪ 1 deterioration. 2 coarseness, vulgarity.

reflect *v* 1 MIRROR, echo, imitate, reproduce, portray, depict, show, reveal, display, exhibit, manifest, demonstrate, indicate, express, communicate. 2 THINK, ponder, consider, mull (over), deliberate, contemplate, meditate, muse.

reflection *n* 1 IMAGE, likeness, echo, impression, indication, sign, manifestation, observation, view, opinion. 2 THINKING, thought, study, consideration, deliberation, contemplation, meditation, musing.

reform v change, amend, improve, ameliorate, better, rectify, correct, mend, repair, rehabilitate, rebuild, reconstruct, remodel, revamp, renovate, restore, regenerate, reconstitute, reorganize, shake up (*infml*), revolutionize, purge.
➤ n change, amendment, revision, improvement, rectification, correction, rehabilitation, renovation, reorganization, shake-up (*infml*), purge.

refrain v stop, cease, quit, leave off, renounce, desist, abstain, forbear, avoid.

refresh v 1 COOL, freshen, enliven, invigorate, fortify, revive, restore, renew, rejuvenate, revitalize, reinvigorate. 2 *refresh one's memory*: jog, stimulate, prompt, prod.
🔁 1 tire, exhaust.

refreshing adj cool, thirst-quenching, bracing, invigorating, energizing, stimulating, inspiring, fresh, new, novel, original.

refreshment n sustenance, food, drink, snack, revival, restoration, renewal, reanimation, reinvigoration, revitalization.

refuge n sanctuary, asylum, shelter, protection, security, retreat, hideout, hideaway, resort, harbour, haven.

refugee n exile, émigré, displaced person, fugitive, runaway, escapee.

refund v repay, reimburse, rebate, return, give back, restore.
➤ n repayment, reimbursement, rebate, return.

refusal n rejection, no, rebuff, repudiation, denial, negation.
🔁 acceptance.

refuse[1] v reject, turn down, knock back (*infml*), decline, spurn, repudiate, rebuff, repel, deny, withhold.
🔁 accept, allow, permit.

refuse[2] n rubbish, waste, trash, garbage, junk, litter.

refute v disprove, rebut, confute, give the lie to, discredit, counter, negate.

regain v recover, get back, recoup, reclaim, repossess, retake, recapture, retrieve, return to.

regal adj majestic, kingly, queenly, princely, imperial, royal, sovereign, stately, magnificent, noble, lordly.

regard v consider, deem, judge, rate, value, think, believe, suppose, imagine, look upon, view, observe, watch.
➤ n care, concern, consideration, attention, notice, heed, respect, deference, honour, esteem, admiration, affection, love, sympathy.
🔁 disregard, contempt.

regarding prep with regard to, as regards, concerning, with reference to, re, about, as to.

regardless adj disregarding, heedless, unmindful, neglectful, inattentive, unconcerned, indifferent.
🔁 heedful, mindful, attentive.
➤ adv anyway, anyhow, nevertheless, nonetheless, despite everything, come what may.

regime n government, rule, administration, management, leadership, command, control, establishment, system.

regimented adj strict, disciplined, controlled, regulated, standardized, ordered, methodical, systematic, organized.
🔁 free, lax, disorganized.

region n land, terrain, territory, country, province, area, district, zone, sector, neighbourhood, range, scope, expanse, domain, realm, sphere, field, division, section, part, place.

> *Types of geographical region and community include*: antarctic, arctic, area, bailiwick, banana republic, basin, belt, Black Country, borough, built-up area, burgh, capital city, catchment area, city, coast, colony, commune, continent, country, countryside, county, county town, desert, development area, diocese, district, dockland, domain, dominion, duchy, East End, emirate, empire,

estate, The Fens, forest, free state, ghetto, ghost town, grassland, green belt, hamlet, health resort, heartland, heath, hemisphere, home town, hundred, industrial park, inner city, interior, jungle, kibbutz, kingdom, lowlands, manor, market town, marshland, metropolis, The Midlands, mission, municipality, nation, new town, no-man's land, old country, orient, outback, outpost, outskirts, pampas, parish, plain, port, postal district, prairie, principality, protectorate, province, quarter, realm, red light district, region, republic, reservation, resort, riding, riviera, rural district, satellite town, savannah, scrubland, seaside, settlement, shanty town, shire, spa, state, steppe, subcontinent, suburb, territory, Third World, time zone, town, township, tract, tropics, tundra, urban district, veld, village, wasteland, West Country, West End, wilderness, woodland, zone. *see also* **park**.

register *n* roll, roster, list, index, catalogue, directory, log, record, chronicle, annals, archives, file, ledger, schedule, diary, almanac.

➤ *v* **1** RECORD, note, log, enter, inscribe, mark, list, catalogue, chronicle, enrol, enlist, sign on, check in. **2** SHOW, reveal, betray, display, exhibit, manifest, express, say, read, indicate, signal.

regret *v* rue, repent, lament, mourn, grieve, deplore.

➤ *n* remorse, contrition, compunction, self-reproach, shame, sorrow, grief, disappointment, bitterness.

regretful *adj* remorseful, rueful, repentant, contrite, penitent, conscience-stricken, ashamed, sorry, apologetic, sad, sorrowful, disappointed.
◪ impenitent, unashamed.

regrettable *adj* unfortunate, unlucky, unhappy, sad, disappointing, upsetting, distressing, lamentable, deplorable, shameful, wrong, ill-advised.
◪ fortunate, happy.

regular *adj* **1** ROUTINE, habitual, typical, usual, customary, time-honoured, conventional, orthodox, correct, official, standard, normal, ordinary, common, commonplace, everyday. **2** PERIODIC, rhythmic, steady, constant, fixed, set, unvarying, uniform, even, level, smooth, balanced, symmetrical, orderly, systematic, methodical.
◪ **1** unusual, unconventional. **2** irregular.

regulate *v* control, direct, guide, govern, rule, administer, manage, handle, conduct, run, organize, order, arrange, settle, square, monitor, set, adjust, tune, moderate, balance.

regulation *n* rule, statute, law, ordinance, edict, decree, order, commandment, precept, dictate, requirement, procedure.
➤ *adj* standard, official, statutory, prescribed, required, orthodox, accepted, customary, usual, normal.

rehearsal *n* practice, drill, exercise, dry run, run-through, preparation, reading, recital, narration, account, enumeration, list.

rehearse *v* practise, drill, train, go over, prepare, try out, repeat, recite, recount, relate.

reign *n* rule, sway, monarchy, empire, sovereignty, supremacy, power, command, dominion, control, influence.
➤ *v* rule, govern, command, prevail, predominate, dominate, influence.

reimburse *v* refund, repay, return, give back, restore, recompense, compensate, indemnify, remunerate.

reinforce *v* strengthen, fortify, toughen, harden, stiffen, steel, brace, support, buttress, shore, prop, stay, supplement, augment, increase, emphasize, stress, underline.
◪ weaken, undermine.

reinforcements *n* auxiliaries, reserves, back-up, support, help.

reinstate *v* restore, return, replace,

recall, reappoint, reinstall, re-establish.

reject v refuse, deny, decline, knock back (*infml*), turn down, blacklist, blackball, veto, disallow, condemn, despise, spurn, rebuff, jilt, exclude, repudiate, repel, renounce, eliminate, scrap, discard, jettison, cast off.
◼ accept, choose, select.
➤ n failure, second, discard, cast-off.

rejection n refusal, denial, veto, dismissal, rebuff, knockback (*infml*), brush-off, exclusion, repudiation, renunciation, elimination.
◼ acceptance, choice, selection.

rejoice v celebrate, revel, delight, glory, exult, triumph.

rejoicing n celebration, revelry, merrymaking, festivity, happiness, gladness, joy, delight, elation, jubilation, exultation, triumph.

relapse v worsen, deteriorate, degenerate, weaken, sink, fail, lapse, revert, regress, backslide.
➤ n worsening, deterioration, degeneration, setback, recurrence, weakening, lapse, reversion, regression, backsliding.

relate v 1 LINK, connect, join, couple, ally, associate, correlate. 2 REFER, apply, concern, pertain, appertain. 3 *relate an anecdote*: tell, recount, narrate, report, describe, recite. 4 IDENTIFY, sympathize, empathize, understand, feel for.

related adj kindred, akin, affiliated, allied, associated, connected, linked, interrelated, interconnected, accompanying, concomitant, joint, mutual.
◼ unrelated, unconnected.

relation n 1 LINK, connection, bond, tie, relationship, correlation, comparison, similarity, affiliation, interrelation, interconnection, interdependence, regard, reference. 2 RELATIVE, family, kin, kindred.

relations n 1 RELATIVES, family, kin, kindred. 2 RELATIONSHIP, terms, rapport, liaison, intercourse, affairs, dealings, interaction, communications, contact, associations, connections, ties.

relationship n bond, link, connection, tie, association, liaison, rapport, affinity, closeness, similarity, parallel, correlation, ratio, proportion.

relative adj comparative, proportional, proportionate, commensurate, corresponding, respective, appropriate, relevant, applicable, related, connected, interrelated, reciprocal, dependent.
➤ n relation, family, kin.

relax v slacken, loosen, lessen, reduce, diminish, weaken, lower, soften, moderate, abate (*fml*), remit, relieve, ease, rest, de-stress, unwind, veg out (*infml*), chill out (*infml*), calm, tranquillize, sedate.
◼ tighten, intensify.

relaxation n 1 REST, repose, refreshment, leisure, recreation, fun, amusement, entertainment, enjoyment, pleasure. 2 SLACKENING, lessening, reduction, moderation, abatement (*fml*), let-up (*infml*), détente, easing.
◼ 2 tension, intensification.

relaxed adj informal, casual, laid-back (*infml*), easy-going (*infml*), carefree, happy-go-lucky, cool, calm, composed, collected, unhurried, leisurely.
◼ tense, nervous, formal.

relay n 1 BROADCAST, transmission, programme, communication, message, dispatch. 2 *work in relays*: shift, turn.
➤ v broadcast, transmit, communicate, send, spread, carry, supply.

release v loose, unloose, unleash, unfasten, extricate, free, liberate, deliver, emancipate, acquit, absolve, exonerate, excuse, exempt, discharge, issue, publish, circulate, distribute, present, launch, unveil.
◼ imprison, detain, check.
➤ n freedom, liberty, liberation, deliverance, emancipation, acquittal, absolution, exoneration, exemption, discharge, issue, publication,

announcement, proclamation.
ⓔ imprisonment, detention.

relent *v* give in, give way, yield, capitulate, unbend, relax, slacken, soften, weaken.

relentless *adj* unrelenting, unremitting, incessant, persistent, unflagging, ruthless, remorseless, implacable, merciless, pitiless, unforgiving, cruel, harsh, fierce, grim, hard, punishing, uncompromising, inflexible, unyielding, inexorable.
ⓔ merciful, yielding.

relevant *adj* pertinent, material, significant, germane, related, applicable, apposite, apt, appropriate, suitable, fitting, proper, admissible.
ⓔ irrelevant, inapplicable, inappropriate, unsuitable.

reliable *adj* unfailing, certain, sure, dependable, responsible, trusty, trustworthy, honest, true, faithful, constant, staunch, solid, safe, sound, stable, predictable, regular.
ⓔ unreliable, doubtful, uncertain, untrustworthy.

reliance *n* dependence, trust, faith, belief, credit, confidence, assurance.

relic *n* memento, souvenir, keepsake, token, survival, remains, remnant, scrap, fragment, vestige, trace.

relief *n* reassurance, consolation, comfort, ease, alleviation, cure, remedy, release, deliverance, help, aid, assistance, support, sustenance, refreshment, diversion, relaxation, rest, respite, break, breather (*infml*), remission, let-up (*infml*), abatement (*fml*).

relieve *v* reassure, console, comfort, ease, soothe, alleviate, mitigate, cure, release, deliver, free, unburden, lighten, soften, slacken, relax, calm, help, aid, assist, support, sustain.
ⓔ aggravate, intensify.

religion

Religions include: Christianity, Church of England (C of E), Church of Scotland, Baptists, Catholicism, Methodism, Protestantism, Presbyterianism, Anglicanism, Congregationalism, Calvinism, evangelicalism, Free Church, Jehovah's Witnesses, Mormonism, Quakerism, Amish; Baha'ism, Buddhism, Confucianism, Hinduism, Islam, Jainism, Judaism, Sikhism, Taoism, Shintoism, Zen, Zoroastrianism, voodoo, druidism, paganism.

religious *adj* **1** SACRED, holy, divine, spiritual, devotional, scriptural, theological, doctrinal. **2** *a religious person*: devout, faithful, godly, pious, God-fearing, church-going, reverent, righteous.
ⓔ **1** secular. **2** irreligious, ungodly.

Religious festivals include:
Buddhist: Buddha Purnima;
Christian: Christmas, Easter, Good Friday, Pentecost;
Hindu: Diwali, Dusserah, Holi, Oram;
Islamic: Id-al-adha, Id-al-fitr;
Jewish: Hanukkah, Passover, Purim, Rosh Hashanah, Shavuot, Yom Kippur;
Pagan: Beltane, Imbolc;
ancient Roman: Bacchanalia, Saturnalia.

Religious officers include: abbess, abbot, archbishop, archdeacon, bishop, canon, cardinal, chancellor, chaplain, clergy, clergyman, clergywoman, curate, deacon, deaconess, dean, elder, father, friar, minister, monk, Monsignor, mother superior, nun, padre, parson, pastor, pope, prelate, priest, prior, proctor, rector, vicar; ayatollah, Dalai Lama, guru, imam, rabbi.

relinquish *v* let go, release, hand over, surrender, yield, cede, give up, resign, renounce, repudiate, waive, forgo, abandon, desert, forsake, drop, discard.
ⓔ keep, retain.

relish *v* like, enjoy, savour, delight in, appreciate, revel in.

➤ *n* **1** SEASONING, condiment, sauce, pickle, spice, piquancy, tang. **2** ENJOYMENT, pleasure, delight, gusto, zest.

reluctant *adj* unwilling, disinclined, indisposed, hesitant, slow, backward, loath, averse, unenthusiastic, grudging.
🖪 willing, ready, eager.

rely *v* depend, lean, count, bank, reckon, trust, swear by.

remain *v* stay, rest, stand, dwell, abide, last, endure, survive, prevail, persist, continue, linger, wait, hang about (*infml*).
🖪 go, leave, depart.

remainder *n* rest, balance, surplus, excess, carry-over, remnant, remains.

remaining *adj* left, unused, unspent, unfinished, residual, outstanding, surviving, persisting, lingering, lasting, abiding.

remains *n* rest, remainder, residue, dregs, leavings, leftovers, scraps, crumbs, fragments, remnants, oddments, traces, vestiges, relics, body, corpse, carcase, ashes, debris.

remark *v* comment, observe, note, mention, say, state, declare.
➤ *n* comment, observation, opinion, reflection, mention, utterance, statement, assertion, declaration.

remarkable *adj* striking, impressive, noteworthy, surprising, amazing, strange, odd, unusual, uncommon, extraordinary, phenomenal, exceptional, outstanding, notable, conspicuous, prominent, distinguished.
🖪 average, ordinary, commonplace, usual.

remedy *n* cure, antidote, corrective, countermeasure, restorative, medicine, treatment, therapy, relief, solution, answer, panacea, elixir.
➤ *v* correct, rectify, put right, redress, counteract, cure, heal, restore, treat, help, relieve, soothe, ease, mitigate, mend, repair, fix, solve.

remember *v* **1** RECALL, recollect, summon up, think back, reminisce, recognize, place. **2** MEMORIZE, learn, retain.
🖪 **1** forget.

remind *v* prompt, nudge, hint, jog one's memory, refresh one's memory, bring to mind, call to mind, call up.

reminder *n* prompt, nudge, hint, suggestion, memorandum, memo, aide-memoire, souvenir, memento.

reminiscence *n* memory, remembrance, memoir, anecdote, recollection, recall, retrospection, review, reflection.

reminiscent *adj* suggestive, evocative, nostalgic.

remit *v* send, transmit, dispatch, post, mail, forward, pay, settle.
➤ *n* brief, orders, instructions, guidelines, terms of reference, scope, authorization, responsibility.

remittance *n* sending, dispatch, payment, fee, allowance, consideration.

remnant *n* scrap, piece, bit, fragment, end, off cut, leftover, remainder, balance, residue, shred, trace, vestige.

remorse *n* regret, compunction, ruefulness, repentance, penitence, contrition, self-reproach, shame, guilt, bad conscience, sorrow, grief.

remote *adj* **1** DISTANT, far, faraway, far-off, outlying, out-of-the-way, inaccessible, godforsaken, isolated, secluded, lonely. **2** DETACHED, aloof, standoffish, uninvolved, reserved, withdrawn. **3** *a remote possibility*: slight, small, slim, slender, faint, negligible, unlikely, improbable.
🖪 **1** close, nearby, accessible. **2** friendly.

remove *v* detach, pull off, amputate, cut off, extract, pull out, withdraw, take away, take off, strip, shed, doff, expunge, efface, erase, delete, strike out, get rid of, abolish, purge, eliminate, dismiss, discharge, eject, throw out, oust, depose, displace, dislodge, shift, move, transport, transfer, relocate.

remuneration *n* pay, wages, salary,

emolument, stipend, fee, retainer, earnings, income, profit, reward, recompense, payment, remittance, repayment, reimbursement, compensation, indemnity.

render v **1** *they rendered it harmless*: make, cause to be, leave. **2** GIVE, provide, supply, tender, present, submit, hand over, deliver. **3** TRANSLATE, transcribe, interpret, explain, clarify, represent, perform, play, sing.

renew v **1** RENOVATE, modernize, refurbish, refit, recondition, mend, repair, overhaul, remodel, reform, transform, recreate, reconstitute, re-establish, regenerate, revive, resuscitate, refresh, rejuvenate, reinvigorate, revitalize, restore, replace, replenish, restock. **2** REPEAT, restate, reaffirm, extend, prolong, continue, recommence, restart, resume.

renounce v abandon, forsake, give up, resign, relinquish, surrender, discard, reject, spurn, disown, repudiate, disclaim, deny, recant, abjure.

renovate v restore, renew, repair, recondition, overhaul, modernize, refurbish, refit, redecorate, do up (*infml*), remodel, reform, revamp, improve.

renown n fame, celebrity, stardom, acclaim, glory, eminence, distinction, illustriousness, note, mark, esteem, reputation, honour.
🖪 obscurity, anonymity.

renowned adj famous, well-known, celebrated, acclaimed, famed, noted, eminent, distinguished, illustrious, notable.
🖪 unknown, obscure.

rent n rental, lease, hire, payment, fee.
➤ v let, sublet, lease, hire, charter.

repair v mend, fix, patch up, overhaul, service, rectify, redress, restore, renovate, renew.
➤ n mend, patch, darn, overhaul, service, maintenance, restoration, adjustment, improvement.

repartee n banter, badinage, jesting, wit, riposte, retort.

repay v refund, reimburse, compensate, recompense, reward, remunerate, pay, pay back, settle, square, get even with, retaliate, reciprocate, revenge, avenge.

repeal v revoke, rescind, abrogate, quash, annul, nullify, void, invalidate, cancel, countermand, reverse, abolish.
🖪 enact.

repeat v restate, reiterate, recapitulate, echo, quote, recite, relate, retell, reproduce, duplicate, renew, rebroadcast, reshow, replay, rerun, redo.
➤ n repetition, echo, reproduction, duplicate, rebroadcast, reshowing, replay, rerun.

repeatedly adv time after time, time and (time) again, again and again, over and over, frequently, often.

repel v **1** DRIVE BACK, repulse, check, hold off, ward off, parry, resist, oppose, fight, refuse, decline, reject, rebuff. **2** DISGUST, revolt, nauseate, sicken, offend, put off.
🖪 **1** attract. **2** delight.

repent v regret, rue, sorrow, lament, deplore, atone.

repentance n penitence, contrition, remorse, compunction, regret, sorrow, grief, guilt, shame.

repentant adj penitent, contrite, sorry, apologetic, remorseful, regretful, rueful, chastened, ashamed.
🖪 unrepentant.

repercussion n result, upshot, consequence, backlash, echo, reverberation, rebound, recoil.

repetition n restatement, reiteration, recapitulation, echo, return, reappearance, recurrence, duplication, tautology.

repetitive adj recurrent, monotonous, tedious, boring, dull, mechanical, unchanging, unvaried.

replace v **1** *replace the lid*: put back, return, restore, make good, reinstate, re-establish. **2** SUPERSEDE, succeed, follow, supplant, oust, deputize, substitute.

replacement n substitute, stand-in, understudy, fill-in, supply, proxy, representative, surrogate, successor.

replenish v refill, restock, reload, recharge, replace, restore, renew, supply, provide, furnish, stock, fill, top up.

replica n model, imitation, facsimile, reproduction, copy, duplicate, clone.

reply v answer, respond, retort, rejoin, react, acknowledge, return, echo, reciprocate, counter, retaliate.
➤ n answer, response, retort, rejoinder, riposte, repartee, reaction, comeback, acknowledgement, return, echo, retaliation.

report n article, piece, write-up, record, account, relation, narrative, description, story, tale, gossip, hearsay, rumour, talk, statement, communiqué, declaration, announcement, release, communication, information, news, word, message, note.
➤ v state, announce, declare, proclaim, air, broadcast, relay, publish, circulate, communicate, notify, tell, recount, relate, narrate, describe, detail, cover, document, record, note.

reporter n journalist, correspondent, columnist, newspaperman, newspaperwoman, hack, newscaster, commentator, announcer.

represent v stand for, symbolize, designate, denote, mean, express, evoke, depict, portray, describe, picture, draw, sketch, illustrate, exemplify, typify, epitomize, embody, personify, appear as, act as, enact, perform, show, exhibit, be, amount to, constitute.

representation n 1 LIKENESS, image, icon, picture, portrait, illustration, sketch, model, statue, bust, depiction, portrayal, description, account, explanation. 2 PERFORMANCE, production, staging, presentation, play, show, spectacle.

representative n delegate, deputy, proxy, stand-in, spokesperson,

spokesman, spokeswoman, ambassador, commissioner, agent, salesman, saleswoman, rep (*infml*), traveller.
➤ adj typical, illustrative, exemplary, archetypal, characteristic, usual, normal, symbolic.
🔁 unrepresentative, atypical.

repress v inhibit, check, control, curb, restrain, suppress, bottle up, hold back, stifle, smother, muffle, silence, quell, crush, quash, subdue, overpower, overcome, master, subjugate, oppress.

repression n inhibition, restraint, suppression, suffocation, gagging, censorship, authoritarianism, despotism, tyranny, oppression, domination, control, constraint, coercion.

repressive adj oppressive, authoritarian, despotic, tyrannical, dictatorial, autocratic, totalitarian, absolute, harsh, severe, tough, coercive.

reprieve v pardon, let off, spare, rescue, redeem, relieve, respite.
➤ n pardon, amnesty, suspension, abeyance, postponement, deferment, remission, respite, relief, let-up (*infml*), abatement (*fml*).

reprimand n rebuke, reproof, reproach, admonition, telling-off (*infml*), ticking-off (*infml*), lecture, talking-to (*infml*), dressing-down (*infml*), censure, blame.
➤ v rebuke, reprove, reproach, admonish, carpet (*infml*), scold, chide, tell off (*infml*), tick off (*infml*), lecture, criticize, slate (*infml*), censure, blame.

reprisal n retaliation, counter-attack, retribution, requital, payback, revenge, vengeance.

reproach v rebuke, reprove, reprimand, upbraid, scold, chide, reprehend, blame, censure, condemn, criticize, disparage, defame.
➤ n rebuke, reproof, reprimand, scolding, blame, censure, condemnation, criticism, disapproval,

scorn, contempt, shame, disgrace.

reproachful *adj* reproving, scolding, upbraiding, censorious, critical, fault-finding, disapproving, scornful.
🔁 complimentary.

reproduce *v* 1 COPY, transcribe, print, duplicate, mirror, echo, repeat, imitate, emulate, match, simulate, recreate, reconstruct. 2 BREED, spawn, procreate, generate, propagate, multiply.

reproduction *n* 1 COPY, print, picture, duplicate, facsimile, replica, clone, imitation. 2 BREEDING, procreation, generation, propagation, multiplication.
🔁 1 original.

reproductive *adj* procreative, generative, sexual, sex, genital.

reproof *n* rebuke, reproach, reprimand, admonition, upbraiding, dressing-down (*infml*), scolding, telling-off (*infml*), ticking-off (*infml*), censure, condemnation, criticism.
🔁 praise.

reprove *v* rebuke, reproach, upbraid, reprimand, scold, chide, tell off (*infml*), reprehend, admonish, censure, condemn, criticize.
🔁 praise.

reptile

> *Reptiles include*: adder, puff adder, grass snake, tree snake, asp, viper, rattlesnake, sidewinder, anaconda, boa constrictor, cobra, king cobra, mamba, python; lizard, frilled lizard, chameleon, gecko, iguana, skink, slow-worm; turtle, green turtle, hawksbill turtle, terrapin, tortoise, giant tortoise; alligator, crocodile. *see also* **dinosaur**.

repugnance *n* reluctance, distaste, dislike, aversion, detestation, hatred, loathing, abhorrence, horror, repulsion, revulsion, disgust.
🔁 liking, pleasure, delight.

repulsive *adj* repellent, repugnant, revolting, disgusting, nauseating,

sickening, offensive, distasteful, objectionable, obnoxious, foul, vile, loathsome, abominable, abhorrent, detestable, hateful, horrid, unpleasant, disagreeable, ugly, hideous, forbidding.
🔁 attractive, pleasant, delightful.

reputable *adj* respectable, reliable, dependable, trustworthy, upright, honourable, creditable, worthy, good, excellent, irreproachable.
🔁 disreputable, infamous.

reputation *n* honour, character, standing, stature, esteem, opinion, credit, repute, fame, renown, celebrity, distinction, name, good name, bad name, infamy, notoriety.

reputed *adj* alleged, supposed, said, rumoured, believed, thought, considered, regarded, estimated, reckoned, held, seeming, apparent, ostensible.
🔁 actual, true.

request *v* ask for, solicit, demand, require, seek, desire, beg, entreat, supplicate (*fml*), petition, appeal.
➤ *n* appeal, call, demand, requisition, desire, application, solicitation, suit, petition, entreaty, supplication (*fml*), prayer.

require *v* 1 NEED, want, wish, desire, lack, miss. 2 *you are required to attend*: oblige, force, compel, constrain, make, ask, request, instruct, direct, order, demand, necessitate, take, involve.

requirement *n* need, necessity, essential, must, requisite, prerequisite, demand, stipulation, condition, term, specification, proviso, qualification, provision.

requisite *adj* required, needed, necessary, essential, obligatory, compulsory, set, prescribed.

requisition *v* request, put in for, demand, commandeer, appropriate, take, confiscate, seize, occupy.

rescue *v* save, recover, salvage, deliver, free, liberate, release, redeem, ransom.
🔁 capture, imprison.
➤ *n* saving, recovery, salvage,

deliverance, liberation, release, redemption, salvation.
F3 capture.

research *n* investigation, inquiry, fact-finding, groundwork, examination, analysis, scrutiny, study, search, probe, exploration, experimentation.
➤ *v* investigate, examine, analyse, scrutinize, study, search, probe, explore, experiment.

resemblance *n* likeness, similarity, sameness, parity, conformity, closeness, affinity, parallel, analogy, comparison, correspondence, image, facsimile.
F3 dissimilarity.

resemble *v* be like, look like, take after, favour, mirror, echo, duplicate, parallel, approach.
F3 differ from.

resent *v* grudge, begrudge, envy, take offence at, take umbrage at, take amiss, object to, grumble at, take exception to, dislike.
F3 accept, like.

resentful *adj* grudging, envious, jealous, bitter, embittered, hurt, wounded, offended, aggrieved, put out, miffed (*infml*), peeved (*infml*), indignant, angry, vindictive.
F3 satisfied, contented.

resentment *n* grudge, envy, jealousy, bitterness, spite, malice, ill-will, ill-feeling, animosity, hurt, umbrage, pique, displeasure, irritation, indignation, vexation, anger, vindictiveness.
F3 contentment, happiness.

reservation *n* **1** DOUBT, scepticism, misgiving, qualm, scruple, hesitation, second thought. **2** PROVISO, stipulation, qualification, condition. **3** RESERVE, preserve, park, sanctuary, homeland, enclave. **4** BOOKING, engagement, appointment.

reserve *v* **1** SET APART, earmark, keep, retain, hold back, save, store, stockpile. **2** *reserve a seat*: book, engage, order, secure, earmark.
F3 **1** use up.
➤ *n* **1** STORE, stock, supply, fund,

stockpile, cache, hoard, savings. **2** SHYNESS, reticence, secretiveness, coolness, aloofness, modesty, restraint. **3** RESERVATION, preserve, park, sanctuary. **4** REPLACEMENT, substitute, stand-in, proxy, understudy.
F3 **2** friendliness, openness.

reserved *adj* **1** BOOKED, engaged, taken, spoken for, set aside, earmarked, meant, intended, designated, destined, saved, held, kept, retained. **2** SHY, retiring, reticent, unforthcoming, uncommunicative, secretive, silent, taciturn, unsociable, cool, aloof, standoffish, unapproachable, modest, restrained, cautious.
F3 **1** unreserved, free, available. **2** friendly, open.

reside *v* live, inhabit, dwell, lodge, stay, sojourn, settle, remain.

residence *n* dwelling, habitation, domicile, abode, seat, place, pad (*infml*), gaff (*sl*), home, house, lodgings, quarters, hall, manor, mansion, palace, villa, country house, country seat.

resident *n* inhabitant, citizen, local, householder, occupier, tenant, lodger, guest.
F3 non-resident.

residual *adj* remaining, left-over, unused, unconsumed, net.

resign *v* stand down, leave, quit, abdicate, vacate, renounce, relinquish, forgo, waive, surrender, yield, abandon, forsake.
F3 join.
◇ **resign oneself** reconcile oneself, accept, bow, submit, yield, comply, acquiesce.
F3 resist.

resignation *n* **1** STANDING-DOWN, abdication, retirement, departure, notice, renunciation, relinquishment, surrender. **2** ACCEPTANCE, compliance, acquiescence, submission, non-resistance, passivity, patience, stoicism, defeatism.
F3 **2** resistance.

resigned adj reconciled, stoical, philosophical, patient, unprotesting, unresisting, compliant, passive, submissive, defeatist.
🔁 resistant.

resilient adj 1 resilient material: flexible, pliable, supple, plastic, elastic, springy, bouncy. 2 STRONG, tough, hardy, adaptable, buoyant.
🔁 1 rigid, brittle.

resist v oppose, defy, confront, fight, combat, weather, withstand, repel, counteract, check, avoid, refuse.
🔁 submit, accept.

resistant adj 1 OPPOSED, antagonistic, defiant, unyielding, intransigent, unwilling. 2 PROOF, impervious, immune, invulnerable, tough, strong.
🔁 1 compliant, yielding.

resolute adj determined, resolved, set, fixed, unwavering, staunch, firm, steadfast, relentless, single-minded, persevering, dogged, tenacious, stubborn, obstinate, strong-willed, undaunted, unflinching, bold.
🔁 irresolute, weak-willed, half-hearted.

resolution n 1 DETERMINATION, resolve, willpower, commitment, dedication, devotion, firmness, steadfastness, persistence, perseverance, doggedness, tenacity, zeal, courage, boldness. 2 DECISION, judgement, finding, declaration, proposition, motion.
🔁 1 half-heartedness, uncertainty, indecision.

resolve v decide, make up one's mind, determine, fix, settle, conclude, sort out, work out, solve.

resort v go, visit, frequent, patronize, haunt.
➤ n recourse, refuge, course (of action), alternative, option, chance, possibility.
◊ **resort to** turn to, use, utilize, employ, exercise.

resound v resonate, reverberate, echo, re-echo, ring, boom, thunder.

resounding adj 1 RESONANT, reverberating, echoing, ringing, sonorous, booming, thunderous, full, rich, vibrant. 2 a resounding victory: decisive, conclusive, crushing, thorough.
🔁 1 faint.

resource n 1 SUPPLY, reserve, stockpile, stash (infml), source, expedient, contrivance, device. 2 RESOURCEFULNESS, initiative, ingenuity, inventiveness, talent, ability, capability.

resourceful adj ingenious, imaginative, creative, inventive, innovative, original, clever, bright, sharp, quick-witted, able, capable, talented.

resources n materials, supplies, reserves, holdings, funds, money, wealth, riches, capital, assets, property, means.

respect n 1 ADMIRATION, esteem, appreciation, recognition, honour, deference, reverence, veneration, politeness, courtesy. 2 in every respect: point, aspect, facet, feature, characteristic, particular, detail, sense, way, regard, reference, relation, connection.
🔁 1 disrespect.
➤ v 1 ADMIRE, esteem, regard, appreciate, value. 2 OBEY, observe, heed, follow, honour, recognize, fulfil.
🔁 1 despise, scorn. 2 ignore, disobey.

respectable adj 1 HONOURABLE, worthy, respected, dignified, upright, honest, decent, clean-living. 2 ACCEPTABLE, tolerable, passable, adequate, fair, reasonable, appreciable, considerable.
🔁 1 dishonourable, disreputable. 2 inadequate, paltry.

respectful adj deferential, reverential, humble, polite, well-mannered, courteous, civil.
🔁 disrespectful.

respective adj corresponding, relevant, various, several, separate, individual, personal, own, particular, special.

respond v answer, reply, retort,

acknowledge, react, return, reciprocate.

response n answer, reply, retort, comeback, acknowledgement, reaction, feedback.
⊟ query.

responsibility n fault, blame, guilt, culpability, answerability, accountability, duty, obligation, burden, onus, charge, care, trust, authority, power.

responsible adj **1** GUILTY, culpable, at fault, to blame, liable, answerable, accountable. **2** a responsible citizen: dependable, reliable, conscientious, trustworthy, honest, sound, steady, sober, mature, sensible, rational. **3** IMPORTANT, authoritative, executive, decision-making.
⊟ **2** irresponsible, unreliable, untrustworthy.

rest[1] n **1** LEISURE, relaxation, repose, lie-down, sleep, snooze, forty winks (**infml**), nap, siesta, idleness, inactivity, motionlessness, standstill, stillness, tranquillity, calm. **2** BREAK, pause, breathing-space, breather (**infml**), intermission, interlude, interval, recess, holiday, vacation, halt, cessation (**fml**), lull, respite, let-up (**infml**). **3** SUPPORT, prop, stand, base.
⊟ **1** action, activity. **2** work.
➤ v **1** PAUSE, halt, stop, cease. **2** RELAX, repose, sit, recline, lounge, laze, lie down, sleep, snooze, doze. **3** DEPEND, rely, hinge, hang, lie. **4** LEAN, prop, support, stand.
⊟ **1** continue. **2** work.

rest[2] n remainder, others, balance, surplus, excess, residue, remains, leftovers, remnants.

restaurant

> *Types of restaurant include*: bistro, brasserie, buffet, burger bar, café, cafeteria, canteen, carvery, chippy (**infml**), coffee bar, diner (**US**), dining car, dining room, eating house, fish and chip shop, greasy spoon (**sl**), grill, grill room, health food restaurant, ice-cream parlour, Internet café, luncheonette (**US**), McDonald's, mess

> room, milk bar, motorway café, NAAFI (Navy, Army and Air Force Institutes), pizzeria, pull-in, refectory, sandwich bar, self-service restaurant, snack bar, steakhouse, sushi bar, teahouse, tea room, tea shop, transport café, trattoria.

restful adj relaxing, soothing, calm, tranquil, serene, peaceful, quiet, undisturbed, relaxed, comfortable, leisurely, unhurried.
⊟ tiring, restless.

restless adj fidgety, unsettled, disturbed, troubled, agitated, nervous, anxious, worried, uneasy, fretful, edgy, jumpy (**infml**), restive, unruly, turbulent, sleepless.
⊟ calm, relaxed, comfortable.

restore v **1** REPLACE, return, reinstate, rehabilitate, re-establish, reintroduce, re-enforce. **2** restore a building: renovate, renew, rebuild, reconstruct, refurbish, retouch, recondition, repair, mend, fix. **3** REVIVE, refresh, rejuvenate, revitalize, strengthen.
⊟ **1** remove. **2** damage. **3** weaken.

restrain v hold back, keep back, suppress, subdue, repress, inhibit, check, curb, bridle, stop, arrest, prevent, bind, tie, chain, fetter, manacle, imprison, jail, confine, restrict, regulate, control, govern.
⊟ encourage, liberate.

restrained adj moderate, temperate, mild, subdued, muted, quiet, soft, low-key, unobtrusive, discreet, tasteful, calm, controlled, steady, self-controlled.
⊟ unrestrained.

restraint n moderation, inhibition, self-control, self-discipline, hold, grip, check, curb, rein, bridle, suppression, bondage, captivity, confinement, imprisonment, bonds, chains, fetters, straitjacket, restriction, control, constraint, limitation, tie, hindrance, prevention.
⊟ liberty.

restrict v limit, bound, demarcate,

control, regulate, confine, contain, cramp, constrain, impede, hinder, hamper, handicap, tie, restrain, curtail.
🔁 broaden, free.

restriction *n* limit, bound, confine, limitation, constraint, handicap, check, curb, restraint, ban, embargo, control, regulation, rule, stipulation, condition, proviso.
🔁 freedom.

result *n* effect, consequence, sequel, repercussion, reaction, outcome, upshot, issue, end-product, fruit, score, answer, verdict, judgement, decision, conclusion.
🔁 cause.
➤ *v* follow, ensue, happen, occur, issue, emerge, arise, spring, derive, stem, flow, proceed, develop, end, finish, terminate, culminate.
🔁 cause.

resume *v* restart, recommence, reopen, reconvene, continue, carry on, go on, proceed.
🔁 cease.

resumption *n* recommencement, restart, reopening, renewal, resurgence, continuation.
🔁 cessation.

resurrect *v* restore, revive, resuscitate, reactivate, bring back, reintroduce, reinstate, re-establish, renew.
🔁 kill, bury.

resurrection *n* restoration, revival, resuscitation, renaissance, rebirth, renewal, resurgence, reappearance, return, comeback.

resuscitate *v* revive, resurrect, save, rescue, reanimate, quicken, reinvigorate, revitalize, restore, renew.

retain *v* **1** KEEP, hold, reserve, hold back, save, preserve. **2** *retain information*: remember, memorize. **3** EMPLOY, engage, hire, commission.
🔁 **1** release. **2** forget. **3** dismiss.

retaliate *v* reciprocate, counter, counter-attack, hit back, strike back, fight back, get one's own back, get even with, take revenge.

retaliation *n* reprisal, counter-attack, revenge, vengeance, retribution.

reticent *adj* reserved, shy, inhibited, uncommunicative, unforthcoming, tight-lipped, secretive, taciturn, silent, quiet.
🔁 communicative, forward, frank.

retire *v* leave, depart, withdraw, retreat, recede.
🔁 join, enter, advance.

retirement *n* withdrawal, retreat, solitude, loneliness, seclusion, privacy, obscurity.

retiring *adj* shy, bashful, timid, shrinking, inhibited, quiet, reticent, reserved, self-effacing, unassertive, modest, unassuming, humble.
🔁 bold, forward, assertive.

retort *v* answer, reply, respond, rejoin, return, counter, retaliate.
➤ *n* answer, reply, response, rejoinder, riposte, repartee, quip.

retract *v* take back, withdraw, recant, reverse, revoke, rescind, cancel, repeal, repudiate, disown, disclaim, deny.
🔁 assert, maintain.

retreat *v* draw back, recoil, shrink, turn tail (*infml*), do a U-turn (*infml*), withdraw, retire, leave, depart, quit.
🔁 advance.
➤ *n* **1** WITHDRAWAL, departure, evacuation, flight. **2** SECLUSION, privacy, hideaway, den, refuge, asylum, shelter, sanctuary, haven.
🔁 **1** advance, charge.

retrieve *v* fetch, bring back, regain, get back, recapture, repossess, recoup, recover, salvage, save, rescue, redeem, restore, return.
🔁 lose.

retrograde *adj* retrogressive, backward, reverse, negative, downward, declining, deteriorating.
🔁 progressive.

retrospect *n* hindsight, afterthought, re-examination, review, recollection, remembrance.
🔁 prospect.

return v **1** COME BACK, reappear, recur, go back, backtrack, regress, revert. **2** GIVE BACK, hand back, send back, deliver, put back, replace, restore. **3** *return a favour*: reciprocate, requite, repay, refund, reimburse, recompense, pay back.
▪ **1** leave, depart. **2** take.
➤ n **1** REAPPEARANCE, recurrence, comeback, homecoming. **2** REPAYMENT, recompense, replacement, restoration, reinstatement, reciprocation. **3** REVENUE, income, proceeds, takings, yield, gain, profit, reward, advantage, benefit.
▪ **1** departure, disappearance. **2** removal. **3** payment, expense, loss.

reveal v expose, uncover, unveil, unmask, show, display, exhibit, manifest, disclose, divulge, betray, leak, tell, impart, communicate, broadcast, publish, announce, proclaim.
▪ hide, conceal, mask.

revel in enjoy, relish, savour, delight in, thrive on, bask in, glory in, lap up, indulge in, wallow in, luxuriate in.

revelation n uncovering, unveiling, exposure, unmasking, show, display, exhibition, manifestation, disclosure, confession, admission, betrayed, giveaway, leak, news, information, communication, broadcasting, publication, announcement, proclamation.

revelry n celebration, festivity, party, merrymaking, jollity, fun, carousal, debauchery.
▪ sobriety.

revenge n vengeance, satisfaction, reprisal, retaliation, requital, payback, retribution.
➤ v avenge, repay, pay back, retaliate, get one's own back.

revenue n income, return, yield, interest, profit, gain, proceeds, receipts, takings.
▪ expenditure.

reverberate v echo, re-echo, resound, resonate, ring, boom, vibrate.

revere v respect, esteem, honour, pay homage to, venerate, worship, idolize, adore, exalt.
▪ despise, scorn.

reverence n respect, deference, honour, homage, admiration, awe, veneration, worship, adoration, devotion.
▪ contempt, scorn.

reverent adj reverential, respectful, deferential, humble, dutiful, awed, solemn, pious, devout, adoring, loving.
▪ irreverent, disrespectful.

reversal n negation, cancellation, annulment, nullification, revocation, countermanding (*fml*), rescinding, repeal, reverse, turnabout, turnaround, U-turn, volte-face, upset.
▪ advancement, progress.

reverse v **1** BACK, retreat, backtrack, do a U-turn (*infml*), undo, negate, cancel, annul, invalidate, countermand (*fml*), overrule, revoke, rescind, repeal, retract, quash, overthrow. **2** TRANSPOSE, turn round, invert, up-end, overturn, upset, change, alter.
▪ **1** advance, enforce.
➤ n **1** UNDERSIDE, back, rear, inverse, converse, contrary, opposite, antithesis. **2** MISFORTUNE, mishap, misadventure, adversity, affliction, hardship, trial, blow, disappointment, setback, check, delay, problem, difficulty, failure, defeat.
➤ adj opposite, contrary, converse, inverse, inverted, backward, back, rear.

revert v return, go back, resume, lapse, relapse, regress.

review v **1** CRITICIZE, assess, evaluate, judge, weigh, discuss, examine, inspect, scrutinize, study, survey, recapitulate. **2** *review the situation*: reassess, re-evaluate, re-examine, reconsider, rethink, revise.
➤ n **1** CRITICISM, critique, assessment, evaluation, judgement, report, commentary, examination, scrutiny, analysis, study, survey, recapitulation, reassessment, re-evaluation, re-examination, revision. **2** MAGAZINE, periodical, journal.

revise v 1 *revise one's opinion*: change, alter, modify, amend, correct, update, edit, rewrite, reword, recast, revamp, reconsider, re-examine, review. 2 STUDY, learn, swot up (*infml*), cram (*infml*).

revival n resuscitation, revitalization, restoration, renewal, renaissance, rebirth, reawakening, resurgence, upsurge.

revive v resuscitate, reanimate, revitalize, restore, renew, refresh, animate, invigorate, quicken, rouse, awaken, recover, rally, reawaken, rekindle, reactivate.
🔁 weary.

revoke v repeal, rescind, quash, abrogate, annul, nullify, invalidate, negate, cancel, countermand (*fml*), reverse, retract, withdraw.
🔁 enforce.

revolt n revolution, rebellion, mutiny, rising, uprising, insurrection, putsch, coup (d'état), secession, defection.
➤ v 1 REBEL, mutiny, rise up, riot, resist, dissent, disobey, defect. 2 DISGUST, sicken, nauseate, repel, offend, shock, outrage, scandalize.
🔁 1 submit. 2 please, delight.

revolting adj disgusting, sickening, nauseating, repulsive, repugnant, repellent, obnoxious, odious, nasty, horrible, foul, vile, loathsome, abhorrent, distasteful, offensive, shocking, appalling.
🔁 pleasant, delightful, attractive, palatable.

revolution n 1 REVOLT, rebellion, mutiny, rising, uprising, insurrection, putsch, coup (d'état), reformation, change, transformation, innovation, upheaval, cataclysm. 2 ROTATION, turn, spin, cycle, circuit, round, circle, orbit, gyration.

revolutionary n rebel, mutineer, insurgent, dissenter, anarchist, revolutionist.
➤ adj 1 REBEL, rebellious, mutinous, insurgent, subversive, seditious, anarchistic. 2 *revolutionary ideas*: new,

innovative, avant-garde, cutting-edge, different, drastic, radical, thoroughgoing.
🔁 1 conservative.

revolve v rotate, turn, pivot, swivel, spin, wheel, whirl, gyrate, circle, orbit.

revulsion n repugnance, disgust, distaste, dislike, aversion, hatred, detestation, loathing, abhorrence, abomination.
🔁 delight, pleasure, approval.

reward n prize, honour, medal, decoration, bounty, pay-off, bonus, premium, payment, remuneration, recompense, repayment, requital, compensation, gain, profit, return, benefit, merit, desert, retribution.
🔁 punishment.
➤ v pay, remunerate, recompense, repay, requite, compensate, honour, decorate.
🔁 punish.

rewarding adj profitable, profit-making, remunerative, lucrative, productive, fruitful, worthwhile, valuable, advantageous, beneficial, satisfying, gratifying, pleasing, fulfilling, enriching.
🔁 unrewarding.

rhetoric n eloquence, oratory, grandiloquence, magniloquence, bombast, pomposity, hyperbole, verbosity, wordiness, floridness.

Rhetorical devices include:
abscission, alliteration, amplification, anacoluthon, anadiplosis, anaphora, anastrophe, anticlimax, antimetabole, antimetathesis, antiphrasis, antithesis, antonomasia, aporia, apostrophe, asyndeton, auxesis, bathos, catachresis, cataphora, chiasmus, climax, diallage, diegesis, dissimile, double entendre, dramatic irony, dysphemism, ellipsis, enantiosis, enumeration, epanadiplosis, epanalepsis, epanaphora, epanodos, epanorthosis, epigram, epiphonema, epistrophe, epizeuxis, erotema, erotetic,

euphemism, figure of speech, hendiadys, hypallage, hyperbole, hypostrophe, hypotyposis, hysteron-proteron, increment, innuendo, irony, litotes, meiosis, metalepsis, metaphor, mixed metaphor, metonymy, onomatopoeia, oxymoron, parabole, paradox, paraleipsis, parenthesis, pathetic fallacy, personification, prolepsis, pun, rhetorical question, simile, syllepsis, symploce, synchoresis, synchrysis, synecdoche, synoeciosis, tautology, transferred epithet, trope, vicious circle, zeugma.

rhetorical *adj* oratorical, grandiloquent, magniloquent, bombastic, declamatory, pompous, high-sounding, grand, high-flown, flowery, florid, flamboyant, showy, pretentious, artificial, insincere.
E3 simple.

rhyme *n* poetry, verse, poem, ode, limerick, jingle, song, ditty.

rhythm *n* beat, pulse, time, tempo, metre, measure, movement, flow, lilt, swing, accent, cadence, pattern.

rhythmic *adj* rhythmical, metric, metrical, pulsating, throbbing, flowing, lilting, periodic, regular, steady.

rich *adj* 1 WEALTHY, affluent, moneyed, prosperous, well-to-do, well-off, loaded (*sl*). 2 PLENTIFUL, abundant, copious, profuse, prolific, ample, full. 3 FERTILE, fruitful, productive, lush. 4 *rich food*: creamy, fatty, full-bodied, heavy, full-flavoured, strong, spicy, savoury, tasty, delicious, luscious, juicy, sweet. 5 *rich colours*: deep, intense, vivid, bright, vibrant, warm. 6 EXPENSIVE, precious, valuable, lavish, sumptuous, opulent, luxurious, splendid, gorgeous, fine, elaborate, ornate.
E3 1 poor, impoverished. 3 barren. 4 plain, bland. 5 dull, soft. 6 plain, simple.

riches *n* wealth, affluence, money, gold, treasure, fortune, assets, property, substance, resources, means.
E3 poverty.

rickety *adj* unsteady, wobbly, shaky, unstable, insecure, flimsy, jerry-built, decrepit, ramshackle, broken-down, dilapidated, derelict.
E3 stable, strong.

rid *v* clear, purge, free, deliver, relieve, unburden.

riddle¹ *n* enigma, mystery, conundrum, brain-teaser, puzzle, poser, problem.

riddle² *v* 1 PERFORATE, pierce, puncture, pepper, fill, permeate, pervade, infest. 2 SIFT, sieve, strain, filter, mar, winnow.

ride *v* sit, move, progress, travel, journey, gallop, trot, pedal, drive, steer, control, handle, manage.
➤ *n* journey, trip, outing, jaunt, spin, drive, lift.

ridicule *n* satire, irony, sarcasm, mockery, jeering, scorn, derision, taunting, teasing, chaff, banter, badinage, laughter.
E3 praise.
➤ *v* satirize, send up (*infml*), caricature, lampoon, burlesque, parody, mock, make fun of, jeer, scoff, deride, sneer, tease, rib (*infml*), humiliate, taunt.
E3 praise.

ridiculous *adj* ludicrous, absurd, nonsensical, silly, foolish, stupid, contemptible, derisory, laughable, farcical, comical, funny, hilarious, outrageous, preposterous, incredible, unbelievable.
E3 sensible.

rife *adj* abundant, rampant, teeming, raging, epidemic, prevalent, widespread, general, common, frequent.
E3 scarce.

rift *n* 1 SPLIT, breach, break, fracture, crack, fault, chink, cleft, cranny, crevice, gap, divide, space, opening. 2 DISAGREEMENT, difference, separation, division, divide, schism, alienation.
E3 2 unity.

rig *n* equipment, kit, outfit, gear, tackle, apparatus, machinery, fittings, fixtures.
◇ **rig out** equip, kit out, outfit, fit (out), supply, furnish, clothe, dress (up).

right adj 1 the right answer: correct, accurate, exact, precise, true, factual, actual, real. 2 PROPER, fitting, seemly, becoming, appropriate, meet (fml), suitable, fit, admissible, satisfactory, reasonable, desirable, favourable, advantageous. 3 FAIR, just, equitable, lawful, honest, upright, good, virtuous, righteous, moral, ethical, honourable. 4 RIGHT-WING, conservative, Tory.
🔁 1 wrong, incorrect. 2 improper, unsuitable. 3 unfair, wrong. 4 left-wing.
➤ adv 1 CORRECTLY, accurately, exactly, precisely, factually, properly, satisfactorily, well, fairly. 2 right to the bottom: straight, directly, completely, utterly.
🔁 1 wrongly, incorrectly, unfairly.
➤ n 1 PRIVILEGE, prerogative, due, claim, business, authority, power. 2 JUSTICE, legality, good, virtue, righteousness, morality, honour, integrity, uprightness.
🔁 2 wrong.
➤ v rectify, correct, put right, fix, repair, redress, vindicate, avenge, pay back, settle, straighten, stand up.
◇ **right away** straight away, immediately, at once, now, instantly, directly, forthwith, without delay, promptly.
🔁 later, eventually.

rightful adj legitimate, lawful, legal, just, bona fide, true, real, genuine, valid, authorized, correct, proper, suitable, due.
🔁 wrongful, unlawful.

rigid adj stiff, inflexible, unbending, immutable, cast-iron, hard, firm, set, fixed, unalterable, invariable, austere, harsh, severe, unrelenting, strict, rigorous, stringent, stern, uncompromising, unyielding.
🔁 flexible, elastic.

rigorous adj strict, stringent, rigid, firm, exact, precise, accurate, meticulous, painstaking, scrupulous, conscientious, thorough.
🔁 lax, superficial.

rile v annoy, irritate, nettle, pique, peeve (infml), put out, upset, irk, vex, anger,

aggravate (infml), exasperate.
🔁 calm, soothe.

rim n lip, edge, brim, brink, verge, margin, border, circumference.
🔁 centre, middle.

rind n peel, skin, husk, crust.

ring[1] n 1 CIRCLE, round, loop, hoop, halo, band, girdle, collar, circuit, arena, enclosure. 2 GROUP, cartel, syndicate, association, organization, gang, crew, mob, band, cell, clique, coterie.
➤ v surround, encircle, gird, circle, circumscribe, encompass, enclose.

ring[2] v 1 CHIME, peal, toll, tinkle, clink, jingle, clang, sound, resound, resonate, reverberate, buzz. 2 TELEPHONE, phone, call, ring up.
➤ n 1 CHIME, peal, toll, tinkle, clink, jingle, clang. 2 PHONE CALL, call, buzz (infml), tinkle (infml).

rinse v swill, bathe, wash, clean, cleanse, flush, wet, dip.

riot n insurrection, rising, uprising, revolt, rebellion, mutiny, anarchy, lawlessness, affray, disturbance, turbulence, disorder, confusion, commotion, tumult, turmoil, uproar, row, quarrel, strife.
🔁 order, calm.
➤ v revolt, rebel, rise up, run riot, run wild, rampage.

rip v tear, rend, split, separate, rupture, burst, cut, slit, slash, gash, lacerate, hack.
➤ n tear, rent, split, cleavage, rupture, cut, slit, slash, gash, hole.
◇ **rip off** (sl) overcharge, swindle, defraud, cheat, diddle (infml), do (infml), fleece, sting (sl), con (infml), trick, dupe, exploit.

ripe adj 1 RIPENED, mature, mellow, seasoned, grown, developed, complete, finished, perfect. 2 READY, suitable, right, favourable, auspicious, propitious, timely, opportune.
🔁 2 untimely, inopportune.

ripen v develop, mature, mellow, season, age.

rise v 1 GO UP, ascend, climb, mount,

slope (up), soar, tower, grow, increase, escalate, intensify. **2** STAND UP, get up, arise, jump up, spring up. **3** ADVANCE, progress, get on, improve, prosper. **4** ORIGINATE, spring, flow, issue, emerge, appear.

▪ **1** fall, descend. **2** sit down. **3** decline.

➤ *n* **1** ASCENT, climb, slope, incline, hill, elevation. **2** INCREASE, increment, upsurge, upturn, advance, progress, improvement, advancement, promotion.

▪ **1** descent, valley. **2** fall, decline.

risk *n* danger, peril, jeopardy, hazard, chance, possibility, uncertainty, gamble, speculation, venture, adventure.

▪ safety, certainty.

➤ *v* endanger, imperil, jeopardize, hazard, chance, gamble, venture, dare.

risky *adj* dangerous, unsafe, perilous, hazardous, chancy, uncertain, touch-and-go, dicey (*infml*), tricky, precarious.

▪ safe.

risqué *adj* indecent, improper, indelicate, suggestive, coarse, crude, earthy, bawdy, racy, saucy (*infml*), naughty, blue.

▪ decent, proper.

ritual *n* custom, tradition, convention, usage, practice, habit, wont, routine, procedure, ordinance, prescription, form, formality, ceremony, ceremonial, solemnity, rite, sacrament, service, liturgy, observance, act.

➤ *adj* customary, traditional, habitual, conventional, routine, procedural, prescribed, set, formal, ceremonial.

▪ informal.

rival *n* competitor, contestant, contender, challenger, opponent, adversary, antagonist, match, equal, peer.

▪ colleague, associate.

➤ *adj* competitive, competing, opposed, opposing, conflicting.

▪ associate.

➤ *v* compete with, contend with, vie with, oppose, emulate, match, equal.

▪ co-operate.

rivalry *n* competitiveness, competition, contest, contention, conflict, struggle, strife, opposition, antagonism.

▪ co-operation.

river *n* waterway, watercourse.

Forms of river or watercourse include: beck, billabong, bourn, broads, brook, burn, canal, channel, confluence, creek, cut, delta, estuary, firth, frith, inlet, mountain stream, mouth, rill, rillet, rivulet, runnel, source, stream, tributary, wadi.

The world's longest rivers include: Nile (Africa), Amazon (South America), Yangtze (Asia), Mississippi-Missouri (North America), Yenisey-Angara-Selenga (Asia), Amur-Argun-Kerulen (Asia), Ob-Irtysh (Asia), Plata-Parena-Grande (South America), Yellow (Asia), Zaire (Africa).

---

road *n* roadway, motorway, bypass, highway, thoroughfare, street, avenue, boulevard, crescent, drive, lane, track, route, course, way, direction.

roam *v* wander, rove, range, travel, walk, ramble, stroll, amble, prowl, drift, stray.

▪ stay.

roar *v, n* bellow, yell, shout, cry, bawl, howl, hoot, guffaw, thunder, crash, blare, rumble, boom.

▪ whisper.

rob *v* steal from, hold up, raid, burgle, loot, pillage, plunder, sack, rifle, ransack, swindle, rip off (*sl*), do (*infml*), cheat, defraud, deprive.

robbery *n* theft, stealing, larceny, hold-up, stick-up (*sl*), heist (*sl*), raid, burglary, pillage, plunder, fraud, embezzlement, swindle, rip-off (*sl*).

robot *n* automaton, machine, android, zombie.

robust *adj* strong, sturdy, tough, hardy, vigorous, powerful, muscular, athletic, fit, healthy, well.

▪ weak, feeble, unhealthy.

rock[1] *n* boulder, stone, pebble, crag, outcrop.

> *Rocks include*: basalt, breccia, chalk, coal, conglomerate, flint, gabbro, gneiss, granite, gravel, lava, limestone, marble, marl, obsidian, ore, porphyry, pumice stone, sandstone, schist, serpentine, shale, slate.

rock[2] *v* **1** SWAY, swing, tilt, tip, shake, wobble, roll, pitch, toss, lurch, reel, stagger, totter. **2** *news that rocked the nation*: shock, stun, daze, dumbfound, astound, astonish, surprise, startle.

rocky[1] *adj* stony, pebbly, craggy, rugged, rough, hard, flinty.
Fa smooth, soft.

rocky[2] *adj* unsteady, shaky, wobbly, staggering, tottering, unstable, unreliable, uncertain, weak.
Fa steady, stable, dependable, strong.

rod *n* bar, shaft, strut, pole, stick, baton, wand, cane, switch, staff, mace, sceptre.

rodent

> *Rodents include*: agouti, bandicoot, beaver, black rat, brown rat, cane rat, capybara, cavy, chinchilla, chipmunk, cony, coypu, dormouse, fieldmouse, ferret, gerbil, gopher, grey squirrel, groundhog, guinea pig, hamster, hare, harvest mouse, hedgehog, jerboa, kangaroo rat, lemming, marmot, meerkat, mouse, muskrat, musquash, pika, porcupine, prairie dog, rabbit, rat, red squirrel, sewer rat, squirrel, vole, water rat, water vole, woodchuck.

rogue *n* scoundrel, rascal, scamp, villain, miscreant (*fml*), crook (*infml*), swindler, fraud, cheat, con man (*infml*), reprobate, wastrel, ne'er-do-well.

role *n* part, character, representation, portrayal, impersonation, function, capacity, task, duty, job, post, position.

roll *v* **1** ROTATE, revolve, turn, spin, wheel, twirl, whirl, gyrate, move, run, pass. **2** WIND, coil, furl, twist, curl, wrap, envelop, enfold, bind. **3** *the ship rolled*: rock, sway, swing, pitch, toss, lurch, reel,

wallow, undulate. **4** PRESS, flatten, smooth, level. **5** RUMBLE, roar, thunder, boom, resound, reverberate.

➤ *n* **1** ROLLER, cylinder, drum, reel, spool, bobbin, scroll. **2** REGISTER, roster, census, list, inventory, index, catalogue, directory, schedule, record, chronicle, annals. **3** ROTATION, revolution, cycle, turn, spin, wheel, twirl, whirl, gyration, undulation. **4** RUMBLE, roar, thunder, boom, resonance, reverberation.

◇ **roll up** (*infml*) arrive, assemble, gather, congregate, convene.
Fa leave.

romance *n* **1** LOVE AFFAIR, affair, relationship, liaison, fling (*infml*), intrigue, passion. **2** LOVE STORY, novel, story, tale, fairytale, legend, idyll, fiction, fantasy. **3** ADVENTURE, excitement, melodrama, mystery, charm, fascination, glamour, sentiment.
➤ *v* lie, fantasize, exaggerate, overstate.

romantic *adj* **1** IMAGINARY, fictitious, fanciful, fantastic, legendary, fairy-tale, idyllic, utopian, idealistic, quixotic, visionary, starry-eyed, dreamy, unrealistic, impractical, improbable, wild, extravagant, exciting, fascinating. **2** SENTIMENTAL, loving, amorous, passionate, tender, fond, lovey-dovey (*infml*), soppy, mushy, sloppy.
Fa 1 real, practical. **2** unromantic, unsentimental.
➤ *n* sentimentalist, daydreamer, dreamer, visionary, idealist, utopian.
Fa realist.

roof

> *Types of roof include*: bell roof, conical broach roof, cupola, dome, flat roof, French roof, gable roof, gable-and-valley roof, gambrel roof, geodesic dome, helm roof, hip roof, imbricated roof, imperial roof, lean-to roof, mansard roof, monitor roof, ogee roof, onion dome, pavilion roof, pendentive dome, pitched roof, saddle roof, saucer dome, sawtooth roof, sloped turret, span roof, thatched roof.

room *n* space, volume, capacity,

headroom, legroom, elbow-room, scope, range, extent, leeway, latitude, margin, allowance, chance, opportunity.

Types of room include: attic, loft, boxroom, bedroom, boudoir, spare room, dressing-room, guest room, nursery, playroom, sitting-room, lounge, front room, living room, drawing-room, salon, reception room, chamber, lounge-diner, dining room, study, den (*infml*), library, kitchen, kitchen-diner, kitchenette, breakfast room, larder, pantry, scullery, bathroom, en suite bathroom, toilet, lavatory, restroom (*US*), WC, loo (*infml*), cloakroom, laundry, utility room, porch, hall, landing, conservatory, sun lounge, cellar, basement; classroom, music room, laboratory, office, sick-room, dormitory, workroom, studio, workshop, storeroom, waiting room, anteroom, foyer, mezzanine, family room, day room, games room.

roomy *adj* spacious, capacious, large, sizable, broad, wide, extensive, ample, generous.
E3 cramped, small, tiny.

root[1] *n* **1** TUBER, rhizome, stem. **2** ORIGIN, source, derivation, cause, starting point, fount, fountainhead, seed, germ, nucleus, heart, core, nub, essence, seat, base, bottom, basis, foundation.
➤ *v* anchor, moor, fasten, fix, set, stick, implant, embed, entrench, establish, ground, base.
◇ **root out** unearth, dig out, uncover, discover, uproot, eradicate, extirpate, eliminate, exterminate, destroy, abolish, clear away, remove.

root[2] *v* dig, delve, burrow, forage, hunt, rummage, ferret, poke, pry, nose.

roots *n* beginning(s), origins, family, heritage, background, birthplace, home.

rope

Kinds of rope include: bobstay,

bowline, brace, bridle, buntline, cable, clew-line, cord, cordage, cringle, dragline, dragrope, gantline, guy, guy-rope, hackamore, halter, halyard, hawser, head rope, hobble, lanyard, lariat, lashing, lasso, line, marline, noose, painter, ratline, stay, strand, string, tack, tackle, tether, towrope, vang, warp, widdy.

➤ *v* tie, bind, lash, fasten, hitch, moor, tether.
◇ **rope in** enlist, engage, involve, persuade, inveigle.

roster *n* rota, schedule, register, roll, list.

rostrum *n* platform, stage, dais, podium.

rot *v* decay, decompose, putrefy, fester, perish, corrode, spoil, go bad, go off, degenerate, deteriorate, crumble, disintegrate, taint, corrupt.
➤ *n* **1** DECAY, decomposition, putrefaction, corrosion, rust, mould. **2** (*infml*) NONSENSE, rubbish, twaddle, poppycock (*infml*), drivel, claptrap (*infml*), balderdash (*infml*).

rotary *adj* rotating, revolving, turning, spinning, whirling, gyrating.
E3 fixed.

rotate *v* revolve, turn, spin, wheel, gyrate, pivot, swivel, roll.

rotation *n* revolution, turn, spin, gyration, orbit, cycle, sequence, succession, turning, spinning.

rotten *adj* **1** DECAYED, decomposed, putrid, addled, bad, off, mouldy, fetid, rancid, stinking, rank, foul, rotting, decaying, disintegrating. **2** INFERIOR, bad, poor, inadequate, low-grade, low-rent (*sl*), lousy, crummy (*sl*), ropy (*sl*), mean, nasty, beastly, dirty, despicable, contemptible, dishonourable, wicked. **3** (*infml*) ILL, sick, unwell, poorly, grotty (*sl*), rough (*infml*), off-colour.
E3 1 fresh. **2** good. **3** well.

rough *adj* **1** UNEVEN, bumpy, lumpy, rugged, craggy, jagged, irregular, coarse, bristly, scratchy. **2** HARSH, severe, tough, hard, cruel, brutal, drastic, extreme, brusque, curt, sharp. **3** APPROXIMATE, estimated, imprecise, inexact, vague, general, cursory, hasty, incomplete, unfinished, crude, rudimentary. **4** *rough sea*: choppy, agitated, turbulent, stormy, tempestuous, violent, wild. **5** (*infml*) ILL, sick, unwell, poorly, off-colour, rotten (*infml*).

fa 1 smooth. **2** mild. **3** accurate. **4** calm. **5** well.

round *adj* **1** SPHERICAL, globular, ball-shaped, circular, ring-shaped, disc-shaped, cylindrical, rounded, curved. **2** ROTUND, plump, stout, portly.

➤ *n* **1** CIRCLE, ring, band, disc, sphere, ball, orb. **2** CYCLE, series, sequence, succession, period, bout, session. **3** BEAT, circuit, lap, course, routine.

➤ *v* circle, skirt, flank, bypass.

◇ **round off** finish (off), complete, end, close, conclude, cap, crown.

fa begin.

◇ **round on** turn on, attack, lay into, abuse.

◇ **round up** herd, marshal, assemble, gather, rally, collect, group.

fa disperse, scatter.

roundabout *adj* circuitous, tortuous, twisting, winding, indirect, oblique, devious, evasive.

fa straight, direct.

rouse *v* wake (up), awaken, arouse, call, stir, move, start, disturb, agitate, anger, provoke, stimulate, instigate, incite, inflame, excite, galvanize, whip up.

fa calm.

rout *n* defeat, conquest, overthrow, vanquishment, beating, thrashing, flight, stampede.

fa win.

➤ *v* defeat, conquer, overthrow, vanquish, crush, beat, hammer (*infml*), thrash, lick, put to flight, chase, dispel, scatter.

route *n* course, run, path, road, avenue, way, direction, itinerary, journey, passage, circuit, round, beat.

routine *n* **1** PROCEDURE, way, method, system, order, pattern, formula, practice, usage, custom, habit. **2** *comedy routine*: act, piece, programme, performance.

➤ *adj* customary, habitual, usual, typical, ordinary, run-of-the-mill, normal, standard, bog-standard (*infml*), conventional, unoriginal, predictable, familiar, everyday, banal, humdrum, dull, boring, monotonous, tedious.

fa unusual, different, exciting.

row[1] *n* line, tier, bank, rank, range, column, file, queue, string, series, sequence.

row[2] *n* **1** ARGUMENT, quarrel, dispute, controversy, squabble, tiff, slanging match (*infml*), fight, brawl, scrap (*infml*). **2** NOISE, racket, din, uproar, commotion, disturbance, rumpus, fracas.

fa 2 calm.

➤ *v* argue, quarrel, wrangle, bicker, squabble, fight, scrap (*infml*).

rowdy *adj* noisy, loud, rough, boisterous, disorderly, unruly, riotous, wild.

fa quiet, peaceful.

royal *adj* regal, majestic, kingly, queenly, princely, imperial, monarchical, sovereign, august, grand, stately, magnificent, splendid, superb.

rub *v* apply, spread, smear, stroke, caress, massage, knead, chafe, grate, scrape, abrade, scour, scrub, clean, wipe, smooth, polish, buff, shine.

◇ **rub out** erase, efface, obliterate, delete, cancel.

rubbish *n* **1** REFUSE, garbage, trash, junk, litter, waste, dross, debris, flotsam and jetsam. **2** NONSENSE, drivel, claptrap (*infml*), twaddle, gibberish, gobbledygook, balderdash, poppycock (*infml*), rot (*infml*), cobblers (*sl*).

fa 2 sense.

ruddy *adj* red, scarlet, crimson, blushing, flushed, rosy, apple-cheeked, glowing, healthy, blooming, florid, sunburnt.

fa pale.

rude *adj* **1** IMPOLITE, discourteous,

disrespectful, impertinent, impudent, cheeky (*infml*), insolent, offensive, insulting, abusive, ill-mannered, ill-bred, uncouth, uncivilized, unrefined, unpolished, uneducated, untutored, uncivil, curt, brusque, abrupt, sharp, short. **2** *a rude joke*: obscene, vulgar, coarse, dirty, naughty, gross.
≠ 1 polite, courteous, civil. **2** clean, decent.

rudimentary *adj* primary, initial, introductory, elementary, basic, fundamental, primitive, undeveloped, embryonic.
≠ advanced, developed.

rudiments *n* basics, fundamentals, essentials, principles, elements, ABC, beginnings, foundations.

rugged *adj* **1** ROUGH, bumpy, uneven, irregular, jagged, rocky, craggy, stark. **2** STRONG, robust, hardy, tough, muscular, weather-beaten.
≠ 1 smooth.

ruin *n* destruction, devastation, wreckage, havoc, damage, disrepair, decay, disintegration, breakdown, collapse, fall, downfall, failure, defeat, overthrow, ruination, undoing, insolvency, bankruptcy, crash.
≠ development, reconstruction.
➤ *v* spoil, mar, botch, mess up (*infml*), screw up (*sl*), damage, break, smash, shatter, wreck, destroy, demolish, raze, devastate, overwhelm, overthrow, defeat, crush, impoverish, bankrupt.
≠ develop, restore.

rule *n* **1** REGULATION, law, statute, ordinance, decree, order, direction, guide, precept, tenet, canon, maxim, axiom, principle, formula, guideline, standard, criterion. **2** REIGN, sovereignty, supremacy, dominion, mastery, power, authority, command, control, influence, regime, government, leadership. **3** CUSTOM, convention, practice, routine, habit, wont.
➤ *v* **1** *rule a country*: reign, govern, command, lead, administer, manage, direct, guide, control, regulate, prevail, dominate. **2** JUDGE, adjudicate, decide,

find, determine, resolve, establish, decree, pronounce.
◇ as a rule usually, normally, ordinarily, generally.
◇ rule out exclude, eliminate, reject, dismiss, preclude, prevent, ban, prohibit, forbid, disallow.

ruler

> *Titles of rulers include*: Aga, begum, caesar, caliph, consul, duce, emir, emperor, empress, Führer, governor, governor-general, head of state, Kaiser, khan, king, maharajah, maharani, mikado, monarch, nawab, nizam, pharaoh, president, prince, princess, queen, rajah, rani, regent, shah, sheikh, shogun, sovereign, sultan, sultana, suzerain, tsar, viceroy.

ruling *n* judgement, adjudication, verdict, decision, finding, resolution, decree, pronouncement.
➤ *adj* reigning, sovereign, supreme, governing, commanding, leading, main, chief, principal, dominant, predominant, controlling.

rumour *n* hearsay, gossip, talk, whisper, word, news, report, story, grapevine, bush telegraph.

run *v* **1** SPRINT, jog, race, career, tear, dash, hurry, rush, speed, bolt, dart, scoot, scuttle. **2** GO, pass, move, proceed, issue. **3** FUNCTION, work, operate, perform. **4** *run a company*: head, lead, administer, direct, manage, superintend, supervise, oversee, control, regulate. **5** COMPETE, contend, stand, challenge. **6** LAST, continue, extend, reach, stretch, spread, range. **7** FLOW, stream, pour, gush.
➤ *n* **1** JOG, gallop, race, sprint, spurt, dash, rush. **2** DRIVE, ride, spin, jaunt, excursion, outing, trip, journey. **3** SEQUENCE, series, string, chain, course.
◇ run after chase, pursue, follow, tail.
≠ flee.
◇ run away escape, flee, abscond, bolt, scarper (*sl*), beat it (*infml*), run off, make off, clear off (*infml*).
≠ stay.

◇ **run down 1** CRITICIZE, belittle, disparage, denigrate, defame. **2** RUN OVER, knock over, hit, strike. **3** TIRE, weary, exhaust, weaken. **4** *run down production*: reduce, decrease, drop, cut, trim, curtail.
🔄 **1** praise. **4** increase.

◇ **run into** meet, encounter, run across, bump into (*infml*), hit, strike, collide with.
🔄 miss.

◇ **run out** expire, terminate, end, cease, close, finish, dry up, fail.

runaway *n* escaper, escapee, fugitive, absconder, deserter, refugee.
➤ *adj* escaped, fugitive, loose, uncontrolled.

rundown *n* **1** REDUCTION, decrease, decline, drop, cut. **2** SUMMARY, résumé, synopsis, outline, review, recap, run-through.

runner *n* jogger, sprinter, athlete, competitor, participant, courier, messenger.

running *adj* successive, consecutive, unbroken, uninterrupted, non-stop, continuous, constant, perpetual, incessant, unceasing, moving, flowing.
🔄 broken, occasional.
➤ *n* **1** ADMINISTRATION, direction, management, organization, co-ordination, superintendency, supervision, leadership, charge, control, regulation, functioning, working, operation, performance, conduct. **2** *out of the running*: contention, contest, competition.

runny *adj* flowing, fluid, liquid, liquefied, melted, molten, watery, diluted.
🔄 solid.

run-of-the-mill *adj* ordinary, common, everyday, average, bog-standard (*infml*), unexceptional, unremarkable, undistinguished, unimpressive, mediocre.
🔄 exceptional.

rupture *n* split, tear, burst, puncture, break, breach, fracture, crack, separation, division, estrangement, schism, rift, disagreement, quarrel, row, falling-out, bust-up (*infml*).
➤ *v* split, tear, burst, puncture, break, fracture, crack, sever, separate, divide.

rural *adj* country, rustic, pastoral, agricultural, agrarian.
🔄 urban.

rush *v* hurry, hasten, quicken, accelerate, speed (up), press, push, dispatch, bolt, dart, shoot, fly, tear, career, dash, race, run, sprint, scramble, stampede, charge.
➤ *n* hurry, haste, urgency, speed, swiftness, dash, race, scramble, stampede, charge, flow, surge.

rust *n* corrosion, oxidation.
➤ *v* corrode, decay, rot, oxidize, tarnish, deteriorate, decline.

rustic *adj* **1** PASTORAL, sylvan, bucolic, countrified, country, rural. **2** PLAIN, simple, rough, crude, coarse, rude, clumsy, awkward, artless, unworldly, unsophisticated, unrefined, uncultured, provincial, uncouth, boorish, oafish.
🔄 **1** urban. **2** urbane, sophisticated, cultivated, polished.

rustle *v, n* crackle, whoosh, swish, whisper.

rusty *adj* **1** CORRODED, rusted, rust-covered, oxidized, tarnished, discoloured, dull. **2** UNPRACTISED, weak, poor, deficient, dated, old-fashioned, outmoded, antiquated, stale, stiff, creaking.

ruthless *adj* merciless, pitiless, hard-hearted, hard, heartless, unfeeling, callous, cruel, vicious, inhuman, brutal, savage, cut-throat, fierce, ferocious, relentless, unrelenting, inexorable, implacable, harsh, severe.
🔄 merciful, compassionate.

Ss

sabotage *v* damage, spoil, mar, disrupt, vandalize, wreck, destroy, thwart, scupper, cripple, incapacitate, disable, undermine, weaken.
➤ *n* vandalism, damage, impairment, disruption, wrecking, destruction.

sack (*infml*) *v* dismiss, fire, discharge, axe (*infml*), lay off, make redundant.
➤ *n* dismissal, discharge, one's cards, notice, the boot (*infml*), the push (*infml*), the elbow (*infml*), the axe (*infml*), the chop (*infml*).

sacred *adj* holy, divine, heavenly, blessed, hallowed, sanctified, consecrated, dedicated, religious, devotional, ecclesiastical, priestly, saintly, godly, venerable, revered, sacrosanct, inviolable.
🔳 temporal, profane.

> *Sacred writings include*: Holy Bible, the Gospel, Old Testament, New Testament, Epistle, Torah, Pentateuch, Talmud, Koran, Bhagavad-Gita, Veda, Granth, Zend-Avesta.

sacrifice *v* surrender, forfeit, relinquish, let go, abandon, renounce, give up, forgo, offer, slaughter.
➤ *n* offering, immolation, slaughter, destruction, surrender, renunciation, loss.

sacrilege *n* blasphemy, profanity, heresy, desecration, profanation, violation, outrage, irreverence, disrespect, mockery.
🔳 piety, reverence, respect.

sacrosanct *adj* sacred, hallowed, untouchable, inviolable, impregnable, protected, secure.

sad *adj* **1** UNHAPPY, sorrowful, tearful, grief-stricken, heavy-hearted, upset, distressed, miserable, low-spirited, downcast, glum, long-faced, crestfallen, dejected, downhearted, despondent, melancholy, depressed, low, gloomy, dismal. **2** *sad news*: upsetting, distressing, painful, depressing, touching, poignant, heart-rending, tragic, grievous, lamentable, regrettable, sorry, unfortunate, serious, grave, disastrous.
🔳 **1** happy, cheerful. **2** fortunate, lucky.

sadden *v* upset, distress, grieve, depress, dismay, discourage, dishearten.
🔳 cheer, please, gratify, delight.

saddle *v* burden, encumber, lumber, impose, tax, charge, load (*infml*).

sadistic *adj* cruel, inhuman, brutal, savage, malicious, vicious, merciless, pitiless, barbarous, bestial, unnatural, perverted.

safe *adj* **1** HARMLESS, innocuous, non-toxic, non-poisonous, uncontaminated. **2** UNHARMED, undamaged, unscathed, uninjured, unhurt, intact, secure, protected, guarded, impregnable, invulnerable, immune. **3** CAUTIOUS, unadventurous, prudent, conservative, sure, proven, tried, tested, sound, dependable, reliable, trustworthy.
🔳 **1** dangerous, harmful. **2** vulnerable, exposed. **3** risky.

safeguard *v* protect, preserve, defend, guard, shield, screen, shelter, secure.
🔳 endanger, jeopardize.
➤ *n* protection, defence, shield, security, surety, guarantee, assurance, insurance, cover, precaution.

safekeeping *n* protection, care,

custody, keeping, charge, trust, guardianship, surveillance, supervision.

safety *n* protection, refuge, sanctuary, shelter, cover, security, safeguard, immunity, impregnability, safeness, harmlessness, reliability, dependability.
Ea danger, jeopardy, risk.

sag *v* bend, give, bag, droop, hang, fall, drop, sink, dip, decline, slump, flop, fail, flag, weaken, wilt.
Ea bulge, rise.

sail *v* **1** *sail for France*: embark, set sail, weigh anchor, put to sea, cruise, voyage. **2** CAPTAIN, skipper, pilot, navigate, steer. **3** GLIDE, plane, sweep, float, skim, scud, fly.

Types of sail include: Bermuda rig, canvas, course, foreroyal, foresail, forestaysail, foretop, fore-topgallant, fore-topsail, gaff sail, gaff-topsail, genoa, headsail, jib, jigger, kite, lateen sail, lugsail, main course, mainsail, maintopsail, mizzen, moonraker, rig, fore-and-aft rig, jury rig, royal, skysail, spanker, spinnaker, spritsail, square sail, staysail, studdingsail, topgallant, topsail, trysail.

sailing *n* boating, yachting.

Terms used in sailing include: abaft, across the wind, alongside, astern, backing, bearing, beat, beating, bending on (a sail), blanketing effect, breaking out (the anchor), casting off/ letting go, close-hauled, coming about, downwind, fetch, fitting out, fixing a position, going about, gybe, handing (a sail), hard on the wind, heeling (to the wind), in irons/in stays, knockdown (by the wind), laying off (a course), lay up, lee helm, lee-oh!, leeway, lift, points of sailing, port, reaching, beam reach, broad reach, close reach, ready about!, running, running goose-winged, sailing by the lee, sail trimming, sheeting in a sail, spilling wind, standing on, starboard, stepping/unstepping (the mast), tacking, port tack, starboard tack,

steerage way, taking soundings, unbending (a sail), under way, upwind, veer (the anchor cable), weathering, weather helm, windward, yawing.

sailor *n* seafarer, mariner, seaman.

Types of sailor include: AB, able seaman, bargee, bluejacket, boatman, boatswain, bosun, buccaneer, cabin boy, captain, cox, coxswain, crewman, deck hand, fisherman, galiogee, gob (*US*), hearty, helmsman, Jack tar, lascar, leatherneck, limey (*US sl*), marine, master, mate, matelot (*sl*), navigator, oarsman, pilot, pirate, purser, rating, rower, salt, sculler, sea dog, skipper, tar (*infml*), tarry-breeks, water rat, Wren, yachtsman, yachtswoman.

saintly *adj* godly, pious, devout, God-fearing, holy, religious, blessed, angelic, pure, spotless, innocent, blameless, sinless, virtuous, upright, worthy, righteous.
Ea godless, unholy, wicked.

sake *n* benefit, advantage, good, welfare, wellbeing, gain, profit, behalf, interest, account, regard, respect, cause, reason.

salary *n* pay, remuneration, emolument (*fml*), stipend, wages, earnings, income.

sale *n* selling, marketing, dealing, vending, disposal, trade, traffic, transaction, deal, auction.

Types of sale include: auction, autumn sale, bargain offer, bazaar, bazumble, boot sale, bring-and-buy, car boot sale, charity sale, church bazaar, clearance sale, closing-down sale, cold-call, e-auction, end-of-line sale, end-of-season sale, exhibition, exposition, fair, fleamarket, forced sale, garage sale, grand opening sale, introductory offer, January sale, jumble sale, mail order, market, mid-season sale, online sale, on-promotion, open market, private sale, public sale, pyramid selling, remainder sale, rummage sale, sale of bankrupt stock, sale of the century, sale of work, second-hand sale, special offer, spring sale, stocktaking sale, summer sale, tabletop sale, telesales, trade show, trash and treasure sale, warrant sale, winter sale.

salesperson *n* salesman, saleswoman, sales assistant, shop assistant, shop-boy, shop-girl, shopkeeper, representative, rep (*infml*).

salient *adj* important, significant, chief, main, principal, striking, conspicuous, noticeable, obvious, prominent, outstanding, remarkable.

sallow *adj* yellowish, pale, pallid, wan, pasty, sickly, unhealthy, anaemic, colourless.
🔳 rosy, healthy.

salt *n* seasoning, taste, flavour, savour, relish, piquancy.

salty *adj* salt, salted, saline, briny, brackish, savoury, spicy, piquant, tangy.
🔳 fresh, sweet.

salubrious *adj* sanitary, hygienic, health-giving, healthy, wholesome, pleasant.

salutary *adj* good, beneficial, advantageous, profitable, valuable, helpful, useful, practical, timely.

salute *v* greet, acknowledge, recognize, wave, hail, address, nod, bow, honour.
➤ *n* greeting, acknowledgement, recognition, wave, gesture, hail, address, handshake, nod, bow, tribute, reverence.

salvage *v* save, preserve, conserve, rescue, recover, recuperate, retrieve, reclaim, redeem, repair, restore.
🔳 waste, abandon.

salvation *n* deliverance, liberation, rescue, saving, preservation, redemption, reclamation.
🔳 loss, damnation.

salve *n* ointment, lotion, cream, balm, liniment, embrocation, medication, preparation, application.

same *adj* identical, twin, duplicate, indistinguishable, equal, selfsame, very, alike, like, similar, comparable, equivalent, matching, corresponding, mutual, reciprocal, interchangeable, substitutable, synonymous, consistent, uniform, unvarying, changeless, unchanged.
🔳 different, inconsistent, variable, changeable.

sample *n* specimen, example, cross-section, model, pattern, swatch, piece, demonstration, demo (*infml*), illustration, instance, sign, indication, foretaste.
➤ *v* try, test, taste, sip, inspect, experience.
➤ *adj* representative, specimen, demonstrative, illustrative, dummy, trial, test, pilot.

sanctify *v* hallow, consecrate, venerate, bless, anoint, dedicate, cleanse, purify, exalt, canonize.
🔳 desecrate, defile.

sanctimonious *adj* self-righteous, holier-than-thou, pious, moralizing, smug, superior, hypocritical, pharisaical.
🔳 humble.

sanction *n* authorization, permission, agreement, OK (*infml*), approval, go-ahead, green light, ratification, confirmation, support, backing, endorsement, licence, authority.
🔳 veto, disapproval.
➤ *v* authorize, allow, permit, approve, ratify, confirm, support, back, endorse, underwrite, accredit, license, warrant.
🔳 veto, forbid, disapprove.

sanctions *n* restrictions, boycott, embargo, ban, prohibition, penalty.

sanctity *n* holiness, sacredness, inviolability, piety, godliness, religiousness, devotion, grace, spirituality, purity, goodness, righteousness.
🔳 unholiness, secularity, worldliness, godlessness, impurity.

sanctuary *n* 1 CHURCH, temple, tabernacle, shrine, altar. 2 ASYLUM, refuge, protection, shelter, haven, retreat.

sand *n* beach, shore, strand, sands, grit.

sane *adj* normal, rational, right-minded, all there (*infml*), balanced, stable, sound, sober, level-headed, sensible, judicious, reasonable, moderate.
🖃 insane, mad, crazy, foolish.

sanitary *adj* clean, pure, uncontaminated, unpolluted, aseptic, germ-free, disinfected, hygienic, salubrious, healthy, wholesome.
🖃 insanitary, unwholesome.

sanity *n* normality, rationality, reason, sense, common sense, balance of mind, stability, soundness, level-headedness, judiciousness.
🖃 insanity, madness.

sap *v* bleed, drain, exhaust, weaken, undermine, deplete, reduce, diminish, impair.
🖃 strengthen, build up, increase.

sarcasm *n* irony, satire, mockery, sneering, derision, scorn, contempt, cynicism, bitterness.

sarcastic *adj* ironical, satirical, mocking, taunting, sneering, derisive, scathing, disparaging, cynical, incisive, cutting, biting, caustic, mordant.

sardonic *adj* mocking, jeering, sneering, derisive, scornful, sarcastic, biting, cruel, heartless, malicious, cynical, bitter.

sash *n* belt, girdle, cummerbund, waistband.

satanic *adj* satanical, diabolical, devilish, demonic, fiendish, hellish, infernal, inhuman, malevolent, wicked, evil, black.
🖃 holy, divine, godly, saintly, benevolent.

satire *n* ridicule, irony, sarcasm, wit, burlesque, skit, send-up (*infml*), spoof (*infml*), take-off (*infml*), parody, caricature, travesty.

satirical *adj* ironical, sarcastic, mocking, irreverent, taunting, derisive, sardonic, incisive, cutting, biting, mordant, caustic, cynical, bitter.

satirize *v* ridicule, mock, make fun of, burlesque, lampoon, send up (*infml*), take off (*infml*), parody, caricature, criticize, deride.
🖃 acclaim, honour.

satisfaction *n* 1 GRATIFICATION, contentment, happiness, pleasure, enjoyment, comfort, ease, well-being, fulfilment, self-satisfaction, pride. 2 SETTLEMENT, compensation, reimbursement, indemnification, damages, reparation, amends, redress, recompense, requital, payback, vindication.
🖃 1 dissatisfaction, displeasure.

satisfactory *adj* acceptable, passable, up to the mark, all right, OK (*infml*), fair, average, competent, adequate, sufficient, suitable, proper.
🖃 unsatisfactory, unacceptable, inadequate.

satisfy *v* 1 GRATIFY, indulge, content, appease, please, delight, quench, slake, sate, satiate, surfeit. 2 *satisfy requirements*: meet, fulfil, discharge, settle, answer, fill, suffice, serve, qualify. 3 ASSURE, convince, persuade.
🖃 1 dissatisfy. 2 fail.

saturate *v* soak, steep, souse, drench, waterlog, impregnate, permeate, imbue, suffuse, fill.

saucy (*infml*) *adj* cheeky, impertinent, impudent, insolent, disrespectful, pert, forward, presumptuous, flippant.
🖃 polite, respectful.

saunter *v* stroll, amble, mosey (*infml*), mooch (*infml*), wander, ramble (*sl*), meander.
➤ *n* stroll, walk, constitutional, ramble.

savage *adj* wild, untamed, undomesticated, uncivilized, primitive, barbaric, barbarous, fierce, ferocious, vicious, beastly, cruel, inhuman, brutal, sadistic, bloodthirsty, bloody, murderous, pitiless, merciless, ruthless, harsh.

🔁 tame, civilized, humane, mild.
➤ *n* brute, beast, barbarian.
➤ *v* attack, bite, claw, tear, maul, mangle.

save *v* **1** ECONOMIZE, cut back, conserve, preserve, keep, retain, hold, reserve, store, lay up, set aside, put by, hoard, stash (*infml*), collect, gather. **2** RESCUE, deliver, liberate, free, salvage, recover, reclaim. **3** PROTECT, guard, screen, shield, safeguard, spare, prevent, hinder.
🔁 **1** spend, squander, waste, discard.
➤ *n* economy, thrift, discount, reduction, bargain, cut, conservation, preservation.
🔁 expense, waste, loss.

savings *n* capital, investments, nest egg, fund, store, reserves, resources.

saviour *n* rescuer, deliverer, redeemer, liberator, emancipator, guardian, protector, defender, champion.
🔁 destroyer.

savour *n* taste, flavour, smack, smell, tang, piquancy, salt, spice, relish, zest.
➤ *v* relish, enjoy, delight in, revel in, like, appreciate.
🔁 shrink from.

savoury *adj* **1** TASTY, appetizing, delicious, mouthwatering, luscious, palatable. **2** *savoury pancakes*: salty, spicy, aromatic, piquant, tangy.
🔁 **1** unappetizing, tasteless, insipid. **2** sweet.

saw

> *Kinds of saw include*: bandsaw, bench saw, chainsaw, circular saw, compass saw, coping saw, crosscut saw, fretsaw, hacksaw, handsaw, jigsaw, panel saw, power-driven saw, pruning saw, rabbet saw, radial-arm saw, ripsaw, scroll saw, tenon saw.

say *v* **1** EXPRESS, phrase, put, render, utter, voice, articulate, enunciate, pronounce, deliver, speak, orate (*fml*), recite, repeat, read, indicate. **2** ANSWER, reply, respond, rejoin, retort, exclaim, ejaculate, comment, remark, observe, mention, add, drawl, mutter, grunt. **3** TELL, instruct, order, communicate, convey, intimate, report, announce, declare, state, assert, affirm, maintain, claim, allege, rumour, suggest, imply, signify, reveal, disclose, divulge. **4** GUESS, estimate, reckon, judge, imagine, suppose, assume, presume, surmise.

> *Words for say include*: accuse, acknowledge, add, admit, admonish, advise, affirm, agree, allege, announce, answer, argue, ask, assert, assume, babble, banter, bark, bawl, beg, begin, bellow, blare, blaspheme, blurt, boast, brag, call, chant, chatter, claim, coax, command, comment, complain, conclude, confide, continue, contradict, correct, counter, croak, cry, curse, declare, demand, deny, describe, detail, disclose, dispute, divulge, echo, elaborate, elucidate, emphasize, enjoin, enquire, estimate, exclaim, expostulate, express, falter, finish, flounder, gasp, greet, groan, growl, grumble, grunt, guess, hint, howl, imagine, implore, imply, indicate, infer, inform, insinuate, instruct, interrogate, interrupt, intervene, intimate, jeer, jest, joke, laugh, lecture, lie, mention, mimic, moan, mock, mouth, mumble, murmur, mutter, nag, observe, offer, orate, order, persist, persuade, phrase, pipe, plead, point out, predict, press, presume, proclaim, profess, proffer, prompt, pronounce, propose, protest, query, question, quote, rage, rail, rant, read, reassure, rebuke, recite, recommend, reckon, rehearse, reiterate, rejoice, relate, remark, remonstrate, renounce, repeat, reply, report, respond, request, resolve, respond, retaliate, retort, retract, reveal, roar, scoff, scold, scream, screech, shout, shriek, snap, snarl, speak, specify, squeak, stammer, state, storm, stutter, submit, suggest, surmise, swear, sympathize, taunt, tease, tell, testify, thunder, urge, utter, venture, voice, volunteer, vow, whine, whisper, wonder, yell.

saying *n* adage, proverb, dictum, precept, axiom, aphorism, maxim, motto, slogan, phrase, expression, quotation, statement, remark.

scale¹ *n* ratio, proportion, measure, degree, extent, spread, reach, range, scope, compass, spectrum, gamut, sequence, series, progression, order, hierarchy, ranking, ladder, steps, gradation, graduation, calibration, register.
➤ *v* climb, ascend, mount, clamber, scramble, shin up, conquer, surmount.

scale² *n* encrustation, deposit, crust, layer, film, lamina, plate, flake, scurf.

scamp *n* rogue, rascal, scallywag, monkey, imp, devil.

scamper *v* scuttle, scurry, scoot, dart, dash, run, sprint, rush, hurry, hasten (*fml*), fly, romp, frolic, gambol.

scan *v* **1** EXAMINE, scrutinize, study, search, survey, sweep, investigate, check. **2** SKIM, glance at, flick through, thumb through.
➤ *n* screening, examination, scrutiny, search, probe, check, investigation, survey, review.

scandal *n* outrage, offence, outcry, uproar, furore, gossip, rumours, smear, dirt, discredit, dishonour, sleaze (*infml*), disgrace, shame, embarrassment, ignominy.

scandalize *v* shock, horrify, appal, dismay, disgust, repel, revolt, offend, affront, outrage.

scandalous *adj* shocking, appalling, atrocious, abominable, monstrous, unspeakable, outrageous, disgraceful, shameful, disreputable, infamous, improper, unseemly, defamatory, scurrilous, slanderous, libellous, untrue.

scanty *adj* deficient, short, inadequate, insufficient, scant, little, limited, restricted, narrow, poor, meagre, insubstantial, thin, skimpy, sparse, bare.
◨ adequate, sufficient, ample, plentiful, substantial.

scar *n* mark, lesion, wound, injury, blemish, disfigurement, stigma.
➤ *v* mark, disfigure, spoil, damage, brand, stigmatize.

scarce *adj* few, rare, infrequent, uncommon, unusual, sparse, scanty, insufficient, deficient, lacking.
◨ plentiful, common.

scarcely *adv* hardly, barely, only just.

scarcity *n* lack, shortage, dearth, deficiency, insufficiency, paucity, rareness, rarity, infrequency, uncommonness, sparseness, scantiness.
◨ glut, plenty, abundance, sufficiency, enough.

scare *v* frighten, startle, alarm, dismay, daunt, intimidate, unnerve, threaten, menace, terrorize, shock, appal, panic, terrify.
◨ reassure, calm.
➤ *n* fright, start, shock, alarm, panic, hysteria, terror.
◨ reassurance, comfort.

scared *adj* frightened, fearful, afraid, nervous, anxious, worried, startled, shaken, panic-stricken, terrified.
◨ confident, reassured.

scary *adj* frightening, alarming, daunting, intimidating, disturbing, shocking, horrifying, terrifying, hair-raising, bloodcurdling, spine-chilling, chilling, creepy, eerie, spooky (*infml*).

scathing *adj* sarcastic, scornful, critical, trenchant, cutting, biting, mordant, caustic, acid, vitriolic, bitter, harsh, brutal, savage, unsparing.
◨ complimentary.

scatter *v* disperse, dispel, dissipate, disband, disunite, separate, divide, break up, disintegrate, diffuse, broadcast, disseminate, spread, sprinkle, sow, strew, fling, shower.
◨ gather, collect.

scatterbrained *adj* forgetful, absent-minded, empty-headed, air-headed (*infml*), feather-brained, dizzy (*infml*), scatty (*infml*), flaky (*US infml*), ditsy (*US sl*), careless, inattentive, thoughtless, unreliable, irresponsible, frivolous.

F3 sensible, sober, efficient, careful.

scattering n sprinkling, few, handful, smattering.

F3 mass, abundance.

scavenge v forage, rummage, rake, search, scrounge.

scenario n outline, synopsis, summary, résumé, storyline, plot, scheme, plan, programme, projection, sequence, situation, scene.

scene n 1 PLACE, area, spot, locale, site, situation, position, whereabouts, location, locality, environment, milieu, setting, contact, background, backdrop, set, stage. **2** LANDSCAPE, panorama, view, vista, prospect, sight, spectacle, picture, tableau, pageant. **3** EPISODE, incident, part, division, act, clip. **4** *don't make a scene*: fuss, commotion, to-do (*infml*), performance, drama, exhibition, display, show.

scenery n landscape, terrain, panorama, view, vista, outlook, scene, background, setting, surroundings, backdrop, set.

scenic *adj* panoramic, picturesque, attractive, pretty, beautiful, grand, striking, impressive, spectacular, breathtaking, awe-inspiring.

F3 dull, dreary.

scent n 1 PERFUME, fragrance, aroma, bouquet, smell, odour. **2** *follow the scent*: track, trail.

F3 1 stink.

➤ v smell, sniff (out), nose (out), sense, perceive, detect, discern, recognize.

scented *adj* perfumed, fragrant, sweet-smelling, aromatic.

F3 malodorous, stinking.

sceptic n doubter, unbeliever, disbeliever, agnostic, atheist, rationalist, questioner, scoffer, cynic.

F3 believer.

sceptical *adj* doubting, doubtful, unconvinced, unbelieving, disbelieving, questioning, distrustful, mistrustful, hesitating, dubious, suspicious, scoffing, cynical, pessimistic.

F3 convinced, confident, trusting.

scepticism n doubt, unbelief, disbelief, agnosticism, atheism, rationalism, distrust, suspicion, cynicism, pessimism.

F3 belief, faith.

schedule n timetable, programme, agenda, diary, calendar, itinerary, plan, scheme, list, inventory, catalogue, table, form.

➤ v timetable, time, table, programme, plan, organize, arrange, appoint, assign, book, list.

schematic *adj* diagrammatic, representational, symbolic, illustrative, graphic.

scheme n 1 PROGRAMME, schedule, plan, project, idea, proposal, proposition, suggestion, draft, outline, blueprint, schema, diagram, chart, layout, pattern, design, shape, configuration, arrangement. **2** INTRIGUE, plot, conspiracy, device, stratagem, ruse, ploy, shift, manoeuvre, tactic(s), strategy, procedure, system, method.

➤ v plot, conspire, connive, collude, intrigue, machinate, manoeuvre, manipulate, pull strings, mastermind, plan, project, contrive, devise, frame, work out.

schism n 1 DIVISION, split, rift, rupture, break, breach, disunion, separation, severance, divide, estrangement, discord. **2** SPLINTER GROUP, faction, sect.

scholar n pupil, student, academic, intellectual, egghead (*infml*), boffin (*infml*), authority, expert.

F3 dunce, ignoramus.

scholarly *adj* learned, erudite (*fml*), lettered, academic, scholastic, school, intellectual, highbrow, bookish, studious, knowledgeable, well-read, analytical, scientific.

F3 uneducated, illiterate.

scholarship n 1 ERUDITION (*fml*), learnedness, learning, knowledge, wisdom, education, schooling. **2** *a* *scholarship to a public school*: grant, award, bursary, endowment, fellowship, exhibition.

school *n* college, academy, institute, institution, seminary, faculty, department, discipline, class, group, pupils, students.

➤ *v* educate, teach, instruct, tutor, coach, train, discipline, drill, verse, prime, prepare, indoctrinate.

schooling *n* education, book-learning, teaching, instruction, tuition, coaching, training, drill, preparation, grounding, guidance, indoctrination.

science *n* technology, discipline, specialization, knowledge, skill, proficiency, technique, art.

Sciences include: acoustics, aerodynamics, aeronautics, agricultural science, agriscience, anatomy, anthropology, archaeology, astronomy, astrophysics, behavioural science, biochemistry, biology, biophysics, botany, chemistry, chemurgy, climatology, computer science, cybernetics, diagnostics, dietetics, domestic science, dynamics, earth science, ecology, economics, electrodynamics, electronics, engineering, entomology, environmental science, food science, genetics, geochemistry, geographical science, geology, geophysics, graphology, hydraulics, information technology, inorganic chemistry, life science, linguistics, macrobiotics, materials science, mathematics, mechanical engineering, mechanics, medical science, metallurgy, meteorology, microbiology, mineralogy, morphology, natural science, nuclear physics, organic chemistry, ornithology, pathology, pharmacology, physics, physiology, political science, psychology, radiochemistry, robotics, sociology, space technology, telecommunications, thermodynamics, toxicology, ultrasonics, veterinary science, zoology.

Types of scientific instrument include: absorptiometer, barostat, cathode ray oscilloscope, centrifuge, chronograph, coherer, collimator, cryostat, decoherer, dephlegmator, dipleidoscope, electromyograph, electrosonde, eudiometer, fluoroscope, Fresnel lens, Geissler tube, heliograph, heliostat, hodoscope, humidistat, hydrophone, hydroscope, hydrostat, hygrograph, hygrostat, iconoscope, image converter, image tube, interferometer, microtome, nephograph, optical character reader, oscillograph, oscilloscope, pantograph, parametric amplifier, phonendoscope, radarscope, radiosonde, rheocord, rheostat, slide-rule, spectroscope, stactometer, stauroscope, strobe, stroboscope, tachistoscope, tachograph, teinoscope, telemeter, telethermoscope, tesla coil, thermostat, thyratron, torsion-balance, transformer, transponder, tunnel diode, vernier, zymoscope. *see also* **laboratory**; **measure**; **medical**.

---

scientific *adj* methodical, systematic, controlled, regulated, analytical, mathematical, exact, precise, accurate, scholarly, thorough.

scintillating *adj* sparkling, glittering, flashing, bright, shining, brilliant, dazzling, exciting, stimulating, lively, animated, vivacious, ebullient, witty.
🖪 dull.

scoff[1] *v* mock, ridicule, poke fun, taunt, tease, rib (*sl*), jeer, sneer, pooh-pooh, scorn, despise, revile, deride, belittle, disparage, knock (*infml*).
🖪 praise, compliment, flatter.

scoff[2] *v* eat, consume, devour, put away (*infml*), gobble, guzzle, wolf (*infml*), snarf (*infml*), bolt, gulp.
🖪 fast, abstain.

scold *v* chide, tell off (*infml*), tick off (*infml*), reprimand, reprove, rebuke, take to task, admonish, upbraid, reproach,

blame, censure, lecture, nag.
🖪 praise, commend.

scolding n castigation (*fml*), telling-off (*infml*), ticking-off (*infml*), dressing-down (*infml*), reprimand, reproof, rebuke, lecture, talking-to (*infml*), earful (*infml*), earbashing (*infml*).
🖪 praise, commendation.

scoop n 1 LADLE, spoon, dipper, bailer, bucket, shovel. 2 EXCLUSIVE, coup, inside story, revelation, exposé, sensation, latest (*infml*).
➤ v gouge, scrape, hollow, empty, excavate, dig, shovel, ladle, spoon, dip, bail.

scope n 1 RANGE, compass, field, area, sphere, ambit, terms of reference, confines, reach, extent, span, breadth, coverage. 2 *scope for improvement*: room, space, capacity, elbow-room, latitude, leeway, freedom, liberty, opportunity.

scorch v burn, singe, char, blacken, scald, roast, sear, parch, shrivel, wither.

scorching adj burning, boiling, baking, roasting, sizzling, blistering, sweltering, torrid, tropical, searing, red-hot.

score n 1 RESULT, total, sum, tally, points, marks. 2 SCRATCH, line, groove, mark, nick, notch.
➤ v 1 RECORD, register, chalk up, notch up, count, total, make, earn, gain, achieve, attain, win, have the advantage, have the edge, be one up. 2 SCRATCH, scrape, graze, scuff, mark, groove, gouge, cut, incise, engrave, indent, nick, slash.

scorn n contempt, scornfulness, disdain, sneering, derision, mockery, ridicule, sarcasm, disparagement, disgust.
🖪 admiration, respect.
➤ v despise, look down on, disdain, sneer at, scoff at, deride, mock, laugh at, slight, spurn, refuse, reject, dismiss.
🖪 admire, respect.

scornful adj contemptuous, disdainful, supercilious, haughty,

arrogant, sneering, scoffing, derisive, mocking, jeering, sarcastic, scathing, disparaging, insulting, slighting, dismissive.
🖪 admiring, respectful.

scour¹ v scrape, abrade (*fml*), rub, polish, burnish, scrub, clean, wash, cleanse, purge, flush.

scour² v search, hunt, comb, drag, ransack, rummage, forage, rake.

scourge n 1 AFFLICTION, misfortune, torment, terror, bane, evil, curse, plague, penalty, punishment. 2 WHIP, lash.
🖪 1 blessing, godsend, boon.
➤ v 1 AFFLICT, torment, curse, plague, devastate, punish, chastise, discipline. 2 WHIP, flog, beat, lash, cane, flail, thrash.

scout v spy out, reconnoitre, explore, investigate, check out, survey, case (*sl*), spy, snoop, search, seek, hunt, probe, look, watch, observe.
➤ n spy, reconnoitre, vanguard, outrider, escort, lookout, recruiter, spotter.

scowl v, n frown, glower, glare, grimace, pout, moue.
🖪 smile, grin, beam.

scraggy adj scrawny, skinny, thin, lean, lanky, bony, angular, gaunt, emaciated, undernourished, wasted.
🖪 plump, sleek.

scramble v 1 CLIMB, scale, clamber, crawl, shuffle, scrabble, grope. 2 RUSH, hurry, hasten (*fml*), run, push, jostle, struggle, strive, vie, contend.
➤ n rush, hurry, race, dash, hustle, bustle, commotion, confusion, muddle, struggle, free-for-all, mêlée.

scrap¹ n bit, piece, fragment, part, fraction, crumb, morsel, bite, mouthful, sliver, shred, snippet, atom, iota, grain, particle, mite, trace, vestige, remnant, leftover, waste, junk.
➤ v discard, throw away, jettison, shed, abandon, drop, dump, ditch (*sl*), cancel, axe, demolish, break up, write off.
🖪 recover, restore.

scrap² n fight, scuffle, brawl, dust-up

(*infml*), quarrel, row, argument, squabble, wrangle, dispute, disagreement.

Ea peace, agreement.

➤ *v* fight, brawl, quarrel, argue, fall out, squabble, bicker, wrangle, disagree.

Ea agree.

scrape *v* grate, grind, rasp, file, abrade, scour, rub, clean, remove, erase, scrabble, claw, scratch, graze, skin, bark, scuff.

scrappy *adj* bitty, disjointed, piecemeal, fragmentary, incomplete, sketchy, superficial, slapdash, slipshod.

Ea complete, finished.

scratch *v* claw, gouge, score, mark, cut, incise, etch, engrave, scrape, rub, scuff, graze, gash, lacerate.

➤ *n* mark, line, scrape, scuff, abrasion, graze, gash, laceration.

scrawny *adj* scraggy, skinny, thin, lean, lanky, angular, bony, underfed, undernourished, emaciated, wasted.

Ea fat, plump.

scream *v, n* shriek, screech, cry, shout, yell, bawl, roar, howl, wail, squeal, yelp.

screen *v* 1 *screen a film*: show, present, broadcast. 2 SHIELD, protect, safeguard, defend, guard, cover, mask, veil, cloak, shroud, hide, conceal, shelter, shade. 3 SORT, grade, sift, sieve, filter, process, evaluate, gauge, examine, scan, vet.

Ea 2 uncover, expose.

➤ *n* partition, divider, shield, guard, cover, mask, veil, cloak, shroud, concealment, shelter, shade, awning, canopy, net, mesh.

screw *v* fasten, adjust, tighten, contract, compress, squeeze, extract, extort, force, constrain, pressurize, turn, wind, twist, wring, distort, wrinkle.

scribble *v* write, pen, jot, dash off, scrawl, doodle.

scribe *n* writer, copyist, amanuensis, secretary, clerk.

script *n* 1 *a film script*: text, lines, words, dialogue, screenplay, libretto, book. 2 WRITING, handwriting, hand,

longhand, calligraphy, letters, manuscript, copy.

scrounge *v* cadge, beg, sponge.

scrounger *n* cadger, sponger, parasite.

scrub *v* 1 *scrub the floor*: rub, brush, clean, wash, cleanse, scour. 2 (*infml*) ABOLISH, cancel, delete, rub out, abandon, give up, drop, discontinue.

scruffy *adj* untidy, messy, unkempt, dishevelled, bedraggled, run-down, tattered, shabby, disreputable, worn-out, ragged, seedy, squalid, slovenly.

Ea tidy, well-dressed.

scruple *n* reluctance, hesitation, doubt, qualm, misgiving, uneasiness, difficulty, perplexity.

➤ *v* hesitate, think twice, hold back, shrink.

scruples *n* standards, principles, morals, ethics.

scrupulous *adj* 1 PAINSTAKING, meticulous, conscientious, careful, rigorous, strict, exact, precise, minute, nice. 2 PRINCIPLED, moral, ethical, honourable, upright.

Ea 1 superficial, careless, reckless. 2 unscrupulous, unprincipled.

scrutinize *v* examine, inspect, study, scan, analyse, sift, investigate, probe, search, explore.

scrutiny *n* examination, inspection, study, analysis, investigation, inquiry, search, exploration.

scuff *v* scrape, scratch, graze, abrade, rub, brush, drag.

scuffle *v* fight, scrap (*infml*), tussle, brawl, grapple, struggle, contend, clash.

➤ *n* fight, scrap (*infml*), tussle, brawl, fray, set-to, rumpus, commotion, disturbance, affray.

sculpt *v* sculpture, carve, chisel, hew, cut, model, mould, cast, form, shape, fashion.

sculpture

Types of sculpture include: bas-relief, bronze, bust, carving, caryatid, cast, effigy, figure, figurine, group, head, herm, high-relief, maquette, marble, moulding, plaster cast, relief, statue, statuette, telamon, waxwork.

scum *n* froth, foam, film, impurities, dross, dregs, rubbish, trash.

scurrilous *adj* rude, vulgar, coarse, foul, obscene, indecent, salacious, offensive, abusive, insulting, disparaging, defamatory, slanderous, libellous, scandalous.
🔳 polite, courteous, complimentary.

scurry *v* dash, rush, hurry, hasten (*fml*), bustle, scramble, scuttle, scamper, scoot, dart, run, sprint, trot, race, fly, skim, scud.

sea *n* **1** OCEAN, main, deep, briny (*infml*). **2** *a sea of faces*: multitude, abundance, profusion, mass.

> *The world's oceans and largest seas include*: Pacific Ocean, Atlantic Ocean, Indian Ocean, Arctic Ocean, Antarctic (Southern) Ocean, South China Sea, Caribbean Sea, Mediterranean Sea, Bering Sea, Gulf of Mexico, Sea of Okhotsk.

➤ *adj* marine, maritime, ocean, oceanic, salt, saltwater, aquatic, seafaring.
🔳 land, air.
◇ **at sea** adrift, lost, confused, bewildered, baffled, puzzled, flummoxed (*infml*), perplexed, mystified.

seafaring *adj* sea-going, ocean-going, sailing, nautical, naval, marine, maritime.

seal *v* **1** *seal a jar*: close, shut, stop, plug, cork, waterproof, fasten, secure. **2** SETTLE, conclude, finalize, stamp.
🔳 **1** open, unseal.
➤ *n* **1** LID, stopper, plug, cork. **2** STAMP, signet, insignia, imprimatur, validation, authentication, assurance, attestation, confirmation, ratification.
◇ **seal off** block up, close off, shut off, fence off, cut off, segregate, isolate, quarantine.
🔳 open up.

seam *n* **1** JOIN, joint, weld, closure, line. **2** *coal seam*: layer, stratum, vein, lode.

seamy *adj* disreputable, sleazy, sordid, squalid, unsavoury, rough, dark, low, nasty, unpleasant.
🔳 respectable, wholesome, pleasant.

sear *v* burn, scorch, brown, fry, sizzle, seal, cauterize, brand, parch, shrivel, wither.

search *v* seek, look, hunt, rummage, rifle, ransack, scour, comb, sift, probe, explore, frisk (*sl*), examine, scrutinize, inspect, check, investigate, inquire, pry.
➤ *n* hunt, quest, pursuit, rummage, probe, exploration, examination, scrutiny, inspection, investigation, inquiry, research, survey.

searching *adj* penetrating, piercing, keen, sharp, close, intent, probing, thorough, minute.
🔳 vague, superficial.

seaside *n* coast, shore, front, strand, beach, sands.

season *n* period, spell, phase, term, time, span, interval.
➤ *v* **1** *season food*: flavour, spice, salt. **2** AGE, mature, ripen, harden, toughen, train, prepare, condition, treat, temper.

seasonable *adj* timely, well-timed, welcome, opportune, convenient, suitable, appropriate, fitting.
🔳 unseasonable, inopportune.

seasoned *adj* mature, experienced, practised, well-versed, veteran, old, hardened, toughened, conditioned, acclimatized, weathered.
🔳 inexperienced, novice.

seasoning *n* flavouring, spice, condiment, salt, pepper, relish, sauce, dressing.

seat *n* **1** CHAIR, bench, pew, stool, throne. **2** *country seat*: residence, abode, house, mansion. **3** PLACE, site, situation, location, headquarters, centre, heart, hub, axis, source, cause, bottom, base, foundation, footing, ground.
➤ *v* sit, place, set, locate, install, fit, fix,

settle, accommodate, hold, contain, take.

seating n seats, chairs, places, room, accommodation.

secluded adj private, cloistered, sequestered, shut away, cut off, isolated, lonely, solitary, remote, out-of-the-way, sheltered, hidden, concealed.
🖃 public, accessible.

seclusion n privacy, retirement, retreat, isolation, solitude, remoteness, shelter, hiding, concealment.

second¹ adj duplicate, twin, double, repeated, additional, further, extra, supplementary, alternative, other, alternate, next, following, subsequent, succeeding, secondary, subordinate, lower, inferior, lesser, supporting.
➤ n helper, assistant, backer, supporter.
➤ v approve, agree with, endorse, back, support, help, assist, aid, further, advance, forward, promote, encourage.

second² n minute, tick (*infml*), moment, mo (*infml*), instant, flash, jiffy (*infml*).

secondary adj subsidiary, subordinate, lower, inferior, lesser, minor, unimportant, ancillary, auxiliary, supporting, relief, back-up, reserve, spare, extra, second, alternative, indirect, derived, resulting.
🖃 primary, main, major.

second-hand adj used, old, worn, hand-me-down, pre-owned, borrowed, derivative, secondary, indirect, vicarious.
🖃 new.

second-rate adj inferior, substandard, second-class, second-best, poor, low-grade, low-rent (*sl*), shoddy, cheap, tawdry, mediocre, undistinguished, uninspired, uninspiring.
🖃 first-rate.

secrecy n privacy, seclusion, confidentiality, confidence, covertness, concealment, disguise, camouflage, furtiveness, surreptitiousness, stealthiness, stealth, mystery.
🖃 openness.

secret adj 1 PRIVATE, discreet, covert, hidden, concealed, unseen, shrouded, covered, disguised, camouflaged, undercover, furtive, surreptitious, stealthy, sly, underhand, under-the-counter, hole-and-corner, cloak-and-dagger, clandestine, underground, backstairs, back-door. 2 CLASSIFIED, restricted, confidential, hush-hush (*infml*), unpublished, undisclosed, unrevealed, unknown. 3 CRYPTIC, mysterious, occult, arcane, recondite, deep. 4 SECRETIVE, close, retired, secluded, out-of-the-way.
🖃 1 public, open. 2 well-known.
➤ n confidence, mystery, enigma, code, key, formula, recipe.

secretary n personal assistant, PA, typist, stenographer, clerk.

secrete¹ v hide, conceal, stash away (*infml*), bury, cover, screen, shroud, veil, disguise, take, appropriate.
🖃 uncover, reveal, disclose.

secrete² v exude, discharge, release, give off, emit, emanate, produce.

secretion n exudation (*fml*), discharge, release, emission.

secretive adj tight-lipped, close, cagey (*infml*), uncommunicative, unforthcoming, reticent, reserved, withdrawn, quiet, deep, cryptic, enigmatic.
🖃 open, communicative, forthcoming.

sect n denomination, cult, division, subdivision, group, splinter group, faction, camp, wing, party, school.

sectarian adj factional, partisan, cliquish, exclusive, narrow, limited, parochial, insular, narrow-minded, bigoted, fanatical, doctrinaire, dogmatic, rigid.
🖃 non-sectarian, cosmopolitan, broad-minded.

section n division, subdivision, chapter, paragraph, passage, instalment, part, component, fraction, fragment, bit, piece, slice, portion, segment, sector, zone, district, area,

sector _n_ region, department, branch, wing.
◾ whole.

sector _n_ zone, district, quarter, area, region, section, division, subdivision, part.
◾ whole.

secular _adj_ lay, temporal, worldly, earthly, civil, state, non-religious, profane.
◾ religious.

secure _adj_ **1** SAFE, unharmed, undamaged, protected, sheltered, shielded, immune, impregnable, fortified, fast, tight, fastened, locked, fixed, immovable, stable, steady, solid, firm, well-founded, reliable, dependable, steadfast, certain, sure, conclusive, definite. **2** CONFIDENT, assured, reassured.
◾ **1** insecure, vulnerable. **2** uneasy, ill at ease.
➤ _v_ **1** OBTAIN, acquire, gain, get. **2** FASTEN, attach, fix, make fast, tie, moor, lash, chain, lock (up), padlock, bolt, batten down, nail, rivet.
◾ **1** lose. **2** unfasten.

security _n_ **1** SAFETY, immunity, asylum, sanctuary, refuge, cover, protection, defence, surveillance, safekeeping, preservation, care, custody. **2** _security for a loan_: collateral, surety, pledge, guarantee, warranty, assurance, insurance, precautions, safeguards. **3** CONFIDENCE, conviction, certainty, positiveness.
◾ **1** insecurity.

sedate _adj_ staid, dignified, solemn, grave, serious, sober, decorous, proper, seemly, demure, composed, unruffled, serene, tranquil, calm, quiet, cool, collected, imperturbable, unflappable (_infml_), deliberate, slow-moving.
◾ undignified, lively, agitated.

sedative _adj_ calming, soothing, anodyne, lenitive, tranquillizing, relaxing, soporific, depressant.
◾ rousing.
➤ _n_ tranquillizer, sleeping pill, narcotic, barbiturate.

sedentary _adj_ sitting, seated, desk-bound, inactive, still, stationary, immobile, unmoving.
◾ active.

sediment _n_ deposit, residue, grounds, lees, dregs.

sedition _n_ agitation, rabble-rousing, subversion, disloyalty, treachery, treason, insubordination, mutiny, rebellion, revolt.
◾ calm, loyalty.

seduce _v_ entice, lure, allure, attract, tempt, charm, beguile, ensnare, lead astray, mislead, deceive, corrupt, dishonour, ruin.
◾ repel.

seduction _n_ enticement, lure, attraction, temptation, come-on (_infml_), corruption, ruin.

seductive _adj_ enticing, alluring, attractive, tempting, tantalizing, inviting, come-hither (_infml_), flirtatious, sexy, provocative, beguiling, captivating, bewitching, irresistible.
◾ unattractive, repulsive.

see _v_ **1** PERCEIVE, glimpse, discern, spot, make out, distinguish, identify, sight, notice, observe, watch, view, look at, mark, note. **2** IMAGINE, picture, visualize, envisage, foresee, anticipate. **3** _I see your point_: understand, comprehend, grasp, fathom, follow, realize, recognize, appreciate, regard, consider, deem. **4** DISCOVER, find out, learn, ascertain, determine, decide. **5** LEAD, usher, accompany, escort, court, go out with, date. **6** VISIT, consult, interview, meet.
◇ **see to** attend to, deal with, take care of, look after, arrange, organize, manage, do, fix, repair, sort out.

seed _n_ pip, stone, kernel, nucleus, grain, germ, sperm, ovum, egg, ovule, spawn, embryo, source, start, beginning.

seedy _adj_ **1** SHABBY, scruffy, tatty, mangy, sleazy, squalid, grotty (_infml_), crummy (_sl_), run-down, dilapidated, decaying. **2** UNWELL, ill, sick, poorly, ailing, off-colour, under the weather (_infml_).
◾ **2** well.

seek v look for, search for, hunt, pursue, follow, inquire, ask, invite, request, solicit, petition, entreat, want, desire, aim, aspire, try, attempt, endeavour, strive.

seem v appear, look, feel, sound, pretend to be.

seeming adj apparent, ostensible, outward, superficial, surface, quasi-, pseudo, specious.
E3 real.

seep v ooze, leak, exude, well, trickle, dribble, percolate, permeate, soak.

seethe v 1 BOIL, simmer, bubble, effervesce, fizz, foam, froth, ferment, rise, swell, surge, teem, swarm. 2 RAGE, fume, smoulder, storm.

see-through adj transparent, translucent, sheer, fine, filmy, gauzy, gossamer(y), flimsy.
E3 opaque.

segment n section, division, compartment, part, bit, piece, slice, portion, wedge.
E3 whole.

segregate v separate, keep apart, cut off, isolate, quarantine, set apart, exclude.
E3 unite, join.

segregation n separation, isolation, quarantine, apartheid, discrimination.
E3 unification.

seize v grab, snatch, grasp, clutch, grip, hold, take, confiscate, impound, appropriate, commandeer, hijack, annex, abduct, catch, capture, arrest, apprehend, nab (*infml*), nick (*sl*), collar (*infml*).
E3 let go, release, hand back.

seizure n 1 FIT, attack, convulsion, paroxysm, spasm. 2 TAKING, confiscation, appropriation, hijack, annexation, abduction, capture, arrest, apprehension.
E3 2 release, liberation.

seldom adv rarely, infrequently, occasionally, hardly ever.
E3 often, usually.

select v choose, pick, single out, decide on, appoint, elect, prefer, opt for.
➤ adj selected, choice, top, prime, first-class, first-rate, hand-picked, elite, exclusive, limited, privileged, special, excellent, superior, posh (*infml*), up-market.
E3 second-rate, ordinary, general.

selection n choice, pick, option, preference, assortment, variety, range, line-up, miscellany, medley, potpourri, collection, anthology.

selective adj particular, choosy (*infml*), fussy (*infml*), careful, discerning, discriminating.
E3 indiscriminate.

self n ego, personality, identity, person.

self-centred adj selfish, self-seeking, self-serving, self-interested, egotistic(al), narcissistic, self-absorbed, egocentric.
E3 altruistic.

self-confident adj confident, self-reliant, self-assured, assured, self-possessed, cool, fearless.
E3 unsure, self-conscious.

self-conscious adj uncomfortable, ill at ease, awkward, embarrassed, shamefaced, sheepish, shy, bashful, coy, retiring, shrinking, self-effacing, nervous, insecure.
E3 natural, unaffected, confident.

self-control n calmness, composure, cool (*infml*), patience, self-restraint, restraint, self-denial, temperance, self-discipline, self-mastery, willpower.

self-denial n moderation, temperance, abstemiousness, asceticism, self-sacrifice, unselfishness, selflessness.
E3 self-indulgence.

self-evident adj obvious, manifest, clear, plain, undeniable, axiomatic, unquestionable, incontrovertible, inescapable.

self-government n autonomy, independence, home rule, democracy.
E3 subjection.

self-indulgent *adj* hedonistic, dissolute, dissipated, profligate, extravagant, intemperate, immoderate. **Ea** abstemious.

selfish *adj* self-interested, self-seeking, self-serving, mean, miserly, mercenary, greedy, covetous, self-centred, egocentric, egotistic(al). **Ea** unselfish, selfless, generous, considerate.

selfless *adj* unselfish, altruistic, self-denying, self-sacrificing, generous, philanthropic. **Ea** selfish, self-centred.

self-respect *n* pride, dignity, self-esteem, self-assurance, self-confidence.

self-righteous *adj* smug, complacent, superior, goody-goody (*infml*), pious, sanctimonious, holier-than-thou, pietistic, hypocritical, pharisaical.

self-sacrifice *n* self-denial, self-renunciation, selflessness, altruism, unselfishness, generosity. **Ea** selfishness.

self-satisfied *adj* smug, smart, complacent, self-congratulatory, self-righteous. **Ea** humble.

self-styled *adj* self-appointed, professed, so-called, would-be.

self-supporting *adj* self-sufficient, self-financing, independent, self-reliant. **Ea** dependent.

sell *v* barter, exchange, trade, auction, vend, retail, stock, handle, deal in, trade in, traffic in, merchandise, hawk, peddle, push, advertise, promote, market. **Ea** buy.

seller *n* vendor, merchant, trader, supplier, dealer, stockist. **Ea** buyer, purchaser.

Types of seller include: agent, auctioneer, bagman, barrow-boy, broker, cold caller, colporteur, commercial traveller, costermonger, dealer, demonstrator, door-to-door salesman/saleswoman, estate agent, factor, hawker, huckster, jobber, knight of the road, market trader, merchandiser, milklady, milkman, pedlar, peddler (*US*), rep (*infml*), representative, retailer, sales assistant, sales clerk, sales executive, saleslady, salesman, salesperson, saleswoman, sales staff, shop assistant, shopkeeper, store clerk, storekeeper, street trader, tallyman, telephone salesperson, ticket agent, tout, tradesman, tradeswoman, traveller, wholesaler. *see also* **shop**.

semblance *n* appearance, air, show, pretence, guise, mask, front, façade, veneer, apparition, image, resemblance, likeness, similarity.

send *v* **1** POST, mail, dispatch, consign, remit, forward, convey, deliver. **2** TRANSMIT, broadcast, communicate. **3** PROPEL, drive, move, throw, fling, hurl, launch, fire, shoot, discharge, emit, direct.
◊ **send for** summon, call for, request, order, command. **Ea** dismiss.
◊ **send up** (*infml*) satirize, mock, ridicule, parody, take off (*infml*), mimic, imitate.

send-off *n* farewell, leave-taking, departure, start, goodbye. **Ea** arrival.

senile *adj* old, aged, doddering, decrepit, failing, confused.

senior *adj* older, elder, higher, superior, high-ranking, major, chief. **Ea** junior.

seniority *n* priority, precedence, rank, standing, status, age, superiority, importance.

sensation *n* **1** FEELING, sense, impression, perception, awareness, consciousness, emotion. **2** *the report caused a sensation*: commotion, stir, agitation, excitement, thrill, furore, outrage, scandal.

sensational *adj* **1** EXCITING, thrilling, electrifying, breathtaking, startling,

jaw-dropping (*infml*), amazing, astounding, staggering, dramatic, spectacular, impressive, exceptional, excellent, wonderful, marvellous, smashing (*infml*). **2** SCANDALOUS, shocking, horrifying, revealing, melodramatic, lurid.
F3 **1** ordinary, run-of-the-mill.

sense *n* **1** FEELING, sensation, impression, perception, awareness, consciousness, appreciation, faculty. **2** REASON, logic, mind, brain(s), wit(s), wisdom, intelligence, cleverness, understanding, discernment, judgement, intuition, nous (*sl*). **3** MEANING, significance, definition, interpretation, implication, point, purpose, substance.
F3 **2** foolishness. **3** nonsense.
➤ *v* feel, suspect, intuit, perceive, detect, notice, observe, realize, appreciate, understand, comprehend, grasp.

senseless *adj* **1** FOOLISH, stupid, unwise, silly, idiotic, mad, crazy, daft (*infml*), ridiculous, ludicrous, absurd, meaningless, nonsensical, fatuous, irrational, illogical, unreasonable, pointless, purposeless, futile. **2** UNCONSCIOUS, out, stunned, anaesthetized, deadened, numb, unfeeling.
F3 **1** sensible, meaningful. **2** conscious.

sensible *adj* wise, prudent, judicious, well-advised, clued-up (*infml*), shrewd, far-sighted, intelligent, level-headed, down-to-earth, commonsense, sober, sane, rational, logical, reasonable, realistic, practical, functional, sound.
F3 senseless, foolish, unwise.

sensitive *adj* **1** SUSCEPTIBLE, vulnerable, impressionable, tender, emotional, thin-skinned, touchy (*infml*), temperamental, irritable, sensitized, responsive, aware, perceptive, discerning, appreciative. **2** DELICATE, fine, exact, precise, accurate.
F3 **1** insensitive, thick-skinned. **2** imprecise, approximate.

sensual *adj* self-indulgent,

voluptuous, worldly, physical, animal, carnal, fleshly, bodily, sexual, erotic, sexy, lustful, randy (*infml*), horny (*sl*), lecherous, lewd, licentious.
F3 ascetic.

sensuous *adj* pleasurable, gratifying, voluptuous, rich, lush, luxurious, sumptuous.
F3 ascetic, plain, simple.

sentence *n* judgement, decision, verdict, condemnation, ruling, pronouncement, decree, order.
➤ *v* judge, pass judgement on, condemn, doom, punish, penalize.

sentiment *n* **1** THOUGHT, idea, feeling, opinion, view, judgement, belief, persuasion, attitude. **2** EMOTION, sensibility, tenderness, soft-heartedness, romanticism, sentimentality, mawkishness.

sentimental *adj* tender, soft-hearted, emotional, gushing, touchy-feely (*infml*), touching, pathetic, tear-jerking, weepy (*infml*), maudlin, mawkish, nostalgic, romantic, lovey-dovey (*infml*), slushy, mushy, sloppy, schmaltzy, soppy, corny (*infml*).
F3 unsentimental, realistic, cynical.

sentry *n* sentinel, guard, picket, watchman, watch, lookout.

separable *adj* divisible, detachable, removable, distinguishable, distinct.
F3 inseparable.

separate *v* divide, sever, part, split (up), divorce, part company, diverge, disconnect, uncouple, disunite, disaffiliate, disentangle, segregate, isolate, cut off, abstract, remove, detach, withdraw, secede.
F3 join, unite, combine.
➤ *adj* single, individual, particular, independent, alone, solitary, isolated, segregated, apart, divorced, divided, disunited, disconnected, disjointed, detached, unattached, unconnected, unrelated, different, disparate, distinct, discrete, several, sundry.
F3 together, attached.

separation *n* division, severance,

parting, leave-taking, farewell, split-up, break-up, divorce, split, rift, divide, gap, divergence, disconnection, dissociation, disengagement, estrangement, segregation, isolation, detachment.
E3 unification.

septic *adj* infected, poisoned, festering, putrefying, putrid.

sequel *n* follow-up, continuation, development, result, consequence, outcome, issue, upshot, pay-off, end, conclusion.

sequence *n* succession, series, run, progression, chain, string, train, line, procession, order, arrangement, course, track, cycle, set.

serene *adj* calm, tranquil, cool, composed, placid, untroubled, undisturbed, still, quiet, peaceful.
E3 troubled, disturbed.

series *n* set, cycle, succession, sequence, run, progression, chain, string, line, train, order, arrangement, course.

serious *adj* 1 IMPORTANT, significant, weighty, momentous, crucial, critical, urgent, pressing, acute, grave, worrying, difficult, dangerous, grim, severe, deep, far-reaching. 2 UNSMILING, long-faced, humourless, solemn, sober, stern, thoughtful, pensive, earnest, sincere.
E3 1 trivial, slight. 2 smiling, facetious, frivolous.

sermon *n* address, discourse, lecture, harangue, homily, talking-to (*infml*).

serrated *adj* toothed, notched, indented, jagged.
E3 smooth.

servant *n* attendant, retainer, hireling, menial, skivvy (*infml*), help, helper, assistant, ancillary.
E3 master, mistress.

Kinds of servant include: au pair, barmaid, barman, batman, bell-hop (*US*), boots, butler, care assistant, carer, chambermaid, char (*infml*), charlady, chauffeur, chauffeuse, chef,

cleaner, coachman, commissionaire, cook, daily (*infml*), dogsbody (*infml*), domestic, domestic help, drudge, equerry, errand boy, factotum, fag, flunkey, footman, governess, groom, henchman, henchperson, henchwoman, home help, house boy, housekeeper, housemaid, kitchen-maid, lackey, lady-in-waiting, lady's maid, maid, manservant, menial, nanny, ostler, page, page boy, parlourmaid, scullery maid, scullion, seneschal, slave, steward, stewardess, tweeny (*infml*), valet, waiter, waitress, wet nurse.

serve *v* 1 WAIT ON, attend, minister to, work for, help, aid, assist, benefit, further. 2 *serve a purpose*: fulfil, complete, answer, satisfy, discharge, perform, act, function. 3 DISTRIBUTE, dole out, mete out, present, deliver, provide, supply.

service *n* 1 EMPLOYMENT, work, labour, business, duty, function, performance. 2 USE, usefulness, utility, advantage, benefit, help, assistance. 3 SERVICING, maintenance, overhaul, check. 4 *church service*: worship, observance, ceremony, rite.
➤ *v* maintain, overhaul, check, repair, recondition, tune.

serviceable *adj* usable, useful, helpful, profitable, advantageous, beneficial, utilitarian, simple, plain, unadorned, strong, tough, durable, hard-wearing, dependable, efficient, functional, practical, convenient.
E3 unserviceable, unusable.

servile *adj* obsequious, sycophantic, toadying, cringing, fawning, grovelling, bootlicking (*infml*), slavish, subservient, subject, submissive, humble, abject, low, mean, base, menial.
E3 assertive, aggressive.

session *n* sitting, hearing, meeting, assembly, convention, conference, discussion, period, time, term, semester, year.

set *v* 1 PUT, place, locate, situate,

position, arrange, prepare, lodge, fix, stick, park, deposit. **2** SCHEDULE, appoint, designate, specify, name, prescribe, ordain, assign, allocate, impose, fix, establish, determine, decide, conclude, settle, resolve. **3** ADJUST, regulate, synchronize, co-ordinate. **4** *the sun sets*: go down, sink, dip, subside, disappear, vanish. **5** CONGEAL, thicken, gel, stiffen, solidify, harden, crystallize.

F3 4 rise.

➤ *n* batch, series, sequence, kit, outfit, compendium, assortment, collection, class, category, group, band, gang, crowd, circle, clique, faction.

➤ *adj* scheduled, appointed, arranged, prepared, prearranged, fixed, established, definite, decided, agreed, settled, firm, strict, rigid, inflexible, prescribed, formal, conventional, traditional, customary, usual, routine, regular, standard, stock, stereotyped, hackneyed.

F3 movable, free, spontaneous, undecided.

◇ **set about** begin, start, embark on, undertake, tackle, attack.

◇ **set aside 1** PUT ASIDE, lay aside, keep (back), save, reserve, set apart, separate, select, earmark. **2** ANNUL, abrogate, cancel, revoke, reverse, overturn, overrule, reject, discard.

◇ **set back** delay, hold up, slow, retard, hinder, impede.

◇ **set off 1** LEAVE, depart, set out, start (out), begin. **2** DETONATE, light, ignite, touch off, trigger off, explode. **3** DISPLAY, show off, enhance, contrast.

◇ **set on** set upon, attack, turn on, go for, fall upon, lay into, beat up (*infml*).

◇ **set out 1** LEAVE, depart, set off, start (out), begin. **2** LAY OUT, arrange, display, exhibit, present, describe, explain.

◇ **set up** raise, elevate, erect, build, construct, assemble, compose, form, create, establish, institute, found, inaugurate, initiate, begin, start, introduce, organize, arrange, prepare.

setback *n* delay, hold-up, problem, snag, hitch, hiccup, reverse, upset,

misfortune, whammy (*infml*), disappointment, defeat.

F3 boost, advance, help, advantage.

setting *n* mounting, frame, surroundings, milieu, environment, background, context, perspective, period, position, location, locale, site, scene, scenery.

settle *v* **1** ARRANGE, order, adjust, reconcile, resolve, complete, conclude. **2** SINK, subside, drop, fall, descend, land, alight. **3** CHOOSE, appoint, fix, establish, determine, decide, agree, confirm. **4** COLONIZE, occupy, populate, people, inhabit, live, reside. **5** *settle a bill*: pay, clear, discharge.

settlement *n* **1** RESOLUTION, agreement, arrangement, decision, conclusion, termination, satisfaction. **2** PAYMENT, clearance, clearing, discharge. **3** COLONY, outpost, community, kibbutz, camp, encampment, hamlet, village.

settler *n* colonist, colonizer, pioneer, frontiersman, frontierswoman, planter, immigrant, incomer, newcomer, squatter.

F3 native.

set-up *n* system, structure, organization, arrangement, business, conditions, circumstances.

sever *v* cut, cleave, split, rend, part, separate, divide, cut off, amputate, detach, disconnect, disjoin, disunite, dissociate, estrange, alienate, break off, dissolve, end, terminate.

F3 join, unite, combine, attach.

several *adj* some, many, various, assorted, sundry, diverse, different, distinct, separate, particular, individual.

severe *adj* **1** STERN, disapproving, sober, strait-laced, button-down (*infml*), strict, rigid, unbending, harsh, tough, hard, difficult, demanding, arduous, punishing, rigorous, grim, forbidding, cruel, biting, cutting, scathing, pitiless, merciless, oppressive, relentless, inexorable, acute, bitter, intense, extreme, fierce, violent, distressing, serious, grave, critical, dangerous. **2**

PLAIN, simple, unadorned, stark, unembellished, functional, restrained, austere, ascetic.

☒ **1** kind, compassionate, sympathetic, lenient, mild. **2** decorated, ornate.

sew *v* stitch, tack, baste, hem, darn, embroider.

sex *n* **1** GENDER, sexuality. **2** SEXUAL INTERCOURSE, intercourse, sexual relations, copulation, coitus, lovemaking, fornication, reproduction, union, intimacy.

sexual *adj* sex, reproductive, procreative, genital, coital, venereal, carnal, sensual, erotic.

sexy *adj* sensual, voluptuous, nubile, beddable (*infml*), horny (*sl*), seductive, inviting, flirtatious, arousing, provoking, provocative, titillating, pornographic, erotic, salacious, suggestive.

☒ sexless.

shabby *adj* **1** RAGGED, tattered, frayed, worn, worn-out, mangy, moth-eaten, scruffy, tatty, disreputable, dilapidated, run-down, seedy, dirty, dingy, poky. **2** *a shabby trick*: contemptible, despicable, rotten, mean, low, cheap, shoddy, shameful, dishonourable.

☒ **1** smart. **2** honourable, fair.

shack *n* hut, cabin, shanty, hovel, shed, lean-to.

shade *n* **1** SHADINESS, shadow, darkness, obscurity, semi-darkness, dimness, gloom, gloominess, twilight, dusk, gloaming. **2** AWNING, canopy, cover, shelter, screen, blind, curtain, shield, visor, umbrella, parasol. **3** COLOUR, hue, tint, tone, tinge. **4** TRACE, dash, hint, suggestion, suspicion, soupçon, nuance, gradation, degree, amount, variety. **5** GHOST, spectre, phantom, spirit, apparition, semblance.

➤ *v* shield, screen, protect, cover, shroud, veil, hide, conceal, obscure, cloud, dim, darken, shadow, overshadow.

shadow *n* **1** SHADE, darkness, obscurity, semi-darkness, dimness, gloom, twilight, dusk, gloaming, cloud,

cover, protection. **2** SILHOUETTE, shape, image, representation. **3** TRACE, hint, suggestion, suspicion, vestige, remnant.

➤ *v* **1** OVERSHADOW, overhang, shade, shield, screen, obscure, darken. **2** FOLLOW, tail, dog, stalk, trail, watch.

shadowy *adj* dark, gloomy, murky, obscure, dim, faint, indistinct, ill-defined, vague, hazy, nebulous, intangible, unsubstantial, ghostly, spectral, illusory, dreamlike, imaginary, unreal.

shady *adj* **1** SHADED, shadowy, dim, dark, cool, leafy. **2** (*infml*) DUBIOUS, questionable, suspect, suspicious, fishy (*infml*), dishonest, crooked (*infml*), unreliable, untrustworthy, disreputable, unscrupulous, unethical, underhand.

☒ **1** sunny, sunlit, bright. **2** honest, trustworthy, honourable.

shaft *n* handle, shank, stem, upright, pillar, pole, rod, bar, stick, arrow, dart, beam, ray, duct, passage.

shaggy *adj* hairy, long-haired, hirsute, bushy, woolly, unshorn, dishevelled, unkempt.

☒ bald, shorn, close-cropped.

shake *v* **1** WAVE, flourish, brandish, wag, waggle, agitate, rattle, joggle, jolt, jerk, twitch, convulse, heave, throb, vibrate, oscillate, fluctuate, waver, wobble, totter, sway, rock, tremble, quiver, quake, shiver, shudder. **2** *the news shook her*: upset, distress, shock, frighten, unnerve, intimidate, disturb, discompose, unsettle, agitate, stir, rouse.

◇ **shake off** get rid of, dislodge, lose, elude, give the slip, leave behind, outdistance, outstrip.

shake-up (*infml*) *n* reorganization, rearrangement, reshuffle, reform, disturbance, upheaval.

shaky *adj* **1** TREMBLING, quivering, faltering, tentative, uncertain. **2** UNSTABLE, unsteady, unsafe, insecure, precarious, wobbly, rocky, tottery, rickety, weak. **3** DUBIOUS, questionable,

suspect, unreliable, unsound, unsupported.
🔁 **2** firm, strong.

shallow *adj* superficial, surface, skin-deep, slight, flimsy, trivial, frivolous, foolish, idle, empty, meaningless, unscholarly, ignorant, simple.
🔁 deep, profound.

sham *n* pretence, fraud, counterfeit, forgery, fake, imitation, simulation, charade, hoax, humbug.
➤ *adj* false, fake, counterfeit, spurious, bogus, phoney (*infml*), pretended, feigned, put-on, simulated, artificial, mock, imitation, synthetic.
🔁 genuine, authentic, real.
➤ *v* pretend, feign, affect, put on, simulate, imitate, fake, counterfeit.

shame *n* disgrace, dishonour, discredit, stain, stigma, disrepute, infamy, scandal, ignominy, humiliation, degradation, shamefacedness, remorse, guilt, embarrassment, mortification.
🔁 honour, credit, distinction, pride.
➤ *v* embarrass, mortify, abash, confound, humiliate, ridicule, humble, put to shame, show up, disgrace, dishonour, discredit, debase, degrade, sully, taint, stain.

shamefaced *adj* ashamed, conscience-stricken, remorseful, contrite, repentant, apologetic, sorry, sheepish, red-faced, blushing, embarrassed, mortified, abashed, humiliated, uncomfortable.
🔁 unashamed, proud.

shameful *adj* **1** *a shameful waste of money*: disgraceful, outrageous, scandalous, indecent, abominable, atrocious, wicked, mean, low, vile, reprehensible, contemptible, unworthy, ignoble. **2** EMBARRASSING, mortifying, humiliating, ignominious.
🔁 **1** honourable, creditable, worthy.

shameless *adj* **1** UNASHAMED, unabashed, unrepentant, impenitent, barefaced, flagrant, blatant, brazen, brash, audacious, insolent, defiant,

hardened, incorrigible. **2** IMMODEST, indecent, improper, unprincipled, wanton, dissolute, corrupt, depraved.
🔁 **1** ashamed, shamefaced, contrite. **2** modest.

shape *n* **1** FORM, outline, silhouette, profile, model, mould, pattern, cut, lines, contours, figure, physique, build, frame, format, configuration. **2** APPEARANCE, guise, likeness, semblance. **3** *in good shape*: condition, state, form, health, trim, fettle.

> *Geometrical shapes include*: polygon, circle, semicircle, quadrant, oval, ellipse, crescent, triangle, equilateral triangle, isosceles triangle, scalene triangle, quadrilateral, square, rectangle, oblong, rhombus, diamond, kite, trapezium, parallelogram, pentagon, hexagon, heptagon, octagon, nonagon, decagon; polyhedron, cube, cuboid, prism, pyramid, tetrahedron, pentahedron, octahedron, cylinder, cone, sphere, hemisphere.

➤ *v* form, fashion, model, mould, cast, forge, sculpt, carve, whittle, make, produce, construct, create, devise, frame, plan, prepare, adapt, adjust, regulate, accommodate, modify, remodel.

shapeless *adj* formless, amorphous, unformed, nebulous, unstructured, irregular, misshapen, deformed, dumpy.

share *v* divide, split, go halves, partake, participate, share out, distribute, dole out, give out, deal out, mete out, apportion, allot, allocate, assign.
➤ *n* portion, ration, quota, allowance, allocation, allotment, lot, part, division, proportion, percentage, cut (*infml*), dividend, due, contribution, whack (*infml*).

shark

> *Types of shark include*: basking, blue, dogfish, fox, ghost, goblin, great white, Greenland, grey reef, hammerhead, leopard, mackerel, mako, man-eating,

nurse, porbeagle, requiem, saw, thresher, tiger, whale.

sharp adj 1 a sharp needle: pointed, keen, edged, knife-edged, razor-sharp, cutting, serrated, jagged, barbed, spiky. 2 CLEAR, clear-cut, well-defined, distinct, marked, crisp. 3 QUICK-WITTED, alert, shrewd, astute, perceptive, observant, discerning, penetrating, clever, crafty, cunning, artful, sly. 4 SUDDEN, abrupt, violent, fierce, intense, extreme, severe, acute, piercing, stabbing. 5 PUNGENT, piquant, sour, tart, vinegary, bitter, acerbic, acid. 6 TRENCHANT, incisive, cutting, biting, mordant, caustic, sarcastic, sardonic, scathing, vitriolic, acrimonious.
🔄 1 blunt. 2 blurred. 3 slow, stupid. 4 gentle. 5 bland. 6 mild.
➤ adv punctually, promptly, on the dot, exactly, precisely, abruptly, suddenly, unexpectedly.
🔄 approximately, roughly.

sharpen v edge, whet, hone, grind, file.
🔄 blunt.

shatter v break, smash, splinter, shiver, crack, split, burst, explode, blast, crush, demolish, destroy, devastate, wreck, ruin, overturn, upset.

sheath n 1 SCABBARD, case, sleeve, envelope, shell, casing, covering. 2 CONDOM, rubber (sl), johnnie (sl), French letter (sl).

shed[1] v cast (off), moult, slough, discard, drop, spill, pour, shower, scatter, diffuse, emit, radiate, shine, throw.

shed[2] n outhouse, lean-to, hut, shack, cabin.

sheen n lustre, gloss, shine, shimmer, brightness, brilliance, shininess, polish, burnish.
🔄 dullness, tarnish.

sheepish adj ashamed, shamefaced, embarrassed, mortified, chastened, abashed, uncomfortable, self-conscious, silly, foolish.
🔄 unabashed, brazen, bold.

sheer adj 1 UTTER, complete, total, absolute, thorough, mere, pure, unadulterated, downright, out-and-out, rank, thoroughgoing, unqualified, unmitigated. 2 a sheer drop: vertical, perpendicular, precipitous, abrupt, steep. 3 THIN, fine, flimsy, gauzy, gossamer, translucent, transparent, see-through.
🔄 2 gentle, gradual. 3 thick, heavy.

sheet n cover, blanket, covering, coating, coat, film, layer, stratum, skin, membrane, lamina, veneer, overlay, plate, leaf, page, folio, piece, panel, slab, pane, expanse, surface.

shelf n ledge, mantelpiece, sill, step, bench, counter, bar, bank, sandbank, reef, terrace.

shell n covering, hull, husk, pod, rind, crust, case, casing, body, chassis, frame, framework, structure, skeleton.
➤ v 1 shell nuts: hull, husk, pod. 2 BOMB, bombard, barrage, blitz, attack.

shelter v cover, shroud, screen, shade, shadow, protect, safeguard, defend, guard, shield, harbour, hide, accommodate, put up.
🔄 expose.
➤ n cover, roof, shade, shadow, protection, defence, guard, security, safety, sanctuary, asylum, haven, refuge, retreat, accommodation, lodging.
🔄 exposure.

sheltered adj covered, shaded, shielded, protected, cosy, snug, warm, quiet, secluded, isolated, retired, withdrawn, reclusive, cloistered, unworldly.
🔄 exposed.

shelve v postpone, defer, put off, suspend, halt, put aside, pigeonhole, put on ice, mothball.
🔄 expedite, implement.

shield n buckler, escutcheon, defence, bulwark, rampart, screen, guard, cover, shelter, protection, safeguard.
➤ v defend, guard, protect, safeguard, screen, shade, shadow, cover, shelter.
🔄 expose.

shift *v* change, vary, fluctuate, alter, adjust, move, budge, remove, dislodge, displace, relocate, reposition, rearrange, transpose, transfer, switch, swerve, veer.
➤ *n* change, fluctuation, alteration, modification, move, removal, displacement, rearrangement, transposition, transfer, switch.

shifty *adj* untrustworthy, dishonest, deceitful, scheming, contriving, artful, tricky, wily, crafty, cunning, devious, sly, evasive, slippery, furtive, underhand, dubious, shady (*infml*).
🔁 dependable, honest, open.

shimmer *v* glisten, gleam, glimmer, glitter, scintillate, twinkle.
➤ *n* lustre, gleam, glimmer, glitter, glow.

shine *v* **1** BEAM, radiate, glow, flash, glare, gleam, glint, glitter, sparkle, twinkle, shimmer, glisten, glimmer. **2** POLISH, burnish, buff, brush, rub. **3** *shine at athletics*: excel, stand out.
➤ *n* **1** LIGHT, radiance, glow, brightness, glare, gleam, sparkle, shimmer. **2** GLOSS, polish, burnish, sheen, lustre, glaze.

shining *adj* **1** BRIGHT, radiant, glowing, beaming, flashing, gleaming, glittering, glistening, shimmering, twinkling, sparkling, brilliant, resplendent, splendid, glorious. **2** *a shining example*: conspicuous, outstanding, leading, prime, eminent, celebrated, distinguished, illustrious.
🔁 **1** dark.

shiny *adj* polished, burnished, sheeny, lustrous, glossy, sleek, bright, gleaming, glistening.
🔁 dull, matt.

ship *n* vessel, craft, liner, steamer, tanker, trawler, ferry, boat.

Parts of a ship include: anchor, berth, bilge, boiler room, bollard, bridge, brig, bulkhead, bulwarks, bunk, cabin, capstan, chain locker, chart room, cleat, companion ladder, companionway, crow's nest, davit, deck, after deck, boat deck, flight deck, gun deck, lower deck, main deck, poop deck, promenade deck, quarter deck, top deck, engine room, figurehead, forecastle (fo'c'sle), funnel, galley, gangplank, gangway, gunwale (gunnel), hammock, hatch, hatchway, hawser, head, hold, keel, landing, mast, oar, paddle wheel, pilot house, Plimsoll line, port, porthole, prow, quarter, radio room, rigger, rowlock, rudder, sail, stabilizer, stanchion, starboard, stateroom, stern, superstructure, tiller, transom, wardroom, waterline, wheel, winch.
see also **boat**; **sail**.

shirk *v* dodge, evade, avoid, duck (*infml*), shun, slack, skive (*infml*).

shiver *v* shudder, tremble, quiver, quake, shake, vibrate, palpitate, flutter.
➤ *n* shudder, quiver, shake, tremor, twitch, start, vibration, flutter.

shock *v* disgust, revolt, sicken, offend, appal, outrage, scandalize, horrify, astound, stagger, stun, stupefy, numb, paralyse, traumatize, jolt, jar, shake, agitate, unsettle, disquiet, unnerve, confound, dismay.
🔁 delight, please, gratify, reassure.
➤ *n* fright, start, jolt, impact, collision, surprise, bombshell, thunderbolt, whammy (*infml*), blow, trauma, upset, distress, dismay, consternation, disgust, outrage.
🔁 delight, pleasure, reassurance.

shocking *adj* appalling, outrageous, scandalous, horrifying, disgraceful, deplorable, intolerable, unbearable, atrocious, abominable, monstrous, unspeakable, detestable, abhorrent, dreadful, awful, terrible, frightful, ghastly, hideous, horrible, disgusting, revolting, repulsive, sickening, nauseating, offensive, distressing.
🔁 acceptable, satisfactory, pleasant, delightful.

shoddy *adj* inferior, second-rate, cheap, tawdry, tatty, trashy, rubbishy, poor, careless, slipshod, slapdash.
🔁 superior, well-made.

shoot *v* **1** FIRE, discharge, launch,

propel, hurl, fling, project. **2** DART, bolt, dash, tear, rush, race, sprint, speed, charge, hurtle. **3** HIT, kill, blast, bombard, gun down, snipe at, pick off.
➤ *n* sprout, bud, offshoot, branch, twig, sprig, slip, scion.

shop

Types of shop include: bazaar, market, indoor market, mini-market, corner shop, charity shop, shopping mall, department store, supermarket, superstore, hypermarket, cash-and-carry, online shop, e-shop; butcher, baker, grocer, greengrocer, fishmonger, dairy, delicatessen, health food shop, farm shop, fish and chip shop, takeaway, off-licence, tobacconist, sweet shop, candy store (*US*), confectioner, tuck shop; bookshop, bookstore (*US*), newsagent, stationer, chemist, pharmacy, drugstore (*US*), tailor, outfitter, dress shop, boutique, milliner, shoe shop, haberdasher, draper, florist, jeweller, toy shop, hardware shop, ironmonger, saddler, computer shop, phone shop, radio and TV shop, video shop; launderette, hairdresser, barber, betting shop, bookmaker, bookie (*infml*), pawnbroker, post office.

shore¹ *n* seashore, beach, sand(s), shingle, strand, waterfront, front, promenade, coast, seaboard, lakeside, bank.

shore² *v* support, hold, prop, stay, underpin, buttress, brace, strengthen, reinforce.

short *adj* **1** BRIEF, cursory, fleeting, momentary, transitory, ephemeral, concise, succinct, terse, pithy, epigrammatic, compact, compressed, shortened, curtailed, abbreviated, abridged, summarized. **2** BRUSQUE, curt, gruff, snappy, sharp, abrupt, laconic, blunt, direct, rude, impolite, discourteous, uncivil. **3** SMALL, little, low, petite, diminutive, squat, dumpy. **4** INADEQUATE, insufficient, deficient,

lacking, wanting, low, poor, meagre, scant, sparse.
F3 1 long, lasting. **2** polite. **3** tall. **4** adequate, ample.

shortage *n* inadequacy, insufficiency, deficiency, shortfall, deficit, lack, want, need, scarcity, paucity, poverty, dearth, absence.
F3 sufficiency, abundance, surplus.

shortcoming *n* defect, imperfection, fault, flaw, drawback, failing, weakness, foible.

shorten *v* cut, trim, prune, crop, dock, curtail, truncate, abbreviate, abridge, reduce, lessen, decrease, diminish, take up.
F3 lengthen, enlarge, amplify.

shortly *adv* soon, before long, presently, by and by.

short-sighted *adj* **1** MYOPIC, near-sighted. **2** IMPROVIDENT, imprudent, injudicious, unwise, impolitic, ill-advised, careless, hasty, ill-considered.
F3 1 long-sighted, far-sighted.

shot *n* **1** BULLET, missile, projectile, ball, pellet, slug (*infml*), discharge, blast. **2** (*infml*) ATTEMPT, try, effort, endeavour, go (*infml*), bash (*infml*), crack (*infml*), stab (*infml*), guess, turn.

shoulder *v* **1** PUSH, shove, jostle, thrust, press. **2** ACCEPT, assume, take on, bear, carry, sustain.

shout *n*, *v* call, cry, scream, shriek, yell, roar, bellow, bawl, howl, bay, cheer.

shove *v* push, thrust, drive, propel, force, barge, jostle, elbow, shoulder, press, crowd.

shovel *n* spade, scoop, bucket.
➤ *v* dig, scoop, dredge, clear, move, shift, heap.

show *v* **1** REVEAL, expose, uncover, disclose, divulge, present, offer, exhibit, manifest, display, indicate, register, demonstrate, prove, illustrate, exemplify, explain, instruct, teach, clarify, elucidate. **2** *show him out*: lead, guide, conduct, usher, escort, accompany, attend.

🔀 **1** hide, cover.

➤ *n* **1** OSTENTATION, parade, display, flamboyance, panache, pizzazz (*infml*), glitz (*infml*), showiness, exhibitionism, affectation, pose, charade, pretence, illusion, semblance, façade, impression, appearance, air. **2** DEMONSTRATION, presentation, exhibition, exposition, fair, display, array, parade, pageant, extravaganza, spectacle, sight, entertainment, performance, production, staging, showing, representation.

◇ **show off** parade, strut, swagger, brag, boast, swank (*infml*), flaunt, brandish, display, exhibit, demonstrate, advertise, set off, enhance.

◇ **show up 1** (*infml*) ARRIVE, come, turn up, appear, materialize (*infml*). **2** HUMILIATE, embarrass, mortify, shame, disgrace, let down. **3** REVEAL, show, expose, unmask, lay bare, highlight, pinpoint.

showdown *n* confrontation, clash, crisis, climax, culmination.

shower *n* rain, stream, torrent, deluge, hail, volley, barrage.

➤ *v* spray, sprinkle, rain, pour, deluge, inundate, overwhelm, load, heap, lavish.

show-off *n* swaggerer, braggart, boaster, exhibitionist, peacock, poser, poseur, egotist.

showy *adj* flashy, flamboyant, ostentatious, gaudy, garish, loud, tawdry, fancy, ornate, pretentious, pompous, swanky (*infml*), flash (*infml*), glitzy (*infml*).

🔀 quiet, restrained.

shred *n* ribbon, tatter, rag, scrap, snippet, sliver, bit, piece, fragment, jot, iota, atom, grain, mite, whit, trace.

shrewd *adj* astute, judicious, well-advised, calculated, far-sighted, smart, clever, intelligent, clued-up (*infml*), sharp, keen, acute, alert, perceptive, observant, discerning, discriminating, knowing, calculating, cunning, crafty, artful, wily, sly.

🔀 unwise, obtuse, naïve, unsophisticated.

shriek *v, n* scream, screech, squawk, squeal, cry, shout, yell, wail, howl.

shrill *adj* high, high-pitched, treble, sharp, acute, piercing, penetrating, screaming, screeching, strident, ear-splitting.

🔀 deep, low, soft, gentle.

shrink *v* **1** CONTRACT, shorten, narrow, decrease, lessen, diminish, dwindle, shrivel, wrinkle, wither. **2** RECOIL, back away, shy away, withdraw, retire, balk, quail, cower, cringe, wince, flinch, shun.

🔀 **1** expand, stretch. **2** accept, embrace.

shrivel *v* wrinkle, pucker, wither, wilt, shrink, dwindle, parch, dehydrate, desiccate, scorch, sear, burn, frizzle.

shroud *v* wrap, envelop, swathe, cloak, veil, screen, hide, conceal, blanket, cover.

🔀 uncover, expose.

➤ *n* winding-sheet, pall, mantle, cloak, veil, screen, blanket, covering.

shrub

Shrubs include: azalea, berberis, broom, buddleia, camellia, carabana, clematis, cotoneaster, daphne, dogwood, eucryphia, euonymus, firethorn, flowering currant, forsythia, fuchsia, heather, hebe, holly, honeysuckle, hydrangea, ivy, japonica, jasmine, laburnum, laurel, lavender, lilac, magnolia, mallow, mimosa, mock orange, peony, privet, musk rose, rhododendron, rose, spiraea, viburnum, weigela, witch hazel, wisteria. *see also* **flower**; **plant**.

shudder *v* shiver, shake, tremble, quiver, quake, heave, convulse.

➤ *n* shiver, quiver, tremor, spasm, convulsion.

shuffle *v* **1** MIX (UP), intermix, jumble, confuse, disorder, rearrange, reorganize, shift around, switch. **2** *shuffle across the room*: shamble, scuffle, scrape, drag, limp, hobble.

shun *v* avoid, evade, elude, steer clear of, shy away from, spurn, ignore, cold-shoulder, ostracize.

▰ accept, embrace.

shut v close, slam, seal, fasten, secure, lock, latch, bolt, bar.

▰ open.

◇ **shut down** close, stop, cease, terminate, halt, discontinue, suspend, switch off, inactivate.

◇ **shut in** enclose, box in, hem in, fence in, immure, confine, imprison, cage.

◇ **shut off** seclude, isolate, cut off, separate, segregate.

◇ **shut out 1** EXCLUDE, bar, debar, lock out, ostracize, banish. **2** HIDE, conceal, cover, mask, screen, veil.

◇ **shut up 1** SILENCE, gag, quiet, hush up, pipe down (*infml*), hold one's tongue, clam up (*infml*). **2** CONFINE, coop up, imprison, incarcerate, jail, intern.

shy adj timid, bashful, reticent, reserved, retiring, diffident, coy, self-conscious, inhibited, modest, self-effacing, shrinking, hesitant, cautious, chary, suspicious, nervous.

▰ bold, assertive, confident.

sick adj **1** ILL, unwell, indisposed (*fml*), laid up, poorly, ailing, sickly, off-colour, below par (*infml*), under the weather (*infml*), weak, feeble. **2** VOMITING, queasy, bilious, seasick, airsick. **3** sick of waiting: bored, fed up (*infml*), tired, weary, disgusted, nauseated.

▰ **1** well, healthy.

sicken v nauseate, revolt, disgust, repel, put off, turn off (*sl*), turn one's stomach (*infml*).

▰ delight, attract.

sickening adj nauseating, revolting, stomach-turning (*infml*), disgusting, offensive, distasteful, foul, vile, loathsome, repulsive.

▰ delightful, pleasing, attractive.

sickly adj **1** UNHEALTHY, infirm, delicate, weak, feeble, frail, wan, pallid, ailing, indisposed, sick, bilious, faint, languid. **2** NAUSEATING, revolting, sweet, syrupy, cloying, mawkish.

▰ **1** healthy, robust, sturdy, strong.

sickness n **1** ILLNESS, disease, malady,

ailment, complaint, affliction, ill-health, indisposition, infirmity. **2** VOMITING, nausea, queasiness, biliousness.

▰ **1** health.

side n **1** EDGE, margin, fringe, periphery, border, boundary, limit, verge, brink, bank, shore, quarter, region, flank, hand, face, facet, surface. **2** STANDPOINT, viewpoint, view, aspect, angle, slant. **3** TEAM, party, faction, camp, cause, interest.

➤ adj lateral, flanking, marginal, secondary, subsidiary, subordinate, lesser, minor, incidental, indirect, oblique.

◇ **side with** agree with, team up with, support, vote for, favour, prefer.

sidestep v avoid, dodge, duck, evade, elude, skirt, bypass.

▰ tackle, deal with.

sidetrack v deflect, head off, divert, distract.

sideways adv sidewards, edgeways, laterally, obliquely.

➤ adj sideward, side, lateral, slanted, oblique, indirect, sidelong.

sidle v slink, edge, inch, creep, sneak.

sieve v sift, strain, separate, remove.

➤ n colander, strainer, sifter, riddle, screen.

sift v **1** SIEVE, strain, filter, riddle, screen, winnow, separate, sort. **2** EXAMINE, scrutinize, investigate, analyse, probe, review.

sigh v breathe, exhale, moan, complain, lament, grieve.

sight n **1** VISION, eyesight, seeing, observation, perception. **2** VIEW, look, glance, glimpse, range, field of vision, visibility. **3** APPEARANCE, spectacle, show, display, exhibition, scene, eyesore, monstrosity, fright (*infml*).

➤ v see, observe, notice, spot, glimpse, perceive, discern, distinguish, make out.

sightseer n tourist, visitor, holidaymaker, tripper, excursionist.

sign n **1** SYMBOL, token, character, figure, representation, emblem, badge, insignia, logo. **2** INDICATION, mark, signal, gesture, evidence, clue, manifestation, pointer, hint, suggestion, trace. **3** NOTICE, poster, board, placard. **4** PORTENT, omen, forewarning, foreboding.

➤ v autograph, initial, endorse, write.

◇ **sign up** enlist, enrol, join (up), volunteer, register, sign on, recruit, take on, hire, engage, employ.

signal n sign, indication, mark, gesture, light, alert, warning, tip-off.

> *Kinds of signal and warning include*: alarm, burglar alarm, car alarm, fire alarm, personal alarm, security alarm; alarm bell, alarm clock, amber light, beacon, Belisha beacon, lighthouse beacon; bell, bicycle bell, curfew bell; bleeper, bugle, buoy, buzzer, cue, distress signal, drumbeat, final warning, fire, flag, flare, flashing light, foghorn, gale warning, go-ahead, gong, green light, hand signal, heliograph, honk, hooter, horn, car horn, hurricane warning, indicator, klaxon, knell, larum, larum-bell, Lutine bell, mayday, Morse code, pager, password, red alert, red card, red flag, red light, reveille, rocket, semaphore signal, a shot across the bows, shout, signal box, signal letters, siren, smoke signal, SOS, starter's gun, storm cone, storm signal, storm warning, tattoo, time signal (pips), tocsin, toot, trafficator, traffic lights, Very light, vigia, warning light, whistle, police whistle, winker, written warning, yellow card, yellow flag.

➤ v wave, gesticulate, gesture, beckon, motion, nod, sign, indicate, communicate.

signature n autograph, initials, mark, endorsement, inscription.

significance n importance, relevance, consequence, matter, interest, consideration, weight, force, meaning, implication, sense, point, message.
🔳 insignificance, unimportance, pettiness.

significant adj **1** IMPORTANT, relevant, consequential, momentous, weighty, serious, noteworthy, critical, vital, marked, considerable, appreciable. **2** MEANINGFUL, symbolic, expressive, suggestive, indicative, symptomatic.
🔳 **1** insignificant, unimportant, trivial. **2** meaningless.

signify v **1** MEAN, denote, symbolize, represent, stand for, indicate, show, express, convey, communicate, transmit, intimate, imply, suggest. **2** MATTER, count.

silence n quiet, quietness, hush, peace, stillness, calm, lull, noiselessness, soundlessness, muteness, dumbness, speechlessness, taciturnity, uncommunicativeness, reticence, reserve.
🔳 noise, sound, din, uproar.
➤ v quiet, quieten, hush, mute, deaden, muffle, stifle, gag, muzzle, suppress, subdue, quell, still, dumbfound.

silent adj inaudible, noiseless, soundless, quiet, peaceful, still, hushed, muted, mute, dumb, speechless, tongue-tied, taciturn, mum, reticent, reserved, tacit, unspoken, unexpressed, understood, voiceless, wordless.
🔳 noisy, loud, talkative.

silhouette n outline, contour, delineation, shape, form, configuration, profile, shadow.

silky adj silken, fine, sleek, lustrous, glossy, satiny, smooth, soft, velvety.

silly adj foolish, stupid, imprudent, unwise, senseless, pointless, idiotic, daft (*infml*), ridiculous, ludicrous, preposterous, absurd, meaningless, irrational, illogical, childish, puerile, immature, irresponsible, reckless, scatterbrained, air-headed (*infml*).
🔳 wise, sensible, sane, mature, clever, intelligent.

silt n sediment, deposit, alluvium, sludge, mud, ooze.
◇ **silt up** block, clog, choke.

similar adj like, alike, close, related, akin, corresponding, equivalent, analogous, comparable, uniform, homogeneous.

E3 dissimilar, different.

similarity n likeness, resemblance, similitude (*fml*), closeness, relation, correspondence, congruence, equivalence, analogy, comparability, compatibility, agreement, affinity, homogeneity (*fml*), uniformity.

E3 dissimilarity, difference.

simmer v boil, bubble, seethe, stew, burn, smoulder, fume, rage.

◇ **simmer down** calm down, cool down, control oneself, collect oneself.

simple adj **1** *a simple question*: easy, elementary, straightforward, clear, uncomplicated, uninvolved, lucid, plain, understandable, comprehensible. **2** UNSOPHISTICATED, natural, innocent, artless, guileless, ingenuous, naïve, green, foolish, stupid, silly, idiotic, half-witted, simple-minded, feeble-minded, backward.

E3 1 difficult, hard, complicated, intricate. **2** sophisticated, worldly, artful, clever.

simplicity n simpleness, ease, straightforwardness, clarity, uncomplicatedness, purity, plainness, restraint, naturalness, innocence, artlessness, candour, openness, sincerity, directness.

E3 difficulty, complexity, intricacy, sophistication.

simplify v disentangle, untangle, decipher, clarify, paraphrase, abridge, reduce, streamline.

E3 complicate, elaborate.

simplistic adj oversimplified, superficial, shallow, sweeping, facile, simple, naïve.

E3 analytical, detailed.

simply adv **1** MERELY, just, only, solely, purely, utterly, completely, totally, wholly, absolutely, quite, really, undeniably, unquestionably, clearly, plainly, obviously. **2** EASILY, straightforwardly, directly, intelligibly.

simulate v pretend, affect, assume,

put on, act, feign, sham, fake, counterfeit, reproduce, duplicate, copy, imitate, mimic, parrot, echo, reflect.

simultaneous adj synchronous, synchronic, concurrent, coexistent, contemporaneous, coinciding, parallel.

E3 asynchronous.

sin n wrong, offence, transgression, trespass (*fml*), misdeed, lapse, fault, error, crime, wrongdoing, sinfulness, wickedness, iniquity, evil, impiety, ungodliness, unrighteousness, guilt.

➤ v offend, transgress, trespass (*fml*), lapse, err, misbehave, stray, go astray, fall, fall from grace.

sincere adj honest, truthful, candid, frank, open, direct, straightforward, plain-spoken, serious, earnest, heartfelt, wholehearted, real, true, genuine, pure, unadulterated, unmixed, natural, unaffected, artless, guileless, simple.

E3 insincere, hypocritical, affected.

sincerity n honour, integrity, probity, uprightness, honesty, truthfulness, candour, frankness, openness, directness, straightforwardness, seriousness, earnestness, wholeheartedness, genuineness.

E3 1, 3 insincerity.

sinewy adj muscular, brawny, strong, sturdy, robust, powerful, vigorous, athletic, wiry, stringy.

sinful adj wrong, wrongful, criminal, bad, wicked, iniquitous, erring, fallen, immoral, corrupt, depraved, impious, ungodly, unholy, irreligious, guilty.

E3 sinless, righteous, godly.

sing v chant, intone, vocalize, croon, serenade, yodel, trill, warble, chirp, pipe, whistle, hum.

singe v scorch, char, blacken, burn, sear.

singer

Singers include: balladeer, minstrel, troubadour, opera singer, diva, prima donna, soloist, precentor, choirboy, choirgirl, chorister, chorus, folk-singer, pop star, crooner, carol-singer; soprano, coloratura soprano, castrato, tenor, treble, contralto, alto, baritone, bass; songster, vocalist.

single *adj* one, unique, singular, individual, particular, exclusive, sole, only, lone, solitary, separate, distinct, free, unattached, unmarried, celibate, unshared, undivided, unbroken, simple, one-to-one, man-to-man.
🖪 multiple.
◇ **single out** choose, select, pick, hand-pick, distinguish, identify, separate, set apart, isolate, highlight, pinpoint.

single-handed *adj, adv* solo, alone, unaccompanied, unaided, unassisted, independent(ly).

single-minded *adj* determined, resolute, dogged, obstinate, persevering, tireless, unwavering, fixed, unswerving, undeviating, steadfast, dedicated, devoted.

sinister *adj* ominous, menacing, threatening, disturbing, disquieting, unlucky, inauspicious, malevolent, evil.
🖪 auspicious, harmless, innocent.

sink *v* 1 DESCEND, slip, fall, drop, slump, lower, stoop, succumb, lapse, droop, sag, dip, set, disappear, vanish. 2 DECREASE, lessen, subside, abate (*fml*), dwindle, diminish, ebb, fade, flag, weaken, fail, decline, worsen, degenerate, degrade, decay, collapse. 3 FOUNDER, dive, plunge, plummet, submerge, immerse, engulf, drown. 4 *sink a well*: bore, drill, penetrate, dig, excavate, lay, conceal.
🖪 1 rise. 2 increase. 3 float.

sinner *n* wrongdoer, miscreant (*fml*), offender, transgressor, trespasser (*fml*), backslider, reprobate, evil-doer, malefactor.

sinuous *adj* lithe, slinky, curved, wavy, undulating, tortuous, twisting, winding, meandering, serpentine, coiling.
🖪 straight.

sip *v* taste, sample, drink, sup.

➤ *n* taste, drop, spoonful, mouthful.

sit *v* 1 SETTLE, rest, perch, roost, brood, pose. 2 SEAT, accommodate, hold, contain, carry. 3 MEET, assemble, gather, convene, deliberate.

site *n* location, place, spot, position, situation, station, setting, scene, plot, lot, ground, area.
➤ *v* locate, place, position, situate, station, set, install.

sitting *n* session, period, spell, meeting, assembly, hearing, consultation.

situation *n* 1 SITE, location, position, place, spot, seat, locality, locale, setting, scenario. 2 STATE OF AFFAIRS, case, circumstances, predicament, state, condition, status, rank, station, post, office, job, employment.

sizable *adj* large, substantial, considerable, respectable, goodly, largish, biggish, decent, generous.
🖪 small, tiny.

size *n* magnitude, measurement(s), dimensions, proportions, volume, bulk, mass, height, length, extent, range, scale, amount, greatness, largeness, bigness, vastness, immensity.
◇ **size up** gauge, assess, evaluate, weigh up, measure.

sizzle *v* hiss, crackle, spit, sputter, fry, frizzle.

skeleton *n* bones, frame, structure, framework, bare bones, outline, draft, sketch.

sketch *v* draw, depict, portray, represent, pencil, paint, outline, delineate, draft, rough out, block out.
➤ *n* drawing, vignette, design, plan, diagram, outline, delineation, skeleton, draft.

sketchy *adj* rough, vague, incomplete, unfinished, scrappy, bitty, imperfect, inadequate, insufficient, slight, superficial, cursory, hasty.
🖪 full, complete.

skilful *adj* able, capable, adept, competent, proficient, deft, adroit,

handy, expert, masterly, accomplished, skilled, practised, experienced, professional, clever, tactical, cunning, crafty.
⊟ inept, clumsy, awkward.

skill *n* skilfulness, ability, aptitude, facility, handiness, talent, knack, art, technique, training, experience, know-how (*infml*), expertise, expertness, mastery, proficiency, competence, accomplishment, cleverness, intelligence.

skilled *adj* trained, schooled, qualified, professional, experienced, practised, accomplished, expert, masterly, proficient, able, skilful.
⊟ unskilled, inexperienced.

skim *v* 1 BRUSH, touch, skate, plane, float, sail, glide, fly. 2 SCAN, look through, skip. 3 CREAM, separate.

skimp *v* economize, scrimp, pinch, cut corners, stint, withhold, hold back.
⊟ squander, waste.

skin *n* hide, pelt, membrane, film, coating, surface, outside, peel, rind, husk, casing, crust.
➤ *v* flay, fleece, strip, peel, scrape, graze.

skinny *adj* thin, lean, scrawny, scraggy, skeletal, skin-and-bone, bony, emaciated, wasted, underfed, undernourished.
⊟ fat, plump.

skip *v* 1 HOP, jump, leap, dance, gambol, frisk, caper, prance. 2 *skip a page*: miss, omit, leave out, cut.

skirmish *n* fight, combat, battle, engagement, encounter, conflict, clash, brush, scrap (*infml*), scuffle, tussle, set-to, dust-up (*infml*).

skirt *v* circle, circumnavigate, border, edge, flank, bypass, avoid, evade, circumvent.

skit *n* satire, parody, caricature, spoof, take-off, sketch.

skulk *v* lurk, hide, prowl, sneak, creep, slink.

sky *n* space, atmosphere, air, ether, heavens, blue.

slab *n* piece, block, lump, chunk, hunk, wodge (*infml*), wedge, slice, portion.

slack *adj* 1 LOOSE, limp, sagging, baggy. 2 LAZY, sluggish, slow, quiet, idle, inactive. 3 NEGLECTFUL, negligent, careless, inattentive, remiss, permissive, lax, relaxed, easy-going.
⊟ 1 tight, taut, stiff, rigid. 2 busy. 3 diligent.
➤ *n* looseness, give, play, room, leeway, excess.
➤ *v* idle, do nothing, shirk, skive (*infml*), neglect.

slacken off loosen, release, relax, ease, moderate, reduce, lessen, decrease, diminish, abate (*fml*), slow (down).
⊟ tighten, increase, intensify, quicken.

slacker *n* idler, shirker, skiver (*infml*), dawdler, clock-watcher, good-for-nothing, layabout.

slam *v* 1 BANG, crash, dash, smash, throw, hurl, fling. 2 (*infml*) CRITICIZE, slate (*infml*), pan (*infml*).

slander *n* defamation, calumny (*fml*), misrepresentation, libel, scandal, smear, slur, aspersion (*fml*), backbiting.
➤ *v* defame, vilify (*fml*), malign, denigrate (*fml*), disparage, libel, smear, slur, cast aspersions, backbite.
⊟ praise, compliment.

slanderous *adj* defamatory, false, untrue, libellous, damaging, malicious, abusive, insulting.

slant *v* 1 TILT, slope, incline, lean, list, skew, angle. 2 DISTORT, twist, warp, bend, weight, bias, colour.
➤ *n* 1 SLOPE, incline, gradient, ramp, camber, pitch, tilt, angle, diagonal. 2 BIAS, emphasis, attitude, viewpoint.

slanting *adj* sloping, tilted, oblique, diagonal.

slap *n* smack, spank, cuff, blow, bang, clap, clout (*infml*).
➤ *v* 1 SMACK, spank, hit, strike, cuff, clout (*infml*), bang, clap. 2 DAUB, plaster, spread, apply.

slash *v* cut, slit, gash, lacerate, rip, tear, rend.

➤ *n* cut, incision, slit, gash, laceration, rip, tear, rent.

slate *v* scold, reprove, rebuke, reprimand, berate, censure, blame, criticize, slam (*infml*), knock (*infml*).
🔁 praise.

slaughter *n* killing, murder, massacre, extermination, butchery, carnage, bloodbath, bloodshed.
➤ *v* kill, slay, murder, massacre, exterminate, liquidate, butcher.

slave *n* servant, drudge, vassal, serf, villein, captive.
➤ *v* toil, labour, drudge, sweat, grind, slog, skivvy (*infml*).

slaver *v* dribble, drivel, slobber, drool, salivate.

slavery *n* servitude, bondage, captivity, enslavement, serfdom, thraldom, subjugation (*fml*).
🔁 freedom, liberty.

slavish *adj* **1** UNORIGINAL, imitative, unimaginative, uninspired, literal, strict. **2** SERVILE, abject, submissive, sycophantic, grovelling, cringing, fawning, menial, low, mean.
🔁 **1** original, imaginative. **2** independent, assertive.

sleek *adj* shiny, glossy, lustrous, smooth, silky, well-groomed.
🔁 rough, unkempt.

sleep *v* doze, snooze, slumber, kip (*sl*), doss (down) (*sl*), hibernate, drop off, nod off, rest, repose.
➤ *n* doze, snooze, nap, forty winks (*infml*), shut-eye (*infml*), kip (*sl*), slumber, hibernation, rest, repose, siesta.

sleepless *adj* unsleeping, awake, wide-awake, alert, vigilant, watchful, wakeful, restless, disturbed, insomniac.

sleepy *adj* drowsy, somnolent, tired, weary, heavy, slow, sluggish, torpid, lethargic, inactive, quiet, dull, soporific, hypnotic.
🔁 awake, alert, wakeful, restless.

slender *adj* **1** SLIM, thin, lean, slight, svelte, graceful. **2** *a slender chance*: faint, remote, slight, inconsiderable, tenuous, flimsy, feeble, inadequate, insufficient, meagre, scanty.
🔁 **1** fat. **2** appreciable, considerable, ample.

slice *n* piece, sliver, wafer, rasher, tranche, slab, wedge, segment, section, share, portion, helping, cut (*infml*), whack (*infml*).
➤ *v* carve, cut, chop, divide, segment.

slick *adj* **1** GLIB, plausible, deft, adroit, dexterous, skilful, professional, smooth, suave. **2** SMOOTH, sleek, glossy, shiny, polished.

slide *v* slip, slither, skid, skate, ski, toboggan, glide, plane, coast, skim.

slight *adj* **1** MINOR, unimportant, insignificant, negligible, trivial, paltry, modest, small, little, inconsiderable, insubstantial. **2** SLENDER, slim, diminutive, petite, delicate.
🔁 **1** major, significant, noticeable, considerable. **2** large, muscular.
➤ *v* scorn, despise, disdain, disparage, insult, affront, offend, snub, cut, cold-shoulder, ignore, disregard, neglect.
🔁 respect, praise, compliment, flatter.
➤ *n* insult, affront, slur, snub, rebuff, rudeness, discourtesy, disrespect, contempt, disdain, indifference, disregard, neglect.

slim *adj* **1** SLENDER, thin, lean, svelte, trim. **2** SLIGHT, remote, faint, poor.
🔁 **1** fat, chubby. **2** strong, considerable.
➤ *v* lose weight, diet, reduce.

slimy *adj* **1** MUDDY, miry, mucous, viscous, oily, greasy, slippery. **2** SERVILE, obsequious, sycophantic, toadying, smarmy (*infml*), oily, unctuous.

sling *v* **1** THROW, hurl, fling, catapult, heave, pitch, lob, toss, chuck (*infml*). **2** HANG, suspend, dangle, swing.

slink *v* sneak, steal, creep, sidle, slip, prowl, skulk.

slinky *adj* close-fitting, figure-hugging, clinging, skintight, sleek, sinuous.

slip[1] *v* slide, glide, skate, skid, stumble, trip, fall, slither, slink, sneak, steal, creep.

➤ *n* mistake, error, howler (*infml*), slip-up (*infml*), bloomer (*infml*), blunder, fault, gaffe, indiscretion, boob (*infml*), omission, oversight, failure.

slip² *n* piece, strip, voucher, chit, coupon, certificate.

slippery *adj* 1 SLIPPY, icy, greasy, glassy, smooth, dangerous, treacherous, perilous. 2 *a slippery character*: dishonest, untrustworthy, false, duplicitous, two-faced, crafty, cunning, devious, shifty (*infml*), evasive, smooth, smarmy (*infml*).
🔁 1 rough. 2 trustworthy, reliable.

slipshod *adj* careless, slapdash, sloppy, slovenly, untidy, negligent, lax, casual.
🔁 careful, fastidious, neat, tidy.

slit *v* cut, gash, slash, slice, split, rip, tear.
➤ *n* opening, aperture, vent, cut, incision, gash, slash, split, tear, rent.

slither *v* slide, slip, glide, slink, creep, snake, worm.

sliver *n* flake, shaving, paring, slice, wafer, shred, fragment, chip, splinter, shiver, shard.

slobber *v* dribble, drivel, slaver, drool, salivate.

slogan *n* jingle, motto, catchphrase, catchword, watchword, battle-cry, war cry.

slop *v* spill, overflow, slosh, splash, splatter, spatter.

slope *v* slant, lean, tilt, tip, pitch, incline, rise, fall.

Ways of describing slopes include:
up: acclivity, ascent, climb, incline, rise, uphill, upward;
down: decline, declivity, descent, dip, downgrade, downhill, downward, drop, fall;
up or down: bajada, brae, cant, escalator, escarp, glacis, gradient, inclination, pitch, ramp, scarp, slant, staircase, stairs, stairway, steps, tilt, versant.

---

sloppy *adj* 1 WATERY, wet, liquid, runny, mushy, slushy. 2 *sloppy work*: careless, hit-or-miss, slapdash, slipshod, slovenly, untidy, messy, clumsy, amateurish. 3 SOPPY, sentimental, schmaltzy, slushy, mushy.
🔁 1 solid. 2 careful, exact, precise.

slot *n* hole, opening, aperture, slit, vent, groove, channel, gap, space, time, vacancy, place, spot, position, niche.
➤ *v* insert, fit, place, position, assign, pigeonhole.

slouch *v* stoop, hunch, droop, slump, lounge, loll, shuffle, shamble.

slovenly *adj* sloppy, careless, slipshod, untidy, scruffy, slatternly, sluttish.
🔁 neat, smart.

slow *adj* 1 LEISURELY, unhurried, lingering, loitering, dawdling, lazy, sluggish, slow-moving, creeping, gradual, deliberate, measured, plodding, delayed, late, unpunctual. 2 STUPID, slow-witted, dim, dull, thick (*infml*), dense (*sl*). 3 PROLONGED, protracted, long-drawn-out, tedious, boring, dull, uninteresting, uneventful.
🔁 1 quick, fast, swift, rapid, speedy. 2 clever, intelligent. 3 brisk, lively, exciting.
➤ *v* brake, decelerate, delay, hold up, retard, handicap, check, curb, restrict.
🔁 speed, accelerate.

sluggish *adj* lethargic, listless, torpid, heavy, dull, slow, slow-moving, slothful, lazy, idle, inactive, lifeless, unresponsive.
🔁 brisk, vigorous, lively, dynamic.

slump *v* 1 COLLAPSE, fall, drop, plunge, plummet, sink, decline, deteriorate, worsen, crash, fail. 2 DROOP, sag, bend, stoop, slouch, loll, lounge, flop.
➤ *n* recession, depression, stagnation, downturn, low, trough, decline, deterioration, worsening, fall, drop, collapse, crash, failure.
🔁 boom.

sly *adj* wily, foxy, crafty, cunning, artful, guileful, clever, canny, shrewd, astute, knowing, subtle, devious, shifty, tricky, furtive, stealthy, surreptitious, underhand, covert, secretive, scheming,

conniving, mischievous, roguish.
F3 honest, frank, candid, open.

smack v hit, strike, slap, spank, whack (*infml*), thwack (*infml*), clap, clout (*infml*), box, cuff, pat, tap.
➤ n blow, slap, spank, whack (*infml*), thwack (*infml*), box, cuff, pat, tap.
➤ adv bang, slap-bang, right, plumb, straight, directly, exactly, precisely.

small adj 1 LITTLE, tiny, minute, minuscule, short, slight, puny, petite, diminutive, pint-size(d) (*infml*), miniature, mini (*infml*), pocket, pocket-sized, young. 2 PETTY, trifling, trivial, unimportant, insignificant, minor, inconsiderable, negligible. 3 INADEQUATE, insufficient, scanty, meagre, paltry, mean, limited.
F3 1 large, big, huge. 2 great, considerable. 3 ample.

small-minded adj petty, mean, ungenerous, illiberal, intolerant, bigoted, narrow-minded, parochial, insular, rigid, hidebound.
F3 liberal, tolerant, broad-minded.

smarmy adj smooth, oily, unctuous, servile, obsequious, sycophantic, toadying, ingratiating, crawling, fawning.

smart adj 1 *smart clothes*: elegant, stylish, chic, fashionable, modish, neat, tidy, spruce, trim, well-groomed. 2 CLEVER, intelligent, bright, sharp, acute, shrewd, astute.
F3 1 dowdy, unfashionable, untidy, scruffy. 2 stupid, slow.
➤ v sting, hurt, prick, burn, tingle, twinge, throb.

smarten v neaten, tidy, spruce up, groom, clean, polish, beautify.

smash v 1 *smash a window*: break, shatter, shiver, ruin, wreck, demolish, destroy, defeat, crush. 2 CRASH, collide, strike, bang, bash, thump.
➤ n accident, crash, collision, pile-up.

smattering n bit, modicum, dash, sprinkling, basics, rudiments, elements.

smear v 1 DAUB, plaster, spread, cover, coat, rub, smudge, streak. 2 DEFAME, malign, vilify, blacken, sully, stain, tarnish.
➤ n 1 STREAK, smudge, blot, blotch, splodge, daub. 2 DEFAMATION, slander, libel, mudslinging, muck-raking.

smell v 1 SNIFF, nose, scent, sense, detect. 2 STINK, reek, pong (*infml*).

Ways of describing smells include:
pleasant: aroma, bouquet, fragrance, incense, nose, odour, potpourri, perfume, redolence, scent;
unpleasant: b.o. (body odour), fetor, funk (*US*), hum, malodour, mephitis, miasma, niff (*sl*), pong (*infml*), pungency, reek, sniff, stench, stink, whiff.

---

smelly adj malodorous, pongy (*infml*), stinking, reeking, foul, bad, off, fetid, putrid, high, strong.

smile n, v grin, beam, simper, smirk, leer, laugh.

smoke n fumes, exhaust, gas, vapour, mist, fog, smog.
➤ v fume, smoulder, cure, dry.

smoky adj sooty, black, grey, grimy, murky, cloudy, hazy, foggy.

smooth adj 1 LEVEL, plane, even, flat, horizontal, flush. 2 STEADY, unbroken, flowing, regular, uniform, rhythmic, easy, effortless. 3 SHINY, polished, glossy, silky, glassy, calm, undisturbed, serene, tranquil, peaceful. 4 SUAVE, agreeable, smooth-talking, glib, plausible, persuasive, slick, smarmy, unctuous, ingratiating.
F3 1 rough, lumpy. 2 irregular, erratic, unsteady. 3 rough, choppy.
➤ v 1 IRON, press, roll, flatten, level, plane, file, sand, polish. 2 EASE, alleviate, assuage, allay, mitigate, calm, mollify.
F3 1 roughen, wrinkle, crease.

smother v suffocate, asphyxiate, strangle, throttle, choke, stifle, extinguish, snuff, muffle, suppress, repress, hide, conceal, cover, shroud, envelop, wrap.

smoulder v burn, smoke, fume, rage, seethe, simmer.

smudge *v* blur, smear, daub, mark, spot, stain, dirty, soil.

➤ *n* blot, stain, spot, blemish, blur, smear, streak.

smug *adj* complacent, self-satisfied, superior, holier-than-thou, self-righteous, priggish, conceited.
🖃 humble, modest.

snack *n* refreshment(s), bite, nibble, titbit, elevenses (*infml*).

snag *n* disadvantage, inconvenience, drawback, catch, problem, difficulty, complication, setback, hitch, obstacle, stumbling block.

➤ *v* catch, rip, tear, hole, ladder.

snap *v* **1** *the twig snapped*: break, crack, split, separate, divide. **2** BITE, nip, bark, growl, snarl, retort, crackle, pop. **3** SNATCH, seize, catch, grasp, grip.

➤ *n* break, crack, bite, nip, flick, fillip, crackle, pop.

➤ *adj* immediate, instant, on-the-spot, abrupt, sudden.

snappy *adj* **1** SMART, stylish, chic, fashionable, modish, trendy (*infml*). **2** QUICK, hasty, brisk, lively, energetic. **3** CROSS, irritable, grouchy (*infml*), edgy, touchy (*infml*), brusque, quick-tempered, ill-natured, crabbed, testy.
🖃 **1** dowdy. **2** slow.

snare *v* trap, ensnare, entrap, catch, net.

➤ *n* trap, wire, net, noose, catch, pitfall.

snarl[1] *v* growl, grumble, complain.

snarl[2] *v* tangle, knot, ravel, entangle, enmesh, embroil, confuse, muddle, complicate.

snatch *v* grab, seize, kidnap, take, nab (*infml*), pluck, pull, wrench, wrest, gain, win, clutch, grasp, grip.

sneak *v* **1** CREEP, steal, slip, slink, sidle, skulk, lurk, prowl, smuggle, spirit. **2** TELL TALES, split (*sl*), inform on, grass on (*sl*).

➤ *n* tell-tale, informer, grass (*sl*).

sneaking *adj* private, secret, furtive, surreptitious, hidden, lurking, suppressed, grudging, nagging, niggling, persistent, worrying, uncomfortable, intuitive.

sneer *v* scorn, disdain, look down on, deride, scoff, jeer, mock, ridicule, gibe, laugh, snigger.

➤ *n* scorn, disdain, derision, jeer, mockery, ridicule, gibe, snigger.

snide *adj* derogatory, disparaging, sarcastic, cynical, scornful, sneering, hurtful, unkind, nasty, mean, spiteful, malicious, ill-natured.
🖃 complimentary.

sniff *v* breathe, inhale, snuff, snuffle, smell, nose, scent.

snigger *v, n* laugh, giggle, titter, chuckle, sneer.

snip *v* cut, clip, trim, crop, dock, slit, nick, notch.

snippet *n* piece, scrap, cutting, clipping, fragment, particle, shred, snatch, part, portion, segment, section.

snobbery *n* snobbishness, superciliousness, snootiness (*infml*), airs, loftiness, arrogance, pride, pretension, condescension.

snobbish *adj* supercilious, disdainful, snooty (*infml*), stuck-up (*infml*), toffee-nosed (*infml*), superior, lofty, high and mighty, arrogant, pretentious, affected, condescending, patronizing.

snoop *v* spy, sneak, pry, nose, interfere, meddle.

snooze *v* nap, doze, sleep, kip (*sl*).
➤ *n* nap, catnap, forty winks (*infml*), doze, siesta, sleep, kip (*sl*).

snub *v* rebuff, brush off, cut, cold-shoulder, slight, rebuke, put down, squash, humble, shame, humiliate, mortify.

➤ *n* rebuff, brush-off, cold-shoulder, slight, affront, insult, rebuke, put-down, humiliation.

snug *adj* cosy, warm, comfortable, homely, friendly, intimate, sheltered, secure, tight, close-fitting.

soak *v* wet, drench, saturate, penetrate, permeate, infuse, bathe, marinate, souse, steep, submerge, immerse.

soaking *adj* soaked, drenched, sodden, waterlogged, saturated, sopping, wringing, dripping, streaming.
F3 dry.

soar *v* fly, wing, glide, plane, tower, rise, ascend, climb, mount, escalate, rocket.
F3 fall, plummet.

sob *v* cry, weep, bawl, howl, blubber, snivel.

sober *adj* **1** TEETOTAL, temperate, moderate, abstinent, abstemious. **2** SOLEMN, dignified, serious, staid, steady, sedate, quiet, serene, calm, composed, unruffled, unexcited, cool, dispassionate, level-headed, pragmatic, practical, realistic, reasonable, rational, clear-headed. **3** *sober dress*: sombre, drab, dull, plain, subdued, restrained, button-down (*infml*).
F3 1 drunk, intemperate. **2** frivolous, excited, unrealistic, irrational. **3** flashy, garish.

so-called *adj* alleged, supposed, purported, ostensible, nominal, self-styled, professed, would-be, pretended.

sociable *adj* outgoing, gregarious, friendly, affable, companionable, genial, convivial, cordial, warm, hospitable, neighbourly, approachable, accessible, familiar.
F3 unsociable, withdrawn, unfriendly, hostile.

social *adj* communal, public, community, common, general, collective, group, organized.
➤ *n* party, do (*infml*), get-together, gathering.

socialize *v* mix, mingle, fraternize, get together, go out, entertain.

society *n* **1** COMMUNITY, population, culture, civilization, nation, people, mankind, humanity. **2** CLUB, circle, group, association, organization, company, corporation, league, union, guild, fellowship, fraternity, brotherhood, sisterhood, sorority. **3** FRIENDSHIP, companionship,

camaraderie, fellowship, company. **4** UPPER CLASSES, aristocracy, gentry, nobility, elite.

soft *adj* **1** YIELDING, pliable, flexible, elastic, plastic, malleable, spongy, squashy, pulpy. **2** *soft colours*: pale, light, pastel, delicate, subdued, muted, quiet, low, dim, faint, diffuse, mild, bland, gentle, soothing, sweet, mellow, melodious, dulcet, pleasant. **3** FURRY, downy, velvety, silky, smooth. **4** LENIENT, lax, permissive, indulgent, tolerant, easy-going (*infml*), kind, generous, gentle, merciful, soft-hearted, tender, sensitive. **5** WEAK, spineless, feeble, wimpy (*infml*), wimpish (*infml*), cowardly, wet, submissive.
F3 1 hard, rigid. **2** harsh, strong. **3** rough, coarse. **4** strict, severe.

soften *v* **1** MODERATE, temper, mitigate, lessen, diminish, abate, alleviate, ease, soothe, palliate, quell, assuage, subdue, mollify, appease, calm, still, relax. **2** MELT, liquefy, dissolve, reduce. **3** CUSHION, pad, muffle, quicken, lower, lighten.

soft-hearted *adj* sympathetic, compassionate, kind, benevolent, charitable, generous, warm-hearted, tender, sentimental.
F3 hard-hearted, callous.

soggy *adj* wet, damp, moist, soaked, drenched, sodden, waterlogged, saturated, sopping, dripping, heavy, boggy, spongy, pulpy.

soil[1] *n* earth, clay, loam, humus, dirt, dust, ground, land, region, country.

soil[2] *v* dirty, begrime, stain, spot, smudge, smear, foul, muddy, pollute, defile, besmirch, blemish, sully, tarnish.

solace *n* comfort, consolation, relief, alleviation, support, cheer.

soldier *n* warrior, fighter.

Types of soldier include: cadet, private, sapper, NCO, orderly, officer, gunner, infantryman, trooper, fusilier, rifleman, paratrooper, sentry, guardsman, marine, commando, tommy, dragoon, cavalryman, lancer, hussar, conscript, recruit, regular, Territorial, GI (*US*), mercenary, legionnaire, guerrilla, partisan, centurion; serviceman, servicewoman. *see also* **rank**[1].

sole *adj* only, unique, exclusive, individual, single, singular, one, lone, solitary, alone.
F3 shared, multiple.

solemn *adj* 1 *a solemn expression*: serious, grave, sober, sedate, sombre, glum, thoughtful, earnest, awed, reverential. 2 GRAND, stately, majestic, ceremonial, ritual, formal, ceremonious, pompous, dignified, august, venerable, awe-inspiring, impressive, imposing, momentous.
F3 1 light-hearted. 2 frivolous.

solicit *v* ask, request, seek, crave, beg, beseech, entreat, implore, pray, supplicate (*fml*), sue, petition, canvass, importune (*fml*).

solicitor *n* lawyer, advocate, attorney, barrister, QC.

solicitous *adj* caring, attentive, considerate, concerned, anxious, worried.

solid *adj* 1 HARD, firm, dense, compact, strong, sturdy, substantial, sound, unshakable. 2 *a solid white line*: unbroken, continuous, uninterrupted. 3 RELIABLE, dependable, trusty, worthy, decent, upright, sensible, level-headed, stable, serious, sober. 4 REAL, genuine, pure, concrete, tangible.
F3 1 liquid, gaseous, hollow. 2 broken, dotted. 3 unreliable, unstable. 4 unreal, intangible.

solidarity *n* unity, agreement, accord, unanimity, consensus, harmony, concord, cohesion, like-mindedness, camaraderie, team spirit, esprit de corps, soundness, stability.
F3 discord, division, schism.

solidify *v* harden, set, jell, congeal, coagulate, clot, cake, crystallize.
F3 soften, liquefy, dissolve.

solitary *adj* sole, single, lone, alone,

lonely, lonesome, friendless, unsociable, reclusive, withdrawn, retired, sequestered, cloistered, secluded, separate, isolated, remote, out-of-the-way, inaccessible, unfrequented, unvisited, untrodden.
F3 accompanied, gregarious, busy.

solitude *n* aloneness, loneliness, reclusiveness, retirement, privacy, seclusion, isolation, remoteness.
F3 companionship.

solution *n* 1 ANSWER, result, key, explanation, resolution, remedy. 2 MIXTURE, blend, compound, suspension, emulsion, liquid.

solve *v* work out, figure out, puzzle out, decipher, crack, disentangle, unravel, answer, resolve, settle, clear up, clarify, explain, interpret.

sombre *adj* dark, funereal, drab, dull, dim, obscure, shady, shadowy, gloomy, dismal, melancholy, sad, mournful, joyless, sober, serious, grave.
F3 bright, cheerful, happy.

someday *adv* sometime, one day, eventually, ultimately.
F3 never.

sometimes *adv* occasionally, now and again, now and then, once in a while, from time to time.
F3 always, never.

song *n* tune, melody, lyric, number, ditty.

Types of song include: air, anthem, aria, ballad, barcarole, bird call, bird song, blues, calypso, cantata, canticle, cantilena, canzone, canzonet, carol, chanson, chansonette, chant, chorus, descant, dirge, ditty, elegy, epinikion, epithalamium, folk song, gospel song, hymn, jingle, love song, Lied, lilt, lullaby, madrigal, nursery rhyme, ode, plainchant, plainsong, pop song, psalm, recitative, requiem, rock and roll, roundelay, serenade, shanty, spiritual, Negro spiritual, torch song, war song, wassail, yodel.

soon *adv* shortly, presently, in a minute, before long, in the near future.

soothe *v* alleviate, relieve, ease, salve, comfort, allay, calm, compose, tranquillize, settle, still, quiet, hush, lull, pacify, appease, mollify, assuage, mitigate, soften.
E3 aggravate, irritate, annoy, vex.

sophisticated *adj* **1** URBANE, cosmopolitan, worldly, worldly-wise, cultured, cultivated, refined, polished. **2** *sophisticated technology*: advanced, highly-developed, high-end, complicated, complex, intricate, elaborate, delicate, subtle.
E3 1 unsophisticated, naïve. **2** primitive, simple.

soporific *adj* sleep-inducing, hypnotic, sedative, tranquillizing, sleepy, somnolent.
E3 stimulating, invigorating.

soppy *adj* sentimental, lovey-dovey (*infml*), weepy, sloppy, slushy, mushy, corny (*infml*), mawkish, cloying, touchy-feely (*sl*), soft, silly, daft (*infml*).

sorcery *n* magic, black magic, witchcraft, wicca, wizardry, necromancy (*fml*), voodoo, spell, incantation, charm, enchantment.

sordid *adj* dirty, filthy, unclean, foul, vile, squalid, sleazy, seamy, seedy, disreputable, shabby, tawdry, corrupt, degraded, degenerate, debauched, low, base, despicable, shameful, wretched, mean, miserly, niggardly, grasping, mercenary, selfish, self-seeking.
E3 pure, honourable, upright.

sore *adj* **1** PAINFUL, hurting, aching, smarting, stinging, tender, sensitive, inflamed, red, raw. **2** ANNOYED, irritated, vexed, angry, upset, hurt, wounded, afflicted, aggrieved, resentful.
E3 2 pleased, happy.
➤ *n* wound, lesion, swelling, inflammation, boil, abscess, ulcer.

sorrow *n* sadness, unhappiness, grief, mourning, misery, woe, distress, affliction, anguish, heartache, heartbreak, misfortune, hardship, trouble, worry, trial, tribulation, regret, remorse.
E3 happiness, joy.

sorry *adj* **1** APOLOGETIC, regretful, remorseful, contrite, penitent, repentant, conscience-stricken, guilt-ridden, shamefaced. **2** *in a sorry state*: pathetic, pitiful, poor, wretched, miserable, sad, unhappy, dismal. **3** SYMPATHETIC, compassionate, understanding, pitying, concerned, moved.
E3 1 impenitent, unashamed. **2** happy, cheerful. **3** uncaring.

sort *n* kind, type, genre, ilk, family, race, breed, species, genus, variety, order, class, category, group, denomination, style, make, brand, stamp, quality, nature, character, description.
➤ *v* class, group, categorize, distribute, divide, separate, segregate, sift, screen, grade, rank, order, classify, catalogue, arrange, organize, systematize.
◇ **sort out** resolve, clear up, clarify, tidy up, neaten, choose, select.

soul *n* **1** SPIRIT, psyche, mind, reason, intellect, character, inner being, essence, life, vital force. **2** INDIVIDUAL, person, man, woman, creature.

sound[1] *n* noise, din, report, resonance, reverberation, tone, timbre, tenor, description.

Sounds include: bang, blare, blast, bleep, boom, buzz, chime, chink, chug, clack, clang, clank, clap, clash, clatter, click, clink, crack, crackle, crash, creak, crunch, cry, drone, echo, explode, fizz, grate, grizzle, groan, gurgle, hiccup, hiss, honk, hoot, hum, jangle, jingle, knock, moan, murmur, patter, peal, ping, pip, plop, pop, rattle, report, reverberate, ring, rumble, rustle, scream, sigh, sizzle, skirl, slam, slurp, smack, snap, sniff, snore, snort, sob, splash, splosh, splutter, squeak, squeal, squelch, swish, tap, throb, thud, thump, thunder, tick, ting, tinkle, toot, twang, wail, whimper, whine, whirr, whistle, whoop, yell.

Animal sounds include: bark, bay, bellow, bleat, bray, cackle, caw, chirp, chirrup, cluck, coo, croak, crow, gobble, growl, grunt, hiss, hoot, howl, low, mew, miaow, moo, neigh, purr, quack, roar, screech, snarl, squawk, squeak, tweet, twitter, warble, whinny, woof, yap, yelp, yowl.

➤ *v* **1** RING, toll, chime, peal, resound, resonate, reverberate, echo. **2** ARTICULATE, enunciate, pronounce, voice, express, utter, say, declare, announce.

sound^2 *adj* **1** FIT, well, healthy, vigorous, robust, sturdy, firm, solid, whole, complete, intact, perfect, unbroken, undamaged, unimpaired, unhurt, uninjured. **2** VALID, well-founded, reasonable, rational, logical, orthodox, right, true, proven, reliable, trustworthy, secure, substantial, thorough, good.
E3 1 unfit, ill, shaky. **2** unsound, unreliable, poor.

sound^3 *v* measure, plumb, fathom, probe, examine, test, inspect, investigate.

sour *adj* **1** TART, sharp, acid, pungent, vinegary, bitter, rancid. **2** EMBITTERED, acrimonious, ill-tempered, peevish, crabbed, crusty, disagreeable, grumpy.
E3 1 sweet, sugary. **2** good-natured, generous.

source *n* origin, derivation, beginning, start, commencement, cause, root, rise, spring, fountainhead, wellhead, supply, mine, originator, authority, informant.

souvenir *n* memento, reminder, remembrance, keepsake, relic, token.

sovereign *n* ruler, monarch, king, queen, emperor, empress, potentate, chief.
➤ *adj* ruling, royal, imperial, absolute, unlimited, supreme, paramount, predominant, principal, chief, dominant, independent, autonomous.

sow *v* plant, seed, scatter, strew, spread, disseminate, lodge, implant.

space *n* **1** ROOM, place, seat, accommodation, capacity, volume, extent, expansion, scope, range, play, elbow-room, leeway, margin. **2** BLANK, omission, gap, opening, divide, lacuna, interval, intermission, chasm.

spacious *adj* roomy, capacious, ample, big, large, sizable, broad, wide, huge, vast, extensive, open, uncrowded.
E3 small, narrow, cramped, confined.

span *n* spread, stretch, reach, range, scope, compass, extent, length, distance, duration, term, period, spell.
➤ *v* arch, vault, bridge, link, cross, traverse, extend, cover.

spank *v* smack, slap, wallop (*infml*), whack (*infml*), thrash, slipper, cane.

spare *adj* reserve, emergency, extra, additional, leftover, remaining, unused, over, surplus, superfluous, supernumerary, unwanted, free, unoccupied.
E3 necessary, vital, used.
➤ *v* **1** PARDON, let off, reprieve, release, free. **2** GRANT, allow, afford, part with.

sparing *adj* economical, thrifty, careful, prudent, frugal, meagre, miserly, mean.
E3 unsparing, liberal, lavish.

spark *n* flash, flare, gleam, glint, flicker, hint, trace, vestige, scrap, atom, jot.
➤ *v* kindle, set off, trigger, start, cause, occasion, prompt, provoke, incite, stimulate, stir, excite, inspire.

sparkle *v* **1** TWINKLE, glitter, scintillate, flash, gleam, glint, glisten, shimmer, coruscate, shine, beam. **2** EFFERVESCE, fizz, bubble.
➤ *n* twinkle, glitter, flash, gleam, glint, flicker, spark, radiance, brilliance, dazzle, spirit, vitality, life, animation.

sparse *adj* scarce, scanty, meagre, scattered, infrequent, sporadic.
E3 plentiful, thick, dense.

spartan *adj* austere, harsh, severe, rigorous, strict, disciplined, ascetic, abstemious, temperate, frugal, plain, simple, bleak, joyless.
E3 luxurious, self-indulgent.

spasm *n* burst, eruption, outburst, frenzy, fit, convulsion, seizure, attack, contraction, jerk, twitch, tic.

spasmodic *adj* sporadic, occasional, intermittent, erratic, irregular, fitful, jerky.
🖪 continuous, uninterrupted.

spate *n* flood, deluge, torrent, rush, outpouring, flow.

speak *v* talk, converse (*fml*), say, state, declare, express, utter, voice, articulate, enunciate, pronounce, tell, communicate, address, lecture, harangue, hold forth, declaim, argue, discuss.

speaker *n* lecturer, orator, spokesperson, spokesman, spokeswoman.

special *adj* **1** *a special occasion*: important, significant, momentous, major, noteworthy, distinguished, memorable, remarkable, extraordinary, exceptional. **2** DIFFERENT, distinctive, characteristic, peculiar, singular, individual, unique, exclusive, select, choice, particular, specific, unusual, precise, detailed.
🖪 **1** normal, ordinary, usual. **2** general, common.

specialist *n* consultant, authority, expert, master, professional, connoisseur.

speciality *n* strength, forte, talent, field, area, line, specialty, pièce de résistance.

specific *adj* precise, exact, fixed, limited, particular, special, definite, unequivocal, clear-cut, explicit, express, unambiguous.
🖪 vague, approximate.

specification *n* requirement, condition, qualification, description, listing, item, particular, detail.

specify *v* stipulate, spell out, define, particularize, detail, itemize, enumerate, list, mention, cite, name, designate, indicate, describe, delineate.

specimen *n* sample, example, instance, illustration, model, pattern, paradigm, exemplar, representative, copy, exhibit.

spectacle *n* show, performance, display, exhibition, parade, pageant, extravaganza, scene, sight, curiosity, wonder, marvel, phenomenon.

spectacles

> *Types of spectacles include*: bifocals, contact lens, diving mask, eyeglass, goggles, half-glasses, lorgnette, monocle, pince-nez, Polaroid glasses, quizzing glass, reading glasses, safety glasses, shooting glasses, sports spex, sunglasses, trifocals, varifocals.

spectacular *adj* grand, splendid, magnificent, sensational, impressive, striking, stunning, staggering, amazing, remarkable, dramatic, daring, breathtaking, dazzling, eye-catching, colourful.
🖪 unimpressive, ordinary.

spectator *n* watcher, viewer, onlooker, looker-on, bystander, passer-by, witness, eyewitness, observer.
🖪 player, participant.

spectre *n* ghost, phantom, spirit, wraith, apparition, vision, presence.

speculate *v* wonder, contemplate, meditate, muse, reflect, consider, deliberate, theorize, suppose, guess, conjecture, surmise, gamble, risk, hazard, venture.

speculative *adj* conjectural, hypothetical, theoretical, notional, abstract, academic, tentative, risky, hazardous, uncertain, unpredictable.

speech *n* **1** DICTION, articulation, enunciation, elocution, delivery, utterance, voice, language, tongue, parlance, dialect, jargon. **2** *make a speech*: oration (*fml*), address, discourse, talk, lecture, harangue, spiel (*sl*), conversation, dialogue, monologue, soliloquy.

speechless *adj* dumbfounded, thunderstruck, amazed, aghast,

tongue-tied, inarticulate, mute, dumb, silent, mum, shtoom (*sl*).
🔀 talkative.

speed *n* velocity, rate, pace, tempo, quickness, swiftness, rapidity, celerity (*fml*), alacrity, haste, hurry, dispatch, rush, acceleration.
🔀 slowness, delay.
➤ *v* race, tear, belt (*infml*), zoom, career, bowl along, sprint, gallop, hurry, rush, hasten (*fml*), accelerate, quicken, put one's foot down (*infml*), step on it (*infml*).
🔀 slow, delay.

speedy *adj* fast, quick, swift, rapid, nimble, express, prompt, immediate, hurried, hasty, precipitate, cursory.
🔀 slow, leisurely.

spell[1] *n* period, time, bout, session, term, season, interval, stretch, patch, turn, stint.

spell[2] *n* charm, incantation, magic, sorcery, witchery, bewitchment, enchantment, fascination, glamour.

spellbound *adj* transfixed, gripped, hypnotized, mesmerized, fascinated, enthralled, entranced, captivated, bewitched, enchanted, charmed.

spend *v* **1** *spend money*: disburse, pay out, fork out (*infml*), shell out (*infml*), invest, lay out, splash out (*infml*), waste, squander, fritter, expend, consume, use up, exhaust. **2** PASS, fill, occupy, use, employ, apply, devote.
🔀 **1** save, hoard.

spendthrift *n* squanderer, prodigal, profligate, wastrel.
🔀 miser.
➤ *adj* improvident, extravagant, prodigal, wasteful.

sphere *n* **1** BALL, globe, orb, round. **2** DOMAIN, realm, province, department, territory, field, range, scope, compass, rank, function, capacity.

spherical *adj* round, rotund, ball-shaped, globe-shaped.

spicy *adj* **1** PIQUANT, hot, pungent, tangy, seasoned, aromatic, fragrant. **2** RACY, risqué, ribald, saucy (*infml*), suggestive, indelicate, improper, indecorous, unseemly, scandalous, sensational.
🔀 **1** bland, insipid. **2** decent.

spike *n* point, prong, tine, spine, barb, nail, stake.
➤ *v* impale, stick, spear, skewer, spit.

spill *v* overturn, upset, slop, overflow, disgorge, pour, tip, discharge, shed, scatter.

spin *v* turn, revolve, rotate, twist, gyrate, twirl, pirouette, wheel, whirl, swirl, reel.
➤ *n* **1** TURN, revolution, twist, gyration, twirl, pirouette, whirl, swirl. **2** COMMOTION, agitation, panic, flap (*infml*), state (*infml*), tizzy (*infml*). **3** DRIVE, ride, run.
◇ **spin out** prolong, protract, extend, lengthen, amplify, pad out.

spindle *n* axis, pivot, pin, rod, axle.

spine *n* **1** BACKBONE, spinal column, vertebral column, vertebrae. **2** THORN, barb, prickle, bristle, quill.

spineless *adj* weak, feeble, wimpy (*infml*), wimpish (*infml*), irresolute, ineffective, cowardly, faint-hearted, lily-livered, yellow (*sl*), soft, wet (*infml*), submissive, weak-kneed.
🔀 strong, brave.

spiral *adj* winding, coiled, corkscrew, helical, whorled, scrolled, circular.
➤ *n* coil, helix, corkscrew, screw, whorl, convolution.

spire *n* steeple, pinnacle, peak, summit, top, tip, point, spike.

spirit *n* **1** SOUL, psyche, mind, breath, life. **2** GHOST, spectre, phantom, angel, apparition, demon, fairy, sprite. **3** LIVELINESS, vivacity, animation, sparkle, vigour, energy, zest, fire, ardour, motivation, enthusiasm, zeal, enterprise, resolution, willpower, courage, backbone, mettle. **4** *the spirit of the law*: meaning, sense, substance, essence, gist, tenor, character, quality. **5** MOOD, humour, temper, disposition, temperament, feeling, morale, attitude, outlook.

spirited *adj* lively, vivacious, animated, sparkling, high-spirited, vigorous, energetic, active, ardent, zealous, bold, courageous, mettlesome, plucky, feisty.
🖪 spiritless, lethargic, cowardly.

spiritual *adj* unworldly, incorporeal, immaterial, otherwordly, heavenly, divine, holy, sacred, religious, ecclesiastical.
🖪 physical, material.

spit *v* expectorate, eject, discharge, splutter, hiss.
➤ *n* spittle, saliva, slaver, drool, dribble, sputum, phlegm, expectoration.

spite *n* spitefulness, malice, venom, gall, bitterness, rancour, animosity, ill feeling, grudge, malevolence, malignity, ill nature, hate, hatred.
🖪 goodwill, compassion, affection.
➤ *v* annoy, irritate, irk, vex, provoke, gall, hurt, injure, offend, put out.

spiteful *adj* malicious, venomous, catty, bitchy, snide, barbed, cruel, vindictive, vengeful, malevolent, malignant, ill-natured, ill-disposed, nasty.
🖪 charitable, affectionate.

splash *v* 1 BATHE, wallow, paddle, wade, dabble, plunge, wet, wash, shower, spray, squirt, sprinkle, spatter, splatter, splodge, spread, daub, plaster, slop, slosh, splosh, plop, surge, break, dash, strike, buffet, smack. 2 PUBLICIZE, flaunt, blazon, trumpet.
➤ *n* 1 SPOT, patch, splatter, splodge, burst, touch, dash. 2 PUBLICITY, display, ostentation, effect, impact, stir, excitement, sensation.

splendid *adj* brilliant, dazzling, glittering, lustrous, bright, radiant, glowing, glorious, magnificent, gorgeous, resplendent, sumptuous, luxurious, lavish, rich, fine, grand, stately, imposing, impressive, great, outstanding, remarkable, exceptional, sublime, supreme, superb, excellent, first-class, wonderful, marvellous, admirable.

🖪 drab, ordinary, run-of-the-mill.

splendour *n* brightness, radiance, brilliance, dazzle, lustre, glory, resplendence, magnificence, richness, grandeur, majesty, solemnity, pomp, ceremony, display, show, spectacle.
🖪 drabness, squalor.

splice *v* join, unite, wed, marry, bind, tie, plait, braid, interweave, interlace, intertwine, entwine, mesh, knit, graft.

splinter *n* sliver, shiver, chip, shard, fragment, flake, shaving, paring.
➤ *v* split, fracture, smash, shatter, shiver, fragment, disintegrate.

split *v* divide, separate, partition, part, disunite, disband, open, gape, fork, diverge, break, splinter, shiver, snap, crack, burst, rupture, tear, rend, rip, slit, slash, cleave, halve, slice up, share, distribute, parcel out.
➤ *n* 1 DIVISION, separation, partition, break, breach, gap, cleft, crevice, crack, fissure, rupture, tear, rent, rip, rift, slit, slash. 2 SCHISM, disunion, dissension, discord, difference, divergence, break-up.
➤ *adj* divided, cleft, cloven, bisected, dual, twofold, broken, fractured, cracked, ruptured.
◇ **split up** part, part company, disband, break up, separate, divorce.

spoil *v* 1 MAR, upset, wreck, ruin, destroy, damage, impair, harm, hurt, injure, deface, disfigure, blemish. 2 *spoil a child*: indulge, pamper, cosset, coddle, mollycoddle, baby, spoon-feed. 3 DETERIORATE, go bad, go off, sour, turn, curdle, decay, decompose.

spoils *n* plunder, loot, booty, haul, swag (*sl*), pickings, gain, acquisitions, prizes, winnings.

sponge *v* 1 WIPE, mop, clean, wash. 2 CADGE, scrounge, wheedle.

sponger *n* cadger, scrounger, wheedler, parasite, hanger-on.

spongy *adj* soft, cushioned, yielding, elastic, springy, porous, absorbent, light.

sponsor *n* patron, backer, angel (*infml*), promoter, underwriter, guarantor, surety.

➤ *v* finance, fund, bankroll, subsidize, patronize, back, promote, underwrite, guarantee.

spontaneous *adj* natural, unforced, untaught, instinctive, impulsive, unpremeditated, free, willing, unhesitating, voluntary, unprompted, impromptu, extempore, ad-lib.

🔁 forced, studied, planned, deliberate.

sporadic *adj* occasional, intermittent, infrequent, isolated, spasmodic, erratic, irregular, uneven, random, scattered.

🔁 frequent, regular.

sport *n* **1** GAME, exercise, activity, pastime, amusement, entertainment, diversion, recreation, play. **2** FUN, mirth, humour, joking, jesting, banter, teasing, mockery, ridicule.

Sports include: badminton, fives, lacrosse, squash, table-tennis, ping-pong (*infml*), tennis; American football, Australian Rules football, baseball, basketball, billiards, boules, bowls, Canadian football, cricket, croquet, football, futsal, Gaelic football, golf, handball, hockey, netball, pétanque, pitch and putt, polo, pool, putting, rounders, Rugby, shinty, snooker, soccer, tenpin bowling, volleyball; athletics, cross-country, decathlon, discus, high jump, hurdling, javelin, long jump, marathon, pentathlon, pole vault, running, shot put, triple jump; angling, canoeing, diving, fishing, rowing, sailing, skin-diving, surfing, swimming, synchronized swimming, water polo, water-skiing, windsurfing, yachting; bobsleigh, curling, ice hockey, ice-skating, skeleton bob, cross-country skiing, downhill skiing, skiing, slalom, snowboarding, speed skating, tobogganing (luging); aerobics, aqua aerobics, fencing, gymnastics, jogging, keep-fit, roller-skating, trampolining; archery, darts, quoits; boxing, judo, jujitsu, karate, tae kwon do, weightlifting, wrestling; climbing, mountaineering, rock climbing, walking, orienteering, pot-holing; cycle racing, drag racing, go-karting, motor racing, speedway racing, stock car racing, greyhound racing, horse racing, showjumping, trotting, hunting, shooting, clay pigeon shooting; gliding, paragliding, skydiving. *see also* **martial arts**.

Types of sports equipment include: ball, basketball, boule, bowl, jack, wood, football, netball, rugby ball, tenpin bowling ball, volleyball; fishing-rod, fly rod, spinning rod, fishing-line, paternoster, reel, fly reel, hook, gaff, gang-hook, jig, trace, lure, bait, fly, float, net, keep-net, priest, disgorger; bow, arrow, crossbow, bolt; badminton racket, shuttlecock, net; baseball bat, baseball, mitt, catcher's glove; boxing glove, gum shield, punchbag, punchball; cricket bat, cricket ball, wicket, stump, bail, nets; épée, foil, sabre, face-guard, mask; discus, hammer, javelin, shot; golf club, golf ball, tee, golfing glove; asymmetrical bars, horizontal bar, isometric bar, parallel-bars, beam, balance-beam, mat, pommel horse, vaulting horse, rings, rope, springboard, trampoline; hockey stick, hockey ball, ice hockey stick, puck, hockey skate; curling stone; ice-skate, roller-skate, rollerblade, roller boot, speed skate, skateboard; ski, ski stick, snow board, toboggan; snooker ball, billiard ball, cue ball, table, cue, rest, bridge, rack, chalk; squash racket, squash ball; table-tennis bat, table-tennis ball, net; tennis racket, tennis ball, net, racket press; oar, aqualung, snorkel, water-ski, sailboard, surfboard.

➤ *v* wear, display, exhibit, show off.

sporting *adj* sportsmanlike, gentlemanly, decent, considerate, fair.

🔁 unsporting, ungentlemanly, unfair.

sporty *adj* **1** ATHLETIC, fit, energetic,

outdoor. **2** STYLISH, trendy (*infml*), jaunty, natty (*infml*), snazzy (*infml*), showy, loud, flashy. **3** CASUAL, informal.

spot *n* **1** DOT, speckle, fleck, mark, speck, blotch, blot, smudge, daub, splash, stain, discoloration, blemish, flaw, pimple. **2** PLACE, point, position, situation, location, site, scene, locality. **3** (*infml*) PLIGHT, predicament, quandary, dilemma, difficulty, trouble, mess.
➤ *v* see, notice, observe, detect, discern, identify, recognize.

spotless *adj* immaculate, clean, white, gleaming, spick and span, unmarked, unstained, unblemished, unsullied, pure, chaste, virgin, untouched, innocent, blameless, faultless, irreproachable.
◪ dirty, impure.

spotted *adj* dotted, speckled, flecked, mottled, dappled, pied.

spotty *adj* pimply, pimpled, blotchy, spotted.

spouse *n* husband, wife, partner, mate, other half (*infml*), better half (*infml*).

spout *v* jet, spurt, squirt, spray, shoot, gush, stream, surge, erupt, emit, discharge.
➤ *n* jet, fountain, geyser, gargoyle, outlet, nozzle, rose, spray.

sprawl *v* spread, straggle, trail, ramble, flop, slump, slouch, loll, lounge, recline, repose.

spray[1] *v* shower, spatter, sprinkle, scatter, diffuse, wet, drench.
➤ *n* **1** MOISTURE, drizzle, mist, foam, froth. **2** AEROSOL, atomizer, sprinkler.

spray[2] *n* sprig, branch, corsage, posy, bouquet, garland, wreath.

spread *v* **1** STRETCH, extend, sprawl, broaden, widen, dilate, expand, swell, mushroom, proliferate, escalate, open, unroll, unfurl, unfold, fan out, cover, lay out, arrange. **2** SCATTER, strew, diffuse, radiate, disseminate, broadcast, transmit, communicate, promulgate, propagate, publicize, advertise, publish, circulate, distribute.

◪ **1** close, fold. **2** suppress.
➤ *n* **1** STRETCH, reach, span, extent, expanse, sweep, compass. **2** *the spread of disease*: advance, development, expansion, increase, proliferation, propagation, escalation, diffusion, dissemination, dispersion.

spree *n* bout, fling, binge, splurge, orgy, revel.

sprightly *adj* agile, nimble, spry, active, energetic, lively, spirited, vivacious, hearty, brisk, jaunty, cheerful, blithe, airy.
◪ doddering, inactive, lifeless.

spring[1] *v* **1** JUMP, leap, vault, bound, hop, bounce, rebound, recoil. **2** ORIGINATE, derive, come, stem, arise, start, proceed, issue, emerge, emanate, appear, sprout, grow, develop.
➤ *n* **1** JUMP, leap, vault, bound, bounce. **2** SPRINGINESS, resilience, give, flexibility, elasticity, buoyancy.

spring[2] *n* source, origin, beginning, cause, root, fountainhead, wellhead, wellspring, well, geyser, spa.

springy *adj* bouncy, resilient, flexible, elastic, stretchy, rubbery, spongy, buoyant.
◪ hard, stiff.

sprinkle *v* shower, spray, spatter, scatter, strew, dot, pepper, dust, powder.

sprint *v* run, race, dash, tear, belt (*infml*), dart, shoot.

sprout *v* shoot, bud, germinate, grow, develop, come up, spring up.

spruce *adj* smart, elegant, neat, trim, dapper, well-dressed, well-turned-out, well-groomed, sleek.
◪ scruffy, untidy.
◊ **spruce up** neaten, tidy, smarten up, groom.

spur *v* goad, prod, poke, prick, stimulate, prompt, incite, drive, propel, impel, urge, encourage, motivate.
◪ curb, discourage.
➤ *n* incentive, encouragement, inducement, motive, stimulus,

incitement, impetus, fillip.
☒ curb, disincentive.

spurious *adj* false, fake, counterfeit, forged, bogus, phoney (*infml*), mock, sham, feigned, pretended, simulated, imitation, artificial.
☒ genuine, authentic, real.

spurn *v* reject, turn down, knock back (*infml*), scorn, despise, disdain, rebuff, repulse, slight, snub, cold-shoulder, ignore, disregard.
☒ accept, embrace.

spurt *v* gush, squirt, jet, shoot, burst, erupt, surge.
➤ *n* burst, rush, surge, spate, fit, access.

spy *n* secret agent, undercover agent, double agent, mole (*infml*), fifth columnist, scout, snooper.
➤ *v* spot, glimpse, notice, observe, discover.

squabble *v* bicker, wrangle, quarrel, row, argue, dispute, clash, brawl, scrap (*infml*), fight.

squad *n* crew, team, gang, band, group, company, brigade, troop, force, outfit.

squalid *adj* dirty, filthy, unclean, foul, disgusting, repulsive, sordid, seedy, dingy, untidy, slovenly, unkempt, broken-down, run-down, neglected, uncared-for, low, mean, nasty.
☒ clean, pleasant, attractive.

squander *v* waste, misspend, misuse, lavish, blow (*sl*), fritter away, throw away, dissipate, scatter, spend, expend, consume.

square *v* settle, reconcile, tally, agree, accord, harmonize, correspond, match, balance, straighten, level, align, adjust, regulate, adapt, tailor, fit, suit.
➤ *adj* **1** QUADRILATERAL, rectangular, right-angled, perpendicular, straight, true, even, level. **2** FAIR, equitable, just, ethical, honourable, honest, genuine, above-board, on the level (*infml*).

squash *v* **1** CRUSH, flatten, press, squeeze, compress, crowd, trample, stamp, pound, pulp, smash, distort. **2** SUPPRESS, silence, quell, quash,

annihilate, put down, snub, humiliate.
☒ **1** stretch, expand.

squat *adj* short, stocky, thickset, dumpy, chunky, stubby.
☒ slim, lanky.
➤ *v* crouch, stoop, bend, sit.

squawk *v, n* screech, shriek, cry, croak, cackle, crow, hoot.

squeak *v, n* squeal, whine, creak, peep, cheep, pipe.

squeal *v, n* cry, shout, yell, yelp, wail, scream, screech, shriek, squawk.

squeamish *adj* queasy, nauseated, sick, delicate, fastidious, particular, prudish.

squeeze *v* **1** PRESS, squash, crush, pinch, nip, compress, grip, clasp, clutch, hug, embrace, enfold, cuddle. **2** *squeeze into a corner*: cram, stuff, pack, crowd, wedge, jam, force, ram, push, thrust, shove, jostle. **3** WRING, wrest, extort, milk, bleed, force, lean on (*infml*).
➤ *n* **1** PRESS, squash, crush, crowd, congestion, jam. **2** HUG, embrace, hold, grasp, clasp.

squirt *v* spray, spurt, jet, shoot, spout, gush, ejaculate, discharge, emit, eject, expel.
➤ *n* spray, spurt, jet.

stab *v* pierce, puncture, cut, wound, injure, gore, knife, spear, stick, jab, thrust.
➤ *n* **1** ACHE, pang, twinge, prick, puncture, cut, incision, gash, wound, jab, jag. **2** (*infml*) TRY, attempt, endeavour, bash (*infml*).

stability *n* steadiness, firmness, soundness, constancy, steadfastness, strength, sturdiness, solidity, durability, permanence.
☒ instability, unsteadiness, insecurity, weakness.

stable *adj* steady, firm, secure, fast, sound, sure, constant, steadfast, reliable, established, well-founded, deep-rooted, strong, sturdy, durable, lasting, enduring, abiding, permanent, unchangeable, unalterable, invariable,

immutable, fixed, static, balanced.
⊠ unstable, wobbly, shaky, weak.

stack n heap, pile, mound, mass, load, accumulation, hoard, stockpile, cache, stash (*infml*).

➤ v heap, pile, load, amass, accumulate, assemble, gather, save, hoard, stockpile.

staff n **1** *member of staff*: personnel, workforce, employees, workers, crew, team, teachers, officers. **2** STICK, cane, rod, baton, wand, pole, prop.

stage n point, juncture, step, phase, period, division, lap, leg, length, level, floor.

➤ v mount, put on, present, produce, give, do, perform, arrange, organize, stage-manage, orchestrate, engineer.

stagger v **1** LURCH, totter, teeter, wobble, sway, rock, reel, falter, hesitate, waver. **2** SURPRISE, amaze, astound, astonish, stun, stupefy, dumbfound, flabbergast (*infml*), shake, shock, confound, overwhelm.

stagnant adj still, motionless, standing, brackish, stale, sluggish, torpid, lethargic.
⊠ fresh, moving.

stagnate v vegetate, idle, languish, decline, deteriorate, degenerate, decay, rot, rust.

staid adj sedate, calm, composed, sober, demure, solemn, serious, grave, quiet, steady.
⊠ jaunty, debonair, frivolous, adventurous.

stain v **1** MARK, spot, blemish, blot, smudge, discolour, dirty, soil, taint, contaminate, sully, tarnish, blacken, disgrace. **2** DYE, tint, tinge, colour, paint, varnish.

➤ n mark, spot, blemish, blot, smudge, discoloration, smear, slur, disgrace, shame, dishonour.

stake¹ n post, pole, standard, picket, pale, paling, spike, stick.

stake² n bet, wager, pledge, interest, concern, involvement, share, investment, claim.

➤ v gamble, bet, wager, pledge, risk, chance, hazard, venture.

stale adj **1** *stale bread*: dry, hard, old, musty, fusty, flat, insipid, tasteless. **2** OVERUSED, hackneyed, clichéed, stereotyped, jaded, worn-out, unoriginal, trite, banal, commonplace.
⊠ 1 crisp. **2** new.

stalemate n draw, tie, deadlock, gridlock, impasse, standstill, halt.
⊠ progress.

stalk¹ v track, trail, hunt, follow, pursue, shadow, tail, haunt.

stalk² n stem, twig, branch, trunk.

stall v temporize, play for time, delay, hedge, equivocate, obstruct, stonewall.

stalwart adj strong, sturdy, robust, rugged, stout, strapping, muscular, athletic, vigorous, valiant, daring, intrepid, indomitable, determined, resolute, staunch, steadfast, reliable, dependable.
⊠ weak, feeble, timid.

stamina n energy, vigour, strength, power, force, grit, resilience, resistance, endurance, indefatigability, staying power.
⊠ weakness.

stammer v stutter, stumble, falter, hesitate, splutter.

stamp v **1** TRAMPLE, crush, beat, pound. **2** IMPRINT, impress, print, inscribe, engrave, emboss, mark, brand, label, categorize, identify, characterize.

➤ n print, imprint, impression, seal, signature, authorization, mark, hallmark, attestation, brand, cast, mould, cut, form, fashion, sort, kind, type, breed, character, description.

stampede n charge, rush, dash, sprint, flight, rout.

➤ v charge, rush, dash, tear, run, sprint, gallop, shoot, fly, flee, scatter.

stance n posture, deportment, carriage, bearing, position, standpoint, viewpoint, angle, point of view, attitude.

stand v **1** PUT, place, set, erect, up-end, position, station. **2** *I can't stand it*: bear, tolerate, abide, endure, hack (*infml*), suffer, experience, undergo, withstand, weather. **3** RISE, get up, stand up.

➤ *n* base, mount, pedestal, plinth, support, frame, rack, table, stage, platform, podium, place, stall, booth.

◊ **stand by** support, back, champion, defend, stick up for, uphold, adhere to, hold to, stick by.

🔁 let down.

◊ **stand down** step down, resign, abdicate, quit, give up, retire, withdraw.

🔁 join.

◊ **stand for** represent, symbolize, mean, signify, denote, indicate.

◊ **stand in for** deputize for, cover for, understudy, replace, substitute for.

◊ **stand out** show, catch the eye, stick out, jut out, project, protrude.

◊ **stand up for** defend, stick up for, side with, fight for, support, protect, champion, uphold.

🔁 attack.

◊ **stand up to** defy, oppose, resist, withstand, endure, face, confront, brave.

🔁 give in to.

standard *n* **1** NORM, average, type, model, pattern, example, sample, guideline, benchmark, touchstone, yardstick, rule, measure, gauge, level, criterion, requirement, specification, grade, quality. **2** FLAG, ensign, pennant, pennon, colours, banner.

➤ *adj* normal, average, typical, stock, classic, basic, staple, usual, customary, popular, prevailing, regular, approved, accepted, recognized, official, orthodox, set, established, definitive.

🔁 abnormal, unusual, irregular.

standardize *v* normalize, equalize, homogenize, stereotype, mass-produce.

🔁 differentiate.

standards *n* principles, ideals, morals, ethics.

standoffish *adj* aloof, remote, distant, unapproachable, unsociable, uncommunicative, reserved, cold.

🔁 friendly.

standpoint *n* position, station,

vantagepoint, stance, viewpoint, angle, point of view.

standstill *n* stop, halt, pause, lull, rest, stoppage, jam, log-jam, hold-up, impasse, deadlock, gridlock, stalemate.

🔁 advance, progress.

staple *adj* basic, fundamental, primary, key, main, chief, major, principal, essential, necessary, standard.

🔁 minor.

star *n* celebrity, personage, luminary, idol, lead, leading man, leading lady, superstar, big name.

> *Types of star include*: nova, supernova, pulsar, falling star, shooting star, red giant, supergiant, white dwarf, red dwarf, brown dwarf, neutron star, Pole Star, Polaris, North Star. *see also* **constellation**.

stare *v* gaze, look, watch, gape, gawp, gawk, goggle, glare.

➤ *n* gaze, look, glare.

stark *adj* **1** *stark landscape*: bare, barren, bleak, bald, plain, simple, austere, harsh, severe, grim, dreary, gloomy, depressing. **2** UTTER, unmitigated, total, consummate, absolute, complete, sheer, downright, out-and-out, flagrant, arrant.

start *v* **1** BEGIN, commence, originate, initiate, introduce, pioneer, create, found, establish, set up, institute, inaugurate, launch, open, kick off (*infml*), instigate, activate, trigger, set off, set out, leave, depart, appear, arise, issue. **2** JUMP, jerk, twitch, flinch, recoil.

🔁 **1** stop, finish, end.

➤ *n* **1** BEGINNING, commencement, outset, inception, dawn, birth, break, outburst, onset, origin, initiation, introduction, foundation, inauguration, launch, opening, kick-off (*infml*). **2** JUMP, jerk, twitch, spasm, convulsion, fit.

🔁 **1** stop, finish, end.

startle *v* surprise, amaze, astonish, astound, shock, scare, frighten,

alarm, agitate, upset, disturb.
ᴇᴀ calm.

starvation *n* hunger,
undernourishment, malnutrition,
famine.
ᴇᴀ plenty, excess.

starve *v* hunger, fast, diet, deprive,
refuse, deny, die, perish.
ᴇᴀ feed, gorge.

starving *adj* hungry, underfed,
undernourished, ravenous, famished.

state *v* say, declare, announce, report,
communicate, claim, assert, aver,
affirm, specify, present, express, put,
formulate, articulate, voice.
➤ *n* **1** CONDITION, shape, situation,
position, circumstances, case. **2**
NATION, country, land, territory,
kingdom, republic, government. **3**
(*infml*) PANIC, flap (*infml*), tizzy (*infml*),
bother, plight, predicament. **4** POMP,
ceremony, dignity, majesty, grandeur,
glory, splendour.
➤ *adj* national, governmental, public,
official, formal, ceremonial, pompous,
stately.

stately *adj* grand, imposing,
impressive, elegant, majestic, regal,
royal, imperial, noble, august, lofty,
pompous, dignified, measured,
deliberate, solemn, ceremonious.
ᴇᴀ informal, unimpressive.

statement *n* account, report, bulletin,
communiqué, release, announcement,
declaration, proclamation,
communication, utterance, testimony.

static *adj* stationary, motionless,
immobile, unmoving, still, inert, resting,
fixed, constant, changeless, unvarying,
stable, immutable.
ᴇᴀ dynamic, mobile, varying.

station *n* place, location, position,
post, headquarters, base, depot.
➤ *v* locate, set, establish, install,
garrison, post, send, appoint, assign.

stationary *adj* motionless, immobile,
unmoving, still, static, inert, standing,
resting, parked, moored, fixed.
ᴇᴀ mobile, moving, active.

stationery

Items of stationery include: account
book, address book, adhesive tape,
blotter, bulldog clip, calendar, carbon
paper, card index, cartridge ribbon,
cash book, clipboard, computer disk,
copying paper, correcting paper,
correction fluid, correction ribbon,
desk diary, diary, divider, document
folder, document wallet, drawing pin,
dry-transfer lettering, elastic band,
envelope, brown manila envelope,
reply-paid envelope, self-seal
envelope, window envelope, eraser,
expanding file, file, file tab, filing tray,
Filofax®, flip chart, floppy disk, folder,
graph paper, headed notepaper, index
card, ink, Jiffy bag®, label, lever arch
file, marker, memo pad, notepaper,
paper clip, paper fastener, paper knife,
pen, pencil, pencil sharpener, personal
organizer, pin, pocket calculator,
pocket folder, Post-it® note, printer
label, printer paper, printer ribbon,
reinforcement ring, ring binder, rubber,
rubber band, rubber stamp, ruler,
scissors, Sellotape®, shorthand
notebook, spiral notebook, stamp
pad, staple, suspension file, tape
dispenser, Tipp-Ex®, toner, treasury
tag, typewriter ribbon, wall chart,
writing paper. *see also* **paper**.

---

statue *n* figure, head, bust, effigy, idol,
statuette, carving, bronze.

status *n* rank, grade, degree, level,
class, station, standing, position, state,
condition, prestige, eminence,
distinction, importance, consequence,
weight.
ᴇᴀ unimportance, insignificance.

staunch *adj* loyal, faithful, hearty,
strong, stout, firm, sound, sure, true,
trusty, reliable, dependable, steadfast.
ᴇᴀ unfaithful, weak, unreliable.

stay *v* **1** LAST, continue, endure, abide,
remain, linger, hang on, persist. **2**
RESIDE, dwell, live, settle, sojourn, stop,
halt, pause, wait.
ᴇᴀ **1** go, leave.

➤ *n* visit, holiday, stopover, sojourn.

steady *adj* stable, balanced, poised, fixed, immovable, firm, poised, settled, still, calm, imperturbable, equable, even, uniform, consistent, unvarying, unchanging, constant, immutable, persistent, unremitting, incessant, uninterrupted, unbroken, regular, rhythmic, steadfast, unwavering. ▣ unsteady, unstable, variable, wavering.

➤ *v* balance, stabilize, fix, secure, brace, support.

steal *v* **1** *steal a car*: thieve, pilfer, filch, pinch (*infml*), nick (*sl*), take, appropriate (*fml*), snatch, swipe (*infml*), shoplift, poach, embezzle, lift (*infml*), plagiarize. **2** CREEP, tiptoe, slip, slink, sneak. ▣ **1** return, give back.

stealthy *adj* surreptitious, covert, clandestine, secret, unobtrusive, secretive, quiet, furtive, sly, cunning, sneaky, underhand. ▣ open.

steam *n* vapour, mist, haze, condensation, moisture, dampness.

steep *adj* **1** *a steep slope*: sheer, precipitous, headlong, abrupt, sudden, sharp. **2** (*infml*) EXCESSIVE, extreme, stiff, unreasonable, high, exorbitant, extortionate, overpriced. ▣ **1** gentle, gradual. **2** moderate, low.

steer *v* pilot, guide, direct, control, govern, conduct.

stem[1] *n* stalk, shoot, stock, branch, trunk.

stem[2] *v* stop, halt, arrest, stanch, staunch, block, dam, check, curb, restrain, contain, resist, oppose. ▣ encourage.

stench *n* stink, reek, pong (*infml*), whiff, niff (*sl*), smell, odour.

step *n* **1** PACE, stride, footstep, tread, footprint, print, trace, track. **2** MOVE, act, action, deed, measure, procedure, process, proceeding, progression, movement, stage, phase, degree. **3** RUNG, stair, level, rank, point.

➤ *v* pace, stride, tread, stamp, walk, move.

◇ **step down** stand down, resign, abdicate, quit, leave, retire, withdraw. ▣ join.

◇ **step up** increase, raise, augment, boost, build up, intensify, escalate, accelerate, speed up. ▣ decrease.

stereotype *n* formula, convention, mould, pattern, model.

➤ *v* categorize, pigeonhole, typecast, standardize, formalize, conventionalize, mass-produce. ▣ differentiate.

sterile *adj* **1** GERM-FREE, aseptic, sterilized, sanitized, disinfected, antiseptic, uncontaminated. **2** INFERTILE, barren, arid, bare, unproductive, fruitless, pointless, useless, abortive. ▣ **1** septic. **2** fertile, fruitful.

sterilize *v* disinfect, fumigate, purify, sanitize, clean, cleanse. ▣ contaminate, infect.

stern *adj* strict, severe, authoritarian, rigid, inflexible, unyielding, hard, tough, rigorous, stringent, harsh, cruel, unsparing, relentless, unrelenting, grim, forbidding, stark, austere. ▣ kind, gentle, mild, lenient.

stew *v* boil, simmer, braise, casserole.

stick[1] *v* **1** THRUST, poke, stab, jab, pierce, penetrate, puncture, spear, transfix. **2** GLUE, gum, paste, cement, bond, fuse, weld, solder, adhere, cling, hold. **3** ATTACH, affix, fasten, secure, fix, pin, join, bind. **4** PUT, place, position, set, install, deposit, drop.

◇ **stick at** persevere, plug away (*infml*), persist, continue, hang in (*infml*). ▣ give up.

◇ **stick out** protrude, jut out, project, extend.

◇ **stick up for** stand up for, speak up for, defend, champion, support, uphold. ▣ attack.

stick[2] *n* branch, twig.

Types of stick include: alpenstock, baton, birch, bludgeon, cane, club, cosh, crook, crutch, cudgel, hockey stick, lathi, lug, pike, pole, post, rod, sceptre, shillelagh, staff, stake, tripod stick, truncheon, waddy, walking frame, walking stick, wand, whip, Zimmer frame®.

sticky *adj* **1** ADHESIVE, gummed, tacky, gluey, gummy, viscous, glutinous, gooey (*infml*). **2** (*infml*) *a sticky situation*: difficult, tricky, thorny, unpleasant, awkward, embarrassing, delicate. **3** HUMID, clammy, muggy, close, oppressive, sultry.
🗲 **1** dry. **2** easy. **3** fresh, cool.

stiff *adj* **1** RIGID, inflexible, unbending, unyielding, hard, solid, hardened, solidified, firm, tight, taut, tense. **2** FORMAL, ceremonious, pompous, standoffish, cold, prim, priggish, austere, strict, severe, harsh. **3** DIFFICULT, hard, tough, arduous, laborious, awkward, exacting, rigorous.
🗲 **1** flexible. **2** informal. **3** easy.

stiffen *v* harden, solidify, tighten, tense, brace, reinforce, starch, thicken, congeal, coagulate, gel, set.

stifle *v* smother, suffocate, asphyxiate, strangle, choke, extinguish, muffle, dampen, deaden, silence, hush, suppress, quell, check, curb, restrain.
🗲 encourage.

stigma *n* brand, mark, stain, blot, spot, blemish, disgrace, shame, dishonour.
🗲 credit, honour.

still *adj* stationary, motionless, lifeless, stagnant, smooth, undisturbed, unruffled, calm, tranquil, serene, restful, peaceful, hushed, quiet, silent.
🗲 active, disturbed, agitated, noisy.
➤ *v* calm, soothe, allay, tranquillize, subdue, restrain, hush, quieten, silence, pacify, settle, smooth.
🗲 agitate, stir up.
➤ *adv* yet, even so, nevertheless, nonetheless, notwithstanding (*fml*), however.

stilted *adj* artificial, unnatural, stiff, wooden, forced, constrained.
🗲 fluent, flowing.

stimulate *v* rouse, arouse, turn on (*sl*), animate, quicken, fire, inflame, inspire, motivate, encourage, induce, urge, impel, spur, prompt, goad, provoke, incite, instigate, trigger off.
🗲 discourage, hinder, prevent.

stimulus *n* incentive, encouragement, inducement, spur, goad, provocation, incitement.
🗲 discouragement.

sting *v* **1** *bees sting*: bite, prick, jag, hurt, injure, wound. **2** SMART, tingle, burn, pain.
➤ *n* bite, nip, prick, jag, smart, tingle.

stingy *adj* mean, miserly, niggardly, tight-fisted (*infml*), parsimonious, penny-pinching.
🗲 generous, liberal.

stink *v* smell, reek, pong (*infml*), hum (*sl*).
➤ *n* smell, odour, stench, pong (*infml*), niff (*sl*).

stint *n* spell, stretch, period, time, shift, turn, bit, share, quota.

stipulate *v* specify, lay down, require, demand, insist on.

stipulation *n* specification, requirement, demand, condition, proviso.

stir *v* **1** MOVE, budge, touch, affect, inspire, excite, thrill, disturb, agitate, shake, tremble, quiver, flutter, rustle. **2** MIX, blend, beat.
➤ *n* activity, movement, bustle, flurry, commotion, ado, fuss, to-do (*infml*), uproar, tumult, disturbance, disorder, agitation, excitement, ferment.
🗲 calm.
◇ **stir up** rouse, arouse, awaken, animate, quicken, kindle, fire, inflame, stimulate, spur, prompt, provoke, incite, instigate, agitate.
🗲 calm, discourage.

stock *n* **1** GOODS, merchandise, wares, commodities, capital, assets, inventory, repertoire, range, variety, assortment, source, supply, fund, reservoir, store, reserve, stockpile, hoard. **2** PARENTAGE, ancestry, descent, extraction, family, line, lineage, pedigree, race, breed, species, blood. **3** LIVESTOCK, animals, cattle, horses, sheep, herds, flocks.

➤ *adj* standard, basic, regular, routine, ordinary, run-of-the-mill, bog-standard (*infml*), usual, customary, traditional, conventional, set, stereotyped, hackneyed, overused, banal, trite.

🃏 original, unusual.

➤ *v* keep, carry, sell, trade in, deal in, handle, supply, provide.

◇ **stock up** gather, accumulate, amass, lay in, provision, fill, replenish, store (up), save, hoard, stash (away)(*infml*), pile up.

stocky *adj* sturdy, solid, thickset, chunky, short, squat, dumpy, stubby, stumpy.

🃏 tall, skinny.

stoical *adj* patient, long-suffering, uncomplaining, resigned, philosophical, indifferent, impassive, unemotional, phlegmatic, dispassionate, cool, calm, imperturbable.

🃏 excitable, anxious.

stolid *adj* slow, heavy, dull, bovine, wooden, blockish, lumpish, impassive, phlegmatic, unemotional.

🃏 lively, interested.

stomach *n* tummy (*infml*), tum (*infml*), gut, inside(s), belly, abdomen, paunch, pot.

➤ *v* tolerate, bear, stand, abide, hack (*infml*), endure, suffer, submit to, take.

stony *adj* **1** BLANK, expressionless, hard, cold, frigid, icy, indifferent, unfeeling, heartless, callous, merciless, pitiless, inexorable, hostile. **2** *stony beach*: pebbly, shingly, rocky.

🃏 **1** warm, soft-hearted, friendly.

stoop *v* **1** HUNCH, bow, bend, incline, lean, duck, squat, crouch, kneel. **2** *stoop to blackmail*: descend, sink, lower oneself, resort, go so far as, condescend, deign.

stop *v* **1** HALT, cease, end, finish, conclude, terminate, discontinue, suspend, interrupt, pause, quit, refrain, desist, pack in (*sl*). **2** PREVENT, bar, frustrate, thwart, intercept, hinder, impede, check, restrain. **3** SEAL, close, plug, block, obstruct, arrest, stem, stanch.

🃏 **1** start, continue.

➤ *n* **1** STATION, terminus, destination. **2** REST, break, pause, stage. **3** HALT, standstill, stoppage, cessation, end, finish, conclusion, termination, discontinuation.

🃏 **3** start, beginning, continuation.

stoppage *n* stop, halt, standstill, arrest, blockage, obstruction, check, hindrance, interruption, shutdown, closure, strike, walk-out, sit-in.

🃏 start, continuation.

stopper *n* cork, bung, plug.

store *v* save, keep, put aside, lay by, reserve, stock, lay in, deposit, lay down, lay up, accumulate, hoard, salt away, stockpile, stash (*infml*).

🃏 use.

➤ *n* **1** STOCK, supply, provision, fund, reserve, mine, reservoir, hoard, cache, stockpile, accumulation, quantity, abundance, plenty, lot. **2** STOREROOM, storehouse, warehouse, repository, depository.

🃏 **1** scarcity.

storey *n* floor, level, stage, tier, flight, deck.

storm *n* **1** TEMPEST, thunderstorm, squall, blizzard, gale, hurricane, whirlwind, tornado, cyclone. **2** OUTBURST, uproar, furore, outcry, row, rumpus, commotion, tumult, disturbance, turmoil, stir, agitation, rage, outbreak, attack, assault.

🃏 **2** calm.

Kinds of storm include: blizzard, buran, cloudburst, cyclone, downpour, dust-devil, dust-storm, electrical storm, gale, haboob, hailstorm, hurricane, ice storm, monsoon, rainstorm, sandstorm, snowstorm, squall, tempest, thunderstorm, tornado, typhoon, whirlwind. *see also* **wind**.

➤ *v* charge, rush, attack, assault, assail, roar, thunder, rage, rant, rave, fume.

stormy *adj* tempestuous, squally, rough, choppy, turbulent, wild, raging, windy, gusty, blustery, foul.
🖪 calm.

story *n* **1** TALE, fiction, yarn, anecdote, episode, plot, narrative, history, chronicle, record, account, relation, recital, report, article, feature. **2** LIE, falsehood, untruth.

Types of story include: adventure story, Aga saga, bedtime story, blockbuster (*infml*), children's story, comedy, black comedy, crime story, detective story, fable, fairy tale, fantasy, folk tale, ghost story, historical novel, horror story, interactive story, legend, love story, Mills & Boon®, mystery, myth, novelization, parable, romance, saga, science fiction, sci-fi (*infml*), short story, spiel, spine-chiller, spy story, supernatural tale, tall story, thriller, western, whodunit (*infml*).

stout *adj* **1** FAT, plump, fleshy, portly, corpulent, overweight, heavy, bulky, big, brawny, beefy, hulking, burly, muscular, athletic. **2** *stout packaging*: strong, tough, durable, thick, sturdy, robust, hardy, vigorous. **3** BRAVE, courageous, valiant, plucky, fearless, bold, intrepid, dauntless, resolute, stalwart.
🖪 **1** thin, lean, slim. **2** weak. **3** cowardly, timid.

stow *v* put away, store, load, pack, cram, stuff, stash (*infml*).
🖪 unload.

straight *adj* **1** *a straight line*: level, even, flat, horizontal, upright, vertical, aligned, direct, undeviating, unswerving, true, right. **2** TIDY, neat, orderly, shipshape, organized. **3** HONOURABLE, honest, law-abiding, respectable, upright, trustworthy, reliable, straightforward, fair, just. **4**

FRANK, candid, blunt, forthright, direct. **5** *straight whisky*: undiluted, neat, unadulterated, unmixed.
🖪 **1** bent, crooked. **2** untidy. **3** dishonest. **4** evasive. **5** diluted.
➤ *adv* directly, point-blank, honestly, frankly, candidly.
◇ **straight away** at once, immediately, instantly, right away, directly, now, there and then.
🖪 later, eventually.

straighten *v* unbend, align, tidy, neaten, order, arrange.
🖪 bend, twist.
◇ **straighten out** clear up, sort out, settle, resolve, correct, rectify, disentangle, regularize.
🖪 confuse, muddle.

straightforward *adj* **1** EASY, simple, uncomplicated, clear, elementary. **2** HONEST, truthful, sincere, genuine, open, frank, candid, direct, forthright.
🖪 **1** complicated, difficult. **2** evasive, devious.

strain¹ *v* **1** PULL, wrench, twist, sprain, tear, stretch, extend, tighten, tauten. **2** SIEVE, sift, screen, separate, filter, purify, drain, wring, squeeze, compress, express. **3** WEAKEN, tire, tax, overtax, overwork, labour, try, endeavour, struggle, strive, exert, force, drive, push.
➤ *n* stress, anxiety, burden, pressure, tension, tautness, pull, sprain, wrench, injury, exertion, effort, struggle, force.
🖪 relaxation.

strain² *n* **1** STOCK, ancestry, descent, extraction, family, lineage, line, pedigree, blood, variety, type. **2** TRAIT, streak, vein, tendency, trace, suggestion, suspicion, hint.

strained *adj* forced, constrained, laboured, false, artificial, unnatural, stiff, tense, unrelaxed, uncomfortable, uneasy, awkward, embarrassed, self-conscious.
🖪 natural, relaxed.

strait-laced *adj* prudish, stuffy, starchy, prim, proper, strict, narrow, narrow-minded, puritanical, moralistic.
🖪 broad-minded.

strand *n* fibre, filament, wire, thread, string, piece, length.

stranded *adj* marooned, high and dry, abandoned, forsaken, in the lurch, helpless, aground, grounded, beached, shipwrecked, wrecked.

strange *adj* **1** ODD, peculiar, funny (*infml*), curious, queer, weird, bizarre, left-field, eccentric, abnormal, irregular, uncommon, unusual, exceptional, remarkable, extraordinary, mystifying, perplexing, unexplained. **2** NEW, novel, untried, unknown, unheard-of, unfamiliar, unacquainted, foreign, alien, exotic.
⊟ 1 ordinary, common. **2** well-known, familiar.

stranger *n* newcomer, visitor, guest, non-member, outsider, foreigner, alien.
⊟ local, native.

strangle *v* throttle, choke, asphyxiate, suffocate, stifle, smother, suppress, gag, repress, inhibit.

strap *n* thong, tie, band, belt, leash.
➤ *v* **1** BEAT, lash, whip, flog, belt. **2** FASTEN, secure, tie, bind.

stratagem *n* plan, scheme, plot, intrigue, ruse, ploy, trick, dodge, manoeuvre, device, artifice, wile, subterfuge.

strategic *adj* important, key, critical, decisive, crucial, vital, tactical, planned, calculated, deliberate, politic, diplomatic.
⊟ unimportant.

strategy *n* tactics, planning, policy, approach, procedure, plan, programme, design, scheme.

stray *v* wander (off), get lost, err, ramble, roam, rove, range, meander, straggle, drift, diverge, deviate, digress.
➤ *adj* **1** LOST, abandoned, homeless, wandering, roaming. **2** RANDOM, chance, accidental, freak, odd, erratic.

streak *n* line, stroke, smear, band, stripe, strip, layer, vein, trace, dash, touch, element, strain.
➤ *v* **1** BAND, stripe, fleck, striate, smear, daub. **2** SPEED, tear, hurtle, sprint, gallop, fly, dart, flash, whistle, zoom, whizz, sweep.

stream *n* **1** RIVER, creek, brook, beck, burn, rivulet, tributary. **2** CURRENT, drift, flow, run, gush, flood, deluge, cascade, torrent.
➤ *v* issue, well, surge, run, flow, course, pour, spout, gush, flood, cascade.

streamer *n* ribbon, banner, pennant, pennon, flag, ensign, standard.

streamlined *adj* aerodynamic, smooth, sleek, graceful, efficient, well-run, smooth-running, rationalized, time-saving, well-organized, slick.
⊟ clumsy, inefficient.

strength *n* toughness, robustness, sturdiness, lustiness, brawn, muscle, sinew, power, might, force, vigour, energy, stamina, health, fitness, courage, fortitude, spirit, resolution, firmness, effectiveness, potency, concentration, intensity, vehemence.
⊟ weakness, feebleness, impotence.

strengthen *v* reinforce, brace, steel, fortify, buttress, bolster, support, toughen, harden, stiffen, consolidate, substantiate, corroborate, confirm, encourage, hearten, refresh, restore, invigorate, nourish, increase, heighten, intensify.
⊟ weaken, undermine.

strenuous *adj* **1** *strenuous work*: hard, tough, demanding, gruelling, taxing, laborious, uphill, arduous, tiring, exhausting. **2** ACTIVE, energetic, vigorous, eager, earnest, determined, resolute, spirited, tireless, indefatigable.
⊟ 1 easy, effortless.

stress *n* **1** PRESSURE, strain, tension, worry, anxiety, weight, burden, trauma, hassle (*infml*). **2** EMPHASIS, accent, accentuation, beat, force, weight, importance, significance.
⊟ 1 relaxation.
➤ *v* emphasize, accentuate, highlight, underline, underscore, repeat.
⊟ understate, downplay.

stretch n 1 EXPANSE, spread, sweep, reach, extent, distance, space, area, tract. 2 PERIOD, time, term, spell, stint, run.
➤ v pull, tighten, tauten, strain, tax, extend, lengthen, elongate, expand, spread, unfold, unroll, inflate, swell, reach.
☒ compress.
◇ **stretch out** extend, relax, hold out, put out, lie down, reach.
☒ draw back.

strict adj 1 a strict teacher: stern, authoritarian, no-nonsense, firm, rigid, inflexible, stringent, rigorous, harsh, severe, austere. 2 EXACT, precise, accurate, literal, faithful, true, absolute, utter, total, complete, thoroughgoing, meticulous, scrupulous, particular, religious.
☒ 1 easy-going, flexible. 2 loose.

strident adj loud, blaring, clamorous, vociferous, harsh, raucous, grating, rasping, shrill, screeching, unmusical, discordant, clashing, jarring, jangling.
☒ quiet, soft.

strife n conflict, discord, dissension, controversy, animosity, friction, rivalry, contention, quarrel, row, wrangling, struggle, fighting, combat, battle, warfare.
☒ peace.

strike n 1 INDUSTRIAL ACTION, work-to-rule, go-slow, stoppage, sit-in, walk-out, mutiny, revolt. 2 HIT, blow, stroke, raid, attack.
➤ v 1 STOP WORK, down tools, work to rule, walk out, protest, mutiny, revolt. 2 HIT, knock, collide with, slap, smack, cuff, clout (*infml*), thump, wallop (*infml*), beat, pound, hammer, buffet, raid, attack, afflict. 3 IMPRESS, affect, touch, register. 4 FIND, discover, unearth, uncover, encounter, reach.
◇ **strike out** cross out, delete, strike through, cancel, strike off, remove.
☒ add.

striking adj noticeable, conspicuous, salient, outstanding, remarkable, extraordinary, memorable, impressive, dazzling, arresting, astonishing, stunning.
☒ unimpressive.

string n 1 a piece of string: twine, cord, rope, cable, line, strand, fibre. 2 SERIES, succession, sequence, chain, line, row, file, queue, procession, train.
➤ v thread, link, connect, tie up, hang, suspend, festoon, loop.

stringent adj binding, strict, severe, rigorous, tough, rigid, inflexible, tight.
☒ lax, flexible.

strip[1] v peel, skin, flay, denude, divest, deprive, undress, disrobe, unclothe, uncover, expose, lay bare, bare, empty, clear, gut, ransack, pillage, plunder, loot.
☒ dress, clothe, cover.

strip[2] n ribbon, thong, strap, belt, sash, band, stripe, lath, slat, piece, bit, slip, shred.

stripe n band, line, bar, chevron, flash, streak, fleck, strip, belt.

strive v try, attempt, undertake, endeavour, struggle, strain, work, toil, labour, fight, contend, compete.

stroke n 1 CARESS, pat, rub. 2 BLOW, hit, knock, swipe. 3 SWEEP, flourish, movement, action, move, line.
➤ v caress, fondle, pet, touch, pat, rub, massage.

stroll v saunter, amble, dawdle, ramble, wander.
➤ n saunter, amble, walk, wander, constitutional, turn, ramble.

strong adj 1 TOUGH, resilient, durable, hard-wearing, heavy-duty, robust, sturdy, firm, sound, lusty, strapping, stout, burly, well-built, beefy (*infml*), brawny (*infml*), muscular, sinewy, athletic, fit, healthy, hardy, powerful, mighty, potent. 2 INTENSE, deep, vivid. 3 strong character: fierce, violent, vehement, keen, eager, zealous, fervent, ardent, dedicated, staunch, stalwart, determined, resolute, tenacious, strong-minded, strong-willed, self-assertive. 4 HIGHLY-FLAVOURED, piquant, hot, spicy, highly-seasoned, sharp, pungent, undiluted, concentrated.

5 *strong argument*: convincing, persuasive, cogent, effective, telling, forceful, weighty, compelling, urgent. **ⓕ 1** weak, feeble. **2** indecisive. **3** mild, bland. **4** unconvincing.

stronghold *n* citadel, bastion, fort, fortress, castle, keep, refuge.

structure *n* construction, erection, building, edifice, fabric, framework, form, shape, design, configuration, conformation, make-up, formation, arrangement, organization, set-up.
➤ *v* construct, assemble, build, form, shape, design, arrange, organize.

struggle *v* strive, work, toil, labour, strain, agonize, fight, battle, wrestle, grapple, contend, compete, vie.
ⓕ yield, give in.
➤ *n* difficulty, problem, effort, exertion, pains, agony, work, labour, toil, clash, conflict, strife, fight, battle, skirmish, encounter, combat, hostilities, contest.
ⓕ ease, submission, co-operation.

stub *n* end, stump, remnant, fag-end (*infml*), dog-end (*infml*), butt, counterfoil.

stubborn *adj* obstinate, stiff-necked, mulish, pig-headed (*infml*), obdurate (*fml*), intransigent (*fml*), rigid, inflexible, unbending, unyielding, dogged, persistent, tenacious, headstrong, self-willed, wilful, refractory (*fml*), difficult, unmanageable.
ⓕ compliant, flexible, yielding.

stuck *adj* **1** FAST, jammed, firm, fixed, fastened, joined, glued, cemented. **2** BEATEN, stumped (*infml*), baffled, bamboozled (*infml*).
ⓕ 1 loose.

stuck-up (*infml*) *adj* snobbish, toffee-nosed (*infml*), supercilious, snooty (*infml*), haughty, high and mighty, condescending, proud, arrogant, conceited, bigheaded (*infml*).
ⓕ humble, modest.

student *n* undergraduate, postgraduate, scholar, schoolboy, schoolgirl, pupil, disciple, learner, trainee, apprentice.

studied *adj* deliberate, conscious, wilful, intentional, premeditated, planned, calculated, contrived, forced, unnatural, over-elaborate.
ⓕ unplanned, impulsive, natural.

studio *n* workshop, workroom.

studious *adj* scholarly, academic, intellectual, bookish, serious, thoughtful, reflective, diligent, hard-working, industrious, assiduous, careful, attentive, earnest, eager.
ⓕ lazy, idle, negligent.

study *v* read, learn, revise, cram, swot (*infml*), mug up (*infml*), read up, research, investigate, analyse, survey, scan, examine, scrutinize, peruse, pore over, contemplate, meditate, ponder, consider, deliberate.
➤ *n* **1** READING, homework, preparation, learning, revision, cramming, swotting (*infml*), research, investigation, inquiry, analysis, examination, scrutiny, inspection, contemplation, attention, consideration. **2** REPORT, essay, thesis, paper, monograph, survey, review, critique, analysis. **3** OFFICE, den (*infml*).

Subjects of study include:
accountancy, agriculture, anatomy, anthropology, archaeology, architecture, art, astrology, astronomy, biology, botany, building studies, business studies, calligraphy, chemistry, CDT (craft, design and technology), civil engineering, the Classics, commerce, computer studies, cosmology, craft, dance, design, domestic science, drama, dressmaking, driving, ecology, economics, education, electronics, engineering, environmental studies, erotology, ethnology, eugenics, fashion, fitness, food technology, forensics, gender studies, genetics, geography, geology, heraldry, history, home economics, horticulture, hospitality management, hotel management, information and communication technology (ICT), information technology (IT), journalism, languages, law, leisure

studies, lexicography, librarianship, linguistics, literature, logistics, management studies, marine studies, marketing, mathematics, mechanics, media studies, medicine, metallurgy, metaphysics, meteorology, music, mythology, natural history, oceanography, ornithology, pathology, penology, personal and social education (PSE); personal, health and social education (PHSE), pharmacology, philosophy, photography, physics, physiology, politics, pottery, psychology, publishing, religious studies, science, shorthand, social sciences, sociology, sport, statistics, surveying, technology, theology, typewriting, visual arts, web design, women's studies, word processing, writing, zoology.

stuff v **1** PACK, stow, load, fill, cram, crowd, force, push, shove, ram, wedge, jam, squeeze, compress. **2** GORGE, gormandize, overindulge, guzzle, gobble, sate, satiate.
🔁 **1** unload, empty. **2** nibble.
➤ n **1** MATERIAL, fabric, matter, substance, essence. **2** (*infml*) BELONGINGS, possessions, things, objects, articles, goods, luggage, paraphernalia, gear (*infml*), clobber (*infml*), kit, tackle, equipment, materials.

stuffing n padding, wadding, quilting, filling, force-meat.

stuffy adj **1** *a stuffy room*: musty, stale, airless, unventilated, suffocating, stifling, oppressive, heavy, close, muggy, sultry. **2** STAID, strait-laced, prim, button-down (*infml*), conventional, old-fashioned, pompous, dull, dreary, uninteresting, stodgy.
🔁 **1** airy, well-ventilated. **2** informal, modern, lively.

stumble v **1** TRIP, slip, fall, lurch, reel, stagger, flounder, blunder. **2** STAMMER, stutter, hesitate, falter.
◇ **stumble on** come across, chance upon, happen upon, find, discover, encounter.

stumbling block obstacle, hurdle, barrier, bar, obstruction, hindrance, impediment, difficulty, problem, snag.

stump n end, remnant, trunk, stub.
➤ v (*infml*) defeat, outwit, confound, perplex, puzzle, baffle, mystify, confuse, bewilder, flummox (*infml*), bamboozle (*infml*), dumbfound.
🔁 assist.
◇ **stump up** (*infml*) pay, hand over, fork out (*infml*), shell out (*infml*), donate, contribute, cough up (*infml*).
🔁 receive.

stun v amaze, astonish, astound, stagger, shock, daze, stupefy, dumbfound, flabbergast (*infml*), overcome, confound, confuse, bewilder.

stunning (*infml*) adj beautiful, lovely, gorgeous, ravishing, dazzling, brilliant, striking, impressive, spectacular, remarkable, wonderful, marvellous, great, sensational.
🔁 ugly, awful.

stunt[1] n feat, exploit, act, deed, enterprise, trick, turn, performance.

stunt[2] v stop, arrest, check, restrict, slow, retard, hinder, impede, dwarf.
🔁 promote, encourage.

stupefy v daze, stun, numb, dumbfound, flabbergast (*infml*), shock, stagger, amaze, astound.

stupendous adj huge, enormous, gigantic, colossal, vast, prodigious, phenomenal, tremendous, breathtaking, overwhelming, staggering, stunning, amazing, astounding, fabulous, fantastic (*infml*), superb, wonderful, marvellous.
🔁 ordinary, unimpressive.

stupid adj **1** SILLY, foolish, irresponsible, ill-advised, unwise, indiscreet, foolhardy, rash, senseless, mad, lunatic, brainless, half-witted, idiotic, imbecilic, moronic, feeble-minded, simple-minded, slow, dim, dull, dense, thick (*infml*), dumb, dopey (*infml*), crass, inane, puerile, mindless, futile, pointless, meaningless, nonsensical, absurd, ludicrous, ridiculous, laughable. **2** DAZED, groggy, stupefied, stunned, sluggish, semiconscious.

F∃ 1 sensible, wise, clever, intelligent. **2** alert.

stupor *n* daze, stupefaction, torpor, lethargy, inertia, inactivity, trance, coma, numbness, insensibility, unconsciousness.

F∃ alertness, consciousness.

sturdy *adj* strong, robust, durable, well-made, stout, substantial, solid, well-built, powerful, muscular, athletic, hardy, vigorous, flourishing, hearty, staunch, stalwart, steadfast, firm, resolute, determined.

F∃ weak, flimsy, puny.

stutter *v* stammer, hesitate, falter, stumble, mumble.

style *n* **1** APPEARANCE, cut, design, pattern, shape, form, sort, type, kind, genre, variety, category. **2** ELEGANCE, smartness, chic, flair, panache, stylishness, taste, polish, refinement, sophistication, urbanity, fashion, vogue, trend, mode, dressiness, flamboyance, affluence, luxury, grandeur. **3** *style of working*: technique, approach, method, manner, mode, fashion, way, custom. **4** WORDING, phrasing, turn of phrase, expression, tone, tenor.

F∃ 2 inelegance, tastelessness.

➤ *v* **1** DESIGN, cut, tailor, fashion, shape, adapt. **2** DESIGNATE, term, name, call, address, title, dub, label.

stylish *adj* chic, fashionable, à la mode, modish, in vogue, voguish, trendy (*infml*), snappy, natty (*infml*), snazzy (*infml*), dressy, smart, elegant, classy (*infml*), polished, refined, sophisticated, urbane.

F∃ old-fashioned, shabby.

suave *adj* polite, courteous, charming, agreeable, affable, soft-spoken, smooth, unctuous, sophisticated, urbane, worldly.

F∃ rude, unsophisticated.

subconscious *adj* subliminal, unconscious, intuitive, inner, innermost, hidden, latent, repressed, suppressed.

F∃ conscious.

subdue *v* overcome, quell, suppress, repress, overpower, crush, defeat, conquer, vanquish, overrun, subject, subjugate, humble, break, tame, master, discipline, control, check, moderate, reduce, soften, quieten, damp, mellow.

F∃ arouse, awaken.

subdued *adj* **1** SAD, downcast, dejected, crestfallen, quiet, serious, grave, solemn. **2** QUIET, muted, hushed, soft, dim, shaded, sombre, sober, restrained, unobtrusive, low-key, subtle.

F∃ 1 lively, excited. **2** striking, obtrusive.

subject *n* **1** TOPIC, theme, matter, issue, question, point, case, affair, business, discipline, field. **2** NATIONAL, citizen, participant, client, patient, victim.

F∃ 2 monarch, ruler, master.

➤ *adj* **1** LIABLE, disposed, prone, susceptible, vulnerable, open, exposed. **2** SUBJUGATED, captive, bound, obedient, answerable, subordinate, inferior, subservient, submissive. **3** DEPENDENT, contingent, conditional.

F∃ 1 vulnerable. **2** free, superior. **3** unconditional.

➤ *v* expose, lay open, submit, subjugate, subdue.

subjection *n* subjugation, defeat, captivity, bondage, chains, shackles, slavery, enslavement, oppression, domination, mastery.

subjective *adj* biased, prejudiced, personal, individual, idiosyncratic, emotional, intuitive, instinctive.

F∃ objective, unbiased, impartial.

sublime *adj* exalted, elevated, high, lofty, noble, majestic, great, grand, imposing, magnificent, glorious, transcendent, spiritual.

F∃ lowly, base.

submerge *v* submerse, immerse, plunge, duck, dip, sink, drown, engulf,

overwhelm, swamp, flood, inundate, deluge.
☒ surface.

submerged *adj* submersed, immersed, underwater, sunk, sunken, drowned, swamped, inundated, deluged, hidden, concealed, covered, unseen.

submission *n* **1** SURRENDER, capitulation, resignation, acquiescence, assent, compliance, obedience, deference, submissiveness, meekness, passivity. **2** PRESENTATION, offering, contribution, entry, suggestion, proposal.
☒ **1** intransigence, intractability.

submissive *adj* yielding, unresisting, resigned, patient, uncomplaining, accommodating, compliant, biddable, obedient, deferential, ingratiating, subservient, humble, meek, docile, subdued, passive.
☒ intransigent, intractable.

submit *v* **1** YIELD, give in, surrender, capitulate, knuckle under, bow, bend, stoop, succumb, agree, comply. **2** PRESENT, tender, offer, put forward, suggest, propose, table, state, claim, argue.
☒ **1** resist. **2** withdraw.

subordinate *adj* secondary, auxiliary, ancillary, subsidiary, dependent, inferior, lower, junior, minor, lesser.
☒ superior, senior.
➤ *n* inferior, junior, assistant, attendant, second, aide, dependant, underling (*infml*).
☒ superior, boss (*infml*).

subscribe *v* **1** *subscribe to a theory*: support, endorse, back, advocate, approve, agree. **2** GIVE, donate, contribute.

subscription *n* membership fee, dues, payment, donation, contribution, offering, gift.

subsequent *adj* following, later, future, next, succeeding, consequent, resulting, ensuing.
☒ previous, earlier.

subside *v* sink, collapse, settle, descend, fall, drop, lower, decrease, lessen, diminish, dwindle, decline, wane, ebb, recede, moderate, abate, die down, quieten, slacken, ease.
☒ rise, increase.

subsidiary *adj* auxiliary, supplementary, additional, ancillary, assistant, supporting, contributory, secondary, subordinate, lesser, minor.
☒ primary, chief, major.
➤ *n* branch, offshoot, division, section, part.

subsidize *v* support, back, sponsor, underwrite, finance, fund, aid, assist, promote.

subsidy *n* grant, allowance, assistance, help, aid, contribution, sponsorship, finance, support, backing.

subsistence *n* living, survival, existence, livelihood, maintenance, support, keep, sustenance, food, nourishment, provisions, rations.

substance *n* **1** MATTER, material, stuff, fabric, essence, pith, entity, body, solidity, concreteness, reality, actuality, ground, foundation. **2** SUBJECT, subject-matter, theme, gist, meaning, significance, force.

substandard *adj* second-rate, inferior, imperfect, damaged, shoddy, poor, inadequate, unacceptable.
☒ first-rate, superior, perfect.

substantial *adj* large, big, sizable, ample, generous, great, mega (*infml*), considerable, significant, important, worthwhile, massive, bulky, hefty, well-built, stout, sturdy, strong, sound, durable.
☒ small, insignificant, weak.

substantiate *v* prove, verify, confirm, support, corroborate (*fml*), validate, authenticate.
☒ disprove, refute.

substitute *v* **1** CHANGE, exchange, swap, switch, interchange, replace. **2** STAND IN, fill in (*infml*), cover, deputize, understudy, relieve.
➤ *n* reserve, standby, temp (*infml*),

supply, locum, understudy, stand-in, replacement, relief, surrogate, proxy, agent, deputy, makeshift, stopgap.
➤ *adj* reserve, temporary, acting, surrogate, proxy, replacement, alternative.

subterfuge *n* trick, stratagem, scheme, ploy, ruse, dodge, manoeuvre, machination, deviousness, evasion, deception, artifice, pretence, excuse.
🖪 openness, honesty.

subtle *adj* 1 DELICATE, understated, implied, indirect, slight, tenuous, faint, mild, fine, nice, refined, sophisticated, deep, profound. 2 ARTFUL, cunning, crafty, sly, devious, shrewd, astute.
🖪 1 blatant, obvious. 2 artless, open.

subtract *v* deduct, take away, remove, withdraw, debit, detract, diminish.
🖪 add.

suburbs *n* suburbia, commuter belt, residential area, outskirts, dormitory town.
🖪 centre, heart.

subversive *adj* seditious, treasonous, treacherous, traitorous, inflammatory, incendiary, disruptive, riotous, weakening, undermining, destructive.
🖪 loyal.
➤ *n* seditionist, terrorist, freedom fighter, dissident, traitor, quisling, fifth columnist.

succeed *v* 1 TRIUMPH, make it, get on, thrive, flourish, prosper, make good, manage, work. 2 *winter succeeds autumn*: follow, replace, result, ensue.
🖪 1 fail. 2 precede.

succeeding *adj* following, next, subsequent, ensuing, coming, to come, later, successive.
🖪 previous, earlier.

success *n* 1 TRIUMPH, victory, luck, fortune, prosperity, fame, eminence, happiness. 2 CELEBRITY, star, somebody, winner, bestseller, hit, sensation.
🖪 1 failure, disaster.

successful *adj* 1 VICTORIOUS, winning, lucky, fortunate, prosperous, wealthy, thriving, flourishing, booming,

moneymaking, lucrative, profit-making, profitable, rewarding, satisfying, fruitful, productive. 2 *a successful writer*: famous, well-known, popular, leading, bestselling, top, unbeaten.
🖪 1 unsuccessful, unprofitable, fruitless. 2 unknown.

succession *n* sequence, series, order, progression, run, chain, string, cycle, continuation, flow, course, line, train, procession.

successive *adj* consecutive, sequential, following, succeeding.

succinct *adj* short, brief, terse, pithy, epigrammatic, concise, compact, condensed, summary.
🖪 long, lengthy, wordy, verbose.

succulent *adj* fleshy, juicy, moist, luscious, mouthwatering, lush, rich, mellow.
🖪 dry.

succumb *v* give way, yield, give in, submit, knuckle under, surrender, capitulate, collapse, fall.
🖪 overcome, master.

suck *v* draw in, imbibe, absorb, soak up, extract, drain.

sudden *adj* unexpected, unforeseen, surprising, startling, abrupt, sharp, quick, swift, rapid, prompt, hurried, hasty, rash, impetuous, impulsive, snap (*infml*).
🖪 expected, predictable, gradual, slow.

sue *v* prosecute, charge, take to court, litigate, indict, summon, solicit, appeal.

suffer *v* 1 HURT, ache, agonize, grieve, sorrow. 2 BEAR, support, tolerate, endure, sustain, experience, undergo, go through, feel.

suffering *n* pain, discomfort, agony, anguish, affliction, distress, sorrow, grief, misery, hardship, ordeal, torment, torture.
🖪 ease, comfort.

sufficient *adj* enough, adequate, satisfactory, effective.
🖪 insufficient, inadequate.

suffocate *v* asphyxiate, smother, stifle, choke, strangle, throttle.

sugar

Kinds of sugar include: beet sugar, brown sugar, cane sugar, caster sugar, crystallized sugar, demerara, dextrose, fructose, glucose, golden syrup, granulated sugar, icing sugar, invert sugar, jaggery, lactose, maltose, maple syrup, molasses, powdered sugar, refined sugar, sucrose, sugar loaf, sugar lump, sweets, candy (*US*), sugar candy (*US*), syrup, treacle, unrefined sugar. *see also* **sweet**.

Artificial sweeteners include: acesulfame K, aspartame, Canderel®, cyclamate, Hermesetas®, NutraSweet®, saccharin, sorbitol, Sweetex®.

suggest *v* **1** PROPOSE, put forward, advocate, recommend, advise, counsel. **2** IMPLY, insinuate, hint, intimate, evoke, indicate.

suggestion *n* **1** PROPOSAL, motion, proposition, idea, plan, scheme, recommendation. **2** IMPLICATION, insinuation, innuendo, hint, intimation, suspicion, trace, indication.

suggestive *adj* **1** EVOCATIVE, reminiscent, expressive, meaning, indicative. **2** *a suggestive remark*: indecent, immodest, improper, indelicate, off colour, risqué, bawdy, dirty, smutty, provocative.
☒ **1** inexpressive. **2** decent, clean.

suit *v* **1** SATISFY, gratify, please, answer, match, tally, agree, correspond, harmonize. **2** FIT, befit, become, tailor, adapt, adjust, accommodate, modify.
☒ **1** displease, clash.
➤ *n* outfit, costume, dress, clothing.

suitable *adj* appropriate, fitting, convenient, opportune, suited, due, apt, apposite, relevant, applicable, fit, adequate, satisfactory, acceptable, befitting, becoming, seemly, proper, right.
☒ unsuitable, inappropriate.

sulk *v* mope, brood, pout.

sulky *adj* brooding, moody, morose, resentful, grudging, disgruntled, put out, cross, bad-tempered, sullen, surly, aloof, unsociable.
☒ cheerful, good-tempered, sociable.

sullen *adj* **1** SULKY, moody, morose, glum, gloomy, silent, surly, sour, perverse, obstinate, stubborn. **2** DARK, gloomy, sombre, dismal, cheerless, dull, leaden, heavy.
☒ **1** cheerful, happy. **2** fine, clear.

sully *v* dirty, soil, defile, pollute, contaminate, taint, spoil, mar, spot, blemish, besmirch, stain, tarnish, disgrace, dishonour.
☒ cleanse, honour.

sultry *adj* hot, sweltering, stifling, stuffy, oppressive, close, humid, muggy, sticky.
☒ cool, cold.

sum *n* total, sum total, aggregate, whole, entirety, number, quantity, amount, tally, reckoning, score, result.
◇ **sum up** summarize, review, recapitulate, recap, conclude, close.

summarize *v* outline, précis, condense, abridge, abbreviate, shorten, sum up, encapsulate, review.
☒ expand (on).

summary *n* synopsis, résumé, outline, abstract, précis, sketch, condensation, digest, compendium, abridgement, summing-up, review, recapitulation, recap.
➤ *adj* short, succinct, brief, cursory, hasty, prompt, direct, unceremonious, arbitrary.
☒ lengthy, careful.

summit *n* top, peak, pinnacle, apex, point, crown, head, zenith, acme, culmination, height.
☒ bottom, foot, nadir.

summon *v* call, send for, invite, bid, beckon, gather, assemble, convene, rally, muster, mobilize, rouse, arouse.
☒ dismiss.

sumptuous *adj* luxurious, plush, lavish, extravagant, opulent, rich, costly, expensive, dear, splendid, magnificent,

gorgeous, superb, grand.
☒ plain, poor.

sunbathe *v* sun, bask, tan, brown, bake.

sunburnt *adj* red, blistered, peeling, weather-beaten, burnt.
☒ pale.

sundry *adj* various, diverse, miscellaneous, assorted, varied, different, several, some, a few.

sunken *adj* submerged, buried, recessed, lower, depressed, concave, hollow, haggard, drawn.

sunny *adj* **1** FINE, cloudless, clear, summery, sunshiny, sunlit, bright, brilliant. **2** CHEERFUL, happy, joyful, smiling, beaming, radiant, light-hearted, buoyant, optimistic, pleasant.
☒ **1** sunless, dull. **2** gloomy.

sunrise *n* dawn, crack of dawn, daybreak, daylight.

sunset *n* sundown, dusk, twilight, gloaming, evening, nightfall.

suntanned *adj* brown, bronzed, tanned.

superb *adj* excellent, first-rate, first-class, superior, choice, fine, exquisite, gorgeous, magnificent, splendid, grand, wonderful, marvellous, admirable, impressive, breathtaking.
☒ bad, poor, inferior.

superficial *adj* surface, external, exterior, outward, apparent, seeming, cosmetic, skin-deep, shallow, slight, trivial, lightweight, frivolous, casual, cursory, sketchy, hasty, hurried, passing.
☒ internal, deep, thorough.

superfluous *adj* extra, spare, excess, surplus, remaining, left-over, redundant, supernumerary, unneeded, unnecessary, needless, unwanted, uncalled-for, excessive.
☒ necessary, needed, wanted.

superintend *v* supervise, oversee, overlook, inspect, run, manage, administer, direct, control, handle.

superior *adj* **1** EXCELLENT, first-class, first-rate, top-notch (*infml*), top-flight

(*infml*), high-class, exclusive, choice, select, fine, de luxe, admirable, distinguished, exceptional, unrivalled, par excellence. **2** BETTER, preferred, greater, higher, senior. **3** HAUGHTY, lordly, pretentious, snobbish, snooty (*infml*), lofty, supercilious, disdainful, high and mighty, condescending, patronizing.
☒ **1** inferior, average. **2** worse, lower. **3** humble.
➤ *n* senior, elder, better, boss (*infml*), chief, principal, director, manager, foreman, supervisor.
☒ inferior, junior, assistant.

superiority *n* advantage, lead, edge, supremacy, ascendancy, pre-eminence, predominance.
☒ inferiority.

superlative *adj* best, greatest, highest, supreme, transcendent, unbeatable, unrivalled, unparalleled, matchless, peerless, unsurpassed, unbeaten, consummate, excellent, outstanding, top-drawer (*infml*).
☒ poor, average.

supernatural *adj* paranormal, unnatural, abnormal, metaphysical, spiritual, psychic, mystic, occult, hidden, mysterious, miraculous, magical, phantom, ghostly.
☒ natural, normal.

supersede *v* succeed, replace, supplant, usurp, oust, displace, remove.

superstition *n* myth, old wives' tale, fallacy, delusion, illusion.

superstitious *adj* mythical, false, fallacious, irrational, groundless, delusive, illusory.
☒ rational, logical.

supervise *v* oversee, watch over, look after, superintend, run, manage, administer, direct, conduct, preside over, control, handle.

supervision *n* surveillance, care, charge, superintendence, oversight, running, management, handling, administration, direction, control, guidance, instruction.

supervisor *n* overseer, inspector,

superintendent, boss, chief, director, administrator, manager, foreman, forewoman.

supplant v replace, supersede, usurp, oust, displace, remove, overthrow, topple, unseat.

supple adj flexible, bending, pliant, pliable, plastic, lithe, graceful, loose-limbed, double-jointed, elastic.
🎱 stiff, rigid, inflexible.

supplement n addition, extra, add-on, insert, pull-out, addendum, appendix, codicil, postscript, sequel.
➤ v add to, augment, boost, reinforce, fill up, top up, complement, extend, eke out.
🎱 deplete, use up.

supplementary adj additional, added, extra, auxiliary, secondary, complementary, accompanying.

supplier n dealer, seller, vendor, wholesaler, retailer.

supplies n stores, provisions, food, equipment, materials, necessities.

supply v provide, furnish, equip, outfit, stock, fill, replenish, give, donate, grant, endow, contribute, yield, produce, sell.
🎱 take, receive.
➤ n source, amount, quantity, stock, fund, reservoir, store, reserve, stockpile, hoard, cache.
🎱 lack.

support v 1 BACK, second, defend, champion, advocate, promote, foster, help, aid, assist, rally round, finance, fund, subsidize, underwrite. 2 HOLD UP, bear, carry, sustain, brace, reinforce, strengthen, prop, buttress, bolster. 3 MAINTAIN, keep, provide for, feed, nourish. 4 support a statement: endorse, confirm, verify, authenticate, corroborate (fml), substantiate, document.
🎱 1 oppose. 3 live off. 4 contradict.
➤ n 1 BACKING, allegiance, loyalty, defence, protection, patronage, sponsorship, approval, favour, encouragement, comfort, relief, help, aid, assistance. 2 PROP, stay, post, pillar,

brace, bracket, crutch, foundation, underpinning.
🎱 1 opposition, hostility.

supporter n fan, follower, adherent, advocate, champion, defender, seconder, patron, sponsor, helper, ally, friend.
🎱 opponent.

supportive adj helpful, caring, attentive, sympathetic, understanding, comforting, reassuring, encouraging.
🎱 discouraging.

suppose v assume, presume, expect, infer, conclude, guess, conjecture, surmise, believe, think, consider, judge, imagine, conceive, fancy, pretend, postulate, hypothesize.
🎱 know.

supposed adj alleged, reported, rumoured, assumed, presumed, reputed, putative, imagined, hypothetical.
🎱 known, certain.
◇ **supposed to** meant to, intended to, expected to, required to, obliged to.

supposition n assumption, presumption, guess, conjecture, speculation, theory, hypothesis, idea, notion.
🎱 knowledge.

suppress v crush, stamp out, quash, quell, subdue, stop, silence, censor, stifle, smother, strangle, conceal, withhold, hold back, contain, restrain, check, repress, inhibit.
🎱 encourage, incite.

supreme adj best, greatest, highest, top, crowning, culminating, first, leading, foremost, chief, principal, head, sovereign, pre-eminent, predominant, prevailing, world-beating, unsurpassed, second-to-none, incomparable, matchless, consummate, transcendent, superlative, optimum, premium, prime, ultimate, extreme, final.
🎱 lowly, poor.

sure adj 1 CERTAIN, convinced, assured, confident, decided, positive, definite, unmistakable, clear, accurate, precise,

unquestionable, indisputable, undoubted, undeniable, irrevocable, inevitable, bound. **2** SAFE, secure, fast, solid, firm, steady, stable, guaranteed, reliable, dependable, trustworthy, steadfast, unwavering, unerring, unfailing, infallible, effective.
🖛 **1** unsure, uncertain, doubtful. **2** unsafe, insecure.

surface *n* outside, exterior, façade, veneer, covering, skin, top, side, face, plane.
🖛 inside, interior.
➤ *v* rise, arise, come up, emerge, appear, materialise, come to light.
🖛 sink, disappear, vanish.

surgeon

> *Types of surgeon include*: brain surgeon, cosmetic surgeon, dental surgeon, eye surgeon, general surgeon, heart surgeon, house surgeon, neurosurgeon, oral surgeon, plastic surgeon, tree surgeon, veterinary surgeon.

surly *adj* gruff, brusque, churlish, ungracious, resentful, bad-tempered, cross, crabbed, grouchy, crusty, sullen, sulky, morose, brooding.
🖛 friendly, polite.

surpass *v* beat, outdo, exceed, outstrip, better, excel, transcend, outshine, eclipse.

surplus *n* excess, residue, leftover, remainder, balance, superfluity, glut, surfeit.
🖛 lack, shortage.
➤ *adj* excess, superfluous, redundant, extra, spare, remaining, left-over, unused.

surprise *v* startle, amaze, astonish, astound, stagger, flabbergast (*infml*), bewilder, confuse, nonplus, shock, disconcert, dismay.
➤ *n* amazement, astonishment, incredulity, wonder, bewilderment, dismay, shock, start, bombshell, revelation.
🖛 composure.

surprised *adj* startled, amazed, astonished, astounded, staggered, flabbergasted (*infml*), thunderstruck, dumbfounded, speechless, shocked, nonplussed.
🖛 unsurprised, composed.

surprising *adj* amazing, astonishing, astounding, jaw-dropping (*infml*), staggering, stunning, incredible, extraordinary, remarkable, startling, unexpected, unforeseen.
🖛 unsurprising, expected.

surrender *v* capitulate, submit, resign, concede, yield, give in, cede, give up, quit, relinquish, abandon, renounce, forgo, waive.
➤ *n* capitulation, resignation, submission, yielding, relinquishment, renunciation.

surreptitious *adj* furtive, stealthy, sly, covert, veiled, hidden, secret, clandestine, underhand, unauthorized.
🖛 open, obvious.

surround *v* encircle, ring, girdle, encompass, envelop, encase, enclose, hem in, besiege.

surrounding *adj* encircling, bordering, adjacent, adjoining, neighbouring, nearby.

surroundings *n* neighbourhood, vicinity, locality, setting, environment, background, milieu, ambience.

survey *v* view, contemplate, observe, supervise, scan, scrutinize, examine, inspect, study, research, review, consider, estimate, evaluate, assess, measure, plot, plan, map, chart, reconnoitre.
➤ *n* review, overview, scrutiny, examination, inspection, study, pull, appraisal, assessment, measurement.

survive *v* outlive, outlast, endure, last, stay, remain, live, exist, withstand, weather.
🖛 succumb, die.

susceptible *adj* liable, prone, inclined, disposed, given, subject, receptive, responsive, suggestible, impressionable, weak, vulnerable,

open, sensitive, tender.
🔳 resistant, immune.

suspect v 1 DOUBT, distrust, mistrust, call into question. 2 *I suspect you're right*: believe, fancy, feel, guess, conjecture, speculate, surmise, suppose, consider, conclude, infer.
➤ *adj* suspicious, doubtful, dubious, questionable, debatable, unreliable, iffy (*sl*), dodgy (*infml*), fishy (*infml*).
🔳 acceptable, reliable.

suspend v 1 HANG, dangle, swing. 2 ADJOURN, interrupt, discontinue, cease, delay, defer, postpone, put off, shelve. 3 EXPEL, dismiss, exclude, debar.
🔳 2 continue. 3 restore, reinstate.

suspense n uncertainty, insecurity, anxiety, tension, apprehension, anticipation, expectation, expectancy, excitement.
🔳 certainty, knowledge.

suspension n adjournment, interruption, break, intermission, respite, remission, stay, moratorium, delay, deferral, postponement, abeyance.
🔳 continuation.

suspicion n 1 DOUBT, scepticism, distrust, mistrust, wariness, caution, misgiving, apprehension. 2 TRACE, hint, suggestion, soupçon, touch, tinge, shade, glimmer, shadow. 3 IDEA, notion, hunch, impression.
🔳 1 trust.

suspicious adj 1 DOUBTFUL, sceptical, unbelieving, suspecting, distrustful, mistrustful, wary, chary, apprehensive, uneasy. 2 DUBIOUS, questionable, suspect, irregular, shifty, shady (*infml*), dodgy (*infml*), fishy (*infml*), iffy (*infml*).
🔳 1 trustful, confident. 2 trustworthy, innocent.

sustain v 1 NOURISH, provide for, nurture, foster, help, aid, assist, comfort, relieve, support, uphold, endorse, bear, carry. 2 MAINTAIN, keep going, keep up, continue, prolong, hold.

sustained adj prolonged, protracted, long-drawn-out, steady, continuous,

constant, perpetual, unremitting.
🔳 broken, interrupted, intermittent, spasmodic.

sustenance n nourishment, food, provisions, fare, maintenance, subsistence, livelihood.

swagger v bluster, boast, crow, brag, swank (*infml*), parade, strut.
➤ n bluster, show, ostentation, arrogance.

swallow v 1 CONSUME, devour, eat, gobble up, guzzle (*infml*), snarf (*infml*), drink, quaff, knock back (*infml*), gulp down (*infml*). 2 ENGULF, enfold, envelop, swallow up, absorb, assimilate, accept, believe.

swamp n bog, marsh, fen, slough, quagmire, quicksand, mire, mud.
➤ v flood, inundate, deluge, engulf, submerge, sink, drench, saturate, waterlog, overload, overwhelm, besiege, beset.

swap, swop v exchange, transpose, switch, interchange, barter, trade, traffic.

swarm n crowd, throng, mob, mass, multitude, myriad, host, army, horde, herd, flock, drove, shoal.
➤ v 1 flock, flood, stream, mass, crowd, congregate, throng. 2 *swarming with tourists*: teem, crawl, bristle, abound, crowd.

swarthy adj dark, dark-skinned, dark-complexioned, dusky, black, brown, tanned.
🔳 fair, pale.

sway v 1 ROCK, roll, lurch, swing, wave, oscillate, fluctuate, bend, incline, lean, divert, veer, swerve. 2 INFLUENCE, affect, persuade, induce, convince, convert, overrule, dominate, govern.

swear v 1 VOW, promise, pledge, avow (*fml*), attest (*fml*), asseverate (*fml*), testify, affirm, assert, declare, insist. 2 CURSE, blaspheme.

swear-word n expletive, four-letter word, curse, oath, imprecation, obscenity, profanity, blasphemy, swearing, bad language.

sweat *n* 1 PERSPIRATION, moisture, stickiness. 2 ANXIETY, worry, agitation, panic. 3 TOIL, labour, drudgery, chore.
➤ *v* perspire, swelter, exude (*fml*).

sweaty *adj* damp, moist, clammy, sticky, sweating, perspiring.
🔁 dry, cool.

sweep *v* 1 *sweep the floor*: brush, dust, clean, clear, remove. 2 PASS, sail, fly, glide, scud, skim, glance, whisk, tear, hurtle.
➤ *n* arc, curve, bend, swing, stroke, movement, gesture, compass, scope, range, extent, span, stretch, expanse, vista.

sweeping *adj* general, global, universal, all-inclusive, all-embracing, blanket, across-the-board, broad, wide-ranging, extensive, far-reaching, comprehensive, thoroughgoing, radical, wholesale, indiscriminate, simplistic, oversimplified.
🔁 specific, narrow.

sweet *adj* 1 SUGARY, syrupy, honeyed, sweetened, saccharine, luscious, delicious. 2 PLEASANT, delightful, lovely, attractive, beautiful, pretty, winsome, cute, appealing, lovable, charming, agreeable, amiable, affectionate, tender, kind, treasured, precious, dear, darling. 3 FRESH, clean, wholesome, pure, clear, perfumed, fragrant, aromatic, balmy. 4 *sweet music*: melodious, tuneful, harmonious, euphonious, musical, dulcet, soft, mellow.
🔁 1 savoury, salty, sour, bitter. 2 unpleasant, nasty, ugly. 3 foul. 4 discordant.
➤ *n* dessert, pudding, afters (*infml*).

Sweets include: aniseed ball, barley sugar, bull's eye, butterscotch, caramel, chewing gum, chocolate, fondant, fruit pastille, fudge, gobstopper, gumdrop, humbug, jelly, jelly bean, liquorice, liquorice allsort, lollipop, marshmallow, marzipan, nougat, peppermint, praline, puff candy, rock, Edinburgh rock, toffee, toffee apple, truffle, Turkish delight.

sweeten *v* sugar, honey, mellow, soften, soothe, appease, temper, cushion.
🔁 sour, embitter.

swell *v* expand, dilate, inflate, blow up, puff up, bloat, distend, fatten, bulge, balloon, billow, surge, rise, mount, increase, enlarge, extend, grow, augment, heighten, intensify.
🔁 shrink, contract, decrease, dwindle.
➤ *n* billow, wave, undulation, surge, rise, increase, enlargement.

swelling *n* lump, tumour, bump, bruise, blister, boil, inflammation, bulge, protuberance, puffiness, distension, enlargement.

sweltering *adj* hot, tropical, baking, scorching, stifling, suffocating, airless, oppressive, sultry, steamy, sticky, humid.
🔁 cold, cool, fresh, breezy, airy.

swerve *v* turn, bend, incline, veer, swing, shift, deviate, stray, wander, diverge, deflect, sheer.

swift *adj* fast, quick, rapid, speedy, express, flying, hurried, hasty, short, brief, sudden, prompt, ready, agile, nimble, nippy (*infml*).
🔁 slow, sluggish, unhurried.

swim *v* bathe, float, bob, tread water.

The main swimming strokes include: backstroke, breaststroke, butterfly, crawl, doggy-paddle, sidestroke.

swimsuit *n* swimming costume, bathing costume, bathing suit, bikini, trunks.

swindle *v* cheat, defraud, diddle, do (*infml*), overcharge, fleece, rip off (*sl*), sting (*sl*), trick, deceive, dupe, con (*infml*), bamboozle (*infml*).
➤ *n* fraud, fiddle, racket, scam (*infml*), sharp practice, double-dealing, trickery, deception, con (*infml*), rip-off (*sl*), clean-out (*infml*), sting (*sl*).

swindler n cheat, fraud, impostor, con man (*infml*), fraudster, trickster, shark, rogue, rascal.

swing v hang, suspend, dangle, wave, brandish, sway, rock, oscillate, vibrate, fluctuate, vary, veer, swerve, turn, whirl, twirl, spin, rotate.
➤ n sway, rock, oscillation, vibration, fluctuation, variation, change, shift, movement, motion, rhythm.

swingeing adj harsh, severe, stringent, drastic, punishing, devastating, excessive, extortionate, oppressive, heavy.
🖙 mild.

swipe v 1 HIT, strike, lunge, lash out, slap, whack (*infml*), wallop (*infml*), sock (*sl*). 2 (*infml*) STEAL, pilfer, lift, pinch (*infml*).
➤ n stroke, blow, slap, smack, clout, whack (*infml*), wallop (*infml*).

swirl v churn, agitate, spin, twirl, whirl, wheel, eddy, twist, curl.

switch v change, exchange, swap, trade, interchange, alternate, transpose, substitute, replace, shift, rearrange, turn, veer, deviate, divert, deflect.
➤ n change, alteration, shift, exchange, swap, interchange, substitution, replacement.

swivel v pivot, spin, rotate, revolve, turn, twirl, pirouette, gyrate, wheel.

swollen adj bloated, distended, inflated, tumid, puffed up, puffy, inflamed, enlarged, bulbous, bulging.
🖙 shrunken, shrivelled.

swoop v dive, plunge, drop, fall, descend, stoop, pounce, lunge, rush.
➤ n dive, plunge, drop, descent, pounce, lunge, rush, attack, onslaught.

swop see **swap**.

sword n blade, foil, rapier, sabre, scimitar.

swot (*infml*) v study, work, learn, memorize, revise, cram, mug up (*infml*), bone up (*sl*).

syllabus n curriculum, course, programme, schedule, plan.

symbol n sign, token, representation, mark, character, ideograph, figure, image.

> *Symbols include*: badge, brand, cipher, coat of arms, crest, emblem, hieroglyph, icon, ideogram, insignia, logo, logogram, monogram, motif, pictograph, swastika, token, totem, trademark, watermark; ampersand, asterisk, at sign, caret, dagger, double-dagger, hash, obelus; emoticon, smiley.

symbolic adj symbolical, representative, emblematic, token, figurative, metaphorical, allegorical, meaningful, significant.

symbolize v represent, stand for, denote, mean, signify, typify, exemplify, epitomize, personify.

symmetrical adj balanced, even, regular, parallel, corresponding, proportional.
🖙 asymmetrical, irregular.

symmetry n balance, evenness, regularity, parallelism, correspondence, proportion, harmony, agreement.
🖙 asymmetry, irregularity.

sympathetic adj understanding, appreciative, supportive, comforting, consoling, commiserating, pitying, interested, concerned, solicitous, caring, compassionate, tender, kind, warm-hearted, well-disposed, affectionate, agreeable, friendly, congenial, like-minded, compatible.
🖙 unsympathetic, indifferent, callous, antipathetic.

sympathize v understand, comfort, commiserate, pity, feel for, empathize, identify with, respond to.
🖙 ignore, disregard.

sympathy n 1 UNDERSTANDING, comfort, consolation, condolences, commiseration, pity, compassion, tenderness, kindness, warmth, thoughtfulness, empathy, fellow-feeling, affinity, rapport. 2 AGREEMENT, accord, correspondence, harmony.

▣ **1** indifference, insensitivity, callousness. **2** disagreement.

symptom *n* sign, indication, evidence, manifestation, expression, feature, characteristic, mark, token, warning.

symptomatic *adj* indicative, typical, characteristic, associated, suggestive.

synonymous *adj* interchangeable, substitutable, the same, identical, similar, comparable, tantamount, equivalent, corresponding.
▣ antonymous, opposite.

synopsis *n* outline, abstract, summary, résumé, précis, sketch, condensation, digest, abridgement, review, recapitulation.

synthesize *v* unite, combine, amalgamate, integrate, merge, blend, compound, alloy, fuse, weld, coalesce, unify.

▣ separate, analyse, resolve.

synthetic *adj* manufactured, man-made, simulated, artificial, ersatz, imitation, fake, bogus, mock, sham, pseudo.
▣ genuine, real, natural.

system *n* **1** METHOD, mode, technique, procedure, process, routine, practice, usage, rule. **2** ORGANIZATION, structure, set-up, systematization, co-ordination, orderliness, methodology, logic, classification, arrangement, order, plan, scheme.

systematic *adj* methodical, logical, ordered, well-ordered, planned, well-planned, organized, well-organized, structured, systematized, regular, standardized, orderly, businesslike, efficient.
▣ unsystematic, arbitrary, disorderly, inefficient.

Tt

tab *n* flap, tag, marker, label, sticker, ticket.

table *n* **1** BOARD, slab, counter, worktop, desk, bench, stand. **2** DIAGRAM, chart, graph, timetable, schedule, programme, list, inventory, catalogue, index, register, record.
➤ *v* propose, suggest, submit, put forward.

taboo *adj* forbidden, prohibited, banned, proscribed, unacceptable, unmentionable, unthinkable.
🖪 permitted, acceptable.
➤ *n* ban, interdiction, prohibition, restriction, anathema, curse.

tacit *adj* unspoken, unexpressed, unvoiced, silent, understood, implicit, implied, inferred.
🖪 express, explicit.

taciturn *adj* silent, quiet, uncommunicative, unforthcoming, reticent, reserved, withdrawn, aloof, distant, cold.
🖪 talkative, communicative, forthcoming.

tack *n* **1** NAIL, pin, drawing-pin, staple. **2** COURSE, path, bearing, heading, direction, line, approach, method, way, technique, procedure, plan, tactic, attack.
➤ *v* add, append, attach, affix, fasten, fix, nail, pin, staple, stitch, baste.

tackle *n* **1** *a rugby tackle*: attack, challenge, interception, intervention, block. **2** EQUIPMENT, implements, tools, apparatus, rig, outfit, gear, trappings, paraphernalia.
➤ *v* **1** BEGIN, embark on, set about, try, attempt, undertake, take on, challenge, confront, encounter, face up to, grapple with, deal with, attend to, handle, grab,

seize, grasp. **2** INTERCEPT, block, halt, stop, check.
🖪 **1** avoid, sidestep.

tact *n* tactfulness, diplomacy, discretion, prudence, delicacy, sensitivity, perception, discernment, judgement, understanding, thoughtfulness, consideration, skill, adroitness, finesse.
🖪 tactlessness, indiscretion.

tactful *adj* diplomatic, discreet, politic, judicious, prudent, careful, delicate, subtle, sensitive, perceptive, discerning, understanding, thoughtful, considerate, polite, skilful, adroit.
🖪 tactless, indiscreet, thoughtless, rude.

tactic *n* approach, course, way, means, method, procedure, plan, stratagem, scheme, ruse, ploy, subterfuge, trick, device, shift, move, manoeuvre.

tactical *adj* strategic, planned, calculated, artful, cunning, shrewd, skilful, clever, smart, prudent, politic, judicious.

tactics *n* strategy, campaign, plan, scheme, policy, approach, line of attack, moves, manoeuvres.

tactless *adj* undiplomatic, indiscreet, indelicate, inappropriate, impolitic, imprudent, careless, clumsy, blundering, insensitive, unfeeling, hurtful, unkind, thoughtless, inconsiderate, rude, impolite, discourteous.
🖪 tactful, diplomatic, discreet.

tag *n* label, sticker, tab, ticket, mark, identification, note, slip, docket.
➤ *v* **1** LABEL, mark, identify, designate, term, call, name, christen, nickname,

style, dub. **2** ADD, append, annex, adjoin, affix, fasten.

◇ **tag along** follow, shadow, tail, trail, accompany.

tail *n* end, extremity, rear, rear end, rump, backside (*infml*), behind (*infml*), posterior (*infml*), appendage.

➤ *v* follow, pursue, shadow, dog, stalk, track, trail.

◇ **tail off** decrease, decline, drop, fall away, fade, wane, dwindle, taper off, peter out, die (out).

▣ increase, grow.

tailor *n* outfitter, dressmaker.

➤ *v* fit, suit, cut, trim, style, fashion, shape, mould, alter, modify, adapt, adjust, accommodate.

tailor-made *adj* made-to-measure, custom-built, bespoke, ideal, perfect, right, suited, fitted.

▣ unsuitable.

taint *v* contaminate, infect, pollute, adulterate, corrupt, deprave, stain, blemish, blot, smear, tarnish, blacken, dirty, soil, muddy, defile, sully, harm, damage, blight, spoil, ruin, shame, disgrace, dishonour.

➤ *n* contamination, infection, pollution, corruption, stain, blemish, fault, flaw, defect, spot, blot, smear, stigma, shame, disgrace, dishonour.

take *v* **1** SEIZE, grab, snatch, grasp, hold, catch, capture, get, obtain, acquire, secure, gain, win, derive, adopt, assume, pick, choose, select, accept, receive. **2** REMOVE, eliminate, take away, withdraw, subtract, deduct, steal, filch, purloin, nick (*sl*), pinch (*infml*), appropriate, abduct, kidnap, carry off. **3** NEED, necessitate, require, demand, call for. **4** *take me home*: convey, carry, bring, transport, ferry, accompany, escort, lead, guide, conduct, usher. **5** BEAR, tolerate, stand, stomach, abide, hack (*infml*), endure, suffer, undergo, withstand.

▣ **1** leave, refuse. **2** replace, put back.

◇ **take aback** surprise, astonish, astound, stagger, stun, startle, disconcert, bewilder, dismay, upset.

◇ **take apart** take to pieces, dismantle, disassemble, analyse.

◇ **take back** reclaim, repossess, withdraw, retract, recant, repudiate, deny, eat one's words.

◇ **take down 1** DISMANTLE, disassemble, demolish, raze, level, lower. **2** NOTE, record, write down, put down, set down, transcribe.

◇ **take in 1** ABSORB, assimilate, digest, realize, appreciate, understand, comprehend, grasp, admit, receive, shelter, accommodate, contain, include, comprise, incorporate, embrace, encompass, cover. **2** DECEIVE, fool, dupe, con (*infml*), mislead, trick, hoodwink, bamboozle (*infml*), cheat, swindle.

◇ **take off 1** REMOVE, doff, divest, shed, discard, drop. **2** LEAVE, depart, go, decamp, disappear. **3** IMITATE, mimic, parody, caricature, satirize, mock, send up.

◇ **take on 1** ACCEPT, assume, acquire, undertake, tackle, face, contend with, fight, oppose. **2** *take on staff*: employ, hire, enlist, recruit, engage, retain.

◇ **take up 1** OCCUPY, fill, engage, engross, absorb, monopolize, use up. **2** *take up a hobby*: start, begin, embark on, pursue, carry on, continue. **3** RAISE, lift. **4** ACCEPT, adopt, assume.

take-off *n* (*infml*) imitation, mimicry, impersonation, parody, caricature, spoof, send-up (*infml*), travesty.

takeover *n* merger, amalgamation, combination, incorporation, coup.

takings *n* receipts, gate, proceeds, profits, gain, returns, revenue, yield, income, earnings, pickings.

tale *n* story, yarn, anecdote, spiel (*sl*), narrative, account, report, rumour, tall story, old wives' tale, superstition, fable, myth, legend, saga, lie, fib, falsehood, untruth, fabrication.

talent *n* gift, endowment, genius, flair, feel, knack, bent, aptitude, faculty, skill, ability, capacity, power, strength, forte.

▣ inability, weakness.

talented *adj* gifted, brilliant, well-endowed, versatile, accomplished, able, capable, proficient, adept, adroit, deft, clever, skilful.
F3 inept.

talk *v* speak, utter, articulate, say, communicate, converse, chat, gossip, natter (*infml*), chatter, discuss, confer, negotiate.
➤ *n* **1** CONVERSATION, dialogue, discussion, conference, meeting, consultation, negotiation, chat, chatter, natter (*infml*), gossip, hearsay, rumour, tittle-tattle. **2** *give a talk*: lecture, seminar, symposium, speech, address, discourse, sermon, spiel (*sl*). **3** LANGUAGE, dialect, slang, jargon, speech, utterance, words.
◊ **talk into** encourage, coax, sway, persuade, convince, bring round, win over.
◊ **talk out of** discourage, deter, put off, dissuade.

talkative *adj* garrulous, loquacious (*fml*), voluble, vocal, communicative, forthcoming, unreserved, expansive, chatty, gossipy, verbose, wordy.
F3 taciturn, quiet, reserved.

talking-to (*infml*) *n* lecture, dressing-down (*infml*), telling-off (*infml*), ticking-off (*infml*), scolding, reprimand, rebuke, reproof, reproach, criticism.
F3 praise, commendation.

tall *adj* high, lofty, elevated, soaring, towering, big, great, giant, gigantic.
F3 short, low, small.

tally *v* **1** AGREE, concur, tie in, square, accord, harmonize, coincide, match, correspond, conform, suit, fit. **2** ADD (UP), total, count, reckon, figure.
F3 1 disagree, differ.
➤ *n* record, count, total, score, reckoning, account.

tame *adj* **1** *a tame rabbit*: domesticated, broken in, trained, disciplined, manageable, tractable, amenable, gentle, docile, meek, submissive, passive, unresisting, obedient, biddable. **2** DULL, boring, tedious, uninteresting, humdrum, flat,

bland, insipid, weak, feeble, uninspired, unadventurous, unenterprising, lifeless, spiritless.
F3 1 wild, unmanageable, rebellious. **2** exciting.
➤ *v* domesticate, house-train, break in, train, discipline, master, subjugate, conquer, bridle, curb, repress, suppress, quell, subdue, temper, soften, mellow, calm, pacify, humble.

tamper *v* interfere, meddle, mess (*infml*), tinker, fiddle, fix, rig, manipulate, juggle, alter, damage.

tang *n* sharpness, bite, piquancy, pungency, taste, flavour, savour, smack, smell, aroma, scent, whiff, tinge, touch, trace, hint, suggestion, soupçon, overtone.

tangible *adj* touchable, tactile, palpable, solid, concrete, material, substantial, physical, real, actual, perceptible, discernible, evident, manifest, definite, positive.
F3 intangible, abstract, unreal.

tangle *n* knot, snarl-up, twist, coil, convolution, mesh, web, maze, labyrinth, mess, muddle, jumble, mix-up, confusion, entanglement, embroilment, complication.
➤ *v* entangle, knot, snarl, ravel, twist, coil, interweave, interlace, intertwine, catch, ensnare, entrap, enmesh, embroil, implicate, involve, muddle, confuse.
F3 disentangle.

tangled *adj* knotty, snarled, matted, tousled, dishevelled, messy, muddled, jumbled, confused, twisted, convoluted, tortuous, involved, complicated, complex, intricate.

tangy *adj* sharp, biting, acid, tart, spicy, nippy (*infml*), piquant, pungent, strong, fresh.
F3 tasteless, insipid.

tank *n* container, vessel, reservoir, cistern, aquarium, vat, basin.

tantalize *v* tease, taunt, torment, torture, provoke, lead on, titillate,

tempt, entice, bait, balk, frustrate, thwart.
☒ gratify, satisfy, fulfil.

tantamount *adj* as good as, equivalent, commensurate, equal, synonymous, the same as.

tantrum *n* temper, rage, fury, storm, outburst, fit, scene, paddy (*infml*).

tap[1] *v* hit, strike, knock, rap, beat, drum, pat, touch.
➤ *n* knock, rap, beat, pat, touch.

tap[2] *n* 1 STOPCOCK, valve, faucet, spigot, spout. 2 STOPPER, plug, bung.
➤ *v* use, utilize, exploit, mine, quarry, siphon, bleed, milk, drain.

tape *n* 1 BAND, strip, binding, ribbon. 2 CASSETTE, video.
➤ *v* 1 BIND, secure, stick, seal. 2 RECORD, video.

taper *v* narrow, attenuate, thin, slim, decrease, reduce, lessen, dwindle, fade, wane, peter out, tail off, die away.
☒ widen, flare, swell, increase.
➤ *n* spill, candle, wick.

target *n* aim, object, end, purpose, intention, ambition, goal, objective, destination, butt, mark, victim, prey, quarry.

tariff *n* price list, schedule, charges, rate, toll, tax, levy, customs, excise, duty.

tarnish *v* discolour, corrode, rust, dull, dim, darken, blacken, sully, taint, stain, blemish, spot, blot, mar, spoil.
☒ polish, brighten.

tart[1] *n* pie, flan, pastry, tartlet, patty.

tart[2] *adj* sharp, acid, sour, bitter, vinegary, tangy, piquant, pungent, biting, cutting, trenchant, incisive, caustic, astringent, acerbic, scathing, sardonic, mordant.
☒ bland, sweet.

task *n* job, chore, duty, charge, imposition, assignment, exercise, mission, errand, undertaking, enterprise, business, occupation, activity, employment, work, labour, toil, burden.

taste *n* 1 FLAVOUR, savour, relish, smack, tang. 2 SAMPLE, bit, piece, morsel, titbit, bite, nibble, mouthful, sip, drop, dash, soupçon. 3 *a taste for adventure*: liking, fondness, partiality, preference, inclination, leaning, penchant, desire, appetite. 4 DISCRIMINATION, discernment, judgement, perception, appreciation, sensitivity, refinement, polish, culture, cultivation, breeding, decorum, finesse, style, elegance, tastefulness.
☒ 1 blandness. 3 distaste. 4 tastelessness.

Ways of describing taste include:
acid, acrid, appetizing, bitter, bittersweet, citrus, creamy, delicious, flavoursome, fruity, hot, meaty, moreish, peppery, piquant, pungent, salty, savoury, scrumptious (*infml*), sharp, sour, spicy, sugary, sweet, tangy, tart, tasty, yummy (*infml*).

➤ *v* savour, relish, sample, nibble, sip, try, test, differentiate, distinguish, discern, perceive, experience, undergo, feel, encounter, meet, know.

tasteful *adj* refined, polished, cultured, cultivated, elegant, smart, stylish, aesthetic, artistic, harmonious, beautiful, exquisite, delicate, graceful, restrained, well-judged, judicious, correct, fastidious, discriminating.
☒ tasteless, garish, tawdry.

tasteless *adj* 1 FLAVOURLESS, insipid, bland, mild, weak, watery, flat, stale, dull, boring, uninteresting, vanilla (*infml*), vapid. 2 INELEGANT, graceless, unseemly, improper, indiscreet, crass, rude, crude, vulgar, kitsch, naff (*sl*), cheesy (*sl*), cheap, tawdry, flashy, gaudy, garish, loud.
☒ 1 tasty. 2 tasteful, elegant.

tasty *adj* luscious, palatable, appetizing, mouthwatering, delicious, flavoursome, succulent, scrumptious (*infml*), yummy (*infml*), tangy, piquant, savoury, sweet.
☒ tasteless, insipid.

tattered *adj* ragged, frayed,

threadbare, ripped, torn, tatty, shabby, scruffy.
🔁 smart, neat.

tatters *n* rags, shreds, ribbons, pieces.

taunt *v* tease, torment, harass, provoke, bait, goad, jeer, mock, ridicule, gibe, rib (*sl*), deride, sneer, insult, revile, reproach.
➤ *n* jeer, catcall, gibe, dig, sneer, insult, reproach, taunting, teasing, provocation, ridicule, sarcasm, derision, censure.

taut *adj* tight, stretched, contracted, strained, tense, unrelaxed, stiff, rigid.
🔁 slack, loose, relaxed.

tautological *adj* repetitive, superfluous, redundant, pleonastic, verbose, wordy.
🔁 succinct, economical.

tautology *n* repetition, duplication, superfluity, redundancy, pleonasm.

tawdry *adj* cheap, vulgar, tasteless, fancy, showy, flashy, gaudy, garish, tinselly, glittering.
🔁 fine, tasteful.

tax *n* levy, charge, rate, tariff, customs, contribution, imposition, burden, load.

> *Taxes include*: airport tax, capital gains tax, capital transfer tax, corporation tax, council tax, customs, death duty, estate duty, excise, income tax, inheritance tax, PAYE, poll tax, property tax, rates, surtax, tithe, toll, value added tax (VAT).

➤ *v* levy, charge, demand, exact, assess, impose, burden, load, strain, stretch, try, tire, weary, exhaust, drain, sap, weaken.

tea *n* infusion, tisane, char (*sl*).

> *Types of tea include*: black tea, green tea, oolong; pekoe, orange pekoe, broken orange pekoe (BOP), CTC (crush, tear, curl); Assam, Ceylon, Darjeeling, Earl Grey, English Breakfast, Irish Breakfast, Jasmine, Keemun, Lapsang Souchong, Russian Caravan, Scottish Breakfast; chai, decaffeinated tea, fruit tea, herbal tea, iced tea, instant tea, lemon tea, mint tea.

teach *v* instruct, train, coach, tutor, lecture, drill, ground, verse, discipline, school, educate, enlighten, edify, inform, impart, inculcate, advise, counsel, guide, direct, show, demonstrate.
🔁 learn.

teacher *n* schoolteacher, tutor, educator, guide, instructor.
🔁 pupil.

> *Kinds of teacher include*: adviser, coach, college lecturer, counsellor, crammer, dean, demonstrator, deputy head, doctor, don, duenna, fellow, form teacher, governess, guru, head of department, head of year, headmaster, headmistress, headteacher, housemaster, housemistress, instructor, lecturer, maharishi, master, mentor, middle school teacher, mistress, nursery school teacher, pastoral head, pedagogue, pedant, preceptor, preceptress, primary school teacher, principal, private tutor, professor, pundit, reception teacher, schoolma'am, schoolmaster, schoolmistress, schoolteacher, secondary school teacher, senior lecturer, student teacher, subject co-ordinator, supply teacher, trainer, tutor, university lecturer, upper school teacher.

teaching *n* **1** INSTRUCTION, tuition, education, pedagogy. **2** DOGMA, doctrine, tenet, precept, principle.

> *Methods of teaching include*: apprenticeship, briefing, coaching, computer-aided learning, correspondence course, counselling, demonstration, distance learning, drilling, familiarization, grounding, guidance, hands-on training, home-learning, indoctrination, induction training, in-service training, instruction, job training, lecturing,

lesson, masterclass, on-the-job training, practical, preaching, private tuition, role play, rote learning, schooling, seminar, shadowing, special tuition, theory, training, tuition, tutelage, tutorial, vocational training, work experience.

team *n* side, line-up, squad, shift, crew, gang, band, group, company, stable.
◇ **team up** join, unite, couple, combine, band together, co-operate, collaborate, work together.

tear *v* **1** RIP, rend, divide, rupture, sever, shred, scratch, claw, gash, lacerate, mutilate, mangle. **2** PULL, snatch, grab, seize, wrest. **3** *tear down the street*: dash, rush, hurry, speed, race, run, sprint, fly, shoot, dart, bolt, belt (*infml*), career, charge.
➤ *n* rip, rent, slit, hole, split, rupture, scratch, gash, laceration.

tearful *adj* crying, weeping, sobbing, whimpering, blubbering, sad, sorrowful, upset, distressed, emotional, weepy (*infml*).
🔁 happy, smiling, laughing.

tears *n* crying, weeping, sobbing, wailing, whimpering, blubbering, sorrow, distress.

tease *v* taunt, provoke, bait, annoy, irritate, aggravate (*infml*), needle (*infml*), badger, worry, pester, plague, harass, torment, tantalize, mock, ridicule, gibe, banter, rag (*sl*), rib (*sl*).

technical *adj* mechanical, scientific, technological, electronic, computerized, specialized, expert, professional.

technique *n* method, system, procedure, manner, fashion, style, mode, way, means, approach, course, performance, execution, delivery, artistry, craftsmanship, skill, facility, proficiency, expertise, know-how (*infml*), art, craft, knack, touch.

tedious *adj* boring, monotonous, uninteresting, unexciting, dull, dreary, drab, banal, humdrum, tiresome, wearisome, tiring, laborious, long-winded, long-drawn-out.
🔁 lively, interesting, exciting.

teeming *adj* swarming, crawling, alive, bristling, seething, full, packed, crowded, brimming, overflowing, bursting, replete, abundant, fruitful, thick.
🔁 lacking, sparse, rare.

teenage *adj* teenaged, adolescent, young, youthful, juvenile, immature.

teenager *n* adolescent, youth, youngster, boy, girl, minor, juvenile.

teetotal *adj* temperate, abstinent, abstemious, sober, on the wagon (*sl*).

telepathy *n* mind-reading, thought transference, sixth sense, ESP, clairvoyance.

telephone *n* phone, handset, receiver, blower (*infml*).

Types of telephone include:
Ansaphone, answering machine, caller display phone, cardphone, carphone, cashphone, cellphone, cellular phone, corded phone, cordless phone, dual-band phone, fax, fax-phone, hands-free phone, hazardous area phone, Minicom, mobile phone, pager, payphone, push-button telephone, system phone, textphone, 3G phone, tone-dialling phone, Touchtone, triband, Uniphone, videophone, WAP phone, weather-resistant phone.

➤ *v* phone, ring (up), call (up), dial, buzz (*infml*), contact, get in touch.

telescope *v* contract, shrink, compress, condense, abridge, squash, crush, shorten, curtail, truncate, abbreviate, reduce, cut, trim.

television *n* TV, receiver, set, telly (*infml*), the box (*infml*), goggle-box (*infml*), idiot box (*infml*), small screen.

Parts of a television set include: aerial, aerial socket, amplifier, cathode-ray tube, chrominance signal extractor, colour decoder module, deflector coil, electron gun, horizontal synchronizing module, intermediate frequency amplifier module, loudspeaker, luminance signal amplifier, phosphor dots, picture tube, remote control, scanning current generator, screen, set-top-box, shadow mask, sound demodulator, stand-by switch, synchronizing pulse separator, tuner.

tell *v* **1** INFORM, notify, let know, acquaint, impart, communicate, speak, utter, say, state, confess, divulge, disclose, reveal. **2** *tell a story*: narrate, recount, relate, report, announce, describe, portray, mention. **3** ORDER, command, direct, instruct, authorize. **4** DIFFERENTIATE, distinguish, discriminate, discern, recognize, identify, discover, see, understand, comprehend.

◇ **tell off** (*infml*) scold, chide, tick off (*infml*), upbraid, reprimand, rebuke, reprove, lecture, berate, dress down (*infml*), carpet (*infml*), reproach, censure.

temerity *n* impudence, impertinence, cheek, gall, nerve (*infml*), audacity, boldness, chutzpah, daring, rashness, recklessness, impulsiveness.
🔳 caution, prudence.

temper *n* **1** MOOD, humour, nature, temperament, character, disposition, constitution. **2** ANGER, rage, fury, storm, passion, tantrum, paddy (*infml*), annoyance, irritability, ill-humour. **3** CALM, composure, self-control, cool (*infml*).
🔳 **2** calmness, self-control. **3** anger, rage.

➤ *v* **1** MODERATE, lessen, reduce, calm, soothe, allay, assuage, palliate, mitigate, modify, soften, sweeten. **2** HARDEN, toughen, strengthen.

temperament *n* nature, character, personality, disposition, tendency, bent, constitution, make-up, soul, spirit, mood, humour, temper, state of mind, mindset, attitude, outlook.

temperamental *adj* **1** MOODY, emotional, neurotic, highly-strung, sensitive, touchy (*infml*), irritable,

impatient, passionate, fiery, excitable, explosive, volatile, mercurial, capricious, unpredictable, unreliable. **2** NATURAL, inborn, innate, inherent, constitutional, ingrained.
🔳 **1** calm, level-headed, steady.

temperance *n* teetotalism, prohibition, abstinence, sobriety, abstemiousness, continence, moderation, restraint, self-restraint, self-control, self-discipline, self-denial.
🔳 intemperance, excess.

temperate *adj* **1** *temperate climate*: mild, clement, balmy, fair, equable, balanced, stable, gentle, pleasant, agreeable. **2** TEETOTAL, abstinent, abstemious, sober, continent, moderate, restrained, controlled, even-tempered, calm, composed, reasonable, sensible.
🔳 **2** intemperate, extreme, excessive.

tempestuous *adj* stormy, windy, gusty, blustery, squally, turbulent, tumultuous, rough, wild, violent, furious, raging, heated, passionate, intense.
🔳 calm.

temple *n* shrine, sanctuary, church, tabernacle, mosque, mandir, pagoda.

tempo *n* time, rhythm, metre, beat, pulse, speed, velocity, rate, pace.

temporal *adj* secular, profane, worldly, earthly, terrestrial, material, carnal, fleshly, bodily, mortal.
🔳 spiritual.

temporary *adj* impermanent, provisional, interim, makeshift, stopgap, temporal, transient, transitory, passing, ephemeral, evanescent, fleeting, brief, short-lived, momentary.
🔳 permanent, everlasting.

tempt *v* entice, coax, persuade, woo, bait, lure, allure, attract, draw, seduce, invite, tantalize, provoke, incite.
🔳 discourage, dissuade, repel.

temptation *n* enticement, inducement, coaxing, persuasion, bait, lure, allure, appeal, attraction, draw, pull, seduction, invitation.

tenable *adj* credible, defensible, justifiable, reasonable, rational, sound, arguable, believable, defendable, plausible, viable, feasible, possible.
🡒 untenable, indefensible, unjustifiable.

tenant *n* renter, lessee, leaseholder, occupier, occupant, resident, inhabitant.

tend[1] *v* incline, lean, bend, bear, head, aim, lead, go, move, gravitate.

tend[2] *v* look after, care for, cultivate, keep, maintain, manage, handle, guard, protect, watch, mind, nurture, nurse, minister to, serve, attend.
🡒 neglect, ignore.

tendency *n* trend, drift, movement, course, direction, bearing, heading, bias, partiality, predisposition, propensity, readiness, liability, susceptibility, proneness, inclination, leaning, bent, disposition.

tender[1] *adj* 1 KIND, gentle, caring, humane, considerate, warm-hearted, compassionate, sympathetic, warm, fond, affectionate, loving, amorous, romantic, sentimental, emotional, sensitive, tender-hearted, soft-hearted. 2 YOUNG, youthful, immature, green, raw, new, callow, inexperienced, impressionable, vulnerable. 3 SOFT, succulent, fleshy, dainty, delicate, fragile, frail, weak, feeble. 4 SORE, painful, aching, smarting, bruised, inflamed, raw, swollen.
🡒 1 hard-hearted, callous. 2 mature. 3 tough, hard.

tender[2] *v* offer, proffer, extend, give, present, submit, propose, suggest, advance, volunteer.
🡒 *n* 1 *legal tender*: currency, money. 2 OFFER, bid, estimate, quotation, proposal, proposition, suggestion, submission.

tense *adj* 1 TIGHT, taut, stretched, strained, stiff, rigid. 2 NERVOUS, anxious, worried, jittery, uneasy, apprehensive, edgy, fidgety, restless, jumpy, keyed up, overwrought, wired (*infml*). 3 STRESSFUL, exciting, worrying, fraught.

🡒 1 loose, slack. 2 calm, relaxed.
🡒 *v* tighten, contract, brace, stretch, strain.
🡒 loosen, relax.

tension *n* 1 TIGHTNESS, tautness, stiffness, strain, stress, pressure. 2 NERVOUSNESS, anxiety, worry, uneasiness, apprehension, edginess, restlessness, suspense.
🡒 1 looseness. 2 calm(ness), relaxation.

tent

Types of tent include: barrel-vaulted tent, bell tent, big top, bivvy, black tent, box tent, canopy, canvas, conical tent, crossover pole tent, dome tent, double-A pole mountain tent, frame tent, hooped bivvy, kata, lodge, marquee, mat tent, ridge tent, single hoop tent, sloping ridge tent, sloping wedge tent, tabernacle, tepee, touring tent, trailer tent, tunnel tent, tupik, wigwam, yaranga.

tentative *adj* experimental, exploratory, speculative, hesitant, faltering, cautious, unsure, uncertain, doubtful, undecided, provisional, indefinite, unconfirmed.
🡒 definite, decisive, conclusive, final.

tenuous *adj* thin, slim, slender, fine, slight, insubstantial, flimsy, fragile, delicate, faint, weak, shaky, doubtful, dubious, questionable.
🡒 strong, substantial.

tepid *adj* lukewarm, cool, half-hearted, unenthusiastic, apathetic.
🡒 cold, hot, passionate.

term *n* 1 WORD, name, designation, appellation, title, epithet, phrase, expression. 2 TIME, period, course, duration, spell, span, stretch, interval, space, semester, session, season.
🡒 *v* call, name, dub, style, designate, label, tag, title, entitle.

terminal *adj* 1 LAST, final, concluding, ultimate, extreme, utmost. 2 *terminal illness*: FATAL, deadly, lethal, mortal, incurable.
🡒 1 initial.

terminate *v* finish, complete, conclude, cease, end, stop, close, discontinue, wind up, cut off, abort, lapse, expire.
🔁 begin, start, initiate.

terminology *n* language, jargon, phraseology, vocabulary, words, terms, nomenclature.

terminus *n* end, close, termination, extremity, limit, boundary, destination, goal, target, depot, station, garage, terminal.

terms *n* **1** *on good terms*: relations, relationship, footing, standing, position. **2** CONDITIONS, requirements, specifications, stipulations, provisos, provisions, qualifications, particulars. **3** RATES, charges, fees, prices, tariff.

terrain *n* land, ground, territory, country, countryside, landscape, topography.

terrestrial *adj* earthly, worldly, global, mundane.
🔁 cosmic, heavenly.

terrible *adj* bad, awful, frightful, dreadful, shocking, appalling, outrageous, disgusting, revolting, repulsive, offensive, abhorrent, detestable, hateful, horrid, horrible, unpleasant, obnoxious, foul, vile, hideous, gruesome, horrific, harrowing, distressing, grave, serious, severe, extreme, desperate.
🔁 excellent, wonderful, superb.

terribly (*infml*) *adv* very, much, greatly, extremely, exceedingly, awfully, frightfully, decidedly, seriously.

terrific (*infml*) *adj* **1** EXCELLENT, wonderful, marvellous, super, smashing (*infml*), outstanding, brilliant (*infml*), magnificent, superb, fabulous (*infml*), fantastic (*infml*), mega (*sl*), sensational, amazing, stupendous, breathtaking. **2** HUGE, enormous, gigantic, tremendous, great, intense, extreme, excessive.
🔁 **1** awful, terrible, appalling.

terrify *v* petrify, horrify, appal, shock, terrorize, intimidate, frighten, scare, alarm, dismay.

territory *n* country, land, state, dependency, province, domain, preserve, jurisdiction, sector, region, area, district, zone, tract, terrain.

terror *n* fear, panic, dread, trepidation, horror, shock, fright, alarm, dismay, consternation, terrorism, intimidation.

terrorize *v* threaten, menace, intimidate, oppress, coerce, bully, browbeat, frighten, scare, alarm, terrify, petrify, horrify, shock.

terse *adj* short, brief, succinct, concise, compact, condensed, epigrammatic, pithy, incisive, snappy, curt, brusque, abrupt, laconic.
🔁 long-winded, verbose.

test *v* try, experiment, examine, assess, evaluate, check, investigate, analyse, screen, prove, verify.
➤ *n* trial, try-out, experiment, examination, assessment, evaluation, check, investigation, analysis, proof, probation, ordeal.

testify *v* give evidence, depose (*fml*), state, declare, assert, swear, avow (*fml*), attest, vouch, certify, corroborate, affirm, show, bear witness.

testimonial *n* reference, character, credential, certificate, accolade, recommendation, endorsement, commendation, tribute.

testimony *n* evidence, statement, affidavit, submission, deposition (*fml*), declaration, profession, attestation (*fml*), affirmation, support, proof, verification, confirmation, witness, demonstration, manifestation, indication.

tether *n* chain, rope, cord, line, lead, leash, bond, fetter, shackle, restraint, fastening.
➤ *v* tie, fasten, secure, restrain, chain, rope, leash, bind, lash, fetter, shackle, manacle.

text *n* words, wording, content, matter, body, subject, topic, theme, reading, passage, paragraph, sentence, book, textbook, source.

texture *n* consistency, feel, surface, grain, weave, tissue, fabric, structure, composition, constitution, character, quality.

thank *v* say thank you, be grateful, appreciate, acknowledge, recognize, credit.

thankful *adj* grateful, appreciative, obliged, obligated, indebted, pleased, contented, relieved.
F3 ungrateful, unappreciative.

thankless *adj* unrecognized, unappreciated, unrequited, unrewarding, unprofitable, fruitless.
F3 rewarding, worthwhile.

thanks *n* gratitude, gratefulness, thankfulness, appreciation, acknowledgement, recognition, credit, thanksgiving, thank-offering.
◇ **thanks to** because of, owing to, due to, on account of, as a result of, through.

thaw *v* melt, defrost, defreeze, de-ice, soften, liquefy, dissolve, warm, heat up.
F3 freeze.

theatre *n* **1** *go to the theatre*: playhouse, auditorium, hall, amphitheatre. **2** DRAMA, the stage, dramatics, theatrics, show business.

> *Parts of a theatre include*: apron, auditorium, backstage, balcony, border, box, bridge, catwalk, circle, coulisse, cut drop, cyclorama, decor, downstage, flat, flies, forestage, fourth wall, gallery, the gods (*infml*), green room, grid, leg drop, lights, floats, floods, footlights, spots, loge, loggia, logum, mezzanine, open stage, opposite prompt, orchestra pit, picture-frame stage, pit, prompt side, proscenium, proscenium arch, revolving stage, rostrum, safety curtain, scruto, set, stage, stalls, tormentor, trapdoor, upper circle, upstage, wings.

theatrical *adj* **1** DRAMATIC, thespian.

> *Theatrical forms include*: ballet, burlesque, cabaret, circus, comedy, black comedy, comedy of humours, comedy of manners, comedy of menace, commedia dell'arte, duologue, farce, fringe theatre, Grand Guignol, kabuki, Kensington gore, Kitchen-Sink, legitimate drama, masque, melodrama, mime, miracle play, monologue, morality play, mummery, musical, musical comedy, music hall, mystery play, Noh, opera, operetta, pageant, pantomime, play, Punch and Judy, puppet theatre, revue, street theatre, tableau, theatre-in-the-round, Theatre of the Absurd, Theatre of Cruelty, tragedy. *see also* **performance**.

2 MELODRAMATIC, histrionic, mannered, affected, artificial, pompous, ostentatious, showy, extravagant, exaggerated, overdone, over-the-top, OTT (*infml*).

theft *n* robbery, thieving, stealing, pilfering, larceny, shoplifting, kleptomania, fraud, embezzlement.

theme *n* subject, topic, thread, motif, keynote, idea, gist, essence, burden, argument, thesis, dissertation, composition, essay, text, matter.

theorem *n* formula, principle, rule, statement, deduction, proposition, hypothesis.

theoretical *adj* hypothetical, conjectural, speculative, abstract, academic, doctrinaire, pure, ideal.
F3 practical, applied, concrete.

theorize *v* hypothesize, suppose, guess, conjecture, speculate, postulate, propound, formulate.

theory *n* hypothesis, supposition, assumption, presumption, surmise, guess, conjecture, speculation, idea, notion, abstraction, philosophy, thesis, plan, proposal, scheme, system.
F3 certainty, practice.

therapeutic *adj* remedial, curative, healing, restorative, tonic, medicinal, corrective, good, beneficial.
F3 harmful, detrimental.

therapy *n* treatment, remedy, cure, healing, tonic.

Types of therapy include:
acupressure, acupuncture, Alexander technique, aromatherapy, art therapy, aversion therapy, beauty therapy, behaviour therapy, biofeedback, chemotherapy, chiropractic, cognitive therapy, confrontation therapy, drama therapy, electro-convulsive therapy, electrotherapy, faith healing, family therapy, Gestalt therapy, group therapy, heat treatment, herbalism, homeopathy, hormone-replacement therapy, horticulture therapy, hydrotherapy, hypnotherapy, irradiation, moxibustion, music therapy, naturopathy, occupational therapy, osteopathy, phototherapy, physiotherapy, play therapy, primal therapy, psychotherapy, radiotherapy, reflexology, regression therapy, reminiscence therapy, Rolfing, sex therapy, shiatsu, speech therapy, ultrasound, zone therapy. *see also* supplement **Words Grouped by Ending**.

---

therefore *adv* so, then, consequently, as a result.

thesis *n* **1** *doctoral thesis*: dissertation, essay, composition, study, analysis, treatise, paper, monograph. **2** SUBJECT, topic, theme, idea, opinion, view, theory, hypothesis, proposal, proposition, premise, statement, argument, contention.

thick *adj* **1** WIDE, broad, fat, heavy, solid, dense, impenetrable, close, compact, concentrated, condensed, viscous, coagulated, clotted. **2** FULL, packed, crowded, chock-a-block, chockfull, chocker (*infml*), swarming, teeming, bristling, brimming, bursting, numerous, abundant. **3** (*infml*) STUPID, foolish, dense (*sl*), slow, dull, dim-witted, brainless, simple.
1 thin, slim, slender, slight. **2** sparse. **3** clever, brainy (*infml*).

thicken *v* condense, stiffen, congeal, coagulate, clot, cake, gel, jell, set.
thin.

thicket *n* wood, copse, coppice, grove, spinney.

thickness *n* **1** WIDTH, breadth, diameter, density, viscosity, bulk, body. **2** LAYER, stratum, ply, sheet, coat.
1 thinness.

thick-skinned *adj* insensitive, unfeeling, callous, tough, hardened, case-hardened, hard-boiled.
thin-skinned, sensitive.

thief *n* robber, bandit, mugger, pickpocket, shoplifter, burglar, housebreaker, plunderer, poacher, stealer, pilferer, filcher, kleptomaniac, swindler, embezzler.

thin *adj* **1** LEAN, slim, slender, narrow, attenuated, slight, skinny, bony, skeletal, scraggy, scrawny, lanky, gaunt, spare, underweight, undernourished, emaciated. **2** *thin fabric*: fine, delicate, light, flimsy, filmy, gauzy, gossamer, sheer, see-through, transparent, translucent. **3** SPARSE, scarce, scattered, scant, meagre, poor, inadequate, deficient, scanty, skimpy. **4** WEAK, feeble, runny, watery, diluted.
1 fat, broad. **2** thick, dense, solid. **3** plentiful, abundant. **4** strong.
➤ *v* **1** NARROW, attenuate, diminish, reduce, trim, weed out. **2** WEAKEN, dilute, water down, rarefy, refine.

thing *n* **1** ARTICLE, object, entity, creature, body, substance, item, detail, particular, feature, factor, element, point, fact, concept, thought. **2** DEVICE, contrivance, gadget, tool, implement, instrument, apparatus, machine, mechanism. **3** ACT, deed, feat, action, task, responsibility, problem. **4** CIRCUMSTANCE, eventuality, happening, occurrence, event, incident, phenomenon, affair, proceeding. **5** (*infml*) OBSESSION, preoccupation, fixation, fetish, mania, phobia, hang-up (*infml*).

things *n* belongings, possessions, effects, paraphernalia, stuff (*infml*), goods, luggage, baggage, equipment, gear (*infml*), clobber (*infml*), odds and ends, bits and pieces.

think v 1 BELIEVE, hold, consider, regard, esteem, deem, judge, estimate, reckon, calculate, determine, conclude, reason. 2 CONCEIVE, imagine, suppose, presume, surmise, expect, foresee, envisage, anticipate. 3 *think it over*: ponder, mull over, chew over (*infml*), ruminate, meditate, contemplate, muse, cogitate, reflect, deliberate, weigh up, recall, recollect, remember.
◇ **think up** devise, contrive, dream up, imagine, conceive, visualize, invent, design, create, concoct.

thinker n philosopher, theorist, ideologist, brain, intellect, mastermind.

thinking n reasoning, philosophy, thoughts, conclusions, theory, idea, opinion, view, outlook, position, judgement, assessment.
➤ adj reasoning, rational, intellectual, intelligent, cultured, sophisticated, philosophical, analytical, reflective, contemplative, thoughtful.

third-rate adj low-grade, poor, bad, inferior, mediocre, indifferent, shoddy, cheap and nasty, low-rent (*sl*).
🖪 first-rate.

thirst n 1 THIRSTINESS, dryness, drought. 2 DESIRE, longing, yearning, hankering, craving, hunger, appetite, lust, passion, eagerness, keenness.

thirsty adj 1 DRY, parched (*infml*), gasping (*infml*), dehydrated, arid. 2 *thirsty for knowledge*: desirous, longing, yearning, hankering, craving, hungry, burning, itching, dying, eager, avid, greedy.

thorn n spike, point, barb, prickle, spine, bristle, needle.

thorough adj full, complete, total, entire, utter, absolute, perfect, pure, sheer, unqualified, unmitigated, out-and-out, downright, sweeping, all-embracing, comprehensive, all-inclusive, exhaustive, thoroughgoing, intensive, in-depth, conscientious, efficient, painstaking, scrupulous, meticulous, careful.
🖪 partial, superficial, careless.

though conj although, even if, notwithstanding, while, allowing, granted.
➤ adv however, nevertheless, nonetheless, yet, still, even so, all the same, for all that.

thought n 1 THINKING, attention, heed, regard, consideration, study, scrutiny, introspection, meditation, cogitation, reflection, contemplation, deliberation. 2 IDEA, notion, concept, conception, belief, conviction, opinion, view, judgement, assessment, conclusion, plan, design, intention, purpose, aim, hope, dream, expectation, anticipation. 3 THOUGHTFULNESS, consideration, kindness, care, concern, compassion, sympathy, gesture, touch.

thoughtful adj 1 PENSIVE, wistful, dreamy, abstracted, reflective, contemplative, introspective, thinking, absorbed, studious, serious, solemn. 2 CONSIDERATE, kind, unselfish, helpful, caring, attentive, heedful, mindful, careful, prudent, cautious, wary.
🖪 2 thoughtless, insensitive, selfish.

thoughtless adj 1 INCONSIDERATE, unthinking, insensitive, unfeeling, tactless, undiplomatic, unkind, selfish, uncaring. 2 ABSENT-MINDED, inattentive, heedless, mindless, foolish, stupid, silly, rash, reckless, ill-considered, careless, imprudent, negligent, remiss.
🖪 1 thoughtful, considerate. 2 careful.

thrash v 1 PUNISH, beat, whip, lash, flog, scourge, cane, belt (*infml*), spank, clobber (*infml*), wallop (*infml*), lay into. 2 DEFEAT, beat, trounce, hammer (*infml*), slaughter (*infml*), crush, overwhelm, rout. 3 THRESH, flail, toss, jerk.
◇ **thrash out** discuss, debate, negotiate, settle, resolve.

thread n 1 YARN, strand, fibre, filament, string, line. 2 COURSE, direction, drift, tenor, theme, motif, plot, storyline.

Types of thread include: button thread, cotton, coton à broder, mercerized cotton, pearl cotton, machine twist, quick-match, stranded cotton, embroidery thread, machine embroidery thread, embroidery silk, embroidery wool, floss, metallic thread, nylon thread, polyester, purl, silk.

threadbare *adj* **1** *threadbare clothes*: worn, worn-out, frayed, ragged, moth-eaten, scruffy, shabby, tatty. **2** HACKNEYED, overused, old, stale, tired, trite, clichéd, commonplace, stock, stereotyped.
₤ **1** new. **2** fresh.

threat *n* menace, warning, omen, portent, presage, foreboding, danger, risk, hazard, peril.

threaten *v* menace, intimidate, browbeat, pressurize, bully, terrorize, warn, portend, presage, forebode, foreshadow, endanger, jeopardize, imperil.

threatening *adj* menacing, intimidatory, warning, cautionary, ominous, inauspicious, sinister, grim, looming, impending.

threshold *n* doorstep, sill, doorway, door, entrance, brink, verge, starting-point, dawn, beginning, start, outset, opening.

thrift *n* economy, husbandry, saving, conservation, frugality, prudence, carefulness.
₤ extravagance, waste.

thrifty *adj* economical, saving, frugal, sparing, prudent, careful.
₤ extravagant, profligate, prodigal, wasteful.

thrill *n* excitement, adventure, pleasure, stimulation, charge, kick, buzz (*sl*), hit (*sl*), sensation, glow, tingle, throb, shudder, quiver, tremor.
➤ *v* excite, electrify, galvanize, exhilarate, rouse, arouse, move, stir, stimulate, flush, glow, tingle, throb, shudder, tremble, quiver, shake.
₤ bore.

thrilling *adj* exciting, stimulating, stirring, rousing, sensational, exhilarating, high-octane (*infml*),

gripping, electrifying, heart-stirring, hair-raising (*infml*).

thrive *v* flourish, prosper, boom, grow, increase, advance, develop, bloom, blossom, gain, profit, succeed.
₤ languish, stagnate, fail, die.

throb *v* pulse, pulsate, beat, palpitate, vibrate, pound, thump.
➤ *n* pulse, pulsation, beat, palpitation, vibration, pounding, thumping.

throttle *v* strangle, choke, asphyxiate, suffocate, smother, stifle, gag, silence, suppress, inhibit.

through *prep* **1** BETWEEN, by, via, by way of, by means of, using. **2** *all through the night*: throughout, during, in. **3** BECAUSE OF, as a result of, thanks to.
➤ *adj* **1** FINISHED, ended, completed, done. **2** *through train*: direct, express, non-stop.

throw *v* **1** HURL, heave, lob, pitch, chuck (*infml*), sling, cast, fling, toss, launch, propel, send. **2** *throw light*: shed, cast, project, direct. **3** BRING DOWN, floor, upset, overturn, dislodge, unseat, unsaddle, unhorse. **4** (*infml*) PERPLEX, baffle, confound, confuse, disconcert, astonish, dumbfound.
➤ *n* heave, lob, pitch, sling, fling, toss, cast.
◇ **throw away 1** DISCARD, jettison, dump, ditch (*sl*), scrap, dispose of, throw out. **2** WASTE, squander, fritter away, blow (*sl*).
₤ **1** keep, preserve, salvage, rescue.
◇ **throw off** shed, cast off, drop, abandon, shake off, get rid of, elude.
◇ **throw out 1** EVICT, turn out, expel, turf out (*infml*), eject, emit, radiate, give off. **2** REJECT, discard, dismiss, turn down, jettison, dump, ditch (*sl*), throw away, scrap.
◇ **throw up 1** (*infml*) VOMIT, spew, regurgitate, disgorge, retch, heave. **2** GIVE UP, abandon, renounce, relinquish, resign, quit, leave.

thrust *v* push, shove, butt, ram, jam, wedge, stick, poke, prod, jab, lunge, pierce, stab, plunge, press, force, impel, drive, propel.

➤ *n* push, shove, poke, prod, lunge, stab, drive, impetus, momentum.

thud *n, v* thump, clump, knock, clunk, smack, wallop (*infml*), crash, bang, thunder.

thug *n* ruffian, tough, robber, bandit, mugger, killer, murderer, assassin, gangster, hooligan.

thump *n* knock, blow, punch, clout (*infml*), box, cuff, smack, whack (*infml*), wallop (*infml*), crash, bang, thud, beat, throb.

➤ *v* hit, strike, knock, punch, clout (*infml*), box, cuff, smack, thrash, whack (*infml*), wallop (*infml*), crash, bang, thud, batter, pound, hammer, beat, throb.

thunder *n* boom, reverberation, crash, bang, crack, clap, peal, rumble, roll, roar, blast, explosion.

➤ *v* boom, resound, reverberate, resonate, resound, echo, crash, bang, crack, clap, peal, rumble, roll, roar, blast.

thunderous *adj* booming, resounding, reverberating, roaring, loud, noisy, deafening, ear-splitting.

thus *adv* so, hence, therefore, consequently, then, accordingly, like this, in this way, as follows.

thwart *v* frustrate, foil, stymie, hobble (*infml*), defeat, hinder, impede, obstruct, block, check, baffle, stop, prevent, oppose.

🔁 help, assist, aid.

tick *n* **1** CLICK, tap, stroke, tick-tock. **2** (*infml*) *wait a tick*: moment, instant, flash, jiffy (*infml*), second, minute.

➤ *v* **1** MARK, indicate, choose, select. **2** CLICK, tap, beat.

◊ **tick off** (*infml*) scold, chide, reprimand, rebuke, reproach, reprove, upbraid, tell off (*infml*).

🔁 praise, compliment.

ticket *n* pass, card, certificate, token, voucher, coupon, docket, slip, label, tag, sticker.

tickle *v* excite, thrill, delight, please, gratify, amuse, entertain, divert.

ticklish *adj* sensitive, touchy, delicate, thorny, awkward, difficult, tricky, critical, risky, hazardous, dodgy (*infml*).

🔁 easy, simple.

tide *n* current, ebb, flow, stream, flux, movement, course, direction, drift, trend, tendency.

tidy *adj* **1** NEAT, orderly, methodical, systematic, organized, clean, spick-and-span, shipshape, smart, spruce, trim, well-kept, ordered, uncluttered. **2** (*infml*) *a tidy sum*: large, substantial, sizable, considerable, good, generous, ample.

🔁 **1** untidy, messy, disorganized. **2** small, insignificant.

➤ *v* neaten, straighten, order, arrange, clean, smarten, spruce up, groom.

tie *v* knot, fasten, secure, moor, anchor, tether, attach, join, connect, link, unite, rope, lash, strap, bind, restrain, restrict, confine, limit, hamper, hinder.

➤ *n* **1** KNOT, fastening, joint, connection, link, liaison, relationship, bond, affiliation, obligation, commitment, duty, restraint, restriction, limitation, hindrance. **2** DRAW, dead heat, stalemate, deadlock.

◊ **tie up 1** MOOR, tether, attach, secure, rope, lash, bind, truss, wrap up, restrain. **2** CONCLUDE, terminate, wind up, settle. **3** OCCUPY, engage, engross, involve.

tier *n* floor, storey, level, stage, stratum, layer, belt, zone, band, echelon, rank, row, line.

tight *adj* **1** TAUT, stretched, tense, rigid, stiff, firm, fixed, fast, secure, close, cramped, constricted, compact, snug, close-fitting. **2** SEALED, hermetic, -proof, impervious, airtight, watertight. **3** (*infml*) MEAN, stingy, miserly, niggardly, sparing, parsimonious, tight-fisted (*infml*). **4** *tight security*: strict, severe, stringent, rigorous.

🔁 **1** loose, slack. **2** open. **3** generous. **4** lax.

tighten *v* tauten, stretch, tense, stiffen, fix, fasten, secure, narrow, close, cramp,

constrict, crush, squeeze.
🖃 loosen, relax.

tight-fisted (*infml*) *adj* mean, stingy, miserly, mingy (*infml*), niggardly, penny-pinching, sparing, parsimonious, tight (*infml*), grasping.
🖃 generous, charitable.

till *v* cultivate, work, plough, dig, farm.

tilt *v* slope, incline, slant, pitch, list, tip, lean.
➤ *n* slope, incline, angle, inclination, slant, pitch, list.

timber *n* wood, trees, forest, beam, lath, plank, board, log.

time *n* **1** SPELL, stretch, period, term, season, session, span, duration, interval, space, while. **2** TEMPO, beat, rhythm, beat, measure. **3** MOMENT, point, juncture, stage, instance, occasion, date, day, hour. **4** AGE, era, epoch, life, lifetime, generation, heyday, peak.

Periods of time include: eternity, eon, era, age, generation, epoch, millennium, chiliad, century, lifetime, decade, decennium, quinquennium, year, light-year, yesteryear, quarter, month, fortnight, week, midweek, weekend, long weekend, day, today, tonight, yesterday, tomorrow, morrow, weekday, hour, minute, second, moment, instant, millisecond, microsecond, nanosecond; dawn, sunrise, sun-up, the early hours, wee small hours (*infml*), morning, morn, a.m., daytime, midday, noon, high noon, p.m., afternoon, tea-time, evening, twilight, dusk, sunset, nightfall, bedtime, night, night-time; season, spring, summer, midsummer, autumn, fall (*US*), winter.

➤ *v* clock, measure, meter, regulate, control, set, schedule, timetable.

timeless *adj* ageless, immortal, everlasting, eternal, endless, permanent, changeless, unchanging.

timely *adj* well-timed, seasonable, suitable, appropriate, convenient,

opportune, propitious, prompt, punctual.
🖃 ill-timed, unsuitable, inappropriate.

timetable *n* schedule, programme, agenda, calendar, diary, rota, roster, list, listing, curriculum.

timid *adj* shy, bashful, modest, shrinking, retiring, nervous, apprehensive, afraid, timorous, fearful, cowardly, yellow (*sl*), faint-hearted, lily-livered (*sl*), spineless, irresolute.
🖃 brave, bold, audacious.

tinge *n* tint, dye, colour, shade, touch, trace, suggestion, hint, smack, flavour, pinch, drop, dash, bit, sprinkling, smattering.
➤ *v* tint, dye, stain, colour, shade, suffuse, imbue.

tingle *v* sting, prickle, tickle, itch, thrill, throb, quiver, vibrate.
➤ *n* stinging, pricking, prickling, pins and needles, tickle, tickling, itch, itching, thrill, throb, quiver, shiver, gooseflesh, goose-pimples.

tinker *v* fiddle, play, toy, trifle, potter, dabble, meddle, tamper.

tint *n* dye, stain, rinse, wash, colour, hue, shade, tincture, tinge, tone, cast, streak, trace, touch.
➤ *v* dye, colour, tinge, streak, stain, taint, affect.

tiny *adj* minute, minuscule, microscopic, infinitesimal, teeny (*infml*), small, little, slight, negligible, insignificant, diminutive, petite, dwarfish, pint-size(d) (*infml*), pocket, miniature, mini (*infml*).
🖃 huge, enormous, immense.

tip[1] *n* end, extremity, point, nib, apex, peak, pinnacle, summit, acme, top, cap, crown, head.
➤ *v* cap, crown, top, surmount.

tip[2] *v* lean, incline, slant, list, tilt, topple over, capsize, upset, overturn, spill, pour out, empty, unload, dump.
➤ *n* dump, rubbish-heap, refuse-heap.

tip[3] *n* **1** CLUE, pointer, hint, suggestion, advice, warning, tip-off, information, inside information, forecast. **2** GRATUITY, gift, perquisite.

➤ v **1** ADVISE, suggest, warn, caution, forewarn, tip off, inform, tell. **2** *tip the driver*: reward, remunerate.

tire v weary, fatigue, wear out, exhaust, drain, enervate.
🔁 enliven, invigorate, refresh.

tired adj **1** WEARY, drowsy, sleepy, flagging, fatigued, worn out, exhausted, dog-tired, drained, jaded, fagged (*sl*), bushed (*infml*), whacked (*infml*), shattered (*infml*), beat (*infml*), dead-beat (*infml*), all in (*infml*), knackered (*infml*). **2** *tired of waiting*: fed up, bored, sick. **3** STALE, overused, jaded, unoriginal, hackneyed.
🔁 **1** lively, energetic, rested, refreshed. **3** new, original.

tireless adj untiring, unwearied, unflagging, indefatigable, energetic, vigorous, diligent, industrious, resolute, determined.
🔁 tired, lazy.

tiresome adj troublesome, trying, annoying, irritating, exasperating, wearisome, dull, boring, tedious, monotonous, uninteresting, tiring, fatiguing, laborious.
🔁 interesting, stimulating, easy.

tiring adj wearying, fatiguing, exhausting, draining, demanding, exacting, taxing, wearing, arduous, strenuous, laborious.

tissue n substance, matter, material, fabric, stuff, gauze, web, mesh, network, structure, texture.

titbit n morsel, scrap, appetizer, snack, delicacy, dainty, treat.

titillate v stimulate, arouse, turn on (*sl*), excite, thrill, tickle, provoke, tease, tantalize, intrigue, interest.

title n **1** NAME, appellation, denomination, term, designation, label, epithet, nickname, moniker (*sl*), pseudonym, rank, status, office, position. **2** HEADING, headline, caption, legend, inscription. **3** RIGHT, prerogative, privilege, claim, entitlement, ownership, deeds.

➤ v entitle, name, call, dub, style, term, designate, label.

titter v laugh, chortle, chuckle, giggle, snigger, mock.

titular adj honorary, formal, official, so-called, nominal, token.

toadstool *see panel at* **mushroom**.

toast v grill, brown, roast, heat, warm.
➤ n drink, pledge, tribute, salute, compliment, health.

tobacco

Forms of tobacco include: baccy (*infml*), cheroot, chewing tobacco, cigar, Havana cigar, cigarette, cork-tipped cigarette, filter-tip cigarette, king-size cigarette, menthol cigarette, Russian cigarette, ciggie (*infml*), coffin nail (*sl*), fag (*infml*), cigarette end, cigarette butt, dog-end (*sl*), fag end (*sl*), cigarillo, corona, high-tar, low-tar, panatella, plug, snuff, flake tobacco, pipe tobacco, shag tobacco, Turkish tobacco, Virginia tobacco, the weed (*infml*).

Tobacco accessories include: ashtray, cigar box, cigar case, cigar cutter, cigar holder, cigarette box, cigarette case, cigarette holder, cigarette lighter, gas lighter, petrol lighter, cigarette machine, cigarette paper, cigarette roller, humidor, match, matchbook, box of matches, match striker, pipe, chibouk, church-warden, clay pipe, hookah, meerschaum, narghile, peace pipe (pipe of peace), tobacco pipe, pipe-cleaner, pipe-rack, pipe-rest, smoker's companion, snuffbox, tobacco pouch, vesta.

toddler n infant, baby, babe, child, tot, rugrat (*sl*), ankle-biter (*sl*).

together adv jointly, in concert, side by side, shoulder to shoulder, in unison, as one, simultaneously, at the same time, all at once, collectively, en masse, closely, continuously, consecutively, successively, in succession, in a row, hand in hand.

separately, individually, alone.

toil *n* labour, hard work, donkey-work, spadework, drudgery, sweat, graft (*infml*), industry, application, effort, exertion, elbow grease (*infml*).
➤ *v* labour, work, slave, drudge, sweat, grind, slog, graft (*infml*), plug away (*infml*), persevere, strive, struggle.

toilet *n* lavatory, WC, loo (*infml*), bog (*sl*), can (*sl*), john (*US sl*), bathroom, cloakroom, washroom, restroom (*US*), public convenience, Ladies (*infml*), Gents (*infml*), urinal, convenience, powder room.

token *n* **1** SYMBOL, emblem, representation, mark, sign, indication, manifestation, demonstration, expression, evidence, proof, clue, warning, reminder, memorial, memento, souvenir, keepsake. **2** *gift token*: voucher, coupon, counter, disc.
➤ *adj* symbolic, emblematic, nominal, minimal, perfunctory, superficial, cosmetic, hollow, insincere.

tolerable *adj* bearable, endurable, sufferable, acceptable, passable, adequate, reasonable, fair, average, all right, OK (*infml*), not bad (*infml*), mediocre, indifferent, so-so (*infml*), unexceptional, ordinary, run-of-the-mill.
intolerable, unbearable, insufferable.

tolerance *n* **1** TOLERATION, patience, forbearance, open-mindedness, broad-mindedness, magnanimity, sympathy, understanding, lenity, indulgence, permissiveness. **2** VARIATION, fluctuation, play, allowance, clearance. **3** RESISTANCE, resilience, toughness, endurance, stamina.
1 intolerance, prejudice, bigotry, narrow-mindedness.

tolerant *adj* patient, forbearing, open-minded, fair, unprejudiced, broad-minded, liberal, charitable, kind-hearted, sympathetic, understanding, forgiving, lenient, indulgent, easy-going, permissive, lax, soft.
intolerant, biased, prejudiced, bigoted, unsympathetic.

tolerate *v* endure, suffer, put up with, bear, stand, abide, hack (*infml*), take, stomach, swallow, receive, accept, admit, allow, permit, condone, countenance, indulge.

toll[1] *v* ring, peal, chime, knell, sound, strike, announce, call.

toll[2] *n* charge, fee, payment, levy, tax, duty, tariff, rate, cost, penalty, demand, loss.

tomb *n* grave, burial-place, vault, crypt, sepulchre, catacomb, mausoleum, cenotaph.

tone *n* **1** *tone of voice*: note, timbre, pitch, volume, intonation, modulation, inflection, accent, stress, emphasis, force, strength. **2** TINT, tinge, colour, hue, shade, cast, tonality. **3** AIR, manner, attitude, mood, spirit, humour, temper, character, quality, feel, style, expression, effect, vein, tenor, drift.
➤ *v* match, co-ordinate, blend, harmonize.
◇ **tone down** moderate, temper, subdue, restrain, soften, dim, dampen, play down, reduce, alleviate, assuage, mitigate.

tongue *n* language, speech, discourse, talk, utterance, articulation, parlance, vernacular, idiom, dialect, idiolect, patois.

tongue-tied *adj* speechless, dumbstruck, inarticulate, silent, mute, dumb, voiceless.
talkative, garrulous, voluble.

tonic *n* cordial, pick-me-up, restorative, refresher, bracer, stimulant, shot in the arm (*infml*), boost, fillip.

too *adv* **1** ALSO, as well, in addition, besides, moreover, likewise. **2** EXCESSIVELY, inordinately, unduly, over, overly, unreasonably, ridiculously, extremely, very.

tool *n* **1** IMPLEMENT, instrument, utensil, gadget, device, doodah (*infml*), contrivance, contraption, apparatus, appliance, machine, means, vehicle, medium, agency, agent, intermediary. **2** PUPPET, pawn, dupe, stooge, minion, hireling.

Types of tool include: bolster, caulking iron, crowbar, hod, jackhammer, jointer, mattock, pick, pickaxe, plumb line, sledgehammer; chaser, clamp, dividers, dolly, drill, hacksaw, jack, pincers, pliers, protractor, punch, rule, sander, scriber, snips, socket-wrench, soldering iron, spraygun, tommy bar, vice; auger, awl, brace and bit, bradawl, chisel, file, fretsaw, hammer, handsaw, jack plane, jig-saw, level, mallet, plane, rasp, saw, screwdriver, set square, spirit level, tenon saw, T-square; billhook, chainsaw, chopper, dibber, fork, grass rake, hay fork, hoe, pitchfork, plough, pruning knife, pruning shears, rake, scythe, secateurs, shears, shovel, sickle, spade, thresher, trowel; needle, scissors, pinking shears, bodkin, crochet hook, forceps, scalpel, tweezers, tongs, cleaver, steel, gimlet, mace, mortar, pestle, paper-cutter, paper-knife, stapler, pocket knife, penknife.

tooth

Types of tooth include: baby tooth, back tooth, bicuspid, bucktooth, canine, carnassial, dog-tooth, eye tooth, fang, first tooth, gold tooth, grinder, incisor, central incisor, lateral incisor, milk tooth, molar, first molar, second molar, third molar, premolar, first premolar, second premolar, snaggletooth, tush, tusk, wisdom tooth; false tooth, false teeth, bridge, cap, crown, denture, dentures, plate.

top *n* **1** HEAD, tip, vertex, apex, crest, crown, peak, pinnacle, summit, acme, zenith, culmination, height. **2** LID, cap, cover, cork, stopper.
🔁 **1** bottom, base, nadir.
➤ *adj* highest, topmost, upmost, uppermost, upper, superior, head, chief, leading, first, foremost, principal, sovereign, ruling, pre-eminent, dominant, prime, premium, paramount, greatest, maximum, best, finest,

supreme, optimum, crowning, culminating.
🔁 bottom, lowest, inferior.
➤ *v* **1** TIP, cap, crown, cover, finish (off), decorate, garnish. **2** BEAT, exceed, outstrip, better, excel, best, surpass, eclipse, outshine, outdo, surmount, transcend. **3** HEAD, lead, rule, command.

topic *n* subject, theme, issue, question, matter, point, thesis, text.

topical *adj* current, contemporary, up to date, up to the minute, recent, newsworthy, relevant, popular, familiar.

topple *v* totter, overbalance, tumble, fall, collapse, upset, overturn, capsize, overthrow, oust.

torment *v* tease, provoke, annoy, vex, trouble, worry, harass, hassle (*infml*), hound, pester, bother, bedevil, plague, afflict, distress, harrow, pain, torture, persecute.
➤ *n* provocation, annoyance, vexation, bane, scourge, trouble, bother, nuisance, harassment, worry, anguish, distress, misery, affliction, suffering, pain, agony, ordeal, torture, persecution.

torrent *n* stream, volley, outburst, gush, rush, flood, spate, deluge, cascade, downpour.
🔁 trickle.

tortuous *adj* twisting, winding, meandering, serpentine, zigzag, circuitous, roundabout, indirect, convoluted, complicated, involved.
🔁 straight, straightforward.

torture *v* pain, hurt, agonize, excruciate, crucify, rack, martyr, persecute, torment, afflict, distress.
➤ *n* pain, hurt, agony, suffering, affliction, distress, misery, anguish, torment, martyrdom, persecution.

toss *v* **1** FLIP, cast, fling, throw, chuck (*infml*), sling, hurl, lob. **2** ROLL, heave, pitch, lurch, jolt, shake, agitate, rock, thrash, squirm, wriggle.
➤ *n* flip, cast, fling, throw, pitch.

total *n* sum, whole, entirety, totality, all, lot, mass, aggregate, amount.

➤ *adj* full, complete, entire, whole, integral, all-out, full-on (*sl*), utter, absolute, unconditional, unqualified, outright, undisputed, perfect, consummate, thoroughgoing, sheer, downright, thorough.

⊟ partial, limited, restricted.

➤ *v* add (up), sum (up), tot (up), count (up), reckon, amount to, come to, reach.

totter *v* stagger, reel, lurch, stumble, falter, waver, teeter, sway, rock, shake, quiver, tremble.

touch *n* **1** FEEL, texture, brush, stroke, caress, pat, tap, contact. **2** *a touch of garlic*: trace, spot, dash, pinch, soupçon, suspicion, hint, suggestion, speck, jot, tinge, smack. **3** SKILL, art, knack, flair, style, method, manner, technique, approach.

➤ *v* **1** FEEL, handle, finger, brush, graze, stroke, caress, fondle, pat, tap, hit, strike, contact, meet, abut (*fml*), adjoin, border. **2** MOVE, stir, upset, disturb, impress, inspire, influence, affect, concern, regard. **3** REACH, attain, equal, match, rival, better.

◊ **touch on** mention, broach, speak of, remark on, refer to, allude to, cover, deal with.

touched *adj* **1** MOVED, stirred, affected, disturbed, troubled, impressed. **2** MAD, crazy, deranged, disturbed, eccentric, dotty (*infml*), daft (*infml*), barmy (*infml*).

touching *adj* moving, stirring, affecting, poignant, pitiable, pitiful, pathetic, sad, emotional, tender.

touchy *adj* irritable, irascible, quick-tempered, bad-tempered, stroppy (*infml*), grumpy, grouchy, crabbed, cross, peevish, captious, edgy, over-sensitive.

⊟ calm, imperturbable.

tough *adj* **1** STRONG, durable, resilient, resistant, hardy, sturdy, solid, rigid, stiff, inflexible, hard, leathery. **2** *tough criminal*: rough, violent, vicious, callous, hardened, obstinate. **3** HARSH, severe, strict, stern, firm, resolute, determined, tenacious. **4** ARDUOUS, laborious,

exacting, challenging, hard, difficult, puzzling, perplexing, baffling, knotty, thorny, troublesome.

⊟ **1** fragile, delicate, weak, tender. **2** gentle, soft. **3** gentle. **4** easy, simple.

➤ *n* brute, thug, bully, ruffian, hooligan, lout, yob (*sl*).

tour *n* circuit, round, visit, expedition, journey, trip, outing, excursion, drive, ride, course.

➤ *v* visit, go round, sightsee, explore, travel, journey, drive, ride.

tourist *n* holidaymaker, visitor, sightseer, tripper, excursionist, traveller, voyager, globetrotter.

tournament *n* championship, series, competition, contest, match, event, meeting.

tow *v* pull, tug, draw, trail, drag, lug, haul, transport.

towards *prep* **1** TO, approaching, nearing, close to, nearly, almost. **2** *his feelings towards her*: regarding, with regard to, with respect to, about, concerning, for.

tower *n* steeple, spire, belfry, turret, fortification, bastion, citadel, fort, fortress, castle, keep.

Types of tower and famous towers include: barbican, bastille, bastion, belfry, bell tower, belvedere, campanile, castle, church tower, citadel, column, demi-bastion, donjon, Eiffel Tower, fort, fortification, fortress, gate-tower, high-rise building, hill fort, keep, lookout tower, martello tower, minar, minaret, mirador, pagoda, peel-tower, scaffold tower, skyscraper, smock mill, spire, steeple, tower block, tower mill, Tower of London, Tower of Pisa, turret, watchtower, water tower.

➤ *v* rise, rear, ascend, mount, soar, loom, overlook, dominate, surpass, transcend, exceed, top.

towering *adj* soaring, tall, high, lofty, elevated, monumental, colossal, gigantic, great, magnificent, imposing, impressive, sublime, supreme, surpassing, overpowering, extreme, inordinate.

🔁 small, tiny, minor, trivial.

toxic *adj* poisonous, harmful, noxious, unhealthy, dangerous, deadly, lethal.

🔁 harmless, safe.

toy *n* plaything, knick-knack.

Kinds of toy include: Action Man®, activity centre, aeroplane, baby-bouncer, baby-walker, ball, balloon, bicycle, bike (*infml*), mountain bike, blackboard and easel, boxing gloves, building block, building brick, catapult, climbing frame, computer game, crayon, doll, Barbie® doll, kewpie doll, rag doll, Sindy® doll, Tiny Tears® doll, doll's buggy, doll's cot, doll's house, doll's pram, dreidel, drum set, electronic game, executive toy, farm, fivestones, football, fort, Frisbee®, game, garage, glove puppet, go-kart, golliwog, guitar, gun, cap-gun, pop-gun, gyroscope, hobby-horse, hula-hoop, jack-in-the-box, jigsaw puzzle, kaleidoscope, kite, box kite, Lego®, marble, Meccano®, model car, model kit, model railway, modelling clay, musical box, ocarina, paddling-pool, paints, pantograph, pedal-car, peashooter, Plasticene®, Play-Doh®, playhouse, pogo stick, Pokemon, Power Rangers®, puzzle, rattle, rocker, rocking horse, Rubik's Cube®, sandpit, Scalextric®, scooter, seesaw, sewing machine, shape-sorter, skateboard, skipping rope, slide, soft-toy, spacehopper, spinning top, Subbuteo®, swing, swingball, teaset, teddy bear, toy soldier, train set, trampoline, tricycle, trike (*infml*), Turtles, typewriter, video game, Game Boy®, Game Cube®, PlayStation®, Xbox®, walkie-talkie (*infml*), water pistol, Wendy house, yo-yo. *see also* **game**.

➤ *v* play, tinker, fiddle, sport, trifle, dally.

trace *n* trail, track, spoor, footprint, footmark, mark, token, sign, indication, evidence, record, relic, remains, remnant, vestige, shadow, hint, suggestion, suspicion, soupçon, dash, drop, spot, bit, jot, touch, tinge, smack.

➤ *v* **1** COPY, draw, sketch, outline, delineate, depict, mark, record, map, chart. **2** FIND, discover, detect, unearth, track (down), trail, stalk, hunt, seek, follow, pursue, shadow.

track *n* footstep, footprint, footmark, scent, spoor, trail, wake, mark, trace, slot, groove, rail, path, way, route, orbit, line, course, drift, sequence.

➤ *v* stalk, trail, hunt, trace, follow, pursue, chase, dog, tail, shadow.

◇ **track down** find, discover, trace, hunt down, run to earth, sniff out, ferret out, dig up, unearth, expose, catch, capture.

tract *n* stretch, extent, expanse, plot, lot, territory, area, region, zone, district, quarter.

trade *n* **1** COMMERCE, traffic, business, dealing, buying, selling, shopkeeping, barter, exchange, transactions, custom. **2** OCCUPATION, job, business, profession, line, calling, craft, skill.

➤ *v* traffic, peddle, do business, deal, transact, buy, sell, vend, barter, exchange, swap, switch, bargain.

trademark *n* brand, label, name, sign, symbol, logo, insignia, crest, emblem, badge, hallmark.

trader *n* merchant, tradesman, broker, dealer, buyer, seller, vendor, supplier, wholesaler, retailer, shopkeeper, trafficker, peddler.

tradition *n* convention, custom, usage, way, habit, routine, ritual, institution, folklore.

traditional *adj* conventional, customary, habitual, usual, accustomed, established, fixed, long-established, time-honoured, old, historic, folk, oral, unwritten.

🔁 unconventional, innovative, new, modern, contemporary.

traffic *n* **1** VEHICLES, shipping, transport, transportation, freight,

passengers. **2** TRADE, commerce, business, dealing, trafficking, barter, exchange. **3** COMMUNICATION, dealings, relations.
➤ v peddle, buy, sell, trade, do business, deal, bargain, barter, exchange.

tragedy n adversity, misfortune, unhappiness, affliction, blow, calamity, disaster, catastrophe.

tragic adj sad, sorrowful, miserable, unhappy, unfortunate, unlucky, ill-fated, pitiable, pathetic, heart-rending, heartbreaking, shocking, appalling, dreadful, awful, dire, calamitous, disastrous, catastrophic, deadly, fatal.
⊟ happy, comic, successful.

trail v **1** DRAG, pull, tow, droop, dangle, extend, stream, straggle, dawdle, lag, loiter, linger. **2** TRACK, stalk, hunt, follow, pursue, chase, shadow, tail.
➤ n track, footprints, footmarks, scent, trace, path, footpath, road, route, way.

train v **1** TEACH, instruct, coach, tutor, educate, improve, school, discipline, prepare, drill, exercise, work out, practise, rehearse. **2** POINT, direct, aim, level.
➤ n **1** *train of events*: sequence, succession, series, progression, order, string, chain, line, file, procession, convoy, cortège, caravan. **2** RETINUE, entourage, attendants, court, household, staff, followers, following.

trainer n teacher, instructor, coach, tutor, handler.

training n teaching, instruction, coaching, tuition, education, schooling, discipline, preparation, grounding, drill, exercise, working-out, practice, learning, apprenticeship.

trait n feature, attribute, quality, characteristic, idiosyncrasy, peculiarity, quirk.

traitor n betrayer, informer, deceiver, double-crosser, turncoat, renegade, deserter, defector, quisling, collaborator.
⊟ loyalist, supporter, defender.

tramp v walk, march, tread, stamp,

stomp, stump, plod, trudge, traipse, trail, trek, hike, ramble, roam, rove.
➤ n vagrant, vagabond, hobo, down-and-out, dosser (*sl*).

trample v tread, tramp, stamp, crush, squash, flatten.

trance n dream, daydream, reverie, daze, stupor, unconsciousness, spell, ecstasy, rapture.

tranquil adj calm, composed, cool, imperturbable, unexcited, placid, easy-going (*infml*), sedate, relaxed, laid-back (*infml*), serene, peaceful, restful, still, undisturbed, untroubled, quiet, hushed, silent.
⊟ agitated, disturbed, troubled, noisy.

tranquillizer n sedative, opiate, narcotic, barbiturate.

transaction n deal, bargain, agreement, arrangement, negotiation, business, affair, matter, proceeding, enterprise, undertaking, deed, action, execution, discharge.

transcend v surpass, excel, outshine, eclipse, outdo, outstrip, beat, surmount, exceed, overstep.

transcribe v write out, copy, reproduce, rewrite, transliterate, translate, render, take down, note, record.

transcript n transcription, copy, reproduction, duplicate, transliteration, translation, version, note, record, manuscript.

transfer v change, transpose, move, shift, remove, relocate, transplant, transport, carry, convey, transmit, consign, grant, hand over.
➤ n change, changeover, transposition, move, shift, removal, relocation, displacement, transmission, handover, transference.

transfix v **1** FASCINATE, spellbind, mesmerize, hypnotize, paralyse. **2** IMPALE, spear, skewer, spike, stick.

transform v change, alter, adapt, convert, remodel, reconstruct, remake, transfigure, revolutionize.
⊟ preserve, maintain.

transformation *n* change, alteration, mutation, conversion, metamorphosis, transfiguration, revolution.
⊟ preservation, conservation.

transient *adj* transitory, passing, flying, fleeting, brief, short, momentary, ephemeral, short-lived, temporary, short-term.
⊟ lasting, permanent.

transit *n* passage, journey, travel, movement, transfer, transportation, conveyance, carriage, haulage, shipment.

transition *n* passage, passing, progress, progression, development, evolution, flux, change, alteration, conversion, transformation, shift.

transitional *adj* provisional, temporary, passing, intermediate, developmental, changing, fluid, unsettled.
⊟ initial, final.

translate *v* interpret, render, paraphrase, simplify, decode, decipher, transliterate, transcribe, change, alter, convert, transform, improve.

translation *n* rendering, version, interpretation, gloss, crib, rewording, rephrasing, paraphrase, explanation, simplification, transliteration, transcription, change, alteration, conversion, transformation.

transmission *n* **1** BROADCASTING, diffusion, spread, communication, conveyance, carriage, transport, shipment, sending, dispatch, relaying, transfer. **2** *a live transmission*: broadcast, show, programme, signal.

transmit *v* communicate, impart, convey, carry, bear, transport, send, dispatch, forward, relay, transfer, broadcast, radio, disseminate, network, diffuse, spread.
⊟ receive.

transparency *n* slide, photograph, picture.

transparent *adj* **1** *transparent plastic*: clear, see-through, translucent, sheer. **2** PLAIN, distinct, clear, lucid, explicit, unambiguous, unequivocal, apparent, visible, obvious, evident, manifest, patent, undisguised, open, candid, straightforward.
⊟ **1** opaque. **2** unclear, ambiguous.

transplant *v* move, shift, displace, remove, uproot, transfer, relocate, resettle, repot.
⊟ leave.

transport *v* convey, carry, bear, take, fetch, bring, move, shift, transfer, ship, haul, remove, deport.
➤ *n* conveyance, carriage, transfer, transportation, shipment, shipping, haulage, removal.

transpose *v* swap, exchange, switch, interchange, transfer, shift, rearrange, reorder, change, alter, move, substitute, replace.

transverse *adj* cross, crosswise, transversal, diagonal, oblique.

trap *n* snare, net, noose, springe, gin, booby-trap, pitfall, danger, hazard, ambush, trick, wile, ruse, stratagem, device, trickery, artifice, deception.
➤ *v* snare, net, entrap, ensnare, enmesh, catch, take, ambush, corner, trick, deceive, dupe.

trash *n* rubbish, garbage, refuse, junk, waste, litter, sweepings, offscourings, scum, dregs.

trauma *n* injury, wound, hurt, damage, pain, suffering, anguish, agony, torture, ordeal, shock, jolt, upset, disturbance, upheaval, strain, stress.
⊟ healing.

traumatic *adj* painful, hurtful, injurious, wounding, shocking, upsetting, distressing, disturbing, unpleasant, frightening, stressful.
⊟ healing, relaxing.

travel *v* journey, voyage, go, wend, move, proceed, progress, wander, ramble, roam, rove, tour, cross, traverse.
⊟ stay, remain.

Methods of travel include: fly, aviate, pilot, shuttle, sail, cruise, punt, paddle, row, steam, ride, cycle, bike (*infml*), scooter, skate, skateboard, ski, freewheel, drive, motor, bus, walk, hike, march, ramble, trek, orienteer, hitch-hike, commute.

➤ *n* travelling, touring, tourism, globetrotting.

Forms of travel include: flight, cruise, sail, voyage, ride, drive, march, walk, hike, ramble, excursion, holiday, jaunt, outing, tour, trip, visit, expedition, safari, trek, circumnavigation, exploration, journey, migration, mission, pilgrimage.

traveller *n* **1** TOURIST, explorer, voyager, globetrotter, holidaymaker, tripper (*infml*), excursionist, passenger, commuter, wanderer, rambler, hiker, wayfarer, migrant, refugee, nomad, gypsy, itinerant, tinker, vagrant. **2** SALESMAN, saleswoman, representative, rep (*infml*), agent.

travelling *adj* touring, wandering, roaming, roving, wayfaring, migrant, migratory, nomadic, itinerant, peripatetic, mobile, moving, vagrant, homeless.
🖪 fixed.

travels *n* voyage, expedition, passage, journey, trip, excursion, tour, wanderings.

travesty *n* mockery, parody, take-off (*infml*), send-up (*infml*), farce, caricature, distortion, sham, apology.

treacherous *adj* **1** TRAITOROUS, disloyal, unfaithful, faithless, unreliable, untrustworthy, false, untrue, deceitful, double-crossing. **2** *treacherous roads*: dangerous, hazardous, risky, perilous, precarious, icy, slippery.
🖪 **1** loyal, faithful, dependable. **2** safe, stable.

treachery *n* treason, betrayal, disloyalty, unfaithfulness, infidelity, falseness, duplicity, double-dealing.
🖪 loyalty, dependability.

tread *v* walk, step, pace, stride, march,

tramp, hike, trudge, plod, stamp, trample, walk on, press, crush, squash.
➤ *n* walk, footfall, footstep, step, pace, stride.

treason *n* treachery, perfidy, disloyalty, duplicity, subversion, sedition, mutiny, rebellion.
🖪 loyalty.

treasonable *adj* traitorous, perfidious, disloyal, false, subversive, seditious, mutinous.
🖪 loyal.

treasure *n* fortune, wealth, riches, money, cash, gold, jewels, hoard, cache.
➤ *v* prize, value, esteem, revere, worship, love, adore, idolize, cherish, preserve, guard.
🖪 disparage, belittle.

treat *n* indulgence, gratification, pleasure, delight, joy, enjoyment, fun, entertainment, excursion, outing, party, celebration, feast, banquet, gift, surprise, thrill.
➤ *v* **1** DEAL WITH, manage, handle, use, regard, consider, discuss, cover. **2** TEND, nurse, minister to, attend to, care for, look after, heal, cure. **3** PAY FOR, buy, stand, give, provide, entertain, regale, feast.

treatise *n* essay, dissertation, thesis, monograph, paper, pamphlet, tract, study, exposition.

treatment *n* **1** HEALING, cure, remedy, medication, therapy, surgery, care, nursing. **2** MANAGEMENT, handling, use, usage, conduct, discussion, coverage.

treaty *n* pact, convention, agreement, covenant, compact, negotiation, contract, bond, alliance.

tree

Trees include: acacia, acer, alder, almond, apple, ash, aspen, balsa, bay, beech, birch, blackthorn, blue gum, box, cedar, cherry, chestnut, coconut palm, cottonwood, cypress, date palm, dogwood, Dutch elm, ebony, elder, elm, eucalyptus, fig, fir, gum, hawthorn, hazel, hickory, hornbeam, horse chestnut, Japanese maple, larch, laurel, lime, linden, mahogany, maple, monkey puzzle, mountain ash, oak, palm, pear, pine, plane, plum, poplar, prunus, pussy willow, redwood, rowan, rubber tree, sandalwood, sapele, sequoia, silver birch, silver maple, spruce, sycamore, teak, walnut, weeping willow, whitebeam, willow, witch hazel, yew, yucca; bonsai, conifer, deciduous, evergreen, fruit, hardwood, ornamental, palm, softwood.

trek *n* hike, walk, march, tramp, journey, expedition, safari.
➤ *v* hike, walk, march, tramp, trudge, plod, journey, rove, roam.

tremble *v* shake, vibrate, quake, shiver, shudder, quiver, wobble, rock.
➤ *n* shake, vibration, quake, shiver, shudder, quiver, tremor, wobble.
🔁 steadiness.

tremendous *adj* wonderful, marvellous, stupendous, sensational, spectacular, extraordinary, amazing, incredible, terrific (*infml*), impressive, huge, mega (*sl*), immense, vast, colossal, gigantic, towering, formidable.
🔁 ordinary, unimpressive.

tremor *n* shake, quiver, tremble, shiver, quake, quaver, wobble, vibration, agitation, thrill, shock, earthquake.
🔁 steadiness.

trend *n* course, flow, drift, tendency, inclination, leaning, craze, rage (*infml*), fashion, vogue, mode, style, look.

trespass *v* invade, intrude, encroach, poach, infringe, violate, offend, wrong.
🔁 obey, keep to.
➤ *n* invasion, intrusion, encroachment, poaching, infringement, violation, contravention, offence, misdemeanour.

trespasser *n* intruder, encroacher, poacher, offender, criminal.

trial *n* **1** LITIGATION, lawsuit, hearing, inquiry, tribunal. **2** EXPERIMENT, test, examination, check, dry run, dummy run, practice, rehearsal, audition,

contest. **3** AFFLICTION, suffering, grief, misery, distress, adversity, hardship, ordeal, trouble, nuisance, vexation, tribulation.
🔁 **3** relief, happiness.
➤ *adj* experimental, test, pilot, exploratory, provisional, probationary.

triangle

> *Types of triangle include*: acute-angled, congruent, equilateral, isosceles, obtuse-angled, right-angled, scalene, similar.

tribe *n* race, nation, people, clan, family, line, house, dynasty, blood, stock, group, caste, class, division, branch.

tribute *n* **1** PRAISE, commendation, compliment, accolade, homage, respect, honour, credit, testimony, acknowledgement, recognition, gratitude. **2** PAYMENT, levy, charge, tax, duty, gift, offering, contribution.

trick *n* fraud, swindle, sting (*sl*), deception, deceit, artifice, illusion, hoax, practical joke, joke, jape, leg-pull (*infml*), prank, antic, caper, frolic, feat, stunt, ruse, wile, dodge, subterfuge, trap, device, knack, technique, secret.
➤ *adj* false, mock, artificial, imitation, ersatz, fake, forged, counterfeit, feigned, sham, bogus.
🔁 real, genuine.
➤ *v* deceive, delude, dupe, fool, hoodwink, beguile, mislead, bluff, hoax, pull someone's leg (*infml*), cheat, swindle, diddle, defraud, con (*infml*), sting (*sl*), trap, outwit.

trickery *n* deception, illusion, sleight-of-hand, pretence, artifice, guile, deceit, dishonesty, cheating, swindling, fraud, imposture, double-dealing, monkey business, funny business (*sl*), chicanery, skulduggery, hocus-pocus.
🔁 straightforwardness, honesty.

trickle *v* dribble, run, leak, seep, ooze, exude, drip, drop, filter, percolate.
🔁 stream, gush.
➤ *n* dribble, drip, drop, leak, seepage.
🔁 stream, gush.

tricky *adj* **1** *a tricky problem*: difficult, awkward, problematic, complicated, knotty, thorny, delicate, ticklish. **2** CRAFTY, artful, cunning, sly, wily, foxy, subtle, devious, slippery, scheming, deceitful.
☒ **1** easy, simple. **2** honest.

trifle *n* **1** LITTLE, bit, spot, drop, dash, touch, trace, tad. **2** TOY, plaything, trinket, bauble, knick-knack, triviality, nothing.
➤ *v* toy, play, sport, flirt, dally, dabble, fiddle, meddle, fool.

trifling *adj* small, paltry, slight, negligible, inconsiderable, unimportant, insignificant, minor, trivial, petty, silly, frivolous, idle, empty, worthless.
☒ important, significant, serious.

trigger *v* cause, start, initiate, activate, set off, spark off, provoke, incite, prompt, elicit, generate, produce.
➤ *n* lever, catch, switch, spur, stimulus.

trim *adj* **1** NEAT, tidy, orderly, shipshape, spick-and-span, spruce, smart, dapper. **2** SLIM, slender, streamlined, compact.
☒ **1** untidy, scruffy.
➤ *v* **1** CUT, clip, crop, dock, prune, pare, shave. **2** DECORATE, ornament, embellish, garnish, dress, array, adjust, arrange, order, neaten, tidy.
➤ *n* condition, state, order, form, shape, fitness, health.

trimmings *n* **1** GARNISH, decorations, ornaments, frills, extras, accessories. **2** CUTTINGS, clippings, parings, ends.

trinket *n* bauble, jewel, ornament, knick-knack, trifle.

trio *n* threesome, triad, triumvirate, trinity, triplet, trilogy.

trip *n* outing, excursion, tour, jaunt, ride, drive, spin, journey, voyage, expedition, foray.
➤ *v* stumble, slip, fall, tumble, stagger, totter, blunder.

triple *adj* treble, triplicate, threefold, three-ply, three-way.
➤ *v* treble, triplicate.

trite *adj* banal, commonplace,

ordinary, run-of-the-mill, humdrum, stale, tired, worn, threadbare, unoriginal, unimaginative, hackneyed, overused, stock, stereotyped, clichéd, corny (*infml*).
☒ original, new, fresh.

triumph *n* **1** WIN, victory, conquest, walkover, success, achievement, accomplishment, feat, coup, masterstroke, hit, sensation. **2** EXULTATION, jubilation, rejoicing, celebration, elation, joy, happiness, delight.
☒ **1** failure.
➤ *v* win, succeed, prosper, conquer, vanquish, overcome, overwhelm, prevail, dominate, celebrate, rejoice, delight, glory, gloat.
☒ lose, fail.

triumphant *adj* winning, victorious, conquering, successful, exultant, jubilant, rejoicing, celebratory, glorious, elated, joyful, proud, boastful, gloating, swaggering.
☒ defeated, humble.

trivial *adj* unimportant, insignificant, inconsequential, incidental, minor, petty, paltry, trifling, small, little, inconsiderable, negligible, worthless, meaningless, frivolous, banal, trite, commonplace, everyday.
☒ important, significant, profound.

triviality *n* unimportance, insignificance, pettiness, smallness, worthlessness, meaninglessness, frivolity, trifle, nothing, detail, technicality.
☒ importance, essential.

troop *n* contingent, squadron, unit, division, company, squad, team, crew, gang, band, bunch, group, body, pack, herd, flock, horde, crowd, throng, multitude.
➤ *v* go, march, parade, stream, flock, swarm, throng.

troops *n* army, military, soldiers, servicemen, servicewomen.

trophy *n* cup, prize, award, souvenir, memento.

tropical *adj* hot, torrid, sultry, sweltering, stifling, steamy, humid.
🔁 arctic, cold, cool, temperate.

trot *v* jog, run, scamper, scuttle, scurry.

trouble *n* **1** PROBLEM, difficulty, struggle, annoyance, irritation, bother, nuisance, inconvenience, misfortune, adversity, trial, tribulation, pain, suffering, affliction, distress, grief, woe, heartache, concern, uneasiness, worry, anxiety, agitation. **2** UNREST, strife, tumult, commotion, disturbance, disorder, upheaval. **3** *back trouble*: disorder, complaint, ailment, illness, disease, disability, defect. **4** EFFORT, exertion, pains, care, attention, thought.
🔁 **1** relief, calm. **2** order. **3** health.
➤ *v* annoy, vex, harass, torment, bother, inconvenience, disturb, upset, distress, sadden, pain, afflict, burden, worry, agitate, disconcert, perplex.
🔁 reassure, help.

troublemaker *n* agitator, rabble-rouser, incendiary, instigator, ringleader, stirrer, mischief-maker, rebel.
🔁 peacemaker.

troublesome *adj* **1** ANNOYING, irritating, vexatious, irksome, bothersome, inconvenient, difficult, hard, tricky, thorny, taxing, demanding, laborious, tiresome, wearisome. **2** UNRULY, rowdy, turbulent, trying, unco-operative, insubordinate, rebellious.
🔁 **1** easy, simple. **2** helpful.

trough *n* gutter, conduit, trench, ditch, gully, channel, groove, furrow, hollow, depression.

trousers *n* pants (*US*), slacks, jeans, denims, Levis®, chinos, corduroys, flannels, bags (*infml*), dungarees, breeches, shorts.

truancy *n* absence, absenteeism, shirking, skiving (*infml*), non-attendance.
🔁 attendance.

truant *n* absentee, deserter, runaway, idler, shirker, skiver (*infml*), dodger.
➤ *adj* absent, missing, runaway.

truce *n* ceasefire, peace, armistice, cessation, moratorium, suspension, stay, respite, let-up (*infml*), lull, rest, break, interval, intermission.
🔁 war, hostilities.

truck *n* lorry, van, wagon, trailer, float, cart, barrow.

trudge *v* tramp, plod, clump, stump, lumber, traipse, slog, labour, trek, hike, walk, march.
➤ *n* tramp, traipse, slog, haul, trek, hike, walk, march.

true *adj* **1** REAL, genuine, authentic, actual, veritable, exact, precise, accurate, correct, right, factual, truthful, veracious, sincere, honest, legitimate, valid, rightful, proper. **2** FAITHFUL, loyal, constant, steadfast, staunch, firm, trustworthy, trusty, honourable, dedicated, devoted.
🔁 **1** false, wrong, incorrect, inaccurate. **2** unfaithful, faithless.

truism *n* truth, platitude, cliché, commonplace, bromide, chestnut.

truly *adv* very, greatly, extremely, really, genuinely, sincerely, honestly, truthfully, undeniably, indubitably, indeed, in fact, in reality, exactly, precisely, correctly, rightly, properly.
🔁 slightly, falsely, incorrectly.

trumpet *n* bugle, horn, clarion, klaxon, blare, blast, roar, bellow, cry, call.
➤ *v* blare, blast, roar, bellow, shout, proclaim, announce, broadcast, advertise.

truncate *v* shorten, abbreviate, curtail, cut, lop, dock, prune, pare, clip, trim, crop.
🔁 lengthen, extend.

trunk *n* **1** CASE, suitcase, chest, coffer, box, crate. **2** TORSO, body, frame, shaft, stock, stem, stalk.

truss *v* tie, strap, bind, pinion, fasten, secure, bundle, pack.
🔁 untie, loosen.
➤ *n* binding, bandage, support, brace, prop, stay, shore, strut, joist.

trust *n* **1** FAITH, belief, credence, credit,

hope, expectation, reliance, confidence, assurance, conviction, certainty. **2** CARE, charge, custody, safekeeping, security, guardianship, protection, responsibility, duty.
🔳 **1** distrust, mistrust, scepticism, doubt.
➤ *v* **1** BELIEVE, imagine, assume, presume, suppose, surmise, hope, expect, rely on, depend on, count on, bank on, swear by. **2** ENTRUST, commit, consign, confide, give, assign, delegate.
🔳 **1** distrust, mistrust, doubt, disbelieve.

trusting *adj* trustful, credulous, gullible, naïve, innocent, unquestioning, unsuspecting, unguarded, unwary.
🔳 distrustful, suspicious, cautious.

trustworthy *adj* honest, upright, honourable, principled, dependable, reliable, steadfast, true, responsible, sensible.
🔳 untrustworthy, dishonest, unreliable, irresponsible.

truth *n* **1** TRUTHFULNESS, veracity, candour, frankness, honesty, sincerity, genuineness, authenticity, realism, exactness, precision, accuracy, validity, legitimacy, honour, uprightness, integrity, faithfulness, fidelity, loyalty, constancy. **2** *tell the truth*: facts, reality, actuality, fact, axiom, maxim, principle, truism.
🔳 **1** deceit, dishonesty, falseness. **2** lie, falsehood.

truthful *adj* veracious, frank, candid, straight, honest, sincere, true, veritable, exact, precise, accurate, correct, realistic, faithful, trustworthy, reliable.
🔳 untruthful, deceitful, false, untrue.

try *v* **1** ATTEMPT, endeavour, venture, undertake, seek, strive. **2** HEAR, judge. **3** EXPERIMENT, test, sample, taste, inspect, examine, investigate, evaluate, appraise.
➤ *n* **1** ATTEMPT, endeavour, effort, go (*infml*), bash (*infml*), crack (*infml*), shot (*infml*), stab (*infml*). **2** EXPERIMENT, test, trial, ample, taste.

trying *adj* annoying, irritating, aggravating (*infml*), vexatious,

exasperating, troublesome, tiresome, wearisome, difficult, hard, tough, arduous, taxing, demanding, testing.
🔳 easy.

tub *n* bath, basin, vat, tun, butt, cask, barrel, keg.

tube *n* hose, pipe, cylinder, duct, conduit, spout, channel.

tuck *v* **1** INSERT, push, thrust, stuff, cram. **2** FOLD, pleat, gather, crease.
➤ *n* fold, pleat, gather, pucker, crease.

tuft *n* crest, beard, tassel, knot, clump, cluster, bunch, group.

tug *v* pull, draw, tow, haul, drag, lug, heave, wrench, jerk, pluck.
➤ *n* pull, tow, haul, heave, wrench, jerk, pluck.

tuition *n* teaching, instruction, coaching, training, lessons, schooling, education.

tumble *v* fall, stumble, trip, topple, overthrow, drop, flop, collapse, plummet, pitch, roll, toss.
➤ *n* fall, stumble, trip, drop, plunge, roll, toss.

tumult *n* commotion, turmoil, disturbance, upheaval, stir, agitation, unrest, disorder, chaos, pandemonium, noise, clamour, din, racket, hubbub, hullabaloo, row, rumpus, uproar, riot, fracas, brawl, affray, strife.
🔳 peace, calm, composure.

tumultuous *adj* turbulent, stormy, raging, fierce, violent, wild, hectic, boisterous, rowdy, noisy, disorderly, unruly, riotous, restless, agitated, troubled, disturbed, excited.
🔳 calm, peaceful, quiet.

tune *n* melody, theme, motif, song, number, air, strain.
➤ *v* pitch, harmonize, set, regulate, adjust, adapt, temper, attune, synchronize.

tuneful *adj* melodious, melodic, catchy, musical, euphonious, harmonious, pleasant, mellow, sonorous.
🔳 tuneless, discordant.

tunnel *n* passage, passageway, gallery, subway, underpass, burrow, hole, mine, shaft, chimney.

➤ *v* burrow, dig, excavate, mine, bore, penetrate, undermine, sap.

turbulent *adj* rough, choppy, stormy, blustery, tempestuous, raging, furious, violent, wild, tumultuous, unbridled, boisterous, rowdy, disorderly, unruly, undisciplined, obstreperous, rebellious, mutinous, riotous, agitated, unsettled, unstable, confused, disordered.
🔁 calm, composed.

turmoil *n* confusion, disorder, tumult, commotion, disturbance, riot, trouble, disquiet, agitation, turbulence, upheaval, stir, ferment, flurry, bustle, chaos, pandemonium, bedlam, noise, din, racket, hubbub, row, uproar.
🔁 calm, peace, quiet.

turn *v* **1** REVOLVE, circle, spin, twirl, whirl, twist, gyrate, pivot, hinge, swivel, rotate, roll, move, shift, invert, reverse, bend, veer, swerve, divert. **2** MAKE, transform, transmute, change, alter, modify, convert, adapt, adjust, fit, mould, shape, form, fashion, remodel. **3** *turn cold*: go, become, grow. **4** RESORT, have recourse, apply, appeal. **5** SOUR, curdle, spoil, go off, go bad.

➤ *n* **1** REVOLUTION, cycle, round, circle, rotation, spin, twirl, twist, gyration, bend, curve, loop, reversal. **2** CHANGE, alteration, shift, deviation. **3** *it's your turn*: go, chance, opportunity, occasion, stint, period, spell. **4** ACT, performance, performer.

◇ **turn away** reject, knock back (*infml*), avert, deflect, deviate, depart.
🔁 accept, receive.

◇ **turn down 1** *turn down an offer*: reject, decline, refuse, knock back (*infml*), spurn, rebuff, repudiate. **2** LOWER, lessen, quieten, soften, mute, muffle.
🔁 **1** accept. **2** turn up.

◇ **turn in 1** GO TO BED, retire. **2** HAND OVER, give up, surrender, deliver, hand in, tender, submit, return, give back.
🔁 **1** get up. **2** keep.

◇ **turn off 1** BRANCH OFF, leave, quit, depart from, deviate, divert. **2** SWITCH OFF, turn out, stop, shut down, unplug, disconnect. **3** (*sl*) REPEL, sicken, nauseate, disgust, revolt, offend, displease, disenchant, alienate, bore, discourage, put off.
🔁 **1** join. **2** turn on. **3** turn on (*sl*).

◇ **turn on 1** SWITCH ON, start (up), activate, kick-start (*infml*), connect. **2** (*sl*) AROUSE, stimulate, excite, thrill, please, attract. **3** HINGE ON, depend on, rest on. **4** ATTACK, round on, fall on.
🔁 **1** turn off. **2** turn off (*sl*).

◇ **turn out 1** HAPPEN, come about, transpire, ensue, result, end up, become, develop, emerge. **2** SWITCH OFF, turn off, unplug, disconnect. **3** APPEAR, present, dress, clothe. **4** PRODUCE, make, manufacture, fabricate, assemble. **5** EVICT, throw out, expel, deport, banish, dismiss, discharge, drum out, kick out (*infml*), sack (*infml*). **6** *turn out the attic*: empty, clear, clean out.
🔁 **2** turn on. **5** admit. **6** fill.

◇ **turn over 1** THINK OVER, think about, mull over, ponder, deliberate, reflect on, contemplate, consider, examine. **2** HAND OVER, surrender, deliver, transfer. **3** OVERTURN, upset, upend, invert, capsize, keel over.

◇ **turn up 1** ATTEND, come, arrive, appear, show up (*infml*). **2** AMPLIFY, intensify, raise, increase. **3** DISCOVER, find, unearth, dig up, expose, disclose, reveal, show.
🔁 **1** stay away. **2** turn down.

turning *n* turn-off, junction, crossroads, fork, bend, curve, turn.

turning-point *n* crossroads, watershed, crux, crisis, crunch (*infml*).

turnout *n* **1** ATTENDANCE, audience, gate, crowd, assembly, congregation. **2** APPEARANCE, outfit, dress, clothes.

tutor *n* teacher, instructor, coach, educator, lecturer, supervisor, guide, mentor, guru, guardian.

➤ *v* teach, instruct, train, drill, coach, educate, school, lecture, supervise, direct, guide.

tweak *v, n* twist, pinch, squeeze, nip, pull, tug, jerk, twitch.

twee (*infml*) *adj* sweet, cute, pretty, dainty, quaint, sentimental, affected, precious.

twiddle *v* turn, twirl, swivel, twist, wiggle, adjust, fiddle, finger.

twilight *n* dusk, half-light, gloaming, gloom, dimness, sunset, evening.

twin *n* double, look-alike, likeness, duplicate, clone, match, counterpart, corollary, fellow, mate.
➤ *adj* identical, corresponding, matching, co-ordinating, symmetrical, parallel, matched, paired, double, dual, duplicate, twofold.
➤ *v* match, pair, couple, link, join.

twine *n* string, cord, thread, yarn.
➤ *v* wind, coil, spiral, loop, curl, bend, twist, wreathe, wrap, surround, encircle, entwine, plait, braid, knit, weave.

twinge *n* pain, pang, throb, spasm, throe, stab, jab, stitch, pinch, prick.

twinkle *v* sparkle, glitter, shimmer, glisten, glimmer, flicker, wink, flash, glint, gleam, shine.
➤ *n* sparkle, scintillation, glitter, shimmer, glisten, glimmer, flicker, wink, flash, glint, gleam, light.

twirl *v* spin, whirl, pirouette, wheel, rotate, revolve, swivel, pivot, turn, twist, gyrate, wind, coil.
➤ *n* spin, whirl, pirouette, rotation, revolution, turn, twist, gyration, convlution, spiral, coil.

twist *v* **1** TURN, screw, wring, spin, swivel, wind, zigzag, bend, coil, spiral, curl, wreathe, twine, entwine, intertwine, weave, entangle, wriggle, squirm, writhe. **2** *twist one's ankle*: wrench, rick, sprain, strain. **3** CHANGE, alter, garble, misquote, misrepresent, distort, contort, warp, pervert.
➤ *n* **1** TURN, screw, spin, roll, bend, curve, arc, curl, loop, zigzag, coil, spiral, convolution, squiggle, tangle. **2** CHANGE, variation, break. **3** PERVERSION, distortion, contortion, interpretation,

spin. **4** SURPRISE, quirk, peculiarity.

twisted *adj* warped, perverted, deviant, unnatural.
🔄 straight.

twitch *v* jerk, jump, start, blink, tremble, shake, pull, tug, tweak, snatch, pluck.
➤ *n* spasm, convulsion, tic, tremor, jerk, jump, start.

two-faced *adj* hypocritical, insincere, false, lying, deceitful, treacherous, double-dealing, devious, untrustworthy.
🔄 honest, candid, frank.

tycoon *n* industrialist, entrepreneur, captain of industry, magnate, mogul, baron, supremo, capitalist, financier.

type *n* **1** SORT, kind, form, genre, variety, strain, species, breed, group, class, category, subdivision, classification, description, designation, stamp, mark, order, standard, make, brand. **2** ARCHETYPE, embodiment, prototype, original, model, pattern, specimen, example. **3** PRINT, printing, characters, letters, lettering, face, fount, font.

typical *adj* standard, normal, usual, average, vanilla (*infml*), conventional, orthodox, stock, model, representative, illustrative, indicative, characteristic.
🔄 atypical, unusual.

typify *v* embody, epitomize, personify, encapsulate, characterize, exemplify, symbolize, represent, illustrate.

tyrannical *adj* dictatorial, despotic, autocratic, absolute, authoritarian, domineering, overbearing, high-handed, imperious, magisterial, ruthless, harsh, severe, strict, oppressive, overpowering, unjust, unreasonable.
🔄 liberal, tolerant.

tyranny *n* dictatorship, despotism, autocracy, absolutism, authoritarianism, imperiousness, ruthlessness, harshness, severity, oppression, injustice.
🔄 democracy, freedom.

tyrant *n* dictator, despot, autocrat, absolutist, authoritarian, bully, oppressor, slave-driver, taskmaster.

Uu

ubiquitous *adj* omnipresent, ever-present, widespread, everywhere, universal, global, pervasive, common, frequent.
🔁 rare, scarce.

ugly *adj* **1** UNATTRACTIVE, unsightly, plain, unprepossessing, ill-favoured, hideous, repulsive, monstrous, misshapen, deformed. **2** UNPLEASANT, disagreeable, nasty, horrid, objectionable, offensive, disgusting, revolting, repulsive, vile, frightful, terrible.
🔁 **1** attractive, beautiful, handsome, pretty. **2** pleasant.

ulterior *adj* secondary, hidden, concealed, undisclosed, unseen, unexpressed, covert, secret, private, personal, selfish.
🔁 overt.

ultimate *adj* final, last, closing, concluding, eventual, terminal, furthest, remotest, extreme, utmost, greatest, highest, supreme, superlative, perfect, radical, fundamental, primary.

ultimately *adv* finally, eventually, at last, in the end, after all.

umpire *n* referee, linesman, judge, adjudicator, arbiter, arbitrator, mediator, moderator.
➤ *v* referee, judge, adjudicate, arbitrate, mediate, moderate, control.

umpteen (*infml*) *adj* a good many, numerous, plenty, lots of (*infml*), millions (*infml*), countless, innumerable.
🔁 few.

unabashed *adj* unashamed, unembarrassed, brazen, blatant, bold, confident, undaunted, unconcerned, undismayed.
🔁 abashed, sheepish.

unable *adj* incapable, powerless, impotent, unequipped, unqualified, unfit, incompetent, inadequate.
🔁 able, capable.

unacceptable *adj* intolerable, inadmissible, unsatisfactory, undesirable, unwelcome, unwanted, objectionable, offensive, unpleasant.
🔁 acceptable, satisfactory.

unaccompanied *adj* alone, unescorted, unattended, lone, solo, single-handed.
🔁 accompanied.

unaccountable *adj* inexplicable, unexplainable, unfathomable, impenetrable, incomprehensible, baffling, puzzling, mysterious, astonishing, extraordinary, strange, odd, peculiar, singular, unusual, uncommon, unheard-of.
🔁 explicable, explainable.

unaccustomed *adj* **1** *unaccustomed to such luxury*: unused, unacquainted, unfamiliar, unpractised, inexperienced. **2** STRANGE, unusual, uncommon, different, new, unexpected, surprising, uncharacteristic, unprecedented.
🔁 **1** accustomed, familiar. **2** customary.

unaffected *adj* **1** UNMOVED, unconcerned, indifferent, impervious, untouched, unchanged, unaltered. **2** UNSOPHISTICATED, artless, naïve, ingenuous, unspoilt, plain, simple, straightforward, unpretentious, unassuming, sincere, honest, genuine.
🔁 **1** moved, influenced. **2** affected, pretentious, insincere.

unalterable *adj* unchangeable, invariable, unchanging, immutable, final, inflexible, unyielding, rigid,

fixed, permanent.
🔁 alterable, flexible.

unanimity *n* consensus, unity, agreement, concurrence, accord, like-mindedness, concord, harmony, unison, concert.
🔁 disagreement, disunity.

unanimous *adj* united, concerted, joint, common, as one, in agreement, in accord, harmonious.
🔁 disunited, divided.

unapproachable *adj* inaccessible, remote, distant, aloof, standoffish, withdrawn, reserved, unsociable, unfriendly, forbidding.
🔁 approachable, friendly.

unarmed *adj* defenceless, unprotected, exposed, open, vulnerable, weak, helpless.
🔁 armed, protected.

unashamed *adj* shameless, unabashed, impenitent, unrepentant, unconcealed, undisguised, open, blatant, brazen.

unasked *adj* uninvited, unbidden, unrequested, unsought, unsolicited, unwanted, voluntary, spontaneous.
🔁 invited, wanted.

unassuming *adj* unassertive, self-effacing, retiring, modest, humble, meek, unobtrusive, unpretentious, simple, restrained.
🔁 presumptuous, assertive, pretentious.

unattached *adj* unmarried, single, free, available, footloose, fancy-free, independent, unaffiliated.
🔁 engaged, committed.

unattended *adj* ignored, disregarded, unguarded, unwatched, unsupervised, unaccompanied, unescorted, alone.
🔁 attended, escorted.

unauthorized *adj* unofficial, unlawful, illegal, illicit, illegitimate, irregular, unsanctioned.
🔁 authorized, legal.

unavoidable *adj* inevitable,

inescapable, inexorable, certain, sure, fated, destined, obligatory, compulsory, mandatory, necessary.
🔁 avoidable.

unaware *adj* oblivious, unconscious, ignorant, uninformed, unknowing, unsuspecting, unmindful, heedless, blind, deaf.
🔁 aware, conscious.

unbalanced *adj* 1 INSANE, mad, crazy, lunatic, deranged, disturbed, demented, irrational, unsound. 2 *an unbalanced report*: biased, prejudiced, one-sided, partisan, unfair, unjust, unequal, uneven, asymmetrical, lopsided, unsteady, unstable.
🔁 1 sane. 2 unbiased.

unbearable *adj* intolerable, unacceptable, insupportable, insufferable, unendurable, excruciating.
🔁 bearable, acceptable.

unbeatable *adj* invincible, insuperable, unconquerable, unsurmountable, indomitable, unstoppable, unsurpassable, matchless, supreme, excellent.

unbecoming *adj* unseemly, improper, unsuitable, inappropriate, unbefitting, ungentlemanly, unladylike, unattractive, unsightly.
🔁 suitable, attractive.

unbelief *n* atheism, agnosticism, scepticism, doubt, incredulity, disbelief.
🔁 belief, faith.

unbelievable *adj* incredible, inconceivable, unthinkable, unimaginable, astonishing, staggering, extraordinary, impossible, improbable, unlikely, implausible, unconvincing, far-fetched, preposterous.
🔁 believable, credible.

unborn *adj* embryonic, expected, awaited, coming, future.

unbounded *adj* boundless, limitless, unlimited, unrestricted, unrestrained, unchecked, unbridled, infinite, endless, immeasurable, vast.
🔁 limited, restrained.

unbreakable *adj* indestructible, shatterproof, toughened, resistant, proof, durable, strong, tough, rugged, solid.
E3 breakable, fragile.

unbridled *adj* immoderate, excessive, uncontrolled, full-on (*sl*), unrestrained, unchecked.

unbroken *adj* **1** INTACT, whole, entire, complete, solid, undivided. **2** UNINTERRUPTED, continuous, non-stop, endless, ceaseless, incessant, unceasing, constant, perpetual, progressive, successive. **3** *unbroken record*: unbeaten, unsurpassed, unequalled, unmatched.
E3 **1** broken. **2** intermittent, fitful.

uncalled-for *adj* gratuitous, unprovoked, unjustified, unwarranted, undeserved, unnecessary, needless.
E3 timely.

uncanny *adj* weird, strange, queer, bizarre, mysterious, unaccountable, incredible, remarkable, extraordinary, fantastic, unnatural, unearthly, supernatural, eerie, creepy, spooky (*infml*).

uncaring *adj* unconcerned, unmoved, unsympathetic, inconsiderate, unfeeling, cold, callous, indifferent, uninterested.
E3 caring, concerned.

unceasing *adj* ceaseless, incessant, unending, endless, never-ending, non-stop, continuous, unbroken, constant, perpetual, continual, persistent, relentless, unrelenting, unremitting.
E3 intermittent, spasmodic.

uncertain *adj* **1** UNSURE, unconvinced, doubtful, dubious, undecided, ambivalent, hesitant, wavering, vacillating. **2** INCONSTANT, changeable, mutable, variable, erratic, irregular, shaky, unsteady, unreliable. **3** UNPREDICTABLE, unforeseeable, undetermined, unsettled, unresolved, unconfirmed, indefinite, vague, insecure, risky, iffy (*sl*).
E3 **1** certain, sure. **2** steady. **3** known, predictable.

uncertainty *n* doubt, scepticism, irresolution, dilemma, hesitation, misgiving, confusion, bewilderment, perplexity, puzzlement, unreliability, unpredictability, insecurity.
E3 certainty.

unchanging *adj* unvarying, changeless, steady, steadfast, constant, perpetual, lasting, enduring, abiding, eternal, permanent.
E3 changing, changeable.

uncharitable *adj* unkind, cruel, hard-hearted, callous, unfeeling, insensitive, unsympathetic, unfriendly, mean, ungenerous.
E3 kind, sensitive, charitable, generous.

uncharted *adj* unexplored, undiscovered, unplumbed, foreign, alien, strange, unfamiliar, new, virgin.
E3 familiar.

uncivilized *adj* primitive, barbaric, savage, wild, untamed, uncultured, unsophisticated, unenlightened, uneducated, illiterate, uncouth, antisocial.
E3 civilized, cultured.

unclean *adj* dirty, soiled, filthy, foul, polluted, contaminated, tainted, impure, unhygienic, unwholesome, corrupt, defiled, sullied, blemished.
E3 clean, hygienic.

unclear *adj* indistinct, hazy, dim, obscure, vague, indefinite, ambiguous, equivocal, uncertain, unsure, doubtful, dubious.
E3 clear, evident.

uncomfortable *adj* **1** CRAMPED, hard, cold, ill-fitting, irritating, painful, disagreeable. **2** AWKWARD, self-conscious, embarrassed, abashed, uneasy, troubled, worried, disturbed, distressed, disquieted, conscience-stricken.
E3 **1** comfortable. **2** relaxed.

uncommon *adj* rare, scarce, infrequent, unusual, abnormal, atypical, unfamiliar, strange, odd, curious, bizarre, extraordinary, remarkable, notable, outstanding, exceptional, distinctive, special.

☒ common, usual, normal.

uncommunicative *adj* silent, taciturn, tight-lipped, close, secretive, unforthcoming, unresponsive, curt, brief, reticent, reserved, shy, retiring, withdrawn, unsociable.

☒ communicative, forthcoming.

uncompromising *adj* unyielding, unbending, adamant, inflexible, unaccommodating, rigid, firm, strict, tough, hardline, inexorable, intransigent, stubborn, obstinate, diehard.

☒ flexible.

unconcealed *adj* open, patent, obvious, evident, manifest, blatant, conspicuous, noticeable, visible, apparent.

☒ hidden, secret.

unconcerned *adj* indifferent, apathetic, uninterested, nonchalant, carefree, relaxed, complacent, cool, composed, untroubled, unworried, unruffled, unmoved, uncaring, unsympathetic, callous, aloof, remote, distant, detached, dispassionate, uninvolved, oblivious.

☒ concerned, worried, interested.

unconditional *adj* unqualified, unreserved, unrestricted, unlimited, absolute, utter, full, total, complete, entire, wholehearted, thoroughgoing, downright, outright, positive, categorical, unequivocal.

☒ conditional, qualified, limited.

unconnected *adj* 1 IRRELEVANT, unrelated, unattached, detached, separate, discrete, independent. 2 DISCONNECTED, incoherent, irrational, illogical.

☒ 1 connected, relevant.

unconscious *adj* 1 STUNNED, knocked out, out, out cold, out for the count, concussed, comatose, senseless, insensible. 2 UNAWARE, oblivious, blind, deaf, heedless, unmindful, ignorant. 3 *an unconscious reaction*: involuntary, automatic, reflex, instinctive, impulsive,

innate, subconscious, subliminal, repressed, suppressed, latent, unwitting, inadvertent, accidental, unintentional.

☒ 1 conscious. 2 aware. 3 intentional.

uncontrollable *adj* ungovernable, unmanageable, unruly, wild, mad, furious, violent, strong, irrepressible.

☒ controllable, manageable.

uncontrolled *adj* unrestrained, unbridled, unchecked, rampant, wild, unruly, undisciplined.

☒ controlled, restrained.

unconventional *adj* unorthodox, alternative, different, offbeat, eccentric, idiosyncratic, individual, original, odd, unusual, irregular, abnormal, bizarre, left-field, way-out (*sl*).

☒ conventional, orthodox.

unconvincing *adj* implausible, unlikely, improbable, questionable, doubtful, dubious, suspect, weak, feeble, flimsy, lame.

☒ convincing, plausible.

unco-ordinated *adj* clumsy, awkward, ungainly, ungraceful, inelegant, inept, disjointed.

☒ graceful.

uncouth *adj* coarse, crude, vulgar, rude, ill-mannered, unseemly, improper, clumsy, awkward, gauche, graceless, unrefined, uncultivated, uncultured, uncivilized, rough.

☒ polite, refined, urbane.

uncover *v* unveil, unmask, unwrap, strip, bare, open, expose, reveal, show, disclose, divulge, leak, unearth, exhume, discover, detect.

☒ cover, conceal, suppress.

uncritical *adj* undiscerning, undiscriminating, unselective, unquestioning, credulous, accepting, trusting, gullible, naïve.

☒ discerning, discriminating, sceptical.

uncultivated *adj* fallow, wild, rough, natural.

☒ cultivated.

uncultured *adj* unsophisticated,

unrefined, uncultivated, uncivilized, unenlightened, rough, uncouth, boorish, rustic, coarse, crude, ill-bred.
F3 cultured, sophisticated.

undaunted *adj* undeterred, undiscouraged, undismayed, unbowed, resolute, steadfast, brave, courageous, fearless, bold, intrepid, dauntless, indomitable.
F3 discouraged, timorous.

undecided *adj* uncertain, unsure, in two minds, ambivalent, doubtful, hesitant, wavering, irresolute, uncommitted, indefinite, vague, dubious, debatable, moot, unsettled, open.
F3 decided, certain, definite.

undemonstrative *adj* aloof, standoffish, distant, remote, withdrawn, reserved, reticent, uncommunicative, stiff, formal, cool, cold, unemotional, restrained, impassive, phlegmatic.
F3 demonstrative, communicative.

undeniable *adj* irrefutable (*fml*), unquestionable, incontrovertible, sure, certain, undoubted, indubitable, proven, clear, obvious, patent, evident, manifest, unmistakable.
F3 questionable.

under *prep* below, underneath, beneath, lower than, less than, inferior to, subordinate to.
F3 over, above.
◇ **under way** moving, in motion, going, in operation, started, begun, in progress, afoot.

undercover *adj* secret, hush-hush (*infml*), private, confidential, spy, intelligence, underground, clandestine, surreptitious, furtive, covert, hidden, concealed.
F3 open, unconcealed.

undercurrent *n* undertone, overtone, hint, suggestion, tinge, flavour, aura, atmosphere, feeling, sense, movement, tendency, trend, drift.

underestimate *v* underrate, undervalue, misjudge, miscalculate, minimize, belittle, disparage, dismiss.
F3 overestimate, exaggerate.

undergo *v* experience, suffer, sustain, submit to, bear, stand, endure, weather, withstand.

underground *adj* **1** *an underground passage*: subterranean, buried, sunken, covered, hidden, concealed. **2** SECRET, covert, undercover, surreptitious, clandestine, revolutionary, subversive, radical, experimental, avant-garde, alternative, unorthodox, unofficial.

undergrowth *n* brush, scrub, vegetation, ground cover, bracken, bushes, brambles, briars.

underhand *adj* unscrupulous, unethical, immoral, improper, sly, crafty, sneaky, stealthy, surreptitious, furtive, clandestine, devious, dishonest, deceitful, deceptive, fraudulent, crooked (*infml*), shady (*infml*).
F3 honest, open, above board.

underline *v* mark, underscore, stress, emphasize, accentuate, italicize, highlight, point up.
F3 play down, soft-pedal.

underlying *adj* basic, fundamental, essential, primary, elementary, root, core, intrinsic, latent, hidden, lurking, veiled.

undermine *v* mine, tunnel, excavate, erode, wear away, weaken, sap, sabotage, subvert, vitiate (*fml*), mar, impair.
F3 strengthen, fortify.

underprivileged *adj* deprived, disadvantaged, poor, needy, impoverished, destitute, oppressed.
F3 privileged, fortunate, affluent.

underrate *v* underestimate, undervalue, belittle, disparage, depreciate, dismiss.
F3 overrate, exaggerate.

undersized *adj* small, tiny, minute, minuscule, miniature, pygmy, dwarf, stunted, underdeveloped, underweight, puny.
F3 oversized, big, overweight.

understand *v* **1** *I don't understand*: grasp, comprehend, take in, follow, get

(*infml*), cotton on (*infml*), fathom, penetrate, make out, discern, perceive, see, realize, recognize, appreciate, accept. **2** SYMPATHIZE, empathize, relate, commiserate. **3** BELIEVE, think, know, hear, learn, gather, assume, presume, suppose, conclude.
1 misunderstand.

understanding *n* **1** GRASP, comprehension, knowledge, wisdom, intelligence, intellect, sense, judgement, discernment, insight, appreciation, awareness, impression, interpretation, perception, belief, idea, notion, opinion. **2** AGREEMENT, arrangement, pact, accord, harmony. **3** SYMPATHY, empathy.
➤ *adj* sympathetic, compassionate, kind, considerate, sensitive, tender, loving, patient, tolerant, forbearing, forgiving.
unsympathetic, insensitive, impatient, intolerant.

understate *v* underplay, play down, soft-pedal, minimize, make light of, belittle, dismiss.
exaggerate.

understood *adj* accepted, believed, assumed, presumed, implied, implicit, inferred, tacit, unstated, unspoken, unwritten.

understudy *n* stand-in, double, substitute, replacement, reserve, deputy, proxy.

undertake *v* **1** PLEDGE, promise, guarantee, agree, contract, covenant. **2** BEGIN, commence, embark on, tackle, try, attempt, endeavour, take on, accept, assume.

undertaking *n* **1** ENTERPRISE, venture, business, affair, task, project, operation, attempt, endeavour, effort. **2** PLEDGE, commitment, promise, vow, word, assurance.

undertone *n* hint, suggestion, whisper, murmur, trace, tinge, touch, flavour, feeling, atmosphere, undercurrent.

undervalue *v* underrate, underestimate, misjudge, minimize,

depreciate, disparage, dismiss.
overrate, exaggerate.

underwater *adj* subaquatic, undersea, submarine, submerged, sunken.

underwear *n* underclothes, undergarments, lingerie, undies (*infml*), smalls (*infml*).

underweight *adj* thin, undersized, underfed, undernourished, half-starved, emaciated.
overweight.

underwrite *v* endorse, authorize, sanction, approve, back, guarantee, insure, sponsor, fund, finance, subsidize, assist, subscribe, sign, initial, countersign.

undesirable *adj* unwanted, unwelcome, unacceptable, unsuitable, unpleasant, disagreeable, distasteful, repugnant, offensive, objectionable, obnoxious.
desirable, pleasant.

undignified *adj* inelegant, ungainly, clumsy, foolish, unseemly, improper, unsuitable, inappropriate.
dignified, elegant.

undisguised *adj* unconcealed, open, overt, explicit, frank, genuine, apparent, patent, obvious, evident, manifest, blatant, naked, unadorned, stark, utter, outright, thoroughgoing.
secret, concealed, hidden.

undisputed *adj* uncontested, unchallenged, unquestioned, undoubted, indisputable, incontrovertible, undeniable, irrefutable, accepted, acknowledged, recognized, sure, certain, conclusive.
debatable, uncertain.

undistinguished *adj* unexceptional, unremarkable, unimpressive, ordinary, run-of-the-mill, everyday, banal, vanilla (*infml*), indifferent, mediocre, inferior.
distinguished, exceptional.

undivided *adj* solid, unbroken, intact, whole, entire, full, complete, combined, united, unanimous, concentrated, exclusive, wholehearted.

undo v **1** UNFASTEN, untie, unbuckle, unbutton, unzip, unlock, unwrap, unwind, open, loose, loosen, separate. **2** ANNUL, nullify, invalidate, cancel, offset, neutralize, reverse, overturn, upset, quash, defeat, undermine, subvert, mar, spoil, ruin, wreck, shatter, destroy.
E3 1 fasten, do up.

undoing n downfall, ruin, ruination, collapse, destruction, defeat, overthrow, reversal, weakness, shame, disgrace.

undone adj **1** UNACCOMPLISHED, unfulfilled, unfinished, uncompleted, incomplete, outstanding, left, omitted, neglected, forgotten. **2** UNFASTENED, untied, unlaced, unbuttoned, unlocked, open, loose.
E3 1 done, accomplished, complete. **2** fastened.

undoubted adj unchallenged, undisputed, acknowledged, unquestionable, indisputable, incontrovertible, undesirable, indubitable, sure, certain, definite, obvious, patent.

undress v strip, peel off (*infml*), disrobe, take off, divest, remove, shed.

undressed adj unclothed, disrobed, stripped, naked, stark naked, nude, bare.
E3 clothed.

undue adj unnecessary, needless, uncalled-for, unwarranted, undeserved, unreasonable, disproportionate, excessive, immoderate, inordinate, extreme, extravagant, improper.
E3 reasonable, moderate, proper.

unduly adv too, over, excessively, immoderately, inordinately, disproportionately, unreasonably, unjustifiably, unnecessarily.
E3 moderately, reasonably.

unearth v dig up, exhume, disinter, excavate, uncover, expose, reveal, find, discover, detect.
E3 bury.

unearthly adj **1** SUPERNATURAL, ghostly, eerie, spooky (*infml*), uncanny, weird, strange, bizarre, spine-chilling. **2** *at this unearthly hour*: unreasonable, outrageous, ungodly.
E3 2 reasonable.

uneasy adj uncomfortable, anxious, worried, apprehensive, tense, strained, nervous, agitated, shaky, jittery, on tenterhooks, edgy, upset, troubled, disturbed, unsettled, restless, impatient, unsure, insecure.
E3 calm, composed.

uneducated adj unschooled, untaught, unread, ignorant, illiterate, unenlightened, uncultivated, uncultured, philistine, benighted.
E3 educated.

unemotional adj cool, cold, unfeeling, impassive, indifferent, apathetic, unresponsive, undemonstrative, unexcitable, phlegmatic, objective, dispassionate.
E3 emotional, excitable.

unemployed adj jobless, out of work, laid off, redundant, unwaged, on the dole (*infml*), idle, unoccupied.
E3 employed, occupied.

unending adj endless, never-ending, unceasing, ceaseless, incessant, interminable, constant, continual, non-stop, perpetual, everlasting, eternal, undying.
E3 transient, intermittent.

unenviable adj undesirable, unpleasant, unfortunate, disagreeable, uncongenial, uncomfortable, thankless, difficult.
E3 enviable, desirable.

unequal adj different, varying, dissimilar, unlike, unmatched, uneven, unbalanced, disproportionate, asymmetrical, irregular, unfair, unjust, biased, discriminatory.
E3 equal.

unequivocal adj unambiguous, explicit, clear, plain, evident, distinct, unmistakable, express, direct, straight, definite, positive, categorical, incontrovertible, absolute, unqualified, unreserved.

🔁 ambiguous, vague, qualified.

unethical *adj* unprofessional, immoral, improper, wrong, unscrupulous, unprincipled, dishonourable, disreputable, illegal, illicit, dishonest, underhand, shady (*infml*).

🔁 ethical.

uneven *adj* 1 *uneven ground*: rough, bumpy, rugged. 2 ODD, unequal, inequitable, unfair, unbalanced, one-sided, asymmetrical, lopsided, crooked. 3 IRREGULAR, intermittent, spasmodic, fitful, jerky, unsteady, variable, changeable, fluctuating, erratic, inconsistent, patchy.

🔁 1 flat, level. 2 even, equal. 3 regular.

uneventful *adj* uninteresting, unexciting, quiet, unvaried, boring, monotonous, tedious, dull, routine, humdrum, ordinary, commonplace, unremarkable, unexceptional, unmemorable.

🔁 eventful, memorable.

unexceptional *adj* unremarkable, unmemorable, typical, average, normal, usual, ordinary, vanilla (*infml*), indifferent, mediocre, unimpressive.

🔁 exceptional, impressive.

unexpected *adj* unforeseen, unanticipated, unpredictable, chance, accidental, fortuitous, sudden, abrupt, surprising, startling, amazing, astonishing, unusual.

🔁 expected, predictable.

unfair *adj* unjust, inequitable, partial, biased, prejudiced, bigoted, discriminatory, unbalanced, one-sided, partisan, arbitrary, undeserved, unmerited, undue, unwarranted, uncalled-for, unreasonable, unethical, unscrupulous, unprincipled, wrongful, dishonest.

🔁 fair, just, unbiased, deserved.

unfaithful *adj* disloyal, treacherous, perfidious, false, untrue, deceitful, dishonest, untrustworthy, unreliable,

fickle, inconstant, adulterous, two-timing, duplicitous, double-dealing, faithless, unbelieving, godless.

🔁 faithful, loyal, reliable.

unfamiliar *adj* strange, unusual, uncommon, curious, alien, foreign, uncharted, unexplored, unknown, different, new, novel, unaccustomed, unacquainted, inexperienced, unpractised, unskilled, unversed.

🔁 familiar, customary, conversant.

unfashionable *adj* outmoded, dated, out of date, out, passé, old-fashioned, antiquated, obsolete, old-fangled.

🔁 fashionable.

unfasten *v* undo, untie, loosen, unlock, open, uncouple, disconnect, separate, detach.

🔁 fasten.

unfavourable *adj* inauspicious (*fml*), unpromising, ominous, threatening, discouraging, inopportune, untimely, unseasonable, ill-suited, unfortunate, unlucky, disadvantageous, bad, poor, adverse, contrary, negative, hostile, unfriendly, uncomplimentary.

🔁 favourable, auspicious, promising.

unfeeling *adj* insensitive, cold, hard, stony, callous, heartless, hard-hearted, mean, cruel, inhuman, pitiless, uncaring, unsympathetic, apathetic.

🔁 sensitive, sympathetic.

unfinished *adj* incomplete, uncompleted, half-done, sketchy, rough, crude, imperfect, lacking, wanting, deficient, undone, unaccomplished, unfulfilled.

🔁 finished, perfect.

unfit *adj* 1 UNSUITABLE, inappropriate, unsuited, ill-equipped, unqualified, ineligible, untrained, unprepared, unequal, incapable, incompetent, inadequate, ineffective, useless. 2 UNHEALTHY, out of condition, out of shape, flabby, feeble, decrepit.

🔁 1 fit, suitable, competent. 2 healthy.

unfold *v* 1 DEVELOP, evolve. 2 REVEAL, disclose, show, present, describe,

explain, clarify, elaborate. **3** *unfold a map*: open, spread, flatten, straighten, stretch out, undo, unfurl, unroll, uncoil, unwrap, uncover.
Ea 2 withhold, suppress. **3** fold, wrap.

unforeseen *adj* unpredicted, unexpected, unanticipated, surprising, startling, sudden, unavoidable.
Ea expected, predictable.

unforgettable *adj* memorable, momentous, historic, noteworthy, notable, impressive, remarkable, exceptional, extraordinary.
Ea unmemorable, unexceptional.

unforgivable *adj* unpardonable, inexcusable, unjustifiable, indefensible, reprehensible, shameful, disgraceful, deplorable, abominable.
Ea forgivable, venial.

unfortunate *adj* **1** UNLUCKY, luckless, hapless, unsuccessful, poor, wretched, unhappy, doomed, ill-fated, hopeless, calamitous, disastrous, ruinous. **2** REGRETTABLE, lamentable, deplorable, adverse, unfavourable, unsuitable, inappropriate, inopportune, untimely, ill-timed.
Ea 1 fortunate, happy. **2** favourable, appropriate.

unfounded *adj* baseless, groundless, unsupported, unsubstantiated, unproven, unjustified, idle, false, spurious, trumped-up, fabricated.
Ea substantiated, justified.

unfriendly *adj* unsociable, standoffish, aloof, unapproachable, distant, inhospitable, uncongenial, unneighbourly, unwelcoming, cold, chilly, hostile, aggressive, quarrelsome, inimical, antagonistic, ill-disposed, disagreeable, surly, sour.
Ea friendly, amiable, agreeable.

ungainly *adj* clumsy, awkward, gauche, ungraceful, inelegant, gawky, unco-ordinated, lumbering, unwieldy.
Ea graceful, elegant.

ungodly *adj* **1** UNREASONABLE, outrageous, intolerable, unearthly, unsocial. **2** IMPIOUS, irreligious, godless,

blasphemous, profane, immoral, corrupt, depraved, sinful, wicked.

ungrateful *adj* unthankful, unappreciative, ill-mannered, ungracious, selfish, heedless.
Ea grateful, thankful.

unguarded *adj* **1** *in an unguarded moment*: unwary, careless, incautious, imprudent, impolitic, indiscreet, undiplomatic, thoughtless, unthinking, heedless, foolish, foolhardy, rash, ill-considered. **2** UNDEFENDED, unprotected, exposed, vulnerable, defenceless.
Ea 1 guarded, cautious. **2** defended, protected.

unhappy *adj* **1** SAD, sorrowful, miserable, melancholy, depressed, down, dispirited, despondent, dejected, downcast, crestfallen, long-faced, gloomy. **2** UNFORTUNATE, unlucky, ill-fated, unsuitable, inappropriate, inapt, ill-chosen, tactless, awkward, clumsy.
Ea 1 happy. **2** fortunate, suitable.

unharmed *adj* undamaged, unhurt, uninjured, unscathed, whole, intact, safe, sound.
Ea harmed, damaged.

unhealthy *adj* **1** UNWELL, sick, ill, poorly, ailing, sickly, infirm, invalid, weak, feeble, frail, unsound. **2** UNWHOLESOME, insanitary, unhygienic, harmful, detrimental, morbid, unnatural.
Ea 1 healthy, fit. **2** wholesome, hygienic, natural.

unheard-of *adj* **1** UNTHINKABLE, inconceivable, unimaginable, undreamed-of, unprecedented, unacceptable, offensive, shocking, outrageous, preposterous. **2** UNKNOWN, little-known, unfamiliar, new, unusual, obscure.
Ea 1 normal, acceptable. **2** famous.

unheeded *adj* ignored, disregarded, disobeyed, unnoticed, unobserved, unremarked, overlooked, neglected, forgotten.
Ea noted, observed.

unhesitating *adj* immediate, instant, instantaneous, prompt, ready, swift, automatic, spontaneous, instinctive, unquestioning, unwavering, unfaltering, wholehearted, implicit.
◼ hesitant, tentative.

unholy *adj* 1 IMPIOUS, irreligious, ungodly, sinful, iniquitous, immoral, corrupt, depraved, wicked, evil. 2 (*infml*) *an unholy mess*: unreasonable, shocking, outrageous, ungodly, unearthly.
◼ 1 holy, pious, godly. 2 reasonable.

unhurried *adj* slow, leisurely, deliberate, easy, relaxed, calm, easy-going (*infml*), laid-back (*infml*).
◼ hurried, hasty, rushed.

unidentified *adj* unknown, unrecognized, unmarked, unnamed, nameless, anonymous, incognito, unfamiliar, strange, mysterious.
◼ identified, known, named.

uniform *n* outfit, costume, livery, insignia, regalia, robes, dress, suit, apparel (*fml*).
➤ *adj* same, identical, like, alike, similar, homogeneous, consistent, regular, equal, smooth, even, flat, monotonous, unvarying, unchanging, constant, unbroken.
◼ different, varied, changing.

unify *v* unite, join, bind, combine, integrate, merge, amalgamate, consolidate, coalesce, fuse, weld.
◼ separate, divide, split.

unimaginable *adj* inconceivable, mind-boggling (*infml*), unbelievable, incredible, impossible, fantastic, undreamed-of, unthinkable, unheard-of.

unimaginative *adj* uninspired, unoriginal, predictable, hackneyed, banal, ordinary, ho-hum (*infml*), dull, boring, routine, matter-of-fact, dry, barren, lifeless, unexciting, tame, bland.
◼ imaginative, creative, original.

unimportant *adj* insignificant, inconsequential, irrelevant, immaterial, minor, trivial, trifling, petty, slight, negligible, worthless.

◼ important, significant, relevant, vital.

unimpressive *adj* unspectacular, undistinguished, unexceptional, unremarkable, uninteresting, ho-hum (*infml*), dull, average, commonplace, indifferent, mediocre.
◼ impressive, memorable, notable.

uninhabited *adj* unoccupied, vacant, empty, deserted, abandoned, unpeopled, unpopulated.

uninhibited *adj* unconstrained, unreserved, unselfconscious, liberated, free, unrestricted, uncontrolled, unrestrained, abandoned, natural, spontaneous, frank, candid, open, relaxed, informal.
◼ inhibited, repressed, constrained, restrained.

unintelligible *adj* incomprehensible, incoherent, inarticulate, double Dutch (*infml*), garbled, scrambled, jumbled, muddled, indecipherable, illegible.
◼ intelligible, comprehensible, clear.

unintentional *adj* unintended, accidental, fortuitous, inadvertent, unplanned, unpremeditated, involuntary, unconscious, unwitting.
◼ intentional, deliberate.

uninterested *adj* indifferent, unconcerned, uninvolved, bored, listless, apathetic, unenthusiastic, blasé, impassive, unresponsive.
◼ interested, concerned, enthusiastic, responsive.

uninteresting *adj* boring, tedious, monotonous, humdrum, dull, drab, dreary, dry, flat, tame, uneventful, unexciting, uninspiring, unimpressive.
◼ interesting, exciting.

uninterrupted *adj* unbroken, continuous, non-stop, unending, never-ending, constant, continual, steady, sustained, undisturbed, peaceful.
◼ broken, intermittent.

uninvited *adj* unasked, unsought, unsolicited, unwanted, unwelcome.
◼ invited, welcome.

union *n* alliance, coalition, league,

association, federation, confederation, confederacy, merger, combination, amalgamation, blend, mixture, synthesis, fusion, unification, unity.
F3 separation, alienation, estrangement.

unique *adj* single, one-off, sole, only, lone, solitary, unmatched, matchless, peerless, unequalled, unparalleled, unrivalled, incomparable, inimitable.
F3 common.

unison *n* concert, co-operation, unanimity, unity.

unit *n* item, part, element, constituent, piece, component, module, section, segment, portion, entity, whole, one, system, assembly.

unite *v* join, link, couple, marry, ally, co-operate, band, associate, federate, confederate, combine, pool, amalgamate, merge, blend, unify, consolidate, coalesce, fuse.
F3 separate, sever.

united *adj* allied, affiliated, corporate, unified, combined, pooled, collective, concerted, one, unanimous, agreed, in agreement, in accord, like-minded.
F3 disunited.

unity *n* agreement, accord, concord, harmony, peace, consensus, unanimity, solidarity, integrity, oneness, wholeness, union, unification.
F3 disunity, disagreement, discord, strife.

universal *adj* worldwide, global, all-embracing, all-inclusive, general, common, widespread, across-the-board, total, whole, entire, all-round, unlimited.

unjust *adj* unfair, inequitable, wrong, partial, biased, prejudiced, one-sided, partisan, unreasonable, unjustified, undeserved.
F3 just, fair, reasonable.

unjustifiable *adj* indefensible, inexcusable, unforgivable, unreasonable, unwarranted, uncalled-for, immoderate, excessive, unacceptable, outrageous.
F3 justifiable, acceptable.

unkempt *adj* dishevelled, tousled, rumpled, uncombed, ungroomed, untidy, messy, scruffy, shabby, slovenly.
F3 well-groomed, tidy.

unkind *adj* cruel, inhuman, inhumane, callous, hard-hearted, unfeeling, insensitive, thoughtless, inconsiderate, uncharitable, nasty, malicious, spiteful, mean, malevolent, unfriendly, uncaring, unsympathetic.
F3 kind, considerate.

unknown *adj* unfamiliar, unheard-of, strange, alien, foreign, mysterious, dark, obscure, hidden, concealed, undisclosed, secret, untold, new, uncharted, unexplored, undiscovered, unidentified, unnamed, nameless, anonymous, incognito.
F3 known, familiar.

unlawful *adj* illegal, criminal, illicit, illegitimate, unconstitutional, outlawed, banned, prohibited, forbidden, unauthorized.
F3 lawful, legal.

unlikely *adj* 1 IMPROBABLE, implausible, far-fetched, unconvincing, unbelievable, incredible, unimaginable, unexpected, doubtful, dubious, questionable, suspect, suspicious. 2 SLIGHT, faint, remote, distant.
F3 1 likely, plausible.

unlimited *adj* limitless, unrestricted, unbounded, boundless, infinite, endless, countless, incalculable, immeasurable, vast, immense, extensive, great, indefinite, absolute, unconditional, unqualified, all-encompassing, all-embracing, total, complete, full, unconstrained, unhampered.
F3 limited.

unload *v* unpack, empty, discharge, dump, offload, unburden, relieve.
F3 load.

unlock *v* unbolt, unlatch, unfasten, undo, open, free, release.
F3 lock, fasten.

unloved *adj* unpopular, disliked, hated, detested, unwanted, rejected,

spurned, loveless, uncared-for, neglected.
☒ loved.

unlucky *adj* unfortunate, luckless, unhappy, miserable, wretched, ill-fated, ill-starred, jinxed, doomed, cursed, hopeless, unfavourable, inauspicious, ominous, unsuccessful, disastrous, calamitous.
☒ lucky.

unmanageable *adj* 1 UNWIELDY, bulky, cumbersome, awkward, inconvenient, impractical, unhandy. 2 UNCONTROLLABLE, wild, unruly, disorderly, difficult.
☒ 1 manageable. 2 controllable.

unmarried *adj* single, unwed, celibate, unattached, available.
☒ married.

unmask *v* unveil, uncloak, uncover, bare, expose, reveal, show, disclose, discover, detect.
☒ mask, conceal.

unmentionable *adj* unspeakable, unutterable, taboo, immodest, indecent, shocking, scandalous, shameful, disgraceful, abominable.

unmistakable *adj* clear, plain, distinct, pronounced, obvious, evident, manifest, patent, glaring, explicit, unambiguous, unequivocal, positive, definite, sure, certain, unquestionable, indisputable, undeniable, indubitable.
☒ unclear, ambiguous.

unmoved *adj* unaffected, untouched, unshaken, dry-eyed, unfeeling, cold, dispassionate, indifferent, impassive, unresponsive, unimpressed, firm, adamant, inflexible, unbending, undeviating, unwavering, steady, unchanged, resolute, resolved, determined.
☒ moved, affected, shaken.

unnatural *adj* 1 ABNORMAL, anomalous, freakish, irregular, unusual, strange, odd, peculiar, queer, bizarre, extraordinary, uncanny, supernatural, unearthly, inhuman, perverted. 2 AFFECTED, feigned, artificial, false,

insincere, unspontaneous, contrived, laboured, stilted, forced, strained, self-conscious, stiff, awkward.
☒ 1 natural, normal. 2 sincere, fluent.

unnecessary *adj* unneeded, needless, uncalled-for, unwanted, unwarranted, non-essential, dispensable, expendable, superfluous, redundant, tautological.
☒ necessary, essential, indispensable.

unnerve *v* daunt, intimidate, frighten, scare, discourage, dishearten, demoralize, dismay, disconcert, upset, worry, shake, rattle (*infml*), confound, fluster.
☒ nerve, brace, steel.

unnoticed *adj* unobserved, unremarked, unseen, unrecognized, undiscovered, overlooked, ignored, disregarded, neglected, unheeded.
☒ noticed, noted.

unobtrusive *adj* inconspicuous, unnoticeable, unassertive, self-effacing, humble, modest, unostentatious, unpretentious, restrained, low-key, subdued, quiet, retiring.
☒ obtrusive, ostentatious.

unoccupied *adj* uninhabited, vacant, empty, free, idle, inactive, workless, jobless, unemployed.
☒ occupied, busy.

unofficial *adj* unauthorized, illegal, informal, off-the-record, personal, private, confidential, undeclared, unconfirmed.
☒ official.

unorthodox *adj* unconventional, nonconformist, heterodox, alternative, fringe, irregular, abnormal, unusual, left-field.
☒ orthodox, conventional.

unpaid *adj* 1 *unpaid bills*: overdue, outstanding, unsettled, owing, due, payable. 2 *unpaid work*: voluntary, honorary, unsalaried, unwaged, unremunerative, free.
☒ 1 paid.

unpalatable *adj* 1 UNAPPETIZING, distasteful, insipid, bitter, uneatable,

inedible. **2** UNPLEASANT, disagreeable, unattractive, offensive, repugnant.
Ea 1 palatable. **2** pleasant.

unparalleled *adj* unequalled, unmatched, matchless, peerless, incomparable, unrivalled, unsurpassed, supreme, superlative, rare, exceptional, unprecedented.

unpleasant *adj* disagreeable, ill-natured, nasty, objectionable, offensive, distasteful, unpalatable, unattractive, repulsive, bad, troublesome.
Ea pleasant, agreeable, nice.

unpopular *adj* disliked, hated, detested, unloved, unsought-after, unfashionable, undesirable, unwelcome, unwanted, rejected, shunned, avoided, neglected.
Ea popular, fashionable.

unprecedented *adj* new, original, revolutionary, ground-breaking, unknown, unheard-of, exceptional, remarkable, extraordinary, abnormal, unusual, freakish, unparalleled, unrivalled.
Ea usual.

unpredictable *adj* unforeseeable, unexpected, changeable, variable, inconstant, unreliable, fickle, unstable, erratic, random, chance.
Ea predictable, foreseeable, constant.

unprepared *adj* unready, surprised, unsuspecting, ill-equipped, unfinished, incomplete, half-baked, unplanned, unrehearsed, spontaneous, improvised, ad-lib, off-the-cuff.
Ea prepared, ready.

unpretentious *adj* unaffected, natural, plain, simple, restrained, unobtrusive, honest, straightforward, humble, modest, unassuming, unostentatious.
Ea pretentious.

unproductive *adj* infertile, sterile, barren, dry, arid, unfruitful, fruitless, pointless, futile, vain, idle, useless, ineffective, unprofitable, unremunerative, unrewarding.
Ea productive, fertile.

unprofessional *adj* amateurish, inexpert, unskilled, sloppy, incompetent, inefficient, casual, negligent, lax, unethical, unprincipled, improper, unseemly, unacceptable, inadmissible.
Ea professional, skilful.

unprotected *adj* unguarded, unattended, undefended, unfortified, unarmed, unshielded, unsheltered, uncovered, exposed, open, naked, vulnerable, defenceless, helpless.
Ea protected, safe, immune.

unqualified *adj* **1** UNTRAINED, inexperienced, amateur, ineligible, unfit, incompetent, incapable, unprepared, ill-equipped. **2** ABSOLUTE, categorical, utter, total, complete, thorough, consummate (*fml*), downright, unmitigated, unreserved, outright, wholehearted, unconditional, unrestricted.
Ea 1 qualified, professional. **2** conditional, tentative.

unravel *v* unwind, undo, untangle, disentangle, free, extricate, separate, resolve, sort out, solve, work out, figure out, puzzle out, penetrate, interpret, explain.
Ea tangle, complicate.

unreal *adj* false, artificial, synthetic, mock, faux, fake, sham, imaginary, visionary, fanciful, make-believe, pretend (*infml*), fictitious, made-up, fairy-tale, legendary, mythical, fantastic, illusory, immaterial, insubstantial, hypothetical.
Ea real, genuine.

unrealistic *adj* impractical, idealistic, romantic, quixotic, impracticable, unworkable, unreasonable, impossible.
Ea realistic, pragmatic.

unreasonable *adj* **1** UNFAIR, unjust, biased, unjustifiable, unjustified, unwarranted, undeserved, undue, uncalled-for. **2** IRRATIONAL, illogical, inconsistent, arbitrary, absurd, nonsensical, far-fetched, preposterous, mad, senseless, silly, foolish, stupid, headstrong, opinionated, perverse. **3**

unreasonable prices: excessive, immoderate, extravagant, exorbitant, extortionate.
₤ 1 reasonable, fair. **2** rational, sensible. **3** moderate.

unrecognizable *adj* unidentifiable, disguised, incognito, changed, altered.

unrefined *adj* raw, untreated, unprocessed, unfinished, unpolished, crude, coarse, vulgar, unsophisticated, uncultivated, uncultured.
₤ refined, finished.

unrelated *adj* unconnected, unassociated, irrelevant, extraneous, different, dissimilar, unlike, disparate, distinct, separate, independent.
₤ related, similar.

unrelenting *adj* relentless, unremitting, uncompromising, inexorable, incessant, unceasing, ceaseless, endless, unbroken, continuous, constant, continual, perpetual, steady, unabated, remorseless, unmerciful, merciless, pitiless, unsparing.
₤ spasmodic, intermittent.

unreliable *adj* unsound, fallible, deceptive, false, mistaken, erroneous, inaccurate, unconvincing, implausible, uncertain, undependable, untrustworthy, unstable, fickle, irresponsible.
₤ reliable, dependable, trustworthy.

unrepentant *adj* impenitent, unapologetic, unabashed, unashamed, shameless, brazen, incorrigible, confirmed, hardened, obdurate.
₤ repentant, penitent, ashamed.

unrest *n* protest, rebellion, turmoil, agitation, restlessness, disquiet, dissatisfaction, dissension, disaffection, worry.
₤ peace, calm.

unrestricted *adj* unlimited, unbounded, unopposed, unhindered, unimpeded, unobstructed, clear, free, open, public, unconditional, absolute.
₤ restricted, limited.

unripe *adj* unripened, green,

immature, undeveloped, unready.
₤ ripe, mature.

unrivalled *adj* unequalled, unparalleled, unmatched, matchless, peerless, incomparable, inimitable, unsurpassed, supreme, superlative.

unruffled *adj* undisturbed, untroubled, imperturbable, collected, composed, cool, calm, tranquil, serene, peaceful, smooth, level, even.
₤ troubled, anxious.

unruly *adj* uncontrollable, unmanageable, ungovernable, intractable, disorderly, wild, rowdy, riotous, rebellious, mutinous, lawless, insubordinate, disobedient, wayward, wilful, headstrong, obstreperous.
₤ manageable, orderly.

unsafe *adj* dangerous, perilous, risky, hazardous, treacherous, unreliable, uncertain, unsound, unstable, precarious, insecure, vulnerable, exposed.
₤ safe, secure.

unsatisfactory *adj* unacceptable, imperfect, defective, flawed, faulty, shoddy, inferior, poor, weak, inadequate, insufficient, deficient, unsuitable, displeasing, dissatisfying, unsatisfying, frustrating, disappointing.
₤ satisfactory, pleasing.

unscathed *adj* unhurt, uninjured, unharmed, undamaged, untouched, whole, intact, safe, sound.
₤ hurt, injured.

unscrupulous *adj* unprincipled, ruthless, shameless, dishonourable, dishonest, crooked (*infml*), corrupt, immoral, unethical, improper.
₤ scrupulous, ethical, proper.

unseemly *adj* improper, indelicate, indecorous (*fml*), unbecoming, undignified, unrefined, disreputable, discreditable, undue, inappropriate, unsuitable.
₤ seemly, decorous.

unseen *adj* unnoticed, unobserved, undetected, invisible, hidden, concealed, veiled, obscure.
₤ visible.

unselfish *adj* selfless, altruistic, self-denying, self-sacrificing, disinterested, noble, magnanimous, generous, liberal, charitable, philanthropic, public-spirited, humanitarian, kind.
🔁 selfish.

unsentimental *adj* realistic, practical, pragmatic, hard-headed, tough, unromantic, level-headed.
🔁 sentimental, idealistic.

unsettle *v* disturb, upset, trouble, bother, discompose, ruffle, fluster, unbalance, shake, agitate, rattle (*infml*), disconcert, confuse, throw.

unsettled *adj* 1 DISTURBED, upset, troubled, agitated, anxious, uneasy, tense, on tenterhooks, edgy, flustered, shaken, unnerved, disoriented, confused. 2 UNRESOLVED, undecided, undetermined, open, uncertain, doubtful. 3 *unsettled weather*: changeable, variable, unpredictable, inconstant, unstable, insecure, unsteady, shaky. 4 UNPAID, outstanding, owing, payable, overdue.
🔁 1 composed. 2 certain. 3 settled. 4 paid.

unshakable *adj* firm, well-founded, fixed, stable, immovable, unassailable, unwavering, constant, steadfast, staunch, sure, resolute, determined.
🔁 insecure.

unsightly *adj* ugly, unattractive, unprepossessing, hideous, repulsive, repugnant, off-putting, unpleasant, disagreeable.
🔁 attractive.

unskilled *adj* untrained, unqualified, inexperienced, unpractised, inexpert, amateur, unprofessional, amateurish, incompetent.
🔁 skilled.

unsociable *adj* unfriendly, aloof, distant, standoffish, withdrawn, introverted, reclusive, retiring, reserved, taciturn, unforthcoming, silent, sullen, uncommunicative, cold, chilly, uncongenial, unneighbourly, inhospitable, hostile.
🔁 sociable, friendly.

unsolicited *adj* unrequested, unsought, uninvited, unasked, unwanted, unwelcome, uncalled-for, gratuitous, voluntary, spontaneous.
🔁 requested, invited.

unsophisticated *adj* artless, guileless, innocent, ingenuous, naïve, inexperienced, green, unworldly, childlike, natural, unaffected, unpretentious, unrefined, plain, simple, straightforward, uncomplicated, uninvolved.
🔁 sophisticated, worldly, complex.

unsound *adj* 1 *unsound reasoning*: faulty, flawed, defective, ill-founded, fallacious, false, erroneous, invalid, illogical. 2 UNHEALTHY, unwell, ill, diseased, weak, frail, unbalanced, deranged, unhinged. 3 UNSTABLE, unsteady, wobbly, shaky, insecure, unsafe.
🔁 1 sound. 2 well. 3 stable.

unspeakable *adj* unutterable, inexpressible, indescribable, awful, dreadful, frightful, terrible, horrible, shocking, appalling, monstrous, inconceivable, unbelievable.

unspoilt *adj* preserved, conserved, unchanged, untouched, natural, unaffected, unsophisticated, unharmed, undamaged, unimpaired, unblemished, perfect.
🔁 spoilt, affected.

unspoken *adj* unstated, undeclared, unuttered, unexpressed, unsaid, voiceless, wordless, silent, tacit, implicit, implied, inferred, understood, assumed.
🔁 stated, explicit.

unstable *adj* 1 CHANGEABLE, variable, mutable, fluctuating, vacillating, wavering, fitful, erratic, inconsistent, volatile, capricious, inconstant, unpredictable, unreliable, untrustworthy. 2 UNSTEADY, wobbly, shaky, rickety, insecure, unsafe, risky, precarious, tottering, unbalanced.
🔁 1 stable. 2 steady.

unsteady *adj* unstable, wobbly, shaky,

rickety, insecure, unsafe, treacherous, precarious, tottering, unreliable, inconstant, irregular, flickering.
☒ steady, firm.

unsuccessful *adj* failed, abortive, vain, futile, useless, ineffective, unavailing, fruitless, unproductive, sterile, luckless, unlucky, unfortunate, losing, beaten, defeated, frustrated, thwarted.
☒ successful, effective, fortunate, winning.

unsuitable *adj* inappropriate, inapt, unsuited, unfit, unacceptable, improper, unseemly, unbecoming, incompatible, incongruous.
☒ suitable, appropriate.

unsung *adj* unhonoured, unpraised, unacknowledged, unrecognized, overlooked, disregarded, neglected, forgotten, unknown, obscure, unnamed, anonymous.
☒ honoured, famous, renowned.

unsure *adj* uncertain, doubtful, dubious, suspicious, sceptical, unconvinced, unpersuaded, undecided, hesitant, tentative.
☒ sure, certain, confident.

unsurpassed *adj* surpassing, supreme, transcendent, unbeaten, unexcelled, unequalled, unparalleled, unrivalled, incomparable, matchless, superlative, exceptional.

unsuspecting *adj* unwary, unaware, unconscious, trusting, trustful, unsuspicious, credulous, gullible, ingenuous, naïve, innocent.
☒ suspicious, knowing.

unsympathetic *adj* unpitying, unconcerned, unmoved, unresponsive, indifferent, insensitive, unfeeling, cold, heartless, soulless, hard-hearted, callous, cruel, inhuman, unkind, hard, stony, hostile, antagonistic.
☒ sympathetic, compassionate.

untangle *v* disentangle, extricate, unravel, undo, resolve, solve.
☒ tangle, complicate.

unthinkable *adj* inconceivable,

unimaginable, unheard-of, unbelievable, incredible, impossible, improbable, unlikely, implausible, unreasonable, illogical, absurd, preposterous, outrageous, shocking.

unthinking *adj* thoughtless, inconsiderate, insensitive, tactless, indiscreet, ill-considered, rude, heedless, careless, negligent, rash, impulsive, instinctive, unconscious, automatic, mechanical.
☒ considerate, conscious.

untidy *adj* messy, cluttered, disorderly, muddled, jumbled, unsystematic, chaotic, topsy-turvy, scruffy, unkempt, dishevelled, slovenly, sloppy, slipshod.
☒ tidy, neat.

untie *v* undo, unfasten, unknot, unbind, free, release, loose, loosen.
☒ tie, fasten.

untimely *adj* early, premature, unseasonable, ill-timed, inopportune, inconvenient, awkward, unsuitable, inappropriate, unfortunate, inauspicious.
☒ timely, opportune.

untiring *adj* unflagging, tireless, indefatigable, dogged, persevering, persistent, tenacious, determined, resolute, devoted, dedicated, constant, incessant, unremitting, steady, staunch, unfailing.
☒ inconstant, wavering.

untold *adj* uncounted, unnumbered, unreckoned, incalculable, innumerable, uncountable, countless, infinite, measureless, boundless, inexhaustible, undreamed-of, unimaginable, inconceivable.

untouched *adj* unharmed, undamaged, unimpaired, unhurt, uninjured, unscathed, safe, safe and sound, intact, unchanged, unaltered, unaffected.
☒ damaged, affected.

untrained *adj* unskilled, untaught, unschooled, uneducated, unqualified, inexperienced, inexpert, amateur, unprofessional.
☒ trained, expert.

untried *adj* untested, unproved, experimental, exploratory, new, novel, innovative, innovatory, ground-breaking.
⊟ tried, tested, proven.

untrue *adj* **1** FALSE, fallacious, deceptive, misleading, wrong, incorrect, inaccurate, mistaken, erroneous. **2** UNFAITHFUL, disloyal, untrustworthy, dishonest, deceitful, untruthful.
⊟ **1** true, correct. **2** faithful, honest.

untrustworthy *adj* dishonest, deceitful, untruthful, disloyal, unfaithful, faithless, treacherous, perfidious, false, untrue, capricious, fickle, fly-by-night, unreliable, untrusty.
⊟ trustworthy, reliable.

untruth *n* lie, fib, whopper (*infml*), porkie (*infml*), story, tale, fiction, invention, fabrication, falsehood, lying, untruthfulness, deceit, perjury.
⊟ truth.

untruthful *adj* lying, deceitful, dishonest, crooked (*infml*), hypocritical, two-faced, insincere, false, untrue.
⊟ truthful, honest.

unused *adj* leftover, remaining, surplus, extra, spare, available, new, fresh, blank, clean, untouched, unexploited, unemployed, idle.
⊟ used.

unusual *adj* uncommon, rare, unfamiliar, strange, odd, curious, queer, bizarre, left-field, unconventional, irregular, abnormal, extraordinary, remarkable, exceptional, different, surprising, unexpected.
⊟ usual, normal, ordinary.

unveil *v* uncover, expose, bare, reveal, disclose, divulge, discover.
⊟ cover, hide.

unwanted *adj* undesired, unsolicited, uninvited, unwelcome, outcast, rejected, unrequired, unneeded, unnecessary, surplus, extra, superfluous, redundant.
⊟ wanted, needed, necessary.

unwarranted *adj* unjustified, undue, undeserved, unprovoked, uncalled-for,

groundless, unreasonable, unjust, wrong.
⊟ warranted, justifiable, deserved.

unwary *adj* unguarded, incautious, careless, imprudent, indiscreet, thoughtless, unthinking, heedless, reckless, rash, hasty.
⊟ wary, cautious.

unwelcome *adj* **1** UNWANTED, undesirable, unpopular, uninvited, excluded, rejected. **2** *unwelcome news*: unpleasant, disagreeable, upsetting, worrying, distasteful, unpalatable, unacceptable.
⊟ **1** welcome, desirable. **2** pleasant.

unwell *adj* ill, sick, poorly, indisposed, off-colour, under the weather (*infml*), ailing, sickly, unhealthy.
⊟ well, healthy.

unwieldy *adj* unmanageable, inconvenient, awkward, clumsy, ungainly, bulky, massive, hefty, weighty, ponderous, cumbersome, clunky (*infml*).
⊟ handy, dainty.

unwilling *adj* reluctant, disinclined, indisposed, resistant, opposed, averse, loath, slow, unenthusiastic, grudging.
⊟ willing, enthusiastic.

unwind *v* **1** UNROLL, unreel, unwrap, undo, uncoil, untwist, unravel, disentangle. **2** (*infml*) RELAX, wind down, calm down, chill out (*infml*).
⊟ **1** wind, roll.

unwitting *adj* unaware, unknowing, unsuspecting, unthinking, unconscious, involuntary, accidental, chance, inadvertent, unintentional, unintended, unplanned.
⊟ knowing, conscious, deliberate.

unworldly *adj* spiritual, transcendental, metaphysical, otherworldly, visionary, idealistic, impractical, unsophisticated, inexperienced, innocent, naïve.
⊟ worldly, materialistic, sophisticated.

unworthy *adj* undeserving, inferior, ineligible, unsuitable, inappropriate, unfitting, unbecoming, unseemly,

improper, unprofessional, shameful, disgraceful, dishonourable, ignoble, discreditable, base, contemptible, despicable.
☒ worthy, commendable.

unwritten *adj* verbal, oral, word-of-mouth, unrecorded, tacit, implicit, understood, accepted, recognized, traditional, customary, conventional.
☒ written, recorded.

upbraid *v* reprimand, admonish, rebuke, reprove, reproach, scold, chide, castigate (*fml*), berate, criticize, censure.
☒ praise, commend.

upbringing *n* bringing-up, raising, rearing, breeding, parenting, care, nurture, cultivation, education, training, instruction, teaching.

update *v* modernize, revise, amend, correct, renew, renovate, revamp.

upgrade *v* promote, advance, elevate, raise, improve, enhance.
☒ downgrade, demote.

upheaval *n* disruption, disturbance, upset, chaos, confusion, disorder, trouble, turmoil, strife, shake-up (*infml*), revolution, overthrow.

uphill *adj* hard, difficult, arduous, tough, taxing, strenuous, laborious, tiring, wearisome, exhausting, gruelling, punishing.
☒ easy.

uphold *v* support, maintain, hold to, stand by, defend, champion, advocate, promote, back, endorse, sustain, fortify (*fml*), strengthen, justify, vindicate.
☒ abandon, reject.

upkeep *n* maintenance, preservation, conservation, care, running, repair, support, sustenance, subsistence, keep.
☒ neglect.

upper *adj* higher, loftier, superior, senior, top, topmost, uppermost, high, elevated, exalted, eminent, important.
☒ lower, inferior, junior.

uppermost *adj* highest, loftiest, top, topmost, greatest, supreme, first,

primary, foremost, leading, principal, main, chief, dominant, predominant, paramount, pre-eminent.
☒ lowest.

upright *adj* **1** VERTICAL, plumb, perpendicular, erect, straight. **2** RIGHTEOUS, good, virtuous, upstanding, noble, honourable, ethical, principled, incorruptible, honest, trustworthy.
☒ **1** horizontal, flat. **2** dishonest.

uprising *n* rebellion, revolt, mutiny, rising, insurgence, insurrection, revolution.

uproar *n* noise, din, racket, hubbub, hullabaloo, pandemonium, tumult, turmoil, turbulence, commotion, confusion, strife, disorder, trouble, clamour, outcry, furore, riot, rumpus.

uproot *v* pull up, rip up, root out, weed out, remove, displace, eradicate, destroy, wipe out.

upset *v* **1** DISTRESS, grieve, dismay, trouble, worry, vex, agitate, disturb, bother, fluster, ruffle, discompose, shake, unnerve, disconcert, confuse, disorganize. **2** TIP, spill, overturn, capsize, topple, overthrow, destabilize, unsteady.
➤ *n* **1** TROUBLE, worry, agitation, disturbance, bother, disruption, upheaval, shake-up (*infml*), reverse, surprise, shock, whammy (*infml*). **2** *stomach upset*: disorder, complaint, bug (*infml*), illness, sickness.
➤ *adj* distressed, grieved, hurt, annoyed, dismayed, troubled, worried, agitated, vexed, disturbed, bothered, shaken, disconcerted, confused.

upshot *n* result, consequence, outcome, issue, end, conclusion, finish, culmination.

upside down inverted, upturned, wrong way up, upset, overturned, disordered, muddled, jumbled, confused, topsy-turvy, chaotic.

up to date *adj* current, contemporary, modern, fashionable, trendy (*infml*), latest, recent, new.
☒ out of date, old-fashioned.

upturn *n* revival, recovery, upsurge, upswing, rise, increase, boost, improvement.
▪ downturn, drop.

urban *adj* town, city, inner-city, metropolitan, municipal, civic, built-up.
▪ country, rural.

urge *v* advise, counsel, recommend, advocate, encourage, exhort, implore, beg, beseech, entreat, plead, press, constrain, compel, force, push, drive, impel, goad, spur, hasten, induce, incite, instigate.
▪ discourage, dissuade, deter, hinder.
➤ *n* desire, wish, inclination, fancy, longing, yearning, itch, yen (*infml*), impulse, compulsion, impetus, drive, eagerness.
▪ disinclination.

urgency *n* hurry, haste, pressure, stress, importance, seriousness, gravity, imperativeness, need, necessity.

urgent *adj* immediate, instant, top-priority, important, critical, crucial, imperative, exigent, pressing, compelling, persuasive, earnest, eager, insistent, persistent.
▪ unimportant.

usable *adj* working, operational, serviceable, functional, practical, exploitable, available, current, valid.
▪ unusable, useless.

usage *n* **1** TREATMENT, handling, management, control, running, operation, employment, application, use. **2** TRADITION, custom, practice, habit, convention, etiquette, rule, regulation, form, routine, procedure, method.

use *v* utilize, employ, exercise, practise, operate, work, apply, wield, handle, treat, manipulate, exploit, enjoy, consume, exhaust, expend, spend.
➤ *n* utility, usefulness, value, worth, profit, advantage, benefit, good, avail, help, service, point, object, end, purpose, reason, cause, occasion, need, necessity, usage, application, employment, operation, exercise.

◇ **use up** finish, exhaust, drain, sap, deplete, consume, devour, absorb, waste, squander, fritter.

used *adj* second-hand, pre-owned, cast-off, hand-me-down, nearly new, worn, dog-eared, soiled.
▪ unused, new, fresh.

useful *adj* handy, convenient, all-purpose, practical, effective, productive, fruitful, profitable, valuable, worthwhile, advantageous, beneficial, helpful.
▪ useless, ineffective, worthless.

useless *adj* futile, fruitless, unproductive, vain, idle, unavailing, hopeless, pointless, worthless, unusable, broken-down, clapped-out (*sl*), unworkable, impractical, ineffective, inefficient, incompetent, weak.
▪ useful, helpful, effective.

usher *n* usherette, doorkeeper, attendant, escort, guide.
➤ *v* escort, accompany, conduct, lead, direct, guide, show, pilot, steer.

usual *adj* normal, typical, stock, standard, regular, routine, habitual, customary, conventional, accepted, recognized, accustomed, familiar, common, everyday, general, ordinary, unexceptional, bog-standard (*infml*), expected, predictable.
▪ unusual, strange, rare.

usually *adv* normally, generally, as a rule, ordinarily, typically, traditionally, regularly, commonly, by and large, on the whole, mainly, chiefly, mostly.
▪ exceptionally.

usurp *v* take over, assume, arrogate, seize, take, annex, appropriate, commandeer, steal.

utensil *n* tool, implement, instrument, device, contrivance, gadget, apparatus, appliance.

Kitchen utensils include: baster, bottle opener, breadbin, breadboard, butter curler, butter dish, can opener, cheese board, cheese slicer, chopping board, colander, corer, corkscrew, cruet set, dough hook, egg separator, egg slicer, egg timer, fish slice, flour dredger, fork,

garlic press, grater, herb mill, ice-cream scoop, icing syringe, jelly mould, kitchen scales, knife block, lemon squeezer, mandolin, measuring jug, meat thermometer, mincer, mixing bowl, nutcracker, nutmeg grater, pasta maker, pastry board, pastry brush, pastry cutter, peeler, pepper mill, pie funnel, potato masher, pudding basin, punch bowl, rolling pin, salad spinner, scissors, shears, sharpening steel, sieve, sifter, skewer, spatula, spice rack, stoner, storage jar, tea caddy, tea infuser, tea strainer, toast rack, tongs, tureen, vegetable brush, whisk, wine cooler, wine rack, yoghurt maker, zester;
types of knife: boning knife, bread knife, butter knife, carving knife, cheese knife, cleaver, cocktail knife, cook's knife, fish knife, grapefruit knife, palette knife, paring knife, vegetable knife;
types of spoon: dessertspoon, draining spoon, ladle, measuring spoon, serving spoon, skimmer, straining spoon, tablespoon, teaspoon, wooden spoon. *see also* **cutlery**.

Cooking utensils include: baking sheet, bun tin, cake tin, flan tin, loaf tin, muffin tin, pie plate, quiche dish; bain-marie, brochette, casserole, cocotte, deep-fat fryer, egg coddler, egg poacher, fish kettle, fondue set, frying pan, grill pan, milk pan, preserving pan, pressure cooker,

ramekin, roasting pan, saucepan, skillet, slow cooker, soufflé dish, steamer, stockpot, terrine, vegetable steamer, wok.

utility *n* usefulness, use, value, profit, advantage, benefit, avail, service, convenience, practicality, efficacy, efficiency, fitness, serviceableness.

utmost *adj* **1** *with the utmost care*: extreme, maximum, greatest, highest, supreme, paramount. **2** FARTHEST, furthermost, remotest, outermost, ultimate, final, last.
➤ *n* best, hardest, most, maximum.

utter[1] *adj* absolute, complete, total, entire, thoroughgoing, out-and-out, downright, sheer, stark, arrant (*fml*), unmitigated, unqualified, perfect, consummate (*fml*).

utter[2] *v* speak, say, voice, vocalize, verbalize, express, articulate, enunciate, sound, pronounce, deliver, state, declare, announce, proclaim, tell, reveal, divulge.

utterance *n* statement, remark, comment, expression, articulation, delivery, speech, declaration, announcement, proclamation, pronouncement.

utterly *adv* absolutely, completely, totally, fully, entirely, wholly, thoroughly, downright, perfectly.

U-turn *n* about-turn, volte-face, reversal, backtrack.

Vv

vacancy *n* opportunity, opening, position, post, job, place, room, situation.

vacant *adj* 1 EMPTY, unoccupied, unfilled, free, available, void, not in use, unused, uninhabited. 2 BLANK, expressionless, vacuous, inane, inattentive, absent, absent-minded, air-headed (*infml*), unthinking, dreamy.
🔁 1 occupied, engaged.

vacate *v* leave, depart, evacuate, abandon, withdraw, quit.

vacuum *n* emptiness, void, nothingness, vacuity, space, chasm, gap.

vague *adj* 1 ILL-DEFINED, blurred, indistinct, hazy, dim, shadowy, misty, fuzzy, nebulous, obscure. 2 INDEFINITE, imprecise, unclear, uncertain, undefined, undetermined, unspecific, generalized, inexact, ambiguous, evasive, loose, woolly.
🔁 1 clear. 2 definite.

vain *adj* 1 *a vain attempt*: useless, worthless, futile, abortive, fruitless, pointless, unproductive, unprofitable, unavailing, hollow, groundless, empty, trivial, unimportant. 2 CONCEITED, proud, self-satisfied, arrogant, self-important, egotistical, bigheaded (*infml*), swollen-headed (*infml*), stuck-up (*infml*), affected, pretentious, ostentatious, swaggering.
🔁 1 fruitful, successful. 2 modest, self-effacing.

valiant *adj* brave, courageous, gallant, fearless, intrepid, bold, dauntless, heroic, plucky, indomitable, staunch.
🔁 cowardly, fearful.

valid *adj* 1 LOGICAL, well-founded, well-grounded, sound, good, cogent, convincing, telling, conclusive, reliable, substantial, weighty, powerful, just. 2 OFFICIAL, legal, lawful, legitimate, authentic, bona fide, genuine, binding, proper.
🔁 1 false, weak. 2 unofficial, invalid.

valley *n* dale, vale, dell, glen, hollow, cwm, depression, gulch.

valuable *adj* 1 *valuable necklace*: precious, prized, valued, costly, expensive, dear, high-priced, treasured, cherished, estimable. 2 *valuable suggestions*: helpful, worthwhile, useful, beneficial, invaluable, constructive, fruitful, profitable, important, serviceable, worthy, handy.
🔁 1 worthless. 2 useless.

value *n* 1 COST, price, rate, worth. 2 WORTH, use, usefulness, utility, merit, importance, desirability, benefit, advantage, significance, good, profit.
➤ *v* 1 PRIZE, appreciate, treasure, esteem, hold dear, respect, cherish. 2 EVALUATE, assess, estimate, gauge, price, appraise, survey, rate.
🔁 1 disregard, neglect. 2 undervalue.

vanish *v* disappear, fade, dissolve, evaporate, disperse, melt, die out, depart, exit, fizzle out, peter out.
🔁 appear, materialize.

vanity *n* 1 CONCEIT, conceitedness, pride, arrogance, self-conceit, self-love, self-satisfaction, narcissism, egotism, pretension, ostentation, affectation, airs, bigheadedness (*infml*), swollen-headedness (*infml*). 2 WORTHLESSNESS, uselessness, emptiness, futility, pointlessness, unreality, hollowness, fruitlessness, triviality.
🔁 1 modesty, worth.

vapour *n* steam, mist, fog, smoke,

breath, fumes, haze, damp, dampness, exhalation.

variable *adj* changeable, inconstant, varying, shifting, mutable, unpredictable, fluctuating, fitful, unstable, unsteady, wavering, vacillating, temperamental, fickle, flexible.
🖛 fixed, invariable, stable.

variance *n* 1 VARIATION, difference, discrepancy, disparity, divergence, inconsistency, disagreement. 2 DISAGREEMENT, disharmony, disunity, conflict, discord, division, dissent, dissension, quarrelling, strife.
🖛 1 agreement. 2 harmony.

variation *n* diversity, variety, deviation, discrepancy, disparity, diversification, alteration, change, difference, departure, modification, modulation, inflection, novelty, innovation.
🖛 monotony, uniformity.

varied *adj* assorted, diverse, miscellaneous, mixed, various, sundry, heterogeneous (*fml*), different, wide-ranging.
🖛 standardized, uniform.

variegated *adj* multicoloured, many-coloured, parti-coloured, varicoloured, speckled, mottled, dappled, pied, streaked, motley.
🖛 monochrome, plain.

variety *n* 1 ASSORTMENT, miscellany, mixture, collection, medley, potpourri, range. 2 DIFFERENCE, diversity, dissimilarity, discrepancy, variation, multiplicity. 3 SORT, kind, class, category, species, type, breed, brand, make, strain.
🖛 2 uniformity, similitude (*fml*).

various *adj* different, differing, diverse, varied, varying, assorted, miscellaneous, heterogeneous (*fml*), distinct, diversified, mixed, many, several.

varnish *n* lacquer, glaze, resin, polish, gloss, coating.

vary *v* 1 CHANGE, alter, modify,

modulate, diversify, reorder, transform, alternate, inflect, permutate. 2 DIVERGE, differ, disagree, depart, fluctuate.

vast *adj* huge, immense, massive, gigantic, enormous, great, colossal, extensive, tremendous, sweeping, unlimited, fathomless, innumerable, immeasurable, never-ending, monumental, monstrous, far-flung.

vault¹ *v* leap, spring, bound, clear, jump, hurdle, leap-frog.

vault² *n* 1 CELLAR, crypt, strongroom, repository, cavern, depository, wine-cellar, tomb, mausoleum. 2 ARCH, roof, span, concave.

vaunt (*fml*) *v* boast, brag, exult in, flaunt, show off, parade, trumpet, crow.
🖛 belittle, minimize.

veer *v* swerve, swing, change, shift, diverge, deviate, wheel, turn, sheer, tack.

vegetable

Vegetables include: asparagus, artichoke, aubergine, baby corn, bean, beetroot, bok choy, broad bean, broccoli, Brussels sprout, butter bean, cabbage, calabrese, capsicum, carrot, cassava (or manioc), cauliflower, celeriac, celery, chicory, courgette, cress, cucumber, daikon, eggplant (*US*), endive, fennel, French bean, garlic, Jerusalem artichoke, jicama, kale, kohlrabi, leek, lentil, lettuce, mangetout, marrow, mushroom, okra, onion, parsnip, pea, pepper, petit pois, potato, spud (*infml*), pumpkin, radish, runner bean, shallot, soya bean, spinach, spring onion, squash, swede, sweetcorn, sweet potato, turnip, water chestnut, watercress, yam, zucchini (*US*).

vegetate *v* stagnate, degenerate, deteriorate, rusticate, go to seed, idle, rust, languish.

vehement *adj* impassioned, passionate, ardent, fervent, intense, forceful, emphatic, heated, strong, powerful, urgent, enthusiastic, animated, eager, earnest, forcible, fierce, violent, zealous.

🗷 apathetic, indifferent.

vehicle n **1** CONVEYANCE, transport. **2** MEANS, agency, channel, medium, mechanism, organ.

Vehicles include: plane, boat, ship, car, taxi, cab, hackney carriage, bicycle, bike (*infml*), cycle, tandem, tricycle, boneshaker (*infml*), penny farthing, motorcycle, motorbike, scooter, bus, omnibus, minibus, double-decker (*infml*), coach, charabanc, caravan, caravanette, camper, recreational vehicle (or RV), winnebago (*US*), train, Pullman, sleeper, wagon-lit, tube, tram, monorail, maglev, trolleybus; van, Transit®, lorry, truck, juggernaut, pantechnicon, trailer, tractor, fork-lift truck, steamroller, tank, wagon; bobsleigh, sled, sledge, sleigh, toboggan, troika; barouche, brougham, dog-cart, dray, four-in-hand, gig, hansom, landau, phaeton, post-chaise, stagecoach, sulky, surrey, trap; rickshaw, sedan chair, litter. *see also* **aircraft**; **boat**; **car**.

veil v screen, cloak, cover, mask, shadow, shield, obscure, conceal, hide, disguise, shade.

🗷 expose, uncover.

➤ n cover, cloak, curtain, mask, screen, disguise, film, blind, shade, shroud.

vein n **1** STREAK, stripe, stratum, seam, lode, blood vessel. **2** MOOD, tendency, bent, strain, temper, tenor, tone, frame of mind, mode, style.

Veins and arteries include: aorta, axillary, brachial, carotid, femoral, frontal, gastric, hepatic, iliac, jugular, portal, pulmonary, radial, renal, saphena, subclavian, superior, temporal, tibial.

vendetta n feud, blood-feud, enmity, rivalry, quarrel, bad blood, bitterness.

veneer n front, façade, appearance, coating, surface, show, mask, gloss, pretence, guise, finish.

venerable adj respected, revered, esteemed, honoured, venerated, dignified, grave, wise, august, aged, worshipped.

venerate v revere, respect, honour, esteem, worship, hallow (*fml*), adore.

🗷 despise, anathematize.

vengeance n retribution, revenge, retaliation, reprisal, requital, tit for tat.

🗷 forgiveness.

venom n **1** POISON, toxin. **2** RANCOUR, ill-will, malice, malevolence, spite, bitterness, acrimony, hate, virulence.

venomous adj **1** POISONOUS, toxic, virulent, harmful, noxious. **2** MALICIOUS, spiteful, vicious, vindictive, baleful, hostile, malignant, rancorous, baneful.

🗷 **1** harmless.

vent n opening, hole, aperture, outlet, passage, orifice, duct, channel.

➤ v air, express, voice, utter, release, discharge, emit.

ventilate v **1** *ventilate a room*: air, aerate, freshen. **2** *ventilate one's feelings*: air, broadcast, debate, discuss.

venture v **1** DARE, advance, make bold, put forward, proffer, presume, suggest, volunteer. **2** RISK, hazard, endanger, imperil, jeopardize, speculate, wager, stake.

➤ n risk, chance, hazard, speculation, gamble, undertaking, project, adventure, endeavour, enterprise, operation, fling.

verbal adj spoken, oral, verbatim, unwritten, word-of-mouth.

verbatim adv word for word, exactly, literally, to the letter, precisely.

verbose adj long-winded, wordy, prolix (*fml*), loquacious (*fml*), diffuse, circumlocutory.

🗷 succinct, brief.

verdict n decision, judgement, conclusion, finding, adjudication, assessment, opinion, sentence.

verge n border, edge, margin, limit, rim,

brim, brink, boundary, threshold, extreme, edging, periphery.

◇ **verge on** approach, border on, come close to, near.

verify v confirm, corroborate, substantiate, authenticate, bear out, prove, support, validate, testify, attest.
🔁 invalidate, discredit.

vernacular adj indigenous, local, native, popular, vulgar, informal, colloquial, common.
➤ n language, speech, tongue, parlance, dialect, idiom, jargon.

versatile adj adaptable, flexible, all-round, multipurpose, multifaceted, adjustable, many-sided, general-purpose, functional, resourceful, handy, variable.
🔁 inflexible.

verse n poetry, rhyme, stanza, metre, doggerel, jingle.

versed adj skilled, proficient, practised, experienced, familiar, acquainted, learned, knowledgeable, conversant, seasoned, qualified, competent, accomplished.

version n **1** RENDERING, reading, take, interpretation, account, translation, paraphrase, adaptation, portrayal. **2** TYPE, kind, variant, form, model, style, design.

vertical adj upright, perpendicular, plumb, upstanding, erect, on end.
🔁 horizontal.

vertigo n dizziness, giddiness, light-headedness.

verve n vitality, vivacity, animation, energy, dash, élan, liveliness, zest, sparkle, vigour, enthusiasm, gusto, life, relish, spirit, force.
🔁 apathy, lethargy.

very adv extremely, greatly, highly, deeply, truly, terribly (*infml*), majorly (*sl*), remarkably, excessively, exceeding(ly), acutely, particularly, really, absolutely, noticeably, unusually.
🔁 slightly, scarcely.
➤ adj actual, real, same, selfsame, identical, true, genuine, simple, utter,

sheer, pure, perfect, plain, mere, bare, exact, appropriate.

vestige n trace, suspicion, indication, sign, hint, evidence, whiff, inkling, glimmer, token, scrap, leftovers, remains, remainder, remnant, residue.

vet v investigate, examine, check, scrutinize, scan, inspect, survey, review, appraise, audit.

veteran n master, pastmaster, old hand, old stager, old-timer, pro (*infml*), war-horse.
🔁 novice, recruit.
➤ adj experienced, practised, seasoned, long-serving, long-time, expert, adept, proficient, old.
🔁 inexperienced.

veto v reject, turn down, knock back (*infml*), forbid, disallow, ban, prohibit, rule out, block.
🔁 approve, sanction.
➤ n rejection, ban, embargo, prohibition, thumbs down (*infml*), knockback (*infml*).
🔁 approval, assent.

vex v irritate, annoy, provoke, pester, trouble, upset, worry, bother, put out (*infml*), harass, hassle (*infml*), aggravate (*infml*), needle (*infml*), disturb, distress, agitate, exasperate, torment, fret.
🔁 calm, soothe.

vexed adj **1** IRRITATED, annoyed, provoked, upset, troubled, worried, nettled, put out, exasperated, bothered, confused, perplexed, aggravated (*infml*), harassed, hassled (*infml*), ruffled, riled, disturbed, distressed, displeased, agitated. **2** a vexed question: difficult, moot, controversial, contested, disputed.

viable adj feasible, practicable, possible, workable, usable, operable, achievable, sustainable.
🔁 impossible, unworkable.

vibrant adj **1** ANIMATED, vivacious, vivid, bright, brilliant, colourful, lively, responsive, sparkling, spirited, sensitive. **2** THRILLING, dynamic, electrifying, electric.

vibrate v quiver, pulsate, shudder, shiver, resonate, reverberate, throb, oscillate, tremble, undulate, sway, swing, shake.

vice n **1** EVIL, evil-doing, depravity, immorality, wickedness, sin, corruption, sleaze (*infml*), iniquity (*fml*), profligacy (*fml*), degeneracy. **2** FAULT, failing, flaw, defect, shortcoming, weakness, imperfection, blemish, bad habit, besetting sin.
✴ 1 virtue, morality.

vicinity n neighbourhood, area, locality, district, precincts, environs, proximity.

vicious adj **1** WICKED, bad, wrong, immoral, depraved, unprincipled, diabolical, corrupt, debased, perverted, profligate (*fml*), vile, heinous. **2** MALICIOUS, spiteful, vindictive, virulent, cruel, mean, nasty, slanderous, venomous, defamatory. **3** SAVAGE, wild, violent, barbarous, brutal, dangerous.
✴ 1 virtuous. **2** kind.

victim n sufferer, casualty, prey, scapegoat, Aunt Sally, martyr, sacrifice, fatality.
✴ offender, attacker.

victimize v **1** OPPRESS, persecute, discriminate against, pick on, prey on, bully, exploit. **2** CHEAT, deceive, defraud, swindle (*infml*), dupe, trick, hoodwink, fool.

victorious adj conquering, champion, triumphant, winning, unbeaten, successful, prize-winning, top, first.
✴ defeated, unsuccessful.

victory n conquest, win, triumph, success, superiority, mastery, vanquishment, subjugation, overcoming.
✴ defeat, loss.

vie v strive, compete, contend, struggle, contest, fight, rival.

view n **1** OPINION, attitude, belief, judgement, estimation, feeling, sentiment, impression, notion. **2** SIGHT, scene, vision, vista, outlook, prospect, perspective, panorama, landscape. **3** SURVEY, inspection, examination, observation, scrutiny, scan. **4** GLIMPSE, look, sight, perception.
➤ v **1** CONSIDER, regard, contemplate, judge, think about, speculate. **2** OBSERVE, watch, see, examine, inspect, look at, scan, survey, witness, perceive.

viewer n spectator, watcher, observer, onlooker, witness.

viewpoint n attitude, position, perspective, slant, standpoint, stance, opinion, angle, feeling.

vigilant adj watchful, alert, attentive, observant, on one's guard, on the lookout, cautious, wide-awake, sleepless, unsleeping.
✴ careless.

vigorous adj energetic, active, lively, healthy, strong, strenuous, robust, lusty, sound, vital, brisk, dynamic, forceful, forcible, powerful, stout, spirited, full-blooded, effective, efficient, enterprising, flourishing, intense.
✴ weak, feeble.

vigour n energy, vitality, liveliness, zest, health, robustness, stamina, strength, resilience, soundness, spirit, verve, gusto, activity, animation, power, potency, force, forcefulness, might, dash, dynamism.
✴ weakness.

vile adj **1** *a vile sinner*: base, contemptible, debased, depraved, degenerate, bad, wicked, wretched, worthless, sinful, miserable, mean, evil, impure, corrupt, despicable, disgraceful, degrading, vicious, appalling. **2** *a vile meal*: disgusting, foul, nauseating, sickening, repulsive, repugnant, revolting, noxious, offensive, nasty, loathsome, horrid.
✴ 1 pure, worthy. **2** pleasant, lovely.

villain n evil-doer, wrongdoer, miscreant (*fml*), scoundrel, rogue, malefactor (*fml*), criminal, reprobate, rascal.

villainous adj wicked, bad, criminal, evil, sinful, vicious, notorious, cruel, inhuman, vile, depraved, disgraceful, terrible.
✴ good.

vindicate v 1 CLEAR, acquit, excuse, exonerate, absolve, rehabilitate. 2 JUSTIFY, uphold, support, maintain, defend, establish, advocate, assert, verify.

vindictive adj spiteful, unforgiving, implacable, vengeful, relentless, unrelenting, revengeful, resentful, punitive, venomous, malevolent, malicious.
🖅 forgiving.

vintage n year, period, era, epoch, generation, origin, harvest, crop.
➤ adj choice, best, fine, prime, select, superior, rare, mature, old, ripe, classic, venerable, veteran.

violate v 1 CONTRAVENE, disobey, disregard, transgress, break, flout, infringe. 2 OUTRAGE, debauch, defile, rape, ravish, dishonour, desecrate, profane, invade.
🖅 1 observe.

violence n 1 FORCE, strength, power, vehemence, might, intensity, ferocity, fierceness, severity, tumult, turbulence, wildness. 2 BRUTALITY, destructiveness, cruelty, bloodshed, murderousness, savagery, passion, fighting, frenzy, fury, hostilities.

violent adj 1 INTENSE, strong, severe, sharp, acute, extreme, harmful, destructive, devastating, injurious, powerful, painful, agonizing, forceful, forcible, harsh, ruinous, rough, vehement, tumultuous, turbulent. 2 CRUEL, brutal, aggressive, bloodthirsty, impetuous, hot-headed, headstrong, murderous, savage, wild, vicious, unrestrained, uncontrollable, ungovernable, passionate, furious, intemperate, maddened, outrageous, riotous, fiery.
🖅 1 calm, moderate. 2 peaceful, gentle.

virgin n maiden, girl, celibate, vestal.
➤ adj virginal, chaste, intact, immaculate, maidenly, pure, modest, new, fresh, spotless, stainless, undefiled, untouched, unsullied.

virile adj man-like, masculine, male, manly, macho (*infml*), robust, vigorous, potent, lusty, red-blooded, forceful, strong, rugged.
🖅 effeminate, impotent.

virtual adj effective, essential, practical, implied, implicit, potential.

virtually adv practically, in effect, almost, nearly, as good as, in essence.

virtue n 1 GOODNESS, morality, rectitude, uprightness, worthiness, righteousness, probity (*fml*), integrity, honour, incorruptibility, justice, high-mindedness, excellence. 2 QUALITY, worth, merit, advantage, asset, credit, strength.
🖅 1 vice.

virtuoso n expert, master, maestro, prodigy, genius.

virtuous adj good, moral, righteous, upright, worthy, honourable, irreproachable, incorruptible, exemplary, unimpeachable, high-principled, blameless, clean-living, excellent, innocent, squeaky-clean (*infml*).
🖅 immoral, vicious.

virulent adj 1 POISONOUS, toxic, venomous, deadly, lethal, malignant, injurious, pernicious, intense. 2 HOSTILE, resentful, spiteful, acrimonious, bitter, vicious, vindictive, malevolent, malicious.
🖅 1 harmless.

visible adj perceptible, discernible, detectable, apparent, noticeable, observable, distinguishable, discoverable, evident, unconcealed, undisguised, unmistakable, conspicuous, clear, obvious, manifest, open, palpable, plain, patent.
🖅 invisible, indiscernible, hidden.

vision n 1 APPARITION, hallucination, illusion, delusion, mirage, phantom, ghost, chimera, spectre, wraith. 2 IDEA, ideal, conception, insight, view, picture, image, fantasy, dream, daydream. 3 SIGHT, seeing, eyesight, perception, discernment, far-sightedness, foresight, penetration.

visionary *adj* idealistic, impractical, romantic, dreamy, unrealistic, utopian, unreal, fanciful, prophetic, speculative, unworkable, illusory, imaginary.
➤ *n* idealist, romantic, dreamer, daydreamer, fantasist, prophet, mystic, seer, utopian, rainbow-chaser, theorist.
🖘 pragmatist.

visit *v* call on, call in, call round, stay with, stay at, drop in on (*infml*), stop by (*infml*), look in, look up, pop in (*infml*), see.
➤ *n* call, stay, stop, excursion, sojourn (*fml*).

visitor *n* caller, guest, company, tourist, holidaymaker.

vista *n* view, prospect, panorama, perspective, outlook, scene.

visualize *v* picture, envisage, imagine, conceive.

vital *adj* 1 CRITICAL, crucial, important, imperative, key, significant, basic, fundamental, essential, necessary, mission-critical (*infml*), requisite, indispensable, urgent, life-or-death, decisive, forceful. 2 LIVING, alive, lively, life-giving, invigorating, spirited, vivacious, vibrant, vigorous, dynamic, animated, energetic, quickening (*fml*).
🖘 1 inessential, peripheral. 2 dead.

vitality *n* life, liveliness, animation, vigour, energy, vivacity, zest, spirit, sparkle, exuberance, go (*infml*), strength, stamina.

vitamin

Vitamins include: aneurin (thiamine), ascorbic acid, bioflavonoid/citrin, biotin, calciferol, cholecalciferol, cyanocobalamin, ergocalciferol, folic acid, linoleic acid, linolenic acid, menadione, nicotinic acid (niacin), pantothenic acid, phylloquinone, pteroic acid, pyridoxine (adermin), retinol, riboflavin, tocopherol.

vitriolic *adj* bitter, abusive, virulent, vicious, venomous, malicious, caustic, biting, sardonic, mordant, scathing, destructive.

vivacious *adj* lively, animated, spirited, high-spirited, effervescent, ebullient, cheerful, sparkling, bubbly, light-hearted.

vivid *adj* 1 BRIGHT, colourful, intense, strong, rich, vibrant, brilliant, glowing, dazzling, vigorous, expressive, dramatic, flamboyant, animated, lively, lifelike, spirited. 2 MEMORABLE, powerful, graphic, clear, distinct, striking, sharp, realistic.
🖘 1 colourless, dull. 2 vague.

vocabulary *n* language, words, idiom, glossary, lexicon, dictionary, word-book, thesaurus.

vocal *adj* 1 SPOKEN, said, oral, uttered, voiced. 2 ARTICULATE, eloquent, expressive, noisy, clamorous, shrill, strident, loud, outspoken, frank, forthright, plain-spoken.
🖘 1 unspoken. 2 inarticulate.

vocation *n* calling, pursuit, career, métier, mission, profession, trade, line, employment, work, role, post, job, business, office.

vociferous *adj* noisy, vocal, clamorous, loud, obstreperous, strident, vehement, thundering, shouting.
🖘 quiet.

vogue *n* fashion, mode, style, craze, popularity, trend, prevalence, acceptance, custom, fad (*infml*), the latest (*infml*), the rage (*infml*), the thing (*infml*).

voice *n* 1 SPEECH, utterance, articulation, language, words, sound, tone, intonation, inflection, expression, mouthpiece, medium, instrument, organ. 2 SAY, vote, opinion, view, decision, option, will.
➤ *v* express, say, utter, air, articulate, speak of, verbalize, assert, convey, disclose, divulge, declare, enunciate.

void *adj* 1 EMPTY, emptied, free, unfilled, unoccupied, vacant, clear, bare, blank, drained. 2 ANNULLED, inoperative, invalid, cancelled, ineffective, futile, useless, vain, worthless.

■ **1** full. **2** valid.

➤ *n* emptiness, vacuity, vacuum, chasm, blank, blankness, space, lack, want, cavity, gap, hollow, opening.

volatile *adj* changeable, inconstant, unstable, variable, mutable, erratic, temperamental, unsteady, unsettled, fickle, mercurial, unpredictable, capricious, restless, giddy, flighty, up and down (*infml*), lively.
■ constant, steady.

volcano

> *The world's active volcanoes include*: Mayon (Philippines); Hudson (Chile); Kilauea (Hawaii); Pinatubo, Mt (Philippines); Vulcano (Italy), St Helens, Mt (USA); Etna (Italy); Ruapehu (New Zealand); Stromboli (Italy); Klyuchevskoy (Russia); Mauna Loa (Hawaii); Nyamuragira (Zaire); Hekla (Iceland); Krakatoa (Sumatra); Taal (Philippines); Vesuvius (Italy).

volley *n* barrage, bombardment, hail, shower, burst, blast, discharge, explosion.

voluble *adj* fluent, glib, articulate, loquacious (*fml*), talkative, forthcoming, garrulous.

volume *n* **1** BULK, size, capacity, dimensions, amount, mass, quantity, aggregate, amplitude, body. **2** BOOK, tome, publication.

voluminous *adj* roomy, capacious, ample, spacious, billowing, vast, bulky, huge, large.

voluntary *adj* **1** FREE, gratuitous, optional, spontaneous, unforced, willing, unpaid, honorary. **2** CONSCIOUS, deliberate, purposeful, intended, intentional, wilful.
■ **1** compulsory. **2** involuntary.

volunteer *v* offer, propose, put forward, proffer, present, suggest, step forward, advance.

voluptuous *adj* **1** SENSUAL, licentious, luxurious. **2** EROTIC, shapely, curvy (*infml*), sexy (*infml*), seductive, provocative, enticing.

vomit *v* be sick, bring up, heave, retch, throw up (*infml*), puke (*infml*), hurl (*sl*).

vote *n* ballot, poll, election, franchise, referendum.

➤ *v* elect, ballot, choose, opt, plump for, declare, return.

vouch for guarantee, support, back, endorse, confirm, certify, affirm, assert, attest to, speak for, swear to, uphold.

vow *v* promise, pledge, swear, dedicate, devote, profess, consecrate, affirm.

➤ *n* promise, oath, pledge.

voyage *n* journey, trip, passage, expedition, crossing.

vulgar *adj* **1** TASTELESS, flashy, gaudy, tawdry, cheap and nasty (*infml*), trashy. **2** UNREFINED, uncouth, coarse, common, crude, ill-bred, impolite, indecorous. **3** INDECENT, suggestive, risqué, rude, indelicate. **4** ORDINARY, general, popular, vernacular.
■ **1** tasteful. **2** refined, correct. **3** decent.

vulnerable *adj* unprotected, exposed, defenceless, susceptible, weak, sensitive, wide open.
■ protected, strong.

Ww

wad *n* chunk, plug, roll, ball, wodge (*infml*), lump, hunk, mass, block.

waddle *v* toddle, totter, wobble, sway, rock, shuffle, shamble.

waffle *v* jabber, prattle, blather, rabbit on (*infml*), witter on (*infml*).
➤ *n* blather, prattle, wordiness, padding, nonsense, gobbledygook (*infml*), hot air (*infml*).

waft *v* drift, float, blow, transport, transmit.
➤ *n* breath, puff, draught, current, breeze, scent, whiff.

wag *v* shake, waggle, wave, sway, swing, bob, nod, wiggle, oscillate, flutter, vibrate, quiver, rock.

wage *n* pay, fee, earnings, salary, wage-packet, payment, stipend, remuneration, emolument (*fml*), allowance, reward, hire, compensation, recompense.
➤ *v* carry on, conduct, engage in, undertake, practise, pursue.

waif *n* orphan, stray, foundling.

wail *v* moan, cry, howl, lament, weep, complain, yowl (*infml*).
➤ *n* moan, cry, howl, lament, complaint, weeping.

wait *v* delay, linger, hold back, hesitate, pause, hang around, hang fire, remain, rest, stay.
E3 proceed, go ahead.
➤ *n* hold-up, hesitation, delay, interval, pause, halt.

waive *v* renounce, relinquish, forgo, resign, surrender, yield.

wake¹ *v* **1** RISE, get up, arise, rouse, came to, bring round. **2** STIMULATE, stir, activate, arouse, animate, excite, fire, galvanize.
E3 **1** sleep.
➤ *n* funeral, death-watch, vigil, watch.

wake² *n* trail, track, path, aftermath, backwash, wash, rear, train, waves.

walk

> *Ways to describe walking include*: amble, clump, crawl, creep, dodder, go by shanks's pony (*infml*), hike, hobble, hoof it (*infml*), limp, lope, lurch, march, mince, mooch (*infml*), pace, pad, paddle, parade, patter, perambulate (*fml*), plod, potter, promenade, prowl, ramble, roam, saunter, scuttle, shamble, shuffle, slink, sneak, stagger, stalk, steal, step, stomp, stretch one's legs (*infml*), stride, stroll, strut, stumble, swagger, tiptoe, toddle (*infml*), totter, traipse, tramp, trample, tread, trek, trip, troop, trot, trudge, trundle, waddle, wade, wander, yomp (*infml*).

n **1** *he has an odd walk*: carriage, gait, step, pace, stride. **2** *go for a walk*: stroll, amble, ramble, saunter, march, hike, tramp, trek, traipse, trudge, trail. **3** *a tree-lined walk*: footpath, path, walkway, avenue, pathway, promenade, alley, esplanade, lane, pavement, sidewalk.
◇ **walk of life** field, area, sphere, line, activity, arena, course, pursuit, calling, métier, career, vocation, profession, trade.

walker *n* pedestrian, rambler, hiker.

walk-out *n* strike, stoppage, industrial action, protest, rebellion, revolt.

walkover *n* pushover (*infml*), doddle (*infml*), child's play, piece of cake (*infml*), cinch (*infml*).

wall

> **Types of wall and famous walls include**: abutment, Antonine Wall, bailey, barricade, barrier, Berlin Wall, block, breeze-block wall, brick wall, bulkhead, bulwark, buttress, cavity wall, curtain wall, dam, dike, divider, embankment, enclosure wall, fence, flying buttress, fortification, garden wall, Great Wall of China, Hadrian's Wall, hedge, inner wall, load-bearing wall, mural, obstacle, outer bailey, paling, palisade, parapet, partition, party wall, rampart, retaining wall, screen, sea wall, shield wall, stockade, stud partition, wall of death, Western Wall (or Wailing Wall).

wallow *v* **1** *wallow in mud*: loll, lie, roll, wade, welter, lurch, flounder, splash. **2** *wallow in nostalgia*: indulge, luxuriate, relish, revel, bask, enjoy, glory, delight.

wand *n* rod, baton, staff, stick, sprig, mace, sceptre, twig.

wander *v* **1** ROAM, rove, ramble, meander, saunter, stroll, prowl, drift, range, stray, straggle. **2** DIGRESS, diverge, deviate, depart, go astray, swerve, veer, err. **3** RAMBLE, rave, babble, gibber.
> *n* excursion, ramble, stroll, saunter, meander, prowl, cruise.

wanderer *n* itinerant, traveller, voyager, drifter, rover, rambler, stroller, stray, straggler, ranger, nomad, gypsy, vagrant, vagabond, rolling stone (*infml*).

wane *v* diminish, decrease, decline, weaken, subside, fade, dwindle, ebb, lessen, abate, sink, drop, taper off, dim, droop, contract, shrink, fail, wither.
₽ increase, wax.

wangle (*infml*) *v* manipulate, arrange, contrive, engineer, fix, scheme, manoeuvre, work, pull off, manage, fiddle (*infml*).

want *v* **1** DESIRE, wish, crave, covet, fancy, long for, pine for, yearn for, hunger for, thirst for. **2** NEED, require, demand, lack, miss, call for.

> *n* **1** DESIRE, demand, longing, requirement, wish, need, appetite. **2** LACK, dearth, insufficiency, deficiency, shortage, inadequacy. **3** POVERTY, privation, destitution.

wanting *adj* **1** ABSENT, missing, lacking, short, insufficient. **2** INADEQUATE, imperfect, faulty, defective, flawed, shoddy, substandard, poor, deficient, unsatisfactory.
₽ **1** sufficient. **2** adequate.

wanton *adj* malicious, immoral, shameless, arbitrary, unprovoked, unjustifiable, unrestrained, rash, reckless, wild.

war *n* warfare, hostilities, fighting, battle, combat, conflict, strife, struggle, bloodshed, contest, contention, enmity.
₽ peace, ceasefire.

> **Types of war include**: ambush, armed conflict, assault, attack, battle, biological warfare, blitz, blitzkrieg, bombardment, chemical warfare, civil war, Cod wars, cold war, counter-attack, engagement, germ warfare, guerrilla warfare, holy war, hot war, invasion, jihad, jungle warfare, limited war, manoeuvres, nuclear war, Opium Wars, private war, resistance, skirmish, state of siege, struggle, total war, trade war, trench warfare, war of attrition, war of nerves, world war.

> **Famous wars include**: American Civil War (Second American Revolution), American Revolution (War of Independence), Boer War, Crimean War, Crusades, English Civil War, Falklands War, Franco-Prussian War, Gulf War, Hundred Years War, Indian Wars, Iran-Iraq War, Korean War, Mexican War, Napoleonic War, Peasants' War, Russo-Finnish War (Winter War), Russo-Japanese War, Russo-Turkish Wars, Seven Years War, Six-Day War, Spanish-American War, Spanish-American Wars of Independence, Spanish Civil War, Suez Crisis, Thirty Years War, Vietnam War, War of 1812, War of the Pacific, Wars of

the Roses, World War I (the Great War), World War II.

➤ *v* wage war, fight, take up arms, battle, clash, combat, strive, skirmish, struggle, contest, contend.

ward *n* 1 ROOM, apartment, unit. 2 DIVISION, area, district, quarter, precinct, zone. 3 CHARGE, dependant, protégé(e), minor.

◇ **ward off** avert, fend off, deflect, parry, repel, stave off, thwart, beat off, forestall, evade, turn away, block, avoid.

warden *n* keeper, custodian, guardian, warder, caretaker, curator, ranger, steward, watchman, superintendent, administrator, janitor.

warder *n* jailer, keeper, prison officer, guard, wardress, custodian.

wardrobe *n* 1 CUPBOARD, closet. 2 CLOTHES, outfit, attire.

warehouse *n* store, storehouse, depot, depository, repository, stockroom, entrepot.

wares *n* goods, merchandise, commodities, stock, products, produce, stuff.

warfare *n* war, fighting, hostilities, battle, arms, combat, strife, struggle, passage of arms, contest, conflict, contention, discord, blows.
🖪 peace.

warlike *adj* belligerent, aggressive, bellicose, pugnacious, combative, bloodthirsty, war-mongering, hawkish, militaristic, hostile, antagonistic, unfriendly.
🖪 friendly, peaceable.

warm *adj* 1 HEATED, tepid, lukewarm. 2 ARDENT, passionate, fervent, vehement, earnest, zealous. 3 *warm colours*: rich, intense, mellow, cheerful. 4 FRIENDLY, amiable, cordial, affable, kindly, genial, hearty, hospitable, sympathetic, affectionate, tender. 5 FINE, sunny, balmy, temperate, close.
🖪 1 cool. 2 indifferent. 3 cold. 4 unfriendly. 5 cool.

➤ *v* 1 HEAT (UP), reheat, melt, thaw. 2

ANIMATE, interest, please, delight, stimulate, stir, rouse, excite.
🖪 1 cool.

warmth *n* 1 WARMNESS, heat. 2 FRIENDLINESS, affection, cordiality, geniality, hospitality, tenderness. 3 ARDOUR, enthusiasm, passion, fervour, zeal, eagerness.
🖪 1 coldness. 2 unfriendliness. 3 indifference.

warn *v* caution, alert, admonish, advise, notify, counsel, put on one's guard, inform, tip off (*infml*).

warning *n* 1 CAUTION, alert, admonition, advice, notification, notice, advance notice, counsel, hint, lesson, alarm, threat, tip-off (*infml*). 2 OMEN, augury, premonition, presage, sign, signal, portent.

warp *v* twist, bend, contort, deform, distort, kink, misshape, pervert, corrupt, deviate.
🖪 straighten.

➤ *n* twist, bend, contortion, deformation, distortion, bias, kink, irregularity, turn, bent, defect, deviation, quirk, perversion.

warrant *n* authorization, authority, sanction, permit, permission, licence, guarantee, warranty, security, pledge, commission, voucher.

➤ *v* 1 GUARANTEE, pledge, certify, assure, declare, affirm, vouch for, answer for, underwrite, uphold, endorse. 2 AUTHORIZE, entitle, empower, sanction, permit, allow, license, justify, excuse, approve, call for, commission, necessitate, require.

wary *adj* cautious, guarded, careful, chary, on one's guard, on the lookout, prudent, distrustful, suspicious, heedful, attentive, alert, watchful, vigilant, wide-awake.
🖪 unwary, careless, heedless.

wash *v* 1 CLEAN, cleanse, launder, scrub, swab down, rinse, swill. 2 BATHE, bath, shower, douche, shampoo.

➤ *n* 1 CLEANING, cleansing, bath, bathe, laundry, laundering, scrub, shower, shampoo, washing, rinse. **2** FLOW, sweep, wave, swell.

wash-out (*infml*) *n* failure, disaster, disappointment, fiasco, flop (*infml*), debacle.

🖃 success, triumph.

waste *v* **1** SQUANDER, misspend, misuse, fritter away, dissipate, lavish, spend, throw away, blow (*infml*). **2** CONSUME, erode, exhaust, drain, destroy, spoil.

🖃 **1** economize. **2** preserve.

➤ *n* **1** SQUANDERING, dissipation, prodigality, wastefulness, extravagance, loss. **2** MISAPPLICATION, misuse, abuse, neglect. **3** RUBBISH, refuse, trash, garbage, leftovers, debris, dregs, effluent, litter, scrap, slops, offscouring(s), dross.

➤ *adj* **1** USELESS, worthless, unwanted, unused, left-over, superfluous, supernumerary, extra, unnecessary. **2** BARREN, desolate, empty, uninhabited, bare, devastated, uncultivated, unprofitable, wild, dismal, dreary.

wasted *adj* **1** UNNECESSARY, needless, useless, pointless. **2** EMACIATED, gaunt, withered, shrivelled, washed-out, spent.

🖃 **1** necessary. **2** robust.

wasteful *adj* extravagant, spendthrift, prodigal, profligate, uneconomical, thriftless, unthrifty, ruinous, lavish, improvident.

🖃 economical, thrifty.

wasteland *n* wilderness, desert, barrenness, waste, wild(s), void.

watch *v* **1** OBSERVE, see, look at, regard, note, notice, mark, stare at, peer at, gaze at, view. **2** GUARD, look after, keep an eye on, mind, protect, superintend, take care of, keep. **3** PAY ATTENTION, be careful, take heed, look out.

➤ *n* **1** TIMEPIECE, chronometer. **2** VIGILANCE, watchfulness, vigil, observation, surveillance, notice, lookout, attention, heed, alertness, inspection, supervision.

Types of watch include: chronograph, digital watch, fob watch, pendant watch, repeating watch, ring watch, stopwatch, wristwatch.

◇ **watch out** notice, be vigilant, look out, keep one's eyes open.

◇ **watch over** guard, protect, stand guard over, keep an eye on, look after, mind, shield, defend, shelter, preserve.

watchdog *n* **1** GUARD DOG, house-dog. **2** MONITOR, inspector, scrutineer, vigilante, ombudsman, guardian, custodian, protector.

watcher *n* spectator, observer, onlooker, looker-on, viewer, lookout, spy, witness.

watchful *adj* vigilant, attentive, heedful, observant, alert, guarded, on one's guard, wide awake, suspicious, wary, chary, cautious.

🖃 unobservant, inattentive.

watchman *n* guard, security guard, caretaker, custodian.

water *n* rain, sea, ocean, lake, river, stream.

➤ *v* wet, moisten, dampen, soak, spray, sprinkle, irrigate, drench, flood, hose.

🖃 dry out, parch.

◇ **water down** dilute, thin, water, weaken, adulterate, mix, tone down, soften, qualify.

waterfall *n* fall, cascade, chute, cataract, torrent.

watertight *adj* **1** WATERPROOF, sound, hermetic. **2** IMPREGNABLE, unassailable, airtight, flawless, foolproof, firm, incontrovertible.

🖃 **1** leaky.

watery *adj* **1** LIQUID, liquefied, fluid, moist, wet, damp. **2** WEAK, watered-down, diluted, insipid, tasteless, thin, runny, soggy, flavourless, bland, washy, wishy-washy (*infml*).

🖃 **1** dry.

wave *v* **1** BECKON, gesture, gesticulate, indicate, sign, signal, direct. **2** BRANDISH, flourish, flap, flutter, shake, sway, swing, waft, quiver, ripple.

➤ *n* **1** BREAKER, roller, billow, ripple, tidal

wave, wavelet, undulation, white horse (*infml*). **2** SURGE, sweep, swell, upsurge, ground swell, current, drift, movement, rush, tendency, trend, stream, flood, outbreak, rash.

waver *v* **1** VACILLATE, falter, hesitate, dither, dodder, fluctuate, vary, seesaw. **2** OSCILLATE, shake, sway, wobble, tremble, totter, rock.
⊟ 1 decide.

wavy *adj* undulating, rippled, curly, curvy, ridged, sinuous, winding, zigzag.

wax *v* grow, increase, rise, swell, balloon, develop, enlarge, expand, magnify, mount, fill out, become.
⊟ decrease, wane.

way *n* **1** METHOD, approach, manner, technique, procedure, means, mode, system, fashion. **2** CUSTOM, practice, habit, usage, characteristic, trait, idiosyncrasy, style, conduct, nature. **3** DIRECTION, course, route, path, road, channel, access, avenue, track, passage, highway, street, thoroughfare, lane.
◇ **by the way** incidentally, in passing.

wayward *adj* wilful, capricious, perverse, contrary, changeable, fickle, unpredictable, stubborn, self-willed, unmanageable, headstrong, obstinate, disobedient, rebellious, insubordinate, intractable (*fml*), unruly, incorrigible.
⊟ tractable, good-natured.

weak *adj* **1** FEEBLE, frail, infirm, unhealthy, sickly, delicate, debilitated, exhausted, run-down, fragile, flimsy. **2** VULNERABLE, unprotected, unguarded, defenceless, exposed. **3** POWERLESS, impotent, spineless, cowardly, lily-livered (*infml*), indecisive, ineffectual, irresolute, poor, lacking, lame, inadequate, defective, deficient, inconclusive, unconvincing, untenable. **4** FAINT, slight, low, soft, muffled, dull, imperceptible. **5** INSIPID, tasteless, watery, thin, diluted, runny.
⊟ 1 strong. **2** secure. **3** powerful. **4** strong. **5** strong.

weaken *v* **1** ENFEEBLE, exhaust, debilitate, sap, undermine, dilute,

diminish, lower, lessen, reduce, moderate, mitigate, temper, soften (up), thin, water down. **2** TIRE, flag, fail, give way, droop, fade, abate, ease up, dwindle.
⊟ 1 strengthen.

weakness *n* **1** FEEBLENESS, debility, infirmity, impotence, frailty, powerlessness, vulnerability. **2** FAULT, failing, flaw, shortcoming, blemish, defect, deficiency, foible. **3** LIKING, inclination, fondness, penchant, passion, soft spot (*infml*).
⊟ 1 strength. **2** strength. **3** dislike.

wealth *n* **1** MONEY, cash, riches, assets, affluence, prosperity, funds, mammon, fortune, capital, opulence, means, substance, resources, goods, possessions, property, estate. **2** ABUNDANCE, plenty, bounty, fullness, profusion, store.
⊟ 1 poverty.

wealthy *adj* rich, prosperous, affluent, well-off, moneyed, opulent, comfortable, well-heeled, well-to-do, flush (*infml*), loaded (*sl*), rolling in it (*infml*).
⊟ poor, impoverished.

weapon

Weapons include: gun, airgun, pistol, revolver, automatic, Colt®, Luger®, magnum, Mauser, six-gun, six-shooter, rifle, air rifle, Winchester® rifle, carbine, shotgun, blunderbuss, musket, elephant gun, machine-gun, kalashnikov, submachine gun, Uzi, tommy-gun, sten gun, Bren gun, cannon, field gun, Gatling gun, howitzer, mortar, turret gun; knife, bowie knife, flick-knife, stiletto, dagger, dirk, poniard, sword, épée, foil, rapier, sabre, scimitar, bayonet, broadsword, claymore, lance, spear, pike, machete; bomb, atom bomb, H-bomb, cluster bomb, depth-charge, incendiary bomb, Mills bomb, mine, landmine, napalm bomb, thermobaric bomb, time bomb; bow and arrow, longbow, crossbow, blowpipe, catapult, boomerang, sling, harpoon, bolas, rocket, bazooka, ballistic missile, Cruise missile, Exocet®, Scud (*infml*), torpedo, hand grenade, flame-thrower; battleaxe, pole-axe, halberd, tomahawk, cosh, cudgel, knuckleduster, shillelagh, truncheon; gas, CS gas, mustard gas, nerve gas, tear gas.

wear *v* **1** DRESS IN, have on, put on, don, sport, carry, bear, display, show. **2** DETERIORATE, erode, corrode, consume, fray, rub, abrade, waste, grind.
➤ *n* **1** CLOTHES, clothing, dress, outfit, garments, costume, attire, apparel (*fml*). **2** DETERIORATION, erosion, corrosion, wear and tear, friction, abrasion.
◇ **wear off** decrease, abate, dwindle, diminish, subside, wane, weaken, fade, lessen, ebb, peter out, disappear.
🖙 increase.
◇ **wear out 1** EXHAUST, fatigue, tire (out), enervate, sap. **2** DETERIORATE, wear through, erode, impair, consume, fray.

wearing *adj* exhausting, fatiguing, tiresome, tiring, wearisome, trying, taxing, oppressive, irksome, annoying, exasperating.
🖙 refreshing.

weary *adj* tired, exhausted, fatigued, sleepy, worn out, drained, drowsy, jaded, all in (*infml*), done in (*infml*), fagged out (*infml*), knackered (*infml*), dead beat (*sl*), dog-tired (*infml*), whacked (*infml*).
🖙 refreshed.

wearying *adj* tiring, fatiguing, exhausting, wearisome, wearing, taxing, trying.
🖙 refreshing.

weather *n* climate, conditions, temperature.

Types of weather include: breeze, wind, squall, gale, hurricane, tornado, typhoon, monsoon, cyclone, whirlwind, chinook, mistral, cloud, mist, dew, fog, smog, rain, drizzle, shower, deluge, downpour, rainbow, sunshine, heatwave, haze, drought,

storm, tempest, thunder, lightning, frost, hoar frost, hail, sleet, snow, snowstorm, ice, black ice, thaw, slush. *see also* **precipitation**; **wind**.

➤ *v* **1** ENDURE, survive, live through, come through, ride out, rise above, stick out, withstand, surmount, stand, brave, overcome, resist, pull through, suffer. **2** EXPOSE, toughen, season, harden.
🖙 **1** succumb.

weave *v* **1** INTERLACE, lace, plait, braid, intertwine, spin, knit, entwine, intercross, fuse, merge, unite. **2** CREATE, compose, construct, contrive, put together, fabricate. **3** WIND, twist, zigzag, criss-cross.

web *n* network, net, netting, lattice, mesh, meshwork, webbing, interlacing, weft, snare, tangle, trap.

wedding *n* marriage, matrimony, nuptials (*fml*), wedlock.
🖙 divorce.

wedge *n* lump, block, chunk, wodge, chock.
➤ *v* jam, cram, pack, ram, squeeze, stuff, push, lodge, block, thrust, crowd, force.

weed

Weeds include: annual nettle, bindweed, birdsfoot trefoil, bracken, broad-leaved dock, burnet saxifrage, Canadian pondweed, chickweed, cinquefoil, coltsfoot, common burdock, common chickweed, common persicaria, common plantain, common reed, couch grass, creeping buttercup, creeping thistle, creeping yellow cress, cudweed, curled dock, daisy, dandelion, deadnettle, dock, duckweed, fat hen, field wood rush, greater or rat-tailed plantain, ground elder, ground ivy, groundsel, hairy bittercress, horsetail, Japanese knotgrass, knapweed, knotgrass, large bindweed, lesser celandine, lesser yellow trefoil, liverwort, meadow grass, mind your own business, moss, mouse-ear chickweed, oxalis, pearlwort, perennial nettle, perennial oat-grass, petty spurge, pineapple weed, ragweed, ribwort, rough hawkbit, salad burnet, self-heal, shepherd's purse, sheep's sorrel, small bindweed, snakeweed, sow thistle, speedwell, spurge, stemless thistle, sun spurge, thale cress, vetch, white clover, willowherb, yarrow. *see also* **wild flowers**.

weedy (*infml*) *adj* thin, skinny, puny, scrawny, undersized, weak, feeble, frail, weak-kneed, insipid, wet (*infml*), wimpish (*infml*), wimpy (*infml*).
Ea strong.

weep *v* cry, sob, moan, lament, wail, mourn, grieve, bawl, blubber, snivel, whimper, blub (*infml*).
Ea rejoice.

weigh *v* **1** BEAR DOWN, oppress, burden. **2** CONSIDER, contemplate, evaluate, meditate on, mull over, ponder, think over, examine, reflect on, deliberate.
◇ **weigh down** oppress, overload, load, burden, bear down, weigh upon, press down, get down (*infml*), depress, afflict, trouble, worry.
Ea lighten, hearten.
◇ **weigh up** assess, examine, size up, balance, consider, contemplate, deliberate, mull over, ponder, think over, discuss, chew over (*infml*).

weight *n* **1** HEAVINESS, gravity, burden, load, pressure, mass, force, ballast, tonnage, poundage. **2** IMPORTANCE, gravitas, seriousness, significance, substance, consequence, impact, moment, influence, value, authority, clout (*infml*), power, preponderance, consideration.
Ea 1 lightness.
➤ *v* **1** LOAD, weigh down, oppress, burden, handicap. **2** BIAS, unbalance, slant, prejudice.

weighty *adj* **1** HEAVY, burdensome, substantial, bulky. **2** IMPORTANT, significant, consequential, crucial, critical, momentous, serious, grave, solemn. **3** DEMANDING, difficult, exacting, taxing.
Ea 1 light. **2** unimportant.

weird *adj* strange, uncanny, bizarre, eerie, creepy, supernatural, unnatural, ghostly, freakish, mysterious, queer, grotesque, spooky (*infml*), far-out (*infml*), way-out (*infml*).
Ea normal, usual.

welcome *adj* acceptable, desirable, pleasing, pleasant, agreeable, gratifying, appreciated, delightful, refreshing.
Ea unwelcome.
➤ *n* reception, greeting, salutation (*fml*), acceptance, hospitality, red carpet (*infml*).
➤ *v* greet, hail, receive, salute, meet, accept, approve of, embrace.
Ea reject, snub.

weld *v* fuse, unite, bond, join, solder, bind, connect, seal, link, cement.
Ea separate.

welfare *n* well-being, health, prosperity, happiness, benefit, good, advantage, interest, profit, success.

well¹ *n* spring, well-spring, fountain, fount, source, reservoir, well-head, waterhole.

Types of well include: artesian well, borehole, draw-well, gas well, geyser, gusher, hot spring, inkwell, lift shaft, mineral spring, oil well, pump-well, stairwell, thermal spring, waterhole, wishing well.

➤ *v* flow, spring, surge, gush, stream, brim over, jet, spout, spurt, swell, pour, flood, ooze, run, trickle, rise, seep.

well² *adv* rightly, correctly, properly, skilfully, ably, expertly, successfully, adequately, sufficiently, suitably, easily, satisfactorily, thoroughly, greatly, fully, considerably, completely, agreeably, pleasantly, happily, kindly, favourably, splendidly, substantially, comfortably, readily, carefully, clearly, highly, deeply, justly.
Ea badly, inadequately, incompetently, wrongly.
➤ *adj* **1** HEALTHY, in good health, fit, able-bodied, sound, robust, strong, thriving,

flourishing. **2** SATISFACTORY, right, all right, good, pleasing, proper, agreeable, fine, lucky, fortunate.
☒ **1** ill. **2** bad.

well-balanced *adj* **1** RATIONAL, reasonable, level-headed, well-adjusted, stable, sensible, sane, sound, sober, together (*sl*). **2** SYMMETRICAL, even, harmonious.
☒ **1** unbalanced. **2** asymmetrical.

well-being *n* welfare, happiness, comfort, good.

well-bred *adj* well-mannered, polite, well-brought-up, mannerly, courteous, civil, refined, cultivated, cultured, genteel.
☒ ill-bred.

well-dressed *adj* smart, well-groomed, elegant, fashionable, chic, stylish, neat, trim, spruce, tidy.
☒ badly dressed, scruffy.

well-known *adj* famous, renowned, celebrated, famed, eminent, notable, noted, illustrious, familiar.
☒ unknown.

well-off *adj* rich, wealthy, affluent, prosperous, well-to-do, moneyed, loaded (*infml*), thriving, successful, comfortable, fortunate.
☒ poor, badly-off.

well-thought-of *adj* respected, highly regarded, esteemed, admired, honoured, revered.
☒ despised.

well-worn *adj* timeworn, stale, tired, trite, overused, unoriginal, hackneyed, commonplace, stereotyped, threadbare, corny (*infml*).
☒ original.

wet *adj* **1** DAMP, moist, soaked, soaking, sodden, saturated, soggy, sopping, watery, waterlogged, drenched, dripping, spongy, dank, clammy. **2** RAINING, rainy, showery, teeming, pouring, drizzling, humid. **3** (*infml*) WEAK, feeble, weedy (*infml*), wimpish (*infml*), wimpy (*infml*), spineless, soft, ineffectual, namby-pamby, irresolute, timorous.

☒ **1** dry, arid. **2** dry, fine. **3** strong.
➤ *n* wetness, moisture, damp, dampness, liquid, water, clamminess, condensation, humidity, rain, drizzle.
☒ dryness.
➤ *v* moisten, damp, dampen, soak, saturate, drench, steep, water, irrigate, spray, splash, sprinkle, imbue, dip.
☒ dry.

whack *v* hit, strike, smack, thrash, slap, beat, bash (*infml*), bang, cuff, thump, box, buffet, rap, wallop (*infml*), belt (*infml*), clobber (*infml*), clout (*infml*), sock (*infml*).
➤ *n* smack, slap, blow, hit, rap, stroke, thump, cuff, box, bang, clout (*infml*), bash (*infml*), wallop (*infml*).

wharf *n* dock, quay, quayside, jetty, landing-stage, dockyard, marina, pier.

wheedle *v* cajole, coax, persuade, inveigle, charm, flatter, entice, court, draw.
☒ force.

wheel *n* turn, revolution, circle, rotation, gyration, pivot, roll, spin, twirl, whirl.

> *Types of wheel include*: balance wheel, big wheel, buff wheel, cartwheel, castor, Catherine wheel, charka, cogwheel, crown wheel, drive wheel, escape wheel, Ferris wheel, flywheel, gearwheel, idle wheel, mill wheel, paddle wheel, potter's wheel, prayer wheel, ratchet wheel, roulette wheel, spinning jenny, spinning wheel, sprocket, spur gear, steering wheel, wagon wheel, water wheel, wheel of fortune, worm wheel.

➤ *v* turn, rotate, circle, gyrate, orbit, spin, twirl, whirl, swing, roll, revolve, swivel.

wheeze *v* pant, gasp, cough, hiss, rasp, whistle.

whereabouts *n* location, position, place, situation, site, vicinity.

whet *v* **1** SHARPEN, hone, file, grind. **2** STIMULATE, stir, rouse, arouse, provoke, kindle, quicken, incite, awaken, increase.
☒ **1** blunt. **2** dampen.

whiff *n* breath, puff, hint, trace, blast, draught, odour, smell, aroma, sniff, scent, reek, stink, stench.

whim *n* fancy, caprice, notion, quirk, freak, humour, conceit, fad, vagary, urge.

whimper *v* cry, sob, weep, snivel, whine, grizzle, mewl, moan, whinge (*infml*).
➤ *n* sob, snivel, whine, moan.

whimsical *adj* fanciful, capricious, playful, impulsive, eccentric, funny, droll, curious, queer, unusual, weird, odd, peculiar, quaint, dotty (*infml*).

whine *n* **1** CRY, sob, whimper, moan, wail. **2** COMPLAINT, grumble, grouse, gripe (*infml*), grouch (*infml*).
➤ *v* **1** CRY, sob, whimper, grizzle, moan, wail. **2** COMPLAIN, carp, grumble, whinge (*infml*), gripe (*infml*), grouch (*infml*), kvetch (*US sl*).

whip *v* **1** BEAT, flog, lash, flagellate, scourge, birch, cane, strap, thrash, punish, chastise, discipline, castigate (*fml*). **2** PULL, jerk, snatch, whisk, dash, dart, rush, tear, flit, flash, fly. **3** GOAD, drive, spur, push, urge, stir, rouse, agitate, incite, provoke, instigate.
➤ *n* lash, scourge, switch, birch, cane, horsewhip, riding-crop, cat-o'-nine-tails.

whirl *v* swirl, spin, turn, twist, twirl, pivot, pirouette, swivel, wheel, rotate, revolve, reel, roll, gyrate, circle.
➤ *n* **1** SPIN, twirl, twist, gyration, revolution, pirouette, swirl, turn, wheel, rotation, circle, reel, roll. **2** CONFUSION, daze, flurry, commotion, agitation, bustle, hubbub, hurly-burly, giddiness, tumult, uproar, turmoil.

whirlwind *n* tornado, cyclone, vortex.
➤ *adj* hasty, impulsive, quick, rapid, speedy, swift, lightning, headlong, impetuous, rash.
F3 deliberate, slow.

whisk *v* **1** WHIP, beat. **2** DART, dash, rush, hurry, speed, hasten, race. **3** BRUSH, sweep, flick, wipe, twitch.

whisper *v* **1** MURMUR, mutter, mumble, breathe, hiss, rustle, sigh. **2** HINT, intimate, insinuate, gossip, divulge.
F3 **1** shout.
➤ *n* **1** MURMUR, undertone, sigh, hiss, rustle. **2** HINT, suggestion, suspicion, breath, whiff, rumour, report, innuendo, insinuation, trace, tinge, soupçon, buzz.

white *adj* **1** PALE, pallid, wan, ashen, colourless, anaemic, pasty. **2** LIGHT, snowy, milky, creamy, ivory, hoary, silver, grey. **3** PURE, immaculate, spotless, stainless, undefiled.
F3 **1** ruddy. **2** dark. **3** defiled.

whiten *v* bleach, blanch, whitewash, pale, fade.
F3 blacken, darken.

whittle *v* **1** CARVE, cut, scrape, shave, trim, pare, hew, shape. **2** ERODE, eat away, wear away, diminish, consume, reduce, undermine.

whole *adj* **1** COMPLETE, entire, integral, full, total, unabridged, uncut, undivided, unedited. **2** INTACT, unharmed, undamaged, unbroken, inviolate, perfect, in one piece, mint, unhurt. **3** WELL, healthy, fit, sound, strong.
F3 **1** partial. **2** damaged. **3** ill.
➤ *n* total, aggregate, sum total, entirety, all, fullness, totality, ensemble, entity, unit, lot, piece, everything.
F3 part.
◊ **on the whole** generally, mostly, in general, generally speaking, as a rule, for the most part, all in all, all things considered, by and large.

wholehearted *adj* unreserved, unstinting, unqualified, passionate, eager, zealous, enthusiastic, earnest, committed, dedicated, devoted, heartfelt, emphatic, warm, sincere, unfeigned, genuine, complete, true, real.
F3 half-hearted.

wholesale *adj* comprehensive, far-reaching, extensive, sweeping, wide-ranging, mass, broad, outright, total, massive, indiscriminate.
F3 partial.

wholesome *adj* **1** *wholesome food*:

healthy, hygienic, salubrious, sanitary, nutritious, nourishing, beneficial, salutary, invigorating, bracing. **2** *wholesome entertainment*: moral, decent, clean, proper, improving, edifying, uplifting, pure, virtuous, righteous, honourable, respectable. ☒ **1** unhealthy. **2** unwholesome.

wholly *adv* completely, entirely, fully, purely, absolutely, totally, utterly, comprehensively, altogether, perfectly, thoroughly, all, exclusively, only. ☒ partly.

wicked *adj* **1** EVIL, sinful, immoral, depraved, corrupt, vicious, unprincipled, iniquitous, heinous, debased, abominable, ungodly, unrighteous, shameful. **2** BAD, unpleasant, harmful, offensive, vile, worthless, difficult, dreadful, distressing, awful, atrocious, severe, intense, nasty, injurious, troublesome, terrible, foul, fierce. **3** NAUGHTY, mischievous, roguish. ☒ **1** good, upright. **2** harmless.

wide *adj* **1** BROAD, roomy, spacious, vast, immense. **2** DILATED, expanded, full. **3** EXTENSIVE, wide-ranging, comprehensive, far-reaching, general, universal. **4** LOOSE, baggy. **5** OFF-TARGET, distant, remote. ☒ **1** narrow. **3** restricted. **5** near.
➤ *adv* **1** ASTRAY, off course, off target, off the mark. **2** FULLY, completely, all the way. ☒ **1** on target.

widen *v* distend, dilate, expand, extend, spread, stretch, enlarge, broaden. ☒ narrow.

widespread *adj* extensive, prevalent, rife, general, sweeping, universal, wholesale, far-reaching, unlimited, broad, common, pervasive, far-flung. ☒ limited.

width *n* breadth, diameter, wideness, compass, thickness, span, scope, range, measure, girth, beam, amplitude, extent, reach.

wield *v* **1** *wield a weapon*: brandish, flourish, swing, wave, handle, ply, manage, manipulate. **2** *wield power*: have, hold, possess, employ, exert, exercise, use, utilize, maintain, command.

wife *n* partner, spouse, mate, other half (*infml*), better half (*infml*), bride.

wild *adj* **1** UNTAMED, unbroken, undomesticated, feral, savage, barbarous, primitive, uncivilized, natural, ferocious, fierce. **2** UNCULTIVATED, desolate, waste, uninhabited. **3** UNRESTRAINED, unruly, unmanageable, violent, turbulent, rowdy, lawless, disorderly, riotous, boisterous. **4** STORMY, tempestuous, rough, blustery, choppy. **5** UNTIDY, unkempt, messy, dishevelled, tousled. **6** RECKLESS, rash, imprudent, foolish, foolhardy, impracticable, irrational, outrageous, preposterous, wayward, extravagant. **7** MAD, crazy (*infml*), frenzied, distraught, demented. ☒ **1** civilized, tame. **2** cultivated. **3** restrained. **4** calm. **5** tidy. **6** sensible. **7** sane.

wilderness *n* desert, wasteland, waste, wilds, jungle.

wild flower

> *Wild flowers include*: Aaron's rod, ale hoof, bird's foot trefoil, birthwort, bistort, black-eyed susan, bladder campion, bluebell, broomrape, butter-and-eggs, buttercup, campion, celandine, clary, clustered bellflower, clover, columbine, comfrey, common evening primrose, common mallow, common toadflax, cowslip, crane's bill, crowfoot, cuckoo flower, daisy, edelweiss, field cow-wheat, foxglove, goatsbeard, goldcup, goldenrod, great mullein, harebell, heartsease, heather, horsetail, lady's slipper, lady's smock, lungwort, marguerite, masterwort, moneywort, multiflora rose, New England aster, oxeye daisy, oxslip, pennyroyal, poppy, primrose, ragged robin, rock rose, rough-fruited cinquefoil, selfheal, shepherd's club, solomon's seal, stiff-haired sunflower,

stonecrop, teasel, toadflax, violet, water lily, white campion, wild chicory, wild endive, wild gladiolus, wild iris, wild orchid, wild pansy, wood anemone, yarrow, yellow rocket. *see also* **weed**.

wiles *n* trick, stratagem, ruse, ploy, device, contrivance, guile, stealth, manoeuvre, subterfuge, cunning, dodge (*infml*), deceit, cheating, trickery, fraud, craftiness, chicanery.
⊟ guilelessness.

wilful *adj* 1 DELIBERATE, conscious, intentional, voluntary, premeditated. 2 SELF-WILLED, obstinate, stubborn, pig-headed (*infml*), obdurate (*fml*), intransigent, inflexible, perverse, wayward, contrary.
⊟ 1 unintentional. 2 good-natured.

will *n* 1 VOLITION, choice, option, preference, decision, discretion. 2 WISH, desire, inclination, feeling, fancy, disposition, mind. 3 PURPOSE, resolve, resolution, determination, willpower, aim, intention, command.
➤ *v* 1 WANT, desire, choose, compel, command, decree, order, ordain. 2 BEQUEATH, leave, hand down, pass on, transfer, confer, dispose of.

willing *adj* disposed, inclined, agreeable, compliant, ready, prepared, consenting, content, amenable, biddable, pleased, well-disposed, favourable, happy, eager, enthusiastic.
⊟ unwilling, disinclined, reluctant.

wilt *v* droop, sag, wither, shrivel, flop, flag, dwindle, weaken, diminish, fail, fade, languish, ebb, sink, wane.
⊟ perk up.

wily *adj* shrewd, cunning, scheming, artful, crafty, foxy, intriguing, tricky, underhand, shifty, deceitful, deceptive, astute, sly, guileful, designing, crooked (*infml*), fly (*infml*).
⊟ guileless.

win *v* 1 BE VICTORIOUS, triumph, succeed, prevail, overcome, conquer, come first, carry off, finish first. 2 GAIN,

acquire, achieve, attain, accomplish, receive, procure, secure, obtain, get, earn, catch, net.
⊟ 1 fail, lose.
➤ *n* victory, triumph, conquest, success, mastery.
⊟ defeat.
◇ **win over** persuade, prevail upon, convince, influence, convert, sway, talk round, charm, allure, attract.

wind[1] *n* air, breeze, draught, gust, puff, breath, air-current, blast, current, bluster, gale, hurricane, tornado, cyclone.

> *Types of wind include*: anticyclone, austral wind, berg wind, bise, bora, Cape doctor, chinook, cyclone, doctor, east wind, El Niño, etesian, Favonian wind, föhn, gregale, harmattan, helm wind, khamsin, levant, libeccio, meltemi, mistral, monsoon, north wind, nor'wester, pampero, prevailing wind, samiel, simoom, sirocco, snoweater, southerly, southerly buster, trade wind, tramontana, westerly, wet chinook, williwaw, willy-willy, zephyr, zonda. *see also* **storm**.

wind[2] *v* coil, twist, turn, curl, curve, bend, loop, spiral, zigzag, twine, encircle, furl, deviate, meander, ramble, wreathe, roll, reel.
◇ **wind down** 1 SLOW (DOWN), slacken off, lessen, reduce, subside, diminish, dwindle, decline. 2 RELAX, unwind, quieten down, ease up, calm down, chill out (*infml*).
⊟ 1 increase.
◇ **wind up** 1 CLOSE (DOWN), end, conclude, terminate, finalize, finish, liquidate. 2 END UP, finish up, find oneself, settle. 3 (*infml*) ANNOY, irritate, disconcert, fool, trick, kid (*infml*).
⊟ 1 begin.

windfall *n* bonanza, godsend, jackpot, treasure-trove, stroke of luck, find.

window *n* pane, windowpane, light, opening.

> *Types of window include*: astragal, bay, bow, bull's eye, casement,

Catherine wheel, compass, decorated, dormer, double-glazed, early English, fanlight, French, lancet, louvre window, lucarne, mullioned window, Norman, oeil-de-boeuf, oriel, patio door, perpendicular, porthole, quarterlight, rose window, sash, secondary-glazed, shop window, skylight, sliding window, stained glass window, ticket window, windscreen.

windy *adj* breezy, blowy, blustery, squally, gusty, windswept, stormy, tempestuous.
⊟ calm.

wine

Types of wine include: alcohol-free, dry, brut, sec, demi-sec, sweet, sparkling, table wine, house wine; red wine, white wine, rosé, blush wine, fortified wine, mulled wine, tonic wine, vintage wine, plonk (*infml*); sherry, dry sherry, fino, medium sherry, amontillado, sweet sherry, oloroso; port, ruby, tawny, white port, vintage port.

Varieties of wine include: Alsace, Asti, Auslese, Beaujolais, Beaujolais Nouveau, Beaune, Bordeaux, Burgundy, cabernet sauvignon, Chablis, Chambertin, champagne, Chardonnay, Chianti, claret, Côtes du Rhône, Dão, Douro, Fitou, Frascati, Gewurztraminer, Graves, hock, Lambrusco, Liebfraumilch, Mâcon, Madeira, Malaga, Marsala, Mateus, Médoc, Merlot, moselle, Muscadet, muscatel, Niersteiner, retsina, Riesling, Rioja, Sauternes, Sekt, Shiraz, Soave, Spätlese, Tarragona, Valpolicella, vinho verde, Vouvray.

Sizes of wine bottles include: magnum, flagon, jeroboam, methuselah, rehoboam, salmanazar, balthazar, nebuchadnezzar.

wing *n* branch, arm, section, faction, group, grouping, flank, circle, coterie, set, segment, side, annexe, adjunct, extension.

wink *v* blink, flutter, glimmer, glint, twinkle, gleam, sparkle, flicker, flash.
➤ *n* **1** BLINK, flutter, sparkle, twinkle, glimmering, gleam, glint. **2** INSTANT, second, split second, flash.

winner *n* champion, victor, prizewinner, medallist, title-holder, world-beater, conqueror.
⊟ loser.

winning *adj* **1** CONQUERING, triumphant, unbeaten, undefeated, victorious, successful. **2** WINSOME, charming, attractive, captivating, taking, engaging, fetching, enchanting, endearing, delightful, amiable, alluring, lovely, pleasing, sweet.
⊟ 1 losing. **2** unappealing.

winnow *v* sift, separate, screen, divide, cull, select, part, fan.

wintry *adj* cold, chilly, bleak, cheerless, desolate, dismal, harsh, snowy, frosty, freezing, frozen, icy.

wipe *v* **1** RUB, clean, dry, dust, brush, mop, swab, sponge, clear. **2** REMOVE, erase, take away, take off.
◇ **wipe out** eradicate, obliterate, destroy, massacre, exterminate, annihilate, erase, expunge, raze, abolish, blot out, efface.

wiry *adj* muscular, sinewy, lean, tough, strong.
⊟ puny.

wisdom *n* discernment, penetration, sagacity, reason, sense, astuteness, comprehension, enlightenment, judgement, judiciousness, understanding, knowledge, learning, intelligence, erudition, foresight, prudence.
⊟ folly, stupidity.

wise *adj* **1** DISCERNING, sagacious, perceptive, rational, informed, well-informed, understanding, erudite, enlightened, knowing, intelligent, clever, aware, experienced. **2** WELL-ADVISED, judicious, prudent, reasonable, sensible, sound, long-sighted, shrewd, smart.

E 1 foolish, stupid. 2 ill-advised.

wish v 1 DESIRE, want, yearn, long, hanker, covet, crave, aspire, hope, hunger, thirst, prefer, need. 2 ASK, bid, require, order, instruct, direct, command.
➤ n 1 DESIRE, want, hankering, aspiration, inclination, hunger, thirst, liking, preference, yearning, yen (*infml*), urge, whim, hope. 2 REQUEST, bidding, order, command, will.

wisp n shred, strand, thread, twist, piece, lock.

wispy adj thin, straggly, frail, fine, attenuated, insubstantial, light, flimsy, fragile, delicate, ethereal, gossamer, faint.
E substantial.

wistful adj 1 THOUGHTFUL, pensive, musing, reflective, wishful, contemplative, dreamy, dreaming, meditative. 2 MELANCHOLY, sad, forlorn, disconsolate, longing, mournful.

wit n 1 HUMOUR, repartee, banter, facetiousness, drollery, jocularity, levity. 2 INTELLIGENCE, cleverness, brains, sense, reason, common sense, nous (*sl*), wisdom, understanding, judgement, insight, intellect. 3 HUMORIST, comedian, comic, satirist, joker, wag.
E 1 seriousness. 2 stupidity.

witch n sorceress, enchantress, occultist, magician, hag.

witchcraft n sorcery, magic, wizardry, wicca, occultism, the occult, the black art, black magic, enchantment, necromancy (*fml*), voodoo, spell, incantation, divination, conjuration.

withdraw v 1 RECOIL, shrink back, draw back, pull back. 2 RECANT, disclaim, take back, do a U-turn (*infml*), revoke, rescind, retract, cancel, abjure, recall, take away. 3 DEPART, go (away), absent oneself, retire, remove, leave, back out, fall back, drop out, retreat, secede. 4 DRAW OUT, extract, pull out.

withdrawal n 1 REPUDIATION, recantation, disclaimer, disavowal, revocation, recall, secession, abjuration. 2 DEPARTURE, exit, exodus, retirement, retreat. 3 EXTRACTION, removal.

withdrawn adj 1 RESERVED, unsociable, shy, introvert, quiet, retiring, aloof, detached, shrinking, uncommunicative, unforthcoming, taciturn, silent. 2 REMOTE, isolated, distant, secluded, out-of-the-way, private, hidden, solitary.
E 1 extrovert, outgoing.

wither v shrink, shrivel, dry, wilt, droop, decay, disintegrate, wane, perish, fade, languish, decline, waste.
E flourish, thrive.

withering adj 1 DESTRUCTIVE, deadly, death-dealing, devastating. 2 SCORNFUL, contemptuous, scathing, snubbing, humiliating, mortifying, wounding.
E 2 encouraging, supportive.

withhold v keep back, retain, hold back, suppress, restrain, repress, control, check, reserve, deduct, refuse, hide, conceal.
E give, accord.

withstand v resist, oppose, stand fast, stand one's ground, stand, stand up to, confront, brave, face, cope with, take on, thwart, defy, hold one's ground, hold out, last out, hold off, endure, bear, tolerate, put up with, survive, weather.
E give in, yield.

witness n 1 TESTIFIER, attestant, deponent (*fml*). 2 ONLOOKER, eyewitness, looker-on, observer, spectator, viewer, watcher, bystander.
➤ v 1 SEE, observe, notice, note, view, watch, look on, mark, perceive. 2 TESTIFY, attest (*fml*), bear witness, depose (*fml*), confirm, bear out, corroborate (*fml*). 3 ENDORSE, sign, countersign.

witty adj humorous, amusing, comic, sharp-witted, droll, whimsical, original, brilliant, clever, ingenious, lively, sparkling, funny, facetious, fanciful, jocular.
E dull, unamusing.

wizard n 1 SORCERER, magician,

warlock, enchanter, necromancer (*fml*), occultist, witch, conjurer. **2** (*infml*) EXPERT, adept, virtuoso, ace, master, maestro, prodigy, genius, star (*infml*), whiz (*infml*), hotshot (*infml*).

wizened *adj* shrivelled, shrunken, dried up, withered, wrinkled, gnarled, thin, worn, lined.

wobble *v* shake, oscillate, tremble, quake, sway, teeter, totter, rock, seesaw, vibrate, waver, dodder, fluctuate, hesitate, dither, vacillate, shilly-shally.

wobbly *adj* unstable, shaky, rickety, unsteady, wonky (*infml*), teetering, tottering, doddering, doddery, uneven, unbalanced, unsafe.
⊟ stable, steady.

woman *n* female, lady, girl, matriarch, maiden, maid.

womanly *adj* feminine, female, ladylike, womanish.

wonder *n* **1** MARVEL, phenomenon, miracle, prodigy, sight, spectacle, sensation, rarity, curiosity. **2** AWE, amazement, astonishment, admiration, wonderment, fascination, surprise, bewilderment.

> *The seven wonders of the world are*: Pyramids of Egypt, Hanging Gardens of Babylon, Statue of Zeus at Olympia, Temple of Artemis at Ephesus, Mausoleum of Halicarnassus, Colossus of Rhodes, Pharos of Alexandria.

➤ *v* **1** MEDITATE, speculate, ponder, ask oneself, question, conjecture (*fml*), puzzle, enquire, query, doubt, think. **2** MARVEL, gape, be amazed, be surprised.

wonderful *adj* **1** MARVELLOUS, magnificent, oustanding, excellent, superb, admirable, delightful, phenomenal, sensational, stupendous, tremendous, super (*infml*), terrific (*infml*), brilliant (*infml*), great (*infml*), fabulous (*infml*), fantastic (*infml*), stellar (*sl*). **2** AMAZING, astonishing, astounding, startling, surprising,

extraordinary, incredible, remarkable, staggering, jaw-dropping (*infml*), strange.
⊟ 1 appalling, dreadful. **2** ordinary.

woo *v* **1** *woo a lover*: court, chase, pursue. **2** *woo custom*: encourage, cultivate, attract, look for, seek.

wood *n* **1** TIMBER, lumber, planks. **2** FOREST, woods, woodland, trees, plantation, thicket, grove, coppice, copse, spinney.

> *Types of wood include*: timber, lumber (*US*), hardwood, softwood, heartwood, sapwood, seasoned wood, green wood, bitterwood, brushwood, cordwood, firewood, kindling, matchwood, plywood, pulpwood, whitewood, chipboard, hardboard; afrormosia, ash, balsa, beech, cedar, cherry, chestnut, cottonwood, deal, ebony, elm, iroko, mahogany, African mahogany, maple, oak, pine, redwood, rosewood, rubberwood, sandalwood, sapele, satinwood, sheesham, teak, walnut, willow. *see also* **tree**.

wooded *adj* forested, timbered, woody, tree-covered, sylvan (*fml*).

wooden *adj* **1** TIMBER, woody. **2** EMOTIONLESS, expressionless, awkward, clumsy, stilted, lifeless, spiritless, unemotional, stiff, rigid, leaden, deadpan, blank, empty, slow.
⊟ 2 lively.

wool *n* fleece, down, yarn.

woolly *adj* **1** WOOLLEN, fleecy, woolly-haired, downy, shaggy, fuzzy, frizzy.
2 UNCLEAR, ill-defined, hazy, blurred, confused, muddled, vague, indefinite, nebulous.
⊟ 2 clear, distinct.
➤ *n* jumper, sweater, jersey, pullover, cardigan.

word *n* **1** NAME, lexeme, term, expression, designation, utterance, vocable (*fml*). **2** CONVERSATION, chat, talk, discussion, consultation. **3** INFORMATION, news, report, communication, notice, message, bulletin, communiqué, statement, dispatch, declaration, comment, assertion, account, remark, advice, warning. **4** PROMISE, pledge, oath, assurance, vow, guarantee. **5** COMMAND, order, decree, commandment, authorization, go-ahead (*infml*), green light (*infml*).

➤ *v* phrase, express, couch, put, say, explain, write.

words *n* **1** ARGUMENT, dispute, quarrel, disagreement, altercation, bickering, row, squabble. **2** LYRICS, libretto, text, book.

wordy *adj* verbose, long-winded, loquacious (*fml*), garrulous, prolix (*fml*), rambling, diffuse, discursive.
▪ concise.

work *n* **1** OCCUPATION, employment, job, profession, trade, business, career, calling, vocation, line, field, métier, livelihood, craft, skill. **2** TASK, assignment, undertaking, job, chore, responsibility, duty, commission. **3** TOIL, labour, drudgery, effort, exertion, industry, slog (*infml*), graft (*infml*), elbow grease (*infml*). **4** CREATION, production, achievement, composition, opus.
▪ **1** play, rest, hobby.

➤ *v* **1** BE EMPLOYED, have a job, earn one's living. **2** LABOUR, toil, drudge, slave. **3** FUNCTION, go, operate, perform, run, handle, manage, use, control. **4** BRING ABOUT, accomplish, achieve, create, cause, pull off (*infml*). **5** CULTIVATE, farm, dig, till, plough. **6** MANIPULATE, knead, mould, shape, form, fashion, make, process.
▪ **1** be unemployed. **2** play, rest. **3** fail, break down.

◇ **work out 1** SOLVE, resolve, calculate, figure out, puzzle out, sort out, clear up, understand. **2** DEVELOP, evolve, go well, go to plan, succeed, prosper, turn out, pan out (*infml*). **3** PLAN, devise, arrange, contrive, invent, construct, put together. **4** ADD UP TO, amount to, total, come out.

◇ **work up** incite, provoke, stir up, rouse, arouse, animate, excite, move, stimulate, inflame, spur, instigate, agitate, generate.

worker *n* employee, labourer, working man, working woman, artisan, craftsman, tradesman, hand, operative, wage-earner, breadwinner, proletarian.

workforce *n* workers, employees, personnel, human resources, labour force, staff, labour, work-people, shopfloor.

working *n* functioning, operation, running, routine, manner, method, action.

➤ *adj* **1** FUNCTIONING, operational, running, operative, going. **2** EMPLOYED, active.
▪ **1** inoperative. **2** idle.

workmanship *n* skill, craft, craftsmanship, expertise, art, handicraft, handiwork, technique, execution, manufacture, work, finish.

works *n* **1** FACTORY, plant, workshop, mill, foundry, shop, assembly shop. **2** ACTIONS, acts, doings. **3** PRODUCTIONS, output, oeuvre, writings, books. **4** MACHINERY, mechanism, workings, action, movement, parts, installations.

workshop *n* **1** WORKS, workroom, atelier, studio, factory, plant, mill, shop. **2** STUDY GROUP, seminar, symposium, discussion group, class.

world *n* **1** EARTH, globe, planet, star, universe, cosmos, creation, nature. **2** EVERYBODY, everyone, people, human race, humankind, humanity. **3** SPHERE, realm, field, area, domain, division, system, society, province, kingdom. **4** TIMES, epoch, era, period, age, days, life.

worldly *adj* **1** TEMPORAL, earthly, mundane, terrestrial, physical, secular, unspiritual, profane. **2** WORLDLY-WISE, sophisticated, urbane, cosmopolitan, experienced, knowing, streetwise (*infml*), sussed (*infml*). **3** MATERIALISTIC, selfish, ambitious, grasping, greedy, covetous, avaricious.
▪ **1** spiritual, eternal. **2** naïve, unsophisticated.

worn *adj* **1** SHABBY, threadbare, worn-out, tatty, tattered, frayed, ragged. **2** EXHAUSTED, tired, weary, spent, fatigued,

careworn, drawn, haggard, jaded.
F3 1 new, unused. **2** fresh.
◇ **worn out 1** SHABBY, threadbare,
useless, used, tatty, tattered, on its last
legs, ragged, frayed, moth-eaten,
decrepit, dilapidated. **2** TIRED OUT,
exhausted, weary, done in (*infml*),
all in (*infml*), dog-tired (*infml*),
knackered (*infml*).
F3 1 new, unused. **2** fresh.

worried *adj* anxious, troubled, uneasy,
ill at ease, apprehensive, concerned,
bothered, upset, fearful, afraid,
frightened, on edge, overwrought,
tense, strained, nervous, disturbed,
distraught, distracted, fretful,
distressed, agonized.
F3 calm, unworried, unconcerned.

worry *v* **1** BE ANXIOUS, be troubled, be
distressed, agonize, fret. **2** IRRITATE,
plague, pester, torment, upset, unsettle,
annoy, bother, disturb, vex, tease, nag,
harass, harry, perturb, hassle (*infml*). **3**
ATTACK, go for, savage.
F3 1 be unconcerned. **2** comfort.
➤ *n* **1** PROBLEM, trouble, responsibility,
burden, concern, care, trial, annoyance,
irritation, vexation. **2** ANXIETY,
apprehension, unease, misgiving, fear,
disturbance, agitation, torment, misery,
perplexity.
F3 2 comfort, reassurance.

worsen *v* **1** EXACERBATE, aggravate,
intensify, heighten. **2** GET WORSE,
weaken, deteriorate, degenerate,
decline, sink, go downhill (*infml*).
F3 improve.

worship *v* venerate, revere, reverence,
adore, exalt, glorify, honour, praise,
idolize, adulate, love, respect, pray to,
deify.
F3 despise, hate.
➤ *n* veneration, reverence, adoration,
devotion(s), homage, honour, glory,
glorification, exaltation, praise,
prayer(s), respect, regard, love,
adulation, deification, idolatry.

Places of worship include: abbey,
bethel, cathedral, chantry, church,
fane, gurdwara, kirk, mandir, masjid,
meeting-house, minster, mosque,
pagoda, shrine, shul, synagogue,
tabernacle, temple, wat. *see also*
religion, **religious**.

worth *n* worthiness, merit, value, benefit,
advantage, importance, significance, use,
usefulness, utility, quality, good, virtue,
excellence, credit, desert(s), cost, rate,
price, help, assistance, avail.
F3 worthlessness.

worthless *adj* **1** VALUELESS, useless,
pointless, meaningless, futile, unavailing,
unimportant, insignificant, trivial,
unusable, cheap, poor, rubbishy, trashy,
trifling, paltry. **2** CONTEMPTIBLE,
despicable, good-for-nothing, vile.
F3 1 valuable. **2** worthy.

worthwhile *adj* profitable, useful,
valuable, worthy, good, helpful,
beneficial, constructive, gainful,
justifiable, productive.
F3 worthless.

worthy *adj* praiseworthy, laudable,
creditable, commendable, valuable,
worthwhile, admirable, fit, deserving,
appropriate, respectable, reputable,
good, honest, honourable, excellent,
decent, upright, righteous.
F3 unworthy, disreputable.

wound *n* **1** INJURY, trauma, hurt, cut,
gash, lesion, laceration, scar. **2** HURT,
distress, trauma, torment, pain,
heartbreak, harm, damage, anguish,
grief, shock.
➤ *v* **1** DAMAGE, harm, hurt, injure, hit,
cut, gash, lacerate, slash, pierce. **2**
DISTRESS, offend, insult, pain, mortify,
upset, slight, grieve.

wrangle *n* argument, quarrel, dispute,
controversy, squabble, tiff, row,
bickering, disagreement, clash,
altercation (*fml*), contest, slanging
match (*infml*), set-to (*infml*).
F3 agreement.
➤ *v* argue, quarrel, disagree, dispute,
bicker, altercate (*fml*), contend, fall out
(*infml*), row, squabble, scrap (*infml*),
fight, spar.
F3 agree.

wrap v envelop, fold, enclose, cover, pack, shroud, wind, surround, package, muffle, cocoon, cloak, roll up, bind, bundle up, immerse.
🔳 unwrap.
◇ **wrap up 1** WRAP, pack up, package, parcel. **2** (*infml*) CONCLUDE, finish off, end, bring to a close, terminate, wind up, complete, round off.

wrapper n wrapping, packaging, envelope, cover, jacket, dust jacket, sheath, sleeve, paper.

wreak v inflict, exercise, create, cause, bring about, perpetrate, vent, unleash, express, execute, carry out, bestow.

wreath n garland, coronet, chaplet, festoon, crown, band, ring.

wreck v destroy, ruin, demolish, devastate, shatter, smash, break, spoil, play havoc with, ravage, write off.
🔳 conserve, repair.
➤ n ruin, destruction, devastation, mess, demolition, ruination, write-off, disaster, loss, disruption.

wreckage n debris, remains, rubble, ruin, fragments, flotsam, pieces.

wrench v yank, wrest, jerk, pull, tug, force, sprain, strain, rick, tear, twist, wring, rip, distort.
➤ v struggle, strive, fight, scuffle, grapple, tussle, combat, contend, contest, vie, battle.

wretch n scoundrel, rogue, villain, good-for-nothing, ruffian, rascal, vagabond, miscreant (*fml*), outcast.

wretched adj **1** ATROCIOUS, awful, deplorable, appalling. **2** UNHAPPY, sad, miserable, melancholy, depressed, dejected, disconsolate, downcast, forlorn, gloomy, doleful, distressed, broken-hearted, crestfallen. **3** PATHETIC, pitiable, pitiful, unfortunate, sorry, hopeless, poor. **4** CONTEMPTIBLE, despicable, vile, worthless, shameful, inferior, low, mean, paltry.
🔳 **1** excellent. **2** happy. **3** enviable. **4** worthy.

wriggle v squirm, writhe, wiggle, worm, twist, snake, slink, crawl, edge, sidle, manoeuvre, squiggle, dodge, extricate, zigzag, waggle, turn.
➤ n wiggle, twist, squirm, jiggle, jerk, turn, twitch.

wring v **1** SQUEEZE, twist, wrench, wrest, extract, mangle, screw. **2** EXACT, extort, coerce, force. **3** DISTRESS, grieve, pain, hurt, rack, rend, pierce, torture, wound, stab, tear.

wrinkle n furrow, crease, corrugation, line, fold, gather, pucker, crumple.
➤ v crease, corrugate, furrow, fold, crinkle, crumple, shrivel, gather, pucker.

write v pen, inscribe, record, jot down, set down, take down, transcribe, scribble, scrawl, correspond, communicate, draft, draw up, copy, compose, create.
◇ **write off 1** DELETE, cancel, cross out, disregard. **2** WRECK, destroy, crash, smash up.

writer n wordsmith, scribbler.

Writers include: annalist, author, autobiographer, bard, biographer, calligraphist, chronicler, clerk, columnist, composer, contributor, copyist, copywriter, correspondent, court reporter, diarist, dramatist, editor, essayist, fabler, fiction writer, ghost writer, hack, historian, journalist, leader writer, lexicographer, librettist, lyricist, novelist, pen-friend, penman, pen-pal, penpusher (*infml*), penwoman, playwright, poet, poet laureate, reporter, rhymer, satirist, scribe, scriptwriter, short story writer, sonneteer, stenographer, storyteller (*infml*), technical writer, web author.

---

writhe v squirm, wriggle, thresh, thrash, twist, wiggle, toss, coil, contort, struggle.

writing n **1** HANDWRITING, calligraphy, script, penmanship, scrawl, scribble, hand, print. **2** DOCUMENT, letter, book, composition, letters, literature, work, publication.

Types of writing include: account, advertising copy, annals, article, autobiography, biography, book, chronicle, commentary, confessions, copywriting, correspondence, criticism, critique, curriculum vitae, diary, discourse, dissertation, documentary, drama, editorial, epistle, essay, feature, history, journal, legal document, letter, life story, literature, lyric, memoir, monograph, narrative, news, newspaper column, paper, parable, poem, profile, propaganda, record, report, review, satire, scientific writing, script, sketch, sonnet, statement, story, study, tale, thesis, travelogue, treatise, yearbook. *see also* **book**; **literature**; **poem**; **story**; **sacred**.

Types of writing instrument include: pen, ballpoint, Biro®, calligraphy pen, cartridge pen, dip pen, eraser pen, felt-tip pen, fountain pen, marker pen, rollerball pen, writing brush, pencil, chinagraph pencil, coloured pencil, crayon, ink pencil, lead pencil, propelling pencil, board marker, laundry marker, permanent marker, highlighter; cane pen, quill, reed, Roman metal pen, steel pen, stylus; brailler, typewriter, word-processor.

---

wrong *adj* **1** INACCURATE, incorrect, mistaken, erroneous, false, fallacious, in error, imprecise. **2** INAPPROPRIATE, unsuitable, unseemly, improper, indecorous, unconventional, unfitting, incongruous, inapt. **3** UNJUST, unethical, unfair, unlawful, immoral, illegal, illicit, dishonest, criminal, crooked (*infml*), reprehensible, blameworthy, guilty, to blame, bad, wicked, sinful, iniquitous, evil. **4** DEFECTIVE, faulty, out of order, amiss, awry.

1 correct, right. **2** suitable, right. **3** good, moral.

➤ *adv* amiss, astray, awry, inaccurately, incorrectly, wrongly, mistakenly, faultily, badly, erroneously, improperly.

 right.

➤ *n* sin, misdeed, offence, crime, immorality, sinfulness, transgression, wickedness, wrongdoing, trespass (*fml*), injury, grievance, abuse, injustice, iniquity, inequity, infringement, unfairness, error.

 right.

➤ *v* abuse, ill-treat, mistreat, maltreat, injure, ill-use, hurt, harm, discredit, dishonour, misrepresent, malign, oppress, cheat.

wrongdoer *n* offender, law-breaker, transgressor, criminal, crook (*infml*), delinquent, felon, miscreant (*fml*), evil-doer, sinner, trespasser, culprit.

wrongful *adj* immoral, improper, unfair, unethical, unjust, unlawful, illegal, illegitimate, illicit, dishonest, criminal, blameworthy, wrong, dishonourable, reprehensible, wicked, evil.

 rightful.

wry *adj* **1** *wry humour*: ironic, sardonic, dry, sarcastic, mordant, mocking, droll. **2** TWISTED, distorted, deformed, contorted, warped, uneven, crooked.

2 straight.

Yy

yank *v, n* jerk, tug, pull, wrench, snatch, haul, heave.

yap *v* **1** BARK, yelp. **2** (*infml*) CHATTER, jabber, babble, prattle, yatter, jaw (*infml*).

yardstick *n* measure, gauge, criterion, standard, benchmark, touchstone, comparison.

yarn *n* **1** THREAD, fibre, strand. **2** STORY, tale, anecdote, fable, fabrication, tall story, cock-and-bull story (*infml*).

yawning *adj* gaping, wide, wide-open, huge, vast, cavernous.

yearly *adj* annual, per year, per annum, perennial.
➤ *adv* annually, every year, once a year, perennially.

yearn for long for, pine for, desire, want, wish for, crave, covet, hunger for, hanker for, ache for, languish for, itch for.

yell *v* shout, call, scream, bellow, roar, bawl, shriek, squeal, howl, holler (*infml*), screech, squall, yelp, yowl, whoop.
🔁 whisper.
➤ *n* shout, call, scream, cry, roar, bellow, shriek, howl, screech, squall, whoop.
🔁 whisper.

yelp *v* yap, bark, squeal, cry, yell, yowl, bay.
➤ *n* yap, bark, yip, squeal, cry, yell, yowl.

yield *v* **1** SURRENDER, renounce, abandon, abdicate, cede, part with, relinquish. **2** GIVE WAY, capitulate, concede, submit, succumb, give (in), admit defeat, bow, cave in, knuckle under, resign oneself, go along with, permit, allow, acquiesce, accede, agree, comply, consent. **3** PRODUCE, bear, supply, provide, generate, bring in, bring forth, furnish, return, earn, pay.
🔁 **1** hold. **2** resist, withstand.
➤ *n* return, product, earnings, harvest, crop, produce, output, profit, revenue, takings, proceeds, income.

yoke *n* **1** HARNESS, bond, link. **2** BURDEN, bondage, enslavement, slavery, oppression, subjugation, servility.
➤ *v* couple, link, join, tie, harness, hitch, bracket, connect, unite.

young *adj* **1** YOUTHFUL, juvenile, baby, infant, junior, adolescent. **2** IMMATURE, early, new, recent, green, growing, fledgling, unfledged, inexperienced.
🔁 **1** adult, old. **2** mature, old.
➤ *n* offspring, babies, issue, litter, progeny (*fml*), brood, children, family.

youngster *n* child, boy, girl, toddler, youth, teenager, kid (*infml*).

youth *n* **1** ADOLESCENT, youngster, juvenile, teenager, kid (*infml*), boy, young man. **2** YOUNG PEOPLE, the young, younger generation. **3** ADOLESCENCE, childhood, immaturity, boyhood, girlhood.
🔁 **3** adulthood.

youthful *adj* young, boyish, girlish, childish, immature, juvenile, inexperienced, fresh, active, lively, well-preserved.
🔁 aged.

Zz

zany (*infml*) *adj* comical, funny, amusing, eccentric, droll, crazy (*infml*), madcap (*infml*), clownish, loony (*infml*), wacky (*infml*).
🔁 serious.

zeal *n* ardour, fervour, passion, warmth, fire, enthusiasm, devotion, spirit, keenness, zest, eagerness, earnestness, dedication, fanaticism, gusto, verve.
🔁 apathy, indifference.

zealot *n* fanatic, extremist, bigot, militant, partisan.

zealous *adj* ardent, fervent, impassioned, passionate, devoted, burning, enthusiastic, intense, fanatical, militant, keen, eager, earnest, spirited.
🔁 apathetic, indifferent.

zenith *n* summit, peak, height, pinnacle, apex, high point, top, optimum, climax, culmination, acme, meridian, vertex.
🔁 nadir.

zero *n* nothing, nought, nil, nadir, bottom, cipher, zilch (*infml*), duck, love.

zest *n* **1** GUSTO, appetite, enthusiasm, enjoyment, keenness, zeal, exuberance, interest. **2** FLAVOUR, taste, relish, savour, spice, tang, piquancy.
🔁 **1** apathy.

zigzag *v* meander, snake, wind, twist, curve.
➤ *adj* meandering, crooked, serpentine, sinuous, twisting, winding.
🔁 straight.

zodiac

> *The signs of the zodiac (with their symbols) are*: Aries (Ram), Taurus (Bull), Gemini (Twins), Cancer (Crab), Leo (Lion), Virgo (Virgin), Libra (Balance), Scorpio (Scorpion), Sagittarius (Archer), Capricorn (Goat), Aquarius (Water-bearer), Pisces (Fishes).

zone *n* region, area, district, territory, section, sector, belt, sphere, tract.

zoom *v* race, rush, tear, dash, speed, fly, hurtle, streak, flash, shoot, whirl, dive, buzz, zip.

Using Words Well

This supplement is aimed to help you get maximum benefit from *Chambers Paperback Thesaurus*. It gives advice on choosing the right vocabulary for the context and avoiding potential pitfalls so you can express yourself creatively and accurately.

CHOOSING THE RIGHT WORD

> 'The difference between the almost right word and the right word is really a large matter – it's the difference between the lightning bug* and the lightning.'
>
> *Mark Twain*

Our choice of word in any situation is subconsciously influenced by several factors:

- *Context* – where we are, and in what kind of situation

- *Audience* – who we are communicating with, and their relationship to us

- *Aim* – what effect we wish to have on our audience, and the desired end result

and many others. All these are taken into account before we even open our mouths, or put pen to paper.

When we use a thesaurus, this process of selecting the appropriate word becomes a conscious one. This is especially true as we may be using words with which we are unfamiliar.

Context

The most important factor to remember when choosing a word from the *Paperback Thesaurus* is the context in which you will use it. No matter how apt a word may appear, if it is used out of context it will be inappropriate, and may even have the opposite effect to the one that you hoped for.

Examples of the right and wrong context are given throughout this section to help you choose the right word for the situation.

Audience

> 'A politician's words reveal less about what he thinks about his subject than what he thinks about his audience.'
>
> *George F. Will*

Your audience is the person or people who will be hearing or reading your words: a tutor, your colleagues, the manager of a business for which you want to work, your bank manager, or anyone else that you wish to communicate with. Ask yourself:

* a firefly

- What is the audience's prior knowledge and level of understanding of the subject?

- Will they understand and appreciate simple or more complicated vocabulary?

- What is their relationship to you – are they in authority, or is it an informal relationship?

Think about who your audience is, and then tailor your choice of words to them.

Aim

Your aim in speaking or writing might be to convey the right information so you get a good mark in an essay, to receive a pay rise, to make people laugh, or to persuade people that your point of view is the right one. Consider your aim when choosing words so that you have the best chance of achieving it.

✗ 'I *deserve* praise for this presentation because I *worked* hard on it.'

✓ 'I have *earned* praise for this presentation because I *researched* it, *studied* the issues closely, and have *presented* them clearly.'

The first example says what you think. The second example has more chance of persuading someone, because the words emphasize *why* you think this – and so you have a better chance of achieving your aim.

Appropriateness

Bearing in mind the context, your audience, and your aim will help you to choose the right word. But it is also important to check the meaning of any word that you are unsure about in a dictionary, such as *Chambers Paperback Dictionary*, before using it. Not all synonyms listed are interchangeable, and so not all can be used in the same situation.

Although in their own way each of these words means *harden*, each only applies to certain forms of hardening, and if you use them inappropriately your sentence can become gobbledygook:

✗ She was *caked* to his whining by now, so ignored him as they drove along the rough track, the mud becoming *reinforced* on the *accustomed* tyres.

✓ She was *accustomed* to his whining by now, so ignored him as they drove along the rough track, the mud becoming *caked* on the *reinforced* tyres.

USING THE LABELS

The italic labels used in the *Paperback Thesaurus* indicate, for example, the register of a term, eg formal (*fml*) or slang (*sl*), or the geographical location where it is most used, eg the United States (*US*). Because language is fluid, there is frequently some overlap between different language types. The distinction between *informal* language and *slang*, for example, can be a subtle one. Also, a word may have more than one element in its label, for example *US sl*.

So the labels are there as a *guide* to help you in your choice of words, and to help you choose the most appropriate word for any situation.

REGISTER LABELS

Register is the style of language suitable for certain situations or subjects. People use different words in a formal situation, for example at work or in a report, from those that they use with friends. Most of the time this choice of language is made instinctively. But when using a thesaurus to choose words that might be unfamiliar to you, it is important to be careful. If a word is used in the wrong context, the result may be incongruous or inappropriate.

Most of the words in the *Paperback Thesaurus* are Standard English. However, some words are marked by register labels, which indicate in which context the word might be used.

- *fml* (formal) – words which would be used in a more formal context
- *infml* (informal) – words which would be suitable in an informal context
- *sl* (slang) – words which should only be used in a very informal context

The synonyms given for a word in the *Paperback Thesaurus* may include words from several different registers:

Standard	✓ Linzi fondly *kissed* her brothers goodbye as she waved them off at the station.
formal	✓ 'Male kissing gouramis, *Helostoma temmincki*, press lips and appear to *osculate*, but this is actually attempting to establish territorial dominance,' explained the tropical fish expert.
informal	✓ 'You'll never guess who I saw Ben *smooching* with at the cinema last night!' gossiped Fozia.
slang	✓ 'Ooh, I love Robbie,' squealed Alix, 'I'd *snog* him any time!'

These different registers are discussed in detail below.

Standard English

Standard English is the form of English generally used throughout the English-speaking world in education, business, official bodies, the media, and in all other everyday conventional speech and writing. It is understood by all speakers of English, and exists with very little variation from one English-speaking country to another. It can be seen as the 'common core' of English, what would remain if all the other variations were removed.

Standard English terms are not labelled in the *Paperback Thesaurus*.

Formal language

Formal language is frequently used in official or business situations. Like Standard English, it is strictly correct with regard to grammar, style and choice of words. However, formal language varies both in terms of the words used, and the way the language is structured. Standard English words that are not markedly formal can still be used in a formal context, but informal or slang words should not be used.

Structure

Formal language is more restrictive in its structure than conversational language. Contractions and abbreviations are little used. Passive and impersonal constructions are used more. Both the words and sentences may be longer:

✗ We hope that he'll phone in, as we don't have much time to put this right.

✓ It is to be hoped that he will telephone the office, given the time constraints within which the situation must be rectified.

Vocabulary

Formal words are not frequently used in everyday conversation. However, they may come in useful when addressing authority, or for adding weight to your words.

✗ 'Your Honour, I solemnly swear that on the night in question I was neither *sloshed* nor *plastered*.'

✓ 'Your Honour, I solemnly swear that on the night in question I was not *inebriated*.'

Potential pitfalls

It is important not to overuse formal words, as there is a risk of sounding pompous or pretentious, or losing sight of the meaning of the sentence:

✗ He had a *propensity* for *loquaciousness* and for *prolixity* in his *oration*, for which he was *denigrated*.

✓ He was *criticized* for being too *talkative* and *long-winded*.

Context

The context of formal words is also very important. They are unlikely, for example, to be used by children, or to be dropped casually into conversation:

✗ My brother is a real *miscreant* and always getting into *altercations*!' laughed four-year-old Debbie.

✓ 'It was wrong of you *miscreants* to become involved in this *altercation*,' lectured the headmaster, as John and Jo stared out the window.

Informal language

Informal language, which is also sometimes called colloquial language, is used when you are familiar with your audience, in a more relaxed or everyday situation. It uses vocabulary, idioms and structures characteristic of conversational speech. It is characterized by a lack of formality and tends to be more flexible in its construction and more expressive than formal language. It should not be used in a formal context.

✗ 'Prince Charles Edward Stuart *did a bunk* to Skye,' said the eminent historian.

✓ The red wine stain wouldn't come out of the carpet, so Kieran *did a bunk* before his partner came home.

Remember that not only should informal words only be used in an informal context, but that not all the words listed mean exactly the same thing:

✗ 'The train will *clear out* at 16.20 – so we'd better run!' he shouted.

✓ They grabbed the box of chocolates and *cleared out* as fast as their legs could carry them.

Idioms

Informal language often contains idioms. An idiom is an expression with a meaning that cannot be understood from the usual meanings of the words which form it. Idioms can add colour to your speech and writing, making it more lively and interesting. However, as with all informal language, such idioms are often inappropriate in more formal situations.

✗ The Chief Executive shocked the Board of Directors when she *lost the place* on seeing the sales figures.

✓ Caitlin *lost the place* when the guests arrived just as there was a burning smell from the kitchen.

Slang

> 'Slang is a language that rolls up its sleeves, spits on its hands, and goes to work.'
>
> *Carl Sandburg*

The most informal of all language is slang. Slang has been around for hundreds of years, but the words that are considered to be slang are constantly changing, and many terms that were once slang are now thought to be Standard English. (*Donkey*, for example, was a slang term in the 1800s.) As a general rule, slang should not be used in a formal context, and should always be used with caution. It can also be very specific to one region or group of people.

✗ 'I should invest your *spondulicks* in a high-interest, fixed-rate savings account,' said the financial adviser.

✓ 'Swindle the store, hit the highway, and we'll visit Vegas to spend the *spondulicks*,' growled the infamous gangster 'Red' Rogers.

GEOGRAPHICAL LABELS

> 'We have really everything in common with America nowadays, except, of course, language.'
>
> *Oscar Wilde*

English is spoken by millions of people around the globe, but varies slightly from country to country, as it is influenced by the other languages spoken there and the particular culture of each country. For example, there are differences between the English spoken in the United Kingdom and the English spoken in the United States of America. Terms that are used primarily in the United States are labelled *US* in the *Paperback Thesaurus*.

There are many differences of meaning, pronunciation, spelling and syntax between British and US English. This means that the context in which a word is used is very important. In the example below, 'pants' is an American term meaning trousers, and it is acceptable to use the word in this way if writing in an American context or style. However, if you are writing outside the US it has a different meaning, and should not be used in this sense:

✗ An English gentleman must always carry an umbrella and wear a bowler hat, and his shirt and *pants* should be immaculate.

✓ Movie star Brock Beagle looked gorgeous as he cruised through New York City in casual T-shirt and *pants*.

TECHNICAL AND SPECIALIST LANGUAGE

Technical words may sometimes be found in the panels that list language specific to a certain subject or item.

It is always important to look up technical or specialist terms in a dictionary before you use them. For example, although *convex*, *ogee* and *trefoil* are all kinds of arch, they each have their own characteristics.

Technical language is sometimes called jargon. Jargon is the specialized vocabulary of a particular trade, activity, group or profession. Be careful if you use jargon; even if you are sure what it means, your audience might not be. It is also important not to use jargon in a pretentious or meaningless way.

SENSITIVE LANGUAGE

'There is a wonderful cliché – sticks and stones may break my bones but words can never hurt me. That is nonsense. Words can and do hurt people every day of their lives... Words are all important... Words have influence. Words have power.'

Gurbux Singh, Chair of the Commission for Racial Equality

Sometimes language can be a minefield. Even seemingly innocent language can have unwanted effects if it is used without sensitivity. Language can reinforce unhelpful stereotypes, promote negative opinions and patronize people. It is useful to be aware that there are occasions when you risk causing offence if you do not use language with care.

Sensitive use of language is a complicated and emotive area. There are no fixed rules about what is acceptable and what is inappropriate, and people often disagree. However, the following general principles may be helpful.

- Some traditional ways of referring to people may reinforce stereotypical (and often incorrect) notions, for example that men naturally hold positions of authority in society, or that members of minority groups are inferior or abnormal.

- People usually prefer to be treated as individuals rather than merely as members of a group.

- It is often not relevant to refer to people's race, gender or disabilities if you wish to talk about them. Consider whether such information is really appropriate.

- Try to be aware of terms people use to describe themselves and respect the right of people to choose how they are called.

- Terms which are regarded as appropriate in one country or region may sometimes be regarded as offensive in another.

- Terms which were formerly regarded as acceptable may now be regarded as derogatory, and it is possible that terms which are now acceptable may in time come to be regarded as offensive.

- Sometimes a group may use within itself a term which may still be regarded as offensive when used by people who are not part of the group.

- Although it is often used out of the best of motives, politically correct language can impair clarity of expression or appear ridiculous when taken to extremes.

Following these general principles may help you to use language carefully. These principles are reinforced below by some more specific suggestions on how to use language sensitively with reference to gender, race and religion, disability, and sexuality. However, these are only a few of the areas which call for sensitivity. You should also be careful when speaking, for example, about age, marital or family status, nationality, and political beliefs.

Gender

You risk offending many of your readers if you use language in a way that implies that there is only one gender, or that one gender is superior to the other. This can sometimes be difficult to achieve, however, as many traditional uses of language treat the masculine gender as a privileged form.

- Some people disapprove of the words *he*, *his* and *him* being used to refer to someone who could be of either sex.

    ✗ Every applicant for the job should include *his* curriculum vitae.

    Some people prefer to use the plural words *they*, *their* and *them* (which imply no specific gender) in such situations. This usage is becoming widely acceptable, although some people still regard it as ungrammatical.

    Every applicant for the job should include *their* curriculum vitae.

    Other people prefer to use *he* or *she*, *his* or *hers*, and *him* or *her*, but this can be clumsy, especially when these phrases have to be repeated frequently.

    Every applicant for the job should include *his* or *her* curriculum vitae.

    The best solution in many cases is to rewrite the sentence in such a way that the problem is avoided altogether. This can often be done by making the subject into a plural:

    ✓ Every applicant for the job should include *a* curriculum vitae.
    ✓ All applicants for the job should include *their* curriculum vitae.

- Some people object to words such as *man*, *men* or *mankind* as terms to denote both men and women. There are plenty of alternative terms, such as *people*, *humanity*, or *human beings* which can avoid this usage.

- Be careful about using words which reinforce stereotypical images of the sexes, such as saying that men *converse* while women *gossip*, or that a woman is *hysterical* whilst a man is *angry*.

- If you are talking about two people, you should, other things being equal, use equivalent terms to refer to each of them. Beware of defining women by appearance, age and the number of children they have, and men by career or achievement:

    *✗ Famous actor Brock Beagle was accompanied by his sister, a stunningly attractive blonde mother-of-two.
    *✓ Famous actor Brock Beagle was accompanied by his sister Brenda Beagle, the award-winning photographer.

- Many occupations have traditional titles which imply that they are done only by one sex. There is usually a non-gender-specific term which can be used instead: for example, *flight attendant* in place of *air stewardess*, and *firefighter* in place of *fireman*. These titles should be used consistently – if you use the title *police officer* when talking about men, you should use the same term when talking about women who do the same job, and vice versa.

- Do not make assumptions about people's gender from their occupations. The job titles *nurse*, *doctor* and *secretary*, for example, can refer to people of both sexes. There is no need to use *male nurse, female doctor,* or *male secretary.*

Race and Religion

Sensitive use of language with reference to race and religion does not refer solely to avoiding deliberately offensive terms for racial and religious groups. It can involve respecting the wishes of people to use their own preferred names and by using language in a way that does not perpetuate negative or stereotypical images.

- It is advisable to avoid language which suggests that one group of people are normal and that all others are abnormal. Beware of defining minority groups solely in terms of their differences from the majority group.

- People generally prefer to be identified positively rather than be defined by what they are not. Terms such as *non-white* are best used only when the context makes them relevant.

  ✗ *Non-whites* took to the streets today to protest against racism.
  ✓ An investigation into equal opportunities at the company found that *non-white* employees were paid less than their *white* colleagues.

- People are likely to be offended by over-generalizations, such as using *black* as a generic word for everyone who is not white.

- You risk causing offence if you use words inaccurately. For example, *immigrants* are people who have come to a foreign country with the intention of settling in it. The term is not appropriate to describe people of a different racial group who were born in the country.

- Try to avoid describing people by using stereotypical images of the race or religion to which they belong. For example, people of Chinese origin are likely to be offended if they are associated with adjectives such as *inscrutable,* especially if such words would not be used of other people in the same situation. Even associations that might be intended to be positive, such as regarding people of Indian origin as *industrious* or Germans as *efficient,* can cause offence because they relate to stereotypes rather than individuals.

  ✗ Bruce looks after the company's finances with *typical Scottish thrift.*
  ✓ Bruce keeps tight control over the company's finances.

- Be aware of the names by which different racial groups prefer to be called. In Britain, terms such as *Afro/Caribbean* or *Afro-Caribbean* are preferable to *West Indian,* whilst *British Asian* is preferred for British citizens whose families originate from the Indian subcontinent. In the United States, words like *African American* or *Chinese American* are preferred, as these indicate a person's ethnic group whilst still denoting that someone is an American. In Australia, it is normal to use *Aboriginal people* or the individual group name (for example *Pitjantjatjara*) in preference to *Aborigine.*

It is increasingly common to respect peoples' own preferred names for themselves and for local places rather than using names imposed by colonizers – for example, *Inuit* is now preferred to *Eskimo, Ayers Rock* is now known by its Aboriginal name *Uluru,* and *Mount McKinley* is known as *Denali,* the name given to it by the

Athabascan native people of Alaska. Similarly, the spelling and pronunciation of place names increasingly reflects the usage of indigenous peoples – for example *Makkah* being preferred to *Mecca*, when referring to the holy city of Islam.

Disability

> 'The language we use reflects the way we think. It also shapes the way we think. The language we use about disability is an important way of influencing our own and society's attitudes.'
>
> *Scope (British cerebral palsy charity)*

Some of the language traditionally used when referring to people with disabilities frequently has associations of passivity, pity and limitation. It often stresses the disability at the expense of the person. Sensitive use of language recognizes the abilities as well as the disabilities of a person, and avoids making judgements that may be at odds with the facts.

- Beware of describing someone solely in terms of the disability they have. It is preferable to talk of *a person with a disability* or *a disabled person* rather than *a cripple* or *an invalid*. Similarly, it is preferable to talk of *people with epilepsy* or *deaf people* rather than *epileptics* or *the deaf*.

- Many *disabled people* dislike being referred to as *handicapped* on the grounds that a handicap is created by external surroundings or by other people's attitudes (for example a building without a lift for a wheelchair user, or discrimination in the workplace) and not by the disability itself.

- You may cause offence if you use terms which imply some judgement, such as *sufferer* or *victim*. It is preferable to say that someone *has* a certain disability, rather than making the judgement that they are *afflicted* by it or *suffer* as a result. Similarly, it is preferable to refer to a *wheelchair user* or someone who *uses a wheelchair*, rather than saying that they are *confined to a wheelchair* or *wheelchair bound*, which implies restriction and passivity.

  ✗ Sam is afflicted by cerebral palsy. How the poor woman must suffer!
  ✓ Paul uses a wheelchair to go out with his friends.

- Beware of using inaccurate or outdated terms. Where a recognized scientific term exists, such as *cerebral palsy* or *Down's syndrome*, it is advisable to use this.

- It is usually best to use precise terms to describe disabilities rather than vague and evasive constructions such as *differently abled*, *physically challenged* and *special*.

- You may cause offence if you refer to people who do not have a particular disability as *normal*, when in fact they are just people without that disability.

- Remember that people may have individual preferences. Some people who are deaf dislike being called *hearing impaired*. Some people dislike the terms *blind* or *partially sighted*, and prefer *people with impaired vision* or *people with a visual disability*. Respect a person's wish if they express a preference for a certain term.

Sexuality

As is the case with language relating to race and religion, using sensitive language with regard to sexuality goes beyond simply avoiding terms of abuse. It takes account of differences and avoids crude categorizations.

- Many people prefer to use the term *partner*, as this is regarded as inclusive, whereas terms like *husband*, *wife*, *boyfriend*, *girlfriend* or *spouse* make assumptions about people's sexuality.

- Try to avoid language which stereotypes people, or which makes assumptions based on prejudice or misinformation about their character or lifestyle.

Words Grouped by Ending

-cide
aborticide
acaricide
algicide
aphicide
aphidicide
bacillicide
bactericide
biocide
deicide
ecocide
ethnocide
feticide
filicide
foeticide
fratricide
fungicide
genocide
germicide
giganticide
herbicide
homicide
infanticide
insecticide
larvicide
liberticide
matricide
menticide
miticide
molluscicide
ovicide
parasiticide
parasuicide
parricide
patricide
pesticide
prolicide
pulicide
raticide
regicide
rodenticide
sororicide
speciocide
spermicide
suicide
taeniacide
trypanocide
tyrannicide
uxoricide
vaticide
verbicide
vermicide
viricide
viticide
vulpicide
weedicide

-cracy
aristocracy
autocracy
bureaucracy
chrysocracy
cottonocracy
democracy
demonocracy
despotocracy
dollarocracy
doulocracy
dulocracy
ergatocracy
Eurocracy
gerontocracy
gynaecocracy
hagiocracy
hierocracy
isocracy
kakistocracy
kleptocracy
meritocracy
millocracy
mobocracy
monocracy
nomocracy
ochlocracy
pantisocracy
pedantocracy
physiocracy
plantocracy
plutocracy
plutodemocracy
pornocracy
ptochocracy
quangocracy
slavocracy
snobocracy
squattocracy
stratocracy
stratocracy
technocracy
thalassocracy
thalattocracy
theocracy
thugocracy
timocracy

-culture
agriculture
apiculture
aquaculture
aquiculture
arboriculture
aviculture
citriculture
counter-culture
culture
electroculture
floriculture
horticulture
mariculture
monoculture
ostreiculture
permaculture
pisciculture
polyculture
pomiculture
self-culture
sericiculture
sericulture
silviculture
stirpiculture
subculture
sylviculture

vermiculture
viniculture
viticulture
water-culture
zooculture

-dom

Anglo-Saxondom
apedom
archdukedom
attorneydom
babeldom
babudom
bachelordom
beadledom
beggardom
bestsellerdom
birthdom
bishopdom
boredom
Bumbledom
chiefdom
chefdom
Christendom
clerkdom
cockneydom
crippledom
cuckoldom
czardom
demirepdom
devildom
Dogberrydom
dogdom
dolldom
dufferdom
dukedom
duncedom
earldom
enthraldom
fairydom
fandom
fiefdom
filmdom
flunkeydom
fogydom
freedom
fresherdom
Gaeldom
gangsterdom
Greekdom
gurudom
gypsydom

halidom
heathendom
heirdom
hippiedom
hobodom
jarldom
junkerdom
kaiserdom
kingdom
kitchendom
leechdom
liegedom
mandom
Maoridom
martyrdom
masterdom
moviedom
newspaperdom
noveldom
officialdom
overfreedom
pagandom
pashadom
pauperdom
penny-wisdom
popedom
princedom
puppydom
puzzledom
Quakerdom
queendom
queerdom
rascaldom
rebeldom
sachemdom
saintdom
savagedom
Saxondom
scoundreldom
selfdom
serfdom
shahdom
sheikdom
sheikhdom
sheriffdom
Slavdom
spinsterdom
squiredom
stardom
subkingdom
superstardom
swelldom

thanedom
thraldom
thralldom
topsyturvydom
tsardom
underkingdom
unwisdom
villadom
whoredom
wisdom
Yankeedom
yuppiedom

-gamy

allogamy
anisogamy
apogamy
autogamy
bigamy
chalazogamy
chasmogamy
cleistogamy
clistogamy
cryptogamy
deuterogamy
dichogamy
digamy
endogamy
exogamy
geitonogamy
hercogamy
herkogamy
heterogamy
hologamy
homogamy
hypergamy
isogamy
karyogamy
misogamy
monogamy
oogamy
pangamy
pantagamy
plasmogamy
plastogamy
polygamy
porogamy
siphonogamy
syngamy
trigamy
xenogamy
zoogamy

-genesis
abiogenesis
agamogenesis
angiogenesis
anthropogenesis
atherogenesis
autogenesis
biogenesis
blastogenesis
caenogenesis
carcinogenesis
chondrogenesis
crystallogenesis
cytogenesis
diagenesis
diplogenesis
dynamogenesis
ectogenesis
electrogenesis
embryogenesis
epeirogenesis
epigenesis
frontogenesis
gametogenesis
gamogenesis
gluconeogenesis
glycogenesis
haematogenesis
heterogenesis
histogenesis
homogenesis
hylogenesis
hypnogenesis
merogenesis
metagenesis
monogenesis
morphogenesis
mutagenesis
mythogenesis
neogenesis
neurogenesis
neuropathogenesis
noogenesis
oncogenesis
ontogenesis
oogenesis
organogenesis
orogenesis
orthogenesis
osteogenesis
paedogenesis
palingenesis

pangenesis
paragenesis
parthenogenesis
pathogenesis
perigenesis
petrogenesis
phylogenesis
phytogenesis
polygenesis
psychogenesis
pyogenesis
schizogenesis
spermatogenesis
sporogenesis
syngenesis
taphrogenesis
teratogenesis
thermogenesis
transgenesis
tumorigenesis
xenogenesis

-graphy
aerography
ampelography
anemography
angiography
anthropogeography
anthropography
areography
arteriography
autobiography
autography
autoradiography
autotypography
ballistocardiography
bibliography
biogeography
biography
biostratigraphy
brachygraphy
bronchography
cacography
calligraphy
cardiography
cartography
cathodography
ceramography
cerography
cervicography
chalcography
chartography

cheirography
chirography
cholangiography
cholesystography
choregraphy
choreography
chorography
chromatography
chromolithography
chromotypography
chromoxylography
chronography
cineangiography
cinematography
cinemicrography
climatography
cometography
cosmography
cryptography
crystallography
dactyliography
dactylography
demography
dermatography
dermography
discography
dittography
doxography
echocardiography
ectypography
electrocardiography
electroencephalography
electrography
electromyography
electrophotography
encephalography
enigmatography
epigraphy
epistolography
ethnography
ferrography
filmography
flexography
fractography
geography
glossography
glyphography
glyptography
hagiography
haplography
heliography
heresiography

hierography
historiography
holography
horography
hydrography
hyetography
hymnography
hypsography
ichnography
ichthyography
iconography
ideography
lexicography
lexigraphy
lipography
lithography
logography
lymphography
mammography
metallography
microcosmography
micrography
microphotography
mimography
monography
morphography
myography
mythography
nomography
nosography
oceanography
odontography
oleography
opisthography
orchesography
oreography
organography
orography
orthography
osteography
palaeogeography
palaeography
palaeontography
pantography
paroemiography
pasigraphy
pathography
petrography
phonography
photography
photolithography
photomacrography

photomicrography
phototelegraphy
photoxylography
photozincography
physiography
phytogeography
phytography
pictography
polarography
polygraphy
pornography
prosopography
psaligraphy
pseudepigraphy
pseudography
psychobiography
psychography
pterylography
pyelography
pyrography
pyrophotography
radiography
radiotelegraphy
reflectography
reprography
rhyparography
röntgenography
scenography
scintigraphy
seismography
selenography
serigraphy
sialography
snobography
sonography
spectrography
sphygmography
steganography
stenography
stereography
stratigraphy
stylography
symbolography
tachygraphy
technography
telautography
telegraphy
telephotography
thalassography
thanatography
thaumatography
thermography

tomography
topography
typography
ultrasonography
uranography
urography
venography
ventriculography
xerography
xeroradiography
xylography
xylopyrography
zincography
zoogeography
zoography

-hood

adulthood
angelhood
apehood
apprenticehood
aunthood
babyhood
bachelorhood
beadlehood
beasthood
bountihood
boyhood
brotherhood
cathood
childhood
Christhood
companionhood
cousinhood
cubhood
daughterhood
deaconhood
dollhood
drearihood
elfhood
fairyhood
falsehood
fatherhood
flapperhood
flesh-hood
gawkihood
gentlehood
gentlemanhood
gianthood
girlhood
godhood
hardihood

high-priesthood
hobbledehoyhood
hoghood
husbandhood
idlehood
infanthood
invalidhood
jealoushood
kinghood
kinglihood
kittenhood
knighthood
ladyhood
likelihood
livelihood
lustihood
maidenhood
maidhood
manhood
masterhood
matronhood
misshood
monkhood
motherhood
nationhood
needy-hood
neighbourhood
novicehood
nunhood
old-maidhood
orphanhood
pagehood
parenthood
personhood
popehood
priesthood
princehood
prophethood
puppyhood
queenhood
sainthood
selfhood
serfhood
singlehood
sisterhood
sonhood
spinsterhood
squirehood
statehood
swinehood
tabbyhood
thanehood

thinghood
toddlerhood
traitorhood
unclehood
unlikelihood
victimhood
virginhood
waiterhood
widowerhood
widowhood
wifehood
wivehood
womanhood
youthhood

-iatry
chemopsychiatry
geriatry
gyniatry
hippiatry
neuropsychiatry
orthopsychiatry
paediatry
podiatry
psychiatry

-ics
acoustics
acrobatics
aerobatics
aerobics
aerodynamics
aeronautics
aerostatics
aesthetics
agogics
agonistics
agronomics
ambisonics
anaesthetics
animatronics
apologetics
aquabatics
aquanautics
aquarobics
aquatics
architectonics
astrodynamics
astronautics
astrophysics
athletics
atmospherics

autonomics
avionics
axiomatics
ballistics
barodynamics
bioastronautics
biodynamics
bioethics
biomathematics
biomechanics
biometrics
bionics
bionomics
biophysics
biorhythmics
biosystematics
cacogenics
calisthenics
callanetics
callisthenics
catacoustics
catallactics
cataphonics
catechetics
catoptrics
ceroplastics
chemotherapeutics
chiropractics
chrematistics
chromatics
civics
classics
cliometrics
conics
cosmonautics
cosmopolitics
cryogenics
cryonics
cryophysics
cybernetics
cytogenetics
demotics
deontics
dermatoglyphics
diacoustics
diagnostics
dialectics
dianetics
didactics
dietetics
dioptrics
diplomatics

dogmatics
dramatics
dynamics
dysgenics
Ebonics
eclectics
econometrics
economics
ecumenics
ekistics
electroacoustics
electrodynamics
electrokinetics
electromechanics
electronics
electrostatics
electrotechnics
electrotherapeutics
electrothermics
energetics
entoptics
environics
epigenetics
epistemics
epizootics
ergonomics
ethics
ethnolinguistics
eudaemonics
eudemonics
eugenics
eurhythmics
euthenics
exegetics
floristics
fluidics
forensics
genetics
geodetics
geodynamics
geophysics
geopolitics
geoponics
geostatics
geotechnics
geotectonics
geriatrics
gerontotherapeutics
glyptics
gnomonics
gnotobiotics
graphemics

graphics
gyrostatics
halieutics
haptics
harmonics
hedonics
hermeneutics
hermetics
heuristics
hippiatrics
histrionics
homiletics
hydraulics
hydrodynamics
hydrokinetics
hydromagnetics
hydromechanics
hydroponics
hydrostatics
hydrotherapeutics
hygienics
hypersonics
hysterics
immunodiagnostics
immunogenetics
informatics
irenics
iridodiagnostics
isagogics
isometrics
kinematics
kinesiatrics
kinesics
kinetics
linguistics
lithochromatics
liturgics
logistics
logopedics
loxodromics
macaronics
macrobiotics
macroeconomics
magnetics
magneto-
  hydrodynamics
magneto-optics
maieutics
mathematics
mechanics
mechatronics
melodics

metalinguistics
metamathematics
metaphysics
metapsychics
metempirics
meteoritics
microeconomics
microelectronics
microphysics
mnemonics
mnemotechnics
mole-electronics
monostrophics
morphemics
morphophonemics
nautics
nucleonics
numismatics
obstetrics
olympics
onomastics
operatics
optics
optoelectronics
orchestics
orthodontics
orthodromics
orthogenics
orthopaedics
orthopedics
orthoptics
orthotics
paedeutics
paediatrics
paedodontics
paideutics
pantopragmatics
paralinguistics
party-politics
pataphysics
patristics
pedagogics
peptics
periodontics
petrophysics
pharmaceutics
pharmacodynamics
pharmacokinetics
phelloplastics
phonemics
phonetics
phonics

phonocamptics
phonotactics
photics
photochromics
photoelectronics
photonics
phototherapeutics
photovoltaics
physiatrics
physics
physiotherapeutics
plastics
pneumatics
pneumodynamics
poetics
polemics
politico-economics
politics
power-politics
pragmatics
problematics
prognostics
prosthetics
prosthodontics
proxemics
psionics
psychics
psychodynamics
psychogeriatrics
psychographics
psycholinguistics
psychometrics
psychonomics
psychophysics
psychosomatics
psychotherapeutics
pyrotechnics
quadraphonics
quadrophonics
radionics
radiophonics
radiotherapeutics
rhythmics
robotics
scholastics
semantics
semeiotics
semiotics
Semitics
sferics
significs
sociolinguistics

sonics
sophistics
spherics
sphragistics
statics
statistics
stereoptics
strategics
stylistics
subatomics
subtropics
supersonics
syllabics
symbolics
synectics
systematics
tactics
technics
tectonics
telearchics
telematics
thaumaturgics
theatrics
theoretics
therapeutics
thermionics
thermodynamics
thermoplastics
thermotics
toponymics
toreutics
transonics
transsonics
ultrasonics
vitrics
zoiatrics
zootechnics
zymotechnics

-ism
abnormalism
abolitionism
aboriginalism
absenteeism
absolutism
academicalism
academicism
accidentalism
achromatism
acosmism
acrobatism
acrotism

actinism
activism
Adamitism
adiaphorism
adoptianism
Adoptionism
adventurism
aeroembolism
aerotropism
aestheticism
Africanism
ageism
agnosticism
agrammatism
agrarianism
Albigensianism
albinism
albinoism
alcoholism
algorism
alienism
allelomorphism
allotropism
alpinism
altruism
amateurism
Americanism
ametabolism
amoralism
amorism
amorphism
anabaptism
anabolism
anachronism
anagrammatism
anarchism
anastigmatism
androdioecism
andromonoecism
aneurism
Anglicanism
anglicism
Anglo-Catholicism
aniconism
animalism
animatism
animism
annihilationism
antagonism
anthropomorphism
anthropomorphitism
anthropopathism

anthropophuism
anthropopsychism
antichristianism
anticivism
anticlericalism
antidisestablish-
  mentarianism
anti-federalism
anti-Gallicanism
anti-Jacobinism
antinomianism
antiochianism
antiquarianism
anti-Semitism
antisepticism
antisocialism
antitheism
antitrinitarianism
antivaccinationism
antivivisectionism
anythingarianism
apheliotropism
aphorism
apism
aplanatism
apochromatism
apogeotropism
apoliticism
Apollinarianism
apostolicism
apriorism
Arabism
Aramaism
Arcadianism
archaicism
archaism
Arianism
aristocratism
Aristotelianism
Aristotelism
Arminianism
asceticism
asepticism
Asiaticism
aspheterism
asteism
asterism
astigmatism
asynchronism
asystolism
atavism
atheism

athleticism
Atlanticism
atomism
atonalism
atropism
Atticism
attorneyism
Augustinianism
Australianism
authorism
authoritarianism
autism
autochthonism
autoeroticism
autoerotism
automatism
automobilism
automorphism
autotheism
avant-gardism
Averrhoism
Averroism
Baalism
Baathism
Ba'athism
Babbitism
Babeeism
babelism
Babiism
Babism
babuism
bacchanalianism
bachelorism
Baconianism
Bahaism
bantingism
baptism
barbarism
bashawism
bastardism
bathmism
bedlamism
behaviourism
Benthamism
Bergsonism
Berkeleianism
bestialism
betacism
biblicism
bibliophilism
bilateralism
bilingualism

bimetallism
bipedalism
blackguardism
Blairism
blepharism
bogeyism
bogyism
Bohemianism
bolshevism
Bonapartism
bonism
boobyism
Boswellism
botulism
Bourbonism
bowdlerism
bradyseism
braggartism
Brahmanism
Brahminism
Braidism
Briticism
Britishism
Brownism
bruxism
Buchmanism
Buddhism
bullyism
Burschenism
Byronism
Byzantinism
cabalism
cabbalism
Caesarism
caesaropapism
caffeinism
caffeism
Calvinism
cambism
Camorrism
cannibalism
capitalism
Carbonarism
careerism
Carlism
Carlylism
carnalism
Cartesianism
casualism
catabolism
catastrophism
catechism

catechumenism
Catharism
catheterism
catholicism
causationism
cauterism
cavalierism
Celticism
centenarianism
centralism
centripetalism
centrism
cerebralism
ceremonialism
chaldaism
characterism
charism
charlatanism
chartism
Chasidism
Chassidism
Chaucerism
chauvinism
chemism
chemotropism
chloralism
Christianism
chromaticism
churchism
Ciceronianism
cicisbeism
cinchonism
civism
cladism
classicism
clericalism
cliquism
clubbism
coalitionism
Cobdenism
cocainism
cockneyism
coenobitism
cognitivism
collectivism
collegialism
colloquialism
colonialism
commensalism
commercialism
communalism
communism

compatriotism
comstockism
Comtism
conacreism
conceptualism
concettism
concretism
confessionalism
confrontationism
Confucianism
Congregationalism
conservatism
consortism
constitutionalism
constructionism
constructivism
consubstantialism
consumerism
contact-metamorphism
continentalism
contortionism
contrabandism
conventionalism
conversationism
convictism
copyism
corporatism
corporealism
corybantism
cosmeticism
cosmism
cosmopolitanism
cosmopolitism
cosmotheism
cottierism
Couéism
courtierism
creatianism
creationism
cretinism
cretism
criticism
cronyism
crotalism
cubism
cultism
curialism
cyclicism
cynicism
czarism
Dadaism
Daltonism

dandyism
Darwinism
deaf-mutism
decimalism
defeatism
deism
demagogism
demagoguism
demoniacism
demonianism
demonism
denominationalism
departmentalism
descriptivism
despotism
deteriorism
determinism
deviationism
devilism
diabolism
diachronism
diageotropism
diaheliotropism
dialecticism
diamagnetism
diaphototropism
diastrophism
diatropism
dichroism
dichromatism
dichromism
diclinism
dicrotism
didacticism
diffusionism
dilettanteism
dilettantism
dimerism
dimorphism
dioecism
diorism
diothelism
diphysitism
dirigism
dissenterism
dissolutionism
disyllabism
ditheism
ditheletism
dithelism
dithelitism
divisionism

Docetism
doctrinairism
doctrinarianism
Dogberryism
dogmatism
do-goodism
dolichocephalism
donatism
donnism
do-nothingism
Doricism
Dorism
dowdyism
draconism
dragonism
dramaticism
drudgism
druidism
dualism
dudism
dufferism
dunderheadism
dynamism
dyotheletism
dyothelism
dysphemism
ebionism
ebionitism
echoism
eclecticism
ecoterrorism
ecumenicalism
ecumenicism
ecumenism
Edwardianism
egalitarianism
egoism
egotheism
egotism
electromagnetism
electromerism
elementalism
elitism
Elizabethanism
embolism
emotionalism
emotivism
empiricism
enantiomorphism
Encratism
encyclopaedism
endemism

Englishism
entrism
environmentalism
eonism
epicism
Epicureanism
epicurism
epiphenomenalism
epiphytism
epipolism
episcopalianism
episcopalism
equalitarianism
equestrianism
Erastianism
eremitism
erethism
ergotism
eroticism
erotism
erythrism
escapism
esotericism
esoterism
Essenism
essentialism
etacism
etherism
ethicism
ethnicism
ethnocentrism
eudaemonism
eugenism
euhemerism
eumerism
eunuchism
eunuchoidism
euphemism
euphuism
Eurocommunism
Europeanism
evangelicalism
evangelicism
evangelism
evolutionism
exclusionism
exclusivism
exhibitionism
existentialism
ex-librism
exorcism
exotericism

exoticism
expansionism
experientialism
experimentalism
expressionism
extensionalism
externalism
extremism
Fabianism
factionalism
faddism
fairyism
fakirism
falangism
familism
fanaticism
fantasticism
faradism
fascism
fatalism
Fauvism
favism
favouritism
Febronianism
federalism
femininism
feminism
Fenianism
fetichism
fetishism
feudalism
feuilletonism
fideism
fifth-monarchism
filibusterism
finalism
fissiparism
flagellantism
flunkeyism
fogyism
formalism
fortuitism
Fourierism
fractionalism
Froebelism
functionalism
fundamentalism
fusionism
futurism
gaelicism
Galenism
Gallicanism

gallicism
galvanism
gamotropism
ganderism
gangsterism
Gargantuism
gargarism
gargoylism
Gasconism
Gaullism
generationism
Genevanism
genteelism
gentilism
geocentricism
geomagnetism
geophagism
geotropism
Germanism
Ghandi-ism
giantism
gigantism
Gironism
Gnosticism
Gongorism
gormandism
Gothicism
gourmandism
gradualism
Graecism
grammaticism
Grangerism
Grecism
gregarianism
griffinism
Grobianism
Grundyism
gynandrism
gynandromorphism
gynodioecism
gynomonoecism
gypsyism
gyromagnetism
haptotropism
Hasidism
Hassidism
heathenism
Hebraicism
Hebrewism
hectorism
hedonism
Hegelianism

hegemonism
heliotropism
Hellenism
helotism
hemihedrism
hemimorphism
henotheism
hermaphroditism
heroism
hetaerism
hetairism
heterochronism
heteroecism
heteromorphism
heterostylism
heterothallism
heurism
Hibernianism
Hibernicism
hidalgoism
hierarchism
highbrowism
High-Churchism
Hildebrandism
Hinduism
Hippocratism
hispanicism
historicism
historism
histrionicism
histrionism
Hitlerism
Hobbesianism
Hobbianism
Hobbism
hobbledehoyism
hobbyism
hobgoblinism
hoboism
holism
holohedrism
holometabolism
holophytism
homeomorphism
homoeomorphism
homoeroticism
homoerotism
homomorphism
homothallism
hooliganism
hoydenism
humanism

humanitarianism
Humism
humoralism
hybridism
hydrargyrism
hdyrotropism
hylicism
hylism
hylomorphism
hylopathism
hylotheism
hylozoism
hyperadrenalism
hyperbolism
hypercriticism
hyperthyroidism
hyphenism
hypnotism
hypochondriacism
hypocorism
hypognathism
hypothyroidism
Ibsenism
iconomaticism
iconophilism
idealism
idiotism
idolism
illuminism
illusionism
imagism
immanentism
immaterialism
immediatism
immersionism
immobilism
immoralism
imperialism
impossibilism
impressionism
incendiarism
incivism
incorporealism
indeterminism
indifferentism
individualism
industrialism
infallibilism
infantilism
inflationism
Infralapsarianism
inquilinism

inspirationism
institutionalism
instrumentalism
insularism
insurrectionism
intellectualism
interactionism
internationalism
interventionism
intimism
intransigentism
intuitionalism
intuitionism
intuitivism
invalidism
iodism
Ionism
iotacism
irenicism
Irishism
irrationalism
irredentism
Irvingism
Islamism
Ismailism
isochronism
isodimorphism
isolationism
isomerism
isomorphism
isotropism
itacism
Italianism
italicism
Jacobinism
Jacobitism
Jainism
Jansenism
Jesuitism
jingoism
jockeyism
Johnsonianism
Johnsonism
journalism
Judaism
junkerism
kaiserism
Kantianism
Kantism
karaism
katabolism
Kelticism

Keynesianism
klephitism
know-nothingism
Krishnaism
labdacism
labialism
labourism
laconicism
laconism
ladyism
Lamaism
Lamarckianism
Lamarckism
lambdacism
landlordism
Laodiceanism
larrikinism
lathyrism
Latinism
latitudinarianism
laxism
leftism
legalism
leggism
Leibnitzianism
Leibnizianism
Leninism
lesbianism
liberalism
liberationism
libertarianism
libertinism
lichenism
lionism
lipogrammatism
Listerism
literalism
literaryism
localism
Lollardism
Londonism
Low-Churchism
Luddism
luminarism
Lutheranism
Lutherism
lyricism
lyrism
Lysenkoism
macarism
Machiavellianism
Machiavellism

Magianism
Magism
magnetism
Magyarism
Mahdiism
Mahdism
maidism
malapropism
Malthusianism
mammonism
Manichaeanism
Manichaeism
Manicheanism
Manicheism
mannerism
Maoism
Marcionitism
Marinism
martialism
martinetism
Marxianism
Marxism
masochism
materialism
mathematicism
matriarchalism
maudlinism
Mazdaism
Mazdeism
McCarthyism
mechanism
mediaevalism
medievalism
Medism
melanism
meliorism
memoirism
Mendelism
mentalism
mephitism
mercantilism
mercenarism
mercurialism
merism
merycism
mescalism
mesmerism
mesocephalism
mesomerism
Messianism
metabolism
metachromatism

metachronism
metamerism
metamorphism
metasomatism
metempiricism
meteorism
methodism
metopism
Micawberism
Michurinism
micro-organism
microseism
militarism
millenarianism
millenarism
millennianism
millennairism
Miltonism
minimalism
minimism
misoneism
Mithraicism
Mithraism
mithridatism
modalism
moderatism
modernism
Mohammedanism
Mohammedism
Molinism
monachism
monadism
monarchianism
monarchism
monasticism
monergism
monetarism
mongolism
mongrelism
monism
monkeyism
monochromatism
monoecism
monogenism
monolingualism
monometallism
monophysitism
monorchism
monosyllabism
monotheism
monotheletism
monothelism

monothelitism
Monroeism
Montanism
moralism
Moravianism
Morisonianism
Mormonism
morphinism
mosaicism
Mosaism
Moslemism
mountebankism
multiracialism
Munichism
municipalism
Muslimism
mutism
mutualism
myalism
mysticism
mythicism
mythism
namby-pambyism
nanism
Napoleonism
narcissism
narcotism
nationalism
nativism
naturalism
naturism
navalism
Nazaritism
Naziism
Nazism
necessarianism
necessitarianism
necrophilism
negativism
negroism
negrophilism
neoclassicism
neocolonialism
Neo-Darwinism
Neofascism
Neohellenism
Neo-Impressionism
Neo-Kantianism
Neo-Lamarckism
neologism
Neo-Malthusianism
neo-Nazism

neonomianism
neopaganism
neoplasticism
Neo-Plasticism
Neoplatonism
Neopythagoreanism
neoterism
neovitalism
nephalism
Nestorianism
neuroticism
neutralism
newspaperism
nicotinism
Nietzscheanism
nihilism
noctambulism
Noetianism
nomadism
nominalism
nomism
northernism
notaphilism
nothingarianism
nothingism
Novationism
novelism
nudism
nyctitropism
obeahism
obeism
obiism
objectivism
obscurantism
obsoletism
Occamism
occasionalism
Occidentalism
occultism
Ockhamism
odism
odylism
oecumenicalism
oecumenicism
oecumenism
officialism
old-maidism
onanism
oneirocriticism
onirocriticism
operationalism
Ophism

Ophitism
opportunism
optimism
Orangeism
Orangism
organicism
organism
Orientalism
Origenism
Orleanism
orphanism
Orphism
orthognathism
orthotropism
ostracism
ostrichism
Owenism
pacificism
pacifism
paedobaptism
paedomorphism
paganism
palaeomagnetism
palladianism
paludism
panaesthetism
Pan-Africanism
Pan-Americanism
Pan-Arabism
panchromatism
pancosmism
panderism
panegoism
Pan-Germanism
Panhellenism
panislamism
panlogism
panpsychism
pansexualism
Pan-Slavism
pansophism
panspermatism
panspermism
Pantagruelism
pantheism
papalism
papism
parabaptism
parachronism
paragnathism
paraheliotropism
parallelism

paralogism
paramagnetism
paramorphism
parapsychism
parasitism
Parkinsonism
parliamentarism
Parnassianism
Parnellism
parochialism
Parseeism
Parsiism
Parsism
partialism
particularism
partyism
passivism
pasteurism
pastoralism
paternalism
patrialism
patriarchalism
patriarchism
patriotism
Patripassianism
patristicism
Paulinism
pauperism
pedagogism
pedagoguism
pedanticism
pedantism
pedestrianism
Pelagianism
pelmanism
pelorism
pennalism
pentadactylism
pentamerism
pentaprism
peonism
perfectibilism
perfectionism
peripateticism
perpetualism
Persism
personalism
perspectivism
pessimism
petalism
Petrarchianism
Petrarchism

Petrinism
phaeism
phagocystism
phalansterianism
phalansterism
phallicism
phallism
pharisaism
phariseeism
phenakism
phenomenalism
phenomenism
phihellenism
philistinism
philosophism
phobism
phoneticism
phonetism
phosphorism
photism
photochromism
photoperiodism
phototropism
physicalism
physicism
physitheism
pianism
pietism
piezomagnetism
Pindarism
Pittism
plagiarism
plagiotropism
Plantonicism
Platonism
plebeianism
pleiotropism
pleochroism
pleomorphism
plumbism
pluralism
Plutoism
Plymouthism
pococuranteism
pococurantism
poeticism
pointillism
polonism
polychrism
polycroitism
polydactylism
polygenism

polymastism
polymerism
polymorphism
polynomialism
polysyllabicism
polysyllabism
polysyllogism
polysyntheticism
polysynthetism
polytheism
Pooterism
populism
porism
Porphyrogentism
positivism
possibilism
Post-Impressionism
post-millennialism
Poujadism
Powellism
practicalism
pragmatism
precisianism
predestinarianism
predeterminism
preferentialism
preformationism
prelatism
premillenarianism
premillennialism
Pre-Raphaelism
Pre-Raphaelitism
Presbyterianism
prescriptivism
presentationism
preternaturalism
prettyism
priapism
priggism
primitivism
primordialism
probabiliorism
probabilism
prochronism
professionalism
prognathism
progressionism
progressism
progressivism
prohibitionism
proleterianism
propagandism

prophetism
prosaicism
prosaism
proselytism
prostatism
prosyllogism
protectionism
Protestantism
proverbialism
provincialism
prudentialism
Prussianism
psellism
psephism
pseudo-archaism
pseudoclassicism
pseudomorphism
psilanthropism
psychism
psychologism
psychopannychism
psychoticism
ptyalism
peurillism
pugilism
puppyism
purism
puritanism
Puseyism
pyrrhonism
Pythagoreanism
Pythagorism
Quakerism
quattrocentism
quietism
quixotism
rabbinism
Rabelaisianism
racemism
Rachmanism
racialism
radicalism
Ramism
ranterism
rascalism
rationalism
reactionarism
realism
rebaptism
Rebeccaism
Rechabitism
recidivism

red-tapism
reductionism
reformism
regalism
regionalism
reincarnationism
relationism
relativism
religionism
Rembrandtism
representationalism
representationism
republicanism
restitutionism
restorationism
resurrectionism
reunionism
revanchism
revisionism
revivalism
revolutionism
rheotropism
rheumatism
rhopalism
rhotacism
Ribbonism
rigorism
ritualism
Romanism
romanticism
Rosicrucianism
Rosminianism
Rotarianism
routinism
rowdyism
royalism
ruffianism
ruralism
Russianism
Russophilism
Sabaism
Sabbatarianism
sabbatism
Sabellianism
Sabianism
sacerdotalism
sacramentalism
sacramentarianism
Sadduceeism
Sadducism
sadism
sado-masochism

saintism
Saint-Simonianism
Saint-Simonism
Saivism
Saktism
salvationism
Samaritanism
sanitarianism
sansculottism
sapphism
saprophytism
Saracenism
satanism
saturnism
Saxonism
scepticism
schematism
scholasticism
scientism
sciolism
Scotism
Scotticism
scoundrelism
scribism
scipturalism
scripturism
secessionism
sectarianism
sectionalism
secularism
self-criticism
self-hypnotism
selfism
semi-Arianism
semi-barbarism
Semi-Pelagianism
Semitism
sensationalism
sensationism
sensism
sensualism
sensuism
sentimentalism
separatism
serialism
servillism
servo-mechanism
sesquipedalianism
sexism
sexualism
Shaivism
shakerism

Shaktism
shamanism
shamateurism
Shiism
Shintoism
Shivaism
shunamitism
sigmatism
Sikhism
simplism
sinapism
sinecurism
singularism
Sinicism
Sinophilism
Sivaism
Slavism
snobbism
socialism
Socinianism
sociologism
Sofism
solarism
solecism
sol-faism
solidarism
solidism
solifidianism
solipsism
somatism
somnambulism
somniloquism
sophism
southernism
sovietism
specialism
speciesism
Spencerianism
Spinozism
spiritism
spirtualism
spoonerism
spread-eagleism
Stahlianism
Stahlism
Stakhanovism
Stalinism
stand-pattism
statism
stercoranism
stereoisomerism
stereotropism

stibialism
stigmatism
stoicism
strabism
structuralism
strychninism
strychnism
Stundism
subjectivism
sublapsarianism
subordinationism
substantialism
suburbanism
suffragism
Sufiism
Sufism
suggestionism
supernationalism
supernaturalism
superrealism
Supralapsarianism
supremacism
suprematism
surrealism
sutteeism
Swadeshism
swarajism
Swedenborgianism
swingism
sybaritism
sybotism
syllabism
syllogism
symbolism
symphilism
synaposematism
synchronism
syncretism
syndactylism
syndicalism
synecdochism
synergism
synoecism
syntheticism
Syriacism
Syrianism
systematism
tachism
tactism
Tammanyism
tantalism
Tantrism

Taoism
tarantism
Tartuffism
Tartufism
tautochronism
tautologism
tautomerism
teetotalism
telelogism
tenebrism
teratism
terminism
territorialism
terrorism
tetramerism
tetratheism
Teutonicism
Teutonism
textualism
thanatism
Thatcherism
thaumaturgism
theanthropism
theatricalism
theatricism
theism
theomorphism
Theopaschitism
theophilanthropism
theosophism
therianthropism
theriomorphism
thermotropism
thigmotropism
Thomism
thrombo-embolism
thuggism
tigerism
Timonism
Titanism
Titoism
toadyism
tokenism
Toryism
totalitarianism
totemism
tourism
tractarianism
trade-unionism
traditionalism
Traducianism
traitorism

transcendentalism
transformism
transmigrationism
transsexualism
transvestism
transvestitism
traumatism
trialism
tribadism
tribalism
trichroism
trichromatism
tricotism
triliteralism
trimorphism
Trinitarianism
trinomialism
tripersonalism
tritheism
triticism
trituberculism
trivialism
troglodytism
troilism
trophotropism
tropism
Trotskyism
truism
tsarism
tuism
Turcophilism
tutiorism
tutorism
tychism
ultra-Conservatism
ultraism
ultramontanism
undenominationalism
unicameralism
unidealism
uniformatiarianism
unilateralism
unionism
unitarianism
universalism
unrealism
unsectarianism
unsocialism
untruism
uranism
utilitarianism
utopianism

utopism
Utraquism
vagabondism
Valentinianism
valetudinarianism
vampirism
vandalism
Vansittartism
Vaticanism
Vedism
veganism
vegetarianism
ventriloqism
verbalism
verism
vernacularism
Victorianism
vigilantism
vikingism
virilism
virtualism
vitalism
viviparism
vocalism
vocationalism
volcanism
Voltaireanism
Voltairianism
Voltairism
voltaism
voltinism
voluntarism
voluntaryism
voodooism
vorticism
voyeurism
vulcanism
vulgarism
vulpinism
vulturism
Wagnerianism
Wagnerism
Whabiism
Wahabism
welfarism
werewolfism
Wertherism
werwolfism
Wesleyanism
westernism
Whiggism
whiteboyism

wholism
witticism
Wodenism
Wolfianism
xanthochroism
Yankeeism
yogism
zanyism
Zarathustrianism
Zarathustrism
zealotism
Zionism
Zoilism
zoism
Zolaism
zombiism
zoomagnetism
zoomorphism
zoophilism
zootheism
Zoroastrianism
Zwinglianism
zygodactylism
zygomorphism

-itis
adenitis
alveolitis
antiaditis
aortitis
appendicitis
arachnoiditis
arteritis
arthritis
balanitis
barotitis
blepharitis
bronchitis
bursitis
caecitis
carditis
cellulitis
cephalitis
ceratitis
cerebritis
cervicitis
cheilitis
cholecystitis
chondritis
choroditis
colititis
conchitis

conjunctivitis
crystallitis
cystitis
dermatitis
diaphragmatitis
diphtheritis
diverticulitis
duodenitis
encephalitis
encephalomyelitis
endarteritis
endocarditis
endometritis
enteritis
epiconditis
fibrositis
gastritis
gastroenteritis
gingivitis
glossitis
hamarthritis
hepatitis
hysteritis
ileitis
iritis
keratitis
labyrinthitis
laminitis
laryngitis
lymphadenitis
lymphangitis
mastitis
mastoiditis
meningitis
metritis
myelitis
myocarditis
myositis
myringitis
nephritis
neuritis
oesophagitis
onychitis
oophoritis
ophthalmitis
orchitis
osteitis
osteo-arthritis
osteomyelitis
otitis
ovaritis
panarthritis

pancreatitis
panophthalmitis
papillitis
parotiditis
parotitis
pericarditis
perigastritis
perihepatitis
perinephritis
perineuritis
periodontitis
periostitis
peritonitis
perityphlitis
pharyngitis
phlebitis
phrenitis
pleuritis
pneumonitis
poliomyelitis
polyneuritis
proctitis
prostatitis
pruritis
pseudofolliculitis
pyelitis
pyelonephitis
rachitis
rectitis
retinitis
rhachitis
rhinitis
rhinopharyngitis
sacroliitis
salpingitis
scleritis
sclerotitis
sinuitis
sinusitis
splenitis
spondylitis
staphylitis
stomatitis
strumitis
synovitis
syringitis
tendonitis
tenosynovitis
tenovaginitis
thrombo-phlebitis
thyroiditis
tonsilitis

tonsillitis
tracheitis
trachitis
tympanitis
typhlitis
ulitis
ureteritis
urethritis
uteritis
uveitis
uvulitis
vaginitis
valvulitis
vestibulitis
vulvitis

-latry
angelolatry
anthropolatry
astrolatry
autolatry
bardolatry
bibliolatry
Christolatry
cosmolatry
demonolatry
dendrolatry
ecclesiolatry
epeolatry
geolatry
gyniolatry
hagiolatry
heliolatry
hierolatry
ichthyolatry
iconolatry
idolatry
litholatry
lordolatry
Mariolatry
Maryolatry
monolatry
necrolatry
ophiolatry
physiolatry
plutolatry
pyrolatry
symbololatry
thaumatolatry
theriolatry
zoolatry

-logy
acarology
aerobiology
aerolithology
aerology
aetiology
agriology
agrobiology
agrology
agrostology
algology
amphibology
anaesthesiology
analogy
andrology
anemology
angelology
anthology
anthropobiology
anthropology
antilogy
apology
arachnology
archaeology
archeology
archology
aristology
Assyriology
astacology
astrogeology
astrology
atheology
atmology
audiology
autecology
autology
axiology
bacteriology
balneology
batology
battology
bibliology
bioecology
biology
biotechnology
brachylogy
bryology
bumpology
cacology
caliology
campanology
carcinology

cardiology
carphology
cartology
cetology
characterology
cheirology
chirology
choreology
chorology
Christology
chronobiology
chronology
cine-biology
climatology
codicology
cometology
conchology
coprology
cosmetology
cosmology
craniology
criminology
cryobiology
cryptology
cytology
dactyliology
dactylology
deltiology
demology
demonology
dendrochronology
dendrology
deontology
dermatology
diabology
diabolology
dialectology
diplomatology
dittology
docimology
dogmatology
dosiology
dosology
doxology
dyslogy
dysteleology
ecclesiology
eccrinology
ecology
edaphology
Egyptology
electrobiology

electrology
electrophysiology
electrotechnology
elogy
embryology
emmenology
endemiology
endocrinology
entomology
enzymology
epidemiology
epistemology
erotology
escapology
eschatology
ethnology
ethnomusicology
ethology
Etruscology
etymology
euchology
eulogy
exobiology
festilogy
festology
folk-etymology
futurology
gastroenterology
gastrology
gemmology
gemology
genealogy
genethlialogy
geochronology
geology
geomorphology
gerontology
gigantology
glaciology
glossology
glottology
gnomonology
gnoseology
gnosiology
gnotobiology
graphology
gynaecology
haematology
hagiology
hamartiology
haplology
heliology

helminthology
heortology
hepaticology
hepatology
heresiology
herpetology
heterology
hierlogy
hippology
histiology
histology
histopathology
historiology
homology
hoplology
horology
hydrobiology
hydrogeology
hydrology
hydrometeorology
hyetology
hygrology
hymnology
ichnology
ichthyology
iconology
ideology
immunology
insectology
irenology
kidology
kinesiology
koniology
Kremlinology
larynglogy
lepidopterology
lexicology
lichenology
limacology
limnology
lithology
liturgiology
macrology
malacology
malariology
mammalogy
Mariology
martyrology
Maryology
Mayology
menology
mereology

metapsychology
meteorology
methodology
microbiology
microclimatology
micrology
micro-meteorology
microtechnology
mineralogy
misology
missiology
monadology
monology
morphology
muscology
museology
musicology
mycetology
mycology
myology
myrmecology
mythology
necrology
nematology
neology
nephology
nephrology
neurobiology
neurohypnology
neurology
neuropathology
neurophysiology
neuroradiology
neurypnology
nomology
noology
nosology
nostology
numerology
numismatology
oceanology
odonatology
odontology
oenology
olfactology
oncology
oneirology
onirology
onomasiology
ontology
oology
ophiology

ophthalmology
optology
orchidology
oreology
ornithology
orology
orthopterology
oryctology
osteology
otolaryngology
otology
otorhinolaryngology
ourology
paedology
palaeanthropology
palaeethnology
palaeichthyology
palaeoclimatology
palaeolimnology
palaeontology
palaeopedology
palaeophytology
palaeozoology
palillogy
palynology
pantheology
papyrology
paradoxology
parapsychology
parasitology
paroemiology
pathology
patrology
pedology
pelology
penology
pentalogy
periodontology
perissology
pestology
petrology
phaenology
pharmacology
pharyngology
phenology
phenomenology
philology
phonology
photobiology
photogeology
phraseology

phrenology
phycology
physiology
phytology
phytopathology
planetology
plutology
pneumatology
podology
poenology
pomology
ponerology
posology
potamology
primatology
proctology
protistology
protozoology
psephology
pseudology
psychobiology
psychology
psychopathology
psychophysiology
pteridology
pyramidology
pyretology
pyroballogy
radiobiology
radiology
reflexology
rheology
rheumatology
rhinology
röntgenology
sarcology
satanology
scatology
Scientology
sedimentology
seismology
selenology
selenomorphology
semasiology
semeiology
semiology
serology
sexology
sindonology
Sinology
sitiology
sitology

skatology
sociobiology
sociology
somatology
soteriology
spectrology
spelaeology
sphagnology
sphygmology
spongology
stichology
stoechiology
stoicheiology
stoichiology
stomatology
storiology
symbology
symbolology
symptomatology
synchronology
synecology
synoecology
syphilology
systematology
tautology
technology
teleology
teratology
terminology
terotechnology
tetralogy
thanatology
theology
thermology
therology
thremmatology
timbrology
tocology
tokology
topology
toxicology
traumatology
tribology
trichology
trilogy
trophology
tropology
typhlology
typology
ufology
uranology
urbanology

urinology
urology
venereology
vexillology
victimology
vinology
virology
volcanology
vulcanology
xylology
zoopathology
zoophytology
zoopsychology
zymology

-lysis
analysis
atmolysis
autocatalysis
autolysis
bacteriolysis
biolysis
catalysis
cryptanalysis
cyclodialysis
cytolysis
dialysis
electroanalysis
electrolysis
emphlysis
frontolysis
glycolysis
haematolysis
haemodialysis
haemolysis
histolysis
homolysis
hydrolysis
hypno-analysis
karyolysis
leucocytolysis
lipolysis
microanalysis
narco-analysis
neurolysis
oncolysis
paralysis
photocatalysis
photolysis
plasmolysis
pneumatolysis
proteolysis

psephoanalysis
psychoanalysis
pyrolysis
radiolysis
thermolysis
uranalysis
urinalysis
zincolysis
xymolysis

-mancy
aeromancy
axinomancy
belomancy
bibliomancy
botanomancy
capnomancy
cartomancy
ceromancy
cheiromancy
chiromancy
cleromancy
coscinomancy
crithomancy
crystallomancy
dactyliomancy
gastromancy
geomancy
gyromancy
hieromancy
hydromancy
lampadomancy
lithomancy
myomancy
necromancy
nigromancy
oenomancy
omphalomancy
oneiromancy
oniromancy
onychomancy
ornithomancy
pyromancy
rhabdomancy
scapulimancy
spodomancy
tephromancy
theormancy
zoomancy

-mania
ablutomania

acronymania
ailuromania
anglomania
anthomania
arithmomania
balletomania
bibliomania
Celtomania
cynomania
demomania
demonomania
dipsomania
dromomania
egomania
eleutheromania
ergomania
erotomania
etheromania
flagellomania
francomania
gallomania
graphomania
hedonomania
hippomania
hodomania
hydromania
hypomania
hysteromania
kleptomania
logomania
megalomania
melomania
methomania
metromania
monomania
morphinomania
mythomania
narcomania
necromania
nostomania
nymphomania
oenomania
opsomania
orchidomania
petalomania
phagomania
phyllomania
potichomania
pteridomania
pyromania
squandermania
technomania

thanatomania
theatromania
theomania
timbromania
tomomania
toxicomania
trichotillomania
tulipomania
typomania
verbomania
xenomania

-mathy
chrestomathy
opsimathy
philomathy
polymathy

-metry
acidimetry
aerometry
alcoholometry
alkalimetry
allometry
altimetry
anthropometry
araeometry
archaeometry
astrometry
asymmetry
barometry
bathymetry
biometry
bolometry
calorimetry
campimetry
cephalometry
chlorimetry
chlorometry
chronometry
clinometry
colorimetry
coulometry
craniometry
cytometry
cytophotometry
densimetry
densitometry
dissymmetry
dosimetry
dynamometry
electrometry

galvanometry
gasometry
geometry
goniometry
gravimetry
hodometry
horometry
hydrometry
hygrometry
hypsometry
iconometry
interferometry
iodometry
isometry
isoperimetry
magnetometry
mammetry
micrometry
microseismometry
nanometry
nephelometry
noometry
odometry
odorimetry
olfactometry
ophthalmometry
optometry
pelvimetry
perimetry
photogrammetry
photometry
planimetry
plessimetry
pleximetry
polarmetry
pseudosymmetry
psychometry
psychrometry
pyrometry
saccharimetry
seismometry
sociometry
spectrometry
spectrophotometry
spirometry
stalagmometry
stereometry
stichometry
stoechiometry
stoicheiometry
stoichiometry
stylometry

symmetry
tacheometry
tachometry
tachymetry
telemetry
tensiometry
thermometry
tonometry
trigonometry
udometry
unsymmetry
uranometry
velocimetry
viscometry
viscosimetry
zoometry

-morphy
ectomorphy
enantiomorphy
endomorphy
gynandromorphy
heteromorphy
homoeomorphy
homeomorphy
mesomorphy
pleomorphy
stasimorphy
zoomorphy
zygomorphy

-osis
abiosis
acidosis
actinobacillosis
actinomycosis
adenosis
adiposis
aerobiosis
aeroneurosis
agranulocytosis
alkalosis
alphosis
amaurosis
ameiosis
amitosis
amyloidosis
anabiosis
anadiplosis
anaerobiosis
anamorphosis
anaplerosis

anastomosis
anchylosis
ankylosis
anthracosis
anthropomorphosis
antibiosis
apodosis
aponeurosis
apoptosis
apotheosis
arteriosclerosis
arthrosis
asbestosis
aspergillosis
ateleiosis
atherosclerosis
athetosis
autohypnosis
avitaminosis
babesiosis
bacteriosis
bagassosis
berylliosis
bilharziosis
biocoenosis
bromhidrosis
bromidrosis
brucellosis
byssinosis
carcinomatosis
carcinosis
chlorosis
chondromatosis
cirrhosis
coccidiosis
cryptococcosis
cryptosporidiosis
cyanosis
cyclosis
cystericerosis
cystinosis
dermatosis
diarthrosis
diorthosis
diplosis
diverticulosis
dulosis
ecchymosis
ectostosis
enantiosis
enarthrosis
endometriosis

endomitosis
endosmosis
endosymbiosis
enosis
enteroptosis
epanadiplosis
epanorthosis
erythroblastosis
exocytosis
exosmosis
exostosis
fibrosis
fluorosis
furunculosis
gliomatosis
gliosis
gnosis
gnotobiosis
gomphosis
gummosis
haematosis
haemochromatosis
halitosis
hallucinosis
haplosis
heliosis
heterosis
hidrosis
histoplasmosis
homeosis
homoeosis
homomorphosis
homozygosis
hydrarthrosis
hydronephrosis
hyperhidrosis
hyperidrosis
hyperinosis
hypersarcosis
hypervitaminosis
hypinosis
hypnosis
hypotyposis
ichthyosis
kaolinosis
kenosis
keratosis
ketosis
kurtosis
kyllosis
kyphosis
leishmaniosis

leptospirosis
leucocytosis
leukosis
limosis
lipomatosis
listeriosis
lordosis
madarosis
marmarosis
meiosis
melanosis
metachrosis
metamorphosis
metempsychosis
miosis
mitosis
molybdosis
mononucleosis
monosis
morphosis
mucoviscidosis
mycosis
mycotoxicosis
myosis
myxomatosis
narcohypnosis
narcosis
necrobiosis
necrosis
nephroptosis
nephroptosis
nephrosis
neurofibromatosis
neurosis
onychocryptosis
ornithosis
osmidrosis
osmosis
osteoarthrosis
osteopetrosis
osteoporosis
osteosis
ostosis
otosclerosis
paedomorphosis
parabiosis
paraphimosis
parapsychosis
parasitosis
pasteurellosis
pediculosis
phagocytosis

phimosis
pholidosis
phytosis
pinocytosis
pneumoconiosis
pneumokoniosis
pneumonokiniosis
pneumonoultracmicro-
  scopicsilicovolcano-
  coniosis
podoconiosis
pollenosis
polyposis
porosis
proptosis
psilosis
psittacosis
psychoneurosis
psychosis
pterylosis
ptilosis
ptosis
pycnodysostosis
pycnosis
pyrosis
resinosis
salmonellosis
sarcoidosis
sarcomatosis
sclerosis
scoliosis
self-hypnosis
semiosis
shigellosis
siderosis
silicosis
sorosis
spherocytosis
spirillosis
spirochaetosis
spondylosis
sporotrichosis
steatosis
stegnosis
stenosis
strongylosis
sycosis
symbiosis
symptosis
synarthrosis
synchondrosis
syndesmosis

synoeciosis
synostosis
syntenosis
syssarcosis
thanatosis
theriomorphosis
thrombosis
thylosis
thyrotoxicosis
torulosis
toxicosis
toxoplasmosis
trichinosis
trichophytosis
trichosis
trophobiosis
trophoneurosis
tuberculosis
tylosis
ulosis
urosis
vibriosis
virosis
visceroptosis
xerosis
yersiniosis
zoonosis
zygosis
zymosis

-pathy
allopathy
anthropopathy
antipathy
apathy
arthropathy
cardiomyopathy
dyspathy
empathy
enantiopathy
encephalopathy
enteropathy
haemoglobinopathy
homeopathy
homoeopathy
hydropathy
idiopathy
kinesipathy
lymphadenopathy
myocardiopathy
myopathy
naturopathy

nephropathy
neuropathy
nostopathy
osteopathy
protopathy
psychopathy
sociopathy
sympathy
telepathy
theopathy
zoopathy

-phagy
anthropophagy
autocoprophagy
autophagy
coprophagy
dysphagy
endophagy
entomophagy
exophagy
geophagy
hippophagy
ichthyophagy
monophagy
mycophagy
omophagy
onychophagy
ostreophagy
pantophagy
polyphagy
sarcophagy
scatophagy
theophagy
xerophagy
zoophagy

-philia
ailurophilia
Anglophilia
arctophilia
biophilia
canophilia
coprophilia
cynophilia
eosinophilia
ephebophilia
Germanophilia
gerontophilia
haemophilia
necrophilia
neophilia

paedophilia
paraphilia
retrophilia
scopophilia
scoptophilia
stigmatophilia
thrombophilia
topophilia
zoophilia

-phily
acarophily
arctophily
anemophily
bibliophily
cartophily
entomophily
halophily
hydrophily
malacophily
maximaphily
myrmecophily
necrophily
notaphily
oenophily
ornithophily
photophily
psychophily
scripophily
Sinophily
symphily
timbrophily
toxophily
xerophily
zoophily

-phobia
acrophobia
aerophobia
agoraphobia
aichmophobia
ailurophobia
algophobia
anemophobia
anglophobia
anthropophobia
apiphobia
aquaphobia
arachnophobia
arithmophobia
astraphobia
astrapophobia

autophobia
bathophobia
batrachophobia
bibliophobia
brontophobia
cancerophobia
canophobia
claustrophobia
clinophobia
cynophobia
dromophobia
dysmorphophobia
ecophobia
eleutherophobia
emetophobia
entomophobia
ergophobia
erotophobia
erythrophobia
euphobia
Francophobia
gallophobia
genophobia
gerontophobia
graphophobia
gynophobia
herpetophobia
hierophobia
hippophobia
homophobia
hydrophobia
hypsophobia
kenophobia
monophobia
mysophobia
necrophobia
negrophobia
neophobia
nosophobia
nyctophobia
ochlophobia
odontophobia
ophthalmophobia
ornithophobia
panophobia
panphobia
pantophobia
pathophobia
phagophobia
phasmophobia
phengophobia
phonophobia

photophobia
pyrophobia
Russophobia
satanophobia
scopophobia
scoptophobia
Scotophobia
sitiophobia
sitophobia
symmetrophobia
syphilophobia
tachophobia
taphephobia
taphophobia
technophobia
thanatophobia
theophobia
toxicophobia
toxiphobia
triskaidecaphobia
triskaidekaphobia
xenophobia
zelophobia
zoophobia

-phony
acrophony
antiphony
aphony
apophony
autophony
cacophony
ciphony
colophony
diaphony
dodecaphony
euphony
gramophony
homophony
laryngophony
monophony
photophony
polyphony
quadraphony
quadrophony
radiophony
radiotelephony
stereophony
symphony
tautophony
telephony

-scopy
arthroscopy
autoscopy
bioscopy
bronchoscopy
colonoscopy
colposcopy
cranioscopy
cryoscopy
cystoscopy
dactyloscopy
deuteroscopy
ebullioscopy
endoscopy
episcopy
fluoroscopy
foetoscopy
hepatoscopy
hieroscopy
horoscopy
laparoscopy
laryngoscopy
metoposcopy
microscopy
necroscopy
omoplatoscopy
oneiroscopy
oniroscopy
ophthalmoscopy
ornithoscopy
otoscopy
ouroscopy
peritoneoscopy
pharyngoscopy
poroscopy
proctoscopy
radioscopy
retinoscopy
rhinoscopy
röntgenoscopy
sigmoidoscopy
skiascopy
spectroscopy
stereoscopy
stethoscopy
telescopy
tracheoscopy
ultramicroscopy
urethroscopy
urinoscopy
uroscopy
zooscopy

-ship
abbotship
accountantship
acquaintanceship
administratorship
admiralship
advisership
aedileship
airmanship
aldermanship
amateurship
ambassadorship
apostleship
apprenticeship
archonship
assessorship
associateship
attorneyship
auditorship
augurship
authorship
bachelorship
bailieship
baillieship
bardship
barristership
bashawship
batsmanship
beadleship
bedellship
bedelship
benchership
bondmanship
brinkmanship
bursarship
bushmanship
butlership
cadetship
Caesarship
candidateship
captainship
cardinalship
catechumenship
censorship
chairmanship
chamberlainship
championship
chancellorship
chaplainship
chelaship
chiefship
chieftainship

citizenship
clanship
clerkship
clientship
clownship
coadjutorship
colleagueship
collectorship
colonelship
commandantship
commandership
commissaryship
commissionership
committeeship
companionship
compotationship
comradeship
conductorship
confessorship
connoisseurship
conservatorship
constableship
consulship
controllership
copartnership
co-rivalship
corporalship
counsellorship
countship
courtship
cousinship
cowardship
craftmanship
craftsmanship
creatorship
creatureship
curateship
curatorship
custodianship
deaconship
dealership
deanship
demyship
denizenship
devilship
dictatorship
directorship
discipleship
disfellowship
doctorship
dogeship
dogship

dollarship
donship
draftsmanship
dukeship
editorship
eldership
electorship
emperorship
endship
ensignship
entrepreneurship
envoyship
executorship
factorship
fathership
fellowship
foxship
freshmanship
friendship
gamesmanship
generalship
gentlemanship
giantship
gladiatorship
goddess-ship
godship
good-fellowship
governor-generalship
governorship
grandeeship
guardianship
guideship
hardship
headship
hectorship
heirship
heraldship
heroship
hership
hetmanship
horsemanship
hostess-ship
housewifeship
huntsmanship
inspectorship
interpretership
interrelationship
janitorship
jockeyship
judgeship
justiceship
kaisership

keepership
kindredship
kingship
kinship
knaveship
ladyship
lairdship
land-ownership
laureateship
leadership
lectorship
lectureship
legateship
legislatorship
librarianship
lieutenant-commandership
lieutenant-generalship
lieutenant-governorship
lieutenantship
lifemanship
logship
lordship
ludship
mageship
major-generalship
majorship
managership
marshalship
mastership
matronship
mayorship
mediatorship
membership
Messiaship
milk-kinship
minorship
mistress-ship
moderatorship
monitorship
multi-ownership
musicianship
noviceship
nunship
oarsmanship
one-upmanship
overlordship
ownership
partisanship
partnership
pastorship
patroonship
peatship

pendragonship
penmanship
physicianship
poetship
popeship
possessorship
postmastership
praetorship
preachership
precentorship
prefectship
prelateship
premiership
prenticeship
presbytership
presidentship
pretendership
priestship
primateship
primogenitureship
principalship
priorship
probationership
proconsulship
proctorship
procuratorship
professorship
progenitorship
prolocutorship
prophetship
proprietorship
prosectorship
protectorship
provostship
pursership
quaestorship
queenship
rajahship
rajaship
rangership
readership
recordership
rectorship
regentship
registrarship
relationship
residentiaryship
residentship
retainership
rivalship
rogueship
rulership

sachemship
saintship
salesmanship
scholarship
schoolmastership
scrivenership
seamanship
secretaryship
seigniorship
sempstress-ship
senatorship
seneschalship
serfship
sergeantship
serjeantship
servantship
servitorship
sextonship
sheriffship
showmanship
sibship
sizarship
soldiership
solicitorship
sonship
speakership
spectatorship
spinstership
sponsorship
sportsmanship
squireship
statesmanship
stewardship
studentship
subahship
subdeaconship
subeditorship
subinspectorship
subjectship
successorship
suffraganship
sultanship
superintendentship
superiorship
supervisorship
suretyship
surgeonship
surrogateship
surveyorship
survivorship
swordsmanship
teachership

tellership
tenantship
thaneship
thwartship
tide-waitership
township
traineeship
traitorship
treasurership
treeship
tribuneship
truantship
trusteeship
tutorship
twinship
umpireship
uncleship
under-clerkship
undergraduateship
under-secretaryship
unfriendship
ushership
vaivodeship
vergership
vicarship
vice-chairmanship
vice-chancellorship
vice-consulship
viceroyship
virtuosoship
viscountship
viziership
vizirship
voivodeship
waivodeship
wardenship
wardship
watermanship
Whigship
workmanship
worship
wrangership
writership
yachtsmanship

-sophy
anthroposophy
gastrosophy
gymnosophy
pansophy
philosophy
sciosophy

theosophy

-therapy
actinotherapy
apitherapy
aromatherapy
balneotherapy
chemotherapy
chromotherapy
crymotherapy
cryotherapy
curietherapy
electrotherapy
heliotherapy
hydrotherapy
hypnotherapy
immunotherapy
kinesitherapy
musicotherapy
narcotherapy
opotherapy
organotherapy
pelotherapy
phototherapy
physiotherapy
psychotherapy
pyretotherapy
radiotherapy
röntgenotherapy
serotherapy
thermotherapy
zootherapy

-tomy
adenectomy
adenoidectomy
amniotomy
anatomy
anthropotomy
appendectomy
appendicectomy
arteriotomy
autotomy
cephalotomy
cholecystectomy
cholecystotomy
cliterodectomy
colectomy
colostomy
colotomy
cordectomy
cordotomy

craniectomy
craniotomy
cystectomy
cystotomy
dichotomy
duodenectomy
embryotomy
encephalotomy
enterctomy
enterostomy
enterotomy
episiotomy
gastrectomy
gastrotomy
gingivectomy
glossectomy
hepatectomy
herniotomy
hypophysectomy
hysterectomy
hysterotomy
ileostomy
iridectomy
iridotomy
keratotomy
laparotomy
laryngectomy
laryngotomy
leucotomy
lipectomy
lithotomy
lobectomy
lobotomy
lumpectomy
mammectomy
mastectomy
meniscectomy
microanatomy

microtomy
myringotomy
necrotomy
nephrectomy
nephrotomy
neurectomy
neuroanatomy
neurotomy
oncotomy
oophorectomy
orchidectomy
orchiectomy
osteotomy
ovariotomy
pancreatectomy
patellectomy
pharyngotomy
phlebotomy
phytotomy
pinealectomy
pleurotomy
pneumonectomy
pogonotomy
prostatectomy
rhizotomy
rhytidectomy
salpingectomy
sclerotomy
scotomy
splenectomy
stapedectomy
stereotomy
strabotomy
sympathectomy
symphyseotomy
symphysiotomy
syringotomy
tenotomy

tetrachotomy
thoracotomy
thymectomy
thyroidectomy
tonsilectomy
tonsillectomy
tonsillotomy
tonsilotomy
topectomy
tracheostomy
tracheotomy
trichotomy
tubectomy
tylectomy
ultramicrotomy
urostomy
uterectomy
utertomy
vagotomy
varicotomy
vasectomy
vasotomy
zootomy

-urgy

chemurgy
dramaturgy
electrometallurgy
hierurgy
hydrometallurgy
liturgy
metallurgy
micrurgy
thaumaturgy
theurgy
zymurgy